THE ASTRONOMICAL ALMANAC

FOR THE YEAR

2025

Data for Astronomy, Space Sciences, Geodesy, Surveying, Navigation and other applications

WASHINGTON

Issued by the
Nautical Almanac Office
United States
Naval Observatory
by direction of the
Secretary of the Navy
and under the
authority of Congress

TAUNTON

Issued
by
His Majesty's
Nautical Almanac Office
on behalf
of
The UK Hydrographic Office

WASHINGTON: U.S. GOVERNMENT PUBLISHING OFFICE
TAUNTON: THE UK HYDROGRAPHIC OFFICE

ISBN 978-0-7077-46494

ISSN 0737-6421

UNITED STATES

For sale by the Superintendent of Documents, U.S. Government Publishing Office
Internet: bookstore.gpo.gov Phone: toll free (866) 512-1800; DC area (202) 512-1800
Fax: (202) 512-2104 Mail: Stop IDCC, Washington, DC 20402-0001

UNITED KINGDOM

Published by the United Kingdom Hydrographic Office

http://www.gov.uk/UKHO

Telephone: +44 (0)1823 484 444

E-mail: customerservices@ukho.gov.uk

NOTE

Every care is taken to prevent errors in the production of this publication. As a final precaution it is recommended that the sequence of pages in this copy be examined on receipt. If faulty it should be returned for replacement.

Printed in the United States of America
by the U.S. Government Publishing Office

Beginning with the edition for 1981, the title *The Astronomical Almanac* replaced both the title *The American Ephemeris and Nautical Almanac* and the title *The Astronomical Ephemeris*. The changes in title symbolise the unification of the two series, which until 1980 were published separately in the United States of America since 1855 and in the United Kingdom since 1767. *The Astronomical Almanac* is prepared jointly by the Nautical Almanac Office, United States Naval Observatory, and H.M. Nautical Almanac Office, United Kingdom Hydrographic Office, and is published jointly by the United States Government Publishing Office and the United Kingdom Hydrographic Office; it is printed only in the United States of America using reproducible material from both offices.

By international agreement the tasks of computation and publication of astronomical ephemerides are shared among the ephemeris offices of several countries. The contributors of the basic data for this Almanac are listed on page vii. This volume was designed in consultation with other astronomers of many countries, and is intended to provide current, accurate astronomical data for use in the making and reduction of observations and for general purposes. (The other publications listed on pages viii-ix give astronomical data for particular applications, such as navigation and surveying.)

Beginning with the 1984 edition, most of the data tabulated in *The Astronomical Almanac* have been based on the fundamental ephemerides of the planets and the Moon prepared at the Jet Propulsion Laboratory (JPL). In particular, the 2003 through 2014 editions utilized the JPL Planetary and Lunar Ephemerides DE405/LE405 whereas the 2015 through 2023 editions utilized DE430/LE430. Beginning with the 2024 edition, JPL's DE440/LE440 are the basis of the tabulations.

The 2009 edition implemented the relevant International Astronomical Union (IAU) resolutions passed at the 2003 and 2006 IAU General Assemblies. This includes the adoption of the report by the IAU Working Group on Precession and the Ecliptic which affects a significant fraction of the tabulated data (see Section L for more details). *U.S. Naval Observatory Circular No. 179* (see page ix) gives a detailed explanation of the relevant IAU resolutions. Beginning with the 2014 edition, all sections reflect the IAU 2006 resolution that formally defined planets, dwarf planets, and small solar system bodies. Beginning with the 2015 edition, the 2012 IAU resolution re-defining the astronomical unit has been implemented. Beginning with the 2025 edition, data tables describing lunarcentric celestial objects have been included.

Suggestions for further improvement of this Almanac would be welcomed; they should be sent to the Chief, Nautical Almanac Office, United States Naval Observatory or to the Head, H.M. Nautical Almanac Office, United Kingdom Hydrographic Office.

KIMBERLY M. FREITAS
Captain, U.S. Navy,
Superintendent, U.S. Naval Observatory
3450 Massachusetts Avenue, NW
Washington, D.C. 20392–5420
U.S.A.

RADM PETER SPARKES
Chief Executive Officer
UK Hydrographic Office
Admiralty Way, Taunton
Somerset, TA1 2DN
United Kingdom

July 2024

Changes to The Astronomical Almanac, 2025

Section H: Replaced the bright stars table with a reduced table of navigational stars; Removed most other data tables and replaced them with web references to equivalent online sources.

Section J: New section highlighting lunarcentric celestial object positions and lunar orientation parameters.

Section L: Significant textual changes to reflect the updates to Sections H and J.

Section M: Various entries have been updated or added.

AsA Online: The web companion to *The Astronomical Almanac* has been withdrawn as of January 2023.

PRELIMINARIES

The pagination within each section is given in full on the first page of each section.

U.S. NAVAL OBSERVATORY

CAPT Kimberly M. Freitas, *U.S.N., Superintendent*
CDR, Matthew S. Cushanick *U.S.N., Deputy Superintendent*

CELESTIAL REFERENCE FRAME DEPARTMENT

Claire E. Cramer, *Department Head*
Susan G. Stewart, *Chief, U.S. Nautical Almanac Office*

George H. Kaplan
Michael Efroimsky
Emily Laos
Mark T. Stollberg
Andrew J. Kopf

THE UNITED KINGDOM HYDROGRAPHIC OFFICE

RAdm Peter Sparkes, *Chief Executive Officer*
Amy Northern, *Head of the Scientific Analysis Group*

HIS MAJESTY'S NAUTICAL ALMANAC OFFICE

Steven A. Bell, *Head*

Donald B. Taylor
Antonia J. Wilmot
Gareth Davie
James A. Whittaker
Mark Moffett
Nicola S. Loaring

The data in this volume have been prepared as follows:

By H.M. Nautical Almanac Office, United Kingdom Hydrographic Office:

Section A—phenomena, rising, setting of Sun and Moon, lunar eclipses; B—ephemerides and tables relating to time-scales and coordinate reference frames; D—physical ephemerides and geocentric coordinates of the Moon; F—ephemerides for sixteen of the major planetary satellites; G—opposition dates, finding charts, geocentric coordinates, transit times, and osculating orbital elements, of selected dwarf planets and small solar system bodies; K—tables and data.

By the Nautical Almanac Office, United States Naval Observatory:

Section A—eclipses of the Sun; C—physical ephemerides, geocentric and rectangular coordinates of the Sun; E—physical ephemerides, orbital elements, heliocentric and geocentric coordinates, and transit times of the planets; F—phenomena and ephemerides of satellites, except Jupiter I–IV; H—navigation stars, spectrophotometric standard stars and ICRF3 radio source positions; J—lunarcentric celestial objects; L—notes and references; M—glossary; N—index.

By the Jet Propulsion Laboratory, California Institute of Technology:

The planetary and lunar ephemerides DE440/LE440. The ephemerides of the dwarf planets and the largest and/or brightest 92 minor planets.

By the IAU Standards Of Fundamental Astronomy (SOFA) initiative:

Software implementation of fundamental quantities used in sections A, B, D and G.

By the Institut de Mécanique Céleste et de Calcul des Éphémérides, Paris Observatory:

Section F—ephemerides and phenomena of satellites I–IV of Jupiter.

By the Minor Planet Center, Cambridge, Massachusetts:

Section G—orbital elements of periodic comets.

In general the Office responsible for the preparation of the data has drafted the related explanatory notes and auxiliary material, but both have contributed to the final form of the material. The preliminaries, Section A, except the solar eclipses, and Sections B, D, G and K have been composed in the United Kingdom, while the rest of the material has been composed in the United States. The work of proofreading has been shared, but no attempt has been made to eliminate the differences in spelling and style between the contributions of the two Offices.

Joint publications of HM Nautical Almanac Office (UKHO) and the United States Naval Observatory

These publications are available from UKHO distributors and the Superintendent of Documents, U.S. Government Publishing Office (USGPO) except where noted.

Astronomical Phenomena contains extracts from *The Astronomical Almanac* and is published annually in advance of the main volume. Included are dates and times of planetary and lunar phenomena and other astronomical data of general interest. (UKHO GP200)

The Nautical Almanac contains ephemerides at an interval of one hour and auxiliary astronomical data for marine navigation. (UKHO NP314)

The Air Almanac contains ephemerides at an interval of ten minutes and auxiliary astronomical data for air navigation. This publication is now distributed solely on CD-ROM and is only available from USGPO.

Rapid Sight Reduction Tables for Navigation (AP 3270 / NP 303), 3 volumes, formerly entitled *Sight Reduction Tables for Air Navigation.* Volume 1, selected stars for epoch 2020·0, containing the altitude to 1′ and true azimuth to 1° for the seven stars most suitable for navigation, for all latitudes and hour angles of Aries.

Other publications of HM Nautical Almanac Office (UKHO)

The Star Almanac for Land Surveyors (NP 321) contains the Greenwich hour angle of Aries and the position of the Sun, tabulated for every six hours, and represented by monthly polynomial coefficients. Positions of all stars brighter than magnitude 4·0 are tabulated monthly to a precision of $0^{s}.1$ in right ascension and 1″ in declination. A CD-ROM is included which contains the electronic edition plus coefficients, in ASCII format, representing the data.

NavPac and Compact Data for 2021–2025 (DP 330) is an e-book and software, containing algorithms and data, which are mainly in the form of polynomial coefficients, for calculating the positions of the Sun, Moon, navigational planets and bright stars. It enables navigators to compute their position at sea from sextant observations using Windows OS 8 and 10 for the period 1986–2025. The tabular data are also supplied as ASCII files on the CD-ROM. Upgrades and updates are available from https://astro.ukho.gov.uk/nao/navpacfour/.

Rapid Sight Reduction Tables for Navigation (AP 3270 / NP 303), 3 volumes, formerly entitled *Sight Reduction Tables for Air Navigation.* Volumes 2 and 3 contain altitudes to 1′ and azimuths to 1° for integral degrees of declination from N 29° to S 29°, for relevant latitudes and all hour angles at which the zenith distance is less than 95° providing for sights of the Sun, Moon and planets.

The UK Air Almanac (AP1602) contains data useful in the planning of activities where the level of illumination is important, particularly aircraft movements, and is produced to the general requirements of the Royal Air Force. It may be downloaded from the website https://astro.ukho.gov.uk/nao/publicat/ukaa.html.

NAO Technical Notes are issued irregularly to disseminate astronomical data concerning ephemerides or astronomical phenomena.

Other publications of the United States Naval Observatory

Astronomical Papers of the American Ephemeris† are issued irregularly and contain reports of research in celestial mechanics with particular relevance to ephemerides.

U.S. Naval Observatory Circulars† are issued irregularly to disseminate astronomical data concerning ephemerides or astronomical phenomena.

U.S. Naval Observatory Circular No. 179, The IAU Resolutions on Astronomical Reference Systems, Time Scales, and Earth Rotation Models explains resolutions and their effects on the data (see Web Links).

Explanatory Supplement to The Astronomical Almanac edited by Sean E. Urban, U.S. Naval Observatory and P. Kenneth Seidelmann, University of Virginia. This third edition is completely updated and offers an authoritative source on the basis and derivation of information contained in *The Astronomical Almanac*, and contains material that is relevant to positional and dynamical astronomy and to chronology. The publication is a collaborative work with authors from the U.S. Naval Observatory, H.M. Nautical Almanac Office, the Jet Propulsion Laboratory and others. It is published by, and available from University Science Books, Mill Valley, California, whose UK distributor is Macmillan Distribution.

MICA is an interactive astronomical almanac for professional applications. Software for both PC systems with Intel processors and Apple Macintosh computers is provided on a single CD-ROM. *MICA* allows a user to compute, to full precision, much of the tabular data contained in *The Astronomical Almanac*, as well as data for specific times and locations. All calculations are made in real time and data are not interpolated from tables. MICA is a product of the U.S. Naval Observatory. The latest version covers the interval 1800-2050.

† Many of these publications are available from the Nautical Almanac Office, U.S. Naval Observatory, Washington, DC 20392-5420, see Web Links on the next page for availability.

Publications of other countries

Apparent Places of Fundamental Stars is prepared by the Astronomisches Rechen-Institut, Zentrum für Astronomie der Universität Heidelberg (https://zah.uni-heidelberg.de/institutes/ari). The printed version of APFS gives the data for a few fundamental stars only, together with the explanation and examples. The apparent places of stars using the FK6 or Hipparcos catalogues are provided by the on-line database ARIAPFS (https://wwwadd.zah.uni heidelberg.de/datenbanken/ariapfs/index.php.en). The printed booklet also contains the so-called '10-Day-Stars' and the 'Circumpolar Stars' and is available from dpunkt.verlag GmbH, Wieblinger Weg 17, 69123 Heidelberg, Germany.

Ephemerides of Minor Planets is prepared annually by the Institute of Applied Astronomy (http://iaaras.ru/en/). Included in this volume are elements, opposition dates and opposition ephemerides of all numbered minor planets. This volume is available from the Institute of Applied Astronomy, Naberezhnaya Kutuzova 10, St. Petersburg, 191187 Russia and can be downloaded from http://iaaras.ru/html/emp2020/emp2020.html.

Please refer to the relevant World Wide Web address for further details about the publications and services provided by the following organisations.

U.S. Naval Observatory

- U.S. Naval Observatory at https://www.cnmoc.usff.navy.mil/usno
- USNO Publications at https://aa.usno.navy.mil/publications
- USNO Online Data at https://aa.usno.navy.mil/data
- NOVAS Astrometry Software at https://aa.usno.navy.mil/software/novas_info
- *USNO Circular 179* at https://aa.usno.navy.mil/publications/usnopubs

H.M. Nautical Almanac Office

- General information at https://astro.ukho.gov.uk or http://www.gov.uk/HMNAO
- Eclipses Online at https://astro.ukho.gov.uk/eclipse/
- Online data services at https://astro.ukho.gov.uk/websurf2/
- Crescent MoonWatch at https://astro.ukho.gov.uk/moonwatch/

International Astronomical Organizations

- IAU: International Astronomical Union at https://www.iau.org
- IERS: International Earth Rotation and Reference Systems Service at https://www.iers.org
- SOFA: IAU Standards of Fundamental Astronomy at https://www.iausofa.org
- NSFA: Numerical Standards for Fundamental Astronomy at https://iau-a3.gitlab.io/NSFA
- MPC: Minor Planet Centre at https://minorplanetcenter.net/
- CDS: Centre de Données astronomiques de Strasbourg at https://cdsweb.u-strasbg.fr

Products provided by International Astronomical Organizations

- IERS Products https://www.iers.org/ : then
  Orientation data, time, follow, Data / Products → Earth Orientation Data
  Bulletins A, B, C, D and descriptions follow, Publications → IERS Bulletins
  Technical Notes follow, Publications → IERS Technical Notes
- IERS Conventions Centre, updates at http://iers-conventions.obspm.fr

Publishers and Suppliers

- The UK Hydrographic Office (UKHO) at https://www.gov.uk/UKHO
- U.S. Government Publishing Office (USGPO) at https://bookstore.gpo.gov
- University Science Books at https://www.uscibooks.com
- Macmillan Distribution at https://www.palgrave.com

CONTENTS OF SECTION A

NOTE: All the times in this section are expressed in Universal Time (UT).

THE SUN

		d h			d h m		d h m
Perigee	Jan.	4 13	Equinoxes	Mar.	20 09 01	Sept.	22 18 19
Apogee	July	3 20	Solstices	June	21 02 42	Dec.	21 15 03

PHASES OF THE MOON

Lunation	New Moon		First Quarter		Full Moon		Last Quarter	
		d h m		d h m		d h m		d h m
1262			Jan.	6 23 56	Jan.	13 22 27	Jan.	21 20 31
1263	Jan.	29 12 36	Feb.	5 08 02	Feb.	12 13 53	Feb.	20 17 33
1264	Feb.	28 00 45	Mar.	6 16 32	Mar.	14 06 55	Mar.	22 11 29
1265	Mar.	29 10 58	Apr.	5 02 15	Apr.	13 00 22	Apr.	21 01 36
1266	Apr.	27 19 31	May	4 13 52	May	12 16 56	May	20 11 59
1267	May	27 03 02	June	3 03 41	June	11 07 44	June	18 19 19
1268	June	25 10 32	July	2 19 30	July	10 20 37	July	18 00 38
1269	July	24 19 11	Aug.	1 12 41	Aug.	9 07 55	Aug.	16 05 12
1270	Aug.	23 06 07	Aug.	31 06 25	Sept.	7 18 09	Sept.	14 10 33
1271	Sept.	21 19 54	Sept.	29 23 54	Oct.	7 03 48	Oct.	13 18 13
1272	Oct.	21 12 25	Oct.	29 16 21	Nov.	5 13 19	Nov.	12 05 28
1273	Nov.	20 06 47	Nov.	28 06 59	Dec.	4 23 14	Dec.	11 20 52
1274	Dec.	20 01 43	Dec.	27 19 10				

ECLIPSES

A total eclipse of the Moon	Mar. 14	Parts of Antarctica, western half of Africa, western Europe, Atlantic Ocean, Americas, Pacific Ocean, eastern Australia, northern Japan, eastern Russia
A partial eclipse of the Sun	March. 29	North-eastern North America, Greenland, Iceland, north Atlantic Ocean, most of Europe, north-western Russia
A total eclipse of the Moon	Sep. 7	Parts of Antarctica, western Pacific Ocean, Australasia, Asia, Indian Ocean, Europe, eastern Atlantic Ocean
A partial eclipse of the Sun	Sep. 21	New Zealand, eastern Melanesia, southern Polynesia, western Antarctica

MOON AT PERIGEE

	d h		d h		d h
Jan.	8 00	May	26 02	Oct.	8 13
Feb.	2 03	June	23 05	Nov.	5 22
Mar.	1 21	July	20 14	Dec.	4 11
Mar.	30 05	Aug.	14 18		
Apr.	27 16	Sept.	10 12		

MOON AT APOGEE

	d h		d h		d h
Jan.	21 05	June	7 11	Oct.	24 00
Feb.	18 01	July	5 02	Nov.	20 03
Mar.	17 17	Aug.	1 21	Dec.	17 06
Apr.	13 23	Aug.	29 16		
May	11 01	Sept.	26 10		

OCCULTATIONS OF PLANETS AND BRIGHT STARS BY THE MOON

Date (d h)	Body	Areas of Visibility
Jan. 1 12	Pluto	Most of Antarctica except easternmost
Jan. 4 17	Saturn	N.W South America, S. half of Central America, S.E. tip of USA, Cape Verde Is., N.W. Africa, most of Europe, N.E. Greenland.
Jan. 5 15	Neptune	Azores, north-westernmost Africa, Europe except S.E., Iceland, most of Greenland, Severnaya Zemlya.
Jan. 14 04	Mars	North America except N.W., Azores, Cape Verde Is., N.W. Africa.
Jan. 21 05	*Spica*	Cape Verde Is., parts of western and southern Africa, S. half of Madagascar.
Jan. 25 00	*Antares*	Most of Madagascar, S. Australia, S. Polynesia (including New Zealand).
Feb. 1 05	Saturn	Northern parts of S.E. Asia, China, Japan, E. Russia.
Feb. 1 23	Neptune	Extreme W. tip of Alaska, extreme E. tip of Russia.
Feb. 9 20	Mars	N.E. tip of USA, N. Canada, Greenland, Iceland, most of Scandanavia, most of Russia, E. Kazakhstan, Mongolia, most of China.
Feb. 17 13	*Spica*	E. Micronesia, E. Melanesia, central Polynesia, S. part of South America.
Feb. 21 09	*Antares*	Easter Is., southern South America, easternmost Antarctica, S. tip of Africa.
Feb. 25 10	Pluto	Most of Antarctica, Kerguelen Is.
Mar. 1 04	Mercury	Kerguelen Is., Australia, Melanesia, most of Micronesia, N.W. Polynesia.
Mar. 16 20	*Spica*	E. central parts of Africa, Madagascar, S. tips of Australia, S. New Zealand, E. tip of Antarctica.
Mar. 20 17	*Antares*	S.E. Indonesia, most of Australia, S. New Zealand, westernmost Antarctica, S. tip of South America.
Mar. 24 21	Pluto	Antarctica, south-easternmost Polynesia.
Apr. 13 02	*Spica*	Central America, most of South America, South Georgia & the South Sandwich Is., southernmost tip of Africa.
Apr. 16 23	*Antares*	S. part of Africa, Kerguelen Is., E. Antarctica, southern and central Australia.
Apr. 21 06	Pluto	S. tip of South America, most of Antarctica, Kerguelen Is., S. half of Madagascar.
May 10 08	*Spica*	Micronesia, Melanesia, S.W. Polynesia, tip of Antarctic Peninsula, extreme southern tip of South America.
May 14 05	*Antares*	Easternmost Polynesia, southern South America, tip of Antarctic Peninsula, S.E. edge of Africa.
May 18 12	Pluto	New Zealand, Easter Is., most of South America.
June 6 15	*Spica*	S. half of Africa, Madagascar, Kerguelen Is., E. Antarctica, southernmost New Zealand.
June 10 11	*Antares*	Indonesia, W. Melanesia, Australia, New Zealand, Easter Is.
June 14 17	Pluto	Most of Australia, E. Melanesia, south-easternmost Micronesia, N.E. Polynesia.

continued on page A90 . . .

GEOCENTRIC PHENOMENA

MERCURY

	d h	d h	d h
Superior conjunction . . .	Feb. 9 12	May 30 04	Sept. 13 11
Greatest elongation East	Mar. 8 06 (18°)	July 4 05 (26°)	Oct. 29 22 (24°)
Stationary	Mar. 14 21	July 17 07	Nov. 9 23
Inferior conjunction . . .	Mar. 24 20	Aug. 1 00	Nov. 20 09
Stationary	Apr. 6 06	Aug. 10 18	Nov. 29 15
Greatest elongation West	Apr. 21 19 (27°)	Aug. 19 10 (19°)	Dec. 7 21 (21°)

VENUS

	d h		d h
Greatest elongation East	Jan. 10 05 (47°)	Stationary	Apr. 10 15
Greatest illuminated extent	Feb. 14 22	Greatest illuminated extent	Apr. 27 17
Stationary	Feb. 28 03	Greatest elongation West	June 1 04 (46°)
Inferior conjunction . . .	Mar. 23 01		

SUPERIOR PLANETS

	Conjunction	Stationary	Opposition		Stationary
	d h	d h	d h		d h
Mars	—	—	Jan. 16 03		Feb. 24 10
Jupiter	June 24 15	Nov. 11 20	—	|	Feb. 4 13
Saturn	Mar. 12 10	July 14 08	Sept. 21 06		Nov. 29 01
Uranus	May 18 00	Sept. 6 05	Nov. 21 12	|	Jan. 30 19
Neptune	Mar. 19 23	July 5 15	Sept. 23 13		Dec. 11 00

The vertical bars indicate where the dates for the planet are not in chronological order.

OCCULTATIONS BY PLANETS AND SATELLITES

Details of predictions of occultations of stars by planets, minor planets and satellites are given in *The Handbook of the British Astronomical Association*.

HELIOCENTRIC PHENOMENA

	Aphelion	Perihelion	Descending Node	Greatest Lat. South		Ascending Node	Greatest Lat. North
Mercury	Jan. 19	Mar. 4	Jan. 9	Feb. 8		Feb. 27	Mar. 14
	Apr. 17	May 31	Apr. 7	May 7		May 26	June 10
	July 14	Aug. 27	July 4	Aug. 3		Aug. 22	Sept. 6
	Oct. 10	Nov. 23	Sept. 30	Oct. 30		Nov. 18	Dec. 3
	—	—	Dec. 27	—		—	—
Venus	—	Feb. 19	May 8	July 4	|	Jan. 16	Mar. 13
	June 12	Oct. 2	Dec. 19	—	|	Aug. 29	Oct. 24
Mars	Apr. 16	—	Sept. 23	—		—	Mar. 9

Jupiter: Ascending Node, Sept. 19
Saturn, Uranus, Neptune: None in 2025

ELONGATIONS AND MAGNITUDES OF PLANETS AT 0^{h} UT

Date		Mercury Elong.	Mercury Mag.	Venus Elong.	Venus Mag.
		°		°	
Jan.	**0**	W. 21	−0·4	E. 47	−4·4
	5	W. 20	−0·4	E. 47	−4·5
	10	W. 18	−0·4	E. 47	−4·5
	15	W. 16	−0·4	E. 47	−4·6
	20	W. 13	−0·5	E. 47	−4·6
	25	W. 10	−0·7	E. 46	−4·7
	30	W. 8	−0·9	E. 46	−4·7
Feb.	**4**	W. 4	−1·2	E. 44	−4·8
	9	W. 2	−1·5	E. 43	−4·8
	14	E. 4	−1·5	E. 41	−4·9
	19	E. 8	−1·4	E. 38	−4·9
	24	E. 12	−1·3	E. 35	−4·9
Mar.	**1**	E. 16	−1·0	E. 31	−4·8
	6	E. 18	−0·6	E. 26	−4·7
	11	E. 18	+0·1	E. 20	−4·5
	16	E. 14	+1·4	E. 14	−4·2
	21	E. 8	+3·9	E. 9	−4·2
	26	W. 4	·	W. 9	−4·2
	31	W. 11	+3·3	W. 15	−4·2
Apr.	**5**	W. 18	+1·8	W. 21	−4·5
	10	W. 23	+1·0	W. 26	−4·6
	15	W. 26	+0·7	W. 31	−4·7
	20	W. 27	+0·5	W. 35	−4·8
	25	W. 27	+0·3	W. 38	−4·8
	30	W. 26	+0·1	W. 40	−4·7
May	**5**	W. 24	−0·1	W. 42	−4·7
	10	W. 21	−0·3	W. 44	−4·7
	15	W. 17	−0·7	W. 45	−4·6
	20	W. 12	−1·1	W. 45	−4·5
	25	W. 6	−1·7	W. 46	−4·5
	30	W. 1	·	W. 46	−4·4
June	**4**	E. 6	−1·7	W. 46	−4·4
	9	E. 12	−1·2	W. 46	−4·3
	14	E. 17	−0·7	W. 45	−4·3
	19	E. 21	−0·3	W. 45	−4·2
	24	E. 23	0·0	W. 44	−4·2
	29	E. 25	+0·3	W. 44	−4·2
July	**4**	E. 26	+0·5	W. 43	−4·1

Date		Mercury Elong.	Mercury Mag.	Venus Elong.	Venus Mag.
		°		°	
July	**4**	E. 26	+0·5	W. 43	−4·1
	9	E. 25	+0·8	W. 42	−4·1
	14	E. 23	+1·1	W. 41	−4·1
	19	E. 19	+1·8	W. 41	−4·0
	24	E. 14	+2·9	W. 40	−4·0
	29	E. 7	+4·7	W. 39	−4·0
Aug.	**3**	W. 6	+5·0	W. 38	−4·0
	8	W. 12	+2·8	W. 37	−4·0
	13	W. 16	+1·2	W. 36	−4·0
	18	W. 18	+0·2	W. 34	−3·9
	23	W. 18	−0·5	W. 33	−3·9
	28	W. 15	−1·0	W. 32	−3·9
Sept.	**2**	W. 11	−1·4	W. 31	−3·9
	7	W. 6	−1·6	W. 30	−3·9
	12	W. 2	−1·8	W. 29	−3·9
	17	E. 3	−1·5	W. 27	−3·9
	22	E. 7	−1·0	W. 26	−3·9
	27	E. 11	−0·7	W. 25	−3·9
Oct.	**2**	E. 14	−0·5	W. 24	−3·9
	7	E. 16	−0·4	W. 23	−3·9
	12	E. 19	−0·3	W. 21	−3·9
	17	E. 21	−0·2	W. 20	−3·9
	22	E. 23	−0·2	W. 19	−3·9
	27	E. 24	−0·1	W. 18	−3·9
Nov.	**1**	E. 24	−0·1	W. 16	−3·9
	6	E. 22	+0·1	W. 15	−3·9
	11	E. 18	+0·6	W. 14	−3·9
	16	E. 10	+2·5	W. 13	−3·9
	21	W. 2	·	W. 11	−3·9
	26	W. 12	+1·5	W. 10	−3·9
Dec.	**1**	W. 18	+0·1	W. 9	−3·9
	6	W. 21	−0·3	W. 8	−3·9
	11	W. 20	−0·5	W. 6	−3·9
	16	W. 19	−0·5	W. 5	−3·9
	21	W. 17	−0·5	W. 4	−3·9
	26	W. 15	−0·5	W. 3	−3·9
	31	W. 12	−0·6	W. 2	−3·9
	36	W. 10	−0·7	W. 1	·

SELECTED DWARF AND MINOR PLANETS

	Conjunction	Stationary	Opposition	Stationary
Ceres	Feb. 14	Aug. 16	Oct. 2	Nov. 27
Pallas	Jan. 3	June 3	Aug. 7	Sept. 25
Juno	Dec. 17	Mar. 22	May 14	July 14
Vesta	—	Mar. 23	May 2	June 18
Pluto	Jan. 21	May 6	July 25	Oct. 14

ELONGATIONS AND MAGNITUDES OF PLANETS AT 0^h UT

Date		Mars		Jupiter		Saturn		Uranus		Neptune	
		Elong.	Mag.	Elong.	Mag.	Elong.	Mag.	Elong.	Mag.	Elong.	Mag.
		°		°		°		°		°	
Jan.	**−5**	W. 151	−1·1	E. 159	−2·8	E. 69	+1·0	E. 139	+5·7	E. 83	+7·8
	5	W. 164	−1·3	E. 148	−2·7	E. 60	+1·0	E. 129	+5·7	E. 72	+7·8
	15	W. 175	−1·4	E. 137	−2·7	E. 51	+1·1	E. 118	+5·7	E. 62	+7·8
	25	E. 167	−1·3	E. 126	−2·6	E. 41	+1·1	E. 108	+5·7	E. 53	+7·8
Feb.	**4**	E. 154	−1·0	E. 116	−2·5	E. 32	+1·1	E. 98	+5·7	E. 43	+7·8
	14	E. 142	−0·7	E. 106	−2·4	E. 23	+1·1	E. 88	+5·7	E. 33	+7·8
	24	E. 131	−0·4	E. 96	−2·3	E. 15	+1·1	E. 78	+5·8	E. 23	+7·8
Mar.	**6**	E. 122	−0·2	E. 87	−2·3	E. 6	+1·1	E. 68	+5·8	E. 13	+7·8
	16	E. 114	+0·1	E. 78	−2·2	W. 4	+1·1	E. 58	+5·8	E. 4	+7·8
	26	E. 106	+0·3	E. 70	−2·1	W. 12	+1·2	E. 49	+5·8	W. 6	+7·8
Apr.	**5**	E. 99	+0·5	E. 61	−2·1	W. 21	+1·2	E. 39	+5·8	W. 15	+7·8
	15	E. 93	+0·7	E. 53	−2·0	W. 29	+1·2	E. 30	+5·8	W. 25	+7·8
	25	E. 88	+0·8	E. 45	−2·0	W. 38	+1·2	E. 21	+5·8	W. 34	+7·8
May	**5**	E. 83	+1·0	E. 37	−2·0	W. 47	+1·2	E. 12	+5·8	W. 44	+7·8
	15	E. 78	+1·1	E. 30	−1·9	W. 55	+1·1	E. 3	+5·8	W. 53	+7·8
	25	E. 73	+1·2	E. 22	−1·9	W. 64	+1·1	W. 6	+5·8	W. 62	+7·8
June	**4**	E. 69	+1·3	E. 15	−1·9	W. 73	+1·1	W. 15	+5·8	W. 72	+7·8
	14	E. 65	+1·4	E. 8	−1·9	W. 82	+1·0	W. 24	+5·8	W. 81	+7·8
	24	E. 61	+1·4	0	−1·9	W. 91	+1·0	W. 33	+5·8	W. 91	+7·8
July	**4**	E. 57	+1·5	W. 7	−1·9	W. 100	+0·9	W. 42	+5·8	W. 100	+7·7
	14	E. 54	+1·5	W. 14	−1·9	W. 110	+0·9	W. 52	+5·8	W. 110	+7·7
	24	E. 50	+1·6	W. 21	−1·9	W. 120	+0·8	W. 61	+5·8	W. 119	+7·7
Aug.	**3**	E. 47	+1·6	W. 29	−1·9	W. 129	+0·8	W. 70	+5·8	W. 129	+7·7
	13	E. 43	+1·6	W. 36	−1·9	W. 139	+0·7	W. 79	+5·8	W. 139	+7·7
	23	E. 40	+1·6	W. 44	−2·0	W. 149	+0·7	W. 89	+5·7	W. 149	+7·7
Sept.	**2**	E. 37	+1·6	W. 52	−2·0	W. 160	+0·6	W. 98	+5·7	W. 158	+7·7
	12	E. 34	+1·6	W. 60	−2·0	W. 170	+0·6	W. 108	+5·7	W. 168	+7·7
	22	E. 31	+1·6	W. 68	−2·1	E. 177	+0·6	W. 118	+5·7	W. 178	+7·7
Oct.	**2**	E. 27	+1·6	W. 76	−2·1	E. 168	+0·6	W. 128	+5·7	E. 171	+7·7
	12	E. 24	+1·5	W. 85	−2·2	E. 158	+0·7	W. 138	+5·6	E. 161	+7·7
	22	E. 22	+1·5	W. 94	−2·2	E. 147	+0·7	W. 148	+5·6	E. 151	+7·7
Nov.	**1**	E. 19	+1·4	W. 104	−2·3	E. 137	+0·8	W. 159	+5·6	E. 141	+7·7
	11	E. 16	+1·4	W. 114	−2·4	E. 127	+0·8	W. 169	+5·6	E. 131	+7·7
	21	E. 13	+1·4	W. 124	−2·5	E. 116	+0·9	W. 179	+5·6	E. 121	+7·7
Dec.	**1**	E. 10	+1·3	W. 135	−2·5	E. 106	+0·9	E. 170	+5·6	E. 110	+7·7
	11	E. 8	+1·2	W. 145	−2·6	E. 96	+0·9	E. 159	+5·6	E. 100	+7·7
	21	E. 5	+1·2	W. 157	−2·6	E. 86	+1·0	E. 149	+5·6	E. 90	+7·8
	31	E. 3	+1·1	W. 168	−2·7	E. 77	+1·0	E. 138	+5·6	E. 80	+7·8
	41	W. 1	+1·1	W. 180	−2·7	E. 67	+1·0	E. 128	+5·7	E. 70	+7·8

VISUAL MAGNITUDES OF SELECTED DWARF & MINOR PLANETS

	Jan. 5	Feb. 14	Mar. 26	May 5	June 14	July 24	Sept. 2	Oct. 12	Nov. 21	Dec. 31
Ceres	9·2	9·0	9·2	9·3	9·1	8·7	8·0	7·6	8·3	8·8
Pallas	10·4	10·5	10·5	10·3	9·9	9·5	9·5	10·0	10·3	10·4
Juno	11·4	11·2	10·8	10·1	10·5	11·0	11·4	11·5	11·3	11·2
Vesta	8·0	7·4	6·6	5·7	6·6	7·3	7·8	8·0	8·1	7·9
Pluto	15·2	15·2	15·2	15·2	15·1	15·0	15·1	15·2	15·3	15·2

VISIBILITY OF PLANETS

The planet diagram on page A7 shows, in graphical form for any date during the year, the local mean times of meridian passage of the Sun, of the five planets, Mercury, Venus, Mars, Jupiter and Saturn, and of every 2^h of right ascension. Intermediate lines, corresponding to particular stars, may be drawn in by the user if desired. The diagram is intended to provide a general picture of the availability of planets and stars for observation during the year.

On each side of the line marking the time of meridian passage of the Sun, a band 45^m wide is shaded to indicate that planets and most stars crossing the meridian within 45^m of the Sun are generally too close to the Sun for observation.

For any date the diagram provides immediately the local mean time of meridian passage of the Sun, planets and stars, and thus the following information:

a) whether a planet or star is too close to the Sun for observation;
b) visibility of a planet or star in the morning or evening;
c) location of a planet or star during twilight;
d) proximity of planets to stars or other planets.

When the meridian passage of a body occurs at midnight, it is close to opposition to the Sun and is visible all night, and may be observed in both morning and evening twilights. As the time of meridian passage decreases, the body ceases to be observable in the morning, but its altitude above the eastern horizon during evening twilight gradually increases until it is on the meridian at evening twilight. From then onwards the body is observable above the western horizon, its altitude at evening twilight gradually decreasing, until it becomes too close to the Sun for observation. When it again becomes visible, it is seen in the morning twilight, low in the east. Its altitude at morning twilight gradually increases until meridian passage occurs at the time of morning twilight, then as the time of meridian passage decreases to 0^h, the body is observable in the west in the morning twilight with a gradually decreasing altitude, until it once again reaches opposition.

Notes on the visibility of the planets are given on page A8. Further information on the visibility of planets may be obtained from the diagram below which shows, in graphical form for any date during the year, the declinations of the bodies plotted on the planet diagram on page A7.

DECLINATION OF SUN AND PLANETS, 2025

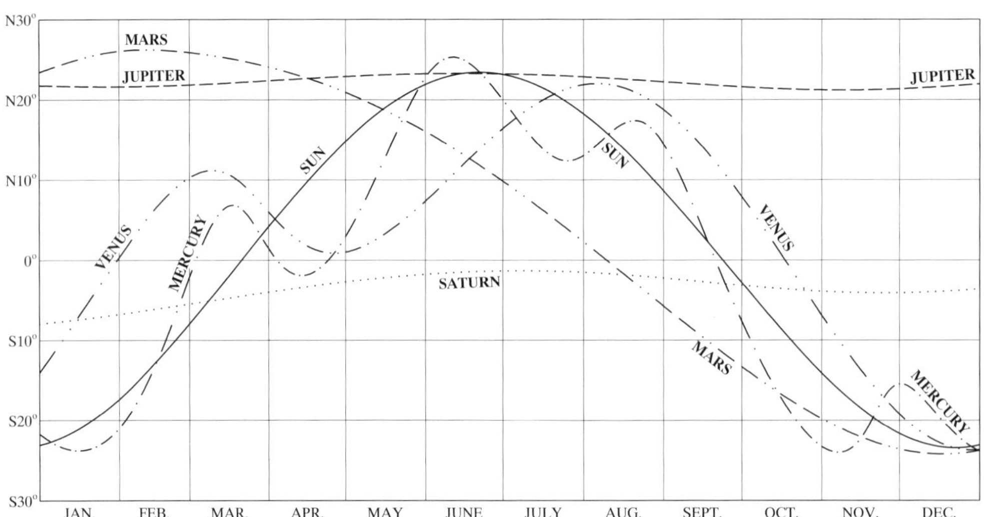

LOCAL MEAN TIME OF MERIDIAN PASSAGE

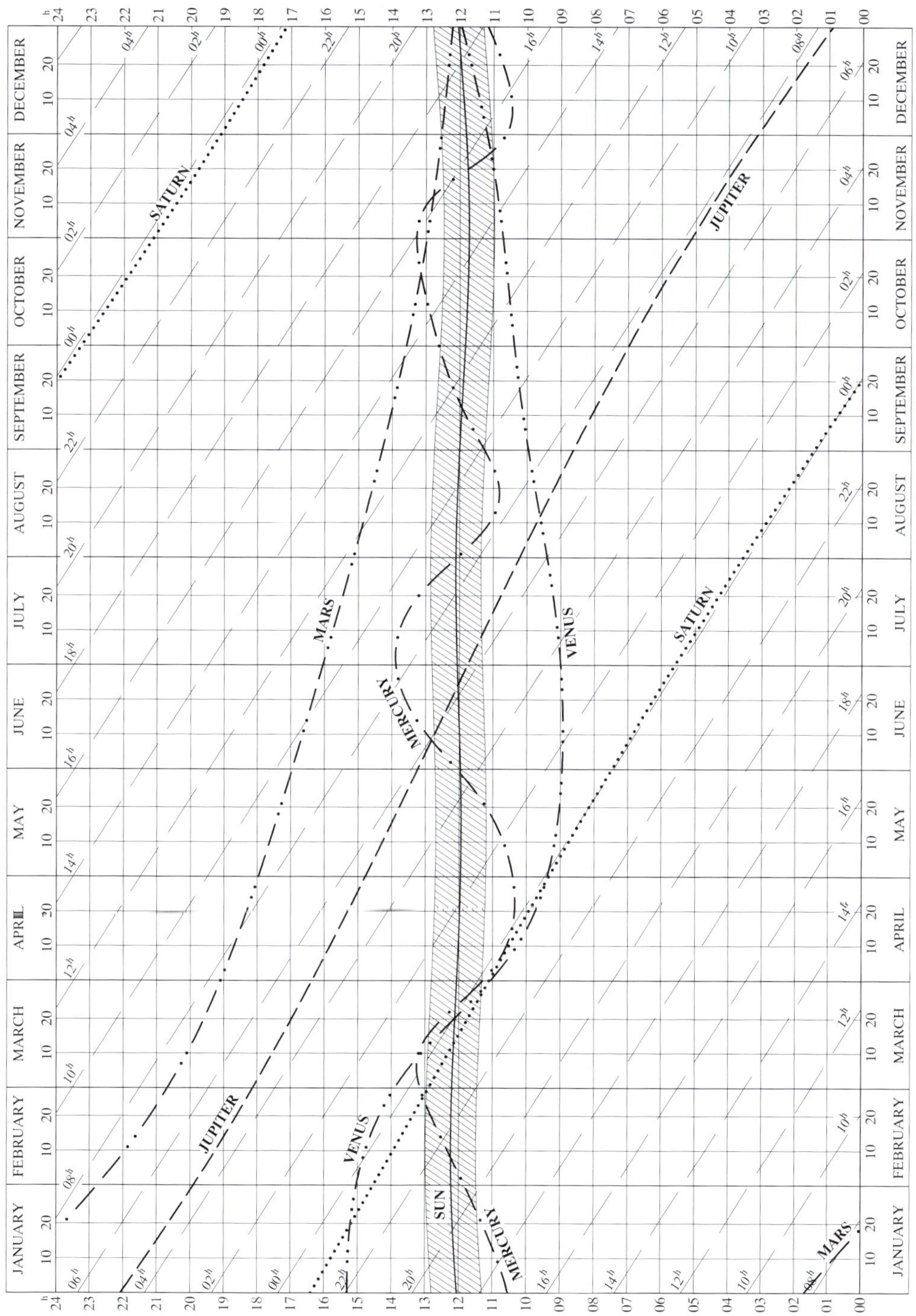

LOCAL MEAN TIME OF MERIDIAN PASSAGE

VISIBILITY OF PLANETS

MERCURY can only be seen low in the east before sunrise, or low in the west after sunset (about the time of beginning or end of civil twilight). It is visible in the mornings between the following approximate dates: January 1 to January 26, April 2 to May 22, August 9 to September 4 and November 26 to December 31. The planet is brighter at the end of each period, (the best conditions in northern latitudes occur in the second half of August and in the first half of December and in southern latitudes from mid-April to early May). It is visible in the evenings between the following approximate dates: February 21 to March 17, June 7 to July 24 and September 25 to November 14. The planet is brighter at the beginning of each period, (the best conditions in northern latitudes occur in the first half of March and in southern latitudes from late June to mid-July and mid-October to early November).

VENUS is a brilliant object in the evening sky until in the second half of March when it becomes too close to the Sun for observation. It reappears in late March as a morning star and can be seen in the morning sky until late November when it again becomes too close to the Sun for observation. Venus is in conjunction with Saturn on January 20, March 30 and April 29, with Mercury on March 9 and November 25 and with Jupiter on August 12.

MARS can be seen in Cancer from the beginning of the year and then from mid-January in Gemini. On January 16 it is at opposition when it can be seen throughout the night, its eastward elongation gradually decreases (passing 2° S of *Pollux* on January 21 and then 4° S of *Pollux* on April 3), returns to Cancer in mid-April and from early May it can only be seen in the evening sky. It then continues through Leo (passing 0.8° N of *Regulus* on June 17), Virgo (passing 2° N of *Spica* on September 12), Libra and Scorpius in early November; from mid-November until the end of the year it is too close to the Sun for observation. Mars is in conjunction with Mercury on October 21 and November 12.

JUPITER is in Taurus at the beginning of the year, and can be seen for more than half the night until early March after which it can only be seen in the evening sky. In the second week of June it becomes too close to the Sun for observation. It reappears in the morning sky in the second week of July in Gemini (passing 7° S of *Pollux* on October 27 and November 26) and remains in this constellation throughout the rest of the year. Jupiter is in conjunction with Mercury on June 8 and with Venus on August 12.

SATURN can be seen in the evening sky in Aquarius until late February when it becomes too close to the Sun for observation. It reappears in the morning sky in late March and passes into Pisces in mid-April. Its westward elongation gradually increases and is at opposition on September 21 when it is visible throughout the night. It returns into Aquarius in late September and its eastward elongation then gradually decreases until in the second half of December it can only be seen in the evening sky. Saturn is in conjunction with Venus on January 20, March 30 and April 29.

URANUS is visible at the beginning of the year in Aries moving into Taurus at the start of March in which constellation it remains throughout the rest of the year. From mid-February until late April it can only be seen in the evening sky. It then becomes too close to the Sun for observation reappearing in the first half of June in the morning sky. It is at opposition on November 21 when it is visible throughout the night, after which its eastward elongation gradually decreases.

NEPTUNE is visible at the beginning of the year in the evening sky in Pisces, in which constellation it remains throughout the year. At the end of February it becomes too close to the Sun for observation and reappears in the first half of April in the morning sky. Neptune is at opposition on September 23 when it is visible throughout the night. Its eastward elongation gradually decreases and in late December can only be seen in the evening sky.

DO NOT CONFUSE (1) Venus with Saturn in mid-January and again from late April to early May, with Jupiter in mid-August and with Mercury in late November; on all occasions Venus is the brighter object. (2) Mercury with Saturn in the second half of February and again in the first half of April and with Mars in the second half of October and again in the first half of November; on all occasions Mercury is the brighter object. (3) Jupiter with Mercury in the first half of June when Jupiter is the brighter object.

VISIBILITY OF PLANETS IN MORNING AND EVENING TWILIGHT

	Morning		Evening	
Venus			January 1	– March 19
	March 27	– November 26		
Mars	January 1	– January 16	January 16	– November 13
Jupiter			January 1	– June 10
	July 9	– December 31		
Saturn			January 1	– February 23
	March 30	– September 21	September 21	– December 31

CONFIGURATIONS OF SUN, MOON AND PLANETS

	d h		
Jan.	1 12	Pluto 1°1 N. of Moon	Occn.
	3 08	Pallas in conjunction with Sun	
	3 15	Venus 1°4 N. of Moon	
	4 13	Earth at perihelion	
	4 17	Saturn 0°7 S. of Moon	Occn.
	5 15	Neptune 1°1 S. of Moon	Occn.
	7 00	FIRST QUARTER	
	8 00	Moon at perigee	
	9 16	Uranus 4° S. of Moon	
	10 05	Venus greatest elong. E. (47°)	
	10 23	Jupiter 5° S. of Moon	
	12 14	Mars closest approach	
	13 22	FULL MOON	
	14 04	Mars 0°2 S. of Moon	Occn.
	16 03	Mars at opposition	
	20 05	Venus 3° N. of Saturn	
	21 05	Moon at apogee	
	21 05	Spica 0°1 N. of Moon	Occn.
	21 12	Pluto in conjunction with Sun	
	21 17	Mars 2° S. of *Pollux*	
	21 21	LAST QUARTER	
	25 00	Antares 0°3 N. of Moon	Occn.
	29 13	NEW MOON	
	30 19	Uranus stationary	
Feb.	1 05	Saturn 1°1 S. of Moon	Occn.
	1 20	Venus 2° N. of Moon	
	1 23	Neptune 1°4 S. of Moon	Occn.
	2 03	Moon at perigee	
	3 20	Venus 4° N. of Neptune	
	4 13	Jupiter stationary	
	5 08	FIRST QUARTER	
	5 21	Uranus 5° S. of Moon	
	7 04	Jupiter 5° S. of Moon	
	9 12	Mercury in superior conjunction	
	9 20	Mars 0°8 S. of Moon	Occn.
	12 14	FULL MOON	
	14 22	Ceres in conjunction with Sun	
	14 22	Venus greatest illuminated extent	
	17 13	Spica 0°3 N. of Moon	Occn.
	18 01	Moon at apogee	
	20 18	LAST QUARTER	
	21 09	Antares 0°4 N. of Moon	Occn.
	24 10	Mars stationary	
	25 10	Pluto 1°0 N. of Moon	Occn.
	28 01	NEW MOON	
	28 03	Venus stationary	
Mar.	1 04	Mercury 0°4 N. of Moon	Occn.
	1 09	Neptune 1°6 S. of Moon	
	1 21	Moon at perigee	
	1 23	Venus 6° N. of Moon	
	5 04	Uranus 5° S. of Moon	
	6 12	Jupiter 6° S. of Moon	

	d h		
Mar.	6 17	FIRST QUARTER	
	8 06	Mercury greatest elong. E. (18°)	
	9 00	Mars 1°7 S. of Moon	
	9 11	Mercury 6° S. of Venus	
	12 10	Saturn in conjunction with Sun	
	14 07	FULL MOON	Eclipse
	14 21	Mercury stationary	
	16 20	Spica 0°4 N. of Moon	Occn.
	17 17	Moon at apogee	
	19 23	Neptune in conjunction with Sun	
	20 09	Equinox	
	20 17	Antares 0°5 N. of Moon	Occn.
	22 11	LAST QUARTER	
	22 18	Juno stationary	
	23 01	Venus in inferior conjunction	
	23 05	Vesta stationary	
	24 20	Mercury in inferior conjunction	
	24 21	Pluto 0°9 N. of Moon	Occn.
	28 14	Venus 9° N. of Moon	
	29 11	NEW MOON	Eclipse
	30 05	Moon at perigee	
	30 06	Venus 10° N. of Saturn	
Apr.	1 14	Uranus 5° S. of Moon	
	3 00	Jupiter 6° S. of Moon	
	3 03	Mars 4° S. of *Pollux*	
	5 02	FIRST QUARTER	
	5 19	Mars 2° S. of Moon	
	6 06	Mercury stationary	
	10 15	Venus stationary	
	13 00	FULL MOON	
	13 02	Spica 0°3 N. of Moon	Occn.
	13 23	Moon at apogee	
	16 19	Mercury 0°7 S. of Neptune	
	16 23	Antares 0°4 N. of Moon	Occn.
	21 02	LAST QUARTER	
	21 06	Pluto 0°7 N. of Moon	Occn.
	21 19	Mercury greatest elong. W. (27°)	
	25 01	Venus 2° N. of Moon	
	25 04	Saturn 2° S. of Moon	
	25 10	Neptune 1°9 S. of Moon	
	26 01	Mercury 4° S. of Moon	
	27 16	Moon at perigee	
	27 17	Venus greatest illuminated extent	
	27 20	NEW MOON	
	29 02	Uranus 5° S. of Moon	
	29 02	Venus 4° N. of Saturn	
	30 18	Jupiter 5° S. of Moon	
May	2 06	Vesta at opposition	
	3 23	Mars 2° S. of Moon	
	4 03	Venus 2° N. of Neptune	
	4 14	FIRST QUARTER	

CONFIGURATIONS OF SUN, MOON AND PLANETS

	d h		
May	6 06	Pluto stationary	
	10 08	Spica 0°.4 N. of Moon	Occn.
	11 01	Moon at apogee	
	12 17	FULL MOON	
	14 05	Antares 0°.3 N. of Moon	Occn.
	14 18	Juno at opposition	
	18 00	Uranus in conjunction with Sun	
	18 12	Pluto 0°.4 N. of Moon	Occn.
	20 12	LAST QUARTER	
	22 18	Saturn 3° S. of Moon	
	22 21	Neptune 2° S. of Moon	
	24 00	Venus 4° S. of Moon	
	26 02	Moon at perigee	
	27 03	NEW MOON	
	28 13	Jupiter 5° S. of Moon	
	30 04	Mercury in superior conjunction	
June	1 04	Venus greatest elong. W. (46°)	
	1 10	Mars 1°.4 S. of Moon	
	3 04	FIRST QUARTER	
	3 21	Pallas stationary	
	6 15	Spica 0°.5 N. of Moon	Occn.
	7 11	Moon at apogee	
	8 20	Mercury 2° N. of Jupiter	
	10 11	Antares 0°.3 N. of Moon	Occn.
	11 08	FULL MOON	
	14 17	Pluto 0°.1 N. of Moon	Occn.
	17 04	Mars 0°.8 N. of *Regulus*	
	18 19	LAST QUARTER	
	18 19	Vesta stationary	
	19 04	Neptune 2° S. of Moon	
	19 04	Saturn 3° S. of Moon	
	21 03	Solstice	
	22 09	Venus 7° S. of Moon	
	22 20	Mercury 5° S. of *Pollux*	
	23 04	Uranus 5° S. of Moon	
	23 05	Moon at perigee	
	24 15	Jupiter in conjunction with Sun	
	25 11	NEW MOON	
	27 06	Mercury 3° S. of Moon	
	29 08	Saturn 1°.0 S. of Neptune	
	30 01	Mars 0°.2 S. of Moon	Occn.
July	2 20	FIRST QUARTER	
	3 20	Earth at aphelion	
	3 22	Spica 0°.8 N. of Moon	Occn.
	4 01	Venus 2° S. of Uranus	
	4 05	Mercury greatest elong. E. (26°)	
	5 02	Moon at apogee	
	5 15	Neptune stationary	
	7 18	Antares 0°.4 N. of Moon	Occn.
	10 21	FULL MOON	

	d h		
July	11 23	Pluto 0°.02 S. of Moon	Occn.
	14 04	Venus 3° N. of *Aldebaran*	
	14 08	Saturn stationary	
	14 10	Juno stationary	
	16 10	Neptune 3° S. of Moon	
	16 11	Saturn 4° S. of Moon	
	17 07	Mercury stationary	
	18 01	LAST QUARTER	
	20 13	Uranus 5° S. of Moon	
	20 14	Moon at perigee	
	21 19	Venus 7° S. of Moon	
	23 04	Jupiter 5° S. of Moon	
	24 19	NEW MOON	
	25 07	Pluto at opposition	
	26 20	Regulus 1°.3 S. of Moon	Occn.
	28 20	Mars 1°.3 N. of Moon	Occn.
	31 06	Spica 1°.0 N. of Moon	Occn.
Aug.	1 00	Mercury in inferior conjunction	
	1 13	FIRST QUARTER	
	1 21	Moon at apogee	
	4 02	Antares 0°.6 N. of Moon	Occn.
	6 10	Saturn 1°.1 S. of Neptune	
	7 21	Pallas at opposition	
	8 05	Pluto 0°.009 S. of Moon	Occn.
	9 08	FULL MOON	
	10 18	Mercury stationary	
	12 08	Venus 0°.9 S. of Jupiter	
	12 15	Saturn 4° S. of Moon	
	12 16	Neptune 3° S. of Moon	
	14 18	Moon at perigee	
	16 01	Ceres stationary	
	16 05	LAST QUARTER	
	16 20	Uranus 5° S. of Moon	
	19 10	Mercury greatest elong. W. (19°)	
	19 21	Jupiter 5° S. of Moon	
	20 11	Venus 5° S. of Moon	
	21 09	Venus 7° S. of *Pollux*	
	21 16	Mercury 4° S. of Moon	
	23 06	NEW MOON	
	26 17	Mars 3° N. of Moon	
	27 15	Spica 1°.2 N. of Moon	Occn.
	29 16	Moon at apogee	
	31 06	FIRST QUARTER	
	31 11	Antares 0°.7 N. of Moon	Occn.
Sept.	2 10	Mercury 1°.2 N. of *Regulus*	
	4 14	Pluto 0°.06 N. of Moon	Occn.
	6 05	Uranus stationary	
	7 18	FULL MOON	Eclipse
	8 20	Saturn 4° S. of Moon	
	8 22	Neptune 3° S. of Moon	
	10 12	Moon at perigee	

CONFIGURATIONS OF SUN, MOON AND PLANETS

	d h		
Sept.	12 08	Mars 2° N. of *Spica*	
	13 02	Uranus 5° S. of Moon	
	13 11	Mercury in superior conjunction	
	14 11	LAST QUARTER	
	16 11	Jupiter 5° S. of Moon	
	19 12	Regulus 1°.3 S. of Moon	Occn.
	19 12	Venus 0°.8 S. of Moon	Occn.
	19 13	Venus 0°.5 N. of *Regulus*	
	21 06	Saturn at opposition	
	21 20	NEW MOON	Eclipse
	22 18	Equinox	
	23 13	Neptune at opposition	
	23 22	Spica 1°.1 N. of Moon	Occn.
	24 15	Mars 4° N. of Moon	
	25 11	Pallas stationary	
	26 10	Moon at apogee	
	27 18	Antares 0°.6 N. of Moon	Occn.
	30 00	FIRST QUARTER	
Oct.	1 22	Pluto 0°.05 N. of Moon	Occn.
	2 11	Mercury 1°.9 N. of *Spica*	
	2 13	Ceres at opposition	
	6 03	Saturn 4° S. of Moon	
	6 07	Neptune 3° S. of Moon	
	7 04	FULL MOON	
	8 13	Moon at perigee	
	10 09	Uranus 5° S. of Moon	
	13 18	LAST QUARTER	
	13 22	Jupiter 4° S. of Moon	
	14 08	Pluto stationary	
	16 18	Regulus 1°.2 S. of Moon	Occn.
	19 22	Venus 4° N. of Moon	
	21 06	Mercury 2° S. of Mars	
	21 12	NEW MOON	
	23 13	Mars 5° N. of Moon	
	23 16	Mercury 2° N. of Moon	
	24 00	Moon at apogee	
	25 01	Antares 0°.5 N. of Moon	Occn.
	27 15	Jupiter 7° S. of *Pollux*	
	29 07	Pluto 0°.1 S. of Moon	Occn.
	29 16	FIRST QUARTER	
	29 22	Mercury greatest elong. E. (24°)	
Nov.	1 04	Venus 4° N. of *Spica*	
	2 11	Saturn 4° S. of Moon	
	2 17	Neptune 3° S. of Moon	
Nov.	5 13	FULL MOON	
	5 22	Moon at perigee	
	6 17	Uranus 5° S. of Moon	
	9 23	Mercury stationary	
	10 08	Jupiter 4° S. of Moon	
	11 20	Jupiter stationary	
	12 05	LAST QUARTER	
	12 19	Mercury 1°.3 S. of Mars	
	13 00	Regulus 1°.0 S. of Moon	Occn.
	17 11	Spica 1°.2 N. of Moon	Occn.
	19 09	Venus 6° N. of Moon	
	20 03	Moon at apogee	
	20 07	NEW MOON	
	20 09	Mercury in inferior conjunction	
	21 12	Uranus at opposition	
	25 05	Mercury 1°.1 N. of Venus	
	25 14	Pluto 0°.4 S. of Moon	Occn.
	26 19	Jupiter 7° S. of *Pollux*	
	27 23	Ceres stationary	
	28 07	FIRST QUARTER	
	29 01	Saturn stationary	
	29 15	Mercury stationary	
	29 19	Saturn 4° S. of Moon	
	30 02	Neptune 3° S. of Moon	
Dec.	4 03	Uranus 5° S. of Moon	
	4 11	Moon at perigee	
	4 23	FULL MOON	
	7 16	Jupiter 4° S. of Moon	
	7 21	Mercury greatest elong. W. (21°)	
	10 07	Regulus 0°.7 S. of Moon	Occn.
	11 00	Neptune stationary	
	11 21	LAST QUARTER	
	17 06	Juno in conjunction with Sun	
	17 06	Moon at apogee	
	18 12	Mercury 6° N. of Moon	
	18 13	Antares 0°.4 N. of Moon	Occn.
	18 21	Mercury 6° N. of *Antares*	
	20 02	NEW MOON	
	21 15	Solstice	
	22 21	Pluto 0°.6 S. of Moon	Occn.
	27 04	Saturn 4° S. of Moon	
	27 09	Neptune 3° S. of Moon	
	27 19	FIRST QUARTER	
	31 12	Uranus 5° S. of Moon	

Arrangement and basis of the tabulations

The tabulations of risings, settings and twilights on pages A14–A77 refer to the instants when the true geocentric zenith distance of the central point of the disk of the Sun or Moon takes the value indicated in the following table. The tabular times are in universal time (UT) for selected latitudes on the meridian of Greenwich; the times for other latitudes and longitudes may be obtained by interpolation as described below and as exemplified on page A13.

	Phenomena	*Zenith distance*	*Pages*
SUN (interval 4 days):	sunrise and sunset	$90^\circ\ 50'$	A14–A21
	civil twilight	96°	A22–A29
	nautical twilight	102°	A30–A37
	astronomical twilight	108°	A38–A45
MOON (interval 1 day): (s = semidiameter, π =horizontal parallax)	moonrise and moonset	$90^\circ\ 34' + s - \pi$	A46–A77

The zenith distance at the times for rising and setting is such that under normal conditions the upper limb of the Sun and Moon appears to be on the horizon of an observer at sea-level. The parallax of the Sun is ignored. The observed time may differ from the tabular time because of a variation of the atmospheric refraction from the adopted value (34′) and because of a difference in height of the observer and the actual horizon.

Use of tabulations

The following procedure may be used to obtain times of the phenomena for a non-tabular place and date.

Step 1: Interpolate linearly for latitude. The differences between adjacent values are usually small and so the required interpolates can often be obtained by inspection.

Step 2: Interpolate linearly for date and longitude in order to obtain the local mean times of the phenomena at the longitude concerned. For the Sun the variations with longitude of the local mean times of the phenomena are small, but to obtain better precision the interpolation factor for date should be increased by

$$\text{west longitude in degrees } /1440$$

since the interval of tabulation is 4 days. For the Moon, the interpolating factor to be used is simply

$$\text{west longitude in degrees } /360$$

since the interval of tabulation is 1 day; backward interpolation should be carried out for east longitudes.

Step 3: Convert the times so obtained (which are on the scale of local mean time for the local meridian) to universal time (UT) or to the appropriate clock time, which may differ from the time of the nearest standard meridian according to the customs of the country concerned. The UT of the phenomenon is obtained from the local mean time by applying the longitude expressed in time measure (1 hour for each 15° of longitude), adding for west longitudes and subtracting for east longitudes. The times so obtained may require adjustment by 24^h; if so, the corresponding date must be changed accordingly.

Approximate formulae for direct calculation

The approximate UT of rising or setting of a body with right ascension α and declination δ at latitude ϕ and *east* longitude λ may be calculated from

$$\text{UT} = 0{\cdot}997\,27\,\{\alpha - \lambda \pm \cos^{-1}(-\tan\phi\tan\delta) - (\text{GMST at } 0^h \text{ UT})\}$$

where each term is expressed in time measure and the GMST at 0^h UT is given in the tabulations on pages B13–B20. The negative sign corresponds to rising and the positive sign to setting. The formula ignores refraction, semi-diameter and any changes in α and δ during the day. If $\tan\phi\tan\delta$ is numerically greater than 1, there is no phenomenon.

Examples

The following examples of the calculations of the times of rising and setting phenomena use the procedure described on page A12.

1. Find the times of sunrise and sunset for Paris on 2025 July 18. Paris is at latitude N 48° 52′ (= +48°.87), longitude E 2° 20′ (= E 2°.33 = E 0^h 09^m), and in the summer the clocks are kept two hours in advance of UT. The relevant portions of the tabulation on page A19 and the results of the interpolation for latitude are as follows, where the interpolation factor is (48·87 – 48)/2 = 0·43:

	Sunrise			Sunset		
	+48°	+50°	+48°.87	+48°	+50°	+48°.87
	h m	h m	h m	h m	h m	h m
July 17	04 18	04 10	04 15	19 53	20 02	19 57
July 21	04 23	04 15	04 20	19 49	19 57	19 52

The interpolation factor for date and longitude is (18 – 17)/4 – 2·33/1440 = 0·25

	Sunrise	Sunset
	d h m	d h m
Interpolate to obtain local mean time:	18 04 16	18 19 56
Subtract 0^h 09^m to obtain universal time:	18 04 07	18 19 47
Add 2^h to obtain clock time:	18 06 07	18 21 47

2. Find the times of beginning and end of astronomical twilight for Canberra, Australia on 2025 November 4. Canberra is at latitude S 35° 18′ (= –35°.30), longitude E 149° 08′(= E 149°.13 = E 9^h 57^m), and in the summer the clocks are kept eleven hours in advance of UT. The relevant portions of the tabulation on page A44 and the results of the interpolation for latitude are as follows, where the interpolation factor is (–35·30 – (–40))/5 = 0·94:

	Astronomical Twilight					
	beginning			end		
	–40°	–35°	–35°.30	–40°	–35°	–35°.30
	h m	h m	h m	h m	h m	h m
Nov. 2	03 05	03 23	03 22	20 24	20 05	20 06
Nov. 6	02 58	03 18	03 17	20 30	20 10	20 11

The interpolation factor for date and longitude is (4 – 2)/4 – 149·13/1440 = 0·40

	Astronomical Twilight	
	beginning	end
	d h m	d h m
Interpolation to obtain local mean time:	4 03 20	4 20 08
Subtract 9^h 57^m to obtain universal time:	3 17 23	4 10 11
Add 11^h to obtain clock time:	4 04 23	4 21 11

3. Find the times of moonrise and moonset for Washington, D.C. on 2025 January 22. Washington is at latitude N 38° 55′ (= +38°.92), longitude W 77° 00′ (= W 77°.00 = W 5^h 08^m), and in the winter the clocks are kept five hours behind UT. The relevant portions of the tabulation on page A46 and the results of the interpolation for latitude are as follows, where the interpolation factor is (38·92 – 35)/5 = 0·78:

	Moonrise			Moonset		
	+35°	+40°	+38°.92	+35°	+40°	+38°.92
	h m	h m	h m	h m	h m	h m
Jan. 22	00 43	00 52	00 50	11 23	11 12	11 14
Jan. 23	01 42	01 55	01 52	11 53	11 39	11 42

The interpolation factor for longitude is 77·0/360 = 0·21

	Moonrise	Moonset
	d h m	d h m
Interpolate to obtain local mean time:	22 01 03	22 11 20
Add 5^h 08^m to obtain universal time:	22 06 11	22 16 28
Subtract 5^h to obtain clock time:	22 01 11	22 11 28

UNIVERSAL TIME FOR MERIDIAN OF GREENWICH

SUNRISE

Lat.	−55°	−50°	−45°	−40°	−35°	−30°	−20°	−10°	0°	+10°	+20°	+30°	+35°	+40°
	h m	h m	h m	h m	h m	h m	h m	h m	h m	h m	h m	h m	h m	h m
Jan. −2	3 23	3 53	4 15	4 33	4 48	5 00	5 22	5 41	5 58	6 16	6 34	6 55	7 07	7 21
2	3 28	3 57	4 18	4 36	4 51	5 03	5 25	5 43	6 00	6 17	6 36	6 56	7 08	7 22
6	3 33	4 01	4 22	4 40	4 54	5 06	5 27	5 45	6 02	6 19	6 37	6 57	7 09	7 22
10	3 39	4 06	4 27	4 44	4 57	5 09	5 30	5 48	6 04	6 20	6 37	6 57	7 08	7 21
14	3 46	4 12	4 32	4 48	5 01	5 13	5 33	5 50	6 05	6 21	6 38	6 57	7 08	7 20
18	3 54	4 18	4 37	4 52	5 05	5 16	5 35	5 52	6 07	6 22	6 38	6 56	7 07	7 19
22	4 02	4 25	4 43	4 57	5 09	5 20	5 38	5 54	6 08	6 22	6 38	6 55	7 05	7 16
26	4 10	4 32	4 48	5 02	5 13	5 23	5 41	5 55	6 09	6 23	6 37	6 53	7 03	7 13
30	4 19	4 39	4 54	5 07	5 18	5 27	5 43	5 57	6 10	6 23	6 36	6 51	7 00	7 10
Feb. 3	4 27	4 46	5 00	5 12	5 22	5 30	5 45	5 58	6 10	6 22	6 35	6 49	6 57	7 06
7	4 36	4 53	5 06	5 17	5 26	5 34	5 48	6 00	6 11	6 22	6 33	6 46	6 54	7 02
11	4 45	5 00	5 12	5 22	5 30	5 37	5 50	6 01	6 11	6 21	6 31	6 43	6 50	6 58
15	4 53	5 07	5 17	5 26	5 34	5 40	5 52	6 02	6 11	6 20	6 29	6 40	6 46	6 53
19	5 02	5 14	5 23	5 31	5 38	5 44	5 54	6 02	6 10	6 18	6 27	6 36	6 41	6 47
23	5 10	5 21	5 29	5 36	5 42	5 47	5 55	6 03	6 10	6 17	6 24	6 32	6 37	6 42
27	5 19	5 28	5 35	5 40	5 45	5 50	5 57	6 03	6 09	6 15	6 21	6 28	6 32	6 36
Mar. 3	5 27	5 34	5 40	5 45	5 49	5 52	5 58	6 04	6 09	6 13	6 18	6 24	6 27	6 30
7	5 35	5 41	5 45	5 49	5 52	5 55	6 00	6 04	6 08	6 11	6 15	6 19	6 21	6 24
11	5 43	5 48	5 51	5 53	5 56	5 58	6 01	6 04	6 07	6 09	6 12	6 14	6 16	6 18
15	5 51	5 54	5 56	5 58	5 59	6 00	6 02	6 04	6 06	6 07	6 08	6 10	6 10	6 11
19	5 59	6 00	6 01	6 02	6 02	6 03	6 04	6 04	6 04	6 05	6 05	6 05	6 05	6 05
23	6 07	6 07	6 06	6 06	6 06	6 05	6 05	6 04	6 03	6 02	6 01	6 00	5 59	5 58
27	6 15	6 13	6 11	6 10	6 09	6 08	6 06	6 04	6 02	6 00	5 58	5 55	5 54	5 52
31	6 23	6 19	6 17	6 14	6 12	6 10	6 07	6 04	6 01	5 58	5 54	5 50	5 48	5 45
Apr. 4	6 30	6 26	6 22	6 18	6 15	6 13	6 08	6 04	6 00	5 55	5 51	5 46	5 43	5 39

SUNSET

Lat.	−55°	−50°	−45°	−40°	−35°	−30°	−20°	−10°	0°	+10°	+20°	+30°	+35°	+40°
	h m	h m	h m	h m	h m	h m	h m	h m	h m	h m	h m	h m	h m	h m
Jan. −2	20 41	20 12	19 49	19 32	19 17	19 04	18 42	18 23	18 06	17 49	17 30	17 09	16 57	16 43
2	20 40	20 11	19 50	19 32	19 18	19 05	18 43	18 25	18 08	17 51	17 33	17 12	17 00	16 46
6	20 38	20 10	19 49	19 32	19 18	19 05	18 44	18 26	18 10	17 53	17 35	17 15	17 04	16 50
10	20 35	20 08	19 48	19 31	19 17	19 05	18 45	18 28	18 11	17 55	17 38	17 18	17 07	16 54
14	20 31	20 05	19 46	19 30	19 17	19 05	18 45	18 29	18 13	17 57	17 41	17 22	17 11	16 58
18	20 26	20 02	19 43	19 28	19 15	19 04	18 45	18 29	18 14	17 59	17 43	17 25	17 15	17 03
22	20 20	19 58	19 40	19 26	19 14	19 03	18 45	18 30	18 15	18 01	17 46	17 29	17 19	17 07
26	20 14	19 53	19 36	19 23	19 11	19 01	18 44	18 30	18 16	18 03	17 48	17 32	17 23	17 12
30	20 07	19 47	19 32	19 19	19 09	18 59	18 43	18 30	18 17	18 04	17 51	17 36	17 27	17 17
Feb. 3	19 59	19 41	19 27	19 15	19 05	18 57	18 42	18 29	18 17	18 06	17 53	17 39	17 31	17 22
7	19 51	19 35	19 22	19 11	19 02	18 54	18 40	18 29	18 18	18 07	17 55	17 42	17 35	17 27
11	19 42	19 28	19 16	19 06	18 58	18 51	18 38	18 28	18 18	18 08	17 57	17 46	17 39	17 31
15	19 33	19 20	19 10	19 01	18 54	18 47	18 36	18 26	18 17	18 09	17 59	17 49	17 43	17 36
19	19 24	19 13	19 03	18 56	18 49	18 43	18 34	18 25	18 17	18 09	18 01	17 52	17 47	17 41
23	19 15	19 05	18 57	18 50	18 44	18 39	18 31	18 23	18 17	18 10	18 03	17 55	17 50	17 45
27	19 05	18 57	18 50	18 44	18 39	18 35	18 28	18 22	18 16	18 10	18 04	17 58	17 54	17 50
Mar. 3	18 55	18 48	18 43	18 38	18 34	18 31	18 25	18 20	18 15	18 11	18 06	18 01	17 58	17 54
7	18 45	18 40	18 36	18 32	18 29	18 26	18 22	18 18	18 14	18 11	18 07	18 03	18 01	17 58
11	18 35	18 31	18 28	18 26	18 23	18 22	18 18	18 16	18 13	18 11	18 08	18 06	18 04	18 03
15	18 25	18 23	18 21	18 19	18 18	18 17	18 15	18 13	18 12	18 11	18 10	18 08	18 08	18 07
19	18 15	18 14	18 13	18 13	18 12	18 12	18 11	18 11	18 11	18 11	18 11	18 11	18 11	18 11
23	18 05	18 05	18 06	18 06	18 07	18 07	18 08	18 09	18 10	18 11	18 12	18 13	18 14	18 15
27	17 54	17 57	17 58	18 00	18 01	18 02	18 05	18 07	18 09	18 11	18 13	18 16	18 17	18 19
31	17 44	17 48	17 51	17 53	17 56	17 58	18 01	18 04	18 07	18 11	18 14	18 18	18 21	18 23
Apr. 4	17 34	17 39	17 44	17 47	17 50	17 53	17 58	18 02	18 06	18 10	18 15	18 21	18 24	18 27

UNIVERSAL TIME FOR MERIDIAN OF GREENWICH

SUNRISE

Lat.	+40°	+42°	+44°	+46°	+48°	+50°	+52°	+54°	+56°	+58°	+60°	+62°	+64°	+66°
	h m	h m	h m	h m	h m	h m	h m	h m	h m	h m	h m	h m	h m	h m
Jan. −2	7 21	7 28	7 34	7 42	7 50	7 58	8 08	8 19	8 32	8 46	9 03	9 24	9 52	10 32
2	7 22	7 28	7 35	7 42	7 50	7 58	8 08	8 19	8 31	8 45	9 02	9 22	9 48	10 25
6	7 22	7 28	7 35	7 41	7 49	7 57	8 07	8 17	8 29	8 43	8 59	9 18	9 43	10 17
10	7 21	7 27	7 34	7 40	7 48	7 56	8 05	8 15	8 26	8 39	8 54	9 13	9 36	10 07
14	7 20	7 26	7 32	7 38	7 45	7 53	8 02	8 11	8 22	8 34	8 49	9 06	9 27	9 55
18	7 19	7 24	7 30	7 36	7 43	7 50	7 58	8 07	8 17	8 29	8 42	8 58	9 18	9 43
22	7 16	7 21	7 27	7 33	7 39	7 46	7 54	8 02	8 12	8 22	8 35	8 50	9 07	9 30
26	7 13	7 18	7 23	7 29	7 35	7 41	7 48	7 56	8 05	8 15	8 27	8 40	8 56	9 16
30	7 10	7 15	7 19	7 24	7 30	7 36	7 43	7 50	7 58	8 07	8 18	8 30	8 45	9 02
Feb. 3	7 06	7 11	7 15	7 20	7 25	7 30	7 36	7 43	7 51	7 59	8 08	8 20	8 33	8 48
7	7 02	7 06	7 10	7 14	7 19	7 24	7 30	7 36	7 42	7 50	7 59	8 08	8 20	8 34
11	6 58	7 01	7 05	7 09	7 13	7 17	7 22	7 28	7 34	7 41	7 48	7 57	8 07	8 19
15	6 53	6 56	6 59	7 02	7 06	7 10	7 15	7 19	7 25	7 31	7 37	7 45	7 54	8 04
19	6 47	6 50	6 53	6 56	6 59	7 03	7 07	7 11	7 15	7 21	7 26	7 33	7 41	7 50
23	6 42	6 44	6 47	6 49	6 52	6 55	6 58	7 02	7 06	7 10	7 15	7 21	7 27	7 35
27	6 36	6 38	6 40	6 42	6 45	6 47	6 50	6 53	6 56	7 00	7 04	7 08	7 14	7 20
Mar. 3	6 30	6 32	6 33	6 35	6 37	6 39	6 41	6 43	6 46	6 49	6 52	6 56	7 00	7 05
7	6 24	6 25	6 26	6 28	6 29	6 30	6 32	6 34	6 36	6 38	6 40	6 43	6 46	6 49
11	6 18	6 18	6 19	6 20	6 21	6 22	6 23	6 24	6 25	6 27	6 28	6 30	6 32	6 34
15	6 11	6 12	6 12	6 12	6 13	6 13	6 14	6 14	6 15	6 16	6 16	6 17	6 18	6 19
19	6 05	6 05	6 05	6 05	6 05	6 05	6 05	6 05	6 04	6 04	6 04	6 04	6 04	6 04
23	5 58	5 58	5 58	5 57	5 57	5 56	5 55	5 55	5 54	5 53	5 52	5 51	5 50	5 48
27	5 52	5 51	5 50	5 49	5 48	5 47	5 46	5 45	5 43	5 42	5 40	5 38	5 35	5 33
31	5 45	5 44	5 43	5 42	5 40	5 39	5 37	5 35	5 33	5 30	5 28	5 25	5 21	5 17
Apr. 4	5 39	5 37	5 36	5 34	5 32	5 30	5 28	5 25	5 22	5 19	5 16	5 12	5 07	5 02

SUNSET

Lat.	+40°	+42°	+44°	+46°	+48°	+50°	+52°	+54°	+56°	+58°	+60°	+62°	+64°	+66°
	h m	h m	h m	h m	h m	h m	h m	h m	h m	h m	h m	h m	h m	h m
Jan. −2	16 43	16 37	16 30	16 23	16 15	16 06	15 56	15 45	15 33	15 19	15 01	14 40	14 13	13 33
2	16 46	16 40	16 34	16 27	16 19	16 10	16 01	15 50	15 38	15 24	15 07	14 47	14 21	13 43
6	16 50	16 44	16 38	16 31	16 23	16 15	16 05	15 55	15 43	15 30	15 14	14 54	14 30	13 56
10	16 54	16 48	16 42	16 35	16 28	16 20	16 11	16 01	15 50	15 37	15 21	15 03	14 40	14 09
14	16 58	16 53	16 47	16 40	16 33	16 25	16 17	16 07	15 57	15 44	15 30	15 13	14 52	14 24
18	17 03	16 57	16 52	16 45	16 39	16 31	16 23	16 14	16 04	15 53	15 39	15 23	15 04	14 39
22	17 07	17 02	16 57	16 51	16 45	16 38	16 30	16 22	16 12	16 01	15 49	15 34	15 17	14 54
26	17 12	17 07	17 02	16 57	16 51	16 44	16 37	16 29	16 21	16 11	15 59	15 46	15 30	15 10
30	17 17	17 12	17 08	17 03	16 57	16 51	16 45	16 37	16 29	16 20	16 09	15 57	15 43	15 25
Feb. 3	17 22	17 18	17 13	17 09	17 03	16 58	16 52	16 45	16 38	16 30	16 20	16 09	15 56	15 40
7	17 27	17 23	17 19	17 15	17 10	17 05	16 59	16 53	16 47	16 39	16 31	16 21	16 09	15 56
11	17 31	17 28	17 24	17 20	17 16	17 12	17 07	17 01	16 55	16 49	16 41	16 32	16 22	16 10
15	17 36	17 33	17 30	17 26	17 23	17 19	17 14	17 10	17 04	16 58	16 52	16 44	16 35	16 25
19	17 41	17 38	17 35	17 32	17 29	17 26	17 22	17 18	17 13	17 08	17 02	16 56	16 48	16 39
23	17 45	17 43	17 41	17 38	17 35	17 32	17 29	17 26	17 22	17 17	17 12	17 07	17 01	16 53
27	17 50	17 48	17 46	17 44	17 42	17 39	17 36	17 33	17 30	17 27	17 23	17 18	17 13	17 07
Mar. 3	17 54	17 53	17 51	17 49	17 48	17 46	17 44	17 41	17 39	17 36	17 33	17 29	17 25	17 21
7	17 58	17 57	17 56	17 55	17 54	17 52	17 51	17 49	17 47	17 45	17 43	17 40	17 37	17 34
11	18 03	18 02	18 01	18 01	18 00	17 59	17 58	17 57	17 56	17 54	17 53	17 51	17 49	17 47
15	18 07	18 07	18 06	18 06	18 06	18 05	18 05	18 04	18 04	18 03	18 03	18 02	18 01	18 01
19	18 11	18 11	18 11	18 11	18 11	18 12	18 12	18 12	18 12	18 12	18 13	18 13	18 13	18 14
23	18 15	18 16	18 16	18 17	18 17	18 18	18 19	18 19	18 20	18 21	18 22	18 24	18 25	18 27
27	18 19	18 20	18 21	18 22	18 23	18 24	18 26	18 27	18 28	18 30	18 32	18 34	18 37	18 40
31	18 23	18 25	18 26	18 27	18 29	18 31	18 32	18 34	18 37	18 39	18 42	18 45	18 49	18 53
Apr. 4	18 27	18 29	18 31	18 33	18 35	18 37	18 39	18 42	18 45	18 48	18 52	18 56	19 01	19 06

UNIVERSAL TIME FOR MERIDIAN OF GREENWICH

SUNRISE

Lat.	−55°	−50°	−45°	−40°	−35°	−30°	−20°	−10°	0°	+10°	+20°	+30°	+35°	+40°
	h m	h m	h m	h m	h m	h m	h m	h m	h m	h m	h m	h m	h m	h m
Mar. 31	6 23	6 19	6 17	6 14	6 12	6 10	6 07	6 04	6 01	5 58	5 54	5 50	5 48	5 45
Apr. 4	6 30	6 26	6 22	6 18	6 15	6 13	6 08	6 04	6 00	5 55	5 51	5 46	5 43	5 39
8	6 38	6 32	6 27	6 22	6 18	6 15	6 09	6 04	5 58	5 53	5 48	5 41	5 37	5 33
12	6 46	6 38	6 32	6 26	6 21	6 17	6 10	6 04	5 57	5 51	5 44	5 36	5 32	5 27
16	6 53	6 44	6 37	6 30	6 25	6 20	6 11	6 04	5 56	5 49	5 41	5 32	5 27	5 21
20	7 01	6 50	6 41	6 34	6 28	6 22	6 12	6 04	5 55	5 47	5 38	5 28	5 22	5 15
24	7 09	6 56	6 46	6 38	6 31	6 25	6 14	6 04	5 55	5 45	5 35	5 24	5 17	5 09
28	7 16	7 02	6 51	6 42	6 34	6 27	6 15	6 04	5 54	5 44	5 33	5 20	5 12	5 04
May 2	7 24	7 08	6 56	6 46	6 37	6 30	6 16	6 05	5 54	5 42	5 30	5 16	5 08	4 59
6	7 31	7 14	7 01	6 50	6 41	6 32	6 18	6 05	5 53	5 41	5 28	5 13	5 04	4 54
10	7 38	7 20	7 06	6 54	6 44	6 35	6 19	6 06	5 53	5 40	5 26	5 10	5 00	4 50
14	7 45	7 26	7 10	6 58	6 47	6 37	6 21	6 06	5 53	5 39	5 24	5 07	4 57	4 46
18	7 52	7 31	7 15	7 01	6 50	6 40	6 22	6 07	5 53	5 38	5 23	5 05	4 54	4 42
22	7 58	7 36	7 19	7 05	6 53	6 42	6 24	6 08	5 53	5 38	5 22	5 03	4 52	4 39
26	8 04	7 41	7 23	7 08	6 55	6 45	6 26	6 09	5 53	5 38	5 21	5 01	4 50	4 36
30	8 10	7 45	7 26	7 11	6 58	6 47	6 27	6 10	5 54	5 38	5 20	5 00	4 48	4 34
June 3	8 14	7 49	7 30	7 14	7 01	6 49	6 29	6 11	5 55	5 38	5 20	4 59	4 47	4 32
7	8 19	7 53	7 33	7 16	7 03	6 51	6 30	6 12	5 55	5 38	5 20	4 58	4 46	4 31
11	8 22	7 55	7 35	7 19	7 05	6 52	6 32	6 13	5 56	5 39	5 20	4 58	4 45	4 31
15	8 25	7 58	7 37	7 20	7 06	6 54	6 33	6 14	5 57	5 39	5 20	4 59	4 46	4 31
19	8 26	7 59	7 38	7 22	7 07	6 55	6 34	6 15	5 58	5 40	5 21	4 59	4 46	4 31
23	8 27	8 00	7 39	7 22	7 08	6 56	6 35	6 16	5 59	5 41	5 22	5 00	4 47	4 32
27	8 27	8 00	7 40	7 23	7 09	6 56	6 35	6 17	5 59	5 42	5 23	5 01	4 48	4 33
July 1	8 26	8 00	7 39	7 23	7 09	6 57	6 36	6 17	6 00	5 43	5 24	5 03	4 50	4 35
5	8 24	7 58	7 38	7 22	7 08	6 56	6 36	6 18	6 01	5 44	5 26	5 04	4 52	4 37

SUNSET

Lat.	−55°	−50°	−45°	−40°	−35°	−30°	−20°	−10°	0°	+10°	+20°	+30°	+35°	+40°
	h m	h m	h m	h m	h m	h m	h m	h m	h m	h m	h m	h m	h m	h m
Mar. 31	17 44	17 48	17 51	17 53	17 56	17 58	18 01	18 04	18 07	18 11	18 14	18 18	18 21	18 23
Apr. 4	17 34	17 39	17 44	17 47	17 50	17 53	17 58	18 02	18 06	18 10	18 15	18 21	18 24	18 27
8	17 24	17 31	17 36	17 41	17 45	17 48	17 54	18 00	18 05	18 10	18 16	18 23	18 27	18 31
12	17 15	17 23	17 29	17 35	17 39	17 44	17 51	17 58	18 04	18 10	18 17	18 25	18 30	18 36
16	17 05	17 15	17 22	17 29	17 34	17 39	17 48	17 56	18 03	18 11	18 19	18 28	18 33	18 40
20	16 56	17 07	17 16	17 23	17 29	17 35	17 45	17 54	18 02	18 11	18 20	18 30	18 37	18 44
24	16 47	16 59	17 09	17 17	17 25	17 31	17 42	17 52	18 01	18 11	18 21	18 33	18 40	18 48
28	16 38	16 52	17 03	17 12	17 20	17 27	17 40	17 51	18 01	18 11	18 23	18 36	18 43	18 52
May 2	16 30	16 45	16 57	17 07	17 16	17 24	17 37	17 49	18 00	18 12	18 24	18 38	18 46	18 56
6	16 22	16 38	16 52	17 03	17 12	17 21	17 35	17 48	18 00	18 12	18 25	18 41	18 50	19 00
10	16 14	16 32	16 47	16 59	17 09	17 18	17 33	17 47	18 00	18 13	18 27	18 43	18 53	19 04
14	16 07	16 27	16 42	16 55	17 06	17 15	17 32	17 46	18 00	18 14	18 29	18 46	18 56	19 08
18	16 01	16 21	16 38	16 51	17 03	17 13	17 30	17 46	18 00	18 15	18 30	18 48	18 59	19 11
22	15 55	16 17	16 34	16 48	17 00	17 11	17 29	17 45	18 00	18 15	18 32	18 51	19 02	19 15
26	15 50	16 13	16 31	16 46	16 58	17 09	17 28	17 45	18 01	18 16	18 34	18 53	19 05	19 18
30	15 45	16 10	16 28	16 44	16 57	17 08	17 28	17 45	18 01	18 18	18 35	18 56	19 08	19 21
June 3	15 42	16 07	16 26	16 42	16 56	17 07	17 28	17 45	18 02	18 19	18 37	18 58	19 10	19 24
7	15 39	16 05	16 25	16 41	16 55	17 07	17 28	17 46	18 03	18 20	18 38	19 00	19 12	19 27
11	15 37	16 04	16 24	16 41	16 55	17 07	17 28	17 46	18 03	18 21	18 39	19 01	19 14	19 29
15	15 36	16 03	16 24	16 41	16 55	17 07	17 28	17 47	18 04	18 22	18 41	19 03	19 16	19 31
19	15 36	16 04	16 24	16 41	16 55	17 08	17 29	17 48	18 05	18 23	18 42	19 04	19 17	19 32
23	15 37	16 05	16 25	16 42	16 56	17 09	17 30	17 49	18 06	18 24	18 43	19 05	19 18	19 33
27	15 39	16 06	16 27	16 44	16 58	17 10	17 31	17 49	18 07	18 24	18 43	19 05	19 18	19 33
July 1	15 42	16 09	16 29	16 45	16 59	17 11	17 32	17 50	18 08	18 25	18 44	19 05	19 18	19 33
5	15 46	16 11	16 31	16 47	17 01	17 13	17 34	17 51	18 08	18 25	18 44	19 05	19 17	19 32

UNIVERSAL TIME FOR MERIDIAN OF GREENWICH

SUNRISE

Lat.	+40°	+42°	+44°	+46°	+48°	+50°	+52°	+54°	+56°	+58°	+60°	+62°	+64°	+66°
	h m	h m	h m	h m	h m	h m	h m	h m	h m	h m	h m	h m	h m	h m
Mar. 31	5 45	5 44	5 43	5 42	5 40	5 39	5 37	5 35	5 33	5 30	5 28	5 25	5 21	5 17
Apr. 4	5 39	5 37	5 36	5 34	5 32	5 30	5 28	5 25	5 22	5 19	5 16	5 12	5 07	5 02
8	5 33	5 31	5 29	5 26	5 24	5 21	5 19	5 15	5 12	5 08	5 04	4 59	4 53	4 46
12	5 27	5 24	5 22	5 19	5 16	5 13	5 10	5 06	5 02	4 57	4 52	4 46	4 39	4 31
16	5 21	5 18	5 15	5 12	5 08	5 05	5 01	4 56	4 52	4 46	4 40	4 33	4 25	4 15
20	5 15	5 12	5 08	5 05	5 01	4 57	4 52	4 47	4 42	4 35	4 28	4 20	4 11	4 00
24	5 09	5 06	5 02	4 58	4 54	4 49	4 44	4 38	4 32	4 25	4 17	4 08	3 57	3 44
28	5 04	5 00	4 56	4 51	4 47	4 42	4 36	4 30	4 23	4 15	4 06	3 55	3 43	3 28
May 2	4 59	4 55	4 50	4 45	4 40	4 34	4 28	4 21	4 13	4 05	3 55	3 43	3 29	3 13
6	4 54	4 49	4 45	4 39	4 34	4 28	4 21	4 13	4 05	3 55	3 44	3 31	3 16	2 57
10	4 50	4 45	4 40	4 34	4 28	4 21	4 14	4 06	3 56	3 46	3 34	3 20	3 03	2 41
14	4 46	4 40	4 35	4 29	4 22	4 15	4 07	3 59	3 49	3 37	3 24	3 09	2 50	2 25
18	4 42	4 37	4 31	4 24	4 17	4 10	4 01	3 52	3 41	3 29	3 15	2 58	2 37	2 09
22	4 39	4 33	4 27	4 20	4 13	4 05	3 56	3 46	3 35	3 22	3 07	2 48	2 25	1 53
26	4 36	4 30	4 24	4 17	4 09	4 01	3 51	3 41	3 29	3 15	2 59	2 39	2 13	1 37
30	4 34	4 28	4 21	4 14	4 06	3 57	3 48	3 37	3 24	3 09	2 52	2 31	2 02	1 20
June 3	4 32	4 26	4 19	4 12	4 03	3 54	3 44	3 33	3 20	3 05	2 46	2 23	1 53	1 02
7	4 31	4 25	4 18	4 10	4 02	3 52	3 42	3 30	3 17	3 01	2 42	2 17	1 44	0 44
11	4 31	4 24	4 17	4 09	4 00	3 51	3 40	3 28	3 14	2 58	2 38	2 13	1 37	0 19
15	4 31	4 24	4 17	4 09	4 00	3 50	3 39	3 27	3 13	2 56	2 36	2 10	1 33	▭
19	4 31	4 24	4 17	4 09	4 00	3 50	3 39	3 27	3 13	2 56	2 36	2 09	1 31	▭
23	4 32	4 25	4 18	4 10	4 01	3 51	3 40	3 28	3 14	2 57	2 36	2 10	1 32	▭
27	4 33	4 26	4 19	4 11	4 02	3 53	3 42	3 30	3 16	2 59	2 39	2 13	1 35	▭
July 1	4 35	4 28	4 21	4 13	4 05	3 55	3 44	3 32	3 19	3 02	2 42	2 17	1 42	0 22
5	4 37	4 31	4 23	4 16	4 07	3 58	3 48	3 36	3 22	3 06	2 47	2 23	1 50	0 48

SUNSET

Lat.	+40°	+42°	+44°	+46°	+48°	+50°	+52°	+54°	+56°	+58°	+60°	+62°	+64°	+66°
	h m	h m	h m	h m	h m	h m	h m	h m	h m	h m	h m	h m	h m	h m
Mar. 31	18 23	18 25	18 26	18 27	18 29	18 31	18 32	18 34	18 37	18 39	18 42	18 45	18 49	18 53
Apr. 4	18 27	18 29	18 31	18 33	18 35	18 37	18 39	18 42	18 45	18 48	18 52	18 56	19 01	19 06
8	18 31	18 34	18 36	18 38	18 40	18 43	18 46	18 49	18 53	18 57	19 01	19 07	19 12	19 19
12	18 36	18 38	18 40	18 43	18 46	18 49	18 53	18 57	19 01	19 06	19 11	19 17	19 25	19 33
16	18 40	18 42	18 45	18 49	18 52	18 56	19 00	19 04	19 09	19 15	19 21	19 28	19 37	19 47
20	18 44	18 47	18 50	18 54	18 58	19 02	19 07	19 12	19 17	19 24	19 31	19 39	19 49	20 00
24	18 48	18 51	18 55	18 59	19 03	19 08	19 13	19 19	19 26	19 33	19 41	19 50	20 01	20 15
28	18 52	18 56	19 00	19 04	19 09	19 14	19 20	19 27	19 34	19 42	19 51	20 02	20 14	20 29
May 2	18 56	19 00	19 05	19 09	19 15	19 21	19 27	19 34	19 42	19 51	20 01	20 13	20 27	20 44
6	19 00	19 04	19 09	19 15	19 20	19 27	19 34	19 41	19 50	20 00	20 11	20 24	20 40	20 59
10	19 04	19 09	19 14	19 20	19 26	19 33	19 40	19 48	19 58	20 08	20 21	20 35	20 53	21 15
14	19 08	19 13	19 18	19 24	19 31	19 38	19 46	19 55	20 05	20 17	20 30	20 46	21 06	21 31
18	19 11	19 17	19 23	19 29	19 36	19 44	19 52	20 02	20 13	20 25	20 39	20 57	21 18	21 47
22	19 15	19 21	19 27	19 34	19 41	19 49	19 58	20 08	20 20	20 33	20 48	21 07	21 31	22 04
26	19 18	19 24	19 31	19 38	19 46	19 54	20 03	20 14	20 26	20 40	20 57	21 17	21 43	22 21
30	19 21	19 28	19 34	19 42	19 50	19 59	20 08	20 19	20 32	20 47	21 04	21 26	21 55	22 39
June 3	19 24	19 31	19 38	19 45	19 53	20 03	20 13	20 24	20 37	20 53	21 11	21 35	22 06	22 58
7	19 27	19 33	19 40	19 48	19 57	20 06	20 16	20 28	20 42	20 58	21 17	21 42	22 15	23 19
11	19 29	19 36	19 43	19 51	19 59	20 09	20 20	20 32	20 46	21 02	21 22	21 47	22 23	23 51
15	19 31	19 37	19 45	19 53	20 01	20 11	20 22	20 34	20 48	21 05	21 25	21 52	22 29	▭
19	19 32	19 39	19 46	19 54	20 03	20 13	20 23	20 36	20 50	21 07	21 27	21 54	22 32	▭
23	19 33	19 39	19 47	19 55	20 04	20 13	20 24	20 36	20 51	21 08	21 28	21 54	22 32	▭
27	19 33	19 40	19 47	19 55	20 04	20 13	20 24	20 36	20 50	21 07	21 27	21 53	22 30	▭
July 1	19 33	19 39	19 47	19 54	20 03	20 12	20 23	20 35	20 49	21 05	21 25	21 50	22 25	23 38
5	19 32	19 39	19 46	19 53	20 02	20 11	20 21	20 33	20 46	21 02	21 21	21 45	22 18	23 16

▭ indicates Sun continuously above horizon.

UNIVERSAL TIME FOR MERIDIAN OF GREENWICH

SUNRISE

Lat.	−55°	−50°	−45°	−40°	−35°	−30°	−20°	−10°	0°	+10°	+20°	+30°	+35°	+40°
	h m	h m	h m	h m	h m	h m	h m	h m	h m	h m	h m	h m	h m	h m
July 1	8 26	8 00	7 39	7 23	7 09	6 57	6 36	6 17	6 00	5 43	5 24	5 03	4 50	4 35
5	8 24	7 58	7 38	7 22	7 08	6 56	6 36	6 18	6 01	5 44	5 26	5 04	4 52	4 37
9	8 21	7 56	7 37	7 21	7 07	6 56	6 36	6 18	6 02	5 45	5 27	5 06	4 54	4 40
13	8 17	7 53	7 34	7 19	7 06	6 55	6 35	6 18	6 02	5 46	5 28	5 08	4 56	4 42
17	8 13	7 50	7 32	7 17	7 04	6 54	6 35	6 18	6 03	5 47	5 30	5 10	4 59	4 45
21	8 07	7 46	7 28	7 14	7 02	6 52	6 34	6 18	6 03	5 48	5 31	5 13	5 02	4 49
25	8 01	7 41	7 25	7 11	7 00	6 50	6 33	6 17	6 03	5 49	5 33	5 15	5 04	4 52
29	7 55	7 35	7 20	7 08	6 57	6 47	6 31	6 17	6 03	5 49	5 34	5 17	5 07	4 56
Aug. 2	7 48	7 30	7 15	7 04	6 53	6 45	6 29	6 16	6 03	5 50	5 36	5 20	5 10	4 59
6	7 40	7 23	7 10	6 59	6 50	6 42	6 27	6 14	6 02	5 50	5 37	5 22	5 13	5 03
10	7 32	7 17	7 05	6 54	6 46	6 38	6 25	6 13	6 02	5 51	5 39	5 25	5 16	5 07
14	7 23	7 10	6 59	6 49	6 41	6 34	6 22	6 11	6 01	5 51	5 40	5 27	5 19	5 11
18	7 14	7 02	6 52	6 44	6 37	6 31	6 19	6 10	6 00	5 51	5 41	5 29	5 22	5 15
22	7 05	6 54	6 46	6 38	6 32	6 26	6 17	6 08	6 00	5 51	5 42	5 32	5 25	5 18
26	6 56	6 46	6 39	6 32	6 27	6 22	6 13	6 06	5 58	5 51	5 43	5 34	5 28	5 22
30	6 46	6 38	6 32	6 26	6 22	6 17	6 10	6 04	5 57	5 51	5 44	5 36	5 31	5 26
Sept. 3	6 36	6 30	6 25	6 20	6 16	6 13	6 07	6 01	5 56	5 51	5 45	5 38	5 34	5 30
7	6 26	6 21	6 17	6 14	6 11	6 08	6 03	5 59	5 55	5 50	5 46	5 40	5 37	5 34
11	6 16	6 13	6 10	6 07	6 05	6 03	6 00	5 56	5 53	5 50	5 47	5 42	5 40	5 37
15	6 06	6 04	6 02	6 01	5 59	5 58	5 56	5 54	5 52	5 50	5 47	5 45	5 43	5 41
19	5 56	5 55	5 55	5 54	5 54	5 53	5 52	5 51	5 50	5 49	5 48	5 47	5 46	5 45
23	5 46	5 46	5 47	5 47	5 48	5 48	5 49	5 49	5 49	5 49	5 49	5 49	5 49	5 49
27	5 35	5 38	5 39	5 41	5 42	5 43	5 45	5 46	5 48	5 49	5 50	5 51	5 52	5 53
Oct. 1	5 25	5 29	5 32	5 34	5 36	5 38	5 41	5 44	5 46	5 49	5 51	5 53	5 55	5 56
5	5 15	5 20	5 24	5 28	5 31	5 33	5 38	5 42	5 45	5 48	5 52	5 56	5 58	6 00

SUNSET

Lat.	−55°	−50°	−45°	−40°	−35°	−30°	−20°	−10°	0°	+10°	+20°	+30°	+35°	+40°
	h m	h m	h m	h m	h m	h m	h m	h m	h m	h m	h m	h m	h m	h m
July 1	15 42	16 09	16 29	16 45	16 59	17 11	17 32	17 50	18 08	18 25	18 44	19 05	19 18	19 33
5	15 46	16 11	16 31	16 47	17 01	17 13	17 34	17 51	18 08	18 25	18 44	19 05	19 17	19 32
9	15 50	16 15	16 34	16 50	17 03	17 15	17 35	17 52	18 09	18 26	18 43	19 04	19 17	19 31
13	15 55	16 19	16 37	16 53	17 06	17 17	17 36	17 53	18 09	18 26	18 43	19 03	19 15	19 29
17	16 00	16 23	16 41	16 56	17 08	17 19	17 38	17 54	18 10	18 25	18 42	19 02	19 13	19 27
21	16 06	16 28	16 45	16 59	17 11	17 21	17 39	17 55	18 10	18 25	18 41	19 00	19 11	19 24
25	16 12	16 33	16 49	17 02	17 14	17 24	17 41	17 56	18 10	18 24	18 40	18 58	19 08	19 20
29	16 19	16 38	16 53	17 06	17 17	17 26	17 42	17 57	18 10	18 24	18 38	18 55	19 05	19 17
Aug. 2	16 26	16 43	16 58	17 09	17 19	17 28	17 44	17 57	18 10	18 23	18 36	18 52	19 02	19 13
6	16 32	16 49	17 02	17 13	17 22	17 31	17 45	17 57	18 09	18 21	18 34	18 49	18 58	19 08
10	16 40	16 55	17 07	17 17	17 25	17 33	17 46	17 58	18 09	18 20	18 32	18 46	18 54	19 03
14	16 47	17 00	17 11	17 20	17 28	17 35	17 47	17 58	18 08	18 18	18 29	18 42	18 49	18 58
18	16 54	17 06	17 16	17 24	17 31	17 37	17 48	17 58	18 07	18 16	18 26	18 38	18 45	18 52
22	17 01	17 12	17 21	17 28	17 34	17 40	17 49	17 58	18 06	18 14	18 23	18 34	18 40	18 47
26	17 09	17 18	17 25	17 32	17 37	17 42	17 50	17 58	18 05	18 12	18 20	18 29	18 35	18 41
30	17 16	17 24	17 30	17 35	17 40	17 44	17 51	17 58	18 04	18 10	18 17	18 25	18 29	18 34
Sept. 3	17 23	17 30	17 35	17 39	17 43	17 46	17 52	17 57	18 03	18 08	18 13	18 20	18 24	18 28
7	17 31	17 35	17 39	17 43	17 46	17 48	17 53	17 57	18 01	18 05	18 10	18 15	18 18	18 22
11	17 38	17 41	17 44	17 47	17 49	17 50	17 54	17 57	18 00	18 03	18 06	18 10	18 12	18 15
15	17 45	17 47	17 49	17 50	17 51	17 53	17 55	17 57	17 58	18 00	18 03	18 05	18 07	18 09
19	17 53	17 53	17 54	17 54	17 54	17 55	17 55	17 56	17 57	17 58	17 59	18 00	18 01	18 02
23	18 00	17 59	17 58	17 58	17 57	17 57	17 56	17 56	17 56	17 55	17 55	17 55	17 55	17 55
27	18 08	18 05	18 03	18 02	18 00	17 59	17 57	17 56	17 54	17 53	17 52	17 50	17 49	17 49
Oct. 1	18 15	18 11	18 08	18 06	18 03	18 01	17 58	17 55	17 53	17 50	17 48	17 45	17 44	17 42
5	18 23	18 18	18 13	18 10	18 07	18 04	17 59	17 55	17 52	17 48	17 44	17 40	17 38	17 36

UNIVERSAL TIME FOR MERIDIAN OF GREENWICH

SUNRISE

Lat.	+40°	+42°	+44°	+46°	+48°	+50°	+52°	+54°	+56°	+58°	+60°	+62°	+64°	+66°
	h m	h m	h m	h m	h m	h m	h m	h m	h m	h m	h m	h m	h m	h m
July 1	4 35	4 28	4 21	4 13	4 05	3 55	3 44	3 32	3 19	3 02	2 42	2 17	1 42	0 22
5	4 37	4 31	4 23	4 16	4 07	3 58	3 48	3 36	3 22	3 06	2 47	2 23	1 50	0 48
9	4 40	4 33	4 26	4 19	4 11	4 02	3 51	3 40	3 27	3 12	2 53	2 30	1 59	1 09
13	4 42	4 36	4 30	4 22	4 14	4 06	3 56	3 45	3 32	3 18	3 00	2 39	2 10	1 27
17	4 45	4 39	4 33	4 26	4 18	4 10	4 01	3 50	3 38	3 24	3 08	2 48	2 22	1 45
21	4 49	4 43	4 37	4 30	4 23	4 15	4 06	3 56	3 45	3 32	3 16	2 58	2 34	2 02
25	4 52	4 47	4 41	4 35	4 28	4 20	4 12	4 02	3 52	3 39	3 25	3 08	2 47	2 19
29	4 56	4 51	4 45	4 39	4 33	4 25	4 17	4 09	3 59	3 47	3 34	3 18	2 59	2 35
Aug. 2	4 59	4 55	4 49	4 44	4 38	4 31	4 24	4 15	4 06	3 56	3 44	3 29	3 12	2 50
6	5 03	4 59	4 54	4 49	4 43	4 37	4 30	4 22	4 14	4 04	3 53	3 40	3 25	3 05
10	5 07	5 03	4 58	4 53	4 48	4 43	4 36	4 29	4 22	4 13	4 03	3 51	3 37	3 20
14	5 11	5 07	5 03	4 58	4 54	4 48	4 43	4 36	4 29	4 21	4 12	4 02	3 49	3 35
18	5 15	5 11	5 07	5 03	4 59	4 54	4 49	4 43	4 37	4 30	4 22	4 13	4 02	3 49
22	5 18	5 15	5 12	5 08	5 05	5 00	4 56	4 51	4 45	4 39	4 32	4 23	4 14	4 02
26	5 22	5 19	5 17	5 13	5 10	5 06	5 02	4 58	4 53	4 47	4 41	4 34	4 26	4 16
30	5 26	5 24	5 21	5 18	5 15	5 12	5 09	5 05	5 01	4 56	4 51	4 45	4 37	4 29
Sept. 3	5 30	5 28	5 26	5 23	5 21	5 18	5 15	5 12	5 09	5 05	5 00	4 55	4 49	4 42
7	5 34	5 32	5 30	5 28	5 26	5 24	5 22	5 19	5 16	5 13	5 09	5 05	5 01	4 55
11	5 37	5 36	5 35	5 33	5 32	5 30	5 28	5 26	5 24	5 22	5 19	5 16	5 12	5 08
15	5 41	5 40	5 39	5 38	5 37	5 36	5 35	5 33	5 32	5 30	5 28	5 26	5 24	5 21
19	5 45	5 44	5 44	5 43	5 43	5 42	5 41	5 41	5 40	5 39	5 38	5 36	5 35	5 33
23	5 49	5 49	5 48	5 48	5 48	5 48	5 48	5 48	5 48	5 47	5 47	5 47	5 46	5 46
27	5 53	5 53	5 53	5 53	5 54	5 54	5 55	5 55	5 55	5 56	5 56	5 57	5 58	5 59
Oct. 1	5 56	5 57	5 58	5 59	5 59	6 00	6 01	6 02	6 03	6 05	6 06	6 07	6 09	6 11
5	6 00	6 01	6 03	6 04	6 05	6 06	6 08	6 10	6 11	6 13	6 15	6 18	6 21	6 24

SUNSET

Lat.	+40°	+42°	+44°	+46°	+48°	+50°	+52°	+54°	+56°	+58°	+60°	+62°	+64°	+66°
	h m	h m	h m	h m	h m	h m	h m	h m	h m	h m	h m	h m	h m	h m
July 1	19 33	19 39	19 47	19 54	20 03	20 12	20 23	20 35	20 49	21 05	21 25	21 50	22 25	23 38
5	19 32	19 39	19 46	19 53	20 02	20 11	20 21	20 33	20 46	21 02	21 21	21 45	22 18	23 16
9	19 31	19 37	19 44	19 51	20 00	20 09	20 19	20 30	20 43	20 58	21 16	21 39	22 09	22 58
13	19 29	19 35	19 42	19 49	19 57	20 05	20 15	20 26	20 38	20 53	21 10	21 31	21 59	22 40
17	19 27	19 32	19 39	19 46	19 53	20 02	20 11	20 21	20 33	20 47	21 03	21 23	21 48	22 24
21	19 24	19 29	19 36	19 42	19 49	19 57	20 06	20 16	20 27	20 40	20 55	21 13	21 36	22 07
25	19 20	19 26	19 32	19 38	19 45	19 52	20 01	20 10	20 20	20 32	20 46	21 03	21 24	21 51
29	19 17	19 22	19 27	19 33	19 40	19 47	19 55	20 03	20 13	20 24	20 37	20 53	21 11	21 35
Aug. 2	19 13	19 17	19 22	19 28	19 34	19 41	19 48	19 56	20 05	20 15	20 27	20 41	20 58	21 19
6	19 08	19 12	19 17	19 22	19 28	19 34	19 41	19 48	19 57	20 06	20 17	20 30	20 45	21 04
10	19 03	19 07	19 12	19 16	19 22	19 27	19 33	19 40	19 48	19 56	20 06	20 18	20 31	20 48
14	18 58	19 02	19 06	19 10	19 15	19 20	19 25	19 32	19 39	19 46	19 55	20 06	20 18	20 32
18	18 52	18 56	18 59	19 03	19 08	19 12	19 17	19 23	19 29	19 36	19 44	19 53	20 04	20 16
22	18 47	18 50	18 53	18 56	19 00	19 04	19 09	19 14	19 19	19 26	19 33	19 41	19 50	20 01
26	18 41	18 43	18 46	18 49	18 53	18 56	19 00	19 04	19 09	19 15	19 21	19 28	19 36	19 45
30	18 34	18 37	18 39	18 42	18 45	18 48	18 51	18 55	18 59	19 04	19 09	19 15	19 22	19 30
Sept. 3	18 28	18 30	18 32	18 34	18 37	18 39	18 42	18 45	18 49	18 53	18 57	19 02	19 08	19 14
7	18 22	18 23	18 25	18 27	18 29	18 31	18 33	18 36	18 38	18 41	18 45	18 49	18 53	18 59
11	18 15	18 16	18 18	18 19	18 20	18 22	18 24	18 26	18 28	18 30	18 33	18 36	18 39	18 43
15	18 09	18 09	18 10	18 11	18 12	18 13	18 14	18 16	18 17	18 19	18 21	18 23	18 25	18 28
19	18 02	18 02	18 03	18 03	18 04	18 04	18 05	18 06	18 07	18 07	18 08	18 10	18 11	18 12
23	17 55	17 55	17 55	17 55	17 55	17 56	17 56	17 56	17 56	17 56	17 56	17 56	17 57	17 57
27	17 49	17 48	17 48	17 48	17 47	17 47	17 46	17 46	17 45	17 45	17 44	17 43	17 43	17 42
Oct. 1	17 42	17 41	17 41	17 40	17 39	17 38	17 37	17 36	17 35	17 33	17 32	17 30	17 28	17 26
5	17 36	17 35	17 33	17 32	17 31	17 29	17 28	17 26	17 24	17 22	17 20	17 17	17 14	17 11

UNIVERSAL TIME FOR MERIDIAN OF GREENWICH

SUNRISE

Lat.	−55°	−50°	−45°	−40°	−35°	−30°	−20°	−10°	0°	+10°	+20°	+30°	+35°	+40°
	h m	h m	h m	h m	h m	h m	h m	h m	h m	h m	h m	h m	h m	h m
Oct. 1	5 25	5 29	5 32	5 34	5 36	5 38	5 41	5 44	5 46	5 49	5 51	5 53	5 55	5 56
5	5 15	5 20	5 24	5 28	5 31	5 33	5 38	5 42	5 45	5 48	5 52	5 56	5 58	6 00
9	5 05	5 11	5 17	5 21	5 25	5 29	5 34	5 39	5 44	5 48	5 53	5 58	6 01	6 04
13	4 55	5 03	5 10	5 15	5 20	5 24	5 31	5 37	5 43	5 48	5 54	6 01	6 04	6 08
17	4 45	4 55	5 03	5 09	5 15	5 20	5 28	5 35	5 42	5 49	5 56	6 03	6 08	6 13
21	4 35	4 47	4 56	5 03	5 10	5 15	5 25	5 33	5 41	5 49	5 57	6 06	6 11	6 17
25	4 26	4 39	4 49	4 58	5 05	5 11	5 22	5 32	5 41	5 49	5 58	6 09	6 15	6 21
29	4 17	4 32	4 43	4 53	5 01	5 08	5 20	5 31	5 40	5 50	6 00	6 12	6 18	6 26
Nov. 2	4 08	4 24	4 37	4 48	4 57	5 04	5 18	5 29	5 40	5 51	6 02	6 15	6 22	6 30
6	4 00	4 18	4 32	4 43	4 53	5 01	5 16	5 28	5 40	5 52	6 04	6 18	6 26	6 35
10	3 52	4 11	4 27	4 39	4 49	4 59	5 14	5 28	5 40	5 53	6 06	6 21	6 30	6 40
14	3 45	4 06	4 22	4 35	4 46	4 56	5 13	5 27	5 41	5 54	6 08	6 24	6 34	6 44
18	3 38	4 01	4 18	4 32	4 44	4 54	5 12	5 27	5 42	5 56	6 11	6 28	6 37	6 49
22	3 32	3 56	4 14	4 29	4 42	4 53	5 12	5 28	5 43	5 57	6 13	6 31	6 41	6 53
26	3 27	3 52	4 12	4 27	4 40	4 52	5 11	5 28	5 44	5 59	6 16	6 34	6 45	6 58
30	3 23	3 49	4 09	4 26	4 39	4 51	5 11	5 29	5 45	6 01	6 18	6 38	6 49	7 02
Dec. 4	3 19	3 47	4 08	4 25	4 39	4 51	5 12	5 30	5 47	6 03	6 21	6 41	6 52	7 06
8	3 17	3 45	4 07	4 24	4 39	4 52	5 13	5 31	5 48	6 05	6 23	6 44	6 56	7 09
12	3 16	3 45	4 07	4 25	4 40	4 52	5 14	5 33	5 50	6 07	6 26	6 46	6 59	7 13
16	3 15	3 45	4 08	4 26	4 41	4 54	5 16	5 34	5 52	6 09	6 28	6 49	7 01	7 15
20	3 16	3 46	4 09	4 27	4 42	4 55	5 17	5 36	5 54	6 11	6 30	6 51	7 04	7 18
24	3 19	3 49	4 11	4 29	4 44	4 57	5 19	5 38	5 56	6 13	6 32	6 53	7 06	7 20
28	3 22	3 52	4 14	4 32	4 47	5 00	5 22	5 40	5 58	6 15	6 34	6 55	7 07	7 21
32	3 26	3 55	4 17	4 35	4 50	5 02	5 24	5 43	6 00	6 17	6 35	6 56	7 08	7 22
36	3 31	4 00	4 21	4 38	4 53	5 05	5 27	5 45	6 02	6 18	6 36	6 57	7 08	7 22

SUNSET

Lat.	−55°	−50°	−45°	−40°	−35°	−30°	−20°	−10°	0°	+10°	+20°	+30°	+35°	+40°
	h m	h m	h m	h m	h m	h m	h m	h m	h m	h m	h m	h m	h m	h m
Oct. 1	18 15	18 11	18 08	18 06	18 03	18 01	17 58	17 55	17 53	17 50	17 48	17 45	17 44	17 42
5	18 23	18 18	18 13	18 10	18 07	18 04	17 59	17 55	17 52	17 48	17 44	17 40	17 38	17 36
9	18 31	18 24	18 18	18 14	18 10	18 06	18 00	17 55	17 50	17 46	17 41	17 36	17 33	17 29
13	18 39	18 30	18 24	18 18	18 13	18 09	18 02	17 55	17 49	17 44	17 38	17 31	17 27	17 23
17	18 47	18 37	18 29	18 22	18 16	18 11	18 03	17 55	17 49	17 42	17 35	17 27	17 22	17 17
21	18 55	18 43	18 34	18 27	18 20	18 14	18 04	17 56	17 48	17 40	17 32	17 23	17 18	17 12
25	19 03	18 50	18 40	18 31	18 24	18 17	18 06	17 56	17 47	17 39	17 29	17 19	17 13	17 06
29	19 12	18 57	18 45	18 36	18 27	18 20	18 08	17 57	17 47	17 37	17 27	17 15	17 09	17 01
Nov. 2	19 20	19 04	18 51	18 40	18 31	18 23	18 10	17 58	17 47	17 36	17 25	17 12	17 05	16 56
6	19 29	19 11	18 56	18 45	18 35	18 26	18 12	17 59	17 47	17 35	17 23	17 09	17 01	16 52
10	19 37	19 17	19 02	18 50	18 39	18 30	18 14	18 00	17 47	17 35	17 22	17 06	16 58	16 48
14	19 45	19 24	19 08	18 54	18 43	18 33	18 16	18 02	17 48	17 35	17 20	17 04	16 55	16 44
18	19 53	19 31	19 13	18 59	18 47	18 36	18 19	18 03	17 49	17 35	17 20	17 03	16 53	16 41
22	20 01	19 37	19 19	19 04	18 51	18 40	18 21	18 05	17 50	17 35	17 19	17 01	16 51	16 39
26	20 09	19 43	19 24	19 08	18 55	18 43	18 24	18 07	17 51	17 35	17 19	17 00	16 49	16 37
30	20 16	19 49	19 29	19 12	18 58	18 46	18 26	18 09	17 52	17 36	17 19	17 00	16 48	16 36
Dec. 4	20 22	19 54	19 33	19 16	19 02	18 50	18 29	18 11	17 54	17 37	17 20	17 00	16 48	16 35
8	20 28	19 59	19 37	19 20	19 05	18 53	18 31	18 13	17 56	17 39	17 21	17 00	16 48	16 35
12	20 32	20 03	19 41	19 23	19 08	18 55	18 34	18 15	17 58	17 40	17 22	17 01	16 49	16 35
16	20 36	20 06	19 44	19 26	19 11	18 58	18 36	18 17	17 59	17 42	17 24	17 02	16 50	16 36
20	20 39	20 09	19 46	19 28	19 13	19 00	18 38	18 19	18 01	17 44	17 25	17 04	16 52	16 38
24	20 41	20 11	19 48	19 30	19 15	19 02	18 40	18 21	18 03	17 46	17 27	17 06	16 54	16 40
28	20 41	20 12	19 49	19 31	19 16	19 04	18 42	18 23	18 05	17 48	17 30	17 09	16 56	16 42
32	20 41	20 12	19 50	19 32	19 17	19 05	18 43	18 25	18 07	17 50	17 32	17 11	16 59	16 45
36	20 39	20 11	19 49	19 32	19 18	19 05	18 44	18 26	18 09	17 52	17 35	17 14	17 02	16 49

UNIVERSAL TIME FOR MERIDIAN OF GREENWICH

SUNRISE

Lat.	+40°	+42°	+44°	+46°	+48°	+50°	+52°	+54°	+56°	+58°	+60°	+62°	+64°	+66°
	h m	h m	h m	h m	h m	h m	h m	h m	h m	h m	h m	h m	h m	h m
Oct. 1	5 56	5 57	5 58	5 59	5 59	6 00	6 01	6 02	6 03	6 05	6 06	6 07	6 09	6 11
5	6 00	6 01	6 03	6 04	6 05	6 06	6 08	6 10	6 11	6 13	6 15	6 18	6 21	6 24
9	6 04	6 06	6 07	6 09	6 11	6 13	6 15	6 17	6 19	6 22	6 25	6 29	6 32	6 37
13	6 08	6 10	6 12	6 14	6 17	6 19	6 22	6 24	6 28	6 31	6 35	6 39	6 44	6 50
17	6 13	6 15	6 17	6 20	6 22	6 25	6 28	6 32	6 36	6 40	6 45	6 50	6 56	7 04
21	6 17	6 20	6 22	6 25	6 28	6 32	6 36	6 40	6 44	6 49	6 55	7 01	7 09	7 17
25	6 21	6 24	6 27	6 31	6 34	6 38	6 43	6 47	6 53	6 58	7 05	7 12	7 21	7 31
29	6 26	6 29	6 33	6 36	6 41	6 45	6 50	6 55	7 01	7 08	7 15	7 24	7 33	7 45
Nov. 2	6 30	6 34	6 38	6 42	6 47	6 52	6 57	7 03	7 10	7 17	7 25	7 35	7 46	8 00
6	6 35	6 39	6 43	6 48	6 53	6 58	7 04	7 11	7 18	7 26	7 36	7 46	7 59	8 14
10	6 40	6 44	6 49	6 54	6 59	7 05	7 11	7 18	7 26	7 35	7 46	7 58	8 12	8 29
14	6 44	6 49	6 54	6 59	7 05	7 11	7 18	7 26	7 35	7 45	7 56	8 09	8 25	8 44
18	6 49	6 54	6 59	7 05	7 11	7 18	7 25	7 34	7 43	7 54	8 06	8 20	8 38	8 59
22	6 53	6 58	7 04	7 10	7 17	7 24	7 32	7 41	7 51	8 02	8 16	8 31	8 50	9 15
26	6 58	7 03	7 09	7 15	7 22	7 30	7 38	7 48	7 58	8 11	8 25	8 42	9 02	9 30
30	7 02	7 07	7 14	7 20	7 28	7 36	7 44	7 54	8 05	8 18	8 33	8 51	9 14	9 44
Dec. 4	7 06	7 12	7 18	7 25	7 32	7 41	7 50	8 00	8 12	8 25	8 41	9 00	9 25	9 58
8	7 09	7 15	7 22	7 29	7 37	7 45	7 55	8 05	8 18	8 32	8 48	9 08	9 34	10 10
12	7 13	7 19	7 26	7 33	7 41	7 49	7 59	8 10	8 22	8 37	8 54	9 15	9 42	10 21
16	7 15	7 22	7 29	7 36	7 44	7 53	8 03	8 14	8 26	8 41	8 58	9 20	9 48	10 29
20	7 18	7 24	7 31	7 38	7 47	7 55	8 05	8 16	8 29	8 44	9 02	9 23	9 52	10 34
24	7 20	7 26	7 33	7 40	7 48	7 57	8 07	8 18	8 31	8 46	9 03	9 25	9 53	10 35
28	7 21	7 27	7 34	7 42	7 50	7 58	8 08	8 19	8 32	8 46	9 03	9 25	9 52	10 33
32	7 22	7 28	7 35	7 42	7 50	7 59	8 08	8 19	8 31	8 45	9 02	9 23	9 49	10 28
36	7 22	7 28	7 35	7 42	7 49	7 58	8 07	8 18	8 30	8 43	9 00	9 19	9 44	10 20

SUNSET

Lat.	+40°	+42°	+44°	+46°	+48°	+50°	+52°	+54°	+56°	+58°	+60°	+62°	+64°	+66°
	h m	h m	h m	h m	h m	h m	h m	h m	h m	h m	h m	h m	h m	h m
Oct. 1	17 42	17 41	17 41	17 40	17 39	17 38	17 37	17 36	17 35	17 33	17 32	17 30	17 28	17 26
5	17 36	17 35	17 33	17 32	17 31	17 29	17 28	17 26	17 24	17 22	17 20	17 17	17 14	17 11
9	17 29	17 28	17 26	17 25	17 23	17 21	17 19	17 17	17 14	17 11	17 08	17 05	17 01	16 56
13	17 23	17 21	17 19	17 17	17 15	17 13	17 10	17 07	17 04	17 00	16 56	16 52	16 47	16 41
17	17 17	17 15	17 13	17 10	17 07	17 04	17 01	16 58	16 54	16 50	16 45	16 39	16 33	16 26
21	17 12	17 09	17 06	17 03	17 00	16 57	16 53	16 49	16 44	16 39	16 33	16 27	16 19	16 11
25	17 06	17 03	17 00	16 57	16 53	16 49	16 45	16 40	16 35	16 29	16 22	16 15	16 06	15 56
29	17 01	16 58	16 54	16 50	16 46	16 42	16 37	16 32	16 26	16 19	16 11	16 03	15 53	15 41
Nov. 2	16 56	16 53	16 49	16 44	16 40	16 35	16 29	16 23	16 17	16 09	16 01	15 51	15 40	15 26
6	16 52	16 48	16 44	16 39	16 34	16 28	16 22	16 16	16 09	16 00	15 51	15 40	15 27	15 12
10	16 48	16 44	16 39	16 34	16 28	16 22	16 16	16 09	16 01	15 52	15 41	15 29	15 15	14 58
14	16 44	16 40	16 35	16 29	16 23	16 17	16 10	16 02	15 53	15 44	15 32	15 19	15 03	14 44
18	16 41	16 36	16 31	16 25	16 19	16 12	16 05	15 56	15 47	15 36	15 24	15 09	14 52	14 30
22	16 39	16 34	16 28	16 22	16 15	16 08	16 00	15 51	15 41	15 29	15 16	15 01	14 41	14 17
26	16 37	16 31	16 25	16 19	16 12	16 04	15 56	15 46	15 36	15 24	15 09	14 53	14 32	14 05
30	16 36	16 30	16 24	16 17	16 10	16 02	15 53	15 43	15 32	15 19	15 04	14 46	14 23	13 53
Dec. 4	16 35	16 29	16 22	16 15	16 08	16 00	15 50	15 40	15 28	15 15	14 59	14 40	14 16	13 42
8	16 35	16 28	16 22	16 15	16 07	15 58	15 49	15 38	15 26	15 12	14 56	14 36	14 10	13 33
12	16 35	16 29	16 22	16 15	16 07	15 58	15 48	15 37	15 25	15 11	14 54	14 33	14 06	13 26
16	16 36	16 30	16 23	16 15	16 07	15 59	15 49	15 38	15 25	15 10	14 53	14 32	14 04	13 22
20	16 38	16 31	16 24	16 17	16 09	16 00	15 50	15 39	15 26	15 11	14 54	14 32	14 04	13 21
24	16 40	16 33	16 26	16 19	16 11	16 02	15 52	15 41	15 28	15 14	14 56	14 35	14 06	13 24
28	16 42	16 36	16 29	16 22	16 14	16 05	15 55	15 44	15 32	15 17	15 00	14 39	14 11	13 30
32	16 45	16 39	16 33	16 25	16 17	16 09	15 59	15 48	15 36	15 22	15 05	14 45	14 18	13 40
36	16 49	16 43	16 36	16 29	16 22	16 13	16 04	15 53	15 41	15 28	15 12	14 52	14 27	13 52

UNIVERSAL TIME FOR MERIDIAN OF GREENWICH

BEGINNING OF MORNING CIVIL TWILIGHT

Lat.	−55°	−50°	−45°	−40°	−35°	−30°	−20°	−10°	0°	+10°	+20°	+30°	+35°	+40°
	h m	h m	h m	h m	h m	h m	h m	h m	h m	h m	h m	h m	h m	h m
Jan. −2	2 25	3 08	3 38	4 00	4 18	4 33	4 58	5 18	5 36	5 53	6 10	6 29	6 39	6 51
2	2 31	3 13	3 41	4 03	4 21	4 36	5 00	5 20	5 38	5 55	6 12	6 30	6 40	6 52
6	2 38	3 18	3 46	4 07	4 25	4 39	5 03	5 23	5 40	5 56	6 13	6 31	6 41	6 52
10	2 45	3 24	3 51	4 11	4 28	4 42	5 06	5 25	5 42	5 58	6 14	6 31	6 41	6 51
14	2 54	3 30	3 56	4 16	4 32	4 46	5 09	5 27	5 43	5 59	6 14	6 31	6 40	6 50
18	3 03	3 37	4 02	4 21	4 37	4 50	5 11	5 29	5 45	6 00	6 14	6 30	6 39	6 49
22	3 13	3 45	4 08	4 26	4 41	4 53	5 14	5 31	5 46	6 00	6 14	6 29	6 38	6 47
26	3 23	3 52	4 14	4 31	4 45	4 57	5 17	5 33	5 47	6 00	6 14	6 28	6 36	6 44
30	3 33	4 00	4 21	4 37	4 50	5 01	5 20	5 35	5 48	6 01	6 13	6 26	6 33	6 41
Feb. 3	3 43	4 08	4 27	4 42	4 54	5 05	5 22	5 36	5 49	6 00	6 12	6 24	6 31	6 38
7	3 53	4 16	4 33	4 47	4 59	5 09	5 25	5 38	5 49	6 00	6 10	6 21	6 27	6 34
11	4 03	4 24	4 40	4 52	5 03	5 12	5 27	5 39	5 49	5 59	6 09	6 18	6 24	6 30
15	4 12	4 31	4 46	4 58	5 07	5 16	5 29	5 40	5 49	5 58	6 07	6 15	6 20	6 25
19	4 22	4 39	4 52	5 03	5 11	5 19	5 31	5 41	5 49	5 57	6 04	6 12	6 16	6 20
23	4 31	4 47	4 58	5 08	5 15	5 22	5 33	5 42	5 49	5 56	6 02	6 08	6 11	6 15
27	4 41	4 54	5 04	5 13	5 19	5 25	5 35	5 42	5 48	5 54	5 59	6 04	6 06	6 09
Mar. 3	4 49	5 01	5 10	5 17	5 23	5 28	5 36	5 43	5 48	5 52	5 56	6 00	6 01	6 03
7	4 58	5 08	5 16	5 22	5 27	5 31	5 38	5 43	5 47	5 50	5 53	5 55	5 56	5 57
11	5 07	5 15	5 21	5 26	5 30	5 34	5 39	5 43	5 46	5 48	5 50	5 51	5 51	5 51
15	5 15	5 22	5 27	5 31	5 34	5 36	5 40	5 43	5 45	5 46	5 46	5 46	5 45	5 44
19	5 23	5 28	5 32	5 35	5 37	5 39	5 42	5 43	5 44	5 44	5 43	5 41	5 40	5 38
23	5 31	5 35	5 37	5 39	5 40	5 41	5 43	5 43	5 43	5 41	5 39	5 36	5 34	5 31
27	5 39	5 41	5 42	5 43	5 44	5 44	5 44	5 43	5 41	5 39	5 36	5 31	5 28	5 25
31	5 47	5 47	5 47	5 47	5 47	5 46	5 45	5 43	5 40	5 37	5 32	5 26	5 23	5 18
Apr. 4	5 54	5 53	5 52	5 51	5 50	5 49	5 46	5 43	5 39	5 34	5 29	5 22	5 17	5 12

END OF EVENING CIVIL TWILIGHT

Lat.	−55°	−50°	−45°	−40°	−35°	−30°	−20°	−10°	0°	+10°	+20°	+30°	+35°	+40°
	h m	h m	h m	h m	h m	h m	h m	h m	h m	h m	h m	h m	h m	h m
Jan. −2	21 38	20 56	20 27	20 04	19 46	19 31	19 07	18 46	18 28	18 12	17 54	17 36	17 25	17 14
2	21 36	20 55	20 27	20 05	19 47	19 32	19 08	18 48	18 30	18 14	17 57	17 38	17 28	17 17
6	21 33	20 53	20 26	20 04	19 47	19 33	19 09	18 49	18 32	18 16	17 59	17 41	17 31	17 20
10	21 28	20 51	20 24	20 03	19 47	19 32	19 09	18 50	18 34	18 18	18 02	17 44	17 35	17 24
14	21 23	20 47	20 21	20 02	19 45	19 32	19 10	18 51	18 35	18 20	18 04	17 48	17 38	17 28
18	21 16	20 43	20 18	19 59	19 44	19 31	19 09	18 52	18 36	18 21	18 07	17 51	17 42	17 32
22	21 09	20 37	20 14	19 56	19 42	19 29	19 09	18 52	18 37	18 23	18 09	17 54	17 46	17 37
26	21 01	20 32	20 10	19 53	19 39	19 27	19 08	18 52	18 38	18 25	18 12	17 57	17 50	17 41
30	20 52	20 25	20 05	19 49	19 36	19 25	19 07	18 52	18 39	18 26	18 14	18 01	17 54	17 46
Feb. 3	20 43	20 18	20 00	19 45	19 33	19 22	19 05	18 51	18 39	18 27	18 16	18 04	17 57	17 50
7	20 34	20 11	19 54	19 40	19 29	19 19	19 03	18 50	18 39	18 28	18 18	18 07	18 01	17 55
11	20 24	20 03	19 48	19 35	19 25	19 16	19 01	18 49	18 39	18 29	18 20	18 10	18 05	17 59
15	20 14	19 55	19 41	19 30	19 20	19 12	18 59	18 48	18 39	18 30	18 22	18 13	18 09	18 04
19	20 04	19 47	19 34	19 24	19 15	19 08	18 56	18 46	18 38	18 31	18 23	18 16	18 12	18 08
23	19 54	19 39	19 27	19 18	19 10	19 04	18 53	18 45	18 38	18 31	18 25	18 19	18 16	18 13
27	19 43	19 30	19 20	19 12	19 05	19 00	18 50	18 43	18 37	18 31	18 27	18 22	18 19	18 17
Mar. 3	19 33	19 21	19 13	19 06	19 00	18 55	18 47	18 41	18 36	18 32	18 28	18 25	18 23	18 21
7	19 22	19 13	19 05	18 59	18 54	18 50	18 44	18 39	18 35	18 32	18 29	18 27	18 26	18 26
11	19 12	19 04	18 58	18 53	18 49	18 46	18 40	18 37	18 34	18 32	18 30	18 30	18 30	18 30
15	19 01	18 55	18 50	18 46	18 43	18 41	18 37	18 34	18 33	18 32	18 32	18 32	18 33	18 34
19	18 51	18 46	18 43	18 40	18 38	18 36	18 33	18 32	18 32	18 32	18 33	18 35	18 36	18 38
23	18 41	18 37	18 35	18 33	18 32	18 31	18 30	18 30	18 30	18 32	18 34	18 37	18 40	18 42
27	18 30	18 29	18 27	18 27	18 26	18 26	18 26	18 28	18 29	18 32	18 35	18 40	18 43	18 47
31	18 20	18 20	18 20	18 20	18 21	18 21	18 23	18 25	18 28	18 32	18 36	18 42	18 46	18 51
Apr. 4	18 10	18 12	18 13	18 14	18 15	18 17	18 20	18 23	18 27	18 32	18 37	18 45	18 49	18 55

UNIVERSAL TIME FOR MERIDIAN OF GREENWICH
BEGINNING OF MORNING CIVIL TWILIGHT

Lat.	+40°	+42°	+44°	+46°	+48°	+50°	+52°	+54°	+56°	+58°	+60°	+62°	+64°	+66°
	h m	h m	h m	h m	h m	h m	h m	h m	h m	h m	h m	h m	h m	h m
Jan. −2	6 51	6 56	7 01	7 07	7 13	7 20	7 27	7 36	7 44	7 55	8 06	8 19	8 35	8 54
2	6 52	6 57	7 02	7 08	7 14	7 20	7 27	7 35	7 44	7 54	8 05	8 18	8 33	8 52
6	6 52	6 57	7 02	7 07	7 13	7 20	7 27	7 34	7 43	7 52	8 03	8 16	8 30	8 48
10	6 51	6 56	7 01	7 06	7 12	7 18	7 25	7 32	7 41	7 50	8 00	8 12	8 26	8 43
14	6 50	6 55	7 00	7 05	7 10	7 16	7 23	7 30	7 37	7 46	7 56	8 07	8 20	8 36
18	6 49	6 53	6 58	7 03	7 08	7 13	7 19	7 26	7 33	7 41	7 51	8 01	8 13	8 28
22	6 47	6 51	6 55	7 00	7 05	7 10	7 16	7 22	7 28	7 36	7 45	7 54	8 05	8 19
26	6 44	6 48	6 52	6 56	7 01	7 06	7 11	7 17	7 23	7 30	7 38	7 47	7 57	8 09
30	6 41	6 45	6 49	6 52	6 57	7 01	7 06	7 11	7 17	7 23	7 30	7 38	7 47	7 58
Feb. 3	6 38	6 41	6 44	6 48	6 52	6 56	7 00	7 05	7 10	7 15	7 22	7 29	7 37	7 47
7	6 34	6 37	6 40	6 43	6 46	6 50	6 54	6 58	7 02	7 07	7 13	7 19	7 26	7 35
11	6 30	6 32	6 35	6 38	6 40	6 44	6 47	6 51	6 54	6 59	7 04	7 09	7 15	7 22
15	6 25	6 27	6 29	6 32	6 34	6 37	6 40	6 43	6 46	6 50	6 54	6 58	7 03	7 09
19	6 20	6 22	6 24	6 25	6 28	6 30	6 32	6 35	6 37	6 40	6 43	6 47	6 51	6 56
23	6 15	6 16	6 17	6 19	6 21	6 22	6 24	6 26	6 28	6 30	6 33	6 35	6 38	6 42
27	6 09	6 10	6 11	6 12	6 13	6 15	6 16	6 17	6 19	6 20	6 22	6 23	6 25	6 28
Mar. 3	6 03	6 04	6 04	6 05	6 06	6 07	6 07	6 08	6 09	6 10	6 10	6 11	6 12	6 13
7	5 57	5 57	5 58	5 58	5 58	5 58	5 58	5 59	5 59	5 59	5 59	5 59	5 59	5 58
11	5 51	5 51	5 51	5 50	5 50	5 50	5 49	5 49	5 48	5 48	5 47	5 46	5 45	5 43
15	5 44	5 44	5 43	5 43	5 42	5 41	5 40	5 39	5 38	5 37	5 35	5 33	5 31	5 28
19	5 38	5 37	5 36	5 35	5 34	5 32	5 31	5 29	5 27	5 25	5 23	5 20	5 16	5 12
23	5 31	5 30	5 29	5 27	5 26	5 24	5 22	5 19	5 17	5 14	5 10	5 06	5 02	4 57
27	5 25	5 23	5 21	5 19	5 17	5 15	5 12	5 09	5 06	5 02	4 58	4 53	4 47	4 40
31	5 18	5 16	5 14	5 11	5 09	5 06	5 03	4 59	4 55	4 50	4 45	4 39	4 32	4 24
Apr. 4	5 12	5 09	5 07	5 04	5 00	4 57	4 53	4 49	4 44	4 39	4 32	4 25	4 17	4 07

END OF EVENING CIVIL TWILIGHT

Lat.	+40°	+42°	+44°	+46°	+48°	+50°	+52°	+54°	+56°	+58°	+60°	+62°	+64°	+66°
	h m	h m	h m	h m	h m	h m	h m	h m	h m	h m	h m	h m	h m	h m
Jan. −2	17 14	17 09	17 03	16 57	16 51	16 45	16 37	16 29	16 20	16 10	15 59	15 45	15 30	15 10
2	17 17	17 12	17 07	17 01	16 55	16 48	16 41	16 33	16 24	16 15	16 03	15 50	15 35	15 17
6	17 20	17 15	17 10	17 05	16 59	16 52	16 46	16 38	16 29	16 20	16 09	15 57	15 42	15 24
10	17 24	17 19	17 14	17 09	17 03	16 57	16 51	16 43	16 35	16 26	16 16	16 04	15 50	15 33
14	17 28	17 24	17 19	17 14	17 08	17 02	16 56	16 49	16 41	16 33	16 23	16 12	15 59	15 43
18	17 32	17 28	17 23	17 19	17 14	17 08	17 02	16 55	16 48	16 40	16 31	16 21	16 08	15 54
22	17 37	17 33	17 28	17 24	17 19	17 14	17 08	17 02	16 55	16 48	16 39	16 30	16 19	16 05
26	17 41	17 37	17 33	17 29	17 25	17 20	17 15	17 09	17 03	16 56	16 48	16 39	16 29	16 17
30	17 46	17 42	17 39	17 35	17 31	17 26	17 21	17 16	17 11	17 04	16 57	16 49	16 40	16 30
Feb. 3	17 50	17 47	17 44	17 40	17 37	17 33	17 28	17 24	17 19	17 13	17 07	17 00	16 52	16 42
7	17 55	17 52	17 49	17 46	17 43	17 39	17 35	17 31	17 27	17 22	17 16	17 10	17 03	16 55
11	17 59	17 57	17 54	17 52	17 49	17 46	17 42	17 39	17 35	17 31	17 26	17 21	17 15	17 08
15	18 04	18 02	17 59	17 57	17 55	17 52	17 49	17 46	17 43	17 39	17 36	17 31	17 26	17 21
19	18 08	18 06	18 05	18 03	18 01	17 59	17 56	17 54	17 51	17 48	17 45	17 42	17 38	17 33
23	18 13	18 11	18 10	18 08	18 07	18 05	18 03	18 02	18 00	17 57	17 55	17 52	17 50	17 46
27	18 17	18 16	18 15	18 14	18 13	18 12	18 10	18 09	18 08	18 06	18 05	18 03	18 01	17 59
Mar. 3	18 21	18 21	18 20	18 19	18 19	18 18	18 17	18 17	18 16	18 15	18 15	18 14	18 13	18 12
7	18 26	18 25	18 25	18 25	18 25	18 25	18 24	18 24	18 24	18 24	18 24	18 25	18 25	18 25
11	18 30	18 30	18 30	18 30	18 31	18 31	18 31	18 32	18 33	18 33	18 34	18 35	18 37	18 38
15	18 34	18 34	18 35	18 36	18 37	18 37	18 38	18 40	18 41	18 42	18 44	18 46	18 49	18 52
19	18 38	18 39	18 40	18 41	18 42	18 44	18 45	18 47	18 49	18 52	18 54	18 57	19 01	19 05
23	18 42	18 44	18 45	18 47	18 48	18 50	18 53	18 55	18 58	19 01	19 04	19 08	19 13	19 19
27	18 47	18 48	18 50	18 52	18 54	18 57	19 00	19 03	19 06	19 10	19 14	19 20	19 26	19 33
31	18 51	18 53	18 55	18 58	19 00	19 03	19 07	19 10	19 15	19 19	19 25	19 31	19 38	19 47
Apr. 4	18 55	18 57	19 00	19 03	19 06	19 10	19 14	19 18	19 23	19 29	19 35	19 43	19 51	20 02

UNIVERSAL TIME FOR MERIDIAN OF GREENWICH
BEGINNING OF MORNING CIVIL TWILIGHT

Lat.	−55°	−50°	−45°	−40°	−35°	−30°	−20°	−10°	0°	+10°	+20°	+30°	+35°	+40°
	h m	h m	h m	h m	h m	h m	h m	h m	h m	h m	h m	h m	h m	h m
Mar. 31	5 47	5 47	5 47	5 47	5 47	5 46	5 45	5 43	5 40	5 37	5 32	5 26	5 23	5 18
Apr. 4	5 54	5 53	5 52	5 51	5 50	5 49	5 46	5 43	5 39	5 34	5 29	5 22	5 17	5 12
8	6 02	5 59	5 57	5 55	5 53	5 51	5 47	5 42	5 38	5 32	5 25	5 17	5 11	5 05
12	6 09	6 05	6 02	5 59	5 56	5 53	5 48	5 42	5 36	5 30	5 22	5 12	5 06	4 59
16	6 16	6 11	6 07	6 03	5 59	5 56	5 49	5 42	5 35	5 28	5 19	5 07	5 01	4 52
20	6 24	6 17	6 11	6 06	6 02	5 58	5 50	5 42	5 34	5 26	5 15	5 03	4 55	4 46
24	6 31	6 23	6 16	6 10	6 05	6 00	5 51	5 42	5 33	5 24	5 12	4 59	4 50	4 40
28	6 38	6 28	6 21	6 14	6 08	6 03	5 52	5 43	5 33	5 22	5 10	4 55	4 45	4 35
May 2	6 45	6 34	6 25	6 18	6 11	6 05	5 54	5 43	5 32	5 20	5 07	4 51	4 41	4 29
6	6 51	6 40	6 30	6 21	6 14	6 07	5 55	5 43	5 32	5 19	5 05	4 47	4 37	4 24
10	6 58	6 45	6 34	6 25	6 17	6 10	5 56	5 44	5 31	5 18	5 03	4 44	4 33	4 19
14	7 04	6 50	6 38	6 29	6 20	6 12	5 58	5 44	5 31	5 17	5 01	4 41	4 29	4 15
18	7 10	6 55	6 42	6 32	6 23	6 14	5 59	5 45	5 31	5 16	4 59	4 38	4 26	4 11
22	7 16	7 00	6 46	6 35	6 25	6 16	6 01	5 46	5 31	5 15	4 58	4 36	4 23	4 08
26	7 21	7 04	6 50	6 38	6 28	6 19	6 02	5 47	5 31	5 15	4 57	4 34	4 21	4 05
30	7 26	7 08	6 53	6 41	6 30	6 21	6 03	5 48	5 32	5 15	4 56	4 33	4 19	4 02
June 3	7 30	7 11	6 56	6 44	6 33	6 23	6 05	5 48	5 32	5 15	4 56	4 32	4 17	4 00
7	7 34	7 15	6 59	6 46	6 35	6 25	6 06	5 49	5 33	5 15	4 55	4 31	4 16	3 59
11	7 37	7 17	7 01	6 48	6 36	6 26	6 08	5 50	5 34	5 16	4 56	4 31	4 16	3 58
15	7 39	7 19	7 03	6 50	6 38	6 27	6 09	5 51	5 34	5 16	4 56	4 31	4 16	3 58
19	7 41	7 21	7 05	6 51	6 39	6 29	6 10	5 52	5 35	5 17	4 57	4 32	4 16	3 58
23	7 42	7 22	7 05	6 52	6 40	6 29	6 11	5 53	5 36	5 18	4 57	4 32	4 17	3 59
27	7 42	7 22	7 06	6 52	6 41	6 30	6 11	5 54	5 37	5 19	4 59	4 34	4 18	4 00
July 1	7 41	7 21	7 05	6 52	6 41	6 30	6 12	5 55	5 38	5 20	5 00	4 35	4 20	4 02
5	7 39	7 20	7 05	6 52	6 40	6 30	6 12	5 55	5 39	5 21	5 01	4 37	4 22	4 05

END OF EVENING CIVIL TWILIGHT

Lat.	−55°	−50°	−45°	−40°	−35°	−30°	−20°	−10°	0°	+10°	+20°	+30°	+35°	+40°
	h m	h m	h m	h m	h m	h m	h m	h m	h m	h m	h m	h m	h m	h m
Mar. 31	18 20	18 20	18 20	18 20	18 21	18 21	18 23	18 25	18 28	18 32	18 36	18 42	18 46	18 51
Apr. 4	18 10	18 12	18 13	18 14	18 15	18 17	18 20	18 23	18 27	18 32	18 37	18 45	18 49	18 55
8	18 01	18 03	18 06	18 08	18 10	18 12	18 16	18 21	18 26	18 32	18 39	18 47	18 53	18 59
12	17 51	17 55	17 59	18 02	18 05	18 08	18 13	18 19	18 25	18 32	18 40	18 50	18 56	19 03
16	17 42	17 47	17 52	17 56	18 00	18 03	18 10	18 17	18 24	18 32	18 41	18 53	19 00	19 08
20	17 33	17 40	17 46	17 51	17 55	17 59	18 07	18 15	18 23	18 32	18 43	18 55	19 03	19 12
24	17 25	17 33	17 39	17 45	17 51	17 56	18 05	18 14	18 23	18 33	18 44	18 58	19 07	19 17
28	17 16	17 26	17 34	17 40	17 46	17 52	18 02	18 12	18 22	18 33	18 46	19 01	19 10	19 21
May 2	17 09	17 19	17 28	17 36	17 42	17 49	18 00	18 11	18 22	18 34	18 47	19 04	19 14	19 25
6	17 01	17 13	17 23	17 31	17 39	17 46	17 58	18 10	18 22	18 34	18 49	19 06	19 17	19 30
10	16 54	17 07	17 18	17 27	17 35	17 43	17 56	18 09	18 22	18 35	18 50	19 09	19 21	19 34
14	16 48	17 02	17 14	17 24	17 33	17 40	17 55	18 08	18 22	18 36	18 52	19 12	19 24	19 38
18	16 42	16 58	17 10	17 21	17 30	17 38	17 54	18 08	18 22	18 37	18 54	19 15	19 27	19 42
22	16 37	16 53	17 07	17 18	17 28	17 37	17 53	18 08	18 22	18 38	18 56	19 18	19 31	19 46
26	16 33	16 50	17 04	17 16	17 26	17 35	17 52	18 07	18 23	18 39	18 58	19 20	19 34	19 50
30	16 29	16 47	17 02	17 14	17 25	17 34	17 52	18 08	18 23	18 40	18 59	19 23	19 37	19 54
June 3	16 26	16 45	17 00	17 12	17 24	17 34	17 51	18 08	18 24	18 41	19 01	19 25	19 39	19 57
7	16 24	16 43	16 59	17 12	17 23	17 33	17 52	18 08	18 25	18 43	19 03	19 27	19 42	19 59
11	16 22	16 42	16 58	17 11	17 23	17 33	17 52	18 09	18 26	18 44	19 04	19 29	19 44	20 02
15	16 22	16 42	16 58	17 11	17 23	17 34	17 52	18 10	18 27	18 45	19 05	19 30	19 45	20 03
19	16 22	16 42	16 58	17 12	17 24	17 34	17 53	18 10	18 28	18 46	19 06	19 31	19 47	20 05
23	16 23	16 43	16 59	17 13	17 25	17 35	17 54	18 11	18 29	18 47	19 07	19 32	19 47	20 06
27	16 25	16 45	17 01	17 14	17 26	17 36	17 55	18 12	18 29	18 47	19 08	19 33	19 48	20 06
July 1	16 27	16 47	17 03	17 16	17 27	17 38	17 56	18 13	18 30	18 48	19 08	19 33	19 48	20 05
5	16 30	16 49	17 05	17 18	17 29	17 39	17 57	18 14	18 31	18 48	19 08	19 32	19 47	20 04

UNIVERSAL TIME FOR MERIDIAN OF GREENWICH

BEGINNING OF MORNING CIVIL TWILIGHT

Lat.	+40°	+42°	+44°	+46°	+48°	+50°	+52°	+54°	+56°	+58°	+60°	+62°	+64°	+66°
	h m	h m	h m	h m	h m	h m	h m	h m	h m	h m	h m	h m	h m	h m
Mar. 31	5 18	5 16	5 14	5 11	5 09	5 06	5 03	4 59	4 55	4 50	4 45	4 39	4 32	4 24
Apr. 4	5 12	5 09	5 07	5 04	5 00	4 57	4 53	4 49	4 44	4 39	4 32	4 25	4 17	4 07
8	5 05	5 02	4 59	4 56	4 52	4 48	4 44	4 39	4 33	4 27	4 19	4 11	4 01	3 50
12	4 59	4 55	4 52	4 48	4 44	4 39	4 34	4 28	4 22	4 15	4 06	3 57	3 45	3 32
16	4 52	4 49	4 45	4 40	4 36	4 31	4 25	4 18	4 11	4 03	3 53	3 42	3 29	3 13
20	4 46	4 42	4 38	4 33	4 28	4 22	4 16	4 08	4 00	3 51	3 40	3 28	3 13	2 54
24	4 40	4 36	4 31	4 26	4 20	4 14	4 06	3 59	3 50	3 39	3 27	3 13	2 56	2 34
28	4 35	4 30	4 25	4 19	4 12	4 05	3 58	3 49	3 39	3 28	3 14	2 58	2 38	2 12
May 2	4 29	4 24	4 18	4 12	4 05	3 58	3 49	3 40	3 29	3 16	3 01	2 43	2 20	1 48
6	4 24	4 18	4 12	4 06	3 58	3 50	3 41	3 30	3 18	3 04	2 48	2 27	2 00	1 19
10	4 19	4 13	4 07	4 00	3 52	3 43	3 33	3 22	3 09	2 53	2 35	2 11	1 38	0 38
14	4 15	4 09	4 02	3 54	3 46	3 36	3 25	3 13	2 59	2 42	2 22	1 54	1 14	// //
18	4 11	4 04	3 57	3 49	3 40	3 30	3 19	3 05	2 50	2 32	2 09	1 37	0 40	// //
22	4 08	4 00	3 53	3 44	3 35	3 24	3 12	2 58	2 42	2 22	1 56	1 18	// //	// //
26	4 05	3 57	3 49	3 40	3 30	3 19	3 06	2 52	2 34	2 12	1 43	0 57	// //	// //
30	4 02	3 54	3 46	3 37	3 26	3 15	3 02	2 46	2 27	2 04	1 31	0 28	// //	// //
June 3	4 00	3 52	3 44	3 34	3 23	3 11	2 57	2 41	2 21	1 56	1 20	// //	// //	// //
7	3 59	3 51	3 42	3 32	3 21	3 09	2 54	2 37	2 17	1 50	1 09	// //	// //	// //
11	3 58	3 50	3 41	3 31	3 19	3 07	2 52	2 35	2 13	1 45	1 00	// //	// //	// //
15	3 58	3 49	3 40	3 30	3 19	3 06	2 51	2 33	2 11	1 41	0 53	// //	// //	▭
19	3 58	3 50	3 40	3 30	3 19	3 06	2 51	2 33	2 10	1 40	0 49	// //	// //	▭
23	3 59	3 51	3 41	3 31	3 20	3 07	2 51	2 33	2 11	1 41	0 50	// //	// //	▭
27	4 00	3 52	3 43	3 33	3 21	3 08	2 53	2 36	2 13	1 44	0 55	// //	// //	▭
July 1	4 02	3 54	3 45	3 35	3 24	3 11	2 56	2 39	2 17	1 49	1 04	// //	// //	// //
5	4 05	3 57	3 48	3 38	3 27	3 14	3 00	2 43	2 22	1 55	1 14	// //	// //	// //

END OF EVENING CIVIL TWILIGHT

Lat.	+40°	+42°	+44°	+46°	+48°	+50°	+52°	+54°	+56°	+58°	+60°	+62°	+64°	+66°
	h m	h m	h m	h m	h m	h m	h m	h m	h m	h m	h m	h m	h m	h m
Mar. 31	18 51	18 53	18 55	18 58	19 00	19 03	19 07	19 10	19 15	19 19	19 25	19 31	19 38	19 47
Apr. 4	18 55	18 57	19 00	19 03	19 06	19 10	19 14	19 18	19 23	19 29	19 35	19 43	19 51	20 02
8	18 59	19 02	19 05	19 09	19 12	19 17	19 21	19 26	19 32	19 39	19 46	19 55	20 05	20 17
12	19 03	19 07	19 10	19 14	19 19	19 23	19 29	19 34	19 41	19 48	19 57	20 07	20 19	20 33
16	19 08	19 12	19 16	19 20	19 25	19 30	19 36	19 43	19 50	19 58	20 08	20 19	20 33	20 50
20	19 12	19 16	19 21	19 26	19 31	19 37	19 43	19 51	19 59	20 08	20 19	20 32	20 48	21 07
24	19 17	19 21	19 26	19 31	19 37	19 44	19 51	19 59	20 08	20 19	20 31	20 46	21 04	21 27
28	19 21	19 26	19 31	19 37	19 44	19 51	19 59	20 07	20 18	20 29	20 43	21 00	21 20	21 48
May 2	19 25	19 31	19 37	19 43	19 50	19 58	20 06	20 16	20 27	20 40	20 55	21 14	21 38	22 12
6	19 30	19 35	19 42	19 49	19 56	20 04	20 14	20 24	20 36	20 51	21 08	21 29	21 58	22 42
10	19 34	19 40	19 47	19 54	20 02	20 11	20 21	20 33	20 46	21 02	21 21	21 45	22 19	23 33
14	19 38	19 45	19 52	20 00	20 08	20 18	20 28	20 41	20 55	21 12	21 34	22 02	22 45	// //
18	19 42	19 49	19 57	20 05	20 14	20 24	20 36	20 49	21 04	21 23	21 47	22 20	23 25	// //
22	19 46	19 53	20 01	20 10	20 19	20 30	20 42	20 56	21 13	21 34	22 00	22 40	// //	// //
26	19 50	19 58	20 06	20 15	20 25	20 36	20 49	21 04	21 21	21 44	22 13	23 03	// //	// //
30	19 54	20 01	20 10	20 19	20 29	20 41	20 55	21 10	21 29	21 53	22 27	23 39	// //	// //
June 3	19 57	20 05	20 13	20 23	20 34	20 46	21 00	21 16	21 36	22 02	22 39	// //	// //	// //
7	19 59	20 07	20 16	20 26	20 37	20 50	21 04	21 21	21 42	22 10	22 51	// //	// //	// //
11	20 02	20 10	20 19	20 29	20 40	20 53	21 08	21 25	21 47	22 16	23 02	// //	// //	// //
15	20 03	20 12	20 21	20 31	20 43	20 56	21 11	21 29	21 51	22 20	23 10	// //	// //	▭
19	20 05	20 13	20 22	20 33	20 44	20 57	21 12	21 30	21 53	22 23	23 14	// //	// //	▭
23	20 06	20 14	20 23	20 33	20 45	20 58	21 13	21 31	21 53	22 23	23 14	// //	// //	▭
27	20 06	20 14	20 23	20 33	20 45	20 58	21 13	21 30	21 52	22 22	23 10	// //	// //	▭
July 1	20 05	20 14	20 23	20 33	20 44	20 57	21 11	21 29	21 50	22 18	23 02	// //	// //	// //
5	20 04	20 13	20 21	20 31	20 42	20 54	21 09	21 26	21 46	22 13	22 52	// //	// //	// //

▭ indicates Sun continuously above horizon.
// // indicates continuous twilight.

UNIVERSAL TIME FOR MERIDIAN OF GREENWICH

BEGINNING OF MORNING CIVIL TWILIGHT

Lat.	−55°	−50°	−45°	−40°	−35°	−30°	−20°	−10°	0°	+10°	+20°	+30°	+35°	+40°
	h m	h m	h m	h m	h m	h m	h m	h m	h m	h m	h m	h m	h m	h m
July 1	7 41	7 21	7 05	6 52	6 41	6 30	6 12	5 55	5 38	5 20	5 00	4 35	4 20	4 02
5	7 39	7 20	7 05	6 52	6 40	6 30	6 12	5 55	5 39	5 21	5 01	4 37	4 22	4 05
9	7 37	7 18	7 03	6 51	6 40	6 30	6 12	5 56	5 39	5 22	5 03	4 39	4 25	4 07
13	7 34	7 16	7 01	6 49	6 39	6 29	6 12	5 56	5 40	5 23	5 04	4 41	4 27	4 10
17	7 30	7 13	6 59	6 47	6 37	6 28	6 11	5 56	5 40	5 24	5 06	4 44	4 30	4 14
21	7 25	7 09	6 56	6 45	6 35	6 26	6 10	5 56	5 41	5 25	5 08	4 46	4 33	4 17
25	7 20	7 05	6 52	6 42	6 33	6 24	6 09	5 55	5 41	5 26	5 09	4 49	4 36	4 21
29	7 14	7 00	6 48	6 39	6 30	6 22	6 08	5 54	5 41	5 27	5 11	4 51	4 39	4 25
Aug. 2	7 07	6 55	6 44	6 35	6 27	6 19	6 06	5 54	5 41	5 28	5 12	4 54	4 43	4 29
6	7 00	6 49	6 39	6 31	6 23	6 17	6 04	5 53	5 41	5 28	5 14	4 56	4 46	4 33
10	6 53	6 42	6 34	6 26	6 19	6 13	6 02	5 51	5 40	5 29	5 15	4 59	4 49	4 38
14	6 45	6 36	6 28	6 21	6 15	6 10	6 00	5 50	5 40	5 29	5 17	5 02	4 52	4 42
18	6 37	6 29	6 22	6 16	6 11	6 06	5 57	5 48	5 39	5 29	5 18	5 04	4 56	4 46
22	6 28	6 21	6 16	6 11	6 06	6 02	5 54	5 46	5 38	5 30	5 19	5 07	4 59	4 50
26	6 19	6 14	6 09	6 05	6 01	5 58	5 51	5 44	5 37	5 30	5 21	5 09	5 02	4 54
30	6 10	6 06	6 02	5 59	5 56	5 53	5 48	5 42	5 36	5 30	5 22	5 12	5 05	4 58
Sept. 3	6 00	5 57	5 55	5 53	5 51	5 49	5 45	5 40	5 35	5 29	5 23	5 14	5 08	5 02
7	5 50	5 49	5 48	5 47	5 45	5 44	5 41	5 38	5 34	5 29	5 24	5 16	5 12	5 06
11	5 40	5 40	5 40	5 40	5 40	5 39	5 38	5 35	5 33	5 29	5 24	5 18	5 15	5 10
15	5 30	5 32	5 33	5 34	5 34	5 34	5 34	5 33	5 31	5 29	5 25	5 21	5 18	5 14
19	5 20	5 23	5 25	5 27	5 28	5 29	5 30	5 30	5 30	5 28	5 26	5 23	5 21	5 18
23	5 09	5 14	5 18	5 20	5 23	5 24	5 27	5 28	5 28	5 28	5 27	5 25	5 24	5 22
27	4 59	5 05	5 10	5 14	5 17	5 19	5 23	5 25	5 27	5 28	5 28	5 27	5 27	5 26
Oct. 1	4 48	4 56	5 02	5 07	5 11	5 14	5 19	5 23	5 26	5 28	5 29	5 30	5 30	5 29
5	4 38	4 47	4 55	5 00	5 05	5 09	5 16	5 21	5 24	5 27	5 30	5 32	5 33	5 33

END OF EVENING CIVIL TWILIGHT

Lat.	−55°	−50°	−45°	−40°	−35°	−30°	−20°	−10°	0°	+10°	+20°	+30°	+35°	+40°
	h m	h m	h m	h m	h m	h m	h m	h m	h m	h m	h m	h m	h m	h m
July 1	16 27	16 47	17 03	17 16	17 27	17 38	17 56	18 13	18 30	18 48	19 08	19 33	19 48	20 05
5	16 30	16 49	17 05	17 18	17 29	17 39	17 57	18 14	18 31	18 48	19 08	19 32	19 47	20 04
9	16 34	16 53	17 08	17 20	17 31	17 41	17 59	18 15	18 31	18 48	19 08	19 31	19 46	20 03
13	16 38	16 56	17 11	17 23	17 33	17 43	18 00	18 16	18 32	18 48	19 07	19 30	19 44	20 01
17	16 43	17 00	17 14	17 25	17 36	17 45	18 01	18 17	18 32	18 48	19 06	19 29	19 42	19 58
21	16 48	17 04	17 17	17 28	17 38	17 47	18 03	18 17	18 32	18 48	19 05	19 27	19 40	19 55
25	16 54	17 09	17 21	17 32	17 41	17 49	18 04	18 18	18 32	18 47	19 04	19 24	19 37	19 51
29	17 00	17 14	17 25	17 35	17 43	17 51	18 05	18 19	18 32	18 46	19 02	19 21	19 33	19 47
Aug. 2	17 06	17 19	17 29	17 38	17 46	17 53	18 07	18 19	18 31	18 45	19 00	19 18	19 29	19 43
6	17 12	17 24	17 33	17 42	17 49	17 56	18 08	18 19	18 31	18 43	18 58	19 15	19 25	19 38
10	17 19	17 29	17 38	17 45	17 52	17 58	18 09	18 19	18 30	18 42	18 55	19 11	19 21	19 32
14	17 25	17 34	17 42	17 48	17 54	18 00	18 10	18 20	18 29	18 40	18 52	19 07	19 16	19 27
18	17 32	17 40	17 46	17 52	17 57	18 02	18 11	18 20	18 28	18 38	18 49	19 03	19 11	19 21
22	17 39	17 45	17 51	17 56	18 00	18 04	18 12	18 19	18 27	18 36	18 46	18 58	19 06	19 15
26	17 46	17 51	17 55	17 59	18 03	18 06	18 13	18 19	18 26	18 34	18 43	18 54	19 01	19 09
30	17 53	17 56	18 00	18 03	18 05	18 08	18 14	18 19	18 25	18 31	18 39	18 49	18 55	19 02
Sept. 3	18 00	18 02	18 04	18 06	18 08	18 10	18 14	18 19	18 23	18 29	18 36	18 44	18 49	18 56
7	18 07	18 08	18 09	18 10	18 11	18 12	18 15	18 18	18 22	18 26	18 32	18 39	18 44	18 49
11	18 14	18 14	18 13	18 14	18 14	18 14	18 16	18 18	18 21	18 24	18 28	18 34	18 38	18 42
15	18 21	18 19	18 18	18 17	18 17	18 16	18 17	18 18	18 19	18 21	18 25	18 29	18 32	18 36
19	18 29	18 25	18 23	18 21	18 20	18 19	18 17	18 17	18 18	18 19	18 21	18 24	18 26	18 29
23	18 36	18 32	18 28	18 25	18 23	18 21	18 18	18 17	18 16	18 16	18 17	18 19	18 20	18 22
27	18 44	18 38	18 33	18 29	18 26	18 23	18 19	18 17	18 15	18 14	18 14	18 14	18 15	18 16
Oct. 1	18 52	18 44	18 38	18 33	18 29	18 25	18 20	18 16	18 14	18 11	18 10	18 09	18 09	18 09
5	19 00	18 51	18 43	18 37	18 32	18 28	18 21	18 16	18 12	18 09	18 07	18 04	18 03	18 03

UNIVERSAL TIME FOR MERIDIAN OF GREENWICH
BEGINNING OF MORNING CIVIL TWILIGHT

Lat.	+40°	+42°	+44°	+46°	+48°	+50°	+52°	+54°	+56°	+58°	+60°	+62°	+64°	+66°
	h m	h m	h m	h m	h m	h m	h m	h m	h m	h m	h m	h m	h m	h m
July 1	4 02	3 54	3 45	3 35	3 24	3 11	2 56	2 39	2 17	1 49	1 04	// //	// //	// //
5	4 05	3 57	3 48	3 38	3 27	3 14	3 00	2 43	2 22	1 55	1 14	// //	// //	// //
9	4 07	3 59	3 51	3 41	3 30	3 18	3 05	2 48	2 28	2 03	1 26	// //	// //	// //
13	4 10	4 03	3 54	3 45	3 35	3 23	3 10	2 54	2 35	2 12	1 39	0 34	// //	// //
17	4 14	4 06	3 58	3 49	3 39	3 28	3 16	3 01	2 43	2 21	1 52	1 05	// //	// //
21	4 17	4 10	4 03	3 54	3 45	3 34	3 22	3 08	2 51	2 31	2 05	1 27	// //	// //
25	4 21	4 14	4 07	3 59	3 50	3 40	3 29	3 15	3 00	2 42	2 18	1 46	0 47	// //
29	4 25	4 19	4 12	4 04	3 56	3 46	3 35	3 23	3 09	2 52	2 31	2 04	1 22	// //
Aug. 2	4 29	4 23	4 17	4 09	4 01	3 53	3 43	3 31	3 18	3 03	2 44	2 20	1 47	0 41
6	4 33	4 28	4 21	4 15	4 07	3 59	3 50	3 39	3 27	3 13	2 56	2 35	2 08	1 25
10	4 38	4 32	4 26	4 20	4 13	4 06	3 57	3 47	3 36	3 24	3 08	2 50	2 26	1 54
14	4 42	4 37	4 31	4 26	4 19	4 12	4 04	3 56	3 46	3 34	3 20	3 04	2 44	2 17
18	4 46	4 41	4 36	4 31	4 25	4 19	4 12	4 04	3 55	3 44	3 32	3 17	3 00	2 37
22	4 50	4 46	4 41	4 37	4 31	4 25	4 19	4 12	4 03	3 54	3 43	3 30	3 15	2 56
26	4 54	4 50	4 46	4 42	4 37	4 32	4 26	4 20	4 12	4 04	3 54	3 43	3 30	3 13
30	4 58	4 55	4 51	4 47	4 43	4 38	4 33	4 27	4 21	4 14	4 05	3 55	3 44	3 29
Sept. 3	5 02	4 59	4 56	4 53	4 49	4 45	4 40	4 35	4 29	4 23	4 16	4 07	3 57	3 45
7	5 06	5 04	5 01	4 58	4 55	4 51	4 47	4 43	4 38	4 32	4 26	4 18	4 10	4 00
11	5 10	5 08	5 06	5 03	5 00	4 57	4 54	4 50	4 46	4 41	4 36	4 30	4 22	4 14
15	5 14	5 12	5 10	5 08	5 06	5 04	5 01	4 58	4 54	4 50	4 46	4 41	4 35	4 28
19	5 18	5 16	5 15	5 13	5 12	5 10	5 07	5 05	5 02	4 59	4 56	4 52	4 47	4 41
23	5 22	5 21	5 20	5 19	5 17	5 16	5 14	5 12	5 10	5 08	5 05	5 02	4 59	4 54
27	5 26	5 25	5 24	5 24	5 23	5 22	5 21	5 20	5 18	5 17	5 15	5 13	5 10	5 07
Oct. 1	5 29	5 29	5 29	5 29	5 28	5 28	5 28	5 27	5 26	5 25	5 24	5 23	5 22	5 20
5	5 33	5 34	5 34	5 34	5 34	5 34	5 34	5 34	5 34	5 34	5 34	5 34	5 33	5 33

END OF EVENING CIVIL TWILIGHT

Lat.	+40°	+42°	+44°	+46°	+48°	+50°	+52°	+54°	+56°	+58°	+60°	+62°	+64°	+66°
	h m	h m	h m	h m	h m	h m	h m	h m	h m	h m	h m	h m	h m	h m
July 1	20 05	20 14	20 23	20 33	20 44	20 57	21 11	21 29	21 50	22 18	23 02	// //	// //	// //
5	20 04	20 13	20 21	20 31	20 42	20 54	21 09	21 26	21 46	22 13	22 52	// //	// //	// //
9	20 03	20 11	20 19	20 29	20 39	20 51	21 05	21 21	21 41	22 06	22 42	// //	// //	// //
13	20 01	20 08	20 17	20 26	20 36	20 48	21 01	21 16	21 35	21 58	22 30	23 29	// //	// //
17	19 58	20 05	20 13	20 22	20 32	20 43	20 56	21 10	21 28	21 49	22 18	23 02	// //	// //
21	19 55	20 02	20 10	20 18	20 27	20 38	20 50	21 04	21 20	21 40	22 05	22 42	// //	// //
25	19 51	19 58	20 05	20 13	20 22	20 32	20 43	20 56	21 11	21 29	21 52	22 23	23 16	// //
29	19 47	19 54	20 00	20 08	20 16	20 26	20 36	20 48	21 02	21 19	21 39	22 06	22 45	// //
Aug. 2	19 43	19 49	19 55	20 02	20 10	20 19	20 29	20 40	20 53	21 08	21 26	21 49	22 21	23 17
6	19 38	19 43	19 49	19 56	20 03	20 12	20 21	20 31	20 43	20 57	21 13	21 33	22 00	22 39
10	19 32	19 38	19 43	19 50	19 56	20 04	20 12	20 22	20 33	20 45	21 00	21 18	21 41	22 12
14	19 27	19 32	19 37	19 43	19 49	19 56	20 04	20 12	20 22	20 33	20 47	21 03	21 22	21 48
18	19 21	19 25	19 30	19 36	19 41	19 48	19 55	20 02	20 11	20 22	20 33	20 48	21 05	21 26
22	19 15	19 19	19 23	19 28	19 33	19 39	19 45	19 53	20 01	20 10	20 20	20 33	20 48	21 06
26	19 09	19 12	19 16	19 21	19 25	19 30	19 36	19 43	19 50	19 58	20 07	20 18	20 31	20 47
30	19 02	19 06	19 09	19 13	19 17	19 22	19 27	19 32	19 39	19 46	19 54	20 04	20 15	20 29
Sept. 3	18 56	18 59	19 02	19 05	19 09	19 13	19 17	19 22	19 28	19 34	19 41	19 49	19 59	20 11
7	18 49	18 52	18 54	18 57	19 00	19 04	19 08	19 12	19 17	19 22	19 28	19 35	19 44	19 54
11	18 42	18 44	18 47	18 49	18 52	18 55	18 58	19 02	19 06	19 10	19 15	19 21	19 28	19 37
15	18 36	18 37	18 39	18 41	18 43	18 46	18 48	18 51	18 55	18 58	19 03	19 08	19 13	19 20
19	18 29	18 30	18 32	18 33	18 35	18 37	18 39	18 41	18 44	18 47	18 50	18 54	18 59	19 04
23	18 22	18 23	18 24	18 25	18 26	18 28	18 29	18 31	18 33	18 35	18 38	18 41	18 44	18 48
27	18 16	18 16	18 17	18 17	18 18	18 19	18 20	18 21	18 22	18 24	18 25	18 27	18 30	18 32
Oct. 1	18 09	18 09	18 09	18 10	18 10	18 10	18 11	18 11	18 12	18 12	18 13	18 14	18 16	18 17
5	18 03	18 02	18 02	18 02	18 02	18 02	18 01	18 01	18 01	18 01	18 01	18 02	18 02	18 02

// // indicates continuous twilight.

UNIVERSAL TIME FOR MERIDIAN OF GREENWICH
BEGINNING OF MORNING CIVIL TWILIGHT

Lat.	−55°	−50°	−45°	−40°	−35°	−30°	−20°	−10°	0°	+10°	+20°	+30°	+35°	+40°
	h m	h m	h m	h m	h m	h m	h m	h m	h m	h m	h m	h m	h m	h m
Oct. 1	4 48	4 56	5 02	5 07	5 11	5 14	5 19	5 23	5 26	5 28	5 29	5 30	5 30	5 29
5	4 38	4 47	4 55	5 00	5 05	5 09	5 16	5 21	5 24	5 27	5 30	5 32	5 33	5 33
9	4 27	4 38	4 47	4 54	5 00	5 04	5 12	5 18	5 23	5 27	5 31	5 34	5 36	5 37
13	4 17	4 30	4 39	4 47	4 54	5 00	5 09	5 16	5 22	5 27	5 32	5 37	5 39	5 41
17	4 06	4 21	4 32	4 41	4 49	4 55	5 06	5 14	5 21	5 27	5 33	5 39	5 42	5 45
21	3 56	4 12	4 25	4 35	4 44	4 51	5 03	5 12	5 20	5 28	5 35	5 42	5 45	5 49
25	3 46	4 04	4 18	4 29	4 39	4 47	5 00	5 10	5 20	5 28	5 36	5 44	5 49	5 54
29	3 36	3 56	4 11	4 24	4 34	4 43	4 57	5 09	5 19	5 28	5 38	5 47	5 52	5 58
Nov. 2	3 26	3 48	4 05	4 18	4 30	4 39	4 55	5 08	5 19	5 29	5 39	5 50	5 56	6 02
6	3 16	3 41	3 59	4 13	4 26	4 36	4 53	5 07	5 19	5 30	5 41	5 53	5 59	6 06
10	3 07	3 33	3 53	4 09	4 22	4 33	4 51	5 06	5 19	5 31	5 43	5 56	6 03	6 11
14	2 58	3 27	3 48	4 05	4 19	4 30	4 49	5 05	5 19	5 32	5 45	5 59	6 07	6 15
18	2 50	3 21	3 44	4 01	4 16	4 28	4 48	5 05	5 20	5 34	5 47	6 02	6 10	6 19
22	2 42	3 15	3 39	3 58	4 13	4 26	4 48	5 05	5 21	5 35	5 50	6 05	6 14	6 24
26	2 36	3 11	3 36	3 56	4 12	4 25	4 47	5 05	5 22	5 37	5 52	6 08	6 18	6 28
30	2 30	3 07	3 33	3 54	4 10	4 24	4 47	5 06	5 23	5 39	5 54	6 12	6 21	6 32
Dec. 4	2 25	3 04	3 31	3 53	4 10	4 24	4 48	5 07	5 24	5 40	5 57	6 15	6 24	6 35
8	2 21	3 02	3 30	3 52	4 10	4 24	4 48	5 08	5 26	5 42	5 59	6 17	6 28	6 39
12	2 18	3 01	3 30	3 52	4 10	4 25	4 50	5 10	5 28	5 44	6 02	6 20	6 30	6 42
16	2 18	3 01	3 30	3 53	4 11	4 26	4 51	5 11	5 29	5 47	6 04	6 23	6 33	6 45
20	2 18	3 02	3 32	3 54	4 12	4 28	4 53	5 13	5 31	5 49	6 06	6 25	6 35	6 47
24	2 20	3 04	3 34	3 56	4 15	4 30	4 55	5 15	5 33	5 51	6 08	6 27	6 37	6 49
28	2 24	3 07	3 37	3 59	4 17	4 32	4 57	5 17	5 35	5 52	6 10	6 28	6 39	6 51
32	2 29	3 11	3 40	4 02	4 20	4 35	4 59	5 20	5 37	5 54	6 11	6 30	6 40	6 51
36	2 36	3 16	3 44	4 06	4 23	4 38	5 02	5 22	5 39	5 56	6 12	6 30	6 41	6 52

END OF EVENING CIVIL TWILIGHT

Lat.	−55°	−50°	−45°	−40°	−35°	−30°	−20°	−10°	0°	+10°	+20°	+30°	+35°	+40°
	h m	h m	h m	h m	h m	h m	h m	h m	h m	h m	h m	h m	h m	h m
Oct. 1	18 52	18 44	18 38	18 33	18 29	18 25	18 20	18 16	18 14	18 11	18 10	18 09	18 09	18 09
5	19 00	18 51	18 43	18 37	18 32	18 28	18 21	18 16	18 12	18 09	18 07	18 04	18 03	18 03
9	19 09	18 57	18 48	18 41	18 35	18 30	18 23	18 16	18 11	18 07	18 03	18 00	17 58	17 56
13	19 17	19 04	18 54	18 46	18 39	18 33	18 24	18 17	18 10	18 05	18 00	17 55	17 53	17 50
17	19 26	19 11	18 59	18 50	18 42	18 36	18 25	18 17	18 10	18 03	17 57	17 51	17 48	17 45
21	19 35	19 18	19 05	18 55	18 46	18 39	18 27	18 17	18 09	18 02	17 54	17 47	17 43	17 39
25	19 44	19 25	19 11	19 00	18 50	18 42	18 29	18 18	18 09	18 00	17 52	17 43	17 39	17 34
29	19 54	19 33	19 17	19 05	18 54	18 45	18 31	18 19	18 08	17 59	17 50	17 40	17 35	17 29
Nov. 2	20 03	19 40	19 23	19 10	18 58	18 49	18 33	18 20	18 08	17 58	17 48	17 37	17 31	17 24
6	20 13	19 48	19 29	19 15	19 02	18 52	18 35	18 21	18 09	17 57	17 46	17 34	17 27	17 20
10	20 23	19 56	19 36	19 20	19 07	18 55	18 37	18 22	18 09	17 57	17 45	17 32	17 24	17 17
14	20 32	20 03	19 42	19 25	19 11	18 59	18 40	18 24	18 10	17 57	17 44	17 30	17 22	17 13
18	20 42	20 11	19 48	19 30	19 15	19 03	18 42	18 26	18 11	17 57	17 43	17 28	17 20	17 11
22	20 52	20 18	19 54	19 35	19 19	19 06	18 45	18 27	18 12	17 57	17 43	17 27	17 18	17 08
26	21 01	20 25	19 59	19 40	19 24	19 10	18 48	18 29	18 13	17 58	17 43	17 26	17 17	17 07
30	21 09	20 31	20 05	19 44	19 27	19 13	18 50	18 31	18 15	17 59	17 43	17 26	17 16	17 05
Dec. 4	21 17	20 37	20 10	19 48	19 31	19 17	18 53	18 34	18 16	18 00	17 44	17 26	17 16	17 05
8	21 24	20 43	20 14	19 52	19 35	19 20	18 56	18 36	18 18	18 01	17 45	17 26	17 16	17 05
12	21 30	20 47	20 18	19 56	19 38	19 23	18 58	18 38	18 20	18 03	17 46	17 27	17 17	17 05
16	21 34	20 51	20 21	19 59	19 41	19 25	19 00	18 40	18 22	18 05	17 48	17 29	17 18	17 07
20	21 37	20 54	20 24	20 01	19 43	19 28	19 03	18 42	18 24	18 07	17 49	17 31	17 20	17 08
24	21 39	20 55	20 26	20 03	19 45	19 29	19 05	18 44	18 26	18 09	17 51	17 33	17 22	17 10
28	21 39	20 56	20 26	20 04	19 46	19 31	19 06	18 46	18 28	18 11	17 54	17 35	17 25	17 13
32	21 37	20 55	20 27	20 05	19 47	19 32	19 08	18 47	18 30	18 13	17 56	17 38	17 27	17 16
36	21 34	20 54	20 26	20 04	19 47	19 32	19 09	18 49	18 32	18 15	17 58	17 40	17 30	17 19

UNIVERSAL TIME FOR MERIDIAN OF GREENWICH
BEGINNING OF MORNING CIVIL TWILIGHT

Lat.	+40°	+42°	+44°	+46°	+48°	+50°	+52°	+54°	+56°	+58°	+60°	+62°	+64°	+66°
	h m	h m	h m	h m	h m	h m	h m	h m	h m	h m	h m	h m	h m	h m
Oct. 1	5 29	5 29	5 29	5 29	5 28	5 28	5 28	5 27	5 26	5 25	5 24	5 23	5 22	5 20
5	5 33	5 34	5 34	5 34	5 34	5 34	5 34	5 34	5 34	5 34	5 34	5 34	5 33	5 33
9	5 37	5 38	5 38	5 39	5 40	5 40	5 41	5 41	5 42	5 43	5 43	5 44	5 45	5 45
13	5 41	5 42	5 43	5 44	5 45	5 46	5 48	5 49	5 50	5 51	5 53	5 54	5 56	5 58
17	5 45	5 47	5 48	5 49	5 51	5 53	5 54	5 56	5 58	6 00	6 02	6 05	6 07	6 11
21	5 49	5 51	5 53	5 55	5 57	5 59	6 01	6 03	6 06	6 09	6 12	6 15	6 19	6 23
25	5 54	5 56	5 58	6 00	6 02	6 05	6 08	6 11	6 14	6 17	6 21	6 25	6 30	6 36
29	5 58	6 00	6 03	6 05	6 08	6 11	6 14	6 18	6 22	6 26	6 30	6 36	6 41	6 48
Nov. 2	6 02	6 05	6 08	6 11	6 14	6 18	6 21	6 25	6 30	6 34	6 40	6 46	6 53	7 01
6	6 06	6 10	6 13	6 16	6 20	6 24	6 28	6 32	6 37	6 43	6 49	6 56	7 04	7 13
10	6 11	6 14	6 18	6 22	6 26	6 30	6 35	6 40	6 45	6 51	6 58	7 06	7 15	7 25
14	6 15	6 19	6 23	6 27	6 31	6 36	6 41	6 47	6 53	6 59	7 07	7 16	7 26	7 37
18	6 19	6 23	6 28	6 32	6 37	6 42	6 47	6 53	7 00	7 07	7 16	7 25	7 36	7 49
22	6 24	6 28	6 32	6 37	6 42	6 48	6 54	7 00	7 07	7 15	7 24	7 34	7 46	8 00
26	6 28	6 32	6 37	6 42	6 47	6 53	6 59	7 06	7 14	7 22	7 32	7 43	7 56	8 11
30	6 32	6 36	6 41	6 47	6 52	6 58	7 05	7 12	7 20	7 29	7 39	7 51	8 05	8 21
Dec. 4	6 35	6 40	6 45	6 51	6 57	7 03	7 10	7 17	7 26	7 35	7 46	7 58	8 13	8 30
8	6 39	6 44	6 49	6 55	7 01	7 07	7 14	7 22	7 31	7 41	7 52	8 05	8 20	8 38
12	6 42	6 47	6 53	6 58	7 04	7 11	7 18	7 26	7 35	7 45	7 57	8 10	8 26	8 45
16	6 45	6 50	6 55	7 01	7 08	7 14	7 22	7 30	7 39	7 49	8 01	8 14	8 30	8 50
20	6 47	6 52	6 58	7 04	7 10	7 17	7 24	7 33	7 42	7 52	8 04	8 17	8 33	8 53
24	6 49	6 54	7 00	7 06	7 12	7 19	7 26	7 34	7 44	7 54	8 05	8 19	8 35	8 55
28	6 51	6 56	7 01	7 07	7 13	7 20	7 27	7 35	7 44	7 55	8 06	8 19	8 35	8 55
32	6 51	6 56	7 02	7 08	7 14	7 20	7 28	7 35	7 44	7 54	8 06	8 19	8 34	8 53
36	6 52	6 57	7 02	7 07	7 13	7 20	7 27	7 35	7 43	7 53	8 04	8 16	8 31	8 49

END OF EVENING CIVIL TWILIGHT

Lat.	+40°	+42°	+44°	+46°	+48°	+50°	+52°	+54°	+56°	+58°	+60°	+62°	+64°	+66°
	h m	h m	h m	h m	h m	h m	h m	h m	h m	h m	h m	h m	h m	h m
Oct. 1	18 09	18 09	18 09	18 10	18 10	18 10	18 11	18 11	18 12	18 12	18 13	18 14	18 16	18 17
5	18 03	18 02	18 02	18 02	18 02	18 02	18 01	18 01	18 01	18 01	18 01	18 02	18 02	18 02
9	17 56	17 56	17 55	17 55	17 54	17 53	17 53	17 52	17 51	17 50	17 50	17 49	17 48	17 47
13	17 50	17 49	17 48	17 47	17 46	17 45	17 44	17 43	17 41	17 40	17 38	17 37	17 35	17 33
17	17 45	17 43	17 42	17 40	17 39	17 37	17 35	17 34	17 32	17 30	17 27	17 25	17 22	17 19
21	17 39	17 37	17 36	17 34	17 32	17 30	17 27	17 25	17 22	17 19	17 16	17 13	17 09	17 05
25	17 34	17 32	17 30	17 27	17 25	17 22	17 20	17 17	17 13	17 10	17 06	17 02	16 57	16 51
29	17 29	17 27	17 24	17 21	17 18	17 15	17 12	17 09	17 05	17 01	16 56	16 51	16 45	16 38
Nov. 2	17 24	17 22	17 19	17 16	17 12	17 09	17 05	17 01	16 57	16 52	16 46	16 40	16 33	16 25
6	17 20	17 17	17 14	17 10	17 07	17 03	16 59	16 54	16 49	16 44	16 37	16 30	16 22	16 13
10	17 17	17 13	17 10	17 06	17 02	16 57	16 53	16 48	16 42	16 36	16 29	16 21	16 12	16 02
14	17 13	17 10	17 06	17 02	16 57	16 52	16 47	16 42	16 36	16 29	16 21	16 12	16 02	15 51
18	17 11	17 07	17 02	16 58	16 53	16 48	16 42	16 36	16 30	16 22	16 14	16 04	15 53	15 41
22	17 08	17 04	17 00	16 55	16 50	16 44	16 38	16 32	16 25	16 17	16 08	15 57	15 45	15 31
26	17 07	17 02	16 57	16 52	16 47	16 41	16 35	16 28	16 20	16 12	16 02	15 51	15 38	15 23
30	17 05	17 01	16 56	16 51	16 45	16 39	16 32	16 25	16 17	16 08	15 58	15 46	15 32	15 16
Dec. 4	17 05	17 00	16 55	16 49	16 44	16 37	16 30	16 23	16 14	16 05	15 54	15 42	15 27	15 10
8	17 05	17 00	16 55	16 49	16 43	16 36	16 29	16 21	16 13	16 03	15 52	15 39	15 24	15 05
12	17 05	17 00	16 55	16 49	16 43	16 36	16 29	16 21	16 12	16 02	15 51	15 37	15 22	15 03
16	17 07	17 01	16 56	16 50	16 44	16 37	16 30	16 21	16 12	16 02	15 51	15 37	15 21	15 01
20	17 08	17 03	16 57	16 52	16 45	16 38	16 31	16 23	16 14	16 03	15 52	15 38	15 22	15 02
24	17 10	17 05	17 00	16 54	16 47	16 41	16 33	16 25	16 16	16 06	15 54	15 40	15 24	15 05
28	17 13	17 08	17 02	16 56	16 50	16 43	16 36	16 28	16 19	16 09	15 57	15 44	15 28	15 09
32	17 16	17 11	17 05	17 00	16 54	16 47	16 40	16 32	16 23	16 13	16 02	15 49	15 33	15 15
36	17 19	17 14	17 09	17 04	16 58	16 51	16 44	16 36	16 28	16 18	16 07	15 55	15 40	15 22

UNIVERSAL TIME FOR MERIDIAN OF GREENWICH

BEGINNING OF MORNING NAUTICAL TWILIGHT

Lat.	−55°	−50°	−45°	−40°	−35°	−30°	−20°	−10°	0°	+10°	+20°	+30°	+35°	+40°
	h m	h m	h m	h m	h m	h m	h m	h m	h m	h m	h m	h m	h m	h m
Jan. −2	// //	2 03	2 48	3 18	3 41	4 00	4 29	4 51	5 10	5 27	5 43	5 59	6 08	6 17
2	0 21	2 09	2 52	3 22	3 45	4 03	4 31	4 53	5 12	5 28	5 44	6 00	6 09	6 18
6	0 47	2 16	2 58	3 26	3 48	4 06	4 34	4 56	5 14	5 30	5 45	6 01	6 09	6 18
10	1 07	2 24	3 03	3 31	3 53	4 10	4 37	4 58	5 16	5 31	5 46	6 01	6 09	6 18
14	1 25	2 32	3 10	3 36	3 57	4 14	4 40	5 00	5 17	5 33	5 47	6 01	6 09	6 17
18	1 42	2 41	3 16	3 42	4 02	4 18	4 43	5 03	5 19	5 34	5 47	6 01	6 08	6 16
22	1 58	2 51	3 24	3 48	4 06	4 22	4 46	5 05	5 21	5 34	5 47	6 00	6 07	6 14
26	2 13	3 00	3 31	3 54	4 11	4 26	4 49	5 07	5 22	5 35	5 47	5 59	6 05	6 12
30	2 27	3 10	3 38	4 00	4 16	4 30	4 52	5 09	5 23	5 35	5 46	5 57	6 03	6 09
Feb. 3	2 41	3 19	3 46	4 06	4 21	4 34	4 55	5 11	5 24	5 35	5 45	5 55	6 00	6 06
7	2 54	3 29	3 53	4 11	4 26	4 38	4 57	5 12	5 24	5 35	5 44	5 53	5 57	6 02
11	3 07	3 38	4 00	4 17	4 31	4 42	5 00	5 14	5 25	5 34	5 43	5 50	5 54	5 58
15	3 19	3 47	4 07	4 23	4 36	4 46	5 02	5 15	5 25	5 33	5 41	5 47	5 50	5 53
19	3 31	3 56	4 14	4 29	4 40	4 50	5 05	5 16	5 25	5 32	5 38	5 44	5 46	5 48
23	3 42	4 04	4 21	4 34	4 45	4 53	5 07	5 17	5 25	5 31	5 36	5 40	5 42	5 43
27	3 53	4 13	4 28	4 39	4 49	4 56	5 09	5 17	5 24	5 29	5 33	5 36	5 37	5 38
Mar. 3	4 03	4 21	4 34	4 44	4 53	5 00	5 10	5 18	5 24	5 28	5 30	5 32	5 32	5 32
7	4 13	4 28	4 40	4 49	4 57	5 03	5 12	5 18	5 23	5 26	5 27	5 27	5 27	5 26
11	4 22	4 36	4 46	4 54	5 00	5 06	5 13	5 19	5 22	5 24	5 24	5 23	5 21	5 19
15	4 31	4 43	4 52	4 59	5 04	5 08	5 15	5 19	5 21	5 22	5 21	5 18	5 16	5 13
19	4 40	4 50	4 57	5 03	5 08	5 11	5 16	5 19	5 20	5 19	5 17	5 13	5 10	5 06
23	4 48	4 57	5 03	5 07	5 11	5 14	5 17	5 19	5 19	5 17	5 14	5 08	5 04	5 00
27	4 57	5 03	5 08	5 12	5 14	5 16	5 18	5 18	5 17	5 15	5 10	5 03	4 59	4 53
31	5 04	5 10	5 13	5 16	5 17	5 19	5 19	5 18	5 16	5 12	5 06	4 58	4 53	4 46
Apr. 4	5 12	5 16	5 18	5 20	5 21	5 21	5 20	5 18	5 15	5 10	5 03	4 53	4 47	4 39

END OF EVENING NAUTICAL TWILIGHT

Lat.	−55°	−50°	−45°	−40°	−35°	−30°	−20°	−10°	0°	+10°	+20°	+30°	+35°	+40°
	h m	h m	h m	h m	h m	h m	h m	h m	h m	h m	h m	h m	h m	h m
Jan. −2	// //	22 00	21 16	20 46	20 23	20 05	19 36	19 13	18 55	18 38	18 22	18 06	17 57	17 48
2	23 40	21 58	21 15	20 46	20 23	20 05	19 37	19 15	18 56	18 40	18 24	18 08	18 00	17 51
6	23 20	21 55	21 14	20 45	20 23	20 05	19 38	19 16	18 58	18 42	18 27	18 11	18 03	17 54
10	23 04	21 50	21 11	20 43	20 22	20 05	19 38	19 17	19 00	18 44	18 29	18 14	18 06	17 58
14	22 50	21 45	21 08	20 41	20 21	20 04	19 38	19 18	19 01	18 46	18 31	18 17	18 09	18 01
18	22 36	21 38	21 03	20 38	20 19	20 03	19 38	19 18	19 02	18 47	18 34	18 20	18 13	18 05
22	22 23	21 31	20 59	20 35	20 16	20 01	19 37	19 18	19 03	18 49	18 36	18 23	18 17	18 10
26	22 10	21 23	20 53	20 31	20 13	19 59	19 36	19 18	19 03	18 50	18 38	18 26	18 20	18 14
30	21 57	21 15	20 47	20 26	20 10	19 56	19 34	19 18	19 04	18 52	18 40	18 29	18 24	18 18
Feb. 3	21 44	21 07	20 41	20 21	20 06	19 53	19 33	19 17	19 04	18 53	18 42	18 33	18 28	18 22
7	21 31	20 58	20 34	20 16	20 01	19 49	19 30	19 16	19 04	18 54	18 44	18 36	18 31	18 27
11	21 19	20 49	20 27	20 10	19 57	19 46	19 28	19 15	19 04	18 54	18 46	18 38	18 35	18 31
15	21 07	20 39	20 19	20 04	19 52	19 42	19 25	19 13	19 03	18 55	18 48	18 41	18 38	18 35
19	20 55	20 30	20 12	19 58	19 47	19 37	19 23	19 11	19 03	18 55	18 49	18 44	18 42	18 40
23	20 43	20 21	20 04	19 52	19 41	19 33	19 20	19 10	19 02	18 56	18 51	18 47	18 45	18 44
27	20 31	20 11	19 56	19 45	19 36	19 28	19 16	19 08	19 01	18 56	18 52	18 50	18 49	18 48
Mar. 3	20 19	20 02	19 49	19 38	19 30	19 23	19 13	19 06	19 00	18 56	18 54	18 52	18 52	18 53
7	20 07	19 52	19 41	19 32	19 24	19 19	19 10	19 03	18 59	18 56	18 55	18 55	18 56	18 57
11	19 56	19 43	19 33	19 25	19 19	19 14	19 06	19 01	18 58	18 56	18 56	18 57	18 59	19 01
15	19 45	19 33	19 25	19 18	19 13	19 09	19 03	18 59	18 57	18 56	18 57	19 00	19 02	19 05
19	19 34	19 24	19 17	19 11	19 07	19 04	18 59	18 56	18 56	18 56	18 58	19 03	19 06	19 10
23	19 23	19 15	19 09	19 05	19 01	18 59	18 56	18 54	18 54	18 56	19 00	19 05	19 09	19 14
27	19 13	19 06	19 02	18 58	18 56	18 54	18 52	18 52	18 53	18 56	19 01	19 08	19 13	19 19
31	19 02	18 57	18 54	18 52	18 50	18 49	18 49	18 50	18 52	18 56	19 02	19 10	19 16	19 23
Apr. 4	18 52	18 49	18 47	18 45	18 45	18 44	18 45	18 47	18 51	18 56	19 03	19 13	19 20	19 28

// // indicates continuous twilight.

UNIVERSAL TIME FOR MERIDIAN OF GREENWICH

BEGINNING OF MORNING NAUTICAL TWILIGHT

Lat.	+40°	+42°	+44°	+46°	+48°	+50°	+52°	+54°	+56°	+58°	+60°	+62°	+64°	+66°
	h m	h m	h m	h m	h m	h m	h m	h m	h m	h m	h m	h m	h m	h m
Jan. −2	6 17	6 21	6 25	6 29	6 34	6 39	6 44	6 49	6 56	7 02	7 10	7 18	7 27	7 38
2	6 18	6 22	6 26	6 30	6 34	6 39	6 44	6 50	6 55	7 02	7 09	7 17	7 26	7 37
6	6 18	6 22	6 26	6 30	6 34	6 39	6 44	6 49	6 54	7 01	7 08	7 15	7 24	7 34
10	6 18	6 21	6 25	6 29	6 33	6 38	6 42	6 47	6 53	6 59	7 05	7 12	7 21	7 30
14	6 17	6 21	6 24	6 28	6 32	6 36	6 40	6 45	6 50	6 55	7 02	7 08	7 16	7 25
18	6 16	6 19	6 22	6 26	6 29	6 33	6 37	6 42	6 46	6 52	6 57	7 03	7 11	7 19
22	6 14	6 17	6 20	6 23	6 27	6 30	6 34	6 38	6 42	6 47	6 52	6 58	7 04	7 11
26	6 12	6 14	6 17	6 20	6 23	6 26	6 30	6 33	6 37	6 41	6 46	6 51	6 56	7 03
30	6 09	6 11	6 14	6 16	6 19	6 22	6 25	6 28	6 32	6 35	6 39	6 43	6 48	6 54
Feb. 3	6 06	6 08	6 10	6 12	6 15	6 17	6 20	6 22	6 25	6 28	6 32	6 35	6 39	6 44
7	6 02	6 04	6 06	6 08	6 10	6 12	6 14	6 16	6 18	6 21	6 23	6 26	6 29	6 33
11	5 58	5 59	6 01	6 02	6 04	6 06	6 07	6 09	6 11	6 12	6 14	6 16	6 19	6 21
15	5 53	5 54	5 56	5 57	5 58	5 59	6 00	6 01	6 03	6 04	6 05	6 06	6 08	6 09
19	5 48	5 49	5 50	5 51	5 51	5 52	5 53	5 53	5 54	5 55	5 55	5 55	5 56	5 56
23	5 43	5 44	5 44	5 44	5 45	5 45	5 45	5 45	5 45	5 45	5 45	5 44	5 44	5 43
27	5 38	5 38	5 38	5 38	5 37	5 37	5 37	5 36	5 36	5 35	5 34	5 32	5 31	5 29
Mar. 3	5 32	5 31	5 31	5 31	5 30	5 29	5 28	5 27	5 26	5 24	5 22	5 20	5 17	5 14
7	5 26	5 25	5 24	5 23	5 22	5 21	5 19	5 18	5 16	5 13	5 11	5 07	5 04	4 59
11	5 19	5 18	5 17	5 16	5 14	5 12	5 10	5 08	5 05	5 02	4 58	4 54	4 49	4 43
15	5 13	5 11	5 10	5 08	5 06	5 04	5 01	4 58	4 54	4 50	4 46	4 41	4 34	4 27
19	5 06	5 04	5 02	5 00	4 57	4 55	4 51	4 48	4 43	4 39	4 33	4 27	4 19	4 10
23	5 00	4 57	4 55	4 52	4 49	4 45	4 42	4 37	4 32	4 26	4 20	4 12	4 03	3 52
27	4 53	4 50	4 47	4 44	4 40	4 36	4 32	4 26	4 21	4 14	4 06	3 57	3 46	3 33
31	4 46	4 43	4 39	4 36	4 31	4 27	4 21	4 15	4 09	4 01	3 52	3 41	3 29	3 13
Apr. 4	4 39	4 36	4 32	4 27	4 22	4 17	4 11	4 04	3 57	3 48	3 38	3 25	3 11	2 52

END OF EVENING NAUTICAL TWILIGHT

Lat.	+40°	+42°	+44°	+46°	+48°	+50°	+52°	+54°	+56°	+58°	+60°	+62°	+64°	+66°
	h m	h m	h m	h m	h m	h m	h m	h m	h m	h m	h m	h m	h m	h m
Jan. −2	17 48	17 44	17 40	17 35	17 31	17 26	17 21	17 15	17 09	17 03	16 55	16 47	16 38	16 27
2	17 51	17 47	17 43	17 39	17 34	17 29	17 24	17 19	17 13	17 07	17 00	16 52	16 42	16 32
6	17 54	17 50	17 46	17 42	17 38	17 34	17 29	17 23	17 18	17 12	17 05	16 57	16 48	16 38
10	17 58	17 54	17 50	17 46	17 42	17 38	17 33	17 28	17 23	17 17	17 11	17 03	16 55	16 46
14	18 01	17 58	17 55	17 51	17 47	17 43	17 39	17 34	17 29	17 23	17 17	17 10	17 03	16 54
18	18 05	18 02	17 59	17 56	17 52	17 48	17 44	17 40	17 35	17 30	17 24	17 18	17 11	17 03
22	18 10	18 07	18 04	18 00	17 57	17 54	17 50	17 46	17 42	17 37	17 32	17 26	17 20	17 13
26	18 14	18 11	18 08	18 05	18 02	17 59	17 56	17 52	17 49	17 45	17 40	17 35	17 30	17 23
30	18 18	18 16	18 13	18 11	18 08	18 05	18 02	17 59	17 56	17 52	17 48	17 44	17 39	17 34
Feb. 3	18 22	18 20	18 18	18 16	18 14	18 11	18 09	18 06	18 03	18 00	17 57	17 54	17 50	17 45
7	18 27	18 25	18 23	18 21	18 19	18 17	18 15	18 13	18 11	18 09	18 06	18 03	18 00	17 57
11	18 31	18 30	18 28	18 27	18 25	18 24	18 22	18 20	18 19	18 17	18 15	18 13	18 11	18 09
15	18 35	18 34	18 33	18 32	18 31	18 30	18 29	18 28	18 27	18 25	18 24	18 23	18 22	18 21
19	18 40	18 39	18 38	18 38	18 37	18 36	18 36	18 35	18 35	18 34	18 34	18 33	18 33	18 33
23	18 44	18 44	18 43	18 43	18 43	18 43	18 43	18 43	18 43	18 43	18 43	18 44	18 45	18 46
27	18 48	18 48	18 48	18 48	18 49	18 49	18 49	18 50	18 51	18 52	18 53	18 54	18 56	18 59
Mar. 3	18 53	18 53	18 53	18 54	18 55	18 56	18 57	18 58	18 59	19 01	19 03	19 05	19 08	19 12
7	18 57	18 58	18 58	18 59	19 01	19 02	19 04	19 05	19 08	19 10	19 13	19 16	19 20	19 25
11	19 01	19 02	19 04	19 05	19 07	19 09	19 11	19 13	19 16	19 19	19 23	19 28	19 33	19 39
15	19 05	19 07	19 09	19 11	19 13	19 15	19 18	19 21	19 25	19 29	19 33	19 39	19 46	19 53
19	19 10	19 12	19 14	19 16	19 19	19 22	19 25	19 29	19 33	19 38	19 44	19 51	19 59	20 08
23	19 14	19 16	19 19	19 22	19 25	19 29	19 33	19 37	19 42	19 48	19 55	20 03	20 13	20 24
27	19 19	19 21	19 24	19 28	19 32	19 36	19 40	19 46	19 52	19 59	20 07	20 16	20 27	20 41
31	19 23	19 26	19 30	19 34	19 38	19 43	19 48	19 54	20 01	20 09	20 18	20 29	20 42	20 58
Apr. 4	19 28	19 31	19 35	19 40	19 45	19 50	19 56	20 03	20 11	20 20	20 31	20 43	20 59	21 18

UNIVERSAL TIME FOR MERIDIAN OF GREENWICH

BEGINNING OF MORNING NAUTICAL TWILIGHT

Lat.	−55°	−50°	−45°	−40°	−35°	−30°	−20°	−10°	0°	+10°	+20°	+30°	+35°	+40°
	h m	h m	h m	h m	h m	h m	h m	h m	h m	h m	h m	h m	h m	h m
Mar. 31	5 04	5 10	5 13	5 16	5 17	5 19	5 19	5 18	5 16	5 12	5 06	4 58	4 53	4 46
Apr. 4	5 12	5 16	5 18	5 20	5 21	5 21	5 20	5 18	5 15	5 10	5 03	4 53	4 47	4 39
8	5 20	5 22	5 23	5 24	5 24	5 23	5 21	5 18	5 13	5 07	4 59	4 48	4 41	4 32
12	5 27	5 28	5 28	5 27	5 27	5 25	5 22	5 18	5 12	5 05	4 56	4 43	4 35	4 25
16	5 34	5 34	5 33	5 31	5 29	5 28	5 23	5 18	5 11	5 03	4 52	4 38	4 29	4 19
20	5 41	5 39	5 37	5 35	5 32	5 30	5 24	5 18	5 10	5 01	4 49	4 34	4 24	4 12
24	5 48	5 45	5 42	5 38	5 35	5 32	5 25	5 18	5 09	4 59	4 46	4 29	4 18	4 06
28	5 55	5 50	5 46	5 42	5 38	5 34	5 26	5 18	5 08	4 57	4 43	4 25	4 13	3 59
May 2	6 01	5 56	5 50	5 46	5 41	5 36	5 27	5 18	5 07	4 55	4 40	4 21	4 08	3 53
6	6 08	6 01	5 55	5 49	5 44	5 39	5 29	5 18	5 06	4 53	4 37	4 17	4 04	3 48
10	6 14	6 06	5 59	5 52	5 47	5 41	5 30	5 18	5 06	4 52	4 35	4 13	3 59	3 42
14	6 19	6 11	6 03	5 56	5 49	5 43	5 31	5 19	5 06	4 51	4 33	4 10	3 55	3 37
18	6 25	6 15	6 07	5 59	5 52	5 45	5 32	5 19	5 05	4 50	4 31	4 07	3 51	3 33
22	6 30	6 19	6 10	6 02	5 54	5 47	5 34	5 20	5 05	4 49	4 29	4 04	3 48	3 29
26	6 35	6 23	6 14	6 05	5 57	5 49	5 35	5 21	5 06	4 48	4 28	4 02	3 45	3 25
30	6 39	6 27	6 17	6 08	5 59	5 51	5 36	5 21	5 06	4 48	4 27	4 00	3 43	3 22
June 3	6 43	6 30	6 20	6 10	6 01	5 53	5 38	5 22	5 06	4 48	4 27	3 59	3 41	3 20
7	6 47	6 33	6 22	6 12	6 03	5 55	5 39	5 23	5 07	4 48	4 26	3 58	3 40	3 18
11	6 49	6 36	6 24	6 14	6 05	5 56	5 40	5 24	5 07	4 49	4 26	3 58	3 39	3 17
15	6 52	6 38	6 26	6 16	6 06	5 58	5 41	5 25	5 08	4 49	4 27	3 58	3 39	3 16
19	6 53	6 39	6 27	6 17	6 08	5 59	5 42	5 26	5 09	4 50	4 27	3 58	3 40	3 16
23	6 54	6 40	6 28	6 18	6 08	6 00	5 43	5 27	5 10	4 51	4 28	3 59	3 40	3 17
27	6 54	6 40	6 29	6 18	6 09	6 00	5 44	5 28	5 11	4 52	4 29	4 00	3 42	3 19
July 1	6 53	6 40	6 28	6 18	6 09	6 00	5 44	5 28	5 12	4 53	4 31	4 02	3 44	3 21
5	6 52	6 39	6 28	6 18	6 09	6 00	5 45	5 29	5 13	4 54	4 32	4 04	3 46	3 24

END OF EVENING NAUTICAL TWILIGHT

Lat.	−55°	−50°	−45°	−40°	−35°	−30°	−20°	−10°	0°	+10°	+20°	+30°	+35°	+40°
	h m	h m	h m	h m	h m	h m	h m	h m	h m	h m	h m	h m	h m	h m
Mar. 31	19 02	18 57	18 54	18 52	18 50	18 49	18 49	18 50	18 52	18 56	19 02	19 10	19 16	19 23
Apr. 4	18 52	18 49	18 47	18 45	18 45	18 44	18 45	18 47	18 51	18 56	19 03	19 13	19 20	19 28
8	18 43	18 41	18 40	18 39	18 39	18 40	18 42	18 45	18 50	18 56	19 05	19 16	19 23	19 32
12	18 33	18 33	18 33	18 33	18 34	18 36	18 39	18 43	18 49	18 57	19 06	19 19	19 27	19 37
16	18 24	18 25	18 26	18 28	18 29	18 31	18 36	18 42	18 48	18 57	19 08	19 22	19 31	19 42
20	18 15	18 18	18 20	18 22	18 25	18 27	18 33	18 40	18 48	18 57	19 09	19 25	19 35	19 46
24	18 07	18 10	18 14	18 17	18 20	18 24	18 31	18 38	18 47	18 58	19 11	19 28	19 38	19 51
28	17 59	18 04	18 08	18 12	18 16	18 20	18 28	18 37	18 47	18 58	19 13	19 31	19 42	19 56
May 2	17 52	17 58	18 03	18 08	18 12	18 17	18 26	18 36	18 47	18 59	19 14	19 34	19 46	20 01
6	17 45	17 52	17 58	18 04	18 09	18 14	18 24	18 35	18 47	19 00	19 16	19 37	19 50	20 06
10	17 38	17 46	17 53	18 00	18 06	18 12	18 23	18 34	18 47	19 01	19 18	19 40	19 54	20 11
14	17 33	17 42	17 49	17 57	18 03	18 09	18 22	18 34	18 47	19 02	19 20	19 43	19 58	20 16
18	17 27	17 37	17 46	17 54	18 01	18 07	18 20	18 34	18 47	19 03	19 22	19 47	20 02	20 21
22	17 23	17 34	17 43	17 51	17 59	18 06	18 20	18 33	18 48	19 05	19 24	19 50	20 06	20 25
26	17 19	17 30	17 40	17 49	17 57	18 05	18 19	18 33	18 49	19 06	19 26	19 52	20 09	20 30
30	17 15	17 28	17 38	17 47	17 56	18 04	18 19	18 34	18 49	19 07	19 28	19 55	20 12	20 34
June 3	17 13	17 26	17 37	17 46	17 55	18 03	18 19	18 34	18 50	19 08	19 30	19 58	20 15	20 37
7	17 11	17 24	17 36	17 46	17 55	18 03	18 19	18 35	18 51	19 10	19 32	20 00	20 18	20 41
11	17 10	17 24	17 35	17 45	17 54	18 03	18 19	18 35	18 52	19 11	19 33	20 02	20 20	20 43
15	17 09	17 23	17 35	17 45	17 55	18 03	18 20	18 36	18 53	19 12	19 34	20 03	20 22	20 45
19	17 10	17 24	17 36	17 46	17 55	18 04	18 21	18 37	18 54	19 13	19 36	20 05	20 23	20 47
23	17 11	17 25	17 36	17 47	17 56	18 05	18 22	18 38	18 55	19 14	19 36	20 05	20 24	20 47
27	17 12	17 26	17 38	17 48	17 57	18 06	18 23	18 39	18 56	19 14	19 37	20 06	20 24	20 47
July 1	17 15	17 28	17 40	17 50	17 59	18 07	18 24	18 40	18 56	19 15	19 37	20 06	20 24	20 47
5	17 17	17 31	17 42	17 52	18 01	18 09	18 25	18 40	18 57	19 15	19 37	20 05	20 23	20 45

NAUTICAL TWILIGHT, 2025

UNIVERSAL TIME FOR MERIDIAN OF GREENWICH

BEGINNING OF MORNING NAUTICAL TWILIGHT

Lat.	+40°	+42°	+44°	+46°	+48°	+50°	+52°	+54°	+56°	+58°	+60°	+62°	+64°	+66°
	h m	h m	h m	h m	h m	h m	h m	h m	h m	h m	h m	h m	h m	h m
Mar. 31	4 46	4 43	4 39	4 36	4 31	4 27	4 21	4 15	4 09	4 01	3 52	3 41	3 29	3 13
Apr. 4	4 39	4 36	4 32	4 27	4 22	4 17	4 11	4 04	3 57	3 48	3 38	3 25	3 11	2 52
8	4 32	4 28	4 24	4 19	4 14	4 08	4 01	3 53	3 45	3 34	3 23	3 09	2 51	2 29
12	4 25	4 21	4 16	4 11	4 05	3 58	3 50	3 42	3 32	3 21	3 07	2 51	2 30	2 03
16	4 19	4 14	4 08	4 02	3 56	3 48	3 40	3 30	3 19	3 07	2 51	2 32	2 07	1 31
20	4 12	4 07	4 01	3 54	3 47	3 39	3 29	3 19	3 07	2 52	2 34	2 12	1 41	0 44
24	4 06	4 00	3 53	3 46	3 38	3 29	3 19	3 07	2 53	2 37	2 16	1 49	1 07	// //
28	3 59	3 53	3 46	3 38	3 30	3 20	3 08	2 56	2 40	2 21	1 57	1 22	// //	// //
May 2	3 53	3 47	3 39	3 31	3 21	3 10	2 58	2 44	2 27	2 05	1 36	0 46	// //	// //
6	3 48	3 40	3 32	3 23	3 13	3 01	2 48	2 32	2 13	1 47	1 10	// //	// //	// //
10	3 42	3 34	3 26	3 16	3 05	2 53	2 38	2 20	1 58	1 28	0 33	// //	// //	// //
14	3 37	3 29	3 20	3 09	2 58	2 44	2 28	2 09	1 43	1 06	// //	// //	// //	// //
18	3 33	3 24	3 14	3 03	2 51	2 36	2 19	1 57	1 28	0 36	// //	// //	// //	// //
22	3 29	3 19	3 09	2 57	2 44	2 28	2 10	1 45	1 11	// //	// //	// //	// //	// //
26	3 25	3 15	3 05	2 52	2 38	2 21	2 01	1 34	0 52	// //	// //	// //	// //	// //
30	3 22	3 12	3 01	2 48	2 33	2 15	1 53	1 23	0 25	// //	// //	// //	// //	// //
June 3	3 20	3 09	2 57	2 44	2 29	2 10	1 46	1 13	// //	// //	// //	// //	// //	// //
7	3 18	3 07	2 55	2 41	2 25	2 06	1 40	1 03	// //	// //	// //	// //	// //	// //
11	3 17	3 06	2 53	2 39	2 23	2 02	1 36	0 55	// //	// //	// //	// //	// //	// //
15	3 16	3 05	2 53	2 38	2 21	2 01	1 33	0 48	// //	// //	// //	// //	// //	▭
19	3 16	3 05	2 53	2 38	2 21	2 00	1 32	0 45	// //	// //	// //	// //	// //	▭
23	3 17	3 06	2 54	2 39	2 22	2 01	1 33	0 46	// //	// //	// //	// //	// //	▭
27	3 19	3 08	2 55	2 41	2 24	2 03	1 36	0 51	// //	// //	// //	// //	// //	▭
July 1	3 21	3 10	2 58	2 44	2 27	2 07	1 40	0 59	// //	// //	// //	// //	// //	// //
5	3 24	3 13	3 01	2 47	2 31	2 11	1 46	1 08	// //	// //	// //	// //	// //	// //

END OF EVENING NAUTICAL TWILIGHT

Lat.	+40°	+42°	+44°	+46°	+48°	+50°	+52°	+54°	+56°	+58°	+60°	+62°	+64°	+66°
	h m	h m	h m	h m	h m	h m	h m	h m	h m	h m	h m	h m	h m	h m
Mar. 31	19 23	19 26	19 30	19 34	19 38	19 43	19 48	19 54	20 01	20 09	20 18	20 29	20 42	20 58
Apr. 4	19 28	19 31	19 35	19 40	19 45	19 50	19 56	20 03	20 11	20 20	20 31	20 43	20 59	21 18
8	19 32	19 36	19 41	19 46	19 51	19 57	20 04	20 12	20 21	20 31	20 43	20 58	21 16	21 39
12	19 37	19 41	19 46	19 52	19 58	20 05	20 13	20 21	20 31	20 43	20 57	21 14	21 35	22 05
16	19 42	19 47	19 52	19 58	20 05	20 13	20 21	20 31	20 42	20 55	21 11	21 31	21 57	22 36
20	19 46	19 52	19 58	20 05	20 12	20 21	20 30	20 41	20 53	21 08	21 27	21 50	22 23	23 34
24	19 51	19 57	20 04	20 11	20 19	20 29	20 39	20 51	21 05	21 22	21 43	22 12	22 59	// //
28	19 56	20 03	20 10	20 18	20 27	20 37	20 48	21 01	21 17	21 37	22 02	22 39	// //	// //
May 2	20 01	20 08	20 16	20 25	20 34	20 45	20 58	21 12	21 30	21 52	22 23	23 21	// //	// //
6	20 06	20 14	20 22	20 31	20 42	20 53	21 07	21 23	21 43	22 10	22 50	// //	// //	// //
10	20 11	20 19	20 28	20 38	20 49	21 02	21 17	21 35	21 58	22 29	23 36	// //	// //	// //
14	20 16	20 25	20 34	20 44	20 56	21 10	21 27	21 46	22 13	22 52	// //	// //	// //	// //
18	20 21	20 30	20 40	20 51	21 04	21 18	21 36	21 58	22 29	23 28	// //	// //	// //	// //
22	20 25	20 35	20 45	20 57	21 11	21 26	21 46	22 10	22 47	// //	// //	// //	// //	// //
26	20 30	20 40	20 50	21 03	21 17	21 34	21 55	22 23	23 08	// //	// //	// //	// //	// //
30	20 34	20 44	20 55	21 08	21 23	21 41	22 04	22 35	23 41	// //	// //	// //	// //	// //
June 3	20 37	20 48	21 00	21 13	21 29	21 48	22 12	22 46	// //	// //	// //	// //	// //	// //
7	20 41	20 51	21 03	21 17	21 33	21 53	22 19	22 57	// //	// //	// //	// //	// //	// //
11	20 43	20 54	21 06	21 21	21 37	21 58	22 24	23 07	// //	// //	// //	// //	// //	// //
15	20 45	20 56	21 09	21 23	21 40	22 01	22 29	23 14	// //	// //	// //	// //	// //	▭
19	20 47	20 58	21 10	21 25	21 42	22 03	22 31	23 18	// //	// //	// //	// //	// //	▭
23	20 47	20 58	21 11	21 25	21 43	22 04	22 31	23 18	// //	// //	// //	// //	// //	▭
27	20 47	20 58	21 11	21 25	21 42	22 03	22 30	23 14	// //	// //	// //	// //	// //	▭
July 1	20 47	20 58	21 10	21 24	21 40	22 01	22 27	23 07	// //	// //	// //	// //	// //	// //
5	20 45	20 56	21 08	21 22	21 38	21 57	22 22	22 59	// //	// //	// //	// //	// //	// //

▭ indicates Sun continuously above horizon.
// // indicates continuous twilight.

NAUTICAL TWILIGHT, 2025

UNIVERSAL TIME FOR MERIDIAN OF GREENWICH

BEGINNING OF MORNING NAUTICAL TWILIGHT

Lat.	−55°	−50°	−45°	−40°	−35°	−30°	−20°	−10°	0°	+10°	+20°	+30°	+35°	+40°
	h m	h m	h m	h m	h m	h m	h m	h m	h m	h m	h m	h m	h m	h m
July 1	6 53	6 40	6 28	6 18	6 09	6 00	5 44	5 28	5 12	4 53	4 31	4 02	3 44	3 21
5	6 52	6 39	6 28	6 18	6 09	6 00	5 45	5 29	5 13	4 54	4 32	4 04	3 46	3 24
9	6 50	6 37	6 27	6 17	6 08	6 00	5 45	5 29	5 13	4 55	4 34	4 06	3 48	3 27
13	6 47	6 35	6 25	6 16	6 07	5 59	5 44	5 30	5 14	4 56	4 36	4 09	3 51	3 30
17	6 44	6 32	6 23	6 14	6 06	5 58	5 44	5 30	5 15	4 58	4 37	4 11	3 55	3 34
21	6 40	6 29	6 20	6 12	6 04	5 57	5 43	5 30	5 15	4 59	4 39	4 14	3 58	3 38
25	6 35	6 25	6 17	6 09	6 02	5 55	5 42	5 29	5 16	5 00	4 41	4 17	4 02	3 43
29	6 29	6 21	6 13	6 06	5 59	5 53	5 41	5 29	5 16	5 01	4 43	4 20	4 05	3 47
Aug. 2	6 23	6 16	6 09	6 02	5 56	5 51	5 40	5 28	5 16	5 02	4 45	4 23	4 09	3 52
6	6 17	6 10	6 04	5 58	5 53	5 48	5 38	5 27	5 16	5 03	4 47	4 26	4 13	3 57
10	6 10	6 04	5 59	5 54	5 49	5 45	5 36	5 26	5 16	5 03	4 48	4 29	4 16	4 02
14	6 02	5 58	5 53	5 49	5 45	5 42	5 33	5 25	5 15	5 04	4 50	4 32	4 20	4 06
18	5 54	5 51	5 48	5 44	5 41	5 38	5 31	5 23	5 15	5 04	4 51	4 35	4 24	4 11
22	5 46	5 44	5 41	5 39	5 37	5 34	5 28	5 22	5 14	5 05	4 53	4 37	4 28	4 16
26	5 37	5 36	5 35	5 34	5 32	5 30	5 25	5 20	5 13	5 05	4 54	4 40	4 31	4 20
30	5 28	5 28	5 28	5 28	5 27	5 26	5 22	5 18	5 12	5 05	4 55	4 43	4 35	4 25
Sept. 3	5 18	5 20	5 21	5 22	5 22	5 21	5 19	5 16	5 11	5 05	4 57	4 45	4 38	4 29
7	5 08	5 12	5 14	5 15	5 16	5 16	5 16	5 13	5 10	5 05	4 58	4 48	4 41	4 33
11	4 58	5 03	5 07	5 09	5 10	5 11	5 12	5 11	5 08	5 05	4 59	4 50	4 45	4 38
15	4 48	4 54	4 59	5 02	5 05	5 07	5 08	5 09	5 07	5 04	5 00	4 53	4 48	4 42
19	4 37	4 45	4 51	4 56	4 59	5 02	5 05	5 06	5 06	5 04	5 01	4 55	4 51	4 46
23	4 26	4 36	4 43	4 49	4 53	4 56	5 01	5 04	5 04	5 04	5 02	4 57	4 54	4 50
27	4 15	4 27	4 35	4 42	4 47	4 51	4 57	5 01	5 03	5 03	5 02	5 00	4 57	4 54
Oct. 1	4 04	4 17	4 27	4 35	4 41	4 46	4 54	4 58	5 02	5 03	5 03	5 02	5 00	4 58
5	3 53	4 08	4 19	4 28	4 35	4 41	4 50	4 56	5 00	5 03	5 04	5 04	5 03	5 02

END OF EVENING NAUTICAL TWILIGHT

Lat.	−55°	−50°	−45°	−40°	−35°	−30°	−20°	−10°	0°	+10°	+20°	+30°	+35°	+40°
	h m	h m	h m	h m	h m	h m	h m	h m	h m	h m	h m	h m	h m	h m
July 1	17 15	17 28	17 40	17 50	17 59	18 07	18 24	18 40	18 56	19 15	19 37	20 06	20 24	20 47
5	17 17	17 31	17 42	17 52	18 01	18 09	18 25	18 40	18 57	19 15	19 37	20 05	20 23	20 45
9	17 21	17 34	17 44	17 54	18 03	18 11	18 26	18 41	18 57	19 15	19 37	20 04	20 22	20 43
13	17 25	17 37	17 47	17 56	18 05	18 12	18 27	18 42	18 58	19 15	19 36	20 03	20 20	20 41
17	17 29	17 40	17 50	17 59	18 07	18 14	18 28	18 43	18 58	19 15	19 35	20 01	20 17	20 38
21	17 34	17 44	17 53	18 02	18 09	18 16	18 30	18 43	18 58	19 14	19 33	19 58	20 14	20 34
25	17 39	17 49	17 57	18 05	18 12	18 18	18 31	18 44	18 58	19 13	19 32	19 56	20 11	20 30
29	17 44	17 53	18 01	18 08	18 14	18 20	18 32	18 44	18 57	19 12	19 30	19 53	20 07	20 25
Aug. 2	17 50	17 58	18 04	18 11	18 17	18 22	18 33	18 44	18 57	19 11	19 27	19 49	20 03	20 20
6	17 56	18 02	18 08	18 14	18 19	18 24	18 34	18 45	18 56	19 09	19 25	19 45	19 58	20 14
10	18 02	18 07	18 12	18 17	18 22	18 26	18 35	18 45	18 55	19 07	19 22	19 41	19 53	20 08
14	18 08	18 12	18 16	18 20	18 24	18 28	18 36	18 45	18 54	19 05	19 19	19 37	19 48	20 02
18	18 14	18 18	18 21	18 24	18 27	18 30	18 37	18 44	18 53	19 03	19 16	19 32	19 43	19 56
22	18 21	18 23	18 25	18 27	18 30	18 32	18 38	18 44	18 52	19 01	19 13	19 28	19 37	19 49
26	18 28	18 28	18 29	18 31	18 32	18 34	18 38	18 44	18 50	18 59	19 09	19 23	19 32	19 42
30	18 35	18 34	18 34	18 34	18 35	18 36	18 39	18 44	18 49	18 56	19 05	19 18	19 26	19 35
Sept. 3	18 42	18 39	18 38	18 38	18 38	18 38	18 40	18 43	18 48	18 54	19 02	19 13	19 20	19 29
7	18 49	18 45	18 43	18 41	18 40	18 40	18 41	18 43	18 46	18 51	18 58	19 08	19 14	19 22
11	18 56	18 51	18 47	18 45	18 43	18 42	18 41	18 42	18 45	18 48	18 54	19 02	19 08	19 15
15	19 04	18 57	18 52	18 49	18 46	18 44	18 42	18 42	18 43	18 46	18 50	18 57	19 02	19 08
19	19 12	19 03	18 57	18 53	18 49	18 46	18 43	18 42	18 42	18 43	18 46	18 52	18 56	19 01
23	19 20	19 10	19 02	18 57	18 52	18 49	18 44	18 41	18 40	18 41	18 43	18 47	18 50	18 54
27	19 28	19 16	19 08	19 01	18 55	18 51	18 45	18 41	18 39	18 38	18 39	18 42	18 44	18 47
Oct. 1	19 37	19 23	19 13	19 05	18 59	18 54	18 46	18 41	18 38	18 36	18 36	18 37	18 38	18 40
5	19 46	19 30	19 19	19 09	19 02	18 56	18 47	18 41	18 36	18 34	18 32	18 32	18 33	18 34

UNIVERSAL TIME FOR MERIDIAN OF GREENWICH
BEGINNING OF MORNING NAUTICAL TWILIGHT

Lat.	+40°	+42°	+44°	+46°	+48°	+50°	+52°	+54°	+56°	+58°	+60°	+62°	+64°	+66°
	h m	h m	h m	h m	h m	h m	h m	h m	h m	h m	h m	h m	h m	h m
July 1	3 21	3 10	2 58	2 44	2 27	2 07	1 40	0 59	// //	// //	// //	// //	// //	// //
5	3 24	3 13	3 01	2 47	2 31	2 11	1 46	1 08	// //	// //	// //	// //	// //	// //
9	3 27	3 16	3 05	2 51	2 36	2 17	1 53	1 19	// //	// //	// //	// //	// //	// //
13	3 30	3 20	3 09	2 56	2 41	2 23	2 01	1 31	0 31	// //	// //	// //	// //	// //
17	3 34	3 24	3 14	3 01	2 47	2 30	2 10	1 43	0 59	// //	// //	// //	// //	// //
21	3 38	3 29	3 19	3 07	2 54	2 38	2 19	1 55	1 20	// //	// //	// //	// //	// //
25	3 43	3 34	3 24	3 13	3 00	2 46	2 28	2 06	1 37	0 43	// //	// //	// //	// //
29	3 47	3 39	3 30	3 19	3 08	2 54	2 38	2 18	1 53	1 14	// //	// //	// //	// //
Aug. 2	3 52	3 44	3 35	3 26	3 15	3 02	2 47	2 29	2 07	1 37	0 38	// //	// //	// //
6	3 57	3 49	3 41	3 32	3 22	3 10	2 57	2 41	2 21	1 55	1 17	// //	// //	// //
10	4 02	3 55	3 47	3 39	3 29	3 18	3 06	2 51	2 34	2 12	1 42	0 48	// //	// //
14	4 06	4 00	3 53	3 45	3 36	3 26	3 15	3 02	2 46	2 27	2 02	1 26	// //	// //
18	4 11	4 05	3 59	3 51	3 43	3 34	3 24	3 12	2 58	2 41	2 20	1 52	1 07	// //
22	4 16	4 10	4 04	3 58	3 50	3 42	3 33	3 22	3 09	2 54	2 36	2 13	1 41	0 36
26	4 20	4 15	4 10	4 04	3 57	3 49	3 41	3 31	3 20	3 07	2 51	2 32	2 06	1 28
30	4 25	4 20	4 15	4 10	4 04	3 57	3 49	3 41	3 31	3 19	3 05	2 48	2 27	1 58
Sept. 3	4 29	4 25	4 21	4 16	4 10	4 04	3 57	3 49	3 41	3 30	3 18	3 04	2 46	2 23
7	4 33	4 30	4 26	4 21	4 16	4 11	4 05	3 58	3 50	3 41	3 31	3 18	3 03	2 44
11	4 38	4 34	4 31	4 27	4 23	4 18	4 13	4 06	4 00	3 52	3 42	3 32	3 19	3 02
15	4 42	4 39	4 36	4 33	4 29	4 25	4 20	4 15	4 09	4 02	3 54	3 44	3 33	3 20
19	4 46	4 44	4 41	4 38	4 35	4 31	4 27	4 23	4 17	4 12	4 05	3 57	3 47	3 36
23	4 50	4 48	4 46	4 43	4 41	4 38	4 34	4 31	4 26	4 21	4 15	4 09	4 01	3 51
27	4 54	4 52	4 51	4 49	4 47	4 44	4 41	4 38	4 35	4 30	4 26	4 20	4 13	4 06
Oct. 1	4 58	4 57	4 56	4 54	4 52	4 50	4 48	4 46	4 43	4 40	4 36	4 31	4 26	4 19
5	5 02	5 01	5 00	4 59	4 58	4 57	4 55	4 53	4 51	4 48	4 46	4 42	4 38	4 33

END OF EVENING NAUTICAL TWILIGHT

Lat.	+40°	+42°	+44°	+46°	+48°	+50°	+52°	+54°	+56°	+58°	+60°	+62°	+64°	+66°
	h m	h m	h m	h m	h m	h m	h m	h m	h m	h m	h m	h m	h m	h m
July 1	20 47	20 58	21 10	21 24	21 40	22 01	22 27	23 07	// //	// //	// //	// //	// //	// //
5	20 45	20 56	21 08	21 22	21 38	21 57	22 22	22 59	// //	// //	// //	// //	// //	// //
9	20 43	20 54	21 05	21 19	21 34	21 53	22 16	22 49	// //	// //	// //	// //	// //	// //
13	20 41	20 51	21 02	21 15	21 29	21 47	22 09	22 38	23 32	// //	// //	// //	// //	// //
17	20 38	20 47	20 58	21 10	21 24	21 41	22 01	22 27	23 08	// //	// //	// //	// //	// //
21	20 34	20 43	20 53	21 05	21 18	21 33	21 52	22 16	22 49	// //	// //	// //	// //	// //
25	20 30	20 38	20 48	20 59	21 11	21 26	21 43	22 04	22 33	23 21	// //	// //	// //	// //
29	20 25	20 33	20 42	20 53	21 04	21 18	21 33	21 53	22 17	22 53	// //	// //	// //	// //
Aug. 2	20 20	20 27	20 36	20 46	20 57	21 09	21 23	21 41	22 02	22 32	23 23	// //	// //	// //
6	20 14	20 21	20 29	20 38	20 49	21 00	21 13	21 29	21 48	22 13	22 49	// //	// //	// //
10	20 08	20 15	20 23	20 31	20 40	20 51	21 03	21 17	21 34	21 55	22 24	23 11	// //	// //
14	20 02	20 08	20 15	20 23	20 32	20 41	20 53	21 05	21 21	21 39	22 03	22 37	// //	// //
18	19 56	20 02	20 08	20 15	20 23	20 32	20 42	20 54	21 07	21 24	21 44	22 11	22 52	// //
22	19 49	19 54	20 00	20 07	20 14	20 22	20 31	20 42	20 54	21 09	21 26	21 48	22 19	23 12
26	19 42	19 47	19 53	19 59	20 05	20 13	20 21	20 30	20 41	20 54	21 09	21 28	21 53	22 28
30	19 35	19 40	19 45	19 50	19 56	20 03	20 10	20 19	20 29	20 40	20 53	21 10	21 30	21 57
Sept. 3	19 29	19 33	19 37	19 42	19 47	19 53	20 00	20 07	20 16	20 26	20 38	20 52	21 09	21 31
7	19 22	19 25	19 29	19 33	19 38	19 43	19 49	19 56	20 04	20 13	20 23	20 35	20 50	21 08
11	19 15	19 18	19 21	19 25	19 29	19 34	19 39	19 45	19 52	19 59	20 08	20 19	20 32	20 47
15	19 08	19 10	19 13	19 17	19 20	19 24	19 29	19 34	19 40	19 47	19 54	20 03	20 14	20 27
19	19 01	19 03	19 05	19 08	19 11	19 15	19 19	19 23	19 28	19 34	19 41	19 48	19 58	20 09
23	18 54	18 56	18 58	19 00	19 03	19 06	19 09	19 13	19 17	19 22	19 27	19 34	19 42	19 51
27	18 47	18 49	18 50	18 52	18 54	18 57	18 59	19 02	19 06	19 10	19 14	19 20	19 26	19 34
Oct. 1	18 40	18 42	18 43	18 44	18 46	18 48	18 50	18 52	18 55	18 58	19 02	19 06	19 11	19 17
5	18 34	18 35	18 36	18 37	18 38	18 39	18 40	18 42	18 44	18 47	18 50	18 53	18 57	19 02

// // indicates continuous twilight.

UNIVERSAL TIME FOR MERIDIAN OF GREENWICH
BEGINNING OF MORNING NAUTICAL TWILIGHT

Lat.	−55°	−50°	−45°	−40°	−35°	−30°	−20°	−10°	0°	+10°	+20°	+30°	+35°	+40°
	h m	h m	h m	h m	h m	h m	h m	h m	h m	h m	h m	h m	h m	h m
Oct. 1	4 04	4 17	4 27	4 35	4 41	4 46	4 54	4 58	5 02	5 03	5 03	5 02	5 00	4 58
5	3 53	4 08	4 19	4 28	4 35	4 41	4 50	4 56	5 00	5 03	5 04	5 04	5 03	5 02
9	3 41	3 58	4 11	4 21	4 29	4 36	4 46	4 54	4 59	5 03	5 05	5 06	5 06	5 06
13	3 29	3 49	4 03	4 15	4 24	4 31	4 43	4 51	4 58	5 03	5 06	5 09	5 10	5 10
17	3 17	3 39	3 55	4 08	4 18	4 26	4 39	4 49	4 57	5 03	5 08	5 11	5 13	5 14
21	3 05	3 30	3 47	4 01	4 12	4 22	4 36	4 47	4 56	5 03	5 09	5 14	5 16	5 18
25	2 53	3 20	3 40	3 55	4 07	4 17	4 33	4 45	4 55	5 03	5 10	5 16	5 19	5 22
29	2 41	3 11	3 32	3 49	4 02	4 13	4 30	4 44	4 54	5 03	5 12	5 19	5 23	5 26
Nov. 2	2 29	3 02	3 25	3 43	3 57	4 09	4 28	4 42	4 54	5 04	5 13	5 22	5 26	5 30
6	2 16	2 53	3 18	3 37	3 53	4 05	4 25	4 41	4 54	5 05	5 15	5 24	5 29	5 34
10	2 03	2 44	3 11	3 32	3 49	4 02	4 23	4 40	4 54	5 06	5 17	5 27	5 33	5 38
14	1 50	2 36	3 05	3 27	3 45	3 59	4 22	4 39	4 54	5 07	5 19	5 30	5 36	5 42
18	1 37	2 28	3 00	3 23	3 42	3 57	4 20	4 39	4 54	5 08	5 21	5 33	5 40	5 47
22	1 24	2 20	2 55	3 19	3 39	3 55	4 19	4 39	4 55	5 09	5 23	5 36	5 43	5 51
26	1 10	2 14	2 50	3 16	3 36	3 53	4 19	4 39	4 56	5 11	5 25	5 39	5 47	5 54
30	0 56	2 08	2 46	3 14	3 35	3 52	4 19	4 39	4 57	5 12	5 27	5 42	5 50	5 58
Dec. 4	0 41	2 03	2 44	3 12	3 34	3 51	4 19	4 40	4 58	5 14	5 30	5 45	5 53	6 02
8	0 23	1 59	2 42	3 11	3 33	3 51	4 19	4 41	5 00	5 16	5 32	5 48	5 56	6 05
12	// //	1 57	2 41	3 11	3 33	3 52	4 20	4 43	5 01	5 18	5 34	5 50	5 59	6 08
16	// //	1 56	2 41	3 11	3 34	3 53	4 22	4 44	5 03	5 20	5 36	5 53	6 01	6 11
20	// //	1 56	2 42	3 12	3 36	3 54	4 23	4 46	5 05	5 22	5 38	5 55	6 04	6 13
24	// //	1 58	2 44	3 15	3 38	3 56	4 26	4 48	5 07	5 24	5 40	5 57	6 06	6 15
28	// //	2 02	2 47	3 17	3 40	3 59	4 28	4 50	5 09	5 26	5 42	5 59	6 07	6 17
32	// //	2 07	2 51	3 21	3 44	4 02	4 30	4 53	5 11	5 28	5 44	6 00	6 08	6 18
36	0 41	2 14	2 56	3 25	3 47	4 05	4 33	4 55	5 13	5 30	5 45	6 01	6 09	6 18

END OF EVENING NAUTICAL TWILIGHT

Lat.	−55°	−50°	−45°	−40°	−35°	−30°	−20°	−10°	0°	+10°	+20°	+30°	+35°	+40°
	h m	h m	h m	h m	h m	h m	h m	h m	h m	h m	h m	h m	h m	h m
Oct. 1	19 37	19 23	19 13	19 05	18 59	18 54	18 46	18 41	18 38	18 36	18 36	18 37	18 38	18 40
5	19 46	19 30	19 19	19 09	19 02	18 56	18 47	18 41	18 36	18 34	18 32	18 32	18 33	18 34
9	19 55	19 38	19 24	19 14	19 06	18 59	18 49	18 41	18 35	18 31	18 29	18 27	18 27	18 28
13	20 05	19 45	19 30	19 19	19 09	19 02	18 50	18 41	18 35	18 30	18 26	18 23	18 22	18 22
17	20 15	19 53	19 37	19 24	19 13	19 05	18 52	18 42	18 34	18 28	18 23	18 19	18 17	18 16
21	20 26	20 01	19 43	19 29	19 18	19 08	18 53	18 42	18 33	18 26	18 20	18 15	18 13	18 11
25	20 37	20 10	19 50	19 34	19 22	19 12	18 55	18 43	18 33	18 25	18 18	18 11	18 08	18 06
29	20 49	20 18	19 56	19 40	19 26	19 15	18 58	18 44	18 33	18 24	18 16	18 08	18 04	18 01
Nov. 2	21 01	20 27	20 03	19 45	19 31	19 19	19 00	18 45	18 33	18 23	18 14	18 05	18 01	17 56
6	21 14	20 36	20 10	19 51	19 35	19 23	19 02	18 47	18 34	18 22	18 12	18 02	17 58	17 53
10	21 27	20 46	20 18	19 57	19 40	19 26	19 05	18 48	18 34	18 22	18 11	18 00	17 55	17 49
14	21 41	20 55	20 25	20 02	19 45	19 30	19 08	18 50	18 35	18 22	18 10	17 58	17 52	17 46
18	21 56	21 04	20 32	20 08	19 50	19 34	19 10	18 52	18 36	18 22	18 10	17 57	17 50	17 43
22	22 12	21 14	20 39	20 14	19 54	19 38	19 13	18 54	18 37	18 23	18 10	17 56	17 49	17 41
26	22 28	21 23	20 46	20 19	19 59	19 42	19 16	18 56	18 39	18 24	18 10	17 55	17 48	17 40
30	22 45	21 31	20 52	20 24	20 03	19 46	19 19	18 58	18 41	18 25	18 10	17 55	17 47	17 39
Dec. 4	23 04	21 39	20 58	20 29	20 07	19 50	19 22	19 00	18 42	18 26	18 11	17 56	17 47	17 39
8	23 27	21 46	21 03	20 33	20 11	19 53	19 25	19 03	18 44	18 28	18 12	17 56	17 48	17 39
12	// //	21 52	21 07	20 37	20 14	19 56	19 27	19 05	18 46	18 29	18 13	17 57	17 49	17 39
16	// //	21 56	21 11	20 40	20 17	19 59	19 30	19 07	18 48	18 31	18 15	17 59	17 50	17 41
20	// //	21 59	21 14	20 43	20 20	20 01	19 32	19 09	18 50	18 33	18 17	18 00	17 52	17 42
24	// //	22 01	21 15	20 45	20 22	20 03	19 34	19 11	18 52	18 35	18 19	18 02	17 54	17 44
28	// //	22 01	21 16	20 46	20 23	20 04	19 35	19 13	18 54	18 37	18 21	18 05	17 56	17 47
32	23 49	21 59	21 16	20 46	20 23	20 05	19 37	19 14	18 56	18 39	18 23	18 07	17 59	17 50
36	23 25	21 56	21 14	20 45	20 23	20 05	19 38	19 16	18 58	18 41	18 26	18 10	18 02	17 53

// // indicates continuous twilight.

UNIVERSAL TIME FOR MERIDIAN OF GREENWICH

BEGINNING OF MORNING NAUTICAL TWILIGHT

Lat.	+40°	+42°	+44°	+46°	+48°	+50°	+52°	+54°	+56°	+58°	+60°	+62°	+64°	+66°
	h m	h m	h m	h m	h m	h m	h m	h m	h m	h m	h m	h m	h m	h m
Oct. 1	4 58	4 57	4 56	4 54	4 52	4 50	4 48	4 46	4 43	4 40	4 36	4 31	4 26	4 19
5	5 02	5 01	5 00	4 59	4 58	4 57	4 55	4 53	4 51	4 48	4 46	4 42	4 38	4 33
9	5 06	5 06	5 05	5 04	5 04	5 03	5 02	5 01	4 59	4 57	4 55	4 53	4 50	4 46
13	5 10	5 10	5 10	5 10	5 09	5 09	5 08	5 08	5 07	5 06	5 05	5 03	5 01	4 59
17	5 14	5 14	5 15	5 15	5 15	5 15	5 15	5 15	5 15	5 14	5 14	5 13	5 12	5 11
21	5 18	5 19	5 19	5 20	5 21	5 21	5 22	5 22	5 23	5 23	5 23	5 23	5 23	5 23
25	5 22	5 23	5 24	5 25	5 26	5 27	5 28	5 29	5 30	5 31	5 32	5 33	5 34	5 35
29	5 26	5 27	5 29	5 30	5 32	5 33	5 35	5 36	5 38	5 40	5 41	5 43	5 45	5 47
Nov. 2	5 30	5 32	5 34	5 35	5 37	5 39	5 41	5 43	5 45	5 48	5 50	5 53	5 56	5 59
6	5 34	5 36	5 38	5 41	5 43	5 45	5 48	5 50	5 53	5 56	5 59	6 02	6 06	6 10
10	5 38	5 41	5 43	5 46	5 48	5 51	5 54	5 57	6 00	6 03	6 07	6 11	6 16	6 21
14	5 42	5 45	5 48	5 51	5 54	5 57	6 00	6 03	6 07	6 11	6 15	6 20	6 26	6 32
18	5 47	5 49	5 52	5 56	5 59	6 02	6 06	6 10	6 14	6 18	6 23	6 29	6 35	6 42
22	5 51	5 54	5 57	6 00	6 04	6 08	6 12	6 16	6 20	6 25	6 31	6 37	6 44	6 52
26	5 54	5 58	6 01	6 05	6 09	6 13	6 17	6 22	6 27	6 32	6 38	6 45	6 52	7 01
30	5 58	6 02	6 05	6 09	6 13	6 18	6 22	6 27	6 32	6 38	6 45	6 52	7 00	7 09
Dec. 4	6 02	6 05	6 09	6 13	6 18	6 22	6 27	6 32	6 38	6 44	6 51	6 58	7 07	7 17
8	6 05	6 09	6 13	6 17	6 21	6 26	6 31	6 37	6 42	6 49	6 56	7 04	7 13	7 23
12	6 08	6 12	6 16	6 20	6 25	6 30	6 35	6 40	6 46	6 53	7 00	7 09	7 18	7 29
16	6 11	6 15	6 19	6 23	6 28	6 33	6 38	6 44	6 50	6 57	7 04	7 12	7 22	7 33
20	6 13	6 17	6 21	6 26	6 30	6 35	6 41	6 46	6 52	6 59	7 07	7 15	7 25	7 36
24	6 15	6 19	6 23	6 28	6 32	6 37	6 42	6 48	6 54	7 01	7 09	7 17	7 27	7 38
28	6 17	6 20	6 25	6 29	6 34	6 38	6 44	6 49	6 55	7 02	7 09	7 18	7 27	7 38
32	6 18	6 21	6 25	6 30	6 34	6 39	6 44	6 50	6 56	7 02	7 09	7 17	7 27	7 37
36	6 18	6 22	6 26	6 30	6 34	6 39	6 44	6 49	6 55	7 01	7 08	7 16	7 25	7 35

END OF EVENING NAUTICAL TWILIGHT

Lat.	+40°	+42°	+44°	+46°	+48°	+50°	+52°	+54°	+56°	+58°	+60°	+62°	+64°	+66°
	h m	h m	h m	h m	h m	h m	h m	h m	h m	h m	h m	h m	h m	h m
Oct. 1	18 40	18 42	18 43	18 44	18 46	18 48	18 50	18 52	18 55	18 58	19 02	19 06	19 11	19 17
5	18 34	18 35	18 36	18 37	18 38	18 39	18 40	18 42	18 44	18 47	18 50	18 53	18 57	19 02
9	18 28	18 28	18 29	18 29	18 30	18 31	18 32	18 33	18 34	18 36	18 38	18 40	18 43	18 46
13	18 22	18 22	18 22	18 22	18 22	18 22	18 23	18 23	18 24	18 25	18 26	18 28	18 30	18 32
17	18 16	18 16	18 15	18 15	18 15	18 15	18 15	18 15	18 15	18 15	18 15	18 16	18 17	18 18
21	18 11	18 10	18 09	18 08	18 08	18 07	18 07	18 06	18 05	18 05	18 05	18 04	18 04	18 04
25	18 06	18 04	18 03	18 02	18 01	18 00	17 59	17 58	17 57	17 56	17 55	17 53	17 52	17 51
29	18 01	17 59	17 58	17 56	17 55	17 53	17 52	17 50	17 49	17 47	17 45	17 43	17 41	17 39
Nov. 2	17 56	17 55	17 53	17 51	17 49	17 47	17 45	17 43	17 41	17 38	17 36	17 33	17 30	17 27
6	17 53	17 50	17 48	17 46	17 44	17 41	17 39	17 36	17 34	17 31	17 28	17 24	17 20	17 16
10	17 49	17 47	17 44	17 42	17 39	17 36	17 33	17 30	17 27	17 24	17 20	17 16	17 11	17 06
14	17 46	17 43	17 41	17 38	17 35	17 32	17 28	17 25	17 21	17 17	17 13	17 08	17 02	16 56
18	17 43	17 41	17 38	17 34	17 31	17 28	17 24	17 20	17 16	17 11	17 06	17 01	16 55	16 48
22	17 41	17 38	17 35	17 32	17 28	17 24	17 20	17 16	17 11	17 06	17 01	16 55	16 48	16 40
26	17 40	17 37	17 33	17 29	17 26	17 22	17 17	17 13	17 08	17 02	16 56	16 49	16 42	16 33
30	17 39	17 35	17 32	17 28	17 24	17 20	17 15	17 10	17 05	16 59	16 52	16 45	16 37	16 28
Dec. 4	17 39	17 35	17 31	17 27	17 23	17 18	17 13	17 08	17 03	16 56	16 50	16 42	16 33	16 24
8	17 39	17 35	17 31	17 27	17 22	17 18	17 13	17 07	17 01	16 55	16 48	16 40	16 31	16 20
12	17 39	17 35	17 31	17 27	17 23	17 18	17 13	17 07	17 01	16 54	16 47	16 39	16 30	16 19
16	17 41	17 37	17 32	17 28	17 23	17 19	17 13	17 08	17 01	16 55	16 47	16 39	16 29	16 18
20	17 42	17 38	17 34	17 30	17 25	17 20	17 15	17 09	17 03	16 56	16 49	16 40	16 30	16 19
24	17 44	17 40	17 36	17 32	17 27	17 22	17 17	17 11	17 05	16 58	16 51	16 42	16 33	16 22
28	17 47	17 43	17 39	17 34	17 30	17 25	17 20	17 14	17 08	17 01	16 54	16 46	16 36	16 25
32	17 50	17 46	17 42	17 38	17 33	17 28	17 23	17 18	17 12	17 05	16 58	16 50	16 41	16 30
36	17 53	17 49	17 45	17 41	17 37	17 32	17 27	17 22	17 16	17 10	17 03	16 55	16 46	16 36

UNIVERSAL TIME FOR MERIDIAN OF GREENWICH
BEGINNING OF MORNING ASTRONOMICAL TWILIGHT

Lat.	−55°	−50°	−45°	−40°	−35°	−30°	−20°	−10°	0°	+10°	+20°	+30°	+35°	+40°
	h m	h m	h m	h m	h m	h m	h m	h m	h m	h m	h m	h m	h m	h m
Jan. −2	// //	// //	1 43	2 30	3 01	3 24	3 58	4 24	4 44	5 00	5 16	5 30	5 37	5 44
2	// //	// //	1 49	2 34	3 05	3 27	4 01	4 26	4 46	5 02	5 17	5 31	5 38	5 45
6	// //	// //	1 56	2 39	3 09	3 31	4 04	4 28	4 48	5 04	5 18	5 32	5 39	5 45
10	// //	0 20	2 04	2 45	3 13	3 35	4 07	4 31	4 50	5 05	5 19	5 32	5 39	5 45
14	// //	0 54	2 12	2 51	3 18	3 39	4 10	4 33	4 52	5 07	5 20	5 33	5 39	5 45
18	// //	1 16	2 21	2 58	3 24	3 44	4 14	4 36	4 53	5 08	5 21	5 32	5 38	5 43
22	// //	1 34	2 31	3 05	3 29	3 48	4 17	4 38	4 55	5 09	5 21	5 32	5 37	5 42
26	// //	1 50	2 40	3 12	3 35	3 53	4 20	4 41	4 56	5 09	5 21	5 31	5 35	5 40
30	// //	2 05	2 50	3 19	3 41	3 58	4 24	4 43	4 58	5 10	5 20	5 29	5 33	5 37
Feb. 3	0 54	2 19	2 59	3 26	3 46	4 02	4 27	4 45	4 59	5 10	5 19	5 27	5 31	5 34
7	1 28	2 32	3 08	3 33	3 52	4 07	4 30	4 46	4 59	5 10	5 18	5 25	5 28	5 30
11	1 52	2 45	3 17	3 40	3 57	4 11	4 33	4 48	5 00	5 09	5 17	5 22	5 25	5 26
15	2 11	2 56	3 25	3 46	4 02	4 15	4 35	4 49	5 00	5 09	5 15	5 19	5 21	5 22
19	2 28	3 07	3 33	3 53	4 08	4 20	4 38	4 51	5 00	5 08	5 13	5 16	5 17	5 17
23	2 44	3 18	3 41	3 59	4 12	4 23	4 40	4 52	5 00	5 06	5 10	5 12	5 12	5 12
27	2 58	3 28	3 49	4 05	4 17	4 27	4 42	4 53	5 00	5 05	5 08	5 08	5 08	5 06
Mar. 3	3 10	3 37	3 56	4 10	4 22	4 31	4 44	4 53	4 59	5 03	5 05	5 04	5 03	5 00
7	3 22	3 46	4 03	4 16	4 26	4 34	4 46	4 54	4 59	5 01	5 02	5 00	4 57	4 54
11	3 34	3 54	4 10	4 21	4 30	4 37	4 47	4 54	4 58	4 59	4 59	4 55	4 52	4 48
15	3 44	4 03	4 16	4 26	4 34	4 40	4 49	4 54	4 57	4 57	4 55	4 50	4 46	4 41
19	3 54	4 10	4 22	4 31	4 38	4 43	4 50	4 54	4 56	4 55	4 52	4 45	4 41	4 34
23	4 04	4 18	4 28	4 35	4 41	4 46	4 51	4 54	4 55	4 53	4 48	4 40	4 35	4 27
27	4 13	4 25	4 33	4 40	4 45	4 48	4 53	4 54	4 53	4 50	4 44	4 35	4 28	4 20
31	4 21	4 31	4 39	4 44	4 48	4 51	4 54	4 54	4 52	4 48	4 41	4 30	4 22	4 13
Apr. 4	4 29	4 38	4 44	4 48	4 51	4 53	4 55	4 54	4 51	4 45	4 37	4 24	4 16	4 06

END OF EVENING ASTRONOMICAL TWILIGHT

Lat.	−55°	−50°	−45°	−40°	−35°	−30°	−20°	−10°	0°	+10°	+20°	+30°	+35°	+40°
	h m	h m	h m	h m	h m	h m	h m	h m	h m	h m	h m	h m	h m	h m
Jan. −2	// //	// //	22 21	21 34	21 03	20 40	20 06	19 41	19 21	19 04	18 49	18 35	18 28	18 21
2	// //	// //	22 18	21 33	21 03	20 41	20 07	19 42	19 23	19 06	18 51	18 37	18 31	18 24
6	// //	// //	22 15	21 32	21 03	20 40	20 08	19 43	19 24	19 08	18 54	18 40	18 34	18 27
10	// //	23 44	22 10	21 29	21 01	20 40	20 08	19 44	19 26	19 10	18 56	18 43	18 37	18 30
14	// //	23 19	22 04	21 26	20 59	20 38	20 08	19 45	19 27	19 11	18 58	18 46	18 40	18 34
18	// //	23 01	21 58	21 22	20 56	20 37	20 07	19 45	19 28	19 13	19 00	18 49	18 43	18 38
22	// //	22 46	21 51	21 17	20 53	20 34	20 06	19 45	19 28	19 14	19 03	18 52	18 47	18 42
26	// //	22 32	21 43	21 12	20 49	20 31	20 04	19 44	19 29	19 16	19 05	18 55	18 50	18 46
30	// //	22 19	21 35	21 07	20 45	20 28	20 03	19 44	19 29	19 17	19 07	18 58	18 54	18 50
Feb. 3	23 24	22 06	21 27	21 01	20 40	20 25	20 00	19 43	19 29	19 18	19 09	19 01	18 57	18 54
7	22 55	21 53	21 19	20 54	20 36	20 21	19 58	19 42	19 29	19 19	19 10	19 04	19 01	18 58
11	22 32	21 41	21 10	20 48	20 30	20 16	19 55	19 40	19 28	19 19	19 12	19 06	19 04	19 03
15	22 13	21 30	21 01	20 41	20 25	20 12	19 53	19 38	19 28	19 20	19 14	19 09	19 08	19 07
19	21 56	21 18	20 52	20 34	20 19	20 07	19 49	19 37	19 27	19 20	19 15	19 12	19 11	19 11
23	21 40	21 07	20 44	20 27	20 13	20 02	19 46	19 35	19 26	19 20	19 16	19 15	19 15	19 15
27	21 25	20 56	20 35	20 19	20 07	19 57	19 43	19 32	19 25	19 20	19 18	19 17	19 18	19 20
Mar. 3	21 11	20 45	20 26	20 12	20 01	19 52	19 39	19 30	19 24	19 21	19 19	19 20	19 22	19 24
7	20 57	20 34	20 18	20 05	19 55	19 47	19 36	19 28	19 23	19 21	19 20	19 23	19 25	19 28
11	20 44	20 24	20 09	19 58	19 49	19 42	19 32	19 26	19 22	19 21	19 22	19 25	19 28	19 33
15	20 32	20 14	20 00	19 51	19 43	19 37	19 28	19 23	19 21	19 21	19 23	19 28	19 32	19 37
19	20 19	20 04	19 52	19 44	19 37	19 32	19 25	19 21	19 20	19 21	19 24	19 31	19 36	19 42
23	20 08	19 54	19 44	19 37	19 31	19 27	19 21	19 19	19 18	19 21	19 25	19 33	19 39	19 47
27	19 56	19 45	19 36	19 30	19 25	19 22	19 18	19 16	19 17	19 21	19 27	19 36	19 43	19 51
31	19 45	19 35	19 28	19 23	19 19	19 17	19 14	19 14	19 16	19 21	19 28	19 39	19 47	19 56
Apr. 4	19 35	19 27	19 21	19 17	19 14	19 12	19 11	19 12	19 15	19 21	19 29	19 42	19 51	20 01

// // indicates continuous twilight.

UNIVERSAL TIME FOR MERIDIAN OF GREENWICH

BEGINNING OF MORNING ASTRONOMICAL TWILIGHT

Lat.	+40°	+42°	+44°	+46°	+48°	+50°	+52°	+54°	+56°	+58°	+60°	+62°	+64°	+66°
	h m	h m	h m	h m	h m	h m	h m	h m	h m	h m	h m	h m	h m	h m
Jan. −2	5 44	5 47	5 50	5 53	5 56	5 59	6 03	6 06	6 10	6 14	6 18	6 23	6 28	6 33
2	5 45	5 48	5 51	5 54	5 57	6 00	6 03	6 06	6 10	6 14	6 18	6 22	6 27	6 32
6	5 45	5 48	5 51	5 54	5 57	6 00	6 03	6 06	6 09	6 13	6 17	6 21	6 25	6 30
10	5 45	5 48	5 50	5 53	5 56	5 59	6 02	6 05	6 08	6 11	6 15	6 18	6 22	6 27
14	5 45	5 47	5 49	5 52	5 54	5 57	6 00	6 02	6 05	6 08	6 11	6 15	6 18	6 22
18	5 43	5 46	5 48	5 50	5 52	5 55	5 57	6 00	6 02	6 05	6 07	6 10	6 13	6 17
22	5 42	5 44	5 46	5 48	5 50	5 52	5 54	5 56	5 58	6 00	6 03	6 05	6 07	6 10
26	5 40	5 41	5 43	5 45	5 47	5 48	5 50	5 52	5 53	5 55	5 57	5 59	6 01	6 02
30	5 37	5 39	5 40	5 41	5 43	5 44	5 45	5 47	5 48	5 49	5 50	5 52	5 53	5 54
Feb. 3	5 34	5 35	5 36	5 37	5 38	5 39	5 40	5 41	5 42	5 43	5 43	5 44	5 44	5 44
7	5 30	5 31	5 32	5 33	5 33	5 34	5 35	5 35	5 35	5 35	5 35	5 35	5 34	5 34
11	5 26	5 27	5 27	5 28	5 28	5 28	5 28	5 28	5 28	5 27	5 26	5 25	5 24	5 22
15	5 22	5 22	5 22	5 22	5 22	5 22	5 21	5 21	5 20	5 19	5 17	5 15	5 13	5 10
19	5 17	5 17	5 17	5 16	5 16	5 15	5 14	5 13	5 11	5 09	5 07	5 04	5 01	4 57
23	5 12	5 11	5 11	5 10	5 09	5 07	5 06	5 04	5 02	4 59	4 56	4 53	4 48	4 43
27	5 06	5 05	5 04	5 03	5 02	5 00	4 58	4 55	4 52	4 49	4 45	4 40	4 35	4 28
Mar. 3	5 00	4 59	4 58	4 56	4 54	4 52	4 49	4 46	4 42	4 38	4 33	4 27	4 20	4 12
7	4 54	4 53	4 51	4 48	4 46	4 43	4 40	4 36	4 32	4 27	4 21	4 14	4 05	3 55
11	4 48	4 46	4 43	4 41	4 38	4 34	4 30	4 26	4 21	4 15	4 08	3 59	3 49	3 37
15	4 41	4 39	4 36	4 33	4 29	4 25	4 20	4 15	4 09	4 02	3 54	3 44	3 32	3 18
19	4 34	4 31	4 28	4 24	4 20	4 15	4 10	4 04	3 57	3 49	3 39	3 28	3 14	2 57
23	4 27	4 24	4 20	4 16	4 11	4 06	3 59	3 52	3 44	3 35	3 24	3 11	2 54	2 33
27	4 20	4 16	4 12	4 07	4 02	3 55	3 49	3 41	3 31	3 21	3 08	2 52	2 33	2 06
31	4 13	4 08	4 04	3 58	3 52	3 45	3 37	3 28	3 18	3 06	2 51	2 32	2 08	1 33
Apr. 4	4 06	4 01	3 55	3 49	3 42	3 35	3 26	3 16	3 04	2 50	2 32	2 10	1 39	0 38

END OF EVENING ASTRONOMICAL TWILIGHT

Lat.	+40°	+42°	+44°	+46°	+48°	+50°	+52°	+54°	+56°	+58°	+60°	+62°	+64°	+66°
	h m	h m	h m	h m	h m	h m	h m	h m	h m	h m	h m	h m	h m	h m
Jan. −2	18 21	18 18	18 15	18 12	18 09	18 05	18 02	17 58	17 55	17 51	17 47	17 42	17 37	17 31
2	18 24	18 21	18 18	18 15	18 12	18 09	18 06	18 02	17 59	17 55	17 51	17 46	17 42	17 36
6	18 27	18 24	18 21	18 19	18 16	18 13	18 10	18 06	18 03	17 59	17 56	17 52	17 47	17 42
10	18 30	18 28	18 25	18 22	18 20	18 17	18 14	18 11	18 08	18 05	18 01	17 58	17 53	17 49
14	18 34	18 32	18 29	18 27	18 24	18 22	18 19	18 16	18 14	18 11	18 07	18 04	18 01	17 57
18	18 38	18 36	18 33	18 31	18 29	18 27	18 24	18 22	18 19	18 17	18 14	18 11	18 08	18 05
22	18 42	18 40	18 38	18 36	18 34	18 32	18 30	18 28	18 26	18 24	18 21	18 19	18 17	18 14
26	18 46	18 44	18 42	18 41	18 39	18 37	18 36	18 34	18 32	18 31	18 29	18 27	18 26	18 24
30	18 50	18 49	18 47	18 46	18 44	18 43	18 42	18 41	18 39	18 38	18 37	18 36	18 35	18 34
Feb. 3	18 54	18 53	18 52	18 51	18 50	18 49	18 48	18 47	18 47	18 46	18 46	18 45	18 45	18 45
7	18 58	18 58	18 57	18 56	18 56	18 55	18 55	18 54	18 54	18 54	18 54	18 55	18 55	18 56
11	19 03	19 02	19 02	19 01	19 01	19 01	19 01	19 01	19 02	19 02	19 03	19 04	19 06	19 08
15	19 07	19 07	19 07	19 07	19 07	19 07	19 08	19 09	19 10	19 11	19 12	19 15	19 17	19 20
19	19 11	19 11	19 12	19 12	19 13	19 14	19 15	19 16	19 18	19 20	19 22	19 25	19 28	19 33
23	19 15	19 16	19 17	19 18	19 19	19 20	19 22	19 24	19 26	19 29	19 32	19 36	19 40	19 46
27	19 20	19 21	19 22	19 23	19 25	19 27	19 29	19 31	19 34	19 38	19 42	19 47	19 53	20 00
Mar. 3	19 24	19 25	19 27	19 29	19 31	19 33	19 36	19 39	19 43	19 47	19 52	19 58	20 06	20 14
7	19 28	19 30	19 32	19 34	19 37	19 40	19 43	19 47	19 52	19 57	20 03	20 10	20 19	20 30
11	19 33	19 35	19 38	19 40	19 43	19 47	19 51	19 56	20 01	20 07	20 14	20 23	20 33	20 46
15	19 37	19 40	19 43	19 46	19 50	19 54	19 59	20 04	20 10	20 18	20 26	20 36	20 48	21 03
19	19 42	19 45	19 48	19 52	19 56	20 01	20 07	20 13	20 20	20 29	20 38	20 50	21 05	21 23
23	19 47	19 50	19 54	19 58	20 03	20 09	20 15	20 22	20 31	20 40	20 52	21 05	21 22	21 45
27	19 51	19 55	20 00	20 05	20 10	20 17	20 24	20 32	20 41	20 52	21 05	21 22	21 42	22 10
31	19 56	20 01	20 06	20 11	20 18	20 25	20 33	20 42	20 53	21 05	21 21	21 40	22 05	22 44
Apr. 4	20 01	20 06	20 12	20 18	20 25	20 33	20 42	20 52	21 05	21 19	21 37	22 01	22 34	// //

// // indicates continuous twilight.

UNIVERSAL TIME FOR MERIDIAN OF GREENWICH
BEGINNING OF MORNING ASTRONOMICAL TWILIGHT

Lat.	−55°	−50°	−45°	−40°	−35°	−30°	−20°	−10°	0°	+10°	+20°	+30°	+35°	+40°
	h m	h m	h m	h m	h m	h m	h m	h m	h m	h m	h m	h m	h m	h m
Mar. 31	4 21	4 31	4 39	4 44	4 48	4 51	4 54	4 54	4 52	4 48	4 41	4 30	4 22	4 13
Apr. 4	4 29	4 38	4 44	4 48	4 51	4 53	4 55	4 54	4 51	4 45	4 37	4 24	4 16	4 06
8	4 37	4 44	4 49	4 52	4 54	4 55	4 56	4 54	4 49	4 43	4 33	4 19	4 10	3 58
12	4 45	4 50	4 54	4 56	4 57	4 58	4 57	4 53	4 48	4 40	4 29	4 14	4 04	3 51
16	4 52	4 56	4 59	5 00	5 00	5 00	4 57	4 53	4 47	4 38	4 26	4 09	3 57	3 43
20	4 59	5 02	5 03	5 03	5 03	5 02	4 58	4 53	4 45	4 35	4 22	4 03	3 51	3 36
24	5 06	5 07	5 08	5 07	5 06	5 04	4 59	4 53	4 44	4 33	4 19	3 58	3 45	3 29
28	5 13	5 13	5 12	5 11	5 09	5 06	5 00	4 53	4 43	4 31	4 15	3 54	3 39	3 22
May 2	5 19	5 18	5 16	5 14	5 11	5 08	5 01	4 53	4 42	4 29	4 12	3 49	3 34	3 15
6	5 25	5 23	5 20	5 17	5 14	5 10	5 02	4 53	4 41	4 27	4 09	3 45	3 29	3 08
10	5 31	5 28	5 24	5 21	5 17	5 12	5 03	4 53	4 41	4 26	4 07	3 41	3 23	3 02
14	5 37	5 32	5 28	5 24	5 19	5 15	5 05	4 53	4 40	4 24	4 04	3 37	3 19	2 56
18	5 42	5 37	5 32	5 27	5 22	5 17	5 06	4 54	4 40	4 23	4 02	3 33	3 14	2 50
22	5 47	5 41	5 35	5 30	5 24	5 19	5 07	4 54	4 40	4 22	4 00	3 30	3 10	2 45
26	5 51	5 45	5 38	5 32	5 26	5 20	5 08	4 55	4 40	4 22	3 59	3 28	3 07	2 40
30	5 56	5 48	5 41	5 35	5 29	5 22	5 09	4 56	4 40	4 21	3 58	3 26	3 04	2 36
June 3	5 59	5 51	5 44	5 37	5 31	5 24	5 11	4 56	4 40	4 21	3 57	3 24	3 02	2 33
7	6 02	5 54	5 46	5 39	5 32	5 26	5 12	4 57	4 41	4 21	3 56	3 23	3 00	2 30
11	6 05	5 56	5 49	5 41	5 34	5 27	5 13	4 58	4 41	4 21	3 56	3 22	2 59	2 29
15	6 07	5 58	5 50	5 43	5 35	5 28	5 14	4 59	4 42	4 22	3 56	3 22	2 59	2 28
19	6 09	6 00	5 52	5 44	5 37	5 29	5 15	5 00	4 43	4 22	3 57	3 22	2 59	2 28
23	6 09	6 00	5 52	5 45	5 37	5 30	5 16	5 01	4 44	4 23	3 58	3 23	3 00	2 28
27	6 10	6 01	5 53	5 45	5 38	5 31	5 17	5 01	4 44	4 24	3 59	3 25	3 01	2 30
July 1	6 09	6 01	5 53	5 45	5 38	5 31	5 17	5 02	4 45	4 25	4 01	3 26	3 03	2 33
5	6 08	6 00	5 52	5 45	5 38	5 31	5 18	5 03	4 46	4 27	4 02	3 29	3 06	2 36

END OF EVENING ASTRONOMICAL TWILIGHT

Lat.	−55°	−50°	−45°	−40°	−35°	−30°	−20°	−10°	0°	+10°	+20°	+30°	+35°	+40°
	h m	h m	h m	h m	h m	h m	h m	h m	h m	h m	h m	h m	h m	h m
Mar. 31	19 45	19 35	19 28	19 23	19 19	19 17	19 14	19 14	19 16	19 21	19 28	19 39	19 47	19 56
Apr. 4	19 35	19 27	19 21	19 17	19 14	19 12	19 11	19 12	19 15	19 21	19 29	19 42	19 51	20 01
8	19 25	19 18	19 14	19 11	19 09	19 08	19 08	19 10	19 14	19 21	19 31	19 45	19 55	20 06
12	19 15	19 10	19 07	19 05	19 04	19 03	19 05	19 08	19 14	19 21	19 33	19 48	19 59	20 12
16	19 06	19 02	19 00	18 59	18 59	18 59	19 02	19 06	19 13	19 22	19 34	19 52	20 03	20 17
20	18 57	18 55	18 54	18 54	18 54	18 55	18 59	19 05	19 12	19 23	19 36	19 55	20 07	20 23
24	18 49	18 48	18 48	18 48	18 50	18 52	18 57	19 03	19 12	19 23	19 38	19 58	20 12	20 28
28	18 41	18 41	18 42	18 44	18 46	18 48	18 54	19 02	19 12	19 24	19 40	20 02	20 16	20 34
May 2	18 34	18 35	18 37	18 39	18 42	18 45	18 52	19 01	19 12	19 25	19 42	20 06	20 21	20 40
6	18 27	18 29	18 32	18 35	18 39	18 42	18 51	19 00	19 12	19 26	19 44	20 09	20 26	20 46
10	18 21	18 24	18 28	18 32	18 36	18 40	18 49	19 00	19 12	19 27	19 47	20 13	20 30	20 52
14	18 15	18 20	18 24	18 29	18 33	18 38	18 48	18 59	19 13	19 29	19 49	20 16	20 35	20 58
18	18 10	18 16	18 21	18 26	18 31	18 36	18 47	18 59	19 13	19 30	19 51	20 20	20 39	21 04
22	18 06	18 12	18 18	18 23	18 29	18 35	18 46	18 59	19 14	19 31	19 53	20 24	20 44	21 10
26	18 02	18 09	18 15	18 22	18 28	18 34	18 46	18 59	19 15	19 33	19 56	20 27	20 48	21 15
30	17 59	18 07	18 14	18 20	18 26	18 33	18 46	19 00	19 15	19 34	19 58	20 30	20 52	21 20
June 3	17 57	18 05	18 12	18 19	18 26	18 32	18 46	19 00	19 16	19 36	20 00	20 33	20 55	21 24
7	17 55	18 04	18 11	18 18	18 25	18 32	18 46	19 01	19 17	19 37	20 02	20 35	20 58	21 28
11	17 54	18 03	18 11	18 18	18 25	18 32	18 46	19 01	19 18	19 38	20 03	20 37	21 01	21 31
15	17 54	18 03	18 11	18 18	18 26	18 33	18 47	19 02	19 19	19 39	20 05	20 39	21 03	21 34
19	17 54	18 03	18 11	18 19	18 26	18 33	18 48	19 03	19 20	19 40	20 06	20 40	21 04	21 35
23	17 55	18 04	18 12	18 20	18 27	18 34	18 49	19 04	19 21	19 41	20 07	20 41	21 05	21 36
27	17 57	18 06	18 14	18 21	18 28	18 35	18 50	19 05	19 22	19 42	20 07	20 41	21 05	21 36
July 1	17 59	18 08	18 15	18 23	18 30	18 37	18 51	19 06	19 22	19 42	20 07	20 41	21 04	21 35
5	18 02	18 10	18 17	18 25	18 31	18 38	18 52	19 07	19 23	19 43	20 07	20 40	21 03	21 33

UNIVERSAL TIME FOR MERIDIAN OF GREENWICH

BEGINNING OF MORNING ASTRONOMICAL TWILIGHT

Lat.	+40°	+42°	+44°	+46°	+48°	+50°	+52°	+54°	+56°	+58°	+60°	+62°	+64°	+66°
	h m	h m	h m	h m	h m	h m	h m	h m	h m	h m	h m	h m	h m	h m
Mar. 31	4 13	4 08	4 04	3 58	3 52	3 45	3 37	3 28	3 18	3 06	2 51	2 32	2 08	1 33
Apr. 4	4 06	4 01	3 55	3 49	3 42	3 35	3 26	3 16	3 04	2 50	2 32	2 10	1 39	0 38
8	3 58	3 53	3 47	3 40	3 32	3 24	3 14	3 02	2 49	2 33	2 12	1 44	0 57	// //
12	3 51	3 45	3 38	3 31	3 22	3 13	3 02	2 49	2 33	2 14	1 49	1 10	// //	// //
16	3 43	3 37	3 29	3 21	3 12	3 01	2 49	2 34	2 17	1 54	1 21	// //	// //	// //
20	3 36	3 29	3 21	3 12	3 02	2 50	2 36	2 19	1 58	1 30	0 39	// //	// //	// //
24	3 29	3 21	3 12	3 02	2 51	2 38	2 22	2 03	1 38	0 59	// //	// //	// //	// //
28	3 22	3 13	3 04	2 53	2 41	2 26	2 08	1 46	1 14	// //	// //	// //	// //	// //
May 2	3 15	3 06	2 55	2 44	2 30	2 14	1 54	1 27	0 41	// //	// //	// //	// //	// //
6	3 08	2 58	2 47	2 34	2 19	2 01	1 38	1 03	// //	// //	// //	// //	// //	// //
10	3 02	2 51	2 39	2 25	2 09	1 48	1 20	0 30	// //	// //	// //	// //	// //	// //
14	2 56	2 44	2 31	2 16	1 58	1 34	1 00	// //	// //	// //	// //	// //	// //	// //
18	2 50	2 38	2 24	2 08	1 47	1 20	0 33	// //	// //	// //	// //	// //	// //	// //
22	2 45	2 32	2 17	1 59	1 37	1 05	// //	// //	// //	// //	// //	// //	// //	// //
26	2 40	2 27	2 11	1 52	1 27	0 47	// //	// //	// //	// //	// //	// //	// //	// //
30	2 36	2 22	2 05	1 45	1 17	0 23	// //	// //	// //	// //	// //	// //	// //	// //
June 3	2 33	2 18	2 00	1 38	1 07	// //	// //	// //	// //	// //	// //	// //	// //	// //
7	2 30	2 15	1 57	1 33	0 58	// //	// //	// //	// //	// //	// //	// //	// //	// //
11	2 29	2 13	1 54	1 29	0 50	// //	// //	// //	// //	// //	// //	// //	// //	// //
15	2 28	2 12	1 52	1 26	0 45	// //	// //	// //	// //	// //	// //	// //	// //	▭
19	2 28	2 11	1 52	1 25	0 42	// //	// //	// //	// //	// //	// //	// //	// //	▭
23	2 28	2 12	1 52	1 26	0 43	// //	// //	// //	// //	// //	// //	// //	// //	▭
27	2 30	2 14	1 55	1 29	0 47	// //	// //	// //	// //	// //	// //	// //	// //	▭
July 1	2 33	2 17	1 58	1 33	0 54	// //	// //	// //	// //	// //	// //	// //	// //	// //
5	2 36	2 21	2 02	1 39	1 04	// //	// //	// //	// //	// //	// //	// //	// //	// //

END OF EVENING ASTRONOMICAL TWILIGHT

Lat.	+40°	+42°	+44°	+46°	+48°	+50°	+52°	+54°	+56°	+58°	+60°	+62°	+64°	+66°
	h m	h m	h m	h m	h m	h m	h m	h m	h m	h m	h m	h m	h m	h m
Mar. 31	19 56	20 01	20 06	20 11	20 18	20 25	20 33	20 42	20 53	21 05	21 21	21 40	22 05	22 44
Apr. 4	20 01	20 06	20 12	20 18	20 25	20 33	20 42	20 52	21 05	21 19	21 37	22 01	22 34	// //
8	20 06	20 12	20 18	20 25	20 33	20 42	20 52	21 03	21 17	21 34	21 56	22 26	23 21	// //
12	20 12	20 18	20 25	20 32	20 41	20 51	21 02	21 15	21 31	21 51	22 18	23 01	// //	// //
16	20 17	20 24	20 31	20 40	20 49	21 00	21 13	21 28	21 46	22 10	22 46	// //	// //	// //
20	20 23	20 30	20 38	20 47	20 58	21 10	21 24	21 41	22 03	22 34	23 37	// //	// //	// //
24	20 28	20 36	20 45	20 55	21 07	21 20	21 36	21 56	22 23	23 06	// //	// //	// //	// //
28	20 34	20 43	20 53	21 04	21 16	21 31	21 49	22 13	22 47	// //	// //	// //	// //	// //
May 2	20 40	20 50	21 00	21 12	21 26	21 43	22 04	22 32	23 25	// //	// //	// //	// //	// //
6	20 46	20 56	21 08	21 21	21 36	21 55	22 19	22 56	// //	// //	// //	// //	// //	// //
10	20 52	21 03	21 15	21 29	21 46	22 08	22 37	23 38	// //	// //	// //	// //	// //	// //
14	20 58	21 10	21 23	21 38	21 57	22 21	22 58	// //	// //	// //	// //	// //	// //	// //
18	21 04	21 16	21 30	21 47	22 08	22 36	23 30	// //	// //	// //	// //	// //	// //	// //
22	21 10	21 22	21 38	21 56	22 19	22 52	// //	// //	// //	// //	// //	// //	// //	// //
26	21 15	21 29	21 45	22 04	22 30	23 12	// //	// //	// //	// //	// //	// //	// //	// //
30	21 20	21 34	21 51	22 12	22 41	23 42	// //	// //	// //	// //	// //	// //	// //	// //
June 3	21 24	21 39	21 57	22 20	22 52	// //	// //	// //	// //	// //	// //	// //	// //	// //
7	21 28	21 44	22 02	22 26	23 02	// //	// //	// //	// //	// //	// //	// //	// //	// //
11	21 31	21 47	22 06	22 31	23 11	// //	// //	// //	// //	// //	// //	// //	// //	// //
15	21 34	21 50	22 09	22 35	23 18	// //	// //	// //	// //	// //	// //	// //	// //	▭
19	21 35	21 52	22 11	22 38	23 21	// //	// //	// //	// //	// //	// //	// //	// //	▭
23	21 36	21 52	22 12	22 38	23 21	// //	// //	// //	// //	// //	// //	// //	// //	▭
27	21 36	21 52	22 11	22 37	23 18	// //	// //	// //	// //	// //	// //	// //	// //	▭
July 1	21 35	21 50	22 09	22 34	23 12	// //	// //	// //	// //	// //	// //	// //	// //	// //
5	21 33	21 48	22 06	22 30	23 04	// //	// //	// //	// //	// //	// //	// //	// //	// //

▭ indicates Sun continuously above horizon.
// // indicates continuous twilight.

ASTRONOMICAL TWILIGHT, 2025

UNIVERSAL TIME FOR MERIDIAN OF GREENWICH
BEGINNING OF MORNING ASTRONOMICAL TWILIGHT

Lat.	−55°	−50°	−45°	−40°	−35°	−30°	−20°	−10°	0°	+10°	+20°	+30°	+35°	+40°
	h m	h m	h m	h m	h m	h m	h m	h m	h m	h m	h m	h m	h m	h m
July 1	6 09	6 01	5 53	5 45	5 38	5 31	5 17	5 02	4 45	4 25	4 01	3 26	3 03	2 33
5	6 08	6 00	5 52	5 45	5 38	5 31	5 18	5 03	4 46	4 27	4 02	3 29	3 06	2 36
9	6 06	5 58	5 51	5 44	5 38	5 31	5 18	5 03	4 47	4 28	4 04	3 31	3 09	2 40
13	6 04	5 56	5 50	5 43	5 37	5 30	5 18	5 04	4 48	4 29	4 06	3 34	3 12	2 44
17	6 00	5 54	5 47	5 41	5 35	5 30	5 17	5 04	4 49	4 31	4 08	3 37	3 16	2 49
21	5 56	5 51	5 45	5 39	5 34	5 28	5 17	5 04	4 49	4 32	4 10	3 40	3 20	2 54
25	5 52	5 47	5 42	5 37	5 32	5 27	5 16	5 04	4 50	4 33	4 12	3 44	3 24	3 00
29	5 47	5 42	5 38	5 34	5 29	5 25	5 15	5 03	4 50	4 34	4 14	3 47	3 29	3 06
Aug. 2	5 41	5 38	5 34	5 30	5 27	5 22	5 13	5 03	4 51	4 36	4 16	3 50	3 33	3 11
6	5 35	5 32	5 30	5 27	5 23	5 20	5 12	5 02	4 51	4 37	4 18	3 54	3 38	3 17
10	5 28	5 27	5 25	5 22	5 20	5 17	5 10	5 01	4 51	4 37	4 20	3 57	3 42	3 23
14	5 20	5 20	5 19	5 18	5 16	5 14	5 08	5 00	4 50	4 38	4 22	4 01	3 46	3 28
18	5 12	5 13	5 14	5 13	5 12	5 10	5 05	4 59	4 50	4 39	4 24	4 04	3 51	3 34
22	5 04	5 06	5 08	5 08	5 07	5 06	5 03	4 57	4 49	4 39	4 26	4 07	3 55	3 39
26	4 55	4 59	5 01	5 02	5 03	5 02	5 00	4 55	4 49	4 40	4 27	4 10	3 59	3 45
30	4 46	4 51	4 54	4 56	4 58	4 58	4 57	4 53	4 48	4 40	4 29	4 13	4 03	3 50
Sept. 3	4 36	4 43	4 47	4 50	4 52	4 53	4 53	4 51	4 47	4 40	4 30	4 16	4 07	3 55
7	4 26	4 34	4 40	4 44	4 47	4 49	4 50	4 49	4 46	4 40	4 31	4 19	4 10	4 00
11	4 15	4 25	4 32	4 37	4 41	4 44	4 46	4 47	4 44	4 40	4 33	4 22	4 14	4 04
15	4 04	4 16	4 24	4 31	4 35	4 39	4 43	4 44	4 43	4 40	4 34	4 24	4 17	4 09
19	3 53	4 06	4 16	4 24	4 29	4 34	4 39	4 42	4 42	4 40	4 35	4 27	4 21	4 13
23	3 41	3 57	4 08	4 17	4 23	4 28	4 35	4 39	4 40	4 39	4 36	4 29	4 24	4 18
27	3 29	3 47	4 00	4 09	4 17	4 23	4 32	4 37	4 39	4 39	4 37	4 32	4 28	4 22
Oct. 1	3 16	3 36	3 51	4 02	4 11	4 18	4 28	4 34	4 38	4 39	4 38	4 34	4 31	4 26
5	3 03	3 26	3 42	3 55	4 05	4 12	4 24	4 31	4 36	4 39	4 39	4 36	4 34	4 30

END OF EVENING ASTRONOMICAL TWILIGHT

Lat.	−55°	−50°	−45°	−40°	−35°	−30°	−20°	−10°	0°	+10°	+20°	+30°	+35°	+40°
	h m	h m	h m	h m	h m	h m	h m	h m	h m	h m	h m	h m	h m	h m
July 1	17 59	18 08	18 15	18 23	18 30	18 37	18 51	19 06	19 22	19 42	20 07	20 41	21 04	21 35
5	18 02	18 10	18 17	18 25	18 31	18 38	18 52	19 07	19 23	19 43	20 07	20 40	21 03	21 33
9	18 05	18 13	18 20	18 27	18 33	18 40	18 53	19 07	19 23	19 42	20 06	20 39	21 01	21 30
13	18 08	18 16	18 22	18 29	18 35	18 41	18 54	19 08	19 24	19 42	20 06	20 37	20 59	21 26
17	18 13	18 19	18 25	18 31	18 37	18 43	18 55	19 08	19 24	19 42	20 04	20 35	20 56	21 22
21	18 17	18 23	18 28	18 34	18 39	18 45	18 56	19 09	19 23	19 41	20 03	20 32	20 52	21 17
25	18 22	18 27	18 32	18 37	18 42	18 47	18 57	19 09	19 23	19 40	20 01	20 29	20 48	21 12
29	18 27	18 31	18 35	18 40	18 44	18 49	18 58	19 10	19 23	19 38	19 58	20 25	20 43	21 06
Aug. 2	18 32	18 36	18 39	18 43	18 46	18 50	18 59	19 10	19 22	19 37	19 56	20 22	20 39	21 00
6	18 38	18 40	18 43	18 46	18 49	18 52	19 00	19 10	19 21	19 35	19 53	20 17	20 33	20 54
10	18 44	18 45	18 47	18 49	18 51	18 54	19 01	19 10	19 20	19 33	19 50	20 13	20 28	20 47
14	18 50	18 50	18 51	18 52	18 54	18 56	19 02	19 09	19 19	19 31	19 47	20 08	20 22	20 40
18	18 56	18 55	18 55	18 55	18 56	18 58	19 03	19 09	19 18	19 29	19 43	20 03	20 16	20 32
22	19 03	19 00	18 59	18 59	18 59	19 00	19 03	19 09	19 16	19 26	19 39	19 58	20 10	20 25
26	19 10	19 06	19 03	19 02	19 02	19 02	19 04	19 08	19 15	19 24	19 36	19 53	20 04	20 18
30	19 17	19 11	19 08	19 05	19 04	19 04	19 05	19 08	19 13	19 21	19 32	19 47	19 57	20 10
Sept. 3	19 24	19 17	19 12	19 09	19 07	19 06	19 05	19 08	19 12	19 18	19 28	19 42	19 51	20 03
7	19 32	19 23	19 17	19 13	19 10	19 08	19 06	19 07	19 10	19 16	19 24	19 36	19 45	19 55
11	19 39	19 29	19 22	19 17	19 13	19 10	19 07	19 07	19 09	19 13	19 20	19 31	19 38	19 48
15	19 48	19 36	19 27	19 20	19 16	19 12	19 08	19 06	19 07	19 10	19 16	19 25	19 32	19 40
19	19 56	19 42	19 32	19 25	19 19	19 14	19 09	19 06	19 06	19 08	19 12	19 20	19 26	19 33
23	20 05	19 49	19 38	19 29	19 22	19 17	19 10	19 06	19 04	19 05	19 08	19 15	19 20	19 26
27	20 15	19 57	19 43	19 33	19 25	19 19	19 11	19 05	19 03	19 03	19 05	19 10	19 14	19 19
Oct. 1	20 25	20 04	19 49	19 38	19 29	19 22	19 12	19 05	19 02	19 00	19 01	19 05	19 08	19 12
5	20 36	20 12	19 56	19 43	19 33	19 25	19 13	19 05	19 01	18 58	18 58	19 00	19 02	19 06

UNIVERSAL TIME FOR MERIDIAN OF GREENWICH
BEGINNING OF MORNING ASTRONOMICAL TWILIGHT

Lat.	+40°	+42°	+44°	+46°	+48°	+50°	+52°	+54°	+56°	+58°	+60°	+62°	+64°	+66°
	h m	h m	h m	h m	h m	h m	h m	h m	h m	h m	h m	h m	h m	h m
July 1	2 33	2 17	1 58	1 33	0 54	// //	// //	// //	// //	// //	// //	// //	// //	// //
5	2 36	2 21	2 02	1 39	1 04	// //	// //	// //	// //	// //	// //	// //	// //	// //
9	2 40	2 25	2 07	1 45	1 14	// //	// //	// //	// //	// //	// //	// //	// //	// //
13	2 44	2 30	2 13	1 53	1 24	0 29	// //	// //	// //	// //	// //	// //	// //	// //
17	2 49	2 36	2 20	2 01	1 35	0 55	// //	// //	// //	// //	// //	// //	// //	// //
21	2 54	2 42	2 27	2 09	1 46	1 14	// //	// //	// //	// //	// //	// //	// //	// //
25	3 00	2 48	2 34	2 17	1 57	1 29	0 40	// //	// //	// //	// //	// //	// //	// //
29	3 06	2 54	2 41	2 26	2 08	1 44	1 08	// //	// //	// //	// //	// //	// //	// //
Aug. 2	3 11	3 01	2 49	2 35	2 18	1 57	1 29	0 35	// //	// //	// //	// //	// //	// //
6	3 17	3 07	2 56	2 43	2 28	2 09	1 46	1 10	// //	// //	// //	// //	// //	// //
10	3 23	3 14	3 03	2 51	2 38	2 21	2 01	1 33	0 44	// //	// //	// //	// //	// //
14	3 28	3 20	3 10	2 59	2 47	2 32	2 14	1 51	1 18	// //	// //	// //	// //	// //
18	3 34	3 26	3 17	3 07	2 56	2 43	2 27	2 07	1 41	1 00	// //	// //	// //	// //
22	3 39	3 32	3 24	3 15	3 05	2 53	2 39	2 22	2 00	1 30	0 33	// //	// //	// //
26	3 45	3 38	3 31	3 22	3 13	3 02	2 50	2 35	2 16	1 53	1 18	// //	// //	// //
30	3 50	3 44	3 37	3 29	3 21	3 11	3 00	2 47	2 31	2 11	1 45	1 03	// //	// //
Sept. 3	3 55	3 49	3 43	3 36	3 29	3 20	3 10	2 58	2 44	2 27	2 06	1 36	0 43	// //
7	4 00	3 55	3 49	3 43	3 36	3 28	3 19	3 09	2 57	2 42	2 24	2 01	1 27	// //
11	4 04	4 00	3 55	3 49	3 43	3 36	3 28	3 19	3 08	2 56	2 40	2 21	1 55	1 17
15	4 09	4 05	4 01	3 56	3 50	3 44	3 37	3 29	3 19	3 08	2 55	2 39	2 18	1 50
19	4 13	4 10	4 06	4 02	3 57	3 51	3 45	3 38	3 29	3 20	3 08	2 55	2 37	2 15
23	4 18	4 15	4 11	4 07	4 03	3 58	3 53	3 47	3 39	3 31	3 21	3 09	2 55	2 37
27	4 22	4 19	4 17	4 13	4 09	4 05	4 00	3 55	3 49	3 41	3 33	3 23	3 11	2 55
Oct. 1	4 26	4 24	4 22	4 19	4 16	4 12	4 08	4 03	3 58	3 52	3 44	3 36	3 25	3 13
5	4 30	4 29	4 27	4 24	4 22	4 19	4 15	4 11	4 07	4 01	3 55	3 48	3 39	3 28

END OF EVENING ASTRONOMICAL TWILIGHT

Lat.	+40°	+42°	+44°	+46°	+48°	+50°	+52°	+54°	+56°	+58°	+60°	+62°	+64°	+66°
	h m	h m	h m	h m	h m	h m	h m	h m	h m	h m	h m	h m	h m	h m
July 1	21 35	21 50	22 09	22 34	23 12	// //	// //	// //	// //	// //	// //	// //	// //	// //
5	21 33	21 48	22 06	22 30	23 04	// //	// //	// //	// //	// //	// //	// //	// //	// //
9	21 30	21 45	22 02	22 24	22 55	// //	// //	// //	// //	// //	// //	// //	// //	// //
13	21 26	21 40	21 57	22 18	22 45	23 35	// //	// //	// //	// //	// //	// //	// //	// //
17	21 22	21 36	21 51	22 10	22 35	23 13	// //	// //	// //	// //	// //	// //	// //	// //
21	21 17	21 30	21 45	22 02	22 24	22 56	// //	// //	// //	// //	// //	// //	// //	// //
25	21 12	21 24	21 38	21 54	22 14	22 40	23 25	// //	// //	// //	// //	// //	// //	// //
29	21 06	21 17	21 30	21 45	22 03	22 26	23 00	// //	// //	// //	// //	// //	// //	// //
Aug. 2	21 00	21 11	21 22	21 36	21 53	22 13	22 40	23 27	// //	// //	// //	// //	// //	// //
6	20 54	21 03	21 14	21 27	21 42	22 00	22 23	22 56	// //	// //	// //	// //	// //	// //
10	20 47	20 56	21 06	21 18	21 31	21 47	22 07	22 33	23 16	// //	// //	// //	// //	// //
14	20 40	20 48	20 58	21 08	21 20	21 35	21 52	22 14	22 45	// //	// //	// //	// //	// //
18	20 32	20 40	20 49	20 59	21 10	21 23	21 38	21 57	22 22	22 59	// //	// //	// //	// //
22	20 25	20 32	20 40	20 49	20 59	21 11	21 25	21 41	22 02	22 30	23 18	// //	// //	// //
26	20 18	20 24	20 32	20 40	20 49	20 59	21 12	21 26	21 44	22 07	22 39	// //	// //	// //
30	20 10	20 16	20 23	20 30	20 39	20 48	20 59	21 12	21 27	21 46	22 11	22 49	// //	// //
Sept. 3	20 03	20 08	20 14	20 21	20 28	20 37	20 47	20 58	21 12	21 28	21 48	22 16	23 02	// //
7	19 55	20 00	20 06	20 12	20 18	20 26	20 35	20 45	20 57	21 11	21 28	21 50	22 21	23 21
11	19 48	19 52	19 57	20 02	20 09	20 15	20 23	20 32	20 43	20 55	21 10	21 28	21 52	22 28
15	19 40	19 44	19 49	19 53	19 59	20 05	20 12	20 20	20 29	20 40	20 53	21 08	21 28	21 54
19	19 33	19 36	19 40	19 45	19 49	19 55	20 01	20 08	20 16	20 25	20 36	20 50	21 06	21 27
23	19 26	19 29	19 32	19 36	19 40	19 45	19 50	19 56	20 03	20 12	20 21	20 33	20 47	21 04
27	19 19	19 21	19 24	19 28	19 31	19 35	19 40	19 45	19 51	19 58	20 07	20 16	20 28	20 43
Oct. 1	19 12	19 14	19 17	19 19	19 22	19 26	19 30	19 34	19 40	19 46	19 53	20 01	20 11	20 23
5	19 06	19 07	19 09	19 11	19 14	19 17	19 20	19 24	19 28	19 34	19 40	19 47	19 55	20 05

// // indicates continuous twilight.

UNIVERSAL TIME FOR MERIDIAN OF GREENWICH
BEGINNING OF MORNING ASTRONOMICAL TWILIGHT

Lat.	−55°	−50°	−45°	−40°	−35°	−30°	−20°	−10°	0°	+10°	+20°	+30°	+35°	+40°
	h m	h m	h m	h m	h m	h m	h m	h m	h m	h m	h m	h m	h m	h m
Oct. 1	3 16	3 36	3 51	4 02	4 11	4 18	4 28	4 34	4 38	4 39	4 38	4 34	4 31	4 26
5	3 03	3 26	3 42	3 55	4 05	4 12	4 24	4 31	4 36	4 39	4 39	4 36	4 34	4 30
9	2 49	3 15	3 34	3 48	3 58	4 07	4 20	4 29	4 35	4 38	4 40	4 39	4 37	4 34
13	2 35	3 04	3 25	3 40	3 52	4 02	4 16	4 26	4 34	4 38	4 41	4 41	4 40	4 38
17	2 20	2 53	3 16	3 33	3 46	3 57	4 13	4 24	4 32	4 38	4 42	4 43	4 43	4 43
21	2 05	2 42	3 07	3 26	3 40	3 52	4 09	4 22	4 31	4 38	4 43	4 46	4 47	4 47
25	1 48	2 30	2 58	3 18	3 34	3 47	4 06	4 20	4 30	4 38	4 44	4 48	4 50	4 51
29	1 29	2 19	2 49	3 12	3 29	3 42	4 03	4 18	4 30	4 39	4 46	4 51	4 53	4 55
Nov. 2	1 07	2 07	2 41	3 05	3 23	3 38	4 00	4 16	4 29	4 39	4 47	4 54	4 56	4 59
6	0 40	1 54	2 32	2 58	3 18	3 34	3 57	4 15	4 29	4 40	4 49	4 56	5 00	5 03
10	// //	1 41	2 24	2 52	3 13	3 30	3 55	4 14	4 28	4 40	4 50	4 59	5 03	5 07
14	// //	1 28	2 16	2 46	3 09	3 26	3 53	4 13	4 28	4 41	4 52	5 02	5 06	5 10
18	// //	1 14	2 08	2 41	3 05	3 23	3 52	4 12	4 29	4 42	4 54	5 05	5 10	5 14
22	// //	0 59	2 01	2 36	3 01	3 21	3 50	4 12	4 29	4 44	4 56	5 07	5 13	5 18
26	// //	0 43	1 54	2 32	2 58	3 19	3 49	4 12	4 30	4 45	4 58	5 10	5 16	5 22
30	// //	0 21	1 48	2 28	2 56	3 17	3 49	4 12	4 31	4 47	5 00	5 13	5 19	5 26
Dec. 4	// //	// //	1 43	2 25	2 54	3 16	3 49	4 13	4 32	4 48	5 03	5 16	5 22	5 29
8	// //	// //	1 39	2 24	2 53	3 16	3 49	4 14	4 34	4 50	5 05	5 19	5 25	5 32
12	// //	// //	1 36	2 23	2 53	3 16	3 50	4 15	4 35	4 52	5 07	5 21	5 28	5 35
16	// //	// //	1 35	2 23	2 54	3 17	3 52	4 17	4 37	4 54	5 09	5 23	5 31	5 38
20	// //	// //	1 36	2 24	2 55	3 19	3 53	4 19	4 39	4 56	5 11	5 26	5 33	5 40
24	// //	// //	1 38	2 26	2 57	3 21	3 55	4 21	4 41	4 58	5 13	5 28	5 35	5 42
28	// //	// //	1 42	2 29	3 00	3 23	3 58	4 23	4 43	5 00	5 15	5 29	5 36	5 44
32	// //	// //	1 47	2 33	3 03	3 26	4 00	4 25	4 45	5 02	5 17	5 31	5 38	5 45
36	// //	// //	1 54	2 38	3 07	3 30	4 03	4 28	4 47	5 03	5 18	5 32	5 38	5 45

END OF EVENING ASTRONOMICAL TWILIGHT

Lat.	−55°	−50°	−45°	−40°	−35°	−30°	−20°	−10°	0°	+10°	+20°	+30°	+35°	+40°
	h m	h m	h m	h m	h m	h m	h m	h m	h m	h m	h m	h m	h m	h m
Oct. 1	20 25	20 04	19 49	19 38	19 29	19 22	19 12	19 05	19 02	19 00	19 01	19 05	19 08	19 12
5	20 36	20 12	19 56	19 43	19 33	19 25	19 13	19 05	19 01	18 58	18 58	19 00	19 02	19 06
9	20 47	20 21	20 02	19 48	19 37	19 28	19 15	19 06	19 00	18 56	18 54	18 55	18 57	18 59
13	21 00	20 30	20 09	19 53	19 41	19 31	19 16	19 06	18 59	18 54	18 51	18 51	18 52	18 53
17	21 13	20 39	20 16	19 59	19 45	19 35	19 18	19 07	18 58	18 52	18 48	18 47	18 47	18 47
21	21 28	20 49	20 24	20 05	19 50	19 38	19 20	19 07	18 58	18 51	18 46	18 43	18 42	18 42
25	21 44	21 00	20 31	20 11	19 55	19 42	19 23	19 08	18 58	18 50	18 44	18 39	18 38	18 37
29	22 03	21 11	20 40	20 17	20 00	19 46	19 25	19 10	18 58	18 49	18 42	18 36	18 34	18 32
Nov. 2	22 25	21 23	20 48	20 24	20 05	19 50	19 27	19 11	18 58	18 48	18 40	18 33	18 30	18 28
6	22 56	21 36	20 57	20 30	20 10	19 54	19 30	19 13	18 59	18 48	18 38	18 31	18 27	18 24
10	// //	21 49	21 06	20 37	20 16	19 59	19 33	19 14	19 00	18 47	18 37	18 29	18 25	18 21
14	// //	22 04	21 15	20 44	20 21	20 03	19 36	19 16	19 01	18 48	18 37	18 27	18 22	18 18
18	// //	22 19	21 24	20 51	20 27	20 08	19 39	19 18	19 02	18 48	18 36	18 26	18 21	18 16
22	// //	22 37	21 33	20 58	20 32	20 12	19 42	19 21	19 03	18 49	18 36	18 25	18 19	18 14
26	// //	22 57	21 42	21 04	20 37	20 16	19 46	19 23	19 05	18 50	18 36	18 24	18 18	18 12
30	// //	23 25	21 51	21 10	20 42	20 21	19 49	19 25	19 07	18 51	18 37	18 24	18 18	18 12
Dec. 4	// //	// //	21 59	21 16	20 47	20 25	19 52	19 28	19 08	18 52	18 38	18 25	18 18	18 11
8	// //	// //	22 06	21 21	20 51	20 28	19 55	19 30	19 10	18 54	18 39	18 25	18 18	18 12
12	// //	// //	22 12	21 25	20 55	20 32	19 57	19 32	19 12	18 56	18 41	18 26	18 19	18 12
16	// //	// //	22 17	21 29	20 58	20 34	20 00	19 35	19 15	18 57	18 42	18 28	18 21	18 14
20	// //	// //	22 20	21 32	21 00	20 37	20 02	19 37	19 17	18 59	18 44	18 30	18 23	18 15
24	// //	// //	22 21	21 33	21 02	20 39	20 04	19 39	19 19	19 01	18 46	18 32	18 25	18 17
28	// //	// //	22 21	21 34	21 03	20 40	20 06	19 40	19 20	19 03	18 48	18 34	18 27	18 20
32	// //	// //	22 19	21 34	21 03	20 40	20 07	19 42	19 22	19 05	18 51	18 37	18 30	18 23
36	// //	// //	22 16	21 32	21 03	20 41	20 07	19 43	19 24	19 07	18 53	18 39	18 33	18 26

// // indicates continuous twilight.

UNIVERSAL TIME FOR MERIDIAN OF GREENWICH

BEGINNING OF MORNING ASTRONOMICAL TWILIGHT

Lat.	+40°	+42°	+44°	+46°	+48°	+50°	+52°	+54°	+56°	+58°	+60°	+62°	+64°	+66°
	h m	h m	h m	h m	h m	h m	h m	h m	h m	h m	h m	h m	h m	h m
Oct. 1	4 26	4 24	4 22	4 19	4 16	4 12	4 08	4 03	3 58	3 52	3 44	3 36	3 25	3 13
5	4 30	4 29	4 27	4 24	4 22	4 19	4 15	4 11	4 07	4 01	3 55	3 48	3 39	3 28
9	4 34	4 33	4 31	4 30	4 28	4 25	4 22	4 19	4 15	4 11	4 06	3 59	3 52	3 43
13	4 38	4 38	4 36	4 35	4 33	4 31	4 29	4 27	4 23	4 20	4 16	4 11	4 05	3 57
17	4 43	4 42	4 41	4 40	4 39	4 38	4 36	4 34	4 32	4 29	4 25	4 21	4 17	4 11
21	4 47	4 46	4 46	4 45	4 45	4 44	4 43	4 41	4 40	4 37	4 35	4 32	4 28	4 24
25	4 51	4 51	4 51	4 51	4 50	4 50	4 49	4 48	4 47	4 46	4 44	4 42	4 39	4 36
29	4 55	4 55	4 55	4 56	4 56	4 56	4 56	4 55	4 55	4 54	4 53	4 52	4 50	4 48
Nov. 2	4 59	4 59	5 00	5 01	5 01	5 02	5 02	5 02	5 02	5 02	5 02	5 01	5 01	4 59
6	5 03	5 04	5 05	5 06	5 07	5 07	5 08	5 09	5 09	5 10	5 10	5 11	5 11	5 10
10	5 07	5 08	5 09	5 11	5 12	5 13	5 14	5 15	5 16	5 18	5 19	5 19	5 20	5 21
14	5 10	5 12	5 14	5 15	5 17	5 19	5 20	5 22	5 23	5 25	5 26	5 28	5 30	5 31
18	5 14	5 16	5 18	5 20	5 22	5 24	5 26	5 28	5 30	5 32	5 34	5 36	5 38	5 41
22	5 18	5 20	5 23	5 25	5 27	5 29	5 31	5 34	5 36	5 39	5 41	5 44	5 47	5 50
26	5 22	5 24	5 27	5 29	5 32	5 34	5 37	5 39	5 42	5 45	5 48	5 51	5 55	5 58
30	5 26	5 28	5 31	5 33	5 36	5 39	5 41	5 44	5 47	5 51	5 54	5 58	6 02	6 06
Dec. 4	5 29	5 32	5 34	5 37	5 40	5 43	5 46	5 49	5 52	5 56	6 00	6 04	6 08	6 13
8	5 32	5 35	5 38	5 41	5 44	5 47	5 50	5 53	5 57	6 01	6 05	6 09	6 14	6 19
12	5 35	5 38	5 41	5 44	5 47	5 50	5 54	5 57	6 01	6 05	6 09	6 14	6 18	6 24
16	5 38	5 41	5 44	5 47	5 50	5 53	5 57	6 00	6 04	6 08	6 13	6 17	6 22	6 28
20	5 40	5 43	5 46	5 49	5 53	5 56	5 59	6 03	6 07	6 11	6 15	6 20	6 25	6 31
24	5 42	5 45	5 48	5 51	5 54	5 58	6 01	6 05	6 09	6 13	6 17	6 22	6 27	6 33
28	5 44	5 47	5 50	5 53	5 56	5 59	6 02	6 06	6 10	6 14	6 18	6 23	6 28	6 33
32	5 45	5 47	5 50	5 53	5 56	6 00	6 03	6 06	6 10	6 14	6 18	6 23	6 27	6 33
36	5 45	5 48	5 51	5 54	5 57	6 00	6 03	6 06	6 10	6 13	6 17	6 21	6 26	6 31

END OF EVENING ASTRONOMICAL TWILIGHT

Lat.	+40°	+42°	+44°	+46°	+48°	+50°	+52°	+54°	+56°	+58°	+60°	+62°	+64°	+66°
	h m	h m	h m	h m	h m	h m	h m	h m	h m	h m	h m	h m	h m	h m
Oct. 1	19 12	19 14	19 17	19 19	19 22	19 26	19 30	19 34	19 40	19 46	19 53	20 01	20 11	20 23
5	19 06	19 07	19 09	19 11	19 14	19 17	19 20	19 24	19 28	19 34	19 40	19 47	19 55	20 05
9	18 59	19 00	19 02	19 04	19 06	19 08	19 11	19 14	19 18	19 22	19 27	19 33	19 40	19 49
13	18 53	18 54	18 55	18 56	18 58	19 00	19 02	19 05	19 07	19 11	19 15	19 20	19 26	19 33
17	18 47	18 48	18 49	18 50	18 51	18 52	18 54	18 55	18 58	19 00	19 04	19 07	19 12	19 18
21	18 42	18 42	18 42	18 43	18 44	18 44	18 45	18 47	18 48	18 50	18 53	18 56	18 59	19 03
25	18 37	18 37	18 37	18 37	18 37	18 37	18 38	18 39	18 40	18 41	18 43	18 45	18 47	18 50
29	18 32	18 32	18 31	18 31	18 31	18 31	18 31	18 31	18 31	18 32	18 33	18 34	18 36	18 38
Nov. 2	18 28	18 27	18 26	18 26	18 25	18 25	18 24	18 24	18 24	18 24	18 24	18 24	18 25	18 26
6	18 24	18 23	18 22	18 21	18 20	18 19	18 18	18 18	18 17	18 16	18 16	18 16	18 15	18 15
10	18 21	18 19	18 18	18 17	18 15	18 14	18 13	18 12	18 10	18 09	18 08	18 07	18 06	18 06
14	18 18	18 16	18 15	18 13	18 11	18 10	18 08	18 06	18 05	18 03	18 02	18 00	17 58	17 57
18	18 16	18 14	18 12	18 10	18 08	18 06	18 04	18 02	18 00	17 58	17 56	17 53	17 51	17 49
22	18 14	18 12	18 09	18 07	18 05	18 03	18 00	17 58	17 56	17 53	17 50	17 48	17 45	17 42
26	18 12	18 10	18 08	18 05	18 03	18 00	17 58	17 55	17 52	17 49	17 46	17 43	17 39	17 36
30	18 12	18 09	18 06	18 04	18 01	17 58	17 56	17 53	17 50	17 46	17 43	17 39	17 35	17 31
Dec. 4	18 11	18 09	18 06	18 03	18 00	17 57	17 54	17 51	17 48	17 44	17 40	17 36	17 32	17 27
8	18 12	18 09	18 06	18 03	18 00	17 57	17 54	17 50	17 47	17 43	17 39	17 35	17 30	17 25
12	18 12	18 09	18 06	18 03	18 00	17 57	17 54	17 50	17 46	17 43	17 38	17 34	17 29	17 23
16	18 14	18 11	18 08	18 04	18 01	17 58	17 55	17 51	17 47	17 43	17 39	17 34	17 29	17 23
20	18 15	18 12	18 09	18 06	18 03	18 00	17 56	17 52	17 49	17 44	17 40	17 35	17 30	17 24
24	18 17	18 14	18 11	18 08	18 05	18 02	17 58	17 55	17 51	17 47	17 42	17 38	17 32	17 27
28	18 20	18 17	18 14	18 11	18 08	18 04	18 01	17 57	17 54	17 50	17 45	17 41	17 36	17 30
32	18 23	18 20	18 17	18 14	18 11	18 08	18 04	18 01	17 57	17 53	17 49	17 45	17 40	17 35
36	18 26	18 23	18 20	18 17	18 14	18 11	18 08	18 05	18 02	17 58	17 54	17 50	17 45	17 40

MOONRISE AND MOONSET, 2025

UNIVERSAL TIME FOR MERIDIAN OF GREENWICH

MOONRISE

Lat.	−55°	−50°	−45°	−40°	−35°	−30°	−20°	−10°	0°	+10°	+20°	+30°	+35°	+40°
	h m	h m	h m	h m	h m	h m	h m	h m	h m	h m	h m	h m	h m	h m
Jan. 0	3 02	3 43	4 12	4 35	4 54	5 10	5 38	6 02	6 23	6 45	7 09	7 36	7 52	8 11
1	4 25	4 59	5 24	5 44	6 01	6 15	6 40	7 01	7 20	7 40	8 01	8 25	8 39	8 55
2	5 56	6 21	6 41	6 57	7 10	7 22	7 42	7 59	8 15	8 30	8 47	9 07	9 18	9 31
3	7 28	7 46	7 59	8 10	8 20	8 28	8 42	8 55	9 06	9 18	9 30	9 44	9 52	10 01
4	8 59	9 09	9 16	9 23	9 28	9 33	9 41	9 48	9 55	10 02	10 09	10 17	10 22	10 27
5	10 29	10 31	10 33	10 34	10 36	10 37	10 39	10 41	10 42	10 44	10 46	10 48	10 49	10 51
6	11 58	11 53	11 49	11 46	11 43	11 41	11 36	11 33	11 30	11 26	11 23	11 19	11 17	11 14
7	13 29	13 16	13 07	12 59	12 52	12 46	12 35	12 26	12 18	12 10	12 01	11 51	11 45	11 39
8	15 03	14 42	14 26	14 13	14 02	13 53	13 36	13 22	13 09	12 56	12 42	12 26	12 17	12 07
9	16 39	16 10	15 47	15 29	15 14	15 02	14 40	14 21	14 03	13 46	13 27	13 06	12 54	12 40
10	18 13	17 35	17 07	16 45	16 27	16 11	15 45	15 22	15 01	14 41	14 19	13 53	13 38	13 21
11	19 34	18 50	18 19	17 55	17 35	17 18	16 50	16 25	16 02	15 40	15 16	14 47	14 31	14 12
12	20 32	19 49	19 19	18 55	18 36	18 19	17 51	17 27	17 04	16 41	16 17	15 49	15 32	15 12
13	21 07	20 32	20 05	19 44	19 27	19 12	18 46	18 24	18 03	17 42	17 20	16 54	16 38	16 20
14	21 29	21 01	20 40	20 23	20 09	19 56	19 34	19 16	18 58	18 40	18 21	17 59	17 46	17 31
15	21 42	21 22	21 07	20 54	20 43	20 33	20 16	20 02	19 48	19 34	19 19	19 02	18 52	18 41
16	21 51	21 38	21 28	21 19	21 12	21 05	20 53	20 43	20 34	20 24	20 14	20 02	19 55	19 47
17	21 58	21 51	21 45	21 41	21 37	21 33	21 27	21 21	21 16	21 11	21 05	20 59	20 55	20 51
18	22 04	22 02	22 01	22 01	22 00	21 59	21 58	21 57	21 56	21 55	21 54	21 53	21 53	21 52
19	22 09	22 13	22 17	22 20	22 22	22 25	22 29	22 32	22 35	22 39	22 42	22 46	22 49	22 52
20	22 15	22 25	22 33	22 40	22 45	22 51	23 00	23 07	23 15	23 22	23 31	23 40	23 45	23 51
21	22 22	22 38	22 51	23 01	23 10	23 18	23 32	23 44	23 56	.. ..	.. ..	.. ..	.. ..	.. ..
22	22 32	22 54	23 12	23 26	23 39	23 49	.. ..	.. ..	.. ..	0 07	0 20	0 34	0 43	0 52
23	22 46	23 16	23 38	23 56	.. ..	.. ..	0 08	0 24	0 39	0 55	1 11	1 31	1 42	1 55
24	23 08	23 45	.. ..	.. ..	0 12	0 25	0 48	1 08	1 27	1 45	2 05	2 29	2 43	2 59

MOONSET

Lat.	−55°	−50°	−45°	−40°	−35°	−30°	−20°	−10°	0°	+10°	+20°	+30°	+35°	+40°
	h m	h m	h m	h m	h m	h m	h m	h m	h m	h m	h m	h m	h m	h m
Jan. 0	21 55	21 19	20 53	20 32	20 15	20 00	19 34	19 12	18 51	18 30	18 07	17 41	17 25	17 07
1	22 17	21 50	21 29	21 12	20 58	20 45	20 23	20 04	19 47	19 29	19 09	18 47	18 34	18 19
2	22 32	22 13	21 57	21 45	21 34	21 24	21 08	20 53	20 40	20 26	20 11	19 54	19 44	19 32
3	22 42	22 30	22 21	22 13	22 05	21 59	21 48	21 39	21 30	21 20	21 11	20 59	20 53	20 45
4	22 51	22 45	22 41	22 37	22 34	22 31	22 26	22 22	22 18	22 13	22 09	22 04	22 00	21 57
5	22 58	22 59	23 00	23 01	23 01	23 02	23 03	23 04	23 05	23 05	23 06	23 07	23 08	23 08
6	23 05	23 13	23 19	23 25	23 29	23 33	23 40	23 46	23 52	23 58	.. ..	.. ..	.. ..	.. ..
7	23 14	23 29	23 41	23 51	23 59	.. ..	.. ..	.. ..	.. ..	.. ..	0 04	0 11	0 16	0 20
8	23 26	23 48	.. ..	.. ..	.. ..	0 06	0 19	0 31	0 42	0 52	1 04	1 17	1 25	1 34
9	23 44	.. ..	0 06	0 21	0 33	0 44	1 02	1 19	1 34	1 50	2 06	2 25	2 36	2 49
10	.. ..	0 15	0 38	0 57	1 13	1 27	1 51	2 11	2 31	2 50	3 11	3 35	3 49	4 05
11	0 12	0 52	1 20	1 43	2 02	2 18	2 45	3 08	3 30	3 52	4 16	4 44	5 00	5 19
12	0 59	1 43	2 15	2 39	2 59	3 16	3 44	4 09	4 32	4 55	5 19	5 48	6 05	6 25
13	2 09	2 51	3 21	3 44	4 03	4 19	4 47	5 11	5 33	5 55	6 18	6 45	7 01	7 20
14	3 34	4 08	4 34	4 54	5 11	5 25	5 50	6 10	6 30	6 49	7 10	7 34	7 47	8 03
15	5 03	5 29	5 49	6 05	6 18	6 30	6 50	7 07	7 22	7 38	7 55	8 14	8 25	8 38
16	6 30	6 48	7 02	7 13	7 23	7 31	7 46	7 59	8 10	8 22	8 34	8 48	8 57	9 06
17	7 52	8 03	8 11	8 18	8 24	8 30	8 39	8 47	8 54	9 02	9 09	9 18	9 23	9 29
18	9 10	9 14	9 18	9 20	9 23	9 25	9 29	9 32	9 35	9 38	9 42	9 45	9 47	9 50
19	10 25	10 23	10 22	10 21	10 20	10 19	10 18	10 16	10 15	10 14	10 13	10 11	10 10	10 09
20	11 39	11 32	11 25	11 20	11 16	11 12	11 06	11 00	10 54	10 49	10 43	10 37	10 33	10 29
21	12 55	12 41	12 30	12 21	12 13	12 06	11 54	11 44	11 34	11 25	11 15	11 03	10 57	10 49
22	14 12	13 51	13 35	13 22	13 11	13 01	12 44	12 30	12 17	12 03	11 49	11 32	11 23	11 12
23	15 32	15 04	14 43	14 25	14 11	13 58	13 37	13 19	13 02	12 45	12 26	12 06	11 53	11 39
24	16 53	16 17	15 51	15 30	15 12	14 58	14 32	14 11	13 51	13 30	13 09	12 44	12 30	12 13

.. .. indicates phenomenon will occur the next day.

UNIVERSAL TIME FOR MERIDIAN OF GREENWICH

MOONRISE

Lat.	+40°	+42°	+44°	+46°	+48°	+50°	+52°	+54°	+56°	+58°	+60°	+62°	+64°	+66°
	h m	h m	h m	h m	h m	h m	h m	h m	h m	h m	h m	h m	h m	h m
Jan. 0	8 11	8 19	8 29	8 39	8 50	9 02	9 16	9 33	9 52	10 16	10 47	11 38	▬	▬
1	8 55	9 02	9 10	9 18	9 28	9 38	9 50	10 03	10 18	10 35	10 57	11 24	12 03	▬
2	9 31	9 36	9 43	9 49	9 56	10 04	10 13	10 22	10 33	10 46	11 00	11 17	11 38	12 04
3	10 01	10 05	10 09	10 14	10 19	10 24	10 30	10 36	10 43	10 52	11 01	11 11	11 23	11 38
4	10 27	10 29	10 31	10 34	10 37	10 40	10 43	10 47	10 51	10 55	11 00	11 06	11 12	11 20
5	10 51	10 51	10 52	10 53	10 53	10 54	10 55	10 56	10 57	10 58	10 59	11 01	11 02	11 04
6	11 14	11 13	11 12	11 11	11 09	11 08	11 06	11 05	11 03	11 01	10 58	10 56	10 53	10 50
7	11 39	11 36	11 33	11 30	11 26	11 23	11 19	11 14	11 09	11 04	10 58	10 51	10 43	10 34
8	12 07	12 02	11 57	11 52	11 46	11 40	11 33	11 26	11 18	11 09	10 58	10 46	10 31	10 14
9	12 40	12 34	12 27	12 20	12 12	12 03	11 53	11 43	11 30	11 16	11 00	10 40	10 15	9 42
10	13 21	13 13	13 05	12 55	12 45	12 34	12 22	12 07	11 51	11 31	11 06	10 33	9 38	▭
11	14 12	14 03	13 53	13 43	13 31	13 18	13 03	12 46	12 26	12 00	11 25	10 17	▭	▭
12	15 12	15 03	14 54	14 43	14 31	14 18	14 03	13 45	13 24	12 57	12 18	▭	▭	▭
13	16 20	16 12	16 03	15 54	15 43	15 31	15 18	15 02	14 44	14 21	13 51	13 06	▭	▭
14	17 31	17 24	17 17	17 09	17 00	16 51	16 40	16 28	16 14	15 57	15 37	15 12	14 37	13 28
15	18 41	18 36	18 30	18 24	18 18	18 11	18 03	17 54	17 44	17 33	17 20	17 04	16 45	16 20
16	19 47	19 44	19 40	19 36	19 32	19 27	19 22	19 16	19 10	19 03	18 54	18 45	18 34	18 21
17	20 51	20 49	20 47	20 45	20 42	20 40	20 37	20 34	20 31	20 27	20 23	20 18	20 13	20 06
18	21 52	21 51	21 51	21 51	21 50	21 50	21 50	21 49	21 49	21 48	21 47	21 46	21 46	21 45
19	22 52	22 53	22 54	22 55	22 57	22 59	23 00	23 02	23 04	23 07	23 10	23 13	23 16	23 20
20	23 51	23 54	23 57	.. ..	.. ..	.. ..	.. ..	.. ..	.. ..	.. ..	.. ..	.. ..	.. ..	.. ..
21	.. ..	.. ..	.. ..	0 00	0 04	0 07	0 11	0 16	0 21	0 26	0 32	0 40	0 48	0 58
22	0 52	0 56	1 01	1 06	1 11	1 17	1 24	1 31	1 39	1 48	1 58	2 10	2 25	2 43
23	1 55	2 01	2 07	2 14	2 21	2 29	2 38	2 48	3 00	3 13	3 29	3 48	4 12	4 45
24	2 59	3 06	3 14	3 23	3 32	3 42	3 54	4 08	4 23	4 42	5 05	5 35	6 23	▬

MOONSET

Lat.	+40°	+42°	+44°	+46°	+48°	+50°	+52°	+54°	+56°	+58°	+60°	+62°	+64°	+66°
	h m	h m	h m	h m	h m	h m	h m	h m	h m	h m	h m	h m	h m	h m
Jan. 0	17 07	16 59	16 50	16 40	16 29	16 17	16 03	15 47	15 28	15 05	14 34	13 44	▬	▬
1	18 19	18 12	18 04	17 56	17 47	17 37	17 26	17 14	16 59	16 42	16 21	15 55	15 16	▬
2	19 32	19 27	19 21	19 15	19 09	19 01	18 53	18 44	18 34	18 23	18 09	17 53	17 34	17 08
3	20 45	20 42	20 38	20 34	20 30	20 25	20 20	20 15	20 08	20 02	19 54	19 44	19 34	19 21
4	21 57	21 55	21 54	21 52	21 50	21 48	21 46	21 43	21 40	21 37	21 34	21 30	21 25	21 20
5	23 08	23 09	23 09	23 09	23 10	23 10	23 10	23 11	23 11	23 12	23 12	23 13	23 14	23 14
6	.. ..	.. ..	.. ..	.. ..	.. ..	.. ..	.. ..	.. ..	.. ..	.. ..	.. ..	.. ..	.. ..	.. ..
7	0 20	0 22	0 25	0 27	0 30	0 32	0 35	0 39	0 43	0 47	0 51	0 57	1 03	1 10
8	1 34	1 38	1 42	1 47	1 52	1 57	2 03	2 09	2 17	2 25	2 34	2 45	2 58	3 14
9	2 49	2 55	3 01	3 08	3 15	3 24	3 33	3 43	3 54	4 07	4 23	4 42	5 06	5 38
10	4 05	4 13	4 21	4 30	4 39	4 50	5 02	5 16	5 32	5 52	6 16	6 48	7 43	▭
11	5 19	5 27	5 37	5 47	5 58	6 11	6 26	6 43	7 03	7 28	8 03	9 12	▭	▭
12	6 25	6 34	6 43	6 54	7 06	7 19	7 34	7 52	8 14	8 41	9 20	▭	▭	▭
13	7 20	7 28	7 37	7 47	7 58	8 10	8 24	8 40	8 59	9 21	9 51	10 37	▭	▭
14	8 03	8 10	8 18	8 27	8 36	8 46	8 57	9 10	9 24	9 41	10 02	10 28	11 04	12 14
15	8 38	8 43	8 50	8 56	9 03	9 11	9 19	9 29	9 39	9 51	10 05	10 22	10 42	11 08
16	9 06	9 10	9 14	9 19	9 24	9 29	9 35	9 42	9 49	9 57	10 06	10 17	10 29	10 44
17	9 29	9 32	9 34	9 37	9 40	9 43	9 47	9 51	9 55	10 00	10 06	10 12	10 19	10 27
18	9 50	9 51	9 52	9 53	9 54	9 56	9 57	9 59	10 00	10 02	10 04	10 07	10 10	10 13
19	10 09	10 09	10 08	10 08	10 07	10 07	10 06	10 05	10 05	10 04	10 03	10 02	10 01	10 00
20	10 29	10 27	10 25	10 23	10 20	10 18	10 15	10 12	10 09	10 06	10 02	9 57	9 52	9 46
21	10 49	10 46	10 42	10 39	10 35	10 30	10 25	10 20	10 14	10 08	10 00	9 52	9 42	9 31
22	11 12	11 07	11 02	10 57	10 51	10 44	10 37	10 30	10 21	10 11	10 00	9 46	9 31	9 12
23	11 39	11 33	11 27	11 19	11 11	11 03	10 53	10 42	10 30	10 16	10 00	9 40	9 15	8 41
24	12 13	12 05	11 57	11 48	11 38	11 27	11 15	11 02	10 46	10 26	10 03	9 32	8 43	▬

▭ indicates Moon continuously above horizon.
▬ indicates Moon continuously below horizon.
.. .. indicates phenomenon will occur the next day.

UNIVERSAL TIME FOR MERIDIAN OF GREENWICH

MOONRISE

Lat.	−55°	−50°	−45°	−40°	−35°	−30°	−20°	−10°	0°	+10°	+20°	+30°	+35°	+40°
	h m	h m	h m	h m	h m	h m	h m	h m	h m	h m	h m	h m	h m	h m
Jan. 23	22 46	23 16	23 38	23 56	.. ..	.. ..	0 08	0 24	0 39	0 55	1 11	1 31	1 42	1 55
24	23 08	23 45	.. ..	.. ..	0 12	0 25	0 48	1 08	1 27	1 45	2 05	2 29	2 43	2 59
25	23 44	.. ..	0 12	0 34	0 52	1 07	1 33	1 56	2 18	2 39	3 02	3 29	3 45	4 03
26	.. ..	0 27	0 57	1 21	1 40	1 57	2 25	2 50	3 12	3 35	4 00	4 28	4 45	5 05
27	0 41	1 24	1 54	2 18	2 37	2 54	3 23	3 47	4 09	4 32	4 56	5 25	5 41	6 01
28	1 58	2 36	3 03	3 25	3 43	3 58	4 24	4 46	5 07	5 28	5 50	6 16	6 31	6 49
29	3 28	3 58	4 20	4 38	4 53	5 05	5 27	5 46	6 04	6 21	6 40	7 01	7 14	7 28
30	5 03	5 24	5 40	5 53	6 04	6 14	6 30	6 44	6 58	7 11	7 25	7 41	7 50	8 01
31	6 38	6 50	7 00	7 08	7 15	7 21	7 31	7 41	7 49	7 57	8 06	8 17	8 22	8 29
Feb. 1	8 11	8 15	8 19	8 22	8 25	8 27	8 31	8 35	8 38	8 42	8 45	8 49	8 51	8 54
2	9 42	9 40	9 37	9 36	9 34	9 33	9 30	9 28	9 26	9 25	9 23	9 21	9 19	9 18
3	11 14	11 04	10 56	10 49	10 44	10 38	10 30	10 22	10 15	10 08	10 01	9 53	9 48	9 43
4	12 49	12 30	12 16	12 04	11 54	11 45	11 30	11 18	11 06	10 54	10 41	10 27	10 19	10 09
5	14 24	13 57	13 36	13 20	13 06	12 54	12 33	12 15	11 59	11 43	11 25	11 05	10 54	10 41
6	15 59	15 22	14 56	14 35	14 17	14 02	13 37	13 15	12 55	12 35	12 14	11 49	11 35	11 19
7	17 23	16 40	16 09	15 46	15 26	15 09	14 41	14 17	13 54	13 32	13 08	12 40	12 24	12 05
8	18 28	17 43	17 12	16 48	16 28	16 11	15 42	15 18	14 55	14 32	14 07	13 38	13 21	13 01
9	19 09	18 30	18 02	17 40	17 21	17 05	16 38	16 15	15 53	15 32	15 08	14 41	14 25	14 06
10	19 34	19 03	18 40	18 21	18 05	17 52	17 28	17 08	16 49	16 30	16 09	15 45	15 31	15 15
11	19 49	19 26	19 09	18 54	18 42	18 31	18 12	17 55	17 40	17 25	17 08	16 49	16 37	16 24
12	19 59	19 44	19 31	19 21	19 12	19 04	18 50	18 38	18 27	18 16	18 03	17 49	17 41	17 32
13	20 07	19 57	19 50	19 44	19 38	19 33	19 25	19 17	19 10	19 03	18 56	18 47	18 42	18 37
14	20 13	20 09	20 06	20 04	20 02	20 00	19 57	19 54	19 51	19 49	19 46	19 43	19 41	19 39
15	20 18	20 20	20 22	20 23	20 25	20 26	20 28	20 29	20 31	20 33	20 35	20 37	20 38	20 39
16	20 24	20 31	20 38	20 43	20 47	20 51	20 58	21 05	21 11	21 17	21 23	21 30	21 34	21 39

MOONSET

Lat.	−55°	−50°	−45°	−40°	−35°	−30°	−20°	−10°	0°	+10°	+20°	+30°	+35°	+40°
	h m	h m	h m	h m	h m	h m	h m	h m	h m	h m	h m	h m	h m	h m
Jan. 23	15 32	15 04	14 43	14 25	14 11	13 58	13 37	13 19	13 02	12 45	12 26	12 06	11 53	11 39
24	16 53	16 17	15 51	15 30	15 12	14 58	14 32	14 11	13 51	13 30	13 09	12 44	12 30	12 13
25	18 08	17 26	16 56	16 33	16 14	15 57	15 30	15 06	14 43	14 21	13 57	13 30	13 13	12 54
26	19 10	18 27	17 56	17 32	17 12	16 55	16 27	16 02	15 39	15 17	14 52	14 23	14 06	13 46
27	19 53	19 14	18 46	18 24	18 05	17 50	17 22	16 59	16 37	16 15	15 52	15 24	15 08	14 49
28	20 20	19 50	19 26	19 08	18 52	18 38	18 14	17 54	17 34	17 15	16 54	16 30	16 16	15 59
29	20 38	20 16	19 58	19 44	19 31	19 20	19 02	18 45	18 30	18 14	17 57	17 38	17 27	17 13
30	20 50	20 35	20 24	20 14	20 05	19 58	19 45	19 33	19 22	19 11	19 00	18 46	18 38	18 29
31	20 59	20 51	20 45	20 40	20 36	20 32	20 25	20 18	20 13	20 07	20 00	19 53	19 48	19 44
Feb. 1	21 07	21 06	21 05	21 04	21 04	21 03	21 03	21 02	21 01	21 00	20 59	20 58	20 58	20 57
2	21 14	21 20	21 25	21 29	21 32	21 35	21 40	21 45	21 49	21 54	21 59	22 04	22 07	22 11
3	21 22	21 35	21 45	21 54	22 01	22 08	22 19	22 29	22 39	22 48	22 59	23 10	23 17	23 25
4	21 33	21 53	22 09	22 23	22 34	22 44	23 01	23 16	23 31	23 45	.. ..	.. ..	.. ..	.. ..
5	21 48	22 17	22 39	22 57	23 12	23 25	23 47	.. ..	.. ..	.. ..	0 00	0 18	0 28	0 40
6	22 12	22 49	23 17	23 39	23 57	.. ..	.. ..	0 07	0 25	0 44	1 04	1 26	1 40	1 56
7	22 51	23 35	.. ..	.. ..	.. ..	0 12	0 39	1 02	1 23	1 45	2 08	2 35	2 51	3 09
8	23 52	.. ..	0 06	0 30	0 50	1 07	1 36	2 00	2 23	2 46	3 11	3 39	3 56	4 16
9	.. ..	0 36	1 07	1 31	1 51	2 08	2 36	3 00	3 23	3 46	4 10	4 38	4 54	5 14
10	1 12	1 49	2 17	2 38	2 56	3 12	3 38	4 00	4 20	4 41	5 03	5 28	5 43	6 00
11	2 39	3 08	3 31	3 48	4 03	4 16	4 38	4 56	5 14	5 31	5 50	6 11	6 23	6 37
12	4 07	4 28	4 44	4 57	5 08	5 18	5 35	5 50	6 03	6 16	6 31	6 47	6 56	7 07
13	5 30	5 44	5 55	6 03	6 11	6 18	6 29	6 39	6 48	6 57	7 07	7 18	7 24	7 31
14	6 50	6 57	7 02	7 07	7 11	7 14	7 20	7 25	7 30	7 35	7 40	7 46	7 49	7 53
15	8 06	8 07	8 08	8 08	8 09	8 09	8 10	8 10	8 11	8 11	8 12	8 12	8 12	8 13
16	9 21	9 16	9 12	9 08	9 05	9 03	8 58	8 54	8 50	8 46	8 42	8 38	8 35	8 32

.. .. indicates phenomenon will occur the next day.

UNIVERSAL TIME FOR MERIDIAN OF GREENWICH

MOONRISE

Lat.	+40°	+42°	+44°	+46°	+48°	+50°	+52°	+54°	+56°	+58°	+60°	+62°	+64°	+66°
	h m	h m	h m	h m	h m	h m	h m	h m	h m	h m	h m	h m	h m	h m
Jan. 23	1 55	2 01	2 07	2 14	2 21	2 29	2 38	2 48	3 00	3 13	3 29	3 48	4 12	4 45
24	2 59	3 06	3 14	3 23	3 32	3 42	3 54	4 08	4 23	4 42	5 05	5 35	6 23	▬
25	4 03	4 12	4 21	4 31	4 42	4 54	5 09	5 25	5 45	6 09	6 42	7 41	▬	▬
26	5 05	5 14	5 24	5 35	5 47	6 00	6 16	6 34	6 56	7 25	8 07	▬	▬	▬
27	6 01	6 10	6 19	6 30	6 41	6 55	7 10	7 27	7 48	8 14	8 51	▬	▬	▬
28	6 49	6 56	7 05	7 14	7 24	7 36	7 49	8 03	8 20	8 41	9 06	9 41	10 47	▬
29	7 28	7 35	7 41	7 49	7 57	8 06	8 16	8 27	8 39	8 54	9 11	9 31	9 58	10 34
30	8 01	8 06	8 11	8 16	8 22	8 28	8 35	8 43	8 51	9 01	9 12	9 25	9 40	9 58
31	8 29	8 32	8 35	8 38	8 42	8 46	8 50	8 55	9 00	9 05	9 12	9 19	9 27	9 37
Feb. 1	8 54	8 55	8 56	8 58	8 59	9 01	9 02	9 04	9 06	9 08	9 11	9 13	9 17	9 20
2	9 18	9 17	9 17	9 16	9 15	9 15	9 14	9 13	9 12	9 11	9 10	9 08	9 07	9 05
3	9 43	9 40	9 38	9 35	9 32	9 29	9 26	9 22	9 18	9 14	9 09	9 03	8 57	8 49
4	10 09	10 05	10 01	9 56	9 51	9 46	9 40	9 33	9 26	9 18	9 08	8 58	8 45	8 30
5	10 41	10 35	10 29	10 22	10 14	10 06	9 58	9 48	9 37	9 24	9 09	8 52	8 30	8 03
6	11 19	11 11	11 03	10 54	10 45	10 34	10 22	10 09	9 54	9 35	9 13	8 44	8 02	▭
7	12 05	11 57	11 47	11 37	11 26	11 13	10 59	10 42	10 22	9 58	9 25	8 31	▭	▭
8	13 01	12 52	12 43	12 32	12 20	12 06	11 51	11 33	11 11	10 43	10 03	▭	▭	▭
9	14 06	13 57	13 48	13 38	13 27	13 14	13 00	12 43	12 23	11 58	11 24	10 20	▭	▭
10	15 15	15 08	15 00	14 51	14 41	14 31	14 19	14 05	13 49	13 30	13 07	12 35	11 44	▭
11	16 24	16 19	16 12	16 06	15 58	15 50	15 41	15 31	15 19	15 06	14 50	14 31	14 07	13 34
12	17 32	17 28	17 23	17 19	17 13	17 08	17 01	16 54	16 47	16 38	16 28	16 16	16 02	15 45
13	18 37	18 34	18 31	18 29	18 25	18 22	18 18	18 14	18 10	18 05	17 59	17 52	17 45	17 36
14	19 39	19 38	19 37	19 36	19 35	19 33	19 32	19 31	19 29	19 27	19 25	19 23	19 20	19 17
15	20 39	20 40	20 41	20 41	20 42	20 43	20 44	20 45	20 46	20 47	20 48	20 50	20 52	20 54
16	21 39	21 41	21 44	21 46	21 49	21 52	21 55	21 58	22 02	22 07	22 12	22 17	22 24	22 31

MOONSET

Lat.	+40°	+42°	+44°	+46°	+48°	+50°	+52°	+54°	+56°	+58°	+60°	+62°	+64°	+66°
	h m	h m	h m	h m	h m	h m	h m	h m	h m	h m	h m	h m	h m	h m
Jan. 23	11 39	11 33	11 27	11 19	11 11	11 03	10 53	10 42	10 30	10 16	10 00	9 40	9 15	8 41
24	12 13	12 05	11 57	11 48	11 38	11 27	11 15	11 02	10 46	10 26	10 03	9 32	8 43	▬
25	12 54	12 46	12 36	12 26	12 15	12 02	11 48	11 31	11 11	10 46	10 13	9 14	▬	▬
26	13 46	13 37	13 27	13 17	13 04	12 51	12 35	12 17	11 55	11 26	10 44	▬	▬	▬
27	14 49	14 40	14 30	14 20	14 08	13 55	13 41	13 23	13 03	12 37	12 00	▬	▬	▬
28	15 59	15 51	15 43	15 34	15 24	15 13	15 01	14 47	14 30	14 10	13 45	13 11	12 06	▬
29	17 13	17 07	17 01	16 54	16 47	16 38	16 29	16 19	16 07	15 53	15 37	15 17	14 52	14 17
30	18 29	18 25	18 20	18 16	18 11	18 05	17 59	17 52	17 45	17 36	17 26	17 15	17 01	16 44
31	19 44	19 41	19 39	19 37	19 34	19 31	19 28	19 24	19 20	19 16	19 11	19 05	18 59	18 51
Feb. 1	20 57	20 57	20 57	20 56	20 56	20 55	20 55	20 55	20 54	20 53	20 53	20 52	20 51	20 50
2	22 11	22 12	22 14	22 16	22 18	22 20	22 22	22 25	22 27	22 30	22 34	22 38	22 43	22 48
3	23 25	23 28	23 32	23 36	23 40	23 45	23 50	23 56	.. ..	.. ..	.. ..	.. ..	.. ..	.. ..
4	.. ..	.. ..	.. ..	.. ..	.. ..	.. ..	.. ..	.. ..	0 02	0 09	0 17	0 27	0 38	0 51
5	0 40	0 45	0 51	0 57	1 04	1 11	1 20	1 29	1 39	1 51	2 05	2 21	2 41	3 08
6	1 56	2 03	2 10	2 19	2 28	2 38	2 49	3 02	3 17	3 35	3 56	4 24	5 05	▭
7	3 09	3 17	3 27	3 37	3 48	4 00	4 14	4 30	4 50	5 14	5 46	6 41	▭	▭
8	4 16	4 25	4 35	4 46	4 58	5 11	5 27	5 45	6 06	6 34	7 15	▭	▭	▭
9	5 14	5 22	5 32	5 42	5 54	6 06	6 21	6 38	6 58	7 24	7 58	9 02	▭	▭
10	6 00	6 08	6 16	6 25	6 35	6 46	6 58	7 12	7 29	7 48	8 12	8 44	9 36	▭
11	6 37	6 43	6 50	6 57	7 05	7 14	7 23	7 34	7 46	8 00	8 17	8 37	9 02	9 36
12	7 07	7 11	7 16	7 22	7 28	7 34	7 41	7 49	7 57	8 07	8 18	8 31	8 46	9 04
13	7 31	7 35	7 38	7 41	7 45	7 49	7 54	7 59	8 04	8 11	8 17	8 25	8 34	8 45
14	7 53	7 55	7 56	7 58	8 00	8 02	8 04	8 07	8 10	8 13	8 16	8 20	8 25	8 30
15	8 13	8 13	8 13	8 13	8 13	8 14	8 14	8 14	8 14	8 14	8 15	8 15	8 15	8 16
16	8 32	8 31	8 29	8 28	8 26	8 24	8 23	8 21	8 18	8 16	8 13	8 10	8 06	8 02

▭ indicates Moon continuously above horizon.
▬ indicates Moon continuously below horizon.
.. .. indicates phenomenon will occur the next day.

UNIVERSAL TIME FOR MERIDIAN OF GREENWICH

MOONRISE

Lat.	−55°	−50°	−45°	−40°	−35°	−30°	−20°	−10°	0°	+10°	+20°	+30°	+35°	+40°
	h m	h m	h m	h m	h m	h m	h m	h m	h m	h m	h m	h m	h m	h m
Feb. 15	20 18	20 20	20 22	20 23	20 25	20 26	20 28	20 29	20 31	20 33	20 35	20 37	20 38	20 39
16	20 24	20 31	20 38	20 43	20 47	20 51	20 58	21 05	21 11	21 17	21 23	21 30	21 34	21 39
17	20 30	20 44	20 54	21 04	21 11	21 18	21 30	21 41	21 51	22 01	22 12	22 24	22 32	22 40
18	20 38	20 58	21 14	21 27	21 38	21 48	22 05	22 19	22 33	22 47	23 02	23 20	23 30	23 42
19	20 50	21 17	21 37	21 54	22 09	22 21	22 42	23 01	23 18	23 36	23 55	.. ..	.. ..	.. ..
20	21 08	21 42	22 07	22 28	22 45	23 00	23 25	23 46	.. ..	.. ..	.. ..	0 17	0 30	0 45
21	21 36	22 17	22 46	23 09	23 29	23 45	.. ..	.. ..	0 07	0 27	0 49	1 15	1 30	1 48
22	22 22	23 06	23 37	.. ..	.. ..	.. ..	0 13	0 37	0 59	1 22	1 46	2 14	2 31	2 50
23	23 29	.. ..	.. ..	0 01	0 21	0 38	1 07	1 31	1 54	2 17	2 42	3 11	3 28	3 48
24	.. ..	0 10	0 40	1 03	1 22	1 38	2 06	2 29	2 51	3 13	3 37	4 04	4 20	4 39
25	0 54	1 27	1 53	2 12	2 29	2 43	3 08	3 28	3 48	4 07	4 28	4 52	5 06	5 22
26	2 27	2 52	3 12	3 27	3 40	3 51	4 11	4 28	4 43	4 59	5 15	5 34	5 45	5 57
27	4 04	4 20	4 33	4 43	4 52	5 00	5 14	5 25	5 36	5 47	5 58	6 12	6 19	6 28
28	5 40	5 48	5 54	6 00	6 04	6 08	6 15	6 21	6 27	6 33	6 39	6 46	6 50	6 54
Mar. 1	7 14	7 15	7 15	7 16	7 16	7 16	7 16	7 17	7 17	7 18	7 18	7 19	7 19	7 19
2	8 50	8 42	8 37	8 32	8 28	8 24	8 18	8 12	8 07	8 02	7 57	7 51	7 48	7 44
3	10 27	10 11	9 59	9 49	9 40	9 33	9 20	9 09	8 59	8 49	8 38	8 26	8 19	8 11
4	12 05	11 41	11 22	11 07	10 54	10 43	10 24	10 08	9 53	9 38	9 22	9 04	8 53	8 41
5	13 44	13 10	12 44	12 25	12 08	11 54	11 30	11 09	10 50	10 31	10 10	9 47	9 33	9 18
6	15 14	14 31	14 01	13 38	13 19	13 02	12 35	12 11	11 49	11 27	11 04	10 36	10 21	10 02
7	16 25	15 40	15 08	14 44	14 23	14 06	13 37	13 12	12 49	12 26	12 01	11 33	11 16	10 56
8	17 12	16 31	16 01	15 38	15 19	15 03	14 35	14 11	13 48	13 26	13 02	12 34	12 17	11 58
9	17 41	17 07	16 42	16 22	16 05	15 51	15 26	15 04	14 44	14 24	14 02	13 37	13 22	13 05
10	17 58	17 32	17 13	16 57	16 43	16 31	16 11	15 53	15 36	15 19	15 01	14 40	14 28	14 14
11	18 09	17 51	17 36	17 25	17 14	17 05	16 50	16 36	16 23	16 11	15 57	15 41	15 32	15 21

MOONSET

Lat.	−55°	−50°	−45°	−40°	−35°	−30°	−20°	−10°	0°	+10°	+20°	+30°	+35°	+40°
	h m	h m	h m	h m	h m	h m	h m	h m	h m	h m	h m	h m	h m	h m
Feb. 15	8 06	8 07	8 08	8 08	8 09	8 09	8 10	8 10	8 11	8 11	8 12	8 12	8 12	8 13
16	9 21	9 16	9 12	9 08	9 05	9 03	8 58	8 54	8 50	8 46	8 42	8 38	8 35	8 32
17	10 37	10 25	10 16	10 08	10 02	9 56	9 46	9 38	9 30	9 22	9 13	9 04	8 58	8 52
18	11 53	11 35	11 21	11 09	11 00	10 51	10 36	10 23	10 11	9 59	9 46	9 32	9 23	9 14
19	13 12	12 47	12 27	12 12	11 59	11 47	11 27	11 10	10 55	10 39	10 22	10 03	9 52	9 39
20	14 32	13 59	13 35	13 15	12 59	12 45	12 21	12 00	11 41	11 22	11 02	10 38	10 25	10 09
21	15 50	15 10	14 41	14 18	13 59	13 43	13 16	12 53	12 32	12 10	11 47	11 20	11 04	10 46
22	16 57	16 13	15 42	15 18	14 58	14 41	14 13	13 48	13 25	13 02	12 38	12 09	11 52	11 32
23	17 48	17 06	16 36	16 13	15 53	15 37	15 08	14 44	14 22	13 59	13 34	13 06	12 49	12 29
24	18 21	17 46	17 20	16 59	16 42	16 27	16 01	15 39	15 18	14 58	14 35	14 09	13 53	13 35
25	18 43	18 16	17 55	17 39	17 24	17 12	16 51	16 32	16 14	15 57	15 38	15 16	15 03	14 48
26	18 57	18 38	18 24	18 11	18 01	17 52	17 36	17 22	17 09	16 55	16 41	16 24	16 14	16 03
27	19 07	18 56	18 47	18 40	18 33	18 28	18 18	18 09	18 01	17 52	17 43	17 33	17 27	17 20
28	19 15	19 11	19 08	19 05	19 03	19 01	18 57	18 54	18 51	18 48	18 44	18 41	18 38	18 36
Mar. 1	19 22	19 25	19 28	19 30	19 32	19 33	19 36	19 39	19 41	19 43	19 46	19 48	19 50	19 52
2	19 30	19 40	19 49	19 55	20 01	20 07	20 16	20 24	20 32	20 39	20 47	20 57	21 02	21 08
3	19 40	19 58	20 12	20 24	20 34	20 43	20 58	21 11	21 24	21 37	21 51	22 06	22 15	22 26
4	19 54	20 20	20 40	20 57	21 11	21 23	21 44	22 02	22 19	22 37	22 55	23 17	23 29	23 44
5	20 15	20 50	21 16	21 37	21 54	22 09	22 35	22 57	23 18	23 38	.. ..	.. ..	.. ..	.. ..
6	20 49	21 31	22 02	22 26	22 45	23 02	23 31	23 55	.. ..	.. ..	0 01	0 27	0 42	1 00
7	21 43	22 28	23 00	23 24	23 44	.. ..	.. ..	.. ..	0 18	0 41	1 05	1 34	1 50	2 10
8	22 57	23 38	.. ..	.. ..	.. ..	0 01	0 30	0 55	1 18	1 41	2 05	2 34	2 51	3 11
9	.. ..	.. ..	0 07	0 29	0 48	1 04	1 31	1 54	2 16	2 37	3 00	3 26	3 42	4 00
10	0 22	0 55	1 19	1 38	1 54	2 08	2 31	2 51	3 10	3 28	3 48	4 10	4 24	4 39
11	1 49	2 13	2 31	2 46	2 59	3 10	3 28	3 44	3 59	4 14	4 30	4 48	4 58	5 10

.. .. indicates phenomenon will occur the next day.

UNIVERSAL TIME FOR MERIDIAN OF GREENWICH

MOONRISE

Lat.	+40°	+42°	+44°	+46°	+48°	+50°	+52°	+54°	+56°	+58°	+60°	+62°	+64°	+66°
	h m	h m	h m	h m	h m	h m	h m	h m	h m	h m	h m	h m	h m	h m
Feb. 15	20 39	20 40	20 41	20 41	20 42	20 43	20 44	20 45	20 46	20 47	20 48	20 50	20 52	20 54
16	21 39	21 41	21 44	21 46	21 49	21 52	21 55	21 58	22 02	22 07	22 12	22 17	22 24	22 31
17	22 40	22 44	22 47	22 52	22 56	23 01	23 07	23 13	23 20	23 27	23 36	23 46	23 58	.. ..
18	23 42	23 47	23 52	23 58	.. ..	.. ..	.. ..	.. ..	.. ..	.. ..	.. ..	.. ..	.. ..	0 13
19	.. ..	.. ..	.. ..	.. ..	0 05	0 12	0 20	0 29	0 40	0 51	1 05	1 21	1 41	2 06
20	0 45	0 51	0 59	1 06	1 15	1 25	1 35	1 48	2 02	2 18	2 38	3 03	3 39	4 48
21	1 48	1 56	2 05	2 14	2 25	2 37	2 50	3 06	3 24	3 46	4 15	4 59	▬	▬
22	2 50	2 59	3 09	3 20	3 31	3 45	4 00	4 18	4 40	5 07	5 48	▬	▬	▬
23	3 48	3 57	4 07	4 18	4 30	4 44	4 59	5 18	5 40	6 09	6 51	▬	▬	▬
24	4 39	4 47	4 56	5 07	5 18	5 30	5 44	6 00	6 20	6 43	7 15	8 05	▬	▬
25	5 22	5 29	5 37	5 45	5 54	6 05	6 16	6 29	6 44	7 01	7 22	7 49	8 26	9 48
26	5 57	6 03	6 09	6 15	6 22	6 30	6 38	6 48	6 58	7 10	7 24	7 40	8 00	8 25
27	6 28	6 31	6 35	6 40	6 44	6 50	6 55	7 01	7 08	7 15	7 24	7 33	7 45	7 58
28	6 54	6 56	6 58	7 01	7 03	7 06	7 08	7 12	7 15	7 19	7 23	7 28	7 33	7 39
Mar. 1	7 19	7 19	7 20	7 20	7 20	7 20	7 20	7 21	7 21	7 21	7 22	7 22	7 23	7 23
2	7 44	7 43	7 41	7 39	7 37	7 35	7 32	7 30	7 27	7 24	7 21	7 17	7 12	7 07
3	8 11	8 07	8 04	8 00	7 56	7 51	7 46	7 40	7 34	7 27	7 20	7 11	7 01	6 49
4	8 41	8 36	8 30	8 24	8 18	8 10	8 02	7 54	7 44	7 33	7 20	7 05	6 47	6 25
5	9 18	9 11	9 03	8 55	8 46	8 36	8 25	8 13	7 59	7 42	7 22	6 58	6 24	5 29
6	10 02	9 54	9 45	9 35	9 24	9 12	8 58	8 42	8 23	8 00	7 31	6 46	▭	▭
7	10 56	10 47	10 37	10 26	10 14	10 01	9 45	9 27	9 05	8 37	7 57	▭	▭	▭
8	11 58	11 49	11 39	11 29	11 17	11 04	10 49	10 31	10 10	9 43	9 05	▭	▭	▭
9	13 05	12 57	12 49	12 40	12 29	12 18	12 05	11 50	11 33	11 12	10 45	10 06	▭	▭
10	14 14	14 07	14 01	13 53	13 45	13 36	13 26	13 15	13 02	12 47	12 28	12 06	11 36	10 50
11	15 21	15 16	15 11	15 06	15 00	14 53	14 46	14 38	14 29	14 19	14 07	13 53	13 36	13 15

MOONSET

Lat.	+40°	+42°	+44°	+46°	+48°	+50°	+52°	+54°	+56°	+58°	+60°	+62°	+64°	+66°
	h m	h m	h m	h m	h m	h m	h m	h m	h m	h m	h m	h m	h m	h m
Feb. 15	8 13	8 13	8 13	8 13	8 13	8 14	8 14	8 14	8 14	8 14	8 15	8 15	8 15	8 16
16	8 32	8 31	8 29	8 28	8 26	8 24	8 23	8 21	8 18	8 16	8 13	8 10	8 06	8 02
17	8 52	8 49	8 46	8 43	8 40	8 36	8 32	8 28	8 23	8 18	8 12	8 05	7 57	7 48
18	9 14	9 10	9 05	9 00	8 55	8 49	8 43	8 36	8 29	8 20	8 10	7 59	7 46	7 30
19	9 39	9 33	9 27	9 20	9 13	9 05	8 57	8 47	8 36	8 24	8 10	7 53	7 32	7 05
20	10 09	10 02	9 54	9 46	9 37	9 27	9 16	9 03	8 48	8 31	8 11	7 45	7 09	5 58
21	10 46	10 38	10 29	10 19	10 08	9 56	9 43	9 27	9 08	8 46	8 16	7 32	▬	▬
22	11 32	11 23	11 14	11 03	10 51	10 37	10 22	10 04	9 42	9 14	8 34	▬	▬	▬
23	12 29	12 20	12 10	11 59	11 47	11 34	11 18	11 00	10 38	10 09	9 27	▬	▬	▬
24	13 35	13 27	13 18	13 08	12 57	12 45	12 31	12 15	11 56	11 33	11 02	10 12	▬	▬
25	14 48	14 41	14 33	14 25	14 17	14 07	13 56	13 44	13 30	13 13	12 53	12 27	11 50	10 28
26	16 03	15 58	15 53	15 47	15 41	15 34	15 26	15 18	15 08	14 57	14 44	14 29	14 10	13 47
27	17 20	17 17	17 13	17 10	17 06	17 02	16 57	16 52	16 46	16 40	16 33	16 24	16 15	16 03
28	18 36	18 35	18 33	18 32	18 31	18 29	18 27	18 26	18 24	18 21	18 19	18 16	18 12	18 08
Mar. 1	19 52	19 53	19 53	19 54	19 55	19 56	19 57	19 59	20 00	20 02	20 03	20 05	20 08	20 10
2	21 08	21 11	21 14	21 17	21 21	21 24	21 28	21 33	21 38	21 43	21 50	21 57	22 05	22 15
3	22 26	22 31	22 36	22 41	22 47	22 54	23 01	23 09	23 18	23 28	23 40	23 53	.. ..	.. ..
4	23 44	23 51	23 58	.. ..	.. ..	.. ..	.. ..	.. ..	.. ..	.. ..	.. ..	.. ..	0 10	0 31
5	.. ..	.. ..	.. ..	0 05	0 14	0 23	0 34	0 45	0 59	1 15	1 34	1 58	2 30	3 24
6	1 00	1 08	1 17	1 27	1 37	1 49	2 03	2 18	2 36	2 59	3 28	4 13	▭	▭
7	2 10	2 19	2 29	2 40	2 52	3 05	3 20	3 38	4 00	4 28	5 08	▭	▭	▭
8	3 11	3 19	3 29	3 40	3 52	4 05	4 20	4 38	4 59	5 26	6 05	▭	▭	▭
9	4 00	4 08	4 17	4 26	4 37	4 48	5 02	5 17	5 35	5 56	6 23	7 02	▭	▭
10	4 39	4 46	4 53	5 01	5 09	5 19	5 29	5 41	5 55	6 11	6 29	6 52	7 23	8 10
11	5 10	5 15	5 21	5 27	5 33	5 41	5 48	5 57	6 07	6 18	6 31	6 46	7 04	7 26

▭ indicates Moon continuously above horizon.
▬ indicates Moon continuously below horizon.
.. .. indicates phenomenon will occur the next day.

UNIVERSAL TIME FOR MERIDIAN OF GREENWICH

MOONRISE

Lat.	−55°	−50°	−45°	−40°	−35°	−30°	−20°	−10°	0°	+10°	+20°	+30°	+35°	+40°
	h m	h m	h m	h m	h m	h m	h m	h m	h m	h m	h m	h m	h m	h m
Mar. 9	17 41	17 07	16 42	16 22	16 05	15 51	15 26	15 04	14 44	14 24	14 02	13 37	13 22	13 05
10	17 58	17 32	17 13	16 57	16 43	16 31	16 11	15 53	15 36	15 19	15 01	14 40	14 28	14 14
11	18 09	17 51	17 36	17 25	17 14	17 05	16 50	16 36	16 23	16 11	15 57	15 41	15 32	15 21
12	18 17	18 05	17 56	17 48	17 41	17 35	17 25	17 16	17 07	16 59	16 50	16 39	16 33	16 26
13	18 23	18 17	18 13	18 09	18 06	18 03	17 58	17 53	17 49	17 45	17 40	17 35	17 32	17 28
14	18 28	18 28	18 28	18 28	18 28	18 28	18 28	18 29	18 29	18 29	18 29	18 29	18 29	18 29
15	18 34	18 39	18 44	18 48	18 51	18 54	18 59	19 04	19 08	19 12	19 17	19 22	19 26	19 29
16	18 40	18 51	19 00	19 08	19 14	19 20	19 30	19 39	19 48	19 56	20 06	20 16	20 22	20 29
17	18 47	19 04	19 18	19 30	19 40	19 48	20 04	20 17	20 29	20 42	20 56	21 11	21 20	21 31
18	18 57	19 21	19 40	19 55	20 09	20 20	20 40	20 57	21 13	21 30	21 47	22 07	22 19	22 33
19	19 12	19 43	20 07	20 26	20 42	20 56	21 20	21 41	22 00	22 20	22 41	23 05	23 20	23 36
20	19 35	20 14	20 42	21 04	21 22	21 38	22 05	22 29	22 50	23 12	23 36	.. ..	.. ..	.. ..
21	20 12	20 56	21 26	21 50	22 10	22 27	22 56	23 20	23 43	.. ..	.. ..	0 03	0 19	0 38
22	21 08	21 52	22 23	22 46	23 06	23 23	23 51	.. ..	.. ..	0 06	0 31	1 00	1 17	1 37
23	22 24	23 02	23 29	23 51	.. ..	.. ..	.. ..	0 16	0 38	1 01	1 25	1 53	2 10	2 30
24	23 52	.. ..	.. ..	.. ..	0 09	0 24	0 50	1 13	1 34	1 54	2 17	2 42	2 57	3 15
25	.. ..	0 22	0 44	1 02	1 17	1 30	1 52	2 10	2 28	2 46	3 04	3 26	3 38	3 53
26	1 26	1 47	2 03	2 16	2 27	2 37	2 53	3 08	3 21	3 34	3 48	4 05	4 14	4 25
27	3 01	3 13	3 23	3 31	3 38	3 44	3 55	4 04	4 12	4 21	4 30	4 40	4 46	4 52
28	4 36	4 41	4 44	4 47	4 50	4 52	4 56	4 59	5 03	5 06	5 09	5 13	5 16	5 18
29	6 12	6 09	6 06	6 04	6 02	6 01	5 58	5 55	5 53	5 51	5 49	5 46	5 45	5 43
30	7 51	7 39	7 30	7 23	7 16	7 11	7 01	6 53	6 45	6 38	6 29	6 20	6 15	6 09
31	9 32	9 12	8 56	8 43	8 32	8 23	8 07	7 53	7 40	7 27	7 13	6 58	6 49	6 39
Apr. 1	11 15	10 45	10 22	10 04	9 49	9 36	9 14	8 55	8 37	8 20	8 01	7 40	7 28	7 14
2	12 53	12 14	11 45	11 23	11 05	10 49	10 22	9 59	9 38	9 17	8 55	8 29	8 14	7 56

MOONSET

Lat.	−55°	−50°	−45°	−40°	−35°	−30°	−20°	−10°	0°	+10°	+20°	+30°	+35°	+40°
	h m	h m	h m	h m	h m	h m	h m	h m	h m	h m	h m	h m	h m	h m
Mar. 9	.. ..	.. ..	0 07	0 29	0 48	1 04	1 31	1 54	2 16	2 37	3 00	3 26	3 42	4 00
10	0 22	0 55	1 19	1 38	1 54	2 08	2 31	2 51	3 10	3 28	3 48	4 10	4 24	4 39
11	1 49	2 13	2 31	2 46	2 59	3 10	3 28	3 44	3 59	4 14	4 30	4 48	4 58	5 10
12	3 13	3 29	3 42	3 53	4 01	4 09	4 23	4 34	4 45	4 56	5 07	5 20	5 27	5 36
13	4 33	4 43	4 50	4 56	5 02	5 06	5 14	5 21	5 28	5 34	5 41	5 48	5 53	5 58
14	5 50	5 53	5 56	5 58	6 00	6 01	6 04	6 06	6 08	6 10	6 12	6 15	6 16	6 18
15	7 06	7 03	7 00	6 58	6 56	6 55	6 52	6 50	6 48	6 45	6 43	6 40	6 39	6 37
16	8 21	8 12	8 04	7 58	7 53	7 48	7 40	7 34	7 27	7 21	7 14	7 06	7 02	6 56
17	9 37	9 21	9 09	8 59	8 50	8 43	8 30	8 18	8 08	7 57	7 46	7 33	7 26	7 17
18	10 55	10 33	10 15	10 01	9 49	9 38	9 20	9 05	8 50	8 36	8 20	8 03	7 53	7 41
19	12 15	11 45	11 22	11 04	10 48	10 35	10 13	9 53	9 35	9 18	8 58	8 36	8 24	8 09
20	13 33	12 55	12 28	12 06	11 48	11 33	11 07	10 45	10 24	10 03	9 41	9 15	9 00	8 43
21	14 44	14 01	13 31	13 07	12 47	12 31	12 02	11 38	11 16	10 53	10 29	10 01	9 44	9 25
22	15 41	14 58	14 27	14 03	13 43	13 26	12 57	12 33	12 10	11 47	11 22	10 53	10 36	10 16
23	16 20	15 42	15 14	14 51	14 33	14 17	13 50	13 27	13 05	12 43	12 19	11 52	11 35	11 16
24	16 46	16 15	15 52	15 33	15 17	15 03	14 40	14 19	14 00	13 40	13 20	12 55	12 41	12 24
25	17 02	16 40	16 22	16 08	15 55	15 44	15 25	15 09	14 53	14 38	14 21	14 02	13 50	13 37
26	17 14	16 59	16 47	16 37	16 29	16 21	16 08	15 56	15 46	15 34	15 23	15 09	15 01	14 52
27	17 22	17 15	17 09	17 04	16 59	16 55	16 48	16 42	16 36	16 30	16 24	16 17	16 12	16 07
28	17 30	17 30	17 29	17 29	17 28	17 28	17 28	17 27	17 26	17 26	17 25	17 25	17 24	17 24
29	17 38	17 44	17 50	17 54	17 58	18 01	18 07	18 13	18 17	18 22	18 28	18 34	18 37	18 41
30	17 47	18 01	18 12	18 22	18 30	18 37	18 49	19 00	19 11	19 21	19 32	19 45	19 52	20 01
31	17 59	18 21	18 39	18 53	19 06	19 16	19 35	19 51	20 07	20 22	20 39	20 58	21 09	21 22
Apr. 1	18 17	18 49	19 12	19 32	19 48	20 02	20 26	20 47	21 06	21 26	21 47	22 11	22 25	22 42
2	18 46	19 27	19 56	20 19	20 38	20 54	21 22	21 46	22 08	22 30	22 54	23 22	23 38	23 58

.. .. indicates phenomenon will occur the next day.

UNIVERSAL TIME FOR MERIDIAN OF GREENWICH

MOONRISE

Lat.	+40°	+42°	+44°	+46°	+48°	+50°	+52°	+54°	+56°	+58°	+60°	+62°	+64°	+66°
	h m	h m	h m	h m	h m	h m	h m	h m	h m	h m	h m	h m	h m	h m
Mar. 9	13 05	12 57	12 49	12 40	12 29	12 18	12 05	11 50	11 33	11 12	10 45	10 06	▭	▭
10	14 14	14 07	14 01	13 53	13 45	13 36	13 26	13 15	13 02	12 47	12 28	12 06	11 36	10 50
11	15 21	15 16	15 11	15 06	15 00	14 53	14 46	14 38	14 29	14 19	14 07	13 53	13 36	13 15
12	16 26	16 23	16 19	16 16	16 12	16 08	16 03	15 58	15 52	15 46	15 39	15 31	15 21	15 09
13	17 28	17 27	17 25	17 23	17 22	17 20	17 17	17 15	17 12	17 09	17 06	17 02	16 58	16 52
14	18 29	18 29	18 29	18 29	18 29	18 29	18 29	18 29	18 30	18 30	18 30	18 30	18 30	18 30
15	19 29	19 31	19 32	19 34	19 36	19 38	19 41	19 43	19 46	19 49	19 53	19 57	20 01	20 07
16	20 29	20 33	20 36	20 40	20 43	20 48	20 52	20 57	21 03	21 09	21 17	21 25	21 35	21 46
17	21 31	21 35	21 40	21 46	21 52	21 58	22 05	22 13	22 22	22 32	22 44	22 58	23 14	23 35
18	22 33	22 39	22 46	22 53	23 01	23 10	23 20	23 31	23 43	23 58	.. ..	.. ..	.. ..	.. ..
19	23 36	23 44	23 52	.. ..	.. ..	.. ..	.. ..	.. ..	.. ..	.. ..	0 15	0 36	1 04	1 46
20	.. ..	.. ..	.. ..	0 01	0 11	0 22	0 34	0 49	1 05	1 25	1 51	2 26	3 35	■
21	0 38	0 47	0 56	1 07	1 18	1 31	1 46	2 03	2 24	2 50	3 26	■	■	■
22	1 37	1 46	1 56	2 07	2 19	2 33	2 49	3 07	3 30	3 59	4 43	■	■	■
23	2 30	2 38	2 48	2 59	3 10	3 23	3 38	3 56	4 17	4 43	5 20	■	■	■
24	3 15	3 23	3 31	3 40	3 51	4 02	4 15	4 29	4 46	5 06	5 32	6 07	7 12	■
25	3 53	3 59	4 06	4 13	4 21	4 30	4 40	4 51	5 04	5 18	5 35	5 56	6 22	6 59
26	4 25	4 29	4 34	4 40	4 46	4 52	4 59	5 07	5 15	5 25	5 36	5 49	6 04	6 22
27	4 52	4 55	4 58	5 02	5 05	5 09	5 14	5 18	5 23	5 29	5 35	5 43	5 51	6 00
28	5 18	5 19	5 20	5 22	5 23	5 24	5 26	5 28	5 30	5 32	5 34	5 37	5 40	5 43
29	5 43	5 42	5 42	5 41	5 40	5 39	5 38	5 37	5 36	5 34	5 33	5 31	5 29	5 27
30	6 09	6 07	6 04	6 01	5 58	5 55	5 51	5 47	5 42	5 38	5 32	5 26	5 19	5 10
31	6 39	6 34	6 30	6 24	6 19	6 13	6 06	5 59	5 51	5 42	5 32	5 20	5 06	4 50
Apr. 1	7 14	7 07	7 00	6 53	6 45	6 36	6 27	6 16	6 04	5 50	5 33	5 13	4 49	4 15
2	7 56	7 48	7 40	7 30	7 20	7 09	6 56	6 41	6 24	6 04	5 39	5 04	4 02	▭

MOONSET

Lat.	+40°	+42°	+44°	+46°	+48°	+50°	+52°	+54°	+56°	+58°	+60°	+62°	+64°	+66°
	h m	h m	h m	h m	h m	h m	h m	h m	h m	h m	h m	h m	h m	h m
Mar. 9	4 00	4 08	4 17	4 26	4 37	4 48	5 02	5 17	5 35	5 56	6 23	7 02	▭	▭
10	4 39	4 46	4 53	5 01	5 09	5 19	5 29	5 41	5 55	6 11	6 29	6 52	7 23	8 10
11	5 10	5 15	5 21	5 27	5 33	5 41	5 48	5 57	6 07	6 18	6 31	6 46	7 04	7 26
12	5 36	5 39	5 43	5 47	5 52	5 57	6 02	6 08	6 15	6 22	6 30	6 40	6 51	7 04
13	5 58	6 00	6 02	6 05	6 07	6 10	6 13	6 17	6 20	6 25	6 29	6 34	6 40	6 47
14	6 18	6 18	6 19	6 20	6 21	6 22	6 23	6 24	6 25	6 26	6 28	6 29	6 31	6 33
15	6 37	6 36	6 35	6 35	6 34	6 33	6 31	6 30	6 29	6 27	6 26	6 24	6 22	6 20
16	6 56	6 54	6 52	6 49	6 47	6 44	6 41	6 37	6 33	6 29	6 24	6 19	6 13	6 05
17	7 17	7 14	7 10	7 06	7 01	6 56	6 51	6 45	6 38	6 31	6 23	6 13	6 02	5 49
18	7 41	7 36	7 30	7 24	7 18	7 11	7 03	6 55	6 45	6 34	6 22	6 07	5 50	5 28
19	8 09	8 02	7 55	7 48	7 39	7 30	7 20	7 08	6 55	6 40	6 22	6 00	5 31	4 49
20	8 43	8 35	8 26	8 17	8 07	7 56	7 43	7 28	7 11	6 51	6 25	5 49	4 39	■
21	9 25	9 16	9 06	8 56	8 44	8 31	8 16	7 59	7 38	7 12	6 35	■	■	■
22	10 16	10 07	9 57	9 46	9 34	9 20	9 04	8 45	8 23	7 54	7 09	■	■	■
23	11 16	11 07	10 58	10 48	10 36	10 23	10 08	9 51	9 30	9 04	8 27	■	■	■
24	12 24	12 17	12 08	12 00	11 50	11 39	11 26	11 12	10 56	10 36	10 11	9 37	8 32	■
25	13 37	13 31	13 25	13 18	13 10	13 02	12 52	12 42	12 30	12 16	12 00	11 40	11 15	10 39
26	14 52	14 48	14 43	14 38	14 33	14 28	14 22	14 15	14 07	13 58	13 48	13 37	13 23	13 06
27	16 07	16 05	16 03	16 00	15 58	15 55	15 52	15 48	15 44	15 40	15 35	15 29	15 22	15 15
28	17 24	17 23	17 23	17 23	17 23	17 22	17 22	17 22	17 21	17 21	17 20	17 20	17 19	17 18
29	18 41	18 43	18 45	18 47	18 49	18 51	18 54	18 57	19 00	19 03	19 07	19 12	19 17	19 23
30	20 01	20 04	20 08	20 13	20 18	20 23	20 28	20 35	20 42	20 50	20 59	21 09	21 21	21 36
31	21 22	21 27	21 34	21 40	21 48	21 56	22 05	22 15	22 26	22 40	22 55	23 14	23 38	.. ..
Apr. 1	22 42	22 50	22 58	23 07	23 17	23 28	23 40	23 54	.. ..	.. ..	.. ..	.. ..	.. ..	0 10
2	23 58	.. ..	.. ..	.. ..	.. ..	.. ..	.. ..	.. ..	0 10	0 30	0 55	1 29	2 30	▭

▭ indicates Moon continuously above horizon.
■ indicates Moon continuously below horizon.
.. .. indicates phenomenon will occur the next day.

UNIVERSAL TIME FOR MERIDIAN OF GREENWICH

MOONRISE

Lat.	−55°	−50°	−45°	−40°	−35°	−30°	−20°	−10°	0°	+10°	+20°	+30°	+35°	+40°
	h m	h m	h m	h m	h m	h m	h m	h m	h m	h m	h m	h m	h m	h m
Apr. 1	11 15	10 45	10 22	10 04	9 49	9 36	9 14	8 55	8 37	8 20	8 01	7 40	7 28	7 14
2	12 53	12 14	11 45	11 23	11 05	10 49	10 22	9 59	9 38	9 17	8 55	8 29	8 14	7 56
3	14 15	13 30	12 59	12 34	12 14	11 57	11 28	11 03	10 41	10 18	9 53	9 25	9 08	8 48
4	15 12	14 29	13 58	13 34	13 15	12 58	12 29	12 05	11 42	11 19	10 55	10 26	10 09	9 49
5	15 46	15 10	14 43	14 22	14 04	13 49	13 23	13 01	12 40	12 19	11 56	11 30	11 15	10 56
6	16 06	15 38	15 17	14 59	14 45	14 32	14 10	13 51	13 33	13 15	12 56	12 34	12 21	12 05
7	16 18	15 58	15 42	15 29	15 18	15 08	14 51	14 36	14 22	14 08	13 53	13 35	13 25	13 13
8	16 27	16 14	16 03	15 54	15 46	15 39	15 27	15 16	15 07	14 57	14 46	14 34	14 27	14 18
9	16 34	16 26	16 20	16 15	16 11	16 07	16 00	15 54	15 48	15 43	15 36	15 30	15 26	15 21
10	16 39	16 37	16 36	16 35	16 33	16 33	16 31	16 29	16 28	16 27	16 25	16 24	16 23	16 22
11	16 44	16 48	16 51	16 54	16 56	16 58	17 01	17 04	17 07	17 10	17 13	17 17	17 19	17 21
12	16 50	16 59	17 07	17 13	17 19	17 24	17 32	17 40	17 47	17 54	18 02	18 10	18 15	18 21
13	16 57	17 12	17 24	17 35	17 43	17 51	18 05	18 16	18 28	18 39	18 51	19 05	19 13	19 22
14	17 06	17 28	17 45	17 59	18 11	18 22	18 40	18 56	19 11	19 26	19 42	20 01	20 12	20 24
15	17 19	17 48	18 10	18 28	18 43	18 56	19 19	19 38	19 56	20 15	20 35	20 58	21 11	21 27
16	17 39	18 15	18 42	19 03	19 21	19 36	20 02	20 24	20 45	21 07	21 29	21 56	22 11	22 30
17	18 11	18 53	19 23	19 46	20 05	20 22	20 50	21 15	21 37	22 00	22 24	22 53	23 09	23 29
18	18 59	19 43	20 14	20 38	20 58	21 15	21 43	22 08	22 31	22 54	23 18	23 47	.. ..	.. ..
19	20 07	20 47	21 16	21 38	21 57	22 13	22 40	23 03	23 25	23 46	.. ..	.. ..	0 04	0 23
20	21 29	22 01	22 26	22 45	23 01	23 15	23 39	23 59	.. ..	.. ..	0 09	0 36	0 52	1 10
21	22 58	23 22	23 41	23 56	.. ..	.. ..	.. ..	.. ..	0 18	0 37	0 57	1 20	1 34	1 50
22	.. ..	.. ..	.. ..	.. ..	0 08	0 19	0 38	0 55	1 10	1 25	1 41	2 00	2 10	2 23
23	0 29	0 45	0 58	1 08	1 17	1 25	1 38	1 49	2 00	2 11	2 22	2 35	2 43	2 51
24	2 01	2 09	2 16	2 21	2 26	2 30	2 37	2 43	2 49	2 55	3 01	3 08	3 12	3 17
25	3 34	3 35	3 35	3 36	3 36	3 36	3 37	3 38	3 38	3 39	3 40	3 41	3 41	3 42

MOONSET

Lat.	−55°	−50°	−45°	−40°	−35°	−30°	−20°	−10°	0°	+10°	+20°	+30°	+35°	+40°
	h m	h m	h m	h m	h m	h m	h m	h m	h m	h m	h m	h m	h m	h m
Apr. 1	18 17	18 49	19 12	19 32	19 48	20 02	20 26	20 47	21 06	21 26	21 47	22 11	22 25	22 42
2	18 46	19 27	19 56	20 19	20 38	20 54	21 22	21 46	22 08	22 30	22 54	23 22	23 38	23 58
3	19 34	20 19	20 51	21 16	21 36	21 53	22 22	22 47	23 10	23 33	23 58	.. ..	.. ..	.. ..
4	20 44	21 27	21 57	22 20	22 40	22 56	23 24	23 48	.. ..	.. ..	.. ..	0 27	0 44	1 04
5	22 08	22 43	23 09	23 29	23 46	.. ..	.. ..	.. ..	0 10	0 32	0 56	1 23	1 39	1 58
6	23 36	.. ..	.. ..	.. ..	.. ..	0 01	0 25	0 46	1 06	1 26	1 46	2 10	2 24	2 40
7	.. ..	0 02	0 22	0 38	0 52	1 04	1 24	1 41	1 57	2 13	2 30	2 49	3 01	3 14
8	1 00	1 19	1 33	1 45	1 55	2 04	2 19	2 32	2 44	2 56	3 08	3 23	3 31	3 41
9	2 21	2 32	2 41	2 49	2 55	3 01	3 11	3 19	3 27	3 35	3 43	3 52	3 57	4 03
10	3 38	3 43	3 47	3 50	3 53	3 56	4 00	4 04	4 07	4 11	4 15	4 19	4 21	4 24
11	4 53	4 52	4 51	4 51	4 50	4 49	4 48	4 48	4 47	4 46	4 45	4 44	4 44	4 43
12	6 08	6 01	5 55	5 50	5 46	5 43	5 37	5 31	5 26	5 21	5 16	5 10	5 06	5 02
13	7 23	7 10	6 59	6 51	6 43	6 37	6 25	6 15	6 06	5 57	5 47	5 36	5 30	5 23
14	8 41	8 21	8 05	7 52	7 41	7 32	7 15	7 01	6 48	6 35	6 21	6 05	5 56	5 45
15	10 00	9 32	9 11	8 55	8 40	8 28	8 07	7 49	7 32	7 16	6 58	6 37	6 25	6 12
16	11 19	10 44	10 18	9 57	9 40	9 26	9 01	8 40	8 20	8 00	7 39	7 14	7 00	6 43
17	12 33	11 51	11 22	10 59	10 40	10 23	9 56	9 32	9 10	8 48	8 25	7 57	7 41	7 22
18	13 35	12 51	12 20	11 56	11 36	11 19	10 50	10 26	10 03	9 40	9 15	8 47	8 29	8 10
19	14 19	13 38	13 09	12 46	12 27	12 11	11 43	11 19	10 57	10 34	10 10	9 42	9 25	9 06
20	14 48	14 15	13 49	13 29	13 12	12 58	12 33	12 11	11 51	11 30	11 08	10 42	10 27	10 10
21	15 07	14 42	14 22	14 05	13 51	13 39	13 18	13 00	12 43	12 26	12 07	11 46	11 33	11 18
22	15 20	15 02	14 48	14 36	14 26	14 17	14 01	13 47	13 34	13 21	13 07	12 51	12 41	12 30
23	15 30	15 19	15 10	15 03	14 56	14 51	14 41	14 32	14 24	14 15	14 06	13 56	13 50	13 43
24	15 38	15 34	15 30	15 28	15 25	15 23	15 19	15 16	15 12	15 09	15 06	15 02	14 59	14 56
25	15 45	15 48	15 50	15 52	15 54	15 55	15 58	16 00	16 02	16 04	16 06	16 09	16 10	16 12

.. .. indicates phenomenon will occur the next day.

UNIVERSAL TIME FOR MERIDIAN OF GREENWICH

MOONRISE

Lat.	+40°	+42°	+44°	+46°	+48°	+50°	+52°	+54°	+56°	+58°	+60°	+62°	+64°	+66°
	h m	h m	h m	h m	h m	h m	h m	h m	h m	h m	h m	h m	h m	h m
Apr. 1	7 14	7 07	7 00	6 53	6 45	6 36	6 27	6 16	6 04	5 50	5 33	5 13	4 49	4 15
2	7 56	7 48	7 40	7 30	7 20	7 09	6 56	6 41	6 24	6 04	5 39	5 04	4 02	□
3	8 48	8 39	8 30	8 19	8 07	7 54	7 39	7 21	7 00	6 34	5 57	□	□	□
4	9 49	9 40	9 30	9 20	9 08	8 54	8 39	8 21	7 59	7 31	6 51	□	□	□
5	10 56	10 48	10 39	10 30	10 19	10 07	9 53	9 37	9 19	8 56	8 25	7 38	□	□
6	12 05	11 59	11 51	11 43	11 34	11 25	11 14	11 01	10 47	10 30	10 10	9 44	9 07	7 43
7	13 13	13 08	13 02	12 56	12 50	12 42	12 34	12 25	12 15	12 04	11 50	11 34	11 14	10 49
8	14 18	14 15	14 11	14 07	14 02	13 57	13 52	13 46	13 39	13 32	13 23	13 13	13 02	12 48
9	15 21	15 19	15 17	15 14	15 12	15 09	15 06	15 03	14 59	14 55	14 51	14 46	14 40	14 33
10	16 22	16 21	16 21	16 20	16 20	16 19	16 18	16 17	16 17	16 16	16 15	16 14	16 12	16 11
11	17 21	17 22	17 24	17 25	17 26	17 28	17 29	17 31	17 33	17 35	17 37	17 40	17 43	17 46
12	18 21	18 24	18 27	18 30	18 33	18 36	18 40	18 44	18 49	18 54	19 00	19 07	19 15	19 24
13	19 22	19 26	19 31	19 35	19 41	19 46	19 53	19 59	20 07	20 16	20 26	20 38	20 51	21 08
14	20 24	20 30	20 36	20 43	20 50	20 58	21 07	21 16	21 28	21 40	21 56	22 14	22 37	23 08
15	21 27	21 34	21 42	21 50	22 00	22 10	22 21	22 34	22 49	23 07	23 30	23 59	.. ..	■
16	22 30	22 38	22 47	22 57	23 08	23 20	23 34	23 50	.. ..	.. ..	.. ..	.. ..	0 42	■
17	23 29	23 38	23 48	23 59	.. ..	.. ..	.. ..	.. ..	0 09	0 33	1 05	1 58	■	■
18	.. ..	.. ..	.. ..	.. ..	0 11	0 24	0 40	0 58	1 20	1 48	2 30	■	■	■
19	0 23	0 32	0 42	0 53	1 05	1 18	1 34	1 51	2 13	2 41	3 21	■	■	■
20	1 10	1 18	1 27	1 37	1 48	2 00	2 14	2 29	2 48	3 10	3 39	4 23	■	■
21	1 50	1 57	2 04	2 12	2 21	2 31	2 42	2 54	3 09	3 25	3 45	4 10	4 44	5 43
22	2 23	2 28	2 34	2 40	2 47	2 54	3 03	3 12	3 22	3 33	3 47	4 03	4 22	4 45
23	2 51	2 55	2 59	3 03	3 08	3 13	3 18	3 24	3 31	3 38	3 47	3 56	4 08	4 21
24	3 17	3 19	3 21	3 23	3 26	3 28	3 31	3 34	3 38	3 42	3 46	3 51	3 56	4 03
25	3 42	3 42	3 42	3 42	3 43	3 43	3 43	3 44	3 44	3 44	3 45	3 46	3 46	3 47

MOONSET

Lat.	+40°	+42°	+44°	+46°	+48°	+50°	+52°	+54°	+56°	+58°	+60°	+62°	+64°	+66°
	h m	h m	h m	h m	h m	h m	h m	h m	h m	h m	h m	h m	h m	h m
Apr. 1	22 42	22 50	22 58	23 07	23 17	23 28	23 40	23 54	.. ..	.. ..	.. ..	.. ..	.. ..	0 10
2	23 58	.. ..	.. ..	.. ..	.. ..	.. ..	.. ..	.. ..	0 10	0 30	0 55	1 29	2 30	□
3	.. ..	0 06	0 16	0 26	0 38	0 51	1 06	1 23	1 44	2 11	2 47	□	□	□
4	1 04	1 13	1 23	1 34	1 46	1 59	2 15	2 33	2 55	3 23	4 03	□	□	□
5	1 58	2 06	2 15	2 25	2 36	2 49	3 03	3 19	3 38	4 01	4 32	5 20	□	□
6	2 40	2 47	2 55	3 04	3 13	3 23	3 34	3 47	4 02	4 19	4 40	5 07	5 45	7 10
7	3 14	3 19	3 25	3 32	3 39	3 47	3 56	4 05	4 16	4 29	4 43	5 00	5 21	5 47
8	3 41	3 45	3 49	3 54	3 59	4 05	4 11	4 18	4 25	4 34	4 43	4 54	5 07	5 22
9	4 03	4 06	4 09	4 12	4 15	4 19	4 23	4 27	4 31	4 36	4 42	4 49	4 56	5 05
10	4 24	4 25	4 26	4 28	4 29	4 31	4 32	4 34	4 36	4 38	4 41	4 43	4 47	4 50
11	4 43	4 43	4 43	4 42	4 42	4 41	4 41	4 41	4 40	4 40	4 39	4 38	4 38	4 37
12	5 02	5 01	4 59	4 57	4 55	4 52	4 50	4 47	4 44	4 41	4 37	4 33	4 28	4 23
13	5 23	5 20	5 16	5 12	5 09	5 04	5 00	4 55	4 49	4 43	4 36	4 28	4 19	4 08
14	5 45	5 41	5 36	5 30	5 25	5 18	5 11	5 04	4 55	4 46	4 35	4 22	4 07	3 49
15	6 12	6 06	5 59	5 52	5 44	5 36	5 27	5 16	5 04	4 51	4 35	4 16	3 52	3 20
16	6 43	6 36	6 28	6 19	6 10	5 59	5 47	5 34	5 18	5 00	4 37	4 07	3 23	■
17	7 22	7 14	7 04	6 54	6 43	6 31	6 17	6 00	5 41	5 17	4 44	3 51	■	■
18	8 10	8 01	7 51	7 40	7 28	7 14	6 59	6 40	6 18	5 50	5 08	■	■	■
19	9 06	8 57	8 47	8 37	8 25	8 12	7 56	7 38	7 17	6 49	6 09	■	■	■
20	10 10	10 02	9 53	9 43	9 33	9 21	9 08	8 53	8 34	8 12	7 44	7 00	■	■
21	11 18	11 12	11 05	10 57	10 49	10 39	10 29	10 17	10 03	9 47	9 28	9 04	8 30	7 32
22	12 30	12 25	12 20	12 14	12 08	12 01	11 54	11 45	11 36	11 25	11 13	10 58	10 40	10 17
23	13 43	13 40	13 36	13 33	13 29	13 25	13 20	13 15	13 10	13 03	12 56	12 48	12 38	12 26
24	14 56	14 55	14 54	14 53	14 51	14 49	14 48	14 46	14 44	14 41	14 38	14 35	14 32	14 28
25	16 12	16 12	16 13	16 14	16 15	16 16	16 17	16 18	16 19	16 21	16 22	16 24	16 26	16 28

□ indicates Moon continuously above horizon.
■ indicates Moon continuously below horizon.
.. .. indicates phenomenon will occur the next day.

UNIVERSAL TIME FOR MERIDIAN OF GREENWICH

MOONRISE

Lat.	−55°	−50°	−45°	−40°	−35°	−30°	−20°	−10°	0°	+10°	+20°	+30°	+35°	+40°
	h m	h m	h m	h m	h m	h m	h m	h m	h m	h m	h m	h m	h m	h m
Apr. 24	2 01	2 09	2 16	2 21	2 26	2 30	2 37	2 43	2 49	2 55	3 01	3 08	3 12	3 17
25	3 34	3 35	3 35	3 36	3 36	3 36	3 37	3 38	3 38	3 39	3 40	3 41	3 41	3 42
26	5 09	5 02	4 57	4 52	4 48	4 45	4 39	4 34	4 29	4 24	4 19	4 13	4 10	4 07
27	6 49	6 34	6 22	6 12	6 03	5 56	5 43	5 32	5 22	5 12	5 01	4 49	4 42	4 34
28	8 33	8 08	7 49	7 34	7 21	7 10	6 51	6 34	6 19	6 04	5 48	5 29	5 19	5 07
29	10 17	9 42	9 17	8 56	8 39	8 25	8 00	7 39	7 20	7 00	6 40	6 16	6 02	5 46
30	11 51	11 08	10 38	10 14	9 55	9 38	9 10	8 46	8 24	8 02	7 38	7 10	6 54	6 35
May 1	13 02	12 17	11 46	11 22	11 02	10 45	10 16	9 51	9 28	9 05	8 40	8 12	7 55	7 35
2	13 45	13 07	12 39	12 16	11 58	11 42	11 15	10 52	10 30	10 08	9 45	9 17	9 01	8 42
3	14 11	13 40	13 17	12 59	12 43	12 29	12 06	11 46	11 27	11 08	10 47	10 24	10 10	9 53
4	14 26	14 04	13 46	13 31	13 19	13 08	12 50	12 33	12 18	12 03	11 46	11 27	11 16	11 03
5	14 36	14 21	14 08	13 58	13 49	13 41	13 28	13 16	13 05	12 53	12 41	12 28	12 20	12 10
6	14 43	14 34	14 27	14 20	14 15	14 10	14 02	13 54	13 48	13 41	13 33	13 25	13 20	13 14
7	14 49	14 46	14 43	14 40	14 38	14 37	14 33	14 31	14 28	14 25	14 22	14 19	14 17	14 15
8	14 55	14 57	14 58	15 00	15 01	15 02	15 04	15 05	15 07	15 09	15 10	15 12	15 14	15 15
9	15 00	15 08	15 14	15 19	15 24	15 27	15 34	15 40	15 46	15 52	15 58	16 05	16 10	16 14
10	15 07	15 20	15 31	15 40	15 48	15 54	16 06	16 17	16 27	16 36	16 47	16 59	17 07	17 15
11	15 15	15 35	15 50	16 03	16 14	16 24	16 40	16 55	17 09	17 23	17 38	17 55	18 05	18 16
12	15 27	15 54	16 14	16 31	16 45	16 57	17 18	17 37	17 54	18 11	18 30	18 52	19 04	19 19
13	15 45	16 19	16 44	17 04	17 21	17 35	18 00	18 22	18 42	19 02	19 24	19 50	20 05	20 22
14	16 13	16 53	17 22	17 45	18 04	18 20	18 47	19 11	19 33	19 55	20 19	20 47	21 04	21 23
15	16 56	17 40	18 10	18 34	18 54	19 11	19 39	20 04	20 26	20 49	21 14	21 42	21 59	22 19
16	17 58	18 39	19 09	19 32	19 51	20 07	20 35	20 58	21 20	21 42	22 06	22 33	22 49	23 08
17	19 15	19 50	20 16	20 36	20 53	21 08	21 32	21 53	22 13	22 33	22 54	23 18	23 32	23 49
18	20 41	21 08	21 28	21 44	21 58	22 10	22 31	22 48	23 05	23 21	23 38	23 58	.. ..	.. ..

MOONSET

Lat.	−55°	−50°	−45°	−40°	−35°	−30°	−20°	−10°	0°	+10°	+20°	+30°	+35°	+40°
	h m	h m	h m	h m	h m	h m	h m	h m	h m	h m	h m	h m	h m	h m
Apr. 24	15 38	15 34	15 30	15 28	15 25	15 23	15 19	15 16	15 12	15 09	15 06	15 02	14 59	14 56
25	15 45	15 48	15 50	15 52	15 54	15 55	15 58	16 00	16 02	16 04	16 06	16 09	16 10	16 12
26	15 54	16 03	16 11	16 18	16 24	16 29	16 38	16 46	16 53	17 01	17 09	17 18	17 23	17 30
27	16 04	16 22	16 36	16 48	16 58	17 07	17 22	17 36	17 48	18 01	18 15	18 31	18 40	18 50
28	16 19	16 46	17 06	17 23	17 37	17 50	18 11	18 30	18 47	19 05	19 24	19 45	19 58	20 13
29	16 43	17 19	17 46	18 07	18 25	18 40	19 06	19 29	19 50	20 11	20 34	21 00	21 16	21 34
30	17 23	18 07	18 38	19 02	19 21	19 38	20 07	20 32	20 55	21 17	21 42	22 11	22 28	22 47
May 1	18 27	19 11	19 42	20 06	20 26	20 43	21 11	21 35	21 58	22 21	22 45	23 13	23 29	23 49
2	19 49	20 27	20 54	21 16	21 34	21 49	22 15	22 37	22 58	23 18	23 40	.. ..	.. ..	.. ..
3	21 18	21 47	22 09	22 27	22 42	22 54	23 16	23 35	23 52	.. ..	.. ..	0 05	0 20	0 37
4	22 46	23 07	23 23	23 36	23 47	23 57	.. ..	.. ..	.. ..	0 09	0 27	0 48	1 01	1 14
5	.. ..	.. ..	.. ..	.. ..	.. ..	.. ..	0 13	0 28	0 41	0 54	1 08	1 24	1 33	1 44
6	0 08	0 22	0 33	0 41	0 49	0 55	1 07	1 16	1 26	1 35	1 44	1 55	2 01	2 08
7	1 27	1 34	1 39	1 44	1 48	1 51	1 57	2 02	2 07	2 12	2 17	2 23	2 26	2 30
8	2 42	2 43	2 44	2 44	2 45	2 45	2 46	2 46	2 47	2 47	2 48	2 48	2 49	2 49
9	3 56	3 51	3 47	3 44	3 41	3 38	3 34	3 30	3 26	3 22	3 18	3 14	3 11	3 08
10	5 11	5 00	4 51	4 43	4 37	4 31	4 22	4 13	4 05	3 58	3 49	3 40	3 34	3 28
11	6 28	6 10	5 56	5 44	5 34	5 26	5 11	4 58	4 47	4 35	4 22	4 08	4 00	3 50
12	7 46	7 21	7 02	6 47	6 33	6 22	6 03	5 46	5 30	5 15	4 58	4 39	4 28	4 15
13	9 06	8 33	8 09	7 50	7 33	7 20	6 56	6 36	6 17	5 58	5 38	5 15	5 01	4 45
14	10 22	9 42	9 14	8 52	8 33	8 17	7 51	7 28	7 06	6 45	6 22	5 56	5 40	5 22
15	11 28	10 45	10 14	9 50	9 31	9 14	8 46	8 21	7 59	7 36	7 12	6 43	6 27	6 07
16	12 18	11 36	11 06	10 43	10 24	10 07	9 39	9 15	8 52	8 30	8 05	7 37	7 20	7 01
17	12 51	12 15	11 49	11 28	11 10	10 55	10 29	10 07	9 46	9 25	9 02	8 36	8 20	8 02
18	13 13	12 44	12 23	12 05	11 51	11 38	11 16	10 56	10 38	10 20	10 00	9 37	9 24	9 08

.. .. indicates phenomenon will occur the next day.

UNIVERSAL TIME FOR MERIDIAN OF GREENWICH

MOONRISE

Lat.	+40°	+42°	+44°	+46°	+48°	+50°	+52°	+54°	+56°	+58°	+60°	+62°	+64°	+66°
	h m	h m	h m	h m	h m	h m	h m	h m	h m	h m	h m	h m	h m	h m
Apr. 24	3 17	3 19	3 21	3 23	3 26	3 28	3 31	3 34	3 38	3 42	3 46	3 51	3 56	4 03
25	3 42	3 42	3 42	3 42	3 43	3 43	3 43	3 44	3 44	3 44	3 45	3 46	3 46	3 47
26	4 07	4 05	4 03	4 02	4 00	3 58	3 55	3 53	3 50	3 47	3 44	3 40	3 36	3 31
27	4 34	4 31	4 27	4 23	4 19	4 14	4 09	4 04	3 58	3 51	3 44	3 35	3 25	3 13
28	5 07	5 01	4 56	4 49	4 43	4 35	4 27	4 19	4 09	3 57	3 44	3 29	3 11	2 49
29	5 46	5 39	5 31	5 23	5 14	5 04	4 53	4 40	4 25	4 09	3 48	3 23	2 48	1 46
30	6 35	6 27	6 18	6 08	5 56	5 44	5 30	5 14	4 54	4 31	4 00	3 11	▭	▭
May 1	7 35	7 26	7 16	7 05	6 53	6 40	6 24	6 06	5 45	5 17	4 37	▭	▭	▭
2	8 42	8 34	8 25	8 14	8 03	7 50	7 36	7 19	6 59	6 34	6 00	4 58	▭	▭
3	9 53	9 46	9 38	9 29	9 20	9 09	8 58	8 44	8 28	8 10	7 46	7 15	6 26	▭
4	11 03	10 58	10 51	10 45	10 37	10 29	10 20	10 10	9 59	9 46	9 30	9 12	8 48	8 16
5	12 10	12 06	12 02	11 57	11 52	11 46	11 40	11 33	11 26	11 17	11 07	10 56	10 42	10 25
6	13 14	13 12	13 09	13 06	13 03	13 00	12 56	12 52	12 47	12 42	12 37	12 30	12 23	12 14
7	14 15	14 14	14 13	14 12	14 11	14 10	14 08	14 07	14 05	14 03	14 01	13 59	13 56	13 53
8	15 15	15 15	15 16	15 17	15 18	15 18	15 19	15 20	15 21	15 22	15 24	15 25	15 27	15 29
9	16 14	16 17	16 19	16 21	16 24	16 27	16 30	16 33	16 37	16 41	16 46	16 51	16 58	17 05
10	17 15	17 18	17 22	17 26	17 31	17 36	17 41	17 47	17 54	18 02	18 10	18 20	18 32	18 46
11	18 16	18 21	18 27	18 33	18 40	18 47	18 55	19 03	19 13	19 25	19 38	19 54	20 13	20 38
12	19 19	19 26	19 33	19 41	19 49	19 59	20 09	20 21	20 35	20 51	21 11	21 35	22 09	23 10
13	20 22	20 30	20 39	20 48	20 58	21 10	21 23	21 38	21 56	22 18	22 46	23 27	▬	▬
14	21 23	21 32	21 41	21 52	22 03	22 17	22 32	22 49	23 10	23 37	.. ..	▬	▬	▬
15	22 19	22 28	22 38	22 48	23 00	23 14	23 29	23 47	.. ..	.. ..	0 15	▬	▬	▬
16	23 08	23 16	23 25	23 35	23 47	23 59	.. ..	.. ..	0 09	0 37	1 18	▬	▬	▬
17	23 49	23 56	.. ..	.. ..	.. ..	.. ..	0 13	0 29	0 49	1 13	1 44	2 36	▬	▬
18	.. ..	.. ..	0 04	0 13	0 22	0 33	0 45	0 58	1 13	1 31	1 54	2 22	3 04	▬

MOONSET

Lat.	+40°	+42°	+44°	+46°	+48°	+50°	+52°	+54°	+56°	+58°	+60°	+62°	+64°	+66°
	h m	h m	h m	h m	h m	h m	h m	h m	h m	h m	h m	h m	h m	h m
Apr. 24	14 56	14 55	14 54	14 53	14 51	14 49	14 48	14 46	14 44	14 41	14 38	14 35	14 32	14 28
25	16 12	16 12	16 13	16 14	16 15	16 16	16 17	16 18	16 19	16 21	16 22	16 24	16 26	16 28
26	17 30	17 32	17 35	17 38	17 42	17 45	17 49	17 54	17 58	18 04	18 10	18 17	18 25	18 35
27	18 50	18 55	19 00	19 06	19 12	19 18	19 25	19 33	19 42	19 52	20 04	20 18	20 35	20 56
28	20 13	20 20	20 27	20 35	20 43	20 53	21 03	21 15	21 29	21 45	22 05	22 30	23 04	.. ..
29	21 34	21 42	21 51	22 01	22 12	22 24	22 38	22 54	23 12	23 36	.. ..	.. ..	▭	0 05
30	22 47	22 56	23 06	23 17	23 29	23 42	23 58	.. ..	.. ..	.. ..	0 06	0 54	▭	▭
May 1	23 49	23 57	.. ..	.. ..	.. ..	.. ..	.. ..	0 16	0 37	1 05	1 45	▭	▭	▭
2	.. ..	.. ..	0 07	0 17	0 29	0 42	0 56	1 13	1 34	1 59	2 33	3 36	▭	▭
3	0 37	0 45	0 53	1 02	1 12	1 23	1 35	1 49	2 05	2 25	2 48	3 20	4 10	▭
4	1 14	1 21	1 27	1 35	1 42	1 51	2 00	2 11	2 23	2 37	2 53	3 13	3 37	4 10
5	1 44	1 49	1 54	1 59	2 05	2 11	2 18	2 25	2 34	2 43	2 54	3 07	3 22	3 40
6	2 08	2 11	2 15	2 18	2 22	2 26	2 31	2 36	2 41	2 47	2 54	3 02	3 11	3 21
7	2 30	2 31	2 33	2 35	2 37	2 39	2 41	2 44	2 46	2 49	2 53	2 57	3 01	3 06
8	2 49	2 49	2 49	2 50	2 50	2 50	2 50	2 51	2 51	2 51	2 51	2 52	2 52	2 53
9	3 08	3 07	3 06	3 04	3 03	3 01	2 59	2 57	2 55	2 53	2 50	2 47	2 43	2 39
10	3 28	3 26	3 23	3 20	3 16	3 13	3 09	3 04	3 00	2 54	2 49	2 42	2 34	2 25
11	3 50	3 46	3 42	3 37	3 32	3 26	3 20	3 13	3 06	2 57	2 48	2 37	2 24	2 08
12	4 15	4 10	4 04	3 57	3 50	3 42	3 34	3 24	3 14	3 02	2 48	2 31	2 11	1 45
13	4 45	4 38	4 31	4 23	4 14	4 04	3 53	3 40	3 26	3 09	2 49	2 24	1 50	0 48
14	5 22	5 14	5 05	4 55	4 45	4 33	4 19	4 04	3 46	3 24	2 55	2 14	▬	▬
15	6 07	5 58	5 48	5 38	5 26	5 13	4 58	4 40	4 19	3 52	3 13	▬	▬	▬
16	7 01	6 52	6 42	6 31	6 19	6 06	5 51	5 33	5 11	4 43	4 02	▬	▬	▬
17	8 02	7 54	7 45	7 35	7 24	7 12	6 58	6 42	6 23	5 59	5 28	4 36	▬	▬
18	9 08	9 01	8 54	8 46	8 36	8 26	8 15	8 02	7 47	7 30	7 08	6 40	5 59	▬

▭ indicates Moon continuously above horizon.
▬ indicates Moon continuously below horizon.
.. .. indicates phenomenon will occur the next day.

UNIVERSAL TIME FOR MERIDIAN OF GREENWICH

MOONRISE

Lat.	−55°	−50°	−45°	−40°	−35°	−30°	−20°	−10°	0°	+10°	+20°	+30°	+35°	+40°
	h m	h m	h m	h m	h m	h m	h m	h m	h m	h m	h m	h m	h m	h m
May 17	19 15	19 50	20 16	20 36	20 53	21 08	21 32	21 53	22 13	22 33	22 54	23 18	23 32	23 49
18	20 41	21 08	21 28	21 44	21 58	22 10	22 31	22 48	23 05	23 21	23 38	23 58	.. ..	.. ..
19	22 09	22 28	22 42	22 54	23 04	23 13	23 28	23 42	23 54	.. ..	.. ..	.. ..	0 10	0 23
20	23 37	23 48	23 57	.. ..	.. ..	.. ..	.. ..	.. ..	.. ..	0 06	0 19	0 34	0 43	0 52
21	.. ..	.. ..	.. ..	0 05	0 11	0 16	0 26	0 34	0 42	0 49	0 58	1 07	1 12	1 18
22	1 06	1 10	1 13	1 16	1 18	1 20	1 23	1 26	1 29	1 32	1 35	1 38	1 40	1 42
23	2 37	2 34	2 31	2 29	2 27	2 25	2 22	2 19	2 17	2 15	2 12	2 09	2 08	2 06
24	4 12	4 00	3 51	3 44	3 38	3 32	3 23	3 15	3 07	2 59	2 52	2 43	2 37	2 32
25	5 51	5 31	5 16	5 03	4 52	4 43	4 27	4 14	4 01	3 48	3 35	3 19	3 11	3 01
26	7 35	7 05	6 43	6 25	6 10	5 57	5 35	5 17	4 59	4 42	4 23	4 02	3 50	3 36
27	9 16	8 37	8 08	7 46	7 28	7 12	6 46	6 23	6 02	5 41	5 19	4 53	4 38	4 20
28	10 40	9 56	9 25	9 00	8 41	8 24	7 55	7 30	7 07	6 45	6 20	5 52	5 35	5 16
29	11 37	10 56	10 26	10 03	9 44	9 27	8 59	8 35	8 12	7 50	7 26	6 58	6 41	6 22
30	12 11	11 37	11 12	10 52	10 35	10 20	9 55	9 34	9 13	8 53	8 31	8 06	7 51	7 34
31	12 31	12 05	11 46	11 30	11 16	11 04	10 44	10 26	10 09	9 52	9 34	9 13	9 01	8 47
June 1	12 43	12 25	12 11	11 59	11 49	11 40	11 25	11 11	10 59	10 46	10 32	10 17	10 07	9 57
2	12 52	12 40	12 31	12 24	12 17	12 11	12 01	11 52	11 44	11 36	11 27	11 16	11 10	11 03
3	12 58	12 53	12 49	12 45	12 42	12 39	12 34	12 30	12 26	12 22	12 17	12 12	12 10	12 06
4	13 04	13 04	13 04	13 05	13 05	13 05	13 05	13 05	13 06	13 06	13 06	13 07	13 07	13 07
5	13 10	13 15	13 20	13 24	13 27	13 30	13 36	13 40	13 45	13 49	13 54	14 00	14 03	14 07
6	13 16	13 27	13 37	13 44	13 51	13 57	14 07	14 16	14 25	14 34	14 43	14 53	15 00	15 07
7	13 24	13 41	13 55	14 07	14 17	14 25	14 41	14 54	15 06	15 19	15 33	15 48	15 57	16 08
8	13 35	13 59	14 18	14 33	14 46	14 57	15 17	15 34	15 51	16 07	16 24	16 45	16 57	17 10
9	13 51	14 22	14 45	15 04	15 20	15 34	15 58	16 19	16 38	16 57	17 18	17 42	17 57	18 13
10	14 15	14 53	15 21	15 43	16 01	16 17	16 44	17 07	17 28	17 50	18 13	18 41	18 57	19 15

MOONSET

Lat.	−55°	−50°	−45°	−40°	−35°	−30°	−20°	−10°	0°	+10°	+20°	+30°	+35°	+40°
	h m	h m	h m	h m	h m	h m	h m	h m	h m	h m	h m	h m	h m	h m
May 17	12 51	12 15	11 49	11 28	11 10	10 55	10 29	10 07	9 46	9 25	9 02	8 36	8 20	8 02
18	13 13	12 44	12 23	12 05	11 51	11 38	11 16	10 56	10 38	10 20	10 00	9 37	9 24	9 08
19	13 27	13 06	12 50	12 37	12 25	12 15	11 58	11 43	11 28	11 14	10 58	10 40	10 30	10 18
20	13 37	13 24	13 13	13 04	12 56	12 49	12 37	12 27	12 17	12 07	11 56	11 43	11 36	11 28
21	13 46	13 39	13 33	13 29	13 25	13 21	13 15	13 09	13 04	12 59	12 53	12 47	12 43	12 38
22	13 53	13 53	13 53	13 52	13 52	13 52	13 52	13 52	13 52	13 51	13 51	13 51	13 50	13 50
23	14 01	14 07	14 12	14 17	14 21	14 24	14 30	14 35	14 40	14 45	14 51	14 57	15 00	15 04
24	14 10	14 23	14 34	14 44	14 52	14 59	15 11	15 22	15 32	15 42	15 53	16 06	16 13	16 21
25	14 22	14 44	15 01	15 15	15 28	15 38	15 57	16 13	16 28	16 43	16 59	17 18	17 29	17 42
26	14 41	15 12	15 36	15 55	16 11	16 25	16 48	17 09	17 28	17 48	18 09	18 33	18 47	19 04
27	15 13	15 53	16 22	16 44	17 03	17 20	17 47	18 11	18 33	18 55	19 19	19 47	20 03	20 22
28	16 05	16 50	17 21	17 45	18 05	18 22	18 51	19 16	19 39	20 02	20 26	20 55	21 11	21 31
29	17 22	18 03	18 32	18 55	19 14	19 30	19 57	20 21	20 42	21 04	21 27	21 53	22 09	22 27
30	18 52	19 25	19 49	20 09	20 25	20 38	21 02	21 22	21 41	21 59	22 19	22 42	22 55	23 10
31	20 24	20 48	21 06	21 21	21 33	21 44	22 03	22 19	22 33	22 48	23 04	23 22	23 32	23 44
June 1	21 51	22 07	22 19	22 29	22 38	22 46	22 59	23 10	23 21	23 31	23 43	23 55	.. ..	.. ..
2	23 12	23 21	23 28	23 34	23 39	23 44	23 51	23 58	.. ..	.. ..	.. ..	.. ..	0 02	0 11
3	.. ..	.. ..	.. ..	.. ..	.. ..	.. ..	.. ..	.. ..	0 04	0 10	0 17	0 24	0 29	0 33
4	0 29	0 32	0 34	0 36	0 37	0 39	0 41	0 43	0 45	0 47	0 49	0 51	0 52	0 54
5	1 44	1 41	1 38	1 36	1 34	1 32	1 29	1 27	1 25	1 22	1 20	1 17	1 15	1 13
6	2 59	2 49	2 42	2 36	2 30	2 26	2 18	2 11	2 04	1 57	1 50	1 43	1 38	1 33
7	4 14	3 59	3 46	3 36	3 27	3 20	3 07	2 55	2 45	2 34	2 23	2 10	2 03	1 54
8	5 32	5 10	4 52	4 38	4 26	4 15	3 57	3 42	3 27	3 13	2 58	2 40	2 30	2 18
9	6 52	6 21	5 59	5 41	5 26	5 12	4 50	4 31	4 13	3 55	3 36	3 14	3 01	2 47
10	8 09	7 32	7 05	6 44	6 26	6 11	5 45	5 23	5 02	4 41	4 19	3 54	3 39	3 21

.. .. indicates phenomenon will occur the next day.

UNIVERSAL TIME FOR MERIDIAN OF GREENWICH

MOONRISE

Lat.	+40°	+42°	+44°	+46°	+48°	+50°	+52°	+54°	+56°	+58°	+60°	+62°	+64°	+66°
	h m	h m	h m	h m	h m	h m	h m	h m	h m	h m	h m	h m	h m	h m
May 17	23 49	23 56	.. ..	.. ..	.. ..	.. ..	0 13	0 29	0 49	1 13	1 44	2 36	▬	▬
18	.. ..	.. ..	0 04	0 13	0 22	0 33	0 45	0 58	1 13	1 31	1 54	2 22	3 04	▬
19	0 23	0 29	0 36	0 42	0 50	0 58	1 07	1 17	1 28	1 41	1 57	2 15	2 37	3 06
20	0 52	0 57	1 01	1 06	1 12	1 17	1 24	1 31	1 39	1 47	1 57	2 09	2 22	2 38
21	1 18	1 21	1 24	1 27	1 30	1 33	1 37	1 41	1 46	1 51	1 57	2 03	2 11	2 19
22	1 42	1 43	1 44	1 45	1 46	1 48	1 49	1 51	1 52	1 54	1 56	1 58	2 01	2 04
23	2 06	2 05	2 05	2 04	2 03	2 02	2 01	2 00	1 58	1 57	1 55	1 53	1 51	1 49
24	2 32	2 29	2 26	2 23	2 20	2 17	2 13	2 09	2 05	2 00	1 55	1 49	1 42	1 33
25	3 01	2 56	2 52	2 47	2 41	2 35	2 29	2 22	2 14	2 05	1 55	1 44	1 30	1 14
26	3 36	3 30	3 23	3 16	3 08	3 00	2 50	2 39	2 27	2 14	1 57	1 38	1 14	0 42
27	4 20	4 13	4 04	3 55	3 45	3 33	3 21	3 06	2 50	2 30	2 05	1 31	0 34	▭
28	5 16	5 07	4 57	4 47	4 35	4 22	4 07	3 50	3 29	3 03	2 27	1 13	▭	▭
29	6 22	6 13	6 03	5 53	5 41	5 28	5 13	4 55	4 34	4 08	3 30	▭	▭	▭
30	7 34	7 26	7 17	7 08	6 58	6 46	6 33	6 18	6 01	5 40	5 12	4 33	▭	▭
31	8 47	8 40	8 33	8 26	8 18	8 09	7 59	7 47	7 35	7 19	7 01	6 39	6 09	5 24
June 1	9 57	9 52	9 47	9 42	9 36	9 29	9 22	9 14	9 05	8 55	8 44	8 30	8 13	7 53
2	11 03	11 00	10 57	10 54	10 50	10 46	10 41	10 36	10 31	10 25	10 18	10 10	10 00	9 49
3	12 06	12 05	12 03	12 02	12 00	11 58	11 56	11 54	11 51	11 48	11 45	11 42	11 37	11 32
4	13 07	13 07	13 07	13 07	13 08	13 08	13 08	13 08	13 08	13 08	13 09	13 09	13 09	13 10
5	14 07	14 08	14 10	14 12	14 14	14 16	14 19	14 21	14 24	14 27	14 31	14 35	14 40	14 46
6	15 07	15 10	15 13	15 17	15 21	15 25	15 30	15 35	15 41	15 47	15 54	16 03	16 13	16 24
7	16 08	16 12	16 18	16 23	16 29	16 35	16 42	16 50	16 59	17 09	17 21	17 35	17 51	18 12
8	17 10	17 16	17 23	17 30	17 38	17 47	17 57	18 08	18 20	18 34	18 52	19 13	19 41	20 21
9	18 13	18 21	18 29	18 38	18 48	18 59	19 11	19 25	19 42	20 01	20 26	21 00	22 04	▬
10	19 15	19 24	19 33	19 44	19 55	20 07	20 22	20 39	20 59	21 24	21 59	23 07	▬	▬

MOONSET

Lat.	+40°	+42°	+44°	+46°	+48°	+50°	+52°	+54°	+56°	+58°	+60°	+62°	+64°	+66°
	h m	h m	h m	h m	h m	h m	h m	h m	h m	h m	h m	h m	h m	h m
May 17	8 02	7 54	7 45	7 35	7 24	7 12	6 58	6 42	6 23	5 59	5 28	4 36	▬	▬
18	9 08	9 01	8 54	8 46	8 36	8 26	8 15	8 02	7 47	7 30	7 08	6 40	5 59	▬
19	10 18	10 12	10 06	10 00	9 53	9 45	9 37	9 28	9 17	9 05	8 50	8 33	8 12	7 44
20	11 28	11 24	11 20	11 16	11 11	11 06	11 01	10 54	10 47	10 40	10 31	10 21	10 08	9 54
21	12 38	12 37	12 34	12 32	12 30	12 27	12 24	12 21	12 18	12 14	12 09	12 04	11 59	11 52
22	13 50	13 50	13 50	13 50	13 50	13 49	13 49	13 49	13 49	13 49	13 48	13 48	13 48	13 47
23	15 04	15 06	15 08	15 10	15 12	15 14	15 17	15 20	15 23	15 26	15 30	15 35	15 40	15 46
24	16 21	16 25	16 29	16 33	16 38	16 43	16 48	16 55	17 01	17 09	17 18	17 28	17 40	17 55
25	17 42	17 47	17 54	18 00	18 07	18 15	18 24	18 34	18 45	18 58	19 13	19 32	19 55	20 26
26	19 04	19 11	19 19	19 28	19 38	19 49	20 01	20 15	20 31	20 50	21 15	21 47	22 44	▭
27	20 22	20 31	20 40	20 51	21 02	21 15	21 30	21 47	22 07	22 33	23 09	.. ..	▭	▭
28	21 31	21 40	21 50	22 00	22 12	22 25	22 41	22 58	23 19	23 46	.. ..	0 23	▭	▭
29	22 27	22 35	22 44	22 54	23 04	23 16	23 29	23 45	.. ..	.. ..	0 24	▭	▭	▭
30	23 10	23 17	23 24	23 32	23 41	23 50	.. ..	.. ..	0 03	0 24	0 52	1 32	▭	▭
31	23 44	23 49	23 55	.. ..	.. ..	.. ..	0 01	0 13	0 26	0 42	1 01	1 24	1 55	2 41
June 1	.. ..	.. ..	.. ..	0 01	0 07	0 14	0 22	0 31	0 40	0 51	1 04	1 19	1 36	1 58
2	0 11	0 14	0 18	0 22	0 27	0 32	0 37	0 43	0 49	0 56	1 04	1 14	1 24	1 37
3	0 33	0 35	0 38	0 40	0 43	0 45	0 48	0 52	0 55	0 59	1 04	1 09	1 15	1 21
4	0 54	0 54	0 55	0 56	0 57	0 57	0 58	0 59	1 00	1 01	1 03	1 04	1 06	1 08
5	1 13	1 12	1 12	1 11	1 10	1 09	1 07	1 06	1 05	1 03	1 01	0 59	0 57	0 55
6	1 33	1 31	1 28	1 26	1 23	1 20	1 17	1 13	1 09	1 05	1 00	0 55	0 48	0 41
7	1 54	1 50	1 47	1 42	1 38	1 33	1 27	1 21	1 15	1 07	0 59	0 50	0 39	0 26
8	2 18	2 13	2 08	2 02	1 55	1 48	1 40	1 32	1 22	1 11	0 59	0 44	0 27	{00 05 / 23 28}
9	2 47	2 40	2 33	2 25	2 17	2 08	1 58	1 46	1 33	1 18	1 00	0 38	{00 10 / 23 26}	▬
10	3 21	3 14	3 05	2 56	2 46	2 35	2 22	2 07	1 51	1 30	1 05	0 30	▬	▬

▭ indicates Moon continuously above horizon.
▬ indicates Moon continuously below horizon.
.. .. indicates phenomenon will occur the next day.

UNIVERSAL TIME FOR MERIDIAN OF GREENWICH

MOONRISE

Lat.	−55°	−50°	−45°	−40°	−35°	−30°	−20°	−10°	0°	+10°	+20°	+30°	+35°	+40°
	h m	h m	h m	h m	h m	h m	h m	h m	h m	h m	h m	h m	h m	h m
June 8	13 35	13 59	14 18	14 33	14 46	14 57	15 17	15 34	15 51	16 07	16 24	16 45	16 57	17 10
9	13 51	14 22	14 45	15 04	15 20	15 34	15 58	16 19	16 38	16 57	17 18	17 42	17 57	18 13
10	14 15	14 53	15 21	15 43	16 01	16 17	16 44	17 07	17 28	17 50	18 13	18 41	18 57	19 15
11	14 54	15 36	16 06	16 30	16 49	17 06	17 34	17 59	18 21	18 44	19 09	19 37	19 54	20 14
12	15 51	16 33	17 03	17 26	17 45	18 02	18 30	18 53	19 16	19 38	20 02	20 30	20 46	21 05
13	17 05	17 41	18 08	18 29	18 47	19 02	19 27	19 49	20 10	20 30	20 52	21 17	21 32	21 49
14	18 29	18 57	19 19	19 37	19 51	20 04	20 26	20 44	21 02	21 19	21 37	21 59	22 11	22 25
15	19 56	20 17	20 33	20 46	20 57	21 07	21 24	21 38	21 51	22 05	22 19	22 35	22 45	22 55
16	21 24	21 37	21 47	21 56	22 03	22 09	22 20	22 30	22 39	22 48	22 58	23 08	23 15	23 22
17	22 50	22 56	23 01	23 05	23 08	23 11	23 17	23 21	23 26	23 30	23 34	23 39	23 42	23 46
18	.. ..	.. ..	.. ..	.. ..	.. ..	.. ..	.. ..	.. ..	.. ..	.. ..	.. ..	.. ..	.. ..	.. ..
19	0 18	0 17	0 16	0 15	0 15	0 14	0 13	0 12	0 12	0 11	0 10	0 10	0 09	0 09
20	1 48	1 39	1 33	1 27	1 22	1 18	1 11	1 05	0 59	0 54	0 48	0 41	0 37	0 33
21	3 22	3 05	2 53	2 42	2 33	2 25	2 12	2 00	1 50	1 39	1 28	1 15	1 08	0 59
22	5 01	4 35	4 16	4 00	3 47	3 36	3 16	3 00	2 44	2 29	2 12	1 54	1 43	1 31
23	6 41	6 06	5 40	5 20	5 03	4 49	4 24	4 03	3 43	3 24	3 03	2 39	2 26	2 10
24	8 13	7 31	7 00	6 37	6 18	6 01	5 33	5 09	4 47	4 25	4 01	3 34	3 18	2 59
25	9 24	8 40	8 09	7 45	7 25	7 08	6 40	6 15	5 52	5 29	5 05	4 36	4 19	4 00
26	10 07	9 30	9 02	8 40	8 22	8 07	7 40	7 17	6 56	6 34	6 11	5 44	5 28	5 10
27	10 33	10 04	9 42	9 24	9 09	8 55	8 33	8 13	7 55	7 36	7 16	6 53	6 40	6 24
28	10 48	10 27	10 11	9 57	9 46	9 36	9 18	9 03	8 48	8 34	8 18	8 00	7 49	7 37
29	10 59	10 45	10 34	10 24	10 16	10 09	9 57	9 46	9 36	9 26	9 15	9 03	8 55	8 47
30	11 06	10 59	10 52	10 47	10 43	10 39	10 32	10 26	10 20	10 15	10 09	10 02	9 58	9 53
July 1	11 12	11 10	11 09	11 08	11 07	11 06	11 04	11 03	11 02	11 00	10 59	10 58	10 57	10 56
2	11 18	11 22	11 25	11 28	11 30	11 32	11 36	11 39	11 42	11 45	11 48	11 52	11 54	11 57

MOONSET

Lat.	−55°	−50°	−45°	−40°	−35°	−30°	−20°	−10°	0°	+10°	+20°	+30°	+35°	+40°
	h m	h m	h m	h m	h m	h m	h m	h m	h m	h m	h m	h m	h m	h m
June 8	5 32	5 10	4 52	4 38	4 26	4 15	3 57	3 42	3 27	3 13	2 58	2 40	2 30	2 18
9	6 52	6 21	5 59	5 41	5 26	5 12	4 50	4 31	4 13	3 55	3 36	3 14	3 01	2 47
10	8 09	7 32	7 05	6 44	6 26	6 11	5 45	5 23	5 02	4 41	4 19	3 54	3 39	3 21
11	9 20	8 37	8 07	7 44	7 25	7 08	6 40	6 16	5 54	5 31	5 07	4 40	4 23	4 04
12	10 15	9 33	9 02	8 39	8 19	8 03	7 34	7 10	6 48	6 25	6 01	5 32	5 15	4 56
13	10 53	10 16	9 48	9 26	9 08	8 53	8 26	8 03	7 42	7 20	6 57	6 30	6 14	5 55
14	11 18	10 48	10 25	10 06	9 51	9 37	9 14	8 54	8 35	8 16	7 55	7 31	7 17	7 01
15	11 34	11 12	10 54	10 39	10 27	10 16	9 58	9 41	9 26	9 10	8 54	8 34	8 23	8 10
16	11 45	11 30	11 18	11 08	10 59	10 51	10 38	10 26	10 14	10 03	9 51	9 37	9 29	9 19
17	11 54	11 45	11 38	11 32	11 27	11 23	11 15	11 08	11 01	10 55	10 47	10 39	10 34	10 29
18	12 01	11 59	11 57	11 56	11 54	11 53	11 51	11 49	11 47	11 46	11 44	11 41	11 40	11 38
19	12 08	12 13	12 16	12 19	12 21	12 24	12 27	12 31	12 34	12 37	12 41	12 44	12 47	12 49
20	12 17	12 28	12 36	12 44	12 50	12 56	13 06	13 14	13 23	13 31	13 40	13 50	13 56	14 02
21	12 27	12 45	13 00	13 12	13 23	13 32	13 48	14 02	14 15	14 28	14 42	14 58	15 08	15 19
22	12 42	13 09	13 30	13 47	14 01	14 14	14 35	14 54	15 12	15 29	15 48	16 10	16 23	16 38
23	13 07	13 43	14 09	14 31	14 48	15 04	15 30	15 52	16 13	16 34	16 57	17 23	17 39	17 57
24	13 48	14 31	15 02	15 26	15 45	16 02	16 31	16 55	17 18	17 41	18 05	18 34	18 50	19 10
25	14 54	15 37	16 08	16 32	16 51	17 08	17 36	18 00	18 23	18 45	19 09	19 37	19 53	20 12
26	16 20	16 57	17 24	17 45	18 02	18 17	18 43	19 04	19 24	19 45	20 06	20 31	20 45	21 02
27	17 54	18 22	18 42	18 59	19 13	19 26	19 46	20 04	20 21	20 37	20 55	21 15	21 27	21 40
28	19 25	19 44	19 59	20 11	20 22	20 31	20 46	20 59	21 12	21 24	21 37	21 52	22 00	22 10
29	20 51	21 02	21 12	21 19	21 26	21 31	21 41	21 50	21 58	22 06	22 14	22 23	22 29	22 35
30	22 11	22 16	22 20	22 23	22 26	22 29	22 33	22 37	22 40	22 44	22 48	22 52	22 54	22 57
July 1	23 28	23 27	23 26	23 25	23 24	23 24	23 23	23 22	23 21	23 20	23 19	23 18	23 17	23 17
2	.. ..	.. ..	.. ..	.. ..	.. ..	.. ..	.. ..	.. ..	.. ..	23 56	23 50	23 44	23 41	23 36

.. .. indicates phenomenon will occur the next day.

UNIVERSAL TIME FOR MERIDIAN OF GREENWICH

MOONRISE

Lat.	+40°	+42°	+44°	+46°	+48°	+50°	+52°	+54°	+56°	+58°	+60°	+62°	+64°	+66°
	h m	h m	h m	h m	h m	h m	h m	h m	h m	h m	h m	h m	h m	h m
June 8	17 10	17 16	17 23	17 30	17 38	17 47	17 57	18 08	18 20	18 34	18 52	19 13	19 41	20 21
9	18 13	18 21	18 29	18 38	18 48	18 59	19 11	19 25	19 42	20 01	20 26	21 00	22 04	■
10	19 15	19 24	19 33	19 44	19 55	20 07	20 22	20 39	20 59	21 24	21 59	23 07	■	■
11	20 14	20 23	20 32	20 43	20 55	21 08	21 24	21 42	22 03	22 31	23 12	■	■	■
12	21 05	21 14	21 23	21 33	21 45	21 58	22 12	22 29	22 49	23 14	23 48	■	■	■
13	21 49	21 56	22 05	22 14	22 24	22 35	22 47	23 01	23 18	23 37	.. ..	0 52	■	■
14	22 25	22 31	22 38	22 46	22 54	23 02	23 12	23 23	23 35	23 49	0 02	0 34	1 28	■
15	22 55	23 00	23 05	23 11	23 17	23 23	23 30	23 38	23 47	23 56	0 06	0 26	0 52	1 27
16	23 22	23 25	23 28	23 32	23 36	23 40	23 44	23 49	23 55	.. ..	0 08	0 21	0 36	0 54
17	23 46	23 47	23 49	23 50	23 52	23 54	23 56	23 58	.. ..	0 01	0 08	0 15	0 24	0 35
18	.. ..	.. ..	.. ..	.. ..	.. ..	.. ..	.. ..	.. ..	0 01	0 04	0 07	0 10	0 14	0 19
19	0 09	0 09	0 08	0 08	0 08	0 08	0 07	0 07	0 07	0 06	0 06	0 06	{00 05 / 23 56}	{00 04 / 23 50}
20	0 33	0 31	0 29	0 27	0 24	0 22	0 19	0 16	0 13	0 09	0 05	{00 01 / 23 56}	23 45	23 33
21	0 59	0 56	0 52	0 48	0 43	0 38	0 33	0 27	0 21	0 13	0 05	23 51	23 32	23 09
22	1 31	1 25	1 19	1 13	1 06	0 59	0 51	0 42	0 31	0 20	0 07	23 45	23 10	22 05
23	2 10	2 02	1 55	1 46	1 37	1 27	1 16	1 03	0 49	0 32	0 11	23 37	□	□
24	2 59	2 50	2 41	2 31	2 20	2 08	1 54	1 38	1 19	0 55	0 25	□	□	□
25	4 00	3 51	3 41	3 30	3 18	3 05	2 50	2 32	2 11	1 44	1 05	□	□	□
26	5 10	5 01	4 52	4 42	4 31	4 19	4 05	3 48	3 29	3 05	2 33	1 39	□	□
27	6 24	6 17	6 09	6 01	5 52	5 42	5 30	5 17	5 02	4 45	4 23	3 55	3 13	□
28	7 37	7 32	7 26	7 20	7 13	7 05	6 57	6 48	6 37	6 25	6 11	5 54	5 33	5 06
29	8 47	8 43	8 40	8 35	8 31	8 26	8 20	8 14	8 07	8 00	7 51	7 41	7 29	7 14
30	9 53	9 51	9 49	9 46	9 44	9 41	9 38	9 35	9 31	9 27	9 23	9 17	9 11	9 04
July 1	10 56	10 55	10 55	10 54	10 54	10 53	10 53	10 52	10 51	10 50	10 49	10 48	10 47	10 45
2	11 57	11 58	11 59	12 00	12 01	12 03	12 05	12 06	12 08	12 10	12 13	12 16	12 19	12 23

MOONSET

Lat.	+40°	+42°	+44°	+46°	+48°	+50°	+52°	+54°	+56°	+58°	+60°	+62°	+64°	+66°
	h m	h m	h m	h m	h m	h m	h m	h m	h m	h m	h m	h m	h m	h m
June 8	2 18	2 13	2 08	2 02	1 55	1 48	1 40	1 32	1 22	1 11	0 59	0 44	0 27	{00 05 / 23 28}
9	2 47	2 40	2 33	2 25	2 17	2 08	1 58	1 46	1 33	1 18	1 00	0 38	{00 10 / 23 26}	■
10	3 21	3 14	3 05	2 56	2 46	2 35	2 22	2 07	1 51	1 30	1 05	0 30	■	■
11	4 04	3 55	3 46	3 35	3 24	3 11	2 57	2 39	2 19	1 54	1 19	0 10	■	■
12	4 56	4 47	4 37	4 26	4 14	4 01	3 45	3 27	3 06	2 38	1 57	■	■	■
13	5 55	5 47	5 38	5 27	5 16	5 04	4 49	4 33	4 13	3 48	3 14	2 11	■	■
14	7 01	6 54	6 46	6 37	6 27	6 17	6 05	5 51	5 35	5 16	4 52	4 20	3 27	■
15	8 10	8 04	7 58	7 51	7 43	7 35	7 26	7 16	7 04	6 50	6 34	6 15	5 50	5 16
16	9 19	9 15	9 11	9 06	9 01	8 55	8 49	8 42	8 34	8 25	8 15	8 03	7 49	7 31
17	10 29	10 26	10 24	10 21	10 18	10 15	10 11	10 07	10 03	9 58	9 52	9 46	9 38	9 30
18	11 38	11 38	11 37	11 36	11 35	11 34	11 33	11 32	11 31	11 30	11 28	11 27	11 25	11 22
19	12 49	12 50	12 51	12 53	12 54	12 56	12 57	12 59	13 01	13 03	13 06	13 09	13 12	13 16
20	14 02	14 05	14 09	14 12	14 16	14 20	14 24	14 29	14 34	14 40	14 47	14 55	15 04	15 15
21	15 19	15 24	15 29	15 35	15 41	15 47	15 55	16 03	16 13	16 23	16 35	16 50	17 08	17 30
22	16 38	16 45	16 52	17 00	17 09	17 18	17 29	17 41	17 55	18 11	18 31	18 56	19 31	20 35
23	17 57	18 05	18 14	18 24	18 35	18 47	19 00	19 16	19 35	19 58	20 28	21 15	□	□
24	19 10	19 19	19 29	19 39	19 51	20 05	20 20	20 37	20 59	21 26	22 05	□	□	□
25	20 12	20 21	20 30	20 40	20 52	21 04	21 19	21 35	21 55	22 19	22 52	23 46	□	□
26	21 02	21 09	21 17	21 26	21 35	21 46	21 58	22 11	22 27	22 45	23 07	23 36	□	□
27	21 40	21 46	21 52	21 59	22 06	22 15	22 24	22 34	22 45	22 58	23 13	23 31	{00 19 / 23 53}	□
28	22 10	22 14	22 19	22 24	22 29	22 35	22 41	22 48	22 56	23 04	23 14	23 26	23 39	{00 21 / 23 55}
29	22 35	22 38	22 41	22 44	22 47	22 50	22 54	22 59	23 03	23 08	23 14	23 21	23 28	23 37
30	22 57	22 58	22 59	23 00	23 02	23 03	23 05	23 07	23 09	23 11	23 13	23 16	23 19	23 23
July 1	23 17	23 16	23 16	23 16	23 15	23 15	23 14	23 14	23 13	23 13	23 12	23 11	23 10	23 10
2	23 36	23 35	23 33	23 31	23 29	23 26	23 24	23 21	23 18	23 15	23 11	23 07	23 02	22 56

□ indicates Moon continuously above horizon.
■ indicates Moon continuously below horizon.
.. .. indicates phenomenon will occur the next day.

UNIVERSAL TIME FOR MERIDIAN OF GREENWICH

MOONRISE

Lat.	−55°	−50°	−45°	−40°	−35°	−30°	−20°	−10°	0°	+10°	+20°	+30°	+35°	+40°
	h m	h m	h m	h m	h m	h m	h m	h m	h m	h m	h m	h m	h m	h m
July 1	11 12	11 10	11 09	11 08	11 07	11 06	11 04	11 03	11 02	11 00	10 59	10 58	10 57	10 56
2	11 18	11 22	11 25	11 28	11 30	11 32	11 36	11 39	11 42	11 45	11 48	11 52	11 54	11 57
3	11 24	11 34	11 41	11 48	11 53	11 58	12 07	12 14	12 22	12 29	12 37	12 46	12 51	12 57
4	11 31	11 47	11 59	12 09	12 18	12 26	12 40	12 51	13 03	13 14	13 26	13 40	13 48	13 58
5	11 41	12 03	12 20	12 34	12 46	12 57	13 15	13 31	13 46	14 01	14 17	14 36	14 47	15 00
6	11 55	12 24	12 46	13 03	13 19	13 32	13 54	14 14	14 32	14 50	15 10	15 33	15 47	16 03
7	12 16	12 52	13 18	13 39	13 57	14 12	14 38	15 00	15 21	15 42	16 05	16 32	16 47	17 05
8	12 49	13 30	14 00	14 24	14 43	14 59	15 27	15 51	16 14	16 36	17 01	17 29	17 46	18 05
9	13 40	14 23	14 53	15 17	15 37	15 53	16 21	16 46	17 08	17 31	17 55	18 23	18 40	19 00
10	14 50	15 29	15 57	16 19	16 37	16 53	17 19	17 42	18 03	18 24	18 47	19 13	19 29	19 46
11	16 13	16 44	17 08	17 26	17 42	17 55	18 18	18 38	18 57	19 15	19 35	19 57	20 10	20 26
12	17 41	18 04	18 22	18 36	18 49	18 59	19 18	19 33	19 48	20 03	20 18	20 36	20 46	20 58
13	19 10	19 25	19 37	19 47	19 56	20 03	20 16	20 27	20 37	20 47	20 58	21 11	21 18	21 26
14	20 38	20 46	20 52	20 57	21 02	21 06	21 12	21 18	21 24	21 30	21 35	21 42	21 46	21 50
15	22 05	22 06	22 07	22 07	22 08	22 08	22 09	22 09	22 10	22 11	22 12	22 12	22 13	22 13
16	23 33	23 27	23 22	23 18	23 14	23 11	23 06	23 01	22 57	22 52	22 48	22 43	22 40	22 37
17	.. ..	.. ..	.. ..	.. ..	.. ..	.. ..	.. ..	23 55	23 45	23 36	23 26	23 15	23 09	23 02
18	1 04	0 50	0 40	0 31	0 23	0 16	0 05	.. ..	.. ..	.. ..	.. ..	23 51	23 42	23 31
19	2 39	2 17	2 00	1 46	1 34	1 24	1 06	0 51	0 37	0 23	0 08	.. ..	.. ..	.. ..
20	4 17	3 46	3 22	3 03	2 47	2 34	2 11	1 51	1 33	1 15	0 55	0 33	0 20	0 05
21	5 51	5 11	4 42	4 19	4 01	3 45	3 18	2 55	2 33	2 12	1 49	1 23	1 07	0 49
22	7 09	6 25	5 54	5 30	5 10	4 52	4 24	3 59	3 36	3 13	2 49	2 20	2 04	1 44
23	8 03	7 22	6 52	6 29	6 10	5 54	5 26	5 02	4 39	4 17	3 53	3 25	3 09	2 49
24	8 34	8 01	7 37	7 17	7 00	6 46	6 21	6 00	5 40	5 20	4 58	4 34	4 19	4 02
25	8 53	8 29	8 10	7 54	7 41	7 29	7 09	6 52	6 36	6 19	6 02	5 41	5 29	5 16

MOONSET

Lat.	−55°	−50°	−45°	−40°	−35°	−30°	−20°	−10°	0°	+10°	+20°	+30°	+35°	+40°
	h m	h m	h m	h m	h m	h m	h m	h m	h m	h m	h m	h m	h m	h m
July 1	23 28	23 27	23 26	23 25	23 24	23 24	23 23	23 22	23 21	23 20	23 19	23 18	23 17	23 17
2	.. ..	.. ..	.. ..	.. ..	.. ..	.. ..	.. ..	.. ..	.. ..	23 56	23 50	23 44	23 41	23 36
3	0 43	0 36	0 30	0 26	0 21	0 18	0 12	0 06	0 01	.. ..	.. ..	.. ..	.. ..	23 57
4	1 59	1 46	1 35	1 26	1 19	1 12	1 00	0 51	0 41	0 32	0 22	0 11	0 05	.. ..
5	3 16	2 56	2 40	2 27	2 17	2 07	1 51	1 36	1 23	1 10	0 56	0 40	0 31	0 20
6	4 35	4 08	3 47	3 30	3 16	3 04	2 43	2 25	2 08	1 51	1 33	1 13	1 01	0 47
7	5 54	5 19	4 53	4 33	4 16	4 01	3 37	3 15	2 55	2 36	2 14	1 50	1 36	1 19
8	7 08	6 27	5 58	5 35	5 16	4 59	4 32	4 08	3 46	3 25	3 01	2 34	2 18	1 59
9	8 09	7 26	6 56	6 32	6 12	5 56	5 27	5 03	4 40	4 17	3 53	3 24	3 07	2 48
10	8 53	8 14	7 45	7 23	7 04	6 48	6 20	5 57	5 35	5 13	4 49	4 21	4 05	3 45
11	9 22	8 50	8 25	8 05	7 49	7 35	7 10	6 49	6 29	6 09	5 48	5 23	5 08	4 50
12	9 41	9 16	8 57	8 41	8 28	8 16	7 56	7 38	7 22	7 05	6 47	6 26	6 14	6 00
13	9 53	9 36	9 22	9 11	9 01	8 52	8 37	8 24	8 12	7 59	7 46	7 30	7 21	7 10
14	10 03	9 52	9 44	9 37	9 31	9 25	9 16	9 07	9 00	8 52	8 43	8 33	8 27	8 21
15	10 10	10 06	10 03	10 00	9 58	9 56	9 52	9 49	9 46	9 43	9 39	9 35	9 33	9 31
16	10 17	10 20	10 22	10 23	10 25	10 26	10 28	10 30	10 32	10 34	10 36	10 38	10 39	10 41
17	10 25	10 34	10 41	10 47	10 53	10 57	11 05	11 13	11 19	11 26	11 34	11 42	11 47	11 52
18	10 34	10 50	11 03	11 14	11 23	11 31	11 45	11 58	12 09	12 21	12 34	12 48	12 56	13 06
19	10 47	11 11	11 30	11 45	11 58	12 10	12 30	12 47	13 03	13 19	13 37	13 57	14 09	14 22
20	11 06	11 39	12 04	12 24	12 41	12 55	13 20	13 41	14 01	14 21	14 43	15 08	15 22	15 40
21	11 39	12 20	12 50	13 13	13 32	13 49	14 17	14 41	15 03	15 25	15 49	16 17	16 34	16 53
22	12 33	13 18	13 49	14 13	14 33	14 50	15 19	15 44	16 07	16 29	16 54	17 22	17 39	17 59
23	13 51	14 31	15 00	15 23	15 42	15 57	16 24	16 47	17 09	17 30	17 53	18 19	18 35	18 52
24	15 23	15 54	16 18	16 37	16 53	17 06	17 29	17 49	18 07	18 25	18 45	19 07	19 20	19 35
25	16 56	17 19	17 36	17 50	18 02	18 13	18 31	18 46	19 01	19 15	19 30	19 47	19 57	20 08

.. .. indicates phenomenon will occur the next day.

UNIVERSAL TIME FOR MERIDIAN OF GREENWICH

MOONRISE

Lat.	+40°	+42°	+44°	+46°	+48°	+50°	+52°	+54°	+56°	+58°	+60°	+62°	+64°	+66°
	h m	h m	h m	h m	h m	h m	h m	h m	h m	h m	h m	h m	h m	h m
July 1	10 56	10 55	10 55	10 54	10 54	10 53	10 53	10 52	10 51	10 50	10 49	10 48	10 47	10 45
2	11 57	11 58	11 59	12 00	12 01	12 03	12 05	12 06	12 08	12 10	12 13	12 16	12 19	12 23
3	12 57	12 59	13 02	13 05	13 09	13 12	13 16	13 20	13 25	13 30	13 36	13 43	13 51	14 01
4	13 58	14 02	14 06	14 11	14 16	14 22	14 28	14 35	14 43	14 52	15 02	15 14	15 28	15 45
5	15 00	15 05	15 12	15 18	15 25	15 33	15 42	15 52	16 03	16 16	16 31	16 50	17 13	17 44
6	16 03	16 10	16 18	16 26	16 35	16 45	16 57	17 10	17 25	17 43	18 05	18 34	19 17	▬
7	17 05	17 14	17 23	17 33	17 43	17 56	18 09	18 25	18 44	19 08	19 39	20 31	▬	▬
8	18 05	18 14	18 24	18 35	18 47	19 00	19 15	19 33	19 55	20 22	21 03	▬	▬	▬
9	19 00	19 09	19 18	19 29	19 40	19 54	20 09	20 26	20 47	21 14	21 52	▬	▬	▬
10	19 46	19 55	20 03	20 13	20 23	20 35	20 48	21 03	21 21	21 43	22 10	22 49	▬	▬
11	20 26	20 32	20 40	20 48	20 56	21 06	21 16	21 28	21 42	21 58	22 16	22 40	23 10	23 58
12	20 58	21 03	21 09	21 15	21 21	21 29	21 36	21 45	21 55	22 06	22 18	22 33	22 51	23 13
13	21 26	21 29	21 33	21 37	21 42	21 46	21 52	21 57	22 04	22 11	22 19	22 28	22 38	22 51
14	21 50	21 52	21 54	21 56	21 59	22 01	22 04	22 07	22 10	22 14	22 18	22 23	22 28	22 34
15	22 13	22 14	22 14	22 14	22 15	22 15	22 15	22 16	22 16	22 17	22 17	22 18	22 18	22 19
16	22 37	22 35	22 34	22 32	22 30	22 29	22 27	22 24	22 22	22 19	22 16	22 13	22 09	22 05
17	23 02	22 59	22 55	22 52	22 48	22 44	22 39	22 34	22 29	22 23	22 16	22 08	21 59	21 48
18	23 31	23 26	23 20	23 15	23 09	23 02	22 55	22 47	22 38	22 28	22 16	22 03	21 47	21 28
19	.. ..	23 59	23 52	23 44	23 36	23 26	23 16	23 05	22 52	22 37	22 19	21 57	21 29	20 49
20	0 05	.. ..	.. ..	.. ..	.. ..	.. ..	23 48	23 33	23 15	22 54	22 27	21 50	▭	▭
21	0 49	0 41	0 32	0 23	0 12	0 01	.. ..	.. ..	23 56	23 29	22 52	▭	▭	▭
22	1 44	1 35	1 25	1 15	1 03	0 50	0 35	0 17	.. ..	.. ..	23 59	▭	▭	▭
23	2 49	2 41	2 31	2 21	2 09	1 56	1 41	1 24	1 03	0 36	.. ..	▭	▭	▭
24	4 02	3 54	3 45	3 36	3 26	3 15	3 02	2 48	2 31	2 10	1 44	1 07	▭	▭
25	5 16	5 09	5 03	4 56	4 48	4 39	4 29	4 18	4 06	3 51	3 34	3 13	2 45	2 05

MOONSET

Lat.	+40°	+42°	+44°	+46°	+48°	+50°	+52°	+54°	+56°	+58°	+60°	+62°	+64°	+66°
	h m	h m	h m	h m	h m	h m	h m	h m	h m	h m	h m	h m	h m	h m
July 1	23 17	23 16	23 16	23 16	23 15	23 15	23 14	23 14	23 13	23 13	23 12	23 11	23 10	23 10
2	23 36	23 35	23 33	23 31	23 29	23 26	23 24	23 21	23 18	23 15	23 11	23 07	23 02	22 56
3	23 57	23 54	23 51	23 47	23 43	23 39	23 34	23 29	23 23	23 17	23 10	23 02	22 52	22 41
4	.. ..	.. ..	.. ..	.. ..	23 59	23 53	23 46	23 38	23 30	23 20	23 09	22 57	22 41	22 23
5	0 20	0 16	0 11	0 05	.. ..	.. ..	.. ..	23 51	23 39	23 26	23 10	22 51	22 27	21 55
6	0 47	0 41	0 34	0 27	0 19	0 11	0 02	.. ..	23 54	23 36	23 13	22 44	21 59	▬
7	1 19	1 12	1 04	0 55	0 46	0 35	0 23	0 10	.. ..	23 54	23 22	22 31	▬	▬
8	1 59	1 51	1 41	1 31	1 20	1 08	0 54	0 37	0 18	.. ..	23 50	▬	▬	▬
9	2 48	2 39	2 29	2 18	2 06	1 53	1 38	1 20	0 58	0 30	.. ..	▬	▬	▬
10	3 45	3 37	3 27	3 17	3 05	2 52	2 37	2 20	1 59	1 32	0 55	▬	▬	▬
11	4 50	4 43	4 34	4 25	4 15	4 03	3 51	3 36	3 18	2 57	2 30	1 52	▬	▬
12	6 00	5 53	5 46	5 39	5 31	5 22	5 12	5 00	4 47	4 32	4 14	3 52	3 22	2 35
13	7 10	7 06	7 01	6 55	6 49	6 43	6 36	6 28	6 19	6 09	5 57	5 43	5 26	5 06
14	8 21	8 18	8 15	8 11	8 08	8 04	7 59	7 55	7 49	7 43	7 36	7 29	7 20	7 09
15	9 31	9 29	9 28	9 27	9 25	9 24	9 22	9 20	9 18	9 16	9 13	9 10	9 07	9 03
16	10 41	10 41	10 42	10 43	10 43	10 44	10 45	10 46	10 47	10 49	10 50	10 51	10 53	10 55
17	11 52	11 55	11 57	12 00	12 03	12 06	12 10	12 14	12 18	12 23	12 29	12 35	12 42	12 51
18	13 06	13 10	13 15	13 20	13 25	13 31	13 38	13 45	13 53	14 02	14 13	14 25	14 39	14 57
19	14 22	14 29	14 35	14 42	14 50	14 59	15 08	15 19	15 32	15 46	16 03	16 24	16 51	17 30
20	15 40	15 47	15 56	16 05	16 15	16 26	16 39	16 54	17 11	17 31	17 58	18 35	▭	▭
21	16 53	17 02	17 12	17 22	17 34	17 47	18 02	18 19	18 40	19 07	19 44	▭	▭	▭
22	17 59	18 08	18 17	18 28	18 40	18 53	19 08	19 25	19 46	20 13	20 50	▭	▭	▭
23	18 52	19 01	19 09	19 19	19 29	19 41	19 54	20 09	20 26	20 48	21 14	21 52	▭	▭
24	19 35	19 42	19 49	19 56	20 05	20 14	20 24	20 36	20 49	21 04	21 22	21 44	22 13	22 54
25	20 08	20 13	20 19	20 24	20 31	20 38	20 45	20 53	21 02	21 13	21 25	21 39	21 55	22 16

▭ indicates Moon continuously above horizon.
▬ indicates Moon continuously below horizon.
.. .. indicates phenomenon will occur the next day.

UNIVERSAL TIME FOR MERIDIAN OF GREENWICH

MOONRISE

Lat.	−55°	−50°	−45°	−40°	−35°	−30°	−20°	−10°	0°	+10°	+20°	+30°	+35°	+40°
	h m	h m	h m	h m	h m	h m	h m	h m	h m	h m	h m	h m	h m	h m
July 24	8 34	8 01	7 37	7 17	7 00	6 46	6 21	6 00	5 40	5 20	4 58	4 34	4 19	4 02
25	8 53	8 29	8 10	7 54	7 41	7 29	7 09	6 52	6 36	6 19	6 02	5 41	5 29	5 16
26	9 05	8 48	8 35	8 24	8 14	8 06	7 51	7 39	7 26	7 14	7 01	6 46	6 38	6 28
27	9 14	9 04	8 55	8 49	8 43	8 37	8 28	8 20	8 13	8 05	7 57	7 48	7 42	7 36
28	9 20	9 16	9 13	9 10	9 08	9 06	9 02	8 59	8 56	8 53	8 49	8 46	8 43	8 41
29	9 26	9 28	9 29	9 30	9 31	9 32	9 34	9 35	9 37	9 38	9 40	9 41	9 42	9 43
30	9 32	9 40	9 45	9 50	9 55	9 59	10 05	10 11	10 17	10 23	10 29	10 36	10 40	10 45
31	9 39	9 52	10 03	10 12	10 19	10 26	10 38	10 48	10 58	11 08	11 18	11 30	11 38	11 46
Aug. 1	9 47	10 07	10 22	10 35	10 46	10 55	11 12	11 27	11 40	11 54	12 09	12 26	12 36	12 47
2	9 59	10 25	10 46	11 02	11 16	11 28	11 50	12 08	12 25	12 42	13 01	13 23	13 35	13 50
3	10 17	10 50	11 15	11 35	11 52	12 07	12 31	12 53	13 13	13 33	13 55	14 21	14 36	14 53
4	10 44	11 24	11 53	12 16	12 35	12 51	13 18	13 42	14 04	14 26	14 50	15 18	15 35	15 54
5	11 27	12 11	12 41	13 05	13 25	13 42	14 11	14 35	14 58	15 21	15 45	16 14	16 31	16 51
6	12 30	13 11	13 41	14 04	14 23	14 40	15 07	15 31	15 53	16 15	16 38	17 06	17 22	17 41
7	13 50	14 24	14 50	15 10	15 27	15 42	16 06	16 28	16 47	17 07	17 28	17 52	18 06	18 23
8	15 18	15 44	16 04	16 21	16 34	16 46	17 06	17 24	17 40	17 56	18 14	18 33	18 45	18 58
9	16 49	17 07	17 21	17 33	17 43	17 51	18 06	18 19	18 31	18 43	18 56	19 10	19 18	19 28
10	18 19	18 30	18 38	18 45	18 51	18 56	19 05	19 12	19 20	19 27	19 34	19 43	19 48	19 54
11	19 49	19 52	19 54	19 56	19 58	20 00	20 02	20 05	20 07	20 09	20 12	20 14	20 16	20 18
12	21 18	21 14	21 11	21 08	21 06	21 04	21 00	20 57	20 54	20 51	20 48	20 45	20 43	20 41
13	22 50	22 38	22 29	22 21	22 15	22 09	21 59	21 51	21 43	21 35	21 27	21 17	21 12	21 06
14	.. ..	.. ..	23 49	23 36	23 25	23 16	23 00	22 46	22 34	22 21	22 07	21 52	21 43	21 33
15	0 24	0 04	.. ..	.. ..	.. ..	.. ..	.. ..	23 45	23 28	23 11	22 53	22 32	22 20	22 06
16	2 01	1 32	1 10	0 53	0 38	0 25	0 04	.. ..	.. ..	.. ..	23 44	23 18	23 03	22 46
17	3 36	2 58	2 30	2 09	1 51	1 35	1 09	0 47	0 26	0 06	.. ..	.. ..	23 56	23 36

MOONSET

Lat.	−55°	−50°	−45°	−40°	−35°	−30°	−20°	−10°	0°	+10°	+20°	+30°	+35°	+40°
	h m	h m	h m	h m	h m	h m	h m	h m	h m	h m	h m	h m	h m	h m
July 24	15 23	15 54	16 18	16 37	16 53	17 06	17 29	17 49	18 07	18 25	18 45	19 07	19 20	19 35
25	16 56	17 19	17 36	17 50	18 02	18 13	18 31	18 46	19 01	19 15	19 30	19 47	19 57	20 08
26	18 25	18 40	18 51	19 01	19 09	19 16	19 28	19 39	19 49	19 59	20 09	20 21	20 28	20 35
27	19 49	19 56	20 02	20 08	20 12	20 16	20 22	20 28	20 34	20 39	20 44	20 51	20 54	20 59
28	21 08	21 09	21 10	21 11	21 12	21 13	21 14	21 15	21 15	21 16	21 17	21 18	21 19	21 19
29	22 25	22 20	22 16	22 13	22 10	22 08	22 03	22 00	21 56	21 53	21 49	21 45	21 42	21 39
30	23 41	23 30	23 21	23 14	23 08	23 02	22 53	22 44	22 37	22 29	22 21	22 11	22 06	22 00
31	.. ..	.. ..	.. ..	.. ..	.. ..	23 57	23 43	23 30	23 18	23 06	22 54	22 39	22 31	22 22
Aug. 1	0 59	0 41	0 27	0 15	0 06	.. ..	.. ..	.. ..	.. ..	23 46	23 29	23 10	22 59	22 47
2	2 17	1 52	1 33	1 18	1 05	0 53	0 34	0 17	0 02	.. ..	.. ..	23 46	23 32	23 17
3	3 36	3 04	2 40	2 20	2 04	1 51	1 27	1 07	0 48	0 29	0 09	.. ..	.. ..	23 53
4	4 53	4 13	3 45	3 23	3 04	2 48	2 22	1 59	1 37	1 16	0 53	0 27	0 11	.. ..
5	6 00	5 16	4 46	4 22	4 02	3 45	3 17	2 53	2 30	2 07	1 43	1 14	0 58	0 38
6	6 50	6 09	5 39	5 15	4 56	4 39	4 11	3 47	3 24	3 02	2 37	2 09	1 52	1 32
7	7 24	6 49	6 22	6 01	5 44	5 28	5 03	4 40	4 19	3 58	3 35	3 09	2 53	2 35
8	7 46	7 19	6 57	6 40	6 25	6 12	5 50	5 31	5 13	4 55	4 35	4 12	3 59	3 44
9	8 01	7 41	7 25	7 12	7 01	6 51	6 34	6 19	6 05	5 50	5 35	5 17	5 07	4 55
10	8 11	7 59	7 48	7 40	7 32	7 26	7 14	7 04	6 54	6 45	6 34	6 22	6 15	6 07
11	8 19	8 13	8 08	8 04	8 01	7 57	7 52	7 47	7 42	7 37	7 32	7 26	7 23	7 19
12	8 27	8 27	8 27	8 28	8 28	8 28	8 29	8 29	8 29	8 30	8 30	8 30	8 30	8 30
13	8 34	8 41	8 47	8 52	8 56	8 59	9 06	9 12	9 17	9 22	9 28	9 35	9 38	9 43
14	8 42	8 57	9 08	9 17	9 25	9 33	9 45	9 56	10 06	10 17	10 28	10 41	10 48	10 57
15	8 54	9 16	9 33	9 47	9 59	10 10	10 28	10 44	10 59	11 14	11 30	11 49	12 00	12 12
16	9 11	9 41	10 04	10 23	10 39	10 52	11 16	11 36	11 55	12 14	12 35	12 59	13 13	13 29
17	9 38	10 17	10 45	11 08	11 26	11 43	12 10	12 33	12 55	13 17	13 41	14 08	14 24	14 43

.. .. indicates phenomenon will occur the next day.

UNIVERSAL TIME FOR MERIDIAN OF GREENWICH

MOONRISE

Lat.	+40°	+42°	+44°	+46°	+48°	+50°	+52°	+54°	+56°	+58°	+60°	+62°	+64°	+66°
	h m	h m	h m	h m	h m	h m	h m	h m	h m	h m	h m	h m	h m	h m
July 24	4 02	3 54	3 45	3 36	3 26	3 15	3 02	2 48	2 31	2 10	1 44	1 07	□	□
25	5 16	5 09	5 03	4 56	4 48	4 39	4 29	4 18	4 06	3 51	3 34	3 13	2 45	2 05
26	6 28	6 23	6 18	6 13	6 08	6 02	5 55	5 47	5 39	5 29	5 18	5 06	4 50	4 31
27	7 36	7 33	7 30	7 27	7 24	7 20	7 16	7 12	7 07	7 01	6 55	6 48	6 39	6 29
28	8 41	8 40	8 39	8 37	8 36	8 35	8 33	8 31	8 29	8 27	8 25	8 22	8 19	8 15
29	9 43	9 44	9 44	9 45	9 46	9 46	9 47	9 48	9 49	9 50	9 51	9 52	9 54	9 55
30	10 45	10 47	10 49	10 51	10 54	10 57	11 00	11 03	11 07	11 11	11 15	11 21	11 27	11 34
31	11 46	11 49	11 53	11 57	12 02	12 07	12 12	12 18	12 25	12 32	12 41	12 51	13 02	13 16
Aug. 1	12 47	12 53	12 58	13 04	13 11	13 18	13 26	13 34	13 44	13 56	14 09	14 25	14 44	15 09
2	13 50	13 57	14 04	14 12	14 20	14 30	14 40	14 52	15 06	15 22	15 41	16 06	16 39	17 39
3	14 53	15 01	15 10	15 19	15 29	15 41	15 54	16 09	16 27	16 48	17 16	17 57	■	■
4	15 54	16 03	16 12	16 23	16 35	16 48	17 03	17 20	17 41	18 08	18 47	■	■	■
5	16 51	17 00	17 10	17 20	17 32	17 46	18 01	18 19	18 41	19 10	19 51	■	■	■
6	17 41	17 49	17 58	18 08	18 20	18 32	18 46	19 03	19 22	19 46	20 18	21 11	■	■
7	18 23	18 30	18 38	18 47	18 56	19 07	19 19	19 32	19 47	20 05	20 27	20 56	21 37	■
8	18 58	19 04	19 10	19 17	19 24	19 32	19 41	19 51	20 02	20 15	20 30	20 48	21 10	21 38
9	19 28	19 32	19 36	19 41	19 46	19 52	19 58	20 05	20 13	20 21	20 31	20 42	20 54	21 10
10	19 54	19 56	19 59	20 02	20 05	20 08	20 12	20 16	20 20	20 25	20 30	20 36	20 43	20 51
11	20 18	20 19	20 19	20 20	20 21	20 22	20 23	20 25	20 26	20 27	20 29	20 31	20 33	20 35
12	20 41	20 40	20 39	20 38	20 37	20 36	20 35	20 33	20 32	20 30	20 28	20 26	20 23	20 21
13	21 06	21 03	21 00	20 57	20 54	20 51	20 47	20 43	20 38	20 33	20 27	20 21	20 13	20 05
14	21 33	21 29	21 24	21 19	21 14	21 08	21 01	20 54	20 46	20 37	20 27	20 15	20 02	19 45
15	22 06	22 00	21 53	21 46	21 38	21 30	21 20	21 10	20 58	20 44	20 28	20 09	19 46	19 14
16	22 46	22 38	22 30	22 21	22 11	22 00	21 48	21 34	21 17	20 58	20 34	20 02	19 10	□
17	23 36	23 27	23 18	23 07	22 56	22 43	22 28	22 11	21 51	21 25	20 50	19 43	□	□

MOONSET

Lat.	+40°	+42°	+44°	+46°	+48°	+50°	+52°	+54°	+56°	+58°	+60°	+62°	+64°	+66°
	h m	h m	h m	h m	h m	h m	h m	h m	h m	h m	h m	h m	h m	h m
July 24	19 35	19 42	19 49	19 56	20 05	20 14	20 24	20 36	20 49	21 04	21 22	21 44	22 13	22 54
25	20 08	20 13	20 19	20 24	20 31	20 38	20 45	20 53	21 02	21 13	21 25	21 39	21 55	22 16
26	20 35	20 39	20 42	20 46	20 50	20 55	21 00	21 05	21 11	21 18	21 25	21 34	21 43	21 55
27	20 59	21 00	21 02	21 04	21 06	21 09	21 11	21 14	21 17	21 21	21 24	21 29	21 34	21 39
28	21 19	21 20	21 20	21 20	21 21	21 21	21 21	21 22	21 22	21 23	21 23	21 24	21 25	21 25
29	21 39	21 38	21 37	21 36	21 34	21 32	21 31	21 29	21 27	21 24	21 22	21 19	21 16	21 12
30	22 00	21 57	21 54	21 51	21 48	21 44	21 41	21 36	21 32	21 26	21 21	21 14	21 06	20 58
31	22 22	22 18	22 13	22 09	22 03	21 58	21 52	21 45	21 38	21 29	21 20	21 09	20 56	20 41
Aug. 1	22 47	22 41	22 35	22 29	22 22	22 14	22 06	21 56	21 46	21 34	21 20	21 03	20 43	20 17
2	23 17	23 10	23 02	22 54	22 45	22 35	22 24	22 12	21 58	21 41	21 21	20 56	20 22	19 22
3	23 53	23 45	23 36	23 27	23 16	23 04	22 51	22 35	22 17	21 55	21 27	20 45	■	■
4	.. ..	.. ..	.. ..	.. ..	23 57	23 44	23 29	23 11	22 50	22 22	21 44	■	■	■
5	0 38	0 29	0 19	0 09	.. ..	.. ..	.. ..	.. ..	23 42	23 14	22 32	■	■	■
6	1 32	1 23	1 13	1 03	0 51	0 37	0 22	0 04	.. ..	.. ..	.. ..	23 08	■	■
7	2 35	2 27	2 18	2 08	1 57	1 45	1 31	1 15	0 55	0 32	0 00	.. ..	■	■
8	3 44	3 37	3 29	3 21	3 12	3 02	2 50	2 38	2 23	2 05	1 44	1 16	0 35	■
9	4 55	4 50	4 44	4 38	4 31	4 23	4 15	4 06	3 56	3 44	3 30	3 13	2 52	2 25
10	6 07	6 04	6 00	5 56	5 51	5 46	5 41	5 35	5 28	5 21	5 13	5 03	4 51	4 37
11	7 19	7 17	7 15	7 13	7 11	7 09	7 06	7 03	7 00	6 57	6 53	6 48	6 43	6 37
12	8 30	8 30	8 31	8 31	8 31	8 31	8 31	8 31	8 31	8 31	8 31	8 32	8 32	8 32
13	9 43	9 45	9 47	9 49	9 51	9 54	9 57	10 00	10 03	10 07	10 11	10 16	10 22	10 28
14	10 57	11 00	11 04	11 09	11 14	11 19	11 24	11 31	11 38	11 46	11 55	12 05	12 17	12 32
15	12 12	12 18	12 24	12 31	12 38	12 46	12 55	13 04	13 15	13 28	13 43	14 01	14 24	14 55
16	13 29	13 36	13 44	13 53	14 03	14 13	14 25	14 39	14 55	15 13	15 37	16 08	16 59	□
17	14 43	14 52	15 01	15 11	15 23	15 35	15 50	16 07	16 27	16 52	17 27	18 34	□	□

□ indicates Moon continuously above horizon.
■ indicates Moon continuously below horizon.
.. .. indicates phenomenon will occur the next day.

UNIVERSAL TIME FOR MERIDIAN OF GREENWICH

MOONRISE

Lat.	−55°	−50°	−45°	−40°	−35°	−30°	−20°	−10°	0°	+10°	+20°	+30°	+35°	+40°
	h m	h m	h m	h m	h m	h m	h m	h m	h m	h m	h m	h m	h m	h m
Aug. 16	2 01	1 32	1 10	0 53	0 38	0 25	0 04	.. ..	.. ..	.. ..	23 44	23 18	23 03	22 46
17	3 36	2 58	2 30	2 09	1 51	1 35	1 09	0 47	0 26	0 06	.. ..	.. ..	23 56	23 36
18	4 59	4 15	3 44	3 20	3 00	2 43	2 15	1 50	1 27	1 05	0 40	0 12	.. ..	.. ..
19	6 00	5 17	4 46	4 22	4 02	3 45	3 17	2 52	2 29	2 07	1 42	1 13	0 57	0 37
20	6 37	6 01	5 34	5 12	4 55	4 39	4 13	3 51	3 30	3 09	2 46	2 19	2 04	1 46
21	6 59	6 31	6 10	5 53	5 38	5 25	5 03	4 44	4 26	4 08	3 49	3 26	3 13	2 58
22	7 13	6 53	6 37	6 24	6 13	6 03	5 47	5 32	5 18	5 04	4 49	4 32	4 22	4 10
23	7 22	7 10	6 59	6 51	6 43	6 36	6 25	6 15	6 05	5 56	5 46	5 34	5 27	5 19
24	7 29	7 23	7 18	7 13	7 09	7 06	7 00	6 55	6 50	6 45	6 39	6 33	6 30	6 26
25	7 35	7 35	7 34	7 34	7 33	7 33	7 32	7 32	7 31	7 31	7 30	7 30	7 30	7 29
26	7 41	7 46	7 50	7 54	7 57	7 59	8 04	8 08	8 12	8 16	8 20	8 25	8 28	8 31
27	7 47	7 58	8 07	8 14	8 21	8 26	8 36	8 45	8 53	9 01	9 10	9 20	9 26	9 33
28	7 55	8 12	8 25	8 37	8 46	8 55	9 10	9 23	9 35	9 47	10 00	10 16	10 24	10 35
29	8 05	8 29	8 47	9 02	9 15	9 26	9 46	10 03	10 19	10 35	10 52	11 12	11 24	11 37
30	8 20	8 50	9 14	9 33	9 48	10 02	10 26	10 46	11 05	11 24	11 45	12 09	12 23	12 40
31	8 42	9 20	9 48	10 09	10 28	10 43	11 10	11 33	11 55	12 16	12 39	13 07	13 23	13 41
Sept. 1	9 17	10 00	10 31	10 55	11 14	11 31	11 59	12 24	12 47	13 10	13 34	14 03	14 20	14 40
2	10 11	10 54	11 25	11 49	12 08	12 25	12 54	13 18	13 41	14 03	14 27	14 56	15 12	15 32
3	11 23	12 02	12 30	12 51	13 09	13 25	13 51	14 14	14 35	14 56	15 18	15 44	15 59	16 17
4	12 48	13 19	13 42	14 00	14 15	14 28	14 51	15 10	15 28	15 46	16 05	16 27	16 40	16 55
5	14 19	14 41	14 58	15 11	15 23	15 33	15 51	16 06	16 20	16 34	16 49	17 06	17 16	17 27
6	15 50	16 04	16 15	16 24	16 32	16 39	16 50	17 00	17 10	17 19	17 29	17 41	17 47	17 55
7	17 22	17 28	17 33	17 37	17 41	17 44	17 49	17 54	17 59	18 03	18 08	18 13	18 16	18 20
8	18 54	18 53	18 52	18 51	18 50	18 50	18 49	18 48	18 47	18 46	18 45	18 45	18 44	18 44
9	20 27	20 18	20 11	20 06	20 01	19 56	19 49	19 42	19 36	19 30	19 24	19 17	19 13	19 08

MOONSET

Lat.	−55°	−50°	−45°	−40°	−35°	−30°	−20°	−10°	0°	+10°	+20°	+30°	+35°	+40°
	h m	h m	h m	h m	h m	h m	h m	h m	h m	h m	h m	h m	h m	h m
Aug. 16	9 11	9 41	10 04	10 23	10 39	10 52	11 16	11 36	11 55	12 14	12 35	12 59	13 13	13 29
17	9 38	10 17	10 45	11 08	11 26	11 43	12 10	12 33	12 55	13 17	13 41	14 08	14 24	14 43
18	10 23	11 08	11 39	12 03	12 23	12 40	13 09	13 34	13 57	14 20	14 45	15 13	15 30	15 50
19	11 32	12 15	12 45	13 08	13 28	13 44	14 12	14 36	14 59	15 21	15 44	16 12	16 28	16 47
20	12 58	13 33	13 59	14 20	14 37	14 51	15 16	15 37	15 57	16 17	16 38	17 02	17 16	17 32
21	14 30	14 56	15 16	15 33	15 46	15 58	16 18	16 35	16 51	17 07	17 24	17 44	17 55	18 08
22	16 00	16 18	16 32	16 44	16 53	17 02	17 17	17 29	17 41	17 53	18 05	18 19	18 27	18 37
23	17 25	17 36	17 45	17 52	17 58	18 03	18 12	18 20	18 27	18 34	18 42	18 50	18 55	19 01
24	18 47	18 51	18 54	18 56	18 59	19 01	19 04	19 07	19 10	19 12	19 15	19 19	19 20	19 22
25	20 05	20 03	20 01	19 59	19 58	19 57	19 55	19 53	19 51	19 49	19 47	19 45	19 44	19 43
26	21 22	21 14	21 07	21 01	20 56	20 52	20 44	20 38	20 32	20 26	20 19	20 12	20 08	20 03
27	22 39	22 24	22 12	22 03	21 54	21 47	21 34	21 23	21 13	21 03	20 52	20 39	20 32	20 24
28	23 58	23 36	23 19	23 05	22 53	22 43	22 25	22 10	21 56	21 41	21 26	21 09	20 59	20 48
29	.. ..	.. ..	.. ..	.. ..	23 52	23 39	23 17	22 58	22 41	22 23	22 04	21 43	21 30	21 16
30	1 17	0 48	0 25	0 07	.. ..	.. ..	.. ..	23 49	23 29	23 08	22 46	22 21	22 06	21 49
31	2 35	1 58	1 31	1 10	0 52	0 37	0 11	.. ..	.. ..	23 57	23 33	23 05	22 49	22 30
Sept. 1	3 46	3 04	2 33	2 10	1 50	1 34	1 06	0 42	0 19	.. ..	.. ..	23 56	23 39	23 19
2	4 43	4 00	3 29	3 05	2 45	2 29	2 00	1 35	1 12	0 50	0 25	.. ..	.. ..	.. ..
3	5 24	4 45	4 16	3 54	3 35	3 19	2 52	2 29	2 07	1 45	1 21	0 53	0 37	0 18
4	5 50	5 18	4 55	4 35	4 19	4 05	3 41	3 20	3 01	2 41	2 20	1 55	1 40	1 23
5	6 07	5 44	5 25	5 10	4 57	4 46	4 26	4 09	3 53	3 37	3 20	2 59	2 47	2 34
6	6 19	6 03	5 50	5 40	5 30	5 22	5 08	4 56	4 44	4 32	4 19	4 05	3 56	3 46
7	6 28	6 19	6 12	6 06	6 00	5 56	5 47	5 40	5 33	5 26	5 19	5 10	5 05	4 59
8	6 36	6 33	6 32	6 30	6 29	6 27	6 25	6 23	6 21	6 20	6 18	6 15	6 14	6 12
9	6 43	6 47	6 51	6 54	6 57	6 59	7 03	7 07	7 10	7 13	7 17	7 21	7 23	7 26

.. .. indicates phenomenon will occur the next day.

UNIVERSAL TIME FOR MERIDIAN OF GREENWICH

MOONRISE

Lat.	+40°	+42°	+44°	+46°	+48°	+50°	+52°	+54°	+56°	+58°	+60°	+62°	+64°	+66°
	h m	h m	h m	h m	h m	h m	h m	h m	h m	h m	h m	h m	h m	h m
Aug. 16	22 46	22 38	22 30	22 21	22 11	22 00	21 48	21 34	21 17	20 58	20 34	20 02	19 10	▭
17	23 36	23 27	23 18	23 07	22 56	22 43	22 28	22 11	21 51	21 25	20 50	19 43	▭	▭
18	.. ..	.. ..	.. ..	.. ..	23 55	23 42	23 27	23 09	22 47	22 19	21 39	▭	▭	▭
19	0 37	0 28	0 18	0 07	.. ..	.. ..	.. ..	.. ..	.. ..	23 44	23 13	22 24	▭	▭
20	1 46	1 37	1 28	1 19	1 08	0 56	0 42	0 26	0 07	.. ..	.. ..	.. ..	23 58	▭
21	2 58	2 51	2 44	2 36	2 27	2 17	2 06	1 54	1 39	1 22	1 02	0 36	.. ..	▭
22	4 10	4 05	3 59	3 53	3 47	3 40	3 32	3 23	3 13	3 01	2 48	2 32	2 13	1 47
23	5 19	5 16	5 12	5 08	5 04	4 59	4 54	4 48	4 42	4 35	4 27	4 17	4 06	3 53
24	6 26	6 24	6 22	6 20	6 18	6 15	6 13	6 10	6 07	6 03	5 59	5 55	5 49	5 43
25	7 29	7 29	7 29	7 29	7 28	7 28	7 28	7 28	7 28	7 27	7 27	7 27	7 26	7 26
26	8 31	8 33	8 34	8 36	8 38	8 40	8 42	8 44	8 46	8 49	8 53	8 56	9 00	9 05
27	9 33	9 36	9 39	9 42	9 46	9 50	9 55	10 00	10 05	10 11	10 18	10 26	10 35	10 46
28	10 35	10 39	10 44	10 49	10 55	11 01	11 08	11 16	11 25	11 34	11 46	11 59	12 15	12 34
29	11 37	11 43	11 50	11 57	12 05	12 13	12 23	12 33	12 46	13 00	13 17	13 37	14 04	14 42
30	12 40	12 47	12 55	13 04	13 14	13 25	13 37	13 51	14 07	14 26	14 51	15 24	16 23	▬
31	13 41	13 50	13 59	14 09	14 21	14 33	14 48	15 05	15 25	15 50	16 25	17 33	▬	▬
Sept. 1	14 40	14 49	14 59	15 09	15 21	15 35	15 51	16 09	16 31	17 00	17 43	▬	▬	▬
2	15 32	15 41	15 50	16 01	16 13	16 26	16 41	16 58	17 19	17 46	18 24	▬	▬	▬
3	16 17	16 25	16 34	16 43	16 53	17 05	17 18	17 33	17 50	18 11	18 37	19 14	20 40	▬
4	16 55	17 02	17 09	17 16	17 25	17 34	17 44	17 56	18 09	18 24	18 42	19 04	19 32	20 14
5	17 27	17 32	17 37	17 43	17 49	17 56	18 03	18 11	18 21	18 31	18 43	18 57	19 13	19 33
6	17 55	17 58	18 01	18 05	18 09	18 13	18 18	18 23	18 29	18 35	18 43	18 51	19 00	19 11
7	18 20	18 21	18 23	18 24	18 26	18 28	18 30	18 33	18 35	18 38	18 42	18 45	18 49	18 54
8	18 44	18 43	18 43	18 43	18 43	18 42	18 42	18 42	18 41	18 41	18 40	18 40	18 39	18 39
9	19 08	19 06	19 04	19 02	18 59	18 57	18 54	18 51	18 47	18 44	18 39	18 35	18 29	18 23

MOONSET

Lat.	+40°	+42°	+44°	+46°	+48°	+50°	+52°	+54°	+56°	+58°	+60°	+62°	+64°	+66°
	h m	h m	h m	h m	h m	h m	h m	h m	h m	h m	h m	h m	h m	h m
Aug. 16	13 29	13 36	13 44	13 53	14 03	14 13	14 25	14 39	14 55	15 13	15 37	16 08	16 59	▭
17	14 43	14 52	15 01	15 11	15 23	15 35	15 50	16 07	16 27	16 52	17 27	18 34	▭	▭
18	15 50	15 59	16 09	16 20	16 32	16 45	17 01	17 19	17 40	18 08	18 48	▭	▭	▭
19	16 47	16 55	17 04	17 14	17 26	17 38	17 52	18 08	18 27	18 51	19 22	20 12	▭	▭
20	17 32	17 39	17 47	17 56	18 05	18 15	18 27	18 40	18 54	19 12	19 33	20 00	20 38	▭
21	18 08	18 13	18 20	18 26	18 33	18 41	18 50	18 59	19 10	19 22	19 37	19 53	20 14	20 40
22	18 37	18 41	18 45	18 50	18 55	19 00	19 06	19 13	19 20	19 28	19 37	19 48	20 00	20 15
23	19 01	19 03	19 06	19 09	19 12	19 15	19 19	19 22	19 27	19 31	19 37	19 43	19 49	19 57
24	19 22	19 23	19 24	19 25	19 26	19 28	19 29	19 30	19 32	19 34	19 35	19 38	19 40	19 43
25	19 43	19 42	19 41	19 41	19 40	19 39	19 38	19 37	19 36	19 35	19 34	19 33	19 31	19 29
26	20 03	20 01	19 59	19 56	19 54	19 51	19 48	19 45	19 41	19 37	19 32	19 27	19 22	19 15
27	20 24	20 21	20 17	20 13	20 08	20 04	19 58	19 53	19 46	19 39	19 31	19 22	19 12	18 59
28	20 48	20 43	20 37	20 32	20 25	20 18	20 11	20 03	19 53	19 43	19 31	19 16	18 59	18 39
29	21 16	21 09	21 02	20 55	20 46	20 37	20 27	20 16	20 03	19 49	19 31	19 10	18 42	18 03
30	21 49	21 41	21 33	21 24	21 14	21 02	20 50	20 36	20 19	19 59	19 34	19 01	18 01	▬
31	22 30	22 21	22 11	22 01	21 50	21 37	21 22	21 05	20 45	20 19	19 44	18 36	▬	▬
Sept. 1	23 19	23 10	23 00	22 49	22 37	22 24	22 08	21 50	21 27	20 59	20 16	▬	▬	▬
2	.. ..	.. ..	23 59	23 49	23 37	23 24	23 10	22 52	22 31	22 05	21 28	▬	▬	▬
3	0 18	0 09	.. ..	.. ..	.. ..	.. ..	.. ..	.. ..	23 53	23 33	23 07	22 30	21 05	▬
4	1 23	1 16	1 07	0 58	0 48	0 37	0 25	0 10	.. ..	.. ..	.. ..	.. ..	.. ..	23 23
5	2 34	2 28	2 21	2 14	2 06	1 57	1 48	1 37	1 24	1 10	0 53	0 31	0 04	.. ..
6	3 46	3 42	3 37	3 32	3 26	3 20	3 14	3 06	2 58	2 49	2 38	2 25	2 10	1 51
7	4 59	4 56	4 54	4 51	4 48	4 44	4 40	4 36	4 32	4 26	4 20	4 14	4 06	3 57
8	6 12	6 12	6 11	6 10	6 09	6 08	6 07	6 06	6 05	6 03	6 02	6 00	5 58	5 56
9	7 26	7 27	7 29	7 30	7 31	7 33	7 35	7 37	7 39	7 41	7 44	7 47	7 50	7 54

▭ indicates Moon continuously above horizon.
▬ indicates Moon continuously below horizon.
.. .. indicates phenomenon will occur the next day.

UNIVERSAL TIME FOR MERIDIAN OF GREENWICH

MOONRISE

Lat.	−55°	−50°	−45°	−40°	−35°	−30°	−20°	−10°	0°	+10°	+20°	+30°	+35°	+40°
	h m	h m	h m	h m	h m	h m	h m	h m	h m	h m	h m	h m	h m	h m
Sept. 8	18 54	18 53	18 52	18 51	18 50	18 50	18 49	18 48	18 47	18 46	18 45	18 45	18 44	18 44
9	20 27	20 18	20 11	20 06	20 01	19 56	19 49	19 42	19 36	19 30	19 24	19 17	19 13	19 08
10	22 03	21 46	21 33	21 22	21 13	21 05	20 51	20 39	20 28	20 17	20 05	19 52	19 44	19 35
11	23 43	23 16	22 56	22 40	22 27	22 15	21 55	21 38	21 22	21 06	20 50	20 31	20 19	20 07
12	.. ..	.. ..	.. ..	23 58	23 41	23 27	23 02	22 40	22 20	22 01	21 40	21 15	21 01	20 45
13	1 21	0 45	0 19	.. ..	.. ..	.. ..	.. ..	23 44	23 21	22 59	22 35	22 08	21 51	21 33
14	2 50	2 07	1 36	1 12	0 53	0 36	0 08	.. ..	.. ..	.. ..	23 36	23 07	22 50	22 30
15	3 57	3 13	2 42	2 17	1 57	1 40	1 11	0 46	0 23	0 00	.. ..	.. ..	23 55	23 36
16	4 40	4 01	3 33	3 11	2 52	2 36	2 09	1 46	1 24	1 02	0 39	0 11	.. ..	.. ..
17	5 06	4 35	4 12	3 53	3 37	3 24	3 00	2 40	2 21	2 02	1 41	1 17	1 03	0 47
18	5 21	4 59	4 41	4 27	4 14	4 04	3 45	3 29	3 13	2 58	2 41	2 22	2 11	1 58
19	5 32	5 17	5 04	4 54	4 45	4 38	4 24	4 12	4 01	3 50	3 38	3 24	3 16	3 07
20	5 39	5 31	5 23	5 17	5 12	5 07	4 59	4 52	4 46	4 39	4 32	4 24	4 19	4 13
21	5 46	5 43	5 40	5 38	5 37	5 35	5 32	5 30	5 28	5 26	5 23	5 21	5 19	5 17
22	5 51	5 54	5 56	5 58	6 00	6 01	6 04	6 06	6 09	6 11	6 13	6 16	6 18	6 19
23	5 57	6 06	6 13	6 18	6 23	6 28	6 36	6 43	6 49	6 56	7 03	7 11	7 16	7 21
24	6 04	6 19	6 30	6 40	6 48	6 56	7 09	7 20	7 31	7 41	7 53	8 06	8 14	8 23
25	6 13	6 34	6 51	7 04	7 16	7 26	7 44	7 59	8 14	8 28	8 44	9 02	9 13	9 25
26	6 26	6 54	7 15	7 32	7 47	8 00	8 22	8 41	8 59	9 17	9 37	9 59	10 12	10 28
27	6 45	7 20	7 46	8 06	8 24	8 39	9 04	9 26	9 47	10 08	10 30	10 56	11 12	11 30
28	7 14	7 55	8 25	8 48	9 07	9 23	9 51	10 15	10 38	11 00	11 24	11 53	12 09	12 29
29	7 59	8 43	9 14	9 38	9 57	10 14	10 43	11 07	11 30	11 53	12 18	12 46	13 03	13 23
30	9 02	9 43	10 13	10 36	10 54	11 11	11 38	12 01	12 23	12 45	13 08	13 36	13 52	14 10
Oct. 1	10 21	10 55	11 20	11 40	11 57	12 11	12 35	12 56	13 16	13 35	13 56	14 20	14 34	14 50
2	11 47	12 13	12 33	12 49	13 02	13 14	13 34	13 51	14 07	14 23	14 40	15 00	15 11	15 24

MOONSET

Lat.	−55°	−50°	−45°	−40°	−35°	−30°	−20°	−10°	0°	+10°	+20°	+30°	+35°	+40°
	h m	h m	h m	h m	h m	h m	h m	h m	h m	h m	h m	h m	h m	h m
Sept. 8	6 36	6 33	6 32	6 30	6 29	6 27	6 25	6 23	6 21	6 20	6 18	6 15	6 14	6 12
9	6 43	6 47	6 51	6 54	6 57	6 59	7 03	7 07	7 10	7 13	7 17	7 21	7 23	7 26
10	6 51	7 03	7 12	7 20	7 26	7 32	7 43	7 52	8 00	8 09	8 18	8 29	8 35	8 42
11	7 01	7 21	7 36	7 49	7 59	8 09	8 25	8 40	8 53	9 07	9 21	9 38	9 48	9 59
12	7 16	7 44	8 06	8 23	8 38	8 50	9 12	9 32	9 49	10 07	10 27	10 49	11 02	11 18
13	7 40	8 17	8 44	9 06	9 23	9 39	10 05	10 28	10 49	11 10	11 33	12 00	12 16	12 34
14	8 19	9 03	9 34	9 58	10 18	10 35	11 04	11 28	11 51	12 14	12 39	13 07	13 24	13 44
15	9 21	10 05	10 36	11 00	11 20	11 37	12 06	12 30	12 53	13 15	13 40	14 08	14 24	14 44
16	10 42	11 20	11 48	12 09	12 27	12 43	13 09	13 31	13 52	14 12	14 34	15 00	15 14	15 32
17	12 12	12 41	13 03	13 21	13 36	13 49	14 10	14 29	14 46	15 04	15 22	15 43	15 55	16 09
18	13 41	14 02	14 18	14 32	14 43	14 52	15 09	15 23	15 37	15 50	16 04	16 20	16 29	16 40
19	15 07	15 20	15 31	15 39	15 47	15 53	16 04	16 14	16 23	16 32	16 41	16 52	16 58	17 05
20	16 29	16 35	16 40	16 44	16 48	16 51	16 57	17 02	17 06	17 11	17 15	17 20	17 23	17 27
21	17 47	17 47	17 47	17 47	17 47	17 47	17 47	17 47	17 47	17 47	17 47	17 47	17 47	17 47
22	19 04	18 58	18 53	18 49	18 46	18 42	18 37	18 32	18 28	18 24	18 19	18 14	18 11	18 07
23	20 21	20 09	19 59	19 51	19 44	19 38	19 27	19 18	19 09	19 00	18 51	18 41	18 35	18 28
24	21 40	21 20	21 05	20 53	20 42	20 33	20 17	20 04	19 51	19 38	19 25	19 10	19 01	18 51
25	22 59	22 32	22 12	21 55	21 42	21 30	21 09	20 52	20 35	20 19	20 01	19 42	19 30	19 17
26	.. ..	23 43	23 18	22 58	22 41	22 27	22 02	21 41	21 22	21 02	20 42	20 18	20 04	19 48
27	0 17	.. ..	.. ..	23 59	23 40	23 24	22 56	22 33	22 11	21 50	21 26	20 59	20 43	20 25
28	1 31	0 51	0 21	.. ..	.. ..	.. ..	23 50	23 26	23 03	22 40	22 16	21 47	21 30	21 10
29	2 34	1 50	1 19	0 55	0 36	0 19	.. ..	.. ..	23 56	23 33	23 09	22 41	22 24	22 04
30	3 20	2 39	2 09	1 46	1 27	1 10	0 42	0 18	.. ..	.. ..	.. ..	23 39	23 24	23 06
Oct. 1	3 52	3 16	2 50	2 30	2 12	1 57	1 32	1 09	0 49	0 28	0 05	.. ..	.. ..	.. ..
2	4 12	3 44	3 23	3 06	2 52	2 39	2 17	1 59	1 41	1 23	1 04	0 41	0 28	0 13

.. .. indicates phenomenon will occur the next day.

UNIVERSAL TIME FOR MERIDIAN OF GREENWICH

MOONRISE

Lat.	+40°	+42°	+44°	+46°	+48°	+50°	+52°	+54°	+56°	+58°	+60°	+62°	+64°	+66°
	h m	h m	h m	h m	h m	h m	h m	h m	h m	h m	h m	h m	h m	h m
Sept. 8	18 44	18 43	18 43	18 43	18 43	18 42	18 42	18 42	18 41	18 41	18 40	18 40	18 39	18 39
9	19 08	19 06	19 04	19 02	18 59	18 57	18 54	18 51	18 47	18 44	18 39	18 35	18 29	18 23
10	19 35	19 32	19 28	19 23	19 18	19 13	19 08	19 02	18 55	18 48	18 39	18 29	18 18	18 05
11	20 07	20 01	19 55	19 49	19 42	19 34	19 26	19 16	19 06	18 54	18 40	18 23	18 04	17 39
12	20 45	20 38	20 30	20 21	20 12	20 02	19 50	19 37	19 22	19 05	18 43	18 16	17 38	▭
13	21 33	21 24	21 15	21 05	20 53	20 41	20 27	20 10	19 51	19 27	18 55	18 03	▭	▭
14	22 30	22 21	22 11	22 00	21 48	21 35	21 19	21 01	20 39	20 11	19 31	▭	▭	▭
15	23 36	23 28	23 18	23 08	22 57	22 44	22 29	22 13	21 53	21 27	20 53	19 47	▭	▭
16	.. ..	.. ..	.. ..	.. ..	.. ..	.. ..	23 51	23 37	23 21	23 02	22 39	22 07	21 15	▭
17	0 47	0 40	0 32	0 23	0 13	0 03	.. ..	.. ..	.. ..	.. ..	.. ..	.. ..	23 42	23 10
18	1 58	1 52	1 46	1 39	1 32	1 24	1 15	1 05	0 53	0 40	0 25	0 06	.. ..	.. ..
19	3 07	3 03	2 59	2 54	2 49	2 43	2 37	2 30	2 23	2 14	2 04	1 53	1 39	1 23
20	4 13	4 11	4 08	4 06	4 03	4 00	3 56	3 52	3 48	3 43	3 37	3 31	3 24	3 16
21	5 17	5 16	5 16	5 15	5 14	5 13	5 12	5 10	5 09	5 08	5 06	5 04	5 02	4 59
22	6 19	6 20	6 21	6 22	6 23	6 24	6 25	6 27	6 28	6 30	6 31	6 34	6 36	6 39
23	7 21	7 23	7 26	7 29	7 32	7 35	7 38	7 42	7 46	7 51	7 57	8 03	8 10	8 19
24	8 23	8 27	8 31	8 35	8 40	8 46	8 52	8 58	9 06	9 14	9 23	9 34	9 48	10 03
25	9 25	9 31	9 37	9 43	9 50	9 58	10 06	10 16	10 26	10 39	10 53	11 10	11 32	12 01
26	10 28	10 35	10 42	10 50	10 59	11 09	11 20	11 33	11 48	12 05	12 26	12 53	13 33	▬
27	11 30	11 38	11 47	11 57	12 07	12 19	12 33	12 49	13 07	13 30	14 00	14 48	▬	▬
28	12 29	12 38	12 48	12 58	13 10	13 23	13 39	13 57	14 18	14 46	15 26	▬	▬	▬
29	13 23	13 32	13 42	13 53	14 05	14 18	14 33	14 51	15 13	15 41	16 22	▬	▬	▬
30	14 10	14 19	14 28	14 38	14 49	15 01	15 15	15 31	15 50	16 14	16 45	17 33	▬	▬
Oct. 1	14 50	14 57	15 05	15 14	15 23	15 33	15 45	15 58	16 13	16 30	16 52	17 19	17 58	▬
2	15 24	15 30	15 36	15 43	15 50	15 58	16 06	16 16	16 27	16 40	16 54	17 11	17 33	18 00

MOONSET

Lat.	+40°	+42°	+44°	+46°	+48°	+50°	+52°	+54°	+56°	+58°	+60°	+62°	+64°	+66°
	h m	h m	h m	h m	h m	h m	h m	h m	h m	h m	h m	h m	h m	h m
Sept. 8	6 12	6 12	6 11	6 10	6 09	6 08	6 07	6 06	6 05	6 03	6 02	6 00	5 58	5 56
9	7 26	7 27	7 29	7 30	7 31	7 33	7 35	7 37	7 39	7 41	7 44	7 47	7 50	7 54
10	8 42	8 45	8 48	8 52	8 56	9 00	9 04	9 10	9 15	9 22	9 29	9 37	9 47	9 58
11	9 59	10 04	10 10	10 16	10 22	10 29	10 37	10 45	10 55	11 06	11 19	11 34	11 53	12 17
12	11 18	11 25	11 32	11 40	11 49	11 59	12 10	12 22	12 37	12 53	13 14	13 40	14 18	▭
13	12 34	12 42	12 51	13 01	13 12	13 25	13 38	13 55	14 14	14 37	15 09	16 00	▭	▭
14	13 44	13 53	14 03	14 14	14 26	14 39	14 55	15 13	15 34	16 02	16 43	▭	▭	▭
15	14 44	14 52	15 02	15 12	15 24	15 37	15 51	16 08	16 29	16 54	17 29	18 36	▭	▭
16	15 32	15 39	15 48	15 57	16 07	16 18	16 30	16 44	17 00	17 20	17 44	18 16	19 09	▭
17	16 09	16 16	16 22	16 30	16 37	16 46	16 56	17 06	17 18	17 32	17 49	18 08	18 33	19 07
18	16 40	16 44	16 49	16 55	17 00	17 07	17 13	17 21	17 30	17 39	17 50	18 02	18 17	18 35
19	17 05	17 08	17 11	17 15	17 18	17 22	17 27	17 32	17 37	17 43	17 49	17 57	18 06	18 16
20	17 27	17 28	17 30	17 32	17 33	17 35	17 38	17 40	17 42	17 45	17 48	17 52	17 56	18 01
21	17 47	17 47	17 47	17 47	17 47	17 47	17 47	17 47	17 47	17 47	17 47	17 47	17 47	17 47
22	18 07	18 06	18 04	18 02	18 01	17 59	17 56	17 54	17 51	17 49	17 45	17 42	17 38	17 33
23	18 28	18 25	18 22	18 18	18 15	18 11	18 06	18 02	17 56	17 51	17 44	17 37	17 28	17 18
24	18 51	18 46	18 41	18 36	18 31	18 25	18 18	18 11	18 03	17 54	17 43	17 31	17 17	17 00
25	19 17	19 11	19 04	18 58	18 50	18 42	18 33	18 23	18 11	17 58	17 43	17 25	17 02	16 33
26	19 48	19 40	19 32	19 24	19 15	19 04	18 53	18 40	18 24	18 07	17 45	17 17	16 37	▬
27	20 25	20 17	20 07	19 58	19 47	19 34	19 20	19 04	18 46	18 22	17 52	17 04	▬	▬
28	21 10	21 01	20 51	20 41	20 29	20 15	20 00	19 42	19 20	18 52	18 12	▬	▬	▬
29	22 04	21 55	21 45	21 35	21 23	21 09	20 54	20 36	20 14	19 46	19 05	▬	▬	▬
30	23 06	22 57	22 49	22 39	22 28	22 16	22 02	21 47	21 28	21 05	20 34	19 46	▬	▬
Oct. 1	.. ..	.. ..	23 58	23 50	23 41	23 31	23 20	23 08	22 53	22 36	22 16	21 49	21 11	▬
2	0 13	0 06	.. ..	.. ..	.. ..	.. ..	.. ..	.. ..	.. ..	.. ..	23 59	23 43	23 23	22 57

▭ indicates Moon continuously above horizon.
▬ indicates Moon continuously below horizon.
.. .. indicates phenomenon will occur the next day.

UNIVERSAL TIME FOR MERIDIAN OF GREENWICH

MOONRISE

Lat.	−55°	−50°	−45°	−40°	−35°	−30°	−20°	−10°	0°	+10°	+20°	+30°	+35°	+40°
	h m	h m	h m	h m	h m	h m	h m	h m	h m	h m	h m	h m	h m	h m
Oct. 1	10 21	10 55	11 20	11 40	11 57	12 11	12 35	12 56	13 16	13 35	13 56	14 20	14 34	14 50
2	11 47	12 13	12 33	12 49	13 02	13 14	13 34	13 51	14 07	14 23	14 40	15 00	15 11	15 24
3	13 17	13 35	13 49	14 00	14 10	14 18	14 33	14 45	14 57	15 09	15 21	15 36	15 44	15 53
4	14 48	14 58	15 06	15 12	15 18	15 23	15 31	15 39	15 46	15 53	16 00	16 09	16 13	16 19
5	16 19	16 22	16 24	16 26	16 27	16 28	16 31	16 33	16 34	16 36	16 38	16 41	16 42	16 43
6	17 53	17 48	17 44	17 40	17 38	17 35	17 31	17 27	17 24	17 20	17 17	17 13	17 11	17 08
7	19 30	19 17	19 07	18 58	18 51	18 44	18 33	18 24	18 15	18 07	17 57	17 47	17 41	17 34
8	21 11	20 49	20 32	20 18	20 06	19 56	19 39	19 24	19 10	18 56	18 42	18 25	18 16	18 05
9	22 54	22 22	21 59	21 40	21 24	21 10	20 47	20 27	20 09	19 51	19 31	19 09	18 56	18 41
10	.. ..	23 50	23 21	22 58	22 39	22 23	21 56	21 33	21 11	20 50	20 27	20 00	19 45	19 27
11	0 31	.. ..	.. ..	.. ..	23 49	23 32	23 03	22 38	22 15	21 52	21 28	20 59	20 42	20 22
12	1 49	1 05	0 33	0 09	.. ..	.. ..	.. ..	23 40	23 18	22 55	22 31	22 03	21 47	21 27
13	2 41	2 00	1 31	1 07	0 48	0 32	0 04	.. ..	.. ..	23 57	23 35	23 10	22 55	22 38
14	3 11	2 38	2 13	1 54	1 37	1 23	0 58	0 37	0 17	.. ..	.. ..	.. ..	.. ..	23 50
15	3 29	3 05	2 45	2 30	2 16	2 05	1 44	1 27	1 10	0 54	0 36	0 16	0 04	.. ..
16	3 41	3 24	3 10	2 58	2 49	2 40	2 25	2 12	1 59	1 47	1 34	1 18	1 09	0 59
17	3 49	3 39	3 30	3 23	3 16	3 11	3 01	2 53	2 44	2 36	2 28	2 18	2 12	2 05
18	3 56	3 51	3 47	3 44	3 41	3 39	3 34	3 30	3 27	3 23	3 19	3 15	3 12	3 09
19	4 02	4 03	4 03	4 04	4 04	4 05	4 06	4 07	4 07	4 08	4 09	4 10	4 10	4 11
20	4 08	4 14	4 19	4 24	4 28	4 31	4 37	4 42	4 47	4 53	4 58	5 04	5 08	5 12
21	4 14	4 27	4 36	4 45	4 52	4 58	5 09	5 19	5 28	5 38	5 48	5 59	6 06	6 13
22	4 22	4 41	4 56	5 08	5 18	5 28	5 43	5 57	6 11	6 24	6 38	6 55	7 04	7 15
23	4 34	4 59	5 19	5 35	5 48	6 00	6 21	6 38	6 55	7 12	7 30	7 51	8 04	8 18
24	4 50	5 23	5 47	6 07	6 23	6 37	7 02	7 23	7 42	8 02	8 24	8 48	9 03	9 20
25	5 16	5 55	6 23	6 45	7 04	7 20	7 47	8 10	8 32	8 54	9 17	9 45	10 01	10 20

MOONSET

Lat.	−55°	−50°	−45°	−40°	−35°	−30°	−20°	−10°	0°	+10°	+20°	+30°	+35°	+40°
	h m	h m	h m	h m	h m	h m	h m	h m	h m	h m	h m	h m	h m	h m
Oct. 1	3 52	3 16	2 50	2 30	2 12	1 57	1 32	1 09	0 49	0 28	0 05	.. ..	.. ..	.. ..
2	4 12	3 44	3 23	3 06	2 52	2 39	2 17	1 59	1 41	1 23	1 04	0 41	0 28	0 13
3	4 25	4 06	3 50	3 37	3 26	3 17	3 00	2 45	2 31	2 17	2 02	1 45	1 35	1 23
4	4 36	4 23	4 13	4 05	3 57	3 51	3 40	3 30	3 20	3 11	3 01	2 49	2 42	2 34
5	4 44	4 38	4 33	4 30	4 26	4 23	4 18	4 13	4 09	4 04	4 00	3 54	3 51	3 47
6	4 51	4 52	4 53	4 54	4 54	4 55	4 56	4 57	4 58	4 58	4 59	5 00	5 00	5 01
7	4 59	5 07	5 14	5 19	5 24	5 28	5 35	5 42	5 48	5 54	6 00	6 08	6 12	6 17
8	5 09	5 24	5 37	5 47	5 56	6 04	6 17	6 29	6 41	6 52	7 04	7 18	7 26	7 36
9	5 22	5 46	6 05	6 20	6 33	6 44	7 04	7 21	7 37	7 54	8 11	8 31	8 43	8 57
10	5 42	6 16	6 41	7 01	7 17	7 32	7 57	8 18	8 38	8 58	9 20	9 45	10 00	10 17
11	6 16	6 58	7 28	7 51	8 10	8 27	8 55	9 19	9 42	10 04	10 28	10 57	11 13	11 33
12	7 11	7 56	8 28	8 52	9 12	9 29	9 58	10 22	10 45	11 08	11 33	12 01	12 18	12 38
13	8 29	9 09	9 38	10 00	10 19	10 35	11 02	11 25	11 46	12 08	12 30	12 57	13 12	13 30
14	9 58	10 30	10 53	11 12	11 28	11 42	12 05	12 25	12 43	13 01	13 21	13 43	13 56	14 11
15	11 28	11 51	12 09	12 23	12 35	12 46	13 04	13 20	13 34	13 49	14 04	14 22	14 32	14 43
16	12 54	13 09	13 21	13 31	13 40	13 47	14 00	14 11	14 21	14 32	14 42	14 55	15 02	15 10
17	14 16	14 24	14 31	14 36	14 41	14 45	14 53	14 59	15 05	15 11	15 17	15 24	15 28	15 32
18	15 34	15 36	15 38	15 39	15 40	15 41	15 43	15 45	15 46	15 48	15 49	15 51	15 52	15 53
19	16 50	16 46	16 43	16 40	16 38	16 36	16 33	16 29	16 27	16 24	16 21	16 17	16 15	16 13
20	18 07	17 56	17 48	17 42	17 36	17 31	17 22	17 14	17 07	17 00	16 52	16 44	16 39	16 33
21	19 24	19 07	18 54	18 43	18 34	18 26	18 12	18 00	17 48	17 37	17 25	17 12	17 04	16 55
22	20 43	20 19	20 00	19 45	19 33	19 22	19 03	18 47	18 32	18 17	18 01	17 43	17 32	17 20
23	22 02	21 30	21 07	20 48	20 32	20 19	19 56	19 36	19 18	18 59	18 40	18 17	18 04	17 49
24	23 17	22 39	22 11	21 49	21 31	21 16	20 50	20 27	20 06	19 45	19 23	18 57	18 42	18 24
25	.. ..	23 41	23 11	22 47	22 28	22 11	21 43	21 19	20 57	20 34	20 10	19 42	19 26	19 06

.. .. indicates phenomenon will occur the next day.

UNIVERSAL TIME FOR MERIDIAN OF GREENWICH

MOONRISE

Lat.	+40°	+42°	+44°	+46°	+48°	+50°	+52°	+54°	+56°	+58°	+60°	+62°	+64°	+66°
	h m	h m	h m	h m	h m	h m	h m	h m	h m	h m	h m	h m	h m	h m
Oct. 1	14 50	14 57	15 05	15 14	15 23	15 33	15 45	15 58	16 13	16 30	16 52	17 19	17 58	▬
2	15 24	15 30	15 36	15 43	15 50	15 58	16 06	16 16	16 27	16 40	16 54	17 11	17 33	18 00
3	15 53	15 57	16 01	16 06	16 11	16 17	16 23	16 29	16 37	16 45	16 54	17 05	17 18	17 33
4	16 19	16 21	16 24	16 27	16 30	16 33	16 36	16 40	16 44	16 49	16 54	17 00	17 06	17 14
5	16 43	16 44	16 45	16 46	16 46	16 47	16 48	16 49	16 50	16 52	16 53	16 54	16 56	16 58
6	17 08	17 07	17 06	17 04	17 03	17 02	17 00	16 58	16 56	16 54	16 52	16 49	16 46	16 43
7	17 34	17 31	17 28	17 25	17 21	17 17	17 13	17 09	17 03	16 58	16 51	16 44	16 36	16 26
8	18 05	18 00	17 55	17 49	17 43	17 37	17 30	17 22	17 13	17 03	16 52	16 39	16 23	16 05
9	18 41	18 35	18 27	18 20	18 11	18 02	17 52	17 40	17 27	17 12	16 54	16 33	16 05	15 25
10	19 27	19 18	19 10	19 00	18 49	18 38	18 24	18 09	17 52	17 30	17 03	16 24	▭	▭
11	20 22	20 13	20 04	19 53	19 41	19 28	19 13	18 55	18 34	18 07	17 28	▭	▭	▭
12	21 27	21 19	21 09	20 59	20 47	20 34	20 19	20 02	19 41	19 14	18 37	▭	▭	▭
13	22 38	22 30	22 22	22 13	22 03	21 51	21 39	21 24	21 07	20 46	20 20	19 42	▭	▭
14	23 50	23 43	23 37	23 29	23 21	23 13	23 03	22 52	22 39	22 24	22 07	21 45	21 17	20 35
15	.. ..	.. ..	.. ..	.. ..	.. ..	.. ..	.. ..	.. ..	.. ..	23 59	23 48	23 34	23 18	22 59
16	0 59	0 55	0 50	0 44	0 39	0 32	0 25	0 18	0 09	.. ..	.. ..	.. ..	.. ..	.. ..
17	2 05	2 03	1 59	1 56	1 53	1 49	1 44	1 40	1 34	1 28	1 22	1 14	1 05	0 54
18	3 09	3 08	3 06	3 05	3 03	3 02	3 00	2 58	2 55	2 53	2 50	2 47	2 43	2 39
19	4 11	4 11	4 12	4 12	4 12	4 13	4 13	4 13	4 14	4 15	4 15	4 16	4 17	4 18
20	5 12	5 14	5 16	5 18	5 20	5 23	5 25	5 28	5 32	5 35	5 39	5 44	5 50	5 56
21	6 13	6 17	6 20	6 24	6 28	6 33	6 38	6 44	6 50	6 57	7 05	7 14	7 25	7 38
22	7 15	7 20	7 25	7 31	7 37	7 44	7 52	8 00	8 10	8 20	8 33	8 48	9 06	9 28
23	8 18	8 24	8 31	8 39	8 47	8 56	9 06	9 18	9 31	9 46	10 04	10 27	10 58	11 46
24	9 20	9 28	9 36	9 45	9 55	10 07	10 19	10 34	10 51	11 12	11 38	12 15	▬	▬
25	10 20	10 29	10 38	10 49	11 00	11 13	11 28	11 45	12 05	12 31	13 07	14 37	▬	▬

MOONSET

Lat.	+40°	+42°	+44°	+46°	+48°	+50°	+52°	+54°	+56°	+58°	+60°	+62°	+64°	+66°
	h m	h m	h m	h m	h m	h m	h m	h m	h m	h m	h m	h m	h m	h m
Oct. 1	.. ..	.. ..	23 58	23 50	23 41	23 31	23 20	23 08	22 53	22 36	22 16	21 49	21 11	▬
2	0 13	0 06	.. ..	.. ..	.. ..	.. ..	.. ..	.. ..	.. ..	.. ..	23 59	23 43	23 23	22 57
3	1 23	1 18	1 12	1 06	0 59	0 52	0 44	0 35	0 24	0 13	.. ..	.. ..	.. ..	.. ..
4	2 34	2 31	2 27	2 23	2 19	2 14	2 09	2 03	1 57	1 50	1 41	1 32	1 21	1 07
5	3 47	3 45	3 44	3 42	3 40	3 38	3 35	3 32	3 30	3 26	3 23	3 18	3 13	3 08
6	5 01	5 01	5 01	5 02	5 02	5 02	5 03	5 03	5 03	5 04	5 04	5 05	5 06	5 07
7	6 17	6 19	6 22	6 24	6 27	6 30	6 33	6 36	6 40	6 45	6 50	6 55	7 02	7 09
8	7 36	7 40	7 44	7 49	7 54	8 00	8 06	8 13	8 21	8 30	8 40	8 52	9 06	9 23
9	8 57	9 03	9 10	9 17	9 25	9 33	9 43	9 54	10 06	10 20	10 37	10 58	11 25	12 04
10	10 17	10 25	10 34	10 43	10 53	11 05	11 17	11 32	11 50	12 11	12 37	13 15	▭	▭
11	11 33	11 42	11 51	12 02	12 13	12 27	12 42	12 59	13 21	13 47	14 25	▭	▭	▭
12	12 38	12 47	12 56	13 07	13 19	13 32	13 47	14 05	14 26	14 52	15 30	▭	▭	▭
13	13 30	13 38	13 47	13 56	14 07	14 19	14 32	14 47	15 04	15 25	15 52	16 30	▭	▭
14	14 11	14 18	14 25	14 33	14 41	14 51	15 01	15 13	15 26	15 41	15 59	16 22	16 51	17 34
15	14 43	14 48	14 54	15 00	15 06	15 13	15 21	15 29	15 39	15 49	16 02	16 16	16 33	16 54
16	15 10	15 13	15 17	15 21	15 25	15 30	15 35	15 41	15 47	15 54	16 02	16 11	16 21	16 33
17	15 32	15 34	15 36	15 39	15 41	15 44	15 47	15 50	15 53	15 57	16 01	16 06	16 11	16 17
18	15 53	15 53	15 54	15 54	15 55	15 56	15 56	15 57	15 58	15 59	16 00	16 01	16 02	16 04
19	16 13	16 12	16 11	16 10	16 08	16 07	16 06	16 04	16 02	16 00	15 58	15 56	15 53	15 50
20	16 33	16 31	16 28	16 25	16 22	16 19	16 15	16 11	16 07	16 02	15 57	15 51	15 44	15 36
21	16 55	16 51	16 47	16 42	16 37	16 32	16 26	16 20	16 13	16 05	15 56	15 46	15 34	15 20
22	17 20	17 14	17 09	17 02	16 56	16 48	16 40	16 31	16 21	16 09	15 56	15 40	15 22	14 58
23	17 49	17 42	17 35	17 27	17 18	17 09	16 58	16 46	16 32	16 17	15 58	15 34	15 03	14 14
24	18 24	18 16	18 07	17 58	17 47	17 36	17 23	17 08	16 51	16 30	16 03	15 25	▬	▬
25	19 06	18 57	18 48	18 37	18 26	18 13	17 58	17 41	17 20	16 54	16 18	14 48	▬	▬

▭ indicates Moon continuously above horizon.
▬ indicates Moon continuously below horizon.
.. .. indicates phenomenon will occur the next day.

UNIVERSAL TIME FOR MERIDIAN OF GREENWICH

MOONRISE

Lat.	−55°	−50°	−45°	−40°	−35°	−30°	−20°	−10°	0°	+10°	+20°	+30°	+35°	+40°
	h m	h m	h m	h m	h m	h m	h m	h m	h m	h m	h m	h m	h m	h m
Oct. 24	4 50	5 23	5 47	6 07	6 23	6 37	7 02	7 23	7 42	8 02	8 24	8 48	9 03	9 20
25	5 16	5 55	6 23	6 45	7 04	7 20	7 47	8 10	8 32	8 54	9 17	9 45	10 01	10 20
26	5 55	6 37	7 08	7 32	7 51	8 08	8 36	9 01	9 23	9 46	10 11	10 39	10 56	11 16
27	6 51	7 33	8 03	8 26	8 45	9 02	9 30	9 53	10 16	10 38	11 02	11 29	11 46	12 05
28	8 03	8 39	9 06	9 27	9 45	10 00	10 25	10 47	11 07	11 28	11 50	12 15	12 29	12 47
29	9 24	9 53	10 15	10 33	10 47	11 00	11 22	11 40	11 58	12 15	12 34	12 55	13 07	13 22
30	10 50	11 11	11 27	11 41	11 52	12 02	12 19	12 33	12 47	13 00	13 15	13 31	13 41	13 52
31	12 17	12 30	12 41	12 50	12 57	13 04	13 15	13 25	13 34	13 44	13 53	14 04	14 11	14 18
Nov. 1	13 45	13 51	13 56	14 00	14 04	14 07	14 12	14 17	14 21	14 26	14 31	14 36	14 39	14 42
2	15 15	15 14	15 13	15 13	15 12	15 11	15 11	15 10	15 09	15 09	15 08	15 07	15 07	15 06
3	16 49	16 40	16 33	16 28	16 23	16 19	16 11	16 05	15 59	15 53	15 47	15 40	15 36	15 31
4	18 28	18 11	17 58	17 47	17 37	17 29	17 15	17 03	16 52	16 41	16 29	16 16	16 08	16 00
5	20 12	19 46	19 25	19 09	18 55	18 43	18 23	18 06	17 50	17 34	17 17	16 57	16 46	16 33
6	21 56	21 20	20 53	20 32	20 14	19 59	19 34	19 12	18 52	18 32	18 11	17 46	17 32	17 15
7	23 28	22 44	22 13	21 50	21 30	21 13	20 45	20 20	19 58	19 36	19 12	18 44	18 27	18 08
8	.. ..	23 50	23 20	22 56	22 36	22 20	21 51	21 27	21 04	20 41	20 17	19 49	19 32	19 12
9	0 33	.. ..	.. ..	23 49	23 31	23 16	22 50	22 28	22 07	21 46	21 23	20 57	20 42	20 24
10	1 12	0 36	0 10	.. ..	.. ..	.. ..	23 41	23 22	23 04	22 47	22 28	22 06	21 53	21 38
11	1 35	1 08	0 47	0 29	0 15	0 02	.. ..	.. ..	23 56	23 43	23 28	23 11	23 01	22 50
12	1 49	1 29	1 14	1 01	0 50	0 41	0 24	0 10	.. ..	.. ..	.. ..	.. ..	.. ..	23 58
13	1 58	1 46	1 36	1 27	1 20	1 13	1 02	0 52	0 43	0 34	0 24	0 12	0 06	.. ..
14	2 05	1 59	1 54	1 49	1 46	1 42	1 36	1 31	1 26	1 21	1 16	1 10	1 07	1 03
15	2 12	2 11	2 10	2 10	2 09	2 09	2 08	2 08	2 07	2 07	2 06	2 05	2 05	2 05
16	2 18	2 22	2 26	2 30	2 32	2 35	2 39	2 43	2 47	2 51	2 55	3 00	3 02	3 06
17	2 24	2 34	2 43	2 50	2 56	3 02	3 11	3 20	3 27	3 35	3 44	3 54	4 00	4 06

MOONSET

Lat.	−55°	−50°	−45°	−40°	−35°	−30°	−20°	−10°	0°	+10°	+20°	+30°	+35°	+40°
	h m	h m	h m	h m	h m	h m	h m	h m	h m	h m	h m	h m	h m	h m
Oct. 24	23 17	22 39	22 11	21 49	21 31	21 16	20 50	20 27	20 06	19 45	19 23	18 57	18 42	18 24
25	.. ..	23 41	23 11	22 47	22 28	22 11	21 43	21 19	20 57	20 34	20 10	19 42	19 26	19 06
26	0 24	.. ..	.. ..	23 40	23 20	23 04	22 36	22 11	21 49	21 26	21 02	20 33	20 16	19 57
27	1 16	0 34	0 03	.. ..	.. ..	23 52	23 25	23 02	22 41	22 19	21 56	21 29	21 13	20 54
28	1 52	1 14	0 47	0 25	0 07	.. ..	.. ..	23 51	23 32	23 13	22 52	22 28	22 14	21 58
29	2 15	1 45	1 22	1 03	0 48	0 34	0 11	.. ..	.. ..	.. ..	23 49	23 30	23 18	23 05
30	2 31	2 08	1 50	1 36	1 23	1 12	0 54	0 37	0 22	0 06	.. ..	.. ..	.. ..	.. ..
31	2 42	2 27	2 14	2 04	1 55	1 47	1 33	1 21	1 10	0 58	0 46	0 31	0 23	0 14
Nov. 1	2 51	2 42	2 35	2 29	2 24	2 19	2 11	2 04	1 57	1 50	1 42	1 34	1 29	1 23
2	2 58	2 56	2 54	2 53	2 51	2 50	2 48	2 46	2 44	2 42	2 40	2 37	2 36	2 34
3	3 06	3 10	3 14	3 17	3 19	3 22	3 26	3 29	3 32	3 36	3 39	3 43	3 45	3 48
4	3 15	3 26	3 35	3 43	3 50	3 56	4 06	4 15	4 23	4 32	4 41	4 52	4 58	5 05
5	3 26	3 45	4 01	4 14	4 24	4 34	4 51	5 05	5 19	5 32	5 47	6 04	6 14	6 25
6	3 43	4 11	4 33	4 51	5 06	5 19	5 41	6 01	6 19	6 37	6 57	7 19	7 33	7 48
7	4 11	4 48	5 16	5 38	5 56	6 12	6 39	7 02	7 23	7 45	8 08	8 35	8 51	9 09
8	4 58	5 42	6 13	6 37	6 57	7 14	7 42	8 07	8 30	8 53	9 17	9 46	10 02	10 22
9	6 10	6 52	7 22	7 45	8 04	8 21	8 49	9 13	9 35	9 57	10 20	10 47	11 03	11 22
10	7 39	8 13	8 39	8 59	9 16	9 30	9 55	10 16	10 35	10 54	11 15	11 39	11 53	12 09
11	9 11	9 37	9 57	10 12	10 26	10 37	10 57	11 14	11 30	11 45	12 02	12 21	12 32	12 45
12	10 40	10 58	11 12	11 23	11 32	11 41	11 55	12 08	12 19	12 31	12 43	12 56	13 04	13 13
13	12 04	12 14	12 23	12 29	12 35	12 40	12 49	12 57	13 04	13 11	13 19	13 27	13 32	13 37
14	13 23	13 27	13 30	13 33	13 35	13 37	13 40	13 43	13 46	13 49	13 52	13 55	13 57	13 59
15	14 40	14 37	14 36	14 34	14 33	14 32	14 30	14 28	14 26	14 25	14 23	14 21	14 20	14 19
16	15 55	15 47	15 40	15 35	15 30	15 26	15 19	15 12	15 06	15 01	14 54	14 47	14 43	14 39
17	17 12	16 57	16 45	16 36	16 28	16 20	16 08	15 57	15 47	15 37	15 27	15 15	15 08	15 00

.. .. indicates phenomenon will occur the next day.

UNIVERSAL TIME FOR MERIDIAN OF GREENWICH

MOONRISE

Lat.	+40°	+42°	+44°	+46°	+48°	+50°	+52°	+54°	+56°	+58°	+60°	+62°	+64°	+66°
	h m	h m	h m	h m	h m	h m	h m	h m	h m	h m	h m	h m	h m	h m
Oct. 24	9 20	9 28	9 36	9 45	9 55	10 07	10 19	10 34	10 51	11 12	11 38	12 15	■	■
25	10 20	10 29	10 38	10 49	11 00	11 13	11 28	11 45	12 05	12 31	13 07	14 37	■	■
26	11 16	11 25	11 35	11 45	11 57	12 11	12 26	12 44	13 06	13 34	14 15	■	■	■
27	12 05	12 13	12 23	12 33	12 44	12 57	13 12	13 28	13 49	14 14	14 48	15 50	■	■
28	12 47	12 54	13 03	13 12	13 22	13 33	13 45	13 59	14 16	14 35	14 59	15 32	16 27	■
29	13 22	13 28	13 35	13 42	13 50	13 59	14 09	14 20	14 32	14 47	15 04	15 24	15 50	16 26
30	13 52	13 56	14 02	14 07	14 13	14 20	14 27	14 35	14 44	14 54	15 05	15 18	15 34	15 53
31	14 18	14 21	14 25	14 28	14 32	14 36	14 41	14 46	14 52	14 58	15 05	15 13	15 22	15 33
Nov. 1	14 42	14 44	14 45	14 47	14 49	14 51	14 53	14 56	14 58	15 01	15 04	15 08	15 12	15 17
2	15 06	15 06	15 06	15 06	15 05	15 05	15 05	15 05	15 04	15 04	15 04	15 03	15 03	15 02
3	15 31	15 29	15 27	15 25	15 23	15 20	15 17	15 14	15 11	15 07	15 03	14 58	14 53	14 47
4	16 00	15 56	15 52	15 47	15 43	15 38	15 32	15 26	15 19	15 12	15 03	14 54	14 42	14 29
5	16 33	16 28	16 22	16 15	16 08	16 00	15 52	15 42	15 31	15 19	15 05	14 48	14 28	14 03
6	17 15	17 08	17 00	16 51	16 42	16 31	16 20	16 06	15 51	15 33	15 11	14 43	14 02	□
7	18 08	18 00	17 50	17 40	17 29	17 16	17 02	16 45	16 25	16 01	15 28	14 33	□	□
8	19 12	19 03	18 54	18 43	18 31	18 18	18 03	17 45	17 24	16 57	16 18	□	□	□
9	20 24	20 16	20 07	19 57	19 46	19 34	19 21	19 05	18 47	18 24	17 54	17 08	□	□
10	21 38	21 31	21 24	21 16	21 07	20 58	20 47	20 35	20 21	20 04	19 44	19 19	18 44	17 37
11	22 50	22 45	22 39	22 33	22 27	22 20	22 12	22 03	21 54	21 43	21 30	21 14	20 55	20 32
12	23 58	23 55	23 51	23 47	23 43	23 38	23 33	23 28	23 21	23 15	23 07	22 57	22 47	22 34
13	.. ..	.. ..	.. ..	.. ..	.. ..	.. ..	.. ..	.. ..	.. ..	.. ..	.. ..	.. ..	.. ..	.. ..
14	1 03	1 01	0 59	0 57	0 55	0 52	0 50	0 47	0 44	0 41	0 37	0 32	0 27	0 21
15	2 05	2 05	2 04	2 04	2 04	2 04	2 03	2 03	2 03	2 03	2 02	2 02	2 01	2 01
16	3 06	3 07	3 08	3 10	3 12	3 13	3 15	3 18	3 20	3 23	3 26	3 29	3 33	3 38
17	4 06	4 09	4 12	4 16	4 19	4 23	4 27	4 32	4 37	4 43	4 50	4 58	5 07	5 17

MOONSET

Lat.	+40°	+42°	+44°	+46°	+48°	+50°	+52°	+54°	+56°	+58°	+60°	+62°	+64°	+66°
	h m	h m	h m	h m	h m	h m	h m	h m	h m	h m	h m	h m	h m	h m
Oct. 24	18 24	18 16	18 07	17 58	17 47	17 36	17 23	17 08	16 51	16 30	16 03	15 25	■	■
25	19 06	18 57	18 48	18 37	18 26	18 13	17 58	17 41	17 20	16 54	16 18	14 48	■	■
26	19 57	19 48	19 38	19 27	19 15	19 02	18 46	18 28	18 07	17 39	16 58	■	■	■
27	20 54	20 46	20 37	20 27	20 15	20 03	19 49	19 32	19 12	18 47	18 14	17 12	■	■
28	21 58	21 51	21 43	21 34	21 24	21 14	21 02	20 48	20 32	20 13	19 49	19 17	18 23	■
29	23 05	22 59	22 53	22 46	22 38	22 30	22 21	22 10	21 58	21 45	21 28	21 09	20 43	20 08
30	.. ..	.. ..	.. ..	.. ..	23 54	23 49	23 42	23 35	23 27	23 18	23 07	22 55	22 41	22 23
31	0 14	0 09	0 05	0 00	.. ..	.. ..	.. ..	.. ..	.. ..	.. ..	.. ..	.. ..	.. ..	.. ..
Nov. 1	1 23	1 21	1 18	1 15	1 12	1 09	1 05	1 01	0 56	0 51	0 45	0 39	0 31	0 22
2	2 34	2 34	2 33	2 32	2 31	2 30	2 29	2 28	2 27	2 25	2 24	2 22	2 20	2 17
3	3 48	3 49	3 50	3 52	3 53	3 55	3 56	3 58	4 00	4 02	4 05	4 08	4 11	4 15
4	5 05	5 08	5 11	5 15	5 19	5 23	5 27	5 32	5 38	5 44	5 52	6 00	6 10	6 21
5	6 25	6 31	6 36	6 42	6 48	6 55	7 03	7 12	7 22	7 33	7 46	8 02	8 21	8 45
6	7 48	7 55	8 03	8 11	8 20	8 30	8 41	8 54	9 09	9 26	9 48	10 15	10 55	□
7	9 09	9 18	9 27	9 37	9 48	10 01	10 15	10 31	10 51	11 15	11 47	12 41	□	□
8	10 22	10 31	10 41	10 51	11 03	11 17	11 32	11 50	12 11	12 38	13 16	□	□	□
9	11 22	11 30	11 39	11 49	12 00	12 13	12 27	12 43	13 01	13 25	13 55	14 41	□	□
10	12 09	12 16	12 23	12 32	12 41	12 51	13 02	13 15	13 30	13 47	14 07	14 33	15 09	16 17
11	12 45	12 50	12 56	13 03	13 10	13 17	13 26	13 35	13 46	13 58	14 11	14 28	14 48	15 13
12	13 13	13 17	13 22	13 26	13 31	13 36	13 42	13 49	13 56	14 04	14 13	14 23	14 35	14 49
13	13 37	13 40	13 42	13 45	13 48	13 51	13 55	13 58	14 03	14 07	14 12	14 18	14 25	14 33
14	13 59	13 59	14 00	14 01	14 03	14 04	14 05	14 06	14 08	14 10	14 11	14 14	14 16	14 19
15	14 19	14 18	14 17	14 17	14 16	14 15	14 15	14 14	14 13	14 12	14 10	14 09	14 07	14 06
16	14 39	14 37	14 34	14 32	14 30	14 27	14 24	14 21	14 17	14 14	14 09	14 04	13 59	13 52
17	15 00	14 56	14 53	14 49	14 45	14 40	14 35	14 29	14 23	14 16	14 09	14 00	13 49	13 37

□ indicates Moon continuously above horizon.
■ indicates Moon continuously below horizon.
.. .. indicates phenomenon will occur the next day.

UNIVERSAL TIME FOR MERIDIAN OF GREENWICH

MOONRISE

Lat.	−55°	−50°	−45°	−40°	−35°	−30°	−20°	−10°	0°	+10°	+20°	+30°	+35°	+40°
	h m	h m	h m	h m	h m	h m	h m	h m	h m	h m	h m	h m	h m	h m
Nov. 16	2 18	2 22	2 26	2 30	2 32	2 35	2 39	2 43	2 47	2 51	2 55	3 00	3 02	3 06
17	2 24	2 34	2 43	2 50	2 56	3 02	3 11	3 20	3 27	3 35	3 44	3 54	4 00	4 06
18	2 32	2 48	3 01	3 12	3 22	3 30	3 45	3 57	4 09	4 21	4 34	4 49	4 58	5 07
19	2 42	3 05	3 23	3 38	3 51	4 02	4 21	4 37	4 53	5 09	5 25	5 45	5 56	6 10
20	2 57	3 27	3 50	4 08	4 24	4 37	5 00	5 20	5 39	5 58	6 18	6 42	6 56	7 12
21	3 20	3 56	4 23	4 45	5 03	5 18	5 44	6 07	6 28	6 49	7 12	7 39	7 55	8 13
22	3 54	4 36	5 06	5 29	5 48	6 05	6 33	6 57	7 19	7 42	8 06	8 34	8 51	9 10
23	4 45	5 28	5 58	6 21	6 40	6 57	7 25	7 49	8 11	8 34	8 58	9 25	9 42	10 01
24	5 52	6 30	6 58	7 20	7 38	7 53	8 19	8 42	9 03	9 24	9 46	10 12	10 27	10 45
25	7 10	7 41	8 05	8 23	8 39	8 52	9 15	9 35	9 53	10 12	10 31	10 53	11 07	11 22
26	8 33	8 56	9 15	9 29	9 42	9 52	10 11	10 27	10 42	10 56	11 12	11 30	11 41	11 53
27	9 57	10 13	10 26	10 36	10 45	10 53	11 06	11 17	11 28	11 39	11 50	12 03	12 11	12 19
28	11 22	11 30	11 38	11 43	11 49	11 53	12 01	12 07	12 14	12 20	12 27	12 34	12 38	12 43
29	12 47	12 49	12 51	12 52	12 53	12 54	12 56	12 58	12 59	13 01	13 02	13 04	13 05	13 06
30	14 15	14 10	14 06	14 03	14 00	13 57	13 53	13 49	13 46	13 42	13 39	13 35	13 32	13 30
Dec. 1	15 48	15 36	15 26	15 17	15 10	15 04	14 53	14 44	14 35	14 27	14 18	14 08	14 02	13 55
2	17 28	17 06	16 49	16 36	16 25	16 15	15 58	15 43	15 29	15 16	15 02	14 45	14 36	14 25
3	19 11	18 40	18 17	17 58	17 43	17 29	17 06	16 47	16 29	16 11	15 52	15 30	15 17	15 03
4	20 51	20 11	19 42	19 19	19 01	18 45	18 18	17 55	17 33	17 12	16 49	16 23	16 08	15 50
5	22 12	21 29	20 58	20 34	20 14	19 57	19 28	19 04	18 41	18 18	17 54	17 25	17 09	16 49
6	23 05	22 26	21 57	21 35	21 16	21 00	20 33	20 10	19 48	19 26	19 02	18 35	18 18	18 00
7	23 36	23 05	22 42	22 23	22 07	21 53	21 30	21 09	20 50	20 31	20 10	19 46	19 32	19 16
8	23 54	23 31	23 14	22 59	22 47	22 36	22 18	22 02	21 46	21 31	21 15	20 56	20 45	20 32
9	.. ..	23 50	23 38	23 28	23 20	23 12	22 59	22 48	22 37	22 26	22 14	22 01	21 53	21 44
10	0 05	.. ..	23 58	23 53	23 48	23 43	23 36	23 29	23 23	23 16	23 09	23 02	22 57	22 52

MOONSET

Lat.	−55°	−50°	−45°	−40°	−35°	−30°	−20°	−10°	0°	+10°	+20°	+30°	+35°	+40°
	h m	h m	h m	h m	h m	h m	h m	h m	h m	h m	h m	h m	h m	h m
Nov. 16	15 55	15 47	15 40	15 35	15 30	15 26	15 19	15 12	15 06	15 01	14 54	14 47	14 43	14 39
17	17 12	16 57	16 45	16 36	16 28	16 20	16 08	15 57	15 47	15 37	15 27	15 15	15 08	15 00
18	18 29	18 08	17 51	17 37	17 26	17 16	16 59	16 44	16 30	16 16	16 01	15 45	15 35	15 24
19	19 48	19 19	18 57	18 40	18 25	18 12	17 51	17 32	17 15	16 58	16 39	16 18	16 06	15 51
20	21 05	20 29	20 03	19 42	19 24	19 10	18 44	18 23	18 03	17 42	17 21	16 56	16 41	16 25
21	22 15	21 34	21 04	20 41	20 22	20 06	19 38	19 15	18 53	18 31	18 07	17 40	17 24	17 05
22	23 11	22 29	21 59	21 35	21 16	20 59	20 31	20 07	19 44	19 22	18 57	18 29	18 12	17 53
23	23 52	23 13	22 45	22 23	22 04	21 48	21 21	20 58	20 36	20 14	19 51	19 24	19 07	18 48
24	.. ..	23 47	23 22	23 03	22 46	22 32	22 08	21 47	21 27	21 08	20 46	20 22	20 07	19 50
25	0 19	.. ..	23 52	23 36	23 23	23 11	22 51	22 33	22 17	22 00	21 42	21 21	21 09	20 55
26	0 36	0 12	.. ..	.. ..	23 55	23 46	23 30	23 17	23 04	22 51	22 37	22 21	22 12	22 01
27	0 49	0 31	0 17	0 05	.. ..	.. ..	.. ..	23 58	23 50	23 41	23 32	23 22	23 15	23 08
28	0 58	0 47	0 38	0 30	0 24	0 18	0 07	.. ..	.. ..	.. ..	.. ..	.. ..	.. ..	.. ..
29	1 06	1 01	0 57	0 53	0 50	0 48	0 43	0 39	0 35	0 31	0 27	0 22	0 19	0 16
30	1 13	1 14	1 15	1 16	1 17	1 18	1 19	1 20	1 21	1 22	1 23	1 24	1 25	1 25
Dec. 1	1 21	1 29	1 35	1 41	1 45	1 49	1 57	2 03	2 09	2 15	2 21	2 29	2 33	2 38
2	1 30	1 46	1 58	2 08	2 17	2 24	2 38	2 49	3 00	3 11	3 23	3 37	3 45	3 54
3	1 44	2 07	2 26	2 41	2 54	3 05	3 24	3 41	3 57	4 13	4 30	4 50	5 01	5 15
4	2 05	2 38	3 03	3 22	3 39	3 53	4 18	4 39	4 59	5 19	5 40	6 05	6 20	6 37
5	2 42	3 23	3 52	4 15	4 35	4 51	5 19	5 43	6 05	6 28	6 52	7 20	7 36	7 55
6	3 42	4 26	4 57	5 21	5 41	5 58	6 26	6 50	7 13	7 36	8 00	8 28	8 44	9 04
7	5 07	5 46	6 13	6 35	6 53	7 09	7 35	7 57	8 18	8 39	9 01	9 26	9 41	9 58
8	6 43	7 12	7 35	7 52	8 07	8 20	8 42	9 00	9 18	9 35	9 53	10 14	10 26	10 40
9	8 18	8 38	8 54	9 07	9 18	9 27	9 44	9 58	10 11	10 24	10 38	10 54	11 03	11 13
10	9 46	9 59	10 09	10 17	10 24	10 31	10 41	10 51	10 59	11 08	11 17	11 27	11 33	11 40

.. .. indicates phenomenon will occur the next day.

UNIVERSAL TIME FOR MERIDIAN OF GREENWICH

MOONRISE

Lat.	+40°	+42°	+44°	+46°	+48°	+50°	+52°	+54°	+56°	+58°	+60°	+62°	+64°	+66°
	h m	h m	h m	h m	h m	h m	h m	h m	h m	h m	h m	h m	h m	h m
Nov. 16	3 06	3 07	3 08	3 10	3 12	3 13	3 15	3 18	3 20	3 23	3 26	3 29	3 33	3 38
17	4 06	4 09	4 12	4 16	4 19	4 23	4 27	4 32	4 37	4 43	4 50	4 58	5 07	5 17
18	5 07	5 12	5 17	5 22	5 27	5 33	5 40	5 48	5 56	6 05	6 16	6 29	6 44	7 03
19	6 10	6 16	6 22	6 29	6 36	6 45	6 54	7 04	7 16	7 30	7 46	8 06	8 31	9 06
20	7 12	7 19	7 27	7 36	7 45	7 56	8 08	8 21	8 37	8 56	9 19	9 50	10 39	▬
21	8 13	8 21	8 30	8 40	8 51	9 04	9 18	9 34	9 53	10 17	10 50	11 44	▬	▬
22	9 10	9 19	9 29	9 39	9 51	10 04	10 20	10 37	10 59	11 26	12 05	▬	▬	▬
23	10 01	10 10	10 19	10 30	10 41	10 54	11 09	11 26	11 47	12 13	12 48	14 04	▬	▬
24	10 45	10 53	11 02	11 11	11 21	11 33	11 46	12 01	12 18	12 39	13 05	13 43	▬	▬
25	11 22	11 28	11 36	11 44	11 52	12 02	12 12	12 24	12 37	12 53	13 12	13 35	14 06	14 53
26	11 53	11 58	12 03	12 10	12 16	12 23	12 31	12 40	12 50	13 01	13 14	13 30	13 48	14 11
27	12 19	12 23	12 27	12 31	12 36	12 41	12 46	12 52	12 59	13 06	13 15	13 25	13 36	13 49
28	12 43	12 45	12 48	12 50	12 53	12 56	12 59	13 02	13 06	13 10	13 15	13 20	13 26	13 33
29	13 06	13 07	13 07	13 08	13 09	13 09	13 10	13 11	13 12	13 13	13 14	13 15	13 17	13 18
30	13 30	13 29	13 27	13 26	13 25	13 23	13 22	13 20	13 18	13 16	13 13	13 11	13 08	13 04
Dec. 1	13 55	13 53	13 50	13 46	13 43	13 39	13 35	13 30	13 25	13 20	13 13	13 06	12 58	12 49
2	14 25	14 21	14 16	14 10	14 05	13 58	13 51	13 44	13 35	13 25	13 15	13 02	12 47	12 29
3	15 03	14 56	14 49	14 41	14 33	14 24	14 14	14 03	13 50	13 36	13 18	12 57	12 31	11 53
4	15 50	15 42	15 33	15 23	15 13	15 01	14 48	14 34	14 16	13 55	13 29	12 52	11 35	▭
5	16 49	16 40	16 31	16 20	16 08	15 55	15 40	15 23	15 02	14 36	14 00	12 41	▭	▭
6	18 00	17 51	17 42	17 31	17 20	17 07	16 53	16 36	16 16	15 51	15 17	14 15	▭	▭
7	19 16	19 08	19 00	18 52	18 42	18 31	18 19	18 06	17 50	17 31	17 07	16 36	15 44	▭
8	20 32	20 26	20 20	20 13	20 06	19 58	19 49	19 39	19 28	19 15	18 59	18 41	18 17	17 46
9	21 44	21 40	21 36	21 31	21 26	21 21	21 15	21 08	21 01	20 53	20 43	20 32	20 19	20 03
10	22 52	22 50	22 47	22 45	22 42	22 39	22 36	22 32	22 28	22 23	22 18	22 12	22 05	21 57

MOONSET

Lat.	+40°	+42°	+44°	+46°	+48°	+50°	+52°	+54°	+56°	+58°	+60°	+62°	+64°	+66°
	h m	h m	h m	h m	h m	h m	h m	h m	h m	h m	h m	h m	h m	h m
Nov. 16	14 39	14 37	14 34	14 32	14 30	14 27	14 24	14 21	14 17	14 14	14 09	14 04	13 59	13 52
17	15 00	14 56	14 53	14 49	14 45	14 40	14 35	14 29	14 23	14 16	14 09	14 00	13 49	13 37
18	15 24	15 19	15 14	15 08	15 02	14 55	14 48	14 40	14 30	14 20	14 08	13 55	13 38	13 18
19	15 51	15 45	15 38	15 31	15 23	15 14	15 04	14 53	14 41	14 27	14 10	13 49	13 23	12 47
20	16 25	16 17	16 09	16 00	15 50	15 39	15 27	15 13	14 57	14 38	14 14	13 43	12 52	▬
21	17 05	16 56	16 47	16 37	16 26	16 13	15 59	15 42	15 23	14 59	14 26	13 31	▬	▬
22	17 53	17 44	17 34	17 24	17 12	16 58	16 43	16 25	16 04	15 37	14 57	▬	▬	▬
23	18 48	18 40	18 30	18 20	18 09	17 56	17 41	17 24	17 04	16 38	16 03	14 47	▬	▬
24	19 50	19 42	19 34	19 25	19 15	19 03	18 51	18 36	18 19	17 59	17 33	16 56	▬	▬
25	20 55	20 48	20 42	20 34	20 26	20 17	20 07	19 56	19 43	19 27	19 09	18 47	18 17	17 31
26	22 01	21 56	21 51	21 46	21 40	21 33	21 26	21 18	21 08	20 58	20 46	20 32	20 14	19 53
27	23 08	23 05	23 02	22 58	22 54	22 50	22 45	22 40	22 34	22 28	22 21	22 12	22 02	21 51
28	.. ..	.. ..	.. ..	.. ..	.. ..	.. ..	.. ..	.. ..	.. ..	23 58	23 55	23 51	23 47	23 42
29	0 16	0 15	0 13	0 11	0 10	0 08	0 06	0 03	0 01	.. ..	.. ..	.. ..	.. ..	.. ..
30	1 25	1 26	1 26	1 26	1 27	1 27	1 28	1 28	1 29	1 29	1 30	1 31	1 32	1 33
Dec. 1	2 38	2 40	2 42	2 45	2 47	2 50	2 53	2 57	3 01	3 05	3 10	3 15	3 22	3 29
2	3 54	3 58	4 03	4 07	4 12	4 18	4 24	4 31	4 38	4 47	4 57	5 08	5 22	5 38
3	5 15	5 21	5 27	5 34	5 42	5 50	5 59	6 10	6 22	6 36	6 52	7 12	7 38	8 14
4	6 37	6 45	6 53	7 02	7 12	7 23	7 36	7 50	8 07	8 28	8 54	9 30	10 46	▭
5	7 55	8 04	8 14	8 24	8 36	8 49	9 04	9 21	9 42	10 08	10 44	12 03	▭	▭
6	9 04	9 12	9 22	9 32	9 44	9 57	10 11	10 28	10 49	11 14	11 48	12 51	▭	▭
7	9 58	10 06	10 14	10 23	10 33	10 45	10 57	11 11	11 28	11 47	12 11	12 43	13 36	▭
8	10 40	10 47	10 53	11 00	11 08	11 17	11 26	11 37	11 49	12 03	12 19	12 39	13 03	13 36
9	11 13	11 18	11 22	11 28	11 33	11 40	11 46	11 54	12 02	12 11	12 22	12 34	12 48	13 06
10	11 40	11 43	11 46	11 49	11 53	11 56	12 01	12 05	12 10	12 16	12 22	12 30	12 38	12 48

▭ indicates Moon continuously above horizon.
▬ indicates Moon continuously below horizon.
.. .. indicates phenomenon will occur the next day.

UNIVERSAL TIME FOR MERIDIAN OF GREENWICH

MOONRISE

Lat.	−55°	−50°	−45°	−40°	−35°	−30°	−20°	−10°	0°	+10°	+20°	+30°	+35°	+40°
	h m	h m	h m	h m	h m	h m	h m	h m	h m	h m	h m	h m	h m	h m
Dec. 9	.. ..	23 50	23 38	23 28	23 20	23 12	22 59	22 48	22 37	22 26	22 14	22 01	21 53	21 44
10	0 05	.. ..	23 58	23 53	23 48	23 43	23 36	23 29	23 23	23 16	23 09	23 02	22 57	22 52
11	0 14	0 05	.. ..	.. ..	.. ..	.. ..	.. ..	.. ..	.. ..	.. ..	.. ..	23 59	23 58	23 56
12	0 20	0 18	0 16	0 14	0 13	0 11	0 09	0 07	0 05	0 03	0 01	.. ..	.. ..	.. ..
13	0 26	0 30	0 32	0 34	0 36	0 38	0 41	0 43	0 46	0 48	0 51	0 54	0 56	0 58
14	0 33	0 42	0 49	0 55	1 00	1 04	1 12	1 20	1 26	1 33	1 40	1 49	1 54	1 59
15	0 40	0 55	1 07	1 16	1 25	1 32	1 45	1 57	2 07	2 18	2 30	2 43	2 51	3 00
16	0 50	1 11	1 27	1 41	1 53	2 03	2 20	2 36	2 50	3 05	3 21	3 39	3 50	4 02
17	1 03	1 31	1 52	2 10	2 24	2 37	2 59	3 18	3 36	3 54	4 13	4 36	4 49	5 04
18	1 23	1 58	2 24	2 44	3 01	3 16	3 42	4 04	4 24	4 45	5 07	5 33	5 48	6 06
19	1 54	2 34	3 03	3 26	3 45	4 01	4 29	4 53	5 15	5 37	6 01	6 29	6 45	7 04
20	2 40	3 23	3 53	4 16	4 36	4 52	5 20	5 44	6 07	6 29	6 54	7 22	7 38	7 58
21	3 43	4 23	4 51	5 14	5 32	5 48	6 15	6 38	6 59	7 21	7 44	8 10	8 26	8 44
22	4 59	5 32	5 57	6 17	6 33	6 47	7 11	7 31	7 50	8 09	8 30	8 53	9 07	9 23
23	6 22	6 47	7 06	7 22	7 35	7 47	8 07	8 24	8 39	8 55	9 12	9 31	9 42	9 55
24	7 45	8 03	8 17	8 29	8 38	8 47	9 02	9 14	9 26	9 38	9 51	10 05	10 13	10 23
25	9 08	9 19	9 28	9 35	9 41	9 46	9 56	10 04	10 11	10 19	10 27	10 36	10 41	10 47
26	10 31	10 36	10 39	10 42	10 44	10 46	10 50	10 53	10 56	10 59	11 02	11 05	11 07	11 10
27	11 56	11 53	11 51	11 49	11 48	11 46	11 44	11 42	11 40	11 39	11 37	11 35	11 33	11 32
28	13 23	13 14	13 06	12 59	12 54	12 49	12 41	12 34	12 27	12 20	12 13	12 05	12 01	11 56
29	14 56	14 38	14 24	14 13	14 03	13 55	13 41	13 28	13 17	13 05	12 53	12 39	12 31	12 23
30	16 34	16 07	15 47	15 31	15 17	15 05	14 45	14 27	14 11	13 55	13 38	13 19	13 08	12 55
31	18 14	17 38	17 11	16 50	16 33	16 18	15 53	15 31	15 11	14 52	14 30	14 06	13 52	13 35
32	19 44	19 01	18 31	18 07	17 48	17 31	17 03	16 39	16 16	15 54	15 30	15 03	14 46	14 27
33	20 51	20 09	19 38	19 15	18 55	18 39	18 10	17 46	17 23	17 01	16 36	16 08	15 51	15 32

MOONSET

Lat.	−55°	−50°	−45°	−40°	−35°	−30°	−20°	−10°	0°	+10°	+20°	+30°	+35°	+40°
	h m	h m	h m	h m	h m	h m	h m	h m	h m	h m	h m	h m	h m	h m
Dec. 9	8 18	8 38	8 54	9 07	9 18	9 27	9 44	9 58	10 11	10 24	10 38	10 54	11 03	11 13
10	9 46	9 59	10 09	10 17	10 24	10 31	10 41	10 51	10 59	11 08	11 17	11 27	11 33	11 40
11	11 09	11 15	11 19	11 23	11 27	11 30	11 35	11 39	11 43	11 47	11 52	11 56	11 59	12 02
12	12 27	12 27	12 27	12 26	12 26	12 26	12 25	12 25	12 25	12 24	12 24	12 24	12 23	12 23
13	13 44	13 37	13 32	13 28	13 24	13 21	13 15	13 10	13 05	13 01	12 56	12 50	12 47	12 43
14	15 00	14 47	14 37	14 28	14 21	14 15	14 04	13 55	13 46	13 37	13 28	13 17	13 11	13 04
15	16 17	15 57	15 42	15 30	15 19	15 10	14 54	14 41	14 28	14 15	14 02	13 46	13 37	13 27
16	17 35	17 08	16 48	16 32	16 18	16 06	15 46	15 28	15 12	14 56	14 38	14 18	14 07	13 54
17	18 53	18 19	17 54	17 34	17 17	17 03	16 39	16 18	15 59	15 39	15 19	14 55	14 41	14 25
18	20 05	19 25	18 57	18 34	18 16	18 00	17 33	17 10	16 48	16 27	16 04	15 37	15 21	15 03
19	21 07	20 24	19 54	19 31	19 11	18 55	18 26	18 02	17 40	17 17	16 53	16 25	16 08	15 49
20	21 52	21 12	20 43	20 20	20 02	19 45	19 18	18 54	18 32	18 10	17 46	17 19	17 02	16 43
21	22 23	21 49	21 23	21 03	20 46	20 31	20 06	19 44	19 24	19 04	18 42	18 16	18 01	17 43
22	22 43	22 16	21 55	21 38	21 24	21 12	20 50	20 32	20 14	19 57	19 38	19 16	19 03	18 48
23	22 56	22 37	22 21	22 08	21 57	21 47	21 31	21 16	21 02	20 48	20 33	20 16	20 06	19 54
24	23 06	22 53	22 43	22 34	22 26	22 20	22 08	21 58	21 48	21 38	21 28	21 16	21 09	21 00
25	23 14	23 07	23 02	22 57	22 53	22 50	22 43	22 38	22 33	22 27	22 22	22 15	22 11	22 07
26	23 21	23 20	23 20	23 19	23 19	23 19	23 18	23 17	23 17	23 16	23 15	23 15	23 14	23 14
27	23 28	23 34	23 38	23 42	23 45	23 48	23 53	23 58	.. ..	.. ..	.. ..	.. ..	.. ..	.. ..
28	23 37	23 49	23 59	.. ..	.. ..	.. ..	.. ..	.. ..	0 02	0 06	0 11	0 16	0 19	0 22
29	23 48	.. ..	.. ..	0 07	0 14	0 20	0 31	0 41	0 50	0 59	1 09	1 20	1 27	1 34
30	.. ..	0 07	0 23	0 36	0 47	0 57	1 13	1 28	1 42	1 56	2 11	2 28	2 38	2 50
31	0 04	0 32	0 54	1 12	1 27	1 40	2 02	2 21	2 39	2 57	3 17	3 40	3 53	4 08
32	0 31	1 08	1 36	1 58	2 16	2 31	2 58	3 20	3 42	4 03	4 26	4 53	5 09	5 27
33	1 18	2 01	2 32	2 56	3 16	3 32	4 01	4 25	4 48	5 11	5 35	6 04	6 20	6 40

.. .. indicates phenomenon will occur the next day.

UNIVERSAL TIME FOR MERIDIAN OF GREENWICH

MOONRISE

Lat.	+40°	+42°	+44°	+46°	+48°	+50°	+52°	+54°	+56°	+58°	+60°	+62°	+64°	+66°
	h m	h m	h m	h m	h m	h m	h m	h m	h m	h m	h m	h m	h m	h m
Dec. 9	21 44	21 40	21 36	21 31	21 26	21 21	21 15	21 08	21 01	20 53	20 43	20 32	20 19	20 03
10	22 52	22 50	22 47	22 45	22 42	22 39	22 36	22 32	22 28	22 23	22 18	22 12	22 05	21 57
11	23 56	23 56	23 55	23 54	23 53	23 52	23 52	23 51	23 49	23 48	23 47	23 45	23 43	23 41
12	.. ..	.. ..	.. ..	.. ..	.. ..	.. ..	.. ..	.. ..	.. ..	.. ..	.. ..	.. ..	.. ..	.. ..
13	0 58	0 59	1 00	1 01	1 02	1 03	1 05	1 06	1 08	1 10	1 12	1 14	1 17	1 20
14	1 59	2 02	2 04	2 07	2 10	2 13	2 17	2 21	2 25	2 30	2 36	2 42	2 50	2 58
15	3 00	3 04	3 08	3 13	3 18	3 23	3 29	3 36	3 43	3 52	4 01	4 12	4 26	4 42
16	4 02	4 07	4 13	4 20	4 27	4 34	4 43	4 52	5 03	5 15	5 30	5 47	6 09	6 37
17	5 04	5 11	5 18	5 27	5 35	5 45	5 56	6 09	6 23	6 40	7 01	7 28	8 06	▬
18	6 06	6 14	6 23	6 32	6 43	6 54	7 08	7 23	7 42	8 04	8 33	9 17	▬	▬
19	7 04	7 13	7 23	7 33	7 45	7 58	8 13	8 30	8 51	9 18	9 55	▬	▬	▬
20	7 58	8 06	8 16	8 27	8 38	8 51	9 06	9 24	9 45	10 11	10 49	▬	▬	▬
21	8 44	8 52	9 01	9 11	9 21	9 33	9 47	10 02	10 21	10 43	11 12	11 55	▬	▬
22	9 23	9 30	9 37	9 46	9 55	10 05	10 16	10 29	10 43	11 00	11 21	11 47	12 23	13 33
23	9 55	10 01	10 07	10 13	10 21	10 28	10 37	10 47	10 57	11 10	11 24	11 41	12 02	12 28
24	10 23	10 27	10 31	10 36	10 41	10 47	10 53	11 00	11 07	11 16	11 25	11 36	11 49	12 04
25	10 47	10 50	10 52	10 55	10 59	11 02	11 06	11 10	11 14	11 19	11 25	11 31	11 39	11 47
26	11 10	11 11	11 12	11 13	11 14	11 16	11 17	11 19	11 20	11 22	11 24	11 27	11 30	11 33
27	11 32	11 31	11 31	11 30	11 30	11 29	11 28	11 27	11 26	11 25	11 24	11 22	11 21	11 19
28	11 56	11 54	11 51	11 49	11 46	11 43	11 40	11 36	11 32	11 28	11 23	11 18	11 12	11 05
29	12 23	12 19	12 14	12 10	12 05	12 00	11 54	11 48	11 41	11 33	11 24	11 14	11 02	10 48
30	12 55	12 49	12 43	12 36	12 29	12 21	12 13	12 03	11 52	11 40	11 26	11 09	10 49	10 23
31	13 35	13 28	13 20	13 11	13 02	12 52	12 40	12 27	12 12	11 54	11 32	11 04	10 25	▭
32	14 27	14 19	14 09	13 59	13 48	13 36	13 21	13 05	12 45	12 21	11 50	10 58	▭	▭
33	15 32	15 23	15 13	15 03	14 51	14 38	14 23	14 05	13 44	13 18	12 40	▭	▭	▭

MOONSET

Lat.	+40°	+42°	+44°	+46°	+48°	+50°	+52°	+54°	+56°	+58°	+60°	+62°	+64°	+66°
	h m	h m	h m	h m	h m	h m	h m	h m	h m	h m	h m	h m	h m	h m
Dec. 9	11 13	11 18	11 22	11 28	11 33	11 40	11 46	11 54	12 02	12 11	12 22	12 34	12 48	13 06
10	11 40	11 43	11 46	11 49	11 53	11 56	12 01	12 05	12 10	12 16	12 22	12 30	12 38	12 48
11	12 02	12 04	12 05	12 07	12 08	12 10	12 12	12 14	12 17	12 19	12 22	12 25	12 29	12 33
12	12 23	12 23	12 23	12 23	12 23	12 22	12 22	12 22	12 22	12 21	12 21	12 21	12 20	12 20
13	12 43	12 42	12 40	12 38	12 36	12 34	12 32	12 29	12 27	12 24	12 20	12 16	12 12	12 07
14	13 04	13 01	12 58	12 55	12 51	12 47	12 42	12 37	12 32	12 26	12 20	12 12	12 03	11 53
15	13 27	13 23	13 18	13 13	13 07	13 01	12 55	12 47	12 39	12 30	12 19	12 07	11 53	11 36
16	13 54	13 48	13 41	13 35	13 27	13 19	13 10	13 00	12 48	12 35	12 20	12 02	11 40	11 10
17	14 25	14 18	14 10	14 02	13 52	13 42	13 31	13 18	13 03	12 45	12 24	11 56	11 18	▬
18	15 03	14 55	14 46	14 36	14 25	14 13	13 59	13 44	13 25	13 03	12 33	11 48	▬	▬
19	15 49	15 40	15 31	15 20	15 08	14 55	14 40	14 23	14 02	13 35	12 57	▬	▬	▬
20	16 43	16 34	16 25	16 14	16 03	15 50	15 35	15 17	14 56	14 30	13 53	▬	▬	▬
21	17 43	17 35	17 27	17 17	17 07	16 55	16 42	16 27	16 09	15 47	15 18	14 36	▬	▬
22	18 48	18 41	18 34	18 26	18 17	18 08	17 57	17 45	17 31	17 14	16 54	16 29	15 54	14 44
23	19 54	19 49	19 43	19 37	19 31	19 23	19 15	19 06	18 56	18 45	18 31	18 15	17 55	17 30
24	21 00	20 57	20 53	20 49	20 44	20 39	20 34	20 28	20 22	20 14	20 06	19 56	19 44	19 30
25	22 07	22 05	22 03	22 01	21 58	21 56	21 53	21 50	21 46	21 42	21 38	21 33	21 27	21 21
26	23 14	23 13	23 13	23 13	23 13	23 12	23 12	23 12	23 11	23 11	23 10	23 10	23 09	23 08
27	.. ..	.. ..	.. ..	.. ..	.. ..	.. ..	.. ..	.. ..	.. ..	.. ..	.. ..	.. ..	.. ..	.. ..
28	0 22	0 24	0 25	0 27	0 29	0 31	0 33	0 36	0 38	0 41	0 45	0 48	0 53	0 58
29	1 34	1 37	1 41	1 45	1 49	1 53	1 58	2 04	2 10	2 16	2 24	2 33	2 43	2 56
30	2 50	2 55	3 00	3 06	3 13	3 20	3 28	3 37	3 47	3 58	4 11	4 27	4 46	5 11
31	4 08	4 15	4 23	4 31	4 40	4 50	5 01	5 14	5 28	5 46	6 07	6 34	7 12	▭
32	5 27	5 36	5 45	5 55	6 06	6 18	6 32	6 48	7 07	7 31	8 02	8 53	▭	▭
33	6 40	6 49	6 59	7 09	7 21	7 34	7 49	8 07	8 28	8 55	9 32	▭	▭	▭

▭ indicates Moon continuously above horizon.
▬ indicates Moon continuously below horizon.
.. .. indicates phenomenon will occur the next day.

CONTENTS OF THE ECLIPSE SECTION

SUMMARY OF ECLIPSES AND TRANSITS FOR 2025

There are four eclipses, two of the Sun and two of the Moon. All times are expressed in Universal Time using $\Delta T = +69^{s}.0$. There are no transits of Mercury or Venus across the Sun.

I. *A total eclipse of the Moon*, March 14. See map on page A84. The eclipse begins at $03^{h}\ 55^{m}$ and ends at $10^{h}\ 02^{m}$; the total phase begins at $6^{h}\ 26^{m}$ and ends at $7^{h}\ 32^{m}$. It is visible from Antarctica, North America, South America, Africa, Europe, Australia, eastern Asia, the Pacific Ocean and the Atlantic Ocean.

II. *A partial eclipse of the Sun*, March 29. See map on page A86. The eclipse begins at $08^{h}\ 50^{m}$ and ends at $12^{h}\ 44^{m}$. It is visible from eastern North America, Greenland, western Europe, extreme western Africa, western Asia, and the north Atlantic Ocean.

III. *A total eclipse of the Moon*, September 7. See map on page A87. The eclipse begins at $15^{h}\ 26^{m}$ and ends at $20^{h}\ 57^{m}$; the total phase begins at $17^{h}\ 30^{m}$ and ends at $18^{h}\ 53^{m}$. It is visible from Antarctica, extreme eastern South America, Africa, Europe, Asia, Australia, the eastern Atlantic Ocean, Indian Ocean, and the western Pacific Ocean.

IV. *A partial eclipse of the Sun*, September 21. See map on page A89. The eclipse begins at $17^{h}\ 29^{m}$ and ends at $21^{h}\ 54^{m}$. It is visible from Antarctica, New Zealand, and the south Pacific Ocean.

General Information

The elements and circumstances are computed according to Bessel's method from apparent right ascensions and declinations of the Sun and Moon. Semidiameters of the Sun and Moon used in the calculation of eclipses do not include irradiation. The adopted semidiameter of the Sun at unit distance is $15' \, 59''.64$ from the IAU (1976) Astronomical Constants. The apparent semidiameter of the Moon is equal to arcsin (k sin π), where π is the Moon's horizontal parallax and k is an adopted constant. In 1982, the IAU adopted $k = 0.272\ 5076$, corresponding to the mean radius of Watts' datum as determined by observations of occultations and to the adopted radius of the Earth.

Standard corrections of $+0''.5$ and $-0''.25$ have been applied to the longitude and latitude of the Moon, respectively, to help correct for the difference between the center of figure and the center of mass.

Refraction is neglected in calculating solar and lunar eclipses. Because the circumstances of eclipses are calculated for the surface of the ellipsoid, refraction is not included in Besselian element polynomials. For local predictions, corrections for refraction are unnecessary; they are required only in precise comparisons of theory with observation in which many other refinements are also necessary.

All time arguments are given provisionally in Universal Time, using $\Delta T(A) = +69^{s}.0$. Once an updated value of ΔT is known, the data on these pages may be expressed in Universal Time as follows:

Define $\delta T = \Delta T - \Delta T(A)$, in units of seconds of time.

Change the times of circumstances given in preliminary Universal Time by subtracting δT.

Correct the tabulated longitudes, $\lambda(A)$, using $\lambda = \lambda(A) + 0.00417807 \times \delta T$ (longitudes are in degrees).

Leave all other quantities unchanged.

The correction of δT is included in the Besselian elements.

Longitude is positive to the east, and negative to the west.

Explanation of Solar Eclipse Diagram

The solar eclipse diagrams in *The Astronomical Almanac* show the region over which different phases of each eclipse may be seen and the times at which these phases occur. Each diagram has a series of dashed curves that show the outline of the Moon's penumbra on the Earth's surface at one-hour intervals. Short dashes show the leading edge, and long dashes show the trailing edge. Except for certain extreme cases, the shadow outline moves generally from west to east. The Moon's shadow cone first contacts the Earth's surface where "First Contact" is indicated on the diagram. "Last Contact" is where the Moon's shadow cone last contacts the Earth's surface. The path of the central eclipse, whether for a total, annular, or annular-total eclipse, is marked by two closely spaced curves that cut across all of the dashed curves. These two curves mark the extent of the Moon's umbral shadow on the Earth's surface. Viewers within these boundaries will observe a total, annular, or annular-total eclipse, and viewers outside these boundaries will see a partial eclipse.

Solid curves labeled "Northern" and "Southern Limit of Eclipse" represent the furthest extent north or south of the Moon's penumbra on the Earth's surface. Viewers outside of these boundaries will not experience any eclipse. When only one of these two curves appears, only part of the Moon's penumbra touches the Earth; the other part is projected into space north or south of the Earth. The solid curves labeled "Eclipse begins at Sunset" and "Eclipse ends at Sunrise" define the other limits.

Another set of solid curves appears on some diagrams as two teardrop shapes (or lobes) on either end of the eclipse path, and on other diagrams as a distorted figure eight. These lobes represent in time the intersection of the Moon's penumbra with the Earth's terminator as the eclipse progresses. As time elapses, the Earth's terminator moves east-to-west while the Moon's penumbra moves west-to-east. These lobes connect to form an elongated figure eight on a diagram when part of the Moon's penumbra stays in contact with the Earth's terminator throughout the eclipse. The lobes become two separate teardrop shapes when the Moon's penumbra breaks contact with the Earth's terminator during the beginning of the eclipse and reconnects with it near the end. In the east, the outer portion of the lobe is labeled "Eclipse begins at Sunset" and marks the first contact between the Moon's penumbra and Earth's terminator in the east. Observers on this curve just fail to see the eclipse. The inner part of the lobe is labeled "Eclipse ends at Sunset" and marks the last contact between the Moon's penumbra and the Earth's terminator in the east. Observers on this curve just see the whole eclipse. The curve bisecting this lobe is labeled "Maximum Eclipse at Sunset" and is part of the sunset terminator at maximum eclipse. Viewers in the eastern half of the lobe will see the Sun set before maximum eclipse; *i.e.* see less than half of the eclipse. Viewers in the western half of the lobe will see the Sun set after maximum eclipse; *i.e.* see more than half of the eclipse. A similar description holds for the western lobe except everything occurs at sunrise instead of sunset.

Computing Local Circumstances for Solar Eclipses

The solar eclipse maps show the path of the eclipse, beginning and ending times of the eclipse, and the region of visibility, including restrictions due to rising and setting of the Sun. The short-dash and long-dash lines show, respectively, the progress of the leading and trailing edge of the penumbra; thus, at a given location, the times of the first and last contact may be interpolated. If further precision is desired, Besselian elements can be utilized.

Besselian elements characterize the geometric position of the shadow of the Moon relative to the Earth. The exterior tangents to the surfaces of the Sun and Moon form the umbral cone; the interior tangents form the penumbral cone. The common axis of these two cones is the axis of the shadow. To form a system of geocentric rectangular coordinates, the geocentric plane perpendicular to the axis of the shadow is taken as the xy-plane. This is called the fundamental plane. The x-axis is the intersection of the fundamental plane with the plane of the equator; it is positive toward the east. The y-axis is positive toward the north. The z-axis is parallel to the axis of the shadow and is positive toward the Moon. The tabular values of x and y are the coordinates, in units of the Earth's equatorial radius, of the intersection of the axis of the shadow with the fundamental plane. The direction of the axis of the shadow is specified by the declination d and hour angle μ of the point on the celestial sphere toward which the axis is directed.

The radius of the umbral cone is regarded as positive for an annular eclipse and negative for a total eclipse. The angles f_1 and f_2 are the angles at which the tangents that form the penumbral and umbral cones, respectively, intersect the axis of the shadow.

To predict accurate local circumstances, calculate the geocentric coordinates $\rho \sin \phi'$ and $\rho \cos \phi'$ from the geodetic latitude ϕ and longitude λ, using the relationships given on pages K11–K12 of *The Astronomical Almanac*. Inclusion of the height h in this calculation is all that is necessary to obtain the local circumstances at high altitudes.

Obtain approximate times for the beginning, middle and end of the eclipse from the eclipse map. For each of these three times, compute — from the Besselian element polynomials — the values of x, y, $\sin d$, $\cos d$, μ and l_1 (the radius of the penumbra on the fundamental plane). If the eclipse is central (i.e., total, annular or annular-total), then, at the approximate time of the middle of the eclipse, l_2 (the radius of the umbra on the fundamental plane) is required instead of l_1. The hourly variations x', y' of x and y are needed, and may be obtained by evaluating the derivative of the polynomial expressions for x and y. Values of μ', d', tan f_1 and tan f_2 are nearly constant throughout the eclipse and are given immediately following the Besselian polynomials.

For each of the three approximate times, calculate the coordinates ξ, η, ζ for the observer and the hourly variations ξ' and η' from

$$\begin{aligned}
\xi &= \rho\cos\phi'\sin\theta,\\
\eta &= \rho\sin\phi'\cos d - \rho\cos\phi'\sin d\cos\theta,\\
\zeta &= \rho\sin\phi'\sin d + \rho\cos\phi'\cos d\cos\theta,\\
\xi' &= \mu'\rho\cos\phi'\cos\theta,\\
\eta' &= \mu'\xi\sin d - \zeta d',
\end{aligned}$$

where

$$\theta = \mu + \lambda$$

for longitudes measured positive towards the east.

Next, calculate

$$\begin{aligned}
u &= x - \xi & u' &= x' - \xi'\\
v &= y - \eta & v' &= y' - \eta'\\
m^2 &= u^2 + v^2 & n^2 &= u'^2 + v'^2 \qquad (m, n > 0)
\end{aligned}$$

$$\begin{aligned}
L_i &= l_i - \zeta\tan f_i\\
D &= uu' + vv'\\
\Delta &= \tfrac{1}{n}(uv' - u'v)\\
\sin\psi &= \tfrac{\Delta}{L_i},
\end{aligned}$$

where $i = 1, 2$.

At the approximate times of the beginning and end of the eclipse, L_1 is required. At the approximate time of the middle of the eclipse, L_2 is required if the eclipse is central; L_1 is required if the eclipse is partial.

Neglecting the variation of L, the correction τ to be applied to the approximate time of the middle of the eclipse to obtain the *Universal Time of greatest phase* (in hours) is

$$\tau = -\frac{D}{n^2},$$

which may be expressed in minutes by multiplying by 60. The correction τ to be applied to the approximate times of the beginning and end of the eclipse to obtain the *Universal Times of the penumbral contacts* (in hours) is

$$\tau = \frac{L_1}{n}\cos\psi - \frac{D}{n^2},$$

which may be expressed in minutes by multiplying by 60.

If the eclipse is central, use the approximate time for the middle of the eclipse as a first approximation to the times of umbral contact. The correction τ to be applied to obtain the *Universal Times of the umbral contacts* is

$$\tau = \frac{L_2}{n}\cos\psi - \frac{D}{n^2},$$

which may be expressed in minutes by multiplying by 60.

In the last two equations, the ambiguity in the quadrant of ψ is removed by noting that $\cos\psi$ must be *negative* for the beginning of the eclipse, for the beginning of the annular phase, or for the end of the total phase; $\cos\psi$ must be *positive* for the end of the eclipse, the end of the annular phase, or the beginning of the total phase.

For greater accuracy, the times resulting from the calculation outlined above should be used in place of the original approximate times, and the entire procedure repeated at least once. The calculations for each of the contact times and the time of greatest phase should be performed separately.

The *magnitude of greatest partial eclipse*, in units of the solar diameter, is

$$M_1 = \frac{L_1 - m}{(2L_1 - 0.5459)},$$

where the value of m at the time of greatest phase is used. If the magnitude is negative at the time of greatest phase, no eclipse is visible from the location.

The *magnitude of the central phase*, in the same units, is

$$M_2 = \frac{L_1 - L_2}{(L_1 + L_2)}.$$

The *position angle of a point of contact*, measured eastward (counterclockwise) from the north point of the solar limb, is given by

$$\tan P = \frac{u}{v},$$

where u and v are evaluated at the times of contacts computed in the final approximation. The quadrant of P is determined by noting that $\sin P$ has the algebraic sign of u, except for the contacts of the total phase, for which $\sin P$ has the opposite sign to u.

The position angle of the point of contact measured eastward from the vertex of the solar limb is given by

$$V = P - C,$$

where C, the parallactic angle, is obtained with sufficient accuracy from

$$\tan C = \frac{\xi}{\eta},$$

with $\sin C$ having the same algebraic sign as ξ, and the results of the final approximation again being used. The vertex point of the solar limb lies on a great circle arc drawn from the zenith to the center of the solar disk.

Lunar Eclipses

A calculator to produce local circumstances of recent and upcoming lunar eclipses is provided at https://aa.usno.navy.mil/data/LunarEclipse.

In calculating lunar eclipses, the radius of the geocentric shadow of the Earth is increased by one-fiftieth part to allow for the effect of the atmosphere. Refraction is neglected in calculating solar and lunar eclipses. Standard corrections of $+0''.5$ and $-0''.25$ have been applied to the longitude and latitude of the Moon, respectively, to help correct for the difference between the center of figure and the center of mass.

Explanation of Lunar Eclipse Diagram

Information on lunar eclipses is presented in the form of a diagram consisting of two parts. The upper panel shows the path of the Moon relative to the penumbral and umbral shadows of the Earth. The lower panel shows the visibility of the eclipse from the surface of the Earth. The title of the upper panel includes the type of eclipse, its place in the sequence of eclipses for the year and the Greenwich calendar date of the eclipse. The inner darker circle is the umbral shadow of the Earth and the outer lighter circle is that of the penumbra. The axis of the shadow of the Earth is denoted by (+) with the ecliptic shown for reference purposes. A 30-arcminute scale bar is provided on the right hand side of the diagram and the orientation is given by the cardinal points displayed on the small graphic on the left hand side of the diagram. The position angle (PA) is measured from North point of the lunar disk along the limb of the Moon to the point of contact. It is shown on the graphic by the use of an arc extending anti-clockwise (eastwards) from North terminated with an arrowhead.

Moon symbols are plotted at the principal phases of the eclipse to show its position relative to the umbral and penumbral shadows. The UT times of the different phases of the eclipse to the nearest tenth of a minute are printed above or below the Moon symbols as appropriate. P1 and P4 are the first and last external contacts of the penumbra respectively and denote the beginning and end of the penumbral eclipse respectively. U1 and U4 are the first and last external contacts of the umbra denoting the beginning and end of the partial phase of the eclipse respectively. U2 and U3 are the first and last internal contacts of the umbra and denote the beginning and end of the total phase respectively. MID is the middle of the eclipse. The position angle is given for P1 and P4 for penumbral eclipses and U1 and U4 for partial and total eclipses. The UT time of the geocentric opposition in right ascension of the Sun and Moon and the magnitude of the eclipse are given above or below the Moon symbols as appropriate.

The lower panel is a cylindrical equidistant map projection showing the Earth centered on the longitude at which the Moon is in the zenith at the middle of the eclipse. The visibility of the eclipse is displayed by plotting the Moon rise/set terminator for the principal phases of the eclipse for which timing information is provided in the upper panel. The terminator for the middle of the eclipse is not plotted for the sake of clarity.

The unshaded area indicates the region of the Earth from which all the eclipse is visible, whereas the darkest shading indicates the area from which the eclipse is invisible. The different shades of gray indicate regions where the Moon is either rising or setting during the principal phases of the eclipse. The Moon is rising on the left hand side of the diagram after the eclipse has started and is setting on the right hand side of the diagram before the eclipse ends. Labels are provided to this effect.

Symbols are plotted showing the locations for which the Moon is in the zenith at the principal phases of the eclipse. The points at which the Moon is in the zenith at P1 and P4 are denoted by (+), at U1 and U4 by (⊙) and at U2 and U3 by (⊕). These symbols are also plotted on the upper panel where appropriate. The value of ΔT used for the calculation of the eclipse circumstances is given below the diagram. Country boundaries are also provided to assist the user in determining the visibility of the eclipse at a particular location.

I. - Total Eclipse of the Moon

2025 March 14

UT of geocentric opposition in RA: March 14^{d} 6^{h} 35^{m} 59^{s}.487

Umbral magnitude of the eclipse: 1.183

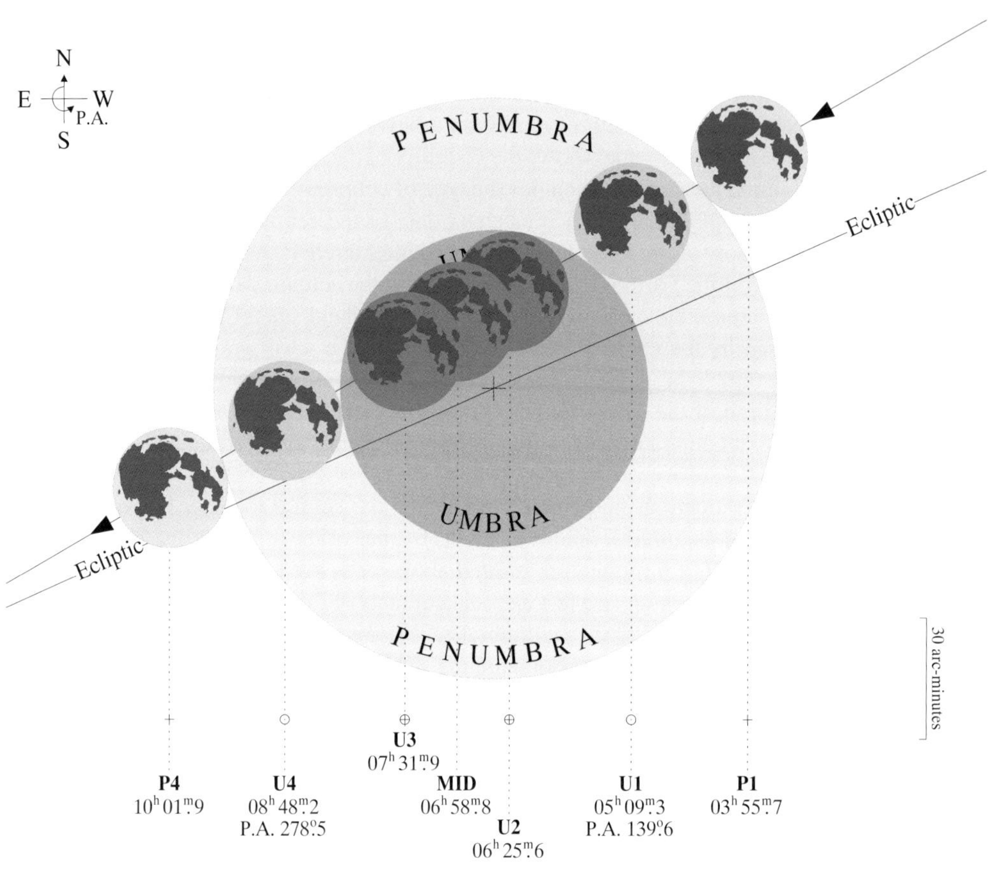

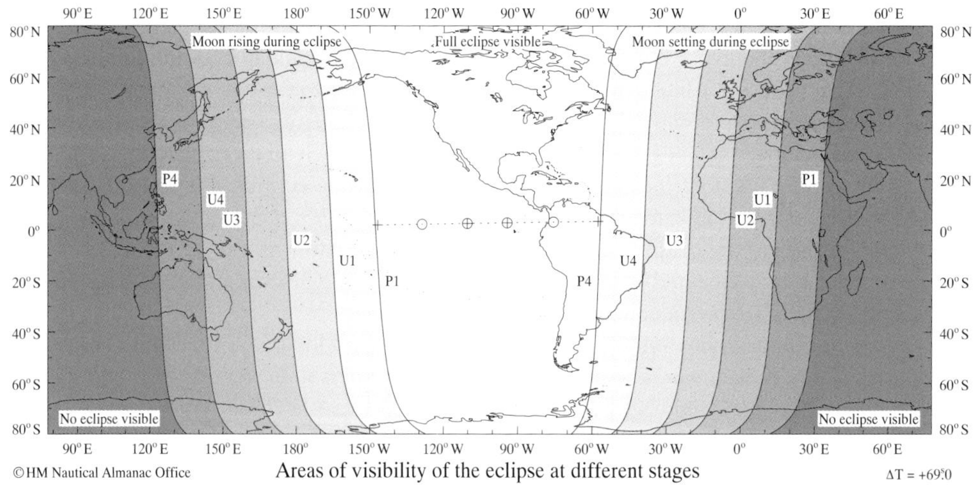

Areas of visibility of the eclipse at different stages

ΔT = +69^{s}.0

II. – Partial Eclipse of the Sun, 2025 March 29

CIRCUMSTANCES OF THE ECLIPSE

Universal Time of geocentric conjunction in right ascension, March 29^{d} 11^{h} 46^{m} 17^{s}.947
Julian Date = 2460763.9904854912

		UT	Longitude	Latitude
		d h m	° ′	° ′
Eclipse begins	March	29 08 50.7	− 42 23.1	+14 00.2
Greatest eclipse		29 10 47.5	− 77 12.8	+61 15.6
Eclipse ends		29 12 43.8	+ 90 52.0	+71 13.3

Magnitude of greatest eclipse: 0.9380

BESSELIAN ELEMENTS

Let $t = (\mathrm{UT} - 9^{h}) + \delta T / 3600$ in units of hours.

These equations are valid over the range $-0^{h}.208 \leq t \leq 3^{h}.900$. Do not use t outside the given range, and do not omit any terms in the series. If μ is greater than 360°, then subtract 360° from its computed value.

Intersection of the axis of shadow with the fundamental plane:

$$x = -1.41170743 + 0.50914890\,t + 0.00009158\,t^2 - 0.00000843\,t^3$$
$$y = +0.41312293 + 0.27906439\,t - 0.00004354\,t^2 - 0.00000484\,t^3$$

Direction of the axis of shadow:

$$\sin d = +0.06166205 + 0.00027076\,t - 0.00000003\,t^2$$
$$\cos d = +0.99809708 - 0.00001672\,t - 0.00000004\,t^2$$
$$\mu = 313^{\circ}.82221012 + 15.00436551\,t - 0.00000003\,t^2 - 0.00000001\,t^3 - 0.00417807\,\delta T$$

Radius of the shadow on the fundamental plane:

$$\text{penumbra } (l_1) = +0.53584366 - 0.00000257\,t - 0.00001272\,t^2 - 0.00000002\,t^3$$
$$\text{umbra } (l_2) = -0.01048966 - 0.00000215\,t - 0.00001287\,t^2 + 0.00000001\,t^3$$

Other important quantities:

$\tan f_1 = +0.004682$

$\mu' = +0.261876$ radians per hour

$d' = +0.000271$ radians per hour

All time arguments are given provisionally in Universal Time, using $\Delta T(A) = 69^{s}.0$.

PARTIAL SOLAR ECLIPSE OF 2025 MARCH 29

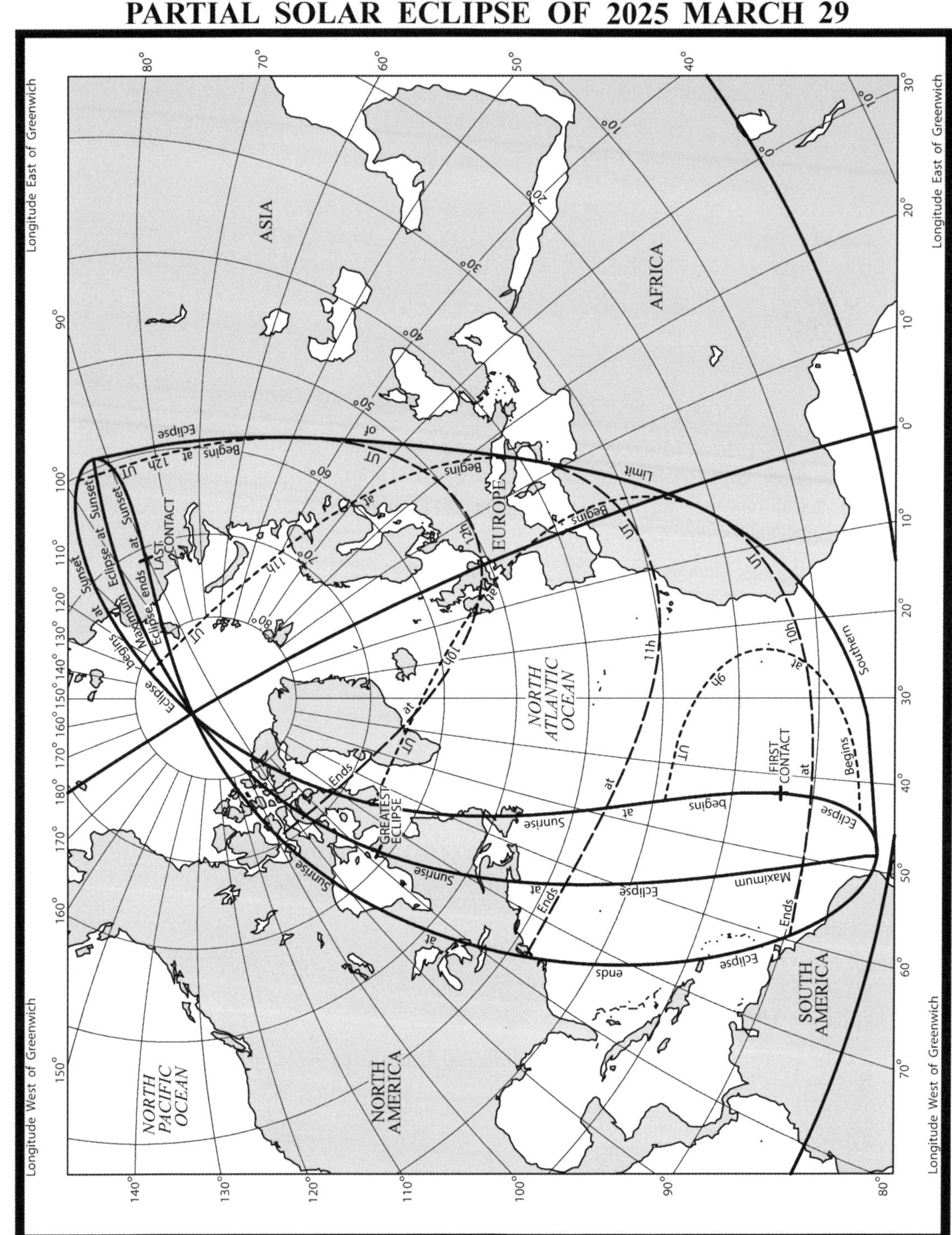

III. - Total Eclipse of the Moon 2025 September 07

U3 $18^{h} 53^{m}.3$

MID $18^{h} 11^{m}.8$

U2 $17^{h} 30^{m}.4$

P4 $20^{h} 56^{m}.6$

U4 $19^{h} 56^{m}.9$ P.A. 257°.2

U1 $16^{h} 26^{m}.8$ P.A. 45°.9

P1 $15^{h} 26^{m}.9$

30 arc-minutes

PENUMBRA

UMBRA

Ecliptic

N E W S P.A.

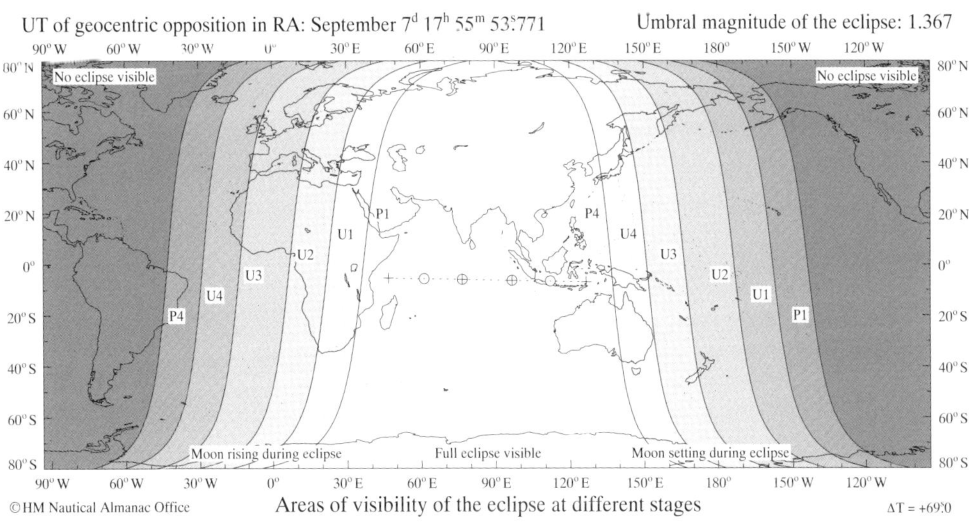

Areas of visibility of the eclipse at different stages

IV. – Partial Eclipse of the Sun, 2025 September 21

CIRCUMSTANCES OF THE ECLIPSE

Universal Time of geocentric conjunction in right ascension, September $21^d\ 20^h\ 50^m\ 29^s.799$
Julian Date = 2460940.3684004503

		UT	Longitude	Latitude
		d h m	° ′	° ′
Eclipse begins	September	21 17 29.7	−174 05.7	−13 58.3
Greatest eclipse		21 19 41.9	+153 24.5	−61 03.9
Eclipse ends		21 21 53.8	− 61 16.8	−72 16.0

Magnitude of greatest eclipse: 0.8554

BESSELIAN ELEMENTS

Let $t = (\text{UT}-17^h) + \delta T/3600$ in units of hours.

These equations are valid over the range $0^h.375 \le t \le 5^h.067$. Do not use t outside the given range, and do not omit any terms in the series.

Intersection of the axis of shadow with the fundamental plane:

$$x = -1.74069072 + 0.45299724\,t + 0.00005128\,t^2 - 0.00000538\,t^3$$
$$y = -0.24985178 - 0.25235167\,t + 0.00001755\,t^2 + 0.00000314\,t^3$$

Direction of the axis of shadow:

$$\sin d = +0.00717725 - 0.00027223\,t$$
$$\cos d = +0.99997411 + 0.00000213\,t - 0.00000010\,t^2 + 0.00000001\,t^3$$
$$\mu = 76^\circ.76690142 + 15.00477142\,t + 0.00000013\,t^2 - 0.00000005\,t^3 - 0.00417807\,\delta T$$

Radius of the shadow on the fundamental plane:

$$\text{penumbra } (l_1) = +0.56215344 + 0.00015216\,t - 0.00001030\,t^2$$
$$\text{umbra } (l_2) = +0.01568940 + 0.00015117\,t - 0.00001015\,t^2 - 0.00000001\,t^3$$

Other important quantities:

$$\tan f_1 = +0.004658$$
$$\mu' = +0.261883 \text{ radians per hour}$$
$$d' = -0.000272 \text{ radians per hour}$$

All time arguments are given provisionally in Universal Time, using $\Delta T(A) = 69^s.0$.

PARTIAL SOLAR ECLIPSE OF 2025 SEPTEMBER 21

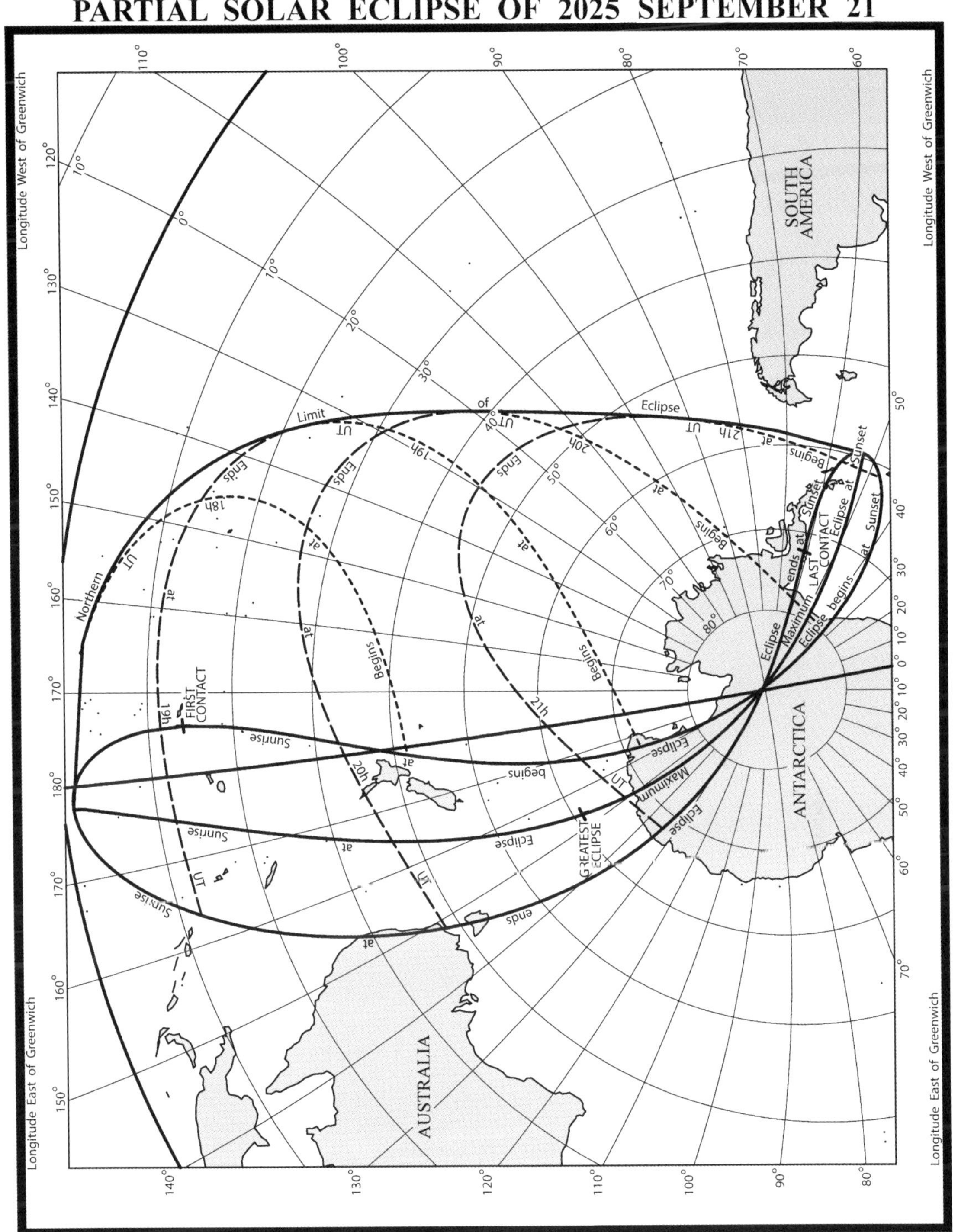

. . . continued from page A2

OCCULTATIONS OF PLANETS AND BRIGHT STARS BY THE MOON

Date (d h)	Body	Areas of Visibility
June 30 01	Mars	N.E. tip of Russia, Hawaii, Galapagos Is., N.W. tip of South America.
July 3 22	*Spica*	Easternmost Polynesia, S. part of South America, most of Antarctica.
July 7 18	*Antares*	S. tip of Africa, Kerguelen Is., easternmost Antarctica, S.W. Australia.
July 11 23	Pluto	St Helena Is., southern Africa, Madagascar, India.
July 26 20	*Regulus*	S.E. Iceland, Faroe Is.
July 28 20	Mars	Westernmost Antarctica.
July 31 06	*Spica*	Extreme S.W. tip of Australia, Kerguelen Is., most of Antarctica.
Aug. 4 02	*Antares*	S. Polynesia (including New Zealand), S. tip of South America, parts of Antarctica.
Aug. 8 05	Pluto	E. Polynesia, N.W. South America, S. Caribbean region
Aug. 27 15	*Spica*	S. tip of South America, W. Antarctica.
Aug. 31 11	*Antares*	S.E. edge of southern Africa, S. Madagascar, Kerguelen Is., most of Antarctica, S. New Zealand.
Sept. 4 14	Pluto	Madagascar, most of Australia, south-easternmost S.E. Asia, Melanesia, most of Micronesia.
Sept. 19 12	*Regulus*	Urals region of Russia.
Sept. 19 12	Venus	N.W. Canada, Greenland, Iceland, Europe, W. Russia, parts of the Middle East, N.E. Africa.
Sept. 23 22	*Spica*	S. New Zealand, Tasmania, parts of Antarctica.
Sept. 27 18	*Antares*	Easter Is., S. part of South America, most of Antarctica, Kerguelen Is., Marion Is.
Oct. 1 22	Pluto	Easter Is., most of southern South America, St Helena Is., W. and middle Africa.
Oct. 16 18	*Regulus*	Greenland, N.E. Canada, extreme N.E. tip of USA.
Oct. 25 01	*Antares*	Australia, New Zealand, W. Antarctica, S. tip of South America.
Oct. 29 07	Pluto	S. parts of S.E. Asia, most of Australia, most of Melanesia, W. Polynesia (except New Zealand).
Nov. 13 00	*Regulus*	N. Greenland, N.E. Russia, most of Alaska, N.E. tip of China, N. Japan.
Nov. 17 11	*Spica*	Southernmost tip of South America, W. Antarctica.
Nov. 25 14	Pluto	Cape Verde Is., Africa except N. and S. parts, most of Arabian Peninsula, S. Asia, parts of Kazakhstan.
Dec. 10 07	*Regulus*	Most of Canada, E. Alaska, Greenland, Iceland, Europe, Azores, most of N. Africa.
Dec. 18 13	*Antares*	Easter Is., southern South America, easternmost Antarctica, S. tip of Africa.
Dec. 22 21	Pluto	Hawaii, most of Central America, most of USA, N. Caribbean, E. Canada.

AVAILABILITY OF PREDICTIONS OF LUNAR OCCULTATIONS

The International Lunar Occultation Centre, Astronomical Division, Hydrographic Department, Tsukiji-5, Chuo-ku, Tokyo, 104 JAPAN is responsible for the predictions and for the reductions of timings of occultations of stars by the Moon.

CONTENTS OF SECTION B

Introduction

The tables and formulae in this section are produced in accordance with the recommendations of the International Astronomical Union at its General Assemblies up to and including 2012 and reviewed before the current edition was prepared. They are intended for use with relativistic coordinate time-scales, the International Celestial Reference System (ICRS), the Geocentric Celestial Reference System (GCRS) and the standard epoch of J2000·0 TT.

Because of its consistency with previous reference systems, implementation of the ICRS will be transparent to any applications with accuracy requirements of no better than 0″1 near epoch J2000·0. At this level of accuracy the distinctions between the International Celestial Reference Frame, FK5, and dynamical equator and equinox of J2000·0 are not significant.

Procedures are given to calculate both intermediate and apparent right ascension, declination and hour angle of planetary and stellar objects which are referred to the ICRS, e.g. the JPL DE440/LE440 Planetary and Lunar Ephemerides or the Hipparcos star catalogue. These procedures include the effects of the differences between time-scales, light-time and the relativistic effects of light-deflection, parallax and aberration, and the rotations, i.e. frame bias, precession and nutation, to give the "of date" system.

The rotations from the GCRS to the Terrestrial Intermediate Reference System are illustrated using both equinox-based and CIO-based techniques. Both of these techniques require the position of the Celestial Intermediate Pole and involve the angles for frame bias, precession and nutation, whether applied individually or amalgamated, directly or indirectly. Within this section the CIO-based techniques are indicated by shading of the text.

The equinox-based and CIO-based techniques only differ in the location of the origin for right ascension, and thus whether Greenwich apparent sidereal time or Earth rotation angle, respectively, is used to calculate hour angle. Equinox-based techniques use the equinox as the origin for right ascension and the system is usually labelled the true equator and equinox of date. CIO-based techniques use the celestial intermediate origin (CIO), and the system is labelled the Celestial Intermediate Reference System. It must be emphasized that the equator of date is the celestial intermediate equator and hour angle is independent of the origin of right ascension. However, the hour angle must be calculated consistently within the system used.

Introduction (continued)

This section includes the long-standing daily tabulations of the nutation angles, $\Delta\psi$ and $\Delta\epsilon$, the true obliquity of the ecliptic, Greenwich mean and apparent sidereal time and the equation of the equinoxes, as well as the parameters that define the Celestial Intermediate Reference System, $\mathcal{X}$, $\mathcal{Y}$, s, the Earth rotation angle and equation of the origins. Also tabulated daily are the matrices, both equinox and CIO based, for reduction from the GCRS.

It should be noted that the IAU 2006 precession parameters are to be used with the IAU 2000A nutation series. However, for the highest precision, adjustments are required to the nutation in longitude and obliquity (see page B55). These adjustments are included in the IAU SOFA code which is used throughout this section.

Background information about time-scales and coordinate reference systems recommended by the IAU and adopted in this almanac are given in Section L, *Notes and References* and in Section M, *Glossary*.

Definitions involving the relationship between universal and sidereal time require knowledge of ΔT. However, accurate values of ΔT (see pages K8–K9) are only available in retrospect via analysis of observations from the IERS (see page x). Therefore the tables adopt the most likely value at the time of production. The value used and the errors are stated in the text.

CALENDAR

Julian date

A Julian date (JD) may be associated with any time scale (see page B6). A tabulation of Julian date (JD) at 0^h UT1 against calendar date is given with the ephemeris of universal and sidereal times on pages B13–B20. Similarly, pages B21–B24 tabulate the UT1 Julian date together with the Earth rotation angle. The following relationship holds during 2025:

$$\text{UT1 Julian date} = \text{JD}_{\text{UT1}} = 246\ 0675{\cdot}5 + \text{day of year} + \text{fraction of day from } 0^h \text{ UT1}$$

$$\text{TT Julian date} = \text{JD}_{\text{TT}} = 246\ 0675{\cdot}5 + d + \text{fraction of day from } 0^h \text{ TT}$$

where the day of the year (d) for the current year of the Gregorian calendar is given on pages B4–B5. The following table gives the Julian dates at day 0 of each month of 2025:

0^h	Julian Date	0^h	Julian Date	0^h	Julian Date	0^h	Julian Date
Jan. 0	246 0675·5	Apr. 0	246 0765·5	July 0	246 0856·5	Oct. 0	246 0948·5
Feb. 0	246 0706·5	May 0	246 0795·5	Aug. 0	246 0887·5	Nov. 0	246 0979·5
Mar. 0	246 0734·5	June 0	246 0826·5	Sept. 0	246 0918·5	Dec. 0	246 1009·5

Tabulations of Julian date against calendar date for other years are given on pages K2–K4.

A date may also be expressed in years as a Julian epoch, or for some purposes as a Besselian epoch, using:

$$\text{Julian epoch} = \text{J}[2000{\cdot}0 + (\text{JD}_{\text{TT}} - 245\ 1545{\cdot}0)/365{\cdot}25]$$

$$\text{Besselian epoch} = \text{B}[1900{\cdot}0 + (\text{JD}_{\text{TT}} - 241\ 5020{\cdot}313\ 52)/365{\cdot}242\ 198\ 781]$$

the prefixes J and B may be omitted only where the context, or precision, make them superfluous.

400-day date, JD 246 0800·5 = 2025 May 5·0

Standard epoch B1900·0 = 1900 Jan. 0·813 52 = JD 241 5020·313 52 TT
B1950·0 = 1950 Jan. 0·923 = JD 243 3282·423 TT
B2025·0 = 2025 Jan. 0·088 TT = JD 246 0675·588 TT

Standard epoch J2000·0 = 2000 Jan. 1·5 TT = JD 245 1545·0 TT
J2025·5 = 2025 July 2·375 TT = JD 246 0858·875 TT

For epochs B1900·0 and B1950·0 the TT time scale is used proleptically.

The *modified Julian date* (MJD) is the Julian date minus 240 0000·5 and in 2025 is given by: MJD = 60675·0 + day of year + fraction of day from 0^h in the time scale being used.

Day of Month	JANUARY Day of Week	Day of Year	FEBRUARY Day of Week	Day of Year	MARCH Day of Week	Day of Year	APRIL Day of Week	Day of Year	MAY Day of Week	Day of Year	JUNE Day of Week	Day of Year
1	Wed.	1	Sat.	32	Sat.	60	Tue.	91	Thu.	121	Sun.	152
2	Thu.	2	Sun.	33	Sun.	61	Wed.	92	Fri.	122	Mon.	153
3	Fri.	3	Mon.	34	Mon.	62	Thu.	93	Sat.	123	Tue.	154
4	Sat.	4	Tue.	35	Tue.	63	Fri.	94	Sun.	124	Wed.	155
5	Sun.	5	Wed.	36	Wed.	64	Sat.	95	Mon.	125	Thu.	156
6	Mon.	6	Thu.	37	Thu.	65	Sun.	96	Tue.	126	Fri.	157
7	Tue.	7	Fri.	38	Fri.	66	Mon.	97	Wed.	127	Sat.	158
8	Wed.	8	Sat.	39	Sat.	67	Tue.	98	Thu.	128	Sun.	159
9	Thu.	9	Sun.	40	Sun.	68	Wed.	99	Fri.	129	Mon.	160
10	Fri.	10	Mon.	41	Mon.	69	Thu.	100	Sat.	130	Tue.	161
11	Sat.	11	Tue.	42	Tue.	70	Fri.	101	Sun.	131	Wed.	162
12	Sun.	12	Wed.	43	Wed.	71	Sat.	102	Mon.	132	Thu.	163
13	Mon.	13	Thu.	44	Thu.	72	Sun.	103	Tue.	133	Fri.	164
14	Tue.	14	Fri.	45	Fri.	73	Mon.	104	Wed.	134	Sat.	165
15	Wed.	15	Sat.	46	Sat.	74	Tue.	105	Thu.	135	Sun.	166
16	Thu.	16	Sun.	47	Sun.	75	Wed.	106	Fri.	136	Mon.	167
17	Fri.	17	Mon.	48	Mon.	76	Thu.	107	Sat.	137	Tue.	168
18	Sat.	18	Tue.	49	Tue.	77	Fri.	108	Sun.	138	Wed.	169
19	Sun.	19	Wed.	50	Wed.	78	Sat.	109	Mon.	139	Thu.	170
20	Mon.	20	Thu.	51	Thu.	79	Sun.	110	Tue.	140	Fri.	171
21	Tue.	21	Fri.	52	Fri.	80	Mon.	111	Wed.	141	Sat.	172
22	Wed.	22	Sat.	53	Sat.	81	Tue.	112	Thu.	142	Sun.	173
23	Thu.	23	Sun.	54	Sun.	82	Wed.	113	Fri.	143	Mon.	174
24	Fri.	24	Mon.	55	Mon.	83	Thu.	114	Sat.	144	Tue.	175
25	Sat.	25	Tue.	56	Tue.	84	Fri.	115	Sun.	145	Wed.	176
26	Sun.	26	Wed.	57	Wed.	85	Sat.	116	Mon.	146	Thu.	177
27	Mon.	27	Thu.	58	Thu.	86	Sun.	117	Tue.	147	Fri.	178
28	Tue.	28	Fri.	59	Fri.	87	Mon.	118	Wed.	148	Sat.	179
29	Wed.	29			Sat.	88	Tue.	119	Thu.	149	Sun.	180
30	Thu.	30			Sun.	89	Wed.	120	Fri.	150	Mon.	181
31	Fri.	31			Mon.	90			Sat.	151		

CHRONOLOGICAL CYCLES AND ERAS

Dominical Letter	E	Julian Period (year of)	6738
Epact	30	Roman Indiction	3
Golden Number (Lunar Cycle)	XII	Solar Cycle	18

All dates are given in terms of the Gregorian calendar in which 2025 January 14 corresponds to 2025 January 1 of the Julian calendar.

ERA	YEAR	BEGINS	ERA	YEAR	BEGINS
Byzantine	7534	Sept. 14	Japanese	2685	Jan. 1
Jewish (A.M.)*	5786	Sept. 22	Seleucidæ (Grecian)	2337	Sept. 14 (or Oct. 14)
Chinese (yǐ sì)		Jan. 29			
Roman (A.U.C.)	2778	Jan. 14	Saka (Indian)	1947	Mar. 22
Nabonassar	2774	Apr. 17	Diocletian (Coptic)	1742	Sept. 11
			Islamic (Hegira)*	1447	June 26

* Year begins at sunset

Day of Month	JULY Day of Week	JULY Day of Year	AUGUST Day of Week	AUGUST Day of Year	SEPTEMBER Day of Week	SEPTEMBER Day of Year	OCTOBER Day of Week	OCTOBER Day of Year	NOVEMBER Day of Week	NOVEMBER Day of Year	DECEMBER Day of Week	DECEMBER Day of Year
1	Tue.	182	Fri.	213	Mon.	244	Wed.	274	Sat.	305	Mon.	335
2	Wed.	183	Sat.	214	Tue.	245	Thu.	275	Sun.	306	Tue.	336
3	Thu.	184	Sun.	215	Wed.	246	Fri.	276	Mon.	307	Wed.	337
4	Fri.	185	Mon.	216	Thu.	247	Sat.	277	Tue.	308	Thu.	338
5	Sat.	186	Tue.	217	Fri.	248	Sun.	278	Wed.	309	Fri.	339
6	Sun.	187	Wed.	218	Sat.	249	Mon.	279	Thu.	310	Sat.	340
7	Mon.	188	Thu.	219	Sun.	250	Tue.	280	Fri.	311	Sun.	341
8	Tue.	189	Fri.	220	Mon.	251	Wed.	281	Sat.	312	Mon.	342
9	Wed.	190	Sat.	221	Tue.	252	Thu.	282	Sun.	313	Tue.	343
10	Thu.	191	Sun.	222	Wed.	253	Fri.	283	Mon.	314	Wed.	344
11	Fri.	192	Mon.	223	Thu.	254	Sat.	284	Tue.	315	Thu.	345
12	Sat.	193	Tue.	224	Fri.	255	Sun.	285	Wed.	316	Fri.	346
13	Sun.	194	Wed.	225	Sat.	256	Mon.	286	Thu.	317	Sat.	347
14	Mon.	195	Thu.	226	Sun.	257	Tue.	287	Fri.	318	Sun.	348
15	Tue.	196	Fri.	227	Mon.	258	Wed.	288	Sat.	319	Mon.	349
16	Wed.	197	Sat.	228	Tue.	259	Thu.	289	Sun.	320	Tue.	350
17	Thu.	198	Sun.	229	Wed.	260	Fri.	290	Mon.	321	Wed.	351
18	Fri.	199	Mon.	230	Thu.	261	Sat.	291	Tue.	322	Thu.	352
19	Sat.	200	Tue.	231	Fri.	262	Sun.	292	Wed.	323	Fri.	353
20	Sun.	201	Wed.	232	Sat.	263	Mon.	293	Thu.	324	Sat.	354
21	Mon.	202	Thu.	233	Sun.	264	Tue.	294	Fri.	325	Sun.	355
22	Tue.	203	Fri.	234	Mon.	265	Wed.	295	Sat.	326	Mon.	356
23	Wed.	204	Sat.	235	Tue.	266	Thu.	296	Sun.	327	Tue.	357
24	Thu.	205	Sun.	236	Wed.	267	Fri.	297	Mon.	328	Wed.	358
25	Fri.	206	Mon.	237	Thu.	268	Sat.	298	Tue.	329	Thu.	359
26	Sat.	207	Tue.	238	Fri.	269	Sun.	299	Wed.	330	Fri.	360
27	Sun.	208	Wed.	239	Sat.	270	Mon.	300	Thu.	331	Sat.	361
28	Mon.	209	Thu.	240	Sun.	271	Tue.	301	Fri.	332	Sun.	362
29	Tue.	210	Fri.	241	Mon.	272	Wed.	302	Sat.	333	Mon.	363
30	Wed.	211	Sat.	242	Tue.	273	Thu.	303	Sun.	334	Tue.	364
31	Thu.	212	Sun.	243			Fri.	304			Wed.	365

RELIGIOUS CALENDARS

Epiphany	Jan.	6	Ascension Day	May	29
Ash Wednesday	Mar.	5	Whit Sunday—Pentecost ...	June	8
Palm Sunday	Apr.	13	Trinity Sunday	June	15
Good Friday	Apr.	18	First Sunday in Advent	Nov.	30
Easter Day	Apr.	20	Christmas Day (Thursday) ...	Dec.	25
First day of Passover (Pesach)	Apr.	13	Day of Atonement (Yom Kippur)	Oct.	2
Feast of Weeks (Shavuot) ...	June	2	First day of Tabernacles (Succoth)	Oct.	7
Jewish New Year (Rosh Hashanah)	Sept.	23	Festival of Lights (Hanukkah)	Dec.	15
First day of Ramadân	Mar.	1	Islamic New Year	June	27
First day of Shawwal (Eid ul-Fitr)	Mar.	31			

The Jewish and Islamic dates above are tabular dates, which begin at sunset on the previous evening and end at sunset on the date tabulated. In practice, the dates of Islamic fasts and festivals are determined by an actual sighting of the appropriate new moon.

Notation for time-scales and related quantities

A summary of the notation for time-scales and related quantities used in this Almanac is given below. Additional information is given in the *Glossary* (Section M) and in the *Notes and References* (Section L).

UT1	universal time (also UT); counted from 0^h (midnight); unit is second of mean solar time, affected by irregularities in the Earth's rate of rotation.
GMST	Greenwich mean sidereal time; GHA of mean equinox of date.
GAST	Greenwich apparent sidereal time; GHA of true equinox of date.
E_e	Equation of the equinoxes: GAST − GMST.
E_o	Equation of the origins: ERA − GAST = θ − GAST.
ERA	Earth rotation angle (θ); the angle between the celestial and terrestrial intermediate origins; it is proportional to UT1.
TAI	International Atomic Time; unit is the SI second on the geoid.
UTC	coordinated universal time; differs from TAI by an integral number of seconds, and is the basis of most radio time signals and national and/or legal time systems.
ΔUT	= UT1−UTC; increment to be applied to UTC to give UT1.
DUT1	predicted value of ΔUT, rounded to $0\overset{s}{.}1$, given in some radio time signals.
TDB	barycentric dynamical time; used as time-scale of ephemerides, referred to the barycentre of the solar system.
TT	terrestrial time; used as time-scale of ephemerides for observations from the Earth's surface (geoid). TT = TAI + $32\overset{s}{.}184$.
ΔT	= TT − UT1; increment to be applied to UT1 to give TT. = TAI + $32\overset{s}{.}184$ − UT1.
ΔAT	= TAI − UTC; increment to be applied to UTC to give TAI; an integral number of seconds.
ΔTT	= TT − UTC = ΔAT+$32\overset{s}{.}184$; increment to be applied to UTC to give TT.
JD_{TT}	= Julian date and fraction, where the time fraction is expressed in the terrestrial time scale, e.g. 2000 January 1, 12^h TT is JD 245 1545·0 TT.
JD_{UT1}	= Julian date and fraction, where the time fraction is expressed in the universal time scale, e.g. 2000 January 1, 12^h UT1 is JD 245 1545·0 UT1.

The following intervals are used in this section.

$$T = (\text{JD}_{\text{TT}} - 245\,1545{\cdot}0)/36\,525 = \text{Julian centuries of } 365\,25 \text{ days from J2000}{\cdot}0$$
$$D = \text{JD} - 245\,1545{\cdot}0 = \text{days and fraction from J2000}{\cdot}0$$
$$D_{\text{U}} = \text{JD}_{\text{UT1}} - 245\,1545{\cdot}0 = \text{days and UT1 fraction from J2000}{\cdot}0$$
$$d = \text{Day of the year, January } 1 = 1, \text{ etc., see B4–B5}$$

Note that the intervals above are based on different time scales. T implies the TT time scale while D_{U} implies the UT1 time scale. This is an important distinction when calculating Greenwich mean sidereal time. T is the number of Julian centuries from J2000·0 to the required epoch (TT), while D, D_{U} and d are all in days.

The name Greenwich mean time (GMT) is not used in this Almanac since it is ambiguous. It is now used, although not in astronomy, in the sense of UTC, in addition to the earlier sense of UT; prior to 1925 it was reckoned for astronomical purposes from Greenwich mean noon (12^h UT).

Relationships between time-scales

The unit of UTC is the SI second on the geoid, but step adjustments of 1 second (leap seconds) are occasionally introduced into UTC so that universal time (UT1) may be obtained directly from it with an accuracy of 1 second or better and so that International Atomic Time (TAI) may be obtained by the addition of an integral number of seconds. The step adjustments, when required, are usually inserted after the 60th second of the last minute of December 31 or June 30. Values of the differences ΔAT for 1972 onwards are given on page K9. Accurate values of the increment ΔUT to be applied to UTC to give UT1 are derived from observations, but predicted values are transmitted in code in some time signals. Wherever UT is used in this volume it always means UT1.

The difference between the terrestrial time scale (TT) and the barycentric dynamical time scale (TDB) is often ignored, since the two time scales differ by no more than 2 milliseconds.

An approximate expression for the relationship between the barycentric and terrestrial time-scales (due to the variations in gravitational potential around the Earth's orbit) is:

$$\mathrm{TDB} = \mathrm{TT} + 0\overset{s}{.}001\,656\,67 \sin g + 0\overset{s}{.}000\,022\,42 \sin(L - L_J)$$

and

$$g = 357\overset{\circ}{.}53 + 0{\cdot}985\,600\,28(\mathrm{JD} - 245\,1545{\cdot}0)$$
$$L - L_J = 246\overset{\circ}{.}11 + 0{\cdot}902\,517\,92(\mathrm{JD} - 245\,1545{\cdot}0)$$

where g is the mean anomaly of the Earth in its orbit around the Sun, and $L - L_J$ is the difference in the mean ecliptic longitudes of the Sun and Jupiter. The above formula for TDB − TT is accurate to about $\pm 30\mu$s over the period 1980 to 2050.

For 2025

$$g = 356\overset{\circ}{.}55 + 0\overset{\circ}{.}985\,60\,d \qquad \text{and} \qquad L - L_J = -153\overset{\circ}{.}45 + 0\overset{\circ}{.}902\,52\,d$$

where d is the day of the year and fraction of the day.

The TDB time scale should be used for quantities such as precession angles and the fundamental arguments. However, for these quantities, the difference between TDB and TT is negligible at the microarcsecond (μas) level.

Relationships between universal time, ERA, GMST and GAST

The following equations show the relationships between the Earth rotation angle (ERA=θ), Greenwich mean (GMST) and apparent (GAST) sidereal time, in terms of the equation of the origins (E_o) and the equation of the equinoxes (E_e):

$$\begin{aligned}\mathrm{GMST}(D_\mathrm{U}, T) &= \theta(D_\mathrm{U}) + \text{polynomial part}(T)\\ \mathrm{GAST}(D_\mathrm{U}, T) &= \theta(D_\mathrm{U}) - \text{equation of the origins}(T)\\ &= \mathrm{GMST}(D_\mathrm{U}, T) + \text{equation of the equinoxes}(T)\end{aligned}$$

The definition of these quantities follow. Note that ERA is a function of UT1, while GMST and GAST are functions of both UT1 and TT. A diagram showing the relationships between these concepts is given on page B9.

ERA is for use with intermediate right ascensions while GAST must be used with apparent (equinox based) right ascensions.

Relationship between universal time and Earth rotation angle

The Earth rotation angle (θ) is measured in the Celestial Intermediate Reference System along its equator (the true equator of date) between the terrestrial and the celestial intermediate origins. It is proportional to UT1, and its time derivative is the Earth's adopted mean angular velocity; it is defined by the following relationship

$$\theta(D_U) = 2\pi(0{\cdot}7790\,5727\,32640 + 1{\cdot}0027\,3781\,1911\,35448\,D_U)\text{ radians}$$
$$= 360^\circ(0{\cdot}7790\,5727\,32640 + 0{\cdot}0027\,3781\,1911\,35448\,D_U + D_U \bmod 1)$$

where D_U is the interval, in days, elapsed since the epoch 2000 January 1^d 12^h UT1 (JD 245 1545·0 UT1), and D_U mod 1 is the fraction of the UT1 day remaining after removing all the whole days. The Earth rotation angle (ERA) is tabulated daily at 0^h UT1 on pages B21–B24.

During 2025, on day d, at t^h UT1, the Earth rotation angle, expressed in arc and time, respectively, is given by:

$$\theta = 99^\circ\!.593\,615 + 0^\circ\!.985\,612\,288\,d + 15^\circ\!.041\,0672\,t$$
$$= 6^h\!.639\,5743 + 0^h\!.065\,707\,4859\,d + 1^h\!.002\,737\,81\,t$$

Relationship between universal and sidereal time

Greenwich Mean Sidereal Time

Universal time is defined in terms of Greenwich mean sidereal time (i.e. the hour angle of the mean equinox of date) by:

$$\text{GMST}(D_U, T) = \theta(D_U) + \text{GMST}_P(T)$$
$$\text{GMST}_P(T) = 0''\!.014\,506 + 4612''\!.156\,534\,T + 1''\!.391\,5817\,T^2 - 0''\!.000\,000\,44\,T^3 - 0''\!.000\,029\,956\,T^4 - 3''\!.68\times10^{-8}\,T^5$$

where θ is the Earth rotation angle. The polynomial part, $\text{GMST}_P(T)$ is due almost entirely to the effect of precession and is given separately as it also forms part of the equation of the origins (see page B10). The time interval D_U is measured in days elapsed since the epoch 2000 January 1^d 12^h UT1 (JD 245 1545·0 UT1), whereas T is measured in the TT scale, in Julian centuries of 36 525 days, from JD 245 1545·0 TT.

The Earth rotation angle is expressed in degrees while the terms of the polynomial part (GMST_P) are in arcseconds. GMST is tabulated on pages B13–B20 and the equivalent expression in time units is

$$\text{GMST}(D_U, T) = 86400^s(0{\cdot}7790\,5727\,32640 + 0{\cdot}0027\,3781\,1911\,35448 D_U + D_U \bmod 1) + 0^s\!.000\,967\,07 + 307^s\!.477\,102\,27\,T + 0^s\!.092\,772\,113\,T^2 - 0^s\!.000\,000\,0293\,T^3 - 0^s\!.000\,001\,997\,07\,T^4 - 2^s\!.453\times10^{-9}\,T^5$$

It is necessary, in this formula, to distinguish TT from UT1 only for the most precise work. The table on pages B13–B20 is calculated assuming $\Delta T = 69^s$. During 2025, an error of $\pm1^s$ in ΔT at 0^h UT1 introduces differences of $\mp1''\!.5\times10^{-6}$ or equivalently $\mp0^s\!.10\times10^{-6}$, in the calculation of GMST.

The following relationship holds during 2025:

on day of year d at t^h UT1, $\text{GMST} = 6^h\!.660\,9270 + 0^h\!.065\,709\,8246\,d + 1^h\!.002\,737\,91\,t$,

where the day of year d is tabulated on pages B4–B5. Add or subtract multiples of 24^h as necessary.

Relationship between universal and sidereal time (continued)

In 2025: 1 mean solar day $= 1{\cdot}002\ 737\ 909\ 36$ mean sidereal days
$= 24^{h}\ 03^{m}\ 56\overset{s}{.}555\ 37$ of mean sidereal time

1 mean sidereal day $= 0{\cdot}997\ 269\ 566\ 32$ mean solar days
$= 23^{h}\ 56^{m}\ 04\overset{s}{.}090\ 53$ of mean solar time

Greenwich Apparent Sidereal Time

The hour angle of the true equinox of date (GAST) is given by:

$$\mathrm{GAST}(D_{\mathrm{U}}, T) = \theta(D_{\mathrm{U}}) - \text{equation of the origins} = \theta(D_{\mathrm{U}}) - E_o(T)$$
$$= \mathrm{GMST}(D_{\mathrm{U}}, T) + \text{equation of the equinoxes} = \mathrm{GMST}(D_{\mathrm{U}}, T) + E_e(T)$$

where θ is the Earth rotation angle (ERA) and GMST, the Greenwich mean sidereal time are given above, while the equation of the origins (E_o) and the equation of the equinoxes (E_e) are given on page B10.

Pages B13–B20 tabulate GAST and the equation of the equinoxes daily at 0^{h} UT1. These quantities have been calculated using the IAU 2000A nutation model together with the tiny (μas level) amendments (see B55); they are expressed in time units and are based on a predicted $\Delta T = 69^{s}$. During 2025, an error of $\pm 1^{s}$ in ΔT at 0^{h} UT1 introduces a maximum error of $\pm 3\overset{''}{.}9 \times 10^{-6}$ or equivalently $\pm 0\overset{s}{.}26 \times 10^{-6}$, in the calculation of GAST.

Interpolation may be used to obtain the equation of the equinoxes for another instant, or if full precision is required.

Relationships between origins

The difference between the CIO and true equinox of date is called the equation of the origins

$$E_o(T) = \theta - \mathrm{GAST}$$

while the difference between the true and mean equinox is called the equation of the equinoxes and is given by

$$E_e(T) = \mathrm{GAST} - \mathrm{GMST}$$

The following schematic diagram shows the relationship between the "zero longitude" defined by the terrestrial intermediate origin, the true equinox and the celestial intermediate origin.

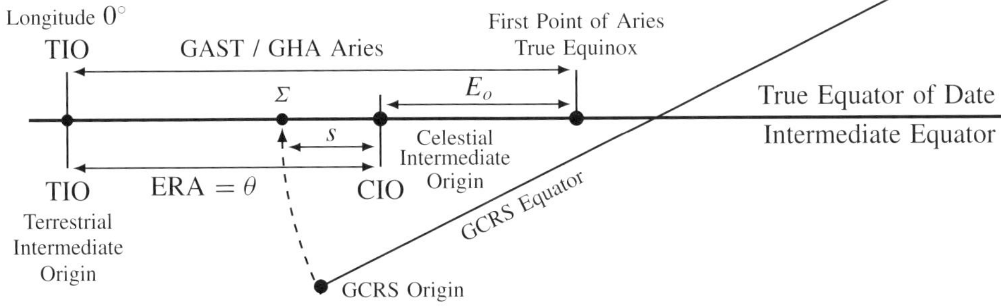

The diagram illustrates that the origin of Greenwich hour angle, the terrestrial intermediate origin (TIO), may be obtained from either Greenwich apparent sidereal time (GAST) or Earth rotation angle (ERA). The quantity s, the CIO locator, positions the GCRS origin (Σ) on the equator (see page B47). Note that the planes of intermediate equator and the true equator of date (the pole of which is the celestial intermediate pole) are identical.

Relationships between origins (continued)

Equation of the origins

The equation of the origins (E_o), the angular difference between the origin of intermediate right ascension (the CIO) and the origin of equinox right ascension (the true equinox) is defined to be

$$E_o(T) = \theta - \mathrm{GAST} = s - \tan^{-1}\frac{\mathbf{M_j} \cdot \mathcal{R}_{\Sigma_i}}{\mathbf{M_i} \cdot \mathcal{R}_{\Sigma_i}}$$

where s is the CIO locator (see page B47). $\mathbf{M_i}$, and $\mathbf{M_j}$ are vectors formed from the top and middle rows of $\mathbf{M}$ (see page B50) which transforms positions from the GCRS to the equator and equinox of date, while the vector $\mathcal{R}_{\Sigma_i}$ which is formed from the top row of $\mathcal{R}_{\Sigma}$ is given on page B49. The symbol $\cdot$ denotes the scalar or dot product of the two vectors.

Alternatively,

$$E_o(T) = -(\mathrm{GMST}_P(T) + E_e(T))$$

where GMST_P is the polynomial part of the Greenwich mean sidereal time formulae (see page B8), and E_e is the equation of the equinoxes given below. E_o is tabulated with the Earth rotation angle (θ) on pages B21–B24, and is calculated in the sense

$$E_o = \theta - \mathrm{GAST} = \alpha_i - \alpha_e$$

and therefore $\qquad \alpha_i = E_o + \alpha_e$

Thus, given an apparent right ascension (α_e) and the equation of the origins, the intermediate right ascension (α_i) may be calculated so that it can be used with the Earth rotation angle (θ) to form an hour angle.

Equation of the equinoxes

The equation of the equinoxes (E_e) is the difference between Greenwich apparent (GAST) and mean (GMST) sidereal time.

$$E_e(T) = \mathrm{GAST} - \mathrm{GMST}$$

which can be expressed, less precisely, in series form as

$$= \Delta\psi\, \cos\epsilon_A + \sum_k S_k \sin A_k - 0''\!.87 \times 10^{-6}\, T\, \sin\Omega$$

GAST and GMST are given on pages B9 and B8, respectively. $\Delta\psi$ is the total nutation in longitude (in seconds of arc) and ϵ_A is the mean obliquity of the ecliptic (see pages B55 and B52, respectively). The coefficients (S_k) are in seconds of arc in the above equation; they are given below (in μas) for all terms exceeding 0·5μas during 1975-2025. This series expression is accurate to $\pm 0''\!.3 \times 10^{-5}$ during this period. The arguments (A_k) l, l', F, D, and Ω are given on page B47.

k	A_k	S_k μas	k	A_k	S_k μas	k	A_k	S_k μas
1	Ω	+2640·96	5	$2F-2D+2\Omega$	−4·55	9	$l'+\Omega$	−1·41
2	2Ω	+63·52	6	$2F+3\Omega$	+2·02	10	$l'-\Omega$	−1·26
3	$2F-2D+3\Omega$	+11·75	7	$2F+\ \Omega$	+1·98	11	$l+\Omega$	−0·63
4	$2F-2D+\ \Omega$	+11·21	8	3Ω	−1·72	12	$l-\Omega$	−0·63

The following approximate expression for the equation of the equinoxes (in seconds), incorporates the two largest terms, and is accurate to better than $2^{\mathrm{s}} \times 10^{-6}$ assuming $\Delta\psi$ and ϵ_A are supplied with sufficient accuracy.

$$E_e^{\mathrm{s}} = \tfrac{1}{15}\,(\Delta\psi\, \cos\epsilon_A + 0''\!.002\,64 \sin\Omega + 0''\!.000\,06 \sin 2\Omega)$$

During 2025, $\Omega = 1^\circ\!.55 - 0^\circ\!.052\,953\,74\, d$, and d is the day of the year and fraction of day (see page D2).

Relationships between local time and hour angle

The local hour angle of an object is the angle between two planes: the plane containing the geocentre, the CIP, and the observer; and the plane containing the geocentre, the CIP, and the object. Hour angle increases with time and is positive when the object is west of the observer as viewed from the geocentre. The plane defining the astronomical zero ("Greenwich") meridian (from which Greenwich hour angles are measured) contains the geocentre, the CIP, and the TIO; there, the observer's longitude λ (not λ_{ITRS}) = 0. This plane is called the TIO meridian and it is a fundamental plane of the Terrestrial Intermediate Reference System.

The following general relationships are used to relate the right ascensions of celestial objects to locations on the Earth and universal time (UT1):

local mean solar time = universal time + east longitude
local hour angle (h) = Greenwich hour angle (H) + east longitude (λ)

Equinox-based

local mean sidereal time = Greenwich mean sidereal time + east longitude
local apparent sidereal time = local mean sidereal time + equation of equinoxes
= Greenwich apparent sidereal time + east longitude
Greenwich hour angle = Greenwich apparent sidereal time − apparent right ascension
local hour angle = local apparent sidereal time − apparent right ascension

CIO-based

Greenwich hour angle = Earth rotation angle − intermediate right ascension
local hour angle = Earth rotation angle − intermediate right ascension + east longitude
= Earth rotation angle − equation of origins − apparent right ascension + east longitude

Note: ensure that the units of all quantities used are compatible.

Alternatively, use the rotation matrix $\mathbf{R}_3$ (see page K19) to rotate the equator and equinox of date system or the Celestial Intermediate Reference System about the z-axis (CIP) to the terrestrial system, resulting in either the TIO meridian and hour angle, or the local meridian and local hour angle.

Equinox-based	*CIO-based*
$\mathbf{r}_e$ = position with respect to the equator and equinox (mean or true) of date	$\mathbf{r}_i$ = position with respect to the Celestial Intermediate Reference System
$\mathbf{r} = \mathbf{R}_3(\text{GST})\,\mathbf{r}_e$ or $\mathbf{R}_3(\text{GST}+\lambda)\,\mathbf{r}_e$	$\mathbf{r} = \mathbf{R}_3(\theta)\,\mathbf{r}_i$ or $\mathbf{R}_3(\theta+\lambda)\,\mathbf{r}_i$

depending on whether the Greenwich (H) or local (h) hour angle is required, and then

$$H \text{ or } h = \tan^{-1}(-\mathbf{r}_y/\mathbf{r}_x) \qquad \text{positive to the west,}$$

and $\mathbf{r}_x$, $\mathbf{r}_y$ are components of $\mathbf{r}$ (see page K18). GST is the Greenwich mean (GMST) or apparent (GAST) sidereal time, as appropriate, and θ is the Earth rotation angle. Greenwich apparent and mean sidereal times, and the equation of the equinoxes are tabulated on pages B13–B20, while Earth rotation angle and equation of the origins are tabulated on pages B21–B24. Both tables are tabulated daily at 0^{h} UT1.

The relationships above, which result in a position with respect to the Terrestrial Intermediate Reference System (see page B26 note 7), require corrections for polar motion (see page B84) when the reduction of very precise observations are made with respect to a standard geodetic system such as the International Terrestrial Reference System (ITRS). These small corrections are (i) the alignment of the terrestrial intermediate origin (TIO) onto the longitude origin (λ_{ITRS} = 0) of the ITRS, and (ii) for positioning the pole (CIP) within the ITRS.

Examples of the use of the ephemeris of universal and sidereal times

1. *Conversion of universal time to local sidereal time*

To find the local apparent sidereal time at $09^{h}\ 44^{m}\ 30^{s}$ UT on 2025 July 8 in longitude $80^{\circ}\ 22'\ 55''\!\cdot79$ west.

	h	m	s
Greenwich mean sidereal time on July 8 at 0^{h} UT (page B17)	19	04	48·3020
Add the equivalent mean sidereal time interval from 0^{h} to $09^{h}\ 44^{m}\ 30^{s}$ UT (multiply UT interval by 1·002 737 9094)	9	46	06·0185
Greenwich mean sidereal time at required UT:	4	50	54·3205
Add equation of equinoxes, interpolated using second-order differences to approximate UT = $0^{d}\!\cdot41$			+0·1863
Greenwich apparent sidereal time:	4	50	54·5068
Subtract west longitude (add east longitude)	5	21	31·7193
Local apparent sidereal time:	23	29	22·7875

The calculation for local mean sidereal time is similar, but omit the step which allows for the equation of the equinoxes.

2. *Conversion of local sidereal time to universal time*

To find the universal time at $23^{h}\ 29^{m}\ 22^{s}\!\cdot7875$ local apparent sidereal time on 2025 July 8 in longitude $80^{\circ}\ 22'\ 55''\!\cdot79$ west.

	h	m	s
Local apparent sidereal time:	23	29	22·7875
Add west longitude (subtract east longitude)	5	21	31·7193
Greenwich apparent sidereal time:	4	50	54·5068
Subtract equation of equinoxes, interpolated using second-order differences to approximate UT = $0^{d}\!\cdot41$			+0·1863
Greenwich mean sidereal time:	4	50	54·3205
Subtract Greenwich mean sidereal time at 0^{h} UT	19	04	48·3020
Mean sidereal time interval from 0^{h} UT:	9	46	06·0185
Equivalent UT interval (multiply mean sidereal time interval by 0·997 269 5663)	9	44	30·0000

The conversion of mean sidereal time to universal time is carried out by a similar procedure; omit the step which allows for the equation of the equinoxes.

Date 0h UT1		Julian Date	G. SIDEREAL TIME (GHA of the Equinox) Apparent	Mean	Equation of Equinoxes at 0h UT1	GSD at 0h GMST	UT1 at 0h GMST (Greenwich Transit of the Mean Equinox)	
		246	h m s	s	s	**246**		h m s
Jan.	0	**0675·5**	6 39 39·3394	39·3373	+0·0021	**7414·0**	Jan. 0	17 17 30·2272
	1	**0676·5**	6 43 35·9047	35·8926	+0·0121	**7415·0**	1	17 13 34·3178
	2	**0677·5**	6 47 32·4678	32·4480	+0·0198	**7416·0**	2	17 09 38·4083
	3	**0678·5**	6 51 29·0276	29·0034	+0·0242	**7417·0**	3	17 05 42·4988
	4	**0679·5**	6 55 25·5837	25·5587	+0·0249	**7418·0**	4	17 01 46·5894
	5	**0680·5**	6 59 22·1368	22·1141	+0·0227	**7419·0**	5	16 57 50·6799
	6	**0681·5**	7 03 18·6883	18·6695	+0·0189	**7420·0**	6	16 53 54·7704
	7	**0682·5**	7 07 15·2402	15·2249	+0·0154	**7421·0**	7	16 49 58·8610
	8	**0683·5**	7 11 11·7943	11·7802	+0·0141	**7422·0**	8	16 46 02·9515
	9	**0684·5**	7 15 08·3520	08·3356	+0·0164	**7423·0**	9	16 42 07·0420
	10	**0685·5**	7 19 04·9136	04·8910	+0·0226	**7424·0**	10	16 38 11·1325
	11	**0686·5**	7 23 01·4785	01·4463	+0·0322	**7425·0**	11	16 34 15·2231
	12	**0687·5**	7 26 58·0453	58·0017	+0·0436	**7426·0**	12	16 30 19·3136
	13	**0688·5**	7 30 54·6120	54·5571	+0·0549	**7427·0**	13	16 26 23·4041
	14	**0689·5**	7 34 51·1769	51·1124	+0·0644	**7428·0**	14	16 22 27·4947
	15	**0690·5**	7 38 47·7386	47·6678	+0·0708	**7429·0**	15	16 18 31·5852
	16	**0691·5**	7 42 44·2968	44·2232	+0·0736	**7430·0**	16	16 14 35·6757
	17	**0692·5**	7 46 40·8516	40·7785	+0·0730	**7431·0**	17	16 10 39·7663
	18	**0693·5**	7 50 37·4039	37·3339	+0·0700	**7432·0**	18	16 06 43·8568
	19	**0694·5**	7 54 33·9548	33·8893	+0·0655	**7433·0**	19	16 02 47·9473
	20	**0695·5**	7 58 30·5054	30·4446	+0·0608	**7434·0**	20	15 58 52·0378
	21	**0696·5**	8 02 27·0569	27·0000	+0·0569	**7435·0**	21	15 54 56·1284
	22	**0697·5**	8 06 23·6101	23·5554	+0·0548	**7436·0**	22	15 51 00·2189
	23	**0698·5**	8 10 20·1657	20·1108	+0·0549	**7437·0**	23	15 47 04·3094
	24	**0699·5**	8 14 16·7239	16·6661	+0·0578	**7438·0**	24	15 43 08·4000
	25	**0700·5**	8 18 13·2848	13·2215	+0·0633	**7439·0**	25	15 39 12·4905
	26	**0701·5**	8 22 09·8478	09·7769	+0·0709	**7440·0**	26	15 35 16·5810
	27	**0702·5**	8 26 06·4120	06·3322	+0·0798	**7441·0**	27	15 31 20·6716
	28	**0703·5**	8 30 02·9760	02·8876	+0·0884	**7442·0**	28	15 27 24·7621
	29	**0704·5**	8 33 59·5383	59·4430	+0·0953	**7443·0**	29	15 23 28·8526
	30	**0705·5**	8 37 56·0973	55·9983	+0·0990	**7444·0**	30	15 19 32·9431
	31	**0706·5**	8 41 52·6526	52·5537	+0·0989	**7445·0**	31	15 15 37·0337
Feb.	1	**0707·5**	8 45 49·2042	49·1091	+0·0951	**7446·0**	Feb. 1	15 11 41·1242
	2	**0708·5**	8 49 45·7537	45·6644	+0·0892	**7447·0**	2	15 07 45·2147
	3	**0709·5**	8 53 42·3029	42·2198	+0·0831	**7448·0**	3	15 03 49·3053
	4	**0710·5**	8 57 38·8540	38·7752	+0·0788	**7449·0**	4	14 59 53·3958
	5	**0711·5**	9 01 35·4084	35·3305	+0·0778	**7450·0**	5	14 55 57·4863
	6	**0712·5**	9 05 31·9666	31·8859	+0·0807	**7451·0**	6	14 52 01·5769
	7	**0713·5**	9 09 28·5281	28·4413	+0·0868	**7452·0**	7	14 48 05·6674
	8	**0714·5**	9 13 25·0917	24·9967	+0·0950	**7453·0**	8	14 44 09·7579
	9	**0715·5**	9 17 21·6556	21·5520	+0·1036	**7454·0**	9	14 40 13·8484
	10	**0716·5**	9 21 18·2182	18·1074	+0·1108	**7455·0**	10	14 36 17·9390
	11	**0717·5**	9 25 14·7781	14·6628	+0·1153	**7456·0**	11	14 32 22·0295
	12	**0718·5**	9 29 11·3346	11·2181	+0·1165	**7457·0**	12	14 28 26·1200
	13	**0719·5**	9 33 07·8877	07·7735	+0·1142	**7458·0**	13	14 24 30·2106
	14	**0720·5**	9 37 04·4381	04·3289	+0·1092	**7459·0**	14	14 20 34·3011
	15	**0721·5**	9 41 00·9866	00·8842	+0·1024	**7460·0**	15	14 16 38·3916

Date 0^h UT1	Julian Date	G. SIDEREAL TIME (GHA of the Equinox) Apparent	Mean	Equation of Equinoxes at 0^h UT1	GSD at 0^h GMST	UT1 at 0^h GMST (Greenwich Transit of the Mean Equinox)
	246	h m s	s	s	**246**	h m s
Feb. 15	**0721·5**	9 41 00·9866	00·8842	+0·1024	**7460·0**	Feb. 15 14 16 38·3916
16	**0722·5**	9 44 57·5345	57·4396	+0·0949	**7461·0**	16 14 12 42·4822
17	**0723·5**	9 48 54·0829	53·9950	+0·0879	**7462·0**	17 14 08 46·5727
18	**0724·5**	9 52 50·6327	50·5503	+0·0824	**7463·0**	18 14 04 50·6632
19	**0725·5**	9 56 47·1847	47·1057	+0·0790	**7464·0**	19 14 00 54·7537
20	**0726·5**	10 00 43·7392	43·6611	+0·0782	**7465·0**	20 13 56 58·8443
21	**0727·5**	10 04 40·2964	40·2164	+0·0799	**7466·0**	21 13 53 02·9348
22	**0728·5**	10 08 36·8558	36·7718	+0·0840	**7467·0**	22 13 49 07·0253
23	**0729·5**	10 12 33·4168	33·3272	+0·0896	**7468·0**	23 13 45 11·1159
24	**0730·5**	10 16 29·9782	29·8826	+0·0956	**7469·0**	24 13 41 15·2064
25	**0731·5**	10 20 26·5386	26·4379	+0·1007	**7470·0**	25 13 37 19·2969
26	**0732·5**	10 24 23·0966	22·9933	+0·1033	**7471·0**	26 13 33 23·3875
27	**0733·5**	10 28 19·6510	19·5487	+0·1024	**7472·0**	27 13 29 27·4780
28	**0734·5**	10 32 16·2016	16·1040	+0·0975	**7473·0**	28 13 25 31·5685
Mar. 1	**0735·5**	10 36 12·7492	12·6594	+0·0898	**7474·0**	Mar. 1 13 21 35·6590
2	**0736·5**	10 40 09·2957	09·2148	+0·0810	**7475·0**	2 13 17 39·7496
3	**0737·5**	10 44 05·8437	05·7701	+0·0735	**7476·0**	3 13 13 43·8401
4	**0738·5**	10 48 02·3948	02·3255	+0·0693	**7477·0**	4 13 09 47·9306
5	**0739·5**	10 51 58·9501	58·8809	+0·0692	**7478·0**	5 13 05 52·0212
6	**0740·5**	10 55 55·5090	55·4362	+0·0728	**7479·0**	6 13 01 56·1117
7	**0741·5**	10 59 52·0704	51·9916	+0·0787	**7480·0**	7 12 58 00·2022
8	**0742·5**	11 03 48·6323	48·5470	+0·0853	**7481·0**	8 12 54 04·2928
9	**0743·5**	11 07 45·1932	45·1023	+0·0908	**7482·0**	9 12 50 08·3833
10	**0744·5**	11 11 41·7516	41·6577	+0·0939	**7483·0**	10 12 46 12·4738
11	**0745·5**	11 15 38·3070	38·2131	+0·0939	**7484·0**	11 12 42 16·5644
12	**0746·5**	11 19 34·8590	34·7685	+0·0906	**7485·0**	12 12 38 20·6549
13	**0747·5**	11 23 31·4082	31·3238	+0·0844	**7486·0**	13 12 34 24·7454
14	**0748·5**	11 27 27·9554	27·8792	+0·0762	**7487·0**	14 12 30 28·8359
15	**0749·5**	11 31 24·5017	24·4346	+0·0671	**7488·0**	15 12 26 32·9265
16	**0750·5**	11 35 21·0482	20·9899	+0·0583	**7489·0**	16 12 22 37·0170
17	**0751·5**	11 39 17·5960	17·5453	+0·0507	**7490·0**	17 12 18 41·1075
18	**0752·5**	11 43 14·1458	14·1007	+0·0452	**7491·0**	18 12 14 45·1981
19	**0753·5**	11 47 10·6982	10·6560	+0·0421	**7492·0**	19 12 10 49·2886
20	**0754·5**	11 51 07·2531	07·2114	+0·0417	**7493·0**	20 12 06 53·3791
21	**0755·5**	11 55 03·8105	03·7668	+0·0437	**7494·0**	21 12 02 57·4697
22	**0756·5**	11 59 00·3695	00·3221	+0·0474	**7495·0**	22 11 59 01·5602
23	**0757·5**	12 02 56·9295	56·8775	+0·0520	**7496·0**	23 11 55 05·6507
24	**0758·5**	12 06 53·4891	53·4329	+0·0562	**7497·0**	24 11 51 09·7412
25	**0759·5**	12 10 50·0470	49·9882	+0·0587	**7498·0**	25 11 47 13·8318
26	**0760·5**	12 14 46·6020	46·5436	+0·0584	**7499·0**	26 11 43 17·9223
27	**0761·5**	12 18 43·1535	43·0990	+0·0545	**7500·0**	27 11 39 22·0128
28	**0762·5**	12 22 39·7016	39·6544	+0·0473	**7501·0**	28 11 35 26·1034
29	**0763·5**	12 26 36·2479	36·2097	+0·0381	**7502·0**	29 11 31 30·1939
30	**0764·5**	12 30 32·7945	32·7651	+0·0294	**7503·0**	30 11 27 34·2844
31	**0765·5**	12 34 29·3439	29·3205	+0·0234	**7504·0**	31 11 23 38·3750
Apr. 1	**0766·5**	12 38 25·8976	25·8758	+0·0218	**7505·0**	Apr. 1 11 19 42·4655
2	**0767·5**	12 42 22·4559	22·4312	+0·0247	**7506·0**	2 11 15 46·5560

Date 0h UT1		Julian Date	G. SIDEREAL TIME (GHA of the Equinox) Apparent			Mean	Equation of Equinoxes at 0h UT1	GSD at 0h GMST	UT1 at 0h GMST (Greenwich Transit of the Mean Equinox)				
		246	h	m	s	s	s	**246**			h	m	s
Apr.	1	**0766·5**	12	38	25·8976	25·8758	+0·0218	**7505·0**	Apr.	1	11	19	42·4655
	2	**0767·5**	12	42	22·4559	22·4312	+0·0247	**7506·0**		2	11	15	46·5560
	3	**0768·5**	12	46	19·0173	18·9866	+0·0307	**7507·0**		3	11	11	50·6465
	4	**0769·5**	12	50	15·5799	15·5419	+0·0379	**7508·0**		4	11	07	54·7371
	5	**0770·5**	12	54	12·1417	12·0973	+0·0444	**7509·0**		5	11	03	58·8276
	6	**0771·5**	12	58	08·7013	08·6527	+0·0487	**7510·0**		6	11	00	02·9181
	7	**0772·5**	13	02	05·2578	05·2080	+0·0498	**7511·0**		7	10	56	07·0087
	8	**0773·5**	13	06	01·8110	01·7634	+0·0476	**7512·0**		8	10	52	11·0992
	9	**0774·5**	13	09	58·3612	58·3188	+0·0425	**7513·0**		9	10	48	15·1897
	10	**0775·5**	13	13	54·9094	54·8741	+0·0352	**7514·0**		10	10	44	19·2803
	11	**0776·5**	13	17	51·4564	51·4295	+0·0269	**7515·0**		11	10	40	23·3708
	12	**0777·5**	13	21	48·0035	47·9849	+0·0186	**7516·0**		12	10	36	27·4613
	13	**0778·5**	13	25	44·5516	44·5402	+0·0114	**7517·0**		13	10	32	31·5518
	14	**0779·5**	13	29	41·1017	41·0956	+0·0061	**7518·0**		14	10	28	35·6424
	15	**0780·5**	13	33	37·6543	37·6510	+0·0033	**7519·0**		15	10	24	39·7329
	16	**0781·5**	13	37	34·2095	34·2064	+0·0032	**7520·0**		16	10	20	43·8234
	17	**0782·5**	13	41	30·7673	30·7617	+0·0055	**7521·0**		17	10	16	47·9140
	18	**0783·5**	13	45	27·3269	27·3171	+0·0098	**7522·0**		18	10	12	52·0045
	19	**0784·5**	13	49	23·8876	23·8725	+0·0152	**7523·0**		19	10	08	56·0950
	20	**0785·5**	13	53	20·4483	20·4278	+0·0205	**7524·0**		20	10	05	00·1856
	21	**0786·5**	13	57	17·0078	16·9832	+0·0246	**7525·0**		21	10	01	04·2761
	22	**0787·5**	14	01	13·5650	13·5386	+0·0264	**7526·0**		22	9	57	08·3666
	23	**0788·5**	14	05	10·1191	10·0939	+0·0251	**7527·0**		23	9	53	12·4571
	24	**0789·5**	14	09	06·6699	06·6493	+0·0206	**7528·0**		24	9	49	16·5477
	25	**0790·5**	14	13	03·2184	03·2047	+0·0137	**7529·0**		25	9	45	20·6382
	26	**0791·5**	14	16	59·7662	59·7600	+0·0062	**7530·0**		26	9	41	24·7287
	27	**0792·5**	14	20	56·3158	56·3154	+0·0004	**7531·0**		27	9	37	28·8193
	28	**0793·5**	14	24	52·8694	52·8708	−0·0014	**7532·0**		28	9	33	32·9098
	29	**0794·5**	14	28	49·4278	49·4261	+0·0017	**7533·0**		29	9	29	37·0003
	30	**0795·5**	14	32	45·9906	45·9815	+0·0090	**7534·0**		30	9	25	41·0909
May	1	**0796·5**	14	36	42·5556	42·5369	+0·0187	**7535·0**	May	1	9	21	45·1814
	2	**0797·5**	14	40	39·1207	39·0923	+0·0284	**7536·0**		2	9	17	49·2719
	3	**0798·5**	14	44	35·6837	35·6476	+0·0361	**7537·0**		3	9	13	53·3624
	4	**0799·5**	14	48	32·2436	32·2030	+0·0406	**7538·0**		4	9	09	57·4530
	5	**0800·5**	14	52	28·7999	28·7584	+0·0416	**7539·0**		5	9	06	01·5435
	6	**0801·5**	14	56	25·3531	25·3137	+0·0393	**7540·0**		6	9	02	05·6340
	7	**0802·5**	15	00	21·9038	21·8691	+0·0347	**7541·0**		7	8	58	09·7246
	8	**0803·5**	15	04	18·4532	18·4245	+0·0287	**7542·0**		8	8	54	13·8151
	9	**0804·5**	15	08	15·0024	14·9798	+0·0226	**7543·0**		9	8	50	17·9056
	10	**0805·5**	15	12	11·5525	11·5352	+0·0173	**7544·0**		10	8	46	21·9962
	11	**0806·5**	15	16	08·1043	08·0906	+0·0137	**7545·0**		11	8	42	26·0867
	12	**0807·5**	15	20	04·6585	04·6459	+0·0126	**7546·0**		12	8	38	30·1772
	13	**0808·5**	15	24	01·2154	01·2013	+0·0141	**7547·0**		13	8	34	34·2677
	14	**0809·5**	15	27	57·7749	57·7567	+0·0182	**7548·0**		14	8	30	38·3583
	15	**0810·5**	15	31	54·3364	54·3120	+0·0244	**7549·0**		15	8	26	42·4488
	16	**0811·5**	15	35	50·8992	50·8674	+0·0318	**7550·0**		16	8	22	46·5393
	17	**0812·5**	15	39	47·4622	47·4228	+0·0394	**7551·0**		17	8	18	50·6299

Date 0h UT1	Julian Date	G. SIDEREAL TIME (GHA of the Equinox) Apparent	Mean	Equation of Equinoxes at 0h UT1	GSD at 0h GMST	UT1 at 0h GMST (Greenwich Transit of the Mean Equinox)
	246	h m s	s	s	**246**	h m s
May 17	**0812·5**	15 39 47·4622	47·4228	+0·0394	**7551·0**	May 17 8 18 50·6299
18	**0813·5**	15 43 44·0241	43·9782	+0·0460	**7552·0**	18 8 14 54·7204
19	**0814·5**	15 47 40·5840	40·5335	+0·0505	**7553·0**	19 8 10 58·8109
20	**0815·5**	15 51 37·1410	37·0889	+0·0521	**7554·0**	20 8 07 02·9015
21	**0816·5**	15 55 33·6950	33·6443	+0·0507	**7555·0**	21 8 03 06·9920
22	**0817·5**	15 59 30·2464	30·1996	+0·0468	**7556·0**	22 7 59 11·0825
23	**0818·5**	16 03 26·7966	26·7550	+0·0416	**7557·0**	23 7 55 15·1730
24	**0819·5**	16 07 23·3475	23·3104	+0·0371	**7558·0**	24 7 51 19·2636
25	**0820·5**	16 11 19·9014	19·8657	+0·0356	**7559·0**	25 7 47 23·3541
26	**0821·5**	16 15 16·4598	16·4211	+0·0387	**7560·0**	26 7 43 27·4446
27	**0822·5**	16 19 13·0229	12·9765	+0·0465	**7561·0**	27 7 39 31·5352
28	**0823·5**	16 23 09·5897	09·5318	+0·0578	**7562·0**	28 7 35 35·6257
29	**0824·5**	16 27 06·1576	06·0872	+0·0704	**7563·0**	29 7 31 39·7162
30	**0825·5**	16 31 02·7243	02·6426	+0·0817	**7564·0**	30 7 27 43·8068
31	**0826·5**	16 34 59·2880	59·1979	+0·0901	**7565·0**	31 7 23 47·8973
June 1	**0827·5**	16 38 55·8479	55·7533	+0·0946	**7566·0**	June 1 7 19 51·9878
2	**0828·5**	16 42 52·4042	52·3087	+0·0955	**7567·0**	2 7 15 56·0783
3	**0829·5**	16 46 48·9576	48·8641	+0·0935	**7568·0**	3 7 12 00·1689
4	**0830·5**	16 50 45·5092	45·4194	+0·0898	**7569·0**	4 7 08 04·2594
5	**0831·5**	16 54 42·0603	41·9748	+0·0855	**7570·0**	5 7 04 08·3499
6	**0832·5**	16 58 38·6119	38·5302	+0·0818	**7571·0**	6 7 00 12·4405
7	**0833·5**	17 02 35·1651	35·0855	+0·0796	**7572·0**	7 6 56 16·5310
8	**0834·5**	17 06 31·7204	31·6409	+0·0796	**7573·0**	8 6 52 20·6215
9	**0835·5**	17 10 28·2784	28·1963	+0·0822	**7574·0**	9 6 48 24·7121
10	**0836·5**	17 14 24·8390	24·7516	+0·0874	**7575·0**	10 6 44 28·8026
11	**0837·5**	17 18 21·4018	21·3070	+0·0948	**7576·0**	11 6 40 32·8931
12	**0838·5**	17 22 17·9661	17·8624	+0·1037	**7577·0**	12 6 36 36·9836
13	**0839·5**	17 26 14·5307	14·4177	+0·1129	**7578·0**	13 6 32 41·0742
14	**0840·5**	17 30 11·0944	10·9731	+0·1213	**7579·0**	14 6 28 45·1647
15	**0841·5**	17 34 07·6562	07·5285	+0·1277	**7580·0**	15 6 24 49·2552
16	**0842·5**	17 38 04·2152	04·0838	+0·1313	**7581·0**	16 6 20 53·3458
17	**0843·5**	17 42 00·7710	00·6392	+0·1318	**7582·0**	17 6 16 57·4363
18	**0844·5**	17 45 57·3241	57·1946	+0·1295	**7583·0**	18 6 13 01·5268
19	**0845·5**	17 49 53·8755	53·7500	+0·1256	**7584·0**	19 6 09 05·6174
20	**0846·5**	17 53 50·4271	50·3053	+0·1218	**7585·0**	20 6 05 09·7079
21	**0847·5**	17 57 46·9808	46·8607	+0·1201	**7586·0**	21 6 01 13·7984
22	**0848·5**	18 01 43·5382	43·4161	+0·1222	**7587·0**	22 5 57 17·8889
23	**0849·5**	18 05 40·1002	39·9714	+0·1287	**7588·0**	23 5 53 21·9795
24	**0850·5**	18 09 36·6661	36·5268	+0·1393	**7589·0**	24 5 49 26·0700
25	**0851·5**	18 13 33·2343	33·0822	+0·1522	**7590·0**	25 5 45 30·1605
26	**0852·5**	18 17 29·8024	29·6375	+0·1649	**7591·0**	26 5 41 34·2511
27	**0853·5**	18 21 26·3683	26·1929	+0·1754	**7592·0**	27 5 37 38·3416
28	**0854·5**	18 25 22·9304	22·7483	+0·1822	**7593·0**	28 5 33 42·4321
29	**0855·5**	18 29 19·4886	19·3036	+0·1850	**7594·0**	29 5 29 46·5227
30	**0856·5**	18 33 16·0433	15·8590	+0·1843	**7595·0**	30 5 25 50·6132
July 1	**0857·5**	18 37 12·5957	12·4144	+0·1813	**7596·0**	July 1 5 21 54·7037
2	**0858·5**	18 41 09·1470	08·9697	+0·1773	**7597·0**	2 5 17 58·7942

Date 0^h UT1	Julian Date	G. SIDEREAL TIME (GHA of the Equinox) Apparent	Mean	Equation of Equinoxes at 0^h UT1	GSD at 0^h GMST	UT1 at 0^h GMST (Greenwich Transit of the Mean Equinox)	
	246	h m s	s	s	**246**		h m s
July 2	**0858·5**	18 41 09·1470	08·9697	+0·1773	**7597·0**	July 2	5 17 58·7942
3	**0859·5**	18 45 05·6985	05·5251	+0·1734	**7598·0**	3	5 14 02·8848
4	**0860·5**	18 49 02·2512	02·0805	+0·1708	**7599·0**	4	5 10 06·9753
5	**0861·5**	18 52 58·8059	58·6359	+0·1701	**7600·0**	5	5 06 11·0658
6	**0862·5**	18 56 55·3631	55·1912	+0·1719	**7601·0**	6	5 02 15·1564
7	**0863·5**	19 00 51·9228	51·7466	+0·1763	**7602·0**	7	4 58 19·2469
8	**0864·5**	19 04 48·4849	48·3020	+0·1830	**7603·0**	8	4 54 23·3374
9	**0865·5**	19 08 45·0487	44·8573	+0·1913	**7604·0**	9	4 50 27·4280
10	**0866·5**	19 12 41·6131	41·4127	+0·2004	**7605·0**	10	4 46 31·5185
11	**0867·5**	19 16 38·1769	37·9681	+0·2089	**7606·0**	11	4 42 35·6090
12	**0868·5**	19 20 34·7390	34·5234	+0·2156	**7607·0**	12	4 38 39·6995
13	**0869·5**	19 24 31·2982	31·0788	+0·2194	**7608·0**	13	4 34 43·7901
14	**0870·5**	19 28 27·8541	27·6342	+0·2199	**7609·0**	14	4 30 47·8806
15	**0871·5**	19 32 24·4070	24·1895	+0·2174	**7610·0**	15	4 26 51·9711
16	**0872·5**	19 36 20·9578	20·7449	+0·2129	**7611·0**	16	4 22 56·0617
17	**0873·5**	19 40 17·5083	17·3003	+0·2081	**7612·0**	17	4 19 00·1522
18	**0874·5**	19 44 14·0604	13·8556	+0·2048	**7613·0**	18	4 15 04·2427
19	**0875·5**	19 48 10·6156	10·4110	+0·2046	**7614·0**	19	4 11 08·3333
20	**0876·5**	19 52 07·1749	06·9664	+0·2085	**7615·0**	20	4 07 12·4238
21	**0877·5**	19 56 03·7381	03·5218	+0·2164	**7616·0**	21	4 03 16·5143
22	**0878·5**	20 00 00·3040	00·0771	+0·2269	**7617·0**	22	3 59 20·6048
23	**0879·5**	20 03 56·8707	56·6325	+0·2382	**7618·0**	23	3 55 24·6954
24	**0880·5**	20 07 53·4359	53·1879	+0·2481	**7619·0**	24	3 51 28·7859
25	**0881·5**	20 11 49·9981	49·7432	+0·2549	**7620·0**	25	3 47 32·8764
26	**0882·5**	20 15 46·5563	46·2986	+0·2577	**7621·0**	26	3 43 36·9670
27	**0883·5**	20 19 43·1107	42·8540	+0·2568	**7622·0**	27	3 39 41·0575
28	**0884·5**	20 23 39·6623	39·4093	+0·2529	**7623·0**	28	3 35 45·1480
29	**0885·5**	20 27 36·2122	35·9647	+0·2475	**7624·0**	29	3 31 49·2386
30	**0886·5**	20 31 32·7618	32·5201	+0·2417	**7625·0**	30	3 27 53·3291
31	**0887·5**	20 35 29·3123	29·0754	+0·2368	**7626·0**	31	3 23 57·4196
Aug. 1	**0888·5**	20 39 25·8645	25·6308	+0·2337	**7627·0**	Aug. 1	3 20 01·5101
2	**0889·5**	20 43 22·4191	22·1862	+0·2329	**7628·0**	2	3 16 05·6007
3	**0890·5**	20 47 18·9762	18·7415	+0·2346	**7629·0**	3	3 12 09·6912
4	**0891·5**	20 51 15·5356	15·2969	+0·2387	**7630·0**	4	3 08 13·7817
5	**0892·5**	20 55 12·0970	11·8523	+0·2447	**7631·0**	5	3 04 17·8723
6	**0893·5**	20 59 08·6593	08·4076	+0·2517	**7632·0**	6	3 00 21·9628
7	**0894·5**	21 03 05·2216	04·9630	+0·2586	**7633·0**	7	2 56 26·0533
8	**0895·5**	21 07 01·7825	01·5184	+0·2641	**7634·0**	8	2 52 30·1439
9	**0896·5**	21 10 58·3408	58·0738	+0·2671	**7635·0**	9	2 48 34·2344
10	**0897·5**	21 14 54·8958	54·6291	+0·2666	**7636·0**	10	2 44 38·3249
11	**0898·5**	21 18 51·4473	51·1845	+0·2628	**7637·0**	11	2 40 42·4154
12	**0899·5**	21 22 47·9964	47·7399	+0·2565	**7638·0**	12	2 36 46·5060
13	**0900·5**	21 26 44·5446	44·2952	+0·2494	**7639·0**	13	2 32 50·5965
14	**0901·5**	21 30 41·0939	40·8506	+0·2433	**7640·0**	14	2 28 54·6870
15	**0902·5**	21 34 37·6461	37·4060	+0·2402	**7641·0**	15	2 24 58·7776
16	**0903·5**	21 38 34·2022	33·9613	+0·2409	**7642·0**	16	2 21 02·8681
17	**0904·5**	21 42 30·7622	30·5167	+0·2455	**7643·0**	17	2 17 06·9586

Date 0h UT1	Julian Date	G. SIDEREAL TIME (GHA of the Equinox) Apparent	Mean	Equation of Equinoxes at 0h UT1	GSD at 0h GMST	UT1 at 0h GMST (Greenwich Transit of the Mean Equinox)	
	246	h m s	s	s	**246**		h m s
Aug. 17	**0904·5**	21 42 30·7622	30·5167	+0·2455	**7643·0**	Aug. 17	2 17 06·9586
18	**0905·5**	21 46 27·3250	27·0721	+0·2529	**7644·0**	18	2 13 11·0492
19	**0906·5**	21 50 23·8889	23·6274	+0·2615	**7645·0**	19	2 09 15·1397
20	**0907·5**	21 54 20·4520	20·1828	+0·2692	**7646·0**	20	2 05 19·2302
21	**0908·5**	21 58 17·0126	16·7382	+0·2745	**7647·0**	21	2 01 23·3207
22	**0909·5**	22 02 13·5697	13·2935	+0·2761	**7648·0**	22	1 57 27·4113
23	**0910·5**	22 06 10·1230	09·8489	+0·2740	**7649·0**	23	1 53 31·5018
24	**0911·5**	22 10 06·6731	06·4043	+0·2688	**7650·0**	24	1 49 35·5923
25	**0912·5**	22 14 03·2211	02·9597	+0·2614	**7651·0**	25	1 45 39·6829
26	**0913·5**	22 17 59·7684	59·5150	+0·2533	**7652·0**	26	1 41 43·7734
27	**0914·5**	22 21 56·3162	56·0704	+0·2458	**7653·0**	27	1 37 47·8639
28	**0915·5**	22 25 52·8655	52·6258	+0·2397	**7654·0**	28	1 33 51·9545
29	**0916·5**	22 29 49·4170	49·1811	+0·2359	**7655·0**	29	1 29 56·0450
30	**0917·5**	22 33 45·9710	45·7365	+0·2345	**7656·0**	30	1 26 00·1355
31	**0918·5**	22 37 42·5275	42·2919	+0·2356	**7657·0**	31	1 22 04·2260
Sept. 1	**0919·5**	22 41 39·0860	38·8472	+0·2387	**7658·0**	Sept. 1	1 18 08·3166
2	**0920·5**	22 45 35·6458	35·4026	+0·2432	**7659·0**	2	1 14 12·4071
3	**0921·5**	22 49 32·2060	31·9580	+0·2481	**7660·0**	3	1 10 16·4976
4	**0922·5**	22 53 28·7654	28·5133	+0·2521	**7661·0**	4	1 06 20·5882
5	**0923·5**	22 57 25·3228	25·0687	+0·2541	**7662·0**	5	1 02 24·6787
6	**0924·5**	23 01 21·8771	21·6241	+0·2530	**7663·0**	6	0 58 28·7692
7	**0925·5**	23 05 18·4280	18·1794	+0·2485	**7664·0**	7	0 54 32·8598
8	**0926·5**	23 09 14·9759	14·7348	+0·2411	**7665·0**	8	0 50 36·9503
9	**0927·5**	23 13 11·5222	11·2902	+0·2320	**7666·0**	9	0 46 41·0408
10	**0928·5**	23 17 08·0691	07·8456	+0·2236	**7667·0**	10	0 42 45·1313
11	**0929·5**	23 21 04·6187	04·4009	+0·2178	**7668·0**	11	0 38 49·2219
12	**0930·5**	23 25 01·1722	00·9563	+0·2159	**7669·0**	12	0 34 53·3124
13	**0931·5**	23 28 57·7299	57·5117	+0·2182	**7670·0**	13	0 30 57·4029
14	**0932·5**	23 32 54·2907	54·0670	+0·2237	**7671·0**	14	0 27 01·4935
15	**0933·5**	23 36 50·8530	50·6224	+0·2306	**7672·0**	15	0 23 05·5840
16	**0934·5**	23 40 47·4149	47·1778	+0·2371	**7673·0**	16	0 19 09·6745
17	**0935·5**	23 44 43·9745	43·7331	+0·2414	**7674·0**	17	0 15 13·7651
18	**0936·5**	23 48 40·5309	40·2885	+0·2424	**7675·0**	18	0 11 17·8556
19	**0937·5**	23 52 37·0837	36·8439	+0·2398	**7676·0**	19	0 07 21·9461
20	**0938·5**	23 56 33·6333	33·3992	+0·2341	**7677·0**	20	0 03 26·0366
					7678·0	20	23 59 30·1272
21	**0939·5**	0 00 30·1806	29·9546	+0·2260	**7679·0**	21	23 55 34·2177
22	**0940·5**	0 04 26·7268	26·5100	+0·2168	**7680·0**	22	23 51 38·3082
23	**0941·5**	0 08 23·2732	23·0653	+0·2079	**7681·0**	23	23 47 42·3988
24	**0942·5**	0 12 19·8210	19·6207	+0·2002	**7682·0**	24	23 43 46·4893
25	**0943·5**	0 16 16·3708	16·1761	+0·1947	**7683·0**	25	23 39 50·5798
26	**0944·5**	0 20 12·9231	12·7315	+0·1917	**7684·0**	26	23 35 54·6704
27	**0945·5**	0 24 09·4780	09·2868	+0·1912	**7685·0**	27	23 31 58·7609
28	**0946·5**	0 28 06·0351	05·8422	+0·1929	**7686·0**	28	23 28 02·8514
29	**0947·5**	0 32 02·5937	02·3976	+0·1961	**7687·0**	29	23 24 06·9420
30	**0948·5**	0 35 59·1530	58·9529	+0·2001	**7688·0**	30	23 20 11·0325
Oct. 1	**0949·5**	0 39 55·7121	55·5083	+0·2038	**7689·0**	Oct. 1	23 16 15·1230

Date 0^h UT1	Julian Date	G. SIDEREAL TIME (GHA of the Equinox) Apparent	Mean	Equation of Equinoxes at 0^h UT1	GSD at 0^h GMST	UT1 at 0^h GMST (Greenwich Transit of the Mean Equinox)
	246	h m s	s	s	**246**	h m s
Oct. 1	**0949·5**	0 39 55·7121	55·5083	+0·2038	**7689·0**	Oct. 1 23 16 15·1230
2	**0950·5**	0 43 52·2696	52·0637	+0·2060	**7690·0**	2 23 12 19·2135
3	**0951·5**	0 47 48·8248	48·6190	+0·2057	**7691·0**	3 23 08 23·3041
4	**0952·5**	0 51 45·3768	45·1744	+0·2024	**7692·0**	4 23 04 27·3946
5	**0953·5**	0 55 41·9257	41·7298	+0·1959	**7693·0**	5 23 00 31·4851
6	**0954·5**	0 59 38·4724	38·2851	+0·1873	**7694·0**	6 22 56 35·5757
7	**0955·5**	1 03 35·0188	34·8405	+0·1783	**7695·0**	7 22 52 39·6662
8	**0956·5**	1 07 31·5672	31·3959	+0·1714	**7696·0**	8 22 48 43·7567
9	**0957·5**	1 11 28·1196	27·9512	+0·1683	**7697·0**	9 22 44 47·8473
10	**0958·5**	1 15 24·6766	24·5066	+0·1700	**7698·0**	10 22 40 51·9378
11	**0959·5**	1 19 21·2377	21·0620	+0·1757	**7699·0**	11 22 36 56·0283
12	**0960·5**	1 23 17·8009	17·6174	+0·1835	**7700·0**	12 22 33 00·1188
13	**0961·5**	1 27 14·3640	14·1727	+0·1913	**7701·0**	13 22 29 04·2094
14	**0962·5**	1 31 10·9252	10·7281	+0·1971	**7702·0**	14 22 25 08·2999
15	**0963·5**	1 35 07·4831	07·2835	+0·1997	**7703·0**	15 22 21 12·3904
16	**0964·5**	1 39 04·0375	03·8388	+0·1987	**7704·0**	16 22 17 16·4810
17	**0965·5**	1 43 00·5886	00·3942	+0·1944	**7705·0**	17 22 13 20·5715
18	**0966·5**	1 46 57·1373	56·9496	+0·1877	**7706·0**	18 22 09 24·6620
19	**0967·5**	1 50 53·6847	53·5049	+0·1798	**7707·0**	19 22 05 28·7526
20	**0968·5**	1 54 50·2321	50·0603	+0·1718	**7708·0**	20 22 01 32·8431
21	**0969·5**	1 58 46·7805	46·6157	+0·1649	**7709·0**	21 21 57 36·9336
22	**0970·5**	2 02 43·3310	43·1710	+0·1600	**7710·0**	22 21 53 41·0241
23	**0971·5**	2 06 39·8839	39·7264	+0·1575	**7711·0**	23 21 49 45·1147
24	**0972·5**	2 10 36·4395	36·2818	+0·1577	**7712·0**	24 21 45 49·2052
25	**0973·5**	2 14 32·9973	32·8371	+0·1602	**7713·0**	25 21 41 53·2957
26	**0974·5**	2 18 29·5570	29·3925	+0·1645	**7714·0**	26 21 37 57·3863
27	**0975·5**	2 22 26·1176	25·9479	+0·1697	**7715·0**	27 21 34 01·4768
28	**0976·5**	2 26 22·6782	22·5033	+0·1749	**7716·0**	28 21 30 05·5673
29	**0977·5**	2 30 19·2377	19·0586	+0·1791	**7717·0**	29 21 26 09·6579
30	**0978·5**	2 34 15·7952	15·6140	+0·1812	**7718·0**	30 21 22 13·7484
31	**0979·5**	2 38 12·3501	12·1694	+0·1807	**7719·0**	31 21 18 17·8389
Nov 1	**0980·5**	2 42 08·9020	08·7247	+0·1773	**7720·0**	Nov. 1 21 14 21·9294
2	**0981·5**	2 46 05·4515	05·2801	+0·1714	**7721·0**	2 21 10 26·0200
3	**0982·5**	2 50 01·9999	01·8355	+0·1644	**7722·0**	3 21 06 30·1105
4	**0983·5**	2 53 58·5493	58·3908	+0·1584	**7723·0**	4 21 02 34·2010
5	**0984·5**	2 57 55·1018	54·9462	+0·1556	**7724·0**	5 20 58 38·2916
6	**0985·5**	3 01 51·6592	51·5016	+0·1577	**7725·0**	6 20 54 42·3821
7	**0986·5**	3 05 48·2215	48·0569	+0·1646	**7726·0**	7 20 50 46·4726
8	**0987·5**	3 09 44·7872	44·6123	+0·1749	**7727·0**	8 20 46 50·5632
9	**0988·5**	3 13 41·3538	41·1677	+0·1861	**7728·0**	9 20 42 54·6537
10	**0989·5**	3 17 37·9189	37·7230	+0·1958	**7729·0**	10 20 38 58·7442
11	**0990·5**	3 21 34·4808	34·2784	+0·2024	**7730·0**	11 20 35 02·8347
12	**0991·5**	3 25 31·0388	30·8338	+0·2050	**7731·0**	12 20 31 06·9253
13	**0992·5**	3 29 27·5933	27·3892	+0·2041	**7732·0**	13 20 27 11·0158
14	**0993·5**	3 33 24·1450	23·9445	+0·2005	**7733·0**	14 20 23 15·1063
15	**0994·5**	3 37 20·6952	20·4999	+0·1953	**7734·0**	15 20 19 19·1969
16	**0995·5**	3 41 17·2450	17·0553	+0·1898	**7735·0**	16 20 15 23·2874

Date 0h UT1	Julian Date	G. SIDEREAL TIME (GHA of the Equinox) Apparent	Mean	Equation of Equinoxes at 0h UT1	GSD at 0h GMST	UT1 at 0h GMST (Greenwich Transit of the Mean Equinox)
	246	h m s	s	s	246	h m s
Nov. 16	**0995·5**	3 41 17·2450	17·0553	+0·1898	**7735·0**	Nov. 16 20 15 23·2874
17	**0996·5**	3 45 13·7958	13·6106	+0·1852	**7736·0**	17 20 11 27·3779
18	**0997·5**	3 49 10·3483	10·1660	+0·1823	**7737·0**	18 20 07 31·4685
19	**0998·5**	3 53 06·9032	06·7214	+0·1819	**7738·0**	19 20 03 35·5590
20	**0999·5**	3 57 03·4608	03·2767	+0·1840	**7739·0**	20 19 59 39·6495
21	**1000·5**	4 00 60·0208	59·8321	+0·1887	**7740·0**	21 19 55 43·7400
22	**1001·5**	4 04 56·5827	56·3875	+0·1952	**7741·0**	22 19 51 47·8306
23	**1002·5**	4 08 53·1457	52·9428	+0·2028	**7742·0**	23 19 47 51·9211
24	**1003·5**	4 12 49·7088	49·4982	+0·2106	**7743·0**	24 19 43 56·0116
25	**1004·5**	4 16 46·2711	46·0536	+0·2175	**7744·0**	25 19 40 00·1022
26	**1005·5**	4 20 42·8316	42·6089	+0·2227	**7745·0**	26 19 36 04·1927
27	**1006·5**	4 24 39·3896	39·1643	+0·2253	**7746·0**	27 19 32 08·2832
28	**1007·5**	4 28 35·9448	35·7197	+0·2251	**7747·0**	28 19 28 12·3738
29	**1008·5**	4 32 32·4975	32·2751	+0·2225	**7748·0**	29 19 24 16·4643
30	**1009·5**	4 36 29·0488	28·8304	+0·2183	**7749·0**	30 19 20 20·5548
Dec. 1	**1010·5**	4 40 25·6001	25·3858	+0·2143	**7750·0**	Dec. 1 19 16 24·6453
2	**1011·5**	4 44 22·1535	21·9412	+0·2123	**7751·0**	2 19 12 28·7359
3	**1012·5**	4 48 18·7109	18·4965	+0·2144	**7752·0**	3 19 08 32·8264
4	**1013·5**	4 52 15·2733	15·0519	+0·2214	**7753·0**	4 19 04 36·9169
5	**1014·5**	4 56 11·8402	11·6073	+0·2329	**7754·0**	5 19 00 41·0075
6	**1015·5**	5 00 08·4095	08·1626	+0·2469	**7755·0**	6 18 56 45·0980
7	**1016·5**	5 04 04·9785	04·7180	+0·2605	**7756·0**	7 18 52 49·1885
8	**1017·5**	5 08 01·5447	01·2734	+0·2713	**7757·0**	8 18 48 53·2791
9	**1018·5**	5 11 58·1068	57·8287	+0·2781	**7758·0**	9 18 44 57·3696
10	**1019·5**	5 15 54·6648	54·3841	+0·2807	**7759·0**	10 18 41 01·4601
11	**1020·5**	5 19 51·2194	50·9395	+0·2799	**7760·0**	11 18 37 05·5506
12	**1021·5**	5 23 47·7719	47·4948	+0·2771	**7761·0**	12 18 33 09·6412
13	**1022·5**	5 27 44·3237	44·0502	+0·2735	**7762·0**	13 18 29 13·7317
14	**1023·5**	5 31 40·8761	40·6056	+0·2705	**7763·0**	14 18 25 17·8222
15	**1024·5**	5 35 37·4300	37·1610	+0·2691	**7764·0**	15 18 21 21·9128
16	**1025·5**	5 39 33·9861	33·7163	+0·2698	**7765·0**	16 18 17 26·0033
17	**1026·5**	5 43 30·5448	30·2717	+0·2731	**7766·0**	17 18 13 30·0938
18	**1027·5**	5 47 27·1058	26·8271	+0·2788	**7767·0**	18 18 09 34·1844
19	**1028·5**	5 51 23·6689	23·3824	+0·2865	**7768·0**	19 18 05 38·2749
20	**1029·5**	5 55 20·2333	19·9378	+0·2955	**7769·0**	20 18 01 42·3654
21	**1030·5**	5 59 16·7979	16·4932	+0·3048	**7770·0**	21 17 57 46·4559
22	**1031·5**	6 03 13·3618	13·0485	+0·3133	**7771·0**	22 17 53 50·5465
23	**1032·5**	6 07 09·9240	09·6039	+0·3201	**7772·0**	23 17 49 54·6370
24	**1033·5**	6 11 06·4836	06·1593	+0·3243	**7773·0**	24 17 45 58·7275
25	**1034·5**	6 15 03·0404	02·7146	+0·3258	**7774·0**	25 17 42 02·8181
26	**1035·5**	6 18 59·5946	59·2700	+0·3245	**7775·0**	26 17 38 06·9086
27	**1036·5**	6 22 56·1469	55·8254	+0·3215	**7776·0**	27 17 34 10·9991
28	**1037·5**	6 26 52·6988	52·3807	+0·3180	**7777·0**	28 17 30 15·0897
29	**1038·5**	6 30 49·2519	48·9361	+0·3158	**7778·0**	29 17 26 19·1802
30	**1039·5**	6 34 45·8082	45·4915	+0·3167	**7779·0**	30 17 22 23·2707
31	**1040·5**	6 38 42·3687	42·0469	+0·3218	**7780·0**	31 17 18 27·3612
32	**1041·5**	6 42 38·9337	38·6022	+0·3315	**7781·0**	32 17 14 31·4518

Date 0^h UT1	Julian Date	Earth Rotation Angle θ	Equation of Origins E_o
	246	° ′ ″	′ ″
Jan. 0	**0675·5**	99 35 37·0131	− 19 13·0772
1	**0676·5**	100 34 45·2174	− 19 13·3536
2	**0677·5**	101 33 53·4216	− 19 13·5956
3	**0678·5**	102 33 01·6258	− 19 13·7875
4	**0679·5**	103 32 09·8301	− 19 13·9250
5	**0680·5**	104 31 18·0343	− 19 14·0175
6	**0681·5**	105 30 26·2386	− 19 14·0865
7	**0682·5**	106 29 34·4428	− 19 14·1607
8	**0683·5**	107 28 42·6470	− 19 14·2679
9	**0684·5**	108 27 50·8513	− 19 14·4282
10	**0685·5**	109 26 59·0555	− 19 14·6478
11	**0686·5**	110 26 07·2597	− 19 14·9175
12	**0687·5**	111 25 15·4640	− 19 15·2152
13	**0688·5**	112 24 23·6682	− 19 15·5120
14	**0689·5**	113 23 31·8725	− 19 15·7808
15	**0690·5**	114 22 40·0767	− 19 16·0026
16	**0691·5**	115 21 48·2809	− 19 16·1705
17	**0692·5**	116 20 56·4852	− 19 16·2886
18	**0693·5**	117 20 04·6894	− 19 16·3689
19	**0694·5**	118 19 12·8936	− 19 16·4282
20	**0695·5**	119 18 21·0979	− 19 16·4839
21	**0696·5**	120 17 29·3021	− 19 16·5519
22	**0697·5**	121 16 37·5063	− 19 16·6457
23	**0698·5**	122 15 45·7106	− 19 16·7747
24	**0699·5**	123 14 53·9148	− 19 16·9439
25	**0700·5**	124 14 02·1191	− 19 17·1526
26	**0701·5**	125 13 10·3233	− 19 17·3935
27	**0702·5**	126 12 18·5275	− 19 17·6524
28	**0703·5**	127 11 26·7318	− 19 17·9084
29	**0704·5**	128 10 34·9360	− 19 18·1379
30	**0705·5**	129 09 43·1402	− 19 18·3200
31	**0706·5**	130 08 51·3445	− 19 18·4440
Feb. 1	**0707·5**	131 07 59·5487	− 19 18·5145
2	**0708·5**	132 07 07·7530	− 19 18·5518
3	**0709·5**	133 06 15·9572	− 19 18·5863
4	**0710·5**	134 05 24·1614	− 19 18·6484
5	**0711·5**	135 04 32·3657	− 19 18·7600
6	**0712·5**	136 03 40·5699	− 19 18·9289
7	**0713·5**	137 02 48·7741	− 19 19·1476
8	**0714·5**	138 01 56·9784	− 19 19·3970
9	**0715·5**	139 01 05·1826	− 19 19·6516
10	**0716·5**	140 00 13·3869	− 19 19·8859
11	**0717·5**	140 59 21·5911	− 19 20·0802
12	**0718·5**	141 58 29·7953	− 19 20·2238
13	**0719·5**	142 57 37·9996	− 19 20·3166
14	**0720·5**	143 56 46·2038	− 19 20·3673
15	**0721·5**	144 55 54·4080	− 19 20·3910

Date 0^h UT1	Julian Date	Earth Rotation Angle θ	Equation of Origins E_o
	246	° ′ ″	′ ″
Feb. 15	**0721·5**	144 55 54·4080	− 19 20·3910
16	**0722·5**	145 55 02·6123	− 19 20·4050
17	**0723·5**	146 54 10·8165	− 19 20·4265
18	**0724·5**	147 53 19·0208	− 19 20·4698
19	**0725·5**	148 52 27·2250	− 19 20·5455
20	**0726·5**	149 51 35·4292	− 19 20·6593
21	**0727·5**	150 50 43·6335	− 19 20·8122
22	**0728·5**	151 49 51·8377	− 19 20·9991
23	**0729·5**	152 49 00·0419	− 19 21·2094
24	**0730·5**	153 48 08·2462	− 19 21·4264
25	**0731·5**	154 47 16·4504	− 19 21·6288
26	**0732·5**	155 46 24·6546	− 19 21·7945
27	**0733·5**	156 45 32·8589	− 19 21·9064
28	**0734·5**	157 44 41·0631	− 19 21·9605
Mar. 1	**0735·5**	158 43 49·2674	− 19 21·9701
2	**0736·5**	159 42 57·4716	− 19 21·9644
3	**0737·5**	160 42 05·6758	− 19 21·9790
4	**0738·5**	161 41 13·8801	− 19 22·0424
5	**0739·5**	162 40 22·0843	− 19 22·1670
6	**0740·5**	163 39 30·2885	− 19 22·3470
7	**0741·5**	164 38 38·4928	− 19 22·5625
8	**0742·5**	165 37 46·6970	− 19 22·7874
9	**0743·5**	166 36 54·9013	− 19 22·9962
10	**0744·5**	167 36 03·1055	− 19 23·1691
11	**0745·5**	168 35 11·3097	− 19 23·2948
12	**0746·5**	169 34 19·5140	− 19 23·3713
13	**0747·5**	170 33 27·7182	− 19 23·4049
14	**0748·5**	171 32 35·9224	− 19 23·4085
15	**0749·5**	172 31 44·1267	− 19 23·3985
16	**0750·5**	173 30 52·3309	− 19 23·3921
17	**0751·5**	174 30 00·5352	− 19 23·4046
18	**0752·5**	175 29 08·7394	− 19 23·4479
19	**0753·5**	176 28 16·9436	− 19 23·5289
20	**0754·5**	177 27 25·1479	− 19 23·6491
21	**0755·5**	178 26 33·3521	− 19 23·8048
22	**0756·5**	179 25 41·5563	− 19 23·9869
23	**0757·5**	180 24 49·7606	− 19 24·1816
24	**0758·5**	181 23 57·9648	− 19 24·3712
25	**0759·5**	182 23 06·1691	− 19 24·5356
26	**0760·5**	183 22 14·3733	− 19 24·6569
27	**0761·5**	184 21 22·5775	− 19 24·7248
28	**0762·5**	185 20 30·7818	− 19 24·7427
29	**0763·5**	186 19 38·9860	− 19 24·7318
30	**0764·5**	187 18 47·1902	− 19 24·7267
31	**0765·5**	188 17 55·3945	− 19 24·7637
Apr. 1	**0766·5**	189 17 03·5987	− 19 24·8660
2	**0767·5**	190 16 11·8029	− 19 25·0348

$$\text{GHA} = \theta - \alpha_i, \qquad \alpha_i = \alpha_e + E_o$$

α_i, α_e are the right ascensions with respect to the CIO and the true equinox of date, respectively.

Date 0^h UT1	Julian Date	Earth Rotation Angle θ	Equation of Origins E_o
	246	° ′ ″	′ ″
Apr. 1	**0766·5**	189 17 03·5987	− 19 24·8660
2	**0767·5**	190 16 11·8029	− 19 25·0348
3	**0768·5**	191 15 20·0072	− 19 25·2516
4	**0769·5**	192 14 28·2114	− 19 25·4867
5	**0770·5**	193 13 36·4157	− 19 25·7104
6	**0771·5**	194 12 44·6199	− 19 25·9000
7	**0772·5**	195 11 52·8241	− 19 26·0428
8	**0773·5**	196 11 01·0284	− 19 26·1362
9	**0774·5**	197 10 09·2326	− 19 26·1858
10	**0775·5**	198 09 17·4368	− 19 26·2035
11	**0776·5**	199 08 25·6411	− 19 26·2048
12	**0777·5**	200 07 33·8453	− 19 26·2066
13	**0778·5**	201 06 42·0496	− 19 26·2246
14	**0779·5**	202 05 50·2538	− 19 26·2717
15	**0780·5**	203 04 58·4580	− 19 26·3561
16	**0781·5**	204 04 06·6623	− 19 26·4807
17	**0782·5**	205 03 14·8665	− 19 26·6424
18	**0783·5**	206 02 23·0707	− 19 26·8329
19	**0784·5**	207 01 31·2750	− 19 27·0394
20	**0785·5**	208 00 39·4792	− 19 27·2455
21	**0786·5**	208 59 47·6835	− 19 27·4335
22	**0787·5**	209 58 55·8877	− 19 27·5869
23	**0788·5**	210 58 04·0919	− 19 27·6940
24	**0789·5**	211 57 12·2962	− 19 27·7529
25	**0790·5**	212 56 20·5004	− 19 27·7756
26	**0791·5**	213 55 28·7046	− 19 27·7889
27	**0792·5**	214 54 36·9089	− 19 27·8289
28	**0793·5**	215 53 45·1131	− 19 27·9277
29	**0794·5**	216 52 53·3173	− 19 28·1002
30	**0795·5**	217 52 01·5216	− 19 28·3367
May 1	**0796·5**	218 51 09·7258	− 19 28·6085
2	**0797·5**	219 50 17·9301	− 19 28·8802
3	**0798·5**	220 49 26·1343	− 19 29·1219
4	**0799·5**	221 48 34·3385	− 19 29·3156
5	**0800·5**	222 47 42·5428	− 19 29·4562
6	**0801·5**	223 46 50·7470	− 19 29·5489
7	**0802·5**	224 45 58·9512	− 19 29·6058
8	**0803·5**	225 45 07·1555	− 19 29·6426
9	**0804·5**	226 44 15·3597	− 19 29·6763
10	**0805·5**	227 43 23·5640	− 19 29·7229
11	**0806·5**	228 42 31·7682	− 19 29·7960
12	**0807·5**	229 41 39·9724	− 19 29·9049
13	**0808·5**	230 40 48·1767	− 19 30·0542
14	**0809·5**	231 39 56·3809	− 19 30·2421
15	**0810·5**	232 39 04·5851	− 19 30·4611
16	**0811·5**	233 38 12·7894	− 19 30·6988
17	**0812·5**	234 37 20·9936	− 19 30·9389

Date 0^h UT1	Julian Date	Earth Rotation Angle θ	Equation of Origins E_o
	246	° ′ ″	′ ″
May 17	**0812·5**	234 37 20·9936	− 19 30·9389
18	**0813·5**	235 36 29·1979	− 19 31·1639
19	**0814·5**	236 35 37·4021	− 19 31·3578
20	**0815·5**	237 34 45·6063	− 19 31·5090
21	**0816·5**	238 33 53·8106	− 19 31·6142
22	**0817·5**	239 33 02·0148	− 19 31·6810
23	**0818·5**	240 32 10·2190	− 19 31·7293
24	**0819·5**	241 31 18·4233	− 19 31·7890
25	**0820·5**	242 30 26·6275	− 19 31·8929
26	**0821·5**	243 29 34·8318	− 19 32·0646
27	**0822·5**	244 28 43·0360	− 19 32·3081
28	**0823·5**	245 27 51·2402	− 19 32·6046
29	**0824·5**	246 26 59·4445	− 19 32·9194
30	**0825·5**	247 26 07·6487	− 19 33·2159
31	**0826·5**	248 25 15·8529	− 19 33·4673
June 1	**0827·5**	249 24 24·0572	− 19 33·6619
2	**0828·5**	250 23 32·2614	− 19 33·8016
3	**0829·5**	251 22 40·4656	− 19 33·8983
4	**0830·5**	252 21 48·6699	− 19 33·9686
5	**0831·5**	253 20 56·8741	− 19 34·0304
6	**0832·5**	254 20 05·0784	− 19 34·1006
7	**0833·5**	255 19 13·2826	− 19 34·1936
8	**0834·5**	256 18 21·4868	− 19 34·3199
9	**0835·5**	257 17 29·6911	− 19 34·4852
10	**0836·5**	258 16 37·8953	− 19 34·6897
11	**0837·5**	259 15 46·0995	− 19 34·9275
12	**0838·5**	260 14 54·3038	− 19 35·1870
13	**0839·5**	261 14 02·5080	− 19 35·4521
14	**0840·5**	262 13 10·7123	− 19 35·7045
15	**0841·5**	263 12 18·9165	− 19 35·9269
16	**0842·5**	264 11 27·1207	− 19 36·1067
17	**0843·5**	265 10 35·3250	− 19 36·2397
18	**0844·5**	266 09 43·5292	− 19 36·3316
19	**0845·5**	267 08 51·7334	− 19 36·3995
20	**0846·5**	268 07 59·9377	− 19 36·4692
21	**0847·5**	269 07 08·1419	− 19 36·5701
22	**0848·5**	270 06 16·3462	− 19 36·7271
23	**0849·5**	271 05 24·5504	− 19 36·9519
24	**0850·5**	272 04 32·7546	− 19 37·2368
25	**0851·5**	273 03 40·9589	− 19 37·5559
26	**0852·5**	274 02 49·1631	− 19 37·8735
27	**0853·5**	275 01 57·3673	− 19 38·1568
28	**0854·5**	276 01 05·5716	− 19 38·3851
29	**0855·5**	277 00 13·7758	− 19 38·5534
30	**0856·5**	277 59 21·9801	− 19 38·6701
July 1	**0857·5**	278 58 30·1843	− 19 38·7516
2	**0858·5**	279 57 38·3885	− 19 38·8171

$$\text{GHA} = \theta - \alpha_i, \qquad \alpha_i = \alpha_e + E_o$$

α_i, α_e are the right ascensions with respect to the CIO and the true equinox of date, respectively.

Date 0^h UT1	Julian Date	Earth Rotation Angle θ	Equation of Origins E_o
	246	° ′ ″	′ ″
July 1	**0857·5**	278 58 30·1843	−19 38·7516
2	**0858·5**	279 57 38·3885	−19 38·8171
3	**0859·5**	280 56 46·5928	−19 38·8853
4	**0860·5**	281 55 54·7970	−19 38·9716
5	**0861·5**	282 55 03·0012	−19 39·0879
6	**0862·5**	283 54 11·2055	−19 39·2411
7	**0863·5**	284 53 19·4097	−19 39·4329
8	**0864·5**	285 52 27·6139	−19 39·6597
9	**0865·5**	286 51 35·8182	−19 39·9116
10	**0866·5**	287 50 44·0224	−19 40·1738
11	**0867·5**	288 49 52·2267	−19 40·4276
12	**0868·5**	289 49 00·4309	−19 40·6540
13	**0869·5**	290 48 08·6351	−19 40·8379
14	**0870·5**	291 47 16·8394	−19 40·9721
15	**0871·5**	292 46 25·0436	−19 41·0607
16	**0872·5**	293 45 33·2478	−19 41·1194
17	**0873·5**	294 44 41·4521	−19 41·1730
18	**0874·5**	295 43 49·6563	−19 41·2496
19	**0875·5**	296 42 57·8606	−19 41·3737
20	**0876·5**	297 42 06·0648	−19 41·5588
21	**0877·5**	298 41 14·2690	−19 41·8027
22	**0878·5**	299 40 22·4733	−19 42·0873
23	**0879·5**	300 39 30·6775	−19 42·3830
24	**0880·5**	301 38 38·8817	−19 42·6574
25	**0881·5**	302 37 47·0860	−19 42·8853
26	**0882·5**	303 36 55·2902	−19 43·0543
27	**0883·5**	304 36 03·4945	−19 43·1666
28	**0884·5**	305 35 11·6987	−19 43·2353
29	**0885·5**	306 34 19·9029	−19 43·2796
30	**0886·5**	307 33 28·1072	−19 43·3195
31	**0887·5**	308 32 36·3114	−19 43·3726
Aug. 1	**0888·5**	309 31 44·5156	−19 43·4521
2	**0889·5**	310 30 52·7199	−19 43·5662
3	**0890·5**	311 30 00·9241	−19 43·7182
4	**0891·5**	312 29 09·1283	−19 43·9059
5	**0892·5**	313 28 17·3326	−19 44·1218
6	**0893·5**	314 27 25·5368	−19 44·3534
7	**0894·5**	315 26 33·7411	−19 44·5835
8	**0895·5**	316 25 41·9453	−19 44·7926
9	**0896·5**	317 24 50·1495	−19 44·9628
10	**0897·5**	318 23 58·3538	−19 45·0826
11	**0898·5**	319 23 06·5580	−19 45·1518
12	**0899·5**	320 22 14·7622	−19 45·1835
13	**0900·5**	321 21 22·9665	−19 45·2024
14	**0901·5**	322 20 31·1707	−19 45·2383
15	**0902·5**	323 19 39·3750	−19 45·3173
16	**0903·5**	324 18 47·5792	−19 45·4545

Date 0^h UT1	Julian Date	Earth Rotation Angle θ	Equation of Origins E_o
	246	° ′ ″	′ ″
Aug. 16	**0903·5**	324 18 47·5792	−19 45·4545
17	**0904·5**	325 17 55·7834	−19 45·6496
18	**0905·5**	326 17 03·9877	−19 45·8874
19	**0906·5**	327 16 12·1919	−19 46·1422
20	**0907·5**	328 15 20·3961	−19 46·3846
21	**0908·5**	329 14 28·6004	−19 46·5893
22	**0909·5**	330 13 36·8046	−19 46·7406
23	**0910·5**	331 12 45·0089	−19 46·8356
24	**0911·5**	332 11 53·2131	−19 46·8829
25	**0912·5**	333 11 01·4173	−19 46·8989
26	**0913·5**	334 10 09·6216	−19 46·9038
27	**0914·5**	335 09 17·8258	−19 46·9165
28	**0915·5**	336 08 26·0300	−19 46·9521
29	**0916·5**	337 07 34·2343	−19 47·0208
30	**0917·5**	338 06 42·4385	−19 47·1268
31	**0918·5**	339 05 50·6428	−19 47·2694
Sept. 1	**0919·5**	340 04 58·8470	−19 47·4426
2	**0920·5**	341 04 07·0512	−19 47·6360
3	**0921·5**	342 03 15·2555	−19 47·8349
4	**0922·5**	343 02 23·4597	−19 48·0216
5	**0923·5**	344 01 31·6639	−19 48·1777
6	**0924·5**	345 00 39·8682	−19 48·2884
7	**0925·5**	345 59 48·0724	−19 48·3472
8	**0926·5**	346 58 56·2766	−19 48·3614
9	**0927·5**	347 58 04·4809	−19 48·3525
10	**0928·5**	348 57 12·6851	−19 48·3519
11	**0929·5**	349 56 20·8894	−19 48·3908
12	**0930·5**	350 55 29·0936	−19 48·4893
13	**0931·5**	351 54 37·2978	−19 48·6502
14	**0932·5**	352 53 45·5021	−19 48·8588
15	**0933·5**	353 52 53·7063	−19 49·0893
16	**0934·5**	354 52 01·9105	−19 49·3123
17	**0935·5**	355 51 10·1148	−19 49·5028
18	**0936·5**	356 50 18·3190	−19 49·6445
19	**0937·5**	357 49 26·5233	−19 49·7323
20	**0938·5**	358 48 34·7275	−19 49·7719
21	**0939·5**	359 47 42·9317	−19 49·7770
22	**0940·5**	0 46 51·1360	−19 49·7660
23	**0941·5**	1 45 59·3402	−19 49·7582
24	**0942·5**	2 45 07·5444	−19 49·7700
25	**0943·5**	3 44 15·7487	−19 49·8133
26	**0944·5**	4 43 23·9529	−19 49·8942
27	**0945·5**	5 42 32·1572	−19 50·0129
28	**0946·5**	6 41 40·3614	−19 50·1645
29	**0947·5**	7 40 48·5656	−19 50·3397
30	**0948·5**	8 39 56·7699	−19 50·5256
Oct. 1	**0949·5**	9 39 04·9741	−19 50·7067

$$\mathrm{GHA} = \theta - \alpha_i, \qquad \alpha_i = \alpha_e + E_o$$

α_i, α_e are the right ascensions with respect to the CIO and the true equinox of date, respectively.

Date 0^h UT1	Julian Date	Earth Rotation Angle θ	Equation of Origins E_o
	246	° ′ ″	′ ″
Oct. 1	**0949·5**	9 39 04·9741	− 19 50·7067
2	**0950·5**	10 38 13·1783	− 19 50·8662
3	**0951·5**	11 37 21·3826	− 19 50·9889
4	**0952·5**	12 36 29·5868	− 19 51·0649
5	**0953·5**	13 35 37·7911	− 19 51·0942
6	**0954·5**	14 34 45·9953	− 19 51·0908
7	**0955·5**	15 33 54·1995	− 19 51·0828
8	**0956·5**	16 33 02·4038	− 19 51·1048
9	**0957·5**	17 32 10·6080	− 19 51·1859
10	**0958·5**	18 31 18·8122	− 19 51·3374
11	**0959·5**	19 30 27·0165	− 19 51·5487
12	**0960·5**	20 29 35·2207	− 19 51·7923
13	**0961·5**	21 28 43·4249	− 19 52·0350
14	**0962·5**	22 27 51·6292	− 19 52·2481
15	**0963·5**	23 26 59·8334	− 19 52·4134
16	**0964·5**	24 26 08·0377	− 19 52·5249
17	**0965·5**	25 25 16·2419	− 19 52·5873
18	**0966·5**	26 24 24·4461	− 19 52·6133
19	**0967·5**	27 23 32·6504	− 19 52·6202
20	**0968·5**	28 22 40·8546	− 19 52·6266
21	**0969·5**	29 21 49·0588	− 19 52·6494
22	**0970·5**	30 20 57·2631	− 19 52·7018
23	**0971·5**	31 20 05·4673	− 19 52·7915
24	**0972·5**	32 19 13·6716	− 19 52·9204
25	**0973·5**	33 18 21·8758	− 19 53·0844
26	**0974·5**	34 17 30·0800	− 19 53·2750
27	**0975·5**	35 16 38·2843	− 19 53·4798
28	**0976·5**	36 15 46·4885	− 19 53·6840
29	**0977·5**	37 14 54·6927	− 19 53·8726
30	**0978·5**	38 14 02·8970	− 19 54·0312
31	**0979·5**	39 13 11·1012	− 19 54·1497
Nov. 1	**0980·5**	40 12 19·3055	− 19 54·2245
2	**0981·5**	41 11 27·5097	− 19 54·2627
3	**0982·5**	42 10 35·7139	− 19 54·2844
4	**0983·5**	43 09 43·9182	− 19 54·3206
5	**0984·5**	44 08 52·1224	− 19 54·4053
6	**0985·5**	45 08 00·3266	− 19 54·5618
7	**0986·5**	46 07 08·5309	− 19 54·7917
8	**0987·5**	47 06 16·7351	− 19 55·0727
9	**0988·5**	48 05 24·9393	− 19 55·3676
10	**0989·5**	49 04 33·1436	− 19 55·6398
11	**0990·5**	50 03 41·3478	− 19 55·8640
12	**0991·5**	51 02 49·5521	− 19 56·0304
13	**0992·5**	52 01 57·7563	− 19 56·1428
14	**0993·5**	53 01 05·9605	− 19 56·2143
15	**0994·5**	54 00 14·1648	− 19 56·2627
16	**0995·5**	54 59 22·3690	− 19 56·3067

Date 0^h UT1	Julian Date	Earth Rotation Angle θ	Equation of Origins E_o
	246	° ′ ″	′ ″
Nov. 16	**0995·5**	54 59 22·3690	− 19 56·3067
17	**0996·5**	55 58 30·5732	− 19 56·3637
18	**0997·5**	56 57 38·7775	− 19 56·4475
19	**0998·5**	57 56 46·9817	− 19 56·5670
20	**0999·5**	58 55 55·1860	− 19 56·7257
21	**1000·5**	59 55 03·3902	− 19 56·9211
22	**1001·5**	60 54 11·5944	− 19 57·1454
23	**1002·5**	61 53 19·7987	− 19 57·3865
24	**1003·5**	62 52 28·0029	− 19 57·6298
25	**1004·5**	63 51 36·2071	− 19 57·8597
26	**1005·5**	64 50 44·4114	− 19 58·0626
27	**1006·5**	65 49 52·6156	− 19 58·2281
28	**1007·5**	66 49 00·8199	− 19 58·3522
29	**1008·5**	67 48 09·0241	− 19 58·4391
30	**1009·5**	68 47 17·2283	− 19 58·5030
Dec. 1	**1010·5**	69 46 25·4326	− 19 58·5682
2	**1011·5**	70 45 33·6368	− 19 58·6652
3	**1012·5**	71 44 41·8410	− 19 58·8225
4	**1013·5**	72 43 50·0453	− 19 59·0547
5	**1014·5**	73 42 58·2495	− 19 59·3537
6	**1015·5**	74 42 06·4538	− 19 59·6889
7	**1016·5**	75 41 14·6580	− 20 00·0191
8	**1017·5**	76 40 22·8622	− 20 00·3082
9	**1018·5**	77 39 31·0665	− 20 00·5361
10	**1019·5**	78 38 39·2707	− 20 00·7013
11	**1020·5**	79 37 47·4749	− 20 00·8161
12	**1021·5**	80 36 55·6792	− 20 00·8997
13	**1022·5**	81 36 03·8834	− 20 00·9727
14	**1023·5**	82 35 12·0876	− 20 01·0541
15	**1024·5**	83 34 20·2919	− 20 01·1585
16	**1025·5**	84 33 28·4961	− 20 01·2959
17	**1026·5**	85 32 36·7004	− 20 01·4710
18	**1027·5**	86 31 44·9046	− 20 01·6827
19	**1028·5**	87 30 53·1088	− 20 01·9247
20	**1029·5**	88 30 01·3131	− 20 02·1860
21	**1030·5**	89 29 09·5173	− 20 02·4518
22	**1031·5**	90 28 17·7215	− 20 02·7062
23	**1032·5**	91 27 25·9258	− 20 02·9341
24	**1033·5**	92 26 34·1300	− 20 03·1242
25	**1034·5**	93 25 42·3343	− 20 03·2717
26	**1035·5**	94 24 50·5385	− 20 03·3798
27	**1036·5**	95 23 58·7427	− 20 03·4606
28	**1037·5**	96 23 06·9470	− 20 03·5346
29	**1038·5**	97 22 15·1512	− 20 03·6280
30	**1039·5**	98 21 23·3554	− 20 03·7672
31	**1040·5**	99 20 31·5597	− 20 03·9708
32	**1041·5**	100 19 39·7639	− 20 04·2421

$$\text{GHA} = \theta - \alpha_i, \qquad \alpha_i = \alpha_e + E_o$$

α_i, α_e are the right ascensions with respect to the CIO and the true equinox of date, respectively.

Purpose, explanation and arrangement

The formulae, tables and ephemerides in the remainder of this section are mainly intended to provide for the reduction of celestial coordinates (especially of right ascension, declination and hour angle) from one reference system to another; in particular from a position in the International Celestial Reference System (ICRS) to a geocentric apparent or intermediate position, but some of the data may be used for other purposes.

Formulae and numerical values are given for the separate steps in such reductions, i.e. for proper motion, parallax, light-deflection, aberration on pages B27–B29, and for frame bias, precession and nutation on pages B50–B56. Formulae are given for full-precision reductions using vectors and rotation matrices on pages B48–B50. The examples given use **both** the long-standing equator and equinox of date system, as well as the Celestial Intermediate Reference System (equator and CIO of date) (see pages B66–B75). Finally, formulae and numerical values are given for the reduction from geocentric to topocentric place on pages B84–B86. Background information is given in Section L, *Notes and References* and in Section M, the *Glossary* while vector and matrix algebra, including the rotation matrices, is given on pages K18–K19.

Notation and units

The following is a list of some frequently used coordinate systems and their designations and include the practical consequences of adoption of the ICRS, IAU 2000 resolutions B1.6, B1.7 and B1.8, and IAU 2006 resolutions 1 and 2.

1. Barycentric Celestial Reference System (BCRS): a system of barycentric space-time coordinates for the solar system within the framework of General Relativity. For all practical applications, the BCRS is assumed to be oriented according to the ICRS axes, the directions of which are realized by the International Celestial Reference Frame. The ICRS is not identical to the system defined by the dynamical mean equator and equinox of J2000·0, although the difference in orientation is only about $0''.02$.
2. The Geocentric Celestial Reference System (GCRS): is a system of geocentric space-time coordinates within the framework of General Relativity. The directions of the GCRS axes are obtained from those of the BCRS (ICRS) by a relativistic transformation. Positions of stars obtained from ICRS reference data, corrected for proper motion, parallax, light-bending, and aberration (for a geocentric observer) are with respect to the GCRS. The same is true for planetary positions, although the corrections are somewhat different.
3. The J2000·0 dynamical reference system; mean equator and equinox of J2000·0; a geocentric system where the origin of right ascension is the intersection of the mean ecliptic and equator of J2000·0; the system in which the IAU 2000 precession-nutation is defined. For precise applications, a small rotation (frame bias, see page B50) should be made to GCRS positions before precession and nutation are applied. The J2000·0 system may also be barycentric, for example as the reference system for catalogues.
4. The mean system of date (m); mean equator and equinox of date.
5. The true system of date (t); true equator and equinox of date: a geocentric system of date, the pole of which is the celestial intermediate pole (CIP), with the origin of right ascension at the equinox on the true equator of date (intermediate equator). It is a system "between" the GCRS and the Terrestrial Intermediate Reference System that separates the components labelled precession-nutation and polar motion.
6. The Celestial Intermediate Reference System (i): the IAU recommended geocentric system of date, the pole of which is the celestial intermediate pole (CIP), with the origin of right ascension at the celestial intermediate origin (CIO) which is located on the intermediate equator (true equator of date). It is a system "between" (*intermediate*) the GCRS and the Terrestrial Intermediate Reference System that separates the components labelled precession-nutation and polar motion.

Notation and units (continued)

7. The Terrestrial Intermediate Reference System: a rotating geocentric system of date, the pole of which is the celestial intermediate pole (CIP), with the origin of longitude at the terrestrial intermediate origin (TIO), which is located on the intermediate equator (true equator of date). The plane containing the geocentre, the CIP, and TIO is the fundamental plane of this system and is called the TIO meridian and corresponds to the astronomical zero meridian.

8. The International Terrestrial Reference System (ITRS): a geodetic system realized by the International Terrestrial Reference Frame (ITRF2020), see page K11. The CIP and TIO of the Terrestrial Intermediate Reference System differ from the geodetic pole and zero-longitude point on the geodetic equator by the effects of polar motion (page B84).

Summary

No.	System	Equator/Pole	Origin on the Equator	Epoch
1	BCRS (ICRS)	ICRS equator and pole	ICRS (RA)	—
2	GCRS	ICRS (see 2 above)	ICRS (RA)	—
3	J2000·0	mean equator	mean equinox (RA)	J2000·0
4	Mean (m)	mean equator	mean equinox (RA)	date
5	True (t)	equator/CIP	true equinox (RA)	date
6	Intermediate (i)	equator/CIP	CIO (RA)	date
7	Terrestrial	equator/CIP	TIO (GHA)	date
8	ITRS	geodetic equator/pole	longitude (λ_{ITRS})	date

- The true equator of date, the intermediate equator, the instantaneous equator are all terms for the plane orthogonal to the direction of the CIP, which in this volume will be referred to as the "equator of date". Declinations, apparent or intermediate, derived using either equinox-based or CIO-based methods, respectively, are identical.
- The origin of the right ascension system may be one of five different locations (ICRS origin, J2000·0, mean equinox, true equinox, or the CIO). The notation will make it clear which is being referred to when necessary.
- The celestial intermediate origin (CIO) is the chosen origin of the Celestial Intermediate Reference System. It has no instantaneous motion along the equator as the equator's orientation in space changes, and is therefore referred to as a "non-rotating" origin. The CIO makes the relationship between UT1 and Earth rotation a simple linear function (see page B8). Right ascensions measured from this origin are called intermediate right ascensions or CIO right ascensions.
- The only difference between apparent and intermediate right ascensions is the position of the origin on the equator. When using the equator and equinox of date system, right ascension is measured from the equinox and is called apparent right ascension. When using the Celestial Intermediate Reference System, right ascension is measured from the CIO, and is called intermediate right ascension.
- Apparent right ascension is subtracted from Greenwich apparent sidereal time to give hour angle (GHA).
- Intermediate right ascension is subtracted from Earth rotation angle to give hour angle (GHA).

Matrices

$\mathbf{R}_1, \mathbf{R}_2, \mathbf{R}_3$ rotation matrices $\mathbf{R}_n(\phi)$, $n = 1, 2, 3$, where the original system is rotated about its x, y, or z-axis by the angle ϕ, counterclockwise as viewed from the $+x$, $+y$ or $+z$ direction, respectively (see page K19 for information on matrices).

$\mathcal{R}_\Sigma$ Matrix transformation of the GCRS to the equator and GCRS origin of date. An intermediary matrix which locates and relates origins, see pages B9 and B49.

Notation and units (continued)

Matrices for Equinox-Based Techniques

B Bias matrix: transformation of the GCRS to J2000·0 system, mean equator and equinox of J2000·0, see page B50.

P Precession matrix: transformation of the J2000·0 system to the mean equator and equinox of date, see page B51.

N Nutation matrix: transformation of the mean equator and equinox of date to equator and equinox of date, see page B55.

M = **NPB** Celestial to equator and equinox of date matrix: transformation of the GCRS to the true equator and equinox of date, see page B56.

$\mathbf{R}_3$(GAST) Earth rotation matrix: transformation of the true equator and equinox of date to the Terrestrial Intermediate Reference System (origin is the TIO).

Matrices for CIO-Based Techniques

C Celestial to Intermediate matrix: transformation of the GCRS to the Celestial Intermediate Reference System (equator and CIO of date). **C** includes frame bias and precession-nutation, see page B49.

$\mathbf{R}_3(\theta)$ Earth rotation matrix: transformation of the Celestial Intermediate Reference System to the Terrestrial Intermediate Reference System (origin is the TIO).

Other terms

t an epoch expressed in terms of the Julian year; (see page B3); the difference between two epochs represents a time-interval expressed in Julian years; subscripts zero and one are used to indicate the epoch of a catalogue place, usually the standard epoch of J2000·0, and the epoch of the middle of a Julian year (here shortened to "epoch of year"), respectively.

T an interval of time expressed in Julian centuries of 36 525 days; usually measured from J2000·0, i.e. from JD 245 1545·0 TT.

$\mathbf{r}_m, \mathbf{r}_t, \mathbf{r}_i$ column position vectors (see page K18), with respect to mean equinox, true equinox, and celestial intermediate system, respectively.

α, δ, π right ascension, declination and annual parallax; in the formulae for computation, right ascension and related quantities are expressed in time-measure ($1^h = 15^\circ$, etc.), while declination and related quantities, including annual parallax, are expressed in angular measure, unless the contrary is indicated.

α_e, α_i equinox and intermediate right ascensions, respectively; α_e is measured from the equinox, while α_i is measured from the CIO.

μ_α, μ_δ components of proper motion in right ascension and declination. **Check the units**. Modern catalogues usually include the $\cos\delta$ factor in μ_α, translating the rate of change of right ascension to great circle units comparable to those of μ_δ.

λ, β ecliptic longitude and latitude.

Ω, i, ω orbital elements referred to the ecliptic; longitude of ascending node, inclination, argument of perihelion.

X, Y, Z rectangular coordinates of the Earth with respect to the barycentre of the solar system, referred to the ICRS and expressed in astronomical units (au).

$\dot{X}, \dot{Y}, \dot{Z}$ first derivatives of X, Y, Z with respect to time expressed in TDB days.

Approximate reduction for proper motion

In its simplest form the reduction for the proper motion is given by:

$$\alpha = \alpha_0 + (t - t_0)\mu_\alpha \qquad \text{or} \qquad \alpha = \alpha_0 + (t - t_0)\mu_\alpha / \cos\delta$$

$$\delta = \delta_0 + (t - t_0)\mu_\delta$$

where the rate of the proper motions are per year. In some cases it is necessary to allow also for second-order terms, radial velocity and orbital motion, but appropriate formulae are usually given in the catalogue (see page B72).

Approximate reduction for annual parallax

The reduction for annual parallax from the catalogue place (α_0, δ_0) to the geocentric place (α, δ) is given by:

$$\alpha = \alpha_0 + (\pi/15 \cos\delta_0)(X \sin\alpha_0 - Y \cos\alpha_0)$$
$$\delta = \delta_0 + \pi(X \cos\alpha_0 \sin\delta_0 + Y \sin\alpha_0 \sin\delta_0 - Z \cos\delta_0)$$

where X, Y, Z are the coordinates of the Earth tabulated on pages B76-B83. Expressions for X, Y, Z may be obtained from page C5, since $X = -x$, $Y = -y$, $Z = -z$.

The times of reception of periodic phenomena, such as pulsar signals, may be reduced to a common origin at the barycentre by adding the light-time corresponding to the component of the Earth's position vector along the direction to the object; that is by adding to the observed times $(X \cos\alpha \cos\delta + Y \sin\alpha \cos\delta + Z \sin\delta)/c$, where the velocity of light, $c = 173{\cdot}14$ au/d, and the light time for 1 au, $1/c = 0^{\mathrm{d}}\!.005\,7755$.

Approximate reduction for light-deflection

The apparent direction of a star or a body in the solar system may be significantly affected by the deflection of light in the gravitational field of the Sun. The elongation (E) from the centre of the Sun is increased by an amount (ΔE) that, for a star, depends on the elongation in the following manner:

$$\Delta E = 0''\!.004\,07/\tan(E/2)$$

E	0°25	0°5	1°	2°	5°	10°	20°	50°	90°
ΔE	1″866	0″933	0″466	0″233	0″093	0″047	0″023	0″009	0″004

The body disappears behind the Sun when E is less than the limiting grazing value of about 0°25. The effects in right ascension and declination may be calculated approximately from:

$$\cos E = \sin\delta \sin\delta_0 + \cos\delta \cos\delta_0 \cos(\alpha - \alpha_0)$$
$$\Delta\alpha = 0^{\mathrm{s}}\!.000\,271 \cos\delta_0 \sin(\alpha - \alpha_0)/(1 - \cos E)\cos\delta$$
$$\Delta\delta = 0''\!.004\,07[\sin\delta \cos\delta_0 \cos(\alpha - \alpha_0) - \cos\delta \sin\delta_0]/(1 - \cos E)$$

where α, δ refer to the star, and α_0, δ_0 to the Sun. See also page B67 *Step 3*.

Approximate reduction for annual aberration

The reduction for annual aberration from a geometric geocentric place (α_0, δ_0) to an apparent geocentric place (α, δ) is given by:

$$\alpha = \alpha_0 + (-\dot{X} \sin\alpha_0 + \dot{Y} \cos\alpha_0)/(c \cos\delta_0)$$
$$\delta = \delta_0 + (-\dot{X} \cos\alpha_0 \sin\delta_0 - \dot{Y} \sin\alpha_0 \sin\delta_0 + \dot{Z} \cos\delta_0)/c$$

where $c = 173{\cdot}14$ au/d, and $\dot{X}$, $\dot{Y}$, $\dot{Z}$ are the velocity components of the Earth given on pages B76-B83. Alternatively, but to lower precision, it is possible to use the expressions

$$\dot{X} = +0{\cdot}0172 \sin\lambda \qquad \dot{Y} = -0{\cdot}0158 \cos\lambda \qquad \dot{Z} = -0{\cdot}0068 \cos\lambda$$

where the apparent longitude of the Sun, λ, is given by the expression on page C5. The reduction may also be carried out by using the vector-matrix technique (see page B67 *Step 4*) when full precision is required.

Measurements of radial velocity may be reduced to a common origin at the barycentre by adding the component of the Earth's velocity in the direction of the object; that is by adding

$$\dot{X} \cos\alpha_0 \cos\delta_0 + \dot{Y} \sin\alpha_0 \cos\delta_0 + \dot{Z} \sin\delta_0$$

Traditional reduction for planetary aberration

In the case of a body in the solar system, the apparent direction at the instant of observation (t) differs from the geometric direction at that instant because of (a) the motion of the body during the light-time and (b) the motion of the Earth relative to the reference system in which light propagation is computed. The reduction may be carried out in two stages: (i) by combining the barycentric position of the body at time $t - \Delta t$, where Δt is the light-time, with the barycentric position of the Earth at time t, and then (ii) by applying the correction for annual aberration as described above. Alternatively, it is possible to interpolate the geometric (geocentric) ephemeris of the body to the time $t - \Delta t$; it is usually sufficient to subtract the product of the light-time and the first derivative of the coordinate. The light-time Δt in days is given by the distance in au between the body and the Earth, multiplied by 0·005 7755; strictly, the light-time corresponds to the distance from the position of the Earth at time t to the position of the body at time $t - \Delta t$ (i.e. some iteration is required), but it is usually sufficient to use the geocentric distance at time t.

Differential aberration

The corrections for differential annual aberration to be added to the observed differences (in the sense moving object minus star) of right ascension and declination to give the true differences are:

in right ascension	$a\,\Delta\alpha + b\,\Delta\delta$	in units of $0\overset{s}{.}001$
in declination	$c\,\Delta\alpha + d\,\Delta\delta$	in units of $0\overset{''}{.}01$

where $\Delta\alpha$, $\Delta\delta$ are the observed differences in units of 1^{m} and $1'$ respectively, and where a, b, c, d are coefficients defined by:

$$a = -5{\cdot}701 \cos(H + \alpha) \sec\delta \qquad b = -0{\cdot}380 \sin(H + \alpha) \sec\delta \tan\delta$$
$$c = +8{\cdot}552 \sin(H + \alpha) \sin\delta \qquad d = -0{\cdot}570 \cos(H + \alpha) \cos\delta$$
$$H^{h} = 23{\cdot}4 - (\text{day of year}/15{\cdot}2)$$

The day of year is tabulated on pages B4–B5.

GCRS positions

For objects with reference data (catalogue coordinates or ephemerides) expressed in the ICRS, the application of corrections for proper motion and parallax (for stars), light-time (for solar system objects), light-deflection, and annual aberration results in a position referred to the GCRS, which is sometimes called the *proper place*.

Astrometric positions

An astrometric place is the direction of a solar system body formed by applying the correction for the barycentric motion of this body during the light time to the geometric geocentric position referred to the ICRS. Such a position is then directly comparable with the astrometric position of a star formed by applying the corrections for proper motion and annual parallax to the ICRS (or J2000) catalog direction. The gravitational deflection of light is ignored since it will generally be similar (although not identical) for the solar system body and background stars. For high-accuracy applications, gravitational light-deflection effects need to be considered, and the adopted policy declared.

MATRIX ELEMENTS FOR CONVERSION FROM GCRS TO EQUATOR AND EQUINOX OF DATE FOR 0^h TERRESTRIAL TIME

Date 0^h TT	$\mathbf{M}_{1,1}-1$	$\mathbf{M}_{1,2}$	$\mathbf{M}_{1,3}$	$\mathbf{M}_{2,1}$	$\mathbf{M}_{2,2}-1$	$\mathbf{M}_{2,3}$	$\mathbf{M}_{3,1}$	$\mathbf{M}_{3,2}$	$\mathbf{M}_{3,3}-1$
Jan. 0	−185751	−5590 2451	−2428 7894	+5590 1455	−156261	−47 7698	+2429 0184	+34 1917	−29507
1	−185840	−5591 5849	−2429 3708	+5591 4849	−156336	−47 9555	+2429 6009	+34 3708	−29521
2	−185918	−5592 7586	−2429 8801	+5592 6579	−156402	−48 2335	+2430 1119	+34 6431	−29533
3	−185980	−5593 6893	−2430 2841	+5593 5878	−156454	−48 5549	+2430 5177	+34 9600	−29543
4	−186024	−5594 3560	−2430 5737	+5594 2538	−156492	−48 8568	+2430 8090	+35 2586	−29550
5	−186054	−5594 8044	−2430 7687	+5594 7017	−156517	−49 0772	+2431 0052	+35 4768	−29555
6	−186076	−5595 1393	−2430 9144	+5595 0363	−156535	−49 1723	+2431 1515	+35 5703	−29559
7	−186100	−5595 4987	−2431 0708	+5595 3958	−156556	−49 1290	+2431 3076	+35 5253	−29563
8	−186135	−5596 0183	−2431 2966	+5595 9158	−156585	−48 9696	+2431 5326	+35 3633	−29568
9	−186187	−5596 7950	−2431 6339	+5596 6930	−156628	−48 7465	+2431 8686	+35 1365	−29576
10	−186257	−5597 8596	−2432 0959	+5597 7581	−156687	−48 5294	+2432 3295	+34 9142	−29587
11	−186344	−5599 1672	−2432 6634	+5599 0661	−156761	−48 3865	+2432 8962	+34 7650	−29601
12	−186440	−5600 6103	−2433 2895	+5600 5092	−156841	−48 3658	+2433 5222	+34 7373	−29616
13	−186536	−5602 0494	−2433 9139	+5601 9479	−156922	−48 4833	+2434 1473	+34 8478	−29631
14	−186623	−5603 3524	−2434 4793	+5603 2504	−156995	−48 7208	+2434 7141	+35 0789	−29645
15	−186695	−5604 4283	−2434 9463	+5604 3255	−157056	−49 0346	+2435 1829	+35 3874	−29657
16	−186749	−5605 2425	−2435 2998	+5605 1389	−157101	−49 3698	+2435 5383	+35 7187	−29666
17	−186787	−5605 8148	−2435 5485	+5605 7104	−157134	−49 6750	+2435 7887	+36 0211	−29672
18	−186813	−5606 2047	−2435 7181	+5606 0997	−157155	−49 9118	+2435 9596	+36 2560	−29676
19	−186832	−5606 4921	−2435 8432	+5606 3868	−157172	−50 0587	+2436 0856	+36 4015	−29679
20	−186850	−5606 7619	−2435 9608	+5606 6564	−157187	−50 1111	+2436 2034	+36 4526	−29682
21	−186872	−5607 0919	−2436 1044	+5606 9865	−157205	−50 0787	+2436 3469	+36 4186	−29686
22	−186902	−5607 5464	−2436 3020	+5607 4413	−157231	−49 9822	+2436 5440	+36 3199	−29690
23	−186944	−5608 1717	−2436 5736	+5608 0669	−157266	−49 8509	+2436 8149	+36 1855	−29697
24	−186999	−5608 9916	−2436 9297	+5608 8871	−157312	−49 7198	+2437 1702	+36 0504	−29706
25	−187066	−5610 0032	−2437 3687	+5609 8989	−157368	−49 6274	+2437 6088	+35 9531	−29716
26	−187144	−5611 1713	−2437 8756	+5611 0670	−157434	−49 6108	+2438 1156	+35 9308	−29729
27	−187228	−5612 4261	−2438 4202	+5612 3216	−157504	−49 6993	+2438 6607	+36 0132	−29742
28	−187311	−5613 6673	−2438 9588	+5613 5623	−157574	−49 9058	+2439 2005	+36 2137	−29755
29	−187385	−5614 7800	−2439 4417	+5614 6742	−157637	−50 2183	+2439 6852	+36 5207	−29767
30	−187444	−5615 6632	−2439 8251	+5615 5564	−157686	−50 5959	+2440 0708	+36 8939	−29777
31	−187484	−5616 2645	−2440 0864	+5616 1568	−157720	−50 9739	+2440 3342	+37 2690	−29783
Feb. 1	−187507	−5616 6066	−2440 2353	+5616 4982	−157740	−51 2807	+2440 4848	+37 5742	−29787
2	−187519	−5616 7878	−2440 3144	+5616 6789	−157750	−51 4600	+2440 5649	+37 7525	−29789
3	−187530	−5616 9546	−2440 3873	+5616 8457	−157759	−51 4893	+2440 6380	+37 7811	−29791
4	−187550	−5617 2555	−2440 5183	+5617 1468	−157776	−51 3878	+2440 7684	+37 6780	−29794
5	−187586	−5617 7966	−2440 7534	+5617 6883	−157806	−51 2080	+2441 0026	+37 4956	−29800
6	−187641	−5618 6151	−2441 1088	+5618 5073	−157852	−51 0198	+2441 3569	+37 3034	−29808
7	−187712	−5619 6754	−2441 5690	+5619 5679	−157912	−50 8904	+2441 8165	+37 1689	−29819
8	−187793	−5620 8845	−2442 0937	+5620 7771	−157980	−50 8684	+2442 3411	+37 1410	−29832
9	−187875	−5622 1188	−2442 6294	+5622 0110	−158049	−50 9746	+2442 8773	+37 2411	−29845
10	−187951	−5623 2550	−2443 1225	+5623 1467	−158113	−51 1996	+2443 3717	+37 4606	−29857
11	−188014	−5624 1969	−2443 5314	+5624 0878	−158166	−51 5097	+2443 7824	+37 7661	−29868
12	−188061	−5624 8934	−2443 8339	+5624 7835	−158206	−51 8560	+2444 0869	+38 1089	−29875
13	−188091	−5625 3434	−2444 0295	+5625 2326	−158231	−52 1871	+2444 2844	+38 4379	−29880
14	−188107	−5625 5896	−2444 1368	+5625 4782	−158245	−52 4594	+2444 3932	+38 7090	−29883
15	−188115	−5625 7042	−2444 1871	+5625 5923	−158252	−52 6443	+2444 4445	+38 8933	−29884

M = NPB. Values are in units of 10^{-10}. Matrix used with GAST (B13–B20). CIP is $\mathcal{X} = \mathbf{M}_{3,1}$, $\mathcal{Y} = \mathbf{M}_{3,2}$.

MATRIX ELEMENTS FOR CONVERSION FROM
GCRS TO EQUATOR & CELESTIAL INTERMEDIATE ORIGIN OF DATE
FOR 0^h TERRESTRIAL TIME

Julian Date	$C_{1,1}-1$	$C_{1,2}$	$C_{1,3}$	$C_{2,1}$	$C_{2,2}-1$	$C_{2,3}$	$C_{3,1}$	$C_{3,2}$	$C_{3,3}-1$
246									
0675·5	−29501	+ 8	−2429 0185	−838	− 6	−34 1916	+2429 0184	+34 1917	−29507
0676·5	−29515	+ 8	−2429 6009	−843	− 6	−34 3707	+2429 6009	+34 3708	−29521
0677·5	−29527	+ 8	−2430 1119	−849	− 6	−34 6430	+2430 1119	+34 6431	−29533
0678·5	−29537	+ 7	−2430 5177	−857	− 6	−34 9599	+2430 5177	+34 9600	−29543
0679·5	−29544	+ 7	−2430 8090	−864	− 6	−35 2585	+2430 8090	+35 2586	−29550
0680·5	−29549	+ 7	−2431 0052	−870	− 6	−35 4767	+2431 0052	+35 4768	−29555
0681·5	−29553	+ 7	−2431 1515	−872	− 6	−35 5702	+2431 1515	+35 5703	−29559
0682·5	−29556	+ 7	−2431 3076	−871	− 6	−35 5252	+2431 3076	+35 5253	−29563
0683·5	−29562	+ 7	−2431 5326	−867	− 6	−35 3632	+2431 5326	+35 3633	−29568
0684·5	−29570	+ 7	−2431 8686	−861	− 6	−35 1364	+2431 8686	+35 1365	−29576
0685·5	−29581	+ 7	−2432 3295	−856	− 6	−34 9141	+2432 3295	+34 9142	−29587
0686·5	−29595	+ 7	−2432 8962	−852	− 6	−34 7648	+2432 8962	+34 7650	−29601
0687·5	−29610	+ 6	−2433 5222	−852	− 6	−34 7372	+2433 5222	+34 7373	−29616
0688·5	−29625	+ 6	−2434 1473	−854	− 6	−34 8477	+2434 1473	+34 8478	−29631
0689·5	−29639	+ 6	−2434 7141	−860	− 6	−35 0788	+2434 7141	+35 0789	−29645
0690·5	−29651	+ 6	−2435 1829	−867	− 6	−35 3873	+2435 1829	+35 3874	−29657
0691·5	−29659	+ 6	−2435 5383	−876	− 6	−35 7186	+2435 5383	+35 7187	−29666
0692·5	−29665	+ 6	−2435 7887	−883	− 6	−36 0210	+2435 7887	+36 0211	−29672
0693·5	−29670	+ 5	−2435 9596	−889	− 7	−36 2559	+2435 9596	+36 2560	−29676
0694·5	−29673	+ 5	−2436 0856	−892	− 7	−36 4014	+2436 0856	+36 4015	−29679
0695·5	−29675	+ 5	−2436 2034	−893	− 7	−36 4525	+2436 2034	+36 4526	−29682
0696·5	−29679	+ 5	−2436 3469	−893	− 7	−36 4185	+2436 3469	+36 4186	−29686
0697·5	−29684	+ 5	−2436 5440	−890	− 7	−36 3198	+2436 5440	+36 3199	−29690
0698·5	−29690	+ 5	−2436 8149	−887	− 7	−36 1854	+2436 8149	+36 1855	−29697
0699·5	−29699	+ 5	−2437 1702	−884	− 6	−36 0503	+2437 1702	+36 0504	−29706
0700·5	−29710	+ 5	−2437 6088	−881	− 6	−35 9530	+2437 6088	+35 9531	−29716
0701·5	−29722	+ 5	−2438 1156	−881	− 6	−35 9307	+2438 1156	+35 9308	−29729
0702·5	−29735	+ 4	−2438 6607	−883	− 6	−36 0131	+2438 6607	+36 0132	−29742
0703·5	−29749	+ 4	−2439 2005	−888	− 7	−36 2136	+2439 2005	+36 2137	−29755
0704·5	−29760	+ 4	−2439 6852	−895	− 7	−36 5206	+2439 6852	+36 5207	−29767
0705·5	−29770	+ 4	−2440 0708	−904	− 7	−36 8938	+2440 0708	+36 8939	−29777
0706·5	−29776	+ 4	−2440 3342	−913	− 7	−37 2689	+2440 3342	+37 2690	−29783
0707·5	−29780	+ 4	−2440 4848	−921	− 7	−37 5741	+2440 4848	+37 5742	−29787
0708·5	−29782	+ 4	−2440 5649	−925	− 7	−37 7524	+2440 5649	+37 7525	−29789
0709·5	−29784	+ 4	−2440 6380	−926	− 7	−37 7810	+2440 6380	+37 7811	−29791
0710·5	−29787	+ 4	−2440 7684	−923	− 7	−37 6779	+2440 7684	+37 6780	−29794
0711·5	−29793	+ 4	−2441 0026	−919	− 7	−37 4955	+2441 0026	+37 4956	−29800
0712·5	−29801	+ 3	−2441 3569	−914	− 7	−37 3033	+2441 3569	+37 3034	−29808
0713·5	−29812	+ 3	−2441 8165	−911	− 7	−37 1687	+2441 8165	+37 1689	−29819
0714·5	−29825	+ 3	−2442 3411	−910	− 7	−37 1409	+2442 3411	+37 1410	−29832
0715·5	−29838	+ 3	−2442 8773	−913	− 7	−37 2410	+2442 8773	+37 2411	−29845
0716·5	−29850	+ 3	−2443 3717	−918	− 7	−37 4605	+2443 3717	+37 4606	−29857
0717·5	−29860	+ 3	−2443 7824	−926	− 7	−37 7659	+2443 7824	+37 7661	−29868
0718·5	−29868	+ 2	−2444 0869	−934	− 7	−38 1088	+2444 0869	+38 1089	−29875
0719·5	−29873	+ 2	−2444 2844	−942	− 7	−38 4377	+2444 2844	+38 4379	−29880
0720·5	−29875	+ 2	−2444 3932	−949	− 7	−38 7089	+2444 3932	+38 7090	−29883
0721·5	−29877	+ 2	−2444 4446	−953	− 8	−38 8932	+2444 4445	+38 8933	−29884

Values are in units of 10^{-10}. Matrix used with ERA (B21–B24). CIP is $\mathcal{X} = C_{3,1}$, $\mathcal{Y} = C_{3,2}$

MATRIX ELEMENTS FOR CONVERSION FROM GCRS TO EQUATOR AND EQUINOX OF DATE FOR 0^h TERRESTRIAL TIME

Date 0^h TT	$M_{1,1}-1$	$M_{1,2}$	$M_{1,3}$	$M_{2,1}$	$M_{2,2}-1$	$M_{2,3}$	$M_{3,1}$	$M_{3,2}$	$M_{3,3}-1$
Feb. 15	−188115	−5625 7042	−2444 1871	+5625 5923	−158252	−52 6443	+2444 4445	+38 8933	−29884
16	−188119	−5625 7722	−2444 2171	+5625 6601	−158255	−52 7305	+2444 4751	+38 9792	−29885
17	−188126	−5625 8762	−2444 2628	+5625 7641	−158261	−52 7232	+2444 5207	+38 9713	−29886
18	−188140	−5626 0861	−2444 3544	+5625 9742	−158273	−52 6408	+2444 6118	+38 8879	−29888
19	−188165	−5626 4529	−2444 5139	+5626 3413	−158294	−52 5112	+2444 7707	+38 7565	−29892
20	−188202	−5627 0049	−2444 7538	+5626 8937	−158325	−52 3682	+2445 0098	+38 6108	−29898
21	−188251	−5627 7456	−2445 0755	+5627 6347	−158366	−52 2481	+2445 3308	+38 4871	−29906
22	−188312	−5628 6519	−2445 4689	+5628 5411	−158417	−52 1865	+2445 7239	+38 4211	−29915
23	−188380	−5629 6715	−2445 9115	+5629 5606	−158475	−52 2139	+2446 1666	+38 4436	−29926
24	−188451	−5630 7235	−2446 3681	+5630 6123	−158534	−52 3498	+2446 6241	+38 5743	−29937
25	−188516	−5631 7050	−2446 7941	+5631 5931	−158589	−52 5948	+2447 0515	+38 8144	−29948
26	−188570	−5632 5082	−2447 1429	+5632 3955	−158635	−52 9236	+2447 4021	+39 1393	−29957
27	−188606	−5633 0511	−2447 3788	+5632 9375	−158665	−53 2827	+2447 6401	+39 4957	−29963
28	−188624	−5633 3133	−2447 4930	+5633 1990	−158680	−53 5987	+2447 7561	+39 8105	−29966
Mar. 1	−188627	−5633 3600	−2447 5138	+5633 2452	−158683	−53 7992	+2447 7781	+40 0108	−29966
2	−188625	−5633 3327	−2447 5026	+5633 2178	−158681	−53 8398	+2447 7670	+40 0515	−29966
3	−188630	−5633 4030	−2447 5337	+5633 2884	−158685	−53 7233	+2447 7975	+39 9347	−29967
4	−188651	−5633 7101	−2447 6674	+5633 5960	−158703	−53 4994	+2447 9299	+39 7093	−29970
5	−188691	−5634 3141	−2447 9298	+5634 2007	−158737	−53 2451	+2448 1909	+39 4520	−29976
6	−188749	−5635 1864	−2448 3085	+5635 0734	−158786	−53 0373	+2448 5685	+39 2399	−29985
7	−188819	−5636 2312	−2448 7620	+5636 1185	−158844	−52 9319	+2449 0214	+39 1294	−29996
8	−188893	−5637 3216	−2449 2352	+5637 2088	−158906	−52 9530	+2449 4948	+39 1452	−30008
9	−188960	−5638 3340	−2449 6746	+5638 2208	−158963	−53 0940	+2449 9351	+39 2812	−30019
10	−189017	−5639 1724	−2450 0387	+5639 0586	−159010	−53 3242	+2450 3004	+39 5073	−30028
11	−189057	−5639 7820	−2450 3035	+5639 6676	−159045	−53 5990	+2450 5668	+39 7790	−30034
12	−189082	−5640 1530	−2450 4649	+5640 0379	−159066	−53 8693	+2450 7298	+40 0476	−30038
13	−189093	−5640 3163	−2450 5363	+5640 2007	−159075	−54 0914	+2450 8024	+40 2688	−30040
14	−189094	−5640 3339	−2450 5445	+5640 2179	−159076	−54 2328	+2450 8114	+40 4101	−30041
15	−189091	−5640 2853	−2450 5240	+5640 1692	−159074	−54 2766	+2450 7911	+40 4542	−30040
16	−189089	−5640 2540	−2450 5110	+5640 1380	−159072	−54 2226	+2450 7778	+40 4004	−30040
17	−189093	−5640 3148	−2450 5379	+5640 1992	−159075	−54 0852	+2450 8040	+40 2627	−30040
18	−189107	−5640 5246	−2450 6295	+5640 4095	−159087	−53 8905	+2450 8945	+40 0669	−30042
19	−189134	−5640 9169	−2450 8001	+5640 8023	−159109	−53 6713	+2451 0639	+39 8458	−30047
20	−189173	−5641 4995	−2451 0532	+5641 3854	−159142	−53 4638	+2451 3158	+39 6354	−30053
21	−189223	−5642 2541	−2451 3809	+5642 1404	−159184	−53 3027	+2451 6427	+39 4707	−30061
22	−189283	−5643 1371	−2451 7643	+5643 0236	−159234	−53 2181	+2452 0255	+39 3818	−30070
23	−189346	−5644 0812	−2452 1741	+5643 9677	−159287	−53 2308	+2452 4355	+39 3898	−30080
24	−189407	−5645 0001	−2452 5730	+5644 8862	−159339	−53 3473	+2452 8350	+39 5017	−30090
25	−189461	−5645 7974	−2452 9192	+5645 6830	−159384	−53 5544	+2453 1825	+39 7050	−30098
26	−189500	−5646 3859	−2453 1749	+5646 2708	−159418	−53 8150	+2453 4396	+39 9627	−30105
27	−189523	−5646 7150	−2453 3181	+5646 5994	−159436	−54 0684	+2453 5843	+40 2144	−30109
28	−189528	−5646 8021	−2453 3565	+5646 6861	−159441	−54 2410	+2453 6237	+40 3866	−30110
29	−189525	−5646 7492	−2453 3341	+5646 6331	−159438	−54 2691	+2453 6015	+40 4150	−30109
30	−189523	−5646 7244	−2453 3239	+5646 6086	−159437	−54 1260	+2453 5905	+40 2720	−30109
31	−189535	−5646 9036	−2453 4022	+5646 7885	−159447	−53 8392	+2453 6671	+39 9844	−30110
Apr. 1	−189569	−5647 3991	−2453 6176	+5647 2849	−159475	−53 4828	+2453 8805	+39 6255	−30116
2	−189624	−5648 2177	−2453 9730	+5648 1043	−159521	−53 1479	+2454 2340	+39 2866	−30124

M = **NPB**. Values are in units of 10^{-10}. Matrix used with GAST (B13–B20). CIP is $\mathcal{X} = \mathbf{M}_{3,1}$, $\mathcal{Y} = \mathbf{M}_{3,2}$.

MATRIX ELEMENTS FOR CONVERSION FROM
GCRS TO EQUATOR & CELESTIAL INTERMEDIATE ORIGIN OF DATE
FOR 0^h TERRESTRIAL TIME

Julian Date	$\mathbf{C}_{1,1}-1$	$\mathbf{C}_{1,2}$	$\mathbf{C}_{1,3}$	$\mathbf{C}_{2,1}$	$\mathbf{C}_{2,2}-1$	$\mathbf{C}_{2,3}$	$\mathbf{C}_{3,1}$	$\mathbf{C}_{3,2}$	$\mathbf{C}_{3,3}-1$
246									
0721·5	−29877	+ 2	−2444 4446	−953	− 8	−38 8932	+2444 4445	+38 8933	−29884
0722·5	−29877	+ 2	−2444 4751	−955	− 8	−38 9791	+2444 4751	+38 9792	−29885
0723·5	−29878	+ 2	−2444 5207	−955	− 8	−38 9712	+2444 5207	+38 9713	−29886
0724·5	−29881	+ 2	−2444 6118	−953	− 8	−38 8878	+2444 6118	+38 8879	−29888
0725·5	−29885	+ 2	−2444 7707	−950	− 8	−38 7564	+2444 7707	+38 7565	−29892
0726·5	−29890	+ 2	−2445 0098	−946	− 7	−38 6107	+2445 0098	+38 6108	−29898
0727·5	−29898	+ 2	−2445 3308	−943	− 7	−38 4870	+2445 3308	+38 4871	−29906
0728·5	−29908	+ 2	−2445 7239	−941	− 7	−38 4210	+2445 7239	+38 4211	−29915
0729·5	−29919	+ 2	−2446 1666	−942	− 7	−38 4434	+2446 1666	+38 4436	−29926
0730·5	−29930	+ 1	−2446 6241	−945	− 7	−38 5742	+2446 6241	+38 5743	−29937
0731·5	−29940	+ 1	−2447 0515	−951	− 8	−38 8143	+2447 0515	+38 8144	−29948
0732·5	−29949	+ 1	−2447 4021	−959	− 8	−39 1392	+2447 4021	+39 1393	−29957
0733·5	−29955	+ 1	−2447 6401	−968	− 8	−39 4956	+2447 6401	+39 4957	−29963
0734·5	−29958	+ 1	−2447 7561	−976	− 8	−39 8104	+2447 7561	+39 8105	−29966
0735·5	−29958	+ 1	−2447 7781	−980	− 8	−40 0107	+2447 7781	+40 0108	−29966
0736·5	−29958	+ 1	−2447 7671	−981	− 8	−40 0514	+2447 7670	+40 0515	−29966
0737·5	−29959	+ 1	−2447 7975	−979	− 8	−39 9345	+2447 7975	+39 9347	−29967
0738·5	−29962	+ 1	−2447 9299	−973	− 8	−39 7091	+2447 9299	+39 7093	−29970
0739·5	−29968	+ 1	−2448 1909	−967	− 8	−39 4518	+2448 1909	+39 4520	−29976
0740·5	−29977	+ 1	−2448 5685	−962	− 8	−39 2398	+2448 5685	+39 2399	−29985
0741·5	−29989	+ 1	−2449 0214	−959	− 8	−39 1293	+2449 0214	+39 1294	−29996
0742·5	−30000	0	−2449 4948	−959	− 8	−39 1450	+2449 4948	+39 1452	−30008
0743·5	−30011	0	−2449 9351	−963	− 8	−39 2811	+2449 9351	+39 2812	−30019
0744·5	−30020	0	−2450 3004	−968	− 8	−39 5072	+2450 3004	+39 5073	−30028
0745·5	−30026	0	−2450 5668	−975	− 8	−39 7789	+2450 5668	+39 7790	−30034
0746·5	−30030	0	−2450 7298	−981	− 8	−40 0475	+2450 7298	+40 0476	−30038
0747·5	−30032	0	−2450 8024	−987	− 8	−40 2687	+2450 8024	+40 2688	−30040
0748·5	−30032	0	−2450 8114	−990	− 8	−40 4100	+2450 8114	+40 4101	−30041
0749·5	−30032	0	−2450 7911	−991	− 8	−40 4541	+2450 7911	+40 4542	−30040
0750·5	−30032	0	−2450 7778	−990	− 8	−40 4002	+2450 7778	+40 4004	−30040
0751·5	−30032	0	−2450 8040	−987	− 8	−40 2626	+2450 8040	+40 2627	−30040
0752·5	−30034	0	−2450 8945	−982	− 8	−40 0668	+2450 8945	+40 0669	−30042
0753·5	−30039	0	−2451 0639	−976	− 8	−39 8457	+2451 0639	+39 8458	−30047
0754·5	−30045	0	−2451 3158	−971	− 8	−39 6353	+2451 3158	+39 6354	−30053
0755·5	−30053	− 1	−2451 6427	−967	− 8	−39 4706	+2451 6427	+39 4707	−30061
0756·5	−30062	− 1	−2452 0255	−965	− 8	−39 3816	+2452 0255	+39 3818	−30070
0757·5	−30072	− 1	−2452 4355	−965	− 8	−39 3897	+2452 4355	+39 3898	−30080
0758·5	−30082	− 1	−2452 8350	−968	− 8	−39 5016	+2452 8350	+39 5017	−30090
0759·5	−30091	− 1	−2453 1825	−973	− 8	−39 7049	+2453 1825	+39 7050	−30098
0760·5	−30097	− 1	−2453 4396	−979	− 8	−39 9626	+2453 4396	+39 9627	−30105
0761·5	−30100	− 1	−2453 5843	−985	− 8	−40 2143	+2453 5843	+40 2144	−30109
0762·5	−30101	− 1	−2453 6237	−990	− 8	−40 3865	+2453 6237	+40 3866	−30110
0763·5	−30101	− 1	−2453 6015	−990	− 8	−40 4149	+2453 6015	+40 4150	−30109
0764·5	−30101	− 1	−2453 5905	−987	− 8	−40 2719	+2453 5905	+40 2720	−30109
0765·5	−30102	− 1	−2453 6671	−980	− 8	−39 9842	+2453 6671	+39 9844	−30110
0766·5	−30108	− 1	−2453 8805	−971	− 8	−39 6254	+2453 8805	+39 6255	−30116
0767·5	−30116	− 1	−2454 2340	−963	− 8	−39 2865	+2454 2340	+39 2866	−30124

Values are in units of 10^{-10}. Matrix used with ERA (B21–B24). CIP is $\mathcal{X} = \mathbf{C}_{3,1}$, $\mathcal{Y} = \mathbf{C}_{3,2}$

MATRIX ELEMENTS FOR CONVERSION FROM GCRS TO EQUATOR AND EQUINOX OF DATE FOR 0^h TERRESTRIAL TIME

Date 0^h TT	$\mathbf{M}_{1,1}-1$	$\mathbf{M}_{1,2}$	$\mathbf{M}_{1,3}$	$\mathbf{M}_{2,1}$	$\mathbf{M}_{2,2}-1$	$\mathbf{M}_{2,3}$	$\mathbf{M}_{3,1}$	$\mathbf{M}_{3,2}$	$\mathbf{M}_{3,3}-1$
Apr. 1	−189569	−5647 3991	−2453 6176	+5647 2849	−159475	−53 4828	+2453 8805	+39 6255	−30116
2	−189624	−5648 2177	−2453 9730	+5648 1043	−159521	−53 1479	+2454 2340	+39 2866	−30124
3	−189694	−5649 2684	−2454 4290	+5649 1555	−159580	−52 9095	+2454 6888	+39 0430	−30135
4	−189771	−5650 4081	−2454 9237	+5650 2955	−159644	−52 8051	+2455 1829	+38 9331	−30147
5	−189843	−5651 4928	−2455 3945	+5651 3801	−159706	−52 8332	+2455 6538	+38 9559	−30159
6	−189905	−5652 4122	−2455 7936	+5652 2992	−159758	−52 9629	+2456 0537	+39 0810	−30169
7	−189952	−5653 1048	−2456 0944	+5652 9913	−159797	−53 1476	+2456 3556	+39 2624	−30176
8	−189982	−5653 5576	−2456 2913	+5653 4436	−159823	−53 3376	+2456 5535	+39 4501	−30181
9	−189998	−5653 7983	−2456 3962	+5653 6839	−159836	−53 4884	+2456 6593	+39 5997	−30184
10	−190004	−5653 8841	−2456 4340	+5653 7696	−159841	−53 5662	+2456 6976	+39 6771	−30185
11	−190005	−5653 8905	−2456 4373	+5653 7760	−159842	−53 5516	+2456 7008	+39 6624	−30185
12	−190005	−5653 8990	−2456 4416	+5653 7848	−159842	−53 4401	+2456 7045	+39 5509	−30185
13	−190011	−5653 9863	−2456 4800	+5653 8726	−159847	−53 2422	+2456 7418	+39 3526	−30186
14	−190026	−5654 2146	−2456 5795	+5654 1015	−159860	−52 9806	+2456 8398	+39 0898	−30188
15	−190054	−5654 6237	−2456 7575	+5654 5113	−159883	−52 6869	+2457 0161	+38 7941	−30192
16	−190095	−5655 2274	−2457 0197	+5655 1157	−159917	−52 3971	+2457 2767	+38 5014	−30199
17	−190147	−5656 0112	−2457 3601	+5655 9002	−159961	−52 1469	+2457 6157	+38 2473	−30207
18	−190209	−5656 9349	−2457 7611	+5656 8243	−160013	−51 9669	+2458 0157	+38 0628	−30216
19	−190277	−5657 9358	−2458 1955	+5657 8254	−160070	−51 8787	+2458 4497	+37 9697	−30227
20	−190344	−5658 9352	−2458 6293	+5658 8247	−160126	−51 8907	+2458 8836	+37 9767	−30238
21	−190405	−5659 8470	−2459 0251	+5659 7362	−160178	−51 9945	+2459 2800	+38 0760	−30248
22	−190455	−5660 5906	−2459 3481	+5660 4795	−160220	−52 1625	+2459 6040	+38 2405	−30256
23	−190490	−5661 1100	−2459 5738	+5660 9983	−160249	−52 3476	+2459 8307	+38 4229	−30261
24	−190509	−5661 3956	−2459 6982	+5661 2836	−160266	−52 4873	+2459 9559	+38 5613	−30264
25	−190517	−5661 5058	−2459 7465	+5661 3937	−160272	−52 5172	+2460 0044	+38 5906	−30266
26	−190521	−5661 5705	−2459 7752	+5661 4588	−160276	−52 3916	+2460 0324	+38 4647	−30266
27	−190534	−5661 7640	−2459 8596	+5661 6529	−160286	−52 1068	+2460 1152	+38 1789	−30268
28	−190566	−5662 2429	−2460 0678	+5662 1328	−160313	−51 7116	+2460 3212	+37 7814	−30273
29	−190623	−5663 0787	−2460 4307	+5662 9696	−160361	−51 2944	+2460 6817	+37 3601	−30282
30	−190700	−5664 2252	−2460 9283	+5664 1170	−160425	−50 9487	+2461 1774	+37 0087	−30294
May 1	−190789	−5665 5431	−2461 5001	+5665 4353	−160500	−50 7378	+2461 7481	+36 7914	−30308
2	−190877	−5666 8605	−2462 0718	+5666 7529	−160575	−50 6782	+2462 3194	+36 7252	−30322
3	−190956	−5668 0322	−2462 5803	+5667 9244	−160641	−50 7443	+2462 8283	+36 7856	−30334
4	−191020	−5668 9713	−2462 9879	+5668 8632	−160694	−50 8865	+2463 2368	+36 9231	−30345
5	−191066	−5669 6531	−2463 2841	+5669 5446	−160733	−51 0486	+2463 5339	+37 0820	−30352
6	−191096	−5670 1029	−2463 4796	+5669 9940	−160759	−51 1813	+2463 7302	+37 2124	−30357
7	−191114	−5670 3789	−2463 5998	+5670 2699	−160774	−51 2476	+2463 8508	+37 2774	−30360
8	−191126	−5670 5576	−2463 6779	+5670 4486	−160784	−51 2261	+2463 9287	+37 2550	−30362
9	−191138	−5670 7208	−2463 7492	+5670 6121	−160794	−51 1102	+2463 9994	+37 1382	−30363
10	−191153	−5670 9467	−2463 8477	+5670 8384	−160806	−50 9075	+2464 0968	+36 9344	−30366
11	−191177	−5671 3007	−2464 0017	+5671 1931	−160826	−50 6377	+2464 2493	+36 6629	−30369
12	−191212	−5671 8289	−2464 2313	+5671 7221	−160856	−50 3303	+2464 4771	+36 3529	−30375
13	−191261	−5672 5522	−2464 5454	+5672 4461	−160897	−50 0204	+2464 7895	+36 0395	−30382
14	−191322	−5673 4629	−2464 9408	+5673 3575	−160949	−49 7447	+2465 1833	+35 7593	−30392
15	−191394	−5674 5249	−2465 4017	+5674 4200	−161009	−49 5359	+2465 6431	+35 5452	−30403
16	−191472	−5675 6770	−2465 9017	+5675 5724	−161074	−49 4176	+2466 1425	+35 4213	−30416
17	−191550	−5676 8410	−2466 4069	+5676 7364	−161140	−49 4003	+2466 6476	+35 3983	−30428

M = **NPB**. Values are in units of 10^{-10}. Matrix used with GAST (B13–B20). CIP is $\mathcal{X} = \mathbf{M}_{3,1}$, $\mathcal{Y} = \mathbf{M}_{3,2}$.

MATRIX ELEMENTS FOR CONVERSION FROM
GCRS TO EQUATOR & CELESTIAL INTERMEDIATE ORIGIN OF DATE
FOR 0^h TERRESTRIAL TIME

Julian Date	$C_{1,1}-1$	$C_{1,2}$	$C_{1,3}$	$C_{2,1}$	$C_{2,2}-1$	$C_{2,3}$	$C_{3,1}$	$C_{3,2}$	$C_{3,3}-1$
246									
0766·5	−30108	− 1	−2453 8805	−971	− 8	−39 6254	+2453 8805	+39 6255	−30116
0767·5	−30116	− 1	−2454 2340	−963	− 8	−39 2865	+2454 2340	+39 2866	−30124
0768·5	−30128	− 2	−2454 6888	−957	− 8	−39 0429	+2454 6888	+39 0430	−30135
0769·5	−30140	− 2	−2455 1829	−954	− 8	−38 9330	+2455 1829	+38 9331	−30147
0770·5	−30151	− 2	−2455 6538	−955	− 8	−38 9557	+2455 6538	+38 9559	−30159
0771·5	−30161	− 2	−2456 0537	−958	− 8	−39 0809	+2456 0537	+39 0810	−30169
0772·5	−30168	− 2	−2456 3556	−962	− 8	−39 2622	+2456 3556	+39 2624	−30176
0773·5	−30173	− 2	−2456 5535	−967	− 8	−39 4500	+2456 5535	+39 4501	−30181
0774·5	−30176	− 2	−2456 6593	−970	− 8	−39 5995	+2456 6593	+39 5997	−30184
0775·5	−30177	− 2	−2456 6976	−972	− 8	−39 6769	+2456 6976	+39 6771	−30185
0776·5	−30177	− 2	−2456 7008	−972	− 8	−39 6623	+2456 7008	+39 6624	−30185
0777·5	−30177	− 2	−2456 7045	−969	− 8	−39 5508	+2456 7045	+39 5509	−30185
0778·5	−30178	− 2	−2456 7418	−964	− 8	−39 3524	+2456 7418	+39 3526	−30186
0779·5	−30180	− 3	−2456 8398	−958	− 8	−39 0897	+2456 8398	+39 0898	−30188
0780·5	−30185	− 3	−2457 0161	−951	− 8	−38 7940	+2457 0161	+38 7941	−30192
0781·5	−30191	− 3	−2457 2767	−943	− 7	−38 5012	+2457 2767	+38 5014	−30199
0782·5	−30199	− 3	−2457 6157	−937	− 7	−38 2472	+2457 6157	+38 2473	−30207
0783·5	−30209	− 3	−2458 0157	−933	− 7	−38 0627	+2458 0157	+38 0628	−30216
0784·5	−30220	− 3	−2458 4497	−930	− 7	−37 9696	+2458 4497	+37 9697	−30227
0785·5	−30231	− 3	−2458 8836	−930	− 7	−37 9766	+2458 8836	+37 9767	−30238
0786·5	−30240	− 3	−2459 2800	−933	− 7	−38 0759	+2459 2800	+38 0760	−30248
0787·5	−30248	− 4	−2459 6040	−937	− 7	−38 2403	+2459 6040	+38 2405	−30256
0788·5	−30254	− 4	−2459 8307	−941	− 7	−38 4228	+2459 8307	+38 4229	−30261
0789·5	−30257	− 4	−2459 9559	−945	− 7	−38 5612	+2459 9559	+38 5613	−30264
0790·5	−30258	− 4	−2460 0044	−946	− 7	−38 5905	+2460 0044	+38 5906	−30266
0791·5	−30259	− 4	−2460 0324	−942	− 7	−38 4646	+2460 0324	+38 4647	−30266
0792·5	−30261	− 4	−2460 1152	−935	− 7	−38 1788	+2460 1152	+38 1789	−30268
0793·5	−30266	− 4	−2460 3212	−926	− 7	−37 7813	+2460 3212	+37 7814	−30273
0794·5	−30275	− 4	−2460 6817	−915	− 7	−37 3600	+2460 6817	+37 3601	−30282
0795·5	−30287	− 4	−2461 1774	−907	− 7	−37 0086	+2461 1774	+37 0087	−30294
0796·5	−30301	− 4	−2461 7481	−901	− 7	−36 7913	+2461 7481	+36 7914	−30308
0797·5	−30315	− 5	−2462 3194	−900	− 7	−36 7251	+2462 3194	+36 7252	−30322
0798·5	−30328	− 5	−2462 8283	−901	− 7	−36 7855	+2462 8283	+36 7856	−30334
0799·5	−30338	− 5	−2463 2368	−905	− 7	−36 9230	+2463 2368	+36 9231	−30345
0800·5	−30345	− 5	−2463 5339	−908	− 7	−37 0819	+2463 5339	+37 0820	−30352
0801·5	−30350	− 5	−2463 7302	−912	− 7	−37 2123	+2463 7302	+37 2124	−30357
0802·5	−30353	− 5	−2463 8508	−913	− 7	−37 2773	+2463 8508	+37 2774	−30360
0803·5	−30355	− 5	−2463 9287	−913	− 7	−37 2549	+2463 9287	+37 2550	−30362
0804·5	−30357	− 5	−2463 9994	−910	− 7	−37 1381	+2463 9994	+37 1382	−30363
0805·5	−30359	− 5	−2464 0968	−905	− 7	−36 9343	+2464 0968	+36 9344	−30366
0806·5	−30363	− 5	−2464 2493	−898	− 7	−36 6628	+2464 2493	+36 6629	−30369
0807·5	−30368	− 5	−2464 4771	−891	− 7	−36 3528	+2464 4771	+36 3529	−30375
0808·5	−30376	− 6	−2464 7895	−883	− 6	−36 0394	+2464 7895	+36 0395	−30382
0809·5	−30386	− 6	−2465 1833	−876	− 6	−35 7592	+2465 1833	+35 7593	−30392
0810·5	−30397	− 6	−2465 6431	−871	− 6	−35 5451	+2465 6431	+35 5452	−30403
0811·5	−30409	− 6	−2466 1425	−868	− 6	−35 4212	+2466 1425	+35 4213	−30416
0812·5	−30422	− 6	−2466 6476	−867	− 6	−35 3981	+2466 6476	+35 3983	−30428

Values are in units of 10^{-10}. Matrix used with ERA (B21–B24). CIP is $\mathcal{X} = \mathbf{C}_{3,1}$, $\mathcal{Y} = \mathbf{C}_{3,2}$

MATRIX ELEMENTS FOR CONVERSION FROM GCRS TO EQUATOR AND EQUINOX OF DATE FOR 0^h TERRESTRIAL TIME

Date 0^h TT	$\mathbf{M}_{1,1}-1$	$\mathbf{M}_{1,2}$	$\mathbf{M}_{1,3}$	$\mathbf{M}_{2,1}$	$\mathbf{M}_{2,2}-1$	$\mathbf{M}_{2,3}$	$\mathbf{M}_{3,1}$	$\mathbf{M}_{3,2}$	$\mathbf{M}_{3,3}-1$
May 17	−191550	−5676 8410	−2466 4069	+5676 7364	−161140	−49 4003	+2466 6476	+35 3983	−30428
18	−191624	−5677 9320	−2466 8804	+5677 8272	−161202	−49 4779	+2467 1215	+35 4704	−30440
19	−191687	−5678 8721	−2467 2885	+5678 7670	−161256	−49 6261	+2467 5305	+35 6140	−30450
20	−191737	−5679 6057	−2467 6070	+5679 5001	−161297	−49 8040	+2467 8501	+35 7883	−30458
21	−191771	−5680 1160	−2467 8288	+5680 0100	−161326	−49 9578	+2468 0728	+35 9396	−30463
22	−191793	−5680 4398	−2467 9698	+5680 3336	−161345	−50 0298	+2468 2141	+36 0100	−30467
23	−191809	−5680 6737	−2468 0718	+5680 5677	−161358	−49 9727	+2468 3158	+35 9517	−30469
24	−191829	−5680 9632	−2468 1978	+5680 8577	−161374	−49 7665	+2468 4407	+35 7440	−30472
25	−191863	−5681 4666	−2468 4166	+5681 3619	−161403	−49 4333	+2468 6576	+35 4084	−30478
26	−191919	−5682 2988	−2468 7780	+5682 1951	−161450	−49 0389	+2469 0168	+35 0099	−30486
27	−191999	−5683 4793	−2469 2903	+5683 3764	−161517	−48 6739	+2469 5270	+34 6391	−30499
28	−192096	−5684 9163	−2469 9138	+5684 8141	−161599	−48 4211	+2470 1491	+34 3792	−30514
29	−192199	−5686 4425	−2470 5759	+5686 3405	−161685	−48 3246	+2470 8108	+34 2751	−30530
30	−192296	−5687 8803	−2471 1997	+5687 7781	−161767	−48 3788	+2471 4349	+34 3222	−30546
31	−192378	−5689 0994	−2471 7288	+5688 9968	−161837	−48 5393	+2471 9650	+34 4767	−30559
June 1	−192442	−5690 0428	−2472 1383	+5689 9397	−161890	−48 7446	+2472 3757	+34 6773	−30569
2	−192488	−5690 7206	−2472 4327	+5690 6170	−161929	−48 9356	+2472 6712	+34 8650	−30577
3	−192520	−5691 1895	−2472 6366	+5691 0856	−161956	−49 0675	+2472 8758	+34 9946	−30582
4	−192543	−5691 5302	−2472 7848	+5691 4261	−161975	−49 1138	+2473 0243	+35 0392	−30585
5	−192563	−5691 8298	−2472 9153	+5691 7258	−161992	−49 0653	+2473 1545	+34 9892	−30589
6	−192586	−5692 1702	−2473 0634	+5692 0666	−162011	−48 9280	+2473 3019	+34 8502	−30592
7	−192617	−5692 6210	−2473 2594	+5692 5179	−162037	−48 7199	+2473 4967	+34 6399	−30597
8	−192658	−5693 2330	−2473 5253	+5693 1305	−162072	−48 4683	+2473 7611	+34 3852	−30603
9	−192712	−5694 0342	−2473 8732	+5693 9323	−162117	−48 2071	+2474 1075	+34 1201	−30612
10	−192779	−5695 0254	−2474 3034	+5694 9241	−162174	−47 9727	+2474 5365	+33 8808	−30622
11	−192857	−5696 1783	−2474 8038	+5696 0775	−162239	−47 7999	+2475 0359	+33 7023	−30635
12	−192943	−5697 4365	−2475 3498	+5697 3359	−162311	−47 7159	+2475 5814	+33 6121	−30648
13	−193030	−5698 7218	−2475 9075	+5698 6211	−162384	−47 7351	+2476 1393	+33 6249	−30662
14	−193112	−5699 9453	−2476 4385	+5699 8443	−162454	−47 8547	+2476 6710	+33 7384	−30675
15	−193186	−5701 0236	−2476 9065	+5700 9221	−162515	−48 0527	+2477 1402	+33 9311	−30687
16	−193245	−5701 8959	−2477 2852	+5701 7938	−162565	−48 2897	+2477 5202	+34 1638	−30696
17	−193288	−5702 5406	−2477 5652	+5702 4379	−162602	−48 5139	+2477 8016	+34 3848	−30703
18	−193319	−5702 9865	−2477 7591	+5702 8834	−162628	−48 6709	+2477 9964	+34 5396	−30708
19	−193341	−5703 3158	−2477 9024	+5703 2126	−162646	−48 7150	+2478 1399	+34 5821	−30712
20	−193364	−5703 6534	−2478 0493	+5703 5505	−162666	−48 6232	+2478 2864	+34 4886	−30716
21	−193397	−5704 1422	−2478 2618	+5704 0398	−162693	−48 4051	+2478 4976	+34 2681	−30721
22	−193449	−5704 9033	−2478 5923	+5704 8016	−162737	−48 1076	+2478 8264	+33 9668	−30729
23	−193522	−5705 9930	−2479 0652	+5705 8920	−162799	−47 8054	+2479 2977	+33 6592	−30740
24	−193616	−5707 3740	−2479 6645	+5707 2736	−162878	−47 5804	+2479 8956	+33 4274	−30755
25	−193721	−5708 9208	−2480 3355	+5708 8205	−162966	−47 4935	+2480 5663	+33 3328	−30772
26	−193826	−5710 4608	−2481 0037	+5710 3604	−163054	−47 5640	+2481 2349	+33 3957	−30788
27	−193919	−5711 8344	−2481 5997	+5711 7335	−163132	−47 7661	+2481 8321	+33 5910	−30803
28	−193994	−5712 9413	−2482 0801	+5712 8397	−163196	−48 0432	+2482 3141	+33 8625	−30815
29	−194049	−5713 7576	−2482 4345	+5713 6552	−163242	−48 3296	+2482 6701	+34 1448	−30824
30	−194088	−5714 3235	−2482 6805	+5714 2206	−163275	−48 5695	+2482 9175	+34 3820	−30830
July 1	−194115	−5714 7187	−2482 8523	+5714 6153	−163297	−48 7267	+2483 0902	+34 5372	−30835
2	−194136	−5715 0365	−2482 9907	+5714 9330	−163316	−48 7859	+2483 2289	+34 5948	−30838

M = **NPB**. Values are in units of 10^{-10}. Matrix used with GAST (B13–B20). CIP is $\mathcal{X} = \mathbf{M}_{3,1}$, $\mathcal{Y} = \mathbf{M}_{3,2}$.

MATRIX ELEMENTS FOR CONVERSION FROM GCRS TO EQUATOR & CELESTIAL INTERMEDIATE ORIGIN OF DATE FOR 0^h TERRESTRIAL TIME

Julian Date	$C_{1,1}-1$	$C_{1,2}$	$C_{1,3}$	$C_{2,1}$	$C_{2,2}-1$	$C_{2,3}$	$C_{3,1}$	$C_{3,2}$	$C_{3,3}-1$
246									
0812·5	−30422	− 6	−2466 6476	−867	− 6	−35 3981	+2466 6476	+35 3983	−30428
0813·5	−30433	− 6	−2467 1216	−869	− 6	−35 4703	+2467 1215	+35 4704	−30440
0814·5	−30444	− 7	−2467 5305	−872	− 6	−35 6139	+2467 5305	+35 6140	−30450
0815·5	−30451	− 7	−2467 8501	−877	− 6	−35 7882	+2467 8501	+35 7883	−30458
0816·5	−30457	− 7	−2468 0728	−880	− 6	−35 9394	+2468 0728	+35 9396	−30463
0817·5	−30460	− 7	−2468 2141	−882	− 6	−36 0099	+2468 2141	+36 0100	−30467
0818·5	−30463	− 7	−2468 3158	−881	− 6	−35 9516	+2468 3158	+35 9517	−30469
0819·5	−30466	− 7	−2468 4407	−876	− 6	−35 7439	+2468 4407	+35 7440	−30472
0820·5	−30471	− 7	−2468 6576	−867	− 6	−35 4083	+2468 6576	+35 4084	−30478
0821·5	−30480	− 7	−2469 0168	−857	− 6	−35 0098	+2469 0168	+35 0099	−30486
0822·5	−30493	− 7	−2469 5270	−848	− 6	−34 6390	+2469 5270	+34 6391	−30499
0823·5	−30508	− 7	−2470 1491	−842	− 6	−34 3791	+2470 1491	+34 3792	−30514
0824·5	−30525	− 8	−2470 8108	−839	− 6	−34 2750	+2470 8108	+34 2751	−30530
0825·5	−30540	− 8	−2471 4349	−840	− 6	−34 3221	+2471 4349	+34 3222	−30546
0826·5	−30553	− 8	−2471 9650	−844	− 6	−34 4766	+2471 9650	+34 4767	−30559
0827·5	−30563	− 8	−2472 3757	−849	− 6	−34 6772	+2472 3757	+34 6773	−30569
0828·5	−30571	− 8	−2472 6712	−854	− 6	−34 8649	+2472 6712	+34 8650	−30577
0829·5	−30576	− 8	−2472 8758	−857	− 6	−34 9945	+2472 8758	+34 9946	−30582
0830·5	−30579	− 8	−2473 0243	−858	− 6	−35 0391	+2473 0243	+35 0392	−30585
0831·5	−30583	− 8	−2473 1545	−857	− 6	−34 9891	+2473 1545	+34 9892	−30589
0832·5	−30586	− 9	−2473 3019	−853	− 6	−34 8501	+2473 3019	+34 8502	−30592
0833·5	−30591	− 9	−2473 4967	−848	− 6	−34 6398	+2473 4967	+34 6399	−30597
0834·5	−30598	− 9	−2473 7611	−842	− 6	−34 3851	+2473 7611	+34 3852	−30603
0835·5	−30606	− 9	−2474 1075	−835	− 6	−34 1200	+2474 1075	+34 1201	−30612
0836·5	−30617	− 9	−2474 5365	−829	− 6	−33 8807	+2474 5365	+33 8808	−30622
0837·5	−30629	− 9	−2475 0359	−825	− 6	−33 7022	+2475 0359	+33 7023	−30635
0838·5	−30643	− 9	−2475 5814	−823	− 6	−33 6120	+2475 5814	+33 6121	30648
0839·5	−30656	− 9	−2476 1393	−823	− 6	−33 6248	+2476 1393	+33 6249	−30662
0840·5	−30670	− 10	−2476 6710	−826	− 6	−33 7383	+2476 6710	+33 7384	−30675
0841·5	−30681	− 10	−2477 1402	−831	− 6	−33 9310	+2477 1402	+33 9311	−30687
0842·5	−30691	− 10	−2477 5202	−836	− 6	−34 1637	+2477 5202	+34 1638	−30696
0843·5	−30698	− 10	−2477 8016	−842	− 6	−34 3847	+2477 8016	+34 3848	−30703
0844·5	−30702	− 10	−2477 9964	−846	− 6	−34 5395	+2477 9964	+34 5396	−30708
0845·5	−30706	− 10	−2478 1399	−847	− 6	−34 5820	+2478 1399	+34 5821	−30712
0846·5	−30710	− 10	−2478 2864	−845	− 6	−34 4884	+2478 2864	+34 4886	−30716
0847·5	−30715	− 10	−2478 4976	−839	− 6	−34 2680	+2478 4976	+34 2681	−30721
0848·5	−30723	− 10	−2478 8264	−832	− 6	−33 9667	+2478 8264	+33 9668	−30729
0849·5	−30735	− 11	−2479 2977	−824	− 6	−33 6591	+2479 2977	+33 6592	−30740
0850·5	−30749	− 11	−2479 8956	−818	− 6	−33 4273	+2479 8956	+33 4274	−30755
0851·5	−30766	− 11	−2480 5663	−816	− 6	−33 3327	+2480 5663	+33 3328	−30772
0852·5	−30783	− 11	−2481 2349	−817	− 6	−33 3956	+2481 2349	+33 3957	−30788
0853·5	−30797	− 11	−2481 8321	−822	− 6	−33 5909	+2481 8321	+33 5910	−30803
0854·5	−30809	− 12	−2482 3141	−829	− 6	−33 8624	+2482 3141	+33 8625	−30815
0855·5	−30818	− 12	−2482 6702	−836	− 6	−34 1447	+2482 6701	+34 1448	−30824
0856·5	−30824	− 12	−2482 9175	−842	− 6	−34 3819	+2482 9175	+34 3820	−30830
0857·5	−30829	− 12	−2483 0902	−846	− 6	−34 5371	+2483 0902	+34 5372	−30835
0858·5	−30832	− 12	−2483 2289	−847	− 6	−34 5947	+2483 2289	+34 5948	−30838

Values are in units of 10^{-10}. Matrix used with ERA (B21–B24). CIP is $\mathcal{X} = \mathbf{C}_{3,1}$, $\mathcal{Y} = \mathbf{C}_{3,2}$

MATRIX ELEMENTS FOR CONVERSION FROM GCRS TO EQUATOR AND EQUINOX OF DATE FOR 0^h TERRESTRIAL TIME

Date 0^h TT	$\mathbf{M}_{1,1}-1$	$\mathbf{M}_{1,2}$	$\mathbf{M}_{1,3}$	$\mathbf{M}_{2,1}$	$\mathbf{M}_{2,2}-1$	$\mathbf{M}_{2,3}$	$\mathbf{M}_{3,1}$	$\mathbf{M}_{3,2}$	$\mathbf{M}_{3,3}-1$
July 1	−194115	−5714 7187	−2482 8523	+5714 6153	−163297	−48 7267	+2483 0902	+34 5372	−30835
2	−194136	−5715 0365	−2482 9907	+5714 9330	−163316	−48 7859	+2483 2289	+34 5948	−30838
3	−194159	−5715 3668	−2483 1344	+5715 2634	−163334	−48 7501	+2483 3725	+34 5574	−30842
4	−194187	−5715 7855	−2483 3165	+5715 6824	−163358	−48 6361	+2483 5540	+34 4413	−30846
5	−194226	−5716 3491	−2483 5614	+5716 2463	−163390	−48 4703	+2483 7979	+34 2727	−30852
6	−194276	−5717 0915	−2483 8838	+5716 9892	−163433	−48 2853	+2484 1193	+34 0840	−30860
7	−194339	−5718 0215	−2484 2875	+5717 9196	−163486	−48 1170	+2484 5221	+33 9112	−30870
8	−194414	−5719 1207	−2484 7646	+5719 0191	−163549	−48 0008	+2484 9985	+33 7894	−30882
9	−194497	−5720 3420	−2485 2946	+5720 2405	−163619	−47 9668	+2485 5283	+33 7493	−30895
10	−194583	−5721 6130	−2485 8461	+5721 5113	−163691	−48 0346	+2486 0803	+33 8109	−30909
11	−194667	−5722 8436	−2486 3801	+5722 7414	−163762	−48 2077	+2486 6153	+33 9779	−30922
12	−194742	−5723 9416	−2486 8567	+5723 8387	−163825	−48 4691	+2487 0934	+34 2338	−30934
13	−194802	−5724 8331	−2487 2437	+5724 7295	−163876	−48 7812	+2487 4822	+34 5415	−30944
14	−194847	−5725 4839	−2487 5264	+5725 3795	−163913	−49 0913	+2487 7667	+34 8483	−30951
15	−194876	−5725 9135	−2487 7132	+5725 8084	−163938	−49 3420	+2487 9549	+35 0969	−30956
16	−194895	−5726 1982	−2487 8372	+5726 0928	−163954	−49 4850	+2488 0798	+35 2385	−30959
17	−194913	−5726 4580	−2487 9504	+5726 3526	−163969	−49 4947	+2488 1930	+35 2468	−30962
18	−194938	−5726 8294	−2488 1120	+5726 7243	−163990	−49 3771	+2488 3540	+35 1274	−30966
19	−194979	−5727 4308	−2488 3733	+5727 3262	−164025	−49 1714	+2488 6141	+34 9187	−30972
20	−195040	−5728 3278	−2488 7627	+5728 2237	−164076	−48 9423	+2489 0022	+34 6852	−30982
21	−195121	−5729 5103	−2489 2759	+5729 4067	−164144	−48 7639	+2489 5144	+34 5009	−30994
22	−195215	−5730 8900	−2489 8745	+5730 7865	−164223	−48 6987	+2490 1127	+34 4288	−31009
23	−195312	−5732 3233	−2490 4964	+5732 2196	−164305	−48 7793	+2490 7351	+34 5023	−31025
24	−195403	−5733 6540	−2491 0738	+5733 5498	−164381	−48 9985	+2491 3138	+34 7149	−31039
25	−195478	−5734 7590	−2491 5534	+5734 6539	−164445	−49 3143	+2491 7952	+35 0251	−31051
26	−195534	−5735 5786	−2491 9092	+5735 4726	−164492	−49 6649	+2492 1531	+35 3717	−31060
27	−195571	−5736 1230	−2492 1458	+5736 0162	−164523	−49 9885	+2492 3916	+35 6925	−31066
28	−195594	−5736 4564	−2492 2909	+5736 3490	−164542	−50 2378	+2492 5381	+35 9402	−31070
29	−195609	−5736 6714	−2492 3847	+5736 5636	−164555	−50 3878	+2492 6327	+36 0891	−31073
30	−195622	−5736 8649	−2492 4692	+5736 7570	−164566	−50 4348	+2492 7175	+36 1351	−31075
31	−195640	−5737 1221	−2492 5812	+5737 0143	−164581	−50 3927	+2492 8293	+36 0917	−31078
Aug. 1	−195666	−5737 5071	−2492 7487	+5737 3996	−164603	−50 2869	+2492 9962	+35 9840	−31082
2	−195704	−5738 0604	−2492 9891	+5737 9532	−164634	−50 1499	+2493 2358	+35 8442	−31088
3	−195754	−5738 7970	−2493 3090	+5738 6901	−164677	−50 0170	+2493 5550	+35 7077	−31096
4	−195816	−5739 7069	−2493 7040	+5739 6002	−164729	−49 9233	+2493 9495	+35 6095	−31105
5	−195887	−5740 7539	−2494 1584	+5740 6473	−164789	−49 9006	+2494 4038	+35 5815	−31117
6	−195964	−5741 8765	−2494 6457	+5741 7697	−164853	−49 9722	+2494 8915	+35 6475	−31129
7	−196040	−5742 9919	−2495 1297	+5742 8846	−164918	−50 1485	+2495 3766	+35 8183	−31141
8	−196109	−5744 0058	−2495 5698	+5743 8979	−164976	−50 4210	+2495 8183	+36 0857	−31152
9	−196166	−5744 8312	−2495 9282	+5744 7224	−165023	−50 7593	+2496 1787	+36 4199	−31161
10	−196205	−5745 4124	−2496 1807	+5745 3027	−165057	−51 1125	+2496 4332	+36 7701	−31168
11	−196228	−5745 7479	−2496 3268	+5745 6374	−165076	−51 4187	+2496 5810	+37 0747	−31172
12	−196239	−5745 9018	−2496 3940	+5745 7908	−165085	−51 6207	+2496 6494	+37 2760	−31173
13	−196245	−5745 9934	−2496 4343	+5745 8823	−165091	−51 6840	+2496 6901	+37 3388	−31174
14	−196257	−5746 1670	−2496 5102	+5746 0561	−165100	−51 6086	+2496 7655	+37 2625	−31176
15	−196283	−5746 5498	−2496 6767	+5746 4393	−165122	−51 4315	+2496 9310	+37 0835	−31180
16	−196328	−5747 2147	−2496 9655	+5747 1048	−165161	−51 2162	+2497 2186	+36 8649	−31187

M = **NPB**. Values are in units of 10^{-10}. Matrix used with GAST (B13–B20). CIP is $\mathcal{X} = \mathbf{M}_{3,1}$, $\mathcal{Y} = \mathbf{M}_{3,2}$.

MATRIX ELEMENTS FOR CONVERSION FROM
GCRS TO EQUATOR & CELESTIAL INTERMEDIATE ORIGIN OF DATE
FOR 0^h TERRESTRIAL TIME

Julian Date	$\mathbf{C}_{1,1}-1$	$\mathbf{C}_{1,2}$	$\mathbf{C}_{1,3}$	$\mathbf{C}_{2,1}$	$\mathbf{C}_{2,2}-1$	$\mathbf{C}_{2,3}$	$\mathbf{C}_{3,1}$	$\mathbf{C}_{3,2}$	$\mathbf{C}_{3,3}-1$
246									
0857·5	−30829	−12	−2483 0902	−846	−6	−34 5371	+2483 0902	+34 5372	−30835
0858·5	−30832	−12	−2483 2289	−847	−6	−34 5947	+2483 2289	+34 5948	−30838
0859·5	−30836	−12	−2483 3725	−846	−6	−34 5573	+2483 3725	+34 5574	−30842
0860·5	−30840	−12	−2483 5540	−843	−6	−34 4412	+2483 5540	+34 4413	−30846
0861·5	−30846	−12	−2483 7979	−839	−6	−34 2726	+2483 7979	+34 2727	−30852
0862·5	−30854	−12	−2484 1193	−835	−6	−34 0839	+2484 1193	+34 0840	−30860
0863·5	−30864	−12	−2484 5221	−830	−6	−33 9111	+2484 5221	+33 9112	−30870
0864·5	−30876	−12	−2484 9985	−827	−6	−33 7893	+2484 9985	+33 7894	−30882
0865·5	−30889	−13	−2485 5283	−826	−6	−33 7492	+2485 5283	+33 7493	−30895
0866·5	−30903	−13	−2486 0803	−828	−6	−33 8108	+2486 0803	+33 8109	−30909
0867·5	−30916	−13	−2486 6153	−832	−6	−33 9778	+2486 6153	+33 9779	−30922
0868·5	−30928	−13	−2487 0934	−838	−6	−34 2337	+2487 0934	+34 2338	−30934
0869·5	−30938	−13	−2487 4822	−846	−6	−34 5413	+2487 4822	+34 5415	−30944
0870·5	−30945	−13	−2487 7667	−854	−6	−34 8482	+2487 7667	+34 8483	−30951
0871·5	−30950	−13	−2487 9549	−860	−6	−35 0968	+2487 9549	+35 0969	−30956
0872·5	−30953	−14	−2488 0798	−863	−6	−35 2384	+2488 0798	+35 2385	−30959
0873·5	−30956	−14	−2488 1930	−863	−6	−35 2467	+2488 1930	+35 2468	−30962
0874·5	−30960	−14	−2488 3540	−860	−6	−35 1273	+2488 3540	+35 1274	−30966
0875·5	−30966	−14	−2488 6141	−855	−6	−34 9186	+2488 6141	+34 9187	−30972
0876·5	−30976	−14	−2489 0022	−849	−6	−34 6851	+2489 0022	+34 6852	−30982
0877·5	−30988	−14	−2489 5144	−845	−6	−34 5007	+2489 5144	+34 5009	−30994
0878·5	−31003	−14	−2490 1127	−843	−6	−34 4287	+2490 1127	+34 4288	−31009
0879·5	−31019	−14	−2490 7351	−845	−6	−34 5022	+2490 7351	+34 5023	−31025
0880·5	−31033	−15	−2491 3138	−850	−6	−34 7147	+2491 3138	+34 7149	−31039
0881·5	−31045	−15	−2491 7952	−858	−6	−35 0250	+2491 7952	+35 0251	−31051
0882·5	−31054	−15	−2492 1531	−867	−6	−35 3716	+2492 1531	+35 3717	−31060
0883·5	−31060	−15	−2492 3916	−875	−6	−35 6924	+2492 3916	+35 6925	−31066
0884·5	−31064	−15	−2492 5381	−881	6	−35 9401	+2492 5381	+35 9402	−31070
0885·5	−31066	−15	−2492 6327	−884	−7	−36 0890	+2492 6327	+36 0891	−31073
0886·5	−31068	−15	−2492 7175	−886	−7	−36 1350	+2492 7175	+36 1351	−31075
0887·5	−31071	−15	−2492 8293	−885	−7	−36 0916	+2492 8293	+36 0917	−31078
0888·5	−31075	−15	−2492 9962	−882	−6	−35 9839	+2492 9962	+35 9840	−31082
0889·5	−31081	−15	−2493 2358	−878	−6	−35 8441	+2493 2358	+35 8442	−31088
0890·5	−31089	−15	−2493 5550	−875	−6	−35 7075	+2493 5550	+35 7077	−31096
0891·5	−31099	−16	−2493 9495	−873	−6	−35 6094	+2493 9495	+35 6095	−31105
0892·5	−31110	−16	−2494 4038	−872	−6	−35 5814	+2494 4038	+35 5815	−31117
0893·5	−31122	−16	−2494 8915	−873	−6	−35 6474	+2494 8915	+35 6475	−31129
0894·5	−31135	−16	−2495 3766	−878	−6	−35 8182	+2495 3766	+35 8183	−31141
0895·5	−31146	−16	−2495 8183	−884	−7	−36 0856	+2495 8183	+36 0857	−31152
0896·5	−31155	−16	−2496 1787	−893	−7	−36 4198	+2496 1787	+36 4199	−31161
0897·5	−31161	−16	−2496 4332	−901	−7	−36 7700	+2496 4332	+36 7701	−31168
0898·5	−31165	−17	−2496 5810	−909	−7	−37 0745	+2496 5810	+37 0747	−31172
0899·5	−31166	−17	−2496 6494	−914	−7	−37 2759	+2496 6494	+37 2760	−31173
0900·5	−31167	−17	−2496 6901	−916	−7	−37 3386	+2496 6901	+37 3388	−31174
0901·5	−31169	−17	−2496 7655	−914	−7	−37 2624	+2496 7655	+37 2625	−31176
0902·5	−31173	−17	−2496 9310	−909	−7	−37 0833	+2496 9310	+37 0835	−31180
0903·5	−31181	−17	−2497 2186	−904	−7	−36 8648	+2497 2186	+36 8649	−31187

Values are in units of 10^{-10}. Matrix used with ERA (B21–B24). CIP is $\mathcal{X} = \mathbf{C}_{3,1}$, $\mathcal{Y} = \mathbf{C}_{3,2}$

MATRIX ELEMENTS FOR CONVERSION FROM GCRS TO EQUATOR AND EQUINOX OF DATE FOR 0^h TERRESTRIAL TIME

Date 0^h TT	$M_{1,1}-1$	$M_{1,2}$	$M_{1,3}$	$M_{2,1}$	$M_{2,2}-1$	$M_{2,3}$	$M_{3,1}$	$M_{3,2}$	$M_{3,3}-1$
Aug. 16	−196328	−5747 2147	−2496 9655	+5747 1048	−165161	−51 2162	+2497 2186	+36 8649	−31187
17	−196393	−5748 1606	−2497 3761	+5748 0510	−165215	−51 0356	+2497 6282	+36 6795	−31198
18	−196472	−5749 3135	−2497 8764	+5749 2041	−165281	−50 9515	+2498 1281	+36 5897	−31210
19	−196556	−5750 5487	−2498 4124	+5750 4392	−165352	−51 0001	+2498 6644	+36 6321	−31223
20	−196637	−5751 7240	−2498 9225	+5751 6141	−165420	−51 1831	+2499 1756	+36 8093	−31236
21	−196705	−5752 7165	−2499 3533	+5752 6058	−165477	−51 4704	+2499 6081	+37 0916	−31247
22	−196755	−5753 4506	−2499 6721	+5753 3390	−165519	−51 8096	+2499 9288	+37 4271	−31255
23	−196786	−5753 9113	−2499 8724	+5753 7989	−165546	−52 1408	+2500 1310	+37 7560	−31260
24	−196802	−5754 1404	−2499 9723	+5754 0273	−165559	−52 4119	+2500 2325	+38 0260	−31263
25	−196807	−5754 2184	−2500 0067	+5754 1049	−165564	−52 5885	+2500 2679	+38 2022	−31264
26	−196809	−5754 2420	−2500 0175	+5754 1284	−165565	−52 6581	+2500 2791	+38 2716	−31264
27	−196813	−5754 3034	−2500 0447	+5754 1898	−165569	−52 6282	+2500 3062	+38 2414	−31265
28	−196825	−5754 4762	−2500 1202	+5754 3629	−165579	−52 5216	+2500 3810	+38 1340	−31267
29	−196848	−5754 8088	−2500 2649	+5754 6959	−165598	−52 3701	+2500 5249	+37 9808	−31270
30	−196883	−5755 3228	−2500 4883	+5755 2102	−165627	−52 2094	+2500 7474	+37 8176	−31276
31	−196930	−5756 0139	−2500 7885	+5755 9017	−165667	−52 0749	+2501 0468	+37 6796	−31283
Sept. 1	−196988	−5756 8537	−2501 1531	+5756 7416	−165715	−51 9985	+2501 4110	+37 5989	−31292
2	−197052	−5757 7912	−2501 5601	+5757 6792	−165769	−52 0053	+2501 8181	+37 6010	−31303
3	−197118	−5758 7555	−2501 9786	+5758 6431	−165825	−52 1100	+2502 2372	+37 7010	−31313
4	−197180	−5759 6606	−2502 3716	+5759 5477	−165877	−52 3125	+2502 6314	+37 8989	−31323
5	−197232	−5760 4178	−2502 7004	+5760 3042	−165921	−52 5928	+2502 9618	+38 1754	−31331
6	−197268	−5760 9544	−2502 9336	+5760 8400	−165952	−52 9094	+2503 1969	+38 4894	−31337
7	−197288	−5761 2399	−2503 0579	+5761 1248	−165968	−53 2028	+2503 3229	+38 7813	−31341
8	−197293	−5761 3087	−2503 0883	+5761 1930	−165972	−53 4078	+2503 3545	+38 9860	−31342
9	−197290	−5761 2654	−2503 0702	+5761 1496	−165970	−53 4738	+2503 3367	+39 0522	−31341
10	−197289	−5761 2624	−2503 0694	+5761 1468	−165970	−53 3849	+2503 3354	+38 9633	−31341
11	−197302	−5761 4507	−2503 1516	+5761 3357	−165980	−53 1695	+2503 4164	+38 7470	−31343
12	−197335	−5761 9283	−2503 3593	+5761 8140	−166008	−52 8927	+2503 6225	+38 4677	−31348
13	−197388	−5762 7081	−2503 6979	+5762 5944	−166053	−52 6341	+2503 9596	+38 2053	−31356
14	−197458	−5763 7195	−2504 1368	+5763 6062	−166111	−52 4634	+2504 3976	+38 0295	−31367
15	−197534	−5764 8367	−2504 6217	+5764 7235	−166175	−52 4212	+2504 8823	+37 9817	−31379
16	−197608	−5765 9181	−2505 0911	+5765 8047	−166238	−52 5132	+2505 3522	+38 0683	−31391
17	−197672	−5766 8417	−2505 4920	+5766 7277	−166291	−52 7133	+2505 7543	+38 2638	−31401
18	−197719	−5767 5288	−2505 7904	+5767 4142	−166331	−52 9744	+2506 0543	+38 5215	−31409
19	−197748	−5767 9548	−2505 9757	+5767 8395	−166355	−53 2408	+2506 2411	+38 7857	−31414
20	−197761	−5768 1468	−2506 0595	+5768 0309	−166367	−53 4606	+2506 3262	+39 0045	−31416
21	−197763	−5768 1716	−2506 0708	+5768 0554	−166368	−53 5955	+2506 3383	+39 1393	−31416
22	−197759	−5768 1186	−2506 0484	+5768 0023	−166365	−53 6261	+2506 3160	+39 1701	−31416
23	−197757	−5768 0805	−2506 0325	+5767 9644	−166363	−53 5528	+2506 2997	+39 0970	−31415
24	−197761	−5768 1377	−2506 0579	+5768 0220	−166366	−53 3931	+2506 3242	+38 9371	−31416
25	−197775	−5768 3476	−2506 1494	+5768 2324	−166378	−53 1766	+2506 4145	+38 7195	−31418
26	−197802	−5768 7394	−2506 3198	+5768 6248	−166401	−52 9387	+2506 5835	+38 4797	−31422
27	−197841	−5769 3147	−2506 5698	+5769 2007	−166434	−52 7159	+2506 8322	+38 2539	−31428
28	−197892	−5770 0497	−2506 8890	+5769 9361	−166476	−52 5407	+2507 1504	+38 0751	−31436
29	−197950	−5770 8992	−2507 2578	+5770 7858	−166525	−52 4393	+2507 5187	+37 9694	−31446
30	−198012	−5771 8004	−2507 6490	+5771 6871	−166577	−52 4282	+2507 9099	+37 9538	−31455
Oct. 1	−198072	−5772 6781	−2508 0301	+5772 5646	−166628	−52 5113	+2508 2914	+38 0325	−31465

M = **NPB**. Values are in units of 10^{-10}. Matrix used with GAST (B13–B20). CIP is $\mathcal{X} = \mathbf{M}_{3,1}$, $\mathcal{Y} = \mathbf{M}_{3,2}$.

MATRIX ELEMENTS FOR CONVERSION FROM GCRS TO EQUATOR & CELESTIAL INTERMEDIATE ORIGIN OF DATE FOR 0^h TERRESTRIAL TIME

Julian Date	$C_{1,1}-1$	$C_{1,2}$	$C_{1,3}$	$C_{2,1}$	$C_{2,2}-1$	$C_{2,3}$	$C_{3,1}$	$C_{3,2}$	$C_{3,3}-1$
246									
0903·5	−31181	− 17	−2497 2186	−904	− 7	−36 8648	+2497 2186	+36 8649	−31187
0904·5	−31191	− 17	−2497 6282	−899	− 7	−36 6794	+2497 6282	+36 6795	−31198
0905·5	−31203	− 17	−2498 1281	−897	− 7	−36 5896	+2498 1281	+36 5897	−31210
0906·5	−31217	− 17	−2498 6644	−898	− 7	−36 6320	+2498 6644	+36 6321	−31223
0907·5	−31229	− 17	−2499 1756	−902	− 7	−36 8092	+2499 1756	+36 8093	−31236
0908·5	−31240	− 18	−2499 6081	−910	− 7	−37 0915	+2499 6081	+37 0916	−31247
0909·5	−31248	− 18	−2499 9288	−918	− 7	−37 4270	+2499 9288	+37 4271	−31255
0910·5	−31253	− 18	−2500 1310	−926	− 7	−37 7559	+2500 1310	+37 7560	−31260
0911·5	−31256	− 18	−2500 2325	−933	− 7	−38 0259	+2500 2325	+38 0260	−31263
0912·5	−31257	− 18	−2500 2679	−937	− 7	−38 2021	+2500 2679	+38 2022	−31264
0913·5	−31257	− 18	−2500 2791	−939	− 7	−38 2715	+2500 2791	+38 2716	−31264
0914·5	−31258	− 18	−2500 3062	−938	− 7	−38 2413	+2500 3062	+38 2414	−31265
0915·5	−31260	− 18	−2500 3810	−936	− 7	−38 1338	+2500 3810	+38 1340	−31267
0916·5	−31263	− 18	−2500 5249	−932	− 7	−37 9807	+2500 5249	+37 9808	−31270
0917·5	−31269	− 18	−2500 7474	−928	− 7	−37 8174	+2500 7474	+37 8176	−31276
0918·5	−31276	− 18	−2501 0468	−924	− 7	−37 6795	+2501 0468	+37 6796	−31283
0919·5	−31285	− 18	−2501 4110	−922	− 7	−37 5988	+2501 4110	+37 5989	−31292
0920·5	−31296	− 18	−2501 8181	−922	− 7	−37 6009	+2501 8181	+37 6010	−31303
0921·5	−31306	− 19	−2502 2373	−925	− 7	−37 7009	+2502 2372	+37 7010	−31313
0922·5	−31316	− 19	−2502 6314	−930	− 7	−37 8988	+2502 6314	+37 8989	−31323
0923·5	−31324	− 19	−2502 9618	−937	− 7	−38 1753	+2502 9618	+38 1754	−31331
0924·5	−31330	− 19	−2503 1969	−944	− 7	−38 4893	+2503 1969	+38 4894	−31337
0925·5	−31333	− 19	−2503 3229	−952	− 8	−38 7812	+2503 3229	+38 7813	−31341
0926·5	−31334	− 19	−2503 3545	−957	− 8	−38 9858	+2503 3545	+38 9860	−31342
0927·5	−31334	− 19	−2503 3367	−959	− 8	−39 0520	+2503 3367	+39 0522	−31341
0928·5	−31333	− 19	−2503 3354	−956	− 8	−38 9632	+2503 3354	+38 9633	−31341
0929·5	−31336	− 19	−2503 4164	−951	− 8	−38 7469	+2503 4164	+38 7470	31343
0930·5	−31341	19	−2503 6225	−944	− 7	−38 4676	+2503 6225	+38 4677	−31348
0931·5	−31349	− 19	−2503 9596	−937	− 7	−38 2052	+2503 9596	+38 2053	−31356
0932·5	−31360	− 19	−2504 3976	−933	− 7	−38 0294	+2504 3976	+38 0295	−31367
0933·5	−31372	− 20	−2504 8823	−932	− 7	−37 9816	+2504 8823	+37 9817	−31379
0934·5	−31384	− 20	−2505 3522	−934	− 7	−38 0681	+2505 3522	+38 0683	−31391
0935·5	−31394	− 20	−2505 7543	−939	− 7	−38 2637	+2505 7543	+38 2638	−31401
0936·5	−31402	− 20	−2506 0543	−945	− 7	−38 5213	+2506 0543	+38 5215	−31409
0937·5	−31406	− 20	−2506 2411	−952	− 8	−38 7856	+2506 2411	+38 7857	−31414
0938·5	−31408	− 20	−2506 3262	−957	− 8	−39 0044	+2506 3262	+39 0045	−31416
0939·5	−31409	− 20	−2506 3383	−961	− 8	−39 1392	+2506 3383	+39 1393	−31416
0940·5	−31408	− 20	−2506 3161	−962	− 8	−39 1700	+2506 3160	+39 1701	−31416
0941·5	−31408	− 20	−2506 2997	−960	− 8	−39 0969	+2506 2997	+39 0970	−31415
0942·5	−31408	− 20	−2506 3242	−956	− 8	−38 9369	+2506 3242	+38 9371	−31416
0943·5	−31411	− 20	−2506 4145	−950	− 7	−38 7194	+2506 4145	+38 7195	−31418
0944·5	−31415	− 20	−2506 5835	−944	− 7	−38 4796	+2506 5835	+38 4797	−31422
0945·5	−31421	− 20	−2506 8322	−939	− 7	−38 2538	+2506 8322	+38 2539	−31428
0946·5	−31429	− 21	−2507 1504	−934	− 7	−38 0750	+2507 1504	+38 0751	−31436
0947·5	−31438	− 21	−2507 5187	−931	− 7	−37 9693	+2507 5187	+37 9694	−31446
0948·5	−31448	− 21	−2507 9099	−931	− 7	−37 9536	+2507 9099	+37 9538	−31455
0949·5	−31458	− 21	−2508 2914	−933	− 7	−38 0324	+2508 2914	+38 0325	−31465

Values are in units of 10^{-10}. Matrix used with ERA (B21–B24). CIP is $\mathcal{X} = \mathbf{C}_{3,1}$, $\mathcal{Y} = \mathbf{C}_{3,2}$

MATRIX ELEMENTS FOR CONVERSION FROM GCRS TO EQUATOR AND EQUINOX OF DATE FOR 0^h TERRESTRIAL TIME

Date 0^h TT	$\mathbf{M}_{1,1}-1$	$\mathbf{M}_{1,2}$	$\mathbf{M}_{1,3}$	$\mathbf{M}_{2,1}$	$\mathbf{M}_{2,2}-1$	$\mathbf{M}_{2,3}$	$\mathbf{M}_{3,1}$	$\mathbf{M}_{3,2}$	$\mathbf{M}_{3,3}-1$
Oct. 1	−198072	−5772 6781	−2508 0301	+5772 5646	−166628	−52 5113	+2508 2914	+38 0325	−31465
2	−198125	−5773 4516	−2508 3660	+5773 3376	−166672	−52 6771	+2508 6283	+38 1944	−31473
3	−198166	−5774 0469	−2508 6246	+5773 9324	−166707	−52 8956	+2508 8882	+38 4099	−31480
4	−198191	−5774 4155	−2508 7850	+5774 3004	−166728	−53 1180	+2509 0499	+38 6305	−31484
5	−198201	−5774 5576	−2508 8472	+5774 4421	−166736	−53 2825	+2509 1130	+38 7943	−31486
6	−198200	−5774 5415	−2508 8407	+5774 4258	−166736	−53 3281	+2509 1068	+38 8399	−31486
7	−198197	−5774 5023	−2508 8243	+5774 3869	−166733	−53 2167	+2509 0898	+38 7288	−31485
8	−198205	−5774 6087	−2508 8710	+5774 4940	−166739	−52 9535	+2509 1350	+38 4650	−31486
9	−198232	−5775 0016	−2509 0419	+5774 8878	−166762	−52 5922	+2509 3038	+38 1018	−31490
10	−198282	−5775 7361	−2509 3609	+5775 6233	−166804	−52 2191	+2509 6207	+37 7249	−31498
11	−198352	−5776 7603	−2509 8055	+5776 6482	−166863	−51 9202	+2510 0635	+37 4209	−31509
12	−198433	−5777 9412	−2510 3180	+5777 8295	−166931	−51 7525	+2510 5751	+37 2473	−31522
13	−198514	−5779 1180	−2510 8286	+5779 0063	−166999	−51 7300	+2511 0857	+37 2189	−31535
14	−198585	−5780 1512	−2511 2771	+5780 0393	−167059	−51 8287	+2511 5347	+37 3124	−31546
15	−198640	−5780 9527	−2511 6251	+5780 8404	−167105	−52 0000	+2511 8838	+37 4797	−31555
16	−198678	−5781 4933	−2511 8600	+5781 3805	−167137	−52 1874	+2512 1198	+37 6643	−31561
17	−198698	−5781 7960	−2511 9918	+5781 6828	−167154	−52 3386	+2512 2525	+37 8140	−31564
18	−198707	−5781 9223	−2512 0472	+5781 8089	−167162	−52 4142	+2512 3082	+37 8890	−31566
19	−198709	−5781 9558	−2512 0623	+5781 8424	−167164	−52 3918	+2512 3232	+37 8664	−31566
20	−198711	−5781 9867	−2512 0762	+5781 8736	−167165	−52 2672	+2512 3364	+37 7416	−31566
21	−198719	−5782 0973	−2512 1247	+5781 9848	−167172	−52 0530	+2512 3837	+37 5269	−31567
22	−198737	−5782 3512	−2512 2354	+5782 2394	−167186	−51 7749	+2512 4928	+37 2475	−31570
23	−198766	−5782 7860	−2512 4245	+5782 6750	−167211	−51 4667	+2512 6801	+36 9372	−31575
24	−198809	−5783 4105	−2512 6958	+5783 3002	−167247	−51 1652	+2512 9496	+36 6325	−31581
25	−198864	−5784 2059	−2513 0411	+5784 0962	−167293	−50 9045	+2513 2935	+36 3678	−31590
26	−198928	−5785 1298	−2513 4422	+5785 0206	−167347	−50 7125	+2513 6935	+36 1711	−31600
27	−198996	−5786 1224	−2513 8730	+5786 0134	−167404	−50 6069	+2514 1238	+36 0606	−31611
28	−199064	−5787 1128	−2514 3029	+5787 0039	−167461	−50 5936	+2514 5536	+36 0423	−31621
29	−199127	−5788 0269	−2514 6998	+5787 9178	−167514	−50 6646	+2514 9509	+36 1088	−31631
30	−199180	−5788 7963	−2515 0339	+5788 6869	−167559	−50 7969	+2515 2858	+36 2371	−31640
31	−199219	−5789 3707	−2515 2834	+5789 2608	−167592	−50 9518	+2515 5363	+36 3892	−31646
Nov. 1	−199244	−5789 7334	−2515 4412	+5789 6232	−167613	−51 0780	+2515 6948	+36 5135	−31650
2	−199257	−5789 9189	−2515 5222	+5789 8086	−167624	−51 1182	+2515 7760	+36 5528	−31652
3	−199264	−5790 0242	−2515 5685	+5789 9142	−167630	−51 0239	+2515 8217	+36 4580	−31653
4	−199276	−5790 1997	−2515 6451	+5790 0903	−167640	−50 7752	+2515 8969	+36 2083	−31655
5	−199305	−5790 6097	−2515 8234	+5790 5012	−167664	−50 3976	+2516 0731	+35 8287	−31660
6	−199357	−5791 3683	−2516 1528	+5791 2609	−167707	−49 9633	+2516 4000	+35 3906	−31668
7	−199434	−5792 4828	−2516 6366	+5792 3764	−167772	−49 5685	+2516 8815	+34 9902	−31680
8	−199527	−5793 8446	−2517 2274	+5793 7389	−167851	−49 2957	+2517 4708	+34 7105	−31694
9	−199626	−5795 2745	−2517 8478	+5795 1690	−167933	−49 1831	+2518 0906	+34 5908	−31710
10	−199717	−5796 5943	−2518 4205	+5796 4887	−168010	−49 2179	+2518 6635	+34 6189	−31724
11	−199792	−5797 6815	−2518 8924	+5797 5755	−168073	−49 3503	+2519 1362	+34 7458	−31736
12	−199847	−5798 4884	−2519 2428	+5798 3821	−168120	−49 5165	+2519 4875	+34 9080	−31745
13	−199885	−5799 0336	−2519 4797	+5798 9269	−168152	−49 6577	+2519 7253	+35 0464	−31751
14	−199909	−5799 3804	−2519 6306	+5799 2735	−168172	−49 7300	+2519 8766	+35 1170	−31755
15	−199925	−5799 6148	−2519 7328	+5799 5080	−168185	−49 7089	+2519 9787	+35 0947	−31758
16	−199940	−5799 8283	−2519 8259	+5799 7218	−168198	−49 5884	+2520 0711	+34 9731	−31760

M = NPB. Values are in units of 10^{-10}. Matrix used with GAST (B13–B20). CIP is $\mathcal{X} = \mathbf{M}_{3,1}$, $\mathcal{Y} = \mathbf{M}_{3,2}$.

MATRIX ELEMENTS FOR CONVERSION FROM GCRS TO EQUATOR & CELESTIAL INTERMEDIATE ORIGIN OF DATE FOR 0^h TERRESTRIAL TIME

Julian Date	$C_{1,1}-1$	$C_{1,2}$	$C_{1,3}$	$C_{2,1}$	$C_{2,2}-1$	$C_{2,3}$	$C_{3,1}$	$C_{3,2}$	$C_{3,3}-1$
246									
0949·5	−31458	− 21	−2508 2914	−933	− 7	−38 0324	+2508 2914	+38 0325	−31465
0950·5	−31466	− 21	−2508 6283	−937	− 7	−38 1943	+2508 6283	+38 1944	−31473
0951·5	−31473	− 21	−2508 8882	−942	− 7	−38 4098	+2508 8882	+38 4099	−31480
0952·5	−31477	− 21	−2509 0499	−948	− 7	−38 6304	+2509 0499	+38 6305	−31484
0953·5	−31478	− 21	−2509 1130	−952	− 8	−38 7941	+2509 1130	+38 7943	−31486
0954·5	−31478	− 21	−2509 1068	−953	− 8	−38 8398	+2509 1068	+38 8399	−31486
0955·5	−31478	− 21	−2509 0898	−950	− 7	−38 7286	+2509 0898	+38 7288	−31485
0956·5	−31479	− 21	−2509 1350	−944	− 7	−38 4648	+2509 1350	+38 4650	−31486
0957·5	−31483	− 21	−2509 3038	−935	− 7	−38 1016	+2509 3038	+38 1018	−31490
0958·5	−31491	− 21	−2509 6207	−925	− 7	−37 7248	+2509 6207	+37 7249	−31498
0959·5	−31502	− 22	−2510 0635	−918	− 7	−37 4208	+2510 0635	+37 4209	−31509
0960·5	−31515	− 22	−2510 5751	−913	− 7	−37 2472	+2510 5751	+37 2473	−31522
0961·5	−31528	− 22	−2511 0857	−913	− 7	−37 2188	+2511 0857	+37 2189	−31535
0962·5	−31539	− 22	−2511 5347	−915	− 7	−37 3122	+2511 5347	+37 3124	−31546
0963·5	−31548	− 22	−2511 8838	−919	− 7	−37 4796	+2511 8838	+37 4797	−31555
0964·5	−31554	− 22	−2512 1198	−924	− 7	−37 6642	+2512 1198	+37 6643	−31561
0965·5	−31557	− 22	−2512 2525	−928	− 7	−37 8139	+2512 2525	+37 8140	−31564
0966·5	−31559	− 22	−2512 3082	−929	− 7	−37 8889	+2512 3082	+37 8890	−31566
0967·5	−31559	− 22	−2512 3232	−929	− 7	−37 8663	+2512 3232	+37 8664	−31566
0968·5	−31559	− 22	−2512 3364	−926	− 7	−37 7415	+2512 3364	+37 7416	−31566
0969·5	−31560	− 22	−2512 3837	−920	− 7	−37 5268	+2512 3837	+37 5269	−31567
0970·5	−31563	− 23	−2512 4928	−913	− 7	−37 2474	+2512 4928	+37 2475	−31570
0971·5	−31568	− 23	−2512 6801	−906	− 7	−36 9371	+2512 6801	+36 9372	−31575
0972·5	−31575	− 23	−2512 9496	−898	− 7	−36 6324	+2512 9496	+36 6325	−31581
0973·5	−31583	− 23	−2513 2935	−891	− 7	−36 3677	+2513 2935	+36 3678	−31590
0974·5	−31593	− 23	−2513 6935	−886	− 7	−36 1710	+2513 6935	+36 1711	−31600
0975·5	−31604	− 23	−2514 1238	−883	− 7	−36 0604	+2514 1238	+36 0606	−31611
0976·5	−31615	− 23	−2514 5536	−883	− 6	−36 0422	+2514 5536	+36 0423	−31621
0977·5	−31625	− 23	−2514 9509	−885	− 7	−36 1087	+2514 9509	+36 1088	−31631
0978·5	−31633	− 24	−2515 2858	−888	− 7	−36 2370	+2515 2858	+36 2371	−31640
0979·5	−31640	− 24	−2515 5363	−892	− 7	−36 3891	+2515 5363	+36 3892	−31646
0980·5	−31644	− 24	−2515 6948	−895	− 7	−36 5134	+2515 6948	+36 5135	−31650
0981·5	−31646	− 24	−2515 7761	−896	− 7	−36 5527	+2515 7760	+36 5528	−31652
0982·5	−31647	− 24	−2515 8217	−893	− 7	−36 4579	+2515 8217	+36 4580	−31653
0983·5	−31649	− 24	−2515 8969	−887	− 7	−36 2082	+2515 8969	+36 2083	−31655
0984·5	−31653	− 24	−2516 0731	−878	− 6	−35 8286	+2516 0731	+35 8287	−31660
0985·5	−31661	− 24	−2516 4000	−867	− 6	−35 3905	+2516 4000	+35 3906	−31668
0986·5	−31674	− 24	−2516 8815	−857	− 6	−34 9901	+2516 8815	+34 9902	−31680
0987·5	−31688	− 24	−2517 4708	−850	− 6	−34 7104	+2517 4708	+34 7105	−31694
0988·5	−31704	− 24	−2518 0906	−847	− 6	−34 5907	+2518 0906	+34 5908	−31710
0989·5	−31718	− 25	−2518 6635	−847	− 6	−34 6188	+2518 6635	+34 6189	−31724
0990·5	−31730	− 25	−2519 1362	−850	− 6	−34 7457	+2519 1362	+34 7458	−31736
0991·5	−31739	− 25	−2519 4875	−855	− 6	−34 9079	+2519 4875	+34 9080	−31745
0992·5	−31745	− 25	−2519 7253	−858	− 6	−35 0463	+2519 7253	+35 0464	−31751
0993·5	−31749	− 25	−2519 8766	−860	− 6	−35 1168	+2519 8766	+35 1170	−31755
0994·5	−31752	− 25	−2519 9787	−859	− 6	−35 0946	+2519 9787	+35 0947	−31758
0995·5	−31754	− 25	−2520 0711	−856	− 6	−34 9730	+2520 0711	+34 9731	−31760

Values are in units of 10^{-10}. Matrix used with ERA (B21–B24). CIP is $\mathcal{X} = \mathbf{C}_{3,1}$, $\mathcal{Y} = \mathbf{C}_{3,2}$

MATRIX ELEMENTS FOR CONVERSION FROM GCRS TO EQUATOR AND EQUINOX OF DATE FOR 0^h TERRESTRIAL TIME

Date 0^h TT	$\mathbf{M}_{1,1}-1$	$\mathbf{M}_{1,2}$	$\mathbf{M}_{1,3}$	$\mathbf{M}_{2,1}$	$\mathbf{M}_{2,2}-1$	$\mathbf{M}_{2,3}$	$\mathbf{M}_{3,1}$	$\mathbf{M}_{3,2}$	$\mathbf{M}_{3,3}-1$
Nov. 16	−199940	−5799 8283	−2519 8259	+5799 7218	−168198	−49 5884	+2520 0711	+34 9731	−31760
17	−199959	−5800 1046	−2519 9462	+5799 9986	−168214	−49 3785	+2520 1903	+34 7618	−31763
18	−199987	−5800 5106	−2520 1228	+5800 4053	−168237	−49 1019	+2520 3652	+34 4832	−31767
19	−200027	−5801 0900	−2520 3746	+5800 9855	−168270	−48 7901	+2520 6152	+34 1685	−31773
20	−200080	−5801 8592	−2520 7086	+5801 7555	−168315	−48 4790	+2520 9474	+33 8535	−31782
21	−200145	−5802 8065	−2521 1198	+5802 7034	−168370	−48 2036	+2521 3571	+33 5733	−31792
22	−200220	−5803 8938	−2521 5917	+5803 7913	−168433	−47 9940	+2521 8278	+33 3582	−31804
23	−200301	−5805 0628	−2522 0990	+5804 9605	−168501	−47 8705	+2522 3344	+33 2289	−31816
24	−200382	−5806 2420	−2522 6108	+5806 1398	−168569	−47 8413	+2522 8460	+33 1937	−31829
25	−200459	−5807 3570	−2523 0947	+5807 2546	−168634	−47 8999	+2523 3303	+33 2467	−31842
26	−200527	−5808 3405	−2523 5216	+5808 2378	−168691	−48 0258	+2523 7580	+33 3676	−31852
27	−200582	−5809 1431	−2523 8701	+5809 0400	−168738	−48 1848	+2524 1074	+33 5226	−31861
28	−200624	−5809 7449	−2524 1315	+5809 6414	−168773	−48 3324	+2524 3697	+33 6672	−31868
29	−200653	−5810 1662	−2524 3147	+5810 0625	−168797	−48 4190	+2524 5535	+33 7516	−31873
30	−200674	−5810 4762	−2524 4497	+5810 3725	−168815	−48 3988	+2524 6883	+33 7299	−31876
Dec. 1	−200696	−5810 7923	−2524 5873	+5810 6890	−168834	−48 2430	+2524 8250	+33 5724	−31879
2	−200729	−5811 2626	−2524 7917	+5811 1600	−168861	−47 9541	+2525 0278	+33 2812	−31884
3	−200781	−5812 0248	−2525 1227	+5811 9232	−168905	−47 5767	+2525 3566	+32 8999	−31893
4	−200859	−5813 1503	−2525 6112	+5813 0496	−168970	−47 1916	+2525 8428	+32 5091	−31905
5	−200959	−5814 5994	−2526 2399	+5814 4995	−169054	−46 8917	+2526 4699	+32 2019	−31920
6	−201072	−5816 2246	−2526 9450	+5816 1251	−169149	−46 7452	+2527 1742	+32 0472	−31938
7	−201182	−5817 8257	−2527 6396	+5817 7260	−169242	−46 7690	+2527 8689	+32 0630	−31956
8	−201279	−5819 2271	−2528 2477	+5819 1270	−169324	−46 9272	+2528 4780	+32 2141	−31971
9	−201356	−5820 3323	−2528 7274	+5820 2317	−169388	−47 1521	+2528 9590	+32 4333	−31983
10	−201411	−5821 1337	−2529 0753	+5821 0325	−169435	−47 3719	+2529 3082	+32 6492	−31992
11	−201450	−5821 6903	−2529 3172	+5821 5887	−169467	−47 5311	+2529 5510	+32 8055	−31999
12	−201478	−5822 0955	−2529 4934	+5821 9937	−169491	−47 5976	+2529 7276	+32 8700	−32003
13	−201502	−5822 4498	−2529 6476	+5822 3481	−169511	−47 5622	+2529 8816	+32 8328	−32007
14	−201530	−5822 8442	−2529 8191	+5822 7428	−169534	−47 4342	+2530 0524	+32 7027	−32011
15	−201565	−5823 3503	−2530 0391	+5823 2495	−169564	−47 2354	+2530 2713	+32 5014	−32017
16	−201611	−5824 0164	−2530 3284	+5823 9161	−169602	−46 9966	+2530 5592	+32 2592	−32024
17	−201669	−5824 8648	−2530 6968	+5824 7651	−169652	−46 7523	+2530 9261	+32 0106	−32033
18	−201740	−5825 8910	−2531 1422	+5825 7919	−169712	−46 5376	+2531 3704	+31 7908	−32044
19	−201822	−5827 0644	−2531 6514	+5826 9656	−169780	−46 3842	+2531 8787	+31 6314	−32057
20	−201909	−5828 3309	−2532 2010	+5828 2323	−169854	−46 3153	+2532 4279	+31 5561	−32071
21	−201999	−5829 6198	−2532 7603	+5829 5212	−169929	−46 3426	+2532 9874	+31 5769	−32085
22	−202084	−5830 8531	−2533 2955	+5830 7541	−170001	−46 4630	+2533 5233	+31 6911	−32099
23	−202161	−5831 9580	−2533 7750	+5831 8585	−170065	−46 6577	+2534 0040	+31 8802	−32111
24	−202225	−5832 8800	−2534 1753	+5832 7799	−170119	−46 8936	+2534 4057	+32 1113	−32121
25	−202274	−5833 5952	−2534 4859	+5833 4945	−170161	−47 1273	+2534 7177	+32 3414	−32129
26	−202311	−5834 1193	−2534 7136	+5834 0181	−170191	−47 3117	+2534 9465	+32 5231	−32135
27	−202338	−5834 5111	−2534 8840	+5834 4097	−170214	−47 4041	+2535 1175	+32 6136	−32139
28	−202363	−5834 8701	−2535 0402	+5834 7687	−170235	−47 3761	+2535 2735	+32 5838	−32143
29	−202394	−5835 3229	−2535 2371	+5835 2219	−170262	−47 2235	+2535 4695	+32 4289	−32148
30	−202441	−5835 9971	−2535 5299	+5835 8967	−170301	−46 9739	+2535 7609	+32 1758	−32156
31	−202509	−5836 9841	−2535 9584	+5836 8845	−170358	−46 6867	+2536 1877	+31 8836	−32166
32	−202601	−5838 2990	−2536 5289	+5838 1999	−170435	−46 4421	+2536 7568	+31 6324	−32181

$\mathbf{M} = \mathbf{NPB}$. Values are in units of 10^{-10}. Matrix used with GAST (B13–B20). CIP is $\mathcal{X} = \mathbf{M}_{3,1}$, $\mathcal{Y} = \mathbf{M}_{3,2}$.

MATRIX ELEMENTS FOR CONVERSION FROM

GCRS TO EQUATOR & CELESTIAL INTERMEDIATE ORIGIN OF DATE

FOR 0^h TERRESTRIAL TIME

Julian Date	$C_{1,1}-1$	$C_{1,2}$	$C_{1,3}$	$C_{2,1}$	$C_{2,2}-1$	$C_{2,3}$	$C_{3,1}$	$C_{3,2}$	$C_{3,3}-1$
246									
0995·5	−31754	− 25	−2520 0711	−856	− 6	−34 9730	+2520 0711	+34 9731	−31760
0996·5	−31757	− 25	−2520 1903	−851	− 6	−34 7617	+2520 1903	+34 7618	−31763
0997·5	−31761	− 25	−2520 3652	−844	− 6	−34 4831	+2520 3652	+34 4832	−31767
0998·5	−31768	− 25	−2520 6152	−836	− 6	−34 1684	+2520 6152	+34 1685	−31773
0999·5	−31776	− 26	−2520 9474	−828	− 6	−33 8534	+2520 9474	+33 8535	−31782
1000·5	−31786	− 26	−2521 3571	−821	− 6	−33 5732	+2521 3571	+33 5733	−31792
1001·5	−31798	− 26	−2521 8278	−815	− 6	−33 3581	+2521 8278	+33 3582	−31804
1002·5	−31811	− 26	−2522 3344	−812	− 6	−33 2288	+2522 3344	+33 2289	−31816
1003·5	−31824	− 26	−2522 8460	−811	− 6	−33 1936	+2522 8460	+33 1937	−31829
1004·5	−31836	− 26	−2523 3303	−813	− 6	−33 2466	+2523 3303	+33 2467	−31842
1005·5	−31847	− 26	−2523 7580	−816	− 6	−33 3675	+2523 7580	+33 3676	−31852
1006·5	−31856	− 27	−2524 1074	−820	− 6	−33 5225	+2524 1074	+33 5226	−31861
1007·5	−31862	− 27	−2524 3697	−823	− 6	−33 6671	+2524 3697	+33 6672	−31868
1008·5	−31867	− 27	−2524 5535	−825	− 6	−33 7515	+2524 5535	+33 7516	−31873
1009·5	−31870	− 27	−2524 6883	−825	− 6	−33 7298	+2524 6883	+33 7299	−31876
1010·5	−31874	− 27	−2524 8250	−821	− 6	−33 5723	+2524 8250	+33 5724	−31879
1011·5	−31879	− 27	−2525 0278	−813	− 6	−33 2811	+2525 0278	+33 2812	−31884
1012·5	−31887	− 27	−2525 3566	−804	− 5	−32 8998	+2525 3566	+32 8999	−31893
1013·5	−31899	− 27	−2525 8428	−794	− 5	−32 5090	+2525 8428	+32 5091	−31905
1014·5	−31915	− 27	−2526 4699	−786	− 5	−32 2018	+2526 4699	+32 2019	−31920
1015·5	−31933	− 28	−2527 1742	−782	− 5	−32 0471	+2527 1742	+32 0472	−31938
1016·5	−31951	− 28	−2527 8689	−783	− 5	−32 0629	+2527 8689	+32 0630	−31956
1017·5	−31966	− 28	−2528 4780	−787	− 5	−32 2140	+2528 4780	+32 2141	−31971
1018·5	−31978	− 28	−2528 9590	−792	− 5	−32 4332	+2528 9590	+32 4333	−31983
1019·5	−31987	− 28	−2529 3082	−798	− 5	−32 6491	+2529 3082	+32 6492	−31992
1020·5	−31993	− 28	−2529 5510	−801	− 5	−32 8054	+2529 5510	+32 8055	−31999
1021·5	−31998	− 28	−2529 7276	−803	− 5	−32 8699	+2529 7276	+32 8700	32003
1022·5	−32002	− 28	−2529 8816	−802	− 5	−32 8327	+2529 8816	+32 8328	−32007
1023·5	−32006	− 28	−2530 0524	−799	− 5	−32 7026	+2530 0524	+32 7027	−32011
1024·5	−32011	− 29	−2530 2713	−794	− 5	−32 5013	+2530 2713	+32 5014	−32017
1025·5	−32019	− 29	−2530 5592	−788	− 5	−32 2591	+2530 5592	+32 2592	−32024
1026·5	−32028	− 29	−2530 9261	−781	− 5	−32 0105	+2530 9261	+32 0106	−32033
1027·5	−32039	− 29	−2531 3704	−776	− 5	−31 7907	+2531 3704	+31 7908	−32044
1028·5	−32052	− 29	−2531 8787	−772	− 5	−31 6313	+2531 8787	+31 6314	−32057
1029·5	−32066	− 29	−2532 4279	−770	− 5	−31 5560	+2532 4279	+31 5561	−32071
1030·5	−32080	− 29	−2532 9874	−770	− 5	−31 5768	+2532 9874	+31 5769	−32085
1031·5	−32094	− 30	−2533 5233	−773	− 5	−31 6910	+2533 5233	+31 6911	−32099
1032·5	−32106	− 30	−2534 0040	−778	− 5	−31 8801	+2534 0040	+31 8802	−32111
1033·5	−32116	− 30	−2534 4057	−784	− 5	−32 1112	+2534 4057	+32 1113	−32121
1034·5	−32124	− 30	−2534 7177	−790	− 5	−32 3413	+2534 7177	+32 3414	−32129
1035·5	−32130	− 30	−2534 9465	−794	− 5	−32 5230	+2534 9465	+32 5231	−32135
1036·5	−32134	− 30	−2535 1175	−797	− 5	−32 6135	+2535 1175	+32 6136	−32139
1037·5	−32138	− 30	−2535 2735	−796	− 5	−32 5837	+2535 2735	+32 5838	−32143
1038·5	−32143	− 30	−2535 4695	−792	− 5	−32 4288	+2535 4695	+32 4289	−32148
1039·5	−32150	− 30	−2535 7609	−786	− 5	−32 1757	+2535 7609	+32 1758	−32156
1040·5	−32161	− 30	−2536 1877	−778	− 5	−31 8835	+2536 1877	+31 8836	−32166
1041·5	−32176	− 31	−2536 7568	−772	− 5	−31 6323	+2536 7568	+31 6324	−32181

Values are in units of 10^{-10}. Matrix used with ERA (B21–B24). CIP is $\mathcal{X} = \mathbf{C}_{3,1}$, $\mathcal{Y} = \mathbf{C}_{3,2}$

The Celestial Intermediate Reference System

The IAU 2000 and 2006 resolutions very precisely define the Celestial Intermediate Reference System by the direction of its pole (CIP) and the location of its origin of right ascension (CIO) at any date in the Geocentric Celestial Reference System (GCRS). This system is often denoted as the "equator and CIO of date" which has the same pole and equator as the equator and equinox of date, however, they have different origins for right ascension. This section includes the transformations using both origins and the relationships between them.

Pole of the Celestial Intermediate Reference System

The direction of the celestial intermediate pole (CIP), which is the pole of the Celestial Intermediate Reference System (the true celestial pole of date), at any instant is defined by the transformation from the GCRS that involves the rotations implementing frame bias and precession-nutation.

The unit vector components of the CIP (in radians) are given by elements one and two from the third row of the following rotation matrices, namely

$$\mathcal{X} = \mathbf{C}_{3,1} = \mathbf{M}_{3,1} \qquad \text{and} \qquad \mathcal{Y} = \mathbf{C}_{3,2} = \mathbf{M}_{3,2}$$

and the equations for calculating $\mathbf{C}$ are given on page B49, while those for $\mathbf{M}$ are given on page B50. Alternatively, $\mathcal{X}$ and $\mathcal{Y}$ may be calculated directly using

$$\mathcal{X} = \sin\epsilon \sin\psi \cos\bar{\gamma} - (\sin\epsilon \cos\psi \cos\bar{\phi} - \cos\epsilon \sin\bar{\phi}) \sin\bar{\gamma}$$
$$\mathcal{Y} = \sin\epsilon \sin\psi \sin\bar{\gamma} + (\sin\epsilon \cos\psi \cos\bar{\phi} - \cos\epsilon \sin\bar{\phi}) \cos\bar{\gamma}$$

where $\bar{\gamma}$, $\bar{\phi}$, ψ and ϵ include the effects of frame bias, precession and nutation (see page B56). $\mathcal{X}$ and $\mathcal{Y}$ are tabulated, in radians, at 0^{h} TT on even pages B30–B44, on odd pages B31–B45, and in arcseconds on pages B58–B65. The equations above may also be used to calculate the coordinates of the mean pole by ignoring nutation, that is by replacing ψ by $\bar{\psi}$ and ϵ by ϵ_{A}.

The position ($\mathcal{X}$, $\mathcal{Y}$) of the CIP, expressed in arcseconds, accurate to 0.″0001, may also be calculated from the following series expansions,

$$\begin{aligned} \mathcal{X} = &- 0.''016\,617 + 2004.''191\,898\, T - 0.''429\,7829\, T^2 \\ &- 0.''198\,618\,34\, T^3 + 7.''578 \times 10^{-6}\, T^4 + 5.''9285 \times 10^{-6}\, T^5 \\ &+ \sum_{j,i} [(a_{\text{s},j})_i\, T^j \sin(\text{ARGUMENT}) + (a_{\text{c},j})_i\, T^j \cos(\text{ARGUMENT})] + \cdots \end{aligned}$$

$$\begin{aligned} \mathcal{Y} = &- 0.''006\,951 - 0.''025\,896\, T - 22.''407\,2747\, T^2 \\ &+ 0.''001\,900\,59\, T^3 + 0.''001\,112\,526\, T^4 + 0.''1358 \times 10^{-6}\, T^5 \\ &+ \sum_{j,i} [(b_{\text{c},j})_i\, T^j \cos(\text{ARGUMENT}) + (b_{\text{s},j})_i\, T^j \sin(\text{ARGUMENT})] + \cdots \end{aligned}$$

where T is measured in TT Julian centuries from J2000·0 and the coefficients and arguments may be downloaded from the CDS (see https://cdsweb.u-strasbg.fr).

Approximate formulae for the Celestial Intermediate Pole

The following formulae may be used to compute $\mathcal{X}$ and $\mathcal{Y}$ to a precision of 0.″3 during 2025:

$$\mathcal{X} = 500.''95 + 0.''0549\, d - 6.''8 \sin\Omega - 0.''5 \sin 2L \qquad \mathcal{Y} = - 1.''41 + 9.''2 \cos\Omega + 0.''6 \cos 2L$$

where $\Omega = 1.^\circ6 - 0{\cdot}053\, d$, $L = 279.^\circ9 + 0{\cdot}986\, d$ and d is the day of the year and fraction of the day in the TT time scale.

Origin of the Celestial Intermediate Reference System

The CIO locator s, positions the celestial intermediate origin (CIO) on the equator of the Celestial Intermediate Reference System. It is the difference in the right ascension of the node of the equators in the GCRS and the Celestial Intermediate Reference System (see page B9). The CIO locator s is tabulated daily at 0^h TT, in arcseconds, on pages B58–B65.

The location of the CIO may be represented by $s + \mathcal{X}\mathcal{Y}/2$, the series of which is downloadable from the CDS (see https://cdsweb.u-strasbg.fr). However, the definition below includes all terms exceeding 0·5μas during the interval 1975–2025.

$$
\begin{aligned}
s = & -\mathcal{X}\mathcal{Y}/2 + 94'' \times 10^{-6} + \sum_k C_k \sin A_k \\
& + (+0''\!.003\,808\,65 + 1''\!.73 \times 10^{-6} \sin \Omega + 3''\!.57 \times 10^{-6} \cos 2\Omega)\, T \\
& + (-0''\!.000\,122\,68 + 743''\!.52 \times 10^{-6} \sin \Omega - 8''\!.85 \times 10^{-6} \sin 2\Omega \\
& \quad + 56''\!.91 \times 10^{-6} \sin 2(F - D + \Omega) + 9''\!.84 \times 10^{-6} \sin 2(F + \Omega))\, T^2 \\
& - 0''\!.072\,574\,11\, T^3 + 27''\!.98 \times 10^{-6}\, T^4 + 15''\!.62 \times 10^{-6}\, T^5
\end{aligned}
$$

Terms for $C_k \sin A_k$					
k	Argument A_k	Coefficient C_k	k	Argument A_k	Coefficient C_k
		$''$			$''$
1	Ω	−0·002 640 73	**7**	$2F + \Omega$	−0·000 001 98
2	2Ω	−0·000 063 53	**8**	3Ω	+0·000 001 72
3	$2F - 2D + 3\Omega$	−0·000 011 75	**9**	$l' + \Omega$	+0·000 001 41
4	$2F - 2D + \Omega$	−0·000 011 21	**10**	$l' - \Omega$	+0·000 001 26
5	$2F - 2D + 2\Omega$	+0·000 004 57	**11**	$l + \Omega$	+0·000 000 63
6	$2F + 3\Omega$	−0·000 002 02	**12**	$l - \Omega$	+0·000 000 63

$\mathcal{X}$, $\mathcal{Y}$ (expressed in radians) is the position of the CIP at the required TT instant. The coefficients and arguments (C_k, A_k) are tabulated above and the expressions for the fundamental arguments are

$$
\begin{aligned}
l &= 134^\circ\!.963\,402\,51 + 1\,717\,915\,923''\!.2178T + 31''\!.8792T^2 + 0''\!.051\,635T^3 - 0''\!.000\,244\,70T^4 \\
l' &= 357^\circ\!.529\,109\,18 + 129\,596\,581''\!.0481T - 0''\!.5532T^2 + 0''\!.000\,136T^3 - 0''\!.000\,011\,49T^4 \\
F &= 93^\circ\!.272\,090\,62 + 1\,739\,527\,262''\!.8478T - 12''\!.7512T^2 - 0''\!.001\,037T^3 + 0''\!.000\,004\,17T^4 \\
D &= 297^\circ\!.850\,195\,47 + 1\,602\,961\,601''\!.2090T - 6''\!.3706T^2 + 0''\!.006\,593T^3 - 0''\!.000\,031\,69T^4 \\
\Omega &= 125^\circ\!.044\,555\,01 - 6\,962\,890''\!.5431T + 7''\!.4722T^2 + 0''\!.007\,702T^3 - 0''\!.000\,059\,39T^4
\end{aligned}
$$

where T is the interval in TT Julian centuries from J2000·0 and is used in both the fundamental arguments and the expression for s itself.

These fundamental arguments are also used with the series expression for the complementary terms of the equation of the equinoxes (see page B10).

Approximate position of the Celestial Intermediate Origin

The CIO locator s may be ignored (i.e. set $s = 0$) in the interval 1963 to 2031 if accuracies no better than $0''\!.01$ are acceptable.

During 2025, $s + \mathcal{X}\mathcal{Y}/2$ may be computed to a precision of 13×10^{-5} arcseconds from

$$s + \mathcal{X}\mathcal{Y}/2 = -0''\!.000\,10 - 0''\!.0026 \sin(1^\circ\!.6 - 0{\cdot}053\, d) - 0''\!.0001 \sin(3^\circ\!.1 - 0{\cdot}106\, d)$$

where $\mathcal{X}$ and $\mathcal{Y}$ are expressed in radians (page B46 gives an approximation) and d is the day of the year and fraction of the day in the TT time scale.

Reduction from the GCRS

The transformation from the GCRS to the terrestrial reference system applies rotations implementing frame bias, the effects of precession and nutation, and Earth rotation. It is only the origin of right ascension and whether ERA or GAST is used to obtain a position with respect to the terrestrial system, that differ.

The following shows the matrix transformations to both the Celestial Intermediate Reference System (based on the CIP and CIO) and the traditional equator and equinox of date system (based on the CIP and equinox). This is followed by considering frame bias, precession, nutation, and the angles and rotations that represent these effects.

Summary of the CIP and the relationships between various origins

The CIP is the pole of both the Celestial Intermediate Reference System and the system of the the equator and equinox of date. The transformation from the GCRS to either of these systems and to the Terrestrial Intermediate Reference System may be represented by

$$\mathcal{R}_\beta = \mathbf{R}_3(-\beta)\ \mathcal{R}_\Sigma$$

where the matrix $\mathcal{R}_\Sigma$ transforms position vectors from the GCRS equator and origin (see diagram on page B9) to the "of date" system defined by the CIP and β determines the origin to be used and thus the method (see Capitaine, N., and Wallace, P.T., *Astron. Astrophys.*, **450**, 855-872, 2006). Thus listing the matrix relationships by method (i.e. value of β) gives:

CIO Method	Equinox Method
$\beta = s$	$\beta = s - E_o$
$\mathcal{R}_\beta = \mathbf{R}_3(-s)\ \mathcal{R}_\Sigma$	$\mathcal{R}_\beta = \mathbf{R}_3(-s + E_o)\ \mathcal{R}_\Sigma$
$= \mathbf{C}$	$= \mathbf{M} \equiv \mathbf{NPB}$

where s is the CIO locator (see page B47), E_o is the equation of the origins (see page B10), and the matrices $\mathbf{C}$, $\mathcal{R}_\Sigma$ and $\mathbf{M}$ are defined on pages B49 and B50, respectively.

When β includes the Earth rotation angle, or Greenwich apparent sidereal time, then coordinates with respect to the terrestrial intermediate origin are the result. Finally, longitude may be included, then the coordinates will be relative to the observers prime meridian.

CIO Method	Equinox Method
$\beta = s - \theta - \lambda$	$\beta = s - E_o - \text{GAST} - \lambda$
$\mathcal{R}_\beta = \mathbf{R}_3(\lambda + \theta - s)\ \mathcal{R}_\Sigma$	$\mathcal{R}_\beta = \mathbf{R}_3(\lambda + \text{GAST} - s + E_o)\ \mathcal{R}_\Sigma$
$= \mathbf{R}_3(\lambda + \theta)\ \mathbf{C}$	$= \mathbf{R}_3(\lambda + \text{GAST})\ \mathbf{M}$
$= \mathbf{Q}$	$= \mathbf{Q}$

where east longitudes are positive. The above ignores the small corrections for polar motion that are required in the reduction of very precise observations; they are (i) alignment of the terrestrial intermediate origin onto the longitude origin ($\lambda_{\text{ITRS}} = 0$) of the International Terrestrial Reference System, and (ii) for the positioning of the CIP within ITRS, (see page B84).

The equation of the origins, the relationship between the two systems may be calculated using

$$\mathbf{M} = \mathbf{R}_3(-s + E_o)\ \mathcal{R}_\Sigma \qquad \text{and thus} \qquad E_o = s - \tan^{-1}\frac{\mathbf{M}_\mathrm{j} \cdot \mathcal{R}_{\Sigma_\mathrm{i}}}{\mathbf{M}_\mathrm{i} \cdot \mathcal{R}_{\Sigma_\mathrm{i}}}$$

where $\mathbf{M}_\mathrm{i}$ and $\mathbf{M}_\mathrm{j}$ are the first two rows of $\mathbf{M}$, $\mathcal{R}_{\Sigma_\mathrm{i}}$ is the first row of $\mathcal{R}_\Sigma$ and $\cdot$ denotes the dot or scalar product. See also page B10 for an alternative method.

CIO method of reduction from the GCRS—rigorous formulae

Given an equatorial geocentric position vector $\mathbf{r}$ of an object with respect to the GCRS, then $\mathbf{r}_i$, its position with respect to the Celestial Intermediate Reference System, is given by

$$\mathbf{r}_i = \mathbf{C}\,\mathbf{r} \qquad \text{and} \qquad \mathbf{r} = \mathbf{C}^{-1}\,\mathbf{r}_i = \mathbf{C}'\,\mathbf{r}_i$$

The matrix $\mathbf{C}$ is tabulated daily at 0^h TT on odd numbered pages B31–B45, and is calculated thus

$$\mathbf{C}(\mathcal{X}, \mathcal{Y}, s) = \mathbf{R}_3(-[E+s])\,\mathbf{R}_2(d)\,\mathbf{R}_3(E) = \mathbf{R}_3(-s)\,\mathcal{R}_\Sigma$$

where the quantities $\mathcal{X}$, $\mathcal{Y}$, are the coordinates of the CIP, (expressed in radians), and the relationships between $\mathcal{X}$, $\mathcal{Y}$, $\mathcal{Z}$, E and d are:

$$\mathcal{X} = \sin d \cos E = \mathbf{M}_{3,1} = \mathbf{C}_{3,1} \qquad E = \tan^{-1}(\mathcal{Y}/\mathcal{X})$$

$$\mathcal{Y} = \sin d \sin E = \mathbf{M}_{3,2} = \mathbf{C}_{3,2}$$

$$\mathcal{Z} = \cos d = \sqrt{(1 - \mathcal{X}^2 - \mathcal{Y}^2)} \qquad d = \tan^{-1}\left(\frac{\mathcal{X}^2 + \mathcal{Y}^2}{1 - \mathcal{X}^2 - \mathcal{Y}^2}\right)^{\frac{1}{2}}$$

$\mathcal{X}$, $\mathcal{Y}$ and s are given on pages B46-B47 and tabulated, in arcseconds, daily at 0^h TT on pages B58–B65.

The matrix $\mathbf{C}$ transforms positions to the Celestial Intermediate Reference System, with the CIO being located by the rotation $\mathbf{R}_3(-s)$, and $\mathcal{R}_\Sigma$, the transformation from the GCRS equator to the equator of date being given by

$$\mathcal{R}_\Sigma = \begin{pmatrix} 1 - a\mathcal{X}^2 & -a\mathcal{X}\mathcal{Y} & -\mathcal{X} \\ -a\mathcal{X}\mathcal{Y} & 1 - a\mathcal{Y}^2 & -\mathcal{Y} \\ \mathcal{X} & \mathcal{Y} & 1 - a(\mathcal{X}^2 + \mathcal{Y}^2) \end{pmatrix} = \begin{pmatrix} \mathcal{R}_{\Sigma_\mathrm{i}} \\ \mathcal{R}_{\Sigma_\mathrm{k}} \times \mathcal{R}_{\Sigma_\mathrm{i}} \\ \mathcal{R}_{\Sigma_\mathrm{k}} \end{pmatrix}$$

where $a = 1/(1 + \mathcal{Z})$. $\mathcal{R}_{\Sigma_\mathrm{i}}$ is the unit vector pointing towards Σ (see diagram on page B9) that is obtained from the elements of the first row of $\mathcal{R}_\Sigma$ and similarly $\mathcal{R}_{\Sigma_\mathrm{k}}$ is the unit vector pointing towards the CIP. Note that $\mathcal{R}_{\Sigma_\mathrm{k}} = \mathbf{M}_\mathrm{k}$ (see page B50).

Approximate reduction from GCRS to the Celestial Intermediate Reference System

The matrix $\mathbf{C}$ given below together with the approximate formulae for $\mathcal{X}$ and $\mathcal{Y}$ on page B46 (expressed in radians) may be used when the resulting position is required to no better than 0.″3 during 2025:

$$\mathbf{C} = \begin{pmatrix} 1 - \mathcal{X}^2/2 & 0 & -\mathcal{X} \\ 0 & 1 & -\mathcal{Y} \\ \mathcal{X} & \mathcal{Y} & 1 - \mathcal{X}^2/2 \end{pmatrix}$$

Thus the position vector $\mathbf{r}_i = (x_i, y_i, z_i)$ with respect to the Celestial Intermediate Reference System (equator and CIO of date) may be calculated from the geocentric position vector $\mathbf{r} = (r_x, r_y, r_z)$ with respect to the GCRS using

$$\mathbf{r}_i = \mathbf{C}\,\mathbf{r}$$

therefore using the approximate matrix

$$\begin{aligned} x_i &= (1 - \mathcal{X}^2/2)\,r_x && - \mathcal{X}\,r_z \\ y_i &= \qquad\qquad\quad r_y && - \mathcal{Y}\,r_z \\ z_i &= \mathcal{X}\,r_x + \mathcal{Y}\,r_y && + (1 - \mathcal{X}^2/2)\,r_z \end{aligned}$$

and thus

$$\alpha_i = \tan^{-1}(y_i/x_i) \qquad \delta = \tan^{-1}\left(z_i/\sqrt{(x_i^2 + y_i^2)}\right)$$

where α_i, δ, are the intermediate right ascension and declination, and the quadrant of α_i is determined by the signs of x_i and y_i.

Equinox method of reduction from the GCRS—rigorous formulae

The reduction from a geocentric position $\mathbf{r}$ with respect to the Geocentric Celestial Reference System (GCRS) to a position $\mathbf{r}_t$ with respect to the equator and equinox of date, and vice versa, is given by:

$$\mathbf{r}_t = \mathbf{M}\,\mathbf{r} \qquad \text{and} \qquad \mathbf{r} = \mathbf{M}^{-1}\,\mathbf{r}_t = \mathbf{M}'\,\mathbf{r}_t$$

Using the 4-rotation Fukushima-Willams (F-W) method, the rotation matrix $\mathbf{M}$ may be written as

$$\mathbf{M} = \mathbf{R}_1(-[\epsilon_A + \Delta\epsilon])\,\mathbf{R}_3(-[\bar{\psi} + \Delta\psi])\,\mathbf{R}_1(\bar{\phi})\,\mathbf{R}_3(\bar{\gamma}) = \begin{pmatrix}\mathbf{M}_{\rm i}\\ \mathbf{M}_{\rm j}\\ \mathbf{M}_{\rm k}\end{pmatrix} = \mathbf{N\,P\,B}$$

where the angles $\bar{\gamma}$, $\bar{\phi}$, $\bar{\psi}$ combine the frame bias with the effects of precession (see page B56). Nutation is applied by adding the nutations in longitude ($\Delta\psi$) and obliquity ($\Delta\epsilon$) (see page B55) to $\bar{\psi}$ and ϵ_A, respectively. Pages B50–B56 give the formulae for calculating the matrices $\mathbf{B}$, $\mathbf{P}$ and $\mathbf{N}$ individually using the traditional angles and rotations.

The elements of the rows of $\mathbf{M}$ represent unit vectors pointing in the directions of the x, y and z axes of the equator and equinox of date system. Thus the elements of the first row are the components of the unit vector in the direction of the true equinox,

$$\mathbf{M}_{\rm i} = \begin{pmatrix}\mathbf{M}_{1,1}\\ \mathbf{M}_{1,2}\\ \mathbf{M}_{1,3}\end{pmatrix} = \begin{pmatrix}\cos\psi\cos\bar{\gamma} + \sin\psi\cos\bar{\phi}\sin\bar{\gamma}\\ \cos\psi\sin\bar{\gamma} - \sin\psi\cos\bar{\phi}\cos\bar{\gamma}\\ -\sin\psi\sin\bar{\phi}\end{pmatrix}$$

The second row of elements defines the unit vector in the direction of the y-axis, in the plane 90° from the x-z plane, i.e. the plane of the equator of date, and is given by

$$\begin{aligned}\mathbf{M}_{\rm j} &= \mathbf{M}_{\rm k} \times \mathbf{M}_{\rm i}\\ &= \begin{pmatrix}\mathbf{M}_{2,1}\\ \mathbf{M}_{2,2}\\ \mathbf{M}_{2,3}\end{pmatrix} = \begin{pmatrix}\cos\epsilon\sin\psi\cos\bar{\gamma} - (\cos\epsilon\cos\psi\cos\bar{\phi} + \sin\epsilon\sin\bar{\phi})\sin\bar{\gamma}\\ \cos\epsilon\sin\psi\sin\bar{\gamma} + (\cos\epsilon\cos\psi\cos\bar{\phi} + \sin\epsilon\sin\bar{\phi})\cos\bar{\gamma}\\ \cos\epsilon\cos\psi\sin\bar{\phi} - \sin\epsilon\cos\bar{\phi}\end{pmatrix}\end{aligned}$$

Lastly, the elements of the third row are the components of the unit vector pointing in the direction of the celestial intermediate pole (CIP), thus

$$\mathbf{M}_{\rm k} = \begin{pmatrix}\mathbf{M}_{3,1}\\ \mathbf{M}_{3,2}\\ \mathbf{M}_{3,3}\end{pmatrix} = \begin{pmatrix}\mathcal{X}\\ \mathcal{Y}\\ \mathcal{Z}\end{pmatrix} = \begin{pmatrix}\sin\epsilon\sin\psi\cos\bar{\gamma} - (\sin\epsilon\cos\psi\cos\bar{\phi} - \cos\epsilon\sin\bar{\phi})\sin\bar{\gamma}\\ \sin\epsilon\sin\psi\sin\bar{\gamma} + (\sin\epsilon\cos\psi\cos\bar{\phi} - \cos\epsilon\sin\bar{\phi})\cos\bar{\gamma}\\ \sin\epsilon\cos\psi\sin\bar{\phi} + \cos\epsilon\cos\bar{\phi}\end{pmatrix}$$

Reduction from GCRS to J2000—frame bias—rigorous formulae

Positions of objects with respect to the GCRS must be rotated to the J2000·0 dynamical system before precession and nutation are applied. Objects whose positions are given with respect to another system, e.g. FK5, may first be transformed to the GCRS before using the methods given here. An GCRS position $\mathbf{r}$ may be transformed to a J2000·0 or FK5 position $\mathbf{r}_0$ and vice versa, as follows,

$$\mathbf{r}_0 = \mathbf{B}\mathbf{r} \qquad \text{and} \qquad \mathbf{r} = \mathbf{B}^{-1}\mathbf{r}_0 = \mathbf{B}'\mathbf{r}_0$$

where $\mathbf{B}$ is the frame bias matrix.

Reduction from GCRS to J2000—frame bias—rigorous formulae (continued)

There are two sets of parameters that may be used to generate **B**. There are η_0, ξ_0 and $d\alpha_0$ which appeared in the literature first, or those consistent with the Fukushima-Williams precession parameterization, γ_B, ϕ_B and ψ_B.

Offsets of the Pole and Origin at J2000·0

Rotation From	η_0 mas	ξ_0 mas	$d\alpha_0$ mas	F-W IAU 2006 γ_B mas	ϕ_B mas	ψ_B mas
GCRS to J2000·0	− 6·8192	−16·617	−14·6	52·928	6·819	41·775
GCRS to FK5	−19·9	+ 9·1	−22·9			

where η_0, ξ_0 are the offsets from the pole together with $d\alpha_0$, the shift in right ascension origin. The IAU 2006 offsets, γ_B, ϕ_B and ψ_B are extracted from the IAU WGPE report and are consistent with F-W method of rotations:

$$\mathbf{B} = \mathbf{R}_3(-\psi_B)\ \mathbf{R}_1(\phi_B)\ \mathbf{R}_3(\gamma_B)$$

Alternatively

$$\mathbf{B} = \mathbf{R}_1(-\eta_0)\ \mathbf{R}_2(\xi_0)\ \mathbf{R}_3(d\alpha_0) \qquad \mathbf{B}^{-1} = \mathbf{R}_3(-d\alpha_0)\ \mathbf{R}_2(-\xi_0)\ \mathbf{R}_1(+\eta_0)$$

where in terms of corrections provided by the IAU 2000 precession-nutation theory, $\delta\epsilon_0 = \eta_0$ and $\xi_0 = -41{\cdot}775 \sin(23^\circ\,26'\,21''\!.448) = -16{\cdot}617$ mas.

Evaluating the matrix for GCRS to J2000·0 gives

$$\mathbf{B} = \begin{pmatrix} +0{\cdot}9999\,9999\,9999\,9942 & -0{\cdot}0000\,0007\,1 & +0{\cdot}0000\,0008\,056 \\ +0{\cdot}0000\,0007\,1 & +0{\cdot}9999\,9999\,9999\,9969 & +0{\cdot}0000\,0003\,306 \\ -0{\cdot}0000\,0008\,056 & -0{\cdot}0000\,0003\,306 & +0{\cdot}9999\,9999\,9999\,9962 \end{pmatrix}$$

where the number of digits is determined by the accuracy of the offsets.

Approximate reduction from GCRS to J2000

Since the rotations to orient the GCRS to J2000·0 system are small the following approximate matrix, accurate to $2'' \times 10^{-9}$ (1×10^{-14} radians), may be used:

$$\mathbf{B} = \begin{pmatrix} 1 & d\alpha_0 & -\xi_0 \\ -d\alpha_0 & 1 & -\eta_0 \\ \xi_0 & \eta_0 & 1 \end{pmatrix}$$

where η_0, ξ_0 and $d\alpha_0$ are the offsets of the pole and the origin (expressed in radians) from J2000·0 given in the table above.

Reduction for precession—rigorous formulae

Rigorous formulae for the reduction of mean equatorial positions from J2000·0 (t_0) to epoch of date t, and vice versa, are as follows:

For equatorial rectangular coordinates (x_0, y_0, z_0), or direction cosines ($\mathbf{r}_0$),

$$\mathbf{r}_m = \mathbf{P}\,\mathbf{r}_0 \qquad \mathbf{r}_0 = \mathbf{P}^{-1}\,\mathbf{r}_m = \mathbf{P}'\mathbf{r}_m$$

where

$$\begin{aligned} \mathbf{P} &= \mathbf{R}_1(-\epsilon_A)\ \mathbf{R}_3(-\psi_J)\ \mathbf{R}_1(\phi_J)\ \mathbf{R}_3(\gamma_J) \\ &= \mathbf{R}_3(\chi_A)\ \mathbf{R}_1(-\omega_A)\ \mathbf{R}_3(-\psi_A)\ \mathbf{R}_1(\epsilon_0) \\ &= \mathbf{R}_3(-z_A)\ \mathbf{R}_2(\theta_A)\ \mathbf{R}_3(-\zeta_A) \end{aligned}$$

and $\mathbf{r}_m$ is the position vector precessed from t_0 to the mean equinox at t.

The angles given in this section precess positions from J2000·0 to date and therefore do not include the frame bias, which is only needed when positions are with respect to the GCRS.

Reduction for precession—rigorous formulae (continued)

For all the precession angles given in this section, the time argument T is given by

$$T = (t - 2000{\cdot}0)/100 = (\mathrm{JD_{TT}} - 245\ 1545{\cdot}0)/36\ 525$$

which is a function of TT. Strictly speaking precession angles should be a function of TDB, but this makes no significant difference.

The 4-rotation Fukushima-Williams (F-W) method using angles γ_J, ϕ_J, ψ_J, and ϵ_A, are

$$\gamma_J = 10''556\ 403\ T + 0''493\ 2044\ T^2 - 0''000\ 312\ 38\ T^3 - 2''788 \times 10^{-6}\ T^4 + 2''60 \times 10^{-8}\ T^5$$

$$\phi_J = \epsilon_0 - 46''811\ 015\ T + 0''051\ 1269\ T^2 + 0''000\ 532\ 89\ T^3 - 0''440 \times 10^{-6}\ T^4 - 1''76 \times 10^{-8}\ T^5$$

$$\psi_J = 5038''481\ 507\ T + 1''558\ 4176\ T^2 - 0''000\ 185\ 22\ T^3 - 26''452 \times 10^{-6}\ T^4 - 1''48 \times 10^{-8}\ T^5$$

$$\epsilon_A = \epsilon_0 - 46''836\ 769\ T - 0''000\ 1831\ T^2 + 0''002\ 003\ 40\ T^3 - 0''576 \times 10^{-6}\ T^4 - 4''34 \times 10^{-8}\ T^5$$

where $\epsilon_0 = 84\ 381''406 = 23^\circ\ 26'\ 21''406$ is the obliquity of the ecliptic with respect to the dynamical equinox at J2000 and ϵ_A is the obliquity of the ecliptic with respect to the mean equator of date; equivalently

$$\epsilon_A = 23^\circ439\ 279\ 4444 - 0^\circ013\ 010\ 213\ 61\ T - 5^\circ0861 \times 10^{-8}\ T^2 + 5^\circ565 \times 10^{-7}\ T^3 - 1^\circ6 \times 10^{-10}\ T^4 - 1^\circ2056 \times 10^{-11}\ T^5$$

The precession matrix for the F-W precession angles, which includes how to incorporate the frame bias and nutation, is described on page B56.

The Capitaine *et al.* method, the formulation of which cleanly separates precession of the equator from precession of the ecliptic, is via the precession angles χ_A, ω_A, ψ_A, which are

$$\psi_A = 5038''481\ 507\ T - 1''079\ 0069\ T^2 - 0''001\ 140\ 45\ T^3 + 0''000\ 132\ 851\ T^4 - 9''51 \times 10^{-8}\ T^5$$

$$\omega_A = \epsilon_0 - 0''025\ 754\ T + 0''051\ 2623\ T^2 - 0''007\ 725\ 03\ T^3 - 0''000\ 000\ 467\ T^4 + 33''37 \times 10^{-8}\ T^5$$

$$\chi_A = 10''556\ 403\ T - 2''381\ 4292\ T^2 - 0''001\ 211\ 97\ T^3 + 0''000\ 170\ 663\ T^4 - 5''60 \times 10^{-8}\ T^5$$

where the precession matrix using χ_A, ω_A, ψ_A and ϵ_0 is

$$\mathbf{P} = \begin{pmatrix} C_4C_2 - S_2S_4C_3 & C_4S_2C_1 + S_4C_3C_2C_1 - S_1S_4S_3 & C_4S_2S_1 + S_4C_3C_2S_1 + C_1S_4S_3 \\ -S_4C_2 - S_2C_4C_3 & -S_4S_2C_1 + C_4C_3C_2C_1 - S_1C_4S_3 & -S_4S_2S_1 + C_4C_3C_2S_1 + C_1C_4S_3 \\ S_2S_3 & -S_3C_2C_1 - S_1C_3 & -S_3C_2S_1 + C_3C_1 \end{pmatrix}$$

and

$$S_1 = \sin\epsilon_0 \quad S_2 = \sin(-\psi_A) \quad S_3 = \sin(-\omega_A) \quad S_4 = \sin\chi_A$$
$$C_1 = \cos\epsilon_0 \quad C_2 = \cos(-\psi_A) \quad C_3 = \cos(-\omega_A) \quad C_4 = \cos\chi_A$$

The traditional equatorial precession angles ζ_A, z_A, θ_A are

$$\zeta_A = +2''650\ 545 + 2306''083\ 227\ T + 0''298\ 8499\ T^2 + 0''018\ 018\ 28\ T^3 - 5''971 \times 10^{-6}\ T^4 - 3''173 \times 10^{-7}\ T^5$$

$$z_A = -2''650\ 545 + 2306''077\ 181\ T + 1''092\ 7348\ T^2 + 0''018\ 268\ 37\ T^3 - 28''596 \times 10^{-6}\ T^4 - 2''904 \times 10^{-7}\ T^5$$

$$\theta_A = 2004''191\ 903\ T - 0''429\ 4934\ T^2 - 0''041\ 822\ 64\ T^3 - 7''089 \times 10^{-6}\ T^4 - 1''274 \times 10^{-7}\ T^5$$

Reduction for precession—rigorous formulae (continued)

The precession matrix using ζ_A, z_A, θ_A is

$$\mathbf{P} = \begin{pmatrix} \cos\zeta_A \cos\theta_A \cos z_A - \sin\zeta_A \sin z_A & -\sin\zeta_A \cos\theta_A \cos z_A - \cos\zeta_A \sin z_A & -\sin\theta_A \cos z_A \\ \cos\zeta_A \cos\theta_A \sin z_A + \sin\zeta_A \cos z_A & -\sin\zeta_A \cos\theta_A \sin z_A + \cos\zeta_A \cos z_A & -\sin\theta_A \sin z_A \\ \cos\zeta_A \sin\theta_A & -\sin\zeta_A \sin\theta_A & \cos\theta_A \end{pmatrix}$$

For right ascension and declination in terms of ζ_A, z_A, θ_A:

$$\begin{aligned} \sin(\alpha - z_A)\cos\delta &= \sin(\alpha_0 + \zeta_A)\cos\delta_0 \\ \cos(\alpha - z_A)\cos\delta &= \cos(\alpha_0 + \zeta_A)\cos\theta_A \cos\delta_0 - \sin\theta_A \sin\delta_0 \\ \sin\delta &= \cos(\alpha_0 + \zeta_A)\sin\theta_A \cos\delta_0 + \cos\theta_A \sin\delta_0 \end{aligned}$$

$$\begin{aligned} \sin(\alpha_0 + \zeta_A)\cos\delta_0 &= \sin(\alpha - z_A)\cos\delta \\ \cos(\alpha_0 + \zeta_A)\cos\delta_0 &= \cos(\alpha - z_A)\cos\theta_A \cos\delta + \sin\theta_A \sin\delta \\ \sin\delta_0 &= -\cos(\alpha - z_A)\sin\theta_A \cos\delta + \cos\theta_A \sin\delta \end{aligned}$$

where ζ_A, z_A, θ_A, given above, are angles that serve to specify the position of the mean equator and equinox of date with respect to the mean equator and equinox of J2000·0.

Values of all the angles and the elements of **P** for reduction from J2000·0 to epoch and mean equinox of the middle of the year (J2025·5) are as follows:

F-W Precession Angles γ_J, ϕ_J, ψ_J, and ϵ_A

γ_J	=	+2″72	=	+0°000 757	ϕ_J	=	+843 69″47	=	+23°435 965
ψ_J	=	+128 4″91	=	+0°356 921	ϵ_A	=	23° 26′ 09″46	=	23°435 962

Precession Angles ζ_A, z_A, θ_A					Precession Angles ψ_A, ω_A, χ_A				
ζ_A	=	+590″72	=	+0°164 089	ψ_A	=	+128 4″74	=	+0°356 873
z_A	=	+585″47	=	+0°162 631	ω_A	=	+843 81″40	=	+23°439 279
θ_A	=	+511″04	=	+0°141 956	χ_A	=	+2″54	=	+0°000 705

The rotation matrix for precession from J2000·0 to J2025·5 is

$$\mathbf{P} = \begin{pmatrix} +0{\cdot}999\,980\,672 & -0{\cdot}005\,702\,300 & -0{\cdot}002\,477\,581 \\ +0{\cdot}005\,702\,300 & +0{\cdot}999\,983\,742 & -0{\cdot}000\,007\,032 \\ +0{\cdot}002\,477\,581 & -0{\cdot}000\,007\,096 & +0{\cdot}999\,996\,931 \end{pmatrix}$$

The precessional motion of the ecliptic is specified by the inclination (π_A) and longitude of the node (Π_A) of the ecliptic of date with respect to the ecliptic and equinox of J2000·0; they are given by:

$$\sin\pi_A \sin\Pi_A = +\ 4''199\,094\,T + 0''193\,9873\,T^2 - 0''000\,224\,66\,T^3 - 9''12\times10^{-7}\,T^4 + 1''20\times10^{-8}\,T^5$$

$$\sin\pi_A \cos\Pi_A = -46''811\,015\,T + 0''051\,0283\,T^2 + 0''000\,524\,13\,T^3 - 6''46\times10^{-7}\,T^4 - 1''72\times10^{-8}\,T^5$$

π_A is a small angle, and often π_A replaces $\sin\pi_A$.

For epoch J2025·5 $\quad \pi_A = +11''983 = 0°003\,3285$
$\Pi_A = 174°\ 48'8 = 174°813$

Reduction for precession—approximate formulae

Approximate formulae for the reduction of coordinates and orbital elements referred to the mean equinox and equator or ecliptic of date (t) are as follows:

For reduction to J2000·0	For reduction from J2000·0
$\alpha_0 = \alpha - M - N \sin \alpha_m \tan \delta_m$	$\alpha = \alpha_0 + M + N \sin \alpha_m \tan \delta_m$
$\delta_0 = \delta - N \cos \alpha_m$	$\delta = \delta_0 + N \cos \alpha_m$
$\lambda_0 = \lambda - a + b \cos (\lambda + c') \tan \beta_0$	$\lambda = \lambda_0 + a - b \cos (\lambda_0 + c) \tan \beta$
$\beta_0 = \beta - b \sin (\lambda + c')$	$\beta = \beta_0 + b \sin (\lambda_0 + c)$
$\Omega_0 = \Omega - a + b \sin (\Omega + c') \cot i_0$	$\Omega = \Omega_0 + a - b \sin (\Omega_0 + c) \cot i$
$i_0 = i - b \cos (\Omega + c')$	$i = i_0 + b \cos (\Omega_0 + c)$
$\omega_0 = \omega - b \sin (\Omega + c') \operatorname{cosec} i_0$	$\omega = \omega_0 + b \sin (\Omega_0 + c) \operatorname{cosec} i$

where the subscript zero refers to epoch J2000·0 and α_m, δ_m refer to the mean epoch; with sufficient accuracy:

$$\alpha_m = \alpha - \tfrac{1}{2}(M + N \sin \alpha \tan \delta)$$
$$\delta_m = \delta - \tfrac{1}{2} N \cos \alpha_m$$

or

$$\alpha_m = \alpha_0 + \tfrac{1}{2}(M + N \sin \alpha_0 \tan \delta_0)$$
$$\delta_m = \delta_0 + \tfrac{1}{2} N \cos \alpha_m$$

The precessional constants M, N, etc., are given by:

$$M = 1\overset{\circ}{.}2811\,5566\,89\,T + 0\overset{\circ}{.}0003\,8655\,131\,T^2 + 0\overset{\circ}{.}0000\,1007\,9625\,T^3 - 9\overset{\circ}{.}60194 \times 10^{-9}\,T^4 - 1\overset{\circ}{.}68806 \times 10^{-10}\,T^5$$
$$N = 0\overset{\circ}{.}5567\,1997\,31\,T - 0\overset{\circ}{.}0001\,1930\,372\,T^2 - 0\overset{\circ}{.}0000\,1161\,7400\,T^3 - 1\overset{\circ}{.}96917 \times 10^{-9}\,T^4 - 3\overset{\circ}{.}5389 \times 10^{-11}\,T^5$$
$$a = 1\overset{\circ}{.}3968\,8783\,19\,T + 0\overset{\circ}{.}0003\,0706\,522\,T^2 + 2\overset{\circ}{.}2122 \times 10^{-8}\,T^3 - 6\overset{\circ}{.}62694 \times 10^{-9}\,T^4 + 1\overset{\circ}{.}0639 \times 10^{-11}\,T^5$$
$$b = 0\overset{\circ}{.}0130\,5527\,03\,T - 0\overset{\circ}{.}0000\,0930\,350\,T^2 + 3\overset{\circ}{.}4886 \times 10^{-8}\,T^3 + 3\overset{\circ}{.}13889 \times 10^{-11}\,T^4 - 6\overset{\circ}{.}11 \times 10^{-13}\,T^5$$
$$c = 5\overset{\circ}{.}1258\,9067 + 0\overset{\circ}{.}8189\,93580\,T + 0\overset{\circ}{.}0001\,4256\,094\,T^2 + 2\overset{\circ}{.}971\,04 \times 10^{-8}\,T^3 - 2\overset{\circ}{.}480\,66 \times 10^{-9}\,T^4 + 4\overset{\circ}{.}694 \times 10^{-12}\,T^5$$
$$c' = 5\overset{\circ}{.}1258\,9067 - 0\overset{\circ}{.}5778\,94252\,T - 0\overset{\circ}{.}0001\,6450\,428\,T^2 + 7\overset{\circ}{.}588\,19 \times 10^{-9}\,T^3 + 4\overset{\circ}{.}146\,28 \times 10^{-9}\,T^4 - 5\overset{\circ}{.}944 \times 10^{-12}\,T^5$$

Formulae for the reduction from the mean equinox and equator or ecliptic of the middle of year (t_1) to date (t) are as follows:

$\alpha = \alpha_1 + \tau(m + n \sin \alpha_1 \tan \delta_1)$	$\delta = \delta_1 + \tau n \cos \alpha_1$
$\lambda = \lambda_1 + \tau(p - \pi \cos (\lambda_1 + 6^\circ) \tan \beta)$	$\beta = \beta_1 + \tau\pi \sin (\lambda_1 + 6^\circ)$
$\Omega = \Omega_1 + \tau(p - \pi \sin (\Omega_1 + 6^\circ) \cot i)$	$i = i_1 + \tau\pi \cos (\Omega_1 + 6^\circ)$
$\omega = \omega_1 + \tau\pi \sin (\Omega_1 + 6^\circ) \operatorname{cosec} i$	

where $\tau = t - t_1$ and π is the annual rate of rotation of the ecliptic.

Reduction for precession—approximate formulae (continued)

The precessional constants p, m, etc., are as follows:

Annual	Epoch J2025·5		Epoch J2025·5
general precession	$p = +0^{\circ}\!.013\,9704$	Annual rate of rotation	$\pi = +0^{\circ}\!.000\,1305$
precession in R.A.	$m = +0^{\circ}\!.012\,8135$	Longitude of axis	$\Pi = +174^{\circ}\!.8126$
precession in Dec.	$n = +0^{\circ}\!.005\,5666$		$\gamma = 180^{\circ} - \Pi = +5^{\circ}\!.1874$

where Π is the longitude of the instantaneous rotation axis of the ecliptic, measured from the mean equinox of date.

Reduction for nutation—rigorous formulae

Nutations in longitude ($\Delta\psi$) and obliquity ($\Delta\epsilon$) have been calculated using the IAU 2000A series definitions (order of 1μas) with the following adjustments which are required for use at the highest precision with the IAU 2006 precession, viz:

$$\Delta\psi = \Delta\psi_{2000A} + (0{\cdot}4697 \times 10^{-6} - 2{\cdot}7774 \times 10^{-6}\ T)\ \Delta\psi_{2000A}$$
$$\Delta\epsilon = \Delta\epsilon_{2000A} - 2{\cdot}7774 \times 10^{-6}\ T\ \Delta\epsilon_{2000A}$$

where T is measured in Julian centuries from 245 1545·0 TT. $\Delta\psi$ and $\Delta\epsilon$ together with the true obliquity of the ecliptic (ϵ) are tabulated, daily at 0^{h} TT, on pages B58–B65. Web links are given on page x for series for evaluating $\Delta\psi_{2000A}$, $\Delta\epsilon_{2000A}$, and $\Delta\psi$, $\Delta\epsilon$.

A mean place ($\mathbf{r}_m$) may be transformed to a true place ($\mathbf{r}_t$), and vice versa, as follows:

$$\mathbf{r}_t = \mathbf{N}\,\mathbf{r}_m \qquad \mathbf{r}_m = \mathbf{N}^{-1}\,\mathbf{r}_t = \mathbf{N}'\,\mathbf{r}_t$$

where
$$\mathbf{N} = \mathbf{R}_1(-\epsilon)\ \mathbf{R}_3(-\Delta\psi)\ \mathbf{R}_1(+\epsilon_A)$$
$$\epsilon = \epsilon_A + \Delta\epsilon$$

and ϵ_A is given on page B52. The matrix for nutation is given by

$$\mathbf{N} = \begin{pmatrix} \cos\Delta\psi & -\sin\Delta\psi\cos\epsilon_A & -\sin\Delta\psi\sin\epsilon_A \\ \sin\Delta\psi\cos\epsilon & \cos\Delta\psi\cos\epsilon_A\cos\epsilon + \sin\epsilon_A\sin\epsilon & \cos\Delta\psi\sin\epsilon_A\cos\epsilon - \cos\epsilon_A\sin\epsilon \\ \sin\Delta\psi\sin\epsilon & \cos\Delta\psi\cos\epsilon_A\sin\epsilon - \sin\epsilon_A\cos\epsilon & \cos\Delta\psi\sin\epsilon_A\sin\epsilon + \cos\epsilon_A\cos\epsilon \end{pmatrix}$$

Approximate reduction for nutation

To first order, the contributions of the nutations in longitude ($\Delta\psi$) and in obliquity ($\Delta\epsilon$) to the reduction from mean place to true place are given by:

$$\Delta\alpha = (\cos\epsilon + \sin\epsilon\ \sin\alpha\ \tan\delta)\ \Delta\psi - \cos\alpha\ \tan\delta\ \Delta\epsilon \qquad \Delta\lambda = \Delta\psi$$
$$\Delta\delta = \sin\epsilon\ \cos\alpha\ \Delta\psi + \sin\alpha\ \Delta\epsilon \qquad \Delta\beta = 0$$

The following formulae may be used to compute $\Delta\psi$ and $\Delta\epsilon$ to a precision of about $0^{\circ}\!.0002$ (1″) during 2025.

$$\Delta\psi = -\,0^{\circ}\!.0048\sin(1^{\circ}\!.6 - 0{\cdot}053\,d) - 0^{\circ}\!.0004\sin(199^{\circ}\!.8 + 1{\cdot}971\,d)$$
$$\Delta\epsilon = +\,0^{\circ}\!.0026\cos(1^{\circ}\!.6 - 0{\cdot}053\,d) + 0^{\circ}\!.0002\cos(199^{\circ}\!.8 + 1{\cdot}971\,d)$$

where $d = \mathrm{JD_{TT}} - 246\ 0675{\cdot}5$ is the day of the year and fraction; for this precision

$$\epsilon = 23^{\circ}\!.44 \qquad \cos\epsilon = 0{\cdot}918 \qquad \sin\epsilon = 0{\cdot}398$$

Approximate reduction for nutation (continued)

The corrections to be added to the mean rectangular coordinates (x, y, z) to produce the true rectangular coordinates are given by:

$$\Delta x = -(y\cos\epsilon + z\sin\epsilon)\,\Delta\psi \qquad \Delta y = +x\,\Delta\psi\,\cos\epsilon - z\,\Delta\epsilon \qquad \Delta z = +x\,\Delta\psi\,\sin\epsilon + y\,\Delta\epsilon$$

where $\Delta\psi$ and $\Delta\epsilon$ are expressed in radians. The corresponding rotation matrix is

$$\mathbf{N} = \begin{pmatrix} 1 & -\Delta\psi\,\cos\epsilon & -\Delta\psi\,\sin\epsilon \\ +\Delta\psi\,\cos\epsilon & 1 & -\Delta\epsilon \\ +\Delta\psi\,\sin\epsilon & +\Delta\epsilon & 1 \end{pmatrix}$$

Combined reduction for frame bias, precession and nutation—rigorous formulae

The angles $\bar{\gamma}$, $\bar{\phi}$, $\bar{\psi}$ which combine frame bias with the effects of precession are given by

$$\bar{\gamma} = -0''052\,928 + 10''556\,378\,T + 0''493\,2044\,T^2 - 0''000\,312\,38\,T^3 - 2''788\times10^{-6}\,T^4 + 2''60\times10^{-8}\,T^5$$

$$\bar{\phi} = 84381''412\,819 - 46''811\,016\,T + 0''051\,1268\,T^2 + 0''000\,532\,89\,T^3 - 0''440\times10^{-6}\,T^4 - 1''76\times10^{-8}\,T^5$$

$$\bar{\psi} = -0''041\,775 + 5038''481\,484\,T + 1''558\,4175\,T^2 - 0''000\,185\,22\,T^3 - 26''452\times10^{-6}\,T^4 - 1''48\times10^{-8}\,T^5$$

Nutation (see page B55) is applied by adding the nutations in longitude ($\Delta\psi$) and obliquity ($\Delta\epsilon$) thus

$$\psi = \bar{\psi} + \Delta\psi \qquad \text{and} \qquad \epsilon = \epsilon_A + \Delta\epsilon$$

Values for $\Delta\psi$ and $\Delta\epsilon$ are tabulated daily on pages B58–B65 with ϵ, the true obliquity of the ecliptic, while ϵ_A is given on page B52.

Thus the reduction from a geocentric position $\mathbf{r}$ with respect to the GCRS to a position $\mathbf{r}_t$ with respect to the (true) equator and equinox of date, and vice versa, is given by:

$$\mathbf{r}_t = \mathbf{M}\,\mathbf{r} = \mathbf{N}\,\mathbf{P}\,\mathbf{B}\,\mathbf{r} \qquad \mathbf{r} = \mathbf{B}^{-1}\,\mathbf{P}^{-1}\,\mathbf{N}^{-1}\,\mathbf{r}_t = \mathbf{B}'\,\mathbf{P}'\,\mathbf{N}'\,\mathbf{r}_t$$

or where

$$\mathbf{M} = \mathbf{R}_1(-\epsilon)\,\mathbf{R}_3(-\psi)\,\mathbf{R}_1(\bar{\phi})\,\mathbf{R}_3(\bar{\gamma})$$

and the matrices **B**, **P** and **N** are defined in the preceding sections. The combined matrix **M** (see page B50) is tabulated daily at 0^h TT on even numbered pages B30–B44. There should be no significant difference between the various methods of calculating **M**.

Values for the middle of the year, epoch J2025·5 for $\bar{\gamma}$, $\bar{\phi}$, $\bar{\psi}$, ϵ_A, and the combined bias and precession matrices are

F-W Bias and Precession Angles $\bar{\gamma}$, $\bar{\phi}$, $\bar{\psi}$, and ϵ_A

$$\bar{\gamma} = +2''67 = +0^\circ000\,742 \qquad \bar{\phi} = +843\,69''48 = +23^\circ435\,966$$

$$\bar{\psi} = +128\,4''87 = +0^\circ356\,909 \qquad \epsilon_A = 23^\circ\,26'\,09''46 = 23^\circ435\,962$$

$$\mathbf{PB} = \begin{pmatrix} +0{\cdot}999\,980\,672 & -0{\cdot}005\,702\,371 & -0{\cdot}002\,477\,500 \\ +0{\cdot}005\,702\,371 & +0{\cdot}999\,983\,741 & -0{\cdot}000\,006\,999 \\ +0{\cdot}002\,477\,500 & -0{\cdot}000\,007\,129 & +0{\cdot}999\,996\,931 \end{pmatrix}$$

where the combined frame bias and precession matrix has been calculated by ignoring the nutation terms $\Delta\psi$ and $\Delta\epsilon$.

Approximate reduction for precession and nutation

The following formulae and table may be used for the approximate reduction from the equator and equinox of J2000·0 (or from the GCRS if the small frame bias correction is ignored) to the true equator and equinox of date during 2025:

$$\alpha = \alpha_0 + f + g\ \sin(G + \alpha_0)\tan\delta_0$$
$$\delta = \delta_0 + g\ \cos(G + \alpha_0)$$

where the units of the correction to α_0 and δ_0 are seconds and arcminutes, respectively.

Date	f	g	g	G
	s	s	′	h m
Jan. –5	+76·8	33·4	8·34	23 57
5*	+76·9	33·4	8·36	23 57
15	+77·1	33·5	8·37	23 57
25	+77·1	33·5	8·38	23 57
Feb. 4	+77·2	33·6	8·39	23 56
14*	+77·4	33·6	8·40	23 56
24	+77·4	33·6	8·41	23 56
Mar. 6	+77·5	33·7	8·42	23 56
16	+77·6	33·7	8·43	23 56
26*	+77·6	33·7	8·44	23 56
Apr. 5	+77·7	33·8	8·44	23 56
15	+77·8	33·8	8·45	23 56
25	+77·8	33·8	8·46	23 56
May 5*†	+78·0	33·9	8·47	23 57
15	+78·0	33·9	8·48	23 57
25	+78·1	33·9	8·49	23 57
June 4	+78·3	34·0	8·50	23 57
14*	+78·4	34·1	8·51	23 57
24	+78·5	34·1	8·53	23 57
July 4	+78·6	34·2	8·54	23 57
July 4	+78·6	34·2	8·54	23 57
14	+78·7	34·2	8·55	23 57
24*	+78·8	34·3	8·57	23 57
Aug. 3	+78·9	34·3	8·57	23 57
13	+79·0	34·3	8·58	23 57
23	+79·1	34·4	8·60	23 57
Sept. 2*	+79·2	34·4	8·60	23 57
12	+79·2	34·4	8·61	23 56
22	+79·3	34·5	8·62	23 56
Oct. 2	+79·4	34·5	8·62	23 56
12*	+79·4	34·5	8·63	23 57
22	+79·5	34·6	8·64	23 57
Nov. 1	+79·6	34·6	8·65	23 57
11	+79·7	34·6	8·66	23 57
21*	+79·8	34·7	8·67	23 57
Dec. 1	+79·9	34·7	8·68	23 57
11	+80·0	34·8	8·70	23 57
21	+80·2	34·8	8·71	23 57
31*	+80·3	34·9	8·72	23 57

* 40-day date † 400-day date for osculation epoch

Differential precession and nutation

The corrections for differential precession and nutation are given below. These are to be added to the observed differences of the right ascension and declination, $\Delta\alpha$ and $\Delta\delta$, of an object relative to a comparison star to obtain the differences in the mean place for a standard epoch (e.g. J2000·0 or the beginning of the year). The differences $\Delta\alpha$ and $\Delta\delta$ are measured in the sense "object – comparison star", and the corrections are in the same units as $\Delta\alpha$ and $\Delta\delta$.

In the correction to right ascension the same units must be used for $\Delta\alpha$ and $\Delta\delta$.

correction to right ascension $\quad e\tan\delta\,\Delta\alpha - f\sec^2\delta\,\Delta\delta$

correction to declination $\quad f\,\Delta\alpha$

where
$$e = -\cos\alpha\,(nt + \sin\epsilon\,\Delta\psi) - \sin\alpha\,\Delta\epsilon$$
$$f = +\sin\alpha\,(nt + \sin\epsilon\,\Delta\psi) - \cos\alpha\,\Delta\epsilon$$
$$\epsilon = 23^{\circ}\!.44,\ \sin\epsilon = 0{\cdot}3977,\ n = 0{\cdot}000\,0972 \text{ radians for epoch J2025·5},$$

and t is the time in years *from* the standard epoch *to* the time of observation. $\Delta\psi$, $\Delta\epsilon$ are nutations in longitude and obliquity at the time of observation, *expressed in radians*. ($1'' = 0{\cdot}000\,004\,8481$ rad).

The errors in arc units caused by using these formulae are of order $10^{-8}\,t^2\sec^2\delta$ multiplied by the displacement in arc from the comparison star.

FOR 0^h TERRESTRIAL TIME

Date 0^h TT		NUTATION in Long. $\Delta\psi$	NUTATION in Obl. $\Delta\epsilon$	True Obl. of Ecliptic ϵ 23° 26′	**Julian Date** 0^h TT **246**	CELESTIAL INTERMEDIATE Pole $\mathcal{X}$	CELESTIAL INTERMEDIATE Pole $\mathcal{Y}$	CELESTIAL INTERMEDIATE Origin s
		″	″	″		″	″	″
Jan.	**0**	+ 0·033 81	+ 8·466 23	18·164 01	**0675·5**	+ 501·021 02	+ 7·052 54	− 0·008 73
	1	+ 0·197 39	+ 8·503 86	18·200 37	**0676·5**	+ 501·141 16	+ 7·089 50	− 0·008 77
	2	+ 0·323 59	+ 8·560 60	18·255 82	**0677·5**	+ 501·246 55	+ 7·145 65	− 0·008 84
	3	+ 0·395 18	+ 8·626 44	18·320 38	**0678·5**	+ 501·330 26	+ 7·211 02	− 0·008 92
	4	+ 0·407 42	+ 8·688 37	18·381 03	**0679·5**	+ 501·390 35	+ 7·272 62	− 0·008 99
	5	+ 0·370 58	+ 8·733 61	18·424 98	**0680·5**	+ 501·430 82	+ 7·317 63	− 0·009 04
	6	+ 0·308 21	+ 8·753 06	18·443 15	**0681·5**	+ 501·460 99	+ 7·336 91	− 0·009 07
	7	+ 0·251 36	+ 8·743 95	18·432 77	**0682·5**	+ 501·493 20	+ 7·327 62	− 0·009 05
	8	+ 0·230 53	+ 8·710 80	18·398 33	**0683·5**	+ 501·539 60	+ 7·294 21	− 0·009 01
	9	+ 0·267 50	+ 8·664 40	18·350 65	**0684·5**	+ 501·608 91	+ 7·247 42	− 0·008 95
	10	+ 0·369 18	+ 8·619 09	18·304 06	**0685·5**	+ 501·703 97	+ 7·201 58	− 0·008 90
	11	+ 0·525 52	+ 8·588 96	18·272 64	**0686·5**	+ 501·820 86	+ 7·170 79	− 0·008 86
	12	+ 0·712 30	+ 8·583 97	18·266 37	**0687·5**	+ 501·949 99	+ 7·165 08	− 0·008 85
	13	+ 0·898 16	+ 8·607 49	18·288 61	**0688·5**	+ 502·078 92	+ 7·187 87	− 0·008 87
	14	+ 1·053 46	+ 8·655 82	18·335 65	**0689·5**	+ 502·195 84	+ 7·235 54	− 0·008 93
	15	+ 1·157 69	+ 8·719 99	18·398 55	**0690·5**	+ 502·292 52	+ 7·299 18	− 0·009 01
	16	+ 1·203 07	+ 8·788 73	18·466 01	**0691·5**	+ 502·365 83	+ 7·367 51	− 0·009 09
	17	+ 1·194 10	+ 8·851 41	18·527 40	**0692·5**	+ 502·417 48	+ 7·429 89	− 0·009 16
	18	+ 1·144 09	+ 8·900 04	18·574 75	**0693·5**	+ 502·452 73	+ 7·478 33	− 0·009 22
	19	+ 1·071 07	+ 8·930 20	18·603 63	**0694·5**	+ 502·478 73	+ 7·508 34	− 0·009 26
	20	+ 0·994 07	+ 8·940 89	18·613 03	**0695·5**	+ 502·503 03	+ 7·518 89	− 0·009 27
	21	+ 0·930 60	+ 8·934 04	18·604 90	**0696·5**	+ 502·532 62	+ 7·511 88	− 0·009 26
	22	+ 0·895 14	+ 8·913 91	18·583 48	**0697·5**	+ 502·573 27	+ 7·491 52	− 0·009 23
	23	+ 0·898 07	+ 8·886 50	18·554 79	**0698·5**	+ 502·629 15	+ 7·463 79	− 0·009 20
	24	+ 0·944 76	+ 8·859 05	18·526 07	**0699·5**	+ 502·702 44	+ 7·435 94	− 0·009 16
	25	+ 1·034 52	+ 8·839 49	18·505 22	**0700·5**	+ 502·792 90	+ 7·415 86	− 0·009 14
	26	+ 1·159 47	+ 8·835 47	18·499 92	**0701·5**	+ 502·897 45	+ 7·411 26	− 0·009 13
	27	+ 1·303 92	+ 8·853 10	18·516 26	**0702·5**	+ 503·009 87	+ 7·428 25	− 0·009 15
	28	+ 1·445 32	+ 8·895 07	18·556 96	**0703·5**	+ 503·121 23	+ 7·469 60	− 0·009 20
	29	+ 1·557 83	+ 8·958 97	18·619 57	**0704·5**	+ 503·221 20	+ 7·532 94	− 0·009 27
	30	+ 1·618 72	+ 9·036 40	18·695 72	**0705·5**	+ 503·300 73	+ 7·609 92	− 0·009 37
	31	+ 1·616 27	+ 9·114 07	18·772 11	**0706·5**	+ 503·355 06	+ 7·687 29	− 0·009 46
Feb.	**1**	+ 1·555 52	+ 9·177 19	18·833 95	**0707·5**	+ 503·386 12	+ 7·750 24	− 0·009 54
	2	+ 1·458 61	+ 9·214 07	18·869 54	**0708·5**	+ 503·402 65	+ 7·787 02	− 0·009 58
	3	+ 1·358 47	+ 9·220 04	18·874 23	**0709·5**	+ 503·417 72	+ 7·792 91	− 0·009 59
	4	+ 1·288 46	+ 9·198 94	18·851 85	**0710·5**	+ 503·444 63	+ 7·771 65	− 0·009 56
	5	+ 1·272 45	+ 9·161 59	18·813 22	**0711·5**	+ 503·492 92	+ 7·734 03	− 0·009 51
	6	+ 1·318 82	+ 9·122 36	18·772 70	**0712·5**	+ 503·566 02	+ 7·694 39	− 0·009 46
	7	+ 1·419 55	+ 9·095 13	18·744 19	**0713·5**	+ 503·660 80	+ 7·666 63	− 0·009 43
	8	+ 1·553 72	+ 9·089 99	18·737 77	**0714·5**	+ 503·769 01	+ 7·660 88	− 0·009 42
	9	+ 1·693 56	+ 9·111 27	18·757 77	**0715·5**	+ 503·879 62	+ 7·681 54	− 0·009 44
	10	+ 1·811 34	+ 9·157 12	18·802 33	**0716·5**	+ 503·981 60	+ 7·726 81	− 0·009 50
	11	+ 1·885 45	+ 9·220 59	18·864 52	**0717·5**	+ 504·066 30	+ 7·789 81	− 0·009 57
	12	+ 1·904 39	+ 9·291 67	18·934 32	**0718·5**	+ 504·129 11	+ 7·860 53	− 0·009 66
	13	+ 1·867 90	+ 9·359 74	19·001 11	**0719·5**	+ 504·169 85	+ 7·928 38	− 0·009 74
	14	+ 1·785 60	+ 9·415 80	19·055 88	**0720·5**	+ 504·192 30	+ 7·984 31	− 0·009 81
	15	+ 1·673 72	+ 9·453 88	19·092 68	**0721·5**	+ 504·202 88	+ 8·022 33	− 0·009 85

FOR 0h TERRESTRIAL TIME

Date 0h TT		NUTATION in Long. Δψ	NUTATION in Obl. Δε	True Obl. of Ecliptic ε 23° 26′	Julian Date 0h TT 246	CELESTIAL INTERMEDIATE Pole 𝒳	CELESTIAL INTERMEDIATE Pole 𝒴	CELESTIAL INTERMEDIATE Origin s
		″	″	″		″	″	″
Feb.	**15**	+ 1·673 72	+ 9·453 88	19·092 68	**0721·5**	+ 504·202 88	+ 8·022 33	− 0·009 85
	16	+ 1·551 35	+ 9·471 62	19·109 14	**0722·5**	+ 504·209 18	+ 8·040 03	− 0·009 87
	17	+ 1·437 08	+ 9·470 06	19·106 29	**0723·5**	+ 504·218 59	+ 8·038 41	− 0·009 87
	18	+ 1·346 64	+ 9·452 95	19·087 91	**0724·5**	+ 504·237 39	+ 8·021 20	− 0·009 85
	19	+ 1·291 45	+ 9·426 04	19·059 71	**0725·5**	+ 504·270 15	+ 7·994 10	− 0·009 82
	20	+ 1·277 89	+ 9·396 26	19·028 65	**0726·5**	+ 504·319 46	+ 7·964 05	− 0·009 78
	21	+ 1·306 77	+ 9·371 12	19·002 23	**0727·5**	+ 504·385 68	+ 7·938 53	− 0·009 75
	22	+ 1·372 87	+ 9·357 96	18·987 79	**0728·5**	+ 504·466 77	+ 7·924 92	− 0·009 73
	23	+ 1·464 44	+ 9·363 11	18·991 65	**0729·5**	+ 504·558 09	+ 7·929 55	− 0·009 73
	24	+ 1·563 30	+ 9·390 61	19·017 87	**0730·5**	+ 504·652 44	+ 7·956 52	− 0·009 76
	25	+ 1·646 29	+ 9·440 64	19·066 62	**0731·5**	+ 504·740 60	+ 8·006 05	− 0·009 82
	26	+ 1·689 21	+ 9·508 05	19·132 75	**0732·5**	+ 504·812 93	+ 8·073 06	− 0·009 90
	27	+ 1·673 62	+ 9·581 85	19·205 26	**0733·5**	+ 504·862 01	+ 8·146 58	− 0·009 99
	28	+ 1·594 93	+ 9·646 91	19·269 04	**0734·5**	+ 504·885 94	+ 8·211 50	− 0·010 07
Mar.	**1**	+ 1·467 77	+ 9·688 24	19·309 09	**0735·5**	+ 504·890 47	+ 8·252 81	− 0·010 12
	2	+ 1·323 98	+ 9·696 63	19·316 20	**0736·5**	+ 504·888 20	+ 8·261 21	− 0·010 13
	3	+ 1·202 16	+ 9·672 57	19·290 85	**0737·5**	+ 504·894 47	+ 8·237 11	− 0·010 10
	4	+ 1·133 55	+ 9·626 23	19·243 24	**0738·5**	+ 504·921 79	+ 8·190 62	− 0·010 05
	5	+ 1·131 69	+ 9·573 46	19·189 18	**0739·5**	+ 504·975 63	+ 8·137 55	− 0·009 98
	6	+ 1·190 14	+ 9·530 17	19·144 61	**0740·5**	+ 505·053 50	+ 8·093 82	− 0·009 92
	7	+ 1·287 37	+ 9·507 89	19·121 05	**0741·5**	+ 505·146 92	+ 8·071 01	− 0·009 89
	8	+ 1·394 87	+ 9·511 70	19·123 58	**0742·5**	+ 505·244 57	+ 8·074 27	− 0·009 90
	9	+ 1·484 82	+ 9·540 27	19·150 87	**0743·5**	+ 505·335 38	+ 8·102 33	− 0·009 93
	10	+ 1·535 65	+ 9·587 34	19·196 65	**0744·5**	+ 505·410 74	+ 8·148 97	− 0·009 98
	11	+ 1·535 05	+ 9·643 70	19·251 72	**0745·5**	+ 505·465 69	+ 8·205 02	− 0·010 05
	12	+ 1·480 82	+ 9·699 28	19·306 02	**0746·5**	+ 505·499 30	+ 8·260 41	− 0·010 12
	13	+ 1·379 88	+ 9·745 00	19·350 46	**0747·5**	+ 505·514 28	+ 8·306 05	− 0·010 18
	14	+ 1·246 17	+ 9·774 15	19·378 33	**0748·5**	+ 505·516 13	+ 8·335 19	− 0·010 21
	15	+ 1·097 60	+ 9·783 22	19·386 12	**0749·5**	+ 505·511 96	+ 8·344 28	− 0·010 22
	16	+ 0·952 92	+ 9·772 10	19·373 71	**0750·5**	+ 505·509 22	+ 8·333 17	− 0·010 21
	17	+ 0·828 95	+ 9·743 74	19·344 07	**0751·5**	+ 505·514 62	+ 8·304 78	− 0·010 17
	18	+ 0·738 46	+ 9·703 45	19·302 50	**0752·5**	+ 505·533 27	+ 8·264 39	− 0·010 12
	19	+ 0·689 01	+ 9·658 05	19·255 82	**0753·5**	+ 505·568 21	+ 8·218 79	− 0·010 07
	20	+ 0·682 34	+ 9·614 95	19·211 43	**0754·5**	+ 505·620 19	+ 8·175 39	− 0·010 01
	21	+ 0·714 34	+ 9·581 35	19·176 56	**0755·5**	+ 505·687 60	+ 8·141 41	− 0·009 97
	22	+ 0·775 19	+ 9·563 46	19·157 38	**0756·5**	+ 505·766 57	+ 8·123 07	− 0·009 95
	23	+ 0·849 80	+ 9·565 59	19·158 23	**0757·5**	+ 505·851 13	+ 8·124 72	− 0·009 95
	24	+ 0·918 71	+ 9·589 15	19·180 51	**0758·5**	+ 505·933 55	+ 8·147 82	− 0·009 97
	25	+ 0·960 32	+ 9·631 48	19·221 55	**0759·5**	+ 506·005 20	+ 8·189 74	− 0·010 02
	26	+ 0·954 97	+ 9·684 93	19·273 72	**0760·5**	+ 506·058 25	+ 8·242 90	− 0·010 09
	27	+ 0·891 32	+ 9·737 02	19·324 53	**0761·5**	+ 506·088 10	+ 8·294 82	− 0·010 15
	28	+ 0·773 26	+ 9·772 59	19·358 82	**0762·5**	+ 506·096 21	+ 8·330 34	− 0·010 19
	29	+ 0·623 71	+ 9·778 41	19·363 36	**0763·5**	+ 506·091 63	+ 8·336 19	− 0·010 20
	30	+ 0·480 48	+ 9·748 92	19·332 58	**0764·5**	+ 506·089 36	+ 8·306 71	− 0·010 16
	31	+ 0·383 11	+ 9·689 67	19·272 05	**0765·5**	+ 506·105 17	+ 8·247 37	− 0·010 09
Apr.	**1**	+ 0·356 87	+ 9·615 89	19·196 99	**0766·5**	+ 506·149 19	+ 8·173 34	− 0·010 00
	2	+ 0·403 25	+ 9·546 41	19·126 23	**0767·5**	+ 506·222 11	+ 8·103 45	− 0·009 91

FOR 0^h TERRESTRIAL TIME

Date 0^h TT		NUTATION in Long. $\Delta\psi$	NUTATION in Obl. $\Delta\epsilon$	True Obl. of Ecliptic ϵ 23° 26′	Julian Date 0^h TT 246	CELESTIAL INTERMEDIATE Pole $\mathcal{X}$	CELESTIAL INTERMEDIATE Pole $\mathcal{Y}$	CELESTIAL INTERMEDIATE Origin s
		″	″	″		″	″	″
Apr.	**1**	+ 0·356 87	+ 9·615 89	19·196 99	**0766·5**	+ 506·149 19	+ 8·173 34	− 0·010 00
	2	+ 0·403 25	+ 9·546 41	19·126 23	**0767·5**	+ 506·222 11	+ 8·103 45	− 0·009 91
	3	+ 0·501 81	+ 9·496 70	19·075 23	**0768·5**	+ 506·315 90	+ 8·053 20	− 0·009 85
	4	+ 0·620 40	+ 9·474 60	19·051 85	**0769·5**	+ 506·417 82	+ 8·030 52	− 0·009 82
	5	+ 0·726 61	+ 9·479 85	19·055 81	**0770·5**	+ 506·514 96	+ 8·035 22	− 0·009 82
	6	+ 0·795 65	+ 9·506 12	19·080 81	**0771·5**	+ 506·597 45	+ 8·061 03	− 0·009 85
	7	+ 0·813 71	+ 9·543 88	19·117 29	**0772·5**	+ 506·659 71	+ 8·098 44	− 0·009 90
	8	+ 0·777 85	+ 9·582 85	19·154 97	**0773·5**	+ 506·700 54	+ 8·137 17	− 0·009 94
	9	+ 0·694 31	+ 9·613 81	19·184 65	**0774·5**	+ 506·722 36	+ 8·168 02	− 0·009 98
	10	+ 0·575 96	+ 9·629 82	19·199 38	**0775·5**	+ 506·730 24	+ 8·183 98	− 0·010 00
	11	+ 0·439 75	+ 9·626 80	19·195 08	**0776·5**	+ 506·730 92	+ 8·180 95	− 0·010 00
	12	+ 0·304 02	+ 9·603 81	19·170 80	**0777·5**	+ 506·731 67	+ 8·157 96	− 0·009 97
	13	+ 0·185 99	+ 9·562 94	19·128 66	**0778·5**	+ 506·739 36	+ 8·117 05	− 0·009 92
	14	+ 0·099 65	+ 9·508 87	19·073 29	**0779·5**	+ 506·759 59	+ 8·062 85	− 0·009 85
	15	+ 0·053 99	+ 9·448 08	19·011 22	**0780·5**	+ 506·795 95	+ 8·001 86	− 0·009 78
	16	+ 0·052 05	+ 9·388 00	18·949 86	**0781·5**	+ 506·849 71	+ 7·941 47	− 0·009 70
	17	+ 0·090 62	+ 9·335 99	18·896 57	**0782·5**	+ 506·919 63	+ 7·889 07	− 0·009 64
	18	+ 0·160 64	+ 9·298 41	18·857 71	**0783·5**	+ 507·002 14	+ 7·851 02	− 0·009 59
	19	+ 0·248 01	+ 9·279 71	18·837 73	**0784·5**	+ 507·091 65	+ 7·831 81	− 0·009 56
	20	+ 0·335 03	+ 9·281 67	18·838 40	**0785·5**	+ 507·181 15	+ 7·833 26	− 0·009 56
	21	+ 0·402 36	+ 9·302 61	18·858 07	**0786·5**	+ 507·262 92	+ 7·853 75	− 0·009 59
	22	+ 0·431 90	+ 9·336 90	18·891 07	**0787·5**	+ 507·329 73	+ 7·887 66	− 0·009 63
	23	+ 0·411 00	+ 9·374 81	18·927 70	**0788·5**	+ 507·376 51	+ 7·925 30	− 0·009 67
	24	+ 0·337 57	+ 9·403 49	18·955 10	**0789·5**	+ 507·402 33	+ 7·953 84	− 0·009 71
	25	+ 0·224 69	+ 9·409 60	18·959 93	**0790·5**	+ 507·412 34	+ 7·959 89	− 0·009 71
	26	+ 0·101 60	+ 9·383 66	18·932 70	**0791·5**	+ 507·418 10	+ 7·933 91	− 0·009 68
	27	+ 0·007 44	+ 9·324 81	18·872 57	**0792·5**	+ 507·435 18	+ 7·874 96	− 0·009 61
	28	− 0·022 54	+ 9·243 06	18·789 54	**0793·5**	+ 507·477 67	+ 7·792 97	− 0·009 51
	29	+ 0·027 70	+ 9·156 59	18·701 78	**0794·5**	+ 507·552 03	+ 7·706 08	− 0·009 40
	30	+ 0·147 82	+ 9·084 69	18·628 60	**0795·5**	+ 507·654 27	+ 7·633 60	− 0·009 31
May	**1**	+ 0·306 44	+ 9·040 53	18·583 16	**0796·5**	+ 507·771 99	+ 7·588 76	− 0·009 25
	2	+ 0·464 96	+ 9·027 55	18·568 90	**0797·5**	+ 507·889 83	+ 7·575 12	− 0·009 23
	3	+ 0·590 73	+ 9·040 60	18·580 67	**0798·5**	+ 507·994 80	+ 7·587 58	− 0·009 25
	4	+ 0·664 22	+ 9·069 45	18·608 23	**0799·5**	+ 508·079 07	+ 7·615 94	− 0·009 28
	5	+ 0·679 85	+ 9·102 56	18·640 06	**0800·5**	+ 508·140 34	+ 7·648 71	− 0·009 32
	6	+ 0·643 31	+ 9·129 69	18·665 91	**0801·5**	+ 508·180 83	+ 7·675 61	− 0·009 35
	7	+ 0·567 72	+ 9·143 24	18·678 17	**0802·5**	+ 508·205 71	+ 7·689 01	− 0·009 37
	8	+ 0·470 24	+ 9·138 70	18·672 36	**0803·5**	+ 508·221 78	+ 7·684 39	− 0·009 36
	9	+ 0·369 29	+ 9·114 71	18·647 08	**0804·5**	+ 508·236 37	+ 7·660 31	− 0·009 33
	10	+ 0·282 41	+ 9·072 78	18·603 87	**0805·5**	+ 508·256 44	+ 7·618 27	− 0·009 28
	11	+ 0·224 34	+ 9·016 96	18·546 77	**0806·5**	+ 508·287 90	+ 7·562 27	− 0·009 21
	12	+ 0·205 45	+ 8·953 28	18·481 81	**0807·5**	+ 508·334 89	+ 7·498 32	− 0·009 13
	13	+ 0·230 41	+ 8·889 01	18·416 25	**0808·5**	+ 508·399 33	+ 7·433 68	− 0·009 05
	14	+ 0·297 51	+ 8·831 67	18·357 63	**0809·5**	+ 508·480 56	+ 7·375 88	− 0·008 98
	15	+ 0·398 60	+ 8·788 05	18·312 73	**0810·5**	+ 508·575 39	+ 7·331 72	− 0·008 92
	16	+ 0·519 97	+ 8·763 08	18·286 47	**0811·5**	+ 508·678 40	+ 7·306 16	− 0·008 89
	17	+ 0·644 01	+ 8·758 92	18·281 04	**0812·5**	+ 508·782 58	+ 7·301 41	− 0·008 88

FOR 0^h TERRESTRIAL TIME

Date 0^h TT		NUTATION in Long. $\Delta\psi$	NUTATION in Obl. $\Delta\epsilon$	True Obl. of Ecliptic ϵ 23° 26′	**Julian Date** 0^h TT **246**	CELESTIAL INTERMEDIATE Pole $\mathcal{X}$	CELESTIAL INTERMEDIATE Pole $\mathcal{Y}$	CELESTIAL INTERMEDIATE Origin s
		″	″	″		″	″	″
May	**17**	+ 0·644 01	+ 8·758 92	18·281 04	**0812·5**	+ 508·782 58	+ 7·301 41	− 0·008 88
	18	+ 0·751 64	+ 8·774 36	18·295 19	**0813·5**	+ 508·880 35	+ 7·316 30	− 0·008 89
	19	+ 0·825 33	+ 8·804 47	18·324 01	**0814·5**	+ 508·964 70	+ 7·345 92	− 0·008 93
	20	+ 0·852 60	+ 8·840 79	18·359 05	**0815·5**	+ 509·030 62	+ 7·381 87	− 0·008 97
	21	+ 0·829 67	+ 8·872 24	18·389 23	**0816·5**	+ 509·076 55	+ 7·413 07	− 0·009 01
	22	+ 0·764 81	+ 8·886 94	18·402 64	**0817·5**	+ 509·105 71	+ 7·427 59	− 0·009 03
	23	+ 0·679 76	+ 8·875 03	18·389 45	**0818·5**	+ 509·126 68	+ 7·415 57	− 0·009 01
	24	+ 0·607 20	+ 8·832 35	18·345 49	**0819·5**	+ 509·152 45	+ 7·372 74	− 0·008 96
	25	+ 0·582 71	+ 8·763 38	18·275 23	**0820·5**	+ 509·197 19	+ 7·303 51	− 0·008 87
	26	+ 0·632 17	+ 8·681 60	18·192 17	**0821·5**	+ 509·271 26	+ 7·221 30	− 0·008 77
	27	+ 0·759 91	+ 8·605 72	18·115 01	**0822·5**	+ 509·376 51	+ 7·144 82	− 0·008 67
	28	+ 0·945 33	+ 8·552 84	18·060 85	**0823·5**	+ 509·504 83	+ 7·091 22	− 0·008 61
	29	+ 1·150 78	+ 8·532 15	18·038 87	**0824·5**	+ 509·641 31	+ 7·069 75	− 0·008 58
	30	+ 1·336 36	+ 8·542 60	18·048 04	**0825·5**	+ 509·770 05	+ 7·079 46	− 0·008 59
	31	+ 1·472 80	+ 8·575 09	18·079 25	**0826·5**	+ 509·879 37	+ 7·111 34	− 0·008 62
June	**1**	+ 1·547 24	+ 8·616 95	18·119 83	**0827·5**	+ 509·964 09	+ 7·152 72	− 0·008 67
	2	+ 1·561 97	+ 8·656 00	18·157 60	**0828·5**	+ 510·025 04	+ 7·191 42	− 0·008 72
	3	+ 1·529 73	+ 8·682 97	18·183 29	**0829·5**	+ 510·067 24	+ 7·218 15	− 0·008 75
	4	+ 1·468 68	+ 8·692 35	18·191 38	**0830·5**	+ 510·097 88	+ 7·227 35	− 0·008 76
	5	+ 1·398 38	+ 8·682 20	18·179 95	**0831·5**	+ 510·124 73	+ 7·217 05	− 0·008 75
	6	+ 1·337 27	+ 8·653 70	18·150 17	**0832·5**	+ 510·155 13	+ 7·188 38	− 0·008 71
	7	+ 1·300 95	+ 8·610 54	18·105 72	**0833·5**	+ 510·195 31	+ 7·144 98	− 0·008 66
	8	+ 1·300 89	+ 8·558 34	18·052 24	**0834·5**	+ 510·249 86	+ 7·092 47	− 0·008 59
	9	+ 1·343 36	+ 8·504 04	17·996 66	**0835·5**	+ 510·321 31	+ 7·037 77	− 0·008 53
	10	+ 1·428 56	+ 8·455 20	17·946 54	**0836·5**	+ 510·409 79	+ 6·988 42	− 0·008 46
	11	+ 1·550 10	+ 8·418 97	17·909 02	**0837·5**	+ 510·512 80	+ 6·951 60	− 0·008 42
	12	+ 1·695 32	+ 8·401 00	17·889 77	**0838·5**	+ 510·625 33	+ 6·932 98	− 0·008 39
	13	+ 1·846 61	+ 8·404 30	17·891 79	**0839·5**	+ 510·740 39	+ 6·935 63	− 0·008 39
	14	+ 1·984 04	+ 8·428 34	17·914 55	**0840·5**	+ 510·850 06	+ 6·959 05	− 0·008 42
	15	+ 2·088 81	+ 8·468 64	17·953 57	**0841·5**	+ 510·946 83	+ 6·998 80	− 0·008 47
	16	+ 2·147 26	+ 8·517 08	18·000 72	**0842·5**	+ 511·025 23	+ 7·046 79	− 0·008 52
	17	+ 2·154 54	+ 8·563 01	18·045 37	**0843·5**	+ 511·083 26	+ 7·092 38	− 0·008 58
	18	+ 2·117 14	+ 8·595 15	18·076 23	**0844·5**	+ 511·123 44	+ 7·124 30	− 0·008 62
	19	+ 2·053 52	+ 8·604 09	18·083 89	**0845·5**	+ 511·153 05	+ 7·133 07	− 0·008 63
	20	+ 1·991 78	+ 8·584 97	18·063 48	**0846·5**	+ 511·183 26	+ 7·113 77	− 0·008 60
	21	+ 1·964 02	+ 8·539 75	18·016 98	**0847·5**	+ 511·226 83	+ 7·068 30	− 0·008 55
	22	+ 1·997 48	+ 8·477 98	17·953 93	**0848·5**	+ 511·294 65	+ 7·006 15	− 0·008 47
	23	+ 2·104 80	+ 8·415 10	17·889 77	**0849·5**	+ 511·391 85	+ 6·942 71	− 0·008 39
	24	+ 2·277 63	+ 8·367 98	17·841 37	**0850·5**	+ 511·515 20	+ 6·894 89	− 0·008 33
	25	+ 2·487 71	+ 8·349 27	17·821 38	**0851·5**	+ 511·653 52	+ 6·875 39	− 0·008 30
	26	+ 2·696 30	+ 8·363 03	17·833 85	**0852·5**	+ 511·791 43	+ 6·888 36	− 0·008 32
	27	+ 2·867 44	+ 8·404 02	17·873 55	**0853·5**	+ 511·914 61	+ 6·928 64	− 0·008 36
	28	+ 2·978 64	+ 8·460 59	17·928 85	**0854·5**	+ 512·014 03	+ 6·984 64	− 0·008 43
	29	+ 3·024 50	+ 8·519 24	17·986 22	**0855·5**	+ 512·087 48	+ 7·042 88	− 0·008 50
	30	+ 3·014 09	+ 8·568 45	18·034 14	**0856·5**	+ 512·138 49	+ 7·091 79	− 0·008 56
July	**1**	+ 2·965 27	+ 8·600 66	18·065 07	**0857·5**	+ 512·174 13	+ 7·123 80	− 0·008 60
	2	+ 2·899 07	+ 8·612 71	18·075 84	**0858·5**	+ 512·202 73	+ 7·135 69	− 0·008 62

FOR 0^h TERRESTRIAL TIME

Date		NUTATION		True Obl.	Julian	CELESTIAL INTERMEDIATE		
		in Long.	in Obl.	of Ecliptic	Date	Pole		Origin
0^h TT		$\Delta\psi$	$\Delta\epsilon$	ϵ	0^h TT	$\mathcal{X}$	$\mathcal{Y}$	s
				23° 26′	**246**			
		″	″	″		″	″	″
July	**1**	+ 2·965 27	+ 8·600 66	18·065 07	**0857·5**	+ 512·174 13	+ 7·123 80	− 0·008 60
	2	+ 2·899 07	+ 8·612 71	18·075 84	**0858·5**	+ 512·202 73	+ 7·135 69	− 0·008 62
	3	+ 2·835 69	+ 8·605 17	18·067 01	**0859·5**	+ 512·232 35	+ 7·127 97	− 0·008 61
	4	+ 2·792 17	+ 8·581 44	18·042 00	**0860·5**	+ 512·269 78	+ 7·104 03	− 0·008 57
	5	+ 2·781 22	+ 8·546 95	18·006 23	**0861·5**	+ 512·320 09	+ 7·069 25	− 0·008 53
	6	+ 2·810 47	+ 8·508 42	17·966 42	**0862·5**	+ 512·386 38	+ 7·030 34	− 0·008 48
	7	+ 2·881 91	+ 8·473 23	17·929 95	**0863·5**	+ 512·469 46	+ 6·994 68	− 0·008 44
	8	+ 2·991 37	+ 8·448 69	17·904 12	**0864·5**	+ 512·567 73	+ 6·969 57	− 0·008 40
	9	+ 3·128 30	+ 8·441 04	17·895 19	**0865·5**	+ 512·677 02	+ 6·961 30	− 0·008 39
	10	+ 3·276 38	+ 8·454 39	17·907 26	**0866·5**	+ 512·790 86	+ 6·974 00	− 0·008 40
	11	+ 3·415 38	+ 8·489 47	17·941 06	**0867·5**	+ 512·901 22	+ 7·008 44	− 0·008 45
	12	+ 3·524 58	+ 8·542 81	17·993 12	**0868·5**	+ 512·999 83	+ 7·061 22	− 0·008 51
	13	+ 3·587 37	+ 8·606 74	18·055 76	**0869·5**	+ 513·080 04	+ 7·124 69	− 0·008 59
	14	+ 3·596 02	+ 8·670 37	18·118 11	**0870·5**	+ 513·138 72	+ 7·187 98	− 0·008 66
	15	+ 3·554 95	+ 8·721 86	18·168 31	**0871·5**	+ 513·177 55	+ 7·239 25	− 0·008 73
	16	+ 3·481 32	+ 8·751 21	18·196 38	**0872·5**	+ 513·203 30	+ 7·268 45	− 0·008 76
	17	+ 3·402 07	+ 8·753 07	18·196 97	**0873·5**	+ 513·226 66	+ 7·270 18	− 0·008 77
	18	+ 3·347 92	+ 8·728 62	18·171 23	**0874·5**	+ 513·259 85	+ 7·245 54	− 0·008 73
	19	+ 3·345 47	+ 8·685 89	18·127 22	**0875·5**	+ 513·313 50	+ 7·202 50	− 0·008 68
	20	+ 3·409 48	+ 8·638 18	18·078 22	**0876·5**	+ 513·393 56	+ 7·154 33	− 0·008 62
	21	+ 3·537 68	+ 8·600 77	18·039 53	**0877·5**	+ 513·499 20	+ 7·116 31	− 0·008 57
	22	+ 3·710 20	+ 8·586 62	18·024 10	**0878·5**	+ 513·622 61	+ 7·101 46	− 0·008 55
	23	+ 3·894 78	+ 8·602 50	18·038 70	**0879·5**	+ 513·750 99	+ 7·116 60	− 0·008 57
	24	+ 4·056 30	+ 8·647 04	18·081 95	**0880·5**	+ 513·870 36	+ 7·160 45	− 0·008 62
	25	+ 4·167 06	+ 8·711 60	18·145 24	**0881·5**	+ 513·969 66	+ 7·224 45	− 0·008 70
	26	+ 4·213 67	+ 8·783 51	18·215 86	**0882·5**	+ 514·043 48	+ 7·295 93	− 0·008 78
	27	+ 4·198 42	+ 8·849 97	18·281 04	**0883·5**	+ 514·092 66	+ 7·362 11	− 0·008 87
	28	+ 4·135 72	+ 8·901 23	18·331 02	**0884·5**	+ 514·122 89	+ 7·413 20	− 0·008 93
	29	+ 4·046 40	+ 8·932 05	18·360 55	**0885·5**	+ 514·142 41	+ 7·443 91	− 0·008 97
	30	+ 3·952 26	+ 8·941 65	18·368 87	**0886·5**	+ 514·159 89	+ 7·453 41	− 0·008 98
	31	+ 3·872 42	+ 8·932 83	18·358 77	**0887·5**	+ 514·182 95	+ 7·444 45	− 0·008 97
Aug.	**1**	+ 3·821 34	+ 8·910 82	18·335 48	**0888·5**	+ 514·217 38	+ 7·422 24	− 0·008 94
	2	+ 3·808 07	+ 8·882 27	18·305 64	**0889·5**	+ 514·266 81	+ 7·393 41	− 0·008 90
	3	+ 3·836 03	+ 8·854 47	18·276 57	**0890·5**	+ 514·332 64	+ 7·365 23	− 0·008 86
	4	+ 3·902 93	+ 8·834 70	18·255 51	**0891·5**	+ 514·414 01	+ 7·344 99	− 0·008 84
	5	+ 4·000 67	+ 8·829 46	18·248 99	**0892·5**	+ 514·507 72	+ 7·339 21	− 0·008 83
	6	+ 4·115 40	+ 8·843 66	18·261 90	**0893·5**	+ 514·608 31	+ 7·352 83	− 0·008 84
	7	+ 4·228 50	+ 8·879 45	18·296 41	**0894·5**	+ 514·708 37	+ 7·388 05	− 0·008 89
	8	+ 4·318 80	+ 8·935 14	18·350 82	**0895·5**	+ 514·799 48	+ 7·443 22	− 0·008 95
	9	+ 4·366 72	+ 9·004 49	18·418 88	**0896·5**	+ 514·873 81	+ 7·512 14	− 0·009 04
	10	+ 4·359 73	+ 9·077 04	18·490 15	**0897·5**	+ 514·926 31	+ 7·584 38	− 0·009 13
	11	+ 4·297 50	+ 9·140 02	18·551 86	**0898·5**	+ 514·956 79	+ 7·647 20	− 0·009 21
	12	+ 4·194 44	+ 9·181 63	18·592 18	**0899·5**	+ 514·970 91	+ 7·688 72	− 0·009 26
	13	+ 4·077 40	+ 9·194 63	18·603 90	**0900·5**	+ 514·979 30	+ 7·701 67	− 0·009 27
	14	+ 3·978 79	+ 9·178 99	18·586 98	**0901·5**	+ 514·994 86	+ 7·685 94	− 0·009 25
	15	+ 3·927 19	+ 9·142 26	18·548 96	**0902·5**	+ 515·028 99	+ 7·649 01	− 0·009 21
	16	+ 3·939 03	+ 9·097 52	18·502 94	**0903·5**	+ 515·088 31	+ 7·603 93	− 0·009 15

FOR 0^h TERRESTRIAL TIME

Date 0^h TT	NUTATION in Long. $\Delta\psi$	NUTATION in Obl. $\Delta\epsilon$	True Obl. of Ecliptic ϵ 23° 26′	**Julian Date 0^h TT 246**	CELESTIAL INTERMEDIATE Pole $\mathcal{X}$	CELESTIAL INTERMEDIATE Pole $\mathcal{Y}$	CELESTIAL INTERMEDIATE Origin s
	″	″	″		″	″	″
Aug. 16	+ 3·939 03	+ 9·097 52	18·502 94	**0903·5**	+ 515·088 31	+ 7·603 93	− 0·009 15
17	+ 4·014 01	+ 9·059 77	18·463 90	**0904·5**	+ 515·172 79	+ 7·565 69	− 0·009 10
18	+ 4·135 55	+ 9·041 84	18·444 70	**0905·5**	+ 515·275 90	+ 7·547 17	− 0·009 07
19	+ 4·275 59	+ 9·051 21	18·452 79	**0906·5**	+ 515·386 53	+ 7·555 91	− 0·009 08
20	+ 4·402 18	+ 9·088 37	18·488 66	**0907·5**	+ 515·491 97	+ 7·592 46	− 0·009 13
21	+ 4·487 66	+ 9·147 12	18·546 13	**0908·5**	+ 515·581 17	+ 7·650 70	− 0·009 20
22	+ 4·515 04	+ 9·216 70	18·614 43	**0909·5**	+ 515·647 33	+ 7·719 89	− 0·009 28
23	+ 4·480 97	+ 9·284 78	18·681 23	**0910·5**	+ 515·689 04	+ 7·787 74	− 0·009 37
24	+ 4·394 82	+ 9·340 59	18·735 75	**0911·5**	+ 515·709 97	+ 7·843 42	− 0·009 44
25	+ 4·274 72	+ 9·376 97	18·770 85	**0912·5**	+ 515·717 28	+ 7·879 77	− 0·009 48
26	+ 4·142 38	+ 9·391 31	18·783 91	**0913·5**	+ 515·719 59	+ 7·894 09	− 0·009 50
27	+ 4·018 53	+ 9·385 11	18·776 43	**0914·5**	+ 515·725 16	+ 7·887 86	− 0·009 49
28	+ 3·919 73	+ 9·363 04	18·753 07	**0915·5**	+ 515·740 61	+ 7·865 69	− 0·009 46
29	+ 3·856 85	+ 9·331 62	18·720 37	**0916·5**	+ 515·770 29	+ 7·834 11	− 0·009 42
30	+ 3·834 75	+ 9·298 21	18·685 68	**0917·5**	+ 515·816 18	+ 7·800 43	− 0·009 38
31	+ 3·852 47	+ 9·270 11	18·656 30	**0918·5**	+ 515·877 93	+ 7·771 97	− 0·009 34
Sept. 1	+ 3·903 62	+ 9·253 91	18·638 81	**0919·5**	+ 515·953 06	+ 7·755 34	− 0·009 32
2	+ 3·976 75	+ 9·254 83	18·638 45	**0920·5**	+ 516·037 02	+ 7·755 77	− 0·009 32
3	+ 4·055 87	+ 9·275 94	18·658 28	**0921·5**	+ 516·123 48	+ 7·776 39	− 0·009 34
4	+ 4·121 72	+ 9·317 23	18·698 29	**0922·5**	+ 516·204 78	+ 7·817 21	− 0·009 39
5	+ 4·154 29	+ 9·374 66	18·754 44	**0923·5**	+ 516·272 94	+ 7·874 25	− 0·009 46
6	+ 4·137 28	+ 9·439 70	18·818 19	**0924·5**	+ 516·321 41	+ 7·939 01	− 0·009 54
7	+ 4·063 82	+ 9·500 06	18·877 27	**0925·5**	+ 516·347 41	+ 7·999 22	− 0·009 62
8	+ 3·941 62	+ 9·542 31	18·918 24	**0926·5**	+ 516·353 92	+ 8·041 43	− 0·009 67
9	+ 3·794 26	+ 9·555 94	18·930 59	**0927·5**	+ 516·350 26	+ 8·055 09	− 0·009 69
10	+ 3·655 92	+ 9·537 61	18·910 98	**0928·5**	+ 516·350 00	+ 8·036 75	− 0·009 67
11	+ 3·560 61	+ 9·493 09	18·865 17	**0929·5**	+ 516·366 70	+ 7·992 14	− 0·009 61
12	+ 3·530 34	+ 9·435 74	18·806 54	**0930·5**	+ 516·409 20	+ 7·934 54	− 0·009 54
13	+ 3·568 00	+ 9·382 01	18·751 53	**0931·5**	+ 516·478 74	+ 7·880 41	− 0·009 47
14	+ 3·657 72	+ 9·346 27	18·714 50	**0932·5**	+ 516·569 09	+ 7·844 14	− 0·009 42
15	+ 3·771 24	+ 9·336 99	18·703 94	**0933·5**	+ 516·669 06	+ 7·834 29	− 0·009 41
16	+ 3·876 71	+ 9·355 40	18·721 07	**0934·5**	+ 516·765 99	+ 7·852 14	− 0·009 43
17	+ 3·946 69	+ 9·396 21	18·760 60	**0935·5**	+ 516·848 93	+ 7·892 47	− 0·009 48
18	+ 3·963 52	+ 9·449 72	18·812 82	**0936·5**	+ 516·910 80	+ 7·945 62	− 0·009 54
19	+ 3·921 65	+ 9·504 44	18·866 26	**0937·5**	+ 516·949 33	+ 8·000 12	− 0·009 61
20	+ 3·827 16	+ 9·549 68	18·910 22	**0938·5**	+ 516·966 88	+ 8·045 26	− 0·009 67
21	+ 3·695 09	+ 9·577 50	18·936 76	**0939·5**	+ 516·969 38	+ 8·073 06	− 0·009 70
22	+ 3·545 51	+ 9·583 83	18·941 81	**0940·5**	+ 516·964 79	+ 8·079 42	− 0·009 71
23	+ 3·399 30	+ 9·568 73	18·925 42	**0941·5**	+ 516·961 42	+ 8·064 34	− 0·009 69
24	+ 3·274 52	+ 9·535 76	18·891 18	**0942·5**	+ 516·966 47	+ 8·031 34	− 0·009 65
25	+ 3·184 04	+ 9·490 99	18·845 12	**0943·5**	+ 516·985 09	+ 7·986 46	− 0·009 59
26	+ 3·134 48	+ 9·441 73	18·794 58	**0944·5**	+ 517·019 97	+ 7·937 00	− 0·009 53
27	+ 3·126 17	+ 9·395 46	18·747 03	**0945·5**	+ 517·071 26	+ 7·890 44	− 0·009 47
28	+ 3·153 76	+ 9·358 96	18·709 24	**0946·5**	+ 517·136 90	+ 7·853 55	− 0·009 42
29	+ 3·207 08	+ 9·337 61	18·686 61	**0947·5**	+ 517·212 85	+ 7·831 76	− 0·009 39
30	+ 3·272 04	+ 9·334 84	18·682 56	**0948·5**	+ 517·293 55	+ 7·828 52	− 0·009 39
Oct. 1	+ 3·331 72	+ 9·351 53	18·697 97	**0949·5**	+ 517·372 25	+ 7·844 76	− 0·009 41

FOR 0h TERRESTRIAL TIME

Date 0h TT		NUTATION in Long. $\Delta\psi$	NUTATION in Obl. $\Delta\epsilon$	True Obl. of Ecliptic ϵ 23° 26′	**Julian Date** 0h TT **246**	CELESTIAL INTERMEDIATE Pole $\mathcal{X}$	CELESTIAL INTERMEDIATE Pole $\mathcal{Y}$	CELESTIAL INTERMEDIATE Origin s
		″	″	″		″	″	″
Oct.	**1**	+ 3·331 72	+ 9·351 53	18·697 97	**0949·5**	+ 517·372 25	+ 7·844 76	− 0·009 41
	2	+ 3·367 96	+ 9·385 33	18·730 49	**0950·5**	+ 517·441 73	+ 7·878 16	− 0·009 45
	3	+ 3·364 15	+ 9·430 10	18·773 97	**0951·5**	+ 517·495 34	+ 7·922 61	− 0·009 50
	4	+ 3·309 36	+ 9·475 79	18·818 38	**0952·5**	+ 517·528 68	+ 7·968 11	− 0·009 56
	5	+ 3·203 66	+ 9·509 64	18·850 94	**0953·5**	+ 517·541 71	+ 8·001 89	− 0·009 60
	6	+ 3·062 38	+ 9·519 05	18·859 08	**0954·5**	+ 517·540 44	+ 8·011 31	− 0·009 61
	7	+ 2·915 93	+ 9·496 10	18·834 84	**0955·5**	+ 517·536 92	+ 7·988 38	− 0·009 58
	8	+ 2·802 20	+ 9·441 75	18·779 20	**0956·5**	+ 517·546 24	+ 7·933 97	− 0·009 51
	9	+ 2·752 89	+ 9·367 03	18·703 21	**0957·5**	+ 517·581 07	+ 7·859 05	− 0·009 42
	10	+ 2·780 36	+ 9·289 69	18·624 58	**0958·5**	+ 517·646 42	+ 7·781 33	− 0·009 32
	11	+ 2·872 96	+ 9·227 51	18·561 13	**0959·5**	+ 517·737 76	+ 7·718 62	− 0·009 24
	12	+ 3·000 81	+ 9·192 30	18·524 63	**0960·5**	+ 517·843 28	+ 7·682 80	− 0·009 20
	13	+ 3·127 71	+ 9·187 06	18·518 11	**0961·5**	+ 517·948 60	+ 7·676 95	− 0·009 19
	14	+ 3·222 35	+ 9·206 87	18·536 64	**0962·5**	+ 518·041 23	+ 7·696 23	− 0·009 21
	15	+ 3·264 89	+ 9·241 80	18·570 28	**0963·5**	+ 518·113 22	+ 7·730 74	− 0·009 25
	16	+ 3·248 77	+ 9·280 17	18·607 37	**0964·5**	+ 518·161 90	+ 7·768 83	− 0·009 30
	17	+ 3·179 18	+ 9·311 21	18·637 12	**0965·5**	+ 518·189 27	+ 7·799 70	− 0·009 33
	18	+ 3·069 92	+ 9·326 73	18·651 37	**0966·5**	+ 518·200 77	+ 7·815 16	− 0·009 35
	19	+ 2·939 80	+ 9·322 09	18·645 44	**0967·5**	+ 518·203 86	+ 7·810 50	− 0·009 35
	20	+ 2·809 09	+ 9·296 38	18·618 45	**0968·5**	+ 518·206 59	+ 7·784 77	− 0·009 32
	21	+ 2·696 31	+ 9·252 14	18·572 93	**0969·5**	+ 518·216 34	+ 7·740 48	− 0·009 26
	22	+ 2·615 74	+ 9·194 65	18·514 15	**0970·5**	+ 518·238 83	+ 7·682 85	− 0·009 19
	23	+ 2·575 85	+ 9·130 86	18·449 09	**0971·5**	+ 518·277 47	+ 7·618 84	− 0·009 11
	24	+ 2·578 60	+ 9·068 34	18·385 28	**0972·5**	+ 518·333 07	+ 7·556 00	− 0·009 03
	25	+ 2·619 76	+ 9·014 16	18·329 82	**0973·5**	+ 518·404 00	+ 7·501 41	− 0·008 96
	26	+ 2·689 82	+ 8·974 06	18·288 44	**0974·5**	+ 518·486 51	+ 7·460 83	− 0·008 90
	27	+ 2·775 32	+ 8·951 77	18·264 87	**0975·5**	+ 518·575 25	+ 7·438 02	− 0·008 87
	28	+ 2·860 32	+ 8·948 52	18·260 34	**0976·5**	+ 518·663 92	+ 7·434 26	− 0·008 87
	29	+ 2·928 18	+ 8·962 70	18·273 23	**0977·5**	+ 518·745 86	+ 7·447 97	− 0·008 88
	30	+ 2·963 51	+ 8·989 58	18·298 83	**0978·5**	+ 518·814 94	+ 7·474 44	− 0·008 91
	31	+ 2·954 99	+ 9·021 24	18·329 21	**0979·5**	+ 518·866 60	+ 7·505 81	− 0·008 95
Nov.	**1**	+ 2·898 87	+ 9·047 08	18·353 76	**0980·5**	+ 518·899 30	+ 7·531 45	− 0·008 98
	2	+ 2·802 94	+ 9·055 27	18·360 67	**0981·5**	+ 518·916 06	+ 7·539 55	− 0·008 99
	3	+ 2·688 96	+ 9·035 77	18·339 89	**0982·5**	+ 518·925 48	+ 7·519 99	− 0·008 97
	4	+ 2·590 76	+ 8·984 38	18·287 21	**0983·5**	+ 518·940 99	+ 7·468 51	− 0·008 90
	5	+ 2·545 29	+ 8·906 28	18·207 83	**0984·5**	+ 518·977 32	+ 7·390 19	− 0·008 81
	6	+ 2·578 18	+ 8·816 31	18·116 58	**0985·5**	+ 519·044 76	+ 7·299 84	− 0·008 69
	7	+ 2·691 10	+ 8·734 30	18·033 29	**0986·5**	+ 519·144 07	+ 7·217 25	− 0·008 59
	8	+ 2·859 60	+ 8·677 32	17·975 03	**0987·5**	+ 519·265 63	+ 7·159 56	− 0·008 51
	9	+ 3·043 41	+ 8·653 36	17·949 79	**0988·5**	+ 519·393 47	+ 7·134 86	− 0·008 48
	10	+ 3·202 47	+ 8·659 85	17·954 99	**0989·5**	+ 519·511 64	+ 7·140 66	− 0·008 48
	11	+ 3·309 24	+ 8·686 59	17·980 45	**0990·5**	+ 519·609 13	+ 7·166 84	− 0·008 51
	12	+ 3·353 00	+ 8·720 47	18·013 05	**0991·5**	+ 519·681 61	+ 7·200 30	− 0·008 55
	13	+ 3·337 93	+ 8·749 29	18·040 59	**0992·5**	+ 519·730 65	+ 7·228 84	− 0·008 59
	14	+ 3·278 23	+ 8·764 03	18·054 04	**0993·5**	+ 519·761 86	+ 7·243 39	− 0·008 61
	15	+ 3·193 29	+ 8·759 56	18·048 29	**0994·5**	+ 519·782 92	+ 7·238 80	− 0·008 60
	16	+ 3·103 63	+ 8·734 59	18·022 04	**0995·5**	+ 519·801 98	+ 7·213 72	− 0·008 57

FOR 0^h TERRESTRIAL TIME

Date 0^h TT		NUTATION in Long. $\Delta\psi$	NUTATION in Obl. $\Delta\epsilon$	True Obl. of Ecliptic ϵ 23° 26′	**Julian Date** 0^h TT **246**	CELESTIAL INTERMEDIATE Pole $\mathcal{X}$	CELESTIAL INTERMEDIATE Pole $\mathcal{Y}$	CELESTIAL INTERMEDIATE Origin s
		″	″	″		″	″	″
Nov.	**16**	+ 3·103 63	+ 8·734 59	18·022 04	**0995·5**	+ 519·801 98	+ 7·213 72	− 0·008 57
	17	+ 3·028 09	+ 8·691 15	17·977 32	**0996·5**	+ 519·826 55	+ 7·170 13	− 0·008 51
	18	+ 2·981 72	+ 8·633 89	17·918 78	**0997·5**	+ 519·862 65	+ 7·112 66	− 0·008 44
	19	+ 2·974 33	+ 8·569 29	17·852 89	**0998·5**	+ 519·914 20	+ 7·047 76	− 0·008 36
	20	+ 3·009 62	+ 8·504 70	17·787 02	**0999·5**	+ 519·982 74	+ 6·982 78	− 0·008 28
	21	+ 3·084 93	+ 8·447 42	17·728 45	**1000·5**	+ 520·067 23	+ 6·925 00	− 0·008 20
	22	+ 3·191 73	+ 8·403 61	17·683 37	**1001·5**	+ 520·164 32	+ 6·880 63	− 0·008 14
	23	+ 3·316 88	+ 8·377 54	17·656 02	**1002·5**	+ 520·268 82	+ 6·853 95	− 0·008 11
	24	+ 3·444 33	+ 8·370 89	17·648 08	**1003·5**	+ 520·374 35	+ 6·846 69	− 0·008 10
	25	+ 3·557 36	+ 8·382 41	17·658 32	**1004·5**	+ 520·474 24	+ 6·857 62	− 0·008 11
	26	+ 3·640 81	+ 8·407 86	17·682 49	**1005·5**	+ 520·562 45	+ 6·882 56	− 0·008 14
	27	+ 3·683 60	+ 8·440 24	17·713 59	**1006·5**	+ 520·634 53	+ 6·914 53	− 0·008 18
	28	+ 3·681 24	+ 8·470 38	17·742 44	**1007·5**	+ 520·688 63	+ 6·944 35	− 0·008 22
	29	+ 3·638 31	+ 8·488 03	17·758 81	**1008·5**	+ 520·726 53	+ 6·961 78	− 0·008 24
	30	+ 3·570 35	+ 8·483 70	17·753 20	**1009·5**	+ 520·754 34	+ 6·957 29	− 0·008 23
Dec.	**1**	+ 3·503 76	+ 8·451 39	17·719 60	**1010·5**	+ 520·782 54	+ 6·924 81	− 0·008 19
	2	+ 3·471 84	+ 8·391 57	17·658 50	**1011·5**	+ 520·824 36	+ 6·864 74	− 0·008 11
	3	+ 3·505 56	+ 8·313 31	17·578 96	**1012·5**	+ 520·892 19	+ 6·786 09	− 0·008 01
	4	+ 3·620 93	+ 8·233 30	17·497 67	**1013·5**	+ 520·992 48	+ 6·705 49	− 0·007 91
	5	+ 3·809 07	+ 8·170 68	17·433 76	**1014·5**	+ 521·121 82	+ 6·642 12	− 0·007 83
	6	+ 4·036 79	+ 8·139 61	17·401 42	**1015·5**	+ 521·267 09	+ 6·610 21	− 0·007 78
	7	+ 4·259 07	+ 8·143 70	17·404 22	**1016·5**	+ 521·410 40	+ 6·613 46	− 0·007 79
	8	+ 4·436 49	+ 8·175 60	17·434 84	**1017·5**	+ 521·536 02	+ 6·644 63	− 0·007 82
	9	+ 4·547 31	+ 8·221 40	17·479 36	**1018·5**	+ 521·635 23	+ 6·689 85	− 0·007 88
	10	+ 4·589 83	+ 8·266 34	17·523 01	**1019·5**	+ 521·707 28	+ 6·734 37	− 0·007 93
	11	+ 4·577 31	+ 8·298 89	17·554 28	**1020·5**	+ 521·757 36	+ 6·766 63	− 0·007 97
	12	+ 4·530 74	+ 8·312 39	17·566 50	**1021·5**	+ 521·793 78	+ 6·779 92	− 0·007 99
	13	+ 4·472 76	+ 8·304 91	17·557 74	**1022·5**	+ 521·825 55	+ 6·772 25	− 0·007 98
	14	+ 4·423 78	+ 8·278 28	17·529 83	**1023·5**	+ 521·860 78	+ 6·745 42	− 0·007 95
	15	+ 4·399 91	+ 8·237 03	17·487 29	**1024·5**	+ 521·905 91	+ 6·703 90	− 0·007 89
	16	+ 4·412 01	+ 8·187 41	17·436 39	**1025·5**	+ 521·965 31	+ 6·653 94	− 0·007 83
	17	+ 4·465 09	+ 8·136 58	17·384 28	**1026·5**	+ 522·040 99	+ 6·602 66	− 0·007 76
	18	+ 4·558 15	+ 8·091 78	17·338 19	**1027·5**	+ 522·132 62	+ 6·557 32	− 0·007 70
	19	+ 4·684 29	+ 8·059 50	17·304 64	**1028·5**	+ 522·237 47	+ 6·524 44	− 0·007 66
	20	+ 4·831 38	+ 8·044 64	17·288 49	**1029·5**	+ 522·350 76	+ 6·508 91	− 0·007 64
	21	+ 4·983 49	+ 8·049 60	17·292 17	**1030·5**	+ 522·466 16	+ 6·513 20	− 0·007 64
	22	+ 5·123 11	+ 8·073 80	17·315 09	**1031·5**	+ 522·576 70	+ 6·536 75	− 0·007 67
	23	+ 5·233 85	+ 8·113 38	17·353 38	**1032·5**	+ 522·675 85	+ 6·575 76	− 0·007 72
	24	+ 5·303 48	+ 8·161 55	17·400 27	**1033·5**	+ 522·758 69	+ 6·623 44	− 0·007 78
	25	+ 5·326 63	+ 8·209 38	17·446 82	**1034·5**	+ 522·823 05	+ 6·670 90	− 0·007 84
	26	+ 5·306 78	+ 8·247 14	17·483 29	**1035·5**	+ 522·870 25	+ 6·708 38	− 0·007 88
	27	+ 5·257 22	+ 8·265 99	17·500 87	**1036·5**	+ 522·905 51	+ 6·727 03	− 0·007 91
	28	+ 5·200 29	+ 8·260 03	17·493 63	**1037·5**	+ 522·937 70	+ 6·720 88	− 0·007 90
	29	+ 5·164 42	+ 8·228 33	17·460 64	**1038·5**	+ 522·978 12	+ 6·688 94	− 0·007 86
	30	+ 5·178 35	+ 8·176 48	17·407 51	**1039·5**	+ 523·038 23	+ 6·636 74	− 0·007 79
	31	+ 5·262 60	+ 8·116 73	17·346 47	**1040·5**	+ 523·126 26	+ 6·576 47	− 0·007 71
	32	+ 5·420 55	+ 8·065 59	17·294 05	**1041·5**	+ 523·243 66	+ 6·524 65	− 0·007 64

Planetary reduction overview

Data and formulae are provided for the precise computation of the geocentric apparent right ascension, intermediate right ascension, declination, and hour angle, at an instant of time, for an object within the solar system, ignoring polar motion (see page B84), from a barycentric ephemeris in rectangular coordinates and relativistic coordinate time referred to the International Celestial Reference System (ICRS).

1. Given an instant for which the position of the planet is required, obtain the dynamical time (TDB) to use with the ephemeris. If the position is required at a given Universal Time (UT1), or the hour angle is required, then obtain a value for ΔT, which may have to be predicted.

2. Calculate the geocentric rectangular coordinates of the planet from barycentric ephemerides of the planet and the Earth at coordinate time argument TDB, allowing for light time calculated from heliocentric coordinates.

3. Calculate the geocentric direction of the planet by allowing for light-deflection due to solar gravitation.

4. Calculate the proper direction of the planet by applying the correction for the Earth's orbital velocity about the barycentre (i.e. annual aberration). The resulting vector (from steps 2-4) is in the Geocentric Celestial Reference System (GCRS), and is sometimes called the proper or virtual place.

Equinox Method

5. Apply frame bias, precession and nutation to convert from the GCRS to the system defined by the true equator and equinox of date.

6. Convert to spherical coordinates, giving the geocentric apparent right ascension and declination with respect to the true equator and equinox of date.

7. Calculate Greenwich apparent sidereal time and form the Greenwich hour angle for the given UT1.

CIO Method

5. Rotate from the GCRS to the intermediate system using $\mathcal{X}, \mathcal{Y}$ and s to apply frame bias and precession-nutation.

6. Convert to spherical coordinates, giving the geocentric intermediate right ascension and declination with respect to the CIO and equator of date.

7. Calculate the Earth rotation angle and form the Greenwich hour angle for the given UT1.

Alternatively, if right ascension is not required, combine Steps 5 and 7

***5.** Apply frame bias, precession, nutation, and Greenwich apparent sidereal time to convert from the GCRS to the Terrestrial Intermediate Reference System; with origin of longitude at the TIO, and the equator of date.

***5.** Rotate, using $\mathcal{X}$, $\mathcal{Y}$, s and θ to apply frame bias, precession-nutation and Earth rotation, from the GCRS to the Terrestrial Intermediate Reference System; with origin of longitude at the TIO, and equator of date.

***6.** Convert to spherical coordinates, giving the Greenwich hour angle (H) and declination (δ) with respect Terrestrial Intermediate Reference System (TIO and equator of date).

Note: In *Steps* 7 and *Steps* *5 the effects of polar motion (see page B84) have been ignored; they are the very small difference between the International Terrestrial Reference Frame (ITRF) zero meridian and the TIO, and the position of the CIP within the ITRS.

Formulae and method for planetary reduction

Step 1. Depending on the instant at which the planetary position is required, obtain the terrestrial or proper time (TT) and the barycentric dynamical time (TDB). Terrestrial time is related to UT1, whereas TDB is used as the time argument for the barycentric ephemeris. For calculating an apparent place the following approximate formulae are sufficient for converting from UT1 to TT and TDB:

$$\mathrm{TT} = \mathrm{UT1} + \Delta T, \qquad \mathrm{TDB} = \mathrm{TT} + 0\overset{s}{.}001\,656\,67 \sin g + 0{\cdot}000\,022\,42 \sin(L - L_J)$$

$$g = 357\overset{\circ}{.}53 + 0{\cdot}985\,600\,28\; D \quad \text{and} \quad L - L_J = 246\overset{\circ}{.}11 + 0{\cdot}902\,517\,92\; D$$

where $D = \mathrm{JD} - 245\ 1545{\cdot}0$ and ΔT may be obtained from page K9 and JD is the Julian date to two decimals of a day. The difference between TT and TDB may be ignored.

Step 2. Obtain the Earth's barycentric position $\mathbf{E}_\mathrm{B}(t)$ in au and velocity $\dot{\mathbf{E}}_\mathrm{B}(t)$ in au/d, at coordinate time $t = \mathrm{TDB}$, referred to the ICRS.

Using an ephemeris, obtain the barycentric ICRS position of the planet $\mathbf{Q}_\mathrm{B}$ in au at time $(t - \tau)$ where τ is the light time, so that light emitted by the planet at the event $\mathbf{Q}_\mathrm{B}(t - \tau)$ arrives at the Earth at the event $\mathbf{E}_\mathrm{B}(t)$.

The light time equation is solved iteratively using the heliocentric position of the Earth (**E**) and the planet (**Q**), starting with the approximation $\tau = 0$, as follows:

Form **P**, the vector from the Earth to the planet from the equation:

$$\mathbf{P} = \mathbf{Q}_\mathrm{B}(t - \tau) - \mathbf{E}_\mathrm{B}(t)$$

Form **E** and **Q** from the equations:

$$\mathbf{E} = \mathbf{E}_\mathrm{B}(t) - \mathbf{S}_\mathrm{B}(t)$$

$$\mathbf{Q} = \mathbf{Q}_\mathrm{B}(t - \tau) - \mathbf{S}_\mathrm{B}(t - \tau)$$

where $\mathbf{S}_\mathrm{B}$ is the barycentric position of the Sun.

Calculate τ from: $c\tau = P + (2\mu/c^2) \ln[(E + P + Q)/(E - P + Q)]$

where the light time (τ) includes the effect of gravitational retardation due to the Sun, and

μ = solar mass parameter = GM_S $\qquad$ c = velocity of light = 173·1446 au/d

$\mu/c^2 = 9{\cdot}87 \times 10^{-9}$ au $\qquad$ $P = |\mathbf{P}|,\ Q = |\mathbf{Q}|,\ E = |\mathbf{E}|$

where | | means calculate the square root of the sum of the squares of the components.

After convergence, form unit vectors **p**, **q**, **e** by dividing **P**, **Q**, **E** by P, Q, E respectively.

Step 3. Calculate the geocentric direction ($\mathbf{p}_1$) of the planet, corrected for light-deflection due to solar gravitation, from:

$$\mathbf{p}_1 = \mathbf{p} + (2\mu/c^2 E)((\mathbf{p} \cdot \mathbf{q})\,\mathbf{e} - (\mathbf{e} \cdot \mathbf{p})\,\mathbf{q})/(1 + \mathbf{q} \cdot \mathbf{e})$$

where the dot indicates a scalar product.

The vector $\mathbf{p}_1$ is a unit vector to order μ/c^2.

Step 4. Calculate the proper direction of the planet ($\mathbf{p}_2$) in the GCRS that is moving with the instantaneous velocity (**V**) of the Earth, from:

$$\mathbf{p}_2 = (\beta^{-1}\mathbf{p}_1 + (1 + (\mathbf{p}_1 \cdot \mathbf{V})/(1 + \beta^{-1}))\,\mathbf{V})/(1 + \mathbf{p}_1 \cdot \mathbf{V})$$

where $\mathbf{V} = \dot{\mathbf{E}}_\mathrm{B}/c = 0{\cdot}005\ 7755\,\dot{\mathbf{E}}_\mathrm{B}$ and $\beta = (1 - V^2)^{-1/2}$; the velocity (**V**) is expressed in units of the velocity of light.

Formulae and method for planetary reduction (continued)

Equinox method

Step 5. Apply frame bias, precession and nutation to the proper direction ($\mathbf{p}_2$) by multiplying by the rotation matrix $\mathbf{M} = \mathbf{NPB}$ given on the even pages B30–B44 to obtain the apparent direction $\mathbf{p}_3$ from:

$$\mathbf{p}_3 = \mathbf{M}\,\mathbf{p}_2$$

Step 6. Convert to spherical coordinates α_e, δ using:

$$\alpha_e = \tan^{-1}(\eta/\xi) \quad \delta = \tan^{-1}(\zeta/\beta)$$

Step 7. Calculate Greenwich apparent sidereal time (GAST) for the required UT1 (B13–B20), and then form

$$H = \text{GAST} - \alpha_e$$

Note: H is usually given in arc measure, while GAST and right ascension are given in units of time.

CIO method

Step 5. Apply the rotation from the GCRS to the Celestial Intermediate System by multiplying the proper direction ($\mathbf{p}_2$) by the matrix $\mathbf{C}(\mathcal{X}, \mathcal{Y}, s)$ given on the odd pages B31–B45 to obtain the intermediate direction $\mathbf{p}_3$ from:

$$\mathbf{p}_3 = \mathbf{C}\,\mathbf{p}_2$$

Step 6. Convert to spherical coordinates α_i, δ using:

$$\alpha_i = \tan^{-1}(\eta/\xi) \quad \delta = \tan^{-1}(\zeta/\beta)$$

where $\mathbf{p}_3 = (\xi, \eta, \zeta)$, $\beta = \sqrt{(\xi^2 + \eta^2)}$ and the quadrant of α_e or α_i is determined by the signs of ξ and η.

Step 7. Calculate the Earth rotation angle (θ) for the required UT1 (B21–B24), and then form

$$H = \theta - \alpha_i$$

Note: H and θ are usually given in arc measure, while right ascension is given in units of time.

Alternatively combining steps 5 and 7 before forming spherical coordinates

Equinox method

Step *5. Apply frame bias, precession, nutation, and sidereal time, to the proper direction ($\mathbf{p}_2$) by multiplying by the rotation matrix $\mathbf{R}_3(\text{GAST})\mathbf{M}$ to obtain the position ($\mathbf{p}_4$) measured relative to the Terrestrial Intermediate Reference System:

$$\mathbf{p}_4 = \mathbf{R}_3(\text{GAST})\mathbf{M}\,\mathbf{p}_2$$

CIO method

Step *5. Apply the rotation from the GCRS to the terrestrial system by multiplying the proper direction ($\mathbf{p}_2$) by the matrix $\mathbf{R}_3(\theta)\mathbf{C}(\mathcal{X}, \mathcal{Y}, s)$ to obtain the position ($\mathbf{p}_4$) measured with respect to the Terrestrial Intermediate Reference System:

$$\mathbf{p}_4 = \mathbf{R}_3(\theta)\,\mathbf{C}\,\mathbf{p}_2$$

Step *6. Convert to spherical coordinates Greenwich hour angle (H) and declination δ using:

$$H = \tan^{-1}(-\eta/\xi), \quad \delta = \tan^{-1}(\zeta/\beta)$$

where $\mathbf{p}_4 = (\xi, \eta, \zeta)$, $\beta = \sqrt{(\xi^2 + \eta^2)}$, and H is measured from the TIO meridian positive to the west, and the quadrant is determined by the signs of ξ and $-\eta$.

Example of planetary reduction: Equinox method

Calculate the apparent place, the apparent right ascension (right ascension with respect to the equinox) and declination and the Greenwich hour angle, of Venus on 2025 November 15 at $12^{\text{h}}\ 00^{\text{m}}\ 00^{\text{s}}$ UT1. Assume that $\Delta T = 69\overset{\text{s}}{.}0$.

Example of planetary reduction: Equinox method (continued)

Step 1. From page B19, on 2025 November 15 the tabular JD = 246 0994·5 UT1.

$\Delta T = \mathrm{TT} - \mathrm{UT1} = 69^{\mathrm{s}}\!.0 = 7{\cdot}986\,111 \times 10^{-4}$ days.

At $12^{\mathrm{h}}\,00^{\mathrm{m}}\,00^{\mathrm{s}}$ UT1 the required TT instant is therefore

$$\mathrm{TT} = 246\,0995{\cdot}000\,799 = 246\,0994{\cdot}5 + 0{\cdot}500\,00 + 7{\cdot}986\,111 \times 10^{-4}$$

and the equivalent TDB instant is

$$\mathrm{TDB} = 246\,0995{\cdot}000\,798\,597 = -14{\cdot}19 \times 10^{-9} + \mathrm{TT}$$

where $g = 311^{\circ}\!.45$, and $L - L_J = 134^{\circ}\!.91$. Thus the difference between TDB and TT is small and may be neglected.

Step 2. Tabular values, taken from the JPL DE440/LE440 barycentric ephemeris, referred to the ICRS at J2000·0, which are required for the calculation, are as follows:

Vector	Julian date (0^{h} TDB)	Rectangular components x	y	z
$\mathbf{Q}_{\mathrm{B}}$	246 0992·5	−0·685 213 154	−0·233 293 494	−0·061 606 157
	246 0993·5	−0·678 532 976	−0·250 593 737	−0·069 813 090
	246 0994·5	−0·671 321 025	−0·267 700 627	−0·077 966 662
	246 0995·5	−0·663 583 259	−0·284 600 799	−0·086 060 484
	246 0996·5	−0·655 326 043	−0·301 281 068	−0·094 088 220
	246 0997·5	−0·646 556 149	−0·317 728 437	−0·102 043 593
$\mathbf{S}_{\mathrm{B}}$	246 0993·5	−0·003 414 893	−0·005 129 396	−0·002 073 208
	246 0994·5	−0·003 407 591	−0·005 129 609	−0·002 073 450
	246 0995·5	−0·003 400 291	−0·005 129 813	−0·002 073 688
	246 0996·5	−0·003 392 993	−0·005 130 006	−0·002 073 922

Interpolating to the instant JD 246 0995·000 798 597 TDB gives:

$\mathbf{S}_{\mathrm{B}} = (-0{\cdot}003\,403\,935,\quad -0{\cdot}005\,129\,712,\quad -0{\cdot}002\,073\,570)$

$\mathbf{E}_{\mathrm{B}} = (+0{\cdot}591\,636\,517,\quad +0{\cdot}719\,843\,712,\quad +0{\cdot}312\,186\,861)$

$\dot{\mathbf{E}}_{\mathrm{B}} = (-0{\cdot}014\,015\,450,\quad +0{\cdot}009\,441\,913,\quad +0{\cdot}004\,093\,480)$

where Bessel's interpolation formula (see page K14) has been used up to δ^2 for $\mathbf{S}_{\mathrm{B}}$ and δ^4 for $\mathbf{E}_{\mathrm{B}}$ and $\dot{\mathbf{E}}_{\mathrm{B}}$, the tabular values of which may be found on page B82.

$\mathbf{E} = (+0{\cdot}595\,040\,451,\quad +0{\cdot}724\,973\,425,\quad +0{\cdot}314\,260\,430) \qquad E = 0{\cdot}989\,150\,759$

The first iteration, with $\tau = 0$, gives:

$\mathbf{P} = (-1{\cdot}259\,147\,818,\quad -0{\cdot}996\,034\,590,\quad -0{\cdot}394\,214\,764) \qquad P = 1{\cdot}653\,161\,641$

$\mathbf{Q} = (-0{\cdot}664\,107\,366,\quad -0{\cdot}271\,061\,165,\quad -0{\cdot}079\,954\,334) \qquad Q = 0{\cdot}721\,737\,795$

$\tau = 0^{\mathrm{d}}\!.009\,547\,8658$

The second iteration, with $\tau = 0^{\mathrm{d}}\!.009\,547\,8658$ using Bessel's interpolation formula up to δ^4 to interpolate $\mathbf{Q}_{\mathrm{B}}$, and up to δ^2 to interpolate $\mathbf{S}_{\mathrm{B}}$, gives:

$\mathbf{P} = (-1{\cdot}259\,221\,680,\quad -0{\cdot}995\,873\,216,\quad -0{\cdot}394\,137\,480) \qquad P = 1{\cdot}653\,102\,252$

$\mathbf{Q} = (-0{\cdot}664\,181\,159,\quad -0{\cdot}270\,899\,794,\quad -0{\cdot}079\,877\,052) \qquad Q = 0{\cdot}721\,736\,554$

$\tau = 0^{\mathrm{d}}\!.009\,547\,5228$

Iterate until P changes by less than 10^{-9}. Hence the unit vectors are:

$\mathbf{p} = (-0{\cdot}761\,732\,478,\quad -0{\cdot}602\,426\,873,\quad -0{\cdot}238\,422\,930)$

$\mathbf{q} = (-0{\cdot}920\,254\,285,\quad -0{\cdot}375\,344\,435,\quad -0{\cdot}110\,673\,423)$

$\mathbf{e} = (+0{\cdot}601\,566\,997,\quad +0{\cdot}732\,925\,106,\quad +0{\cdot}317\,707\,314)$

Example of planetary reduction: Equinox method (continued)

Step 3. Calculate the scalar products:

$\mathbf{p}\cdot\mathbf{q} = +0{\cdot}953\ 492\ 233 \quad \mathbf{e}\cdot\mathbf{p} = -0{\cdot}975\ 515\ 608 \quad \mathbf{q}\cdot\mathbf{e} = -0{\cdot}863\ 855\ 723$ then

$$\frac{(2\mu/c^2E)}{1+\mathbf{q}\cdot\mathbf{e}}((\mathbf{p}\cdot\mathbf{q})\mathbf{e} - (\mathbf{e}\cdot\mathbf{p})\mathbf{q}) = (-0{\cdot}000\ 000\ 048, +0{\cdot}000\ 000\ 049, +0{\cdot}000\ 000\ 029)$$

and $\mathbf{p}_1 = (-0{\cdot}761\ 732\ 526, -0{\cdot}602\ 426\ 824, -0{\cdot}238\ 422\ 901)$

Step 4. Take $\dot{\mathbf{E}}_B$, interpolated to JD 246 0995·000 799 TT from *Step* 2 and calculate:

$$\mathbf{V} = 0{\cdot}005\ 775\ 518\,\dot{\mathbf{E}}_B = (-0{\cdot}000\ 080\ 946, \quad +0{\cdot}000\ 054\ 532, \quad +0{\cdot}000\ 023\ 642)$$

Then $V = 0{\cdot}000\ 100\ 424$, $\beta = 1{\cdot}000\ 000\ 005$ and $\beta^{-1} = 0{\cdot}999\ 999\ 995$

Calculate the scalar product $\mathbf{p}_1\cdot\mathbf{V} = +0{\cdot}000\ 023\ 171$

Then $1 + (\mathbf{p}_1\cdot\mathbf{V})/(1+\beta^{-1}) = 1{\cdot}000\ 011\ 586$

Hence $\mathbf{p}_2 = (-0{\cdot}761\ 795\ 818, \quad -0{\cdot}602\ 358\ 331, \quad -0{\cdot}238\ 393\ 734)$

Step 5. From page B42, the bias, precession and nutation matrix **M**, interpolated to the required instant JD 246 0995·000 799 TT, is given by:

$$\mathbf{M} = \mathbf{NPB} = \begin{bmatrix} +0{\cdot}999\ 980\ 007 & -0{\cdot}005\ 799\ 719 & -0{\cdot}002\ 519\ 778 \\ +0{\cdot}005\ 799\ 612 & +0{\cdot}999\ 983\ 181 & -0{\cdot}000\ 049\ 661 \\ +0{\cdot}002\ 520\ 024 & +0{\cdot}000\ 035\ 046 & +0{\cdot}999\ 996\ 824 \end{bmatrix}$$

Hence $\mathbf{p}_3 = \mathbf{M}\,\mathbf{p}_2 = (-0{\cdot}757\ 686\ 379, \ -0{\cdot}606\ 754\ 482, \ -0{\cdot}240\ 333\ 831)$

Step 6. Converting to spherical coordinates $\alpha_e = 14^h\ 34^m\ 45^s.0506, \ \delta = -13°\ 54'\ 22''.479$.

Step 7. From page B19, interpolating in the daily values to the required UT1 instant gives GAST − UT1 = $3^h\ 39^m\ 18^s.9701$, and thus

$$\begin{aligned} H &= (\text{GAST} - \text{UT1}) - \alpha_e + \text{UT1} \\ &= 3^h\ 39^m\ 18^s.9701 - 14^h\ 34^m\ 45^s.0506 + 12^h\ 00^m\ 00^s \\ &= 16°\ 08'\ 28''.791 \end{aligned}$$

where H, the Greenwich hour angle of Venus, is expressed in angular measure.

Example of planetary reduction: CIO method

Step 1-4. Repeat Steps 1-4 of the planetary reduction given on page B66, calculating the proper direction of the planet ($\mathbf{p}_2$) in the GCRS, hence

$$\mathbf{p}_2 = (-0{\cdot}761\ 795\ 818, \quad -0{\cdot}602\ 358\ 331, \quad -0{\cdot}238\ 393\ 734)$$

Step 5. From pages B43 extract **C**, interpolated to the required TT time, that rotates the GCRS to the Celestial Intermediate Reference System, viz:

$$\mathbf{C} = \begin{bmatrix} +0{\cdot}999\ 996\ 825 & -0{\cdot}000\ 000\ 003 & -0{\cdot}002\ 520\ 024 \\ -0{\cdot}000\ 000\ 086 & +0{\cdot}999\ 999\ 999 & -0{\cdot}000\ 035\ 046 \\ +0{\cdot}002\ 520\ 024 & +0{\cdot}000\ 035\ 046 & +0{\cdot}999\ 996\ 824 \end{bmatrix}$$

Hence $\mathbf{p}_3 = \mathbf{C}\,\mathbf{p}_2 = (-0{\cdot}761\ 192\ 640, \ -0{\cdot}602\ 349\ 911, \ -0{\cdot}240\ 333\ 831)$

Example of planetary reduction: CIO method (continued)

Step 6. Converting to spherical coordinates $\alpha_i = 14^{\rm h}\ 33^{\rm m}\ 25^{\rm s}\!.2984$, $\delta = -13°\ 54'\ 22''\!.479$.

Step 7. From page B24, interpolating to the required UT1, gives

$$\theta - \mathrm{UT1} = 54°\ 29'\ 48''\!.267$$

and thus the Greenwich hour angle (H) of Venus is

$$\begin{aligned} H &= (\theta - \mathrm{UT1}) - \alpha_i + \mathrm{UT1} \\ &= 54°\ 29'\ 48''\!.267 - 14^{\rm h}\ 33^{\rm m}\ 25^{\rm s}\!.2984 \times 15 + 12^{\rm h}\ 00^{\rm m}\ 00^{\rm s} \times 15 \\ &= 16°\ 08'\ 28''\!.791 \end{aligned}$$

Summary of planetary reduction examples

Thus on 2025 November 15 at $12^{\rm h}\ 00^{\rm m}\ 00^{\rm s}$ UT1, the position of Venus is

$H = 16°\ 08'\ 28''\!.791$ is the Greenwich hour angle ignoring polar motion,

$\delta = -13°\ 54'\ 22''\!.479$ is the apparent and intermediate declination,

$\alpha_e = 14^{\rm h}\ 34^{\rm m}\ 45^{\rm s}\!.0506$ is the apparent (equinox) right ascension, and

$\alpha_i = 14^{\rm h}\ 33^{\rm m}\ 25^{\rm s}\!.2984$ is the intermediate right ascension

The geometric distance between the Earth and Venus at time $t =$ JD 246 0995·000 799 TT is the value of $P = 1{\cdot}653\ 161\ 641$ au in the first iteration in *Step* 2, where $\tau = 0$. The distance between the Earth at time t and Venus at time $(t - \tau)$ is the value of $P = 1{\cdot}653\ 102\ 254$ au in the final iteration in *Step* 2, where $\tau = 0^{\rm d}\!.009\ 547\ 5228$.

Solar reduction

The method for solar reduction is identical to the method for planetary reduction, except for the following differences:

In *Step* 2 set $\mathbf{Q}_{\rm B} = \mathbf{S}_{\rm B}$ and hence $\mathbf{P} = \mathbf{S}_{\rm B}(t - \tau) - \mathbf{E}_{\rm B}(t)$. Calculate the light time (τ) by iteration from $\tau = P/c$ and form the unit vector $\mathbf{p}$ only.

In *Step* 3 set $\mathbf{p}_1 = \mathbf{p}$ since there is no light-deflection from the centre of the Sun's disk.

Stellar reduction overview

The method for planetary reduction may be applied with some modification to the calculation of the apparent places of stars.

The barycentric direction of a star at a particular epoch is calculated from its right ascension, declination and space motion at the catalogue epoch with respect to the ICRS. If the position of the star is not on the ICRS, and the accuracy of the data warrants it, convert it to the ICRS. See page B50 for FK5 to ICRS conversion.

The main modifications to the planetary reduction in the stellar case are: in *Step* 1, the distinction between TDB and TT is not significant; in *Step* 2, the space motion of the star is included but light time is ignored; in *Step* 3, the relativity term for light-deflection is modified to the asymptotic case where the star is assumed to be at infinity.

Formulae and method for stellar reduction

The steps in the stellar reduction are as follows:

Step 1. Set TDB = TT.

Step 2. Obtain the Earth's barycentric position $\mathbf{E}_B$ in au and velocity $\dot{\mathbf{E}}_B$ in au/d, at coordinate time t = TDB, referred to the ICRS.

The barycentric direction ($\mathbf{q}$) of a star at epoch J2000·0, referred to the ICRS, is given by:

$$\mathbf{q} = (\cos\alpha_0 \cos\delta_0,\ \sin\alpha_0 \cos\delta_0,\ \sin\delta_0)$$

where α_0 and δ_0 are the ICRS right ascension and declination at epoch J2000·0.

The space motion vector $\mathbf{m} = (m_x, m_y, m_z)$ of the star, expressed in radians per century, is given by:

$$\begin{aligned} m_x &= -\mu_\alpha \sin\alpha_0 - \mu_\delta \sin\delta_0 \cos\alpha_0 + v\pi \cos\delta_0 \cos\alpha_0 \\ m_y &= \mu_\alpha \cos\alpha_0 - \mu_\delta \sin\delta_0 \sin\alpha_0 + v\pi \cos\delta_0 \sin\alpha_0 \\ m_z &= \mu_\delta \cos\delta_0 + v\pi \sin\delta_0 \end{aligned}$$

where (μ_α, μ_δ), the proper motion in right ascension and declination, are in radians/century; μ_α is the measurement in units of a great circle, and so **includes** the $\cos\delta_0$ factor. Note: catalogues give proper motions in various units, e.g., arcseconds per century (″/cy), milliarcseconds per year (mas/yr). Use the factor 1/10 to convert from mas/yr to ″/cy. The radial velocity (v) is in au/century (1 km/s = 21·095 au/century), measured positively away from the Earth.

Calculate $\mathbf{P}$, the geocentric vector of the star at the required epoch, as:

$$\mathbf{P} = \mathbf{q} + T\,\mathbf{m} - \pi\,\mathbf{E}_B$$

where $T = (\mathrm{JD_{TT}} - 245\,1545{\cdot}0)/36\,525$, which is the interval in Julian centuries from J2000·0, and $\mathrm{JD_{TT}}$ is the Julian date to one decimal of a day.

Form the heliocentric position of the Earth ($\mathbf{E}$) from:

$$\mathbf{E} = \mathbf{E}_B - \mathbf{S}_B$$

where $\mathbf{S}_B$ is the barycentric position of the Sun at time t.

Form the geocentric direction ($\mathbf{p}$) of the star and the unit vector ($\mathbf{e}$) from $\mathbf{p} = \mathbf{P}/|\mathbf{P}|$ and $\mathbf{e} = \mathbf{E}/|\mathbf{E}|$.

Step 3. Calculate the geocentric direction ($\mathbf{p}_1$) of the star, corrected for light-deflection, as:

$$\mathbf{p}_1 = \mathbf{p} + (2\mu/c^2 E)(\mathbf{e} - (\mathbf{p}\cdot\mathbf{e})\mathbf{p})/(1 + \mathbf{p}\cdot\mathbf{e})$$

where the dot indicates a scalar product, $\mu/c^2 = 9{\cdot}87 \times 10^{-9}$ au and $E = |\mathbf{E}|$. Note that the expression is derived from the planetary case by substituting $\mathbf{q} = \mathbf{p}$ in the equation for light-deflection (*Step* 3) given on page B67.

The vector $\mathbf{p}_1$ is a unit vector to order μ/c^2.

Step 4. Calculate the proper direction ($\mathbf{p}_2$) in the GCRS that is moving with the instantaneous velocity ($\mathbf{V}$) of the Earth, from:

$$\mathbf{p}_2 = (\beta^{-1}\mathbf{p}_1 + (1 + (\mathbf{p}_1\cdot\mathbf{V})/(1+\beta^{-1}))\mathbf{V})/(1 + \mathbf{p}_1\cdot\mathbf{V})$$

where $\mathbf{V} = \dot{\mathbf{E}}_B/c = 0{\cdot}005\,7755\,\dot{\mathbf{E}}_B$ and $\beta = (1 - V^2)^{-1/2}$; the velocity ($\mathbf{V}$) is expressed in units of velocity of light.

Equinox method	*CIO method*
Step 5. Follow the left-hand *Steps 5–7* or *Steps *5–*6* on page B68.	*Step* 5. Follow the right-hand *Steps 5–7* or *Steps *5–*6* on page B68.

Example of stellar reduction: Equinox method

Calculate the apparent position of a fictitious star on 2025 January 1 at $0^h\ 00^m\ 00^s$ TT. The ICRS right ascension (α_0), declination (δ_0), proper motions (μ_α, μ_δ), parallax (π) and radial velocity (v) of the star at J2000·0 are given by:

$\alpha_0 = 14^h\ 39^m\ 36^s\!.4958$ $\quad \delta_0 = -60^\circ\ 50'\ 02''\!.309$ $\quad \pi = 0''\!.742 = 3{\cdot}5973 \times 10^{-6}$ rad

$\mu_\alpha = -367\ 8{\cdot}06$ mas/yr $= -0{\cdot}001\ 783\ 174$ rad/cy, $\quad \mu_\delta = +482{\cdot}87$ mas/yr $= +0{\cdot}000\ 234\ 102$ rad/cy, $\quad v = -21{\cdot}6$ km/s, $\quad v\pi = -0{\cdot}001\ 639\ 121$ rad/cy

Note: $\mu_\alpha = -367\ 8{\cdot}06$ mas/yr is the arc proper motion in right ascension on a great circle in milliarcseconds per year; it includes the $\cos\delta_0$ factor.

Step 1. TDB = TT = JD 246 0676·5 TT.

Step 2. Tabular values of $\mathbf{E}_B$, $\dot{\mathbf{E}}_B$ and $\mathbf{S}_B$, taken from the JPL DE440/LE440 barycentric ephemeris, referred to the ICRS, which are required for the calculation, are as follows:

Vector	Julian date (0^h TDB)	Rectangular components x	y	z
$\mathbf{E}_B$	246 0676·5	−0·184 414 047	+0·882 632 940	+0·382 808 177
$\dot{\mathbf{E}}_B$	246 0676·5	−0·017 197 578	−0·002 933 329	−0·001 271 876
$\mathbf{S}_B$	246 0676·5	−0·005 730 606	−0·004 576 753	−0·001 788 611

From the positional data, calculate:

$$\mathbf{q} = (-0{\cdot}373\ 860\ 494,\ -0{\cdot}312\ 618\ 798,\ -0{\cdot}873\ 211\ 210)$$
$$\mathbf{m} = (-0{\cdot}000\ 687\ 882,\ +0{\cdot}001\ 749\ 237,\ +0{\cdot}001\ 545\ 387)$$

Form $\quad \mathbf{P} = \mathbf{q} + T\,\mathbf{m} - \pi\,\mathbf{E}_B = (-0{\cdot}374\ 031\ 806,\ -0{\cdot}312\ 184\ 652,\ -0{\cdot}872\ 826\ 230)$

where $\quad T = (246\ 0676{\cdot}5 - 245\ 1545{\cdot}0)/36\ 525 = +0{\cdot}250\ 006\ 845,$

and form $\quad \mathbf{E} = \mathbf{E}_B - \mathbf{S}_B = (-0{\cdot}178\ 683\ 441,\ +0{\cdot}887\ 209\ 693,\ +0{\cdot}384\ 596\ 788),$
$E - 0{\cdot}983\ 353\ 193$

Hence the unit vectors are:

$$\mathbf{p} = (-0{\cdot}374\ 184\ 378,\ -0{\cdot}312\ 311\ 996,\ -0{\cdot}873\ 182\ 265)$$
$$\mathbf{e} = (-0{\cdot}181\ 708\ 304,\ +0{\cdot}902\ 228\ 924,\ +0{\cdot}391\ 107\ 479)$$

Step 3. Calculate the scalar product $\mathbf{p}\cdot\mathbf{e} = -0{\cdot}555\ 292\ 622$, then

$$\frac{(2\mu/c^2E)}{(1+\mathbf{p}\cdot\mathbf{e})}(\mathbf{e} - (\mathbf{p}\cdot\mathbf{e})\mathbf{p}) = (-0{\cdot}000\ 000\ 018,\ +0{\cdot}000\ 000\ 033,\ -0{\cdot}000\ 000\ 004)$$

and $\quad \mathbf{p}_1 = (-0{\cdot}374\ 184\ 395,\ -0{\cdot}312\ 311\ 963,\ -0{\cdot}873\ 182\ 270)$

Step 4. Using $\dot{\mathbf{E}}_B$ given in the table in *Step* 2, calculate

$\mathbf{V} = 0{\cdot}005\ 775\ 518\,\dot{\mathbf{E}}_B = (-0{\cdot}000\ 099\ 325,\ -0{\cdot}000\ 016\ 941,\ -0{\cdot}000\ 007\ 346)$

Then $V = 0{\cdot}000\ 101\ 027$, $\beta = 1{\cdot}000\ 000\ 005$ and $\beta^{-1} = 0{\cdot}999\ 999\ 995$

Calculate the scalar product $\mathbf{p}_1\cdot\mathbf{V} = +0{\cdot}000\ 048\ 871$

Then $1 + (\mathbf{p}_1\cdot\mathbf{V})/(1+\beta^{-1}) = 1{\cdot}000\ 024\ 436$

Hence $\quad \mathbf{p}_2 = (-0{\cdot}374\ 265\ 430,\ -0{\cdot}312\ 313\ 640,\ -0{\cdot}873\ 146\ 940)$

Example of stellar reduction: Equinox method (continued)

Step 5. From page B30, the bias, precession and nutation matrix **M** is given by:

$$\mathbf{M} = \mathbf{NPB} = \begin{bmatrix} +0{\cdot}999\,981\,416 & -0{\cdot}005\,591\,585 & -0{\cdot}002\,429\,371 \\ +0{\cdot}005\,591\,485 & +0{\cdot}999\,984\,366 & -0{\cdot}000\,047\,956 \\ +0{\cdot}002\,429\,601 & +0{\cdot}000\,034\,371 & +0{\cdot}999\,997\,048 \end{bmatrix}$$

hence $\mathbf{p}_3 = \mathbf{M}\,\mathbf{p}_2 = (-0{\cdot}370\,390\,949,\ -0{\cdot}314\,359\,585,\ -0{\cdot}874\,064\,412)$

Step 6. Converting to spherical coordinates: $\alpha_e = 14^{\mathrm{h}}\ 41^{\mathrm{m}}\ 17^{\mathrm{s}}\!.2936$, $\delta = -60°\ 56'\ 03''\!.990$

Example of stellar reduction: CIO method

Steps 1-4. Repeat Steps 1-4 above, calculating the proper direction of the star ($\mathbf{p}_2$) in the GCRS. Hence

$$\mathbf{p}_2 = (-0{\cdot}374\,265\,430, \quad -0{\cdot}312\,313\,640, \quad -0{\cdot}873\,146\,940)$$

Step 5. From page B31 extract **C** that rotates the GCRS to the CIO and equator of date,

$$\mathbf{C} = \begin{bmatrix} +0{\cdot}999\,997\,049 & +0{\cdot}000\,000\,001 & -0{\cdot}002\,429\,601 \\ -0{\cdot}000\,000\,084 & +0{\cdot}999\,999\,999 & -0{\cdot}000\,034\,371 \\ +0{\cdot}002\,429\,601 & +0{\cdot}000\,034\,371 & +0{\cdot}999\,997\,048 \end{bmatrix}$$

hence $\mathbf{p}_3 = \mathbf{C}\,\mathbf{p}_2 = (-0{\cdot}372\,142\,927,\ -0{\cdot}312\,283\,598,\ -0{\cdot}874\,064\,412)$

Step 6. Converting to spherical coordinates $\alpha_i = 14^{\mathrm{h}}\ 40^{\mathrm{m}}\ 00^{\mathrm{s}}\!.4034$, $\delta = -60°\ 56'\ 03''\!.990$.

Note: the intermediate right ascension (α_i) may also be calculated thus

$$\alpha_i = \alpha_e + E_o = 14^{\mathrm{h}}\ 41^{\mathrm{m}}\ 17^{\mathrm{s}}\!.2936 - 76^{\mathrm{s}}\!.8902$$

where α_e is the apparent (equinox) right ascension and E_o is the equation of the origins, which is tabulated daily at 0^{h} UT1 on pages B21–B24.

Approximate reduction to apparent geocentric altitude and azimuth

The following example illustrates an approximate procedure based on the CIO method for calculating the altitude and azimuth of a star for a specified UT1 instant. The procedure given is accurate to about $\pm 1''$. It is valid for 2025 as it uses the relevant annual equations given earlier in this section. Strictly, all the parameters, except the Earth rotation angle (θ), should be evaluated for the equivalent TT (UT1+ΔT) instant.

Example On 2025 January 1 at $0^{\mathrm{h}}\ 00^{\mathrm{m}}\ 00^{\mathrm{s}}$ UT1 calculate the local hour angle (h), declination (δ), and altitude and azimuth of the fictitious star given in the example on page B73, for an observer at W 60°0, S 30°0.

Step A The day of the year is 1; the time is $0^{\mathrm{h}}\!.000\ 00$ UT1; the ICRS barycentric direction (**q**) and space motion (**m**) of the star at epoch J2000·0 (see page B73) are

$$\mathbf{q} = (-0{\cdot}373\,860\,494,\ -0{\cdot}312\,618\,798,\ -0{\cdot}873\,211\,210)$$
$$\mathbf{m} = (-0{\cdot}000\,687\,882,\ +0{\cdot}001\,749\,237,\ +0{\cdot}001\,545\,387)$$

Apply space motion and ignore parallax to give the approximate geocentric position of the star at the epoch of date with respect to the GCRS

$$\mathbf{p} = \mathbf{q} + T\mathbf{m} = (-0{\cdot}374\,032\,470,\ -0{\cdot}312\,181\,477,\ -0{\cdot}872\,824\,853)$$

where $T = +0{\cdot}250\,006\,845$ centuries from 245 1545·0 TT and $\mathbf{p} = (p_x, p_y, p_z)$ is a column vector.

Approximate reduction to apparent geocentric altitude and azimuth (continued)

Step B Apply aberration and precession-nutation to form

$$\begin{aligned} x_i &= v_x + (1 - \mathcal{X}^2/2)\, p_x \quad - \quad \mathcal{X}\, p_z = -0{\cdot}372\,009 \\ y_i &= v_y + \quad p_y - \quad \mathcal{Y}\, p_z = -0{\cdot}312\,168 \\ z_i &= v_z + \quad \mathcal{X}\, p_x + \mathcal{Y}\, p_y + (1 - \mathcal{X}^2/2)\, p_z = -0{\cdot}873\,749 \end{aligned}$$

where

$$\mathbf{v} = \frac{1}{c}(0{\cdot}0172 \sin L, -0{\cdot}0158 \cos L, -0{\cdot}0068 \cos L)$$

$$= \frac{1}{173{\cdot}14}(-0{\cdot}016\,89, -0{\cdot}002\,98, -0{\cdot}001\,28)$$

where $\mathbf{v}$ in au/day is the approximate barycentric velocity of the Earth, $L = 280^\circ\!.9$ is the ecliptic longitude of the Sun, and the speed of light is given by $c = 173{\cdot}14$ au/d.

$\mathcal{X}$, $\mathcal{Y}$ are the approximate coordinates of the CIP, given in radians, and are evaluated using the approximate formulae on page B46, with arguments $\Omega = 1^\circ\!.5$ and $2L = 201^\circ\!.8$, giving

$$\mathcal{X} = +0{\cdot}002\,429 \qquad \text{and} \qquad \mathcal{Y} = +0{\cdot}000\,035$$

Therefore (x_i, y_i, z_i) is the position vector of the star with respect to the equator and CIO of date, i.e., the position of the star in the Celestial Intermediate Reference System.

Converting to spherical coordinates gives $\alpha_i = 14^\text{h}\ 40^\text{m}\ 00^\text{s}\!.3$ and $\delta = -60^\circ\ 56'\ 04''$ (see page B68 *Step* 6).

Step C Transform from the celestial intermediate origin and equator of date to the observer's meridian at longitude $\lambda = -60^\circ\!.0$ (west longitudes are negative)

$$\begin{aligned} x_g &= +x_i \cos(\theta + \lambda) + y_i \sin(\theta + \lambda) = -0{\cdot}485\,608 \\ y_g &= -x_i \sin(\theta + \lambda) + y_i \cos(\theta + \lambda) = +0{\cdot}004\,897 \\ z_g &= +z_i = -0{\cdot}873\,749 \end{aligned}$$

where the Earth rotation angle (see page B8) is

$$\theta = 99^\circ\!.593\,615 + 0^\circ\!.985\,6123 \times \text{day of year} + 15^\circ\!.041\,067 \times \text{UT1}$$

$$= 100^\circ\!.579\,227$$

Thus the local hour angle (h) and declination (δ) are calculated using

$$\begin{aligned} h &= \tan^{-1}(-y_g/x_g) \\ &= 180^\circ\ 34'\ 40'' \\ \delta &= -60^\circ\ 56'\ 04'' \end{aligned}$$

h is measured positive to the west of the local meridian and the declination is unchanged (from Step B) by the rotation.

Step D Transform to altitude and azimuth (also see page B86), for the observer at latitude $\phi = -30^\circ\!.0$:

$$\begin{aligned} x_t &= -x_g \sin\phi + z_g \cos\phi = -0{\cdot}999\,493 \\ y_t &= +y_g = +0{\cdot}004\,897 \\ z_t &= +x_g \cos\phi + z_g \sin\phi = +0{\cdot}016\,325 \end{aligned}$$

Thus

$$\text{Altitude} = \tan^{-1}\left(\frac{z_t}{\sqrt{x_t^2 + y_t^2}}\right) = +0^\circ\ 56'\ 09''$$

$$\text{Azimuth} = \tan^{-1}\left(\frac{y_t}{x_t}\right) = 179^\circ\ 43'\ 09''$$

where azimuth is measured from north through east in the plane of the horizon.

ICRS, ORIGIN AT SOLAR SYSTEM BARYCENTRE
FOR 0^h BARYCENTRIC DYNAMICAL TIME

Date 0^h TDB		X	Y	Z	$\dot{X}$	$\dot{Y}$	$\dot{Z}$
Jan.	**0**	−0·167 189 285	+0·885 427 389	+0·384 019 775	−1725 0989	− 265 5414	− 115 1251
	1	−0·184 414 047	+0·882 632 940	+0·382 808 177	−1719 7578	− 293 3329	− 127 1876
	2	−0·201 582 532	+0·879 561 069	+0·381 476 173	−1713 8440	− 321 0230	− 139 2050
	3	−0·218 689 035	+0·876 212 876	+0·380 024 256	−1707 3626	− 348 5946	− 151 1689
	4	−0·235 727 919	+0·872 589 627	+0·378 453 001	−1700 3217	− 376 0314	− 163 0714
	5	−0·252 693 639	+0·868 692 747	+0·376 763 057	−1692 7317	− 403 3185	− 174 9054
	6	−0·269 580 764	+0·864 523 798	+0·374 955 141	−1684 6049	− 430 4433	− 186 6651
	7	−0·286 383 993	+0·860 084 456	+0·373 030 019	−1675 9549	− 457 3956	− 198 3457
	8	−0·303 098 163	+0·855 376 486	+0·370 988 500	−1666 7955	− 484 1678	− 209 9443
	9	−0·319 718 250	+0·850 401 717	+0·368 831 413	−1657 1401	− 510 7550	− 221 4590
	10	−0·336 239 353	+0·845 162 012	+0·366 559 600	−1647 0008	− 537 1546	− 232 8895
	11	−0·352 656 687	+0·839 659 251	+0·364 173 902	−1636 3876	− 563 3662	− 244 2364
	12	−0·368 965 549	+0·833 895 312	+0·361 675 147	−1625 3076	− 589 3904	− 255 5010
	13	−0·385 161 297	+0·827 872 065	+0·359 064 151	−1613 7651	− 615 2283	− 266 6849
	14	−0·401 239 314	+0·821 591 366	+0·356 341 713	−1601 7614	− 640 8804	− 277 7894
	15	−0·417 194 985	+0·815 055 078	+0·353 508 626	−1589 2957	− 666 3460	− 288 8149
	16	−0·433 023 679	+0·808 265 076	+0·350 565 680	−1576 3654	− 691 6225	− 299 7610
	17	−0·448 720 734	+0·801 223 273	+0·347 513 677	−1562 9675	− 716 7052	− 310 6259
	18	−0·464 281 462	+0·793 931 638	+0·344 353 439	−1549 0993	− 741 5879	− 321 4073
	19	−0·479 701 144	+0·786 392 207	+0·341 085 819	−1534 7584	− 766 2630	− 332 1019
	20	−0·494 975 049	+0·778 607 098	+0·337 711 703	−1519 9435	− 790 7219	− 342 7059
	21	−0·510 098 432	+0·770 578 520	+0·334 232 016	−1504 6540	− 814 9555	− 353 2152
	22	−0·525 066 548	+0·762 308 771	+0·330 647 728	−1488 8901	− 838 9544	− 363 6256
	23	−0·539 874 654	+0·753 800 247	+0·326 959 850	−1472 6522	− 862 7088	− 373 9325
	24	−0·554 518 014	+0·745 055 444	+0·323 169 439	−1455 9410	− 886 2087	− 384 1313
	25	−0·568 991 901	+0·736 076 958	+0·319 277 602	−1438 7577	− 909 4433	− 394 2170
	26	−0·583 291 598	+0·726 867 500	+0·315 285 495	−1421 1034	− 932 4012	− 404 1841
	27	−0·597 412 405	+0·717 429 899	+0·311 194 336	−1402 9800	− 955 0697	− 414 0264
	28	−0·611 349 645	+0·707 767 117	+0·307 005 405	−1384 3908	− 977 4348	− 423 7373
	29	−0·625 098 684	+0·697 882 264	+0·302 720 054	−1365 3408	− 999 4814	− 433 3091
	30	−0·638 654 953	+0·687 778 603	+0·298 339 712	−1345 8383	−1021 1938	− 442 7341
	31	−0·652 013 980	+0·677 459 555	+0·293 865 887	−1325 8948	−1042 5564	− 452 0045
Feb.	**1**	−0·665 171 427	+0·666 928 688	+0·289 300 160	−1305 5250	−1063 5552	− 461 1135
	2	−0·678 123 119	+0·656 189 701	+0·284 644 174	−1284 7467	−1084 1788	− 470 0556
	3	−0·690 865 063	+0·645 246 390	+0·279 899 618	−1263 5788	−1104 4190	− 478 8269
	4	−0·703 393 460	+0·634 102 615	+0·275 068 210	−1242 0405	−1124 2710	− 487 4258
	5	−0·715 704 698	+0·622 762 271	+0·270 151 679	−1220 1497	−1143 7330	− 495 8518
	6	−0·727 795 333	+0·611 229 254	+0·265 151 747	−1197 9225	−1162 8056	− 504 1061
	7	−0·739 662 071	+0·599 507 450	+0·260 070 123	−1175 3722	−1181 4910	− 512 1905
	8	−0·751 301 738	+0·587 600 715	+0·254 908 496	−1152 5100	−1199 7922	− 520 1073
	9	−0·762 711 259	+0·575 512 875	+0·249 668 528	−1129 3441	−1217 7126	− 527 8589
	10	−0·773 887 628	+0·563 247 724	+0·244 351 861	−1105 8807	−1235 2549	− 535 4475
	11	−0·784 827 894	+0·550 809 030	+0·238 960 115	−1082 1238	−1252 4214	− 542 8749
	12	−0·795 529 135	+0·538 200 546	+0·233 494 897	−1058 0760	−1269 2129	− 550 1421
	13	−0·805 988 450	+0·525 426 023	+0·227 957 806	−1033 7389	−1285 6289	− 557 2494
	14	−0·816 202 951	+0·512 489 225	+0·222 350 444	−1009 1133	−1301 6675	− 564 1962
	15	−0·826 169 759	+0·499 393 943	+0·216 674 422	− 984 2006	−1317 3251	− 570 9811

$\dot{X}$, $\dot{Y}$, $\dot{Z}$ are in units of 10^{-9} au / d.

ICRS, ORIGIN AT SOLAR SYSTEM BARYCENTRE
FOR 0^h BARYCENTRIC DYNAMICAL TIME

Date 0^h TDB		X	Y	Z	$\dot{X}$	$\dot{Y}$	$\dot{Z}$
Feb.	**15**	−0·826 169 759	+0·499 393 943	+0·216 674 422	− 984 2006	−1317 3251	− 570 9811
	16	−0·835 886 010	+0·486 144 008	+0·210 931 368	− 959 0021	−1332 5973	− 577 6022
	17	−0·845 348 857	+0·472 743 299	+0·205 122 932	− 933 5203	−1347 4787	− 584 0570
	18	−0·854 555 481	+0·459 195 756	+0·199 250 792	− 907 7580	−1361 9633	− 590 3426
	19	−0·863 503 095	+0·445 505 377	+0·193 316 654	− 881 7188	−1376 0448	− 596 4561
	20	−0·872 188 949	+0·431 676 227	+0·187 322 254	− 855 4068	−1389 7166	− 602 3943
	21	−0·880 610 336	+0·417 712 434	+0·181 269 363	− 828 8264	−1402 9718	− 608 1539
	22	−0·888 764 597	+0·403 618 202	+0·175 159 784	− 801 9821	−1415 8033	− 613 7311
	23	−0·896 649 115	+0·389 397 808	+0·168 995 361	− 774 8788	−1428 2029	− 619 1221
	24	−0·904 261 328	+0·375 055 614	+0·162 777 977	− 747 5220	−1440 1617	− 624 3223
	25	−0·911 598 732	+0·360 596 077	+0·156 509 567	− 719 9182	−1451 6696	− 629 3265
	26	−0·918 658 898	+0·346 023 763	+0·150 192 121	− 692 0761	−1462 7152	− 634 1287
	27	−0·925 439 496	+0·331 343 354	+0·143 827 687	− 664 0069	−1473 2865	− 638 7228
	28	−0·931 938 330	+0·316 559 652	+0·137 418 379	− 635 7260	−1483 3719	− 643 1026
Mar.	**1**	−0·938 153 372	+0·301 677 568	+0·130 966 365	− 607 2521	−1492 9616	− 647 2632
	2	−0·944 082 801	+0·286 702 095	+0·124 473 856	− 578 6072	−1502 0489	− 651 2013
	3	−0·949 725 022	+0·271 638 272	+0·117 943 085	− 549 8141	−1510 6316	− 654 9159
	4	−0·955 078 664	+0·256 491 139	+0·111 376 280	− 520 8951	−1518 7116	− 658 4083
	5	−0·960 142 568	+0·241 265 698	+0·104 775 649	− 491 8695	−1526 2942	− 661 6817
	6	−0·964 915 753	+0·225 966 889	+0·098 143 362	− 462 7535	−1533 3866	− 664 7403
	7	−0·969 397 379	+0·210 599 573	+0·091 481 543	− 433 5596	−1539 9971	− 667 5889
	8	−0·973 586 718	+0·195 168 528	+0·084 792 270	− 404 2974	−1546 1334	− 670 2318
	9	−0·977 483 122	+0·179 678 461	+0·078 077 579	− 374 9738	−1551 8028	− 672 6731
	10	−0·981 086 008	+0·164 134 009	+0·071 339 469	− 345 5943	−1557 0111	− 674 9161
	11	−0·984 394 837	+0·148 539 759	+0·064 579 908	− 316 1631	−1561 7633	− 676 9637
	12	−0·987 409 108	+0·132 900 252	+0·057 800 840	− 286 6833	−1566 0630	− 678 8179
	13	−0·990 128 349	+0·117 220 000	+0·051 004 191	− 257 1577	−1569 9127	− 680 4800
	14	−0·992 552 117	+0·101 503 493	+0·044 191 877	− 227 5887	−1573 3139	− 681 9509
	15	−0·994 679 988	+0·085 755 215	+0·037 365 809	− 197 9790	1576 2668	− 683 2308
	16	−0·996 511 571	+0·069 979 652	+0·030 527 899	− 168 3315	−1578 7708	− 684 3192
	17	−0·998 046 502	+0·054 181 299	+0·023 680 065	− 138 6493	−1580 8246	− 685 2154
	18	−0·999 284 454	+0·038 364 669	+0·016 824 235	− 108 9363	−1582 4260	− 685 9183
	19	−1·000 225 140	+0·022 534 295	+0·009 962 349	− 79 1970	−1583 5727	− 686 4264
	20	−1·000 868 323	+0·006 694 739	+0·003 096 362	− 49 4363	−1584 2620	− 686 7381
	21	−1·001 213 812	−0·009 149 411	−0·003 771 753	− 19 6594	−1584 4908	− 686 8518
	22	−1·001 261 475	−0·024 993 530	−0·010 640 006	+ 10 1281	−1584 2555	− 686 7653
	23	−1·001 011 235	−0·040 832 961	−0·017 506 384	+ 39 9201	−1583 5522	− 686 4763
	24	−1·000 463 080	−0·056 662 999	−0·024 368 849	+ 69 7100	−1582 3760	− 685 9821
	25	−0·999 617 068	−0·072 478 885	−0·031 225 331	+ 99 4901	−1580 7210	− 685 2793
	26	−0·998 473 343	−0·088 275 800	−0·038 073 727	+ 129 2509	−1578 5805	− 684 3640
	27	−0·997 032 155	−0·104 048 852	−0·044 911 889	+ 158 9802	−1575 9471	− 683 2320
	28	−0·995 293 897	−0·119 793 076	−0·051 737 631	+ 188 6622	−1572 8139	− 681 8795
	29	−0·993 259 134	−0·135 503 446	−0·058 548 732	+ 218 2775	−1569 1757	− 680 3033
	30	−0·990 928 645	−0·151 174 902	−0·065 342 949	+ 247 8035	−1565 0310	− 678 5027
	31	−0·988 303 439	−0·166 802 389	−0·072 118 043	+ 277 2169	−1560 3830	− 676 4791
Apr.	**1**	−0·985 384 756	−0·182 380 911	−0·078 871 802	+ 306 4956	−1555 2396	− 674 2368
	2	−0·982 174 037	−0·197 905 568	−0·085 602 069	+ 335 6214	−1549 6124	− 671 7818

$\dot{X}$, $\dot{Y}$, $\dot{Z}$ are in units of 10^{-9} au / d.

ICRS, ORIGIN AT SOLAR SYSTEM BARYCENTRE FOR 0^h BARYCENTRIC DYNAMICAL TIME

Date 0^h TDB		X	Y	Z	$\dot{X}$	$\dot{Y}$	$\dot{Z}$
Apr.	**1**	−0·985 384 756	−0·182 380 911	−0·078 871 802	+ 306 4956	−1555 2396	− 674 2368
	2	−0·982 174 037	−0·197 905 568	−0·085 602 069	+ 335 6214	−1549 6124	− 671 7818
	3	−0·978 672 885	−0·213 371 591	−0·092 306 753	+ 364 5804	−1543 5149	− 669 1213
	4	−0·974 883 017	−0·228 774 342	−0·098 983 835	+ 393 3633	−1536 9604	− 666 2625
	5	−0·970 806 225	−0·244 109 316	−0·105 631 363	+ 421 9643	−1529 9612	− 663 2116
	6	−0·966 444 350	−0·259 372 120	−0·112 247 445	+ 450 3797	−1522 5280	− 659 9742
	7	−0·961 799 257	−0·274 558 460	−0·118 830 240	+ 478 6073	−1514 6697	− 656 5547
	8	−0·956 872 835	−0·289 664 121	−0·125 377 945	+ 506 6454	−1506 3934	− 652 9568
	9	−0·951 666 986	−0·304 684 955	−0·131 888 791	+ 534 4924	−1497 7054	− 649 1834
	10	−0·946 183 629	−0·319 616 872	−0·138 361 035	+ 562 1469	−1488 6106	− 645 2368
	11	−0·940 424 694	−0·334 455 825	−0·144 792 955	+ 589 6075	−1479 1132	− 641 1189
	12	−0·934 392 129	−0·349 197 806	−0·151 182 846	+ 616 8727	−1469 2166	− 636 8311
	13	−0·928 087 898	−0·363 838 835	−0·157 529 013	+ 643 9405	−1458 9233	− 632 3743
	14	−0·921 513 985	−0·378 374 955	−0·163 829 770	+ 670 8088	−1448 2352	− 627 7491
	15	−0·914 672 395	−0·392 802 227	−0·170 083 435	+ 697 4753	−1437 1537	− 622 9558
	16	−0·907 565 162	−0·407 116 720	−0·176 288 325	+ 723 9368	−1425 6794	− 617 9943
	17	−0·900 194 353	−0·421 314 508	−0·182 442 758	+ 750 1899	−1413 8128	− 612 8642
	18	−0·892 562 072	−0·435 391 667	−0·188 545 045	+ 776 2307	−1401 5535	− 607 5650
	19	−0·884 670 463	−0·449 344 268	−0·194 593 491	+ 802 0544	−1388 9011	− 602 0958
	20	−0·876 521 723	−0·463 168 374	−0·200 586 391	+ 827 6561	−1375 8543	− 596 4555
	21	−0·868 118 102	−0·476 860 035	−0·206 522 027	+ 853 0296	−1362 4116	− 590 6428
	22	−0·859 461 914	−0·490 415 279	−0·212 398 666	+ 878 1679	−1348 5706	− 584 6557
	23	−0·850 555 557	−0·503 830 109	−0·218 214 553	+ 903 0620	−1334 3283	− 578 4922
	24	−0·841 401 526	−0·517 100 496	−0·223 967 914	+ 927 7006	−1319 6815	− 572 1501
	25	−0·832 002 444	−0·530 222 382	−0·229 656 952	+ 952 0694	−1304 6277	− 565 6274
	26	−0·822 361 096	−0·543 191 691	−0·235 279 857	+ 976 1507	−1289 1662	− 558 9233
	27	−0·812 480 456	−0·556 004 356	−0·240 834 817	+ 999 9242	−1273 2998	− 552 0389
	28	−0·802 363 706	−0·568 656 360	−0·246 320 045	+1023 3692	−1257 0358	− 544 9777
	29	−0·792 014 231	−0·581 143 787	−0·251 733 803	+1046 4664	−1240 3865	− 537 7460
	30	−0·781 435 588	−0·593 462 858	−0·257 074 423	+1069 2007	−1223 3676	− 530 3518
May	**1**	−0·770 631 460	−0·605 609 966	−0·262 340 326	+1091 5621	−1205 9967	− 522 8040
	2	−0·759 605 605	−0·617 581 675	−0·267 530 021	+1113 5458	−1188 2907	− 515 1115
	3	−0·748 361 808	−0·629 374 714	−0·272 642 099	+1135 1505	−1170 2650	− 507 2818
	4	−0·736 903 855	−0·640 985 951	−0·277 675 222	+1156 3772	−1151 9322	− 499 3213
	5	−0·725 235 517	−0·652 412 371	−0·282 628 107	+1177 2278	−1133 3031	− 491 2351
	6	−0·713 360 545	−0·663 651 054	−0·287 499 519	+1197 7044	−1114 3862	− 483 0272
	7	−0·701 282 670	−0·674 699 161	−0·292 288 257	+1217 8087	−1095 1889	− 474 7010
	8	−0·689 005 608	−0·685 553 920	−0·296 993 153	+1237 5421	−1075 7176	− 466 2591
	9	−0·676 533 062	−0·696 212 619	−0·301 613 062	+1256 9056	−1055 9779	− 457 7039
	10	−0·663 868 727	−0·706 672 600	−0·306 146 861	+1275 9000	−1035 9748	− 449 0376
	11	−0·651 016 291	−0·716 931 251	−0·310 593 448	+1294 5259	−1015 7126	− 440 2616
	12	−0·637 979 436	−0·726 986 002	−0·314 951 733	+1312 7837	− 995 1953	− 431 3775
	13	−0·624 761 842	−0·736 834 317	−0·319 220 639	+1330 6735	− 974 4260	− 422 3861
	14	−0·611 367 193	−0·746 473 690	−0·323 399 099	+1348 1949	− 953 4072	− 413 2882
	15	−0·597 799 175	−0·755 901 636	−0·327 486 049	+1365 3470	− 932 1408	− 404 0840
	16	−0·584 061 488	−0·765 115 685	−0·331 480 425	+1382 1283	− 910 6282	− 394 7736
	17	−0·570 157 854	−0·774 113 382	−0·335 381 165	+1398 5363	− 888 8702	− 385 3566

$\dot{X}$, $\dot{Y}$, $\dot{Z}$ are in units of 10^{-9} au / d.

ICRS, ORIGIN AT SOLAR SYSTEM BARYCENTRE
FOR 0^h BARYCENTRIC DYNAMICAL TIME

Date 0^h TDB		X	Y	Z	$\dot{X}$	$\dot{Y}$	$\dot{Z}$
May	**17**	−0·570 157 854	−0·774 113 382	−0·335 381 165	+1398 5363	− 888 8702	− 385 3566
	18	−0·556 092 019	−0·782 892 272	−0·339 187 200	+1414 5676	− 866 8671	− 375 8326
	19	−0·541 867 772	−0·791 449 908	−0·342 897 458	+1430 2178	− 844 6190	− 366 2008
	20	−0·527 488 952	−0·799 783 836	−0·346 510 855	+1445 4810	− 822 1257	− 356 4605
	21	−0·512 959 468	−0·807 891 602	−0·350 026 303	+1460 3494	− 799 3866	− 346 6107
	22	−0·498 283 313	−0·815 770 749	−0·353 442 702	+1474 8133	− 776 4019	− 336 6508
	23	−0·483 464 591	−0·823 418 824	−0·356 758 951	+1488 8604	− 753 1726	− 326 5806
	24	−0·468 507 543	−0·830 833 394	−0·359 973 951	+1502 4760	− 729 7017	− 316 4014
	25	−0·453 416 563	−0·838 012 073	−0·363 086 623	+1515 6440	− 705 9955	− 306 1158
	26	−0·438 196 212	−0·844 952 555	−0·366 095 929	+1528 3477	− 682 0645	− 295 7290
	27	−0·422 851 206	−0·851 652 662	−0·369 000 890	+1540 5727	− 657 9231	− 285 2482
	28	−0·407 386 389	−0·858 110 375	−0·371 800 609	+1552 3086	− 633 5891	− 274 6824
	29	−0·391 806 684	−0·864 323 866	−0·374 494 286	+1563 5498	− 609 0817	− 264 0413
	30	−0·376 117 042	−0·870 291 493	−0·377 081 214	+1574 2962	− 584 4192	− 253 3341
	31	−0·360 322 399	−0·876 011 789	−0·379 560 775	+1584 5509	− 559 6181	− 242 5690
June	**1**	−0·344 427 643	−0·881 483 439	−0·381 932 423	+1594 3197	− 534 6919	− 231 7525
	2	−0·328 437 605	−0·886 705 248	−0·384 195 670	+1603 6086	− 509 6516	− 220 8896
	3	−0·312 357 051	−0·891 676 121	−0·386 350 075	+1612 4237	− 484 5061	− 209 9845
	4	−0·296 190 693	−0·896 395 044	−0·388 395 230	+1620 7703	− 459 2628	− 199 0402
	5	−0·279 943 191	−0·900 861 073	−0·390 330 758	+1628 6530	− 433 9281	− 188 0595
	6	−0·263 619 164	−0·905 073 321	−0·392 156 306	+1636 0761	− 408 5078	− 177 0446
	7	−0·247 223 190	−0·909 030 962	−0·393 871 542	+1643 0430	− 383 0073	− 165 9976
	8	−0·230 759 812	−0·912 733 217	−0·395 476 156	+1649 5574	− 357 4315	− 154 9203
	9	−0·214 233 540	−0·916 179 354	−0·396 969 852	+1655 6224	− 331 7845	− 143 8142
	10	−0·197 648 853	−0·919 368 683	−0·398 352 349	+1661 2410	− 306 0702	− 132 6806
	11	−0·181 010 200	−0·922 300 544	−0·399 623 375	+1666 4159	− 280 2915	− 121 5201
	12	−0·164 322 007	−0·924 974 305	−0·400 782 663	+1671 1491	− 254 4506	− 110 3332
	13	−0·147 588 686	−0·927 389 353	−0·401 829 951	+1675 4418	− 228 5489	− 99 1198
	14	−0·130 814 639	−0·929 545 083	−0·402 764 970	+1679 2940	− 202 5873	87 8796
	15	−0·114 004 278	−0·931 440 901	−0·403 587 452	+1682 7044	− 176 5663	− 76 6122
	16	−0·097 162 035	−0·933 076 213	−0·404 297 121	+1685 6699	− 150 4863	− 65 3168
	17	−0·080 292 378	−0·934 450 433	−0·404 893 695	+1688 1861	− 124 3479	− 53 9933
	18	−0·063 399 833	−0·935 562 979	−0·405 376 892	+1690 2463	− 98 1521	− 42 6414
	19	−0·046 488 999	−0·936 413 290	−0·405 746 429	+1691 8423	− 71 9011	− 31 2617
	20	−0·029 564 566	−0·937 000 830	−0·406 002 037	+1692 9642	− 45 5988	− 19 8556
	21	−0·012 631 332	−0·937 325 115	−0·406 143 462	+1693 6007	− 19 2512	− 8 4259
	22	+0·004 305 790	−0·937 385 734	−0·406 170 489	+1693 7400	+ 7 1325	+ 3 0232
	23	+0·021 241 773	−0·937 182 384	−0·406 082 953	+1693 3710	+ 33 5401	+ 14 4856
	24	+0·038 171 486	−0·936 714 903	−0·405 880 759	+1692 4850	+ 59 9561	+ 25 9534
	25	+0·055 089 733	−0·935 983 295	−0·405 563 896	+1691 0771	+ 86 3625	+ 37 4177
	26	+0·071 991 286	−0·934 987 748	−0·405 132 448	+1689 1467	+ 112 7407	+ 48 8691
	27	+0·088 870 937	−0·933 728 635	−0·404 586 588	+1686 6978	+ 139 0729	+ 60 2986
	28	+0·105 723 538	−0·932 206 497	−0·403 926 573	+1683 7379	+ 165 3433	+ 71 6988
	29	+0·122 544 023	−0·930 422 019	−0·403 152 731	+1680 2763	+ 191 5390	+ 83 0633
	30	+0·139 327 424	−0·928 376 001	−0·402 265 443	+1676 3228	+ 217 6496	+ 94 3874
July	**1**	+0·156 068 872	−0·926 069 337	−0·401 265 129	+1671 8871	+ 243 6672	+ 105 6678
	2	+0·172 763 588	−0·923 502 990	−0·400 152 241	+1666 9779	+ 269 5850	+ 116 9017

$\dot{X}$, $\dot{Y}$, $\dot{Z}$ are in units of 10^{-9} au / d.

ICRS, ORIGIN AT SOLAR SYSTEM BARYCENTRE
FOR 0^h BARYCENTRIC DYNAMICAL TIME

Date 0^h TDB		X	Y	Z	$\dot{X}$	$\dot{Y}$	$\dot{Z}$
July	**1**	+0·156 068 872	−0·926 069 337	−0·401 265 129	+1671 8871	+ 243 6672	+ 105 6678
	2	+0·172 763 588	−0·923 502 990	−0·400 152 241	+1666 9779	+ 269 5850	+ 116 9017
	3	+0·189 406 878	−0·920 677 987	−0·398 927 258	+1661 6029	+ 295 3976	+ 128 0868
	4	+0·205 994 119	−0·917 595 406	−0·397 590 674	+1655 7694	+ 321 0999	+ 139 2214
	5	+0·222 520 759	−0·914 256 372	−0·396 143 003	+1649 4838	+ 346 6873	+ 150 3038
	6	+0·238 982 308	−0·910 662 056	−0·394 584 776	+1642 7523	+ 372 1558	+ 161 3325
	7	+0·255 374 340	−0·906 813 666	−0·392 916 535	+1635 5811	+ 397 5014	+ 172 3064
	8	+0·271 692 484	−0·902 712 447	−0·391 138 833	+1627 9760	+ 422 7212	+ 183 2246
	9	+0·287 932 431	−0·898 359 669	−0·389 252 230	+1619 9424	+ 447 8129	+ 194 0866
	10	+0·304 089 920	−0·893 756 621	−0·387 257 288	+1611 4853	+ 472 7749	+ 204 8925
	11	+0·320 160 737	−0·888 904 604	−0·385 154 566	+1602 6084	+ 497 6068	+ 215 6427
	12	+0·336 140 698	−0·883 804 918	−0·382 944 617	+1593 3142	+ 522 3088	+ 226 3381
	13	+0·352 025 632	−0·878 458 860	−0·380 627 983	+1583 6032	+ 546 8813	+ 236 9797
	14	+0·367 811 367	−0·872 867 722	−0·378 205 199	+1573 4737	+ 571 3248	+ 247 5683
	15	+0·383 493 701	−0·867 032 796	−0·375 676 793	+1562 9223	+ 595 6387	+ 258 1043
	16	+0·399 068 387	−0·860 955 385	−0·373 043 290	+1551 9433	+ 619 8214	+ 268 5874
	17	+0·414 531 118	−0·854 636 817	−0·370 305 227	+1540 5299	+ 643 8693	+ 279 0161
	18	+0·429 877 510	−0·848 078 468	−0·367 463 158	+1528 6743	+ 667 7765	+ 289 3878
	19	+0·445 103 105	−0·841 281 783	−0·364 517 674	+1516 3689	+ 691 5348	+ 299 6985
	20	+0·460 203 366	−0·834 248 305	−0·361 469 411	+1503 6066	+ 715 1331	+ 309 9427
	21	+0·475 173 697	−0·826 979 699	−0·358 319 065	+1490 3822	+ 738 5581	+ 320 1137
	22	+0·490 009 461	−0·819 477 773	−0·355 067 406	+1476 6931	+ 761 7944	+ 330 2038
	23	+0·504 706 012	−0·811 744 496	−0·351 715 287	+1462 5401	+ 784 8253	+ 340 2045
	24	+0·519 258 732	−0·803 782 006	−0·348 263 641	+1447 9279	+ 807 6344	+ 350 1076
	25	+0·533 663 066	−0·795 592 600	−0·344 713 486	+1432 8645	+ 830 2060	+ 359 9053
	26	+0·547 914 555	−0·787 178 723	−0·341 065 908	+1417 3608	+ 852 5265	+ 369 5911
	27	+0·562 008 856	−0·778 542 943	−0·337 322 054	+1401 4292	+ 874 5850	+ 379 1598
	28	+0·575 941 755	−0·769 687 925	−0·333 483 115	+1385 0823	+ 896 3729	+ 388 6076
	29	+0·589 709 161	−0·760 616 409	−0·329 550 315	+1368 3329	+ 917 8836	+ 397 9317
	30	+0·603 307 108	−0·751 331 194	−0·325 524 900	+1351 1923	+ 939 1121	+ 407 1302
	31	+0·616 731 739	−0·741 835 121	−0·321 408 134	+1333 6713	+ 960 0546	+ 416 2018
Aug.	**1**	+0·629 979 299	−0·732 131 067	−0·317 201 290	+1315 7797	+ 980 7077	+ 425 1454
	2	+0·643 046 129	−0·722 221 942	−0·312 905 655	+1297 5266	+1001 0685	+ 433 9602
	3	+0·655 928 656	−0·712 110 681	−0·308 522 519	+1278 9209	+1021 1344	+ 442 6454
	4	+0·668 623 398	−0·701 800 245	−0·304 053 181	+1259 9709	+1040 9032	+ 451 2006
	5	+0·681 126 955	−0·691 293 612	−0·299 498 941	+1240 6851	+1060 3734	+ 459 6256
	6	+0·693 436 008	−0·680 593 775	−0·294 861 102	+1221 0715	+1079 5442	+ 467 9207
	7	+0·705 547 317	−0·669 703 725	−0·290 140 958	+1201 1375	+1098 4159	+ 476 0867
	8	+0·717 457 710	−0·658 626 449	−0·285 339 794	+1180 8892	+1116 9897	+ 484 1249
	9	+0·729 164 068	−0·647 364 917	−0·280 458 880	+1160 3311	+1135 2677	+ 492 0370
	10	+0·740 663 307	−0·635 922 073	−0·275 499 468	+1139 4654	+1153 2523	+ 499 8249
	11	+0·751 952 351	−0·624 300 842	−0·270 462 791	+1118 2918	+1170 9455	+ 507 4901
	12	+0·763 028 107	−0·612 504 131	−0·265 350 073	+1096 8073	+1188 3481	+ 515 0334
	13	+0·773 887 445	−0·600 534 853	−0·260 162 531	+1075 0072	+1205 4586	+ 522 4544
	14	+0·784 527 180	−0·588 395 947	−0·254 901 398	+1052 8857	+1222 2728	+ 529 7512
	15	+0·794 944 069	−0·576 090 407	−0·249 567 933	+1030 4373	+1238 7839	+ 536 9202
	16	+0·805 134 821	−0·563 621 313	−0·244 163 436	+1007 6577	+1254 9820	+ 543 9566

$\dot{X}$, $\dot{Y}$, $\dot{Z}$ are in units of 10^{-9} au / d.

ICRS, ORIGIN AT SOLAR SYSTEM BARYCENTRE FOR 0h BARYCENTRIC DYNAMICAL TIME

Date 0h TDB	X	Y	Z	$\dot{X}$	$\dot{Y}$	$\dot{Z}$
Aug. 16	+0·805 134 821	−0·563 621 313	−0·244 163 436	+1007 6577	+1254 9820	+ 543 9566
17	+0·815 096 111	−0·550 991 850	−0·238 689 264	+ 984 5448	+1270 8553	+ 550 8541
18	+0·824 824 606	−0·538 205 333	−0·233 146 839	+ 961 0990	+1286 3907	+ 557 6061
19	+0·834 316 993	−0·525 265 211	−0·227 537 651	+ 937 3239	+1301 5739	+ 564 2053
20	+0·843 570 008	−0·512 175 075	−0·221 863 265	+ 913 2260	+1316 3910	+ 570 6446
21	+0·852 580 467	−0·498 938 655	−0·216 125 315	+ 888 8146	+1330 8288	+ 576 9172
22	+0·861 345 294	−0·485 559 805	−0·210 325 495	+ 864 1017	+1344 8751	+ 583 0174
23	+0·869 861 540	−0·472 042 490	−0·204 465 558	+ 839 1008	+1358 5202	+ 588 9402
24	+0·878 126 399	−0·458 390 766	−0·198 547 295	+ 813 8268	+1371 7560	+ 594 6820
25	+0·886 137 214	−0·444 608 754	−0·192 572 530	+ 788 2944	+1384 5767	+ 600 2403
26	+0·893 891 476	−0·430 700 627	−0·186 543 107	+ 762 5184	+1396 9786	+ 605 6135
27	+0·901 386 816	−0·416 670 587	−0·180 460 880	+ 736 5124	+1408 9590	+ 610 8010
28	+0·908 621 001	−0·402 522 856	−0·174 327 708	+ 710 2895	+1420 5166	+ 615 8024
29	+0·915 591 922	−0·388 261 667	−0·168 145 452	+ 683 8614	+1431 6506	+ 620 6178
30	+0·922 297 583	−0·373 891 258	−0·161 915 970	+ 657 2396	+1442 3605	+ 625 2477
31	+0·928 736 103	−0·359 415 870	−0·155 641 116	+ 630 4347	+1452 6465	+ 629 6924
Sept. 1	+0·934 905 701	−0·344 839 741	−0·149 322 737	+ 603 4572	+1462 5089	+ 633 9526
2	+0·940 804 705	−0·330 167 101	−0·142 962 675	+ 576 3173	+1471 9487	+ 638 0294
3	+0·946 431 538	−0·315 402 169	−0·136 562 756	+ 549 0247	+1480 9677	+ 641 9241
4	+0·951 784 721	−0·300 549 140	−0·130 124 794	+ 521 5887	+1489 5687	+ 645 6385
5	+0·956 862 860	−0·285 612 176	−0·123 650 579	+ 494 0172	+1497 7553	+ 649 1752
6	+0·961 664 633	−0·270 595 398	−0·117 141 873	+ 466 3162	+1505 5325	+ 652 5370
7	+0·966 188 764	−0·255 502 874	−0·110 600 411	+ 438 4893	+1512 9053	+ 655 7270
8	+0·970 434 000	−0·240 338 623	−0·104 027 897	+ 410 5369	+1519 8785	+ 658 7478
9	+0·974 399 076	−0·225 106 627	−0·097 426 013	+ 382 4566	+1526 4547	+ 661 6011
10	+0·978 082 691	−0·209 810 851	−0·090 796 433	+ 354 2439	+1532 6342	+ 664 2869
11	+0·981 483 495	−0·194 455 278	−0·084 140 839	+ 325 8937	+1538 4132	+ 666 8033
12	+0·984 600 094	−0·179 043 945	−0·077 460 945	+ 297 4023	+1543 7848	+ 669 1463
13	+0·987 431 066	−0·163 580 974	−0·070 758 508	+ 268 7684	+1548 7390	+ 671 3108
14	+0·989 974 994	−0·148 070 593	−0·064 035 345	+ 239 9943	+1553 2646	+ 673 2905
15	+0·992 230 502	−0·132 517 150	−0·057 293 336	+ 211 0855	+1557 3496	+ 675 0791
16	+0·994 196 284	−0·116 925 108	−0·050 534 420	+ 182 0508	+1560 9827	+ 676 6707
17	+0·995 871 137	−0·101 299 037	−0·043 760 595	+ 152 9017	+1564 1536	+ 678 0600
18	+0·997 253 981	−0·085 643 606	−0·036 973 910	+ 123 6515	+1566 8535	+ 679 2424
19	+0·998 343 878	−0·069 963 562	−0·030 176 450	+ 94 3148	+1569 0753	+ 680 2143
20	+0·999 140 042	−0·054 263 712	−0·023 370 333	+ 64 9074	+1570 8137	+ 680 9733
21	+0·999 641 844	−0·038 548 911	−0·016 557 700	+ 35 4454	+1572 0653	+ 681 5176
22	+0·999 848 820	−0·022 824 036	−0·009 740 699	+ 5 9447	+1572 8282	+ 681 8467
23	+0·999 760 661	−0·007 093 977	−0·002 921 483	− 23 5792	+1573 1022	+ 681 9606
24	+0·999 377 210	+0·008 636 382	+0·003 897 799	− 53 1112	+1572 8884	+ 681 8602
25	+0·998 698 457	+0·024 362 171	+0·010 715 011	− 82 6374	+1572 1887	+ 681 5467
26	+0·997 724 525	+0·040 078 546	+0·017 528 029	− 112 1447	+1571 0059	+ 681 0219
27	+0·996 455 667	+0·055 780 689	+0·024 334 750	− 141 6207	+1569 3431	+ 680 2875
28	+0·994 892 255	+0·071 463 821	+0·031 133 089	− 171 0537	+1567 2042	+ 679 3458
29	+0·993 034 774	+0·087 123 198	+0·037 920 982	− 200 4324	+1564 5930	+ 678 1989
30	+0·990 883 823	+0·102 754 121	+0·044 696 392	− 229 7462	+1561 5141	+ 676 8495
Oct. 1	+0·988 440 102	+0·118 351 939	+0·051 457 307	− 258 9846	+1557 9729	+ 675 3005

$\dot{X}$, $\dot{Y}$, $\dot{Z}$ are in units of 10^{-9} au / d.

ICRS, ORIGIN AT SOLAR SYSTEM BARYCENTRE
FOR 0^h BARYCENTRIC DYNAMICAL TIME

Date 0^h TDB		X	Y	Z	$\dot{X}$	$\dot{Y}$	$\dot{Z}$
Oct.	**1**	+0·988 440 102	+0·118 351 939	+0·051 457 307	− 258 9846	+1557 9729	+ 675 3005
	2	+0·985 704 414	+0·133 912 058	+0·058 201 747	− 288 1382	+1553 9754	+ 673 5551
	3	+0·982 677 650	+0·149 429 951	+0·064 927 767	− 317 1986	+1549 5289	+ 671 6172
	4	+0·979 360 775	+0·164 901 165	+0·071 633 464	− 346 1593	+1544 6413	+ 669 4911
	5	+0·975 754 809	+0·180 321 334	+0·078 316 977	− 375 0166	+1539 3210	+ 667 1812
	6	+0·971 860 791	+0·195 686 170	+0·084 976 490	− 403 7699	+1533 5760	+ 664 6916
	7	+0·967 679 749	+0·210 991 459	+0·091 610 219	− 432 4218	+1527 4123	+ 662 0250
	8	+0·963 212 676	+0·226 233 029	+0·098 216 404	− 460 9772	+1520 8323	+ 659 1825
	9	+0·958 460 509	+0·241 406 713	+0·104 793 279	− 489 4413	+1513 8346	+ 656 1628
	10	+0·953 424 143	+0·256 508 309	+0·111 339 058	− 517 8173	+1506 4133	+ 652 9624
	11	+0·948 104 457	+0·271 533 540	+0·117 851 908	− 546 1048	+1498 5600	+ 649 5761
	12	+0·942 502 359	+0·286 478 035	+0·124 329 943	− 574 2987	+1490 2648	+ 645 9985
	13	+0·936 618 825	+0·301 337 331	+0·130 771 223	− 602 3899	+1481 5185	+ 642 2244
	14	+0·930 454 945	+0·316 106 877	+0·137 173 761	− 630 3658	+1472 3137	+ 638 2495
	15	+0·924 011 941	+0·330 782 058	+0·143 535 532	− 658 2121	+1462 6447	+ 634 0706
	16	+0·917 291 187	+0·345 358 213	+0·149 854 487	− 685 9131	+1452 5083	+ 629 6860
	17	+0·910 294 216	+0·359 830 660	+0·156 128 564	− 713 4529	+1441 9030	+ 625 0948
	18	+0·903 022 720	+0·374 194 710	+0·162 355 694	− 740 8153	+1430 8290	+ 620 2969
	19	+0·895 478 553	+0·388 445 685	+0·168 533 817	− 767 9846	+1419 2883	+ 615 2934
	20	+0·887 663 724	+0·402 578 931	+0·174 660 881	− 794 9453	+1407 2839	+ 610 0857
	21	+0·879 580 393	+0·416 589 832	+0·180 734 857	− 821 6826	+1394 8202	+ 604 6759
	22	+0·871 230 864	+0·430 473 821	+0·186 753 735	− 848 1823	+1381 9023	+ 599 0669
	23	+0·862 617 583	+0·444 226 386	+0·192 715 540	− 874 4311	+1368 5366	+ 593 2616
	24	+0·853 743 120	+0·457 843 083	+0·198 618 326	− 900 4165	+1354 7299	+ 587 2638
	25	+0·844 610 169	+0·471 319 540	+0·204 460 185	− 926 1268	+1340 4899	+ 581 0770
	26	+0·835 221 537	+0·484 651 462	+0·210 239 249	− 951 5512	+1325 8244	+ 574 7054
	27	+0·825 580 133	+0·497 834 638	+0·215 953 690	− 976 6794	+1310 7419	+ 568 1530
	28	+0·815 688 966	+0·510 864 940	+0·221 601 722	−1001 5023	+1295 2513	+ 561 4245
	29	+0·805 551 135	+0·523 738 334	+0·227 181 607	−1026 0110	+1279 3618	+ 554 5243
	30	+0·795 169 820	+0·536 450 881	+0·232 691 653	−1050 1978	+1263 0837	+ 547 4575
	31	+0·784 548 273	+0·548 998 748	+0·238 130 221	−1074 0564	+1246 4277	+ 540 2295
Nov.	**1**	+0·773 689 802	+0·561 378 213	+0·243 495 725	−1097 5821	+1229 4051	+ 532 8459
	2	+0·762 597 747	+0·573 585 668	+0·248 786 638	−1120 7729	+1212 0277	+ 525 3122
	3	+0·751 275 458	+0·585 617 621	+0·254 001 487	−1143 6296	+1194 3064	+ 517 6338
	4	+0·739 726 255	+0·597 470 680	+0·259 138 845	−1166 1565	+1176 2503	+ 509 8147
	5	+0·727 953 407	+0·609 141 530	+0·264 197 319	−1188 3597	+1157 8650	+ 501 8571
	6	+0·715 960 118	+0·620 626 887	+0·269 175 524	−1210 2459	+1139 1518	+ 493 7607
	7	+0·703 749 531	+0·631 923 462	+0·274 072 062	−1231 8196	+1120 1075	+ 485 5230
	8	+0·691 324 767	+0·643 027 912	+0·278 885 499	−1253 0808	+1100 7257	+ 477 1397
	9	+0·678 688 974	+0·653 936 828	+0·283 614 356	−1274 0243	+1080 9994	+ 468 6064
	10	+0·665 845 373	+0·664 646 732	+0·288 257 114	−1294 6402	+1060 9225	+ 459 9192
	11	+0·652 797 306	+0·675 154 097	+0·292 812 219	−1314 9151	+1040 4914	+ 451 0757
	12	+0·639 548 258	+0·685 455 377	+0·297 278 104	−1334 8340	+1019 7056	+ 442 0752
	13	+0·626 101 865	+0·695 547 032	+0·301 653 201	−1354 3816	+ 998 5670	+ 432 9182
	14	+0·612 461 914	+0·705 425 555	+0·305 935 953	−1373 5430	+ 977 0800	+ 423 6067
	15	+0·598 632 339	+0·715 087 489	+0·310 124 829	−1392 3041	+ 955 2502	+ 414 1433
	16	+0·584 617 210	+0·724 529 441	+0·314 218 324	−1410 6516	+ 933 0848	+ 404 5313

$\dot{X}$, $\dot{Y}$, $\dot{Z}$ are in units of 10^{-9} au / d.

ICRS, ORIGIN AT SOLAR SYSTEM BARYCENTRE
FOR 0^h BARYCENTRIC DYNAMICAL TIME

Date 0^h TDB	X	Y	Z	$\dot{X}$	$\dot{Y}$	$\dot{Z}$
Nov. 16	+0·584 617 210	+0·724 529 441	+0·314 218 324	−1410 6516	+ 933 0848	+ 404 5313
17	+0·570 420 728	+0·733 748 093	+0·318 214 971	−1428 5729	+ 910 5917	+ 394 7743
18	+0·556 047 211	+0·742 740 212	+0·322 113 342	−1446 0564	+ 887 7797	+ 384 8767
19	+0·541 501 096	+0·751 502 656	+0·325 912 052	−1463 0909	+ 864 6584	+ 374 8430
20	+0·526 786 924	+0·760 032 382	+0·329 609 764	−1479 6662	+ 841 2378	+ 364 6781
21	+0·511 909 334	+0·768 326 452	+0·333 205 193	−1495 7728	+ 817 5291	+ 354 3871
22	+0·496 873 058	+0·776 382 041	+0·336 697 106	−1511 4022	+ 793 5436	+ 343 9758
23	+0·481 682 906	+0·784 196 441	+0·340 084 327	−1526 5467	+ 769 2933	+ 333 4498
24	+0·466 343 761	+0·791 767 066	+0·343 365 739	−1541 1998	+ 744 7908	+ 322 8150
25	+0·450 860 566	+0·799 091 458	+0·346 540 286	−1555 3559	+ 720 0487	+ 312 0777
26	+0·435 238 314	+0·806 167 285	+0·349 606 973	−1569 0106	+ 695 0802	+ 301 2441
27	+0·419 482 036	+0·812 992 352	+0·352 564 869	−1582 1607	+ 669 8988	+ 290 3206
28	+0·403 596 788	+0·819 564 596	+0·355 413 107	−1594 8044	+ 644 5181	+ 279 3137
29	+0·387 587 635	+0·825 882 096	+0·358 150 887	−1606 9418	+ 618 9520	+ 268 2299
30	+0·371 459 633	+0·831 943 064	+0·360 777 470	−1618 5750	+ 593 2142	+ 257 0754
Dec. 1	+0·355 217 799	+0·837 745 849	+0·363 292 179	−1629 7090	+ 567 3171	+ 245 8560
2	+0·338 867 093	+0·843 288 912	+0·365 694 389	−1640 3510	+ 541 2716	+ 234 5763
3	+0·322 412 389	+0·848 570 810	+0·367 983 512	−1650 5101	+ 515 0850	+ 223 2389
4	+0·305 858 469	+0·853 590 154	+0·370 158 978	−1660 1956	+ 488 7609	+ 211 8447
5	+0·289 210 031	+0·858 345 568	+0·372 220 210	−1669 4146	+ 462 2985	+ 200 3918
6	+0·272 471 721	+0·862 835 651	+0·374 166 608	−1678 1701	+ 435 6939	+ 188 8772
7	+0·255 648 183	+0·867 058 956	+0·375 997 537	−1686 4594	+ 408 9424	+ 177 2974
8	+0·238 744 112	+0·871 013 997	+0·377 712 330	−1694 2750	+ 382 0404	+ 165 6498
9	+0·221 764 298	+0·874 699 262	+0·379 310 303	−1701 6059	+ 354 9876	+ 153 9333
10	+0·204 713 651	+0·878 113 254	+0·380 790 770	−1708 4397	+ 327 7866	+ 142 1489
11	+0·187 597 203	+0·881 254 518	+0·382 153 063	−1714 7640	+ 300 4433	+ 130 2991
12	+0·170 420 107	+0·884 121 673	+0·383 396 546	−1720 5674	+ 272 9661	+ 118 3876
13	+0·153 187 624	+0·886 713 426	+0·384 520 624	−1725 8401	+ 245 3646	+ 106 4190
14	+0·135 905 103	+0·889 028 586	+0·385 524 752	−1730 5735	+ 217 6494	+ 94 3983
15	+0·118 577 976	+0·891 066 074	+0·386 408 434	−1734 7601	+ 189 8320	+ 82 3308
16	+0·101 211 746	+0·892 824 925	+0·387 171 231	−1738 3934	+ 161 9241	+ 70 2221
17	+0·083 811 972	+0·894 304 294	+0·387 812 757	−1741 4676	+ 133 9377	+ 58 0779
18	+0·066 384 273	+0·895 503 460	+0·388 332 689	−1743 9778	+ 105 8856	+ 45 9041
19	+0·048 934 310	+0·896 421 831	+0·388 730 762	−1745 9197	+ 77 7810	+ 33 7071
20	+0·031 467 785	+0·897 058 950	+0·389 006 775	−1747 2898	+ 49 6374	+ 21 4932
21	+0·013 990 427	+0·897 414 496	+0·389 160 593	−1748 0859	+ 21 4690	+ 9 2694
22	−0·003 492 016	+0·897 488 296	+0·389 192 152	−1748 3069	− 6 7094	− 2 9576
23	−0·020 973 794	+0·897 280 324	+0·389 101 455	−1747 9530	− 34 8830	− 15 1806
24	−0·038 449 166	+0·896 790 703	+0·388 888 578	−1747 0261	− 63 0368	− 27 3925
25	−0·055 912 416	+0·896 019 703	+0·388 553 664	−1745 5294	− 91 1560	− 39 5866
26	−0·073 357 871	+0·894 967 746	+0·388 096 929	−1743 4680	− 119 2261	− 51 7559
27	−0·090 779 917	+0·893 635 392	+0·387 518 649	−1740 8487	− 147 2329	− 63 8943
28	−0·108 173 014	+0·892 023 341	+0·386 819 166	−1737 6800	− 175 1637	− 75 9958
29	−0·125 531 720	+0·890 132 412	+0·385 998 873	−1733 9723	− 203 0067	− 88 0556
30	−0·142 850 703	+0·887 963 530	+0·385 058 207	−1729 7375	− 230 7527	− 100 0698
31	−0·160 124 756	+0·885 517 703	+0·383 997 635	−1724 9883	− 258 3951	− 112 0365
32	−0·177 348 797	+0·882 795 985	+0·382 817 637	−1719 7371	− 285 9308	− 123 9551

$\dot{X}$, $\dot{Y}$, $\dot{Z}$ are in units of 10^{-9} au / d.

Reduction for polar motion

The rotation of the Earth can be represented by a diurnal rotation about a reference axis whose motion with respect to a space-fixed system is given by the theories of precession and nutation plus very small ($<$ 1 mas) corrections from observations. The pole of the reference axis is the celestial intermediate pole (CIP) and the system within which it moves is the GCRS (see page B25). The equator of date is orthogonal to the axis of the CIP. The axis of the CIP also moves with respect to the standard geodetic coordinate system, the ITRS (see below), which is fixed (in a specifically defined sense) with respect to the crust of the Earth. The motion of the CIP within the ITRS is known as polar motion; the path of the pole is quasi-circular with a maximum radius of about 10 m ($0''\!.3$) and principal periods of 365 and 428 days. The longer period component of the spin axis relative to the mean figure axis is called the Chandler wobble. It is the free nutation of the nonrigid triaxial mantle and crust of the Earth. The Chandler wobble is excited primarily by transfer of angular momentum from the atmosphere and oceans to the Earth's crust and mantle. The annual component is driven by seasonal effects. Polar motion as a whole is affected by unpredictable geophysical forces and must be determined continuously from various kinds of observations.

The origin of the International Terrestrial Reference System (ITRS) is the geocentre and the directions of its axes are defined implicitly by the adoption of a set of coordinates of stations (instruments) used to determine UT1 and polar motion from observations. The ITRS is systematically within a few centimetres of WGS 84, the geodetic system provided by GPS. The orientation of the Terrestrial Intermediate Reference System (see page B26) with respect to the ITRS is given by successive rotations through the three small angles y, x, and $-s'$. The celestial reference system is then obtained by a rotation about the z-axis, either by Greenwich apparent sidereal time (GAST) if the celestial coordinates are with respect to the true equator and equinox of date; or by the Earth rotation angle (θ) if the celestial coordinates are with respect to the Celestial Intermediate Reference System.

The small angle s', called the TIO locator, is a measure of the secular drift of the terrestrial intermediate origin (TIO), with respect to geodetic zero longitude, that is, the very slow systematic rotation of the Terrestrial Intermediate Reference System with respect to the ITRS (due to polar motion). The value of s' (see below) is minuscule and may be set to zero unless very precise results are needed.

The quantities x, y correspond to the coordinates of the CIP with respect to the ITRS, measured along the meridians at longitudes 0° and 270° (90° west). Current values of the coordinates, x, y, of the pole for use in the reduction of observations are published by the Central Bureau of the IERS (see https://www.iers.org/IERS/EN/Publications/Bulletins/bulletins.html). Previous values, from 1970 January 1 onwards, are given on page K10 at 3-monthly intervals. For precise work the values at 5-day intervals from the IERS should be used. The coordinates x and y are usually measured in arcseconds.

The longitude and latitude of a terrestrial observer, λ and ϕ, used in astronomical formulae (e.g., for hour angle or the determination of astronomical time), should be expressed in the Terrestrial Intermediate Reference System, that is, corrected for polar motion:

$$\lambda = \lambda_{\text{ITRS}} + \left(x \sin \lambda_{\text{ITRS}} + y \cos \lambda_{\text{ITRS}}\right) \tan \phi_{\text{ITRS}}$$

$$\phi = \phi_{\text{ITRS}} + \left(x \cos \lambda_{\text{ITRS}} - y \sin \lambda_{\text{ITRS}}\right)$$

where λ_{ITRS} and ϕ_{ITRS} are the ITRS (geodetic) longitude and latitude of the observer, and x and y are the ITRS coordinates of the CIP, in the same units as λ and ϕ. These formulae are approximate and should not be used for places at polar latitudes.

Reduction for polar motion (continued)

The rigorous transformation of a vector $\mathbf{p}_3$ with respect to the celestial system to the corresponding vector $\mathbf{p}_4$ with respect to the ITRS is given by the formula:

$$\mathbf{p}_4 = \mathbf{R}_1(-y)\ \mathbf{R}_2(-x)\ \mathbf{R}_3(s')\ \mathbf{R}_3(\beta)\ \mathbf{p}_3$$

and conversely,

$$\mathbf{p}_3 = \mathbf{R}_3(-\beta)\ \mathbf{R}_3(-s')\ \mathbf{R}_2(x)\ \mathbf{R}_1(y)\ \mathbf{p}_4$$

where the TIO locator

$$s' = -0''.000\,047\,T$$

and T is measured in Julian centuries of 365 25 days from 245 1545·0 TT. Some previous values of x and y are tabulated on page K10. Note, the standard rotation matrices $\mathbf{R}_1$, $\mathbf{R}_2$, $\mathbf{R}_3$ are given on page K19 and correspond to rotations about the x, y and z axes, respectively.

The method to form the vector $\mathbf{p}_3$ for celestial objects is given on page B68. However, the vectors given above could represent, for example, the coordinates of a point on the Earth's surface or of a satellite in orbit around the Earth. The quantity β depends on whether the true equinox or the celestial intermediate origin (CIO) is used, viz:

Equinox method

where β = GAST, Greenwich apparent sidereal time, tabulated daily at 0^h UT1 on pages B13–B20. GAST must be used if $\mathbf{p}_3$ is an equinox based position,

CIO method

or $\beta = \theta$, the Earth rotation angle, tabulated daily at 0^h UT1 on pages B21–B24. ERA must be used when $\mathbf{p}_3$ is a CIO based position.

Reduction for diurnal parallax and diurnal aberration

The computation of diurnal parallax and aberration due to the displacement of the observer from the centre of the Earth requires a knowledge of the geocentric coordinates (ρ, geocentric distance in units of the Earth's equatorial radius, and ϕ', geocentric latitude, see the explanation beginning on page K11) of the place of observation, and the local hour angle (h).

For bodies whose equatorial horizontal parallax (π) normally amounts to only a few arcseconds the corrections for diurnal parallax in right ascension and declination (in the sense geocentric place *minus* topocentric place) are given by:

$$\Delta\alpha = \pi(\rho\cos\phi'\sin h\ \sec\delta)$$
$$\Delta\delta = \pi(\rho\sin\phi'\cos\delta - \rho\cos\phi'\cos h\ \sin\delta)$$

and

$$h = \mathrm{GAST} - \alpha_e + \lambda$$
$$= \theta - \alpha_i + \lambda$$

where λ is the longitude. GAST $-\alpha_e$ is the hour angle calculated from the Greenwich apparent sidereal time and the equinox right ascension, whereas $\theta - \alpha_i$ is the hour angle formed from the Earth rotation angle and the CIO right ascension. π may be calculated from $8''.794$ divided by the geocentric distance of the body (in au). For the Moon (and other very close bodies) more precise formulae are required (see page D3).

The corrections for diurnal aberration in right ascension and declination (in the sense apparent place *minus* mean place) are given by:

$$\Delta\alpha = 0^s.0213\,\rho\ \cos\phi'\ \cos h\ \sec\delta$$
$$\Delta\delta = 0''.319\,\rho\ \cos\phi'\ \sin h\ \sin\delta$$

Reduction for diurnal parallax and diurnal aberration (continued)

For a body at transit the local hour angle (h) is zero and so $\Delta\delta$ is zero, but

$$\Delta\alpha = \pm 0^{s}.0213\, \rho \cos\phi' \sec\delta$$

where the plus and minus signs are used for the upper and lower transits, respectively; this may be regarded as a correction to the time of transit.

Alternatively, the effects may be computed in rectangular coordinates using the following expressions for the geocentric coordinates and velocity components of the observer with respect to the celestial equatorial reference system:

$$\begin{array}{ll} \text{position:} & (\;\; a_e\rho\cos\phi'\cos(\beta+\lambda),\; a_e\rho\cos\phi'\sin(\beta+\lambda),\; a_e\rho\sin\phi') \\ \text{velocity:} & (-a_e\omega\rho\cos\phi'\sin(\beta+\lambda),\; a_e\omega\rho\cos\phi'\cos(\beta+\lambda),\; 0) \end{array}$$

where β is the Greenwich sidereal time (mean or apparent) or the Earth rotation angle (as appropriate), λ is the longitude of the observer (east longitudes are positive), a_e is the equatorial radius of the Earth and ω the angular velocity of the Earth.

$$a_e\omega = 0{\cdot}465\text{ km/s} = 0{\cdot}269 \times 10^{-3}\text{au/d} \qquad c = 2{\cdot}998 \times 10^{5}\text{ km/s} = 173{\cdot}14\text{ au/d}$$

$$a_e\omega/c = 1{\cdot}55 \times 10^{-6}\text{ rad} = 0''.320 = 0^{s}.0213$$

These geocentric position and velocity vectors of the observer are added to the barycentric position and velocity of the Earth's centre, respectively, to obtain the corresponding barycentric vectors of the observer. Then, the procedures on pages B66–B75 may be followed using the barycentric position and velocity of the observer rather than $\mathbf{E}_B$ and $\dot{\mathbf{E}}_B$.

Conversion to altitude and azimuth

It is convenient to use the local hour angle (h) as an intermediary in the conversion from the right ascension (α_e or α_i) and declination (δ) to the azimuth (A_z) and altitude (a).

In order to determine the local hour angle (see page B11) corresponding to the UT1 of the observation, first obtain either Greenwich apparent sidereal time (GAST), see pages B13–B20, or the Earth rotation angle (θ) tabulated on pages B21–B24. This choice depends on whether the right ascension is with respect to the equinox or the CIO, respectively. The formulae are:

$$h = \text{GAST} + \lambda - \alpha_e = \theta + \lambda - \alpha_i$$

Then

$$\begin{aligned} \cos a \sin A_z &= -\cos\delta \sin h \\ \cos a \cos A_z &= \sin\delta\cos\phi - \cos\delta\cos h\sin\phi \\ \sin a &= \sin\delta\sin\phi + \cos\delta\cos h\cos\phi \end{aligned}$$

where azimuth (A_z) is measured from the north through east in the plane of the horizon, altitude (a) is measured perpendicular to the horizon, and λ, ϕ are the astronomical values (see page K13) of the east longitude and latitude of the place of observation. The plane of the horizon is defined to be perpendicular to the apparent direction of gravity. Zenith distance is given by $z = 90^\circ - a$.

For most purposes the values of the geodetic longitude and latitude may be used but in some cases the effects of local gravity anomalies and polar motion (see page B84) must be included. For full precision, the values of α, δ must be corrected for diurnal parallax and diurnal aberration. The inverse formulae are:

$$\begin{aligned} \cos\delta \sin h &= -\cos a \sin A_z \\ \cos\delta\cos h &= \sin a\cos\phi - \cos a\cos A_z\sin\phi \\ \sin\delta &= \sin a\sin\phi + \cos a\cos A_z\cos\phi \end{aligned}$$

Correction for refraction

For most astronomical purposes the effect of refraction in the Earth's atmosphere is to decrease the zenith distance (computed by the formulae of the previous section) by an amount R that depends on the zenith distance and on the meteorological conditions at the site. A simple expression for R for zenith distances less than 75° (altitudes greater than 15°) is:

$$R = 0\overset{\circ}{.}004\,52\,P \tan z/(273 + T)$$
$$= 0\overset{\circ}{.}004\,52\,P/((273 + T)\tan a)$$

where T is the temperature (°C) and P is the barometric pressure (millibars). This formula is usually accurate to about 0′.1 for altitudes above 15°, but the error increases rapidly at lower altitudes, especially in abnormal meteorological conditions. For observed apparent altitudes below 15° use the approximate formula:

$$R = P(0{\cdot}1594 + 0{\cdot}0196a + 0{\cdot}000\,02a^2)/[(273 + T)(1 + 0{\cdot}505a + 0{\cdot}0845a^2)]$$

where the altitude a is in degrees.

DETERMINATION OF LATITUDE AND AZIMUTH

Use of the Polaris table

The table on pages B88-B91 gives data for obtaining latitude from an observed altitude of Polaris (suitably corrected for instrumental errors and refraction) and the azimuth of this star (measured from north, positive to the east and negative to the west), for all hour angles and northern latitudes. The six tabulated quantities, each given to a precision of 0′.1, are a_0, a_1, a_2, referring to the correction to altitude, and b_0, b_1, b_2, to the azimuth.

$$\text{latitude} = \text{corrected observed altitude} + a_0 + a_1 + a_2$$
$$\text{azimuth} = (b_0 + b_1 + b_2)/\cos(\text{latitude})$$

The table is to be entered with the local apparent sidereal time of observation (LAST), and gives the values of a_0, b_0 directly; interpolation, with maximum differences of 0′.7, can be done mentally. To the precision of these tables local mean sidereal time may be used instead of LAST. In the same vertical column, the values of a_1, b_1 are found with the latitude, and those of a_2, b_2 with the date, as argument. Thus all six quantities can, if desired, be extracted together. The errors due to the adoption of a mean value of the local sidereal time for each of the subsidiary tables have been reduced to a minimum, and the total error is not likely to exceed 0′.2. Interpolation between columns should not be attempted.

The observed altitude must be corrected for refraction before being used to determine the astronomical latitude of the place of observation. Both the latitude and the azimuth so obtained are affected by local gravity anomalies if the altitude is measured with respect to a plane orthogonal to the local gravity vector, e.g., a liquid surface.

LST	0^h		1^h		2^h		3^h		4^h		5^h	
	a_0	b_0	a_0	b_0	a_0	b_0	a_0	b_0	a_0	b_0	a_0	b_0
m	′	′	′	′	′	′	′	′	′	′	′	′
0	−26·0	+27·5	−32·2	+19·7	−36·2	+10·7	−37·7	+0·8	−36·6	− 9·1	−33·0	−18·4
3	−26·3	+27·1	−32·4	+19·3	−36·3	+10·2	−37·7	+0·3	−36·5	− 9·6	−32·7	−18·8
6	−26·7	+26·8	−32·7	+18·9	−36·4	+ 9·7	−37·7	−0·2	−36·3	−10·1	−32·5	−19·2
9	−27·0	+26·4	−32·9	+18·5	−36·6	+ 9·2	−37·7	−0·7	−36·2	−10·6	−32·2	−19·7
12	−27·4	+26·1	−33·2	+18·0	−36·7	+ 8·7	−37·7	−1·2	−36·1	−11·0	−32·0	−20·1
15	−27·7	+25·7	−33·4	+17·6	−36·8	+ 8·2	−37·7	−1·7	−35·9	−11·5	−31·7	−20·5
18	−28·0	+25·3	−33·6	+17·1	−36·9	+ 7·7	−37·6	−2·2	−35·8	−12·0	−31·4	−20·9
21	−28·4	+25·0	−33·9	+16·7	−37·0	+ 7·3	−37·6	−2·7	−35·6	−12·5	−31·2	−21·3
24	−28·7	+24·6	−34·1	+16·2	−37·1	+ 6·8	−37·6	−3·2	−35·4	−12·9	−30·9	−21·7
27	−29·0	+24·2	−34·3	+15·8	−37·2	+ 6·3	−37·5	−3·7	−35·3	−13·4	−30·6	−22·2
30	−29·3	+23·8	−34·5	+15·3	−37·3	+ 5·8	−37·5	−4·2	−35·1	−13·9	−30·3	−22·6
33	−29·6	+23·4	−34·7	+14·9	−37·3	+ 5·3	−37·4	−4·7	−34·9	−14·3	−30·0	−23·0
36	−29·9	+23·0	−34·9	+14·4	−37·4	+ 4·8	−37·3	−5·2	−34·7	−14·8	−29·7	−23·3
39	−30·2	+22·6	−35·1	+14·0	−37·5	+ 4·3	−37·3	−5·7	−34·5	−15·2	−29·4	−23·7
42	−30·5	+22·2	−35·2	+13·5	−37·5	+ 3·8	−37·2	−6·2	−34·3	−15·7	−29·1	−24·1
45	−30·8	+21·8	−35·4	+13·0	−37·6	+ 3·3	−37·1	−6·7	−34·1	−16·2	−28·8	−24·5
48	−31·1	+21·4	−35·6	+12·6	−37·6	+ 2·8	−37·0	−7·2	−33·9	−16·6	−28·4	−24·9
51	−31·4	+21·0	−35·7	+12·1	−37·6	+ 2·3	−36·9	−7·6	−33·7	−17·0	−28·1	−25·2
54	−31·7	+20·6	−35·9	+11·6	−37·7	+ 1·8	−36·8	−8·1	−33·4	−17·5	−27·8	−25·6
57	−31·9	+20·2	−36·0	+11·1	−37·7	+ 1·3	−36·7	−8·6	−33·2	−17·9	−27·4	−26·0
60	−32·2	+19·7	−36·2	+10·7	−37·7	+ 0·8	−36·6	−9·1	−33·0	−18·4	−27·1	−26·3

Lat.	a_1	b_1	a_1	b_1	a_1	b_1	a_1	b_1	a_1	b_1	a_1	b_1
°												
0	− 0·1	− 0·2	0·0	− 0·2	0·0	− 0·1	0·0	+0·1	0·0	+ 0·2	− 0·1	+ 0·2
10	− 0·1	− 0·2	0·0	− 0·2	0·0	− 0·1	0·0	0·0	0·0	+ 0·1	− 0·1	+ 0·2
20	− 0·1	− 0·2	0·0	− 0·1	0·0	− 0·1	0·0	0·0	0·0	+ 0·1	− 0·1	+ 0·2
30	0·0	− 0·1	0·0	− 0·1	0·0	0·0	0·0	0·0	0·0	+ 0·1	0·0	+ 0·1
40	0·0	− 0·1	0·0	− 0·1	0·0	0·0	0·0	0·0	0·0	0·0	0·0	+ 0·1
45	0·0	0·0	0·0	0·0	0·0	0·0	0·0	0·0	0·0	0·0	0·0	0·0
50	0·0	0·0	0·0	0·0	0·0	0·0	0·0	0·0	0·0	0·0	0·0	0·0
55	0·0	0·0	0·0	0·0	0·0	0·0	0·0	0·0	0·0	0·0	0·0	0·0
60	0·0	+ 0·1	0·0	+ 0·1	0·0	0·0	0·0	0·0	0·0	− 0·1	0·0	− 0·1
62	+ 0·1	+ 0·1	0·0	+ 0·1	0·0	0·0	0·0	0·0	0·0	− 0·1	0·0	− 0·1
64	+ 0·1	+ 0·2	0·0	+ 0·1	0·0	+ 0·1	0·0	0·0	0·0	− 0·1	+ 0·1	− 0·2
66	+ 0·1	+ 0·2	0·0	+ 0·2	0·0	+ 0·1	0·0	0·0	0·0	− 0·1	+ 0·1	− 0·2

Month	a_2	b_2	a_2	b_2	a_2	b_2	a_2	b_2	a_2	b_2	a_2	b_2
Jan.	+ 0·1	− 0·1	+ 0·2	− 0·1	+ 0·2	− 0·1	+ 0·2	0·0	+ 0·2	0·0	+ 0·2	+ 0·1
Feb.	+ 0·1	− 0·3	+ 0·1	− 0·2	+ 0·2	− 0·2	+ 0·2	−0·1	+ 0·3	− 0·1	+ 0·3	0·0
Mar.	− 0·1	− 0·3	0·0	− 0·3	+ 0·1	− 0·3	+ 0·2	−0·3	+ 0·3	− 0·2	+ 0·3	− 0·2
Apr.	− 0·2	− 0·3	− 0·1	− 0·4	0·0	− 0·4	+ 0·1	−0·4	+ 0·2	− 0·3	+ 0·3	− 0·3
May	− 0·3	− 0·2	− 0·3	− 0·3	− 0·2	− 0·4	− 0·1	−0·4	0·0	− 0·4	+ 0·1	− 0·4
June	− 0·4	− 0·1	− 0·3	− 0·2	− 0·3	− 0·2	− 0·2	−0·3	− 0·1	− 0·4	0·0	− 0·4
July	− 0·3	+ 0·1	− 0·3	0·0	− 0·3	− 0·1	− 0·3	−0·2	− 0·2	− 0·2	− 0·2	− 0·3
Aug.	− 0·2	+ 0·2	− 0·2	+ 0·1	− 0·3	+ 0·1	− 0·3	0·0	− 0·3	− 0·1	− 0·2	− 0·1
Sept.	0·0	+ 0·3	− 0·1	+ 0·3	− 0·2	+ 0·2	− 0·2	+0·2	− 0·3	+ 0·1	− 0·3	+ 0·1
Oct.	+ 0·2	+ 0·3	+ 0·1	+ 0·3	0·0	+ 0·3	− 0·1	+0·3	− 0·2	+ 0·3	− 0·2	+ 0·2
Nov.	+ 0·4	+ 0·2	+ 0·3	+ 0·3	+ 0·2	+ 0·4	+ 0·1	+0·4	0·0	+ 0·4	− 0·1	+ 0·4
Dec.	+ 0·5	+ 0·1	+ 0·4	+ 0·2	+ 0·4	+ 0·3	+ 0·3	+0·4	+ 0·2	+ 0·5	0·0	+ 0·5

Latitude = Corrected observed altitude of *Polaris* + a_0 + a_1 + a_2
Azimuth of *Polaris* = (b_0 + b_1 + b_2) / cos (latitude)

LST	6ʰ		7ʰ		8ʰ		9ʰ		10ʰ		11ʰ	
	a_0	b_0	a_0	b_0	a_0	b_0	a_0	b_0	a_0	b_0	a_0	b_0
m	′	′	′	′	′	′	′	′	′	′	′	′
0	−27·1	−26·3	−19·4	−32·5	−10·3	−36·3	−0·5	−37·7	+9·2	−36·5	+18·4	−32·8
3	−26·7	−26·7	−18·9	−32·7	−9·8	−36·5	−0·1	−37·7	+9·7	−36·4	+18·8	−32·6
6	−26·4	−27·0	−18·5	−33·0	−9·3	−36·6	+0·4	−37·7	+10·2	−36·2	+19·2	−32·3
9	−26·0	−27·4	−18·1	−33·2	−8·9	−36·7	+0·9	−37·7	+10·6	−36·1	+19·6	−32·1
12	−25·7	−27·7	−17·6	−33·4	−8·4	−36·8	+1·4	−37·7	+11·1	−36·0	+20·0	−31·8
15	−25·3	−28·1	−17·2	−33·7	−7·9	−36·9	+1·9	−37·6	+11·6	−35·8	+20·5	−31·6
18	−24·9	−28·4	−16·7	−33·9	−7·4	−37·0	+2·4	−37·6	+12·1	−35·6	+20·9	−31·3
21	−24·6	−28·7	−16·3	−34·1	−6·9	−37·1	+2·9	−37·6	+12·5	−35·5	+21·3	−31·0
24	−24·2	−29·0	−15·9	−34·3	−6·4	−37·2	+3·4	−37·5	+13·0	−35·3	+21·7	−30·7
27	−23·8	−29·4	−15·4	−34·5	−6·0	−37·3	+3·9	−37·5	+13·4	−35·1	+22·1	−30·4
30	−23·4	−29·7	−14·9	−34·7	−5·5	−37·3	+4·4	−37·4	+13·9	−35·0	+22·5	−30·1
33	−23·0	−30·0	−14·5	−34·9	−5·0	−37·4	+4·9	−37·4	+14·4	−34·8	+22·9	−29·9
36	−22·6	−30·3	−14·0	−35·1	−4·5	−37·5	+5·4	−37·3	+14·8	−34·6	+23·3	−29·6
39	−22·2	−30·6	−13·6	−35·3	−4·0	−37·5	+5·8	−37·2	+15·3	−34·4	+23·6	−29·2
42	−21·8	−30·8	−13·1	−35·4	−3·5	−37·6	+6·3	−37·1	+15·7	−34·2	+24·0	−28·9
45	−21·4	−31·1	−12·6	−35·6	−3·0	−37·6	+6·8	−37·0	+16·2	−34·0	+24·4	−28·6
48	−21·0	−31·4	−12·2	−35·8	−2·5	−37·6	+7·3	−36·9	+16·6	−33·7	+24·8	−28·3
51	−20·6	−31·7	−11·7	−35·9	−2·0	−37·7	+7·8	−36·8	+17·0	−33·5	+25·1	−28·0
54	−20·2	−31·9	−11·2	−36·1	−1·5	−37·7	+8·3	−36·7	+17·5	−33·3	+25·5	−27·6
57	−19·8	−32·2	−10·8	−36·2	−1·0	−37·7	+8·7	−36·6	+17·9	−33·1	+25·9	−27·3
60	−19·4	−32·5	−10·3	−36·3	−0·5	−37·7	+9·2	−36·5	+18·4	−32·8	+26·2	−27·0
Lat.	a_1	b_1	a_1	b_1	a_1	b_1	a_1	b_1	a_1	b_1	a_1	b_1
°												
0	−0·2	+0·2	−0·2	+0·2	−0·2	+0·1	−0·2	−0·1	−0·2	−0·2	−0·2	−0·2
10	−0·1	+0·2	−0·2	+0·2	−0·2	+0·1	−0·2	0·0	−0·2	−0·1	−0·1	−0·2
20	−0·1	+0·2	−0·1	+0·1	−0·2	+0·1	−0·2	0·0	−0·1	−0·1	−0·1	−0·2
30	−0·1	+0·1	−0·1	+0·1	−0·1	0·0	−0·1	0·0	−0·1	−0·1	−0·1	−0·1
40	0·0	+0·1	−0·1	+0·1	−0·1	0·0	−0·1	0·0	−0·1	0·0	0·0	−0·1
45	0·0	0·0	0·0	0·0	0·0	0·0	0·0	0·0	0·0	0·0	0·0	0·0
50	0·0	0·0	0·0	0·0	0·0	0·0	0·0	0·0	0·0	0·0	0·0	0·0
55	0·0	0·0	0·0	0·0	0·0	0·0	0·0	0·0	0·0	0·0	0·0	0·0
60	+0·1	−0·1	+0·1	−0·1	+0·1	0·0	+0·1	0·0	+0·1	+0·1	+0·1	+0·1
62	+0·1	−0·1	+0·1	−0·1	+0·1	0·0	+0·1	0·0	+0·1	+0·1	+0·1	+0·1
64	+0·1	−0·2	+0·1	−0·1	+0·2	−0·1	+0·2	0·0	+0·2	+0·1	+0·1	+0·2
66	+0·1	−0·2	+0·2	−0·2	+0·2	−0·1	+0·2	0·0	+0·2	+0·1	+0·1	+0·2
Month	a_2	b_2	a_2	b_2	a_2	b_2	a_2	b_2	a_2	b_2	a_2	b_2
Jan.	+0·1	+0·1	+0·1	+0·2	+0·1	+0·2	0·0	+0·2	0·0	+0·2	−0·1	+0·2
Feb.	+0·3	+0·1	+0·2	+0·1	+0·2	+0·2	+0·1	+0·2	+0·1	+0·3	0·0	+0·3
Mar.	+0·3	−0·1	+0·3	0·0	+0·3	+0·1	+0·3	+0·2	+0·2	+0·3	+0·2	+0·3
Apr.	+0·3	−0·2	+0·4	−0·1	+0·4	0·0	+0·4	+0·1	+0·3	+0·2	+0·3	+0·3
May	+0·2	−0·3	+0·3	−0·3	+0·4	−0·2	+0·4	−0·1	+0·4	0·0	+0·4	+0·1
June	+0·1	−0·4	+0·2	−0·3	+0·2	−0·3	+0·3	−0·2	+0·4	−0·1	+0·4	0·0
July	−0·1	−0·3	0·0	−0·3	+0·1	−0·3	+0·2	−0·3	+0·2	−0·2	+0·3	−0·2
Aug.	−0·2	−0·2	−0·1	−0·2	−0·1	−0·3	0·0	−0·3	+0·1	−0·3	+0·1	−0·2
Sept.	−0·3	0·0	−0·3	−0·1	−0·2	−0·2	−0·2	−0·2	−0·1	−0·3	−0·1	−0·3
Oct.	−0·3	+0·2	−0·3	+0·1	−0·3	0·0	−0·3	−0·1	−0·3	−0·2	−0·2	−0·2
Nov.	−0·2	+0·4	−0·3	+0·3	−0·4	+0·2	−0·4	+0·1	−0·4	0·0	−0·4	−0·1
Dec.	−0·1	+0·5	−0·2	+0·4	−0·3	+0·4	−0·4	+0·3	−0·5	+0·2	−0·5	0·0

Latitude = Corrected observed altitude of *Polaris* + a_0 + a_1 + a_2

Azimuth of *Polaris* = (b_0 + b_1 + b_2) / cos (latitude)

LST	12h a_0	12h b_0	13h a_0	13h b_0	14h a_0	14h b_0	15h a_0	15h b_0	16h a_0	16h b_0	17h a_0	17h b_0
m	′	′	′	′	′	′	′	′	′	′	′	′
0	+26·2	−27·0	+32·3	−19·3	+36·2	−10·4	+37·7	−0·8	+36·6	+ 8·9	+33·1	+18·0
3	+26·6	−26·6	+32·6	−18·9	+36·4	− 9·9	+37·7	−0·3	+36·5	+ 9·3	+32·9	+18·4
6	+26·9	−26·3	+32·8	−18·5	+36·5	− 9·4	+37·7	+0·2	+36·4	+ 9·8	+32·6	+18·8
9	+27·3	−25·9	+33·0	−18·0	+36·6	− 9·0	+37·7	+0·7	+36·2	+10·3	+32·4	+19·2
12	+27·6	−25·6	+33·3	−17·6	+36·7	− 8·5	+37·7	+1·2	+36·1	+10·8	+32·1	+19·6
15	+27·9	−25·2	+33·5	−17·2	+36·8	− 8·0	+37·7	+1·7	+36·0	+11·2	+31·9	+20·1
18	+28·3	−24·8	+33·7	−16·7	+36·9	− 7·5	+37·6	+2·1	+35·8	+11·7	+31·6	+20·5
21	+28·6	−24·5	+33·9	−16·3	+37·0	− 7·1	+37·6	+2·6	+35·7	+12·2	+31·3	+20·9
24	+28·9	−24·1	+34·2	−15·9	+37·1	− 6·6	+37·6	+3·1	+35·5	+12·6	+31·0	+21·3
27	+29·2	−23·7	+34·4	−15·4	+37·2	− 6·1	+37·5	+3·6	+35·3	+13·1	+30·8	+21·7
30	+29·5	−23·3	+34·6	−15·0	+37·3	− 5·6	+37·5	+4·1	+35·2	+13·5	+30·5	+22·1
33	+29·8	−22·9	+34·8	−14·5	+37·3	− 5·1	+37·4	+4·6	+35·0	+14·0	+30·2	+22·5
36	+30·1	−22·6	+34·9	−14·1	+37·4	− 4·7	+37·4	+5·0	+34·8	+14·4	+29·9	+22·9
39	+30·4	−22·2	+35·1	−13·6	+37·5	− 4·2	+37·3	+5·5	+34·6	+14·9	+29·6	+23·3
42	+30·7	−21·8	+35·3	−13·2	+37·5	− 3·7	+37·2	+6·0	+34·4	+15·3	+29·3	+23·6
45	+31·0	−21·4	+35·5	−12·7	+37·6	− 3·2	+37·1	+6·5	+34·2	+15·8	+29·0	+24·0
48	+31·3	−21·0	+35·6	−12·2	+37·6	− 2·7	+37·0	+7·0	+34·0	+16·2	+28·6	+24·4
51	+31·5	−20·6	+35·8	−11·8	+37·6	− 2·2	+36·9	+7·5	+33·8	+16·7	+28·3	+24·8
54	+31·8	−20·1	+35·9	−11·3	+37·7	− 1·8	+36·8	+7·9	+33·6	+17·1	+28·0	+25·1
57	+32·1	−19·7	+36·1	−10·9	+37·7	− 1·3	+36·7	+8·4	+33·3	+17·5	+27·7	+25·5
60	+32·3	−19·3	+36·2	−10·4	+37·7	− 0·8	+36·6	+8·9	+33·1	+18·0	+27·3	+25·8

Lat.	12h a_1	12h b_1	13h a_1	13h b_1	14h a_1	14h b_1	15h a_1	15h b_1	16h a_1	16h b_1	17h a_1	17h b_1
°												
0	− 0·1	− 0·2	0·0	− 0·2	0·0	− 0·1	0·0	+0·1	0·0	+ 0·2	− 0·1	+ 0·2
10	− 0·1	− 0·2	0·0	− 0·2	0·0	− 0·1	0·0	0·0	0·0	+ 0·1	− 0·1	+ 0·2
20	− 0·1	− 0·2	0·0	− 0·1	0·0	− 0·1	0·0	0·0	0·0	+ 0·1	− 0·1	+ 0·2
30	0·0	− 0·1	0·0	− 0·1	0·0	0·0	0·0	0·0	0·0	+ 0·1	0·0	+ 0·1
40	0·0	− 0·1	0·0	− 0·1	0·0	0·0	0·0	0·0	0·0	0·0	0·0	+ 0·1
45	0·0	0·0	0·0	0·0	0·0	0·0	0·0	0·0	0·0	0·0	0·0	0·0
50	0·0	0·0	0·0	0·0	0·0	0·0	0·0	0·0	0·0	0·0	0·0	0·0
55	0·0	0·0	0·0	0·0	0·0	0·0	0·0	0·0	0·0	0·0	0·0	0·0
60	0·0	+ 0·1	0·0	+ 0·1	0·0	0·0	0·0	0·0	0·0	− 0·1	0·0	− 0·1
62	+ 0·1	+ 0·1	0·0	+ 0·1	0·0	0·0	0·0	0·0	0·0	− 0·1	0·0	− 0·1
64	+ 0·1	+ 0·2	0·0	+ 0·1	0·0	+ 0·1	0·0	0·0	0·0	− 0·1	+ 0·1	− 0·2
66	+ 0·1	+ 0·2	0·0	+ 0·2	0·0	+ 0·1	0·0	0·0	0·0	− 0·1	+ 0·1	− 0·2

Month	12h a_2	12h b_2	13h a_2	13h b_2	14h a_2	14h b_2	15h a_2	15h b_2	16h a_2	16h b_2	17h a_2	17h b_2
Jan.	− 0·1	+ 0·1	− 0·2	+ 0·1	− 0·2	+ 0·1	− 0·2	0·0	− 0·2	0·0	− 0·2	− 0·1
Feb.	− 0·1	+ 0·3	− 0·1	+ 0·2	− 0·2	+ 0·2	− 0·2	+0·1	− 0·3	+ 0·1	− 0·3	0·0
Mar.	+ 0·1	+ 0·3	0·0	+ 0·3	− 0·1	+ 0·3	− 0·2	+0·3	− 0·3	+ 0·2	− 0·3	+ 0·2
Apr.	+ 0·2	+ 0·3	+ 0·1	+ 0·4	0·0	+ 0·4	− 0·1	+0·4	− 0·2	+ 0·3	− 0·3	+ 0·3
May	+ 0·3	+ 0·2	+ 0·3	+ 0·3	+ 0·2	+ 0·4	+ 0·1	+0·4	0·0	+ 0·4	− 0·1	+ 0·4
June	+ 0·4	+ 0·1	+ 0·3	+ 0·2	+ 0·3	+ 0·2	+ 0·2	+0·3	+ 0·1	+ 0·4	0·0	+ 0·4
July	+ 0·3	− 0·1	+ 0·3	0·0	+ 0·3	+ 0·1	+ 0·3	+0·2	+ 0·2	+ 0·2	+ 0·2	+ 0·3
Aug.	+ 0·2	− 0·2	+ 0·2	− 0·1	+ 0·3	− 0·1	+ 0·3	0·0	+ 0·3	+ 0·1	+ 0·2	+ 0·1
Sept.	0·0	− 0·3	+ 0·1	− 0·3	+ 0·2	− 0·2	+ 0·2	−0·2	+ 0·3	− 0·1	+ 0·3	− 0·1
Oct.	− 0·2	− 0·3	− 0·1	− 0·3	0·0	− 0·3	+ 0·1	−0·3	+ 0·2	− 0·3	+ 0·2	− 0·2
Nov.	− 0·4	− 0·2	− 0·3	− 0·3	− 0·2	− 0·4	− 0·1	−0·4	0·0	− 0·4	+ 0·1	− 0·4
Dec.	− 0·5	− 0·1	− 0·4	− 0·2	− 0·4	− 0·3	− 0·3	−0·4	− 0·2	− 0·5	0·0	− 0·5

Latitude = Corrected observed altitude of *Polaris* + a_0 + a_1 + a_2

Azimuth of *Polaris* = (b_0 + b_1 + b_2) / cos (latitude)

LST	18h a_0	18h b_0	19h a_0	19h b_0	20h a_0	20h b_0	21h a_0	21h b_0	22h a_0	22h b_0	23h a_0	23h b_0
m	′	′	′	′	′	′	′	′	′	′	′	′
0	+27·3	+25·8	+19·7	+32·0	+10·7	+36·1	+1·0	+37·7	− 8·8	+36·7	−18·0	+33·2
3	+27·0	+26·2	+19·3	+32·3	+10·3	+36·2	+0·5	+37·7	− 9·2	+36·6	−18·4	+33·0
6	+26·6	+26·5	+18·9	+32·5	+ 9·8	+36·3	+0·1	+37·7	− 9·7	+36·5	−18·8	+32·8
9	+26·3	+26·9	+18·4	+32·8	+ 9·3	+36·5	−0·4	+37·7	−10·2	+36·4	−19·3	+32·5
12	+25·9	+27·2	+18·0	+33·0	+ 8·8	+36·6	−0·9	+37·7	−10·7	+36·2	−19·7	+32·3
15	+25·6	+27·6	+17·6	+33·3	+ 8·4	+36·7	−1·4	+37·7	−11·1	+36·1	−20·1	+32·0
18	+25·2	+27·9	+17·1	+33·5	+ 7·9	+36·8	−1·9	+37·7	−11·6	+35·9	−20·5	+31·7
21	+24·9	+28·2	+16·7	+33·7	+ 7·4	+36·9	−2·4	+37·6	−12·1	+35·8	−20·9	+31·5
24	+24·5	+28·6	+16·3	+33·9	+ 6·9	+37·0	−2·9	+37·6	−12·6	+35·6	−21·3	+31·2
27	+24·1	+28·9	+15·8	+34·1	+ 6·4	+37·1	−3·4	+37·6	−13·0	+35·5	−21·8	+30·9
30	+23·7	+29·2	+15·4	+34·3	+ 5·9	+37·2	−3·9	+37·5	−13·5	+35·3	−22·2	+30·6
33	+23·3	+29·5	+14·9	+34·5	+ 5·5	+37·3	−4·4	+37·5	−13·9	+35·1	−22·6	+30·3
36	+23·0	+29·8	+14·5	+34·7	+ 5·0	+37·3	−4·9	+37·4	−14·4	+34·9	−23·0	+30·0
39	+22·6	+30·1	+14·0	+34·9	+ 4·5	+37·4	−5·4	+37·4	−14·9	+34·7	−23·3	+29·7
42	+22·2	+30·4	+13·5	+35·1	+ 4·0	+37·5	−5·9	+37·3	−15·3	+34·5	−23·7	+29·4
45	+21·8	+30·7	+13·1	+35·3	+ 3·5	+37·5	−6·3	+37·2	−15·8	+34·3	−24·1	+29·1
48	+21·4	+31·0	+12·6	+35·4	+ 3·0	+37·6	−6·8	+37·1	−16·2	+34·1	−24·5	+28·8
51	+21·0	+31·2	+12·2	+35·6	+ 2·5	+37·6	−7·3	+37·0	−16·7	+33·9	−24·9	+28·5
54	+20·5	+31·5	+11·7	+35·8	+ 2·0	+37·6	−7·8	+36·9	−17·1	+33·7	−25·2	+28·1
57	+20·1	+31·8	+11·2	+35·9	+ 1·5	+37·7	−8·3	+36·8	−17·5	+33·5	−25·6	+27·8
60	+19·7	+32·0	+10·7	+36·1	+ 1·0	+37·7	−8·8	+36·7	−18·0	+33·2	−26·0	+27·5
Lat.	a_1	b_1	a_1	b_1	a_1	b_1	a_1	b_1	a_1	b_1	a_1	b_1
°												
0	− 0·2	+ 0·2	− 0·2	+ 0·2	− 0·2	+ 0·1	−0·2	− 0·1	− 0·2	− 0·2	− 0·2	− 0·2
10	− 0·1	+ 0·2	− 0·2	+ 0·2	− 0·2	+ 0·1	−0·2	0·0	− 0·2	− 0·1	− 0·1	− 0·2
20	− 0·1	+ 0·2	− 0·1	+ 0·1	− 0·2	+ 0·1	−0·2	0·0	− 0·1	− 0·1	− 0·1	− 0·2
30	− 0·1	+ 0·1	− 0·1	+ 0·1	− 0·1	0·0	−0·1	0·0	− 0·1	− 0·1	− 0·1	− 0·1
40	0·0	+ 0·1	− 0·1	+ 0·1	− 0·1	0·0	−0·1	0·0	− 0·1	0·0	0·0	− 0·1
45	0·0	0·0	0·0	0·0	0·0	0·0	0·0	0·0	0·0	0·0	0·0	0·0
50	0·0	0·0	0·0	0·0	0·0	0·0	0·0	0·0	0·0	0·0	0·0	0·0
55	0·0	0·0	0·0	0·0	0·0	0·0	0·0	0·0	0·0	0·0	0·0	0·0
60	+ 0·1	− 0·1	+ 0·1	− 0·1	+ 0·1	0·0	+0·1	0·0	+ 0·1	+ 0·1	+ 0·1	+ 0·1
62	+ 0·1	− 0·1	+ 0·1	− 0·1	+ 0·1	0·0	+0·1	0·0	+ 0·1	+ 0·1	+ 0·1	+ 0·1
64	+ 0·1	− 0·2	+ 0·1	− 0·1	+ 0·2	− 0·1	+0·2	0·0	+ 0·2	+ 0·1	+ 0·1	+ 0·2
66	+ 0·1	− 0·2	+ 0·2	− 0·2	+ 0·2	− 0·1	+0·2	0·0	+ 0·2	+ 0·1	+ 0·1	+ 0·2
Month	a_2	b_2	a_2	b_2	a_2	b_2	a_2	b_2	a_2	b_2	a_2	b_2
Jan.	− 0·1	− 0·1	− 0·1	− 0·2	− 0·1	− 0·2	0·0	− 0·2	0·0	− 0·2	+ 0·1	− 0·2
Feb.	− 0·3	− 0·1	− 0·2	− 0·1	− 0·2	− 0·2	−0·1	− 0·2	− 0·1	− 0·3	0·0	− 0·3
Mar.	− 0·3	+ 0·1	− 0·3	0·0	− 0·3	− 0·1	−0·3	− 0·2	− 0·2	− 0·3	− 0·2	− 0·3
Apr.	− 0·3	+ 0·2	− 0·4	+ 0·1	− 0·4	0·0	−0·4	− 0·1	− 0·3	− 0·2	− 0·3	− 0·3
May	− 0·2	+ 0·3	− 0·3	+ 0·3	− 0·4	+ 0·2	−0·4	+ 0·1	− 0·4	0·0	− 0·4	− 0·1
June	− 0·1	+ 0·4	− 0·2	+ 0·3	− 0·2	+ 0·3	−0·3	+ 0·2	− 0·4	+ 0·1	− 0·4	0·0
July	+ 0·1	+ 0·3	0·0	+ 0·3	− 0·1	+ 0·3	−0·2	+ 0·3	− 0·2	+ 0·2	− 0·3	+ 0·2
Aug.	+ 0·2	+ 0·2	+ 0·1	+ 0·2	+ 0·1	+ 0·3	0·0	+ 0·3	− 0·1	+ 0·3	− 0·1	+ 0·2
Sept.	+ 0·3	0·0	+ 0·3	+ 0·1	+ 0·2	+ 0·2	+0·2	+ 0·2	+ 0·1	+ 0·3	+ 0·1	+ 0·3
Oct.	+ 0·3	− 0·2	+ 0·3	− 0·1	+ 0·3	0·0	+0·3	+ 0·1	+ 0·3	+ 0·2	+ 0·2	+ 0·2
Nov.	+ 0·2	− 0·4	+ 0·3	− 0·3	+ 0·4	− 0·2	+0·4	− 0·1	+ 0·4	0·0	+ 0·4	+ 0·1
Dec.	+ 0·1	− 0·5	+ 0·2	− 0·4	+ 0·3	− 0·4	+0·4	− 0·3	+ 0·5	− 0·2	+ 0·5	0·0

Latitude = Corrected observed altitude of *Polaris* + a_0 + a_1 + a_2
Azimuth of *Polaris* = (b_0 + b_1 + b_2) / cos (latitude)

Pole star formulae

The formulae below provide a method for obtaining latitude from the observed altitude of one of the pole stars, *Polaris* or σ Octantis, and an assumed *east* longitude of the observer λ. In addition, the azimuth of a pole star may be calculated from an assumed *east* longitude λ and the observed altitude a, or from λ and an assumed latitude ϕ. An error of $0^\circ\!\!.002$ in a or $0^\circ\!\!.1$ in λ will produce an error of about $0^\circ\!\!.002$ in the calculated latitude. Likewise an error of $0^\circ\!\!.03$ in λ, a or ϕ will produce an error of about $0^\circ\!\!.002$ in the calculated azimuth for latitudes below 70°.

Step 1. Calculate the hour angle HA and polar distance p, in degrees, from expressions of the form:

$$\mathrm{HA} = a_0 + a_1 L + a_2 \sin L + a_3 \cos L + 15\,t$$

$$p = a_0 + a_1 L + a_2 \sin L + a_3 \cos L$$

where

$$L = 0^\circ\!\!.985\,65\,d$$

$$d = \text{day of year (from pages B4–B5)} + t/24$$

and where the coefficients a_0, a_1, a_2, a_3 are given in the table below, t is the universal time in hours, d is the interval in days from 2025 January 0 at 0^h UT1 to the time of observation, and the quantity L is in degrees. In the above formulae d is required to two decimals of a day, L to two decimals of a degree and t to three decimals of an hour.

Step 2. Calculate the local hour angle *LHA* from:

$$LHA = \mathrm{HA} + \lambda \quad \text{(add or subtract multiples of 360°)}$$

where λ is the assumed longitude measured east from the Greenwich meridian.

Form the quantities: $S = p \sin(LHA)$ $\quad C = p \cos(LHA)$

Step 3. The latitude of the place of observation, in degrees, is given by:

$$\text{latitude} = a - C + 0{\cdot}0087\, S^2 \tan a$$

where a is the observed altitude of the pole star after correction for instrument error and atmospheric refraction.

Step 4. The azimuth of the pole star, in degrees, is given by:

$$\text{azimuth of } Polaris = -S/\cos a$$

$$\text{azimuth of } \sigma \text{ Octantis} = 180^\circ + S/\cos a$$

where azimuth is measured eastwards around the horizon from north.

In *Step 4*, if a has not been observed, use the quantity:

$$a = \phi + C - 0{\cdot}0087\, S^2 \tan \phi$$

where ϕ is an assumed latitude, taken to be positive in either hemisphere.

POLE STAR COEFFICIENTS FOR 2025

	Polaris		σ Octantis	
	GHA	p	GHA	p
	°	°	°	°
a_0	53·97	0·6303	137·58	1·1484
a_1	0·998 79	−0·0000 102	0·999 47	0·0000 128
a_2	0·39	−0·0029	0·17	0·0038
a_3	−0·31	−0·0045	0·21	−0·0039

CONTENTS OF SECTION C

NOTES AND FORMULAS

Mean orbital elements of the Sun

Mean elements of the orbit of the Sun, referred to the mean equinox and ecliptic of date, are given by the following expressions. The time argument d is the interval in days from 2025 January 0, 0^h TT. These expressions are intended for use only during the year of this volume.

d = JD – 246 0675.5 = day of year (from B4–B5) + fraction of day from 0^h TT.

Geometric mean longitude:	$279^{\circ}\!.919\,671 + 0.985\,647\,36\,d$
Mean longitude of perigee:	$283^{\circ}\!.367\,199 + 0.000\,047\,08\,d$
Mean anomaly:	$356^{\circ}\!.552\,472 + 0.985\,600\,28\,d$
Eccentricity:	$0.016\,698\,12 - 0.000\,000\,0012\,d$
Mean obliquity of the ecliptic (w.r.t. mean equator of date):	$23^{\circ}\!.436\,027 - 0.000\,000\,36\,d$

The position of the ecliptic of date with respect to the ecliptic of the standard epoch is given by formulas on page B53. Osculating elements of the Earth/Moon barycenter are on page E8.

NOTES AND FORMULAS

Lengths of principal years

The lengths of the principal years at 2025.0 as derived from thc Sun's mean motion are:

		d	d h m s
tropical year	(equinox to equinox)	365.242 189	365 05 48 45.1
sidereal year	(fixed star to fixed star)	365.256 363	365 06 09 09.8
anomalistic year	(perigee to perigee)	365.259 637	365 06 13 52.6
eclipse year	(node to node)	346.620 084	346 14 52 55.3

Apparent ecliptic coordinates of the Sun

The apparent ecliptic longitude may be computed from the geometric ecliptic longitude tabulated on pages C6–C20 using:

apparent longitude = tabulated longitude + nutation in longitude $(\Delta\psi)$ – $20''\!.496/R$

where $\Delta\psi$ is tabulated on pages B58–B65 and R is the true geocentric distance tabulated on pages C6–C20. The apparent ecliptic latitude is equal to the geometric ecliptic latitude found on pages C6–C20 to the precision of tabulation.

Time of transit of the Sun

The quantity tabulated as "Ephemeris Transit" on pages C7–C21 is the TT of transit of the Sun over the ephemeris meridian, which is at the longitude 1.002 738 ΔT east of the prime (Greenwich) meridian; in this expression ΔT is the difference TT – UT. The TT of transit of the Sun over a local meridian is obtained by interpolation where the first differences are about 24 hours. The interpolation factor p is given by:

$$p = -\lambda + 1.002\,738\ \Delta T$$

where λ is the east longitude and the right-hand side of the equation is expressed in days. (Divide longitude in degrees by 360 and ΔT in seconds by 86 400). During 2025 it is expected that ΔT will be about 69 seconds, so that the second term is about +0.000 81 days.

The UT of transit is obtained by subtracting ΔT from the TT of transit obtained by interpolation.

Equation of Time

Apparent solar time is the timescale based on the diurnal motion of the true Sun. The rate of solar diurnal motion has seasonal variations caused by the obliquity of the ecliptic and by the eccentricity of the Earth's orbit. Additional small variations arise from irregularities in the rotation of the Earth on its axis. Mean solar time is the timescale based on the diurnal motion of the fictitious mean Sun, a point with uniform motion along the celestial equator. The difference between apparent solar time and mean solar time is the Equation of Time.

Equation of Time = apparent solar time – mean solar time

To obtain the Equation of Time to a precision of about 1 second it is sufficient to use:

Equation of Time at 12^{h} UT = 12^{h} – tabulated value of ephem. transit found on C7–C21.

NOTES AND FORMULAS

Equation of Time (continued)

Alternatively, Equation of Time may be calculated for any instant during 2025 in seconds of time to a precision of about 3 seconds directly from the expression:

$$\text{Equation of Time} = -110.7 \sin L + 595.9 \sin 2L + 4.6 \sin 3L - 12.7 \sin 4L - 427.6 \cos L - 2.2 \cos 2L + 19.2 \cos 3L$$

where L is the mean longitude of the Sun, corrected for aberration, given by:

$$L = 279^{\circ}.914 + 0.985\,647\, d$$

and where d is the interval in days from 2025 January 0 at 0^{h} UT, given by:

$$d = \text{day of year (from B4–B5)} + \text{fraction of day from } 0^{h} \text{ UT.}$$

ICRS geocentric rectangular coordinates of the Sun

The geocentric equatorial rectangular coordinates of the Sun in au, referred to the ICRS axes, are given on pages C22–C25. The direction of these axes have been defined by the International Astronomical Union and are realized in practice by the coordinates of several hundred extragalactic radio sources. A rigorous method of determining the apparent place of a solar system object is described beginning on page B66.

Elements of the rotation of the Sun

The mean elements of the rotation of the Sun for 2025.0 are given below. With the exception of the position of the ascending node of the solar equator on the ecliptic whose rate is 0°.014 per year, the values change less than 0°.01 per year and can be used for the entire year for most applications. Linear interpolation using values found in recent editions can be made if needed.

Position of the ascending node of the solar equator:
on the ecliptic (longitude) = 76°.11
on the mean equator of 2025.0 (right ascension) = 16°.18
Inclination of the solar equator:
with respect to the "Carrington" ecliptic (1850) = 7°.25
with respect to the mean equator of 2025.0 = 26°.09
Position of the pole of the solar equator, w.r.t. the mean equinox and equator of 2025.0:
Right ascension = 286°.18
Declination = 63°.91
Sidereal rotation rate of the prime meridian = 14°.1844 per day.
Mean synodic period of rotation of the prime meridian = 27.2753 days.

These data are derived from elements originally given by R. C. Carrington, 1863, *Observations of the Spots on the Sun*, p. 244. They have been updated using values from Urban and Seidelmann, 2012, *Explanatory Supplement to the Astronomical Almanac*, p. 426, and Archinal et al., Celestial Mech Dyn Astr, 2011, **110** 401.

NOTES AND FORMULAS

Heliographic coordinates

Except for Ephemeris Transit, the quantities on the right-hand pages of C7–C21 are tabulated for 0^h TT. Except for L_0, the values are, to the accuracy given, essentially the same for 0^h UT. The value of L_0 at 0^h TT is approximately $0\overset{\circ}{.}01$ greater than its value at 0^h UT.

If ρ_1, θ are the observed angular distance and position angle of a sunspot from the center of the disk of the Sun as seen from the Earth, and ρ is the heliocentric angular distance of the spot on the solar surface from the center of the Sun's disk, then

$$\sin(\rho + \rho_1) = \rho_1/S$$

where S is the semidiameter of the Sun. The position angle is measured from the north point of the disk towards the east.

The formulas for the computation of the heliographic coordinates (L, B) of a sunspot (or other feature on the surface of the Sun) from (ρ, θ) are as follows:

$$\begin{aligned}\sin B &= \sin B_0 \cos\rho + \cos B_0 \sin\rho \cos(P - \theta)\\ \cos B \sin(L - L_0) &= \sin\rho \sin(P - \theta)\\ \cos B \cos(L - L_0) &= \cos\rho \cos B_0 - \sin B_0 \sin\rho \cos(P - \theta)\end{aligned}$$

where B is measured positive to the north of the solar equator and L is measured from 0° to 360° in the direction of rotation of the Sun, i.e., westwards on the apparent disk as seen from the Earth. Daily values for B_0 and L_0 are tabulated on pages C7–C21.

SYNODIC ROTATION NUMBERS, 2025

Number	Date of Commencement			Number	Date of Commencement		
2292	2024	Dec.	10.49	2300	2025	July	16.71
2293	2025	Jan.	6.82	2301		Aug.	12.93
2294		Feb.	3.16	2302		Sept	9.18
2295		Mar.	2.50	2303		Oct.	6.45
2296		Mar.	29.81	2304		Nov.	2.75
2297		Apr.	26.08	2305		Nov.	30.05
2298		May	23.31	2306	2025	Dec.	27.38
2299		June	19.51	2307	2026	Jan.	23.71

At the date of commencement of each synodic rotation period, the value of L_0 is zero; that is, the prime meridian passes through the central point of the disk.

NOTES AND FORMULAS

Low precision formulas for the Sun

The following are low precision formulas for the Sun. On this page, the time argument n is the number of days of TT from J2000.0. UT can be used with negligible error.

The low precision formulas for the apparent right ascension and declination of the Sun yield a precision better than $1\rlap{.}'0$ between the years 1950 and 2050.

n = JD – 2451545.0 = 9130.5 + day of year (from B4–B5) + fraction of day from 0^{h} TT
Mean longitude of Sun, corrected for aberration: $L = 280\rlap{.}^\circ460 + 0\rlap{.}^\circ985\,6474\, n$
Mean anomaly: $g = 357\rlap{.}^\circ528 + 0\rlap{.}^\circ985\,6003\, n$

Put L and g in the range 0° to 360° by adding multiples of 360°.

Ecliptic longitude: $\lambda = L + 1\rlap{.}^\circ915 \sin g + 0\rlap{.}^\circ020 \sin 2g$
Ecliptic latitude: $\beta = 0^\circ$
Obliquity of ecliptic: $\epsilon = 23\rlap{.}^\circ439 - 0\rlap{.}^\circ000\,0004\, n$
Right ascension: $\alpha = \tan^{-1}(\cos\epsilon \tan\lambda)$; ($\alpha$ in same quadrant as λ)

Alternatively, right ascension, α, may be calculated directly from:

Right ascension: $\alpha = \lambda - ft \sin 2\lambda + (f/2)t^2 \sin 4\lambda$
where $f = 180/\pi$ and $t = \tan^2(\epsilon/2)$
Declination: $\delta = \sin^{-1}(\sin\epsilon \sin\lambda)$

The low precision formula for the distance of the Sun from Earth, R, in au, yields a precision better than 0.0003 au between the years 1950 and 2050.

$R = 1.000\,14 - 0.016\,71 \cos g - 0.000\,14 \cos 2g$

The low precision formulas for the equatorial rectangular coordinates of the Sun, in au, yield a precision better than 0.015 au between the years 1950 and 2050.

$x = R \cos\lambda$
$y = R \cos\epsilon \sin\lambda$
$z = R \sin\epsilon \sin\lambda$

The low precision formula for the Equation of Time, E, in minutes, yields a precision better than $3\rlap{.}^s5$ between 1950 and 2050.

$E = (L - \alpha)$, in degrees, multiplied by 4

Other useful quantities:

Horizontal parallax: $0\rlap{.}^\circ0024$
Semidiameter: $0\rlap{.}^\circ2666/R$
Light-time: $0\rlap{.}^d0058$

FOR 0^h TERRESTRIAL TIME

Date		Julian Date	Geometric Ecliptic Coords. Mn Equinox & Ecliptic of Date		Apparent R. A.	Apparent Declination	True Geocentric Distance
			Longitude	Latitude			
		246	° ′ ″	″	h m s	° ′ ″	au
Jan.	0	0675.5	279 47 56.16	−0.67	18 42 37.09	−23 04 37.6	0.983 3692
	1	0676.5	280 49 06.72	−0.63	18 47 02.21	−22 59 53.8	0.983 3532
	2	0677.5	281 50 17.30	−0.57	18 51 27.02	−22 54 42.5	0.983 3409
	3	0678.5	282 51 27.80	−0.47	18 55 51.46	−22 49 03.7	0.983 3325
	4	0679.5	283 52 38.13	−0.36	19 00 15.50	−22 42 57.8	0.983 3281
	5	0680.5	284 53 48.19	−0.23	19 04 39.11	−22 36 24.8	0.983 3278
	6	0681.5	285 54 57.91	−0.10	19 09 02.27	−22 29 25.0	0.983 3320
	7	0682.5	286 56 07.21	+0.03	19 13 24.94	−22 21 58.5	0.983 3410
	8	0683.5	287 57 16.05	+0.16	19 17 47.09	−22 14 05.7	0.983 3551
	9	0684.5	288 58 24.41	+0.26	19 22 08.71	−22 05 46.7	0.983 3746
	10	0685.5	289 59 32.26	+0.35	19 26 29.78	−21 57 01.8	0.983 3999
	11	0686.5	291 00 39.62	+0.40	19 30 50.26	−21 47 51.3	0.983 4312
	12	0687.5	292 01 46.50	+0.43	19 35 10.15	−21 38 15.5	0.983 4687
	13	0688.5	293 02 52.92	+0.42	19 39 29.42	−21 28 14.6	0.983 5126
	14	0689.5	294 03 58.91	+0.38	19 43 48.05	−21 17 48.9	0.983 5629
	15	0690.5	295 05 04.51	+0.31	19 48 06.02	−21 06 58.7	0.983 6197
	16	0691.5	296 06 09.74	+0.22	19 52 23.33	−20 55 44.3	0.983 6828
	17	0692.5	297 07 14.62	+0.11	19 56 39.95	−20 44 05.9	0.983 7521
	18	0693.5	298 08 19.15	−0.01	20 00 55.88	−20 32 03.9	0.983 8274
	19	0694.5	299 09 23.34	−0.14	20 05 11.11	−20 19 38.6	0.983 9085
	20	0695.5	300 10 27.18	−0.26	20 09 25.61	−20 06 50.2	0.983 9951
	21	0696.5	301 11 30.64	−0.39	20 13 39.39	−19 53 39.1	0.984 0870
	22	0697.5	302 12 33.71	−0.50	20 17 52.42	−19 40 05.7	0.984 1840
	23	0698.5	303 13 36.35	−0.59	20 22 04.71	−19 26 10.3	0.984 2858
	24	0699.5	304 14 38.53	−0.67	20 26 16.24	−19 11 53.2	0.984 3921
	25	0700.5	305 15 40.19	−0.72	20 30 27.00	−18 57 14.9	0.984 5027
	26	0701.5	306 16 41.27	−0.74	20 34 36.98	−18 42 15.7	0.984 6173
	27	0702.5	307 17 41.73	−0.73	20 38 46.18	−18 26 55.9	0.984 7356
	28	0703.5	308 18 41.46	−0.70	20 42 54.58	−18 11 16.1	0.984 8574
	29	0704.5	309 19 40.39	−0.63	20 47 02.17	−17 55 16.6	0.984 9825
	30	0705.5	310 20 38.43	−0.53	20 51 08.95	−17 38 57.8	0.985 1108
	31	0706.5	311 21 35.46	−0.42	20 55 14.90	−17 22 20.1	0.985 2421
Feb.	1	0707.5	312 22 31.38	−0.29	20 59 20.02	−17 05 24.0	0.985 3764
	2	0708.5	313 23 26.08	−0.15	21 03 24.31	−16 48 09.9	0.985 5140
	3	0709.5	314 24 19.49	−0.01	21 07 27.77	−16 30 38.2	0.985 6548
	4	0710.5	315 25 11.51	+0.12	21 11 30.40	−16 12 49.2	0.985 7992
	5	0711.5	316 26 02.09	+0.24	21 15 32.20	−15 54 43.6	0.985 9475
	6	0712.5	317 26 51.19	+0.33	21 19 33.18	−15 36 21.6	0.986 0999
	7	0713.5	318 27 38.78	+0.39	21 23 33.34	−15 17 43.8	0.986 2568
	8	0714.5	319 28 24.86	+0.42	21 27 32.69	−14 58 50.5	0.986 4183
	9	0715.5	320 29 09.43	+0.42	21 31 31.23	−14 39 42.2	0.986 5847
	10	0716.5	321 29 52.51	+0.39	21 35 28.98	−14 20 19.2	0.986 7562
	11	0717.5	322 30 34.13	+0.32	21 39 25.94	−14 00 42.0	0.986 9329
	12	0718.5	323 31 14.32	+0.24	21 43 22.13	−13 40 51.0	0.987 1147
	13	0719.5	324 31 53.11	+0.13	21 47 17.55	−13 20 46.6	0.987 3018
	14	0720.5	325 32 30.52	+0.01	21 51 12.23	−13 00 29.0	0.987 4940
	15	0721.5	326 33 06.59	−0.12	21 55 06.18	−12 39 58.9	0.987 6911

FOR 0^h TERRESTRIAL TIME

Date		Pos. Angle of Axis P	Heliographic Latitude B_0	Heliographic Longitude L_0	Horiz. Parallax	Semi-Diameter	Ephemeris Transit
		°	°	°	″	′ ″	h m s
Jan.	0	+ 2.43	− 2.91	89.85	8.94	16 15.87	12 03 12.13
	1	+ 1.94	− 3.03	76.68	8.94	16 15.89	12 03 40.54
	2	+ 1.46	− 3.14	63.51	8.94	16 15.90	12 04 08.62
	3	+ 0.97	− 3.26	50.34	8.94	16 15.91	12 04 36.31
	4	+ 0.49	− 3.37	37.17	8.94	16 15.92	12 05 03.60
	5	+ 0.01	− 3.49	24.00	8.94	16 15.92	12 05 30.44
	6	− 0.48	− 3.60	10.83	8.94	16 15.91	12 05 56.81
	7	− 0.96	− 3.71	357.66	8.94	16 15.90	12 06 22.68
	8	− 1.44	− 3.82	344.49	8.94	16 15.89	12 06 48.02
	9	− 1.92	− 3.93	331.32	8.94	16 15.87	12 07 12.81
	10	− 2.40	− 4.04	318.16	8.94	16 15.84	12 07 37.03
	11	− 2.88	− 4.14	304.99	8.94	16 15.81	12 08 00.65
	12	− 3.35	− 4.25	291.82	8.94	16 15.78	12 08 23.67
	13	− 3.82	− 4.35	278.65	8.94	16 15.73	12 08 46.05
	14	− 4.30	− 4.45	265.48	8.94	16 15.68	12 09 07.79
	15	− 4.76	− 4.56	252.31	8.94	16 15.63	12 09 28.88
	16	− 5.23	− 4.66	239.15	8.94	16 15.56	12 09 49.29
	17	− 5.69	− 4.75	225.98	8.94	16 15.49	12 10 09.01
	18	− 6.15	− 4.85	212.81	8.94	16 15.42	12 10 28.04
	19	− 6.61	− 4.94	199.64	8.94	16 15.34	12 10 46.35
	20	− 7.07	− 5.04	186.48	8.94	16 15.25	12 11 03.94
	21	− 7.52	− 5.13	173.31	8.94	16 15.16	12 11 20.79
	22	− 7.97	− 5.22	160.14	8.94	16 15.07	12 11 36.90
	23	− 8.41	− 5.31	146.98	8.93	16 14.97	12 11 52.25
	24	− 8.86	− 5.40	133.81	8.93	16 14.86	12 12 06.83
	25	− 9.29	− 5.48	120.64	8.93	16 14.75	12 12 20.64
	26	− 9.73	− 5.56	107.48	8.93	16 14.64	12 12 33.66
	27	− 10.16	− 5.65	94.31	8.93	16 14.52	12 12 45.89
	28	− 10.58	− 5.73	81.14	8.93	16 14.40	12 12 57.32
	29	− 11.01	− 5.80	67.98	8.93	16 14.28	12 13 07.93
	30	11.42	− 5.88	54.81	8.93	16 14.15	12 13 17.74
	31	− 11.84	− 5.95	41.65	8.93	16 14.02	12 13 26.71
Feb.	1	− 12.25	− 6.03	28.48	8.92	16 13.89	12 13 34.86
	2	− 12.65	− 6.10	15.31	8.92	16 13.75	12 13 42.18
	3	− 13.05	− 6.17	2.15	8.92	16 13.61	12 13 48.67
	4	− 13.44	− 6.23	348.98	8.92	16 13.47	12 13 54.32
	5	− 13.83	− 6.30	335.82	8.92	16 13.32	12 13 59.15
	6	− 14.22	− 6.36	322.65	8.92	16 13.17	12 14 03.15
	7	− 14.60	− 6.42	309.48	8.92	16 13.02	12 14 06.33
	8	− 14.97	− 6.48	296.32	8.92	16 12.86	12 14 08.70
	9	− 15.34	− 6.54	283.15	8.91	16 12.69	12 14 10.28
	10	− 15.71	− 6.59	269.98	8.91	16 12.52	12 14 11.06
	11	− 16.07	− 6.64	256.81	8.91	16 12.35	12 14 11.07
	12	− 16.42	− 6.69	243.65	8.91	16 12.17	12 14 10.31
	13	− 16.77	− 6.74	230.48	8.91	16 11.99	12 14 08.80
	14	− 17.11	− 6.79	217.31	8.91	16 11.80	12 14 06.56
	15	− 17.45	− 6.83	204.14	8.90	16 11.60	12 14 03.60

FOR 0^h TERRESTRIAL TIME

Date		Julian Date	Geometric Ecliptic Coords. Mn Equinox & Ecliptic of Date Longitude	Latitude	Apparent R. A.	Apparent Declination	True Geocentric Distance
		246	° ′ ″	″	h m s	° ′ ″	au
Feb.	15	0721.5	326 33 06.59	−0.12	21 55 06.18	−12 39 58.9	0.987 6911
	16	0722.5	327 33 41.34	−0.25	21 58 59.42	−12 19 16.4	0.987 8931
	17	0723.5	328 34 14.78	−0.37	22 02 51.95	−11 58 22.0	0.988 0997
	18	0724.5	329 34 46.92	−0.49	22 06 43.81	−11 37 16.1	0.988 3106
	19	0725.5	330 35 17.77	−0.59	22 10 34.99	−11 15 59.1	0.988 5256
	20	0726.5	331 35 47.31	−0.67	22 14 25.52	−10 54 31.4	0.988 7444
	21	0727.5	332 36 15.54	−0.73	22 18 15.41	−10 32 53.3	0.988 9668
	22	0728.5	333 36 42.45	−0.76	22 22 04.69	−10 11 05.4	0.989 1924
	23	0729.5	334 37 08.01	−0.76	22 25 53.35	− 9 49 08.0	0.989 4209
	24	0730.5	335 37 32.18	−0.72	22 29 41.42	− 9 27 01.5	0.989 6520
	25	0731.5	336 37 54.92	−0.66	22 33 28.91	− 9 04 46.3	0.989 8853
	26	0732.5	337 38 16.16	−0.57	22 37 15.83	− 8 42 23.0	0.990 1205
	27	0733.5	338 38 35.85	−0.46	22 41 02.20	− 8 19 51.8	0.990 3574
	28	0734.5	339 38 53.89	−0.33	22 44 48.02	− 7 57 13.2	0.990 5956
Mar.	1	0735.5	340 39 10.19	−0.18	22 48 33.32	− 7 34 27.7	0.990 8350
	2	0736.5	341 39 24.64	−0.04	22 52 18.10	− 7 11 35.6	0.991 0756
	3	0737.5	342 39 37.16	+0.10	22 56 02.39	− 6 48 37.5	0.991 3175
	4	0738.5	343 39 47.67	+0.22	22 59 46.19	− 6 25 33.7	0.991 5606
	5	0739.5	344 39 56.09	+0.32	23 03 29.54	− 6 02 24.5	0.991 8054
	6	0740.5	345 40 02.37	+0.39	23 07 12.43	− 5 39 10.6	0.992 0520
	7	0741.5	346 40 06.50	+0.43	23 10 54.90	− 5 15 52.2	0.992 3006
	8	0742.5	347 40 08.45	+0.44	23 14 36.96	− 4 52 29.7	0.992 5516
	9	0743.5	348 40 08.24	+0.41	23 18 18.63	− 4 29 03.6	0.992 8052
	10	0744.5	349 40 05.89	+0.36	23 21 59.92	− 4 05 34.2	0.993 0615
	11	0745.5	350 40 01.41	+0.27	23 25 40.87	− 3 42 01.9	0.993 3208
	12	0746.5	351 39 54.85	+0.17	23 29 21.49	− 3 18 27.0	0.993 5829
	13	0747.5	352 39 46.23	+0.05	23 33 01.81	− 2 54 49.9	0.993 8481
	14	0748.5	353 39 35.62	−0.08	23 36 41.85	− 2 31 10.9	0.994 1163
	15	0749.5	354 39 23.03	−0.21	23 40 21.63	− 2 07 30.4	0.994 3874
	16	0750.5	355 39 08.53	−0.34	23 44 01.18	− 1 43 48.7	0.994 6614
	17	0751.5	356 38 52.13	−0.46	23 47 40.53	− 1 20 06.2	0.994 9380
	18	0752.5	357 38 33.89	−0.57	23 51 19.70	− 0 56 23.1	0.995 2171
	19	0753.5	358 38 13.83	−0.66	23 54 58.70	− 0 32 39.9	0.995 4984
	20	0754.5	359 37 51.99	−0.72	23 58 37.57	− 0 08 56.8	0.995 7818
	21	0755.5	0 37 28.37	−0.77	0 02 16.33	+ 0 14 45.7	0.996 0670
	22	0756.5	1 37 03.00	−0.78	0 05 54.99	+ 0 38 27.4	0.996 3536
	23	0757.5	2 36 35.89	−0.76	0 09 33.58	+ 1 02 07.8	0.996 6413
	24	0758.5	3 36 07.04	−0.71	0 13 12.12	+ 1 25 46.5	0.996 9298
	25	0759.5	4 35 36.45	−0.64	0 16 50.62	+ 1 49 23.4	0.997 2187
	26	0760.5	5 35 04.09	−0.54	0 20 29.11	+ 2 12 57.8	0.997 5076
	27	0761.5	6 34 29.93	−0.42	0 24 07.60	+ 2 36 29.6	0.997 7962
	28	0762.5	7 33 53.92	−0.28	0 27 46.11	+ 2 59 58.2	0.998 0841
	29	0763.5	8 33 15.99	−0.14	0 31 24.65	+ 3 23 23.4	0.998 3710
	30	0764.5	9 32 36.06	0.00	0 35 03.25	+ 3 46 44.6	0.998 6566
	31	0765.5	10 31 54.04	+0.13	0 38 41.92	+ 4 10 01.7	0.998 9410
Apr.	1	0766.5	11 31 09.87	+0.23	0 42 20.67	+ 4 33 14.1	0.999 2241
	2	0767.5	12 30 23.46	+0.31	0 45 59.53	+ 4 56 21.5	0.999 5061

FOR 0^h TERRESTRIAL TIME

Date		Pos. Angle of Axis P	Heliographic Latitude B_0	Heliographic Longitude L_0	Horiz. Parallax	Semi-Diameter	Ephemeris Transit
		°	°	°	″	′ ″	h m s
Feb.	15	− 17.45	− 6.83	204.14	8.90	16 11.60	12 14 03.60
	16	− 17.78	− 6.87	190.97	8.90	16 11.41	12 13 59.92
	17	− 18.11	− 6.91	177.81	8.90	16 11.20	12 13 55.56
	18	− 18.43	− 6.95	164.64	8.90	16 11.00	12 13 50.52
	19	− 18.74	− 6.99	151.47	8.90	16 10.78	12 13 44.82
	20	− 19.05	− 7.02	138.30	8.89	16 10.57	12 13 38.47
	21	− 19.35	− 7.05	125.13	8.89	16 10.35	12 13 31.48
	22	− 19.65	− 7.08	111.96	8.89	16 10.13	12 13 23.88
	23	− 19.94	− 7.11	98.79	8.89	16 09.91	12 13 15.68
	24	− 20.22	− 7.13	85.62	8.89	16 09.68	12 13 06.90
	25	− 20.50	− 7.15	72.45	8.88	16 09.45	12 12 57.54
	26	− 20.77	− 7.17	59.28	8.88	16 09.22	12 12 47.62
	27	− 21.04	− 7.19	46.11	8.88	16 08.99	12 12 37.16
	28	− 21.30	− 7.21	32.94	8.88	16 08.76	12 12 26.16
Mar.	1	− 21.55	− 7.22	19.76	8.88	16 08.52	12 12 14.65
	2	− 21.80	− 7.23	6.59	8.87	16 08.29	12 12 02.63
	3	− 22.04	− 7.24	353.42	8.87	16 08.05	12 11 50.13
	4	− 22.28	− 7.25	340.24	8.87	16 07.81	12 11 37.14
	5	− 22.51	− 7.25	327.07	8.87	16 07.57	12 11 23.70
	6	− 22.73	− 7.25	313.90	8.86	16 07.33	12 11 09.82
	7	− 22.94	− 7.25	300.72	8.86	16 07.09	12 10 55.52
	8	− 23.15	− 7.25	287.55	8.86	16 06.85	12 10 40.82
	9	− 23.36	− 7.25	274.37	8.86	16 06.60	12 10 25.74
	10	− 23.55	− 7.24	261.19	8.86	16 06.35	12 10 10.30
	11	− 23.74	− 7.23	248.01	8.85	16 06.10	12 09 54.53
	12	− 23.92	− 7.22	234.84	8.85	16 05.84	12 09 38.44
	13	− 24.10	− 7.20	221.66	8.85	16 05.59	12 09 22.07
	14	− 24.27	− 7.19	208.48	8.85	16 05.32	12 09 05.43
	15	− 24.43	− 7.17	195.30	8.84	16 05.06	12 08 48.55
	16	− 24.59	− 7.15	182.12	8.84	16 04.80	12 08 31.46
	17	− 24.74	− 7.13	168.93	8.84	16 04.53	12 08 14.16
	18	− 24.88	− 7.10	155.75	8.84	16 04.26	12 07 56.70
	19	− 25.02	− 7.08	142.57	8.83	16 03.98	12 07 39.08
	20	− 25.14	− 7.05	129.39	8.83	16 03.71	12 07 21.34
	21	− 25.27	− 7.02	116.20	8.83	16 03.43	12 07 03.49
	22	− 25.38	− 6.99	103.02	8.83	16 03.16	12 06 45.56
	23	− 25.49	− 6.95	89.83	8.82	16 02.88	12 06 27.57
	24	− 25.59	− 6.91	76.65	8.82	16 02.60	12 06 09.53
	25	− 25.68	− 6.88	63.46	8.82	16 02.32	12 05 51.47
	26	− 25.77	− 6.83	50.27	8.82	16 02.04	12 05 33.41
	27	− 25.85	− 6.79	37.09	8.81	16 01.76	12 05 15.36
	28	− 25.92	− 6.75	23.90	8.81	16 01.49	12 04 57.34
	29	− 25.99	− 6.70	10.71	8.81	16 01.21	12 04 39.36
	30	− 26.05	− 6.65	357.52	8.81	16 00.94	12 04 21.45
	31	− 26.10	− 6.60	344.33	8.80	16 00.66	12 04 03.61
Apr.	1	− 26.14	− 6.55	331.14	8.80	16 00.39	12 03 45.87
	2	− 26.18	− 6.49	317.94	8.80	16 00.12	12 03 28.23

FOR 0^h TERRESTRIAL TIME

Date		Julian Date	Geometric Ecliptic Coords. Mn Equinox & Ecliptic of Date Longitude	Latitude	Apparent R. A.	Apparent Declination	True Geocentric Distance
		246	° ′ ″	″	h m s	° ′ ″	au
Apr.	1	0766.5	11 31 09.87	+0.23	0 42 20.67	+ 4 33 14.1	0.999 2241
	2	0767.5	12 30 23.46	+0.31	0 45 59.53	+ 4 56 21.5	0.999 5061
	3	0768.5	13 29 34.76	+0.36	0 49 38.51	+ 5 19 23.5	0.999 7871
	4	0769.5	14 28 43.74	+0.37	0 53 17.62	+ 5 42 19.7	1.000 0674
	5	0770.5	15 27 50.39	+0.35	0 56 56.87	+ 6 05 09.9	1.000 3473
	6	0771.5	16 26 54.72	+0.30	1 00 36.29	+ 6 27 53.6	1.000 6269
	7	0772.5	17 25 56.73	+0.22	1 04 15.89	+ 6 50 30.4	1.000 9066
	8	0773.5	18 24 56.47	+0.12	1 07 55.70	+ 7 13 00.2	1.001 1864
	9	0774.5	19 23 53.96	+0.01	1 11 35.72	+ 7 35 22.4	1.001 4665
	10	0775.5	20 22 49.25	−0.12	1 15 15.99	+ 7 57 36.9	1.001 7470
	11	0776.5	21 21 42.39	−0.26	1 18 56.52	+ 8 19 43.3	1.002 0280
	12	0777.5	22 20 33.43	−0.39	1 22 37.33	+ 8 41 41.3	1.002 3095
	13	0778.5	23 19 22.43	−0.51	1 26 18.45	+ 9 03 30.6	1.002 5914
	14	0779.5	24 18 09.45	−0.62	1 29 59.89	+ 9 25 10.8	1.002 8736
	15	0780.5	25 16 54.54	−0.72	1 33 41.67	+ 9 46 41.8	1.003 1562
	16	0781.5	26 15 37.75	−0.79	1 37 23.82	+10 08 03.0	1.003 4388
	17	0782.5	27 14 19.15	−0.84	1 41 06.34	+10 29 14.4	1.003 7214
	18	0783.5	28 12 58.77	−0.87	1 44 49.26	+10 50 15.4	1.004 0038
	19	0784.5	29 11 36.68	−0.86	1 48 32.59	+11 11 05.8	1.004 2856
	20	0785.5	30 10 12.90	−0.83	1 52 16.35	+11 31 45.3	1.004 5667
	21	0786.5	31 08 47.48	−0.76	1 56 00.54	+11 52 13.6	1.004 8466
	22	0787.5	32 07 20.44	−0.67	1 59 45.19	+12 12 30.2	1.005 1250
	23	0788.5	33 05 51.80	−0.56	2 03 30.30	+12 32 34.9	1.005 4016
	24	0789.5	34 04 21.56	−0.44	2 07 15.89	+12 52 27.3	1.005 6760
	25	0790.5	35 02 49.71	−0.30	2 11 01.97	+13 12 07.0	1.005 9477
	26	0791.5	36 01 16.22	−0.17	2 14 48.54	+13 31 33.8	1.006 2164
	27	0792.5	36 59 41.03	−0.04	2 18 35.62	+13 50 47.2	1.006 4818
	28	0793.5	37 58 04.09	+0.07	2 22 23.22	+14 09 46.9	1.006 7436
	29	0794.5	38 56 25.32	+0.16	2 26 11.33	+14 28 32.6	1.007 0017
	30	0795.5	39 54 44.66	+0.22	2 29 59.97	+14 47 04.0	1.007 2563
May	1	0796.5	40 53 02.05	+0.24	2 33 49.12	+15 05 20.6	1.007 5072
	2	0797.5	41 51 17.45	+0.23	2 37 38.80	+15 23 22.1	1.007 7549
	3	0798.5	42 49 30.85	+0.19	2 41 29.01	+15 41 08.3	1.007 9994
	4	0799.5	43 47 42.23	+0.12	2 45 19.74	+15 58 38.7	1.008 2411
	5	0800.5	44 45 51.61	+0.03	2 49 11.00	+16 15 53.1	1.008 4802
	6	0801.5	45 43 59.03	−0.08	2 53 02.81	+16 32 51.1	1.008 7169
	7	0802.5	46 42 04.51	−0.20	2 56 55.16	+16 49 32.6	1.008 9514
	8	0803.5	47 40 08.11	−0.33	3 00 48.05	+17 05 57.1	1.009 1838
	9	0804.5	48 38 09.86	−0.45	3 04 41.51	+17 22 04.4	1.009 4143
	10	0805.5	49 36 09.84	−0.57	3 08 35.52	+17 37 54.2	1.009 6429
	11	0806.5	50 34 08.10	−0.68	3 12 30.10	+17 53 26.3	1.009 8698
	12	0807.5	51 32 04.71	−0.78	3 16 25.25	+18 08 40.4	1.010 0949
	13	0808.5	52 29 59.73	−0.85	3 20 20.98	+18 23 36.2	1.010 3183
	14	0809.5	53 27 53.25	−0.90	3 24 17.27	+18 38 13.5	1.010 5399
	15	0810.5	54 25 45.32	−0.92	3 28 14.15	+18 52 31.9	1.010 7595
	16	0811.5	55 23 36.02	−0.92	3 32 11.59	+19 06 31.3	1.010 9772
	17	0812.5	56 21 25.42	−0.89	3 36 09.61	+19 20 11.4	1.011 1927

FOR 0^h TERRESTRIAL TIME

Date		Pos. Angle of Axis P	Heliographic Latitude B_0	Heliographic Longitude L_0	Horiz. Parallax	Semi-Diameter	Ephemeris Transit
		°	°	°	″	′ ″	h m s
Apr.	1	− 26.14	− 6.55	331.14	8.80	16 00.39	12 03 45.87
	2	− 26.18	− 6.49	317.94	8.80	16 00.12	12 03 28.23
	3	− 26.21	− 6.44	304.75	8.80	15 59.85	12 03 10.71
	4	− 26.23	− 6.38	291.56	8.79	15 59.58	12 02 53.33
	5	− 26.25	− 6.32	278.36	8.79	15 59.31	12 02 36.11
	6	− 26.26	− 6.25	265.16	8.79	15 59.04	12 02 19.06
	7	− 26.26	− 6.19	251.97	8.79	15 58.78	12 02 02.21
	8	− 26.25	− 6.12	238.77	8.78	15 58.51	12 01 45.57
	9	− 26.24	− 6.06	225.57	8.78	15 58.24	12 01 29.17
	10	− 26.22	− 5.99	212.37	8.78	15 57.97	12 01 13.02
	11	− 26.19	− 5.92	199.17	8.78	15 57.70	12 00 57.15
	12	− 26.15	− 5.84	185.97	8.77	15 57.43	12 00 41.57
	13	− 26.11	− 5.77	172.77	8.77	15 57.16	12 00 26.30
	14	− 26.06	− 5.69	159.57	8.77	15 56.90	12 00 11.36
	15	− 26.00	− 5.62	146.36	8.77	15 56.63	11 59 56.77
	16	− 25.94	− 5.54	133.16	8.76	15 56.36	11 59 42.55
	17	− 25.87	− 5.46	119.95	8.76	15 56.09	11 59 28.71
	18	− 25.79	− 5.37	106.75	8.76	15 55.82	11 59 15.27
	19	− 25.70	− 5.29	93.54	8.76	15 55.55	11 59 02.25
	20	− 25.61	− 5.20	80.33	8.75	15 55.28	11 58 49.67
	21	− 25.50	− 5.12	67.13	8.75	15 55.02	11 58 37.53
	22	− 25.40	− 5.03	53.92	8.75	15 54.75	11 58 25.86
	23	− 25.28	− 4.94	40.71	8.75	15 54.49	11 58 14.65
	24	− 25.16	− 4.85	27.50	8.74	15 54.23	11 58 03.94
	25	− 25.02	− 4.76	14.29	8.74	15 53.97	11 57 53.71
	26	− 24.89	− 4.66	1.07	8.74	15 53.72	11 57 43.99
	27	− 24.74	− 4.57	347.86	8.74	15 53.46	11 57 34.78
	28	− 24.59	− 4.47	334.65	8.74	15 53.22	11 57 26.08
	29	− 24.43	− 4.37	321.44	8.73	15 52.97	11 57 17.89
	30	− 24.26	− 4.27	308.22	8.73	15 52.73	11 57 10.22
May	1	− 24.08	− 4.17	295.01	8.73	15 52.49	11 57 03.07
	2	− 23.90	− 4.07	281.79	8.73	15 52.26	11 56 56.45
	3	− 23.71	− 3.97	268.57	8.72	15 52.03	11 56 50.35
	4	− 23.52	− 3.87	255.35	8.72	15 51.80	11 56 44.79
	5	− 23.31	− 3.76	242.14	8.72	15 51.58	11 56 39.77
	6	− 23.10	− 3.66	228.92	8.72	15 51.35	11 56 35.30
	7	− 22.89	− 3.55	215.70	8.72	15 51.13	11 56 31.37
	8	− 22.66	− 3.45	202.48	8.71	15 50.91	11 56 27.99
	9	− 22.43	− 3.34	189.25	8.71	15 50.69	11 56 25.17
	10	− 22.19	− 3.23	176.03	8.71	15 50.48	11 56 22.92
	11	− 21.95	− 3.12	162.81	8.71	15 50.27	11 56 21.23
	12	− 21.70	− 3.01	149.58	8.71	15 50.05	11 56 20.11
	13	− 21.44	− 2.90	136.36	8.70	15 49.84	11 56 19.56
	14	− 21.17	− 2.78	123.14	8.70	15 49.64	11 56 19.58
	15	− 20.90	− 2.67	109.91	8.70	15 49.43	11 56 20.18
	16	− 20.62	− 2.56	96.68	8.70	15 49.22	11 56 21.35
	17	− 20.34	− 2.44	83.46	8.70	15 49.02	11 56 23.09

FOR 0^h TERRESTRIAL TIME

Date		Julian Date	Geometric Ecliptic Coords. Mn Equinox & Ecliptic of Date Longitude	Latitude	Apparent R. A.	Apparent Declination	True Geocentric Distance
		246	° ′ ″	″	h m s	° ′ ″	au
May	17	0812.5	56 21 25.42	−0.89	3 36 09.61	+19 20 11.4	1.011 1927
	18	0813.5	57 19 13.59	−0.83	3 40 08.20	+19 33 31.8	1.011 4057
	19	0814.5	58 17 00.59	−0.75	3 44 07.36	+19 46 32.4	1.011 6161
	20	0815.5	59 14 46.48	−0.64	3 48 07.08	+19 59 12.8	1.011 8236
	21	0816.5	60 12 31.29	−0.52	3 52 07.35	+20 11 32.8	1.012 0278
	22	0817.5	61 10 15.07	−0.39	3 56 08.18	+20 23 32.2	1.012 2283
	23	0818.5	62 07 57.83	−0.26	4 00 09.55	+20 35 10.6	1.012 4247
	24	0819.5	63 05 39.57	−0.13	4 04 11.46	+20 46 27.7	1.012 6167
	25	0820.5	64 03 20.28	−0.02	4 08 13.89	+20 57 23.5	1.012 8040
	26	0821.5	65 00 59.91	+0.08	4 12 16.83	+21 07 57.6	1.012 9861
	27	0822.5	65 58 38.43	+0.14	4 16 20.27	+21 18 09.8	1.013 1629
	28	0823.5	66 56 15.77	+0.18	4 20 24.19	+21 27 59.8	1.013 3343
	29	0824.5	67 53 51.89	+0.18	4 24 28.55	+21 37 27.5	1.013 5002
	30	0825.5	68 51 26.72	+0.14	4 28 33.35	+21 46 32.6	1.013 6609
	31	0826.5	69 49 00.26	+0.09	4 32 38.56	+21 55 15.0	1.013 8165
June	1	0827.5	70 46 32.48	0.00	4 36 44.16	+22 03 34.4	1.013 9672
	2	0828.5	71 44 03.38	−0.10	4 40 50.14	+22 11 30.6	1.014 1133
	3	0829.5	72 41 32.99	−0.22	4 44 56.47	+22 19 03.5	1.014 2550
	4	0830.5	73 39 01.33	−0.34	4 49 03.14	+22 26 12.9	1.014 3926
	5	0831.5	74 36 28.45	−0.46	4 53 10.14	+22 32 58.8	1.014 5262
	6	0832.5	75 33 54.38	−0.57	4 57 17.44	+22 39 20.8	1.014 6561
	7	0833.5	76 31 19.18	−0.68	5 01 25.03	+22 45 19.1	1.014 7825
	8	0834.5	77 28 42.91	−0.77	5 05 32.90	+22 50 53.3	1.014 9054
	9	0835.5	78 26 05.65	−0.84	5 09 41.03	+22 56 03.5	1.015 0250
	10	0836.5	79 23 27.44	−0.89	5 13 49.40	+23 00 49.4	1.015 1414
	11	0837.5	80 20 48.39	−0.91	5 17 57.98	+23 05 11.2	1.015 2546
	12	0838.5	81 18 08.56	−0.90	5 22 06.77	+23 09 08.5	1.015 3647
	13	0839.5	82 15 28.03	−0.87	5 26 15.74	+23 12 41.5	1.015 4717
	14	0840.5	83 12 46.90	−0.81	5 30 24.88	+23 15 49.9	1.015 5755
	15	0841.5	84 10 05.23	−0.73	5 34 34.15	+23 18 33.8	1.015 6759
	16	0842.5	85 07 23.13	−0.63	5 38 43.55	+23 20 53.1	1.015 7729
	17	0843.5	86 04 40.65	−0.51	5 42 53.05	+23 22 47.6	1.015 8661
	18	0844.5	87 01 57.88	−0.38	5 47 02.63	+23 24 17.4	1.015 9554
	19	0845.5	87 59 14.85	−0.24	5 51 12.28	+23 25 22.4	1.016 0403
	20	0846.5	88 56 31.63	−0.12	5 55 21.96	+23 26 02.6	1.016 1206
	21	0847.5	89 53 48.22	0.00	5 59 31.66	+23 26 17.9	1.016 1959
	22	0848.5	90 51 04.65	+0.10	6 03 41.36	+23 26 08.3	1.016 2658
	23	0849.5	91 48 20.90	+0.17	6 07 51.03	+23 25 33.9	1.016 3300
	24	0850.5	92 45 36.93	+0.21	6 12 00.63	+23 24 34.7	1.016 3882
	25	0851.5	93 42 52.73	+0.22	6 16 10.15	+23 23 10.7	1.016 4402
	26	0852.5	94 40 08.23	+0.19	6 20 19.55	+23 21 22.0	1.016 4860
	27	0853.5	95 37 23.39	+0.14	6 24 28.79	+23 19 08.6	1.016 5256
	28	0854.5	96 34 38.19	+0.06	6 28 37.85	+23 16 30.7	1.016 5590
	29	0855.5	97 31 52.58	−0.04	6 32 46.70	+23 13 28.1	1.016 5866
	30	0856.5	98 29 06.57	−0.15	6 36 55.31	+23 10 01.2	1.016 6084
July	1	0857.5	99 26 20.16	−0.27	6 41 03.66	+23 06 09.8	1.016 6248
	2	0858.5	100 23 33.35	−0.39	6 45 11.74	+23 01 54.3	1.016 6359

FOR 0^h TERRESTRIAL TIME

Date		Pos. Angle of Axis P	Heliographic Latitude B_0	Heliographic Longitude L_0	Horiz. Parallax	Semi-Diameter	Ephemeris Transit
		°	°	°	″	′ ″	h m s
May	17	− 20.34	− 2.44	83.46	8.70	15 49.02	11 56 23.09
	18	− 20.05	− 2.33	70.23	8.69	15 48.82	11 56 25.40
	19	− 19.75	− 2.21	57.00	8.69	15 48.63	11 56 28.28
	20	− 19.45	− 2.10	43.77	8.69	15 48.43	11 56 31.72
	21	− 19.14	− 1.98	30.55	8.69	15 48.24	11 56 35.72
	22	− 18.82	− 1.86	17.32	8.69	15 48.05	11 56 40.26
	23	− 18.50	− 1.75	4.09	8.69	15 47.87	11 56 45.35
	24	− 18.17	− 1.63	350.86	8.68	15 47.69	11 56 50.97
	25	− 17.84	− 1.51	337.63	8.68	15 47.51	11 56 57.10
	26	− 17.50	− 1.39	324.40	8.68	15 47.34	11 57 03.74
	27	− 17.15	− 1.27	311.17	8.68	15 47.18	11 57 10.85
	28	− 16.80	− 1.15	297.94	8.68	15 47.02	11 57 18.43
	29	− 16.45	− 1.03	284.70	8.68	15 46.86	11 57 26.44
	30	− 16.08	− 0.91	271.47	8.68	15 46.71	11 57 34.89
	31	− 15.72	− 0.79	258.24	8.67	15 46.57	11 57 43.73
June	1	− 15.35	− 0.67	245.01	8.67	15 46.43	11 57 52.96
	2	− 14.97	− 0.55	231.77	8.67	15 46.29	11 58 02.56
	3	− 14.59	− 0.43	218.54	8.67	15 46.16	11 58 12.52
	4	− 14.21	− 0.31	205.30	8.67	15 46.03	11 58 22.80
	5	− 13.82	− 0.19	192.07	8.67	15 45.90	11 58 33.40
	6	− 13.42	− 0.07	178.84	8.67	15 45.78	11 58 44.30
	7	− 13.02	+ 0.05	165.60	8.67	15 45.67	11 58 55.49
	8	− 12.62	+ 0.17	152.36	8.66	15 45.55	11 59 06.93
	9	− 12.22	+ 0.29	139.13	8.66	15 45.44	11 59 18.62
	10	− 11.81	+ 0.42	125.89	8.66	15 45.33	11 59 30.54
	11	− 11.39	+ 0.54	112.66	8.66	15 45.23	11 59 42.67
	12	− 10.98	+ 0.66	99.42	8.66	15 45.12	11 59 54.99
	13	− 10.56	+ 0.78	86.18	8.66	15 45.02	12 00 07.48
	14	− 10.13	+ 0.90	72.95	8.66	15 44.93	12 00 20.13
	15	− 9.71	+ 1.02	59.71	8.66	15 44.83	12 00 32.91
	16	− 9.28	+ 1.13	46.47	8.66	15 44.74	12 00 45.80
	17	− 8.84	+ 1.25	33.24	8.66	15 44.66	12 00 58.80
	18	− 8.41	+ 1.37	20.00	8.66	15 44.57	12 01 11.86
	19	− 7.97	+ 1.49	6.76	8.66	15 44.49	12 01 24.98
	20	− 7.53	+ 1.61	353.53	8.65	15 44.42	12 01 38.12
	21	− 7.09	+ 1.72	340.29	8.65	15 44.35	12 01 51.27
	22	− 6.65	+ 1.84	327.05	8.65	15 44.29	12 02 04.40
	23	− 6.20	+ 1.96	313.82	8.65	15 44.23	12 02 17.48
	24	− 5.76	+ 2.07	300.58	8.65	15 44.17	12 02 30.48
	25	− 5.31	+ 2.19	287.34	8.65	15 44.12	12 02 43.37
	26	− 4.86	+ 2.30	274.11	8.65	15 44.08	12 02 56.13
	27	− 4.41	+ 2.42	260.87	8.65	15 44.04	12 03 08.72
	28	− 3.96	+ 2.53	247.64	8.65	15 44.01	12 03 21.12
	29	− 3.51	+ 2.64	234.40	8.65	15 43.99	12 03 33.30
	30	− 3.05	+ 2.76	221.16	8.65	15 43.97	12 03 45.23
July	1	− 2.60	+ 2.87	207.93	8.65	15 43.95	12 03 56.90
	2	− 2.15	+ 2.98	194.69	8.65	15 43.94	12 04 08.27

FOR 0^h TERRESTRIAL TIME

Date		Julian Date	Geometric Ecliptic Coords. Mn Equinox & Ecliptic of Date Longitude	Latitude	Apparent R. A.	Apparent Declination	True Geocentric Distance
		246	° ′ ″	″	h m s	° ′ ″	au
July	1	0857.5	99 26 20.16	−0.27	6 41 03.66	+23 06 09.8	1.016 6248
	2	0858.5	100 23 33.35	−0.39	6 45 11.74	+23 01 54.3	1.016 6359
	3	0859.5	101 20 46.17	−0.50	6 49 19.51	+22 57 14.6	1.016 6422
	4	0860.5	102 17 58.67	−0.61	6 53 26.97	+22 52 10.9	1.016 6437
	5	0861.5	103 15 10.87	−0.70	6 57 34.09	+22 46 43.3	1.016 6407
	6	0862.5	104 12 22.83	−0.77	7 01 40.85	+22 40 52.1	1.016 6335
	7	0863.5	105 09 34.61	−0.82	7 05 47.24	+22 34 37.2	1.016 6222
	8	0864.5	106 06 46.26	−0.84	7 09 53.24	+22 27 59.0	1.016 6071
	9	0865.5	107 03 57.86	−0.83	7 13 58.84	+22 20 57.6	1.016 5883
	10	0866.5	108 01 09.48	−0.80	7 18 04.01	+22 13 33.1	1.016 5659
	11	0867.5	108 58 21.21	−0.74	7 22 08.75	+22 05 45.7	1.016 5401
	12	0868.5	109 55 33.13	−0.66	7 26 13.04	+21 57 35.6	1.016 5109
	13	0869.5	110 52 45.34	−0.55	7 30 16.87	+21 49 03.0	1.016 4784
	14	0870.5	111 49 57.93	−0.43	7 34 20.23	+21 40 08.0	1.016 4423
	15	0871.5	112 47 10.99	−0.30	7 38 23.11	+21 30 50.8	1.016 4027
	16	0872.5	113 44 24.59	−0.16	7 42 25.49	+21 21 11.6	1.016 3593
	17	0873.5	114 41 38.82	−0.03	7 46 27.38	+21 11 10.6	1.016 3119
	18	0874.5	115 38 53.73	+0.09	7 50 28.76	+21 00 47.9	1.016 2602
	19	0875.5	116 36 09.36	+0.19	7 54 29.62	+20 50 03.9	1.016 2038
	20	0876.5	117 33 25.75	+0.27	7 58 29.96	+20 38 58.6	1.016 1425
	21	0877.5	118 30 42.89	+0.32	8 02 29.77	+20 27 32.5	1.016 0759
	22	0878.5	119 28 00.78	+0.33	8 06 29.03	+20 15 45.6	1.016 0036
	23	0879.5	120 25 19.40	+0.31	8 10 27.72	+20 03 38.4	1.015 9256
	24	0880.5	121 22 38.71	+0.27	8 14 25.84	+19 51 11.0	1.015 8416
	25	0881.5	122 19 58.67	+0.19	8 18 23.37	+19 38 23.8	1.015 7517
	26	0882.5	123 17 19.24	+0.09	8 22 20.30	+19 25 17.1	1.015 6557
	27	0883.5	124 14 40.40	−0.02	8 26 16.62	+19 11 51.0	1.015 5539
	28	0884.5	125 12 02.11	−0.14	8 30 12.33	+18 58 05.9	1.015 4464
	29	0885.5	126 09 24.36	−0.26	8 34 07.41	+18 44 02.1	1.015 3335
	30	0886.5	127 06 47.15	−0.38	8 38 01.88	+18 29 39.9	1.015 2153
	31	0887.5	128 04 10.49	−0.49	8 41 55.72	+18 14 59.5	1.015 0921
Aug.	1	0888.5	129 01 34.38	−0.59	8 45 48.93	+18 00 01.3	1.014 9643
	2	0889.5	129 58 58.85	−0.67	8 49 41.52	+17 44 45.5	1.014 8320
	3	0890.5	130 56 23.93	−0.72	8 53 33.49	+17 29 12.5	1.014 6955
	4	0891.5	131 53 49.66	−0.75	8 57 24.84	+17 13 22.6	1.014 5551
	5	0892.5	132 51 16.08	−0.75	9 01 15.58	+16 57 16.0	1.014 4111
	6	0893.5	133 48 43.25	−0.72	9 05 05.70	+16 40 53.1	1.014 2638
	7	0894.5	134 46 11.22	−0.66	9 08 55.22	+16 24 14.2	1.014 1133
	8	0895.5	135 43 40.07	−0.58	9 12 44.13	+16 07 19.6	1.013 9599
	9	0896.5	136 41 09.89	−0.47	9 16 32.45	+15 50 09.4	1.013 8038
	10	0897.5	137 38 40.74	−0.35	9 20 20.19	+15 32 44.2	1.013 6451
	11	0898.5	138 36 12.74	−0.21	9 24 07.35	+15 15 04.0	1.013 4839
	12	0899.5	139 33 45.97	−0.07	9 27 53.95	+14 57 09.2	1.013 3201
	13	0900.5	140 31 20.53	+0.07	9 31 40.00	+14 39 00.0	1.013 1538
	14	0901.5	141 28 56.50	+0.19	9 35 25.51	+14 20 36.8	1.012 9846
	15	0902.5	142 26 33.94	+0.30	9 39 10.51	+14 01 59.7	1.012 8124
	16	0903.5	143 24 12.93	+0.39	9 42 54.99	+13 43 09.1	1.012 6369

FOR 0^h TERRESTRIAL TIME

Date		Pos. Angle of Axis P	Heliographic Latitude B_0	Heliographic Longitude L_0	Horiz. Parallax	Semi-Diameter	Ephemeris Transit
		°	°	°	″	′ ″	h m s
July	1	− 2.60	+ 2.87	207.93	8.65	15 43.95	12 03 56.90
	2	− 2.15	+ 2.98	194.69	8.65	15 43.94	12 04 08.27
	3	− 1.69	+ 3.09	181.46	8.65	15 43.94	12 04 19.34
	4	− 1.24	+ 3.19	168.22	8.65	15 43.93	12 04 30.08
	5	− 0.79	+ 3.30	154.98	8.65	15 43.94	12 04 40.46
	6	− 0.33	+ 3.41	141.75	8.65	15 43.94	12 04 50.48
	7	+ 0.12	+ 3.52	128.51	8.65	15 43.95	12 05 00.12
	8	+ 0.57	+ 3.62	115.28	8.65	15 43.97	12 05 09.36
	9	+ 1.02	+ 3.72	102.04	8.65	15 43.99	12 05 18.18
	10	+ 1.47	+ 3.83	88.81	8.65	15 44.01	12 05 26.57
	11	+ 1.92	+ 3.93	75.57	8.65	15 44.03	12 05 34.53
	12	+ 2.37	+ 4.03	62.34	8.65	15 44.06	12 05 42.02
	13	+ 2.81	+ 4.13	49.11	8.65	15 44.09	12 05 49.06
	14	+ 3.26	+ 4.23	35.87	8.65	15 44.12	12 05 55.62
	15	+ 3.70	+ 4.33	22.64	8.65	15 44.16	12 06 01.70
	16	+ 4.14	+ 4.42	9.41	8.65	15 44.20	12 06 07.29
	17	+ 4.58	+ 4.52	356.17	8.65	15 44.24	12 06 12.37
	18	+ 5.02	+ 4.61	342.94	8.65	15 44.29	12 06 16.94
	19	+ 5.46	+ 4.70	329.71	8.65	15 44.34	12 06 20.98
	20	+ 5.89	+ 4.79	316.48	8.65	15 44.40	12 06 24.49
	21	+ 6.32	+ 4.88	303.25	8.66	15 44.46	12 06 27.46
	22	+ 6.75	+ 4.97	290.02	8.66	15 44.53	12 06 29.87
	23	+ 7.18	+ 5.06	276.79	8.66	15 44.60	12 06 31.71
	24	+ 7.60	+ 5.15	263.56	8.66	15 44.68	12 06 32.97
	25	+ 8.02	+ 5.23	250.33	8.66	15 44.76	12 06 33.63
	26	+ 8.44	+ 5.31	237.10	8.66	15 44.85	12 06 33.70
	27	+ 8.85	+ 5.40	223.88	8.66	15 44.95	12 06 33.16
	28	+ 9.27	+ 5.48	210.65	8.66	15 45.05	12 06 32.00
	29	+ 9.68	+ 5.55	197.42	8.66	15 45.15	12 06 30.23
	30	+ 10.08	+ 5.63	184.19	8.66	15 45.26	12 06 27.82
	31	+ 10.48	+ 5.71	170.97	8.66	15 45.38	12 06 24.80
Aug.	1	+ 10.88	+ 5.78	157.74	8.66	15 45.50	12 06 21.15
	2	+ 11.27	+ 5.85	144.52	8.67	15 45.62	12 06 16.87
	3	+ 11.67	+ 5.92	131.29	8.67	15 45.75	12 06 11.97
	4	+ 12.05	+ 5.99	118.07	8.67	15 45.88	12 06 06.45
	5	+ 12.44	+ 6.06	104.84	8.67	15 46.01	12 06 00.31
	6	+ 12.82	+ 6.13	91.62	8.67	15 46.15	12 05 53.56
	7	+ 13.19	+ 6.19	78.40	8.67	15 46.29	12 05 46.21
	8	+ 13.56	+ 6.25	65.17	8.67	15 46.43	12 05 38.27
	9	+ 13.93	+ 6.31	51.95	8.67	15 46.58	12 05 29.74
	10	+ 14.29	+ 6.37	38.73	8.68	15 46.73	12 05 20.63
	11	+ 14.65	+ 6.43	25.51	8.68	15 46.88	12 05 10.96
	12	+ 15.01	+ 6.48	12.29	8.68	15 47.03	12 05 00.73
	13	+ 15.36	+ 6.54	359.07	8.68	15 47.19	12 04 49.96
	14	+ 15.70	+ 6.59	345.85	8.68	15 47.34	12 04 38.67
	15	+ 16.04	+ 6.64	332.63	8.68	15 47.50	12 04 26.85
	16	+ 16.38	+ 6.69	319.41	8.68	15 47.67	12 04 14.53

FOR 0^h TERRESTRIAL TIME

Date		Julian Date	Geometric Ecliptic Coords. Mn Equinox & Ecliptic of Date Longitude	Latitude	Apparent R. A.	Apparent Declination	True Geocentric Distance
		246	° ′ ″	″	h m s	° ′ ″	au
Aug.	16	0903.5	143 24 12.93	+0.39	9 42 54.99	+13 43 09.1	1.012 6369
	17	0904.5	144 21 53.48	+0.44	9 46 38.98	+13 24 05.4	1.012 4578
	18	0905.5	145 19 35.62	+0.46	9 50 22.48	+13 04 48.7	1.012 2748
	19	0906.5	146 17 19.36	+0.45	9 54 05.50	+12 45 19.6	1.012 0876
	20	0907.5	147 15 04.68	+0.41	9 57 48.04	+12 25 38.2	1.011 8961
	21	0908.5	148 12 51.55	+0.34	10 01 30.11	+12 05 44.9	1.011 6999
	22	0909.5	149 10 39.94	+0.25	10 05 11.73	+11 45 40.1	1.011 4990
	23	0910.5	150 08 29.82	+0.13	10 08 52.89	+11 25 24.2	1.011 2934
	24	0911.5	151 06 21.14	+0.01	10 12 33.62	+11 04 57.4	1.011 0832
	25	0912.5	152 04 13.87	−0.12	10 16 13.92	+10 44 20.1	1.010 8683
	26	0913.5	153 02 07.98	−0.24	10 19 53.79	+10 23 32.6	1.010 6490
	27	0914.5	154 00 03.44	−0.36	10 23 33.27	+10 02 35.3	1.010 4255
	28	0915.5	154 58 00.24	−0.46	10 27 12.36	+ 9 41 28.5	1.010 1980
	29	0916.5	155 55 58.37	−0.55	10 30 51.07	+ 9 20 12.5	1.009 9668
	30	0917.5	156 53 57.83	−0.61	10 34 29.42	+ 8 58 47.7	1.009 7321
	31	0918.5	157 51 58.62	−0.65	10 38 07.43	+ 8 37 14.4	1.009 4943
Sept.	1	0919.5	158 50 00.76	−0.66	10 41 45.11	+ 8 15 33.0	1.009 2535
	2	0920.5	159 48 04.26	−0.64	10 45 22.48	+ 7 53 43.7	1.009 0102
	3	0921.5	160 46 09.15	−0.59	10 48 59.56	+ 7 31 47.0	1.008 7646
	4	0922.5	161 44 15.47	−0.51	10 52 36.35	+ 7 09 43.1	1.008 5171
	5	0923.5	162 42 23.26	−0.41	10 56 12.88	+ 6 47 32.3	1.008 2679
	6	0924.5	163 40 32.59	−0.29	10 59 49.18	+ 6 25 14.9	1.008 0175
	7	0925.5	164 38 43.51	−0.16	11 03 25.25	+ 6 02 51.4	1.007 7659
	8	0926.5	165 36 56.12	−0.01	11 07 01.13	+ 5 40 21.8	1.007 5135
	9	0927.5	166 35 10.51	+0.13	11 10 36.83	+ 5 17 46.6	1.007 2604
	10	0928.5	167 33 26.76	+0.27	11 14 12.38	+ 4 55 06.0	1.007 0065
	11	0929.5	168 31 44.96	+0.38	11 17 47.82	+ 4 32 20.2	1.006 7519
	12	0930.5	169 30 05.19	+0.48	11 21 23.15	+ 4 09 29.6	1.006 4963
	13	0931.5	170 28 27.52	+0.54	11 24 58.41	+ 3 46 34.5	1.006 2396
	14	0932.5	171 26 51.99	+0.57	11 28 33.61	+ 3 23 35.2	1.005 9815
	15	0933.5	172 25 18.62	+0.57	11 32 08.77	+ 3 00 32.0	1.005 7218
	16	0934.5	173 23 47.42	+0.54	11 35 43.92	+ 2 37 25.3	1.005 4601
	17	0935.5	174 22 18.38	+0.47	11 39 19.06	+ 2 14 15.4	1.005 1962
	18	0936.5	175 20 51.49	+0.38	11 42 54.21	+ 1 51 02.7	1.004 9299
	19	0937.5	176 19 26.70	+0.27	11 46 29.40	+ 1 27 47.5	1.004 6611
	20	0938.5	177 18 03.98	+0.15	11 50 04.63	+ 1 04 30.2	1.004 3898
	21	0939.5	178 16 43.30	+0.02	11 53 39.93	+ 0 41 11.2	1.004 1158
	22	0940.5	179 15 24.59	−0.10	11 57 15.32	+ 0 17 50.8	1.003 8393
	23	0941.5	180 14 07.83	−0.23	12 00 50.81	− 0 05 30.7	1.003 5602
	24	0942.5	181 12 52.96	−0.33	12 04 26.42	− 0 28 52.8	1.003 2788
	25	0943.5	182 11 39.95	−0.43	12 08 02.18	− 0 52 15.2	1.002 9952
	26	0944.5	183 10 28.76	−0.50	12 11 38.09	− 1 15 37.6	1.002 7096
	27	0945.5	184 09 19.38	−0.54	12 15 14.18	− 1 38 59.6	1.002 4224
	28	0946.5	185 08 11.76	−0.56	12 18 50.47	− 2 02 20.7	1.002 1336
	29	0947.5	186 07 05.90	−0.56	12 22 26.97	− 2 25 40.8	1.001 8436
	30	0948.5	187 06 01.79	−0.52	12 26 03.70	− 2 48 59.4	1.001 5528
Oct.	1	0949.5	188 04 59.42	−0.45	12 29 40.69	− 3 12 16.1	1.001 2614

FOR 0^h TERRESTRIAL TIME

Date		Pos. Angle of Axis P	Heliographic Latitude B_0	Heliographic Longitude L_0	Horiz. Parallax	Semi-Diameter	Ephemeris Transit
		°	°	°	″	′ ″	h m s
Aug.	16	+ 16.38	+ 6.69	319.41	8.68	15 47.67	12 04 14.53
	17	+ 16.71	+ 6.73	306.19	8.69	15 47.84	12 04 01.71
	18	+ 17.04	+ 6.78	292.98	8.69	15 48.01	12 03 48.40
	19	+ 17.36	+ 6.82	279.76	8.69	15 48.18	12 03 34.62
	20	+ 17.68	+ 6.86	266.54	8.69	15 48.36	12 03 20.37
	21	+ 17.99	+ 6.90	253.33	8.69	15 48.55	12 03 05.66
	22	+ 18.30	+ 6.94	240.11	8.69	15 48.74	12 02 50.49
	23	+ 18.60	+ 6.97	226.90	8.70	15 48.93	12 02 34.88
	24	+ 18.90	+ 7.00	213.69	8.70	15 49.13	12 02 18.85
	25	+ 19.19	+ 7.03	200.47	8.70	15 49.33	12 02 02.39
	26	+ 19.48	+ 7.06	187.26	8.70	15 49.53	12 01 45.52
	27	+ 19.76	+ 7.09	174.05	8.70	15 49.74	12 01 28.25
	28	+ 20.04	+ 7.12	160.84	8.71	15 49.96	12 01 10.60
	29	+ 20.31	+ 7.14	147.63	8.71	15 50.17	12 00 52.59
	30	+ 20.57	+ 7.16	134.41	8.71	15 50.40	12 00 34.21
	31	+ 20.83	+ 7.18	121.20	8.71	15 50.62	12 00 15.50
Sept.	1	+ 21.09	+ 7.19	107.99	8.71	15 50.85	11 59 56.47
	2	+ 21.34	+ 7.21	94.79	8.72	15 51.08	11 59 37.13
	3	+ 21.58	+ 7.22	81.58	8.72	15 51.31	11 59 17.51
	4	+ 21.82	+ 7.23	68.37	8.72	15 51.54	11 58 57.62
	5	+ 22.05	+ 7.24	55.16	8.72	15 51.78	11 58 37.48
	6	+ 22.28	+ 7.25	41.95	8.72	15 52.01	11 58 17.11
	7	+ 22.50	+ 7.25	28.75	8.73	15 52.25	11 57 56.54
	8	+ 22.72	+ 7.25	15.54	8.73	15 52.49	11 57 35.78
	9	+ 22.93	+ 7.25	2.33	8.73	15 52.73	11 57 14.87
	10	+ 23.13	+ 7.25	349.13	8.73	15 52.97	11 56 53.82
	11	+ 23.33	+ 7.25	335.92	8.74	15 53.21	11 56 32.65
	12	+ 23.52	+ 7.24	322.72	8.74	15 53.45	11 56 11.39
	13	+ 23.70	+ 7.23	309.52	8.74	15 53.69	11 55 50.06
	14	+ 23.88	+ 7.22	296.31	8.74	15 53.94	11 55 28.69
	15	+ 24.06	+ 7.21	283.11	8.74	15 54.19	11 55 07.28
	16	+ 24.22	+ 7.19	269.91	8.75	15 54.43	11 54 45.87
	17	+ 24.39	+ 7.18	256.71	8.75	15 54.68	11 54 24.46
	18	+ 24.54	+ 7.16	243.50	8.75	15 54.94	11 54 03.08
	19	+ 24.69	+ 7.14	230.30	8.75	15 55.19	11 53 41.74
	20	+ 24.83	+ 7.11	217.10	8.76	15 55.45	11 53 20.46
	21	+ 24.97	+ 7.09	203.90	8.76	15 55.71	11 52 59.26
	22	+ 25.10	+ 7.06	190.70	8.76	15 55.97	11 52 38.16
	23	+ 25.22	+ 7.03	177.51	8.76	15 56.24	11 52 17.17
	24	+ 25.33	+ 7.00	164.31	8.77	15 56.51	11 51 56.30
	25	+ 25.44	+ 6.97	151.11	8.77	15 56.78	11 51 35.59
	26	+ 25.55	+ 6.93	137.91	8.77	15 57.05	11 51 15.04
	27	+ 25.64	+ 6.89	124.71	8.77	15 57.33	11 50 54.67
	28	+ 25.73	+ 6.85	111.52	8.78	15 57.60	11 50 34.51
	29	+ 25.81	+ 6.81	98.32	8.78	15 57.88	11 50 14.57
	30	+ 25.89	+ 6.77	85.12	8.78	15 58.16	11 49 54.87
Oct.	1	+ 25.96	+ 6.72	71.93	8.78	15 58.44	11 49 35.43

FOR 0h TERRESTRIAL TIME

Date		Julian Date	Geometric Ecliptic Coords. Mn Equinox & Ecliptic of Date		Apparent R. A.	Apparent Declination	True Geocentric Distance
			Longitude	Latitude			
		246	° ′ ″	″	h m s	° ′ ″	au
Oct.	1	0949.5	188 04 59.42	−0.45	12 29 40.69	− 3 12 16.1	1.001 2614
	2	0950.5	189 03 58.78	−0.36	12 33 17.95	− 3 35 30.5	1.000 9698
	3	0951.5	190 02 59.91	−0.25	12 36 55.49	− 3 58 42.5	1.000 6784
	4	0952.5	191 02 02.81	−0.12	12 40 33.35	− 4 21 51.5	1.000 3875
	5	0953.5	192 01 07.54	+0.02	12 44 11.54	− 4 44 57.2	1.000 0974
	6	0954.5	193 00 14.13	+0.16	12 47 50.09	− 5 07 59.4	0.999 8086
	7	0955.5	193 59 22.67	+0.30	12 51 29.02	− 5 30 57.7	0.999 5211
	8	0956.5	194 58 33.23	+0.42	12 55 08.36	− 5 53 51.8	0.999 2354
	9	0957.5	195 57 45.90	+0.53	12 58 48.13	− 6 16 41.3	0.998 9513
	10	0958.5	196 57 00.74	+0.60	13 02 28.37	− 6 39 26.0	0.998 6689
	11	0959.5	197 56 17.84	+0.64	13 06 09.08	− 7 02 05.5	0.998 3879
	12	0960.5	198 55 37.24	+0.65	13 09 50.30	− 7 24 39.5	0.998 1083
	13	0961.5	199 54 58.97	+0.62	13 13 32.04	− 7 47 07.5	0.997 8298
	14	0962.5	200 54 23.03	+0.56	13 17 14.32	− 8 09 29.2	0.997 5520
	15	0963.5	201 53 49.44	+0.48	13 20 57.16	− 8 31 44.3	0.997 2748
	16	0964.5	202 53 18.15	+0.37	13 24 40.57	− 8 53 52.2	0.996 9979
	17	0965.5	203 52 49.15	+0.26	13 28 24.56	− 9 15 52.6	0.996 7212
	18	0966.5	204 52 22.38	+0.13	13 32 09.16	− 9 37 45.1	0.996 4446
	19	0967.5	205 51 57.81	0.00	13 35 54.39	− 9 59 29.3	0.996 1679
	20	0968.5	206 51 35.37	−0.12	13 39 40.24	−10 21 04.8	0.995 8911
	21	0969.5	207 51 15.01	−0.23	13 43 26.75	−10 42 31.2	0.995 6143
	22	0970.5	208 50 56.67	−0.33	13 47 13.92	−11 03 48.0	0.995 3375
	23	0971.5	209 50 40.29	−0.41	13 51 01.77	−11 24 54.9	0.995 0607
	24	0972.5	210 50 25.83	−0.46	13 54 50.31	−11 45 51.4	0.994 7842
	25	0973.5	211 50 13.22	−0.49	13 58 39.55	−12 06 37.1	0.994 5080
	26	0974.5	212 50 02.41	−0.49	14 02 29.49	−12 27 11.7	0.994 2325
	27	0975.5	213 49 53.35	−0.46	14 06 20.16	−12 47 34.7	0.993 9578
	28	0976.5	214 49 46.01	−0.41	14 10 11.56	−13 07 45.7	0.993 6842
	29	0977.5	215 49 40.35	−0.33	14 14 03.69	−13 27 44.2	0.993 4120
	30	0978.5	216 49 36.32	−0.22	14 17 56.57	−13 47 29.9	0.993 1415
	31	0979.5	217 49 33.92	−0.10	14 21 50.21	−14 07 02.4	0.992 8730
Nov.	1	0980.5	218 49 33.12	+0.03	14 25 44.62	−14 26 21.3	0.992 6070
	2	0981.5	219 49 33.92	+0.17	14 29 39.80	−14 45 26.1	0.992 3438
	3	0982.5	220 49 36.35	+0.30	14 33 35.78	−15 04 16.5	0.992 0838
	4	0983.5	221 49 40.43	+0.43	14 37 32.55	−15 22 52.1	0.991 8273
	5	0984.5	222 49 46.22	+0.53	14 41 30.15	−15 41 12.5	0.991 5747
	6	0985.5	223 49 53.77	+0.61	14 45 28.57	−15 59 17.4	0.991 3262
	7	0986.5	224 50 03.16	+0.66	14 49 27.83	−16 17 06.5	0.991 0818
	8	0987.5	225 50 14.46	+0.67	14 53 27.95	−16 34 39.3	0.990 8416
	9	0988.5	226 50 27.72	+0.65	14 57 28.92	−16 51 55.5	0.990 6053
	10	0989.5	227 50 42.97	+0.60	15 01 30.75	−17 08 54.6	0.990 3728
	11	0990.5	228 51 00.23	+0.52	15 05 33.44	−17 25 36.3	0.990 1439
	12	0991.5	229 51 19.49	+0.42	15 09 36.99	−17 42 00.1	0.989 9182
	13	0992.5	230 51 40.75	+0.30	15 13 41.41	−17 58 05.7	0.989 6955
	14	0993.5	231 52 03.95	+0.18	15 17 46.70	−18 13 52.5	0.989 4757
	15	0994.5	232 52 29.06	+0.05	15 21 52.85	−18 29 20.3	0.989 2586
	16	0995.5	233 52 56.03	−0.07	15 25 59.86	−18 44 28.6	0.989 0439

FOR 0^h TERRESTRIAL TIME

Date		Pos. Angle of Axis P	Heliographic Latitude B_0	Heliographic Longitude L_0	Horiz. Parallax	Semi-Diameter	Ephemeris Transit
		°	°	°	″	′ ″	h m s
Oct.	1	+ 25.96	+ 6.72	71.93	8.78	15 58.44	11 49 35.43
	2	+ 26.02	+ 6.68	58.73	8.79	15 58.72	11 49 16.28
	3	+ 26.07	+ 6.63	45.54	8.79	15 58.99	11 48 57.43
	4	+ 26.12	+ 6.57	32.34	8.79	15 59.27	11 48 38.90
	5	+ 26.16	+ 6.52	19.15	8.79	15 59.55	11 48 20.72
	6	+ 26.20	+ 6.46	5.95	8.80	15 59.83	11 48 02.91
	7	+ 26.22	+ 6.41	352.76	8.80	16 00.10	11 47 45.49
	8	+ 26.24	+ 6.35	339.57	8.80	16 00.38	11 47 28.49
	9	+ 26.25	+ 6.29	326.37	8.80	16 00.65	11 47 11.94
	10	+ 26.26	+ 6.22	313.18	8.81	16 00.92	11 46 55.85
	11	+ 26.25	+ 6.16	299.99	8.81	16 01.19	11 46 40.25
	12	+ 26.24	+ 6.09	286.79	8.81	16 01.46	11 46 25.17
	13	+ 26.23	+ 6.02	273.60	8.81	16 01.73	11 46 10.61
	14	+ 26.20	+ 5.95	260.41	8.82	16 02.00	11 45 56.60
	15	+ 26.17	+ 5.88	247.22	8.82	16 02.27	11 45 43.16
	16	+ 26.13	+ 5.80	234.03	8.82	16 02.53	11 45 30.30
	17	+ 26.08	+ 5.73	220.84	8.82	16 02.80	11 45 18.05
	18	+ 26.03	+ 5.65	207.65	8.83	16 03.07	11 45 06.40
	19	+ 25.96	+ 5.57	194.46	8.83	16 03.34	11 44 55.39
	20	+ 25.89	+ 5.49	181.27	8.83	16 03.60	11 44 45.02
	21	+ 25.82	+ 5.40	168.08	8.83	16 03.87	11 44 35.30
	22	+ 25.73	+ 5.32	154.89	8.84	16 04.14	11 44 26.25
	23	+ 25.64	+ 5.23	141.70	8.84	16 04.41	11 44 17.88
	24	+ 25.54	+ 5.15	128.51	8.84	16 04.68	11 44 10.20
	25	+ 25.43	+ 5.06	115.33	8.84	16 04.94	11 44 03.23
	26	+ 25.31	+ 4.96	102.14	8.85	16 05.21	11 43 56.96
	27	+ 25.19	+ 4.87	88.95	8.85	16 05.48	11 43 51.43
	28	+ 25.05	+ 4.78	75.76	8.85	16 05.74	11 43 46.62
	29	+ 24.91	+ 4.68	62.58	8.85	16 06.01	11 43 42.56
	30	+ 24.76	+ 4.58	49.39	8.85	16 06.27	11 43 39.26
	31	+ 24.61	+ 4.49	36.20	8.86	16 06.53	11 43 36.72
Nov.	1	+ 24.45	+ 4.39	23.01	8.86	16 06.79	11 43 34.95
	2	+ 24.27	+ 4.28	9.83	8.86	16 07.05	11 43 33.97
	3	+ 24.09	+ 4.18	356.64	8.86	16 07.30	11 43 33.79
	4	+ 23.91	+ 4.08	343.46	8.87	16 07.55	11 43 34.41
	5	+ 23.71	+ 3.97	330.27	8.87	16 07.80	11 43 35.85
	6	+ 23.51	+ 3.86	317.08	8.87	16 08.04	11 43 38.13
	7	+ 23.30	+ 3.76	303.90	8.87	16 08.28	11 43 41.24
	8	+ 23.08	+ 3.65	290.71	8.88	16 08.51	11 43 45.21
	9	+ 22.85	+ 3.54	277.53	8.88	16 08.75	11 43 50.03
	10	+ 22.62	+ 3.43	264.34	8.88	16 08.97	11 43 55.71
	11	+ 22.38	+ 3.31	251.16	8.88	16 09.20	11 44 02.27
	12	+ 22.13	+ 3.20	237.98	8.88	16 09.42	11 44 09.69
	13	+ 21.87	+ 3.09	224.79	8.89	16 09.64	11 44 17.98
	14	+ 21.61	+ 2.97	211.61	8.89	16 09.85	11 44 27.14
	15	+ 21.33	+ 2.85	198.43	8.89	16 10.06	11 44 37.17
	16	+ 21.06	+ 2.74	185.24	8.89	16 10.28	11 44 48.05

FOR 0^h TERRESTRIAL TIME

Date		Julian Date	Geometric Ecliptic Coords. Mn Equinox & Ecliptic of Date		Apparent R. A.	Apparent Declination	True Geocentric Distance
			Longitude	Latitude			
		246	° ′ ″	″	h m s	° ′ ″	au
Nov.	16	0995.5	233 52 56.03	−0.07	15 25 59.86	−18 44 28.6	0.989 0439
	17	0996.5	234 53 24.80	−0.19	15 30 07.73	−18 59 16.9	0.988 8316
	18	0997.5	235 53 55.30	−0.29	15 34 16.44	−19 13 45.0	0.988 6217
	19	0998.5	236 54 27.46	−0.37	15 38 25.99	−19 27 52.4	0.988 4140
	20	0999.5	237 55 01.22	−0.42	15 42 36.38	−19 41 38.8	0.988 2087
	21	1000.5	238 55 36.49	−0.45	15 46 47.58	−19 55 03.7	0.988 0056
	22	1001.5	239 56 13.21	−0.46	15 50 59.58	−20 08 06.8	0.987 8049
	23	1002.5	240 56 51.30	−0.43	15 55 12.38	−20 20 47.7	0.987 6068
	24	1003.5	241 57 30.69	−0.38	15 59 25.95	−20 33 06.1	0.987 4112
	25	1004.5	242 58 11.30	−0.31	16 03 40.27	−20 45 01.6	0.987 2186
	26	1005.5	243 58 53.08	−0.21	16 07 55.33	−20 56 33.8	0.987 0289
	27	1006.5	244 59 35.95	−0.10	16 12 11.11	−21 07 42.5	0.986 8426
	28	1007.5	246 00 19.86	+0.02	16 16 27.59	−21 18 27.3	0.986 6599
	29	1008.5	247 01 04.76	+0.16	16 20 44.76	−21 28 47.9	0.986 4811
	30	1009.5	248 01 50.62	+0.29	16 25 02.58	−21 38 44.0	0.986 3066
Dec.	1	1010.5	249 02 37.41	+0.41	16 29 21.06	−21 48 15.2	0.986 1367
	2	1011.5	250 03 25.13	+0.51	16 33 40.16	−21 57 21.5	0.985 9719
	3	1012.5	251 04 13.79	+0.60	16 37 59.87	−22 06 02.4	0.985 8125
	4	1013.5	252 05 03.42	+0.65	16 42 20.18	−22 14 17.8	0.985 6588
	5	1014.5	253 05 54.08	+0.67	16 46 41.07	−22 22 07.4	0.985 5110
	6	1015.5	254 06 45.81	+0.65	16 51 02.51	−22 29 31.1	0.985 3692
	7	1016.5	255 07 38.67	+0.60	16 55 24.48	−22 36 28.5	0.985 2333
	8	1017.5	256 08 32.71	+0.52	16 59 46.96	−22 42 59.5	0.985 1033
	9	1018.5	257 09 27.93	+0.42	17 04 09.93	−22 49 03.9	0.984 9790
	10	1019.5	258 10 24.36	+0.30	17 08 33.35	−22 54 41.3	0.984 8600
	11	1020.5	259 11 21.98	+0.18	17 12 57.20	−22 59 51.7	0.984 7462
	12	1021.5	260 12 20.77	+0.05	17 17 21.46	−23 04 34.8	0.984 6372
	13	1022.5	261 13 20.68	−0.08	17 21 46.10	−23 08 50.4	0.984 5329
	14	1023.5	262 14 21.66	−0.19	17 26 11.08	−23 12 38.4	0.984 4330
	15	1024.5	263 15 23.66	−0.30	17 30 36.37	−23 15 58.7	0.984 3373
	16	1025.5	264 16 26.62	−0.38	17 35 01.93	−23 18 51.1	0.984 2457
	17	1026.5	265 17 30.46	−0.43	17 39 27.74	−23 21 15.6	0.984 1580
	18	1027.5	266 18 35.11	−0.47	17 43 53.76	−23 23 12.0	0.984 0741
	19	1028.5	267 19 40.49	−0.47	17 48 19.95	−23 24 40.2	0.983 9940
	20	1029.5	268 20 46.52	−0.45	17 52 46.27	−23 25 40.3	0.983 9176
	21	1030.5	269 21 53.10	−0.40	17 57 12.68	−23 26 12.1	0.983 8449
	22	1031.5	270 23 00.16	−0.33	18 01 39.14	−23 26 15.7	0.983 7759
	23	1032.5	271 24 07.61	−0.24	18 06 05.62	−23 25 51.0	0.983 7106
	24	1033.5	272 25 15.35	−0.12	18 10 32.08	−23 24 58.0	0.983 6493
	25	1034.5	273 26 23.30	0.00	18 14 58.47	−23 23 36.8	0.983 5920
	26	1035.5	274 27 31.38	+0.13	18 19 24.76	−23 21 47.3	0.983 5390
	27	1036.5	275 28 39.52	+0.26	18 23 50.91	−23 19 29.7	0.983 4905
	28	1037.5	276 29 47.65	+0.38	18 28 16.90	−23 16 44.0	0.983 4468
	29	1038.5	277 30 55.74	+0.49	18 32 42.68	−23 13 30.3	0.983 4083
	30	1039.5	278 32 03.73	+0.57	18 37 08.23	−23 09 48.7	0.983 3751
	31	1040.5	279 33 11.61	+0.63	18 41 33.52	−23 05 39.3	0.983 3478
	32	1041.5	280 34 19.40	+0.65	18 45 58.52	−23 01 02.3	0.983 3267

FOR 0^h TERRESTRIAL TIME

Date		Pos. Angle of Axis P	Heliographic Latitude B_0	Heliographic Longitude L_0	Horiz. Parallax	Semi-Diameter	Ephemeris Transit
		°	°	°	″	′ ″	h m s
Nov.	16	+ 21.06	+ 2.74	185.24	8.89	16 10.28	11 44 48.05
	17	+ 20.77	+ 2.62	172.06	8.89	16 10.48	11 44 59.78
	18	+ 20.47	+ 2.50	158.88	8.90	16 10.69	11 45 12.35
	19	+ 20.17	+ 2.38	145.70	8.90	16 10.89	11 45 25.76
	20	+ 19.86	+ 2.26	132.52	8.90	16 11.10	11 45 39.99
	21	+ 19.55	+ 2.14	119.33	8.90	16 11.30	11 45 55.03
	22	+ 19.22	+ 2.01	106.15	8.90	16 11.49	11 46 10.86
	23	+ 18.89	+ 1.89	92.97	8.90	16 11.69	11 46 27.48
	24	+ 18.56	+ 1.77	79.79	8.91	16 11.88	11 46 44.86
	25	+ 18.21	+ 1.64	66.61	8.91	16 12.07	11 47 02.99
	26	+ 17.86	+ 1.52	53.43	8.91	16 12.26	11 47 21.85
	27	+ 17.50	+ 1.39	40.25	8.91	16 12.44	11 47 41.43
	28	+ 17.14	+ 1.27	27.07	8.91	16 12.62	11 48 01.70
	29	+ 16.77	+ 1.14	13.89	8.91	16 12.80	11 48 22.64
	30	+ 16.40	+ 1.02	0.71	8.92	16 12.97	11 48 44.24
Dec.	1	+ 16.01	+ 0.89	347.53	8.92	16 13.14	11 49 06.48
	2	+ 15.63	+ 0.76	334.35	8.92	16 13.30	11 49 29.34
	3	+ 15.23	+ 0.63	321.18	8.92	16 13.46	11 49 52.79
	4	+ 14.83	+ 0.51	308.00	8.92	16 13.61	11 50 16.83
	5	+ 14.43	+ 0.38	294.82	8.92	16 13.75	11 50 41.43
	6	+ 14.02	+ 0.25	281.64	8.92	16 13.89	11 51 06.58
	7	+ 13.60	+ 0.12	268.46	8.93	16 14.03	11 51 32.24
	8	+ 13.18	0.00	255.28	8.93	16 14.16	11 51 58.41
	9	+ 12.76	− 0.13	242.11	8.93	16 14.28	11 52 25.05
	10	+ 12.33	− 0.26	228.93	8.93	16 14.40	11 52 52.15
	11	+ 11.89	− 0.39	215.75	8.93	16 14.51	11 53 19.66
	12	+ 11.45	− 0.52	202.58	8.93	16 14.62	11 53 47.57
	13	+ 11.01	− 0.64	189.40	8.93	16 14.72	11 54 15.83
	14	+ 10.56	− 0.77	176.23	8.93	16 14.82	11 54 44.43
	15	+ 10.11	− 0.90	163.05	8.93	16 14.91	11 55 13.31
	16	+ 9.66	− 1.03	149.88	8.93	16 15.01	11 55 42.46
	17	+ 9.20	− 1.15	136.70	8.94	16 15.09	11 56 11.83
	18	+ 8.74	− 1.28	123.53	8.94	16 15.18	11 56 41.38
	19	+ 8.27	− 1.41	110.35	8.94	16 15.25	11 57 11.09
	20	+ 7.81	− 1.53	97.18	8.94	16 15.33	11 57 40.90
	21	+ 7.34	− 1.66	84.01	8.94	16 15.40	11 58 10.79
	22	+ 6.87	− 1.78	70.83	8.94	16 15.47	11 58 40.71
	23	+ 6.39	− 1.91	57.66	8.94	16 15.54	11 59 10.63
	24	+ 5.92	− 2.03	44.49	8.94	16 15.60	11 59 40.51
	25	+ 5.44	− 2.16	31.32	8.94	16 15.65	12 00 10.31
	26	+ 4.96	− 2.28	18.14	8.94	16 15.71	12 00 40.00
	27	+ 4.48	− 2.40	4.97	8.94	16 15.75	12 01 09.53
	28	+ 4.00	− 2.52	351.80	8.94	16 15.80	12 01 38.87
	29	+ 3.51	− 2.64	338.63	8.94	16 15.84	12 02 08.00
	30	+ 3.03	− 2.76	325.46	8.94	16 15.87	12 02 36.87
	31	+ 2.55	− 2.88	312.29	8.94	16 15.90	12 03 05.47
	32	+ 2.06	− 3.00	299.11	8.94	16 15.92	12 03 33.75

ICRS GEOCENTRIC RECTANGULAR COORDINATES
FOR 0^h TERRESTRIAL TIME

Date		x	y	z	Date		x	y	z
		au	au	au			au	au	au
Jan.	0	+0.161 4515	−0.890 0008	−0.385 8068	Feb.	15	+0.820 7642	−0.504 1083	−0.218 5286
	1	+0.178 6834	−0.887 2097	−0.384 5968		16	+0.830 4877	−0.490 8611	−0.212 7869
	2	+0.195 8591	−0.884 1411	−0.383 2663		17	+0.839 9579	−0.477 4632	−0.206 9798
	3	+0.212 9728	−0.880 7962	−0.381 8160		18	+0.849 1718	−0.463 9184	−0.201 1090
	4	+0.230 0188	−0.877 1763	−0.380 2463		19	+0.858 1266	−0.450 2308	−0.195 1762
	5	+0.246 9917	−0.873 2827	−0.378 5579		20	+0.866 8198	−0.436 4044	−0.189 1831
	6	+0.263 8860	−0.869 1170	−0.376 7515		21	+0.875 2484	−0.422 4433	−0.183 1315
	7	+0.280 6964	−0.864 6809	−0.374 8279		22	+0.883 4100	−0.408 3518	−0.177 0233
	8	+0.297 4178	−0.859 9762	−0.372 7880		23	+0.891 3018	−0.394 1342	−0.170 8602
	9	+0.314 0450	−0.855 0046	−0.370 6324		24	+0.898 9213	−0.379 7947	−0.164 6441
	10	+0.330 5733	−0.849 7682	−0.368 3621		25	+0.906 2659	−0.365 3378	−0.158 3770
	11	+0.346 9979	−0.844 2686	−0.365 9779		26	+0.913 3334	−0.350 7682	−0.152 0608
	12	+0.363 3139	−0.838 5079	−0.363 4807		27	+0.920 1213	−0.336 0904	−0.145 6977
	13	+0.379 5169	−0.832 4878	−0.360 8712		28	+0.926 6274	−0.321 3094	−0.139 2897
	14	+0.395 6021	−0.826 2103	−0.358 1503	Mar.	1	+0.932 8497	−0.306 4300	−0.132 8389
	15	+0.411 5650	−0.819 6771	−0.355 3187		2	+0.938 7864	−0.291 4571	−0.126 3477
	16	+0.427 4009	−0.812 8903	−0.352 3772		3	+0.944 4359	−0.276 3959	−0.119 8182
	17	+0.443 1051	−0.805 8516	−0.349 3267		4	+0.949 7968	−0.261 2514	−0.113 2527
	18	+0.458 6731	−0.798 5631	−0.346 1680		5	+0.954 8680	−0.246 0286	−0.106 6533
	19	+0.474 1000	−0.791 0268	−0.342 9018		6	+0.959 6485	−0.230 7324	−0.100 0223
	20	+0.489 3811	−0.783 2448	−0.339 5292		7	+0.964 1374	−0.215 3676	−0.093 3617
	21	+0.504 5117	−0.775 2193	−0.336 0510		8	+0.968 3340	−0.199 9391	−0.086 6737
	22	+0.519 4870	−0.766 9526	−0.332 4682		9	+0.972 2377	−0.184 4516	−0.079 9602
	23	+0.534 3024	−0.758 4472	−0.328 7817		10	+0.975 8479	−0.168 9097	−0.073 2234
	24	+0.548 9530	−0.749 7054	−0.324 9928		11	+0.979 1640	−0.153 3180	−0.066 4650
	25	+0.563 4341	−0.740 7300	−0.321 1024		12	+0.982 1855	−0.137 6810	−0.059 6872
	26	+0.577 7410	−0.731 5236	−0.317 1117		13	+0.984 9121	−0.122 0033	−0.052 8918
	27	+0.591 8690	−0.722 0890	−0.313 0220		14	+0.987 3431	−0.106 2893	−0.046 0807
	28	+0.605 8135	−0.712 4292	−0.308 8345		15	+0.989 4783	−0.090 5435	−0.039 2558
	29	+0.619 5698	−0.702 5474	−0.304 5506		16	+0.991 3171	−0.074 7704	−0.032 4191
	30	+0.633 1333	−0.692 4467	−0.300 1717		17	+0.992 8593	−0.058 9746	−0.025 5725
	31	+0.646 4996	−0.682 1306	−0.295 6993		18	+0.994 1046	−0.043 1604	−0.018 7179
Feb.	1	+0.659 6643	−0.671 6027	−0.291 1350		19	+0.995 0525	−0.027 3325	−0.011 8572
	2	+0.672 6232	−0.660 8667	−0.286 4804		20	+0.995 7030	−0.011 4954	−0.004 9924
	3	+0.685 3724	−0.649 9263	−0.281 7373		21	+0.996 0557	+0.004 3464	+0.001 8745
	4	+0.697 9081	−0.638 7855	−0.276 9073		22	+0.996 1107	+0.020 1880	+0.008 7416
	5	+0.710 2266	−0.627 4480	−0.271 9921		23	+0.995 8677	+0.036 0251	+0.015 6068
	6	+0.722 3244	−0.615 9179	−0.266 9936		24	+0.995 3268	+0.051 8527	+0.022 4681
	7	+0.734 1984	−0.604 1990	−0.261 9134		25	+0.994 4881	+0.067 6662	+0.029 3234
	8	+0.745 8454	−0.592 2952	−0.256 7531		26	+0.993 3516	+0.083 4607	+0.036 1706
	9	+0.757 2621	−0.580 2102	−0.251 5145		27	+0.991 9177	+0.099 2314	+0.043 0076
	10	+0.768 4458	−0.567 9479	−0.246 1992		28	+0.990 1867	+0.114 9733	+0.049 8322
	11	+0.779 3933	−0.555 5121	−0.240 8089		29	+0.988 1592	+0.130 6813	+0.056 6421
	12	+0.790 1018	−0.542 9064	−0.235 3450		30	+0.985 8360	+0.146 3504	+0.063 4352
	13	+0.800 5684	−0.530 1347	−0.229 8093		31	+0.983 2181	+0.161 9755	+0.070 2091
	14	+0.810 7902	−0.517 2007	−0.224 2033	Apr.	1	+0.980 3067	+0.177 5517	+0.076 9618
	15	+0.820 7642	−0.504 1083	−0.218 5286		2	+0.977 1032	+0.193 0741	+0.083 6909

ICRS GEOCENTRIC RECTANGULAR COORDINATES FOR 0^h TERRESTRIAL TIME

Date		x	y	z	Date		x	y	z
		au	au	au			au	au	au
Apr.	1	+0.980 3067	+0.177 5517	+0.076 9618	May	17	+0.565 4136	+0.769 1863	+0.333 4224
	2	+0.977 1032	+0.193 0741	+0.083 6909		18	+0.551 3550	+0.777 9632	+0.337 2275
	3	+0.973 6093	+0.208 5378	+0.090 3944		19	+0.537 1380	+0.786 5189	+0.340 9367
	4	+0.969 8267	+0.223 9382	+0.097 0704		20	+0.522 7665	+0.794 8509	+0.344 5492
	5	+0.965 7572	+0.239 2709	+0.103 7168		21	+0.508 2443	+0.802 9568	+0.348 0637
	6	+0.961 4026	+0.254 5314	+0.110 3317		22	+0.493 5754	+0.810 8340	+0.351 4791
	7	+0.956 7647	+0.269 7155	+0.116 9134		23	+0.478 7639	+0.818 4802	+0.354 7944
	8	+0.951 8456	+0.284 8189	+0.123 4600		24	+0.463 8141	+0.825 8929	+0.358 0084
	9	+0.946 6470	+0.299 8375	+0.129 9697		25	+0.448 7304	+0.833 0697	+0.361 1201
	10	+0.941 1709	+0.314 7671	+0.136 4409		26	+0.433 5174	+0.840 0083	+0.364 1285
	11	+0.935 4192	+0.329 6038	+0.142 8717		27	+0.418 1796	+0.846 7065	+0.367 0325
	12	+0.929 3939	+0.344 3436	+0.149 2605		28	+0.402 7221	+0.853 1624	+0.369 8313
	13	+0.923 0969	+0.358 9824	+0.155 6055		29	+0.387 1496	+0.859 3740	+0.372 5240
	14	+0.916 5303	+0.373 5163	+0.161 9052		30	+0.371 4673	+0.865 3398	+0.375 1100
	15	+0.909 6960	+0.387 9414	+0.168 1578		31	+0.355 6799	+0.871 0583	+0.377 5886
	16	+0.902 5960	+0.402 2537	+0.174 3616	June	1	+0.339 7924	+0.876 5281	+0.379 9593
	17	+0.895 2324	+0.416 4493	+0.180 5149		2	+0.323 8097	+0.881 7481	+0.382 2217
	18	+0.887 6074	+0.430 5243	+0.186 6161		3	+0.307 7364	+0.886 7172	+0.384 3751
	19	+0.879 7231	+0.444 4747	+0.192 6635		4	+0.291 5773	+0.891 4343	+0.386 4194
	20	+0.871 5816	+0.458 2966	+0.198 6553		5	+0.275 3371	+0.895 8985	+0.388 3540
	21	+0.863 1852	+0.471 9861	+0.204 5899		6	+0.259 0204	+0.900 1090	+0.390 1786
	22	+0.854 5363	+0.485 5392	+0.210 4655		7	+0.242 6317	+0.904 0649	+0.391 8929
	23	+0.845 6372	+0.498 9519	+0.216 2803		8	+0.226 1756	+0.907 7653	+0.393 4966
	24	+0.836 4904	+0.512 2202	+0.222 0326		9	+0.209 6566	+0.911 2097	+0.394 9894
	25	+0.827 0986	+0.525 3399	+0.227 7206		10	+0.193 0792	+0.914 3973	+0.396 3710
	26	+0.817 4645	+0.538 3071	+0.233 3424		11	+0.176 4478	+0.917 3274	+0.397 6412
	27	+0.807 5911	+0.551 1177	+0.238 8963		12	+0.159 7669	+0.919 9994	+0.398 7996
	28	+0.797 4816	+0.563 7676	+0.244 3805		13	+0.143 0409	+0.922 4128	+0.399 8460
	29	+0.787 1394	+0.576 2529	+0.249 7932		14	+0.126 2741	+0.924 5668	+0.400 7801
	30	+0.776 5680	+0.588 5699	+0.255 1328		15	+0.109 4710	+0.926 4609	+0.401 6017
May	1	+0.765 7711	+0.600 7150	+0.260 3977		16	+0.092 6361	+0.928 0945	+0.402 3105
	2	+0.754 7525	+0.612 6846	+0.265 5864		17	+0.075 7737	+0.929 4670	+0.402 9062
	3	+0.743 5160	+0.624 4756	+0.270 6974		18	+0.058 8885	+0.930 5779	+0.403 3885
	4	+0.732 0653	+0.636 0848	+0.275 7295		19	+0.041 9849	+0.931 4265	+0.403 7572
	5	+0.720 4042	+0.647 5092	+0.280 6814		20	+0.025 0678	+0.932 0124	+0.404 0119
	6	+0.708 5365	+0.658 7458	+0.285 5518		21	+0.008 1419	+0.932 3350	+0.404 1525
	7	+0.696 4658	+0.669 7919	+0.290 3395		22	−0.008 7880	+0.932 3940	+0.404 1786
	8	+0.684 1960	+0.680 6446	+0.295 0434		23	−0.025 7166	+0.932 1890	+0.404 0903
	9	+0.671 7307	+0.691 3013	+0.299 6623		24	−0.042 6390	+0.931 7199	+0.403 8872
	10	+0.659 0737	+0.701 7593	+0.304 1951		25	−0.059 5500	+0.930 9867	+0.403 5695
	11	+0.646 2285	+0.712 0160	+0.308 6406		26	−0.076 4442	+0.929 9895	+0.403 1372
	12	+0.633 1989	+0.722 0687	+0.312 9979		27	−0.093 3166	+0.928 7288	+0.402 5905
	13	+0.619 9886	+0.731 9151	+0.317 2658		28	−0.110 1619	+0.927 2050	+0.401 9296
	14	+0.606 6012	+0.741 5525	+0.321 4433		29	−0.126 9751	+0.925 4190	+0.401 1550
	15	+0.593 0404	+0.750 9784	+0.325 5293		30	−0.143 7512	+0.923 3714	+0.400 2669
	16	+0.579 3100	+0.760 1905	+0.329 5227	July	1	−0.160 4853	+0.921 0631	+0.399 2657
	17	+0.565 4136	+0.769 1863	+0.333 4224		2	−0.177 1727	+0.918 4952	+0.398 1520

ICRS GEOCENTRIC RECTANGULAR COORDINATES FOR 0h TERRESTRIAL TIME

Date		x	y	z	Date		x	y	z
		au	au	au			au	au	au
July	1	−0.160 4853	+0.921 0631	+0.399 2657	Aug.	16	−0.809 2132	+0.558 5523	+0.242 1300
	2	−0.177 1727	+0.918 4952	+0.398 1520		17	−0.819 1671	+0.545 9217	+0.236 6552
	3	−0.193 8087	+0.915 6686	+0.396 9262		18	−0.828 8882	+0.533 1340	+0.231 1121
	4	−0.210 3886	+0.912 5845	+0.395 5888		19	−0.838 3732	+0.520 1928	+0.225 5023
	5	−0.226 9079	+0.909 2439	+0.394 1403		20	−0.847 6188	+0.507 1016	+0.219 8273
	6	−0.243 3621	+0.905 6481	+0.392 5813		21	−0.856 6218	+0.493 8640	+0.214 0887
	7	−0.259 7469	+0.901 7982	+0.390 9122		22	−0.865 3793	+0.480 4841	+0.208 2883
	8	−0.276 0577	+0.897 6954	+0.389 1337		23	−0.873 8881	+0.466 9657	+0.202 4277
	9	−0.292 2903	+0.893 3412	+0.387 2463		24	−0.882 1456	+0.453 3129	+0.196 5088
	10	−0.308 4405	+0.888 7366	+0.385 2506		25	−0.890 1490	+0.439 5299	+0.190 5334
	11	−0.324 5040	+0.883 8831	+0.383 1471		26	−0.897 8959	+0.425 6207	+0.184 5034
	12	−0.340 4766	+0.878 7819	+0.380 9363		27	−0.905 3838	+0.411 5896	+0.178 4206
	13	−0.356 3542	+0.873 4344	+0.378 6189		28	−0.912 6106	+0.397 4409	+0.172 2868
	14	−0.372 1326	+0.867 8418	+0.376 1954		29	−0.919 5741	+0.383 1786	+0.166 1040
	15	−0.387 8076	+0.862 0054	+0.373 6662		30	−0.926 2724	+0.368 8072	+0.159 8739
	16	−0.403 3750	+0.855 9266	+0.371 0319		31	−0.932 7035	+0.354 3309	+0.153 5985
	17	−0.418 8303	+0.849 6066	+0.368 2931	Sept.	1	−0.938 8657	+0.339 7538	+0.147 2795
	18	−0.434 1694	+0.843 0468	+0.365 4502		2	−0.944 7573	+0.325 0801	+0.140 9189
	19	−0.449 3877	+0.836 2487	+0.362 5040		3	−0.950 3767	+0.310 3143	+0.134 5184
	20	−0.464 4806	+0.829 2138	+0.359 4550		4	−0.955 7225	+0.295 4603	+0.128 0799
	21	−0.479 4436	+0.821 9438	+0.356 3039		5	−0.960 7932	+0.280 5224	+0.121 6051
	22	−0.494 2720	+0.814 4405	+0.353 0515		6	−0.965 5876	+0.265 5047	+0.115 0958
	23	−0.508 9612	+0.806 7058	+0.349 6986		7	−0.970 1043	+0.250 4112	+0.108 5538
	24	−0.523 5066	+0.798 7419	+0.346 2462		8	−0.974 3422	+0.235 2461	+0.101 9808
	25	−0.537 9035	+0.790 5512	+0.342 6953		9	−0.978 2998	+0.220 0132	+0.095 3783
	26	−0.552 1477	+0.782 1359	+0.339 0470		10	−0.981 9761	+0.204 7165	+0.088 7482
	27	−0.566 2346	+0.773 4988	+0.335 3024		11	−0.985 3695	+0.189 3601	+0.082 0921
	28	−0.580 1602	+0.764 6425	+0.331 4627		12	−0.988 4787	+0.173 9479	+0.075 4117
	29	−0.593 9202	+0.755 5696	+0.327 5292		13	−0.991 3022	+0.158 4841	+0.068 7087
	30	−0.607 5108	+0.746 2831	+0.323 5031		14	−0.993 8388	+0.142 9729	+0.061 9851
	31	−0.620 9281	+0.736 7857	+0.319 3856		15	−0.996 0869	+0.127 4186	+0.055 2425
Aug.	1	−0.634 1683	+0.727 0804	+0.315 1780		16	−0.998 0453	+0.111 8257	+0.048 4831
	2	−0.647 2277	+0.717 1699	+0.310 8817		17	−0.999 7127	+0.096 1989	+0.041 7088
	3	−0.660 1029	+0.707 0574	+0.306 4979		18	−1.001 0882	+0.080 5426	+0.034 9216
	4	−0.672 7903	+0.696 7457	+0.302 0278		19	−1.002 1707	+0.064 8618	+0.028 1237
	5	−0.685 2865	+0.686 2378	+0.297 4729		20	−1.002 9594	+0.049 1612	+0.021 3171
	6	−0.697 5881	+0.675 5367	+0.292 8344		21	−1.003 4538	+0.033 4456	+0.014 5039
	7	−0.709 6921	+0.664 6454	+0.288 1135		22	−1.003 6534	+0.017 7200	+0.007 6865
	8	−0.721 5951	+0.653 5669	+0.283 3117		23	−1.003 5579	+0.001 9892	+0.000 8668
	9	−0.733 2941	+0.642 3042	+0.278 4301		24	−1.003 1670	−0.013 7419	−0.005 9530
	10	−0.744 7859	+0.630 8601	+0.273 4700		25	−1.002 4809	−0.029 4684	−0.012 7707
	11	−0.756 0676	+0.619 2377	+0.268 4326		26	−1.001 4996	−0.045 1855	−0.019 5841
	12	−0.767 1360	+0.607 4398	+0.263 3193		27	−1.000 2233	−0.060 8884	−0.026 3913
	13	−0.777 9879	+0.595 4693	+0.258 1311		28	−0.998 6525	−0.076 5722	−0.033 1901
	14	−0.788 6203	+0.583 3292	+0.252 8693		29	−0.996 7876	−0.092 2322	−0.039 9784
	15	−0.799 0298	+0.571 0225	+0.247 5351		30	−0.994 6293	−0.107 8638	−0.046 7543
	16	−0.809 2132	+0.558 5523	+0.242 1300	Oct.	1	−0.992 1782	−0.123 4623	−0.053 5156

ICRS GEOCENTRIC RECTANGULAR COORDINATES FOR 0^h TERRESTRIAL TIME

Date	x	y	z	Date	x	y	z
	au	au	au		au	au	au
Oct. 1	−0.992 1782	−0.123 4623	−0.053 5156	Nov. 16	−0.588 0175	−0.729 6593	−0.316 2920
2	−0.989 4351	−0.139 0231	−0.060 2605	17	−0.573 8137	−0.738 8781	−0.320 2889
3	−0.986 4010	−0.154 5416	−0.066 9870	18	−0.559 4329	−0.747 8704	−0.324 1875
4	−0.983 0767	−0.170 0134	−0.073 6931	19	−0.544 8795	−0.756 6330	−0.327 9864
5	−0.979 4634	−0.185 4342	−0.080 3770	20	−0.530 1580	−0.765 1629	−0.331 6844
6	−0.975 5620	−0.200 7997	−0.087 0369	21	−0.515 2732	−0.773 4571	−0.335 2800
7	−0.971 3736	−0.216 1056	−0.093 6711	22	−0.500 2296	−0.781 5129	−0.338 7721
8	−0.966 8991	−0.231 3477	−0.100 2777	23	−0.485 0322	−0.789 3274	−0.342 1596
9	−0.962 1396	−0.246 5220	−0.106 8549	24	−0.469 6857	−0.796 8982	−0.345 4412
10	−0.957 0959	−0.261 6241	−0.113 4011	25	−0.454 1953	−0.804 2227	−0.348 6159
11	−0.951 7688	−0.276 6499	−0.119 9144	26	−0.438 5657	−0.811 2986	−0.351 6828
12	−0.946 1593	−0.291 5950	−0.126 3928	27	−0.422 8022	−0.818 1238	−0.354 6409
13	−0.940 2684	−0.306 4548	−0.132 8345	28	−0.406 9097	−0.824 6961	−0.357 4893
14	−0.934 0972	−0.321 2249	−0.139 2374	29	−0.390 8932	−0.831 0137	−0.360 2273
15	−0.927 6468	−0.335 9006	−0.145 5995	30	−0.374 7580	−0.837 0747	−0.362 8540
16	−0.920 9187	−0.350 4772	−0.151 9188	Dec. 1	−0.358 5089	−0.842 8776	−0.365 3689
17	−0.913 9144	−0.364 9502	−0.158 1933	2	−0.342 1509	−0.848 4207	−0.367 7713
18	−0.906 6355	−0.379 3147	−0.164 4208	3	−0.325 6889	−0.853 7026	−0.370 0606
19	−0.899 0840	−0.393 5662	−0.170 5993	4	−0.309 1278	−0.858 7220	−0.372 2362
20	−0.891 2618	−0.407 6999	−0.176 7267	5	−0.292 4721	−0.863 4774	−0.374 2976
21	−0.883 1711	−0.421 7112	−0.182 8010	6	−0.275 7265	−0.867 9675	−0.376 2442
22	−0.874 8143	−0.435 5957	−0.188 8202	7	−0.258 8957	−0.872 1908	−0.378 0752
23	−0.866 1936	−0.449 3487	−0.194 7824	8	−0.241 9844	−0.876 1459	−0.379 7902
24	−0.857 3118	−0.462 9658	−0.200 6855	9	−0.224 9974	−0.879 8311	−0.381 3883
25	−0.848 1715	−0.476 4427	−0.206 5277	10	−0.207 9395	−0.883 2451	−0.382 8689
26	−0.838 7756	−0.489 7750	−0.212 3071	11	−0.190 8158	−0.886 3863	−0.384 2313
27	−0.829 1268	−0.502 9586	−0.218 0218	12	−0.173 6315	−0.889 2534	−0.385 4749
28	−0.819 2283	−0.515 9892	−0.223 6702	13	−0.156 3918	−0.891 8451	0.386 5991
29	−0.809 0831	−0.528 8630	−0.229 2504	14	0.139 1020	−0.894 1602	−0.387 6034
30	−0.798 6945	−0.541 5759	−0.234 7607	15	−0.121 7677	−0.896 1976	−0.388 4872
31	−0.788 0656	−0.554 1242	−0.240 1996	16	−0.104 3942	−0.897 9564	−0.389 2501
Nov. 1	−0.777 1998	−0.566 5040	−0.245 5654	17	−0.086 9872	−0.899 4357	−0.389 8918
2	−0.766 1004	−0.578 7118	−0.250 8566	18	−0.069 5523	−0.900 6348	−0.390 4118
3	−0.754 7708	−0.590 7440	−0.256 0718	19	−0.052 0951	−0.901 5530	−0.390 8100
4	−0.743 2143	−0.602 5974	−0.261 2094	20	−0.034 6214	−0.902 1901	−0.391 0861
5	−0.731 4341	−0.614 2686	−0.266 2682	21	−0.017 1368	−0.902 5455	−0.391 2400
6	−0.719 4335	−0.625 7542	−0.271 2466	22	+0.000 3528	−0.902 6192	−0.391 2716
7	−0.707 2156	−0.637 0511	−0.276 1435	23	+0.017 8418	−0.902 4110	−0.391 1810
8	−0.694 7835	−0.648 1558	−0.280 9572	24	+0.035 3244	−0.901 9213	−0.390 9682
9	−0.682 1404	−0.659 0650	−0.285 6863	25	+0.052 7948	−0.901 1501	−0.390 6334
10	−0.669 2895	−0.669 7752	−0.290 3293	26	+0.070 2475	−0.900 0980	−0.390 1768
11	−0.656 2341	−0.680 2828	−0.294 8847	27	+0.087 6767	−0.898 7655	−0.389 5985
12	−0.642 9778	−0.690 5843	−0.299 3508	28	+0.105 0770	−0.897 1533	−0.388 8991
13	−0.629 5241	−0.700 6762	−0.303 7262	29	+0.122 4429	−0.895 2621	−0.388 0789
14	−0.615 8768	−0.710 5550	−0.308 0092	30	+0.139 7690	−0.893 0931	−0.387 1383
15	−0.602 0399	−0.720 2171	−0.312 1983	31	+0.157 0503	−0.890 6470	−0.386 0778
16	−0.588 0175	−0.729 6593	−0.316 2920	32	+0.174 2815	−0.887 9251	−0.384 8979

CONTENTS OF SECTION D

NOTE: All the times on this page are expressed in Universal Time (UT1).

PHASES OF THE MOON

Lunation	New Moon				First Quarter				Full Moon				Last Quarter			
		d	h	m		d	h	m		d	h	m		d	h	m
1262					Jan.	6	23	56	Jan.	13	22	27	Jan.	21	20	31
1263	Jan.	29	12	36	Feb.	5	08	02	Feb.	12	13	53	Feb.	20	17	33
1264	Feb.	28	00	45	Mar.	6	16	32	Mar.	14	06	55	Mar.	22	11	29
1265	Mar.	29	10	58	Apr.	5	02	15	Apr.	13	00	22	Apr.	21	01	36
1266	Apr.	27	19	31	May	4	13	52	May	12	16	56	May	20	11	59
1267	May	27	03	02	June	3	03	41	June	11	07	44	June	18	19	19
1268	June	25	10	32	July	2	19	30	July	10	20	37	July	18	00	38
1269	July	24	19	11	Aug.	1	12	41	Aug.	9	07	55	Aug.	16	05	12
1270	Aug.	23	06	07	Aug.	31	06	25	Sept.	7	18	09	Sept.	14	10	33
1271	Sept.	21	19	54	Sept.	29	23	54	Oct.	7	03	48	Oct.	13	18	13
1272	Oct.	21	12	25	Oct.	29	16	21	Nov.	5	13	19	Nov.	12	05	28
1273	Nov.	20	06	47	Nov.	28	06	59	Dec.	4	23	14	Dec.	11	20	52
1274	Dec.	20	01	43	Dec.	27	19	10								

MOON AT PERIGEE

	d	h		d	h		d	h
Jan.	8	00	May	26	02	Oct.	8	13
Feb.	2	03	June	23	05	Nov.	5	22
Mar.	1	21	July	20	14	Dec.	4	11
Mar.	30	05	Aug.	14	18			
Apr.	27	16	Sept.	10	12			

MOON AT APOGEE

	d	h		d	h		d	h
Jan.	21	05	June	7	11	Oct.	24	00
Feb.	18	01	July	5	02	Nov.	20	03
Mar.	17	17	Aug.	1	21	Dec.	17	06
Apr.	13	23	Aug.	29	16			
May	11	01	Sept.	26	10			

NOTES AND FORMULAE

Mean elements of the orbit of the Moon

The following expressions for the mean elements of the Moon are based on the fundamental arguments developed by Simon *et al.* (*Astron. & Astrophys.*, **282**, 663, 1994). The angular elements are referred to the mean equinox and ecliptic of date. The time argument (d) is the interval in days from 2025 January 0 at 0^h TT. These expressions are intended for use during 2025 only.

$$d = \text{JD} - 246\,0675{\cdot}5 = \text{day of year (from B4–B5)} + \text{fraction of day from } 0^h \text{ TT}$$

Mean longitude of the Moon, measured in the ecliptic to the mean ascending node and then along the mean orbit:

$$L' = 285^\circ\!\!.404\,556 + 13{\cdot}176\,396\,45\,d$$

Mean longitude of the lunar perigee, measured as for L':

$$\Gamma' = 20^\circ\!\!.522\,454 + 0{\cdot}111\,403\,38\,d$$

Mean longitude of the mean ascending node of the lunar orbit on the ecliptic:

$$\Omega = 1^\circ\!\!.550\,335 - 0{\cdot}052\,953\,74\,d$$

Mean elongation of the Moon from the Sun:

$$D = L' - L = 5^\circ\!\!.484\,885 + 12{\cdot}190\,749\,09\,d$$

Mean inclination of the lunar orbit to the ecliptic: $5^\circ\!\!.156\,6898$.

Mean elements of the rotation of the Moon

The following expressions give the mean elements of the mean equator of the Moon, referred to the true equator of the Earth, during 2025 to a precision of about $0^\circ\!\!.001$; the time-argument d is as defined above for the orbital elements.

Inclination of the mean equator of the Moon to the true equator of the Earth:

$$i = 21^\circ\!\!.8964 - 0{\cdot}000\,039\,d + 0{\cdot}000\,000\,689\,d^2$$

Arc of the mean equator of the Moon from its ascending node on the true equator of the Earth to its ascending node on the ecliptic of date:

$$\Delta = 181^\circ\!\!.6552 - 0{\cdot}056\,526\,d + 0{\cdot}000\,000\,282\,d^2$$

Arc of the true equator of the Earth from the true equinox of date to the ascending node of the mean equator of the Moon:

$$\Omega' = -0^\circ\!\!.1135 + 0{\cdot}003\,873\,d - 0{\cdot}000\,000\,299\,d^2$$

The inclination (I) of the mean lunar equator to the ecliptic: $1^\circ\ 32'\ 33''\!\!.6$

The ascending node of the mean lunar equator on the ecliptic is at the descending node of the mean lunar orbit on the ecliptic, that is at longitude $\Omega + 180^\circ$.

Lengths of mean months

The lengths of the mean months at 2025·0, as derived from the mean orbital elements are:

		d	d h m s
synodic month	(new moon to new moon)	29·530 589	29 12 44 02·9
tropical month	(equinox to equinox)	27·321 582	27 07 43 04·7
sidereal month	(fixed star to fixed star)	27·321 662	27 07 43 11·6
anomalistic month	(perigee to perigee)	27·554 550	27 13 18 33·1
draconic month	(node to node)	27·212 221	27 05 05 35·9

NOTES AND FORMULAE

Geocentric coordinates

The apparent longitude (λ) and latitude (β) of the Moon given on pages D6–D20 are referred to the true ecliptic and equinox of date: the apparent right ascension (α) and declination (δ) are referred to the true equator and equinox of date. These coordinates are primarily intended for planning purposes. The true distance r in kilometres and the horizonal parallax (π) are also tabulated. The semidiameter s may be formed from

$$\sin s = \frac{R_M}{r} = \frac{R_M}{a_E} \sin \pi = 0{\cdot}272\,399 \sin \pi$$

where π is the horizontal parallax, $R_M = 1737{\cdot}4$ km is the mean radius of the Moon, and $a_E = 6\,378{\cdot}1366$ km is the equatorial radius of the Earth. The semidiameter is tabulated on pages D7–D21. The distance r_e in Earth radii may be obtained from

$$r_e = \frac{r}{a_E} = r/6\,378{\cdot}1366$$

More precise values of right ascension, declination and horizontal parallax for any time may be obtained by using the polynomial coefficients given on *The Astronomical Almanac Online.*

The tabulated values are all referred to the centre of the Earth, and may differ from the topocentric values by up to about 1 degree in angle and 2 per cent in distance.

Time of transit of the Moon

The TT of upper (or lower) transit of the Moon over a local meridian may be obtained by interpolation in the tabulation of the time of upper (or lower) transit over the ephemeris meridian given on pages D6–D20, where the first differences are about 25 hours. The interpolation factor p is given by:

$$p = -\lambda + 1{\cdot}002\,738\,\Delta T$$

where λ is the *east* longitude and the right-hand side is expressed in days. (Divide longitude in degrees by 360 and ΔT in seconds by 86 400). During 2025 it is expected that ΔT will be about 69 seconds, so that the second term is about $+0{\cdot}000\,80$ days. In general, second-order differences are sufficient to give times to a few seconds, but higher-order differences must be taken into account if a precision of better than 1 second is required. The UT1 of transit is obtained by subtracting ΔT from the TT of transit, which is obtained by interpolation.

Topocentric coordinates

The topocentric equatorial rectangular coordinates of the Moon (x', y', z'), referred to the true equinox of date, are equal to the geocentric equatorial rectangular coordinates of the Moon *minus* the geocentric equatorial rectangular coordinates of the observer. Hence, the topocentric right ascension (α'), declination (δ') and distance (r') of the Moon may be calculated from the formulae:

$$\begin{aligned} x' &= r' \cos\delta' \cos\alpha' = r \cos\delta \cos\alpha - \rho \cos\phi' \cos\theta_0 \\ y' &= r' \cos\delta' \sin\alpha' = r \cos\delta \sin\alpha - \rho \cos\phi' \sin\theta_0 \\ z' &= r' \sin\delta' \qquad\quad\; = r \sin\delta \qquad\quad\;\; - \rho \sin\phi' \end{aligned}$$

where θ_0 is the local apparent sidereal time (see B11) and ρ and ϕ' are the geocentric distance and latitude of the observer.

Then $\quad r'^2 = x'^2 + y'^2 + z'^2, \quad \alpha' = \tan^{-1}(y'/x'), \quad \delta' = \sin^{-1}(z'/r')$

The topocentric hour angle (h') may be calculated from $h' = \theta_0 - \alpha'$.

Physical ephemeris

See page D4 for notes on the physical ephemeris of the Moon on pages D7–D21.

NOTES AND FORMULAE

Appearance of the Moon

The quantities tabulated in the ephemeris for physical observations of the Moon on odd pages D7–D21 represent the geocentric aspect and illumination of the Moon's disk. The semidiameter of the Moon is also included on these pages. For most purposes it is sufficient to regard the instant of tabulation as 0^h UT1. The fraction illuminated (or phase) is the ratio of the illuminated area to the total area of the lunar disk; it is also the fraction of the diameter illuminated perpendicular to the line of cusps. This quantity indicates the general aspect of the Moon, while the precise times of the four principal phases are given on pages A1 and D1; they are the times when the apparent longitudes of the Moon and Sun differ by 0°, 90°, 180° and 270°.

The position angle of the bright limb is measured anticlockwise around the disk from the north point (of the hour circle through the centre of the apparent disk) to the midpoint of the bright limb. Before full moon the morning terminator is visible and the position angle of the northern cusp is 90° greater than the position angle of the bright limb; after full moon the evening terminator is visible and the position angle of the northern cusp is 90° less than the position angle of the bright limb.

The brightness of the Moon is determined largely by the fraction illuminated, but it also depends on the distance of the Moon, on the nature of the part of the lunar surface that is illuminated, and on other factors. The integrated visual magnitude of the full Moon at mean distance is about −12·7. The crescent Moon is not normally visible to the naked eye when the phase is less than 0·01, but much depends on the conditions of observation.

Selenographic coordinates

The positions of points on the Moon's surface are specified by a system of selenographic coordinates, in which latitude is measured positively to the north from the equator of the pole of rotation, and longitude is measured positively to the east on the selenocentric celestial sphere from the lunar meridian through the mean centre of the apparent disk. Selenographic longitudes are measured positive to the west (towards Mare Crisium) on the apparent disk; this sign convention implies that the longitudes of the Sun and of the terminators are decreasing functions of time, and so for some purposes it is convenient to use colongitude which is 90° (or 450°) minus longitude.

The tabulated values of the Earth's selenographic longitude and latitude specify the sub-terrestrial point on the Moon's surface (that is, the centre of the apparent disk). The position angle of the axis of rotation is measured anticlockwise from the north point, and specifies the orientation of the lunar meridian through the sub-terrestrial point, which is the pole of the great circle that corresponds to the limb of the Moon.

The tabulated values of the Sun's selenographic colongitude and latitude specify the sub-solar point of the Moon's surface (that is at the pole of the great circle that bounds the illuminated hemisphere). The following relations hold approximately:

longitude of morning terminator = 360° − colongitude of Sun
longitude of evening terminator = 180° (or 540°) − colongitude of Sun

The altitude (a) of the Sun above the lunar horizon at a point at selenographic longitude and latitude (l, b) may be calculated from:

$$\sin a = \sin b_0 \sin b + \cos b_0 \cos b \sin (c_0 + l)$$

where (c_0, b_0) are the Sun's colongitude and latitude at the time.

NOTES AND FORMULAE

Librations of the Moon

On average the same hemisphere of the Moon is always turned to the Earth but there is a periodic oscillation or libration of the apparent position of the lunar surface that allows about 59 per cent of the surface to be seen from the Earth. The libration is due partly to a physical libration, which is an oscillation of the actual rotational motion about its mean rotation, but mainly to the much larger geocentric optical libration, which results from the non-uniformity of the revolution of the Moon around the centre of the Earth. Both of these effects are taken into account in the computation of the Earth's selenographic longitude (l) and latitude (b) and of the position angle (C) of the axis of rotation. There is a further contribution to the optical libration due to the difference between the viewpoints of the observer on the surface of the Earth and of the hypothetical observer at the centre of the Earth. These topocentric optical librations may be as much as 1° and have important effects on the apparent contour of the limb.

When the libration in longitude, that is the selenographic longitude of the Earth, is positive the mean centre of the disk is displaced eastwards on the celestial sphere, exposing to view a region on the west limb. When the libration in latitude, or selenographic latitude of the Earth, is positive the mean centre of the disk is displaced towards the south, and a region on the north limb is exposed to view. In a similar way the selenographic coordinates of the Sun show which regions of the lunar surface are illuminated.

Differential corrections to be applied to the tabular geocentric librations to form the topocentric librations may be computed from the following formulae:

$$\begin{aligned}\Delta l &= -\pi' \sin(Q - C) \sec b \\ \Delta b &= +\pi' \cos(Q - C) \\ \Delta C &= +\sin(b + \Delta b)\, \Delta l - \pi' \sin Q \tan \delta\end{aligned}$$

where Q is the geocentric parallactic angle of the Moon and π' is the geocentric parallax (diurnal parallax). The latter is obtained from the Moon's horizontal parallax (π), which is tabulated on even pages D6–D20 by using:

$$\pi' = \pi\,(\sin z + 0{\cdot}0084 \sin 2z)$$

where z is the geocentric zenith distance of the Moon. The values of z and Q may be calculated from the geocentric right ascension (α) and declination (δ) of the Moon by using:

$$\begin{aligned}\sin z \sin Q &= \cos\phi \sin h \\ \sin z \cos Q &= \cos\delta \sin\phi - \sin\delta \cos\phi \cos h \\ \cos z &= \sin\delta \sin\phi + \cos\delta \cos\phi \cos h\end{aligned}$$

where ϕ is the geocentric latitude of the observer and h is the local hour angle of the Moon, given by:

$$h = \text{local apparent sidereal time} - \alpha$$

Second differences must be taken into account in the interpolation of the tabular geocentric librations to the time of observation.

FOR 0^h TERRESTRIAL TIME

Date 0^h TT	Apparent Longitude	Apparent Latitude	Apparent R.A.	Apparent Dec.	True Distance	Horiz. Parallax	Ephemeris Transit for date Upper	Ephemeris Transit for date Lower
	° ′ ″	° ′ ″	h m s	° ′ ″	km	′ ″	h	h
Jan. 0	280 34 19	−4 56 02	18 47 45·76	−27 56 06·9	385 360·849	56 54·06	12·6191	00·1405
1	293 54 10	−4 36 37	19 46 40·48	−25 51 45·9	381 738·398	57 26·46	13·5571	01·0924
2	307 26 42	−4 01 23	20 43 49·97	−22 17 45·7	378 562·630	57 55·38	14·4520	02·0106
3	321 09 10	−3 11 48	21 38 26·37	−17 28 25·5	375 915·241	58 19·85	15·2985	02·8810
4	334 59 03	−2 10 24	22 30 32·09	−11 42 18·4	373 810·685	58 39·56	16·1056	03·7060
5	348 54 25	−1 00 43	23 20 48·00	− 5 19 12·8	372 218·600	58 54·62	16·8917	04·4999
6	2 54 01	+0 13 05	0 10 17·92	+ 1 21 12·0	371 094·301	59 05·32	17·6796	05·2839
7	16 57 10	+1 26 27	1 00 16·27	+ 7 59 27·3	370 408·915	59 11·89	18·4934	06·0818
8	31 03 18	+2 34 49	1 51 58·40	+14 15 28·2	370 170·692	59 14·17	19·3550	06·9171
9	45 11 31	+3 33 49	2 46 29·12	+19 47 47·9	370 431·280	59 11·67	20·2789	07·8088
10	59 20 05	+4 19 42	3 44 24·77	+24 13 49·8	371 274·644	59 03·60	21·2639	08·7647
11	73 26 15	+4 49 36	4 45 30·04	+27 12 02·4	372 790·955	58 49·19	22·2866	09·7729
12	87 26 17	+5 01 53	5 48 23·38	+28 26 38·6	375 042·095	58 28·00	23·3051	10·7993
13	101 16 00	+4 56 16	6 50 53·12	+27 52 48·0	378 028·172	58 00·29	. . .	11·7987
14	114 51 18	+4 33 50	7 50 46·92	+25 38 38·6	381 664·493	57 27·13	00·2758	12·7340
15	128 09 02	+3 56 48	8 46 40·73	+22 02 12·7	385 775·304	56 50·39	01·1718	13·5893
16	141 07 23	+3 08 08	9 38 14·31	+17 25 32·3	390 105·507	56 12·53	01·9877	14·3685
17	153 46 14	+2 11 07	10 25 56·39	+12 09 39·2	394 346·657	55 36·26	02·7340	15·0865
18	166 07 09	+1 09 02	11 10 41·87	+ 6 32 10·2	398 170·719	55 04·21	03·4288	15·7633
19	178 13 06	+0 04 53	11 53 35·42	+ 0 46 59·4	401 264·968	54 38·73	04·0927	16·4195
20	190 08 13	−0 58 41	12 35 43·33	− 4 54 49·8	403 363·174	54 21·68	04·7462	17·0753
21	201 57 23	−1 59 16	13 18 10·70	−10 23 47·6	404 270·514	54 14·35	05·4093	17·7506
22	213 45 57	−2 54 44	14 02 00·31	−15 30 35·5	403 881·433	54 17·49	06·1015	18·4641
23	225 39 22	−3 43 01	14 48 10·42	−20 04 50·6	402 190·557	54 31·19	06·8403	19·2319
24	237 42 52	−4 22 07	15 37 28·83	−23 54 08·0	399 296·722	54 54·90	07·6398	20·0644
25	250 01 07	−4 49 58	16 30 21·49	−26 43 48·5	395 399·663	55 27·37	08·5054	20·9612
26	262 37 50	−5 04 36	17 26 37·54	−28 18 07·4	390 788·180	56 06·64	09·4294	21·9064
27	275 35 21	−5 04 15	18 25 19·47	−28 23 11·1	385 818·323	56 50·01	10·3881	22·8701
28	288 54 19	−4 47 37	19 24 51·88	−26 51 01·4	380 880·815	57 34·22	11·3483	23·8191
29	302 33 31	−4 14 22	20 23 32·74	−23 42 47·5	376 359·105	58 15·73	12·2801	. . .
30	316 29 58	−3 25 21	21 20 09·83	−19 09 10·6	372 583·086	58 51·16	13·1680	00·7299
31	330 39 24	−2 22 56	22 14 19·63	−13 28 02·4	369 787·356	59 17·86	14·0126	01·5951
Feb. 1	344 56 51	−1 10 51	23 06 23·78	− 7 01 05·7	368 084·737	59 34·32	14·8271	02·4225
2	359 17 31	+0 06 09	23 57 14·30	− 0 11 15·0	367 463·308	59 40·36	15·6315	03·2292
3	13 37 16	+1 22 50	0 47 58·71	+ 6 38 48·9	367 808·429	59 37·00	16·4484	04·0370
4	27 53 00	+2 34 04	1 39 48·18	+13 07 01·2	368 943·024	59 26·00	17·2991	04·8683
5	42 02 36	+3 35 21	2 33 45·95	+18 51 44·6	370 673·858	59 09·35	18·1994	05·7425
6	56 04 42	+4 23 09	3 30 32·34	+23 31 55·5	372 831·098	58 48·81	19·1533	06·6701
7	69 58 21	+4 54 57	4 30 05·82	+26 48 19·0	375 292·302	58 25·66	20·1464	07·6466
8	83 42 36	+5 09 26	5 31 29·15	+28 26 24·4	377 987·615	58 00·66	21·1469	08·6482
9	97 16 25	+5 06 20	6 32 56·91	+28 20 11·0	380 888·164	57 34·15	22·1159	09·6375
10	110 38 35	+4 46 31	7 32 31·08	+26 34 17·2	383 983·113	57 06·31	23·0241	10·5788
11	123 47 53	+4 11 44	8 28 44·38	+23 22 38·2	387 252·597	56 37·38	23·8596	11·4509
12	136 43 17	+3 24 31	9 21 02·31	+19 04 18·8	390 643·662	56 07·89	. . .	12·2511
13	149 24 16	+2 27 51	10 09 37·82	+13 59 15·8	394 054·831	55 38·73	00·6270	12·9893
14	161 51 00	+1 24 59	10 55 13·41	+ 8 25 37·2	397 332·305	55 11·19	01·3401	13·6818
15	174 04 33	+0 19 08	11 38 45·13	+ 2 38 44·3	400 277·911	54 46·82	02·0167	14·3471

EPHEMERIS FOR PHYSICAL OBSERVATIONS FOR 0^h TERRESTRIAL TIME

Julian Date	The Earth's Selenographic Long.	The Earth's Selenographic Lat.	The Sun's Selenographic Colong.	The Sun's Selenographic Lat.	Position Angle Axis	Position Angle Bright Limb	Semi-diameter	Fraction Illum.
246	°	°	°	°	°	°	′ ″	
0675·5	−4·813	+6·473	275·61	−1·53	355·482	346·28	15 29·95	0·002
0676·5	−4·628	+6·052	287·80	−1·52	350·251	278·75	15 38·77	0·015
0677·5	−4·243	+5·286	299·99	−1·51	345·736	263·17	15 46·65	0·050
0678·5	−3·709	+4·207	312·17	−1·50	342·207	255·09	15 53·32	0·109
0679·5	−3·069	+2·872	324·35	−1·49	339·765	250·15	15 58·68	0·187
0680·5	−2·351	+1·356	336·52	−1·49	338·407	247·41	16 02·78	0·282
0681·5	−1·571	−0·250	348·69	−1·48	338·109	246·54	16 05·70	0·389
0682·5	−0·730	−1·848	0·85	−1·47	338·872	247·41	16 07·49	0·501
0683·5	+0·170	−3·339	13·00	−1·46	340·737	250·02	16 08·11	0·614
0684·5	+1·121	−4·628	25·15	−1·46	343·761	254·42	16 07·43	0·722
0685·5	+2·097	−5·633	37·29	−1·45	347·944	260·69	16 05·23	0·817
0686·5	+3·049	−6·291	49·42	−1·45	353·127	268·92	16 01·30	0·895
0687·5	+3·909	−6·565	61·55	−1·44	358·920	279·69	15 55·53	0·953
0688·5	+4·599	−6·449	73·68	−1·43	4·748	297·48	15 47·99	0·988
0689·5	+5·041	−5·966	85·80	−1·42	10·040	20·57	15 38·95	0·998
0690·5	+5·176	−5·165	97·93	−1·41	14·415	88·86	15 28·95	0·986
0691·5	+4·972	−4·110	110·06	−1·40	17·730	102·26	15 18·64	0·953
0692·5	+4·427	−2·874	122·19	−1·39	20·013	108·47	15 08·76	0·901
0693·5	+3·572	−1·527	134·33	−1·38	21·361	111·84	15 00·03	0·835
0694·5	+2·462	−0·135	146·47	−1·36	21·870	113·38	14 53·09	0·758
0695·5	+1·170	+1·246	158·61	−1·35	21·602	113·50	14 48·44	0·672
0696·5	−0·216	+2·564	170·76	−1·34	20·573	112·35	14 46·45	0·581
0697·5	−1·602	+3·772	182·92	−1·32	18·759	109·99	14 47·30	0·488
0698·5	−2·896	+4·826	195·09	−1·31	16·109	106·40	14 51·03	0·394
0699·5	−4·007	+5·682	207·26	−1·29	12·581	101·54	14 57·49	0·303
0700·5	−4·859	+6·295	219·43	−1·28	8·195	95·41	15 06·34	0·217
0701·5	−5·394	+6·621	231·61	−1·26	3·095	88·02	15 17·03	0·140
0702·5	−5·576	+6·622	243·80	−1·24	357·601	79·33	15 28·85	0·077
0703·5	−5·404	+6·270	255·99	−1·22	352·172	68·35	15 40·89	0·030
0704·5	−4·904	+5·556	268·18	−1·20	347·290	44·55	15 52·19	0·005
0705·5	−4·132	+4·500	280·37	−1·18	343·316	281·16	16 01·84	0·004
0706·5	−3·163	+3·152	292·57	−1·16	340·439	255·88	16 09·11	0·029
0707·5	−2·077	+1·593	304·76	−1·14	338·702	249·08	16 13·60	0·079
0708·5	−0·946	−0·073	316·94	−1·12	338·086	246·46	16 15·24	0·153
0709·5	+0·170	−1·735	329·12	−1·09	338·575	246·27	16 14·33	0·245
0710·5	+1·228	−3·282	341·30	−1·07	340·182	248·03	16 11·33	0·351
0711·5	+2·200	−4·617	353·47	−1·05	342·937	251·54	16 06·80	0·463
0712·5	+3·066	−5·660	5·63	−1·03	346·829	256·65	16 01·20	0·576
0713·5	+3·808	−6·359	17·78	−1·01	351·725	263·16	15 54·90	0·684
0714·5	+4·404	−6·682	29·93	−0·99	357·300	270·66	15 48·09	0·781
0715·5	+4·829	−6·624	42·08	−0·97	3·053	278·69	15 40·87	0·864
0716·5	+5·054	−6·203	54·22	−0·95	8·443	286·96	15 33·29	0·928
0717·5	+5·052	−5·458	66·35	−0·92	13·057	296·14	15 25·41	0·972
0718·5	+4·802	−4·442	78·49	−0·90	16·688	314·36	15 17·37	0·996
0719·5	+4·296	−3·221	90·63	−0·88	19·307	83·92	15 09·43	0·998
0720·5	+3·540	−1·865	102·76	−0·85	20·975	107·64	15 01·93	0·980
0721·5	+2·556	−0·443	114·90	−0·83	21·780	112·72	14 55·29	0·944

FOR 0^h TERRESTRIAL TIME

Date 0^h TT	Apparent Longitude	Apparent Latitude	Apparent R.A.	Apparent Dec.	True Distance	Horiz. Parallax	Ephemeris Transit for date Upper	Ephemeris Transit for date Lower
	° ′ ″	° ′ ″	h m s	° ′ ″	km	′ ″	h	h
Feb. 15	174 04 33	+0 19 08	11 38 45·13	+ 2 38 44·3	400 277·911	54 46·82	02·0167	14·3471
16	186 06 54	−0 46 44	12 21 13·19	− 3 08 37·0	402 666·550	54 27·32	02·6756	15·0042
17	198 00 53	−1 49 54	13 03 37·75	− 8 45 32·3	404 269·645	54 14·36	03·3354	15·6714
18	209 50 11	−2 48 01	13 46 57·29	−14 01 59·6	404 880·987	54 09·45	04·0142	16·3661
19	221 39 03	−3 38 58	14 32 06·86	−18 47 48·8	404 342·067	54 13·78	04·7290	17·1045
20	233 32 15	−4 20 51	15 19 54·16	−22 51 47·2	402 564·889	54 28·14	05·4941	17·8987
21	245 34 43	−4 51 52	16 10 51·62	−26 01 09·8	399 550·864	54 52·80	06·3186	18·7535
22	257 51 23	−5 10 17	17 05 04·71	−28 01 59·3	395 404·472	55 27·33	07·2021	19·6621
23	270 26 43	−5 14 29	18 02 01·27	−28 40 45·0	390 339·864	56 10·51	08·1308	20·6045
24	283 24 18	−5 03 02	19 00 31·59	−27 47 16·2	384 677·620	57 00·12	09·0795	21·5523
25	296 46 25	−4 35 04	19 59 06·92	−25 17 51·5	378 828·082	57 52·94	10·0198	22·4797
26	310 33 24	−3 50 34	20 56 30·18	−21 17 08·2	373 257·931	58 44·77	10·9308	23·3727
27	324 43 28	−2 50 52	21 52 00·75	−15 57 46·2	368 439·226	59 30·88	11·8058	. . .
28	339 12 30	−1 38 55	22 45 41·16	− 9 38 40·0	364 785·779	60 06·64	12·6514	00·2315
Mar. 1	353 54 35	−0 19 19	23 38 08·75	− 2 42 51·4	362 589·262	60 28·49	13·4836	01·0680
2	8 42 36	+1 02 12	0 30 21·99	+ 4 24 21·8	361 972·813	60 34·67	14·3228	01·9010
3	23 29 21	+2 19 29	1 23 27·10	+11 16 52·4	362 878·076	60 25·61	15·1896	02·7515
4	38 08 22	+3 26 56	2 18 24·85	+17 28 54·7	365 090·898	60 03·63	16·1000	03·6387
5	52 34 42	+4 20 13	3 15 54·48	+22 36 18·8	368 296·609	59 32·26	17·0593	04·5739
6	66 45 03	+4 56 33	4 15 55·13	+26 18 19·5	372 146·286	58 55·30	18·0553	05·5542
7	80 37 51	+5 14 42	5 17 32·71	+28 20 20·7	376 315·129	58 16·13	19·0591	06·5586
8	94 12 48	+5 14 45	6 19 07·36	+28 36 52·7	380 541·094	57 37·31	20·0337	07·5522
9	107 30 32	+4 57 50	7 18 47·03	+27 12 47·3	384 640·496	57 00·45	20·9499	08·5003
10	120 32 12	+4 25 46	8 15 08·27	+24 21 28·1	388 503·687	56 26·44	21·7947	09·3813
11	133 19 14	+3 40 57	9 07 37·33	+20 20 52·3	392 076·974	55 55·57	22·5712	10·1909
12	145 53 03	+2 46 09	9 56 25·73	+15 29 42·9	395 337·608	55 27·90	23·2917	10·9374
13	158 15 08	+1 44 17	10 42 13·61	+10 05 13·3	398 268·059	55 03·41	23·9733	11·6363
14	170 26 55	+0 38 27	11 25 54·40	+ 4 22 24·9	400 834·565	54 42·25	. . .	12·3051
15	182 30 01	−0 28 22	12 08 25·47	− 1 25 41·1	402 973·376	54 24·83	00·6338	12·9617
16	194 26 10	−1 33 19	12 50 43·75	− 7 07 29·0	404 586·440	54 11·81	01·2909	13·6235
17	206 17 31	−2 33 48	13 33 43·99	−12 32 07·8	405 546·581	54 04·11	01·9615	14·3068
18	218 06 35	−3 27 28	14 18 17·05	−17 28 49·9	405 710·897	54 02·80	02·6613	15·0266
19	229 56 24	−4 12 20	15 05 06·79	−21 46 17·1	404 940·253	54 08·97	03·4039	15·7944
20	241 50 27	−4 46 37	15 54 43·85	−25 12 21·8	403 122·468	54 23·62	04·1984	16·6160
21	253 52 40	−5 08 46	16 47 16·75	−27 34 22·7	400 196·872	54 47·48	05·0464	17·4882
22	266 07 17	−5 17 25	17 42 23·38	−28 40 11·0	396 178·016	55 20·84	05·9391	18·3966
23	278 38 40	−5 11 25	18 39 09·95	−28 20 07·9	391 176·188	56 03·30	06·8575	19·3188
24	291 30 53	−4 49 53	19 36 23·51	−26 29 16·8	385 411·717	56 53·61	07·7777	20·2319
25	304 47 21	−4 12 28	20 32 55·57	−23 08 53·1	379 218·854	57 49·36	08·6798	21·1206
26	318 30 11	−3 19 40	21 28 04·48	−18 26 35·9	373 033·805	58 46·89	09·5543	21·9817
27	332 39 37	−2 13 11	22 21 45·49	−12 35 46·6	367 361·396	59 41·35	10·4042	22·8237
28	347 13 26	−0 56 20	23 14 27·63	− 5 54 39·4	362 717·785	60 27·21	11·2424	23·6629
29	2 06 44	+0 25 57	0 07 03·88	+ 1 14 13·2	359 554·090	60 59·13	12·0879	. . .
30	17 12 08	+1 47 28	1 00 39·44	+ 8 24 35·9	358 176·609	61 13·20	12·9620	00·5201
31	32 20 34	+3 01 38	1 56 18·55	+15 07 36·1	358 687·644	61 07·97	13·8833	01·4159
Apr. 1	47 22 43	+4 02 39	2 54 46·97	+20 53 44·9	360 968·842	60 44·78	14·8601	02·3648
2	62 10 15	+4 46 22	3 56 09·51	+25 16 11·1	364 713·984	60 07·35	15·8831	03·3672

EPHEMERIS FOR PHYSICAL OBSERVATIONS FOR 0^h TERRESTRIAL TIME

Julian Date	The Earth's Selenographic Long.	The Earth's Selenographic Lat.	The Sun's Selenographic Colong.	The Sun's Selenographic Lat.	Position Angle Axis	Position Angle Bright Limb	Semi-diameter	Fraction Illum.
246	°	°	°	°	°	°	′ ″	
0721·5	+2·556	−0·443	114·90	−0·83	21·780	112·72	14 55·29	0·944
0722·5	+1·384	+0·980	127·04	−0·80	21·787	114·31	14 49·98	0·891
0723·5	+0·076	+2·346	139·19	−0·78	21·025	114·07	14 46·45	0·826
0724·5	−1·301	+3·604	151·34	−0·76	19·488	112·43	14 45·11	0·749
0725·5	−2·673	+4·710	163·50	−0·73	17·141	109·55	14 46·29	0·663
0726·5	−3·960	+5·620	175·66	−0·71	13·948	105·48	14 50·21	0·571
0727·5	−5·078	+6·297	187·83	−0·69	9·911	100·29	14 56·92	0·475
0728·5	−5·948	+6·703	200·01	−0·66	5·123	94·13	15 06·33	0·379
0729·5	−6·501	+6·800	212·19	−0·64	359·822	87·27	15 18·09	0·284
0730·5	−6·683	+6·560	224·38	−0·62	354·389	80·11	15 31·60	0·196
0731·5	−6·464	+5·962	236·57	−0·59	349·278	73·10	15 45·99	0·118
0732·5	−5·844	+5·006	248·77	−0·57	344·898	66·42	16 00·10	0·056
0733·5	−4·858	+3·722	260·98	−0·54	341·522	58·92	16 12·66	0·015
0734·5	−3·574	+2·174	273·18	−0·51	339·276	352·61	16 22·40	0·000
0735·5	−2·086	+0·459	285·38	−0·48	338·191	248·04	16 28·35	0·013
0736·5	−0·502	−1·298	297·59	−0·45	338·273	244·75	16 30·04	0·055
0737·5	+1·069	−2·965	309·79	−0·42	339·541	245·47	16 27·57	0·123
0738·5	+2·527	−4·423	321·98	−0·39	342·022	248·39	16 21·58	0·211
0739·5	+3·794	−5·577	334·17	−0·36	345·707	253·06	16 13·04	0·314
0740·5	+4·813	−6·365	346·36	−0·34	350·463	259·14	16 02·97	0·424
0741·5	+5·552	−6·761	358·54	−0·31	355·967	266·14	15 52·30	0·536
0742·5	+5·996	−6·767	10·71	−0·28	1·725	273·46	15 41·73	0·643
0743·5	+6·149	−6·404	22·87	−0·25	7·200	280·46	15 31·69	0·741
0744·5	+6·023	−5·715	35·04	−0·22	11·968	286·64	15 22·43	0·827
0745·5	+5·637	−4·751	47·19	−0·19	15·804	291·73	15 14·02	0·897
0746·5	+5·015	−3·570	59·35	−0·16	18·657	295·70	15 06·48	0·950
0747·5	+4·183	−2·238	71·50	−0·13	20·571	298·78	14 59·81	0·984
0748·5	+3·171	−0·821	83·65	−0·10	21·621	304·46	14 51·05	0·999
0749·5	+2·010	+0·619	95·80	−0·07	21·870	116·85	14 49·30	0·995
0750·5	+0·737	+2·018	107·96	−0·04	21·349	117·40	14 45·76	0·973
0751·5	−0·609	+3·321	120·11	−0·01	20·056	115·92	14 43·66	0·934
0752·5	−1·980	+4·479	132·27	+0·02	17·963	113·20	14 43·30	0·880
0753·5	−3·326	+5·447	144·43	+0·04	15·039	109·36	14 44·98	0·813
0754·5	−4·588	+6·187	156·60	+0·07	11·285	104·49	14 48·97	0·733
0755·5	−5·702	+6·665	168·78	+0·09	6·775	98·70	14 55·47	0·645
0756·5	−6·601	+6·852	180·96	+0·11	1·704	92·27	15 04·56	0·549
0757·5	−7·220	+6·721	193·14	+0·14	356·390	85·56	15 16·12	0·449
0758·5	−7·496	+6·256	205·34	+0·16	351·236	79·06	15 29·83	0·348
0759·5	−7·380	+5·448	217·54	+0·18	346·634	73·27	15 45·01	0·250
0760·5	−6·841	+4·308	229·74	+0·21	342·883	68·61	16 00·68	0·161
0761·5	−5·877	+2·874	241·95	+0·24	340·159	65·48	16 15·51	0·086
0762·5	−4·522	+1·218	254·17	+0·26	338·546	64·51	16 28·00	0·031
0763·5	−2·850	−0·554	266·39	+0·29	338·089	70·40	16 36·70	0·003
0764·5	−0·974	−2·309	278·61	+0·32	338·841	234·34	16 40·53	0·005
0765·5	+0·968	−3·906	290·83	+0·35	340·868	242·11	16 39·10	0·037
0766·5	+2·825	−5·220	303·05	+0·38	344·209	247·67	16 32·79	0·096
0767·5	+4·461	−6·160	315·26	+0·41	348·779	254·11	16 22·59	0·178

FOR 0^h TERRESTRIAL TIME

Date 0^h TT	Apparent Longitude	Apparent Latitude	Apparent R.A.	Apparent Dec.	True Distance	Horiz. Parallax	Ephemeris Transit for date Upper	Ephemeris Transit for date Lower
	° ′ ″	° ′ ″	h m s	° ′ ″	km	′ ″	h	h
Apr. 1	47 22 43	+4 02 39	2 54 46·97	+20 53 44·9	360 968·842	60 44·78	14·8601	02·3648
2	62 10 15	+4 46 22	3 56 09·51	+25 16 11·1	364 713·984	60 07·35	15·8831	03·3672
3	76 37 04	+5 10 44	4 59 30·97	+27 55 04·1	369 498·427	59 20·64	16·9217	04·4030
4	90 39 42	+5 15 39	6 03 00·29	+28 41 51·6	374 860·481	58 29·70	17·9337	05·4336
5	104 17 14	+5 02 27	7 04 28·18	+27 41 01·0	380 371·526	57 38·85	18·8835	06·4179
6	117 30 48	+4 33 24	8 02 17·11	+25 07 21·1	385 682·017	56 51·22	19·7542	07·3290
7	130 22 57	+3 51 13	8 55 47·87	+21 20 39·3	390 541·372	56 08·77	20·5480	08·1601
8	142 56 54	+2 58 47	9 45 13·75	+16 40 50·4	394 796·472	55 32·46	21·2786	08·9201
9	155 16 09	+1 59 01	10 31 19·82	+11 25 25·7	398 375·738	55 02·51	21·9642	09·6258
10	167 24 04	+0 54 47	11 15 04·55	+ 5 49 05·7	401 265·441	54 38·73	22·6240	10·2961
11	179 23 42	−0 11 04	11 57 29·16	+ 0 04 17·1	403 483·635	54 20·70	23·2766	10·9501
12	191 17 43	−1 15 50	12 39 33·03	− 5 37 52·6	405 055·912	54 08·04	23·9393	11·6057
13	203 08 27	−2 16 54	13 22 12·00	−11 06 42·0	405 996·119	54 00·52	...	12·2795
14	214 57 58	−3 11 51	14 06 17·04	−16 11 14·4	406 294·267	53 58·14	00·6279	12·9863
15	226 48 14	−3 58 32	14 52 31·27	−20 39 50·8	405 912·863	54 01·19	01·3560	13·7379
16	238 41 18	−4 35 01	15 41 24·29	−24 20 04·9	404 791·916	54 10·16	02·1327	14·5404
17	250 39 24	−4 59 45	16 33 03·99	−26 59 12·0	402 861·878	54 25·73	02·9603	15·3912
18	262 45 10	−5 11 26	17 27 08·86	−28 25 22·4	400 063·003	54 48·58	03·8311	16·2776
19	275 01 34	−5 09 10	18 22 47·46	−28 29 31·1	396 369·014	55 19·23	04·7277	17·1786
20	287 32 00	−4 52 19	19 18 50·26	−27 07 07·9	391 812·512	55 57·84	05·6275	18·0720
21	300 20 05	−4 20 44	20 14 11·62	−24 19 13·5	386 508·994	56 43·92	06·5106	18·9422
22	313 29 20	−3 34 46	21 08 10·76	−20 12 00·6	380 675·412	57 36·09	07·3668	19·7848
23	327 02 46	−2 35 36	22 00 41·78	−14 55 52·9	374 637·913	58 31·79	08·1975	20·6065
24	341 02 13	−1 25 27	22 52 11·72	− 8 44 38·7	368 822·188	59 27·17	09·0142	21·4229
25	355 27 36	−0 07 54	23 43 32·51	− 1 55 30·8	363 720·021	60 17·21	09·8354	22·2548
26	10 16 11	+1 12 04	0 35 51·63	+ 5 10 16·6	359 829·344	60 56·33	10·6839	23·1255
27	25 22 14	+2 28 26	1 30 21·64	+12 06 53·7	357 573·818	61 19·39	11·5821	...
28	40 37 11	+3 34 50	2 28 05·10	+18 24 22·3	357 220·017	61 23·04	12·5466	00·0555
29	55 50 42	+4 25 47	3 29 30·47	+23 31 05·4	358 818·571	61 06·63	13·5779	01·0548
30	70 52 25	+4 57 37	4 34 02·97	+26 58 59·8	362 191·751	60 32·48	14·6510	02·1119
May 1	85 33 35	+5 08 59	5 39 51·82	+28 30 38·2	366 972·514	59 45·15	15·7186	03·1889
2	99 48 22	+5 00 41	6 44 20·68	+28 04 23·6	372 679·344	58 50·24	16·7308	04·2341
3	113 34 15	+4 35 03	7 45 12·37	+25 53 45·8	378 800·574	57 53·19	17·6576	05·2057
4	126 51 44	+3 55 14	8 41 17·40	+22 20 53·1	384 865·375	56 58·46	18·4942	06·0866
5	139 43 29	+3 04 37	9 32 36·71	+17 49 09·6	390 490·039	56 09·21	19·2534	06·8823
6	152 13 36	+2 06 27	10 19 56·21	+12 38 53·6	395 398·845	55 27·38	19·9553	07·6101
7	164 26 46	+1 03 47	11 04 20·93	+ 7 06 12·6	399 424·674	54 53·84	20·6217	08·2916
8	176 27 41	−0 00 38	11 46 59·66	+ 1 23 49·7	402 496·000	54 28·70	21·2734	08·9482
9	188 20 48	−1 04 12	12 28 58·43	− 4 17 35·9	404 616·057	54 11·58	21·9295	09·5997
10	200 09 58	−2 04 29	13 11 18·68	− 9 48 09·3	405 838·570	54 01·78	22·6075	10·2647
11	211 58 25	−2 59 12	13 54 56·16	−14 57 36·5	406 243·338	53 58·55	23·3225	10·9596
12	223 48 43	−3 46 11	14 40 38·56	−19 34 42·2	405 914·298	54 01·17	...	11·6977
13	235 42 54	−4 23 28	15 29 00·02	−23 26 56·2	404 922·343	54 09·12	00·0857	12·4870
14	247 42 32	−4 49 21	16 20 12·46	−26 21 03·0	403 314·766	54 22·07	00·9012	13·3271
15	259 49 00	−5 02 29	17 13 56·77	−28 04 25·6	401 112·729	54 39·98	01·7630	14·2062
16	272 03 41	−5 01 57	18 09 20·59	−28 27 15·4	398 317·278	55 03·00	02·6539	15·1029
17	284 28 12	−4 47 17	19 05 09·51	−27 24 43·3	394 923·451	55 31·39	03·5500	15·9925

EPHEMERIS FOR PHYSICAL OBSERVATIONS FOR 0^{h} TERRESTRIAL TIME

Julian Date	The Earth's Selenographic Long.	The Earth's Selenographic Lat.	The Sun's Selenographic Colong.	The Sun's Selenographic Lat.	Position Angle Axis	Position Angle Bright Limb	Semi-diameter	Fraction Illum.
246	°	°	°	°	°	°	′ ″	
0766·5	+2·825	−5·220	303·05	+0·38	344·209	247·67	16 32·79	0·096
0767·5	+4·461	−6·160	315·26	+0·41	348·779	254·11	16 22·59	0·178
0768·5	+5·765	−6·682	327·47	+0·44	354·275	261·40	16 09·87	0·276
0769·5	+6·673	−6·784	339·67	+0·47	0·175	269·01	15 56·00	0·382
0770·5	+7·158	−6·494	351·87	+0·50	5·877	276·26	15 42·15	0·491
0771·5	+7·233	−5·862	4·06	+0·53	10·897	282·60	15 29·17	0·597
0772·5	+6·935	−4·947	16·25	+0·56	14·975	287·69	15 17·61	0·696
0773·5	+6·318	−3·811	28·43	+0·59	18·050	291·40	15 07·72	0·784
0774·5	+5·442	−2·519	40·60	+0·62	20·174	293·67	14 59·57	0·859
0775·5	+4·367	−1·132	52·78	+0·65	21·429	294·37	14 53·09	0·920
0776·5	+3·150	+0·289	64·95	+0·68	21·883	292·98	14 48·18	0·964
0777·5	+1·840	+1·686	77·12	+0·71	21·572	286·63	14 44·73	0·991
0778·5	+0·483	+3·002	89·29	+0·73	20·494	206·31	14 42·68	1·000
0779·5	−0·884	+4·187	101·45	+0·76	18·622	126·34	14 42·03	0·991
0780·5	−2·224	+5·192	113·63	+0·78	15·921	116·89	14 42·86	0·964
0781·5	−3·505	+5·976	125·80	+0·80	12·384	110·28	14 45·31	0·921
0782·5	−4·690	+6·506	137·98	+0·82	8·075	103·76	14 49·55	0·862
0783·5	−5·739	+6·753	150·16	+0·84	3·167	96·96	14 55·77	0·790
0784·5	−6·608	+6·698	162·34	+0·86	357·956	90·04	15 04·12	0·705
0785·5	−7·247	+6·327	174·53	+0·87	352·817	83·35	15 14·64	0·610
0786·5	−7·602	+5·636	186·73	+0·89	348·124	77·33	15 27·19	0·508
0787·5	−7·618	+4·636	198·94	+0·90	344·167	72·32	15 41·39	0·403
0788·5	−7·248	+3·351	211·15	+0·92	341·128	68·64	15 56·57	0·298
0789·5	−6·460	+1·831	223·37	+0·94	339·103	66·56	16 11·65	0·200
0790·5	−5·251	+0·152	235·59	+0·96	338·149	66·47	16 25·28	0·115
0791·5	−3·655	−1·577	247·82	+0·98	338·332	69·35	16 35·93	0·050
0792·5	−1·759	−3·226	260·06	+1·00	339·754	80·29	16 42·22	0·011
0793·5	+0·303	−4·658	272·29	+1·02	342·518	198·07	16 43·21	0·002
0794·5	+2·365	−5·755	284·53	+1·04	346·650	241·65	16 38·74	0·023
0795·5	+4·248	−6·437	296·76	+1·06	351·960	253·39	16 29·44	0·073
0796·5	+5·798	−6·675	308·99	+1·09	357·967	262·81	16 16·55	0·147
0797·5	+6·907	−6·486	321·22	+1·11	3·996	271·27	16 01·59	0·237
0798·5	+7·524	−5·921	333·44	+1·13	9·431	278·59	15 46·05	0·337
0799·5	+7·652	−5·050	345·66	+1·16	13·905	284·48	15 31·15	0·441
0800·5	+7·335	−3·946	357·87	+1·18	17·313	288·86	15 17·73	0·545
0801·5	+6·642	−2·681	10·07	+1·21	19·706	291·77	15 06·34	0·643
0802·5	+5·657	−1·320	22·27	+1·23	21·186	293·28	14 57·20	0·734
0803·5	+4·462	+0·078	34·46	+1·25	21·844	293·39	14 50·36	0·814
0804·5	+3·138	+1·455	46·65	+1·27	21·731	291·98	14 45·69	0·882
0805·5	+1·754	+2·761	58·84	+1·29	20·858	288·59	14 43·02	0·936
0806·5	+0·369	+3·946	71·03	+1·31	19·198	281·64	14 42·15	0·973
0807·5	−0·973	+4·962	83·21	+1·33	16·710	261·85	14 42·86	0·994
0808·5	−2·237	+5·768	95·39	+1·34	13·372	157·82	14 45·02	0·998
0809·5	−3·398	+6·325	107·57	+1·36	9·228	118·01	14 48·55	0·983
0810·5	−4·437	+6·605	119·76	+1·37	4·428	105·06	14 53·43	0·950
0811·5	−5·335	+6·587	131·95	+1·37	359·256	95·79	14 59·70	0·900
0812·5	−6·073	+6·262	144·14	+1·38	354·087	87·85	15 07·43	0·833

FOR 0^h TERRESTRIAL TIME

Date 0^h TT	Apparent Longitude	Apparent Latitude	Apparent R.A.	Apparent Dec.	True Distance	Horiz. Parallax	Ephemeris Transit for date Upper	Ephemeris Transit for date Lower
	° ′ ″	° ′ ″	h m s	° ′ ″	km	′ ″	h	h
May 17	284 28 12	−4 47 17	19 05 09·51	−27 24 43·3	394 923·451	55 31·39	03·5500	15·9925
18	297 04 30	−4 18 33	20 00 10·47	−24 58 04·0	390 940·913	56 05·33	04·4284	16·8563
19	309 55 01	−3 36 20	20 53 35·23	−21 14 00·4	386 418·438	56 44·72	05·2757	17·6868
20	323 02 26	−2 41 54	21 45 12·20	−16 23 04·1	381 468·462	57 28·90	06·0905	18·4885
21	336 29 32	−1 37 15	22 35 24·73	−10 38 04·5	376 286·737	58 16·40	06·8828	19·2757
22	350 18 34	−0 25 17	23 25 02·77	− 4 13 35·3	371 160·975	59 04·69	07·6700	20·0686
23	4 30 37	+0 50 07	0 15 13·86	+ 2 33 33·3	366 461·711	59 50·15	08·4747	20·8914
24	19 04 49	+2 04 05	1 07 15·02	+ 9 23 02·2	362 609·825	60 28·29	09·3218	21·7687
25	33 57 35	+3 11 04	2 02 22·35	+15 49 55·7	360 019·750	60 54·39	10·2344	22·7202
26	49 02 25	+4 05 34	3 01 32·38	+21 24 48·7	359 026·187	61 04·51	11·2260	23·7501
27	64 10 16	+4 43 00	4 04 51·70	+25 36 38·8	359 812·349	60 56·50	12·2886	. . .
28	79 10 59	+5 00 33	5 11 06·42	+27 59 22·5	362 363·038	60 30·76	13·3842	00·8357
29	93 54 57	+4 57 41	6 17 43·99	+28 20 21·9	366 459·983	59 50·16	14·4554	01·9265
30	108 14 50	+4 35 58	7 21 49·87	+26 45 04·3	371 720·957	58 59·35	15·4529	02·9655
31	122 06 27	+3 58 27	8 21 21·99	+23 33 34·6	377 667·713	58 03·61	16·3546	03·9159
June 1	135 28 57	+3 08 52	9 15 42·82	+19 11 54·6	383 800·552	57 07·94	17·1649	04·7702
2	148 24 11	+2 11 02	10 05 21·72	+14 04 35·0	389 661·228	56 16·38	17·9024	05·5413
3	160 55 56	+1 08 27	10 51 22·07	+ 8 31 18·7	394 875·266	55 31·79	18·5902	06·2510
4	173 09 05	+0 04 13	11 34 57·48	+ 2 46 59·2	399 173·157	54 55·92	19·2513	06·9227
5	185 08 56	−0 59 02	12 17 20·52	− 2 56 56·4	402 394·430	54 29·53	19·9071	07·5786
6	197 00 43	−1 58 55	12 59 39·07	− 8 30 47·5	404 479·637	54 12·67	20·5772	08·2392
7	208 49 14	−2 53 18	13 42 55·25	−13 45 11·0	405 454·597	54 04·85	21·2791	08·9232
8	220 38 38	−3 40 10	14 28 03·79	−18 29 53·2	405 410·079	54 05·21	22·0268	09·6465
9	232 32 18	−4 17 38	15 15 47·41	−22 33 10·7	404 479·243	54 12·68	22·8285	10·4207
10	244 32 43	−4 44 01	16 06 28·29	−25 41 55·2	402 814·829	54 26·12	23·6822	11·2494
11	256 41 38	−4 57 51	16 59 57·47	−27 42 42·1	400 568·126	54 44·44	. . .	12·1246
12	269 00 05	−4 58 04	17 55 28·58	−28 24 07·5	397 872·005	55 06·70	00·5737	13·0263
13	281 28 40	−4 44 07	18 51 45·07	−27 39 34·5	394 830·314	55 32·17	01·4788	13·9278
14	294 07 45	−4 16 05	19 47 23·19	−25 29 07·7	391 515·541	56 00·39	02·3705	14·8048
15	306 57 50	−3 34 43	20 41 19·95	−21 59 28·7	387 975·657	56 31·05	03·2296	15·6444
16	319 59 43	−2 41 31	21 33 10·23	−17 22 05·3	384 249·515	57 03·94	04·0497	16·4467
17	333 14 37	−1 38 42	22 23 07·74	−11 50 57·0	380 388·381	57 38·69	04·8370	17·2229
18	346 44 02	−0 29 11	23 11 56·21	− 5 41 06·8	376 479·376	58 14·61	05·6068	17·9915
19	0 29 29	+0 43 24	0 00 39·16	+ 0 51 33·2	372 665·195	58 50·38	06·3800	18·7754
20	14 31 59	+1 54 51	0 50 31·67	+ 7 29 34·8	369 153·609	59 23·97	07·1809	19·5996
21	28 51 20	+3 00 28	1 42 52·72	+13 52 37·6	366 210·658	59 52·61	08·0345	20·4879
22	43 25 28	+3 55 29	2 38 52·70	+19 36 27·3	364 133·703	60 13·10	08·9614	21·4555
23	58 10 01	+4 35 30	3 39 10·63	+24 13 25·2	363 205·462	60 22·34	09·9689	22·4983
24	72 58 26	+4 57 16	4 43 21·98	+27 16 03·1	363 637·222	60 18·04	11·0387	23·5832
25	87 42 40	+4 59 11	5 49 37·80	+28 24 14·8	365 516·055	59 59·44	12·1244	. . .
26	102 14 28	+4 41 39	6 55 09·24	+27 32 53·9	368 772·700	59 27·65	13·1690	00·6550
27	116 26 49	+4 06 52	7 57 17·79	+24 54 01·8	373 181·102	58 45·50	14·1316	01·6619
28	130 14 59	+3 18 20	8 54 36·22	+20 51 13·6	378 389·417	57 56·97	15·0004	02·5775
29	143 36 58	+2 20 07	9 46 57·56	+15 51 04·1	383 971·812	57 06·41	15·7855	03·4022
30	156 33 26	+1 16 15	10 35 07·74	+10 17 07·6	389 486·011	56 17·90	16·5074	04·1529
July 1	169 07 06	+0 10 20	11 20 15·57	+ 4 27 53·6	394 523·974	55 34·76	17·1894	04·8519
2	181 22 09	−0 54 33	12 03 34·74	− 1 22 43·3	398 748·899	54 59·42	17·8542	05·5226

EPHEMERIS FOR PHYSICAL OBSERVATIONS
FOR 0^h TERRESTRIAL TIME

Julian Date	The Earth's Selenographic Long.	The Earth's Selenographic Lat.	The Sun's Selenographic Colong.	The Sun's Selenographic Lat.	Position Angle Axis	Position Angle Bright Limb	Semi-diameter	Fraction Illum.
246	°	°	°	°	°	°	′ ″	
0812·5	−6·073	+6·262	144·14	+1·38	354·087	87·85	15 07·43	0·833
0813·5	−6·623	+5·631	156·34	+1·38	349·300	80·99	15 16·67	0·752
0814·5	−6·950	+4·707	168·54	+1·39	345·196	75·30	15 27·40	0·658
0815·5	−7·010	+3·519	180·75	+1·39	341·957	70·95	15 39·44	0·555
0816·5	−6·758	+2·111	192·96	+1·39	339·667	68·04	15 52·37	0·446
0817·5	−6·151	+0·544	205·18	+1·40	338·370	66·70	16 05·53	0·337
0818·5	−5·163	−1·095	217·41	+1·40	338·114	67·14	16 17·91	0·233
0819·5	−3·800	−2·702	229·65	+1·41	338·986	69·74	16 28·30	0·141
0820·5	−2·113	−4·157	241·89	+1·42	341·113	75·42	16 35·41	0·068
0821·5	−0·204	−5·340	254·13	+1·43	344·605	87·74	16 38·16	0·021
0822·5	+1·775	−6·151	266·38	+1·44	349·428	148·00	16 35·98	0·002
0823·5	+3·649	−6·528	278·62	+1·45	355·261	243·24	16 28·97	0·013
0824·5	+5·247	−6·461	290·87	+1·46	1·481	261·72	16 17·91	0·053
0825·5	+6·435	−5·982	303·11	+1·47	7·360	272·44	16 04·07	0·115
0826·5	+7·137	−5·161	315·35	+1·48	12·359	280·27	15 48·89	0·196
0827·5	+7·336	−4·077	327·59	+1·50	16·248	285·99	15 33·73	0·288
0828·5	+7·064	−2·815	339·82	+1·51	19·034	289·93	15 19·69	0·386
0829·5	+6·390	−1·451	352·04	+1·52	20·825	292·31	15 07·54	0·486
0830·5	+5·400	−0·052	4·26	+1·53	21·736	293·30	14 57·77	0·584
0831·5	+4·188	+1·324	16·47	+1·55	21·849	293·00	14 50·58	0·677
0832·5	+2·848	+2·628	28·68	+1·56	21·192	291·41	14 45·99	0·762
0833·5	+1·463	+3·812	40·88	+1·57	19·755	288·40	14 43·86	0·837
0834·5	+0·105	+4·833	53·08	+1·57	17·497	283·67	14 43·96	0·900
0835·5	−1·169	+5·649	65·28	+1·58	14·383	276·42	14 45·99	0·949
0836·5	−2·318	+6·224	77·47	+1·58	10·428	263·64	14 49·65	0·982
0837·5	−3·317	+6·526	89·66	+1·58	5·748	222·31	14 54·64	0·997
0838·5	−4·152	+6·530	101·85	+1·58	0·598	123·08	15 00·71	0·994
0839·5	−4·822	+6·226	114·04	+1·58	355·350	98·19	15 07·64	0·971
0840·5	−5·325	+5·614	126·24	+1·57	350·409	86·71	15 15·33	0·928
0841·5	−5·658	+4·712	138·44	+1·56	346·112	78·91	15 23·68	0·867
0842·5	−5·809	+3·553	150·64	+1·55	342·665	73·28	15 32·64	0·788
0843·5	−5·759	+2·184	162·84	+1·54	340·160	69·41	15 42·10	0·695
0844·5	−5·477	+0·670	175·06	+1·53	338·622	67·19	15 51·89	0·591
0845·5	−4·931	−0·911	187·28	+1·52	338·072	66·59	16 01·63	0·479
0846·5	−4·097	−2·469	199·50	+1·51	338·565	67·68	16 10·78	0·367
0847·5	−2·970	−3·900	211·74	+1·50	340·202	70·63	16 18·58	0·259
0848·5	−1·577	−5·102	223·98	+1·49	343·103	75·74	16 24·16	0·163
0849·5	+0·008	−5·978	236·22	+1·49	347·324	83·56	16 26·68	0·085
0850·5	+1·674	−6·457	248·47	+1·48	352·712	95·97	16 25·50	0·031
0851·5	+3·276	−6·502	260·72	+1·48	358·808	128·56	16 20·44	0·005
0852·5	+4·666	−6·123	272·98	+1·48	4·917	243·86	16 11·78	0·006
0853·5	+5·719	−5·368	285·23	+1·47	10·381	270·58	16 00·30	0·034
0854·5	+6·350	−4·313	297·48	+1·47	14·802	281·02	15 47·08	0·085
0855·5	+6·528	−3·047	309·72	+1·47	18·076	287·20	15 33·31	0·154
0856·5	+6·267	−1·658	321·97	+1·47	20·274	290·98	15 20·10	0·237
0857·5	+5·619	−0·224	334·20	+1·47	21·516	293·00	15 08·35	0·328
0858·5	+4·660	+1·188	346·44	+1·47	21·906	293·58	14 58·73	0·423

FOR 0^h TERRESTRIAL TIME

Date 0^h TT		Apparent Longitude	Apparent Latitude	Apparent R.A.	Apparent Dec.	True Distance	Horiz. Parallax	Ephemeris Transit for date Upper	Ephemeris Transit for date Lower
		° ′ ″	° ′ ″	h m s	° ′ ″	km	′ ″	h	h
July	**1**	169 07 06	+0 10 20	11 20 15·57	+ 4 27 53·6	394 523·974	55 34·76	17·1894	04·8519
	2	181 22 09	−0 54 33	12 03 34·74	− 1 22 43·3	398 748·899	54 59·42	17·8542	05·5226
	3	193 23 37	−1 55 50	12 46 16·31	− 7 03 53·4	401 917·259	54 33·41	18·5226	06·1867
	4	205 16 47	−2 51 21	13 29 26·43	−12 26 12·2	403 887·763	54 17·44	19·2138	06·8642
	5	217 06 53	−3 39 13	14 14 05·04	−17 20 13·7	404 620·162	54 11·54	19·9443	07·5732
	6	228 58 43	−4 17 42	15 01 02·56	−21 35 25·4	404 166·500	54 15·19	20·7262	08·3284
	7	240 56 26	−4 45 14	15 50 52·77	−24 59 39·9	402 656·598	54 27·40	21·5634	09·1381
	8	253 03 23	−5 00 20	16 43 42·15	−27 19 44·0	400 279·021	54 46·81	22·4479	10·0008
	9	265 21 54	−5 01 51	17 39 00·04	−28 23 05·3	397 258·553	55 11·80	23·3590	10·9018
	10	277 53 21	−4 49 01	18 35 38·91	−28 00 41·6	393 831·666	55 40·62	. . .	11·8159
	11	290 38 10	−4 21 40	19 32 11·87	−26 09 47·3	390 222·264	56 11·52	00·2691	12·7156
	12	303 36 03	−3 40 23	20 27 21·79	−22 55 01·6	386 620·886	56 42·93	01·1533	13·5809
	13	316 46 14	−2 46 43	21 20 25·30	−18 27 24·5	383 170·997	57 13·57	01·9981	14·4055
	14	330 07 51	−1 43 02	22 11 20·27	−13 01 55·7	379 965·434	57 42·54	02·8040	15·1956
	15	343 40 09	−0 32 35	23 00 39·13	− 6 55 22·8	377 054·296	58 09·28	03·5822	15·9665
	16	357 22 39	+0 40 44	23 49 17·71	− 0 25 10·9	374 462·845	58 33·43	04·3511	16·7389
	17	11 15 08	+1 52 38	0 38 25·45	+ 6 10 43·1	372 215·095	58 54·65	05·1330	17·5363
	18	25 17 19	+2 58 38	1 29 17·48	+12 33 09·9	370 356·662	59 12·39	05·9518	18·3820
	19	39 28 29	+3 54 23	2 23 05·06	+18 20 53·4	368 969·818	59 25·74	06·8293	19·2951
	20	53 47 01	+4 36 02	3 20 39·14	+23 10 13·7	368 174·890	59 33·44	07·7795	20·2815
	21	68 10 03	+5 00 34	4 22 04·89	+26 36 41·6	368 115·176	59 34·02	08·7981	21·3248
	22	82 33 26	+5 06 13	5 26 17·23	+28 19 28·4	368 927·087	59 26·15	09·8557	22·3841
	23	96 52 01	+4 52 43	6 31 03·28	+28 07 55·8	370 702·149	59 09·08	10·9036	23·4086
	24	111 00 16	+4 21 25	7 33 48·70	+26 06 05·0	373 451·223	58 42·95	11·8950	. . .
	25	124 53 13	+3 35 04	8 32 40·14	+22 31 10·7	377 081·633	58 09·03	12·8042	00·3604
	26	138 27 03	+2 37 22	9 26 56·20	+17 47 23·9	381 394·229	57 29·57	13·6299	01·2269
	27	151 39 45	+1 32 26	10 16 56·71	+12 19 18·1	386 101·003	56 47·51	14·3860	02·0155
	28	164 31 10	+0 24 17	11 03 35·91	+ 6 28 04·0	390 857·887	56 06·04	15·0930	02·7443
	29	177 02 55	−0 43 29	11 48 00·89	+ 0 30 30·4	395 304·308	55 28·18	15·7724	03·4348
	30	189 17 59	−1 47 51	12 31 20·18	− 5 20 15·5	399 101·561	54 56·51	16·4451	04·1084
	31	201 20 25	−2 46 21	13 14 39·29	−10 53 31·4	401 964·726	54 33·02	17·1305	04·7851
Aug.	**1**	213 14 54	−3 37 00	13 58 58·79	−15 59 35·7	403 685·899	54 19·07	17·8460	05·4835
	2	225 06 25	−4 18 08	14 45 12·00	−20 28 34·1	404 148·631	54 15·34	18·6058	06·2197
	3	236 59 55	−4 48 16	15 33 59·66	−24 09 30·3	403 334·453	54 21·91	19·4181	07·0052
	4	249 00 06	−5 06 08	16 25 41·13	−26 50 17·2	401 322·354	54 38·26	20·2817	07·8441
	5	261 11 05	−5 10 34	17 20 04·03	−28 18 34·1	398 281·576	55 03·29	21·1830	08·7289
	6	273 36 10	−5 00 40	18 16 19·41	−28 23 54·3	394 457·560	55 35·32	22·0985	09·6407
	7	286 17 40	−4 35 57	19 13 10·74	−27 00 31·4	390 150·737	56 12·14	23·0021	10·5532
	8	299 16 39	−3 56 37	20 09 17·74	−24 09 24·2	385 688·399	56 51·16	23·8748	11·4430
	9	312 32 57	−3 03 45	21 03 43·09	−19 58 34·1	381 391·422	57 29·60	. . .	12·2970
	10	326 05 17	−1 59 29	21 56 07·29	−14 41 41·2	377 539·802	58 04·79	00·7102	13·1153
	11	339 51 25	−0 47 08	22 46 47·91	− 8 36 01·3	374 343·123	58 34·55	01·5141	13·9086
	12	353 48 36	+0 29 06	23 36 30·02	− 2 00 45·7	371 922·780	58 57·43	02·3012	14·6945
	13	7 53 52	+1 44 24	0 26 15·48	+ 4 43 53·6	370 310·969	59 12·83	03·0913	15·4944
	14	22 04 22	+2 53 48	1 17 13·59	+11 16 57·5	369 467·117	59 20·94	03·9065	16·3302
	15	36 17 30	+3 52 45	2 10 31·48	+17 16 32·0	369 307·138	59 22·48	04·7677	17·2207
	16	50 30 56	+4 37 26	3 06 59·98	+22 19 51·2	369 736·945	59 18·34	05·6899	18·1750

EPHEMERIS FOR PHYSICAL OBSERVATIONS
FOR 0^h TERRESTRIAL TIME

Julian Date	The Earth's Selenographic Long.	The Earth's Selenographic Lat.	The Sun's Selenographic Colong.	The Sun's Selenographic Lat.	Position Angle Axis	Position Angle Bright Limb	Semi-diameter	Fraction Illum.
246	°	°	°	°	°	°	′ ″	
0857·5	+5·619	−0·224	334·20	+1·47	21·516	293·00	15 08·35	0·328
0858·5	+4·660	+1·188	346·44	+1·47	21·906	293·58	14 58·73	0·423
0859·5	+3·480	+2·522	358·66	+1·47	21·501	292·88	14 51·64	0·519
0860·5	+2·171	+3·733	10·88	+1·47	20·310	290·95	14 47·29	0·613
0861·5	+0·823	+4·779	23·09	+1·47	18·307	287·79	14 45·68	0·703
0862·5	−0·483	+5·621	35·30	+1·47	15·454	283·33	14 46·68	0·785
0863·5	−1·678	+6·226	47·51	+1·46	11·744	277·44	14 50·00	0·858
0864·5	−2·710	+6·561	59·71	+1·45	7·252	269·86	14 55·29	0·918
0865·5	−3·545	+6·600	71·90	+1·44	2·181	259·66	15 02·10	0·963
0866·5	−4·165	+6·326	84·10	+1·42	356·876	241·27	15 09·95	0·991
0867·5	−4·570	+5·737	96·29	+1·41	351·754	150·06	15 18·36	0·998
0868·5	−4·771	+4·844	108·48	+1·39	347·197	90·92	15 26·92	0·985
0869·5	−4·782	+3·682	120·68	+1·37	343·466	77·91	15 35·26	0·950
0870·5	−4·619	+2·301	132·87	+1·34	340·689	71·44	15 43·15	0·893
0871·5	−4·289	+0·773	145·07	+1·32	338·900	67·83	15 50·44	0·816
0872·5	−3·793	−0·820	157·28	+1·30	338·106	66·25	15 57·01	0·723
0873·5	−3·127	−2·383	169·49	+1·27	338·332	66·45	16 02·79	0·617
0874·5	−2·287	−3·820	181·71	+1·25	339·646	68·36	16 07·62	0·504
0875·5	−1·280	−5·038	193·93	+1·23	342·142	72·02	16 11·26	0·390
0876·5	−0·132	−5·951	206·16	+1·21	345·886	77·45	16 13·36	0·281
0877·5	+1·108	−6·493	218·40	+1·19	350·809	84·62	16 13·52	0·183
0878·5	+2·362	−6·624	230·65	+1·17	356·589	93·40	16 11·37	0·102
0879·5	+3·533	−6·340	242·89	+1·15	2·653	104·13	16 06·72	0·044
0880·5	+4·522	−5·667	255·14	+1·14	8·346	121·68	15 59·61	0·010
0881·5	+5·238	−4·668	267·40	+1·12	13·171	229·81	15 50·37	0·001
0882·5	+5·617	−3·421	279·65	+1·11	16·903	278·64	15 39·62	0·018
0883·5	+5·629	−2·016	291·90	+1·10	19·532	288·03	15 28·17	0·057
0884·5	+5·277	−0·541	304·14	+1·08	21·151	292·20	15 16·87	0·114
0885·5	+4·595	+0·927	316·38	+1·07	21·866	294·00	15 06·56	0·185
0886·5	+3·639	+2·322	328·62	+1·06	21·749	294·17	14 57·93	0·268
0887·5	+2·481	+3·593	340·85	+1·05	20·831	293·00	14 51·53	0·357
0888·5	+1·204	+4·695	353·08	+1·04	19·101	290·61	14 47·73	0·451
0889·5	−0·109	+5·592	5·30	+1·03	16·533	287·05	14 46·72	0·546
0890·5	−1·376	+6·251	17·51	+1·01	13·111	282·35	14 48·51	0·639
0891·5	−2·522	+6·645	29·72	+1·00	8·877	276·58	14 52·96	0·728
0892·5	−3·482	+6·748	41·92	+0·98	3·984	269·89	14 59·78	0·810
0893·5	−4·207	+6·541	54·12	+0·96	358·719	262·47	15 08·50	0·881
0894·5	−4·665	+6·012	66·32	+0·94	353·474	254·39	15 18·53	0·938
0895·5	−4·844	+5·166	78·51	+0·91	348·655	244·57	15 29·16	0·979
0896·5	−4·750	+4·027	90·69	+0·88	344·583	216·89	15 39·63	0·998
0897·5	−4·405	+2·642	102·88	+0·85	341·444	83·22	15 49·21	0·994
0898·5	−3·844	+1·080	115·07	+0·82	339·314	69·83	15 57·32	0·966
0899·5	−3·105	−0·567	127·25	+0·79	338·216	65·98	16 03·55	0·914
0900·5	−2·228	−2·195	139·45	+0·75	338·166	65·11	16 07·74	0·839
0901·5	−1·253	−3·698	151·64	+0·72	339·214	66·29	16 09·95	0·746
0902·5	−0·216	−4·977	163·85	+0·69	341·433	69·26	16 10·37	0·640
0903·5	+0·846	−5·948	176·06	+0·66	344·874	73·90	16 09·25	0·526

FOR 0^h TERRESTRIAL TIME

Date 0^h TT	Apparent Longitude	Apparent Latitude	Apparent R.A.	Apparent Dec.	True Distance	Horiz. Parallax	Ephemeris Transit for date Upper	Ephemeris Transit for date Lower
	° ′ ″	° ′ ″	h m s	° ′ ″	km	′ ″	h	h
Aug. 16	50 30 56	+4 37 26	3 06 59·98	+22 19 51·2	369 736·945	59 18·34	05·6899	18·1750
17	64 42 28	+5 05 04	4 06 52·98	+26 04 25·9	370 680·704	59 09·28	06·6743	19·1847
18	78 49 54	+5 14 08	5 09 26·28	+28 11 07·0	372 096·438	58 55·78	07·7015	20·2195
19	92 50 54	+5 04 25	6 12 54·74	+28 28 48·8	373 975·678	58 38·01	08·7327	21·2359
20	106 43 02	+4 36 58	7 15 03·87	+26 58 19·9	376 328·404	58 16·01	09·7246	22·1958
21	120 23 51	+3 54 00	8 14 01·91	+23 52 19·4	379 158·463	57 49·91	10·6478	23·0802
22	133 51 11	+2 58 38	9 08 54·63	+19 31 04·9	382 436·903	57 20·17	11·4936	23·8897
23	147 03 18	+1 54 35	9 59 45·43	+14 17 12·2	386 080·883	56 47·69	12·2703	...
24	159 59 17	+0 45 47	10 47 15·31	+ 8 31 48·6	389 943·830	56 13·93	12·9945	00·6377
25	172 39 05	−0 23 58	11 32 22·54	+ 2 32 57·6	393 819·101	55 40·73	13·6857	01·3430
26	185 03 41	−1 31 16	12 16 09·97	− 3 24 26·7	397 455·792	55 10·16	14·3635	02·0251
27	197 15 03	−2 33 15	12 59 39·11	− 9 07 58·8	400 582·855	54 44·32	15·0463	02·7032
28	209 16 01	−3 27 33	13 43 47·51	−14 26 45·0	402 936·840	54 25·13	15·7511	03·3950
29	221 10 10	−4 12 22	14 29 26·57	−19 10 25·0	404 289·211	54 14·20	16·4921	04·1163
30	233 01 39	−4 46 13	15 17 17·60	−23 08 25·0	404 470·479	54 12·75	17·2791	04·8794
31	244 54 58	−5 07 56	16 07 45·03	−26 09 36·0	403 389·684	54 21·46	18·1148	05·6910
Sept. 1	256 54 49	−5 16 30	17 00 47·89	−28 02 37·4	401 048·502	54 40·50	18·9917	06·5490
2	269 05 46	−5 11 08	17 55 53·86	−28 37 15·0	397 549·362	55 09·38	19·8926	07·4405
3	281 32 00	−4 51 15	18 52 02·97	−27 46 23·6	393 096·489	55 46·87	20·7947	08·3449
4	294 17 02	−4 16 42	19 48 04·07	−25 28 04·7	387 988·127	56 30·94	21·6781	09·2396
5	307 23 16	−3 27 59	20 42 58·11	−21 46 24·2	382 597·702	57 18·72	22·5321	10·1090
6	320 51 40	−2 26 31	21 36 15·81	−16 51 14·2	377 342·211	58 06·62	23·3579	10·9481
7	334 41 32	−1 14 57	22 28 02·56	−10 57 09·4	372 638·289	58 50·63	...	11·7631
8	348 50 20	+0 02 48	23 18 53·06	− 4 22 22·2	368 850·594	59 26·89	00·1660	12·5686
9	3 13 55	+1 21 43	0 09 41·83	+ 2 32 05·1	366 242·155	59 52·30	00·9737	13·3838
10	17 46 54	+2 36 11	1 01 33·58	+ 9 22 55·2	364 939·568	60 05·12	01·8016	14·2296
11	32 23 19	+3 40 45	1 55 32·62	+15 45 13·3	364 924·045	60 05·28	02·6701	15·1247
12	46 57 23	+4 30 51	2 52 28·35	+21 13 25·8	366 051·829	59 54·17	03·5945	16·0792
13	61 24 08	+5 03 20	3 52 34·96	+25 23 13·6	368 097·385	59 34·19	04·5776	17·0868
14	75 39 45	+5 16 40	4 55 11·18	+27 54 48·2	370 805·650	59 08·09	05·6029	18·1207
15	89 41 48	+5 10 49	5 58 37·38	+28 37 06·8	373 938·666	58 38·35	06·6347	19·1397
16	103 28 59	+4 47 06	7 00 45·03	+27 30 55·5	377 306·366	58 06·95	07·6312	20·1060
17	117 01 00	+4 07 44	7 59 45·87	+24 48 10·9	380 777·796	57 35·16	08·5620	20·9988
18	130 18 04	+3 15 41	8 54 45·80	+20 47 50·2	384 274·639	57 03·71	09·4167	21·8170
19	143 20 48	+2 14 17	9 45 46·18	+15 50 56·7	387 752·396	56 33·00	10·2015	22·5723
20	156 09 57	+1 07 09	10 33 25·39	+10 17 22·1	391 175·942	56 03·30	10·9318	23·2824
21	168 46 20	−0 02 11	11 18 39·25	+ 4 24 30·5	394 496·022	55 35·00	11·6264	23·9662
22	181 10 54	−1 10 18	12 02 28·34	− 1 32 41·8	397 631·951	55 08·69	12·3041	...
23	193 24 48	−2 14 08	12 45 51·90	− 7 21 12·4	400 463·745	54 45·29	12·9828	00·6423
24	205 29 30	−3 11 04	13 29 45·00	−12 49 12·9	402 834·638	54 25·96	13·6787	01·3277
25	217 26 53	−3 58 59	14 14 56·44	−17 45 30·2	404 562·900	54 12·00	14·4056	02·0375
26	229 19 22	−4 36 13	15 02 05·36	−21 58 58·4	405 460·561	54 04·80	15·1732	02·7839
27	241 09 58	−5 01 32	15 51 35·62	−25 18 28·7	405 356·144	54 05·64	15·9854	03·5738
28	253 02 12	−5 14 02	16 43 28·83	−27 33 10·3	404 118·727	54 15·58	16·8371	04·4069
29	265 00 07	−5 13 05	17 37 19·45	−28 33 29·4	401 681·156	54 35·34	17·7148	05·2739
30	277 08 06	−4 58 16	18 32 17·29	−28 12 36·2	398 060·626	55 05·13	18·5993	06·1575
Oct. 1	289 30 42	−4 29 30	19 27 20·54	−26 27 47·4	393 374·820	55 44·50	19·4719	07·0380

EPHEMERIS FOR PHYSICAL OBSERVATIONS
FOR 0^h TERRESTRIAL TIME

Julian Date	The Earth's Selenographic Long.	The Earth's Selenographic Lat.	The Sun's Selenographic Colong.	The Sun's Selenographic Lat.	Position Angle Axis	Position Angle Bright Limb	Semi-diameter	Fraction Illum.
246	°	°	°	°	°	°	′ ″	
0903·5	+0·846	−5·948	176·06	+0·66	344·874	73·90	16 09·25	0·526
0904·5	+1·892	−6·552	188·27	+0·63	349·481	80·02	16 06·78	0·412
0905·5	+2·879	−6·755	200·49	+0·60	354·993	87·26	16 03·10	0·302
0906·5	+3·758	−6·550	212·72	+0·57	0·919	95·04	15 58·26	0·204
0907·5	+4·481	−5·962	224·96	+0·54	6·656	102·75	15 52·27	0·122
0908·5	+4·999	−5·037	237·20	+0·52	11·690	110·06	15 45·16	0·059
0909·5	+5·274	−3·845	249·44	+0·49	15·734	117·74	15 37·06	0·019
0910·5	+5·279	−2·464	261·68	+0·47	18·712	141·90	15 28·21	0·001
0911·5	+5·004	−0·981	273·92	+0·45	20·676	287·34	15 19·02	0·006
0912·5	+4·455	+0·523	286·16	+0·43	21·713	294·32	15 09·98	0·032
0913·5	+3·656	+1·975	298·40	+0·41	21·896	295·82	15 01·65	0·077
0914·5	+2·644	+3·313	310·64	+0·39	21·260	295·34	14 54·61	0·137
0915·5	+1·471	+4·487	322·87	+0·37	19·810	293·48	14 49·38	0·210
0916·5	+0·198	+5·456	335·10	+0·36	17·525	290·42	14 46·41	0·292
0917·5	−1·106	+6·190	347·32	+0·34	14·394	286·26	14 46·01	0·382
0918·5	−2·368	+6·661	359·53	+0·32	10·445	281·09	14 48·39	0·476
0919·5	−3·515	+6·848	11·74	+0·30	5·795	275·11	14 53·57	0·571
0920·5	−4·475	+6·733	23·94	+0·28	0·677	268·60	15 01·44	0·666
0921·5	−5·184	+6·305	36·13	+0·25	355·433	261·96	15 11·65	0·756
0922·5	−5·592	+5·560	48·32	+0·23	350·450	255·64	15 23·65	0·838
0923·5	−5·660	+4·510	60·51	+0·20	346·075	250·05	15 36·66	0·908
0924·5	−5·376	+3·185	72·69	+0·17	342·548	245·41	15 49·71	0·961
0925·5	−4·750	+1·643	84·86	+0·14	339·999	241·43	16 01·70	0·992
0926·5	−3·817	−0·032	97·04	+0·10	338·488	66·13	16 11·57	0·999
0927·5	−2·639	−1·732	109·21	+0·06	338·054	62·03	16 18·49	0·979
0928·5	−1·293	−3·337	121·38	+0·03	338·756	62·97	16 21·99	0·932
0929·5	+0·127	−4·728	133·56	−0·01	340·672	65·75	16 22·03	0·860
0930·5	+1·529	−5·808	145·74	−0·05	343·859	70·19	16 19·00	0·769
0931·5	+2·827	−6·508	157·93	−0·08	348·270	76·09	16 13·56	0·664
0932·5	+3·950	−6·794	170·13	−0·11	353·656	83·07	16 06·45	0·551
0933·5	+4·847	−6·665	182·33	−0·15	359·540	90·52	15 58·35	0·438
0934·5	+5·489	−6·150	194·53	−0·18	5·326	97·75	15 49·80	0·330
0935·5	+5·863	−5·298	206·75	−0·21	10·497	104·12	15 41·14	0·232
0936·5	+5·971	−4·172	218·97	−0·24	14·742	109·23	15 32·58	0·148
0937·5	+5·823	−2·847	231·19	−0·26	17·962	112·82	15 24·21	0·081
0938·5	+5·436	−1·398	243·42	−0·29	20·186	114·60	15 16·12	0·034
0939·5	+4·830	+0·096	255·65	−0·32	21·489	112·82	15 08·41	0·007
0940·5	+4·029	+1·564	267·87	−0·34	21·937	324·70	15 01·25	0·000
0941·5	+3·056	+2·939	280·10	−0·36	21·567	302·42	14 54·88	0·014
0942·5	+1·942	+4·165	292·33	−0·38	20·381	298·63	14 49·61	0·045
0943·5	+0·719	+5·197	304·55	−0·40	18·363	294·98	14 45·81	0·093
0944·5	−0·571	+5·997	316·77	−0·42	15·498	290·64	14 43·85	0·155
0945·5	−1·882	+6·540	328·99	−0·44	11·809	285·50	14 44·08	0·230
0946·5	−3·157	+6·805	341·20	−0·46	7·396	279·64	14 46·78	0·314
0947·5	−4·335	+6·779	353·40	−0·48	2·459	273·28	14 52·16	0·405
0948·5	−5·349	+6·453	5·60	−0·50	357·303	266·78	15 00·28	0·502
0949·5	−6·127	+5·825	17·79	−0·52	352·282	260·56	15 11·00	0·600

FOR 0^h TERRESTRIAL TIME

Date 0^h TT	Apparent Longitude	Apparent Latitude	Apparent R.A.	Apparent Dec.	True Distance	Horiz. Parallax	Ephemeris Transit for date Upper	Ephemeris Transit for date Lower
	° ′ ″	° ′ ″	h m s	° ′ ″	km	′ ″	h	h
Oct. 1	289 30 42	−4 29 30	19 27 20·54	−26 27 47·4	393 374·820	55 44·50	19·4719	07·0380
2	302 12 18	−3 47 00	20 21 35·20	−23 21 05·9	387 851·237	56 32·14	20·3215	07·9000
3	315 16 42	−2 51 38	21 14 31·58	−18 59 08·5	381 826·294	57 25·67	21·1468	08·7369
4	328 46 36	−1 45 09	22 06 10·91	−13 32 30·1	375 729·832	58 21·58	21·9561	09·5526
5	342 42 56	−0 30 26	22 57 02·87	− 7 15 20·8	370 050·850	59 15·32	22·7650	10·3594
6	357 04 20	+0 48 17	23 47 58·52	− 0 25 32·3	365 283·071	60 01·73	23·5937	11·1755
7	11 46 46	+2 05 35	0 40 02·04	+ 6 35 01·9	361 855·506	60 35·85	...	12·0222
8	26 43 35	+3 15 28	1 34 21·01	+13 20 25·9	360 062·005	60 53·96	00·4638	12·9204
9	41 46 17	+4 12 13	2 31 51·63	+19 21 38·9	360 010·300	60 54·49	01·3935	13·8837
10	56 45 42	+4 51 25	3 32 56·05	+24 09 11·4	361 608·733	60 38·33	02·3899	14·9097
11	71 33 28	+5 10 37	4 36 56·43	+27 17 44·6	364 596·212	60 08·52	03·4390	15·9724
12	86 03 13	+5 09 28	5 42 06·01	+28 32 05·8	368 604·401	59 29·28	04·5037	17·0267
13	100 11 08	+4 49 24	6 45 59·16	+27 51 22·9	373 230·794	58 45·03	05·5359	18·0272
14	113 56 00	+4 13 05	7 46 29·79	+25 28 17·3	378 102·109	57 59·61	06·4981	18·9475
15	127 18 36	+3 23 47	8 42 34·08	+21 43 33·1	382 915·837	57 15·86	07·3759	19·7844
16	140 21 05	+2 25 00	9 34 12·78	+16 59 37·4	387 457·407	56 35·58	08·1750	20·5500
17	153 06 15	+1 20 16	10 22 08·63	+11 36 48·2	391 596·775	55 59·69	08·9121	21·2637
18	165 37 06	+0 12 55	11 07 22·82	+ 5 52 06·0	395 270·990	55 28·46	09·6075	21·9459
19	177 56 23	−0 53 54	11 51 00·57	− 0 00 17·6	398 459·439	55 01·82	10·2814	22·6163
20	190 06 30	−1 57 16	12 34 04·39	− 5 48 01·2	401 157·677	54 39·61	10·9528	23·2928
21	202 09 27	−2 54 36	13 17 31·57	−11 19 36·2	403 354·518	54 21·75	11·6384	23·9911
22	214 06 55	−3 43 39	14 02 12·22	−16 23 43·7	405 015·799	54 08·37	12·3525	...
23	226 00 27	−4 22 35	14 48 46·24	−20 48 51·8	406 076·850	53 59·88	13·1056	00·7238
24	237 51 41	−4 49 59	15 37 37·87	−24 23 17·5	406 444·273	53 56·95	13·9020	01·4985
25	249 42 29	−5 04 53	16 28 48·96	−26 55 41·9	406 006·386	54 00·44	14·7377	02·3156
26	261 35 13	−5 06 42	17 21 54·15	−28 16 20·4	404 650·711	54 11·30	15·5998	03·1666
27	273 32 48	−4 55 11	18 16 03·43	−28 18 31·6	402 286·348	54 30·41	16·4694	04·0349
28	285 38 47	−4 30 27	19 10 14·99	−26 59 49·2	398 868·917	54 58·43	17·3275	04·9008
29	297 57 14	−3 52 54	20 03 34·41	−24 22 19·1	394 425·600	55 35·59	18·1619	05·7481
30	310 32 38	−3 03 22	20 55 31·01	−20 31 59·3	389 077·576	56 21·44	18·9700	06·5690
31	323 29 26	−2 03 12	21 46 04·65	−15 37 36·9	383 056·303	57 14·60	19·7589	07·3661
Nov. 1	336 51 37	−0 54 30	22 35 43·59	− 9 50 11·2	376 708·808	58 12·48	20·5434	08·1506
2	350 41 59	+0 19 37	23 25 18·35	− 3 23 06·7	370 485·840	59 11·15	21·3438	08·9402
3	5 01 10	+1 34 53	0 15 54·97	+ 3 26 45·2	364 906·644	60 05·45	22·1835	09·7572
4	19 46 52	+2 45 59	1 08 47·96	+10 17 46·6	360 497·566	60 49·55	23·0860	10·6256
5	34 53 18	+3 47 04	2 05 08·83	+16 42 45·3	357 710·187	61 17·99	...	11·5664
6	50 11 23	+4 32 38	3 05 44·70	+22 09 53·5	356 836·794	61 26·99	00·0675	12·5883
7	65 30 01	+4 58 40	4 10 25·57	+26 06 58·2	357 949·797	61 15·53	01·1259	13·6752
8	80 37 55	+5 03 26	5 17 36·75	+28 09 06·2	360 888·287	60 45·60	02·2296	14·7814
9	95 25 42	+4 47 40	6 24 32·54	+28 07 02·2	365 297·464	60 01·59	03·3231	15·8482
10	109 47 13	+4 14 00	7 28 22·92	+26 10 00·1	370 705·220	59 09·05	04·3520	16·8320
11	123 39 58	+3 26 13	8 27 23·59	+22 40 20·0	376 608·690	58 13·41	05·2874	17·7190
12	137 04 33	+2 28 27	9 21 15·09	+18 04 26·0	382 546·913	57 19·18	06·1287	18·5189
13	150 03 45	+1 24 40	10 10 37·86	+12 46 12·0	388 147·502	56 29·55	06·8924	19·2523
14	162 41 39	+0 18 25	10 56 39·54	+ 7 04 43·7	393 146·464	55 46·44	07·6014	19·9427
15	175 02 46	−0 47 11	11 40 33·91	+ 1 14 47·2	397 386·623	55 10·73	08·2788	20·6124
16	187 11 29	−1 49 24	12 23 31·43	− 4 31 43·7	400 801·758	54 42·52	08·9460	21·2817

EPHEMERIS FOR PHYSICAL OBSERVATIONS
FOR 0^h TERRESTRIAL TIME

Julian Date	The Earth's Selenographic Long.	The Earth's Selenographic Lat.	The Sun's Selenographic Colong.	The Sun's Selenographic Lat.	Position Angle Axis	Position Angle Bright Limb	Semi-diameter	Fraction Illum.
246	°	°	°	°	°	°	′ ″	
0949·5	−6·127	+5·825	17·79	−0·52	352·282	260·56	15 11·00	0·600
0950·5	−6·602	+4·902	29·97	−0·54	347·733	255·03	15 23·98	0·697
0951·5	−6·712	+3·702	42·15	−0·56	343·909	250·59	15 38·56	0·789
0952·5	−6·414	+2·263	54·32	−0·59	340·972	247·59	15 53·79	0·870
0953·5	−5·686	+0·649	66·48	−0·62	339·013	246·58	16 08·42	0·936
0954·5	−4·545	−1·050	78·64	−0·65	338·099	249·41	16 21·06	0·981
0955·5	−3·047	−2·716	90·80	−0·68	338·310	290·41	16 30·36	0·999
0956·5	−1·293	−4·221	102·95	−0·71	339·759	53·31	16 35·29	0·989
0957·5	+0·579	−5·441	115·11	−0·75	342·550	63·06	16 35·43	0·949
0958·5	+2·418	−6·281	127·27	−0·78	346·695	70·38	16 31·03	0·883
0959·5	+4·075	−6·687	139·43	−0·81	351·988	78·06	16 22·91	0·796
0960·5	+5·436	−6·652	151·60	−0·84	357·951	86·04	16 12·22	0·695
0961·5	+6·426	−6·208	163·78	−0·87	3·934	93·74	16 00·17	0·585
0962·5	+7·017	−5·413	175·96	−0·89	9·348	100·52	15 47·80	0·475
0963·5	+7·219	−4·339	188·15	−0·92	13·837	105·98	15 35·89	0·368
0964·5	+7·069	−3·062	200·34	−0·94	17·286	109·93	15 24·92	0·271
0965·5	+6·618	−1·658	212·54	−0·97	19·727	112·32	15 15·14	0·185
0966·5	+5·921	−0·199	224·75	−0·99	21·243	113·05	15 06·63	0·113
0967·5	+5·031	+1·246	236·96	−1·01	21·909	111·73	14 59·38	0·059
0968·5	+3·994	+2·615	249·17	−1·04	21·765	106·71	14 53·33	0·022
0969·5	+2·848	+3·852	261·38	−1·05	20·814	85·08	14 48·46	0·003
0970·5	+1·624	+4·910	273·59	−1·07	19·037	325·25	14 44·82	0·003
0971·5	+0·348	+5·748	285·81	−1·09	16·411	301·94	14 42·51	0·021
0972·5	−0·954	+6·335	298·01	−1·10	12·946	292·81	14 41·71	0·056
0973·5	−2·256	+6·651	310·22	−1·12	8·726	285·40	14 42·66	0·107
0974·5	−3·522	+6·681	322·42	−1·13	3·936	278·26	14 45·62	0·172
0975·5	−4·709	+6·423	334·62	−1·14	358·862	271·26	14 50·82	0·250
0976·5	−5·763	+5·878	346·81	−1·15	353·848	264·65	14 58·45	0·337
0977·5	−6·622	+5·055	358·99	−1·16	349·218	258·72	15 08·58	0·433
0978·5	−7·212	+3·974	11·17	−1·18	345·226	253·77	15 21·06	0·534
0979·5	−7·461	+2·663	23·34	−1·19	342·030	250·04	15 35·54	0·636
0980·5	−7·298	+1·170	35·50	−1·21	339·722	247·73	15 51·31	0·736
0981·5	−6·673	−0·439	47·66	−1·22	338·369	247·13	16 07·29	0·828
0982·5	−5·564	−2·070	59·81	−1·24	338·055	248·80	16 22·08	0·906
0983·5	−4·003	−3·610	71·95	−1·26	338·905	254·44	16 34·09	0·963
0984·5	−2·076	−4·931	84·09	−1·28	341·077	275·42	16 41·83	0·994
0985·5	+0·067	−5·914	96·23	−1·30	344·687	38·65	16 44·29	0·995
0986·5	+2·236	−6·471	108·37	−1·32	349·669	66·46	16 41·16	0·966
0987·5	+4·233	−6·566	120·51	−1·34	355·634	78·56	16 33·01	0·909
0988·5	+5·890	−6·213	132·66	−1·36	1·901	88·23	16 21·02	0·830
0989·5	+7·096	−5·471	144·81	−1·37	7·741	96·38	16 06·71	0·735
0990·5	+7·804	−4·424	156·96	−1·39	12·661	102·89	15 51·56	0·632
0991·5	+8·024	−3·163	169·13	−1·41	16·473	107·72	15 36·79	0·525
0992·5	+7·808	−1·772	181·30	−1·42	19·204	110·93	15 23·27	0·421
0993·5	+7·230	−0·330	193·47	−1·44	20·956	112·62	15 11·53	0·323
0994·5	+6·371	+1·096	205·66	−1·45	21·832	112·86	15 01·81	0·235
0995·5	+5·311	+2·448	217·84	−1·46	21·892	111·60	14 54·12	0·158

FOR 0^h TERRESTRIAL TIME

Date 0^h TT	Apparent Longitude	Apparent Latitude	Apparent R.A.	Apparent Dec.	True Distance	Horiz. Parallax	Ephemeris Transit for date Upper	Ephemeris Transit for date Lower
	° ′ ″	° ′ ″	h m s	° ′ ″	km	′ ″	h	h
Nov. 16	187 11 29	−1 49 24	12 23 31·43	− 4 31 43·7	400 801·758	54 42·52	08·9460	21·2817
17	199 11 41	−2 45 51	13 06 36·16	−10 04 15·9	403 392·805	54 21·44	09·6219	21·9684
18	211 06 37	−3 34 27	13 50 44·32	−15 12 26·5	405 201·140	54 06·88	10·3230	22·6871
19	222 58 47	−4 13 23	14 36 41·69	−19 45 17·6	406 282·808	53 58·23	11·0618	23·4478
20	234 50 06	−4 41 12	15 24 58·48	−23 31 07·1	406 686·748	53 55·02	11·8452	. . .
21	246 42 03	−4 56 48	16 15 41·80	−26 18 01·6	406 439·490	53 56·99	12·6712	00·2534
22	258 35 55	−4 59 30	17 08 29·27	−27 55 18·3	405 538·029	54 04·18	13·5281	01·0969
23	270 33 04	−4 49 04	18 02 29·66	−28 15 17·6	403 951·740	54 16·92	14·3959	01·9620
24	282 35 14	−4 25 43	18 56 35·14	−27 15 02·8	401 633·139	54 35·73	15·2530	02·8270
25	294 44 40	−3 50 04	19 49 42·38	−24 56 50·7	398 536·315	55 01·18	16·0833	03·6721
26	307 04 18	−3 03 11	20 41 11·81	−21 27 20·8	394 640·950	55 33·77	16·8811	04·4862
27	319 37 42	−2 06 35	21 30 56·42	−16 55 57·5	389 979·164	56 13·63	17·6511	05·2689
28	332 28 54	−1 02 15	22 19 19·87	−11 33 28·7	384 661·609	57 00·27	18·4065	06·0295
29	345 42 00	+0 07 12	23 07 09·71	− 5 31 39·0	378 898·267	57 52·30	19·1664	06·7845
30	359 20 34	+1 18 23	23 55 30·59	+ 0 56 14·3	373 008·080	58 47·13	19·9542	07·5552
Dec. 1	13 26 46	+2 27 07	0 45 38·80	+ 7 33 55·7	367 410·332	59 40·88	20·7957	08·3666
2	28 00 22	+3 28 28	1 38 55·51	+14 00 24·2	362 591·075	60 28·48	21·7152	09·2444
3	42 57 49	+4 17 15	2 36 32·75	+19 48 40·0	359 041·843	61 04·35	22·7268	10·2094
4	58 11 55	+4 48 45	3 39 05·30	+24 26 43·9	357 177·185	61 23·48	23·8196	11·2650
5	73 32 19	+4 59 46	4 45 51·27	+27 22 52·0	357 250·014	61 22·73	. . .	12·3836
6	88 47 16	+4 49 22	5 54 30·88	+28 15 18·6	359 292·121	61 01·80	00·9488	13·5064
7	103 45 41	+4 19 08	7 01 46·24	+27 01 20·4	363 102·663	60 23·36	02·0488	14·5700
8	118 19 12	+3 32 36	8 04 50·16	+23 57 55·7	368 289·130	59 32·33	03·0663	15·5366
9	132 23 10	+2 34 22	9 02 27·63	+19 33 11·4	374 344·270	58 34·54	03·9812	16·4019
10	145 56 36	+1 29 12	9 54 50·95	+14 16 09·4	380 732·107	57 35·57	04·8014	17·1827
11	159 01 29	+0 21 24	10 43 01·58	+ 8 30 59·2	386 960·334	56 39·95	05·5490	17·9034
12	171 41 44	−0 45 26	11 28 17·65	+ 2 35 50·9	392 628·013	55 50·86	06·2491	18·5889
13	184 02 18	−1 48 24	12 11 57·11	− 3 15 47·6	397 448·105	55 10·22	06·9258	19·2623
14	196 08 23	−2 45 10	12 55 11·68	− 8 53 17·0	401 249·947	54 38·86	07·6008	19·9437
15	208 04 57	−3 33 49	13 39 05·10	−14 07 02·6	403 968·010	54 16·79	08·2931	20·6507
16	219 56 24	−4 12 47	14 24 31·22	−18 47 17·0	405 622·306	54 03·51	09·0182	21·3966
17	231 46 25	−4 40 42	15 12 09·82	−22 43 18·7	406 294·337	53 58·14	09·7866	22·1882
18	243 37 49	−4 56 30	16 02 19·27	−25 43 36·7	406 101·514	53 59·68	10·6009	23·0233
19	255 32 41	−4 59 27	16 54 48·28	−27 36 53·7	405 172·485	54 07·11	11·4533	23·8884
20	267 32 29	−4 49 11	17 48 52·58	−28 14 03·3	403 625·769	54 19·55	12·3256	. . .
21	279 38 15	−4 25 50	18 43 23·26	−27 30 23·3	401 554·120	54 36·37	13·1941	00·7618
22	291 50 52	−3 50 01	19 37 07·42	−25 26 56·6	399 016·807	54 57·21	14·0381	01·6202
23	304 11 25	−3 02 59	20 29 11·29	−22 10 13·5	396 041·264	55 21·98	14·8463	02·4469
24	316 41 21	−2 06 26	21 19 14·02	−17 50 32·4	392 634·417	55 50·81	15·6188	03·2366
25	329 22 40	−1 02 40	22 07 28·46	−12 40 04·3	388 802·499	56 23·84	16·3653	03·9944
26	342 17 56	+0 05 36	22 54 34·26	− 6 51 36·5	384 576·591	57 01·02	17·1027	04·7339
27	355 30 04	+1 15 07	23 41 29·82	− 0 38 19·6	380 039·706	57 41·87	17·8520	05·4744
28	9 01 53	+2 22 12	0 29 26·36	+ 5 45 28·4	375 349·905	58 25·13	18·6378	06·2388
29	22 55 35	+3 22 44	1 19 42·86	+12 02 57·7	370 752·907	59 08·59	19·4856	07·0524
30	37 11 47	+4 12 24	2 13 38·08	+17 53 08·5	366 577·241	59 49·02	20·4172	07·9400
31	51 48 51	+4 46 58	3 12 12·74	+22 49 59·8	363 206·292	60 22·33	21·4405	08·9179
32	66 42 13	+5 02 56	4 15 37·73	+26 24 05·5	361 026·011	60 44·21	22·5357	09·9817

EPHEMERIS FOR PHYSICAL OBSERVATIONS
FOR 0^h TERRESTRIAL TIME

Julian Date	The Earth's Selenographic Long.	The Earth's Selenographic Lat.	The Sun's Selenographic Colong.	The Sun's Selenographic Lat.	Position Angle Axis	Position Angle Bright Limb	Semi-diameter	Fraction Illum.
246	°	°	°	°	°	°	′ ″	
0995·5	+5·311	+2·448	217·84	−1·46	21·892	111·60	14 54·12	0·158
0996·5	+4·118	+3·674	230·03	−1·48	21·153	108·59	14 48·38	0·095
0997·5	+2·850	+4·729	242·23	−1·49	19·597	102·98	14 44·41	0·047
0998·5	+1·549	+5·574	254·43	−1·50	17·196	91·47	14 42·06	0·016
0999·5	+0·246	+6·177	266·62	−1·50	13·941	47·81	14 41·18	0·002
1000·5	−1·037	+6·513	278·82	−1·51	9·892	312·37	14 41·72	0·006
1001·5	−2·285	+6·567	291·02	−1·51	5·213	289·55	14 43·68	0·028
1002·5	−3·480	+6·336	303·21	−1·52	0·177	278·16	14 47·15	0·067
1003·5	−4·598	+5·823	315·40	−1·52	355·131	269·55	14 52·27	0·122
1004·5	−5·607	+5·042	327·59	−1·52	350·415	262·43	14 59·20	0·192
1005·5	−6·459	+4·018	339·77	−1·52	346·294	256·62	15 08·08	0·275
1006·5	−7·095	+2·782	351·94	−1·52	342·927	252·11	15 18·94	0·369
1007·5	−7·446	+1·380	4·11	−1·52	340·397	248·96	15 31·64	0·471
1008·5	−7·440	−0·134	16·27	−1·52	338·749	247·24	15 45·81	0·577
1009·5	−7·008	−1·685	28·42	−1·52	338·038	247·07	16 00·75	0·683
1010·5	−6·108	−3·182	40·57	−1·52	338·365	248·71	16 15·38	0·783
1011·5	−4·735	−4·520	52·71	−1·52	339·883	252·63	16 28·35	0·871
1012·5	−2·944	−5·584	64·84	−1·52	342·765	259·95	16 38·12	0·940
1013·5	−0·857	−6·271	76·97	−1·53	347·099	275·44	16 43·33	0·984
1014·5	+1·348	−6·511	89·10	−1·53	352·708	357·80	16 43·12	0·998
1015·5	+3·461	−6·284	101·22	−1·53	359·044	71·66	16 37·42	0·982
1016·5	+5·287	−5·623	113·35	−1·53	5·316	88·25	16 26·95	0·938
1017·5	+6·679	−4·608	125·48	−1·53	10·826	98·02	16 13·06	0·870
1018·5	+7·560	−3·338	137·62	−1·53	15·209	104·75	15 57·32	0·786
1019·5	+7·916	−1·918	149·76	−1·53	18·407	109·27	15 41·25	0·690
1020·5	+7·788	−0·441	161·91	−1·53	20·521	111·99	15 26·10	0·589
1021·5	+7·247	+1·016	174·07	−1·53	21·678	113·18	15 12·74	0·488
1022·5	+6·384	+2·388	186·23	−1·53	21·974	113·01	15 01·67	0·390
1023·5	+5·288	+3·626	198·40	−1·53	21·454	111·53	14 53·12	0·299
1024·5	+4·047	+4·689	210·57	−1·53	20·118	108·74	14 47·11	0·216
1025·5	+2·733	+5·541	222·75	−1·53	17·942	104·49	14 43·50	0·144
1026·5	+1·407	+6·153	234·93	−1·53	14·910	98·45	14 42·03	0·085
1027·5	+0·114	+6·502	247·12	−1·52	11·053	89·66	14 42·45	0·041
1028·5	−1·118	+6·570	259·31	−1·52	6·499	73·79	14 44·48	0·012
1029·5	−2·268	+6·350	271·50	−1·51	1·496	10·55	14 47·87	0·002
1030·5	−3·326	+5·845	283·69	−1·50	356·386	288·77	14 52·45	0·010
1031·5	−4·280	+5·068	295·87	−1·49	351·533	270·21	14 58·12	0·036
1032·5	−5·116	+4·047	308·06	−1·48	347·234	260·75	15 04·87	0·081
1033·5	−5·810	+2·818	320·24	−1·47	343·679	254·46	15 12·72	0·143
1034·5	−6·325	+1·432	332·42	−1·45	340·956	250·17	15 21·72	0·221
1035·5	−6·615	−0·052	344·59	−1·44	339·098	247·53	15 31·84	0·313
1036·5	−6·625	−1·566	356·75	−1·42	338·133	246·42	15 42·97	0·415
1037·5	−6·298	−3·028	8·91	−1·41	338·120	246·85	15 54·75	0·523
1038·5	−5·594	−4·350	21·06	−1·39	339·171	248·93	16 06·59	0·634
1039·5	−4·495	−5·438	33·20	−1·38	341·441	252·85	16 17·60	0·740
1040·5	−3·031	−6·199	45·34	−1·36	345·065	258·86	16 26·67	0·836
1041·5	−1·280	−6·556	57·47	−1·35	350·032	267·36	16 32·63	0·914

NOTES AND FORMULAE

Low-precision formulae for geocentric coordinates of the Moon

The following formulae give approximate geocentric coordinates of the Moon. During the period 1900 to 2100 the errors will rarely exceed $0^\circ\!.3$ in ecliptic longitude (λ), $0^\circ\!.2$ in ecliptic latitude (β), $0^\circ\!.003$ in horizontal parallax (π), $0^\circ\!.001$ in semidiameter (SD), 0·2 Earth radii in distance (r), $0^\circ\!.3$ in right ascension (α) and $0^\circ\!.2$ in declination (δ).

On this page the time argument T is the number of Julian centuries from J2000·0.

$$T = (\mathrm{JD} - 245\,1545{\cdot}0)/36\,525 = (9130{\cdot}5 + \text{day of year} + (\mathrm{UT1} + \Delta T)/24)/36\,525$$

where day of year is given on pages B4–B5. The Universal Time (UT1) and $\Delta T = \mathrm{TT} - \mathrm{UT1}$ (see pages K8–K9), are expressed in hours. To the precision quoted ΔT may be ignored.

$$\begin{aligned}
\lambda = {} & 218^\circ\!.32 + 481\,267^\circ\!.881\,T \\
& + 6^\circ\!.29 \sin(135^\circ\!.0 + 477\,198^\circ\!.87\,T) - 1^\circ\!.27 \sin(259^\circ\!.3 - 413\,335^\circ\!.36\,T) \\
& + 0^\circ\!.66 \sin(235^\circ\!.7 + 890\,534^\circ\!.22\,T) + 0^\circ\!.21 \sin(269^\circ\!.9 + 954\,397^\circ\!.74\,T) \\
& - 0^\circ\!.19 \sin(357^\circ\!.5 + 35\,999^\circ\!.05\,T) - 0^\circ\!.11 \sin(186^\circ\!.5 + 966\,404^\circ\!.03\,T)
\end{aligned}$$

$$\begin{aligned}
\beta = {} & + 5^\circ\!.13 \sin(93^\circ\!.3 + 483\,202^\circ\!.02\,T) + 0^\circ\!.28 \sin(228^\circ\!.2 + 960\,400^\circ\!.89\,T) \\
& - 0^\circ\!.28 \sin(318^\circ\!.3 + 6\,003^\circ\!.15\,T) - 0^\circ\!.17 \sin(217^\circ\!.6 - 407\,332^\circ\!.21\,T)
\end{aligned}$$

$$\begin{aligned}
\pi = {} & + 0^\circ\!.9508 + 0^\circ\!.0518 \cos(135^\circ\!.0 + 477\,198^\circ\!.87\,T) + 0^\circ\!.0095 \cos(259^\circ\!.3 - 413\,335^\circ\!.36\,T) \\
& + 0^\circ\!.0078 \cos(235^\circ\!.7 + 890\,534^\circ\!.22\,T) + 0^\circ\!.0028 \cos(269^\circ\!.9 + 954\,397^\circ\!.74\,T)
\end{aligned}$$

$$SD = 0{\cdot}2724\,\pi \qquad \text{and} \qquad r = 1/\sin\pi$$

Form the geocentric direction cosines (l, m, n) from:

$$\begin{aligned}
l &= \cos\beta\cos\lambda &&= \cos\delta\cos\alpha \\
m &= +0{\cdot}9175\cos\beta\sin\lambda - 0{\cdot}3978\sin\beta &&= \cos\delta\sin\alpha \\
n &= +0{\cdot}3978\cos\beta\sin\lambda + 0{\cdot}9175\sin\beta &&= \sin\delta
\end{aligned}$$

Then

$$\alpha = \tan^{-1}(m/l) \qquad \text{and} \qquad \delta = \sin^{-1}(n)$$

where the quadrant of α is determined by the signs of l and m, and where α, δ are referred to the mean equator and equinox of date.

Low-precision formulae for topocentric coordinates of the Moon

The following formulae give approximate topocentric values of right ascension (α'), declination (δ'), distance (r'), parallax (π') and semidiameter (SD').

Form the geocentric rectangular coordinates (x, y, z) from:

$$\begin{aligned}
x &= rl = r\cos\delta\cos\alpha \\
y &= rm = r\cos\delta\sin\alpha \\
z &= rn = r\sin\delta
\end{aligned}$$

Form the topocentric rectangular coordinates (x', y', z') from:

$$\begin{aligned}
x' &= x - \cos\phi'\cos\theta_0 \\
y' &= y - \cos\phi'\sin\theta_0 \\
z' &= z - \sin\phi'
\end{aligned}$$

where (ϕ', λ') are the observer's geocentric latitude and longitude (east positive). The local sidereal time (see page B8) may be approximated by

$$\theta_0 = 100^\circ\!.46 + 36\,000^\circ\!.77\,T_U + \lambda' + 15\,\mathrm{UT1}$$

where $T_U = (\mathrm{JD} - 245\,1545{\cdot}0)/36\,525 = (9130{\cdot}5 + \text{day of year} + \mathrm{UT1}/24)/36\,525$

Then

$$r' = (x'^2 + y'^2 + z'^2)^{1/2} \qquad \alpha' = \tan^{-1}(y'/x') \qquad \delta' = \sin^{-1}(z'/r')$$

$$\pi' = \sin^{-1}(1/r') \qquad SD' = 0{\cdot}2724\pi'$$

CONTENTS OF SECTION E

NOTES AND FORMULAS

Orbital elements

The heliocentric osculating orbital elements for the Earth given on page E8 and the heliocentric coordinates and velocity of the Earth on page E7 actually refer to the Earth-Moon barycenter. The heliocentric coordinates and velocity of the Earth itself are given by:

$$\text{(Earth's center)} = \text{(Earth-Moon barycenter)} - (0.000\,0312 \cos L,\ 0.000\,0286 \sin L,\ 0.000\,0124 \sin L,\ -0.000\,00718 \sin L,\ 0.000\,00657 \cos L,\ 0.000\,00285 \cos L)$$

where $L = 218° + 481\,268°\,T$, with T in Julian centuries from JD 245 1545.0. This estimate is accurate to the fifth decimal place in position and the sixth decimal place in velocity. The position and velocity are with respect to the mean equator and equinox of J2000.0, in units of au and au/day, respectively.

Linear interpolation of the heliocentric osculating orbital elements usually leads to errors of about 1″ or 2″ in the resulting geocentric positions of the Sun and planets; the errors may, however, reach about 7″ for Venus at inferior conjunction and about 3″ for Mars at opposition.

Heliocentric coordinates

The heliocentric ecliptic coordinates of the Earth may be obtained from the geocentric ecliptic coordinates of the Sun given on pages C6–C20 by adding ± 180° to the longitude, and reversing the sign of the latitude.

Invariable plane of the solar system

Approximate coordinates of the north pole of the invariable plane are:

$$\alpha_0 = 273\overset{\circ}{.}85 \qquad \delta_0 = 66\overset{\circ}{.}99$$

from Souami & Souchay (2012, A&A, 543, A133). This is the direction of the total angular momentum vector of the solar system (Sun and major planets) with respect to the ICRS coordinate axes.

Semidiameter and horizontal parallax

The apparent angular semidiameter, s, of a planet is given by:

$$s = \text{semidiameter at 1 au / distance in au}$$

where the distance in au is given in the daily geocentric ephemeris on pages E18–E45. Unless otherwise specified, the semidiameters at unit distance (1 au) are for equatorial radii. They are:

Planet	Semi-diameter	Planet	Semi-diameter	Planet	Semi-diameter
	″		″		″
Mercury	3.36	Jupiter: equatorial	98.57	Uranus: equatorial	35.24
Venus	8.34	Jupiter: polar	92.18	Uranus: polar	34.43
Mars: equatorial	4.68	Saturn: equatorial	83.10	Neptune: equatorial	34.14
Mars: polar	4.65	Saturn: polar	74.96	Neptune: polar	33.56

The difference in transit times of the limb and center of a planet in seconds of time is given approximately by:

$$\text{difference in transit time} = (s \text{ in seconds of arc}) / 15 \cos\delta$$

where the sidereal motion of the planet is ignored.

The equatorial horizontal parallax of a planet is given by $8\overset{''}{.}794\,143$ divided by its distance in au; formulas for the corrections for diurnal parallax are given on page B85.

NOTES AND FORMULAS

Time of transit of a planet

The transit times that are tabulated on pages E46–E53 are expressed in terrestrial time (TT) and refer to the transits over the ephemeris meridian; for most purposes, this may be regarded as giving the universal time (UT) of transit over the Greenwich meridian.

The UT of transit over a local meridian is given by:

$$\text{time of ephemeris transit} - (\lambda/24) \times \text{first difference}$$

with an error that is usually less than 1 second, where λ is the *east* longitude in hours and the first difference is about 24 hours.

Times of rising and setting

Approximate times of the rising and setting of a planet at a place with latitude φ may be obtained from the time of transit by applying the value of the hour angle h of the point on the horizon at the same declination δ as the planet; h is given by:

$$\cos h \;=\; -\tan \varphi \, \tan \delta$$

This ignores the sidereal motion of the planet during the interval between transit and rising or setting and the effects of refraction ($\sim$ 2.25 minutes). Similarly, the time at which a planet reaches a zenith distance z may be obtained by determining the corresponding hour angle h:

$$\cos h \;=\; -\tan \varphi \, \tan \delta + \sec \varphi \, \sec \delta \, \cos z$$

and applying h to the time of transit.

Ephemeris for physical observations

Explanatory information for data presented in the ephemeris for physical observations (E54–E79) of the planets and the planetary central meridians (E80–E87) is given here. Additional information is given in the Notes and References section, on page L12.

The tabulated surface brightness is the average visual magnitude of an area of one square arcsecond of the illuminated portion of the apparent disk. For a few days around inferior and superior conjunctions, the tabulated surface brightness and magnitude of Mercury and Venus are unknown; surface brightness values are given for phase angles $2^{\circ}\!.1 < \phi < 169^{\circ}\!.5$ for Mercury and $2^{\circ}\!.2 < \phi < 179^{\circ}\!.0$ for Venus. For Saturn, the magnitude includes the contribution due to the rings, but the surface brightness applies only to the disk of the planet.

The diagram on the next page illustrates many of the quantities tabulated. The primary reference points are the sub-Earth point, e (center of the apparent disk); the sub-solar point, s; and the north pole of the planet, n. Points e and s are on the lines of sight (taking into account light-time and aberration) between the center of a planet and the centers of the Earth and Sun, respectively. An observer on the body's surface at point e or point s would see the apparent center of the Earth or the Sun at the planetocentric zenith, respectively.

For points e and s, planetographic longitudes, λ_e and λ_s, and planetographic latitudes, β_e and β_s, are given. Planetographic longitude is reckoned from the prime meridian and increases from 0° to 360° in the direction opposite rotation. Planetographic latitude is the angle between the planet's equator and the normal to the reference spheroid at the point. Latitudes north of the equator are positive for planets.

For points s and n, apparent distances from the center of the disk, d_s and d_n, and apparent position angles, p_s and p_n, are given. Position angles are measured east from north on the celestial sphere, with north defined by the great circle on the celestial sphere passing through the center of the planet's apparent disk and the true celestial pole of date. Apparent distances are positive in the visible hemisphere and negative on the far side of the planet, so the sign of the distance may change abruptly for points near the limb. Points close to e may appear to be discontinuous in the tables because distance and position angle can vary rapidly and the tabular interval is fixed.

NOTES AND FORMULAS

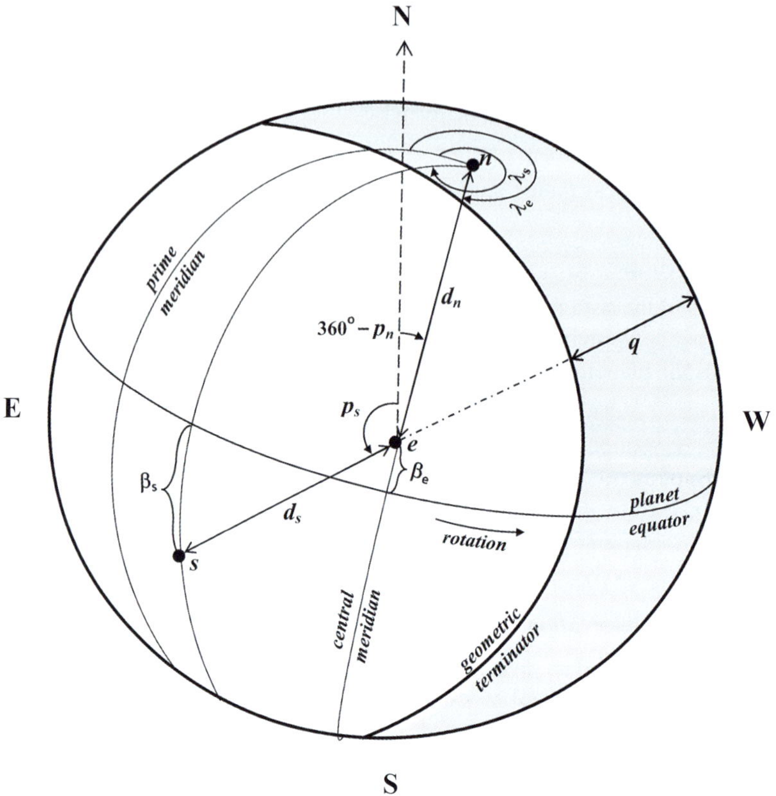

Diagram illustrating many of the physical ephemeris values

The phase is the ratio of the illuminated area of the disk to the total area of the disk, as seen from the Earth. The phase angle, ϕ, is the planetocentric elongation of the Earth from the Sun. The defect of illumination, q, is the length of the unilluminated section of the diameter passing through e and s. The position angle of q can be computed by adding 180° to p_s. Phase and q are based on the geometric terminator, defined by the plane crossing through the planet's center of mass, orthogonal to the direction of the Sun. Both the phase and q assume that the change in their values caused by the flattening of the planet is insignificant.

The planetocentric orbital longitude of the Sun, L_s, is measured eastward in the planet's orbital plane from the planet's vernal equinox. Instantaneous orbital and equatorial planes are used in computing L_s. Values of L_s of 0°, 90°, 180°, and 270° correspond to the beginning of spring, summer, autumn and winter, for the northern hemisphere of a planet. For small solar system bodies, such as dwarf planets and minor planets, L_s=0 corresponds to the beginning of spring in the hemisphere in which the rotation about the pole is counterclockwise.

The angle W of the prime meridian is measured counterclockwise (when viewed from above the planet's north pole) along the planet's equator from the ascending node of the planet's equator on the ICRS equator. For a planet with direct rotation (counterclockwise viewed from the planet's north pole), W increases with time. Values of W and their rates of change are given on page E5.

Longitudes of the planetary central meridians are sub-Earth planetographic longitudes, λ_e, measured from the planet's prime meridian. None are given for Uranus and Neptune since their rotational periods are not well known. Cassini mission data calls into question Saturn's rotation rate.

ROTATION ELEMENTS REFERRED TO THE ICRS
at 2025 JANUARY 0, 0^h TDB

Planet	North Pole Right Ascension α_1	North Pole Declination δ_1	Argument of Prime Meridian at epoch W_0	Argument of Prime Meridian var./day $\dot{W}$	Longitude of Central Meridian λ_e	Inclination of Equator to Orbit
	°	°	°	°	°	°
Mercury	281.00	+ 61.41	217.28	+ 6.1385108	149.22	+ 0.03
Venus	272.76	+ 67.16	314.56	− 1.4813688	189.20	+ 2.64
Mars	317.66	+ 52.87	355.88	+ 350.8919824	96.35	+ 25.19
Jupiter I	268.06	+ 64.50	333.05	+ 877.9000000	57.09	+ 3.12
II	268.06	+ 64.50	123.54	+ 870.2700000	207.76	+ 3.12
III	268.06	+ 64.50	273.90	+ 870.5360000	358.12	+ 3.12
Saturn	40.58	+ 83.54	312.63	+ 810.7939024	229.64	+ 26.73
Uranus	257.31	− 15.18	321.58	− 501.1600928	174.75	+ 82.23
Neptune	299.48	+ 42.96	126.61	+ 541.1397757	237.19	+ 28.35

Rotational elements definitions and formulas

α_1, δ_1 right ascension and declination of the north pole of the planet; variations during one year are negligible.

W_0 the angle measured from the planet's equator in the positive sense with respect to the planet's north pole from the ascending node of the planet's equator on the Earth's mean equator of date to the prime meridian of the planet.

$\dot{W}$ the mean daily rate of change of W_0. Sidereal periods of rotation are given on page E6.

Given:

α, δ: apparent right ascension and declination of planet (pages E18–E45).
s: apparent equatorial diameter (pages E54–E79).
p_n: position angle of north pole (or central meridian or axis) (pages E54–E79).
λ_e: planetographic longitude of the sub-Earth point (or central meridian) (pages E54–E77 or E80–E87).
β_e: planetographic latitude of the sub-Earth point (pages E54–E79).
$\dot{W}$: from the above table.
f: geometric flattening (from page E6).

To compute the displacements $\Delta\alpha$, $\Delta\delta$ in right ascension and declination, measured from the center of the disk, of a feature at planetographic longitude λ and planetographic latitude ϕ, first compute the planetocentric quantities ϕ', β'_e, λ', and λ'_e, and the quantity s'. The formulas on the right may be used for planets where the flattening f is small and can be ignored [1]:

$\tan\phi' = (1-f)^2\tan\phi$	$\phi' = \phi$
$\tan\beta'_e = (1-f)^2\tan\beta_e$	$\beta'_e = \beta_e$
$\lambda' = 360° - \lambda$ if $\dot{W}$ is positive; $\lambda' = \lambda$ if $\dot{W}$ is negative	λ' as at left
$\lambda'_e = 360° - \lambda_e$ if $\dot{W}$ is positive; $\lambda'_e = \lambda_e$ if $\dot{W}$ is negative	λ'_e as at left
$s' = \frac{1}{2}s(1 - f\sin^2\phi')$	$s' = \frac{1}{2}s$

Then compute the quantities X, Y, and Z:

$$X = s'\cos\phi'\sin(\lambda' - \lambda'_e)$$
$$Y = s'\left(\sin\phi'\cos\beta'_e - \cos\phi'\sin\beta'_e\cos(\lambda' - \lambda'_e)\right)$$
$$Z = s'\left(\sin\phi'\sin\beta'_e + \cos\phi'\cos\beta'_e\cos(\lambda' - \lambda'_e)\right)$$

Finally,

$$\Delta\alpha\cos\delta = -X\cos p_n + Y\sin p_n$$
$$\Delta\delta = X\sin p_n + Y\cos p_n$$

If Z is positive, the feature is on the near (visible) side of the planet; if Z is negative, it is on the far side. If $|Z| < 0.1\,s'$, the feature is on or very near the limb.

[1] The flattening is negligible if only one apparent diameter is given, or if the difference between the apparent equatorial and polar diameters is not significant to the precision required.

PHYSICAL AND PHOTOMETRIC DATA

Planet	Mass[1]	Mean Equatorial Radius	Minimum Geocentric Distance[2]	Flattening[3] (geometric)	Coefficients of the Potential J_2	J_3	J_4
	kg	km	au		10^{-3}	10^{-6}	10^{-6}
Mercury	3.3010×10^{23}	2440.53	0.549	0.000 930	0.050333	12.473	17.679
Venus	4.8673×10^{24}	6052	0.265	0	0.004404	– 2.108	– 2.147
Earth	5.9721×10^{24}	6378.1366	—	0.003 352 81	1.082625	– 2.532	– 1.616
(Moon)	7.3458×10^{22}	1737.4	0.002 38	0	0.203216	8.460	– 9.704
Mars	6.4169×10^{23}	3396.2	0.373	0.005 886	1.956609	31.148	– 15.39
Jupiter	1.8981×10^{27}	71492	3.945	0.064 9	14.698	—	– 586.6
Saturn	5.6831×10^{26}	60268	8.032	0.098 0	16.29057	0.06	– 935.31
Uranus	8.6809×10^{25}	25559	17.292	0.023 0	3.5107	—	– 34.0
Neptune	1.0241×10^{26}	24764	28.814	0.017	3.408	—	– 33.0

Planet	Period of Rotation	Mean Density	Maximum Angular Diameter[2]	Geometric Albedo	Visual Magnitude[4] $V(1,0)$	V_0	Color Indices $B-V$	$U-B$
	d	g/cm³	″					
Mercury	58.646 145 9	5.43	12.3	0.142	– 0.61	—	0.97	0.41
Venus	243.018 5	5.24	63.0	0.689	– 4.38	—	0.71	0.50
Earth	0.997 269 566	5.513	—	0.434	– 3.99	—	0.47	– 0.12
(Moon)	27.321 66	3.34	2010.8	0.113	+ 0.23	– 12.72	0.85	0.36
Mars	1.025 956 76	3.93	25.1	0.170	– 1.60	– 2.09	1.36	0.64
Jupiter	0.413 54 (System III)	1.33	49.9	0.538	– 9.40	– 2.70	0.86	0.43
Saturn	0.444 01	0.69	20.7	0.499	– 8.91	+ 0.64	1.07	0.76
Uranus	0.718 33	1.27	4.1	0.488	– 7.11	+ 5.60	0.50	0.33
Neptune	0.665 26	1.64	2.4	0.442	– 7.00	+ 7.11	0.39	0.17

NOTES TO TABLE

[1] Values for the masses include the atmospheres but exclude satellites.

[2] The tabulated minimum geocentric distance applies to the interval 1950 to 2050.

[3] The flattening for Mars is calculated by using the average of its north and south polar radii.

[4] $V(1,0)$ is the visual magnitude at 1 au and phase angle zero; V_0 is the mean opposition magnitude.

HELIOCENTRIC COORDINATES AND VELOCITY COMPONENTS REFERRED TO THE MEAN EQUATOR AND EQUINOX OF J2000.0

Julian Date (TDB) 246	x	y	z	$\dot{x}$	$\dot{y}$	$\dot{z}$
MERCURY	au	au	au	au/day	au/day	au/day
0640.5	+0.326 8633	+ 0.088 5931	+ 0.013 4493	−0.012 656 58	+0.024 715 91	+0.014 515 05
0720.5	+0.353 5778	− 0.113 7722	− 0.097 4231	+0.005 072 27	+0.024 387 65	+0.012 502 22
0800.5	+0.263 6236	− 0.282 5785	− 0.178 2767	+0.016 386 02	+0.017 333 95	+0.007 561 55
0880.5	+0.108 4529	− 0.384 3239	− 0.216 5470	+0.021 670 51	+0.008 035 58	+0.002 046 65
0960.5	−0.069 1272	− 0.409 7638	− 0.211 7324	+0.022 177 66	−0.001 625 68	−0.003 166 96
1040.5	−0.234 1007	− 0.359 7539	− 0.167 9191	+0.018 556 37	−0.010 782 84	−0.007 683 41
1120.5	−0.353 9710	− 0.241 3435	− 0.092 2414	+0.010 813 22	−0.018 618 24	−0.011 066 60
VENUS						
0640.5	+0.721 2437	− 0.056 5938	− 0.071 0964	+0.002 142 45	+0.018 298 94	+0.008 098 35
0720.5	−0.382 0484	+ 0.545 5299	+ 0.269 6408	−0.017 192 47	−0.010 313 70	−0.003 553 10
0800.5	−0.234 0810	− 0.631 8657	− 0.269 5120	+0.019 007 71	−0.005 592 11	−0.003 718 85
0880.5	+0.688 8853	+ 0.219 9378	+ 0.055 3822	−0.006 319 69	+0.017 316 80	+0.008 191 89
0960.5	−0.601 8388	+ 0.342 4247	+ 0.192 1575	−0.011 093 39	−0.015 819 23	−0.006 416 37
1040.5	+0.068 9071	− 0.658 6140	− 0.300 7171	+0.019 999 24	+0.002 141 17	−0.000 301 81
1120.5	+0.533 3556	+ 0.457 1728	+ 0.171 9717	−0.013 713 51	+0.013 217 84	+0.006 815 25
EARTH*						
0640.5	+0.434 5895	+ 0.813 0031	+ 0.352 4227	−0.015 726 86	+0.006 891 61	+0.002 987 51
0720.5	−0.810 8208	+ 0.517 2098	+ 0.224 2081	−0.010 100 86	−0.013 019 59	−0.005 643 75
0800.5	−0.720 4282	− 0.647 4910	− 0.280 6715	+0.011 760 12	−0.011 335 40	−0.004 913 77
0880.5	+0.523 4959	− 0.798 7169	− 0.346 2328	+0.014 464 90	+0.008 075 70	+0.003 500 58
0960.5	+0.946 1616	+ 0.291 6212	+ 0.126 4070	−0.005 757 76	+0.014 904 06	+0.006 460 68
1040.5	−0.157 0320	+ 0.890 6671	+ 0.386 0892	−0.017 263 14	−0.002 580 09	−0.001 118 32
1120.5	−0.995 9968	− 0.000 2993	− 0.000 1236	−0.000 273 86	−0.015 844 26	−0.006 868 20
MARS						
0640.5	−0.047 026	+ 1.429 390	+ 0.656 894	−0.013 458 67	+0.000 569 39	+0.000 624 229
0720.5	−1.034 363	+ 1.154 443	+ 0.557 416	−0.010 359 52	−0.007 009 77	−0.002 935 779
0800.5	−1.599 751	+ 0.399 788	+ 0.226 524	−0.003 319 78	−0.011 178 22	−0.005 037 648
0880.5	−1.524 059	− 0.513 413	− 0.194 382	+0.005 260 77	−0.010 831 99	−0.005 110 284
0960.5	−0.792 493	− 1.196 091	− 0.527 243	+0.012 494 20	−0.005 382 70	−0.002 805 922
1040.5	+0.326 443	− 1.261 867	− 0.587 593	+0.014 153 21	+0.004 137 74	+0.001 516 141
1120.5	+1.227 488	− 0.562 899	− 0.291 296	+0.006 942 77	+0.012 466 10	+0.005 530 657
JUPITER						
0640.5	+1.323 488	+ 4.510 867	+ 1.901 264	−0.007 378 89	+0.002 072 92	+0.001 068 127
0720.5	+0.725 031	+ 4.643 713	+ 1.972 773	−0.007 564 01	+0.001 246 37	+0.000 718 352
0800.5	+0.116 191	+ 4.710 166	+ 2.016 077	−0.007 638 77	+0.000 415 28	+0.000 363 941
0880.5	−0.494 304	+ 4.710 368	+ 2.031 024	−0.007 605 95	−0.000 407 97	+0.000 010 275
0960.5	−1.097 994	+ 4.645 399	+ 2.017 871	−0.007 469 35	−0.001 212 14	−0.000 337 741
1040.5	−1.686 771	+ 4.517 221	+ 1.977 263	−0.007 234 15	−0.001 986 49	−0.000 675 376
1120.5	−2.253 005	+ 4.328 604	+ 1.910 200	−0.006 906 94	0.002 721 69	−0.000 998 459
SATURN						
0640.5	+9.433 510	− 1.663 726	− 1.093 370	+0.000 821 84	+0.005 054 70	+0.002 052 342
0720.5	+9.489 224	− 1.257 762	− 0.928 096	+0.000 570 50	+0.005 092 63	+0.002 078 814
0800.5	+9.524 716	− 0.849 184	− 0.760 872	+0.000 316 33	+0.005 120 09	+0.002 101 093
0880.5	+9.539 763	− 0.438 833	− 0.592 036	+0.000 059 43	+0.005 136 84	+0.002 119 067
0960.5	+9.534 170	− 0.027 588	− 0.421 943	−0.000 199 51	+0.005 142 41	+0.002 132 503
1040.5	+9.507 805	+ 0.383 657	− 0.250 956	−0.000 459 82	+0.005 136 84	+0.002 141 404
1120.5	+9.460 570	+ 0.794 006	− 0.079 441	−0.000 721 14	+0.005 119 94	+0.002 145 674
URANUS						
0640.5	+11.22 120	+ 14.73 240	+ 6.293 54	−0.003 257 62	+0.001 885 64	+0.000 871 936
0720.5	+10.95 916	+ 14.88 134	+ 6.362 48	−0.003 293 09	+0.001 837 74	+0.000 851 473
0800.5	+10.69 433	+ 15.02 643	+ 6.429 77	−0.003 327 50	+0.001 789 42	+0.000 830 805
0880.5	+10.42 678	+ 15.16 764	+ 6.495 40	−0.003 361 25	+0.001 740 66	+0.000 809 936
0960.5	+10.15 656	+ 15.30 491	+ 6.559 35	−0.003 394 13	+0.001 691 19	+0.000 788 741
1040.5	+9.883 74	+ 15.43 821	+ 6.621 60	−0.003 426 00	+0.001 641 26	+0.000 767 329
1120.5	+9.608 41	+ 15.56 750	+ 6.682 12	−0.003 457 05	+0.001 590 84	+0.000 745 696
NEPTUNE						
0640.5	+29.87 830	− 0.418 50	− 0.915 11	+0.000 051 36	+0.002 926 38	+0.001 196 543
0720.5	+29.88 133	− 0.184 41	− 0.819 37	+0.000 024 57	+0.002 925 74	+0.001 196 931
0800.5	+29.88 224	+ 0.049 62	− 0.723 60	−0.000 001 94	+0.002 925 03	+0.001 197 286
0880.5	+29.88 102	+ 0.283 59	− 0.627 80	−0.000 028 57	+0.002 924 21	+0.001 197 608
0960.5	+29.87 767	+ 0.517 48	− 0.531 99	−0.000 055 12	+0.002 923 04	+0.001 197 769
1040.5	+29.87 220	+ 0.751 27	− 0.436 16	−0.000 081 46	+0.002 921 73	+0.001 197 873
1120.5	+29.86 463	+ 0.984 95	− 0.340 33	−0.000 107 80	+0.002 920 24	+0.001 197 912

*Values labeled for the Earth are actually for the Earth-Moon barycenter;

HELIOCENTRIC OSCULATING ORBITAL ELEMENTS REFERRED TO THE MEAN EQUINOX AND ECLIPTIC OF J2000.0

Julian Date (TDB) 246	Inclin-ation i	Longitude Asc. Node Ω	Longitude Perihelion ϖ	Semimajor Axis a	Daily Motion n	Eccen-tricity e	Mean Longitude L
MERCURY	°	°	°	au	°		°
0640.5	7.003 52	48.2998	77.4955	0.387 0986	4.092 339	0. 205 6402	34.117 67
0680.5	7.003 51	48.2998	77.4956	0.387 0988	4.092 337	0. 205 6387	197.811 27
0720.5	7.003 49	48.2996	77.4969	0.387 0986	4.092 340	0. 205 6377	1.504 15
0760.5	7.003 50	48.2995	77.4974	0.387 0996	4.092 325	0. 205 6400	165.197 48
0800.5	7.003 49	48.2994	77.4978	0.387 0972	4.092 363	0. 205 6491	328.890 69
0840.5	7.003 49	48.2993	77.4974	0.387 0973	4.092 360	0. 205 6507	132.585 06
0880.5	7.003 47	48.2992	77.4976	0.387 0976	4.092 356	0. 205 6491	296.279 34
0920.5	7.003 46	48.2990	77.4976	0.387 0975	4.092 358	0. 205 6499	99.973 51
0960.5	7.003 45	48.2989	77.4975	0.387 0975	4.092 357	0. 205 6474	263.668 01
1000.5	7.003 45	48.2988	77.4976	0.387 0977	4.092 355	0. 205 6465	67.362 04
1040.5	7.003 44	48.2988	77.4976	0.387 0980	4.092 350	0. 205 6429	231.056 44
1080.5	7.003 40	48.2982	77.4991	0.387 0985	4.092 341	0. 205 6323	34.748 82
VENUS							
0640.5	3.394 40	76.6117	131.831	0.723 3229	1.602 162	0. 006 7471	354.159 79
0680.5	3.394 40	76.6117	131.753	0.723 3289	1.602 142	0. 006 7464	58.246 04
0720.5	3.394 37	76.6115	131.677	0.723 3334	1.602 127	0. 006 7462	122.330 61
0760.5	3.394 36	76.6087	131.637	0.723 3415	1.602 100	0. 006 7612	186.413 91
0800.5	3.394 43	76.6073	131.548	0.723 3349	1.602 122	0. 006 7705	250.497 17
0840.5	3.394 43	76.6073	131.536	0.723 3277	1.602 146	0. 006 7809	314.582 07
0880.5	3.394 43	76.6072	131.538	0.723 3246	1.602 156	0. 006 7864	18.668 42
0920.5	3.394 42	76.6073	131.454	0.723 3317	1.602 132	0. 006 7885	82.754 23
0960.5	3.394 41	76.6071	131.406	0.723 3297	1.602 139	0. 006 7836	146.838 89
1000.5	3.394 41	76.6070	131.405	0.723 3285	1.602 143	0. 006 7812	210.924 69
1040.5	3.394 40	76.6070	131.478	0.723 3343	1.602 124	0. 006 7811	275.009 66
1080.5	3.394 39	76.6069	131.519	0.723 3316	1.602 133	0. 006 7853	339.094 21
EARTH*							
0640.5	0.003 24	174.2	102.9650	1.000 0200	0.985 580 8	0. 016 7153	65.070 41
0680.5	0.003 24	174.3	102.9302	1.000 0166	0.985 585 9	0. 016 7082	104.492 42
0720.5	0.003 24	174.3	102.9082	0.999 9956	0.985 617 0	0. 016 6879	143.916 67
0760.5	0.003 35	174.2	102.9104	0.999 9852	0.985 632 3	0. 016 6638	183.344 11
0800.5	0.003 41	174.6	102.9689	1.000 0040	0.985 604 5	0. 016 6455	222.770 54
0840.5	0.003 41	174.6	102.9983	1.000 0137	0.985 590 2	0. 016 6396	262.194 13
0880.5	0.003 41	174.7	103.0194	1.000 0091	0.985 597 0	0. 016 6443	301.617 17
0920.5	0.003 41	174.7	103.0635	0.999 9929	0.985 621 0	0. 016 6549	341.041 11
0960.5	0.003 42	174.7	103.1017	0.999 9814	0.985 638 0	0. 016 6579	20.466 30
1000.5	0.003 42	174.8	103.0839	0.999 9873	0.985 629 2	0. 016 6610	59.891 67
1040.5	0.003 42	174.9	103.0325	0.999 9990	0.985 611 9	0. 016 6677	99.315 24
1080.5	0.003 43	174.7	102.9728	0.999 9947	0.985 618 2	0. 016 6681	138.737 94

*Values labeled for the Earth are actually for the Earth-Moon barycenter (see note on page E2).

FORMULAS

Mean anomaly, $M = L - \varpi$

Argument of perihelion, measured from node, $\omega = \varpi - \Omega$

True anomaly, $\nu = M + (2e - e^3/4)\sin M + (5e^2/4)\sin 2M + (13e^3/12)\sin 3M + \ldots$ in radians.

Planet-Sun distance, $r = a(1 - e^2)/(1 + e\cos\nu)$

Heliocentric rectangular coordinates, referred to the ecliptic, may be computed from these elements by:

$$x = r\{\cos(\nu + \omega)\cos\Omega - \sin(\nu + \omega)\cos i\,\sin\Omega\}$$
$$y = r\{\cos(\nu + \omega)\sin\Omega + \sin(\nu + \omega)\cos i\,\cos\Omega\}$$
$$z = r\sin(\nu + \omega)\sin i$$

HELIOCENTRIC OSCULATING ORBITAL ELEMENTS REFERRED TO THE MEAN EQUINOX AND ECLIPTIC OF J2000.0

Julian Date (TDB) 246	Inclination i	Longitude Asc. Node Ω	Longitude Perihelion ϖ	Semimajor Axis a	Daily Motion n	Eccentricity e	Mean Longitude L
MARS	°	°	°	au	°		°
0640.5	1.847 64	49.4882	336.2083	1.523 7727	0.523 992 5	0.093 4065	81.780 49
0680.5	1.847 59	49.4864	336.1939	1.523 7232	0.524 018 1	0.093 4366	102.739 14
0720.5	1.847 57	49.4848	336.1764	1.523 6669	0.524 047 1	0.093 4642	123.701 04
0760.5	1.847 57	49.4836	336.1622	1.523 6243	0.524 069 1	0.093 4875	144.665 07
0800.5	1.847 57	49.4831	336.1541	1.523 5928	0.524 085 3	0.093 5097	165.629 75
0840.5	1.847 57	49.4831	336.1507	1.523 5829	0.524 090 4	0.093 5191	186.594 25
0880.5	1.847 56	49.4834	336.1477	1.523 5897	0.524 086 9	0.093 5168	207.558 10
0920.5	1.847 54	49.4836	336.1408	1.523 6126	0.524 075 1	0.093 5041	228.520 81
0960.5	1.847 53	49.4836	336.1282	1.523 6457	0.524 058 1	0.093 4918	249.482 63
1000.5	1.847 51	49.4834	336.1170	1.523 6708	0.524 045 1	0.093 4845	270.443 61
1040.5	1.847 50	49.4831	336.1092	1.523 6844	0.524 038 1	0.093 4807	291.404 23
1080.5	1.847 49	49.4823	336.1064	1.523 6800	0.524 040 3	0.093 4744	312.364 99
JUPITER							
0640.5	1.303 58	100.5177	14.0132	5.202 336	0.083 102 67	0.048 2898	70.116 88
0680.5	1.303 58	100.5176	14.0306	5.202 385	0.083 101 49	0.048 2839	73.442 34
0720.5	1.303 58	100.5176	14.0296	5.202 349	0.083 102 37	0.048 2711	76.767 68
0760.5	1.303 57	100.5178	14.0103	5.202 241	0.083 104 96	0.048 2584	80.092 46
0800.5	1.303 57	100.5177	13.9899	5.202 159	0.083 106 93	0.048 2594	83.415 96
0840.5	1.303 59	100.5176	13.9918	5.202 182	0.083 106 35	0.048 2687	86.739 25
0880.5	1.303 60	100.5175	14.0093	5.202 270	0.083 104 25	0.048 2779	90.062 79
0920.5	1.303 61	100.5175	14.0362	5.202 388	0.083 101 43	0.048 2785	93.387 23
0960.5	1.303 59	100.5175	14.0452	5.202 422	0.083 100 60	0.048 2724	96.712 06
1000.5	1.303 58	100.5175	14.0468	5.202 428	0.083 100 48	0.048 2688	100.036 50
1040.5	1.303 57	100.5175	14.0442	5.202 416	0.083 100 77	0.048 2683	103.360 59
1080.5	1.303 60	100.5177	14.0539	5.202 458	0.083 099 75	0.048 2702	106.684 31
SATURN							
0640.5	2.487 65	113.6215	91.3058	9.550 266	0.033 415 76	0.055 3588	354.515 95
0680.5	2.487 70	113.6231	91.4754	9.548 685	0.033 424 07	0.055 3931	355.853 33
0720.5	2.487 74	113.6244	91.6468	9.547 102	0.033 432 38	0.055 4089	357.189 28
0760.5	2.487 78	113.6259	91.8051	9.545 651	0.033 440 00	0.055 4061	358.524 01
0800.5	2.487 79	113.6265	91.9286	9.544 520	0.033 445 95	0.055 3958	359.858 96
0840.5	2.487 81	113.6270	92.0460	9.543 439	0.033 451 63	0.055 3932	1.195 38
0880.5	2.487 82	113.6276	92.1714	9.542 282	0.033 457 71	0.055 3939	2.532 63
0920.5	2.487 84	113.6287	92.3222	9.540 890	0.033 465 03	0.055 3931	3.870 11
0960.5	2.487 88	113.6303	92.4805	9.539 422	0.033 472 76	0.055 3751	5.206 24
1000.5	2.487 90	113.6314	92.6270	9.538 054	0.033 479 96	0.055 3475	6.541 95
1040.5	2.487 91	113.6321	92.7615	9.536 787	0.033 486 63	0.055 3130	7.877 46
1080.5	2.487 91	113.6320	92.8893	9.535 580	0.033 492 99	0.055 2809	9.213 82
URANUS							
0640.5	0.772 30	74.0274	165.9635	19.27 881	0.011 651 02	0.045 8594	59.955 79
0720.5	0.772 45	74.0235	166.0496	19.27 602	0.011 653 54	0.046 1563	60.918 02
0800.5	0.772 52	74.0218	166.2549	19.27 175	0.011 657 42	0.046 4077	61.872 27
0880.5	0.772 68	74.0183	166.3677	19.26 907	0.011 659 85	0.046 6223	62.825 59
0960.5	0.772 75	74.0167	166.5609	19.26 501	0.011 663 54	0.046 8840	63.782 46
1040.5	0.772 79	74.0160	166.8453	19.25 970	0.011 668 36	0.047 1192	64.734 64
1120.5	0.772 93	74.0135	167.1241	19.25 454	0.011 673 05	0.047 3416	65.686 27
NEPTUNE							
0640.5	1.769 73	131.7698	42.637	30.15 835	0.005 955 029	0.012 0435	359.533 07
0720.5	1.769 91	131.7764	45.079	30.13 918	0.005 960 713	0.011 6547	0.019 47
0800.5	1.770 09	131.7826	46.995	30.12 297	0.005 965 522	0.011 2838	0.496 08
0880.5	1.770 18	131.7858	48.855	30.10 905	0.005 969 661	0.010 9991	0.977 17
0960.5	1.770 37	131.7929	51.186	30.09 174	0.005 974 814	0.010 6346	1.456 05
1040.5	1.770 55	131.7996	53.220	30.07 596	0.005 979 516	0.010 2656	1.928 06
1120.5	1.770 63	131.8027	55.277	30.06 085	0.005 984 024	0.009 9184	2.400 19

HELIOCENTRIC POSITIONS FOR 0^h BARYCENTRIC DYNAMICAL TIME
MEAN EQUINOX AND ECLIPTIC OF J2000.0

Date	Longitude	Latitude	True Heliocentric Distance	Date	Longitude	Latitude	True Heliocentric Distance
	° ′ ″	° ′ ″	au		° ′ ″	° ′ ″	au
Jan. 0	199 14 31.1	+ 3 24 52.4	0.415 4489	Feb. 15	342 06 54.0	− 6 24 44.5	0.378 2384
1	202 39 49.4	+ 3 02 32.7	0.420 3046	16	346 23 41.0	− 6 11 06.3	0.372 4403
2	206 00 23.5	+ 2 40 05.3	0.424 9629	17	350 48 21.1	− 5 54 53.2	0.366 6328
3	209 16 35.1	+ 2 17 34.9	0.429 4122	18	355 21 14.2	− 5 35 57.7	0.360 8501
4	212 28 45.1	+ 1 55 05.5	0.433 6422	19	0 02 38.4	− 5 14 13.3	0.355 1298
5	215 37 13.2	+ 1 32 40.5	0.437 6441	20	4 52 49.2	− 4 49 35.0	0.349 5129
6	218 42 18.4	+ 1 10 22.8	0.441 4098	21	9 51 58.4	− 4 22 00.3	0.344 0433
7	221 44 18.7	+ 0 48 15.2	0.444 9324	22	15 00 13.6	− 3 51 29.1	0.338 7678
8	224 43 31.5	+ 0 26 19.7	0.448 2058	23	20 17 36.7	− 3 18 05.1	0.333 7358
9	227 40 13.4	+ 0 04 38.3	0.451 2247	24	25 44 03.0	− 2 41 56.3	0.328 9983
10	230 34 40.1	− 0 16 47.2	0.453 9843	25	31 19 20.2	− 2 03 15.6	0.324 6076
11	233 27 06.9	− 0 37 55.4	0.456 4806	26	37 03 06.8	− 1 22 21.5	0.320 6158
12	236 17 48.5	− 0 58 44.8	0.458 7103	27	42 54 51.9	− 0 39 38.0	0.317 0737
13	239 06 59.0	− 1 19 14.4	0.460 6702	28	48 53 54.1	+ 0 04 24.8	0.314 0293
14	241 54 52.2	− 1 39 22.9	0.462 3579	Mar. 1	54 59 21.1	+ 0 49 11.5	0.311 5262
15	244 41 41.3	− 1 59 09.3	0.463 7714	2	61 10 10.5	+ 1 34 02.5	0.309 6019
16	247 27 39.5	− 2 18 32.4	0.464 9089	3	67 25 10.0	+ 2 18 15.1	0.308 2865
17	250 12 59.4	− 2 37 31.4	0.465 7690	4	73 42 59.1	+ 3 01 05.4	0.307 6008
18	252 57 53.6	− 2 56 05.0	0.466 3509	5	80 02 11.3	+ 3 41 50.2	0.307 5561
19	255 42 34.5	− 3 14 12.4	0.466 6538	6	86 21 16.2	+ 4 19 49.5	0.308 1531
20	258 27 14.2	− 3 31 52.3	0.466 6775	7	92 38 42.8	+ 4 54 28.2	0.309 3820
21	261 12 05.0	− 3 49 03.7	0.466 4218	8	98 53 02.2	+ 5 25 17.4	0.311 2232
22	263 57 19.2	− 4 05 45.2	0.465 8871	9	105 02 50.8	+ 5 51 56.0	0.313 6479
23	266 43 08.8	− 4 21 55.4	0.465 0739	10	111 06 52.5	+ 6 14 10.8	0.316 6195
24	269 29 46.4	− 4 37 33.0	0.463 9833	11	117 04 00.9	+ 6 31 56.4	0.320 0952
25	272 17 24.3	− 4 52 36.3	0.462 6164	12	122 53 20.4	+ 6 45 14.6	0.324 0275
26	275 06 15.3	− 5 07 03.5	0.460 9749	13	128 34 07.0	+ 6 54 13.3	0.328 3658
27	277 56 32.3	− 5 20 52.6	0.459 0609	14	134 05 48.3	+ 6 59 05.4	0.333 0583
28	280 48 28.5	− 5 34 01.6	0.456 8767	15	139 28 02.8	+ 7 00 07.4	0.338 0525
29	283 42 17.5	− 5 46 28.0	0.454 4252	16	144 40 39.2	+ 6 57 38.1	0.343 2971
30	286 38 13.3	− 5 58 09.2	0.451 7099	17	149 43 34.9	+ 6 51 57.6	0.348 7426
31	289 36 30.3	− 6 09 02.3	0.448 7346	18	154 36 54.9	+ 6 43 26.7	0.354 3418
Feb. 1	292 37 23.4	− 6 19 04.2	0.445 5039	19	159 20 50.4	+ 6 32 25.5	0.360 0502
2	295 41 08.2	− 6 28 11.2	0.442 0231	20	163 55 37.4	+ 6 19 13.4	0.365 8265
3	298 48 00.6	− 6 36 19.7	0.438 2980	21	168 21 35.7	+ 6 04 08.7	0.371 6328
4	301 58 17.3	− 6 43 25.2	0.434 3356	22	172 39 07.9	+ 5 47 28.0	0.377 4342
5	305 12 15.7	− 6 49 23.2	0.430 1436	23	176 48 38.2	+ 5 29 26.7	0.383 1989
6	308 30 13.8	− 6 54 08.6	0.425 7307	24	180 50 31.8	+ 5 10 18.3	0.388 8982
7	311 52 30.3	− 6 57 35.8	0.421 1070	25	184 45 14.8	+ 4 50 15.2	0.394 5064
8	315 19 24.8	− 6 59 38.9	0.416 2838	26	188 33 13.1	+ 4 29 28.1	0.400 0002
9	318 51 17.3	− 7 00 11.4	0.411 2739	27	192 14 52.2	+ 4 08 06.4	0.405 3589
10	322 28 28.6	− 6 59 06.3	0.406 0917	28	195 50 37.3	+ 3 46 18.5	0.410 5639
11	326 11 20.3	− 6 56 16.3	0.400 7534	29	199 20 52.8	+ 3 24 11.4	0.415 5987
12	330 00 14.3	− 6 51 33.4	0.395 2773	30	202 46 02.1	+ 3 01 51.4	0.420 4488
13	333 55 32.9	− 6 44 49.5	0.389 6837	31	206 06 28.0	+ 2 39 23.8	0.425 1010
14	337 57 38.6	− 6 35 56.0	0.383 9956	Apr. 1	209 22 32.0	+ 2 16 53.4	0.429 5439
15	342 06 54.0	− 6 24 44.5	0.378 2384	2	212 34 34.9	+ 1 54 24.0	0.433 7673

HELIOCENTRIC POSITIONS FOR 0^h BARYCENTRIC DYNAMICAL TIME
MEAN EQUINOX AND ECLIPTIC OF J2000.0

Date	Longitude	Latitude	True Heliocentric Distance	Date	Longitude	Latitude	True Heliocentric Distance
	° ′ ″	° ′ ″	au		° ′ ″	° ′ ″	au
Apr. 1	209 22 32.0	+ 2 16 53.4	0.429 5439	May 17	355 29 39.1	− 5 35 20.5	0.360 6727
2	212 34 34.9	+ 1 54 24.0	0.433 7673	18	0 11 19.2	− 5 13 30.9	0.354 9546
3	215 42 56.6	+ 1 31 59.2	0.437 7622	19	5 01 46.4	− 4 48 47.3	0.349 3412
4	218 47 55.9	+ 1 09 41.8	0.441 5208	20	10 01 12.4	− 4 21 07.1	0.343 8764
5	221 49 50.9	+ 0 47 34.5	0.445 0360	21	15 09 44.6	− 3 50 30.6	0.338 6072
6	224 48 58.8	+ 0 25 39.4	0.448 3019	22	20 27 24.7	− 3 17 01.4	0.333 5829
7	227 45 36.3	+ 0 03 58.5	0.451 3131	23	25 54 07.8	− 2 40 47.7	0.328 8549
8	230 39 59.1	− 0 17 26.5	0.454 0649	24	31 29 41.3	− 2 02 02.6	0.324 4752
9	233 32 22.4	− 0 38 34.1	0.456 5533	25	37 13 43.5	− 1 21 04.6	0.320 4960
10	236 23 01.0	− 0 59 23.0	0.458 7749	26	43 05 43.2	− 0 38 18.2	0.316 9681
11	239 12 08.9	− 1 19 51.9	0.460 7268	27	49 04 58.5	+ 0 05 46.5	0.313 9394
12	241 59 59.8	− 1 39 59.7	0.462 4063	28	55 10 37.1	+ 0 50 34.1	0.311 4532
13	244 46 47.2	− 1 59 45.4	0.463 8116	29	61 21 35.9	+ 1 35 24.7	0.309 5470
14	247 32 43.9	− 2 19 07.8	0.464 9407	30	67 36 42.6	+ 2 19 35.5	0.308 2504
15	250 18 02.8	− 2 38 06.0	0.465 7926	31	73 54 36.3	+ 3 02 22.6	0.307 5841
16	253 02 56.3	− 2 56 38.8	0.466 3661	June 1	80 13 50.4	+ 3 43 03.0	0.307 5591
17	255 47 36.8	− 3 14 45.4	0.466 6606	2	86 32 54.4	+ 4 20 56.7	0.308 1756
18	258 32 16.6	− 3 32 24.4	0.466 6758	3	92 50 17.3	+ 4 55 28.7	0.309 4238
19	261 17 07.8	− 3 49 34.9	0.466 4117	4	99 04 30.3	+ 5 26 10.5	0.311 2835
20	264 02 22.7	− 4 06 15.4	0.465 8686	5	105 14 10.1	+ 5 52 41.2	0.313 7258
21	266 48 13.5	− 4 22 24.7	0.465 0470	6	111 18 00.7	+ 6 14 47.8	0.316 7137
22	269 34 52.6	− 4 38 01.2	0.463 9480	7	117 14 56.0	+ 6 32 25.1	0.320 2044
23	272 22 32.4	− 4 53 03.4	0.462 5727	8	123 04 00.9	+ 6 45 35.1	0.324 1503
24	275 11 25.7	− 5 07 29.4	0.460 9229	9	128 44 31.7	+ 6 54 26.0	0.328 5006
25	278 01 45.4	− 5 21 17.4	0.459 0006	10	134 15 56.3	+ 6 59 10.7	0.333 2034
26	280 53 44.6	− 5 34 25.1	0.456 8082	11	139 37 53.5	+ 7 00 05.8	0.338 2065
27	283 47 37.2	− 5 46 50.1	0.454 3487	12	144 50 12.4	+ 6 57 30.2	0.343 4584
28	286 43 36.9	− 5 58 29.9	0.451 6253	13	149 52 50.5	+ 6 51 44.2	0.348 9098
29	289 41 58.3	− 6 09 21.5	0.448 6421	14	154 45 53.1	+ 6 43 08.3	0.354 5133
30	292 42 56.2	− 6 19 21.7	0.445 4037	15	159 29 31.6	+ 6 32 02.7	0.360 2248
May 1	295 46 46.3	− 6 28 27.0	0.441 9152	16	164 04 02.2	+ 6 18 46.8	0.366 0030
2	298 53 44.5	− 6 36 33.6	0.438 1827	17	168 29 44.7	+ 6 03 38.8	0.371 8100
3	302 04 07.6	− 6 43 37.1	0.434 2131	18	172 47 01.7	+ 5 46 55.4	0.377 6110
4	305 18 12.9	− 6 49 33.0	0.430 0140	19	176 56 17.5	+ 5 28 51.7	0.383 3744
5	308 36 18.4	− 6 54 16.1	0.425 5944	20	180 57 57.5	+ 5 09 41.5	0.389 0717
6	311 58 43.0	− 6 57 40.8	0.420 9643	21	184 52 27.6	+ 4 49 36.8	0.394 6770
7	315 25 46.1	− 6 59 41.3	0.416 1350	22	188 40 13.8	+ 4 28 48.5	0.400 1672
8	318 57 47.9	− 7 00 10.9	0.411 1195	23	192 21 41.5	+ 4 07 25.9	0.405 5216
9	322 35 09.2	− 6 59 02.8	0.405 9320	24	195 57 16.1	+ 3 45 37.2	0.410 7218
10	326 18 11.5	− 6 56 09.4	0.400 5890	25	199 27 21.6	+ 3 23 29.6	0.415 7514
11	330 07 16.7	− 6 51 22.9	0.395 1086	26	202 52 21.8	+ 3 01 09.3	0.420 5957
12	334 02 47.3	− 6 44 35.2	0.389 5115	27	206 12 39.2	+ 2 38 41.6	0.425 2417
13	338 05 05.8	− 6 35 37.7	0.383 8206	28	209 28 35.3	+ 2 16 11.1	0.429 6781
14	342 14 34.5	− 6 24 21.8	0.378 0614	29	212 40 31.1	+ 1 53 41.9	0.433 8947
15	346 31 35.7	− 6 10 39.0	0.372 2622	30	215 48 46.1	+ 1 31 17.2	0.437 8825
16	350 56 30.6	− 5 54 21.1	0.366 4545	July 1	218 53 39.4	+ 1 09 00.1	0.441 6338
17	355 29 39.1	− 5 35 20.5	0.360 6727	2	221 55 28.9	+ 0 46 53.2	0.445 1415

HELIOCENTRIC POSITIONS FOR 0^h BARYCENTRIC DYNAMICAL TIME
MEAN EQUINOX AND ECLIPTIC OF J2000.0

Date	Longitude	Latitude	True Heliocentric Distance	Date	Longitude	Latitude	True Heliocentric Distance
	° ′ ″	° ′ ″	au		° ′ ″	° ′ ″	au
July 1	218 53 39.4	+ 1 09 00.1	0.441 6338	Aug. 16	10 10 40.2	− 4 20 12.5	0.343 7096
2	221 55 28.9	+ 0 46 53.2	0.445 1415	17	15 19 29.4	− 3 49 30.4	0.338 4472
3	224 54 31.9	+ 0 24 58.5	0.448 3996	18	20 37 26.5	− 3 15 56.0	0.333 4314
4	227 51 04.8	+ 0 03 18.1	0.451 4028	19	26 04 26.3	− 2 39 37.4	0.328 7134
5	230 45 23.6	− 0 18 06.4	0.454 1466	20	31 40 16.0	− 2 00 47.9	0.324 3454
6	233 37 43.5	− 0 39 13.4	0.456 6268	21	37 24 33.5	− 1 19 46.1	0.320 3796
7	236 28 18.9	− 1 00 01.7	0.458 8401	22	43 16 47.4	− 0 36 56.8	0.316 8665
8	239 17 24.2	− 1 20 30.0	0.460 7835	23	49 16 15.5	+ 0 07 09.8	0.313 8540
9	242 05 12.9	− 1 40 37.1	0.462 4546	24	55 22 04.9	+ 0 51 58.1	0.311 3854
10	244 51 58.4	− 2 00 22.0	0.463 8513	25	61 33 12.6	+ 1 36 48.0	0.309 4977
11	247 37 53.7	− 2 19 43.7	0.464 9719	26	67 48 25.6	+ 2 20 56.9	0.308 2204
12	250 23 11.6	− 2 38 41.1	0.465 8151	27	74 06 23.2	+ 3 03 40.7	0.307 5739
13	253 08 04.5	− 2 57 13.2	0.466 3799	28	80 25 38.3	+ 3 44 16.5	0.307 5689
14	255 52 44.7	− 3 15 18.8	0.466 6657	29	86 44 40.5	+ 4 22 04.4	0.308 2053
15	258 37 24.6	− 3 32 57.0	0.466 6722	30	93 01 58.7	+ 4 56 29.6	0.309 4728
16	261 22 16.4	− 3 50 06.5	0.466 3994	31	99 16 04.5	+ 5 27 03.8	0.311 3511
17	264 07 32.2	− 4 06 46.1	0.465 8476	Sept. 1	105 25 34.4	+ 5 53 26.4	0.313 8109
18	266 53 24.3	− 4 22 54.4	0.465 0174	2	111 29 13.1	+ 6 15 24.7	0.316 8152
19	269 40 05.1	− 4 38 29.9	0.463 9097	3	117 25 54.5	+ 6 32 53.6	0.320 3208
20	272 27 47.0	− 4 53 30.9	0.462 5259	4	123 14 44.0	+ 6 45 55.4	0.324 2799
21	275 16 42.7	− 5 07 55.8	0.460 8675	5	128 54 58.2	+ 6 54 38.4	0.328 6420
22	278 07 05.3	− 5 21 42.5	0.458 9367	6	134 26 05.4	+ 6 59 15.7	0.333 3549
23	280 59 07.9	− 5 34 48.9	0.456 7360	7	139 47 44.7	+ 7 00 03.9	0.338 3664
24	283 53 04.1	− 5 47 12.6	0.454 2681	8	144 59 45.5	+ 6 57 22.1	0.343 6253
25	286 49 08.0	− 5 58 50.9	0.451 5366	9	150 02 05.6	+ 6 51 30.5	0.349 0820
26	289 47 34.0	− 6 09 40.9	0.448 5454	10	154 54 50.5	+ 6 42 49.6	0.354 6895
27	292 48 37.1	− 6 19 39.5	0.445 2991	11	159 38 11.7	+ 6 31 39.7	0.360 4036
28	295 52 32.8	− 6 28 43.0	0.441 8029	12	164 12 25.5	+ 6 18 20.0	0.366 1833
29	298 59 37.1	− 6 36 47.7	0.438 0629	13	168 37 51.9	+ 6 03 08.8	0.371 9906
30	302 10 06.8	− 6 43 49.2	0.434 0860	14	172 54 53.6	+ 5 46 22.7	0.377 7908
31	305 24 19.3	− 6 49 42.8	0.429 8799	15	177 03 54.8	+ 5 28 16.7	0.383 5526
Aug. 1	308 42 32.6	− 6 54 23.6	0.425 4536	16	181 05 21.1	+ 5 09 04.6	0.389 2473
2	312 05 05.6	− 6 57 45.8	0.420 8171	17	184 59 38.3	+ 4 48 58.5	0.394 8493
3	315 32 17.6	− 6 59 43.5	0.415 9819	18	188 47 12.3	+ 4 28 08.9	0.400 3356
4	319 04 29.0	− 7 00 10.2	0.410 9607	19	192 28 28.7	+ 4 06 45.4	0.405 6854
5	322 42 00.6	− 6 58 58.9	0.405 7682	20	196 03 52.7	+ 3 44 56.0	0.410 8805
6	326 25 13.9	− 6 56 02.1	0.400 4206	21	199 33 48.4	+ 3 22 47.9	0.415 9045
7	330 14 30.8	− 6 51 12.0	0.394 9363	22	202 58 39.5	+ 3 00 27.3	0.420 7428
8	334 10 13.7	− 6 44 20.3	0.389 3359	23	206 18 48.4	+ 2 37 59.5	0.425 3824
9	338 12 45.2	− 6 35 18.6	0.383 6425	24	209 34 36.9	+ 2 15 29.0	0.429 8121
10	342 22 27.7	− 6 23 58.3	0.377 8816	25	212 46 25.4	+ 1 52 59.8	0.434 0217
11	346 39 43.3	− 6 10 10.8	0.372 0817	26	215 54 34.0	+ 1 30 35.3	0.438 0022
12	351 04 53.2	− 5 53 47.9	0.366 2743	27	218 59 21.3	+ 1 08 18.5	0.441 7460
13	355 38 17.3	− 5 34 42.2	0.360 4939	28	222 01 05.4	+ 0 46 11.9	0.445 2460
14	0 20 13.6	− 5 12 47.2	0.354 7785	29	225 00 03.5	+ 0 24 17.7	0.448 4962
15	5 10 57.4	− 4 47 58.1	0.349 1690	30	227 56 32.1	+ 0 02 37.8	0.451 4914
16	10 10 40.2	− 4 20 12.5	0.343 7096	Oct. 1	230 50 47.0	− 0 18 46.2	0.454 2270

MERCURY, 2025

HELIOCENTRIC POSITIONS FOR 0^h BARYCENTRIC DYNAMICAL TIME
MEAN EQUINOX AND ECLIPTIC OF J2000.0

Date		Longitude	Latitude	True Heliocentric Distance	Date		Longitude	Latitude	True Heliocentric Distance
		° ′ ″	° ′ ″	au			° ′ ″	° ′ ″	au
Oct.	1	230 50 47.0	− 0 18 46.2	0.454 2270	Nov.	16	31 50 52.4	− 1 59 32.9	0.324 2165
	2	233 43 03.4	− 0 39 52.7	0.456 6990		17	37 35 25.3	− 1 18 27.4	0.320 2641
	3	236 33 35.9	− 1 00 40.4	0.458 9039		18	43 27 53.3	− 0 35 35.2	0.316 7660
	4	239 22 38.6	− 1 21 08.0	0.460 8389		19	49 27 33.9	+ 0 08 33.2	0.313 7699
	5	242 10 25.2	− 1 41 14.5	0.462 5014		20	55 33 34.1	+ 0 53 22.1	0.311 3189
	6	244 57 09.0	− 2 00 58.7	0.463 8895		21	61 44 50.4	+ 1 38 11.5	0.309 4499
	7	247 43 03.0	− 2 20 19.6	0.465 0015		22	68 00 09.7	+ 2 22 18.3	0.308 1921
	8	250 28 19.9	− 2 39 16.2	0.465 8360		23	74 18 10.8	+ 3 04 58.7	0.307 5655
	9	253 13 12.2	− 2 57 47.5	0.466 3922		24	80 37 26.6	+ 3 45 29.8	0.307 5805
	10	255 57 52.4	− 3 15 52.3	0.466 6693		25	86 56 26.8	+ 4 23 11.9	0.308 2368
	11	258 42 32.5	− 3 33 29.6	0.466 6671		26	93 13 40.2	+ 4 57 30.3	0.309 5236
	12	261 27 24.9	− 3 50 38.2	0.466 3856		27	99 27 38.4	+ 5 27 56.9	0.311 4205
	13	264 12 41.7	− 4 07 16.8	0.465 8251		28	105 36 58.3	+ 5 54 11.4	0.313 8978
	14	266 58 35.1	− 4 23 24.1	0.464 9862		29	111 40 24.7	+ 6 16 01.3	0.316 9182
	15	269 45 17.7	− 4 38 58.5	0.463 8700		30	117 36 52.1	+ 6 33 21.9	0.320 4386
	16	272 33 01.7	− 4 53 58.5	0.462 4776	Dec.	1	123 25 26.0	+ 6 46 15.5	0.324 4110
	17	275 22 00.0	− 5 08 22.2	0.460 8107		2	129 05 23.5	+ 6 54 50.6	0.328 7847
	18	278 12 25.5	− 5 22 07.7	0.458 8715		3	134 36 13.1	+ 6 59 20.5	0.333 5076
	19	281 04 31.4	− 5 35 12.8	0.456 6624		4	139 57 34.5	+ 7 00 01.9	0.338 5274
	20	283 58 31.5	− 5 47 35.1	0.454 1863		5	145 09 17.1	+ 6 57 13.9	0.343 7931
	21	286 54 39.6	− 5 59 11.9	0.451 4467		6	150 11 19.2	+ 6 51 16.7	0.349 2551
	22	289 53 10.3	− 6 10 00.4	0.448 4475		7	155 03 46.3	+ 6 42 30.9	0.354 8664
	23	292 54 18.6	− 6 19 57.3	0.445 1933		8	159 46 50.1	+ 6 31 16.6	0.360 5831
	24	295 58 19.9	− 6 28 59.0	0.441 6895		9	164 20 47.2	+ 6 17 53.3	0.366 3640
	25	299 05 30.5	− 6 37 01.8	0.437 9420		10	168 45 57.6	+ 6 02 38.9	0.372 1715
	26	302 16 06.9	− 6 44 01.2	0.433 9578		11	173 02 43.9	+ 5 45 50.0	0.377 9709
	27	305 30 26.6	− 6 49 52.7	0.429 7448		12	177 11 30.7	+ 5 27 41.8	0.383 7309
	28	308 48 47.8	− 6 54 31.0	0.425 3118		13	181 12 43.2	+ 5 08 27.9	0.389 4230
	29	312 11 29.1	− 6 57 50.7	0.420 6690		14	185 06 47.5	+ 4 48 20.2	0.395 0216
	30	315 38 50.3	− 6 59 45.7	0.415 8278		15	188 54 09.4	+ 4 27 29.5	0.400 5038
	31	319 11 11.3	− 7 00 09.4	0.410 8011		16	192 35 14.5	+ 4 06 05.0	0.405 8491
Nov.	1	322 48 53.3	− 6 58 54.9	0.405 6035		17	196 10 28.0	+ 3 44 15.0	0.411 0390
	2	326 32 17.6	− 6 55 54.7	0.400 2515		18	199 40 13.9	+ 3 22 06.4	0.416 0573
	3	330 21 46.2	− 6 51 00.9	0.394 7633		19	203 04 55.9	+ 2 59 45.5	0.420 8895
	4	334 17 41.5	− 6 44 05.4	0.389 1598		20	206 24 56.5	+ 2 37 17.5	0.425 5228
	5	338 20 26.1	− 6 34 59.5	0.383 4639		21	209 40 37.2	+ 2 14 47.0	0.429 9457
	6	342 30 22.4	− 6 23 34.6	0.377 7014		22	212 52 18.7	+ 1 52 17.9	0.434 1482
	7	346 47 52.5	− 6 09 42.4	0.371 9008		23	216 00 20.8	+ 1 29 53.7	0.438 1214
	8	351 13 17.5	− 5 53 14.5	0.366 0938		24	219 05 02.2	+ 1 07 37.1	0.441 8576
	9	355 46 57.3	− 5 34 03.6	0.360 3150		25	222 06 40.9	+ 0 45 30.9	0.445 3499
	10	0 29 09.8	− 5 12 03.3	0.354 6023		26	225 05 34.2	+ 0 23 37.1	0.448 5922
	11	5 20 10.2	− 4 47 08.7	0.348 9969		27	228 01 58.5	+ 0 01 57.6	0.451 5794
	12	10 20 10.0	− 4 19 17.5	0.343 5430		28	230 56 09.5	− 0 19 25.9	0.454 3068
	13	15 29 16.2	− 3 48 30.1	0.338 2877		29	233 48 22.6	− 0 40 31.8	0.456 7705
	14	20 47 30.2	− 3 14 50.4	0.333 2805		30	236 38 52.1	− 1 01 18.9	0.458 9670
	15	26 14 46.7	− 2 38 26.9	0.328 5727		31	239 27 52.3	− 1 21 45.9	0.460 8935
	16	31 50 52.4	− 1 59 32.9	0.324 2165		32	242 15 36.8	− 1 41 51.6	0.462 5476

HELIOCENTRIC POSITIONS FOR 0^h BARYCENTRIC DYNAMICAL TIME
MEAN EQUINOX AND ECLIPTIC OF J2000.0

Date	Longitude	Latitude	True Heliocentric Distance	Date	Longitude	Latitude	True Heliocentric Distance
	° ′ ″	° ′ ″	au		° ′ ″	° ′ ″	au
Jan. −1	47 54 26.4	− 1 37 54.4	0.722 7769	Apr. 1	196 46 17.0	+ 2 56 08.3	0.721 2547
1	51 06 51.7	− 1 27 45.3	0.722 5065	3	199 59 43.8	+ 2 50 06.7	0.721 5060
3	54 19 23.8	− 1 17 19.3	0.722 2385	5	203 13 00.3	+ 2 43 33.2	0.721 7630
5	57 32 02.8	− 1 06 38.2	0.721 9739	7	206 26 06.2	+ 2 36 29.1	0.722 0248
7	60 44 48.8	− 0 55 44.1	0.721 7135	9	209 39 01.5	+ 2 28 55.7	0.722 2908
9	63 57 42.0	− 0 44 39.1	0.721 4580	11	212 51 45.8	+ 2 20 54.5	0.722 5599
11	67 10 42.2	− 0 33 25.1	0.721 2084	13	216 04 19.3	+ 2 12 27.3	0.722 8314
13	70 23 49.7	− 0 22 04.4	0.720 9653	15	219 16 41.8	+ 2 03 35.5	0.723 1044
15	73 37 04.3	− 0 10 39.0	0.720 7297	17	222 28 53.4	+ 1 54 21.0	0.723 3781
17	76 50 26.2	+ 0 00 48.9	0.720 5021	19	225 40 54.2	+ 1 44 45.5	0.723 6516
19	80 03 55.2	+ 0 12 17.0	0.720 2834	21	228 52 44.3	+ 1 34 50.9	0.723 9239
21	83 17 31.5	+ 0 23 43.2	0.720 0743	23	232 04 23.9	+ 1 24 39.0	0.724 1944
23	86 31 14.8	+ 0 35 05.2	0.719 8755	25	235 15 53.3	+ 1 14 11.9	0.724 4621
25	89 45 05.2	+ 0 46 21.0	0.719 6875	27	238 27 12.7	+ 1 03 31.4	0.724 7262
27	92 59 02.6	+ 0 57 28.2	0.719 5109	29	241 38 22.5	+ 0 52 39.6	0.724 9859
29	96 13 06.6	+ 1 08 24.8	0.719 3465	May 1	244 49 23.0	+ 0 41 38.4	0.725 2404
31	99 27 17.3	+ 1 19 08.6	0.719 1946	3	248 00 14.7	+ 0 30 30.1	0.725 4889
Feb. 2	102 41 34.4	+ 1 29 37.4	0.719 0557	5	251 10 58.0	+ 0 19 16.6	0.725 7306
4	105 55 57.5	+ 1 39 49.4	0.718 9304	7	254 21 33.3	+ 0 07 59.9	0.725 9648
6	109 10 26.5	+ 1 49 42.4	0.718 8190	9	257 32 01.2	− 0 03 17.8	0.726 1908
8	112 25 00.9	+ 1 59 14.5	0.718 7220	11	260 42 22.3	− 0 14 34.5	0.726 4079
10	115 39 40.5	+ 2 08 23.8	0.718 6395	13	263 52 36.9	− 0 25 48.1	0.726 6154
12	118 54 24.8	+ 2 17 08.6	0.718 5719	15	267 02 45.8	− 0 36 56.6	0.726 8126
14	122 09 13.4	+ 2 25 27.1	0.718 5193	17	270 12 49.4	− 0 47 57.9	0.726 9991
16	125 24 05.7	+ 2 33 17.6	0.718 4821	19	273 22 48.4	− 0 58 50.2	0.727 1741
18	128 39 01.4	+ 2 40 38.7	0.718 4602	21	276 32 43.3	− 1 09 31.4	0.727 3373
20	131 53 59.7	+ 2 47 28.8	0.718 4538	23	279 42 34.7	− 1 19 59.5	0.727 4880
22	135 09 00.2	+ 2 53 46.7	0.718 4628	25	282 52 23.1	− 1 30 12.9	0.727 6259
24	138 24 02.2	+ 2 59 31.0	0.718 4874	27	286 02 09.2	− 1 40 09.5	0.727 7505
26	141 39 05.1	+ 3 04 40.7	0.718 5272	29	289 11 53.5	− 1 49 47.6	0.727 8614
28	144 54 08.2	+ 3 09 14.8	0.718 5824	31	292 21 36.5	− 1 59 05.5	0.727 9583
Mar. 2	148 09 10.9	+ 3 13 12.4	0.718 6526	June 2	295 31 18.8	− 2 08 01.5	0.728 0409
4	151 24 12.5	+ 3 16 32.7	0.718 7376	4	298 41 01.0	− 2 16 34.1	0.728 1090
6	154 39 12.2	+ 3 19 15.1	0.718 8372	6	301 50 43.4	− 2 24 41.7	0.728 1624
8	157 54 09.5	+ 3 21 19.1	0.718 9511	8	305 00 26.5	− 2 32 22.8	0.728 2008
10	161 09 03.5	+ 3 22 44.3	0.719 0789	10	308 10 10.9	− 2 39 36.0	0.728 2242
12	164 23 53.5	+ 3 23 30.6	0.719 2201	12	311 19 57.0	− 2 46 20.2	0.728 2325
14	167 38 38.9	+ 3 23 37.7	0.719 3744	14	314 29 45.0	− 2 52 33.9	0.728 2257
16	170 53 19.1	+ 3 23 05.7	0.719 5411	16	317 39 35.6	− 2 58 16.2	0.728 2038
18	174 07 53.3	+ 3 21 54.7	0.719 7199	18	320 49 28.9	− 3 03 25.9	0.728 1668
20	177 22 20.9	+ 3 20 05.2	0.719 9101	20	323 59 25.3	− 3 08 02.1	0.728 1149
22	180 36 41.3	+ 3 17 37.4	0.720 1111	22	327 09 25.1	− 3 12 04.1	0.728 0482
24	183 50 54.0	+ 3 14 31.9	0.720 3223	24	330 19 28.7	− 3 15 30.9	0.727 9670
26	187 04 58.3	+ 3 10 49.4	0.720 5430	26	333 29 36.2	− 3 18 22.0	0.727 8713
28	190 18 53.9	+ 3 06 30.7	0.720 7724	28	336 39 47.9	− 3 20 36.8	0.727 7617
30	193 32 40.3	+ 3 01 36.6	0.721 0099	30	339 50 04.0	− 3 22 14.9	0.727 6383
Apr. 1	196 46 17.0	+ 2 56 08.3	0.721 2547	July 2	343 00 24.7	− 3 23 15.9	0.727 5016

HELIOCENTRIC POSITIONS FOR 0h BARYCENTRIC DYNAMICAL TIME MEAN EQUINOX AND ECLIPTIC OF J2000.0

Date		Longitude	Latitude	True Heliocentric Distance	Date		Longitude	Latitude	True Heliocentric Distance
		° ′ ″	° ′ ″	au			° ′ ″	° ′ ″	au
July	2	343 00 24.7	− 3 23 15.9	0.727 5016	Oct.	2	130 45 42.1	+ 2 45 09.4	0.718 4232
	4	346 10 50.2	− 3 23 39.6	0.727 3519		4	134 00 42.9	+ 2 51 38.7	0.718 4281
	6	349 21 20.6	− 3 23 25.9	0.727 1897		6	137 15 45.3	+ 2 57 34.9	0.718 4486
	8	352 31 56.1	− 3 22 34.8	0.727 0156		8	140 30 48.9	+ 3 02 56.9	0.718 4845
	10	355 42 36.8	− 3 21 06.4	0.726 8299		10	143 45 52.8	+ 3 07 43.5	0.718 5357
	12	358 53 22.8	− 3 19 00.9	0.726 6334		12	147 00 56.5	+ 3 11 53.9	0.718 6022
	14	2 04 14.2	− 3 16 18.6	0.726 4265		14	150 15 59.3	+ 3 15 27.3	0.718 6836
	16	5 15 11.2	− 3 12 59.9	0.726 2099		16	153 31 00.4	+ 3 18 23.0	0.718 7798
	18	8 26 13.8	− 3 09 05.5	0.725 9844		18	156 45 59.1	+ 3 20 40.5	0.718 8903
	20	11 37 22.2	− 3 04 35.9	0.725 7504		20	160 00 54.9	+ 3 22 19.3	0.719 0149
	22	14 48 36.3	− 2 59 32.0	0.725 5089		22	163 15 46.8	+ 3 23 19.1	0.719 1531
	24	17 59 56.3	− 2 53 54.6	0.725 2605		24	166 30 34.4	+ 3 23 39.8	0.719 3045
	26	21 11 22.3	− 2 47 44.6	0.725 0060		26	169 45 16.8	+ 3 23 21.5	0.719 4685
	28	24 22 54.3	− 2 41 03.2	0.724 7461		28	172 59 53.4	+ 3 22 24.1	0.719 6447
	30	27 34 32.5	− 2 33 51.6	0.724 4817		30	176 14 23.6	+ 3 20 48.0	0.719 8325
Aug.	1	30 46 17.0	− 2 26 10.9	0.724 2136	Nov.	1	179 28 46.8	+ 3 18 33.4	0.720 0313
	3	33 58 07.7	− 2 18 02.7	0.723 9426		3	182 43 02.4	+ 3 15 41.0	0.720 2404
	5	37 10 04.9	− 2 09 28.3	0.723 6696		5	185 57 09.8	+ 3 12 11.4	0.720 4592
	7	40 22 08.5	− 2 00 29.2	0.723 3954		7	189 11 08.6	+ 3 08 05.2	0.720 6870
	9	43 34 18.8	− 1 51 07.3	0.723 1209		9	192 24 58.2	+ 3 03 23.4	0.720 9230
	11	46 46 35.7	− 1 41 24.0	0.722 8469		11	195 38 38.3	+ 2 58 06.9	0.721 1665
	13	49 58 59.4	− 1 31 21.3	0.722 5744		13	198 52 08.5	+ 2 52 16.8	0.721 4167
	15	53 11 30.0	− 1 21 01.0	0.722 3041		15	202 05 28.5	+ 2 45 54.3	0.721 6728
	17	56 24 07.5	− 1 10 24.9	0.722 0369		17	205 18 38.1	+ 2 39 00.6	0.721 9341
	19	59 36 52.0	− 0 59 35.1	0.721 7736		19	208 31 36.9	+ 2 31 37.3	0.722 1996
	21	62 49 43.6	− 0 48 33.6	0.721 5152		21	211 44 24.9	+ 2 23 45.7	0.722 4685
	23	66 02 42.4	− 0 37 22.5	0.721 2623		23	214 57 02.0	+ 2 15 27.4	0.722 7401
	25	69 15 48.4	− 0 26 03.8	0.721 0159		25	218 09 28.1	+ 2 06 44.0	0.723 0133
	27	72 29 01.6	− 0 14 39.7	0.720 7767		27	221 21 43.3	+ 1 57 37.3	0.723 2875
	29	75 42 22.1	− 0 03 12.4	0.720 5454		29	224 33 47.6	+ 1 48 08.9	0.723 5617
	31	78 55 49.8	+ 0 08 15.9	0.720 3229	Dec.	1	227 45 41.2	+ 1 38 20.8	0.723 8351
Sept.	2	82 09 24.7	+ 0 19 43.1	0.720 1098		3	230 57 24.2	+ 1 28 14.7	0.724 1068
	4	85 23 06.7	+ 0 31 07.0	0.719 9068		5	234 08 56.8	+ 1 17 52.7	0.724 3760
	6	88 36 55.9	+ 0 42 25.2	0.719 7146		7	237 20 19.4	+ 1 07 16.7	0.724 6418
	8	91 50 52.0	+ 0 53 35.8	0.719 5338		9	240 31 32.2	+ 0 56 28.6	0.724 9035
	10	95 04 55.0	+ 1 04 36.4	0.719 3649		11	243 42 35.7	+ 0 45 30.5	0.725 1601
	12	98 19 04.6	+ 1 15 25.0	0.719 2086		13	246 53 30.1	+ 0 34 24.5	0.725 4110
	14	101 33 20.6	+ 1 25 59.4	0.719 0653		15	250 04 16.0	+ 0 23 12.5	0.725 6554
	16	104 47 42.9	+ 1 36 17.5	0.718 9354		17	253 14 53.8	+ 0 11 56.8	0.725 8924
	18	108 02 11.1	+ 1 46 17.4	0.718 8195		19	256 25 24.0	+ 0 00 39.2	0.726 1215
	20	111 16 44.8	+ 1 55 57.1	0.718 7179		21	259 35 47.0	− 0 10 38.0	0.726 3418
	22	114 31 23.8	+ 2 05 14.7	0.718 6309		23	262 46 03.6	− 0 21 52.9	0.726 5528
	24	117 46 07.7	+ 2 14 08.3	0.718 5588		25	265 56 14.1	− 0 33 03.4	0.726 7537
	26	121 00 55.9	+ 2 22 36.2	0.718 5018		27	269 06 19.3	− 0 44 07.5	0.726 9440
	28	124 15 48.1	+ 2 30 36.7	0.718 4601		29	272 16 19.5	− 0 55 03.1	0.727 1231
	30	127 30 43.7	+ 2 38 08.3	0.718 4339		31	275 26 15.5	− 1 05 48.4	0.727 2904
Oct.	2	130 45 42.1	+ 2 45 09.4	0.718 4232		33	278 36 07.8	− 1 16 21.3	0.727 4455

HELIOCENTRIC POSITIONS FOR 0h BARYCENTRIC DYNAMICAL TIME
MEAN EQUINOX AND ECLIPTIC OF J2000.0

Date	Longitude	Latitude	True Heliocentric Distance	Date	Longitude	Latitude	True Heliocentric Distance
	° ′ ″	° ′ ″	au		° ′ ″	° ′ ″	au
Jan. −3	107 00 51.9	+ 1 33 32.0	1.608 7050	June 30	188 50 57.5	+ 1 12 12.3	1.639 2886
1	108 52 57.2	+ 1 35 25.4	1.612 6065	July 4	190 39 18.8	+ 1 09 31.1	1.636 3920
5	110 44 30.7	+ 1 37 12.2	1.616 3927	8	192 28 03.6	+ 1 06 45.2	1.633 3591
9	112 35 33.6	+ 1 38 52.4	1.620 0601	12	194 17 12.9	+ 1 03 54.5	1.630 1924
13	114 26 07.0	+ 1 40 26.0	1.623 6054	16	196 06 48.1	+ 1 00 59.4	1.626 8947
17	116 16 12.1	+ 1 41 53.0	1.627 0255	20	197 56 50.3	+ 0 57 59.7	1.623 4687
21	118 05 50.3	+ 1 43 13.5	1.630 3174	24	199 47 20.8	+ 0 54 55.7	1.619 9175
25	119 55 02.5	+ 1 44 27.4	1.633 4783	28	201 38 20.7	+ 0 51 47.4	1.616 2442
29	121 43 50.1	+ 1 45 34.7	1.636 5054	Aug. 1	203 29 51.3	+ 0 48 35.0	1.612 4521
Feb. 2	123 32 14.3	+ 1 46 35.4	1.639 3963	5	205 21 53.7	+ 0 45 18.6	1.608 5446
6	125 20 16.2	+ 1 47 29.7	1.642 1485	9	207 14 29.1	+ 0 41 58.4	1.604 5253
10	127 07 57.1	+ 1 48 17.4	1.644 7597	13	209 07 38.8	+ 0 38 34.3	1.600 3980
14	128 55 18.1	+ 1 48 58.6	1.647 2279	17	211 01 23.9	+ 0 35 06.7	1.596 1667
18	130 42 20.4	+ 1 49 33.4	1.649 5510	21	212 55 45.6	+ 0 31 35.7	1.591 8354
22	132 29 05.3	+ 1 50 01.7	1.651 7273	25	214 50 45.0	+ 0 28 01.3	1.587 4085
26	134 15 34.0	+ 1 50 23.6	1.653 7549	29	216 46 23.3	+ 0 24 23.9	1.582 8903
Mar. 2	136 01 47.6	+ 1 50 39.2	1.655 6324	Sept. 2	218 42 41.7	+ 0 20 43.5	1.578 2855
6	137 47 47.4	+ 1 50 48.4	1.657 3582	6	220 39 41.1	+ 0 17 00.4	1.573 5989
10	139 33 34.6	+ 1 50 51.2	1.658 9310	10	222 37 22.8	+ 0 13 14.8	1.568 8354
14	141 19 10.2	+ 1 50 47.8	1.660 3497	14	224 35 47.7	+ 0 09 26.8	1.564 0001
18	143 04 35.7	+ 1 50 38.2	1.661 6131	18	226 34 57.0	+ 0 05 36.7	1.559 0985
22	144 49 52.1	+ 1 50 22.3	1.662 7202	22	228 34 51.7	+ 0 01 44.8	1.554 1359
26	146 35 00.6	+ 1 50 00.3	1.663 6703	26	230 35 32.7	− 0 02 08.7	1.549 1182
30	148 20 02.5	+ 1 49 32.1	1.664 4627	30	232 37 01.0	− 0 06 03.7	1.544 0510
Apr. 3	150 04 58.9	+ 1 48 57.8	1.665 0967	Oct. 4	234 39 17.6	− 0 09 59.7	1.538 9405
7	151 49 51.0	+ 1 48 17.5	1.665 5718	8	236 42 23.3	− 0 13 56.5	1.533 7929
11	153 34 40.0	+ 1 47 31.2	1.665 8878	12	238 46 19.0	− 0 17 53.9	1.528 6146
15	155 19 27.2	+ 1 46 38.8	1.666 0444	16	240 51 05.4	− 0 21 51.4	1.523 4121
19	157 04 13.7	+ 1 45 40.6	1.666 0415	20	242 56 43.4	− 0 25 48.9	1.518 1921
23	158 49 00.6	+ 1 44 36.4	1.665 8790	24	245 03 13.6	− 0 29 45.9	1.512 9616
27	160 33 49.3	+ 1 43 26.4	1.665 5571	28	247 10 36.6	− 0 33 42.0	1.507 7275
May 1	162 18 40.8	+ 1 42 10.6	1.665 0760	Nov. 1	249 18 53.1	− 0 37 37.1	1.502 4971
5	164 03 36.5	+ 1 40 49.0	1.664 4362	5	251 28 03.4	− 0 41 30.6	1.497 2777
9	165 48 37.4	+ 1 39 21.8	1.663 6379	9	253 38 08.2	− 0 45 22.1	1.492 0768
13	167 33 44.8	+ 1 37 48.8	1.662 6819	13	255 49 07.6	− 0 49 11.4	1.486 9020
17	169 18 59.9	+ 1 36 10.3	1.661 5689	17	258 01 02.0	− 0 52 57.9	1.481 7610
21	171 04 23.9	+ 1 34 26.2	1.660 2997	21	260 13 51.6	− 0 56 41.3	1.476 6617
25	172 49 58.0	+ 1 32 36.6	1.658 8753	25	262 27 36.4	− 1 00 21.0	1.471 6121
29	174 35 43.3	+ 1 30 41.5	1.657 2966	29	264 42 16.5	− 1 03 56.8	1.466 6200
June 2	176 21 41.2	+ 1 28 41.1	1.655 5650	Dec. 3	266 57 51.7	− 1 07 28.0	1.461 6937
6	178 07 52.7	+ 1 26 35.3	1.653 6818	7	269 14 21.9	− 1 10 54.3	1.456 8412
10	179 54 19.2	+ 1 24 24.3	1.651 6484	11	271 31 46.7	− 1 14 15.3	1.452 0707
14	181 41 01.8	+ 1 22 08.0	1.649 4664	15	273 50 05.7	− 1 17 30.3	1.447 3904
18	183 28 01.7	+ 1 19 46.6	1.647 1375	19	276 09 18.4	− 1 20 39.0	1.442 8084
22	185 15 20.1	+ 1 17 20.1	1.644 6635	23	278 29 24.0	− 1 23 40.9	1.438 3331
26	187 02 58.3	+ 1 14 48.7	1.642 0465	27	280 50 21.8	− 1 26 35.4	1.433 9723
30	188 50 57.5	+ 1 12 12.3	1.639 2886	31	283 12 10.8	− 1 29 22.3	1.429 7343

JUPITER, SATURN, URANUS, NEPTUNE, 2025

HELIOCENTRIC POSITIONS FOR 0^h BARYCENTRIC DYNAMICAL TIME
MEAN EQUINOX AND ECLIPTIC OF J2000.0

JUPITER

Date	Longitude	Latitude	True Heliocentric Distance
	° ′ ″	° ′ ″	au
Jan. −5	77 29 08.2	− 0 30 36.3	5.080 607
5	78 21 18.8	− 0 29 30.6	5.083 882
15	79 13 25.3	− 0 28 24.5	5.087 181
25	80 05 27.7	− 0 27 18.1	5.090 503
Feb. 4	80 57 26.0	− 0 26 11.4	5.093 847
14	81 49 20.1	− 0 25 04.5	5.097 212
24	82 41 10.1	− 0 23 57.3	5.100 598
Mar. 6	83 32 56.0	− 0 22 49.8	5.104 004
16	84 24 37.7	− 0 21 42.2	5.107 430
26	85 16 15.2	− 0 20 34.3	5.110 873
Apr. 5	86 07 48.5	− 0 19 26.3	5.114 334
15	86 59 17.6	− 0 18 18.1	5.117 812
25	87 50 42.4	− 0 17 09.7	5.121 306
May 5	88 42 03.1	− 0 16 01.2	5.124 815
15	89 33 19.5	− 0 14 52.6	5.128 339
25	90 24 31.6	− 0 13 43.8	5.131 876
June 4	91 15 39.5	− 0 12 35.0	5.135 427
14	92 06 43.2	− 0 11 26.1	5.138 989
24	92 57 42.6	− 0 10 17.2	5.142 563
July 4	93 48 37.7	− 0 09 08.2	5.146 147
14	94 39 28.6	− 0 07 59.2	5.149 741
24	95 30 15.3	− 0 06 50.2	5.153 344
Aug. 3	96 20 57.6	− 0 05 41.2	5.156 955
13	97 11 35.7	− 0 04 32.2	5.160 573
23	98 02 09.6	− 0 03 23.2	5.164 198
Sept. 2	98 52 39.2	− 0 02 14.3	5.167 827
12	99 43 04.6	− 0 01 05.5	5.171 462
22	100 33 25.7	+ 0 00 03.2	5.175 100
Oct. 2	101 23 42.5	+ 0 01 11.9	5.178 742
12	102 13 55.2	+ 0 02 20.4	5.182 386
22	103 04 03.5	+ 0 03 28.8	5.186 031
Nov. 1	103 54 07.7	+ 0 04 37.1	5.189 678
11	104 44 07.7	+ 0 05 45.2	5.193 324
21	105 34 03.4	+ 0 06 53.2	5.196 970
Dec. 1	106 23 55.0	+ 0 08 00.9	5.200 614
11	107 13 42.3	+ 0 09 08.5	5.204 256
21	108 03 25.5	+ 0 10 15.9	5.207 895
31	108 53 04.6	+ 0 11 23.0	5.211 530

SATURN

Date	Longitude	Latitude	True Heliocentric Distance
	° ′ ″	° ′ ″	au
Jan. −5	349 14 17.1	− 2 03 12.3	9.632 250
5	349 33 58.6	− 2 03 41.1	9.629 228
15	349 53 40.8	− 2 04 09.7	9.626 202
25	350 13 23.7	− 2 04 38.1	9.623 173
Feb. 4	350 33 07.3	− 2 05 06.2	9.620 140
14	350 52 51.7	− 2 05 34.2	9.617 104
24	351 12 36.8	− 2 06 01.9	9.614 066
Mar. 6	351 32 22.7	− 2 06 29.3	9.611 024
16	351 52 09.3	− 2 06 56.5	9.607 979
26	352 11 56.6	− 2 07 23.5	9.604 932
Apr. 5	352 31 44.7	− 2 07 50.3	9.601 883
15	352 51 33.5	− 2 08 16.8	9.598 830
25	353 11 23.1	− 2 08 43.1	9.595 776
May 5	353 31 13.5	− 2 09 09.1	9.592 719
15	353 51 04.5	− 2 09 34.9	9.589 660
25	354 10 56.4	− 2 10 00.4	9.586 598
June 4	354 30 49.0	− 2 10 25.7	9.583 534
14	354 50 42.4	− 2 10 50.8	9.580 468
24	355 10 36.5	− 2 11 15.6	9.577 401
July 4	355 30 31.3	− 2 11 40.2	9.574 331
14	355 50 27.0	− 2 12 04.5	9.571 259
24	356 10 23.4	− 2 12 28.5	9.568 185
Aug. 3	356 30 20.5	− 2 12 52.4	9.565 110
13	356 50 18.4	− 2 13 15.9	9.562 032
23	357 10 17.1	− 2 13 39.2	9.558 954
Sept. 2	357 30 16.6	− 2 14 02.3	9.555 874
12	357 50 16.7	− 2 14 25.1	9.552 792
22	358 10 17.7	− 2 14 47.6	9.549 710
Oct. 2	358 30 19.4	− 2 15 09.9	9.546 626
12	358 50 21.9	− 2 15 31.9	9.543 542
22	359 10 25.2	− 2 15 53.6	9.540 457
Nov. 1	359 30 29.2	− 2 16 15.1	9.537 372
11	359 50 34.0	− 2 16 36.3	9.534 286
21	0 10 39.5	− 2 16 57.3	9.531 199
Dec. 1	0 30 45.8	− 2 17 18.0	9.528 112
11	0 50 52.9	− 2 17 38.4	9.525 025
21	1 11 00.8	− 2 17 58.5	9.521 938
31	1 31 09.4	− 2 18 18.4	9.518 851

URANUS

Date	Longitude	Latitude	True Heliocentric Distance
	° ′ ″	° ′ ″	au
Jan. −35	54 59 27.4	− 0 15 06.9	19.559 34
Jan. 5	55 26 36.0	− 0 14 46.1	19.552 59
Feb. 14	55 53 45.8	− 0 14 25.2	19.545 81
Mar. 26	56 20 56.5	− 0 14 04.3	19.538 99
May 5	56 48 08.3	− 0 13 43.3	19.532 13
June 14	57 15 21.2	− 0 13 22.3	19.525 25
July 24	57 42 35.1	− 0 13 01.2	19.518 33
Sept. 2	58 09 50.2	− 0 12 40.0	19.511 37
Oct. 12	58 37 06.3	− 0 12 18.7	19.504 39
Nov. 21	59 04 23.5	− 0 11 57.4	19.497 37
Dec. 31	59 31 41.7	− 0 11 36.0	19.490 32
Dec. 71	59 59 01.0	− 0 11 14.6	19.483 24

NEPTUNE

Date	Longitude	Latitude	True Heliocentric Distance
	° ′ ″	° ′ ″	au
Jan. −35	358 33 57.4	− 1 17 24.7	29.895 24
Jan. 5	358 48 30.0	− 1 17 43.1	29.894 18
Feb. 14	359 03 02.6	− 1 18 01.4	29.893 13
Mar. 26	359 17 35.1	− 1 18 19.6	29.892 08
May 5	359 32 07.5	− 1 18 37.8	29.891 04
June 14	359 46 39.9	− 1 18 55.9	29.889 99
July 24	0 01 12.2	− 1 19 13.9	29.888 96
Sept. 2	0 15 44.5	− 1 19 31.8	29.887 92
Oct. 12	0 30 16.8	− 1 19 49.6	29.886 88
Nov. 21	0 44 48.9	− 1 20 07.3	29.885 85
Dec. 31	0 59 21.1	− 1 20 25.0	29.884 83
Dec. 71	1 13 53.2	− 1 20 42.5	29.883 81

GEOCENTRIC COORDINATES FOR 0^h TERRESTRIAL TIME

Date	Apparent Right Ascension	Apparent Declination	True Geocentric Distance	Date	Apparent Right Ascension	Apparent Declination	True Geocentric Distance
	h m s	° ′ ″	au		h m s	° ′ ″	au
Jan. 0	17 10 51.889	−21 41 56.90	1.130 6345	Feb. 15	22 14 24.993	−12 49 26.43	1.353 7466
1	17 16 16.931	−21 56 28.45	1.148 0425	16	22 21 19.837	−12 05 32.11	1.343 7242
2	17 21 49.828	−22 10 22.90	1.164 8333	17	22 28 13.529	−11 20 21.75	1.332 7291
3	17 27 29.869	−22 23 35.28	1.181 0094	18	22 35 05.742	−10 33 58.79	1.320 7215
4	17 33 16.426	−22 36 01.20	1.196 5756	19	22 41 56.084	− 9 46 27.39	1.307 6622
5	17 39 08.941	−22 47 36.72	1.211 5378	20	22 48 44.083	− 8 57 52.54	1.293 5144
6	17 45 06.917	−22 58 18.34	1.225 9036	21	22 55 29.178	− 8 08 20.20	1.278 2447
7	17 51 09.910	−23 08 02.94	1.239 6808	22	23 02 10.706	− 7 17 57.38	1.261 8247
8	17 57 17.524	−23 16 47.71	1.252 8781	23	23 08 47.891	− 6 26 52.27	1.244 2332
9	18 03 29.399	−23 24 30.14	1.265 5042	24	23 15 19.831	− 5 35 14.37	1.225 4585
10	18 09 45.211	−23 31 07.94	1.277 5679	25	23 21 45.490	− 4 43 14.52	1.205 5002
11	18 16 04.662	−23 36 39.04	1.289 0776	26	23 28 03.691	− 3 51 05.06	1.184 3722
12	18 22 27.483	−23 41 01.55	1.300 0417	27	23 34 13.116	− 2 58 59.72	1.162 1047
13	18 28 53.423	−23 44 13.75	1.310 4680	28	23 40 12.303	− 2 07 13.72	1.138 7464
14	18 35 22.252	−23 46 14.04	1.320 3638	Mar. 1	23 45 59.663	− 1 16 03.58	1.114 3662
15	18 41 53.760	−23 47 00.93	1.329 7357	2	23 51 33.486	− 0 25 47.06	1.089 0544
16	18 48 27.749	−23 46 33.08	1.338 5898	3	23 56 51.970	+ 0 23 17.10	1.062 9223
17	18 55 04.038	−23 44 49.20	1.346 9315	4	0 01 53.248	+ 1 10 49.42	1.036 1020
18	19 01 42.456	−23 41 48.14	1.354 7653	5	0 06 35.418	+ 1 56 29.96	1.008 7441
19	19 08 22.844	−23 37 28.81	1.362 0950	6	0 10 56.591	+ 2 39 58.65	0.981 0152
20	19 15 05.054	−23 31 50.20	1.368 9238	7	0 14 54.926	+ 3 20 55.61	0.953 0944
21	19 21 48.945	−23 24 51.38	1.375 2537	8	0 18 28.682	+ 3 59 01.48	0.925 1691
22	19 28 34.386	−23 16 31.48	1.381 0859	9	0 21 36.262	+ 4 33 57.70	0.897 4308
23	19 35 21.251	−23 06 49.69	1.386 4208	10	0 24 16.261	+ 5 05 26.77	0.870 0714
24	19 42 09.424	−22 55 45.25	1.391 2577	11	0 26 27.506	+ 5 33 12.50	0.843 2787
25	19 48 58.793	−22 43 17.47	1.395 5948	12	0 28 09.108	+ 5 57 00.28	0.817 2339
26	19 55 49.254	−22 29 25.69	1.399 4293	13	0 29 20.504	+ 6 16 37.30	0.792 1083
27	20 02 40.707	−22 14 09.32	1.402 7571	14	0 30 01.496	+ 6 31 52.88	0.768 0614
28	20 09 33.059	−21 57 27.80	1.405 5731	15	0 30 12.298	+ 6 42 38.77	0.745 2393
29	20 16 26.220	−21 39 20.61	1.407 8708	16	0 29 53.570	+ 6 48 49.57	0.723 7733
30	20 23 20.108	−21 19 47.29	1.409 6423	17	0 29 06.444	+ 6 50 23.14	0.703 7793
31	20 30 14.644	−20 58 47.42	1.410 8787	18	0 27 52.551	+ 6 47 21.09	0.685 3565
Feb. 1	20 37 09.756	−20 36 20.61	1.411 5691	19	0 26 14.014	+ 6 39 49.17	0.668 5872
2	20 44 05.377	−20 12 26.53	1.411 7016	20	0 24 13.440	+ 6 27 57.68	0.653 5364
3	20 51 01.447	−19 47 04.92	1.411 2623	21	0 21 53.875	+ 6 12 01.64	0.640 2508
4	20 57 57.904	−19 20 15.56	1.410 2358	22	0 19 18.742	+ 5 52 20.84	0.628 7589
5	21 04 54.691	−18 51 58.33	1.408 6047	23	0 16 31.757	+ 5 29 19.59	0.619 0709
6	21 11 51.751	−18 22 13.18	1.406 3498	24	0 13 36.819	+ 5 03 26.17	0.611 1791
7	21 18 49.022	−17 51 00.17	1.403 4497	25	0 10 37.896	+ 4 35 12.09	0.605 0583
8	21 25 46.440	−17 18 19.44	1.399 8810	26	0 07 38.901	+ 4 05 11.04	0.600 6672
9	21 32 43.934	−16 44 11.29	1.395 6181	27	0 04 43.576	+ 3 33 57.79	0.597 9501
10	21 39 41.424	−16 08 36.15	1.390 6330	28	0 01 55.388	+ 3 02 06.96	0.596 8384
11	21 46 38.819	−15 31 34.64	1.384 8957	29	23 59 17.449	+ 2 30 11.95	0.597 2534
12	21 53 36.012	−14 53 07.62	1.378 3738	30	23 56 52.454	+ 1 58 43.93	0.599 1085
13	22 00 32.878	−14 13 16.23	1.371 0328	31	23 54 42.653	+ 1 28 11.10	0.602 3119
14	22 07 29.266	−13 32 01.89	1.362 8364	Apr. 1	23 52 49.839	+ 0 58 58.17	0.606 7684
15	22 14 24.993	−12 49 26.43	1.353 7466	2	23 51 15.364	+ 0 31 26.14	0.612 3824

GEOCENTRIC COORDINATES FOR 0^h TERRESTRIAL TIME

Date	Apparent Right Ascension	Apparent Declination	True Geocentric Distance	Date	Apparent Right Ascension	Apparent Declination	True Geocentric Distance
	h m s	° ′ ″	au		h m s	° ′ ″	au
Apr. 1	23 52 49.839	+ 0 58 58.17	0.606 7684	May 17	2 38 46.428	+13 45 17.77	1.228 8133
2	23 51 15.364	+ 0 31 26.14	0.612 3824	18	2 46 06.547	+14 28 17.02	1.241 2475
3	23 50 00.165	+ 0 05 52.18	0.619 0591	19	2 53 36.944	+15 11 14.68	1.253 0995
4	23 49 04.810	− 0 17 30.14	0.626 7062	20	3 01 17.786	+15 54 02.93	1.264 2937
5	23 48 29.543	− 0 38 30.65	0.635 2353	21	3 09 09.184	+16 36 33.20	1.274 7493
6	23 48 14.335	− 0 57 02.19	0.644 5624	22	3 17 11.179	+17 18 36.18	1.284 3817
7	23 48 18.934	− 1 13 00.24	0.654 6090	23	3 25 23.717	+18 00 01.86	1.293 1037
8	23 48 42.910	− 1 26 22.49	0.665 3021	24	3 33 46.641	+18 40 39.49	1.300 8267
9	23 49 25.701	− 1 37 08.45	0.676 5745	25	3 42 19.662	+19 20 17.75	1.307 4634
10	23 50 26.646	− 1 45 19.13	0.688 3648	26	3 51 02.352	+19 58 44.77	1.312 9296
11	23 51 45.021	− 1 50 56.67	0.700 6172	27	3 59 54.121	+20 35 48.41	1.317 1477
12	23 53 20.062	− 1 54 04.11	0.713 2811	28	4 08 54.219	+21 11 16.38	1.320 0487
13	23 55 10.989	− 1 54 45.12	0.726 3111	29	4 18 01.729	+21 44 56.56	1.321 5760
14	23 57 17.025	− 1 53 03.81	0.739 6666	30	4 27 15.580	+22 16 37.40	1.321 6874
15	23 59 37.404	− 1 49 04.60	0.753 3111	31	4 36 34.570	+22 46 07.56	1.320 3576
16	0 02 11.388	− 1 42 52.10	0.767 2123	June 1	4 45 57.342	+23 13 17.49	1.317 5798
17	0 04 58.269	− 1 34 30.96	0.781 3412	2	4 55 22.489	+23 37 58.58	1.313 3658
18	0 07 57.380	− 1 24 05.87	0.795 6722	3	5 04 48.534	+24 00 03.82	1.307 7463
19	0 11 08.095	− 1 11 41.45	0.810 1824	4	5 14 13.979	+24 19 27.89	1.300 7694
20	0 14 29.831	− 0 57 22.23	0.824 8516	5	5 23 37.345	+24 36 07.26	1.292 4985
21	0 18 02.052	− 0 41 12.66	0.839 6615	6	5 32 57.200	+24 50 00.17	1.283 0101
22	0 21 44.268	− 0 23 17.01	0.854 5959	7	5 42 12.188	+25 01 06.58	1.272 3904
23	0 25 36.037	− 0 03 39.44	0.869 6401	8	5 51 21.052	+25 09 28.00	1.260 7325
24	0 29 36.960	+ 0 17 36.02	0.884 7808	9	6 00 22.650	+25 15 07.38	1.248 1333
25	0 33 46.685	+ 0 40 25.53	0.900 0056	10	6 09 15.960	+25 18 08.87	1.234 6909
26	0 38 04.906	+ 1 04 45.35	0.915 3033	11	6 18 00.087	+25 18 37.62	1.220 5023
27	0 42 31.356	+ 1 30 31.88	0.930 6630	12	6 26 34.255	+25 16 39.58	1.205 6612
28	0 47 05.813	+ 1 57 41.67	0.946 0743	13	6 34 57.810	+25 12 21.34	1.190 2572
29	0 51 48.091	+ 2 26 11.34	0.961 5271	14	6 43 10.200	+25 05 49.90	1.174 3740
30	0 56 38.047	+ 2 55 57.62	0.977 0111	15	6 51 10.975	+24 57 12.58	1.158 0896
May 1	1 01 35.570	+ 3 26 57.32	0.992 5157	16	6 58 59.768	+24 46 36.84	1.141 4754
2	1 06 40.590	+ 3 59 07.32	1.008 0298	17	7 06 36.287	+24 34 10.23	1.124 5965
3	1 11 53.072	+ 4 32 24.53	1.023 5411	18	7 14 00.305	+24 20 00.30	1.107 5116
4	1 17 13.018	+ 5 06 45.91	1.039 0364	19	7 21 11.644	+24 04 14.52	1.090 2735
5	1 22 40.462	+ 5 42 08.39	1.054 5007	20	7 28 10.169	+23 47 00.25	1.072 9294
6	1 28 15.472	+ 6 18 28.90	1.069 9175	21	7 34 55.775	+23 28 24.73	1.055 5212
7	1 33 58.149	+ 6 55 44.31	1.085 2680	22	7 41 28.379	+23 08 35.06	1.038 0862
8	1 39 48.621	+ 7 33 51.40	1.100 5311	23	7 47 47.913	+22 47 38.17	1.020 6577
9	1 45 47.044	+ 8 12 46.84	1.115 6829	24	7 53 54.314	+22 25 40.87	1.003 2650
10	1 51 53.600	+ 8 52 27.13	1.130 6964	25	7 59 47.517	+22 02 49.80	0.985 9345
11	1 58 08.493	+ 9 32 48.57	1.145 5409	26	8 05 27.455	+21 39 11.46	0.968 6898
12	2 04 31.949	+10 13 47.23	1.160 1821	27	8 10 54.051	+21 14 52.22	0.951 5522
13	2 11 04.209	+10 55 18.89	1.174 5813	28	8 16 07.220	+20 49 58.34	0.934 5413
14	2 17 45.527	+11 37 18.97	1.188 6951	29	8 21 06.859	+20 24 35.99	0.917 6751
15	2 24 36.163	+12 19 42.52	1.202 4750	30	8 25 52.851	+19 58 51.27	0.900 9705
16	2 31 36.379	+13 02 24.10	1.215 8675	July 1	8 30 25.058	+19 32 50.21	0.884 4434
17	2 38 46.428	+13 45 17.77	1.228 8133	2	8 34 43.321	+19 06 38.86	0.868 1095

GEOCENTRIC COORDINATES FOR 0^h TERRESTRIAL TIME

Date	Apparent Right Ascension	Apparent Declination	True Geocentric Distance	Date	Apparent Right Ascension	Apparent Declination	True Geocentric Distance
	h m s	° ′ ″	au		h m s	° ′ ″	au
July 1	8 30 25.058	+19 32 50.21	0.884 4434	Aug. 16	8 29 45.391	+17 07 14.18	0.819 3656
2	8 34 43.321	+19 06 38.86	0.868 1095	17	8 32 32.473	+17 14 49.48	0.843 9459
3	8 38 47.455	+18 40 23.23	0.851 9841	18	8 35 48.254	+17 20 16.52	0.869 2845
4	8 42 37.250	+18 14 09.36	0.836 0826	19	8 39 31.996	+17 23 25.43	0.895 2582
5	8 46 12.469	+17 48 03.35	0.820 4208	20	8 43 42.742	+17 24 07.08	0.921 7336
6	8 49 32.849	+17 22 11.34	0.805 0151	21	8 48 19.323	+17 22 13.21	0.948 5674
7	8 52 38.100	+16 56 39.56	0.789 8828	22	8 53 20.368	+17 17 36.61	0.975 6080
8	8 55 27.907	+16 31 34.37	0.775 0425	23	8 58 44.315	+17 10 11.39	1.002 6967
9	8 58 01.935	+16 07 02.19	0.760 5141	24	9 04 29.428	+16 59 53.12	1.029 6710
10	9 00 19.828	+15 43 09.63	0.746 3194	25	9 10 33.822	+16 46 39.06	1.056 3665
11	9 02 21.219	+15 20 03.36	0.732 4818	26	9 16 55.486	+16 30 28.33	1.082 6214
12	9 04 05.733	+14 57 50.24	0.719 0273	27	9 23 32.322	+16 11 21.98	1.108 2799
13	9 05 32.998	+14 36 37.20	0.705 9840	28	9 30 22.182	+15 49 23.04	1.133 1960
14	9 06 42.657	+14 16 31.28	0.693 3831	29	9 37 22.917	+15 24 36.44	1.157 2371
15	9 07 34.376	+13 57 39.59	0.681 2581	30	9 44 32.419	+14 57 08.90	1.180 2870
16	9 08 07.867	+13 40 09.25	0.669 6459	31	9 51 48.661	+14 27 08.69	1.202 2482
17	9 08 22.898	+13 24 07.36	0.658 5866	Sept. 1	9 59 09.741	+13 54 45.34	1.223 0432
18	9 08 19.320	+13 09 40.89	0.648 1234	2	10 06 33.908	+13 20 09.38	1.242 6146
19	9 07 57.087	+12 56 56.58	0.638 3029	3	10 13 59.586	+12 43 31.99	1.260 9247
20	9 07 16.283	+12 46 00.86	0.629 1750	4	10 21 25.386	+12 05 04.70	1.277 9540
21	9 06 17.149	+12 36 59.63	0.620 7929	5	10 28 50.114	+11 24 59.10	1.293 6995
22	9 05 00.117	+12 29 58.16	0.613 2126	6	10 36 12.760	+10 43 26.61	1.308 1721
23	9 03 25.833	+12 25 00.84	0.606 4928	7	10 43 32.502	+10 00 38.25	1.321 3945
24	9 01 35.196	+12 22 10.99	0.600 6944	8	10 50 48.680	+ 9 16 44.55	1.333 3984
25	8 59 29.376	+12 21 30.65	0.595 8794	9	10 58 00.789	+ 8 31 55.40	1.344 2225
26	8 57 09.838	+12 23 00.39	0.592 1109	10	11 05 08.458	+ 7 46 19.99	1.353 9101
27	8 54 38.351	+12 26 39.12	0.589 4512	11	11 12 11.431	+ 7 00 06.85	1.362 5077
28	8 51 56.992	+12 32 23.97	0.587 9615	12	11 19 09.551	+ 6 13 23.78	1.370 0632
29	8 49 08.128	+12 40 10.18	0.587 7003	13	11 26 02.741	+ 5 26 17.88	1.376 6247
30	8 46 14.392	+12 49 51.13	0.588 7220	14	11 32 50.990	+ 4 38 55.59	1.382 2398
31	8 43 18.644	+13 01 18.35	0.591 0763	15	11 39 34.339	+ 3 51 22.78	1.386 9546
Aug. 1	8 40 23.912	+13 14 21.69	0.594 8064	16	11 46 12.877	+ 3 03 44.78	1.390 8134
2	8 37 33.336	+13 28 49.48	0.599 9483	17	11 52 46.725	+ 2 16 06.35	1.393 8583
3	8 34 50.091	+13 44 28.81	0.606 5303	18	11 59 16.033	+ 1 28 31.76	1.396 1286
4	8 32 17.323	+14 01 05.80	0.614 5717	19	12 05 40.968	+ 0 41 04.88	1.397 6614
5	8 29 58.069	+14 18 25.89	0.624 0828	20	12 12 01.713	− 0 06 10.80	1.398 4909
6	8 27 55.202	+14 36 14.17	0.635 0647	21	12 18 18.460	− 0 53 12.16	1.398 6485
7	8 26 11.369	+14 54 15.57	0.647 5088	22	12 24 31.406	− 1 39 56.36	1.398 1634
8	8 24 48.955	+15 12 15.15	0.661 3975	23	12 30 40.751	− 2 26 20.81	1.397 0619
9	8 23 50.046	+15 29 58.21	0.676 7038	24	12 36 46.694	− 3 12 23.18	1.395 3679
10	8 23 16.419	+15 47 10.46	0.693 3915	25	12 42 49.429	− 3 58 01.31	1.393 1033
11	8 23 09.526	+16 03 38.02	0.711 4155	26	12 48 49.148	− 4 43 13.24	1.390 2874
12	8 23 30.507	+16 19 07.51	0.730 7218	27	12 54 46.033	− 5 27 57.13	1.386 9376
13	8 24 20.190	+16 33 26.06	0.751 2472	28	13 00 40.263	− 6 12 11.28	1.383 0694
14	8 25 39.108	+16 46 21.23	0.772 9193	29	13 06 32.005	− 6 55 54.11	1.378 6964
15	8 27 27.513	+16 57 41.10	0.795 6560	30	13 12 21.419	− 7 39 04.10	1.373 8306
16	8 29 45.391	+17 07 14.18	0.819 3656	Oct. 1	13 18 08.651	− 8 21 39.82	1.368 4822

GEOCENTRIC COORDINATES FOR 0^h TERRESTRIAL TIME

Date	Apparent Right Ascension	Apparent Declination	True Geocentric Distance	Date	Apparent Right Ascension	Apparent Declination	True Geocentric Distance
	h m s	° ′ ″	au		h m s	° ′ ″	au
Oct. 1	13 18 08.651	− 8 21 39.82	1.368 4822	Nov. 16	16 06 14.313	−21 48 34.91	0.698 3493
2	13 23 53.842	− 9 03 39.90	1.362 6603	17	16 01 57.441	−21 17 27.84	0.688 9240
3	13 29 37.116	− 9 45 03.01	1.356 3721	18	15 57 12.185	−20 43 33.14	0.682 1101
4	13 35 18.592	−10 25 47.86	1.349 6241	19	15 52 06.558	−20 07 28.36	0.678 1482
5	13 40 58.370	−11 05 53.19	1.342 4212	20	15 46 50.077	−19 30 03.34	0.677 2205
6	13 46 36.544	−11 45 17.76	1.334 7674	21	15 41 33.176	−18 52 18.00	0.679 4340
7	13 52 13.192	−12 24 00.34	1.326 6655	22	15 36 26.467	−18 15 18.26	0.684 8103
8	13 57 48.376	−13 01 59.71	1.318 1174	23	15 31 39.955	−17 40 10.65	0.693 2814
9	14 03 22.143	−13 39 14.64	1.309 1241	24	15 27 22.349	−17 07 56.62	0.704 6943
10	14 08 54.521	−14 15 43.87	1.299 6854	25	15 23 40.579	−16 39 27.76	0.718 8226
11	14 14 25.515	−14 51 26.11	1.289 8007	26	15 20 39.549	−16 15 22.44	0.735 3833
12	14 19 55.107	−15 26 20.00	1.279 4685	27	15 18 22.151	−15 56 04.62	0.754 0565
13	14 25 23.256	−16 00 24.16	1.268 6864	28	15 16 49.451	−15 41 44.26	0.774 5038
14	14 30 49.892	−16 33 37.11	1.257 4520	29	15 16 01.006	−15 32 19.11	0.796 3864
15	14 36 14.920	−17 05 57.36	1.245 7622	30	15 15 55.224	−15 27 37.24	0.819 3780
16	14 41 38.212	−17 37 23.31	1.233 6135	Dec. 1	15 16 29.713	−15 27 19.67	0.843 1751
17	14 46 59.605	−18 07 53.30	1.221 0024	2	15 17 41.592	−15 31 02.92	0.867 5029
18	14 52 18.899	−18 37 25.59	1.207 9254	3	15 19 27.739	−15 38 21.10	0.892 1191
19	14 57 35.850	−19 05 58.37	1.194 3790	4	15 21 44.983	−15 48 47.52	0.916 8141
20	15 02 50.167	−19 33 29.72	1.180 3599	5	15 24 30.233	−16 01 55.93	0.941 4099
21	15 08 01.504	−19 59 57.60	1.165 8653	6	15 27 40.564	−16 17 21.28	0.965 7586
22	15 13 09.457	−20 25 19.87	1.150 8930	7	15 31 13.275	−16 34 40.19	0.989 7386
23	15 18 13.552	−20 49 34.24	1.135 4418	8	15 35 05.906	−16 53 31.24	1.013 2524
24	15 23 13.243	−21 12 38.30	1.119 5115	9	15 39 16.250	−17 13 35.04	1.036 2230
25	15 28 07.899	−21 34 29.44	1.103 1036	10	15 43 42.342	−17 34 34.22	1.058 5911
26	15 32 56.795	−21 55 04.90	1.086 2215	11	15 48 22.450	−17 56 13.31	1.080 3119
27	15 37 39.103	−22 14 21.69	1.068 8709	12	15 53 15.049	−18 18 18.60	1.101 3534
28	15 42 13.878	−22 32 16.58	1.051 0607	13	15 58 18.808	−18 40 38.01	1.121 6934
29	15 46 40.046	−22 48 46.08	1.032 8034	14	16 03 32.561	−19 03 00.88	1.141 3183
30	15 50 56.391	−23 03 46.40	1.014 1161	15	16 08 55.296	−19 25 17.83	1.160 2207
31	15 55 01.540	−23 17 13.37	0.995 0214	16	16 14 26.130	−19 47 20.60	1.178 3989
Nov. 1	15 58 53.949	−23 29 02.43	0.975 5483	17	16 20 04.292	−20 09 01.93	1.195 8552
2	16 02 31.891	−23 39 08.55	0.955 7340	18	16 25 49.113	−20 30 15.39	1.212 5948
3	16 05 53.441	−23 47 26.16	0.935 6251	19	16 31 40.006	−20 50 55.31	1.228 6257
4	16 08 56.475	−23 53 49.06	0.915 2793	20	16 37 36.460	−21 10 56.64	1.243 9575
5	16 11 38.659	−23 58 10.37	0.894 7676	21	16 43 38.024	−21 30 14.91	1.258 6010
6	16 13 57.465	−24 00 22.42	0.874 1763	22	16 49 44.304	−21 48 46.10	1.272 5678
7	16 15 50.185	−24 00 16.69	0.853 6097	23	16 55 54.950	−22 06 26.64	1.285 8702
8	16 17 13.980	−23 57 43.74	0.833 1921	24	17 02 09.653	−22 23 13.29	1.298 5203
9	16 18 05.948	−23 52 33.30	0.813 0707	25	17 08 28.137	−22 39 03.12	1.310 5305
10	16 18 23.236	−23 44 34.40	0.793 4180	26	17 14 50.156	−22 53 53.48	1.321 9130
11	16 18 03.190	−23 33 35.69	0.774 4334	27	17 21 15.490	−23 07 41.96	1.332 6793
12	16 17 03.565	−23 19 26.12	0.756 3441	28	17 27 43.938	−23 20 26.33	1.342 8408
13	16 15 22.783	−23 01 55.88	0.739 4045	29	17 34 15.320	−23 32 04.56	1.352 4082
14	16 13 00.242	−22 40 57.84	0.723 8929	30	17 40 49.467	−23 42 34.77	1.361 3915
15	16 09 56.643	−22 16 29.42	0.710 1060	31	17 47 26.226	−23 51 55.22	1.369 7999
16	16 06 14.313	−21 48 34.91	0.698 3493	32	17 54 05.451	−24 00 04.28	1.377 6420

GEOCENTRIC COORDINATES FOR 0^h TERRESTRIAL TIME

Date	Apparent Right Ascension	Apparent Declination	True Geocentric Distance	Date	Apparent Right Ascension	Apparent Declination	True Geocentric Distance
	h m s	° ′ ″	au		h m s	° ′ ″	au
Jan. 0	21 57 30.740	−14 01 14.53	0.758 1828	Feb. 15	0 18 02.930	+ 6 32 33.02	0.425 4625
1	22 01 34.569	−13 35 12.26	0.750 8179	16	0 19 35.392	+ 6 54 01.08	0.418 9211
2	22 05 36.223	−13 08 54.70	0.743 4450	17	0 21 01.748	+ 7 14 54.02	0.412 4525
3	22 09 35.685	−12 42 22.72	0.736 0644	18	0 22 21.790	+ 7 35 09.91	0.406 0612
4	22 13 32.937	−12 15 37.19	0.728 6766	19	0 23 35.308	+ 7 54 46.77	0.399 7518
5	22 17 27.962	−11 48 39.00	0.721 2821	20	0 24 42.090	+ 8 13 42.50	0.393 5292
6	22 21 20.740	−11 21 29.03	0.713 8816	21	0 25 41.921	+ 8 31 54.91	0.387 3985
7	22 25 11.253	−10 54 08.17	0.706 4756	22	0 26 34.589	+ 8 49 21.73	0.381 3648
8	22 28 59.481	−10 26 37.31	0.699 0652	23	0 27 19.881	+ 9 06 00.57	0.375 4338
9	22 32 45.404	− 9 58 57.33	0.691 6511	24	0 27 57.589	+ 9 21 48.96	0.369 6110
10	22 36 28.999	− 9 31 09.12	0.684 2343	25	0 28 27.512	+ 9 36 44.33	0.363 9025
11	22 40 10.243	− 9 03 13.59	0.676 8160	26	0 28 49.454	+ 9 50 43.99	0.358 3144
12	22 43 49.112	− 8 35 11.60	0.669 3972	27	0 29 03.234	+10 03 45.17	0.352 8532
13	22 47 25.578	− 8 07 04.04	0.661 9789	28	0 29 08.681	+10 15 45.03	0.347 5256
14	22 50 59.616	− 7 38 51.77	0.654 5624	Mar. 1	0 29 05.645	+10 26 40.62	0.342 3387
15	22 54 31.197	− 7 10 35.64	0.647 1486	2	0 28 53.997	+10 36 28.97	0.337 2999
16	22 58 00.292	− 6 42 16.49	0.639 7386	3	0 28 33.638	+10 45 07.08	0.332 4170
17	23 01 26.872	− 6 13 55.18	0.632 3335	4	0 28 04.498	+10 52 31.95	0.327 6981
18	23 04 50.904	− 5 45 32.53	0.624 9342	5	0 27 26.550	+10 58 40.63	0.323 1518
19	23 08 12.351	− 5 17 09.40	0.617 5418	6	0 26 39.811	+11 03 30.29	0.318 7868
20	23 11 31.175	− 4 48 46.63	0.610 1573	7	0 25 44.350	+11 06 58.23	0.314 6121
21	23 14 47.334	− 4 20 25.09	0.602 7816	8	0 24 40.295	+11 09 01.99	0.310 6368
22	23 18 00.780	− 3 52 05.66	0.595 4159	9	0 23 27.835	+11 09 39.40	0.306 8701
23	23 21 11.461	− 3 23 49.20	0.588 0611	10	0 22 07.230	+11 08 48.63	0.303 3212
24	23 24 19.321	− 2 55 36.64	0.580 7184	11	0 20 38.807	+11 06 28.27	0.299 9992
25	23 27 24.298	− 2 27 28.87	0.573 3889	12	0 19 02.967	+11 02 37.39	0.296 9129
26	23 30 26.325	− 1 59 26.85	0.566 0737	13	0 17 20.186	+10 57 15.62	0.294 0711
27	23 33 25.328	− 1 31 31.52	0.558 7741	14	0 15 31.010	+10 50 23.17	0.291 4819
28	23 36 21.226	− 1 03 43.87	0.551 4912	15	0 13 36.057	+10 42 00.93	0.289 1531
29	23 39 13.932	− 0 36 04.92	0.544 2264	16	0 11 36.008	+10 32 10.48	0.287 0920
30	23 42 03.351	− 0 08 35.71	0.536 9810	17	0 09 31.608	+10 20 54.13	0.285 3052
31	23 44 49.382	+ 0 18 42.66	0.529 7565	18	0 07 23.653	+10 08 14.94	0.283 7987
Feb. 1	23 47 31.916	+ 0 45 49.09	0.522 5545	19	0 05 12.983	+ 9 54 16.72	0.282 5776
2	23 50 10.838	+ 1 12 42.43	0.515 3770	20	0 03 00.476	+ 9 39 04.00	0.281 6461
3	23 52 46.024	+ 1 39 21.48	0.508 2258	21	0 00 47.030	+ 9 22 42.00	0.281 0077
4	23 55 17.345	+ 2 05 45.03	0.501 1032	22	23 58 33.560	+ 9 05 16.61	0.280 6647
5	23 57 44.664	+ 2 31 51.81	0.494 0117	23	23 56 20.979	+ 8 46 54.28	0.280 6186
6	0 00 07.837	+ 2 57 40.53	0.486 9538	24	23 54 10.188	+ 8 27 41.91	0.280 8699
7	0 02 26.712	+ 3 23 09.85	0.479 9323	25	23 52 02.066	+ 8 07 46.84	0.281 4178
8	0 04 41.132	+ 3 48 18.39	0.472 9503	26	23 49 57.456	+ 7 47 16.63	0.282 2609
9	0 06 50.933	+ 4 13 04.75	0.466 0108	27	23 47 57.157	+ 7 26 19.03	0.283 3967
10	0 08 55.946	+ 4 37 27.47	0.459 1172	28	23 46 01.917	+ 7 05 01.82	0.284 8218
11	0 10 55.997	+ 5 01 25.08	0.452 2729	29	23 44 12.423	+ 6 43 32.71	0.286 5322
12	0 12 50.907	+ 5 24 56.04	0.445 4816	30	23 42 29.299	+ 6 21 59.27	0.288 5230
13	0 14 40.492	+ 5 47 58.78	0.438 7468	31	23 40 53.105	+ 6 00 28.82	0.290 7890
14	0 16 24.564	+ 6 10 31.67	0.432 0724	Apr. 1	23 39 24.333	+ 5 39 08.37	0.293 3242
15	0 18 02.930	+ 6 32 33.02	0.425 4625	2	23 38 03.410	+ 5 18 04.57	0.296 1224

GEOCENTRIC COORDINATES FOR 0^h TERRESTRIAL TIME

Date	Apparent Right Ascension	Apparent Declination	True Geocentric Distance
	h m s	° ′ ″	au
Apr. 1	23 39 24.333	+ 5 39 08.37	0.293 3242
2	23 38 03.410	+ 5 18 04.57	0.296 1224
3	23 36 50.695	+ 4 57 23.66	0.299 1768
4	23 35 46.486	+ 4 37 11.45	0.302 4803
5	23 34 51.019	+ 4 17 33.27	0.306 0254
6	23 34 04.472	+ 3 58 33.97	0.309 8044
7	23 33 26.964	+ 3 40 17.89	0.313 8093
8	23 32 58.566	+ 3 22 48.84	0.318 0318
9	23 32 39.296	+ 3 06 10.15	0.322 4637
10	23 32 29.130	+ 2 50 24.63	0.327 0965
11	23 32 28.002	+ 2 35 34.65	0.331 9219
12	23 32 35.810	+ 2 21 42.09	0.336 9316
13	23 32 52.421	+ 2 08 48.43	0.342 1173
14	23 33 17.676	+ 1 56 54.76	0.347 4709
15	23 33 51.389	+ 1 46 01.80	0.352 9844
16	23 34 33.358	+ 1 36 09.95	0.358 6501
17	23 35 23.363	+ 1 27 19.33	0.364 4604
18	23 36 21.171	+ 1 19 29.77	0.370 4079
19	23 37 26.542	+ 1 12 40.91	0.376 4856
20	23 38 39.227	+ 1 06 52.15	0.382 6865
21	23 39 58.972	+ 1 02 02.73	0.389 0041
22	23 41 25.522	+ 0 58 11.74	0.395 4321
23	23 42 58.622	+ 0 55 18.15	0.401 9643
24	23 44 38.016	+ 0 53 20.81	0.408 5950
25	23 46 23.455	+ 0 52 18.47	0.415 3188
26	23 48 14.691	+ 0 52 09.84	0.422 1305
27	23 50 11.484	+ 0 52 53.56	0.429 0253
28	23 52 13.600	+ 0 54 28.24	0.435 9988
29	23 54 20.814	+ 0 56 52.48	0.443 0468
30	23 56 32.909	+ 1 00 04.87	0.450 1657
May 1	23 58 49.678	+ 1 04 04.02	0.457 3517
2	0 01 10.924	+ 1 08 48.53	0.464 6016
3	0 03 36.461	+ 1 14 17.07	0.471 9122
4	0 06 06.112	+ 1 20 28.30	0.479 2803
5	0 08 39.713	+ 1 27 20.90	0.486 7028
6	0 11 17.104	+ 1 34 53.60	0.494 1770
7	0 13 58.139	+ 1 43 05.10	0.501 6999
8	0 16 42.674	+ 1 51 54.15	0.509 2688
9	0 19 30.575	+ 2 01 19.48	0.516 8810
10	0 22 21.714	+ 2 11 19.85	0.524 5338
11	0 25 15.969	+ 2 21 54.03	0.532 2248
12	0 28 13.226	+ 2 33 00.78	0.539 9514
13	0 31 13.373	+ 2 44 38.88	0.547 7114
14	0 34 16.306	+ 2 56 47.13	0.555 5022
15	0 37 21.925	+ 3 09 24.32	0.563 3216
16	0 40 30.135	+ 3 22 29.25	0.571 1675
17	0 43 40.845	+ 3 36 00.73	0.579 0376
May 17	0 43 40.845	+ 3 36 00.73	0.579 0376
18	0 46 53.969	+ 3 49 57.58	0.586 9298
19	0 50 09.427	+ 4 04 18.62	0.594 8421
20	0 53 27.139	+ 4 19 02.67	0.602 7725
21	0 56 47.034	+ 4 34 08.59	0.610 7191
22	1 00 09.042	+ 4 49 35.22	0.618 6800
23	1 03 33.099	+ 5 05 21.43	0.626 6536
24	1 06 59.143	+ 5 21 26.09	0.634 6381
25	1 10 27.118	+ 5 37 48.11	0.642 6323
26	1 13 56.969	+ 5 54 26.38	0.650 6347
27	1 17 28.644	+ 6 11 19.84	0.658 6441
28	1 21 02.095	+ 6 28 27.43	0.666 6597
29	1 24 37.278	+ 6 45 48.13	0.674 6804
30	1 28 14.152	+ 7 03 20.93	0.682 7055
31	1 31 52.685	+ 7 21 04.84	0.690 7341
June 1	1 35 32.848	+ 7 38 58.92	0.698 7656
2	1 39 14.616	+ 7 57 02.24	0.706 7991
3	1 42 57.969	+ 8 15 13.89	0.714 8338
4	1 46 42.891	+ 8 33 32.96	0.722 8688
5	1 50 29.366	+ 8 51 58.57	0.730 9034
6	1 54 17.382	+ 9 10 29.84	0.738 9366
7	1 58 06.927	+ 9 29 05.89	0.746 9676
8	2 01 57.992	+ 9 47 45.85	0.754 9954
9	2 05 50.568	+10 06 28.86	0.763 0192
10	2 09 44.648	+10 25 14.05	0.771 0380
11	2 13 40.224	+10 44 00.55	0.779 0510
12	2 17 37.290	+11 02 47.52	0.787 0571
13	2 21 35.840	+11 21 34.06	0.795 0553
14	2 25 35.868	+11 40 19.33	0.803 0447
15	2 29 37.370	+11 59 02.45	0.811 0243
16	2 33 40.341	+12 17 42.55	0.818 9930
17	2 37 44.775	+12 36 18.76	0.826 9499
18	2 41 50.669	+12 54 50.21	0.834 8939
19	2 45 58.018	+13 13 16.04	0.842 8240
20	2 50 06.820	+13 31 35.39	0.850 7392
21	2 54 17.068	+13 49 47.40	0.858 6388
22	2 58 28.758	+14 07 51.25	0.866 5219
23	3 02 41.882	+14 25 46.08	0.874 3876
24	3 06 56.432	+14 43 31.08	0.882 2356
25	3 11 12.396	+15 01 05.41	0.890 0652
26	3 15 29.766	+15 18 28.25	0.897 8760
27	3 19 48.532	+15 35 38.81	0.905 6678
28	3 24 08.688	+15 52 36.27	0.913 4402
29	3 28 30.229	+16 09 19.87	0.921 1930
30	3 32 53.151	+16 25 48.83	0.928 9260
July 1	3 37 17.451	+16 42 02.40	0.936 6388
2	3 41 43.128	+16 57 59.84	0.944 3312

GEOCENTRIC COORDINATES FOR 0^h TERRESTRIAL TIME

Date	Apparent Right Ascension	Apparent Declination	True Geocentric Distance	Date	Apparent Right Ascension	Apparent Declination	True Geocentric Distance
	h m s	° ′ ″	au		h m s	° ′ ″	au
July 1	3 37 17.451	+16 42 02.40	0.936 6388	Aug. 16	7 19 43.844	+21 26 45.90	1.261 6034
2	3 41 43.128	+16 57 59.84	0.944 3312	17	7 24 47.242	+21 20 05.41	1.267 8716
3	3 46 10.177	+17 13 40.41	0.952 0027	18	7 29 50.521	+21 12 49.01	1.274 0995
4	3 50 38.597	+17 29 03.39	0.959 6531	19	7 34 53.631	+21 04 56.83	1.280 2866
5	3 55 08.381	+17 44 08.06	0.967 2820	20	7 39 56.526	+20 56 29.04	1.286 4327
6	3 59 39.525	+17 58 53.69	0.974 8889	21	7 44 59.157	+20 47 25.80	1.292 5373
7	4 04 12.021	+18 13 19.58	0.982 4733	22	7 50 01.482	+20 37 47.33	1.298 6004
8	4 08 45.861	+18 27 25.03	0.990 0349	23	7 55 03.457	+20 27 33.83	1.304 6216
9	4 13 21.034	+18 41 09.33	0.997 5732	24	8 00 05.043	+20 16 45.56	1.310 6010
10	4 17 57.530	+18 54 31.78	1.005 0875	25	8 05 06.205	+20 05 22.78	1.316 5384
11	4 22 35.335	+19 07 31.69	1.012 5774	26	8 10 06.908	+19 53 25.80	1.322 4339
12	4 27 14.434	+19 20 08.38	1.020 0423	27	8 15 07.121	+19 40 54.92	1.328 2875
13	4 31 54.812	+19 32 21.14	1.027 4814	28	8 20 06.813	+19 27 50.48	1.334 0992
14	4 36 36.450	+19 44 09.32	1.034 8941	29	8 25 05.957	+19 14 12.85	1.339 8690
15	4 41 19.331	+19 55 32.22	1.042 2797	30	8 30 04.527	+19 00 02.40	1.345 5969
16	4 46 03.433	+20 06 29.19	1.049 6374	31	8 35 02.497	+18 45 19.52	1.351 2830
17	4 50 48.735	+20 16 59.59	1.056 9665	Sept. 1	8 39 59.847	+18 30 04.64	1.356 9272
18	4 55 35.212	+20 27 02.80	1.064 2663	2	8 44 56.554	+18 14 18.19	1.362 5295
19	5 00 22.836	+20 36 38.21	1.071 5359	3	8 49 52.599	+17 58 00.59	1.368 0900
20	5 05 11.578	+20 45 45.23	1.078 7749	4	8 54 47.967	+17 41 12.32	1.373 6085
21	5 10 01.403	+20 54 23.31	1.085 9825	5	8 59 42.642	+17 23 53.83	1.379 0852
22	5 14 52.274	+21 02 31.89	1.093 1584	6	9 04 36.611	+17 06 05.60	1.384 5198
23	5 19 44.152	+21 10 10.45	1.100 3020	7	9 09 29.866	+16 47 48.12	1.389 9123
24	5 24 36.995	+21 17 18.46	1.107 4131	8	9 14 22.400	+16 29 01.86	1.395 2625
25	5 29 30.763	+21 23 55.44	1.114 4915	9	9 19 14.209	+16 09 47.33	1.400 5701
26	5 34 25.414	+21 30 00.89	1.121 5369	10	9 24 05.292	+15 50 05.04	1.405 8346
27	5 39 20.910	+21 35 34.39	1.128 5493	11	9 28 55.650	+15 29 55.52	1.411 0558
28	5 44 17.210	+21 40 35.48	1.135 5286	12	9 33 45.282	+15 09 19.33	1.416 2331
29	5 49 14.276	+21 45 03.77	1.142 4746	13	9 38 34.188	+14 48 17.04	1.421 3660
30	5 54 12.067	+21 48 58.90	1.149 3873	14	9 43 22.370	+14 26 49.26	1.426 4541
31	5 59 10.544	+21 52 20.49	1.156 2665	15	9 48 09.827	+14 04 56.60	1.431 4969
Aug. 1	6 04 09.664	+21 55 08.23	1.163 1121	16	9 52 56.560	+13 42 39.67	1.436 4940
2	6 09 09.387	+21 57 21.81	1.169 9240	17	9 57 42.573	+13 19 59.13	1.441 4451
3	6 14 09.670	+21 59 00.94	1.176 7020	18	10 02 27.869	+12 56 55.60	1.446 3499
4	6 19 10.468	+22 00 05.38	1.183 4459	19	10 07 12.457	+12 33 29.72	1.451 2083
5	6 24 11.737	+22 00 34.86	1.190 1555	20	10 11 56.346	+12 09 42.16	1.456 0200
6	6 29 13.433	+22 00 29.19	1.196 8306	21	10 16 39.548	+11 45 33.55	1.460 7851
7	6 34 15.509	+21 59 48.17	1.203 4710	22	10 21 22.077	+11 21 04.57	1.465 5034
8	6 39 17.920	+21 58 31.61	1.210 0762	23	10 26 03.950	+10 56 15.87	1.470 1751
9	6 44 20.620	+21 56 39.36	1.216 6461	24	10 30 45.184	+10 31 08.12	1.474 8002
10	6 49 23.564	+21 54 11.29	1.223 1802	25	10 35 25.797	+10 05 42.01	1.479 3787
11	6 54 26.705	+21 51 07.27	1.229 6780	26	10 40 05.810	+ 9 39 58.21	1.483 9109
12	6 59 30.001	+21 47 27.22	1.236 1390	27	10 44 45.245	+ 9 13 57.40	1.488 3968
13	7 04 33.408	+21 43 11.07	1.242 5627	28	10 49 24.124	+ 8 47 40.26	1.492 8366
14	7 09 36.880	+21 38 18.79	1.248 9484	29	10 54 02.470	+ 8 21 07.50	1.497 2304
15	7 14 40.374	+21 32 50.39	1.255 2955	30	10 58 40.309	+ 7 54 19.78	1.501 5785
16	7 19 43.844	+21 26 45.90	1.261 6034	Oct. 1	11 03 17.666	+ 7 27 17.82	1.505 8809

GEOCENTRIC COORDINATES FOR 0^h TERRESTRIAL TIME

Date	Apparent Right Ascension	Apparent Declination	True Geocentric Distance	Date	Apparent Right Ascension	Apparent Declination	True Geocentric Distance
	h m s	° ′ ″	au		h m s	° ′ ″	au
Oct. 1	11 03 17.666	+ 7 27 17.82	1.505 8809	Nov. 16	14 37 11.377	−14 06 44.49	1.654 2586
2	11 07 54.568	+ 7 00 02.30	1.510 1379	17	14 42 05.331	−14 31 15.04	1.656 4222
3	11 12 31.044	+ 6 32 33.90	1.514 3496	18	14 47 00.411	−14 55 23.77	1.658 5408
4	11 17 07.124	+ 6 04 53.31	1.518 5163	19	14 51 56.635	−15 19 09.87	1.660 6146
5	11 21 42.840	+ 5 37 01.22	1.522 6379	20	14 56 54.016	−15 42 32.55	1.662 6436
6	11 26 18.226	+ 5 08 58.29	1.526 7148	21	15 01 52.566	−16 05 30.98	1.664 6278
7	11 30 53.320	+ 4 40 45.20	1.530 7467	22	15 06 52.296	−16 28 04.38	1.666 5676
8	11 35 28.159	+ 4 12 22.62	1.534 7338	23	15 11 53.212	−16 50 11.93	1.668 4632
9	11 40 02.780	+ 3 43 51.22	1.538 6757	24	15 16 55.320	−17 11 52.86	1.670 3146
10	11 44 37.221	+ 3 15 11.70	1.542 5723	25	15 21 58.622	−17 33 06.35	1.672 1223
11	11 49 11.517	+ 2 46 24.77	1.546 4232	26	15 27 03.120	−17 53 51.64	1.673 8864
12	11 53 45.703	+ 2 17 31.15	1.550 2280	27	15 32 08.813	−18 14 07.94	1.675 6074
13	11 58 19.811	+ 1 48 31.56	1.553 9865	28	15 37 15.700	−18 33 54.48	1.677 2856
14	12 02 53.876	+ 1 19 26.77	1.557 6984	29	15 42 23.776	−18 53 10.52	1.678 9214
15	12 07 27.932	+ 0 50 17.49	1.561 3632	30	15 47 33.036	−19 11 55.29	1.680 5152
16	12 12 02.013	+ 0 21 04.49	1.564 9809	Dec. 1	15 52 43.474	−19 30 08.08	1.682 0673
17	12 16 36.156	− 0 08 11.50	1.568 5513	2	15 57 55.083	−19 47 48.18	1.683 5783
18	12 21 10.397	− 0 37 29.73	1.572 0743	3	16 03 07.852	−20 04 54.90	1.685 0485
19	12 25 44.773	− 1 06 49.45	1.575 5498	4	16 08 21.770	−20 21 27.57	1.686 4781
20	12 30 19.322	− 1 36 09.93	1.578 9778	5	16 13 36.818	−20 37 25.53	1.687 8675
21	12 34 54.082	− 2 05 30.40	1.582 3585	6	16 18 52.977	−20 52 48.11	1.689 2167
22	12 39 29.089	− 2 34 50.12	1.585 6918	7	16 24 10.222	−21 07 34.67	1.690 5257
23	12 44 04.382	− 3 04 08.34	1.588 9779	8	16 29 28.526	−21 21 44.57	1.691 7945
24	12 48 39.996	− 3 33 24.28	1.592 2170	9	16 34 47.860	−21 35 17.15	1.693 0228
25	12 53 15.969	− 4 02 37.21	1.595 4092	10	16 40 08.192	−21 48 11.82	1.694 2105
26	12 57 52.336	− 4 31 46.35	1.598 5549	11	16 45 29.490	−22 00 27.97	1.695 3574
27	13 02 29.135	− 5 00 50.93	1.601 6542	12	16 50 51.717	−22 12 05.03	1.696 4634
28	13 07 06.401	− 5 29 50.19	1.604 7074	13	16 56 14.835	−22 23 02.48	1.697 5282
29	13 11 44.171	− 5 58 43.37	1.607 7148	14	17 01 38.801	−22 33 19.79	1.698 5518
30	13 16 22.480	− 6 27 29.69	1.610 6766	15	17 07 03.572	−22 42 56.48	1.699 5340
31	13 21 01.364	− 6 56 08.39	1.613 5934	16	17 12 29.098	−22 51 52.10	1.700 4749
Nov. 1	13 25 40.861	− 7 24 38.69	1.616 4652	17	17 17 55.329	−23 00 06.21	1.701 3744
2	13 30 21.008	− 7 52 59.83	1.619 2926	18	17 23 22.213	−23 07 38.42	1.702 2324
3	13 35 01.844	− 8 21 11.06	1.622 0758	19	17 28 49.693	−23 14 28.35	1.703 0489
4	13 39 43.407	− 8 49 11.61	1.624 8151	20	17 34 17.713	−23 20 35.68	1.703 8241
5	13 44 25.737	− 9 17 00.76	1.627 5108	21	17 39 46.211	−23 26 00.09	1.704 5579
6	13 49 08.873	− 9 44 37.73	1.630 1628	22	17 45 15.126	−23 30 41.30	1.705 2505
7	13 53 52.849	−10 12 01.77	1.632 7713	23	17 50 44.395	−23 34 39.08	1.705 9021
8	13 58 37.699	−10 39 12.11	1.635 3361	24	17 56 13.955	−23 37 53.20	1.706 5127
9	14 03 23.453	−11 06 07.94	1.637 8570	25	18 01 43.742	−23 40 23.49	1.707 0826
10	14 08 10.141	−11 32 48.47	1.640 3339	26	18 07 13.691	−23 42 09.80	1.707 6121
11	14 12 57.789	−11 59 12.87	1.642 7665	27	18 12 43.740	−23 43 12.03	1.708 1015
12	14 17 46.427	−12 25 20.33	1.645 1545	28	18 18 13.825	−23 43 30.11	1.708 5511
13	14 22 36.079	−12 51 10.04	1.647 4978	29	18 23 43.883	−23 43 03.99	1.708 9613
14	14 27 26.773	−13 16 41.18	1.649 7964	30	18 29 13.855	−23 41 53.70	1.709 3324
15	14 32 18.531	−13 41 52.93	1.652 0499	31	18 34 43.677	−23 39 59.27	1.709 6648
16	14 37 11.377	−14 06 44.49	1.654 2586	32	18 40 13.289	−23 37 20.80	1.709 9589

GEOCENTRIC COORDINATES FOR 0^h TERRESTRIAL TIME

Date	Apparent Right Ascension	Apparent Declination	True Geocentric Distance	Date	Apparent Right Ascension	Apparent Declination	True Geocentric Distance
	h m s	° ′ ″	au		h m s	° ′ ″	au
Jan. 0	8 21 50.094	+23 26 07.90	0.659 2885	Feb. 15	7 18 19.471	+26 12 28.84	0.759 4812
1	8 20 30.247	+23 32 42.50	0.656 7369	16	7 17 49.240	+26 11 44.44	0.766 0430
2	8 19 07.677	+23 39 18.99	0.654 3825	17	7 17 22.487	+26 10 51.77	0.772 7381
3	8 17 42.521	+23 45 56.44	0.652 2289	18	7 16 59.200	+26 09 51.12	0.779 5628
4	8 16 14.925	+23 52 33.86	0.650 2793	19	7 16 39.364	+26 08 42.77	0.786 5135
5	8 14 45.047	+23 59 10.28	0.648 5367	20	7 16 22.958	+26 07 27.01	0.793 5865
6	8 13 13.053	+24 05 44.72	0.647 0036	21	7 16 09.959	+26 06 04.08	0.800 7782
7	8 11 39.114	+24 12 16.22	0.645 6824	22	7 16 00.339	+26 04 34.23	0.808 0851
8	8 10 03.412	+24 18 43.84	0.644 5752	23	7 15 54.069	+26 02 57.69	0.815 5035
9	8 08 26.128	+24 25 06.67	0.643 6837	24	7 15 51.113	+26 01 14.66	0.823 0299
10	8 06 47.449	+24 31 23.84	0.643 0096	25	7 15 51.437	+25 59 25.32	0.830 6609
11	8 05 07.564	+24 37 34.51	0.642 5540	26	7 15 55.001	+25 57 29.86	0.838 3927
12	8 03 26.663	+24 43 37.89	0.642 3182	27	7 16 01.766	+25 55 28.41	0.846 2218
13	8 01 44.939	+24 49 33.22	0.642 3032	28	7 16 11.688	+25 53 21.10	0.854 1446
14	8 00 02.588	+24 55 19.78	0.642 5096	Mar. 1	7 16 24.726	+25 51 08.04	0.862 1573
15	7 58 19.808	+25 00 56.87	0.642 9382	2	7 16 40.834	+25 48 49.33	0.870 2563
16	7 56 36.801	+25 06 23.86	0.643 5895	3	7 16 59.962	+25 46 25.09	0.878 4377
17	7 54 53.772	+25 11 40.14	0.644 4637	4	7 17 22.061	+25 43 55.40	0.886 6980
18	7 53 10.926	+25 16 45.16	0.645 5608	5	7 17 47.072	+25 41 20.39	0.895 0336
19	7 51 28.473	+25 21 38.41	0.646 8807	6	7 18 14.936	+25 38 40.14	0.903 4410
20	7 49 46.619	+25 26 19.46	0.648 4231	7	7 18 45.591	+25 35 54.76	0.911 9169
21	7 48 05.572	+25 30 47.91	0.650 1872	8	7 19 18.971	+25 33 04.31	0.920 4583
22	7 46 25.535	+25 35 03.44	0.652 1721	9	7 19 55.014	+25 30 08.87	0.929 0622
23	7 44 46.708	+25 39 05.78	0.654 3768	10	7 20 33.654	+25 27 08.47	0.937 7257
24	7 43 09.288	+25 42 54.71	0.656 7997	11	7 21 14.831	+25 24 03.16	0.946 4463
25	7 41 33.466	+25 46 30.07	0.659 4393	12	7 21 58.482	+25 20 52.95	0.955 2214
26	7 39 59.426	+25 49 51.76	0.662 2935	13	7 22 44.549	+25 17 37.87	0.964 0485
27	7 38 27.347	+25 52 59.73	0.665 3603	14	7 23 32.975	+25 14 17.92	0.972 9255
28	7 36 57.400	+25 55 53.97	0.668 6372	15	7 24 23.705	+25 10 53.10	0.981 8501
29	7 35 29.748	+25 58 34.50	0.672 1215	16	7 25 16.686	+25 07 23.42	0.990 8201
30	7 34 04.544	+26 01 01.42	0.675 8102	17	7 26 11.864	+25 03 48.85	0.999 8336
31	7 32 41.936	+26 03 14.82	0.679 7001	18	7 27 09.189	+25 00 09.40	1.008 8884
Feb. 1	7 31 22.060	+26 05 14.84	0.683 7876	19	7 28 08.611	+24 56 25.04	1.017 9827
2	7 30 05.042	+26 07 01.68	0.688 0690	20	7 29 10.081	+24 52 35.75	1.027 1145
3	7 28 50.997	+26 08 35.56	0.692 5403	21	7 30 13.550	+24 48 41.51	1.036 2818
4	7 27 40.027	+26 09 56.74	0.697 1973	22	7 31 18.972	+24 44 42.29	1.045 4830
5	7 26 32.222	+26 11 05.52	0.702 0359	23	7 32 26.298	+24 40 38.06	1.054 7160
6	7 25 27.657	+26 12 02.24	0.707 0518	24	7 33 35.485	+24 36 28.76	1.063 9790
7	7 24 26.395	+26 12 47.24	0.712 2407	25	7 34 46.488	+24 32 14.35	1.073 2702
8	7 23 28.487	+26 13 20.89	0.717 5983	26	7 35 59.263	+24 27 54.77	1.082 5878
9	7 22 33.974	+26 13 43.56	0.723 1204	27	7 37 13.768	+24 23 29.95	1.091 9297
10	7 21 42.887	+26 13 55.60	0.728 8029	28	7 38 29.963	+24 18 59.83	1.101 2939
11	7 20 55.250	+26 13 57.38	0.734 6417	29	7 39 47.809	+24 14 24.31	1.110 6786
12	7 20 11.081	+26 13 49.26	0.740 6328	30	7 41 07.269	+24 09 43.34	1.120 0815
13	7 19 30.391	+26 13 31.57	0.746 7723	31	7 42 28.303	+24 04 56.85	1.129 5005
14	7 18 53.188	+26 13 04.66	0.753 0564	Apr. 1	7 43 50.871	+24 00 04.81	1.138 9335
15	7 18 19.471	+26 12 28.84	0.759 4812	2	7 45 14.930	+23 55 07.19	1.148 3785

GEOCENTRIC COORDINATES FOR 0^h TERRESTRIAL TIME

Date	Apparent Right Ascension	Apparent Declination	True Geocentric Distance	Date	Apparent Right Ascension	Apparent Declination	True Geocentric Distance
	h m s	° ′ ″	au		h m s	° ′ ″	au
Apr. 1	7 43 50.871	+24 00 04.81	1.138 9335	May 17	9 05 04.480	+18 27 30.74	1.566 4982
2	7 45 14.930	+23 55 07.19	1.148 3785	18	9 07 04.858	+18 17 48.88	1.575 3063
3	7 46 40.435	+23 50 03.97	1.157 8337	19	9 09 05.578	+18 08 00.79	1.584 0837
4	7 48 07.340	+23 44 55.11	1.167 2972	20	9 11 06.632	+17 58 06.49	1.592 8299
5	7 49 35.600	+23 39 40.60	1.176 7673	21	9 13 08.011	+17 48 05.97	1.601 5445
6	7 51 05.172	+23 34 20.40	1.186 2427	22	9 15 09.708	+17 37 59.23	1.610 2269
7	7 52 36.012	+23 28 54.47	1.195 7219	23	9 17 11.716	+17 27 46.28	1.618 8765
8	7 54 08.083	+23 23 22.77	1.205 2036	24	9 19 14.032	+17 17 27.10	1.627 4925
9	7 55 41.345	+23 17 45.27	1.214 6866	25	9 21 16.649	+17 07 01.71	1.636 0741
10	7 57 15.764	+23 12 01.92	1.224 1698	26	9 23 19.561	+16 56 30.13	1.644 6205
11	7 58 51.305	+23 06 12.69	1.233 6523	27	9 25 22.762	+16 45 52.40	1.653 1308
12	8 00 27.936	+23 00 17.54	1.243 1328	28	9 27 26.240	+16 35 08.57	1.661 6040
13	8 02 05.626	+22 54 16.43	1.252 6106	29	9 29 29.983	+16 24 18.69	1.670 0394
14	8 03 44.344	+22 48 09.34	1.262 0847	30	9 31 33.979	+16 13 22.83	1.678 4361
15	8 05 24.064	+22 41 56.23	1.271 5542	31	9 33 38.215	+16 02 21.04	1.686 7935
16	8 07 04.755	+22 35 37.08	1.281 0183	June 1	9 35 42.680	+15 51 13.37	1.695 1112
17	8 08 46.391	+22 29 11.86	1.290 4761	2	9 37 47.364	+15 39 59.87	1.703 3887
18	8 10 28.946	+22 22 40.53	1.299 9267	3	9 39 52.260	+15 28 40.59	1.711 6256
19	8 12 12.393	+22 16 03.07	1.309 3694	4	9 41 57.361	+15 17 15.57	1.719 8216
20	8 13 56.708	+22 09 19.45	1.318 8031	5	9 44 02.659	+15 05 44.87	1.727 9766
21	8 15 41.867	+22 02 29.63	1.328 2272	6	9 46 08.150	+14 54 08.52	1.736 0903
22	8 17 27.846	+21 55 33.57	1.337 6406	7	9 48 13.827	+14 42 26.59	1.744 1625
23	8 19 14.623	+21 48 31.24	1.347 0424	8	9 50 19.686	+14 30 39.12	1.752 1933
24	8 21 02.178	+21 41 22.58	1.356 4316	9	9 52 25.723	+14 18 46.16	1.760 1823
25	8 22 50.491	+21 34 07.54	1.365 8071	10	9 54 31.932	+14 06 47.78	1.768 1297
26	8 24 39.545	+21 26 46.09	1.375 1677	11	9 56 38.310	+13 54 44.01	1.776 0353
27	8 26 29.322	+21 19 18.17	1.384 5122	12	9 58 44.852	+13 42 34.92	1.783 8990
28	8 28 19.804	+21 11 43.77	1.393 8393	13	10 00 51.554	+13 30 20.56	1.791 7209
29	8 30 10.972	+21 04 02.88	1.403 1477	14	10 02 58.413	+13 18 00.98	1.799 5008
30	8 32 02.802	+20 56 15.51	1.412 4361	15	10 05 05.426	+13 05 36.21	1.807 2386
May 1	8 33 55.270	+20 48 21.68	1.421 7033	16	10 07 12.590	+12 53 06.31	1.814 9343
2	8 35 48.350	+20 40 21.40	1.430 9482	17	10 09 19.906	+12 40 31.31	1.822 5877
3	8 37 42.018	+20 32 14.69	1.440 1700	18	10 11 27.372	+12 27 51.24	1.830 1986
4	8 39 36.251	+20 24 01.55	1.449 3677	19	10 13 34.990	+12 15 06.12	1.837 7665
5	8 41 31.025	+20 15 42.01	1.458 5406	20	10 15 42.761	+12 02 15.99	1.845 2912
6	8 43 26.322	+20 07 16.05	1.467 6881	21	10 17 50.689	+11 49 20.86	1.852 7723
7	8 45 22.123	+19 58 43.69	1.476 8097	22	10 19 58.774	+11 36 20.79	1.860 2090
8	8 47 18.411	+19 50 04.94	1.485 9047	23	10 22 07.018	+11 23 15.81	1.867 6009
9	8 49 15.169	+19 41 19.80	1.494 9727	24	10 24 15.418	+11 10 06.00	1.874 9473
10	8 51 12.383	+19 32 28.29	1.504 0133	25	10 26 23.973	+10 56 51.42	1.882 2475
11	8 53 10.038	+19 23 30.43	1.513 0260	26	10 28 32.678	+10 43 32.16	1.889 5010
12	8 55 08.119	+19 14 26.23	1.522 0106	27	10 30 41.527	+10 30 08.31	1.896 7071
13	8 57 06.615	+19 05 15.70	1.530 9666	28	10 32 50.516	+10 16 39.93	1.903 8653
14	8 59 05.511	+18 55 58.87	1.539 8937	29	10 34 59.644	+10 03 07.11	1.910 9754
15	9 01 04.795	+18 46 35.75	1.548 7916	30	10 37 08.906	+ 9 49 29.91	1.918 0369
16	9 03 04.456	+18 37 06.37	1.557 6599	July 1	10 39 18.303	+ 9 35 48.41	1.925 0498
17	9 05 04.480	+18 27 30.74	1.566 4982	2	10 41 27.834	+ 9 22 02.68	1.932 0139

GEOCENTRIC COORDINATES FOR 0^h TERRESTRIAL TIME

Date	Apparent Right Ascension	Apparent Declination	True Geocentric Distance	Date	Apparent Right Ascension	Apparent Declination	True Geocentric Distance
	h m s	° ′ ″	au		h m s	° ′ ″	au
July 1	10 39 18.303	+ 9 35 48.41	1.925 0498	Aug. 16	12 21 28.304	− 1 50 54.32	2.194 1505
2	10 41 27.834	+ 9 22 02.68	1.932 0139	17	12 23 46.695	− 2 06 34.65	2.198 8138
3	10 43 37.499	+ 9 08 12.79	1.938 9292	18	12 26 05.387	− 2 22 15.56	2.203 4268
4	10 45 47.299	+ 8 54 18.81	1.945 7954	19	12 28 24.386	− 2 37 56.94	2.207 9890
5	10 47 57.232	+ 8 40 20.81	1.952 6128	20	12 30 43.695	− 2 53 38.70	2.212 5001
6	10 50 07.301	+ 8 26 18.87	1.959 3813	21	12 33 03.318	− 3 09 20.72	2.216 9597
7	10 52 17.506	+ 8 12 13.06	1.966 1010	22	12 35 23.259	− 3 25 02.87	2.221 3676
8	10 54 27.846	+ 7 58 03.45	1.972 7720	23	12 37 43.523	− 3 40 45.05	2.225 7236
9	10 56 38.324	+ 7 43 50.13	1.979 3943	24	12 40 04.115	− 3 56 27.15	2.230 0273
10	10 58 48.938	+ 7 29 33.16	1.985 9682	25	12 42 25.039	− 4 12 09.04	2.234 2787
11	11 00 59.691	+ 7 15 12.63	1.992 4937	26	12 44 46.303	− 4 27 50.63	2.238 4778
12	11 03 10.583	+ 7 00 48.59	1.998 9710	27	12 47 07.911	− 4 43 31.80	2.242 6245
13	11 05 21.617	+ 6 46 21.12	2.005 4002	28	12 49 29.869	− 4 59 12.44	2.246 7190
14	11 07 32.795	+ 6 31 50.27	2.011 7814	29	12 51 52.183	− 5 14 52.44	2.250 7612
15	11 09 44.122	+ 6 17 16.10	2.018 1146	30	12 54 14.856	− 5 30 31.67	2.254 7515
16	11 11 55.604	+ 6 02 38.65	2.024 3997	31	12 56 37.895	− 5 46 10.03	2.258 6899
17	11 14 07.245	+ 5 47 57.98	2.030 6367	Sept. 1	12 59 01.303	− 6 01 47.39	2.262 5768
18	11 16 19.054	+ 5 33 14.11	2.036 8253	2	13 01 25.085	− 6 17 23.64	2.266 4124
19	11 18 31.035	+ 5 18 27.12	2.042 9653	3	13 03 49.246	− 6 32 58.65	2.270 1970
20	11 20 43.195	+ 5 03 37.04	2.049 0562	4	13 06 13.789	− 6 48 32.30	2.273 9310
21	11 22 55.538	+ 4 48 43.97	2.055 0977	5	13 08 38.721	− 7 04 04.47	2.277 6147
22	11 25 08.066	+ 4 33 47.97	2.061 0892	6	13 11 04.045	− 7 19 35.04	2.281 2486
23	11 27 20.780	+ 4 18 49.13	2.067 0304	7	13 13 29.768	− 7 35 03.89	2.284 8331
24	11 29 33.681	+ 4 03 47.55	2.072 9207	8	13 15 55.898	− 7 50 30.90	2.288 3686
25	11 31 46.769	+ 3 48 43.34	2.078 7597	9	13 18 22.445	− 8 05 55.99	2.291 8553
26	11 34 00.045	+ 3 33 36.57	2.084 5470	10	13 20 49.419	− 8 21 19.04	2.295 2938
27	11 36 13.512	+ 3 18 27.35	2.090 2824	11	13 23 16.829	− 8 36 39.98	2.298 6840
28	11 38 27.172	+ 3 03 15.76	2.095 9657	12	13 25 44.686	− 8 51 58.71	2.302 0261
29	11 40 41.028	+ 2 48 01.90	2.101 5968	13	13 28 12.998	− 9 07 15.12	2.305 3201
30	11 42 55.085	+ 2 32 45.84	2.107 1756	14	13 30 41.772	− 9 22 29.10	2.308 5659
31	11 45 09.344	+ 2 17 27.69	2.112 7021	15	13 33 11.013	− 9 37 40.52	2.311 7633
Aug. 1	11 47 23.811	+ 2 02 07.52	2.118 1764	16	13 35 40.727	− 9 52 49.25	2.314 9121
2	11 49 38.489	+ 1 46 45.43	2.123 5986	17	13 38 10.919	−10 07 55.15	2.318 0121
3	11 51 53.381	+ 1 31 21.52	2.128 9688	18	13 40 41.594	−10 22 58.08	2.321 0631
4	11 54 08.490	+ 1 15 55.87	2.134 2871	19	13 43 12.757	−10 37 57.88	2.324 0648
5	11 56 23.820	+ 1 00 28.59	2.139 5539	20	13 45 44.413	−10 52 54.43	2.327 0172
6	11 58 39.375	+ 0 44 59.75	2.144 7693	21	13 48 16.571	−11 07 47.57	2.329 9201
7	12 00 55.157	+ 0 29 29.47	2.149 9335	22	13 50 49.234	−11 22 37.16	2.332 7735
8	12 03 11.170	+ 0 13 57.83	2.155 0469	23	13 53 22.409	−11 37 23.07	2.335 5773
9	12 05 27.418	− 0 01 35.07	2.160 1098	24	13 55 56.103	−11 52 05.16	2.338 3317
10	12 07 43.906	− 0 17 09.15	2.165 1223	25	13 58 30.319	−12 06 43.27	2.341 0367
11	12 10 00.641	− 0 32 44.33	2.170 0848	26	14 01 05.062	−12 21 17.27	2.343 6926
12	12 12 17.630	− 0 48 20.54	2.174 9974	27	14 03 40.337	−12 35 47.00	2.346 2995
13	12 14 34.882	− 1 03 57.71	2.179 8603	28	14 06 16.147	−12 50 12.32	2.348 8576
14	12 16 52.405	− 1 19 35.77	2.184 6735	29	14 08 52.497	−13 04 33.08	2.351 3673
15	12 19 10.210	− 1 35 14.67	2.189 4369	30	14 11 29.388	−13 18 49.13	2.353 8290
16	12 21 28.304	− 1 50 54.32	2.194 1505	Oct. 1	14 14 06.825	−13 33 00.30	2.356 2430

GEOCENTRIC COORDINATES FOR 0^h TERRESTRIAL TIME

Date	Apparent Right Ascension	Apparent Declination	True Geocentric Distance	Date	Apparent Right Ascension	Apparent Declination	True Geocentric Distance
	h m s	° ′ ″	au		h m s	° ′ ″	au
Oct. 1	14 14 06.825	−13 33 00.30	2.356 2430	Nov. 16	16 25 43.262	−22 12 40.49	2.420 4166
2	14 16 44.811	−13 47 06.44	2.358 6096	17	16 28 49.416	−22 20 03.04	2.420 8867
3	14 19 23.348	−14 01 07.39	2.360 9295	18	16 31 56.147	−22 27 12.94	2.421 3209
4	14 22 02.442	−14 15 03.00	2.363 2031	19	16 35 03.447	−22 34 10.05	2.421 7195
5	14 24 42.097	−14 28 53.12	2.365 4308	20	16 38 11.308	−22 40 54.21	2.422 0826
6	14 27 22.320	−14 42 37.58	2.367 6133	21	16 41 19.719	−22 47 25.28	2.422 4105
7	14 30 03.119	−14 56 16.26	2.369 7511	22	16 44 28.670	−22 53 43.11	2.422 7035
8	14 32 44.502	−15 09 49.03	2.371 8446	23	16 47 38.150	−22 59 47.56	2.422 9617
9	14 35 26.478	−15 23 15.75	2.373 8942	24	16 50 48.147	−23 05 38.49	2.423 1858
10	14 38 09.053	−15 36 36.31	2.375 9001	25	16 53 58.650	−23 11 15.74	2.423 3759
11	14 40 52.234	−15 49 50.55	2.377 8625	26	16 57 09.645	−23 16 39.19	2.423 5327
12	14 43 36.024	−16 02 58.34	2.379 7815	27	17 00 21.121	−23 21 48.68	2.423 6566
13	14 46 20.426	−16 15 59.50	2.381 6569	28	17 03 33.066	−23 26 44.09	2.423 7482
14	14 49 05.443	−16 28 53.87	2.383 4886	29	17 06 45.467	−23 31 25.27	2.423 8080
15	14 51 51.078	−16 41 41.28	2.385 2767	30	17 09 58.316	−23 35 52.10	2.423 8368
16	14 54 37.334	−16 54 21.56	2.387 0209	Dec. 1	17 13 11.602	−23 40 04.46	2.423 8352
17	14 57 24.214	−17 06 54.52	2.388 7212	2	17 16 25.315	−23 44 02.24	2.423 8039
18	15 00 11.722	−17 19 20.00	2.390 3776	3	17 19 39.448	−23 47 45.34	2.423 7436
19	15 02 59.861	−17 31 37.82	2.391 9899	4	17 22 53.990	−23 51 13.67	2.423 6551
20	15 05 48.634	−17 43 47.83	2.393 5582	5	17 26 08.930	−23 54 27.15	2.423 5388
21	15 08 38.042	−17 55 49.84	2.395 0827	6	17 29 24.255	−23 57 25.69	2.423 3952
22	15 11 28.087	−18 07 43.69	2.396 5633	7	17 32 39.952	−24 00 09.19	2.423 2248
23	15 14 18.770	−18 19 29.22	2.398 0003	8	17 35 56.006	−24 02 37.54	2.423 0276
24	15 17 10.091	−18 31 06.25	2.399 3938	9	17 39 12.405	−24 04 50.65	2.422 8039
25	15 20 02.049	−18 42 34.61	2.400 7442	10	17 42 29.136	−24 06 48.40	2.422 5537
26	15 22 54.643	−18 53 54.13	2.402 0517	11	17 45 46.186	−24 08 30.71	2.422 2770
27	15 25 47.871	−19 05 04.63	2.403 3167	12	17 49 03.544	−24 09 57.47	2.421 9740
28	15 28 41.730	−19 16 05.94	2.404 5395	13	17 52 21.196	−24 11 08.62	2.421 6446
29	15 31 36.218	−19 26 57.88	2.405 7206	14	17 55 39.128	−24 12 04.08	2.421 2890
30	15 34 31.334	−19 37 40.28	2.406 8605	15	17 58 57.327	−24 12 43.78	2.420 9072
31	15 37 27.074	−19 48 12.94	2.407 9597	16	18 02 15.776	−24 13 07.68	2.420 4994
Nov. 1	15 40 23.437	−19 58 35.71	2.409 0187	17	18 05 34.461	−24 13 15.71	2.420 0657
2	15 43 20.422	−20 08 48.40	2.410 0382	18	18 08 53.364	−24 13 07.84	2.419 6064
3	15 46 18.030	−20 18 50.85	2.411 0188	19	18 12 12.468	−24 12 44.02	2.419 1216
4	15 49 16.262	−20 28 42.89	2.411 9612	20	18 15 31.754	−24 12 04.22	2.418 6116
5	15 52 15.119	−20 38 24.39	2.412 8659	21	18 18 51.205	−24 11 08.40	2.418 0767
6	15 55 14.603	−20 47 55.19	2.413 7335	22	18 22 10.802	−24 09 56.54	2.417 5172
7	15 58 14.712	−20 57 15.16	2.414 5645	23	18 25 30.526	−24 08 28.61	2.416 9335
8	16 01 15.446	−21 06 24.16	2.415 3591	24	18 28 50.358	−24 06 44.59	2.416 3261
9	16 04 16.799	−21 15 22.01	2.416 1175	25	18 32 10.281	−24 04 44.46	2.415 6953
10	16 07 18.767	−21 24 08.55	2.416 8399	26	18 35 30.277	−24 02 28.20	2.415 0419
11	16 10 21.346	−21 32 43.60	2.417 5262	27	18 38 50.330	−23 59 55.81	2.414 3663
12	16 13 24.532	−21 41 06.99	2.418 1764	28	18 42 10.425	−23 57 07.29	2.413 6692
13	16 16 28.321	−21 49 18.54	2.418 7905	29	18 45 30.549	−23 54 02.65	2.412 9513
14	16 19 32.708	−21 57 18.08	2.419 3686	30	18 48 50.686	−23 50 41.90	2.412 2133
15	16 22 37.690	−22 05 05.45	2.419 9106	31	18 52 10.825	−23 47 05.08	2.411 4559
16	16 25 43.262	−22 12 40.49	2.420 4166	32	18 55 30.950	−23 43 12.22	2.410 6797

GEOCENTRIC COORDINATES FOR 0^h TERRESTRIAL TIME

Date	Apparent Right Ascension	Apparent Declination	True Geocentric Distance	Date	Apparent Right Ascension	Apparent Declination	True Geocentric Distance
	h m s	° ′ ″	au		h m s	° ′ ″	au
Jan. 0	4 47 59.468	+21 47 50.62	4.183 1179	Feb. 15	4 39 58.641	+21 43 04.89	4.753 1721
1	4 47 31.761	+21 47 14.59	4.190 7348	16	4 40 07.997	+21 43 35.20	4.768 8667
2	4 47 04.652	+21 46 39.44	4.198 6273	17	4 40 18.183	+21 44 06.99	4.784 6260
3	4 46 38.160	+21 46 05.20	4.206 7915	18	4 40 29.197	+21 44 40.23	4.800 4457
4	4 46 12.302	+21 45 31.89	4.215 2236	19	4 40 41.036	+21 45 14.93	4.816 3213
5	4 45 47.096	+21 44 59.56	4.223 9195	20	4 40 53.694	+21 45 51.06	4.832 2485
6	4 45 22.562	+21 44 28.24	4.232 8752	21	4 41 07.167	+21 46 28.62	4.848 2229
7	4 44 58.716	+21 43 57.97	4.242 0862	22	4 41 21.450	+21 47 07.58	4.864 2400
8	4 44 35.576	+21 43 28.80	4.251 5483	23	4 41 36.537	+21 47 47.92	4.880 2956
9	4 44 13.155	+21 43 00.78	4.261 2572	24	4 41 52.421	+21 48 29.62	4.896 3851
10	4 43 51.467	+21 42 33.96	4.271 2086	25	4 42 09.095	+21 49 12.66	4.912 5041
11	4 43 30.524	+21 42 08.38	4.281 3981	26	4 42 26.553	+21 49 56.99	4.928 6480
12	4 43 10.333	+21 41 44.09	4.291 8215	27	4 42 44.787	+21 50 42.58	4.944 8123
13	4 42 50.903	+21 41 21.12	4.302 4745	28	4 43 03.791	+21 51 29.38	4.960 9923
14	4 42 32.242	+21 40 59.49	4.313 3530	Mar. 1	4 43 23.559	+21 52 17.34	4.977 1835
15	4 42 14.358	+21 40 39.22	4.324 4528	2	4 43 44.087	+21 53 06.43	4.993 3811
16	4 41 57.259	+21 40 20.33	4.335 7697	3	4 44 05.371	+21 53 56.62	5.009 5807
17	4 41 40.955	+21 40 02.85	4.347 2995	4	4 44 27.403	+21 54 47.89	5.025 7778
18	4 41 25.456	+21 39 46.78	4.359 0379	5	4 44 50.177	+21 55 40.21	5.041 9681
19	4 41 10.770	+21 39 32.16	4.370 9807	6	4 45 13.684	+21 56 33.57	5.058 1474
20	4 40 56.907	+21 39 19.02	4.383 1236	7	4 45 37.912	+21 57 27.93	5.074 3118
21	4 40 43.875	+21 39 07.39	4.395 4619	8	4 46 02.852	+21 58 23.26	5.090 4574
22	4 40 31.682	+21 38 57.28	4.407 9913	9	4 46 28.493	+21 59 19.52	5.106 5805
23	4 40 20.335	+21 38 48.75	4.420 7071	10	4 46 54.825	+22 00 16.66	5.122 6775
24	4 40 09.841	+21 38 41.80	4.433 6048	11	4 47 21.839	+22 01 14.64	5.138 7449
25	4 40 00.204	+21 38 36.46	4.446 6795	12	4 47 49.525	+22 02 13.41	5.154 7794
26	4 39 51.429	+21 38 32.77	4.459 9265	13	4 48 17.878	+22 03 12.93	5.170 7776
27	4 39 43.519	+21 38 30.73	4.473 3409	14	4 48 46.889	+22 04 13.17	5.186 7362
28	4 39 36.477	+21 38 30.36	4.486 9178	15	4 49 16.553	+22 05 14.07	5.202 6520
29	4 39 30.304	+21 38 31.66	4.500 6520	16	4 49 46.863	+22 06 15.62	5.218 5218
30	4 39 25.002	+21 38 34.62	4.514 5384	17	4 50 17.813	+22 07 17.78	5.234 3424
31	4 39 20.572	+21 38 39.25	4.528 5718	18	4 50 49.396	+22 08 20.53	5.250 1106
Feb. 1	4 39 17.016	+21 38 45.53	4.542 7467	19	4 51 21.606	+22 09 23.83	5.265 8232
2	4 39 14.337	+21 38 53.45	4.557 0578	20	4 51 54.436	+22 10 27.66	5.281 4771
3	4 39 12.536	+21 39 03.01	4.571 4997	21	4 52 27.877	+22 11 31.99	5.297 0691
4	4 39 11.614	+21 39 14.21	4.586 0672	22	4 53 01.922	+22 12 36.79	5.312 5960
5	4 39 11.573	+21 39 27.06	4.600 7550	23	4 53 36.564	+22 13 42.03	5.328 0547
6	4 39 12.408	+21 39 41.56	4.615 5579	24	4 54 11.793	+22 14 47.66	5.343 4420
7	4 39 14.118	+21 39 57.72	4.630 4710	25	4 54 47.601	+22 15 53.66	5.358 7546
8	4 39 16.697	+21 40 15.53	4.645 4892	26	4 55 23.979	+22 16 59.98	5.373 9893
9	4 39 20.140	+21 40 34.98	4.660 6078	27	4 56 00.921	+22 18 06.56	5.389 1428
10	4 39 24.440	+21 40 56.05	4.675 8222	28	4 56 38.417	+22 19 13.35	5.404 2118
11	4 39 29.593	+21 41 18.72	4.691 1277	29	4 57 16.464	+22 20 20.31	5.419 1928
12	4 39 35.593	+21 41 42.96	4.706 5199	30	4 57 55.055	+22 21 27.40	5.434 0827
13	4 39 42.437	+21 42 08.75	4.721 9943	31	4 58 34.186	+22 22 34.58	5.448 8781
14	4 39 50.121	+21 42 36.07	4.737 5465	Apr. 1	4 59 13.848	+22 23 41.84	5.463 5760
15	4 39 58.641	+21 43 04.89	4.753 1721	2	4 59 54.034	+22 24 49.16	5.478 1732

GEOCENTRIC COORDINATES FOR 0^h TERRESTRIAL TIME

Date	Apparent Right Ascension	Apparent Declination	True Geocentric Distance	Date	Apparent Right Ascension	Apparent Declination	True Geocentric Distance
	h m s	° ′ ″	au		h m s	° ′ ″	au
Apr. 1	4 59 13.848	+22 23 41.84	5.463 5760	May 17	5 36 56.832	+23 07 34.97	5.996 4116
2	4 59 54.034	+22 24 49.16	5.478 1732	18	5 37 52.995	+23 08 12.13	6.004 2216
3	5 00 34.732	+22 25 56.50	5.492 6671	19	5 38 49.353	+23 08 48.10	6.011 8505
4	5 01 15.932	+22 27 03.85	5.507 0550	20	5 39 45.899	+23 09 22.88	6.019 2972
5	5 01 57.623	+22 28 11.15	5.521 3343	21	5 40 42.629	+23 09 56.42	6.026 5605
6	5 02 39.794	+22 29 18.36	5.535 5028	22	5 41 39.537	+23 10 28.71	6.033 6393
7	5 03 22.435	+22 30 25.45	5.549 5581	23	5 42 36.620	+23 10 59.71	6.040 5322
8	5 04 05.540	+22 31 32.36	5.563 4982	24	5 43 33.874	+23 11 29.42	6.047 2380
9	5 04 49.100	+22 32 39.05	5.577 3208	25	5 44 31.296	+23 11 57.82	6.053 7555
10	5 05 33.109	+22 33 45.50	5.591 0239	26	5 45 28.882	+23 12 24.91	6.060 0835
11	5 06 17.560	+22 34 51.65	5.604 6056	27	5 46 26.624	+23 12 50.69	6.066 2208
12	5 07 02.448	+22 35 57.49	5.618 0637	28	5 47 24.516	+23 13 15.18	6.072 1666
13	5 07 47.766	+22 37 02.99	5.631 3964	29	5 48 22.547	+23 13 38.36	6.077 9199
14	5 08 33.509	+22 38 08.11	5.644 6017	30	5 49 20.708	+23 14 00.23	6.083 4803
15	5 09 19.671	+22 39 12.85	5.657 6775	31	5 50 18.991	+23 14 20.77	6.088 8471
16	5 10 06.245	+22 40 17.17	5.670 6221	June 1	5 51 17.387	+23 14 39.95	6.094 0200
17	5 10 53.225	+22 41 21.06	5.683 4334	2	5 52 15.891	+23 14 57.75	6.098 9986
18	5 11 40.603	+22 42 24.49	5.696 1095	3	5 53 14.498	+23 15 14.16	6.103 7827
19	5 12 28.372	+22 43 27.43	5.708 6484	4	5 54 13.203	+23 15 29.17	6.108 3721
20	5 13 16.524	+22 44 29.86	5.721 0481	5	5 55 12.002	+23 15 42.77	6.112 7666
21	5 14 05.052	+22 45 31.75	5.733 3066	6	5 56 10.892	+23 15 54.96	6.116 9659
22	5 14 53.948	+22 46 33.05	5.745 4219	7	5 57 09.868	+23 16 05.72	6.120 9698
23	5 15 43.206	+22 47 33.74	5.757 3917	8	5 58 08.926	+23 16 15.08	6.124 7783
24	5 16 32.819	+22 48 33.76	5.769 2142	9	5 59 08.061	+23 16 23.02	6.128 3911
25	5 17 22.781	+22 49 33.09	5.780 8870	10	6 00 07.268	+23 16 29.55	6.131 8080
26	5 18 13.087	+22 50 31.68	5.792 4080	11	6 01 06.542	+23 16 34.67	6.135 0289
27	5 19 03.735	+22 51 29.51	5.803 7750	12	6 02 05.878	+23 16 38.39	6.138 0535
28	5 19 54.719	+22 52 26.55	5.814 9859	13	6 03 05.270	+23 16 40.71	6.140 8815
29	5 20 46.032	+22 53 22.81	5.826 0388	14	6 04 04.711	+23 16 41.62	6.143 5127
30	5 21 37.667	+22 54 18.28	5.836 9318	15	6 05 04.196	+23 16 41.11	6.145 9467
May 1	5 22 29.612	+22 55 12.92	5.847 6632	16	6 06 03.719	+23 16 39.18	6.148 1832
2	5 23 21.858	+22 56 06.74	5.858 2315	17	6 07 03.276	+23 16 35.81	6.150 2217
3	5 24 14.394	+22 56 59.68	5.868 6354	18	6 08 02.861	+23 16 30.99	6.152 0619
4	5 25 07.212	+22 57 51.72	5.878 8735	19	6 09 02.473	+23 16 24.70	6.153 7030
5	5 26 00.305	+22 58 42.82	5.888 9448	20	6 10 02.107	+23 16 16.95	6.155 1448
6	5 26 53.666	+22 59 32.96	5.898 8481	21	6 11 01.761	+23 16 07.72	6.156 3866
7	5 27 47.289	+23 00 22.10	5.908 5824	22	6 12 01.433	+23 15 57.03	6.157 4279
8	5 28 41.169	+23 01 10.22	5.918 1466	23	6 13 01.121	+23 15 44.88	6.158 2683
9	5 29 35.302	+23 01 57.30	5.927 5398	24	6 14 00.836	+23 15 31.13	6.158 9074
10	5 30 29.682	+23 02 43.33	5.936 7610	25	6 15 00.377	+23 15 15.84	6.159 3451
11	5 31 24.305	+23 03 28.29	5.945 8092	26	6 16 00.100	+23 15 00.01	6.159 5813
12	5 32 19.165	+23 04 12.16	5.954 6834	27	6 16 59.756	+23 14 42.27	6.159 6159
13	5 33 14.257	+23 04 54.95	5.963 3828	28	6 17 59.376	+23 14 23.10	6.159 4493
14	5 34 09.576	+23 05 36.64	5.971 9063	29	6 18 58.958	+23 14 02.52	6.159 0817
15	5 35 05.116	+23 06 17.21	5.980 2530	30	6 19 58.498	+23 13 40.51	6.158 5136
16	5 36 00.870	+23 06 56.66	5.988 4217	July 1	6 20 57.991	+23 13 17.08	6.157 7453
17	5 36 56.832	+23 07 34.97	5.996 4116	2	6 21 57.435	+23 12 52.23	6.156 7773

GEOCENTRIC COORDINATES FOR 0^h TERRESTRIAL TIME

Date	Apparent Right Ascension	Apparent Declination	True Geocentric Distance	Date	Apparent Right Ascension	Apparent Declination	True Geocentric Distance
	h m s	° ′ ″	au		h m s	° ′ ″	au
July 1	6 20 57.991	+23 13 17.08	6.157 7453	Aug. 16	7 04 20.287	+22 33 22.99	5.914 5883
2	6 21 57.435	+23 12 52.23	6.156 7773	17	7 05 11.910	+22 32 08.86	5.905 0656
3	6 22 56.825	+23 12 25.98	6.155 6102	18	7 06 03.236	+22 30 54.16	5.895 3784
4	6 23 56.158	+23 11 58.33	6.154 2443	19	7 06 54.256	+22 29 38.94	5.885 5282
5	6 24 55.429	+23 11 29.30	6.152 6803	20	7 07 44.962	+22 28 23.23	5.875 5162
6	6 25 54.635	+23 10 58.89	6.150 9186	21	7 08 35.344	+22 27 07.07	5.865 3439
7	6 26 53.770	+23 10 27.14	6.148 9597	22	7 09 25.394	+22 25 50.48	5.855 0131
8	6 27 52.830	+23 09 54.04	6.146 8042	23	7 10 15.104	+22 24 33.48	5.844 5254
9	6 28 51.810	+23 09 19.63	6.144 4524	24	7 11 04.468	+22 23 16.08	5.833 8827
10	6 29 50.703	+23 08 43.91	6.141 9049	25	7 11 53.480	+22 21 58.33	5.823 0870
11	6 30 49.504	+23 08 06.90	6.139 1621	26	7 12 42.136	+22 20 40.24	5.812 1402
12	6 31 48.206	+23 07 28.60	6.136 2243	27	7 13 30.429	+22 19 21.85	5.801 0444
13	6 32 46.805	+23 06 49.03	6.133 0920	28	7 14 18.356	+22 18 03.19	5.789 8017
14	6 33 45.295	+23 06 08.16	6.129 7653	29	7 15 05.910	+22 16 44.31	5.778 4141
15	6 34 43.672	+23 05 26.02	6.126 2445	30	7 15 53.086	+22 15 25.24	5.766 8838
16	6 35 41.932	+23 04 42.59	6.122 5299	31	7 16 39.877	+22 14 06.03	5.755 2130
17	6 36 40.072	+23 03 57.89	6.118 6214	Sept. 1	7 17 26.277	+22 12 46.71	5.743 4036
18	6 37 38.090	+23 03 11.92	6.114 5194	2	7 18 12.280	+22 11 27.33	5.731 4580
19	6 38 35.981	+23 02 24.70	6.110 2239	3	7 18 57.878	+22 10 07.92	5.719 3782
20	6 39 33.741	+23 01 36.27	6.105 7352	4	7 19 43.063	+22 08 48.52	5.707 1663
21	6 40 31.365	+23 00 46.64	6.101 0536	5	7 20 27.830	+22 07 29.17	5.694 8246
22	6 41 28.844	+22 59 55.85	6.096 1794	6	7 21 12.170	+22 06 09.88	5.682 3549
23	6 42 26.170	+22 59 03.92	6.091 1132	7	7 21 56.078	+22 04 50.69	5.669 7594
24	6 43 23.334	+22 58 10.88	6.085 8556	8	7 22 39.547	+22 03 31.61	5.657 0400
25	6 44 20.328	+22 57 16.74	6.080 4074	9	7 23 22.574	+22 02 12.67	5.644 1986
26	6 45 17.144	+22 56 21.50	6.074 7695	10	7 24 05.154	+22 00 53.89	5.631 2371
27	6 46 13.776	+22 55 25.18	6.068 9429	11	7 24 47.283	+21 59 35.30	5.618 1574
28	6 47 10.219	+22 54 27.77	6.062 9288	12	7 25 28.955	+21 58 16.96	5.604 9613
29	6 48 06.468	+22 53 29.31	6.056 7281	13	7 26 10.165	+21 56 58.91	5.591 6508
30	6 49 02.520	+22 52 29.80	6.050 3422	14	7 26 50.903	+21 55 41.21	5.578 2280
31	6 49 58.371	+22 51 29.28	6.043 7721	15	7 27 31.159	+21 54 23.91	5.564 6951
Aug. 1	6 50 54.015	+22 50 27.75	6.037 0192	16	7 28 10.924	+21 53 07.06	5.551 0544
2	6 51 49.449	+22 49 25.26	6.030 0847	17	7 28 50.186	+21 51 50.70	5.537 3085
3	6 52 44.667	+22 48 21.84	6.022 9698	18	7 29 28.937	+21 50 34.86	5.523 4600
4	6 53 39.664	+22 47 17.50	6.015 6756	19	7 30 07.167	+21 49 19.58	5.509 5115
5	6 54 34.435	+22 46 12.28	6.008 2035	20	7 30 44.870	+21 48 04.88	5.495 4661
6	6 55 28.972	+22 45 06.21	6.000 5547	21	7 31 22.038	+21 46 50.81	5.481 3265
7	6 56 23.271	+22 43 59.31	5.992 7303	22	7 31 58.665	+21 45 37.39	5.467 0960
8	6 57 17.325	+22 42 51.62	5.984 7316	23	7 32 34.745	+21 44 24.67	5.452 7775
9	6 58 11.126	+22 41 43.13	5.976 5596	24	7 33 10.272	+21 43 12.69	5.438 3744
10	6 59 04.671	+22 40 33.88	5.968 2154	25	7 33 45.239	+21 42 01.49	5.423 8897
11	6 59 57.952	+22 39 23.87	5.959 7000	26	7 34 19.639	+21 40 51.12	5.409 3268
12	7 00 50.967	+22 38 13.11	5.951 0145	27	7 34 53.467	+21 39 41.62	5.394 6889
13	7 01 43.712	+22 37 01.62	5.942 1596	28	7 35 26.714	+21 38 33.05	5.379 9793
14	7 02 36.183	+22 35 49.42	5.933 1363	29	7 35 59.373	+21 37 25.45	5.365 2014
15	7 03 28.376	+22 34 36.53	5.923 9456	30	7 36 31.436	+21 36 18.86	5.350 3583
16	7 04 20.287	+22 33 22.99	5.914 5883	Oct. 1	7 37 02.896	+21 35 13.32	5.335 4535

GEOCENTRIC COORDINATES FOR 0^h TERRESTRIAL TIME

Date	Apparent Right Ascension	Apparent Declination	True Geocentric Distance	Date	Apparent Right Ascension	Apparent Declination	True Geocentric Distance
	h m s	° ′ ″	au		h m s	° ′ ″	au
Oct. 1	7 37 02.896	+21 35 13.32	5.335 4535	Nov. 16	7 48 22.393	+21 13 40.38	4.646 3876
2	7 37 33.745	+21 34 08.88	5.320 4902	17	7 48 18.431	+21 13 59.58	4.632 9283
3	7 38 03.975	+21 33 05.56	5.305 4718	18	7 48 13.623	+21 14 20.98	4.619 6088
4	7 38 33.579	+21 32 03.40	5.290 4016	19	7 48 07.971	+21 14 44.56	4.606 4343
5	7 39 02.551	+21 31 02.42	5.275 2827	20	7 48 01.477	+21 15 10.34	4.593 4101
6	7 39 30.884	+21 30 02.65	5.260 1183	21	7 47 54.143	+21 15 38.31	4.580 5415
7	7 39 58.575	+21 29 04.10	5.244 9116	22	7 47 45.972	+21 16 08.44	4.567 8335
8	7 40 25.619	+21 28 06.81	5.229 6656	23	7 47 36.966	+21 16 40.74	4.555 2913
9	7 40 52.013	+21 27 10.81	5.214 3834	24	7 47 27.129	+21 17 15.18	4.542 9200
10	7 41 17.748	+21 26 16.17	5.199 0682	25	7 47 16.464	+21 17 51.75	4.530 7246
11	7 41 42.818	+21 25 22.93	5.183 7232	26	7 47 04.976	+21 18 30.42	4.518 7100
12	7 42 07.212	+21 24 31.15	5.168 3517	27	7 46 52.668	+21 19 11.14	4.506 8811
13	7 42 30.920	+21 23 40.88	5.152 9573	28	7 46 39.549	+21 19 53.89	4.495 2426
14	7 42 53.930	+21 22 52.16	5.137 5436	29	7 46 25.625	+21 20 38.63	4.483 7991
15	7 43 16.234	+21 22 05.02	5.122 1145	30	7 46 10.904	+21 21 25.29	4.472 5552
16	7 43 37.822	+21 21 19.50	5.106 6740	Dec. 1	7 45 55.396	+21 22 13.84	4.461 5153
17	7 43 58.689	+21 20 35.62	5.091 2262	2	7 45 39.113	+21 23 04.24	4.450 6836
18	7 44 18.825	+21 19 53.41	5.075 7752	3	7 45 22.065	+21 23 56.44	4.440 0644
19	7 44 38.227	+21 19 12.90	5.060 3253	4	7 45 04.263	+21 24 50.41	4.429 6617
20	7 44 56.888	+21 18 34.12	5.044 8810	5	7 44 45.714	+21 25 46.14	4.419 4796
21	7 45 14.802	+21 17 57.10	5.029 4465	6	7 44 26.425	+21 26 43.60	4.409 5222
22	7 45 31.965	+21 17 21.89	5.014 0265	7	7 44 06.404	+21 27 42.75	4.399 7937
23	7 45 48.370	+21 16 48.51	4.998 6253	8	7 43 45.656	+21 28 43.57	4.390 2983
24	7 46 04.013	+21 16 17.01	4.983 2476	9	7 43 24.192	+21 29 45.99	4.381 0403
25	7 46 18.887	+21 15 47.42	4.967 8979	10	7 43 02.020	+21 30 49.96	4.372 0240
26	7 46 32.986	+21 15 19.77	4.952 5807	11	7 42 39.156	+21 31 55.41	4.363 2539
27	7 46 46.305	+21 14 54.09	4.937 3007	12	7 42 15.612	+21 33 02.28	4.354 7343
28	7 46 58.838	+21 14 30.42	4.922 0624	13	7 41 51.405	+21 34 10.51	4.346 4695
29	7 47 10.578	+21 14 08.77	4.906 8703	14	7 41 26.550	+21 35 20.06	4.338 4636
30	7 47 21.521	+21 13 49.17	4.891 7290	15	7 41 01.064	+21 36 30.85	4.330 7209
31	7 47 31.662	+21 13 31.63	4.876 6431	16	7 40 34.966	+21 37 42.84	4.323 2453
Nov. 1	7 47 40.996	+21 13 16.16	4.861 6169	17	7 40 08.271	+21 38 55.96	4.316 0407
2	7 47 49.521	+21 13 02.76	4.846 6550	18	7 39 40.999	+21 40 10.17	4.309 1110
3	7 47 57.235	+21 12 51.44	4.831 7616	19	7 39 13.167	+21 41 25.40	4.302 4598
4	7 48 04.136	+21 12 42.20	4.816 9411	20	7 38 44.795	+21 42 41.59	4.296 0906
5	7 48 10.224	+21 12 35.05	4.802 1978	21	7 38 15.901	+21 43 58.69	4.290 0067
6	7 48 15.498	+21 12 30.01	4.787 5357	22	7 37 46.505	+21 45 16.61	4.284 2113
7	7 48 19.954	+21 12 27.11	4.772 9592	23	7 37 16.628	+21 46 35.30	4.278 7075
8	7 48 23.587	+21 12 26.39	4.758 4728	24	7 36 46.290	+21 47 54.68	4.273 4979
9	7 48 26.390	+21 12 27.87	4.744 0807	25	7 36 15.514	+21 49 14.66	4.268 5852
10	7 48 28.357	+21 12 31.57	4.729 7878	26	7 35 44.323	+21 50 35.16	4.263 9718
11	7 48 29.482	+21 12 37.49	4.715 5988	27	7 35 12.741	+21 51 56.11	4.259 6598
12	7 48 29.761	+21 12 45.64	4.701 5186	28	7 34 40.794	+21 53 17.42	4.255 6513
13	7 48 29.192	+21 12 56.01	4.687 5522	29	7 34 08.507	+21 54 39.01	4.251 9478
14	7 48 27.775	+21 13 08.59	4.673 7048	30	7 33 35.907	+21 56 00.81	4.248 5511
15	7 48 25.508	+21 13 23.38	4.659 9816	31	7 33 03.019	+21 57 22.77	4.245 4625
16	7 48 22.393	+21 13 40.38	4.646 3876	32	7 32 29.867	+21 58 44.83	4.242 6832

GEOCENTRIC COORDINATES FOR 0^h TERRESTRIAL TIME

Date	Apparent Right Ascension	Apparent Declination	True Geocentric Distance	Date	Apparent Right Ascension	Apparent Declination	True Geocentric Distance
	h m s	° ′ ″	au		h m s	° ′ ″	au
Jan. 0	23 05 47.397	− 7 56 52.19	10.010 3428	Feb. 15	23 22 35.756	− 6 06 36.57	10.521 5892
1	23 06 03.923	− 7 55 00.40	10.025 2703	16	23 23 01.763	− 6 03 49.02	10.527 7811
2	23 06 20.749	− 7 53 06.81	10.040 0756	17	23 23 27.875	− 6 01 00.88	10.533 7339
3	23 06 37.870	− 7 51 11.45	10.054 7545	18	23 23 54.091	− 5 58 12.18	10.539 4461
4	23 06 55.281	− 7 49 14.36	10.069 3030	19	23 24 20.406	− 5 55 22.94	10.544 9165
5	23 07 12.978	− 7 47 15.55	10.083 7172	20	23 24 46.816	− 5 52 33.18	10.550 1437
6	23 07 30.958	− 7 45 15.04	10.097 9934	21	23 25 13.319	− 5 49 42.93	10.555 1265
7	23 07 49.219	− 7 43 12.84	10.112 1280	22	23 25 39.910	− 5 46 52.22	10.559 8636
8	23 08 07.757	− 7 41 08.98	10.126 1175	23	23 26 06.583	− 5 44 01.09	10.564 3537
9	23 08 26.571	− 7 39 03.48	10.139 9587	24	23 26 33.333	− 5 41 09.56	10.568 5958
10	23 08 45.656	− 7 36 56.35	10.153 6485	25	23 27 00.155	− 5 38 17.68	10.572 5886
11	23 09 05.008	− 7 34 47.65	10.167 1838	26	23 27 27.042	− 5 35 25.48	10.576 3310
12	23 09 24.620	− 7 32 37.41	10.180 5616	27	23 27 53.990	− 5 32 33.00	10.579 8221
13	23 09 44.487	− 7 30 25.65	10.193 7791	28	23 28 20.992	− 5 29 40.27	10.583 0610
14	23 10 04.603	− 7 28 12.43	10.206 8333	Mar. 1	23 28 48.045	− 5 26 47.32	10.586 0469
15	23 10 24.963	− 7 25 57.76	10.219 7213	2	23 29 15.146	− 5 23 54.16	10.588 7792
16	23 10 45.562	− 7 23 41.67	10.232 4402	3	23 29 42.293	− 5 21 00.81	10.591 2577
17	23 11 06.397	− 7 21 24.19	10.244 9870	4	23 30 09.483	− 5 18 07.29	10.593 4820
18	23 11 27.464	− 7 19 05.32	10.257 3589	5	23 30 36.712	− 5 15 13.63	10.595 4522
19	23 11 48.761	− 7 16 45.09	10.269 5527	6	23 31 03.976	− 5 12 19.87	10.597 1684
20	23 12 10.286	− 7 14 23.50	10.281 5656	7	23 31 31.270	− 5 09 26.04	10.598 6307
21	23 12 32.034	− 7 12 00.58	10.293 3945	8	23 31 58.586	− 5 06 32.18	10.599 8394
22	23 12 54.003	− 7 09 36.35	10.305 0364	9	23 32 25.920	− 5 03 38.34	10.600 7948
23	23 13 16.190	− 7 07 10.83	10.316 4884	10	23 32 53.266	− 5 00 44.56	10.601 4971
24	23 13 38.591	− 7 04 44.04	10.327 7476	11	23 33 20.619	− 4 57 50.87	10.601 9466
25	23 14 01.202	− 7 02 16.01	10.338 8111	12	23 33 47.972	− 4 54 57.31	10.602 1436
26	23 14 24.018	− 6 59 46.77	10.349 6759	13	23 34 15.321	− 4 52 03.81	10.602 0883
27	23 14 47.035	− 6 57 16.36	10.360 3391	14	23 34 42.667	− 4 49 10.39	10.601 7811
28	23 15 10.245	− 6 54 44.81	10.370 7981	15	23 35 10.011	− 4 46 17.10	10.601 2221
29	23 15 33.643	− 6 52 12.16	10.381 0500	16	23 35 37.348	− 4 43 24.00	10.600 4117
30	23 15 57.224	− 6 49 38.45	10.391 0921	17	23 36 04.675	− 4 40 31.10	10.599 3499
31	23 16 20.980	− 6 47 03.71	10.400 9218	18	23 36 31.987	− 4 37 38.41	10.598 0371
Feb. 1	23 16 44.909	− 6 44 27.96	10.410 5369	19	23 36 59.282	− 4 34 45.96	10.596 4735
2	23 17 09.005	− 6 41 51.24	10.419 9348	20	23 37 26.556	− 4 31 53.77	10.594 6594
3	23 17 33.267	− 6 39 13.54	10.429 1137	21	23 37 53.805	− 4 29 01.87	10.592 5950
4	23 17 57.692	− 6 36 34.91	10.438 0716	22	23 38 21.024	− 4 26 10.28	10.590 2807
5	23 18 22.276	− 6 33 55.35	10.446 8067	23	23 38 48.209	− 4 23 19.05	10.587 7168
6	23 18 47.015	− 6 31 14.90	10.455 3175	24	23 39 15.353	− 4 20 28.20	10.584 9036
7	23 19 11.904	− 6 28 33.60	10.463 6024	25	23 39 42.453	− 4 17 37.77	10.581 8416
8	23 19 36.938	− 6 25 51.47	10.471 6601	26	23 40 09.502	− 4 14 47.80	10.578 5312
9	23 20 02.110	− 6 23 08.57	10.479 4892	27	23 40 36.496	− 4 11 58.31	10.574 9730
10	23 20 27.415	− 6 20 24.92	10.487 0883	28	23 41 03.429	− 4 09 09.34	10.571 1677
11	23 20 52.846	− 6 17 40.57	10.494 4562	29	23 41 30.300	− 4 06 20.91	10.567 1160
12	23 21 18.400	− 6 14 55.54	10.501 5915	30	23 41 57.105	− 4 03 33.03	10.562 8188
13	23 21 44.072	− 6 12 09.84	10.508 4930	31	23 42 23.844	− 4 00 45.72	10.558 2775
14	23 22 09.858	− 6 09 23.52	10.515 1593	Apr. 1	23 42 50.512	− 3 57 59.00	10.553 4933
15	23 22 35.756	− 6 06 36.57	10.521 5892	2	23 43 17.107	− 3 55 12.90	10.548 4678

GEOCENTRIC COORDINATES FOR 0^h TERRESTRIAL TIME

Date	Apparent Right Ascension	Apparent Declination	True Geocentric Distance	Date	Apparent Right Ascension	Apparent Declination	True Geocentric Distance
	h m s	° ′ ″	au		h m s	° ′ ″	au
Apr. 1	23 42 50.512	− 3 57 59.00	10.553 4933	May 17	0 00 51.717	− 2 08 32.64	10.101 7233
2	23 43 17.107	− 3 55 12.90	10.548 4678	18	0 01 10.674	− 2 06 42.92	10.087 7023
3	23 43 43.621	− 3 52 27.46	10.543 2026	19	0 01 29.380	− 2 04 54.98	10.073 5452
4	23 44 10.051	− 3 49 42.72	10.537 6993	20	0 01 47.830	− 2 03 08.85	10.059 2550
5	23 44 36.389	− 3 46 58.71	10.531 9597	21	0 02 06.020	− 2 01 24.54	10.044 8347
6	23 45 02.631	− 3 44 15.47	10.525 9854	22	0 02 23.946	− 1 59 42.08	10.030 2873
7	23 45 28.771	− 3 41 33.04	10.519 7783	23	0 02 41.607	− 1 58 01.49	10.015 6160
8	23 45 54.806	− 3 38 51.42	10.513 3399	24	0 02 59.001	− 1 56 22.77	10.000 8241
9	23 46 20.733	− 3 36 10.65	10.506 6721	25	0 03 16.126	− 1 54 45.94	9.985 9151
10	23 46 46.550	− 3 33 30.74	10.499 7763	26	0 03 32.979	− 1 53 11.02	9.970 8925
11	23 47 12.252	− 3 30 51.71	10.492 6543	27	0 03 49.558	− 1 51 38.01	9.955 7602
12	23 47 37.839	− 3 28 13.57	10.485 3076	28	0 04 05.857	− 1 50 06.96	9.940 5221
13	23 48 03.308	− 3 25 36.34	10.477 7380	29	0 04 21.871	− 1 48 37.89	9.925 1822
14	23 48 28.656	− 3 23 00.04	10.469 9469	30	0 04 37.595	− 1 47 10.84	9.909 7444
15	23 48 53.880	− 3 20 24.69	10.461 9360	31	0 04 53.023	− 1 45 45.84	9.894 2129
16	23 49 18.976	− 3 17 50.30	10.453 7070	June 1	0 05 08.152	− 1 44 22.92	9.878 5916
17	23 49 43.942	− 3 15 16.91	10.445 2614	2	0 05 22.979	− 1 43 02.07	9.862 8845
18	23 50 08.773	− 3 12 44.54	10.436 6008	3	0 05 37.502	− 1 41 43.32	9.847 0954
19	23 50 33.464	− 3 10 13.23	10.427 7269	4	0 05 51.721	− 1 40 26.67	9.831 2282
20	23 50 58.010	− 3 07 43.00	10.418 6415	5	0 06 05.632	− 1 39 12.13	9.815 2867
21	23 51 22.407	− 3 05 13.90	10.409 3461	6	0 06 19.236	− 1 37 59.70	9.799 2747
22	23 51 46.649	− 3 02 45.94	10.399 8426	7	0 06 32.531	− 1 36 49.39	9.783 1959
23	23 52 10.733	− 3 00 19.17	10.390 1327	8	0 06 45.514	− 1 35 41.21	9.767 0541
24	23 52 34.652	− 2 57 53.60	10.380 2184	9	0 06 58.184	− 1 34 35.17	9.750 8529
25	23 52 58.405	− 2 55 29.28	10.370 1017	10	0 07 10.539	− 1 33 31.27	9.734 5962
26	23 53 21.988	− 2 53 06.20	10.359 7847	11	0 07 22.574	− 1 32 29.55	9.718 2875
27	23 53 45.400	− 2 50 44.39	10.349 2698	12	0 07 34.288	− 1 31 30.01	9.701 9306
28	23 54 08.639	− 2 48 23.85	10.338 5594	13	0 07 45.677	− 1 30 32.68	9.685 5291
29	23 54 31.701	− 2 46 04.62	10.327 6561	14	0 07 56.737	− 1 29 37.57	9.669 0868
30	23 54 54.583	− 2 43 46.72	10.316 5629	15	0 08 07.464	− 1 28 44.71	9.652 6073
May 1	23 55 17.277	− 2 41 30.20	10.305 2826	16	0 08 17.855	− 1 27 54.12	9.636 0945
2	23 55 39.778	− 2 39 15.08	10.293 8182	17	0 08 27.907	− 1 27 05.82	9.619 5521
3	23 56 02.081	− 2 37 01.41	10.282 1727	18	0 08 37.617	− 1 26 19.82	9.602 9840
4	23 56 24.181	− 2 34 49.22	10.270 3490	19	0 08 46.984	− 1 25 36.12	9.586 3942
5	23 56 46.073	− 2 32 38.52	10.258 3501	20	0 08 56.008	− 1 24 54.74	9.569 7869
6	23 57 07.756	− 2 30 29.34	10.246 1788	21	0 09 04.687	− 1 24 15.67	9.553 1662
7	23 57 29.226	− 2 28 21.69	10.233 8380	22	0 09 13.020	− 1 23 38.91	9.536 5365
8	23 57 50.482	− 2 26 15.58	10.221 3305	23	0 09 21.006	− 1 23 04.48	9.519 9023
9	23 58 11.521	− 2 24 11.04	10.208 6592	24	0 09 28.642	− 1 22 32.38	9.503 2682
10	23 58 32.341	− 2 22 08.06	10.195 8269	25	0 09 35.924	− 1 22 02.65	9.486 6390
11	23 58 52.939	− 2 20 06.66	10.182 8362	26	0 09 42.848	− 1 21 35.30	9.470 0193
12	23 59 13.315	− 2 18 06.87	10.169 6901	27	0 09 49.409	− 1 21 10.35	9.453 4141
13	23 59 33.463	− 2 16 08.70	10.156 3912	28	0 09 55.606	− 1 20 47.81	9.436 8280
14	23 59 53.381	− 2 14 12.16	10.142 9423	29	0 10 01.437	− 1 20 27.70	9.420 2658
15	0 00 13.066	− 2 12 17.29	10.129 3461	30	0 10 06.900	− 1 20 10.01	9.403 7321
16	0 00 32.513	− 2 10 24.11	10.115 6056	July 1	0 10 11.997	− 1 19 54.74	9.387 2313
17	0 00 51.717	− 2 08 32.64	10.101 7233	2	0 10 16.727	− 1 19 41.87	9.370 7681

GEOCENTRIC COORDINATES FOR 0^h TERRESTRIAL TIME

Date	Apparent Right Ascension	Apparent Declination	True Geocentric Distance	Date	Apparent Right Ascension	Apparent Declination	True Geocentric Distance
	h m s	° ′ ″	au		h m s	° ′ ″	au
July 1	0 10 11.997	− 1 19 54.74	9.387 2313	Aug. 16	0 07 34.170	− 1 49 48.71	8.739 4926
2	0 10 16.727	− 1 19 41.87	9.370 7681	17	0 07 22.823	− 1 51 15.97	8.729 4471
3	0 10 21.091	− 1 19 31.40	9.354 3469	18	0 07 11.195	− 1 52 44.82	8.719 6370
4	0 10 25.090	− 1 19 23.33	9.337 9720	19	0 06 59.289	− 1 54 15.24	8.710 0660
5	0 10 28.724	− 1 19 17.64	9.321 6478	20	0 06 47.111	− 1 55 47.21	8.700 7379
6	0 10 31.992	− 1 19 14.33	9.305 3786	21	0 06 34.662	− 1 57 20.68	8.691 6566
7	0 10 34.894	− 1 19 13.39	9.289 1687	22	0 06 21.950	− 1 58 55.62	8.682 8255
8	0 10 37.430	− 1 19 14.84	9.273 0223	23	0 06 08.980	− 2 00 31.99	8.674 2482
9	0 10 39.598	− 1 19 18.66	9.256 9436	24	0 05 55.758	− 2 02 09.72	8.665 9280
10	0 10 41.398	− 1 19 24.87	9.240 9368	25	0 05 42.294	− 2 03 48.76	8.657 8680
11	0 10 42.828	− 1 19 33.46	9.225 0061	26	0 05 28.596	− 2 05 29.06	8.650 0713
12	0 10 43.886	− 1 19 44.45	9.209 1556	27	0 05 14.671	− 2 07 10.54	8.642 5407
13	0 10 44.570	− 1 19 57.83	9.193 3895	28	0 05 00.529	− 2 08 53.15	8.635 2789
14	0 10 44.881	− 1 20 13.61	9.177 7120	29	0 04 46.177	− 2 10 36.83	8.628 2884
15	0 10 44.819	− 1 20 31.79	9.162 1273	30	0 04 31.623	− 2 12 21.53	8.621 5718
16	0 10 44.383	− 1 20 52.35	9.146 6397	31	0 04 16.876	− 2 14 07.19	8.615 1312
17	0 10 43.576	− 1 21 15.29	9.131 2537	Sept. 1	0 04 01.941	− 2 15 53.76	8.608 9689
18	0 10 42.399	− 1 21 40.58	9.115 9737	2	0 03 46.827	− 2 17 41.19	8.603 0870
19	0 10 40.854	− 1 22 08.21	9.100 8043	3	0 03 31.540	− 2 19 29.43	8.597 4873
20	0 10 38.942	− 1 22 38.17	9.085 7503	4	0 03 16.086	− 2 21 18.43	8.592 1717
21	0 10 36.664	− 1 23 10.45	9.070 8164	5	0 03 00.472	− 2 23 08.15	8.587 1418
22	0 10 34.020	− 1 23 45.05	9.056 0075	6	0 02 44.706	− 2 24 58.54	8.582 3994
23	0 10 31.007	− 1 24 21.96	9.041 3285	7	0 02 28.794	− 2 26 49.55	8.577 9460
24	0 10 27.625	− 1 25 01.19	9.026 7842	8	0 02 12.745	− 2 28 41.13	8.573 7831
25	0 10 23.874	− 1 25 42.73	9.012 3795	9	0 01 56.567	− 2 30 33.21	8.569 9121
26	0 10 19.756	− 1 26 26.56	8.998 1192	10	0 01 40.271	− 2 32 25.73	8.566 3347
27	0 10 15.272	− 1 27 12.68	8.984 0079	11	0 01 23.867	− 2 34 18.61	8.563 0523
28	0 10 10.425	− 1 28 01.04	8.970 0503	12	0 01 07.364	− 2 36 11.80	8.560 0665
29	0 10 05.220	− 1 28 51.63	8.956 2507	13	0 00 50.770	− 2 38 05.24	8.557 3788
30	0 09 59.660	− 1 29 44.40	8.942 6136	14	0 00 34.093	− 2 39 58.88	8.554 9909
31	0 09 53.750	− 1 30 39.32	8.929 1432	15	0 00 17.341	− 2 41 52.67	8.552 9040
Aug. 1	0 09 47.492	− 1 31 36.37	8.915 8437	16	0 00 00.518	− 2 43 46.57	8.551 1197
2	0 09 40.892	− 1 32 35.51	8.902 7192	17	23 59 43.634	− 2 45 40.51	8.549 6391
3	0 09 33.951	− 1 33 36.71	8.889 7737	18	23 59 26.697	− 2 47 34.46	8.548 4633
4	0 09 26.674	− 1 34 39.95	8.877 0112	19	23 59 09.714	− 2 49 28.34	8.547 5931
5	0 09 19.063	− 1 35 45.20	8.864 4355	20	23 58 52.697	− 2 51 22.08	8.547 0293
6	0 09 11.121	− 1 36 52.44	8.852 0504	21	23 58 35.655	− 2 53 15.63	8.546 7723
7	0 09 02.850	− 1 38 01.65	8.839 8598	22	23 58 18.600	− 2 55 08.90	8.546 8225
8	0 08 54.254	− 1 39 12.80	8.827 8672	23	23 58 01.543	− 2 57 01.83	8.547 1801
9	0 08 45.333	− 1 40 25.88	8.816 0763	24	23 57 44.493	− 2 58 54.33	8.547 8449
10	0 08 36.092	− 1 41 40.87	8.804 4907	25	23 57 27.463	− 3 00 46.35	8.548 8167
11	0 08 26.533	− 1 42 57.72	8.793 1140	26	23 57 10.461	− 3 02 37.82	8.550 0951
12	0 08 16.662	− 1 44 16.41	8.781 9498	27	23 56 53.497	− 3 04 28.67	8.551 6796
13	0 08 06.485	− 1 45 36.90	8.771 0019	28	23 56 36.581	− 3 06 18.85	8.553 5695
14	0 07 56.006	− 1 46 59.14	8.760 2738	29	23 56 19.721	− 3 08 08.31	8.555 7639
15	0 07 45.233	− 1 48 23.09	8.749 7694	30	23 56 02.926	− 3 09 56.98	8.558 2617
16	0 07 34.170	− 1 49 48.71	8.739 4926	Oct. 1	23 55 46.203	− 3 11 44.81	8.561 0620

GEOCENTRIC COORDINATES FOR 0ʰ TERRESTRIAL TIME

Date	Apparent Right Ascension	Apparent Declination	True Geocentric Distance	Date	Apparent Right Ascension	Apparent Declination	True Geocentric Distance
	h m s	° ′ ″	au		h m s	° ′ ″	au
Oct. 1	23 55 46.203	− 3 11 44.81	8.561 0620	Nov. 16	23 46 33.234	− 4 05 34.55	8.980 3502
2	23 55 29.562	− 3 13 31.77	8.564 1634	17	23 46 28.354	− 4 05 53.27	8.994 5724
3	23 55 13.008	− 3 15 17.79	8.567 5647	18	23 46 23.854	− 4 06 09.41	9.008 9468
4	23 54 56.552	− 3 17 02.83	8.571 2643	19	23 46 19.737	− 4 06 22.94	9.023 4683
5	23 54 40.200	− 3 18 46.84	8.575 2607	20	23 46 16.007	− 4 06 33.85	9.038 1319
6	23 54 23.963	− 3 20 29.75	8.579 5523	21	23 46 12.665	− 4 06 42.14	9.052 9325
7	23 54 07.850	− 3 22 11.52	8.584 1377	22	23 46 09.713	− 4 06 47.81	9.067 8648
8	23 53 51.872	− 3 23 52.06	8.589 0151	23	23 46 07.152	− 4 06 50.85	9.082 9237
9	23 53 36.038	− 3 25 31.33	8.594 1832	24	23 46 04.983	− 4 06 51.27	9.098 1039
10	23 53 20.358	− 3 27 09.26	8.599 6403	25	23 46 03.206	− 4 06 49.07	9.113 4001
11	23 53 04.840	− 3 28 45.83	8.605 3850	26	23 46 01.821	− 4 06 44.25	9.128 8070
12	23 52 49.488	− 3 30 20.97	8.611 4157	27	23 46 00.828	− 4 06 36.83	9.144 3193
13	23 52 34.310	− 3 31 54.67	8.617 7307	28	23 46 00.228	− 4 06 26.80	9.159 9318
14	23 52 19.312	− 3 33 26.89	8.624 3281	29	23 46 00.021	− 4 06 14.18	9.175 6392
15	23 52 04.501	− 3 34 57.57	8.631 2062	30	23 46 00.209	− 4 05 58.94	9.191 4363
16	23 51 49.884	− 3 36 26.67	8.638 3626	Dec. 1	23 46 00.792	− 4 05 41.11	9.207 3180
17	23 51 35.471	− 3 37 54.14	8.645 7951	2	23 46 01.773	− 4 05 20.66	9.223 2793
18	23 51 21.270	− 3 39 19.92	8.653 5011	3	23 46 03.153	− 4 04 57.59	9.239 3153
19	23 51 07.291	− 3 40 43.96	8.661 4781	4	23 46 04.932	− 4 04 31.92	9.255 4212
20	23 50 53.543	− 3 42 06.19	8.669 7232	5	23 46 07.111	− 4 04 03.65	9.271 5923
21	23 50 40.034	− 3 43 26.58	8.678 2333	6	23 46 09.685	− 4 03 32.80	9.287 8241
22	23 50 26.773	− 3 44 45.06	8.687 0053	7	23 46 12.653	− 4 02 59.40	9.304 1121
23	23 50 13.769	− 3 46 01.59	8.696 0359	8	23 46 16.011	− 4 02 23.48	9.320 4515
24	23 50 01.028	− 3 47 16.12	8.705 3216	9	23 46 19.757	− 4 01 45.05	9.336 8378
25	23 49 48.557	− 3 48 28.63	8.714 8590	10	23 46 23.890	− 4 01 04.10	9.353 2662
26	23 49 36.363	− 3 49 39.07	8.724 6444	11	23 46 28.412	− 4 00 20.66	9.369 7319
27	23 49 24.452	− 3 50 47.42	8.734 6739	12	23 46 33.323	− 3 59 34.70	9.386 2299
28	23 49 12.828	− 3 51 53.65	8.744 9437	13	23 46 38.623	− 3 58 46.24	9.402 7553
29	23 49 01.496	− 3 52 57.72	8.755 4499	14	23 46 44.313	− 3 57 55.27	9.419 3031
30	23 48 50.462	− 3 53 59.62	8.766 1885	15	23 46 50.392	− 3 57 01.80	9.435 8680
31	23 48 39.731	− 3 54 59.32	8.777 1553	16	23 46 56.861	− 3 56 05.84	9.452 4451
Nov. 1	23 48 29.307	− 3 55 56.80	8.788 3462	17	23 47 03.717	− 3 55 07.40	9.469 0291
2	23 48 19.195	− 3 56 52.02	8.799 7571	18	23 47 10.961	− 3 54 06.49	9.485 6150
3	23 48 09.402	− 3 57 44.96	8.811 3838	19	23 47 18.588	− 3 53 03.13	9.502 1976
4	23 47 59.935	− 3 58 35.57	8.823 2223	20	23 47 26.598	− 3 51 57.35	9.518 7716
5	23 47 50.799	− 3 59 23.83	8.835 2685	21	23 47 34.987	− 3 50 49.16	9.535 3321
6	23 47 42.001	− 4 00 09.70	8.847 5185	22	23 47 43.751	− 3 49 38.60	9.551 8737
7	23 47 33.545	− 4 00 53.17	8.859 9684	23	23 47 52.888	− 3 48 25.68	9.568 3915
8	23 47 25.433	− 4 01 34.23	8.872 6142	24	23 48 02.394	− 3 47 10.44	9.584 8804
9	23 47 17.668	− 4 02 12.87	8.885 4522	25	23 48 12.265	− 3 45 52.89	9.601 3354
10	23 47 10.250	− 4 02 49.08	8.898 4784	26	23 48 22.500	− 3 44 33.06	9.617 7516
11	23 47 03.182	− 4 03 22.86	8.911 6886	27	23 48 33.095	− 3 43 10.97	9.634 1242
12	23 46 56.468	− 4 03 54.19	8.925 0788	28	23 48 44.049	− 3 41 46.63	9.650 4485
13	23 46 50.112	− 4 04 23.05	8.938 6446	29	23 48 55.361	− 3 40 20.05	9.666 7199
14	23 46 44.117	− 4 04 49.42	8.952 3815	30	23 49 07.029	− 3 38 51.26	9.682 9339
15	23 46 38.490	− 4 05 13.26	8.966 2849	31	23 49 19.051	− 3 37 20.27	9.699 0863
16	23 46 33.234	− 4 05 34.55	8.980 3502	32	23 49 31.423	− 3 35 47.10	9.715 1728

GEOCENTRIC COORDINATES FOR 0^h TERRESTRIAL TIME

Date	Apparent Right Ascension	Apparent Declination	True Geocentric Distance	Date	Apparent Right Ascension	Apparent Declination	True Geocentric Distance
	h m s	° ′ ″	au		h m s	° ′ ″	au
Jan. 0	3 25 22.581	+18 26 32.56	18.859 222	Feb. 15	3 24 09.201	+18 23 04.12	19.575 631
1	3 25 16.500	+18 26 11.58	18.871 650	16	3 24 12.569	+18 23 17.83	19.592 649
2	3 25 10.592	+18 25 51.24	18.884 289	17	3 24 16.148	+18 23 32.28	19.609 646
3	3 25 04.860	+18 25 31.54	18.897 135	18	3 24 19.938	+18 23 47.49	19.626 618
4	3 24 59.304	+18 25 12.49	18.910 184	19	3 24 23.939	+18 24 03.46	19.643 559
5	3 24 53.929	+18 24 54.08	18.923 429	20	3 24 28.151	+18 24 20.19	19.660 465
6	3 24 48.738	+18 24 36.33	18.936 866	21	3 24 32.572	+18 24 37.68	19.677 331
7	3 24 43.735	+18 24 19.23	18.950 491	22	3 24 37.201	+18 24 55.94	19.694 151
8	3 24 38.926	+18 24 02.82	18.964 298	23	3 24 42.036	+18 25 14.95	19.710 921
9	3 24 34.311	+18 23 47.12	18.978 282	24	3 24 47.076	+18 25 34.72	19.727 636
10	3 24 29.895	+18 23 32.14	18.992 440	25	3 24 52.317	+18 25 55.23	19.744 291
11	3 24 25.677	+18 23 17.89	19.006 765	26	3 24 57.757	+18 26 16.47	19.760 879
12	3 24 21.657	+18 23 04.40	19.021 253	27	3 25 03.392	+18 26 38.42	19.777 398
13	3 24 17.834	+18 22 51.65	19.035 900	28	3 25 09.223	+18 27 01.06	19.793 840
14	3 24 14.208	+18 22 39.64	19.050 701	Mar. 1	3 25 15.249	+18 27 24.37	19.810 201
15	3 24 10.779	+18 22 28.37	19.065 651	2	3 25 21.470	+18 27 48.35	19.826 477
16	3 24 07.548	+18 22 17.83	19.080 746	3	3 25 27.886	+18 28 12.99	19.842 661
17	3 24 04.517	+18 22 08.02	19.095 981	4	3 25 34.500	+18 28 38.31	19.858 749
18	3 24 01.688	+18 21 58.94	19.111 351	5	3 25 41.308	+18 29 04.31	19.874 737
19	3 23 59.064	+18 21 50.60	19.126 852	6	3 25 48.308	+18 29 30.99	19.890 619
20	3 23 56.647	+18 21 43.02	19.142 479	7	3 25 55.498	+18 29 58.35	19.906 392
21	3 23 54.441	+18 21 36.19	19.158 227	8	3 26 02.872	+18 30 26.38	19.922 051
22	3 23 52.446	+18 21 30.13	19.174 091	9	3 26 10.426	+18 30 55.05	19.937 593
23	3 23 50.665	+18 21 24.86	19.190 065	10	3 26 18.159	+18 31 24.35	19.953 012
24	3 23 49.099	+18 21 20.38	19.206 145	11	3 26 26.065	+18 31 54.27	19.968 307
25	3 23 47.748	+18 21 16.71	19.222 326	12	3 26 34.145	+18 32 24.77	19.983 471
26	3 23 46.615	+18 21 13.85	19.238 602	13	3 26 42.395	+18 32 55.85	19.998 502
27	3 23 45.696	+18 21 11.81	19.254 968	14	3 26 50.816	+18 33 27.50	20.013 397
28	3 23 44.993	+18 21 10.59	19.271 418	15	3 26 59.407	+18 33 59.72	20.028 150
29	3 23 44.504	+18 21 10.17	19.287 948	16	3 27 08.166	+18 34 32.49	20.042 759
30	3 23 44.229	+18 21 10.55	19.304 550	17	3 27 17.094	+18 35 05.81	20.057 220
31	3 23 44.166	+18 21 11.73	19.321 220	18	3 27 26.189	+18 35 39.70	20.071 529
Feb. 1	3 23 44.317	+18 21 13.67	19.337 952	19	3 27 35.449	+18 36 14.13	20.085 683
2	3 23 44.683	+18 21 16.40	19.354 740	20	3 27 44.873	+18 36 49.11	20.099 677
3	3 23 45.267	+18 21 19.90	19.371 579	21	3 27 54.458	+18 37 24.64	20.113 509
4	3 23 46.071	+18 21 24.18	19.388 462	22	3 28 04.201	+18 38 00.72	20.127 174
5	3 23 47.097	+18 21 29.27	19.405 384	23	3 28 14.100	+18 38 37.32	20.140 669
6	3 23 48.343	+18 21 35.17	19.422 341	24	3 28 24.151	+18 39 14.43	20.153 990
7	3 23 49.808	+18 21 41.88	19.439 326	25	3 28 34.349	+18 39 52.05	20.167 133
8	3 23 51.492	+18 21 49.41	19.456 334	26	3 28 44.693	+18 40 30.15	20.180 095
9	3 23 53.390	+18 21 57.75	19.473 361	27	3 28 55.178	+18 41 08.71	20.192 872
10	3 23 55.501	+18 22 06.89	19.490 401	28	3 29 05.804	+18 41 47.70	20.205 461
11	3 23 57.823	+18 22 16.81	19.507 450	29	3 29 16.569	+18 42 27.11	20.217 857
12	3 24 00.354	+18 22 27.51	19.524 502	30	3 29 27.473	+18 43 06.94	20.230 058
13	3 24 03.094	+18 22 38.96	19.541 552	31	3 29 38.517	+18 43 47.18	20.242 059
14	3 24 06.043	+18 22 51.17	19.558 597	Apr. 1	3 29 49.700	+18 44 27.84	20.253 857
15	3 24 09.201	+18 23 04.12	19.575 631	2	3 30 01.017	+18 45 08.93	20.265 451

GEOCENTRIC COORDINATES FOR 0^h TERRESTRIAL TIME

Date	Apparent Right Ascension	Apparent Declination	True Geocentric Distance	Date	Apparent Right Ascension	Apparent Declination	True Geocentric Distance
	h m s	° ′ ″	au		h m s	° ′ ″	au
Apr. 1	3 29 49.700	+18 44 27.84	20.253 857	May 17	3 40 01.999	+19 20 04.33	20.541 129
2	3 30 01.017	+18 45 08.93	20.265 451	18	3 40 16.409	+19 20 50.63	20.541 298
3	3 30 12.466	+18 45 50.44	20.276 835	19	3 40 30.781	+19 21 40.72	20.541 199
4	3 30 24.040	+18 46 32.36	20.288 009	20	3 40 45.215	+19 22 29.01	20.540 832
5	3 30 35.735	+18 47 14.66	20.298 969	21	3 40 59.636	+19 23 17.10	20.540 197
6	3 30 47.546	+18 47 57.33	20.309 713	22	3 41 14.048	+19 24 05.04	20.539 293
7	3 30 59.471	+18 48 40.34	20.320 239	23	3 41 28.450	+19 24 52.84	20.538 120
8	3 31 11.505	+18 49 23.67	20.330 544	24	3 41 42.843	+19 25 40.49	20.536 679
9	3 31 23.648	+18 50 07.32	20.340 627	25	3 41 57.227	+19 26 27.99	20.534 970
10	3 31 35.897	+18 50 51.25	20.350 485	26	3 42 11.599	+19 27 15.36	20.532 992
11	3 31 48.252	+18 51 35.48	20.360 117	27	3 42 25.958	+19 28 02.60	20.530 747
12	3 32 00.710	+18 52 19.98	20.369 519	28	3 42 40.298	+19 28 49.70	20.528 234
13	3 32 13.271	+18 53 04.76	20.378 691	29	3 42 54.613	+19 29 36.66	20.525 456
14	3 32 25.933	+18 53 49.81	20.387 630	30	3 43 08.898	+19 30 23.47	20.522 412
15	3 32 38.694	+18 54 35.12	20.396 334	31	3 43 23.149	+19 31 10.08	20.519 103
16	3 32 51.552	+18 55 20.71	20.404 802	June 1	3 43 37.360	+19 31 56.50	20.515 532
17	3 33 04.504	+18 56 06.55	20.413 031	2	3 43 51.531	+19 32 42.68	20.511 700
18	3 33 17.546	+18 56 52.66	20.421 019	3	3 44 05.659	+19 33 28.64	20.507 607
19	3 33 30.676	+18 57 39.00	20.428 765	4	3 44 19.743	+19 34 14.35	20.503 255
20	3 33 43.889	+18 58 25.58	20.436 266	5	3 44 33.781	+19 34 59.81	20.498 646
21	3 33 57.181	+18 59 12.37	20.443 521	6	3 44 47.773	+19 35 45.02	20.493 781
22	3 34 10.550	+18 59 59.36	20.450 528	7	3 45 01.716	+19 36 29.98	20.488 661
23	3 34 23.991	+19 00 46.53	20.457 285	8	3 45 15.610	+19 37 14.68	20.483 289
24	3 34 37.502	+19 01 33.85	20.463 789	9	3 45 29.451	+19 37 59.14	20.477 664
25	3 34 51.081	+19 02 21.30	20.470 040	10	3 45 43.237	+19 38 43.34	20.471 789
26	3 35 04.728	+19 03 08.88	20.476 034	11	3 45 56.966	+19 39 27.29	20.465 666
27	3 35 18.442	+19 03 56.58	20.481 772	12	3 46 10.633	+19 40 10.98	20.459 295
28	3 35 32.223	+19 04 44.41	20.487 250	13	3 46 24.235	+19 40 54.41	20.452 679
29	3 35 46.068	+19 05 32.37	20.492 468	14	3 46 37.769	+19 41 37.55	20.445 818
30	3 35 59.973	+19 06 20.46	20.497 424	15	3 46 51.230	+19 42 20.41	20.438 714
May 1	3 36 13.934	+19 07 08.67	20.502 118	16	3 47 04.615	+19 43 02.95	20.431 369
2	3 36 27.943	+19 07 56.99	20.506 548	17	3 47 17.922	+19 43 45.17	20.423 783
3	3 36 41.997	+19 08 45.40	20.510 714	18	3 47 31.149	+19 44 27.05	20.415 959
4	3 36 56.091	+19 09 33.87	20.514 616	19	3 47 44.294	+19 45 08.57	20.407 898
5	3 37 10.221	+19 10 22.38	20.518 253	20	3 47 57.356	+19 45 49.74	20.399 602
6	3 37 24.386	+19 11 10.91	20.521 625	21	3 48 10.336	+19 46 30.55	20.391 071
7	3 37 38.583	+19 11 59.46	20.524 731	22	3 48 23.231	+19 47 11.00	20.382 309
8	3 37 52.812	+19 12 48.00	20.527 571	23	3 48 36.041	+19 47 51.12	20.373 316
9	3 38 07.071	+19 13 36.54	20.530 145	24	3 48 48.761	+19 48 30.89	20.364 096
10	3 38 21.358	+19 14 25.08	20.532 452	25	3 49 01.386	+19 49 10.33	20.354 650
11	3 38 35.671	+19 15 13.60	20.534 493	26	3 49 13.911	+19 49 49.40	20.344 980
12	3 38 50.010	+19 16 02.11	20.536 267	27	3 49 26.330	+19 50 28.11	20.335 090
13	3 39 04.371	+19 16 50.61	20.537 774	28	3 49 38.640	+19 51 06.42	20.324 981
14	3 39 18.752	+19 17 39.09	20.539 014	29	3 49 50.837	+19 51 44.32	20.314 658
15	3 39 33.151	+19 18 27.55	20.539 987	30	3 50 02.920	+19 52 21.79	20.304 123
16	3 39 47.565	+19 19 15.98	20.540 691	July 1	3 50 14.888	+19 52 58.83	20.293 378
17	3 40 01.999	+19 20 04.33	20.541 129	2	3 50 26.740	+19 53 35.43	20.282 427

GEOCENTRIC COORDINATES FOR 0^h TERRESTRIAL TIME

Date	Apparent Right Ascension	Apparent Declination	True Geocentric Distance	Date	Apparent Right Ascension	Apparent Declination	True Geocentric Distance
	h m s	° ′ ″	au		h m s	° ′ ″	au
July 1	3 50 14.888	+19 52 58.83	20.293 378	Aug. 16	3 56 46.411	+20 12 34.76	19.627 222
2	3 50 26.740	+19 53 35.43	20.282 427	17	3 56 50.752	+20 12 47.33	19.610 379
3	3 50 38.474	+19 54 11.59	20.271 272	18	3 56 54.894	+20 12 59.32	19.593 500
4	3 50 50.091	+19 54 47.31	20.259 917	19	3 56 58.833	+20 13 10.73	19.576 590
5	3 51 01.587	+19 55 22.60	20.248 364	20	3 57 02.566	+20 13 21.56	19.559 654
6	3 51 12.963	+19 55 57.46	20.236 616	21	3 57 06.091	+20 13 31.79	19.542 697
7	3 51 24.214	+19 56 31.88	20.224 677	22	3 57 09.404	+20 13 41.40	19.525 723
8	3 51 35.340	+19 57 05.88	20.212 549	23	3 57 12.505	+20 13 50.39	19.508 738
9	3 51 46.337	+19 57 39.45	20.200 235	24	3 57 15.394	+20 13 58.74	19.491 746
10	3 51 57.202	+19 58 12.58	20.187 738	25	3 57 18.072	+20 14 06.45	19.474 754
11	3 52 07.930	+19 58 45.26	20.175 061	26	3 57 20.539	+20 14 13.53	19.457 765
12	3 52 18.520	+19 59 17.49	20.162 206	27	3 57 22.796	+20 14 19.98	19.440 785
13	3 52 28.967	+19 59 49.25	20.149 178	28	3 57 24.845	+20 14 25.80	19.423 818
14	3 52 39.270	+20 00 20.53	20.135 977	29	3 57 26.685	+20 14 31.01	19.406 871
15	3 52 49.426	+20 00 51.30	20.122 608	30	3 57 28.317	+20 14 35.61	19.389 947
16	3 52 59.434	+20 01 21.56	20.109 074	31	3 57 29.740	+20 14 39.61	19.373 051
17	3 53 09.295	+20 01 51.31	20.095 376	Sept. 1	3 57 30.954	+20 14 43.01	19.356 189
18	3 53 19.008	+20 02 20.55	20.081 519	2	3 57 31.958	+20 14 45.82	19.339 365
19	3 53 28.572	+20 02 49.28	20.067 505	3	3 57 32.750	+20 14 48.03	19.322 584
20	3 53 37.987	+20 03 17.51	20.053 337	4	3 57 33.330	+20 14 49.65	19.305 850
21	3 53 47.249	+20 03 45.25	20.039 020	5	3 57 33.696	+20 14 50.66	19.289 168
22	3 53 56.354	+20 04 12.50	20.024 556	6	3 57 33.848	+20 14 51.05	19.272 544
23	3 54 05.298	+20 04 39.26	20.009 949	7	3 57 33.785	+20 14 50.82	19.255 980
24	3 54 14.076	+20 05 05.51	19.995 204	8	3 57 33.508	+20 14 49.96	19.239 481
25	3 54 22.684	+20 05 31.24	19.980 323	9	3 57 33.019	+20 14 48.45	19.223 053
26	3 54 31.120	+20 05 56.42	19.965 312	10	3 57 32.322	+20 14 46.31	19.206 699
27	3 54 39.381	+20 06 21.04	19.950 174	11	3 57 31.417	+20 14 43.55	19.190 424
28	3 54 47.467	+20 06 45.10	19.934 914	12	3 57 30.308	+20 14 40.18	19.174 233
29	3 54 55.377	+20 07 08.59	19.919 535	13	3 57 28.993	+20 14 36.22	19.158 129
30	3 55 03.111	+20 07 31.51	19.904 042	14	3 57 27.473	+20 14 31.67	19.142 119
31	3 55 10.670	+20 07 53.86	19.888 440	15	3 57 25.744	+20 14 26.55	19.126 206
Aug. 1	3 55 18.052	+20 08 15.65	19.872 732	16	3 57 23.806	+20 14 20.84	19.110 397
2	3 55 25.256	+20 08 36.89	19.856 922	17	3 57 21.657	+20 14 14.53	19.094 695
3	3 55 32.281	+20 08 57.57	19.841 015	18	3 57 19.297	+20 14 07.62	19.079 106
4	3 55 39.125	+20 09 17.70	19.825 015	19	3 57 16.725	+20 14 00.10	19.063 635
5	3 55 45.786	+20 09 37.29	19.808 926	20	3 57 13.945	+20 13 51.96	19.048 287
6	3 55 52.262	+20 09 56.33	19.792 752	21	3 57 10.957	+20 13 43.20	19.033 068
7	3 55 58.551	+20 10 14.82	19.776 497	22	3 57 07.765	+20 13 33.83	19.017 982
8	3 56 04.649	+20 10 32.75	19.760 165	23	3 57 04.371	+20 13 23.85	19.003 035
9	3 56 10.554	+20 10 50.10	19.743 760	24	3 57 00.778	+20 13 13.28	18.988 231
10	3 56 16.263	+20 11 06.87	19.727 287	25	3 56 56.989	+20 13 02.12	18.973 575
11	3 56 21.777	+20 11 23.04	19.710 748	26	3 56 53.004	+20 12 50.39	18.959 072
12	3 56 27.094	+20 11 38.60	19.694 149	27	3 56 48.827	+20 12 38.10	18.944 726
13	3 56 32.215	+20 11 53.55	19.677 492	28	3 56 44.459	+20 12 25.25	18.930 543
14	3 56 37.142	+20 12 07.88	19.660 783	29	3 56 39.900	+20 12 11.87	18.916 527
15	3 56 41.874	+20 12 21.62	19.644 025	30	3 56 35.152	+20 11 57.94	18.902 682
16	3 56 46.411	+20 12 34.76	19.627 222	Oct. 1	3 56 30.215	+20 11 43.48	18.889 012

GEOCENTRIC COORDINATES FOR 0^h TERRESTRIAL TIME

Date	Apparent Right Ascension	Apparent Declination	True Geocentric Distance	Date	Apparent Right Ascension	Apparent Declination	True Geocentric Distance
	h m s	° ′ ″	au		h m s	° ′ ″	au
Oct. 1	3 56 30.215	+20 11 43.48	18.889 012	Nov. 16	3 50 07.008	+19 52 40.73	18.513 996
2	3 56 25.090	+20 11 28.49	18.875 522	17	3 49 56.613	+19 52 09.13	18.512 454
3	3 56 19.779	+20 11 12.95	18.862 216	18	3 49 46.199	+19 51 37.43	18.511 223
4	3 56 14.283	+20 10 56.87	18.849 098	19	3 49 35.772	+19 51 05.65	18.510 305
5	3 56 08.605	+20 10 40.24	18.836 172	20	3 49 25.335	+19 50 33.82	18.509 700
6	3 56 02.748	+20 10 23.05	18.823 441	21	3 49 14.895	+19 50 01.96	18.509 408
7	3 55 56.716	+20 10 05.32	18.810 910	22	3 49 04.455	+19 49 30.08	18.509 430
8	3 55 50.515	+20 09 47.05	18.798 581	23	3 48 54.020	+19 48 58.21	18.509 766
9	3 55 44.148	+20 09 28.26	18.786 460	24	3 48 43.592	+19 48 26.34	18.510 415
10	3 55 37.618	+20 09 08.99	18.774 549	25	3 48 33.176	+19 47 54.51	18.511 378
11	3 55 30.928	+20 08 49.24	18.762 853	26	3 48 22.775	+19 47 22.70	18.512 654
12	3 55 24.076	+20 08 29.03	18.751 376	27	3 48 12.394	+19 46 50.94	18.514 242
13	3 55 17.063	+20 08 08.36	18.740 122	28	3 48 02.037	+19 46 19.22	18.516 141
14	3 55 09.889	+20 07 47.22	18.729 094	29	3 47 51.709	+19 45 47.55	18.518 351
15	3 55 02.555	+20 07 25.61	18.718 297	30	3 47 41.416	+19 45 15.94	18.520 871
16	3 54 55.065	+20 07 03.53	18.707 735	Dec. 1	3 47 31.165	+19 44 44.41	18.523 699
17	3 54 47.422	+20 06 40.97	18.697 412	2	3 47 20.962	+19 44 12.98	18.526 835
18	3 54 39.629	+20 06 17.93	18.687 332	3	3 47 10.813	+19 43 41.68	18.530 276
19	3 54 31.692	+20 05 54.44	18.677 498	4	3 47 00.725	+19 43 10.54	18.534 021
20	3 54 23.615	+20 05 30.50	18.667 915	5	3 46 50.699	+19 42 39.58	18.538 070
21	3 54 15.403	+20 05 06.12	18.658 587	6	3 46 40.737	+19 42 08.82	18.542 421
22	3 54 07.060	+20 04 41.33	18.649 515	7	3 46 30.841	+19 41 38.27	18.547 072
23	3 53 58.592	+20 04 16.14	18.640 705	8	3 46 21.012	+19 41 07.93	18.552 022
24	3 53 50.000	+20 03 50.56	18.632 158	9	3 46 11.253	+19 40 37.80	18.557 271
25	3 53 41.290	+20 03 24.62	18.623 879	10	3 46 01.567	+19 40 07.88	18.562 816
26	3 53 32.464	+20 02 58.33	18.615 870	11	3 45 51.961	+19 39 38.18	18.568 656
27	3 53 23.525	+20 02 31.70	18.608 134	12	3 45 42.441	+19 39 08.70	18.574 790
28	3 53 14.475	+20 02 04.74	18.600 673	13	3 45 33.012	+19 38 39.48	18.581 216
29	3 53 05.319	+20 01 37.45	18.593 491	14	3 45 23.679	+19 38 10.52	18.587 932
30	3 52 56.059	+20 01 09.84	18.586 589	15	3 45 14.449	+19 37 41.86	18.594 935
31	3 52 46.698	+20 00 41.91	18.579 969	16	3 45 05.327	+19 37 13.51	18.602 224
Nov. 1	3 52 37.241	+20 00 13.66	18.573 635	17	3 44 56.316	+19 36 45.50	18.609 796
2	3 52 27.691	+19 59 45.09	18.567 587	18	3 44 47.420	+19 36 17.85	18.617 649
3	3 52 18.056	+19 59 16.22	18.561 828	19	3 44 38.644	+19 35 50.57	18.625 779
4	3 52 08.341	+19 58 47.05	18.556 359	20	3 44 29.991	+19 35 23.69	18.634 185
5	3 51 58.553	+19 58 17.61	18.551 183	21	3 44 21.464	+19 34 57.20	18.642 862
6	3 51 48.697	+19 57 47.92	18.546 299	22	3 44 13.064	+19 34 31.14	18.651 808
7	3 51 38.777	+19 57 18.03	18.541 712	23	3 44 04.796	+19 34 05.49	18.661 019
8	3 51 28.796	+19 56 47.94	18.537 421	24	3 43 56.661	+19 33 40.26	18.670 493
9	3 51 18.754	+19 56 17.66	18.533 429	25	3 43 48.664	+19 33 15.46	18.680 224
10	3 51 08.652	+19 55 47.21	18.529 737	26	3 43 40.809	+19 32 51.10	18.690 211
11	3 50 58.494	+19 55 16.57	18.526 348	27	3 43 33.099	+19 32 27.18	18.700 448
12	3 50 48.282	+19 54 45.74	18.523 264	28	3 43 25.541	+19 32 03.71	18.710 932
13	3 50 38.022	+19 54 14.73	18.520 485	29	3 43 18.138	+19 31 40.70	18.721 659
14	3 50 27.719	+19 53 43.55	18.518 013	30	3 43 10.896	+19 31 18.19	18.732 624
15	3 50 17.379	+19 53 12.21	18.515 850	31	3 43 03.819	+19 30 56.20	18.743 825
16	3 50 07.008	+19 52 40.73	18.513 996	32	3 42 56.909	+19 30 34.74	18.755 256

GEOCENTRIC COORDINATES FOR 0^h TERRESTRIAL TIME

Date	Apparent Right Ascension	Apparent Declination	True Geocentric Distance	Date	Apparent Right Ascension	Apparent Declination	True Geocentric Distance
	h m s	° ′ ″	au		h m s	° ′ ″	au
Jan. 0	23 52 04.675	− 2 15 35.83	30.091 890	Feb. 15	23 56 09.087	− 1 47 45.11	30.727 267
1	23 52 07.600	− 2 15 14.49	30.108 803	16	23 56 16.411	− 1 46 56.50	30.736 417
2	23 52 10.644	− 2 14 52.39	30.125 646	17	23 56 23.797	− 1 46 07.53	30.745 318
3	23 52 13.807	− 2 14 29.52	30.142 412	18	23 56 31.243	− 1 45 18.20	30.753 969
4	23 52 17.087	− 2 14 05.92	30.159 097	19	23 56 38.748	− 1 44 28.53	30.762 366
5	23 52 20.484	− 2 13 41.57	30.175 695	20	23 56 46.312	− 1 43 38.51	30.770 508
6	23 52 23.998	− 2 13 16.47	30.192 200	21	23 56 53.933	− 1 42 48.17	30.778 391
7	23 52 27.631	− 2 12 50.62	30.208 610	22	23 57 01.608	− 1 41 57.51	30.786 015
8	23 52 31.382	− 2 12 24.02	30.224 917	23	23 57 09.336	− 1 41 06.55	30.793 376
9	23 52 35.252	− 2 11 56.66	30.241 118	24	23 57 17.113	− 1 40 15.32	30.800 472
10	23 52 39.241	− 2 11 28.56	30.257 208	25	23 57 24.936	− 1 39 23.83	30.807 301
11	23 52 43.347	− 2 10 59.71	30.273 183	26	23 57 32.801	− 1 38 32.10	30.813 862
12	23 52 47.568	− 2 10 30.15	30.289 039	27	23 57 40.706	− 1 37 40.16	30.820 152
13	23 52 51.900	− 2 09 59.88	30.304 770	28	23 57 48.649	− 1 36 48.01	30.826 168
14	23 52 56.341	− 2 09 28.94	30.320 374	Mar. 1	23 57 56.628	− 1 35 55.67	30.831 911
15	23 53 00.888	− 2 08 57.33	30.335 845	2	23 58 04.643	− 1 35 03.15	30.837 378
16	23 53 05.539	− 2 08 25.06	30.351 180	3	23 58 12.694	− 1 34 10.42	30.842 567
17	23 53 10.295	− 2 07 52.15	30.366 374	4	23 58 20.781	− 1 33 17.51	30.847 478
18	23 53 15.155	− 2 07 18.58	30.381 423	5	23 58 28.904	− 1 32 24.41	30.852 110
19	23 53 20.118	− 2 06 44.37	30.396 322	6	23 58 37.059	− 1 31 31.15	30.856 462
20	23 53 25.185	− 2 06 09.50	30.411 068	7	23 58 45.244	− 1 30 37.74	30.860 533
21	23 53 30.355	− 2 05 33.99	30.425 656	8	23 58 53.455	− 1 29 44.21	30.864 324
22	23 53 35.630	− 2 04 57.84	30.440 082	9	23 59 01.688	− 1 28 50.58	30.867 833
23	23 53 41.007	− 2 04 21.04	30.454 341	10	23 59 09.940	− 1 27 56.87	30.871 061
24	23 53 46.486	− 2 03 43.61	30.468 429	11	23 59 18.208	− 1 27 03.10	30.874 006
25	23 53 52.065	− 2 03 05.55	30.482 342	12	23 59 26.491	− 1 26 09.28	30.876 669
26	23 53 57.744	− 2 02 26.88	30.496 075	13	23 59 34.788	− 1 25 15.43	30.879 049
27	23 54 03.519	− 2 01 47.61	30.509 625	14	23 59 43.096	− 1 24 21.54	30.881 146
28	23 54 09.388	− 2 01 07.77	30.522 987	15	23 59 51.417	− 1 23 27.62	30.882 960
29	23 54 15.348	− 2 00 27.36	30.536 157	16	23 59 59.748	− 1 22 33.67	30.884 490
30	23 54 21.395	− 1 59 46.42	30.549 131	17	0 00 08.091	− 1 21 39.72	30.885 736
31	23 54 27.528	− 1 59 04.96	30.561 905	18	0 00 16.444	− 1 20 45.77	30.886 699
Feb. 1	23 54 33.745	− 1 58 22.98	30.574 475	19	0 00 24.805	− 1 19 51.89	30.887 377
2	23 54 40.046	− 1 57 40.49	30.586 837	20	0 00 33.161	− 1 18 58.09	30.887 771
3	23 54 46.431	− 1 56 57.49	30.598 988	21	0 00 41.514	− 1 18 04.07	30.887 880
4	23 54 52.900	− 1 56 13.97	30.610 924	22	0 00 49.881	− 1 17 10.02	30.887 705
5	23 54 59.453	− 1 55 29.94	30.622 644	23	0 00 58.250	− 1 16 16.08	30.887 245
6	23 55 06.089	− 1 54 45.41	30.634 142	24	0 01 06.615	− 1 15 22.24	30.886 501
7	23 55 12.805	− 1 54 00.40	30.645 417	25	0 01 14.973	− 1 14 28.51	30.885 472
8	23 55 19.600	− 1 53 14.92	30.656 466	26	0 01 23.320	− 1 13 34.89	30.884 159
9	23 55 26.468	− 1 52 28.99	30.667 287	27	0 01 31.654	− 1 12 41.40	30.882 561
10	23 55 33.408	− 1 51 42.65	30.677 876	28	0 01 39.973	− 1 11 48.06	30.880 680
11	23 55 40.415	− 1 50 55.90	30.688 232	29	0 01 48.276	− 1 10 54.87	30.878 516
12	23 55 47.488	− 1 50 08.76	30.698 351	30	0 01 56.565	− 1 10 01.82	30.876 070
13	23 55 54.625	− 1 49 21.25	30.708 231	31	0 02 04.838	− 1 09 08.91	30.873 342
14	23 56 01.825	− 1 48 33.36	30.717 871	Apr. 1	0 02 13.096	− 1 08 16.15	30.870 334
15	23 56 09.087	− 1 47 45.11	30.727 267	2	0 02 21.337	− 1 07 23.55	30.867 047

GEOCENTRIC COORDINATES FOR 0ʰ TERRESTRIAL TIME

Date	Apparent Right Ascension	Apparent Declination	True Geocentric Distance	Date	Apparent Right Ascension	Apparent Declination	True Geocentric Distance
	h m s	° ′ ″	au		h m s	° ′ ″	au
Apr. 1	0 02 13.096	− 1 08 16.15	30.870 334	May 17	0 07 42.631	− 0 34 01.76	30.461 892
2	0 02 21.337	− 1 07 23.55	30.867 047	18	0 07 48.124	− 0 33 28.82	30.448 103
3	0 02 29.558	− 1 06 31.12	30.863 482	19	0 07 53.522	− 0 32 56.51	30.434 155
4	0 02 37.755	− 1 05 38.90	30.859 642	20	0 07 58.823	− 0 32 24.87	30.420 053
5	0 02 45.924	− 1 04 46.90	30.855 527	21	0 08 04.026	− 0 31 53.89	30.405 800
6	0 02 54.062	− 1 03 55.16	30.851 141	22	0 08 09.130	− 0 31 23.58	30.391 399
7	0 03 02.166	− 1 03 03.67	30.846 483	23	0 08 14.136	− 0 30 53.94	30.376 854
8	0 03 10.235	− 1 02 12.46	30.841 556	24	0 08 19.043	− 0 30 24.97	30.362 169
9	0 03 18.267	− 1 01 21.54	30.836 363	25	0 08 23.853	− 0 29 56.66	30.347 348
10	0 03 26.261	− 1 00 30.90	30.830 904	26	0 08 28.566	− 0 29 29.00	30.332 396
11	0 03 34.216	− 0 59 40.56	30.825 181	27	0 08 33.182	− 0 29 02.00	30.317 316
12	0 03 42.133	− 0 58 50.51	30.819 196	28	0 08 37.698	− 0 28 35.67	30.302 113
13	0 03 50.011	− 0 58 00.77	30.812 951	29	0 08 42.110	− 0 28 10.04	30.286 792
14	0 03 57.849	− 0 57 11.32	30.806 447	30	0 08 46.416	− 0 27 45.13	30.271 357
15	0 04 05.645	− 0 56 22.19	30.799 687	31	0 08 50.613	− 0 27 20.95	30.255 814
16	0 04 13.399	− 0 55 33.37	30.792 672	June 1	0 08 54.699	− 0 26 57.51	30.240 166
17	0 04 21.108	− 0 54 44.88	30.785 404	2	0 08 58.673	− 0 26 34.81	30.224 419
18	0 04 28.772	− 0 53 56.74	30.777 885	3	0 09 02.536	− 0 26 12.87	30.208 576
19	0 04 36.386	− 0 53 08.95	30.770 116	4	0 09 06.287	− 0 25 51.66	30.192 642
20	0 04 43.948	− 0 52 21.54	30.762 101	5	0 09 09.929	− 0 25 31.19	30.176 621
21	0 04 51.457	− 0 51 34.52	30.753 839	6	0 09 13.460	− 0 25 11.45	30.160 519
22	0 04 58.907	− 0 50 47.92	30.745 335	7	0 09 16.882	− 0 24 52.44	30.144 339
23	0 05 06.299	− 0 50 01.74	30.736 589	8	0 09 20.194	− 0 24 34.16	30.128 085
24	0 05 13.629	− 0 49 16.00	30.727 605	9	0 09 23.397	− 0 24 16.61	30.111 762
25	0 05 20.896	− 0 48 30.71	30.718 383	10	0 09 26.489	− 0 23 59.79	30.095 374
26	0 05 28.101	− 0 47 45.87	30.708 928	11	0 09 29.470	− 0 23 43.70	30.078 925
27	0 05 35.244	− 0 47 01.46	30.699 241	12	0 09 32.339	− 0 23 28.35	30.062 420
28	0 05 42.326	− 0 46 17.50	30.689 325	13	0 09 35.094	− 0 23 13.76	30.045 863
29	0 05 49.346	− 0 45 33.98	30.679 184	14	0 09 37.733	− 0 22 59.92	30.029 257
30	0 05 56.302	− 0 44 50.91	30.668 820	15	0 09 40.255	− 0 22 46.87	30.012 607
May 1	0 06 03.190	− 0 44 08.32	30.658 237	16	0 09 42.658	− 0 22 34.59	29.995 918
2	0 06 10.007	− 0 43 26.24	30.647 438	17	0 09 44.941	− 0 22 23.10	29.979 194
3	0 06 16.748	− 0 42 44.68	30.636 427	18	0 09 47.104	− 0 22 12.40	29.962 438
4	0 06 23.412	− 0 42 03.67	30.625 208	19	0 09 49.149	− 0 22 02.48	29.945 656
5	0 06 29.997	− 0 41 23.20	30.613 783	20	0 09 51.075	− 0 21 53.33	29.928 852
6	0 06 36.501	− 0 40 43.30	30.602 156	21	0 09 52.885	− 0 21 44.96	29.912 031
7	0 06 42.924	− 0 40 03.95	30.590 331	22	0 09 54.579	− 0 21 37.34	29.895 197
8	0 06 49.267	− 0 39 25.17	30.578 310	23	0 09 56.158	− 0 21 30.47	29.878 356
9	0 06 55.528	− 0 38 46.95	30.566 098	24	0 09 57.622	− 0 21 24.36	29.861 511
10	0 07 01.709	− 0 38 09.29	30.553 697	25	0 09 58.968	− 0 21 19.02	29.844 670
11	0 07 07.807	− 0 37 32.19	30.541 111	26	0 10 00.193	− 0 21 14.46	29.827 835
12	0 07 13.824	− 0 36 55.66	30.528 343	27	0 10 01.295	− 0 21 10.71	29.811 014
13	0 07 19.757	− 0 36 19.70	30.515 396	28	0 10 02.273	− 0 21 07.76	29.794 211
14	0 07 25.607	− 0 35 44.32	30.502 274	29	0 10 03.127	− 0 21 05.63	29.777 430
15	0 07 31.370	− 0 35 09.53	30.488 981	30	0 10 03.856	− 0 21 04.29	29.760 677
16	0 07 37.046	− 0 34 35.34	30.475 519	July 1	0 10 04.463	− 0 21 03.76	29.743 957
17	0 07 42.631	− 0 34 01.76	30.461 892	2	0 10 04.949	− 0 21 04.01	29.727 274

GEOCENTRIC COORDINATES FOR 0^h TERRESTRIAL TIME

Date	Apparent Right Ascension	Apparent Declination	True Geocentric Distance	Date	Apparent Right Ascension	Apparent Declination	True Geocentric Distance
	h m s	° ′ ″	au		h m s	° ′ ″	au
July 1	0 10 04.463	− 0 21 03.76	29.743 957	Aug. 16	0 08 29.776	− 0 33 39.30	29.087 482
2	0 10 04.949	− 0 21 04.01	29.727 274	17	0 08 25.362	− 0 34 10.37	29.077 249
3	0 10 05.314	− 0 21 05.04	29.710 634	18	0 08 20.869	− 0 34 41.91	29.067 247
4	0 10 05.561	− 0 21 06.84	29.694 040	19	0 08 16.298	− 0 35 13.92	29.057 481
5	0 10 05.690	− 0 21 09.39	29.677 498	20	0 08 11.649	− 0 35 46.39	29.047 954
6	0 10 05.702	− 0 21 12.70	29.661 011	21	0 08 06.921	− 0 36 19.34	29.038 671
7	0 10 05.598	− 0 21 16.76	29.644 585	22	0 08 02.115	− 0 36 52.74	29.029 633
8	0 10 05.377	− 0 21 21.57	29.628 223	23	0 07 57.234	− 0 37 26.60	29.020 844
9	0 10 05.040	− 0 21 27.12	29.611 931	24	0 07 52.278	− 0 38 00.89	29.012 308
10	0 10 04.585	− 0 21 33.43	29.595 713	25	0 07 47.252	− 0 38 35.60	29.004 027
11	0 10 04.012	− 0 21 40.49	29.579 572	26	0 07 42.159	− 0 39 10.70	28.996 004
12	0 10 03.319	− 0 21 48.32	29.563 513	27	0 07 37.002	− 0 39 46.16	28.988 242
13	0 10 02.506	− 0 21 56.91	29.547 540	28	0 07 31.785	− 0 40 21.98	28.980 743
14	0 10 01.574	− 0 22 06.27	29.531 658	29	0 07 26.509	− 0 40 58.12	28.973 509
15	0 10 00.522	− 0 22 16.40	29.515 871	30	0 07 21.178	− 0 41 34.57	28.966 544
16	0 09 59.351	− 0 22 27.27	29.500 183	31	0 07 15.793	− 0 42 11.33	28.959 848
17	0 09 58.065	− 0 22 38.89	29.484 599	Sept. 1	0 07 10.356	− 0 42 48.37	28.953 425
18	0 09 56.665	− 0 22 51.23	29.469 123	2	0 07 04.868	− 0 43 25.69	28.947 275
19	0 09 55.153	− 0 23 04.29	29.453 760	3	0 06 59.331	− 0 44 03.28	28.941 401
20	0 09 53.531	− 0 23 18.04	29.438 514	4	0 06 53.746	− 0 44 41.13	28.935 804
21	0 09 51.799	− 0 23 32.50	29.423 391	5	0 06 48.113	− 0 45 19.23	28.930 486
22	0 09 49.956	− 0 23 47.65	29.408 395	6	0 06 42.434	− 0 45 57.59	28.925 449
23	0 09 48.001	− 0 24 03.51	29.393 530	7	0 06 36.710	− 0 46 36.19	28.920 693
24	0 09 45.933	− 0 24 20.08	29.378 803	8	0 06 30.944	− 0 47 15.01	28.916 221
25	0 09 43.751	− 0 24 37.37	29.364 216	9	0 06 25.138	− 0 47 54.03	28.912 034
26	0 09 41.455	− 0 24 55.38	29.349 776	10	0 06 19.298	− 0 48 33.23	28.908 133
27	0 09 39.046	− 0 25 14.11	29.335 487	11	0 06 13.428	− 0 49 12.57	28.904 520
28	0 09 36.526	− 0 25 33.53	29.321 353	12	0 06 07.530	− 0 49 52.04	28.901 196
29	0 09 33.897	− 0 25 53.63	29.307 378	13	0 06 01.607	− 0 50 31.62	28.898 163
30	0 09 31.163	− 0 26 14.39	29.293 567	14	0 05 55.660	− 0 51 11.30	28.895 423
31	0 09 28.324	− 0 26 35.80	29.279 923	15	0 05 49.690	− 0 51 51.08	28.892 977
Aug. 1	0 09 25.384	− 0 26 57.85	29.266 452	16	0 05 43.697	− 0 52 30.95	28.890 826
2	0 09 22.344	− 0 27 20.51	29.253 156	17	0 05 37.682	− 0 53 10.92	28.888 972
3	0 09 19.205	− 0 27 43.79	29.240 040	18	0 05 31.646	− 0 53 50.96	28.887 415
4	0 09 15.969	− 0 28 07.67	29.227 107	19	0 05 25.592	− 0 54 31.08	28.886 158
5	0 09 12.636	− 0 28 32.14	29.214 361	20	0 05 19.521	− 0 55 11.24	28.885 201
6	0 09 09.207	− 0 28 57.20	29.201 805	21	0 05 13.437	− 0 55 51.43	28.884 544
7	0 09 05.682	− 0 29 22.85	29.189 444	22	0 05 07.345	− 0 56 31.62	28.884 188
8	0 09 02.061	− 0 29 49.10	29.177 279	23	0 05 01.247	− 0 57 11.79	28.884 133
9	0 08 58.344	− 0 30 15.93	29.165 316	24	0 04 55.148	− 0 57 51.92	28.884 381
10	0 08 54.532	− 0 30 43.34	29.153 557	25	0 04 49.051	− 0 58 31.97	28.884 929
11	0 08 50.626	− 0 31 11.33	29.142 006	26	0 04 42.958	− 0 59 11.94	28.885 780
12	0 08 46.627	− 0 31 39.88	29.130 666	27	0 04 36.872	− 0 59 51.81	28.886 932
13	0 08 42.540	− 0 32 08.98	29.119 540	28	0 04 30.796	− 1 00 31.55	28.888 385
14	0 08 38.367	− 0 32 38.59	29.108 631	29	0 04 24.732	− 1 01 11.17	28.890 138
15	0 08 34.112	− 0 33 08.71	29.097 944	30	0 04 18.679	− 1 01 50.65	28.892 191
16	0 08 29.776	− 0 33 39.30	29.087 482	Oct. 1	0 04 12.641	− 1 02 29.97	28.894 543

GEOCENTRIC COORDINATES FOR 0^h TERRESTRIAL TIME

Date	Apparent Right Ascension	Apparent Declination	True Geocentric Distance	Date	Apparent Right Ascension	Apparent Declination	True Geocentric Distance
	h m s	° ′ ″	au		h m s	° ′ ″	au
Oct. 1	0 04 12.641	− 1 02 29.97	28.894 543	Nov. 16	0 00 28.682	− 1 25 54.76	29.298 821
2	0 04 06.619	− 1 03 09.15	28.897 194	17	0 00 25.738	− 1 26 11.81	29.313 054
3	0 04 00.613	− 1 03 48.15	28.900 142	18	0 00 22.904	− 1 26 28.11	29.327 462
4	0 03 54.626	− 1 04 26.98	28.903 386	19	0 00 20.184	− 1 26 43.64	29.342 039
5	0 03 48.659	− 1 05 05.62	28.906 926	20	0 00 17.578	− 1 26 58.39	29.356 781
6	0 03 42.716	− 1 05 44.05	28.910 759	21	0 00 15.088	− 1 27 12.37	29.371 684
7	0 03 36.800	− 1 06 22.25	28.914 886	22	0 00 12.714	− 1 27 25.57	29.386 742
8	0 03 30.917	− 1 07 00.18	28.919 305	23	0 00 10.457	− 1 27 37.98	29.401 950
9	0 03 25.071	− 1 07 37.83	28.924 014	24	0 00 08.316	− 1 27 49.60	29.417 304
10	0 03 19.263	− 1 08 15.16	28.929 014	25	0 00 06.292	− 1 28 00.45	29.432 797
11	0 03 13.497	− 1 08 52.18	28.934 302	26	0 00 04.384	− 1 28 10.51	29.448 426
12	0 03 07.771	− 1 09 28.88	28.939 878	27	0 00 02.593	− 1 28 19.80	29.464 184
13	0 03 02.087	− 1 10 05.26	28.945 741	28	0 00 00.920	− 1 28 28.30	29.480 067
14	0 02 56.445	− 1 10 41.31	28.951 890	29	23 59 59.365	− 1 28 36.01	29.496 069
15	0 02 50.845	− 1 11 17.03	28.958 322	30	23 59 57.930	− 1 28 42.92	29.512 186
16	0 02 45.290	− 1 11 52.42	28.965 038	Dec. 1	23 59 56.616	− 1 28 49.02	29.528 411
17	0 02 39.782	− 1 12 27.44	28.972 034	2	23 59 55.428	− 1 28 54.30	29.544 741
18	0 02 34.325	− 1 13 02.08	28.979 309	3	23 59 54.366	− 1 28 58.73	29.561 169
19	0 02 28.922	− 1 13 36.32	28.986 861	4	23 59 53.433	− 1 29 02.32	29.577 692
20	0 02 23.576	− 1 14 10.14	28.994 688	5	23 59 52.628	− 1 29 05.06	29.594 304
21	0 02 18.292	− 1 14 43.51	29.002 788	6	23 59 51.950	− 1 29 06.96	29.611 001
22	0 02 13.071	− 1 15 16.41	29.011 157	7	23 59 51.396	− 1 29 08.04	29.627 777
23	0 02 07.918	− 1 15 48.83	29.019 794	8	23 59 50.965	− 1 29 08.32	29.644 629
24	0 02 02.834	− 1 16 20.74	29.028 695	9	23 59 50.656	− 1 29 07.80	29.661 551
25	0 01 57.821	− 1 16 52.15	29.037 858	10	23 59 50.469	− 1 29 06.48	29.678 539
26	0 01 52.881	− 1 17 23.03	29.047 280	11	23 59 50.405	− 1 29 04.34	29.695 587
27	0 01 48.014	− 1 17 53.38	29.056 956	12	23 59 50.465	− 1 29 01.39	29.712 690
28	0 01 43.223	− 1 18 23.20	29.066 885	13	23 59 50.653	− 1 28 57.61	29.729 842
29	0 01 38.508	− 1 18 52.48	29.077 063	14	23 59 50.969	− 1 28 52.99	29.747 040
30	0 01 33.869	− 1 19 21.22	29.087 487	15	23 59 51.414	− 1 28 47.52	29.764 276
31	0 01 29.309	− 1 19 49.40	29.098 152	16	23 59 51.990	− 1 28 41.20	29.781 546
Nov. 1	0 01 24.828	− 1 20 17.02	29.109 056	17	23 59 52.696	− 1 28 34.02	29.798 844
2	0 01 20.429	− 1 20 44.06	29.120 194	18	23 59 53.534	− 1 28 25.99	29.816 165
3	0 01 16.115	− 1 21 10.52	29.131 564	19	23 59 54.502	− 1 28 17.11	29.833 502
4	0 01 11.889	− 1 21 36.35	29.143 161	20	23 59 55.599	− 1 28 07.39	29.850 851
5	0 01 07.756	− 1 22 01.55	29.154 983	21	23 59 56.826	− 1 27 56.83	29.868 205
6	0 01 03.718	− 1 22 26.09	29.167 025	22	23 59 58.180	− 1 27 45.44	29.885 560
7	0 00 59.777	− 1 22 49.95	29.179 285	23	23 59 59.660	− 1 27 33.24	29.902 908
8	0 00 55.934	− 1 23 13.15	29.191 758	24	0 00 01.266	− 1 27 20.23	29.920 246
9	0 00 52.186	− 1 23 35.69	29.204 443	25	0 00 02.996	− 1 27 06.41	29.937 566
10	0 00 48.534	− 1 23 57.57	29.217 334	26	0 00 04.851	− 1 26 51.78	29.954 864
11	0 00 44.978	− 1 24 18.80	29.230 429	27	0 00 06.830	− 1 26 36.36	29.972 134
12	0 00 41.517	− 1 24 39.37	29.243 724	28	0 00 08.935	− 1 26 20.12	29.989 371
13	0 00 38.155	− 1 24 59.26	29.257 215	29	0 00 11.166	− 1 26 03.08	30.006 569
14	0 00 34.893	− 1 25 18.47	29.270 897	30	0 00 13.525	− 1 25 45.21	30.023 724
15	0 00 31.734	− 1 25 36.98	29.284 768	31	0 00 16.013	− 1 25 26.52	30.040 830
16	0 00 28.682	− 1 25 54.76	29.298 821	32	0 00 18.628	− 1 25 07.01	30.057 882

Date		Mercury	Venus	Mars	Jupiter	Saturn	Uranus	Neptune
		h m s	h m s	h m s	h m s	h m s	h m s	h m s
Jan.	0	10 31 50	15 17 56	1 41 48	22 04 17	16 23 38	20 42 14	17 09 38
	1	10 33 22	15 18 02	1 36 33	21 59 54	16 19 58	20 38 12	17 05 45
	2	10 35 02	15 18 06	1 31 15	21 55 32	16 16 19	20 34 10	17 01 53
	3	10 36 49	15 18 07	1 25 54	21 51 10	16 12 41	20 30 09	16 58 00
	4	10 38 42	15 18 07	1 20 31	21 46 49	16 09 02	20 26 08	16 54 07
	5	10 40 40	15 18 04	1 15 06	21 42 29	16 05 24	20 22 07	16 50 15
	6	10 42 44	15 17 58	1 09 38	21 38 09	16 01 46	20 18 06	16 46 23
	7	10 44 53	15 17 51	1 04 09	21 33 50	15 58 09	20 14 05	16 42 30
	8	10 47 06	15 17 41	0 58 38	21 29 32	15 54 32	20 10 04	16 38 38
	9	10 49 23	15 17 29	0 53 05	21 25 14	15 50 55	20 06 04	16 34 46
	10	10 51 45	15 17 15	0 47 31	21 20 57	15 47 18	20 02 04	16 30 54
	11	10 54 09	15 16 58	0 41 56	21 16 41	15 43 41	19 58 04	16 27 03
	12	10 56 37	15 16 39	0 36 20	21 12 26	15 40 05	19 54 04	16 23 11
	13	10 59 08	15 16 17	0 30 43	21 08 11	15 36 29	19 50 05	16 19 19
	14	11 01 42	15 15 53	0 25 06	21 03 58	15 32 53	19 46 05	16 15 28
	15	11 04 18	15 15 26	0 19 27	20 59 45	15 29 18	19 42 06	16 11 37
	16	11 06 57	15 14 57	0 13 49	20 55 32	15 25 43	19 38 07	16 07 45
	17	11 09 38	15 14 26	0 08 11	20 51 21	15 22 08	19 34 08	16 03 54
	18	11 12 21	15 13 52	0 02 33	20 47 10	15 18 33	19 30 10	16 00 03
	19	11 15 06	15 13 15	23 51 18	20 43 01	15 14 58	19 26 12	15 56 12
	20	11 17 53	15 12 35	23 45 42	20 38 52	15 11 24	19 22 13	15 52 22
	21	11 20 42	15 11 53	23 40 07	20 34 43	15 07 50	19 18 15	15 48 31
	22	11 23 31	15 11 08	23 34 32	20 30 36	15 04 16	19 14 18	15 44 40
	23	11 26 23	15 10 21	23 29 00	20 26 30	15 00 42	19 10 20	15 40 50
	24	11 29 15	15 09 30	23 23 29	20 22 24	14 57 09	19 06 23	15 36 59
	25	11 32 09	15 08 37	23 17 59	20 18 19	14 53 35	19 02 26	15 33 09
	26	11 35 04	15 07 41	23 12 32	20 14 15	14 50 02	18 58 29	15 29 19
	27	11 37 59	15 06 41	23 07 06	20 10 12	14 46 29	18 54 32	15 25 29
	28	11 40 56	15 05 38	23 01 43	20 06 10	14 42 57	18 50 36	15 21 39
	29	11 43 53	15 04 33	22 56 23	20 02 09	14 39 24	18 46 40	15 17 49
	30	11 46 51	15 03 23	22 51 04	19 58 08	14 35 52	18 42 44	15 13 59
	31	11 49 50	15 02 11	22 45 49	19 54 09	14 32 20	18 38 48	15 10 09
Feb.	1	11 52 49	15 00 55	22 40 36	19 50 10	14 28 48	18 34 52	15 06 20
	2	11 55 49	14 59 35	22 35 27	19 46 12	14 25 16	18 30 57	15 02 30
	3	11 58 49	14 58 11	22 30 20	19 42 15	14 21 44	18 27 02	14 58 41
	4	12 01 49	14 56 43	22 25 17	19 38 19	14 18 12	18 23 07	14 54 51
	5	12 04 50	14 55 12	22 20 16	19 34 24	14 14 41	18 19 12	14 51 02
	6	12 07 51	14 53 36	22 15 19	19 30 29	14 11 10	18 15 18	14 47 13
	7	12 10 52	14 51 55	22 10 26	19 26 36	14 07 39	18 11 23	14 43 23
	8	12 13 54	14 50 11	22 05 35	19 22 43	14 04 08	18 07 29	14 39 34
	9	12 16 55	14 48 21	22 00 48	19 18 52	14 00 37	18 03 35	14 35 45
	10	12 19 56	14 46 27	21 56 05	19 15 01	13 57 06	17 59 42	14 31 56
	11	12 22 57	14 44 27	21 51 25	19 11 10	13 53 36	17 55 48	14 28 07
	12	12 25 58	14 42 22	21 46 48	19 07 21	13 50 05	17 51 55	14 24 18
	13	12 28 59	14 40 12	21 42 15	19 03 33	13 46 35	17 48 02	14 20 30
	14	12 31 58	14 37 57	21 37 45	18 59 45	13 43 05	17 44 09	14 16 41
	15	12 34 58	14 35 35	21 33 19	18 55 58	13 39 35	17 40 17	14 12 52

Second transit: Mars, Jan. $18^{d}23^{h}56^{m}55^{s}$.

Date	Mercury	Venus	Mars	Jupiter	Saturn	Uranus	Neptune
	h m s	h m s	h m s	h m s	h m s	h m s	h m s
Feb. 15	12 34 58	14 35 35	21 33 19	18 55 58	13 39 35	17 40 17	14 12 52
16	12 37 56	14 33 08	21 28 56	18 52 12	13 36 05	17 36 24	14 09 04
17	12 40 52	14 30 34	21 24 36	18 48 27	13 32 35	17 32 32	14 05 15
18	12 43 48	14 27 54	21 20 20	18 44 43	13 29 05	17 28 40	14 01 27
19	12 46 41	14 25 07	21 16 08	18 40 59	13 25 36	17 24 48	13 57 38
20	12 49 31	14 22 13	21 11 59	18 37 17	13 22 06	17 20 57	13 53 50
21	12 52 18	14 19 13	21 07 53	18 33 35	13 18 37	17 17 05	13 50 02
22	12 55 01	14 16 05	21 03 50	18 29 54	13 15 07	17 13 14	13 46 13
23	12 57 39	14 12 50	20 59 51	18 26 14	13 11 38	17 09 23	13 42 25
24	13 00 11	14 09 27	20 55 55	18 22 34	13 08 09	17 05 32	13 38 37
25	13 02 37	14 05 56	20 52 02	18 18 55	13 04 39	17 01 42	13 34 49
26	13 04 54	14 02 17	20 48 13	18 15 17	13 01 10	16 57 51	13 31 01
27	13 07 02	13 58 30	20 44 26	18 11 40	12 57 41	16 54 01	13 27 13
28	13 08 58	13 54 35	20 40 43	18 08 04	12 54 12	16 50 11	13 23 25
Mar. 1	13 10 42	13 50 31	20 37 02	18 04 28	12 50 43	16 46 22	13 19 37
2	13 12 11	13 46 18	20 33 25	18 00 53	12 47 14	16 42 32	13 15 49
3	13 13 24	13 41 57	20 29 51	17 57 19	12 43 45	16 38 43	13 12 01
4	13 14 18	13 37 27	20 26 19	17 53 46	12 40 17	16 34 53	13 08 13
5	13 14 53	13 32 49	20 22 51	17 50 13	12 36 48	16 31 04	13 04 26
6	13 15 05	13 28 02	20 19 25	17 46 41	12 33 19	16 27 16	13 00 38
7	13 14 53	13 23 06	20 16 02	17 43 10	12 29 50	16 23 27	12 56 50
8	13 14 16	13 18 01	20 12 41	17 39 39	12 26 22	16 19 38	12 53 02
9	13 13 12	13 12 49	20 09 23	17 36 09	12 22 53	16 15 50	12 49 15
10	13 11 40	13 07 29	20 06 08	17 32 40	12 19 24	16 12 02	12 45 27
11	13 09 39	13 02 01	20 02 55	17 29 11	12 15 55	16 08 14	12 41 39
12	13 07 08	12 56 26	19 59 45	17 25 43	12 12 27	16 04 26	12 37 52
13	13 04 06	12 50 44	19 56 37	17 22 16	12 08 58	16 00 39	12 34 04
14	13 00 35	12 44 57	19 53 31	17 18 50	12 05 29	15 56 51	12 30 16
15	12 56 34	12 39 04	19 50 27	17 15 24	12 02 01	15 53 04	12 26 29
16	12 52 04	12 33 07	19 47 26	17 11 58	11 58 32	15 49 17	12 22 41
17	12 47 07	12 27 05	19 44 27	17 08 34	11 55 03	15 45 30	12 18 53
18	12 41 44	12 21 01	19 41 30	17 05 10	11 51 34	15 41 43	12 15 06
19	12 35 58	12 14 54	19 38 34	17 01 46	11 48 06	15 37 57	12 11 18
20	12 29 52	12 08 46	19 35 41	16 58 23	11 44 37	15 34 10	12 07 31
21	12 23 30	12 02 37	19 32 50	16 55 01	11 41 08	15 30 24	12 03 43
22	12 16 53	11 56 29	19 30 01	16 51 40	11 37 39	15 26 38	11 59 55
23	12 10 07	11 50 23	19 27 14	16 48 19	11 34 10	15 22 52	11 56 08
24	12 03 15	11 44 18	19 24 28	16 44 58	11 30 41	15 19 06	11 52 20
25	11 56 21	11 38 16	19 21 44	16 41 38	11 27 12	15 15 20	11 48 33
26	11 49 29	11 32 19	19 19 02	16 38 19	11 23 43	15 11 35	11 44 45
27	11 42 42	11 26 26	19 16 22	16 35 00	11 20 14	15 07 50	11 40 57
28	11 36 04	11 20 38	19 13 43	16 31 42	11 16 45	15 04 04	11 37 10
29	11 29 37	11 14 56	19 11 06	16 28 24	11 13 16	15 00 19	11 33 22
30	11 23 24	11 09 21	19 08 30	16 25 07	11 09 47	14 56 34	11 29 34
31	11 17 27	11 03 53	19 05 56	16 21 51	11 06 17	14 52 49	11 25 47
Apr. 1	11 11 47	10 58 32	19 03 24	16 18 34	11 02 48	14 49 05	11 21 59
2	11 06 26	10 53 20	19 00 53	16 15 19	10 59 18	14 45 20	11 18 11

Date		Mercury	Venus	Mars	Jupiter	Saturn	Uranus	Neptune
		h m s	h m s	h m s	h m s	h m s	h m s	h m s
Apr.	1	11 11 47	10 58 32	19 03 24	16 18 34	11 02 48	14 49 05	11 21 59
	2	11 06 26	10 53 20	19 00 53	16 15 19	10 59 18	14 45 20	11 18 11
	3	11 01 25	10 48 15	18 58 23	16 12 04	10 55 49	14 41 36	11 14 24
	4	10 56 43	10 43 19	18 55 55	16 08 49	10 52 19	14 37 51	11 10 36
	5	10 52 21	10 38 32	18 53 28	16 05 35	10 48 49	14 34 07	11 06 48
	6	10 48 19	10 33 54	18 51 02	16 02 21	10 45 20	14 30 23	11 03 00
	7	10 44 36	10 29 25	18 48 37	15 59 08	10 41 50	14 26 39	10 59 12
	8	10 41 13	10 25 05	18 46 14	15 55 56	10 38 20	14 22 55	10 55 24
	9	10 38 07	10 20 53	18 43 52	15 52 43	10 34 49	14 19 11	10 51 36
	10	10 35 20	10 16 51	18 41 31	15 49 31	10 31 19	14 15 28	10 47 49
	11	10 32 49	10 12 58	18 39 11	15 46 20	10 27 49	14 11 44	10 44 01
	12	10 30 35	10 09 14	18 36 52	15 43 09	10 24 18	14 08 01	10 40 12
	13	10 28 36	10 05 38	18 34 34	15 39 59	10 20 48	14 04 17	10 36 24
	14	10 26 52	10 02 11	18 32 17	15 36 49	10 17 17	14 00 34	10 32 36
	15	10 25 22	9 58 52	18 30 02	15 33 39	10 13 46	13 56 51	10 28 48
	16	10 24 05	9 55 41	18 27 47	15 30 29	10 10 15	13 53 08	10 25 00
	17	10 23 01	9 52 38	18 25 33	15 27 21	10 06 44	13 49 25	10 21 12
	18	10 22 09	9 49 43	18 23 20	15 24 12	10 03 13	13 45 42	10 17 23
	19	10 21 28	9 46 55	18 21 07	15 21 04	9 59 41	13 41 59	10 13 35
	20	10 20 58	9 44 14	18 18 56	15 17 56	9 56 10	13 38 17	10 09 47
	21	10 20 38	9 41 41	18 16 45	15 14 49	9 52 38	13 34 34	10 05 58
	22	10 20 27	9 39 13	18 14 36	15 11 42	9 49 06	13 30 51	10 02 10
	23	10 20 27	9 36 53	18 12 27	15 08 35	9 45 34	13 27 09	9 58 21
	24	10 20 35	9 34 38	18 10 18	15 05 29	9 42 02	13 23 26	9 54 32
	25	10 20 52	9 32 30	18 08 11	15 02 23	9 38 30	13 19 44	9 50 44
	26	10 21 17	9 30 27	18 06 04	14 59 17	9 34 57	13 16 02	9 46 55
	27	10 21 50	9 28 29	18 03 58	14 56 12	9 31 24	13 12 20	9 43 06
	28	10 22 32	9 26 37	18 01 53	14 53 07	9 27 52	13 08 37	9 39 17
	29	10 23 21	9 24 50	17 59 48	14 50 02	9 24 19	13 04 55	9 35 28
	30	10 24 18	9 23 07	17 57 44	14 46 58	9 20 45	13 01 13	9 31 39
May	1	10 25 22	9 21 29	17 55 40	14 43 54	9 17 12	12 57 31	9 27 50
	2	10 26 34	9 19 56	17 53 38	14 40 50	9 13 38	12 53 49	9 24 01
	3	10 27 53	9 18 27	17 51 35	14 37 47	9 10 04	12 50 07	9 20 12
	4	10 29 20	9 17 01	17 49 34	14 34 43	9 06 30	12 46 25	9 16 22
	5	10 30 54	9 15 40	17 47 32	14 31 41	9 02 56	12 42 44	9 12 33
	6	10 32 36	9 14 22	17 45 32	14 28 38	8 59 22	12 39 02	9 08 43
	7	10 34 25	9 13 08	17 43 31	14 25 36	8 55 47	12 35 20	9 04 54
	8	10 36 23	9 11 58	17 41 32	14 22 33	8 52 12	12 31 38	9 01 04
	9	10 38 29	9 10 50	17 39 32	14 19 32	8 48 37	12 27 57	8 57 15
	10	10 40 43	9 09 46	17 37 33	14 16 30	8 45 02	12 24 15	8 53 25
	11	10 43 05	9 08 45	17 35 35	14 13 28	8 41 27	12 20 33	8 49 35
	12	10 45 36	9 07 47	17 33 37	14 10 27	8 37 51	12 16 52	8 45 45
	13	10 48 16	9 06 51	17 31 39	14 07 26	8 34 15	12 13 10	8 41 55
	14	10 51 05	9 05 59	17 29 42	14 04 26	8 30 39	12 09 28	8 38 05
	15	10 54 04	9 05 09	17 27 45	14 01 25	8 27 02	12 05 47	8 34 15
	16	10 57 13	9 04 22	17 25 49	13 58 25	8 23 26	12 02 05	8 30 24
	17	11 00 31	9 03 37	17 23 53	13 55 25	8 19 49	11 58 24	8 26 34

Date	Mercury	Venus	Mars	Jupiter	Saturn	Uranus	Neptune
	h m s	h m s	h m s	h m s	h m s	h m s	h m s
May 17	11 00 31	9 03 37	17 23 53	13 55 25	8 19 49	11 58 24	8 26 34
18	11 04 00	9 02 54	17 21 57	13 52 25	8 16 12	11 54 42	8 22 43
19	11 07 39	9 02 14	17 20 02	13 49 25	8 12 34	11 51 01	8 18 53
20	11 11 29	9 01 36	17 18 06	13 46 26	8 08 57	11 47 19	8 15 02
21	11 15 29	9 01 00	17 16 12	13 43 26	8 05 19	11 43 37	8 11 11
22	11 19 40	9 00 26	17 14 17	13 40 27	8 01 41	11 39 56	8 07 21
23	11 24 02	8 59 55	17 12 23	13 37 28	7 58 02	11 36 14	8 03 30
24	11 28 34	8 59 25	17 10 29	13 34 29	7 54 23	11 32 33	7 59 39
25	11 33 16	8 58 57	17 08 36	13 31 31	7 50 44	11 28 51	7 55 47
26	11 38 08	8 58 31	17 06 42	13 28 32	7 47 05	11 25 09	7 51 56
27	11 43 08	8 58 07	17 04 49	13 25 34	7 43 26	11 21 28	7 48 05
28	11 48 17	8 57 44	17 02 56	13 22 35	7 39 46	11 17 46	7 44 13
29	11 53 32	8 57 24	17 01 04	13 19 37	7 36 06	11 14 04	7 40 22
30	11 58 53	8 57 05	16 59 12	13 16 39	7 32 25	11 10 23	7 36 30
31	12 04 19	8 56 47	16 57 20	13 13 41	7 28 45	11 06 41	7 32 38
June 1	12 09 48	8 56 31	16 55 28	13 10 44	7 25 04	11 02 59	7 28 46
2	12 15 18	8 56 17	16 53 36	13 07 46	7 21 23	10 59 17	7 24 54
3	12 20 49	8 56 04	16 51 45	13 04 49	7 17 41	10 55 35	7 21 02
4	12 26 18	8 55 53	16 49 54	13 01 51	7 13 59	10 51 54	7 17 10
5	12 31 45	8 55 44	16 48 03	12 58 54	7 10 17	10 48 12	7 13 18
6	12 37 07	8 55 36	16 46 12	12 55 57	7 06 35	10 44 30	7 09 25
7	12 42 23	8 55 30	16 44 21	12 52 59	7 02 52	10 40 47	7 05 33
8	12 47 33	8 55 25	16 42 31	12 50 02	6 59 09	10 37 05	7 01 40
9	12 52 35	8 55 21	16 40 41	12 47 05	6 55 25	10 33 23	6 57 47
10	12 57 28	8 55 19	16 38 51	12 44 08	6 51 42	10 29 41	6 53 55
11	13 02 11	8 55 19	16 37 01	12 41 11	6 47 58	10 25 59	6 50 02
12	13 06 44	8 55 20	16 35 11	12 38 15	6 44 13	10 22 16	6 46 08
13	13 11 05	8 55 22	16 33 21	12 35 18	6 40 28	10 18 34	6 42 15
14	13 15 15	8 55 26	16 31 32	12 32 21	6 36 43	10 14 51	6 38 22
15	13 19 14	8 55 32	16 29 43	12 29 24	6 32 58	10 11 09	6 34 28
16	13 23 00	8 55 39	16 27 53	12 26 28	6 29 12	10 07 26	6 30 35
17	13 26 33	8 55 47	16 26 04	12 23 31	6 25 26	10 03 44	6 26 41
18	13 29 54	8 55 57	16 24 16	12 20 35	6 21 40	10 00 01	6 22 47
19	13 33 02	8 56 09	16 22 27	12 17 38	6 17 53	9 56 18	6 18 54
20	13 35 57	8 56 21	16 20 38	12 14 41	6 14 06	9 52 35	6 15 00
21	13 38 39	8 56 36	16 18 50	12 11 45	6 10 19	9 48 52	6 11 05
22	13 41 08	8 56 51	16 17 02	12 08 48	6 06 31	9 45 09	6 07 11
23	13 43 24	8 57 08	16 15 14	12 05 52	6 02 43	9 41 26	6 03 17
24	13 45 26	8 57 27	16 13 26	12 02 55	5 58 55	9 37 42	5 59 22
25	13 47 15	8 57 47	16 11 38	11 59 59	5 55 06	9 33 59	5 55 28
26	13 48 51	8 58 08	16 09 50	11 57 02	5 51 17	9 30 15	5 51 33
27	13 50 13	8 58 31	16 08 03	11 54 06	5 47 27	9 26 32	5 47 38
28	13 51 22	8 58 55	16 06 15	11 51 09	5 43 38	9 22 48	5 43 43
29	13 52 18	8 59 20	16 04 28	11 48 12	5 39 47	9 19 04	5 39 48
30	13 52 59	8 59 47	16 02 41	11 45 16	5 35 57	9 15 20	5 35 53
July 1	13 53 27	9 00 16	16 00 54	11 42 19	5 32 06	9 11 36	5 31 57
2	13 53 40	9 00 45	15 59 07	11 39 22	5 28 15	9 07 52	5 28 02

Date	Mercury	Venus	Mars	Jupiter	Saturn	Uranus	Neptune
	h m s	h m s	h m s	h m s	h m s	h m s	h m s
July 1	13 53 27	9 00 16	16 00 54	11 42 19	5 32 06	9 11 36	5 31 57
2	13 53 40	9 00 45	15 59 07	11 39 22	5 28 15	9 07 52	5 28 02
3	13 53 40	9 01 16	15 57 21	11 36 25	5 24 23	9 04 08	5 24 06
4	13 53 24	9 01 49	15 55 34	11 33 29	5 20 31	9 00 23	5 20 11
5	13 52 55	9 02 22	15 53 48	11 30 32	5 16 39	8 56 39	5 16 15
6	13 52 10	9 02 58	15 52 02	11 27 35	5 12 46	8 52 54	5 12 19
7	13 51 10	9 03 34	15 50 15	11 24 37	5 08 53	8 49 09	5 08 23
8	13 49 54	9 04 12	15 48 29	11 21 40	5 04 59	8 45 25	5 04 27
9	13 48 22	9 04 51	15 46 44	11 18 43	5 01 05	8 41 40	5 00 31
10	13 46 34	9 05 31	15 44 58	11 15 46	4 57 11	8 37 54	4 56 34
11	13 44 30	9 06 13	15 43 12	11 12 48	4 53 17	8 34 09	4 52 38
12	13 42 08	9 06 56	15 41 27	11 09 51	4 49 22	8 30 24	4 48 41
13	13 39 29	9 07 41	15 39 42	11 06 53	4 45 26	8 26 38	4 44 44
14	13 36 32	9 08 26	15 37 56	11 03 55	4 41 31	8 22 52	4 40 47
15	13 33 18	9 09 13	15 36 11	11 00 57	4 37 35	8 19 07	4 36 50
16	13 29 45	9 10 01	15 34 27	10 57 59	4 33 38	8 15 21	4 32 53
17	13 25 53	9 10 50	15 32 42	10 55 01	4 29 42	8 11 34	4 28 56
18	13 21 43	9 11 41	15 30 57	10 52 03	4 25 44	8 07 48	4 24 59
19	13 17 15	9 12 32	15 29 13	10 49 05	4 21 47	8 04 02	4 21 01
20	13 12 29	9 13 25	15 27 29	10 46 06	4 17 49	8 00 15	4 17 04
21	13 07 24	9 14 18	15 25 45	10 43 08	4 13 51	7 56 28	4 13 06
22	13 02 02	9 15 13	15 24 01	10 40 09	4 09 52	7 52 41	4 09 08
23	12 56 24	9 16 09	15 22 17	10 37 10	4 05 53	7 48 54	4 05 11
24	12 50 30	9 17 06	15 20 34	10 34 11	4 01 54	7 45 07	4 01 13
25	12 44 21	9 18 03	15 18 51	10 31 12	3 57 54	7 41 20	3 57 14
26	12 38 00	9 19 02	15 17 08	10 28 12	3 53 54	7 37 32	3 53 16
27	12 31 29	9 20 01	15 15 25	10 25 12	3 49 54	7 33 44	3 49 18
28	12 24 48	9 21 01	15 13 42	10 22 13	3 45 53	7 29 56	3 45 19
29	12 18 02	9 22 02	15 12 00	10 19 13	3 41 52	7 26 08	3 41 21
30	12 11 12	9 23 03	15 10 18	10 16 12	3 37 50	7 22 20	3 37 22
31	12 04 22	9 24 06	15 08 36	10 13 12	3 33 48	7 18 32	3 33 24
Aug. 1	11 57 34	9 25 09	15 06 54	10 10 11	3 29 46	7 14 43	3 29 25
2	11 50 52	9 26 12	15 05 12	10 07 11	3 25 44	7 10 54	3 25 26
3	11 44 19	9 27 16	15 03 31	10 04 10	3 21 41	7 07 05	3 21 27
4	11 37 58	9 28 20	15 01 50	10 01 08	3 17 38	7 03 16	3 17 28
5	11 31 51	9 29 25	15 00 09	9 58 07	3 13 34	6 59 27	3 13 28
6	11 26 02	9 30 31	14 58 28	9 55 05	3 09 30	6 55 37	3 09 29
7	11 20 33	9 31 36	14 56 47	9 52 03	3 05 26	6 51 47	3 05 30
8	11 15 26	9 32 42	14 55 07	9 49 01	3 01 22	6 47 58	3 01 30
9	11 10 43	9 33 49	14 53 27	9 45 58	2 57 17	6 44 07	2 57 30
10	11 06 25	9 34 55	14 51 47	9 42 56	2 53 12	6 40 17	2 53 31
11	11 02 35	9 36 02	14 50 08	9 39 53	2 49 06	6 36 27	2 49 31
12	10 59 13	9 37 09	14 48 28	9 36 49	2 45 00	6 32 36	2 45 31
13	10 56 20	9 38 16	14 46 49	9 33 46	2 40 54	6 28 45	2 41 31
14	10 53 56	9 39 23	14 45 11	9 30 42	2 36 48	6 24 54	2 37 31
15	10 52 02	9 40 30	14 43 32	9 27 38	2 32 41	6 21 03	2 33 31
16	10 50 36	9 41 37	14 41 54	9 24 34	2 28 34	6 17 11	2 29 31

Date	Mercury	Venus	Mars	Jupiter	Saturn	Uranus	Neptune
	h m s	h m s	h m s	h m s	h m s	h m s	h m s
Aug. 16	10 50 36	9 41 37	14 41 54	9 24 34	2 28 34	6 17 11	2 29 31
17	10 49 40	9 42 43	14 40 16	9 21 29	2 24 27	6 13 20	2 25 30
18	10 49 12	9 43 50	14 38 38	9 18 24	2 20 20	6 09 28	2 21 30
19	10 49 11	9 44 57	14 37 01	9 15 19	2 16 12	6 05 36	2 17 29
20	10 49 37	9 46 03	14 35 24	9 12 13	2 12 04	6 01 44	2 13 29
21	10 50 29	9 47 09	14 33 48	9 09 07	2 07 56	5 57 51	2 09 28
22	10 51 44	9 48 15	14 32 11	9 06 01	2 03 47	5 53 58	2 05 28
23	10 53 21	9 49 20	14 30 35	9 02 54	1 59 38	5 50 06	2 01 27
24	10 55 19	9 50 25	14 29 00	8 59 48	1 55 29	5 46 13	1 57 26
25	10 57 35	9 51 29	14 27 24	8 56 40	1 51 20	5 42 19	1 53 25
26	11 00 07	9 52 33	14 25 49	8 53 33	1 47 10	5 38 26	1 49 24
27	11 02 54	9 53 37	14 24 15	8 50 25	1 43 00	5 34 32	1 45 23
28	11 05 53	9 54 40	14 22 41	8 47 16	1 38 50	5 30 38	1 41 22
29	11 09 02	9 55 42	14 21 07	8 44 08	1 34 40	5 26 44	1 37 21
30	11 12 19	9 56 44	14 19 33	8 40 59	1 30 30	5 22 50	1 33 20
31	11 15 42	9 57 45	14 18 00	8 37 49	1 26 19	5 18 55	1 29 18
Sept. 1	11 19 08	9 58 46	14 16 27	8 34 39	1 22 09	5 15 00	1 25 17
2	11 22 37	9 59 46	14 14 55	8 31 29	1 17 58	5 11 05	1 21 16
3	11 26 07	10 00 45	14 13 22	8 28 18	1 13 46	5 07 10	1 17 14
4	11 29 37	10 01 44	14 11 51	8 25 07	1 09 35	5 03 15	1 13 13
5	11 33 04	10 02 41	14 10 19	8 21 56	1 05 24	4 59 19	1 09 11
6	11 36 30	10 03 39	14 08 49	8 18 44	1 01 12	4 55 23	1 05 10
7	11 39 52	10 04 35	14 07 18	8 15 31	0 57 00	4 51 27	1 01 08
8	11 43 10	10 05 31	14 05 48	8 12 18	0 52 49	4 47 31	0 57 06
9	11 46 24	10 06 26	14 04 18	8 09 05	0 48 37	4 43 35	0 53 05
10	11 49 33	10 07 20	14 02 49	8 05 52	0 44 24	4 39 38	0 49 03
11	11 52 37	10 08 14	14 01 20	8 02 37	0 40 12	4 35 41	0 45 01
12	11 55 37	10 09 06	13 59 52	7 59 23	0 36 00	4 31 44	0 40 59
13	11 58 31	10 09 58	13 58 24	7 56 08	0 31 47	4 27 47	0 36 58
14	12 01 21	10 10 50	13 56 57	7 52 52	0 27 35	4 23 50	0 32 56
15	12 04 06	10 11 40	13 55 30	7 49 36	0 23 22	4 19 52	0 28 54
16	12 06 45	10 12 30	13 54 03	7 46 20	0 19 10	4 15 54	0 24 52
17	12 09 21	10 13 19	13 52 37	7 43 03	0 14 57	4 11 56	0 20 50
18	12 11 51	10 14 08	13 51 12	7 39 45	0 10 44	4 07 58	0 16 48
19	12 14 18	10 14 56	13 49 47	7 36 27	0 06 31	4 03 59	0 12 46
20	12 16 40	10 15 43	13 48 22	7 33 09	0 02 19	4 00 00	0 08 44
21	12 18 59	10 16 29	13 46 58	7 29 49	23 53 53	3 56 01	0 04 42
22	12 21 13	10 17 15	13 45 35	7 26 30	23 49 40	3 52 02	0 00 41
23	12 23 25	10 18 00	13 44 12	7 23 10	23 45 27	3 48 03	23 52 37
24	12 25 33	10 18 44	13 42 49	7 19 49	23 41 14	3 44 04	23 48 35
25	12 27 37	10 19 28	13 41 27	7 16 28	23 37 02	3 40 04	23 44 33
26	12 29 39	10 20 11	13 40 06	7 13 06	23 32 49	3 36 04	23 40 31
27	12 31 38	10 20 54	13 38 45	7 09 43	23 28 36	3 32 04	23 36 29
28	12 33 35	10 21 36	13 37 25	7 06 20	23 24 23	3 28 04	23 32 27
29	12 35 29	10 22 18	13 36 05	7 02 57	23 20 11	3 24 03	23 28 25
30	12 37 21	10 22 59	13 34 45	6 59 33	23 15 58	3 20 02	23 24 23
Oct. 1	12 39 10	10 23 39	13 33 27	6 56 08	23 11 46	3 16 02	23 20 21

Second transits: Saturn, Sept. $20^{d}23^{h}58^{m}6^{s}$; Neptune, Sept. $22^{d}23^{h}56^{m}39^{s}$.

Date	Mercury	Venus	Mars	Jupiter	Saturn	Uranus	Neptune
	h m s	h m s	h m s	h m s	h m s	h m s	h m s
Oct. 1	12 39 10	10 23 39	13 33 27	6 56 08	23 11 46	3 16 02	23 20 21
2	12 40 58	10 24 20	13 32 08	6 52 42	23 07 33	3 12 01	23 16 19
3	12 42 44	10 24 59	13 30 51	6 49 16	23 03 21	3 07 59	23 12 17
4	12 44 28	10 25 39	13 29 34	6 45 50	22 59 09	3 03 58	23 08 15
5	12 46 11	10 26 18	13 28 17	6 42 23	22 54 57	2 59 56	23 04 14
6	12 47 52	10 26 57	13 27 01	6 38 55	22 50 45	2 55 55	23 00 12
7	12 49 31	10 27 35	13 25 46	6 35 26	22 46 33	2 51 53	22 56 10
8	12 51 09	10 28 13	13 24 31	6 31 57	22 42 22	2 47 51	22 52 08
9	12 52 46	10 28 51	13 23 17	6 28 27	22 38 10	2 43 48	22 48 07
10	12 54 21	10 29 29	13 22 03	6 24 57	22 33 59	2 39 46	22 44 05
11	12 55 55	10 30 07	13 20 50	6 21 25	22 29 47	2 35 43	22 40 03
12	12 57 27	10 30 44	13 19 38	6 17 54	22 25 36	2 31 41	22 36 02
13	12 58 58	10 31 22	13 18 26	6 14 21	22 21 26	2 27 38	22 32 00
14	13 00 27	10 31 59	13 17 15	6 10 48	22 17 15	2 23 35	22 27 59
15	13 01 55	10 32 37	13 16 05	6 07 14	22 13 04	2 19 31	22 23 57
16	13 03 21	10 33 14	13 14 55	6 03 39	22 08 54	2 15 28	22 19 56
17	13 04 44	10 33 52	13 13 45	6 00 04	22 04 44	2 11 25	22 15 55
18	13 06 06	10 34 30	13 12 37	5 56 28	22 00 34	2 07 21	22 11 53
19	13 07 25	10 35 08	13 11 29	5 52 51	21 56 25	2 03 17	22 07 52
20	13 08 41	10 35 46	13 10 21	5 49 14	21 52 15	1 59 13	22 03 51
21	13 09 54	10 36 24	13 09 15	5 45 35	21 48 06	1 55 09	21 59 50
22	13 11 04	10 37 03	13 08 09	5 41 56	21 43 57	1 51 05	21 55 49
23	13 12 09	10 37 42	13 07 03	5 38 17	21 39 49	1 47 00	21 51 48
24	13 13 09	10 38 21	13 05 58	5 34 36	21 35 41	1 42 56	21 47 47
25	13 14 05	10 39 01	13 04 54	5 30 55	21 31 32	1 38 51	21 43 46
26	13 14 53	10 39 41	13 03 51	5 27 13	21 27 25	1 34 47	21 39 45
27	13 15 35	10 40 21	13 02 48	5 23 30	21 23 17	1 30 42	21 35 45
28	13 16 09	10 41 02	13 01 45	5 19 46	21 19 10	1 26 37	21 31 44
29	13 16 33	10 41 43	13 00 44	5 16 02	21 15 03	1 22 32	21 27 44
30	13 16 47	10 42 25	12 59 43	5 12 17	21 10 56	1 18 27	21 23 43
31	13 16 49	10 43 08	12 58 42	5 08 31	21 06 50	1 14 22	21 19 43
Nov. 1	13 16 37	10 43 51	12 57 42	5 04 44	21 02 44	1 10 16	21 15 42
2	13 16 09	10 44 35	12 56 43	5 00 56	20 58 38	1 06 11	21 11 42
3	13 15 24	10 45 20	12 55 45	4 57 08	20 54 33	1 02 05	21 07 42
4	13 14 20	10 46 05	12 54 47	4 53 19	20 50 28	0 58 00	21 03 42
5	13 12 53	10 46 51	12 53 49	4 49 29	20 46 23	0 53 54	20 59 42
6	13 11 01	10 47 38	12 52 53	4 45 38	20 42 19	0 49 49	20 55 42
7	13 08 42	10 48 26	12 51 56	4 41 46	20 38 15	0 45 43	20 51 43
8	13 05 53	10 49 15	12 51 01	4 37 54	20 34 11	0 41 37	20 47 43
9	13 02 30	10 50 05	12 50 06	4 34 00	20 30 08	0 37 31	20 43 43
10	12 58 31	10 50 55	12 49 12	4 30 06	20 26 05	0 33 25	20 39 44
11	12 53 55	10 51 47	12 48 18	4 26 11	20 22 02	0 29 19	20 35 45
12	12 48 38	10 52 39	12 47 25	4 22 16	20 18 00	0 25 13	20 31 45
13	12 42 40	10 53 33	12 46 33	4 18 19	20 13 58	0 21 07	20 27 46
14	12 36 01	10 54 28	12 45 41	4 14 22	20 09 56	0 17 01	20 23 47
15	12 28 42	10 55 23	12 44 50	4 10 23	20 05 55	0 12 54	20 19 48
16	12 20 47	10 56 20	12 43 59	4 06 24	20 01 54	0 08 48	20 15 49

Date	Mercury	Venus	Mars	Jupiter	Saturn	Uranus	Neptune
	h m s	h m s	h m s	h m s	h m s	h m s	h m s
Nov. 16	12 20 47	10 56 20	12 43 59	4 06 24	20 01 54	0 08 48	20 15 49
17	12 12 21	10 57 18	12 43 09	4 02 24	19 57 54	0 04 42	20 11 50
18	12 03 31	10 58 17	12 42 20	3 58 23	19 53 54	0 00 36	20 07 52
19	11 54 26	10 59 17	12 41 31	3 54 22	19 49 54	23 52 23	20 03 53
20	11 45 15	11 00 19	12 40 42	3 50 19	19 45 55	23 48 17	19 59 55
21	11 36 09	11 01 21	12 39 55	3 46 16	19 41 56	23 44 11	19 55 57
22	11 27 17	11 02 25	12 39 07	3 42 12	19 37 57	23 40 04	19 51 58
23	11 18 50	11 03 30	12 38 20	3 38 07	19 33 59	23 35 58	19 48 00
24	11 10 54	11 04 36	12 37 34	3 34 01	19 30 02	23 31 52	19 44 02
25	11 03 37	11 05 44	12 36 48	3 29 54	19 26 04	23 27 45	19 40 05
26	10 57 01	11 06 52	12 36 03	3 25 47	19 22 07	23 23 39	19 36 07
27	10 51 08	11 08 02	12 35 18	3 21 38	19 18 11	23 19 33	19 32 09
28	10 46 00	11 09 13	12 34 34	3 17 29	19 14 14	23 15 27	19 28 12
29	10 41 35	11 10 25	12 33 50	3 13 19	19 10 19	23 11 21	19 24 14
30	10 37 52	11 11 38	12 33 07	3 09 09	19 06 23	23 07 15	19 20 17
Dec. 1	10 34 47	11 12 53	12 32 24	3 04 57	19 02 28	23 03 09	19 16 20
2	10 32 18	11 14 08	12 31 41	3 00 45	18 58 34	22 59 03	19 12 23
3	10 30 22	11 15 25	12 30 59	2 56 32	18 54 39	22 54 57	19 08 26
4	10 28 55	11 16 43	12 30 17	2 52 19	18 50 46	22 50 51	19 04 29
5	10 27 55	11 18 02	12 29 36	2 48 04	18 46 52	22 46 45	19 00 33
6	10 27 19	11 19 22	12 28 55	2 43 49	18 42 59	22 42 39	18 56 36
7	10 27 04	11 20 44	12 28 14	2 39 33	18 39 06	22 38 33	18 52 40
8	10 27 08	11 22 06	12 27 34	2 35 16	18 35 14	22 34 28	18 48 44
9	10 27 29	11 23 29	12 26 54	2 30 59	18 31 22	22 30 22	18 44 48
10	10 28 05	11 24 54	12 26 14	2 26 41	18 27 31	22 26 17	18 40 52
11	10 28 54	11 26 19	12 25 35	2 22 22	18 23 40	22 22 11	18 36 56
12	10 29 55	11 27 45	12 24 56	2 18 03	18 19 49	22 18 06	18 33 00
13	10 31 07	11 29 12	12 24 17	2 13 43	18 15 59	22 14 01	18 29 04
14	10 32 28	11 30 40	12 23 38	2 09 22	18 12 09	22 09 56	18 25 09
15	10 33 58	11 32 09	12 23 00	2 05 01	18 08 19	22 05 51	18 21 14
16	10 35 36	11 33 38	12 22 22	2 00 39	18 04 30	22 01 46	18 17 18
17	10 37 21	11 35 08	12 21 44	1 56 16	18 00 41	21 57 41	18 13 23
18	10 39 12	11 36 39	12 21 07	1 51 53	17 56 53	21 53 37	18 09 28
19	10 41 09	11 38 10	12 20 30	1 47 30	17 53 05	21 49 32	18 05 33
20	10 43 11	11 39 42	12 19 52	1 43 06	17 49 17	21 45 28	18 01 39
21	10 45 19	11 41 14	12 19 15	1 38 41	17 45 30	21 41 23	17 57 44
22	10 47 31	11 42 47	12 18 39	1 34 16	17 41 43	21 37 19	17 53 50
23	10 49 47	11 44 20	12 18 02	1 29 50	17 37 56	21 33 15	17 49 55
24	10 52 07	11 45 53	12 17 25	1 25 24	17 34 10	21 29 11	17 46 01
25	10 54 31	11 47 27	12 16 49	1 20 57	17 30 24	21 25 07	17 42 07
26	10 56 58	11 49 00	12 16 12	1 16 30	17 26 39	21 21 04	17 38 13
27	10 59 29	11 50 34	12 15 36	1 12 03	17 22 54	21 17 00	17 34 19
28	11 02 02	11 52 07	12 14 59	1 07 35	17 19 09	21 12 57	17 30 25
29	11 04 38	11 53 41	12 14 23	1 03 07	17 15 24	21 08 54	17 26 32
30	11 07 18	11 55 14	12 13 46	0 58 39	17 11 40	21 04 51	17 22 38
31	11 09 59	11 56 48	12 13 10	0 54 11	17 07 57	21 00 48	17 18 45
32	11 12 43	11 58 21	12 12 33	0 49 42	17 04 13	20 56 46	17 14 52

Second transit: Uranus, Nov. $18^{d}23^{h}56^{m}29^{s}$.

EPHEMERIS FOR PHYSICAL OBSERVATIONS FOR 0^h TERRESTRIAL TIME

Date		Light-time	Magnitude	Surface Brightness	Diameter	Phase	Phase Angle	Defect of Illumination
		m		mag./arcsec^2	″		°	″
Jan.	−1	9.25	−0.4	+3.0	6.05	0.740	61.3	1.57
	1	9.55	−0.4	+2.9	5.86	0.773	56.9	1.33
	3	9.82	−0.4	+2.9	5.70	0.802	52.9	1.13
	5	10.07	−0.4	+2.9	5.56	0.826	49.3	0.96
	7	10.31	−0.4	+2.8	5.43	0.848	45.9	0.83
	9	10.52	−0.4	+2.8	5.32	0.867	42.8	0.71
	11	10.72	−0.4	+2.8	5.22	0.884	39.9	0.61
	13	10.90	−0.4	+2.7	5.14	0.898	37.2	0.52
	15	11.06	−0.4	+2.7	5.06	0.912	34.6	0.45
	17	11.20	−0.5	+2.7	5.00	0.924	32.1	0.38
	19	11.33	−0.5	+2.6	4.94	0.935	29.6	0.32
	21	11.44	−0.5	+2.6	4.89	0.944	27.3	0.27
	23	11.53	−0.6	+2.5	4.85	0.953	24.9	0.23
	25	11.61	−0.7	+2.5	4.82	0.962	22.6	0.18
	27	11.67	−0.7	+2.4	4.80	0.969	20.2	0.15
	29	11.71	−0.8	+2.3	4.78	0.976	17.8	0.11
	31	11.73	−0.9	+2.2	4.77	0.982	15.3	0.08
Feb.	2	11.74	−1.0	+2.1	4.77	0.988	12.8	0.06
	4	11.73	−1.2	+2.0	4.77	0.992	10.2	0.04
	6	11.70	−1.3	+1.8	4.79	0.995	7.7	0.02
	8	11.64	−1.5	+1.7	4.81	0.998	5.6	0.01
	10	11.57	−1.6	+1.6	4.84	0.998	5.0	0.01
	12	11.46	−1.6	+1.6	4.88	0.996	6.9	0.02
	14	11.34	−1.5	+1.7	4.94	0.992	10.3	0.04
	16	11.18	−1.4	+1.8	5.01	0.984	14.6	0.08
	18	10.99	−1.4	+1.8	5.10	0.971	19.6	0.15
	20	10.76	−1.4	+1.9	5.20	0.952	25.2	0.25
	22	10.50	−1.3	+2.0	5.33	0.926	31.5	0.39
	24	10.19	−1.3	+2.0	5.49	0.891	38.5	0.60
	26	9.85	−1.2	+2.1	5.68	0.846	46.2	0.87
	28	9.47	−1.1	+2.2	5.91	0.790	54.6	1.24
Mar.	2	9.06	−1.0	+2.4	6.18	0.723	63.6	1.71
	4	8.62	−0.8	+2.5	6.49	0.645	73.1	2.30
	6	8.16	−0.6	+2.7	6.86	0.561	83.0	3.01
	8	7.70	−0.3	+2.9	7.27	0.472	93.2	3.84
	10	7.24	0.0	+3.1	7.73	0.383	103.5	4.77
	12	6.80	+0.3	+3.3	8.23	0.298	113.8	5.78
	14	6.39	+0.8	+3.6	8.76	0.219	124.1	6.84
	16	6.02	+1.4	+4.0	9.30	0.150	134.4	7.90
	18	5.70	+2.3	+4.4	9.82	0.093	144.4	8.90
	20	5.44	+3.3	+4.9	10.30	0.050	154.2	9.78
	22	5.23	+4.5	+5.2	10.70	0.021	163.4	10.48
	24	5.08	—	—	11.01	0.007	170.7	10.93
	26	5.00	—	—	11.20	0.007	170.7	11.12
	28	4.96	+4.7	+5.4	11.28	0.019	164.1	11.06
	30	4.98	+3.7	+5.3	11.23	0.042	156.4	10.76
Apr.	1	5.05	+2.9	+5.0	11.09	0.072	148.8	10.29

MERCURY, 2025

EPHEMERIS FOR PHYSICAL OBSERVATIONS
FOR 0ʰ TERRESTRIAL TIME

Date		Sub-Earth Point		Sub-Solar Point			North Pole	
		Long.	Lat.	Long.	Dist.	P.A.	Dist.	P.A.
		°	°	°	″	°	″	°
Jan.	−1	144.34	− 4.78	205.50	+2.65	98.92	−3.01	11.55
	1	154.07	− 4.77	210.82	+2.46	97.23	−2.92	10.35
	3	163.70	− 4.76	216.45	+2.27	95.47	−2.84	9.08
	5	173.25	− 4.76	222.34	+2.10	93.63	−2.77	7.73
	7	182.73	− 4.76	228.45	+1.95	91.72	−2.70	6.33
	9	192.15	− 4.76	234.75	+1.81	89.74	−2.65	4.87
	11	201.52	− 4.77	241.20	+1.67	87.69	−2.60	3.38
	13	210.85	− 4.78	247.77	+1.55	85.56	−2.56	1.85
	15	220.14	− 4.79	254.43	+1.44	83.36	−2.52	0.29
	17	229.39	− 4.80	261.15	+1.33	81.07	−2.49	358.71
	19	238.61	− 4.81	267.90	+1.22	78.69	−2.46	357.11
	21	247.78	− 4.82	274.67	+1.12	76.18	−2.44	355.51
	23	256.92	− 4.83	281.41	+1.02	73.52	−2.42	353.91
	25	266.02	− 4.84	288.11	+0.93	70.66	−2.40	352.32
	27	275.09	− 4.86	294.74	+0.83	67.51	−2.39	350.74
	29	284.11	− 4.87	301.26	+0.73	63.92	−2.38	349.18
	31	293.09	− 4.89	307.65	+0.63	59.64	−2.37	347.64
Feb.	2	302.02	− 4.91	313.88	+0.53	54.16	−2.37	346.14
	4	310.91	− 4.93	319.91	+0.42	46.44	−2.38	344.67
	6	319.74	− 4.95	325.70	+0.32	33.93	−2.38	343.26
	8	328.53	− 4.97	331.21	+0.23	10.45	−2.39	341.89
	10	337.27	− 5.00	336.39	+0.21	330.54	−2.41	340.58
	12	345.95	− 5.03	341.19	+0.29	295.62	−2.43	339.34
	14	354.59	− 5.07	345.57	+0.44	277.10	−2.46	338.16
	16	3.18	− 5.12	349.45	+0.63	267.02	−2.49	337.07
	18	11.74	− 5.18	352.80	+0.85	260.71	−2.53	336.06
	20	20.29	− 5.25	355.57	+1.11	256.33	−2.59	335.14
	22	28.83	− 5.33	357.71	+1.39	253.04	−2.65	334.32
	24	37.41	− 5.44	359.21	+1.71	250.46	−2.73	333.61
	26	46.06	− 5.56	0.11	+2.05	248.35	−2.82	333.00
	28	54.83	− 5.71	0.45	+2.41	246.58	−2.94	332.50
Mar.	2	63.80	− 5.89	0.37	+2.77	245.05	−3.07	332.10
	4	73.02	− 6.10	0.03	+3.11	243.68	−3.23	331.80
	6	82.59	− 6.33	359.63	+3.40	242.39	−3.41	331.58
	8	92.58	− 6.59	359.38	−3.63	241.10	−3.61	331.43
	10	103.05	− 6.87	359.46	−3.76	239.71	−3.84	331.33
	12	114.06	− 7.16	0.02	−3.77	238.13	−4.08	331.27
	14	125.64	− 7.45	1.17	−3.63	236.20	−4.34	331.23
	16	137.81	− 7.71	2.95	−3.32	233.66	−4.60	331.22
	18	150.55	− 7.93	5.35	−2.86	230.05	−4.86	331.22
	20	163.79	− 8.09	8.37	−2.24	224.23	−5.09	331.25
	22	177.44	− 8.15	11.95	−1.53	212.70	−5.29	331.31
	24	191.37	− 8.12	16.06	−0.89	181.64	−5.45	331.41
	26	205.43	7.98	20.62	−0.90	120.19	−5.54	331.54
	28	219.48	− 7.73	25.59	−1.54	90.15	−5.58	331.69
	30	233.38	− 7.39	30.91	−2.25	79.09	−5.57	331.85
Apr.	1	247.03	− 6.99	36.55	−2.87	73.65	−5.50	331.99

MERCURY, 2025

EPHEMERIS FOR PHYSICAL OBSERVATIONS FOR 0^h TERRESTRIAL TIME

Date		Light-time	Magnitude	Surface Brightness	Diameter	Phase	Phase Angle	Defect of Illumination
		m		mag./arcsec^2	″		°	″
Apr.	1	5.05	+2.9	+5.0	11.09	0.072	148.8	10.29
	3	5.15	+2.2	+4.7	10.87	0.108	141.6	9.70
	5	5.28	+1.8	+4.5	10.60	0.147	134.9	9.04
	7	5.44	+1.4	+4.4	10.28	0.187	128.7	8.36
	9	5.63	+1.1	+4.3	9.95	0.227	123.0	7.69
	11	5.83	+0.9	+4.2	9.61	0.267	117.8	7.04
	13	6.04	+0.8	+4.1	9.27	0.305	113.0	6.44
	15	6.26	+0.7	+4.0	8.93	0.342	108.4	5.88
	17	6.50	+0.6	+3.9	8.61	0.377	104.2	5.37
	19	6.74	+0.5	+3.9	8.31	0.411	100.3	4.90
	21	6.98	+0.4	+3.8	8.02	0.443	96.5	4.46
	23	7.23	+0.4	+3.8	7.74	0.475	92.9	4.07
	25	7.48	+0.3	+3.7	7.48	0.505	89.4	3.70
	27	7.74	+0.3	+3.6	7.23	0.535	86.0	3.36
	29	8.00	+0.2	+3.5	7.00	0.565	82.6	3.05
May	1	8.25	+0.1	+3.4	6.78	0.594	79.2	2.75
	3	8.51	0.0	+3.3	6.58	0.624	75.7	2.47
	5	8.77	−0.1	+3.2	6.38	0.654	72.1	2.21
	7	9.02	−0.2	+3.1	6.20	0.684	68.4	1.96
	9	9.28	−0.3	+3.0	6.03	0.715	64.5	1.72
	11	9.53	−0.4	+2.9	5.88	0.748	60.3	1.48
	13	9.77	−0.6	+2.7	5.73	0.781	55.9	1.26
	15	10.00	−0.7	+2.5	5.60	0.814	51.1	1.04
	17	10.22	−0.9	+2.4	5.48	0.848	45.9	0.83
	19	10.42	−1.0	+2.2	5.37	0.882	40.2	0.63
	21	10.60	−1.2	+2.0	5.28	0.914	34.1	0.45
	23	10.75	−1.4	+1.8	5.20	0.944	27.4	0.29
	25	10.87	−1.7	+1.6	5.15	0.969	20.3	0.16
	27	10.95	−1.9	+1.3	5.11	0.988	12.7	0.06
	29	10.99	−2.3	+1.0	5.09	0.998	4.9	0.01
	31	10.98	−2.3	+0.9	5.10	0.999	4.1	0.01
June	2	10.92	−2.0	+1.3	5.12	0.989	12.1	0.06
	4	10.82	−1.7	+1.5	5.17	0.969	20.2	0.16
	6	10.67	−1.5	+1.7	5.25	0.941	28.1	0.31
	8	10.49	−1.3	+2.0	5.34	0.907	35.6	0.50
	10	10.27	−1.1	+2.1	5.45	0.868	42.6	0.72
	12	10.03	−0.9	+2.3	5.58	0.827	49.2	0.97
	14	9.77	−0.7	+2.5	5.73	0.785	55.3	1.23
	16	9.49	−0.6	+2.7	5.90	0.743	61.0	1.52
	18	9.21	−0.4	+2.9	6.08	0.702	66.2	1.81
	20	8.92	−0.3	+3.0	6.27	0.662	71.1	2.12
	22	8.63	−0.1	+3.2	6.48	0.624	75.7	2.44
	24	8.35	0.0	+3.3	6.71	0.586	80.0	2.77
	26	8.06	+0.1	+3.4	6.95	0.550	84.2	3.12
	28	7.77	+0.2	+3.5	7.20	0.515	88.2	3.49
	30	7.49	+0.3	+3.6	7.47	0.481	92.2	3.88
July	2	7.22	+0.4	+3.7	7.75	0.447	96.1	4.28

MERCURY, 2025

EPHEMERIS FOR PHYSICAL OBSERVATIONS FOR 0^h TERRESTRIAL TIME

Date		Sub-Earth Point		Sub-Solar Point			North Pole	
		Long.	Lat.	Long.	Dist.	P.A.	Dist.	P.A.
		°	°	°	″	°	″	°
Apr.	1	247.03	− 6.99	36.55	−2.87	73.65	−5.50	331.99
	3	260.35	− 6.54	42.44	−3.38	70.42	−5.40	332.11
	5	273.31	− 6.06	48.56	−3.75	68.26	−5.26	332.19
	7	285.90	− 5.57	54.86	−4.01	66.71	−5.11	332.22
	9	298.11	− 5.09	61.31	−4.17	65.54	−4.95	332.21
	11	309.98	− 4.61	67.88	−4.25	64.61	−4.78	332.15
	13	321.53	− 4.15	74.54	−4.27	63.85	−4.62	332.07
	15	332.77	− 3.71	81.26	−4.24	63.23	−4.45	331.96
	17	343.75	− 3.30	88.02	−4.17	62.71	−4.30	331.84
	19	354.49	− 2.90	94.78	−4.09	62.28	−4.14	331.72
	21	5.00	− 2.53	101.53	−3.98	61.93	−4.00	331.61
	23	15.31	− 2.18	108.22	−3.86	61.66	−3.86	331.52
	25	25.44	− 1.85	114.85	+3.74	61.47	−3.73	331.46
	27	35.39	− 1.54	121.37	+3.61	61.35	−3.61	331.43
	29	45.19	− 1.24	127.76	+3.47	61.32	−3.50	331.45
May	1	54.83	− 0.97	133.99	+3.33	61.37	−3.39	331.52
	3	64.33	− 0.70	140.01	+3.19	61.52	−3.28	331.66
	5	73.69	− 0.46	145.79	+3.04	61.76	−3.19	331.87
	7	82.91	− 0.22	151.30	+2.88	62.11	−3.10	332.17
	9	92.00	0.00	156.47	+2.72	62.58	−3.01	332.55
	11	100.95	+ 0.21	161.27	+2.55	63.18	+2.94	333.03
	13	109.77	+ 0.41	165.63	+2.37	63.93	+2.86	333.63
	15	118.45	+ 0.60	169.51	+2.18	64.85	+2.80	334.34
	17	126.99	+ 0.78	172.85	+1.97	65.97	+2.74	335.18
	19	135.41	+ 0.96	175.61	+1.73	67.32	+2.68	336.17
	21	143.69	+ 1.13	177.74	+1.48	68.98	+2.64	337.31
	23	151.85	+ 1.29	179.23	+1.20	71.10	+2.60	338.60
	25	159.90	+ 1.46	180.12	+0.89	73.99	+2.57	340.06
	27	167.87	+ 1.62	180.46	+0.56	78.84	+2.55	341.68
	29	175.77	+ 1.79	180.37	+0.22	94.43	+2.54	343.44
	31	183.64	+ 1.97	180.03	+0.18	227.16	+2.54	345.35
June	2	191.51	+ 2.15	179.62	+0.54	247.42	+2.56	347.36
	4	199.43	+ 2.34	179.37	+0.89	253.18	+2.58	349.44
	6	207.42	+ 2.54	179.46	+1.23	256.89	+2.62	351.57
	8	215.52	+ 2.75	180.04	+1.55	259.93	+2.66	353.71
	10	223.75	+ 2.97	181.19	+1.85	262.64	+2.72	355.82
	12	232.12	+ 3.22	182.97	+2.11	265.15	+2.78	357.88
	14	240.64	+ 3.47	185.39	+2.36	267.50	+2.86	359.87
	16	249.32	+ 3.74	188.41	+2.58	269.71	+2.94	1.76
	18	258.16	+ 4.02	192.01	+2.78	271.80	+3.03	3.55
	20	267.16	+ 4.33	196.11	+2.97	273.77	+3.12	5.23
	22	276.33	+ 4.64	200.68	+3.14	275.63	+3.23	6.80
	24	285.67	+ 4.98	205.66	+3.30	277.39	+3.34	8.25
	26	295.17	+ 5.33	210.99	+3.46	279.05	+3.46	9.59
	28	304.84	+ 5.70	216.63	+3.60	280.62	+3.58	10.80
	30	314.70	+ 6.08	222.53	−3.73	282.13	+3.71	11.90
July	2	324.74	+ 6.49	228.65	−3.85	283.57	+3.85	12.88

EPHEMERIS FOR PHYSICAL OBSERVATIONS FOR 0^h TERRESTRIAL TIME

Date		Light-time	Magnitude	Surface Brightness	Diameter	Phase	Phase Angle	Defect of Illumination
		m		mag./arcsec^2	″		°	″
July	2	7.22	+0.4	+3.7	7.75	0.447	96.1	4.28
	4	6.95	+0.5	+3.8	8.05	0.414	100.0	4.72
	6	6.70	+0.6	+3.9	8.36	0.380	103.9	5.18
	8	6.45	+0.7	+4.0	8.68	0.346	108.0	5.68
	10	6.21	+0.8	+4.1	9.02	0.311	112.2	6.21
	12	5.98	+1.0	+4.2	9.36	0.277	116.5	6.77
	14	5.77	+1.1	+4.3	9.70	0.242	121.1	7.36
	16	5.57	+1.3	+4.4	10.05	0.206	126.0	7.98
	18	5.39	+1.6	+4.5	10.38	0.171	131.1	8.60
	20	5.23	+2.0	+4.7	10.70	0.137	136.6	9.23
	22	5.10	+2.4	+4.9	10.97	0.104	142.3	9.83
	24	5.00	+2.9	+5.1	11.20	0.074	148.4	10.37
	26	4.92	+3.6	+5.3	11.37	0.048	154.6	10.81
	28	4.89	+4.3	+5.5	11.45	0.028	160.7	11.12
	30	4.90	+5.1	+5.5	11.43	0.015	165.9	11.25
Aug.	1	4.95	+5.4	+5.5	11.31	0.011	168.2	11.18
	3	5.04	+5.0	+5.5	11.10	0.016	165.6	10.92
	5	5.19	+4.2	+5.3	10.78	0.031	159.7	10.45
	7	5.38	+3.3	+5.0	10.39	0.057	152.4	9.80
	9	5.63	+2.4	+4.6	9.95	0.093	144.5	9.02
	11	5.92	+1.7	+4.2	9.46	0.139	136.3	8.15
	13	6.25	+1.2	+3.9	8.96	0.193	127.9	7.23
	15	6.62	+0.7	+3.6	8.46	0.256	119.2	6.29
	17	7.02	+0.3	+3.3	7.98	0.326	110.3	5.37
	19	7.44	0.0	+3.1	7.52	0.402	101.3	4.49
	21	7.89	−0.3	+2.9	7.10	0.482	92.0	3.67
	23	8.34	−0.5	+2.8	6.71	0.564	82.6	2.93
	25	8.78	−0.7	+2.6	6.37	0.645	73.2	2.26
	27	9.22	−0.9	+2.4	6.07	0.721	63.8	1.69
	29	9.62	−1.1	+2.2	5.82	0.790	54.5	1.22
	31	10.00	−1.2	+2.1	5.60	0.849	45.7	0.84
Sept.	2	10.33	−1.4	+1.9	5.42	0.898	37.3	0.55
	4	10.63	−1.4	+1.8	5.27	0.935	29.6	0.34
	6	10.88	−1.5	+1.7	5.15	0.962	22.4	0.19
	8	11.09	−1.6	+1.6	5.05	0.981	16.0	0.10
	10	11.26	−1.7	+1.5	4.97	0.992	10.4	0.04
	12	11.39	−1.8	+1.4	4.91	0.997	5.9	0.01
	14	11.50	−1.8	+1.4	4.87	0.999	4.4	0.01
	16	11.57	−1.6	+1.6	4.84	0.996	6.9	0.02
	18	11.61	−1.4	+1.8	4.82	0.992	10.4	0.04
	20	11.63	−1.2	+2.0	4.81	0.986	13.8	0.07
	22	11.63	−1.0	+2.1	4.81	0.978	17.1	0.11
	24	11.61	−0.9	+2.2	4.82	0.969	20.2	0.15
	26	11.56	−0.8	+2.3	4.84	0.960	23.2	0.20
	28	11.50	−0.7	+2.4	4.87	0.949	26.0	0.25
	30	11.43	−0.6	+2.5	4.90	0.939	28.7	0.30
Oct.	2	11.33	−0.5	+2.6	4.94	0.927	31.3	0.36

MERCURY, 2025

EPHEMERIS FOR PHYSICAL OBSERVATIONS
FOR 0^h TERRESTRIAL TIME

Date		Sub-Earth Point		Sub-Solar Point			North Pole	
		Long.	Lat.	Long.	Dist.	P.A.	Dist.	P.A.
		°	°	°	″	°	″	°
July	2	324.74	+ 6.49	228.65	−3.85	283.57	+3.85	12.88
	4	334.98	+ 6.91	234.95	−3.96	284.96	+3.99	13.75
	6	345.44	+ 7.35	241.41	−4.06	286.32	+4.14	14.51
	8	356.12	+ 7.80	247.98	−4.13	287.67	+4.30	15.15
	10	7.04	+ 8.27	254.64	−4.18	289.04	+4.46	15.68
	12	18.22	+ 8.75	261.37	−4.19	290.46	+4.62	16.09
	14	29.69	+ 9.23	268.12	−4.15	291.97	+4.79	16.38
	16	41.46	+ 9.72	274.89	−4.07	293.64	+4.95	16.55
	18	53.54	+10.19	281.63	−3.91	295.56	+5.11	16.59
	20	65.95	+10.64	288.33	−3.68	297.89	+5.25	16.51
	22	78.69	+11.06	294.95	−3.35	300.87	+5.38	16.30
	24	91.75	+11.41	301.47	−2.94	304.98	+5.49	15.96
	26	105.09	+11.69	307.86	−2.44	311.17	+5.56	15.51
	28	118.66	+11.88	314.09	−1.90	321.56	+5.60	14.97
	30	132.39	+11.95	320.11	−1.40	341.03	+5.59	14.35
Aug.	1	146.18	+11.90	325.89	−1.16	15.13	+5.53	13.71
	3	159.92	+11.72	331.38	−1.38	49.66	+5.43	13.09
	5	173.50	+11.43	336.55	−1.87	69.61	+5.28	12.53
	7	186.81	+11.04	341.34	−2.41	80.28	+5.10	12.09
	9	199.78	+10.58	345.70	−2.89	86.70	+4.88	11.81
	11	212.34	+10.06	349.57	−3.27	91.07	+4.65	11.71
	13	224.43	+ 9.51	352.90	−3.54	94.38	+4.41	11.83
	15	236.06	+ 8.96	355.65	−3.69	97.13	+4.17	12.16
	17	247.19	+ 8.42	357.77	−3.74	99.57	+3.94	12.70
	19	257.86	+ 7.90	359.25	−3.69	101.87	+3.72	13.45
	21	268.08	+ 7.42	0.12	−3.55	104.11	+3.52	14.38
	23	277.88	+ 6.97	0.46	+3.33	106.36	+3.33	15.46
	25	287.31	+ 6.56	0.36	+3.05	108.63	+3.16	16.66
	27	296.43	+ 6.20	0.02	+2.72	110.97	+3.02	17.93
	29	305.28	+ 5.88	359.62	+2.37	113.39	+2.89	19.24
	31	313.93	+ 5.59	359.37	+2.00	115.95	+2.78	20.53
Sept.	2	322.45	+ 5.34	359.46	+1.64	118.74	+2.69	21.77
	4	330.89	+ 5.12	0.05	+1.30	121.94	+2.62	22.94
	6	339.28	+ 4.92	1.21	+0.98	125.93	+2.56	24.01
	8	347.68	+ 4.75	3.00	+0.70	131.63	+2.51	24.97
	10	356.09	+ 4.59	5.43	+0.45	141.58	+2.48	25.81
	12	4.55	+ 4.44	8.46	+0.25	164.92	+2.45	26.54
	14	13.07	+ 4.31	12.06	+0.19	220.42	+2.43	27.15
	16	21.65	+ 4.18	16.18	+0.29	260.53	+2.41	27.65
	18	30.29	+ 4.06	20.75	+0.43	275.29	+2.40	28.04
	20	39.00	+ 3.94	25.73	+0.58	282.12	+2.40	28.33
	22	47.78	+ 3.83	31.07	+0.71	286.00	+2.40	28.51
	24	56.63	+ 3.72	36.71	+0.83	288.47	+2.40	28.61
	26	65.53	+ 3.61	42.61	+0.95	290.15	+2.41	28.62
	28	74.51	+ 3.50	48.73	+1.07	291.32	+2.43	28.54
	30	83.54	+ 3.39	55.04	+1.18	292.15	+2.44	28.38
Oct.	2	92.63	+ 3.28	61.50	+1.28	292.71	+2.46	28.15

EPHEMERIS FOR PHYSICAL OBSERVATIONS FOR 0^h TERRESTRIAL TIME

Date		Light-time	Magnitude	Surface Brightness	Diameter	Phase	Phase Angle	Defect of Illumination
		m		mag./arcsec^2	″		°	″
Oct.	2	11.33	− 0.5	+ 2.6	4.94	0.927	31.3	0.36
	4	11.23	− 0.4	+ 2.7	4.99	0.915	33.8	0.42
	6	11.10	− 0.4	+ 2.7	5.04	0.903	36.3	0.49
	8	10.96	− 0.3	+ 2.8	5.11	0.889	38.9	0.57
	10	10.81	− 0.3	+ 2.9	5.18	0.875	41.4	0.65
	12	10.64	− 0.3	+ 2.9	5.26	0.860	44.0	0.74
	14	10.46	− 0.2	+ 2.9	5.35	0.843	46.7	0.84
	16	10.26	− 0.2	+ 3.0	5.45	0.825	49.4	0.95
	18	10.05	− 0.2	+ 3.0	5.57	0.805	52.4	1.08
	20	9.82	− 0.2	+ 3.1	5.70	0.784	55.5	1.23
	22	9.57	− 0.2	+ 3.1	5.85	0.759	58.8	1.41
	24	9.31	− 0.2	+ 3.1	6.01	0.732	62.3	1.61
	26	9.04	− 0.1	+ 3.2	6.19	0.702	66.2	1.85
	28	8.74	− 0.1	+ 3.2	6.40	0.667	70.5	2.13
	30	8.44	− 0.1	+ 3.2	6.64	0.628	75.2	2.47
Nov.	1	8.11	− 0.1	+ 3.3	6.90	0.583	80.5	2.88
	3	7.78	0.0	+ 3.3	7.19	0.532	86.3	3.37
	5	7.44	0.0	+ 3.3	7.52	0.474	92.9	3.95
	7	7.10	+ 0.1	+ 3.4	7.88	0.409	100.4	4.66
	9	6.76	+ 0.3	+ 3.5	8.28	0.338	108.9	5.48
	11	6.44	+ 0.6	+ 3.6	8.69	0.261	118.6	6.42
	13	6.15	+ 1.1	+ 3.8	9.10	0.182	129.5	7.44
	15	5.91	+ 1.9	+ 4.1	9.48	0.108	141.7	8.46
	17	5.73	+ 3.3	+ 4.6	9.77	0.046	155.2	9.32
	19	5.64	—	—	9.92	0.008	169.6	9.84
	21	5.65	—	—	9.91	0.002	174.8	9.88
	23	5.77	+ 3.8	+ 4.7	9.71	0.031	159.8	9.41
	25	5.98	+ 2.1	+ 4.1	9.36	0.090	145.0	8.52
	27	6.27	+ 1.1	+ 3.6	8.93	0.172	131.1	7.40
	29	6.62	+ 0.4	+ 3.4	8.45	0.263	118.2	6.23
Dec.	1	7.01	+ 0.1	+ 3.2	7.98	0.357	106.6	5.13
	3	7.42	− 0.2	+ 3.1	7.55	0.445	96.3	4.19
	5	7.83	− 0.3	+ 3.0	7.15	0.525	87.1	3.39
	7	8.23	− 0.4	+ 3.0	6.80	0.596	79.0	2.75
	9	8.62	− 0.4	+ 2.9	6.50	0.656	71.8	2.23
	11	8.98	− 0.5	+ 2.9	6.23	0.708	65.4	1.82
	13	9.33	− 0.5	+ 2.8	6.00	0.752	59.7	1.49
	15	9.65	− 0.5	+ 2.8	5.80	0.789	54.7	1.22
	17	9.94	− 0.5	+ 2.7	5.63	0.820	50.1	1.01
	19	10.22	− 0.5	+ 2.7	5.48	0.847	46.0	0.84
	21	10.47	− 0.5	+ 2.7	5.35	0.870	42.3	0.70
	23	10.69	− 0.5	+ 2.7	5.23	0.889	38.9	0.58
	25	10.90	− 0.5	+ 2.6	5.14	0.906	35.7	0.48
	27	11.08	− 0.5	+ 2.6	5.05	0.921	32.7	0.40
	29	11.25	− 0.6	+ 2.6	4.98	0.933	30.0	0.33
	31	11.39	− 0.6	+ 2.5	4.91	0.944	27.3	0.27
	33	11.52	− 0.6	+ 2.5	4.86	0.954	24.8	0.22

MERCURY, 2025

EPHEMERIS FOR PHYSICAL OBSERVATIONS FOR 0h TERRESTRIAL TIME

Date		Sub-Earth Point		Sub-Solar Point			North Pole	
		Long.	Lat.	Long.	Dist.	P.A.	Dist.	P.A.
		°	°	°	″	°	″	°
Oct.	2	92.63	+ 3.28	61.50	+1.28	292.71	+2.46	28.15
	4	101.77	+ 3.17	68.07	+1.39	293.08	+2.49	27.84
	6	110.97	+ 3.06	74.73	+1.49	293.28	+2.51	27.46
	8	120.23	+ 2.94	81.46	+1.60	293.33	+2.55	27.02
	10	129.54	+ 2.82	88.22	+1.71	293.28	+2.58	26.51
	12	138.90	+ 2.70	94.98	+1.83	293.11	+2.62	25.95
	14	148.33	+ 2.58	101.72	+1.95	292.86	+2.67	25.33
	16	157.81	+ 2.45	108.42	+2.07	292.52	+2.72	24.66
	18	167.36	+ 2.32	115.04	+2.21	292.11	+2.78	23.94
	20	176.99	+ 2.18	121.56	+2.35	291.64	+2.85	23.18
	22	186.69	+ 2.04	127.95	+2.50	291.12	+2.92	22.39
	24	196.49	+ 1.89	134.17	+2.66	290.56	+3.00	21.58
	26	206.40	+ 1.73	140.19	+2.83	289.97	+3.09	20.76
	28	216.45	+ 1.56	145.96	+3.02	289.36	+3.20	19.95
	30	226.66	+ 1.39	151.46	+3.21	288.76	+3.31	19.16
Nov.	1	237.07	+ 1.20	156.62	+3.40	288.18	+3.44	18.42
	3	247.73	+ 0.99	161.41	+3.59	287.65	+3.59	17.75
	5	258.70	+ 0.77	165.76	−3.76	287.20	+3.76	17.18
	7	270.06	+ 0.52	169.63	−3.88	286.84	+3.94	16.77
	9	281.88	+ 0.25	172.95	−3.91	286.61	+4.13	16.54
	11	294.26	− 0.05	175.68	−3.82	286.50	−4.34	16.55
	13	307.28	− 0.38	177.79	−3.51	286.49	−4.55	16.81
	15	320.98	− 0.74	179.27	−2.94	286.41	−4.73	17.35
	17	335.32	− 1.11	180.13	−2.05	285.74	−4.88	18.12
	19	350.16	− 1.48	180.45	−0.90	281.02	−4.96	19.05
	21	5.20	− 1.83	180.36	−0.45	130.48	−4.95	20.01
	23	20.10	− 2.14	180.01	−1.68	116.63	−4.85	20.88
	25	34.52	− 2.39	179.61	−2.68	114.92	−4.67	21.55
	27	48.25	− 2.59	179.37	−3.37	114.20	−4.45	21.99
	29	61.20	− 2.75	179.47	−3.72	113.62	−4.22	22.18
Dec.	1	73.40	− 2.87	180.06	−3.82	112.97	−3.98	22.14
	3	84.95	− 2.97	181.23	−3.75	112.20	−3.76	21.91
	5	95.95	− 3.05	183.04	+3.57	111.31	−3.57	21.50
	7	106.53	− 3.12	185.47	+3.34	110.30	−3.39	20.93
	9	116.77	− 3.19	188.52	+3.09	109.16	−3.24	20.24
	11	126.76	− 3.26	192.12	+2.83	107.91	−3.11	19.42
	13	136.56	− 3.33	196.25	+2.59	106.54	−2.99	18.50
	15	146.22	− 3.40	200.83	+2.37	105.06	−2.89	17.48
	17	155.77	− 3.46	205.81	+2.16	103.47	−2.81	16.37
	19	165.23	− 3.53	211.15	+1.97	101.78	−2.73	15.19
	21	174.64	− 3.60	216.80	+1.80	99.97	−2.67	13.93
	23	184.00	− 3.66	222.70	+1.64	98.06	−2.61	12.60
	25	193.31	− 3.73	228.83	+1.50	96.03	−2.56	11.22
	27	202.60	− 3.80	235.14	+1.37	93.88	−2.52	9.78
	29	211.86	− 3.87	241.60	+1.24	91.60	−2.48	8.29
	31	221.09	− 3.93	248.17	+1.13	89.17	−2.45	6.76
	33	230.30	− 4.00	254.84	+1.02	86.56	−2.42	5.19

VENUS, 2025

EPHEMERIS FOR PHYSICAL OBSERVATIONS FOR 0h TERRESTRIAL TIME

Date		Light-time	Magnitude	Surface Brightness	Diameter	Phase	Phase Angle	Defect of Illumination
		m		mag./arcsec^2	″		°	″
Jan.	−3	6.49	−4.4	+1.4	21.39	0.573	81.6	9.13
	1	6.25	−4.4	+1.4	22.22	0.555	83.7	9.89
	5	6.00	−4.5	+1.4	23.13	0.536	85.9	10.74
	9	5.75	−4.5	+1.4	24.13	0.516	88.2	11.68
	13	5.51	−4.5	+1.4	25.21	0.495	90.5	12.72
	17	5.26	−4.6	+1.4	26.39	0.473	93.1	13.90
	21	5.01	−4.6	+1.4	27.68	0.450	95.7	15.22
	25	4.77	−4.7	+1.5	29.10	0.426	98.5	16.71
	29	4.53	−4.7	+1.5	30.66	0.400	101.5	18.39
Feb.	2	4.29	−4.8	+1.5	32.38	0.373	104.7	20.31
	6	4.05	−4.8	+1.5	34.27	0.344	108.2	22.48
	10	3.82	−4.8	+1.4	36.34	0.313	111.9	24.96
	14	3.59	−4.9	+1.4	38.62	0.281	116.0	27.77
	18	3.38	−4.9	+1.4	41.09	0.247	120.4	30.96
	22	3.17	−4.9	+1.4	43.76	0.211	125.3	34.53
	26	2.98	−4.8	+1.3	46.57	0.174	130.7	38.46
Mar.	2	2.81	−4.8	+1.3	49.47	0.137	136.5	42.69
	6	2.65	−4.7	+1.2	52.35	0.101	142.9	47.06
	10	2.52	−4.5	+1.0	55.02	0.068	149.8	51.28
	14	2.42	−4.3	+0.7	57.25	0.040	156.9	54.96
	18	2.36	−4.1	+0.3	58.80	0.020	163.6	57.61
	22	2.33	—	—	59.46	0.011	168.0	58.81
	26	2.35	—	—	59.12	0.013	166.9	58.36
	30	2.40	−4.1	+0.5	57.84	0.026	161.4	56.33
Apr.	3	2.49	−4.4	+0.8	55.78	0.049	154.5	53.06
	7	2.61	−4.5	+1.1	53.18	0.078	147.5	49.01
	11	2.76	−4.7	+1.2	50.28	0.112	140.8	44.63
	15	2.94	−4.7	+1.3	47.28	0.148	134.7	40.26
	19	3.13	−4.8	+1.4	44.33	0.185	129.0	36.13
	23	3.34	−4.8	+1.4	41.52	0.221	123.9	32.35
	27	3.57	−4.8	+1.4	38.90	0.256	119.2	28.95
May	1	3.80	−4.7	+1.5	36.49	0.289	115.0	25.95
	5	4.05	−4.7	+1.5	34.29	0.321	111.0	23.30
	9	4.30	−4.7	+1.5	32.29	0.350	107.4	20.97
	13	4.55	−4.6	+1.5	30.47	0.379	104.0	18.93
	17	4.82	−4.6	+1.5	28.82	0.406	100.9	17.13
	21	5.08	−4.5	+1.5	27.33	0.431	97.9	15.55
	25	5.34	−4.5	+1.5	25.97	0.455	95.1	14.15
	29	5.61	−4.4	+1.5	24.74	0.478	92.5	12.90
June	2	5.88	−4.4	+1.5	23.61	0.500	89.9	11.80
	6	6.14	−4.4	+1.4	22.59	0.522	87.5	10.80
	10	6.41	−4.3	+1.4	21.65	0.542	85.2	9.92
	14	6.68	−4.3	+1.4	20.78	0.561	82.9	9.12
	18	6.94	−4.2	+1.4	19.99	0.580	80.8	8.39
	22	7.21	−4.2	+1.4	19.26	0.598	78.7	7.74
	26	7.47	−4.2	+1.4	18.59	0.616	76.6	7.14
	30	7.72	−4.2	+1.4	17.97	0.633	74.6	6.60

VENUS, 2025

EPHEMERIS FOR PHYSICAL OBSERVATIONS FOR 0^h TERRESTRIAL TIME

Date	L_s	Sub-Earth Point		Sub-Solar Point				North Pole	
		Long.	Lat.	Long.	Lat.	Dist.	P.A.	Dist.	P.A.
	°	°	°	°	°	″	°	″	°
Jan. −3	166.93	181.51	+1.18	263.13	+0.60	+10.58	252.24	+10.69	341.81
1	173.35	191.76	+0.84	275.47	+0.31	+11.05	251.08	+11.11	340.86
5	179.77	201.93	+0.46	287.82	+0.01	+11.54	250.01	+11.57	340.03
9	186.21	212.01	+0.05	300.17	−0.29	+12.06	249.04	+12.06	339.33
13	192.66	221.99	−0.39	312.54	−0.58	−12.60	248.16	−12.60	338.74
17	199.11	231.84	−0.87	324.91	−0.86	−13.18	247.35	−13.19	338.26
21	205.58	241.55	−1.39	337.30	−1.14	−13.77	246.59	−13.84	337.88
25	212.05	251.11	−1.94	349.69	−1.40	−14.39	245.88	−14.54	337.59
29	218.52	260.47	−2.52	2.09	−1.64	−15.02	245.18	−15.32	337.37
Feb. 2	225.01	269.63	−3.13	14.50	−1.87	−15.66	244.47	−16.16	337.23
6	231.49	278.53	−3.78	26.91	−2.06	−16.28	243.71	−17.10	337.14
10	237.99	287.13	−4.46	39.33	−2.24	−16.86	242.87	−18.12	337.09
14	244.48	295.38	−5.17	51.75	−2.38	−17.36	241.88	−19.23	337.07
18	250.97	303.23	−5.89	64.18	−2.49	−17.71	240.67	−20.44	337.07
22	257.47	310.60	−6.62	76.61	−2.58	−17.85	239.14	−21.73	337.06
26	263.97	317.45	−7.35	89.03	−2.62	−17.66	237.15	−23.09	337.04
Mar. 2	270.46	323.69	−8.04	101.46	−2.64	−17.01	234.48	−24.49	337.00
6	276.95	329.28	−8.67	113.88	−2.62	−15.77	230.76	−25.87	336.94
10	283.44	334.21	−9.19	126.30	−2.57	−13.83	225.27	−27.15	336.88
14	289.92	338.50	−9.54	138.71	−2.48	−11.22	216.41	−28.23	336.83
18	296.40	342.28	−9.68	151.12	−2.36	− 8.30	200.07	−28.98	336.82
22	302.87	345.76	−9.58	163.52	−2.22	− 6.18	167.67	−29.31	336.86
26	309.33	349.18	−9.21	175.91	−2.04	− 6.70	125.86	−29.18	336.95
30	315.78	352.82	−8.63	188.29	−1.84	− 9.24	100.55	−28.59	337.08
Apr. 3	322.23	356.88	−7.88	200.66	−1.62	−12.02	88.03	−27.63	337.20
7	328.67	1.52	−7.02	213.02	−1.37	−14.30	81.07	−26.39	337.31
11	335.09	6.80	−6.12	225.37	−1.11	−15.88	76.71	−25.00	337.37
15	341.51	12.73	−5.22	237.70	−0.84	−16.81	73.75	−23.54	337.38
19	347.92	19.27	−4.36	250.03	−0.55	−17.21	71.62	−22.10	337.35
23	354.32	26.36	−3.56	262.35	−0.26	−17.23	70.01	−20.72	337.30
27	0.70	33.94	−2.83	274.65	+0.03	−16.97	68.78	−19.43	337.23
May 1	7.08	41.93	−2.16	286.95	+0.32	−16.54	67.83	−18.23	337.18
5	13.45	50.27	−1.57	299.24	+0.61	−16.00	67.10	−17.14	337.16
9	19.81	58.91	−1.04	311.52	+0.89	−15.41	66.57	−16.14	337.18
13	26.17	67.81	−0.57	323.80	+1.16	−14.78	66.20	−15.24	337.26
17	32.52	76.94	−0.16	336.06	+1.42	−14.15	66.00	−14.41	337.41
21	38.86	86.25	+0.19	348.33	+1.65	−13.53	65.95	+13.66	337.64
25	45.19	95.73	+0.50	0.59	+1.87	−12.93	66.04	+12.99	337.97
29	51.52	105.35	+0.75	12.84	+2.07	−12.36	66.29	+12.37	338.39
June 2	57.85	115.08	+0.97	25.10	+2.23	+11.81	66.68	+11.81	338.92
6	64.17	124.92	+1.14	37.35	+2.37	+11.28	67.22	+11.29	339.55
10	70.50	134.85	+1.28	49.60	+2.49	+10.79	67.90	+10.82	340.29
14	76.82	144.86	+1.38	61.86	+2.57	+10.31	68.73	+10.39	341.15
18	83.14	154.94	+1.46	74.11	+2.62	+ 9.87	69.70	+ 9.99	342.11
22	89.46	165.09	+1.50	86.37	+2.64	+ 9.44	70.81	+ 9.63	343.20
26	95.79	175.30	+1.52	98.63	+2.63	+ 9.04	72.05	+ 9.29	344.39
30	102.12	185.55	+1.51	110.89	+2.58	+ 8.66	73.44	+ 8.98	345.69

EPHEMERIS FOR PHYSICAL OBSERVATIONS
FOR 0^h TERRESTRIAL TIME

Date		Light-time	Magnitude	Surface Brightness	Diameter	Phase	Phase Angle	Defect of Illumination
		m		mag./arcsec²	″		°	″
June	30	7.72	−4.2	+1.4	17.97	0.633	74.6	6.60
July	4	7.98	−4.1	+1.3	17.39	0.649	72.7	6.10
	8	8.23	−4.1	+1.3	16.86	0.665	70.7	5.65
	12	8.48	−4.1	+1.3	16.36	0.680	68.8	5.23
	16	8.73	−4.1	+1.3	15.90	0.695	67.0	4.84
	20	8.97	−4.0	+1.3	15.47	0.710	65.2	4.49
	24	9.21	−4.0	+1.3	15.07	0.724	63.4	4.16
	28	9.44	−4.0	+1.2	14.70	0.738	61.6	3.85
Aug.	1	9.67	−4.0	+1.2	14.35	0.751	59.8	3.57
	5	9.90	−4.0	+1.2	14.02	0.764	58.1	3.30
	9	10.12	−4.0	+1.2	13.72	0.777	56.3	3.06
	13	10.33	−4.0	+1.2	13.43	0.789	54.6	2.83
	17	10.54	−3.9	+1.1	13.16	0.801	52.9	2.61
	21	10.75	−3.9	+1.1	12.91	0.813	51.3	2.42
	25	10.95	−3.9	+1.1	12.68	0.824	49.6	2.23
	29	11.14	−3.9	+1.1	12.46	0.835	47.9	2.05
Sept.	2	11.33	−3.9	+1.1	12.25	0.846	46.3	1.89
	6	11.51	−3.9	+1.1	12.05	0.856	44.6	1.74
	10	11.69	−3.9	+1.0	11.87	0.866	43.0	1.59
	14	11.86	−3.9	+1.0	11.70	0.875	41.4	1.46
	18	12.03	−3.9	+1.0	11.54	0.884	39.8	1.33
	22	12.19	−3.9	+1.0	11.39	0.893	38.2	1.22
	26	12.34	−3.9	+1.0	11.25	0.902	36.6	1.11
	30	12.49	−3.9	+1.0	11.11	0.910	35.0	1.00
Oct.	4	12.63	−3.9	+0.9	10.99	0.917	33.4	0.91
	8	12.76	−3.9	+0.9	10.87	0.925	31.9	0.82
	12	12.89	−3.9	+0.9	10.77	0.932	30.3	0.74
	16	13.01	−3.9	+0.9	10.66	0.938	28.8	0.66
	20	13.13	−3.9	+0.9	10.57	0.944	27.3	0.59
	24	13.24	−3.9	+0.9	10.48	0.950	25.8	0.52
	28	13.35	−3.9	+0.9	10.40	0.956	24.3	0.46
Nov.	1	13.44	−3.9	+0.8	10.32	0.961	22.8	0.40
	5	13.54	−3.9	+0.8	10.25	0.966	21.3	0.35
	9	13.62	−3.9	+0.8	10.19	0.970	19.9	0.30
	13	13.70	−3.9	+0.8	10.13	0.974	18.4	0.26
	17	13.78	−3.9	+0.8	10.08	0.978	17.0	0.22
	21	13.84	−3.9	+0.8	10.03	0.982	15.6	0.18
	25	13.91	−3.9	+0.8	9.98	0.985	14.2	0.15
	29	13.96	−3.9	+0.8	9.94	0.988	12.8	0.12
Dec.	3	14.01	−3.9	+0.8	9.90	0.990	11.4	0.10
	7	14.06	−3.9	+0.8	9.87	0.992	10.1	0.08
	11	14.10	−3.9	+0.8	9.84	0.994	8.7	0.06
	15	14.13	−3.9	+0.8	9.82	0.996	7.4	0.04
	19	14.16	−3.9	+0.8	9.80	0.997	6.1	0.03
	23	14.19	−3.9	+0.8	9.78	0.998	4.8	0.02
	27	14.21	−3.9	+0.8	9.77	0.999	3.5	0.01
	31	14.22	−3.9	+0.8	9.76	1.000	2.3	0.00

VENUS, 2025

EPHEMERIS FOR PHYSICAL OBSERVATIONS FOR 0^h TERRESTRIAL TIME

Date		L_s	Sub-Earth Point		Sub-Solar Point				North Pole	
			Long.	Lat.	Long.	Lat.	Dist.	P.A.	Dist.	P.A.
		°	°	°	°	°	″	°	″	°
June	30	102.12	185.55	+1.51	110.89	+2.58	+ 8.66	73.44	+ 8.98	345.69
July	4	108.46	195.85	+1.49	123.15	+2.50	+ 8.30	74.95	+ 8.69	347.10
	8	114.80	206.20	+1.44	135.42	+2.40	+ 7.96	76.58	+ 8.43	348.62
	12	121.14	216.58	+1.38	147.70	+2.26	+ 7.63	78.34	+ 8.18	350.22
	16	127.50	227.00	+1.31	159.98	+2.09	+ 7.32	80.20	+ 7.95	351.92
	20	133.86	237.46	+1.22	172.27	+1.90	+ 7.02	82.16	+ 7.73	353.69
	24	140.23	247.94	+1.12	184.56	+1.69	+ 6.74	84.20	+ 7.53	355.53
	28	146.61	258.46	+1.02	196.87	+1.45	+ 6.46	86.31	+ 7.35	357.41
Aug.	1	152.99	269.01	+0.91	209.17	+1.20	+ 6.20	88.48	+ 7.17	359.34
	5	159.39	279.58	+0.79	221.49	+0.93	+ 5.95	90.68	+ 7.01	1.28
	9	165.80	290.17	+0.67	233.82	+0.65	+ 5.71	92.90	+ 6.86	3.23
	13	172.22	300.79	+0.55	246.16	+0.36	+ 5.48	95.11	+ 6.72	5.16
	17	178.64	311.43	+0.44	258.50	+0.06	+ 5.25	97.30	+ 6.58	7.05
	21	185.08	322.10	+0.32	270.85	−0.23	+ 5.04	99.46	+ 6.46	8.90
	25	191.52	332.79	+0.21	283.22	−0.53	+ 4.83	101.55	+ 6.34	10.68
	29	197.98	343.50	+0.10	295.59	−0.81	+ 4.62	103.57	+ 6.23	12.38
Sept.	2	204.44	354.22	0.00	307.97	−1.09	+ 4.43	105.49	+ 6.12	13.98
	6	210.91	4.97	−0.09	320.36	−1.35	+ 4.23	107.31	− 6.03	15.47
	10	217.38	15.73	−0.17	332.76	−1.60	+ 4.05	109.00	− 5.94	16.84
	14	223.86	26.51	−0.24	345.17	−1.83	+ 3.87	110.57	− 5.85	18.08
	18	230.35	37.31	−0.31	357.58	−2.03	+ 3.69	112.00	− 5.77	19.19
	22	236.84	48.12	−0.36	10.00	−2.21	+ 3.52	113.27	− 5.69	20.15
	26	243.34	58.95	−0.40	22.42	−2.36	+ 3.35	114.40	− 5.62	20.98
	30	249.83	69.79	−0.43	34.85	−2.48	+ 3.19	115.36	− 5.56	21.65
Oct.	4	256.33	80.64	−0.44	47.27	−2.56	+ 3.03	116.16	− 5.50	22.17
	8	262.82	91.51	−0.45	59.70	−2.62	+ 2.87	116.79	− 5.44	22.55
	12	269.32	102.38	−0.44	72.13	−2.64	+ 2.72	117.24	− 5.38	22.77
	16	275.81	113.27	−0.42	84.55	−2.63	+ 2.57	117.52	− 5.33	22.84
	20	282.30	124.17	−0.39	96.97	−2.58	+ 2.42	117.61	− 5.28	22.75
	24	288.78	135.07	−0.36	109.38	−2.50	+ 2.28	117.53	− 5.24	22.51
	28	295.26	145.99	−0.31	121.79	−2.39	+ 2.14	117.25	− 5.20	22.12
Nov.	1	301.73	156.91	−0.25	134.19	−2.24	+ 2.00	116.78	− 5.16	21.57
	5	308.19	167.83	−0.18	146.58	−2.07	+ 1.86	116.11	− 5.13	20.87
	9	314.65	178.77	−0.11	158.96	−1.88	+ 1.73	115.25	− 5.09	20.02
	13	321.09	189.70	−0.03	171.34	−1.66	+ 1.60	114.18	− 5.06	19.02
	17	327.53	200.65	+0.05	183.70	−1.42	+ 1.47	112.89	+ 5.04	17.86
	21	333.96	211.59	+0.14	196.05	−1.16	+ 1.35	111.39	+ 5.01	16.57
	25	340.38	222.54	+0.23	208.39	−0.89	+ 1.22	109.66	+ 4.99	15.13
	29	346.79	233.50	+0.32	220.72	−0.60	+ 1.10	107.70	+ 4.97	13.55
Dec.	3	353.19	244.45	+0.41	233.03	−0.31	+ 0.98	105.49	+ 4.95	11.86
	7	359.58	255.41	+0.50	245.34	−0.02	+ 0.86	102.99	+ 4.94	10.05
	11	5.96	266.37	+0.59	257.64	+0.27	+ 0.75	100.18	+ 4.92	8.13
	15	12.33	277.33	+0.67	269.93	+0.56	+ 0.63	96.95	+ 4.91	6.14
	19	18.69	288.29	+0.75	282.22	+0.85	+ 0.52	93.14	+ 4.90	4.07
	23	25.05	299.26	+0.82	294.49	+1.12	+ 0.41	88.39	+ 4.89	1.96
	27	31.40	310.22	+0.89	306.76	+1.37	+ 0.30	81.75	+ 4.88	359.83
	31	37.74	321.18	+0.94	319.03	+1.61	+ 0.19	70.30	+ 4.88	357.70

EPHEMERIS FOR PHYSICAL OBSERVATIONS FOR 0^h TERRESTRIAL TIME

Date		Light-time	Magnitude	Surface Brightness	Diameter Eq.	Diameter Polar	Phase	Phase Angle	Defect of Illumination
		m		mag./arcsec^2	″	″		°	″
Jan.	−3	5.56	− 1.1	+ 4.3	14.02	13.94	0.981	15.9	0.27
	1	5.46	− 1.2	+ 4.3	14.26	14.18	0.987	12.9	0.18
	5	5.39	− 1.3	+ 4.2	14.44	14.36	0.993	9.7	0.10
	9	5.35	− 1.4	+ 4.2	14.55	14.47	0.997	6.6	0.05
	13	5.34	− 1.4	+ 4.1	14.58	14.50	0.999	3.7	0.02
	17	5.36	− 1.4	+ 4.1	14.53	14.45	0.999	2.7	0.01
	21	5.41	− 1.4	+ 4.2	14.40	14.32	0.998	4.9	0.03
	25	5.48	− 1.3	+ 4.2	14.20	14.12	0.995	7.9	0.07
	29	5.59	− 1.2	+ 4.3	13.93	13.85	0.991	11.0	0.13
Feb.	2	5.72	− 1.0	+ 4.3	13.61	13.53	0.985	13.9	0.20
	6	5.88	− 0.9	+ 4.4	13.25	13.17	0.979	16.7	0.28
	10	6.06	− 0.8	+ 4.4	12.85	12.78	0.972	19.3	0.36
	14	6.26	− 0.7	+ 4.5	12.44	12.36	0.965	21.7	0.44
	18	6.48	− 0.6	+ 4.5	12.01	11.94	0.957	23.9	0.51
	22	6.72	− 0.5	+ 4.5	11.59	11.52	0.950	25.8	0.58
	26	6.97	− 0.4	+ 4.5	11.17	11.11	0.943	27.6	0.63
Mar.	2	7.24	− 0.3	+ 4.6	10.76	10.70	0.937	29.2	0.68
	6	7.51	− 0.2	+ 4.6	10.37	10.31	0.931	30.5	0.72
	10	7.80	− 0.1	+ 4.6	9.99	9.93	0.925	31.8	0.75
	14	8.09	0.0	+ 4.6	9.63	9.57	0.920	32.8	0.77
	18	8.39	+ 0.1	+ 4.6	9.28	9.23	0.916	33.7	0.78
	22	8.70	+ 0.2	+ 4.6	8.96	8.91	0.912	34.5	0.79
	26	9.00	+ 0.3	+ 4.6	8.65	8.60	0.909	35.2	0.79
	30	9.32	+ 0.4	+ 4.6	8.36	8.31	0.906	35.7	0.78
Apr.	3	9.63	+ 0.5	+ 4.6	8.09	8.04	0.904	36.1	0.78
	7	9.94	+ 0.5	+ 4.6	7.83	7.79	0.902	36.5	0.77
	11	10.26	+ 0.6	+ 4.6	7.59	7.55	0.901	36.8	0.75
	15	10.58	+ 0.7	+ 4.6	7.36	7.32	0.900	36.9	0.74
	19	10.89	+ 0.8	+ 4.6	7.15	7.11	0.899	37.1	0.72
	23	11.20	+ 0.8	+ 4.6	6.95	6.91	0.899	37.1	0.70
	27	11.52	+ 0.9	+ 4.6	6.76	6.73	0.899	37.1	0.68
May	1	11.82	+ 0.9	+ 4.6	6.59	6.55	0.899	37.0	0.66
	5	12.13	+ 1.0	+ 4.6	6.42	6.39	0.900	36.9	0.64
	9	12.43	+ 1.0	+ 4.6	6.26	6.23	0.900	36.8	0.62
	13	12.73	+ 1.1	+ 4.6	6.12	6.08	0.901	36.6	0.60
	17	13.03	+ 1.1	+ 4.6	5.98	5.95	0.903	36.4	0.58
	21	13.32	+ 1.2	+ 4.6	5.85	5.82	0.904	36.1	0.56
	25	13.61	+ 1.2	+ 4.6	5.72	5.69	0.906	35.8	0.54
	29	13.89	+ 1.2	+ 4.6	5.61	5.58	0.907	35.5	0.52
June	2	14.17	+ 1.3	+ 4.6	5.50	5.47	0.909	35.1	0.50
	6	14.44	+ 1.3	+ 4.6	5.39	5.37	0.911	34.7	0.48
	10	14.71	+ 1.4	+ 4.6	5.30	5.27	0.913	34.3	0.46
	14	14.97	+ 1.4	+ 4.6	5.20	5.18	0.915	33.9	0.44
	18	15.22	+ 1.4	+ 4.6	5.12	5.09	0.917	33.4	0.42
	22	15.47	+ 1.4	+ 4.6	5.03	5.01	0.919	33.0	0.41
	26	15.72	+ 1.5	+ 4.6	4.96	4.93	0.922	32.5	0.39
	30	15.95	+ 1.5	+ 4.6	4.88	4.86	0.924	32.0	0.37

EPHEMERIS FOR PHYSICAL OBSERVATIONS FOR 0^h TERRESTRIAL TIME

Date		L_s	Sub-Earth Point		Sub-Solar Point				North Pole	
			Long.	Lat.	Long.	Lat.	Dist.	P.A.	Dist.	P.A.
		°	°	°	°	°	″	°	″	°
Jan.	–3	22.02	122.83	+13.42	138.53	+ 9.29	+ 1.92	96.15	+6.78	352.94
	1	23.89	87.54	+12.83	100.38	+10.04	+ 1.59	93.23	+6.92	352.19
	5	25.75	52.39	+12.20	62.23	+10.78	+ 1.22	88.63	+7.02	351.34
	9	27.60	17.35	+11.54	24.07	+11.50	+ 0.83	80.02	+7.09	350.41
	13	29.44	342.38	+10.86	345.90	+12.22	+ 0.47	57.90	+7.12	349.43
	17	31.27	307.42	+10.19	307.72	+12.91	+ 0.34	354.76	+7.11	348.44
	21	33.10	272.43	+ 9.56	269.54	+13.60	+ 0.62	312.37	+7.06	347.46
	25	34.92	237.37	+ 8.96	231.34	+14.26	+ 0.98	298.67	+6.97	346.54
	29	36.73	202.21	+ 8.43	193.13	+14.92	+ 1.32	292.33	+6.85	345.68
Feb.	2	38.54	166.89	+ 7.98	154.92	+15.55	+ 1.64	288.58	+6.70	344.93
	6	40.34	131.41	+ 7.62	116.69	+16.17	+ 1.90	286.04	+6.53	344.28
	10	42.13	95.74	+ 7.36	78.45	+16.78	+ 2.12	284.21	+6.34	343.77
	14	43.92	59.88	+ 7.19	40.20	+17.37	+ 2.30	282.83	+6.13	343.38
	18	45.70	23.82	+ 7.12	1.94	+17.94	+ 2.43	281.79	+5.93	343.11
	22	47.48	347.57	+ 7.14	323.67	+18.49	+ 2.52	281.01	+5.72	342.98
	26	49.26	311.13	+ 7.25	285.40	+19.02	+ 2.59	280.43	+5.51	342.96
Mar.	2	51.03	274.51	+ 7.44	247.11	+19.54	+ 2.62	280.03	+5.30	343.06
	6	52.79	237.72	+ 7.71	208.81	+20.03	+ 2.63	279.78	+5.11	343.27
	10	54.55	200.77	+ 8.04	170.50	+20.51	+ 2.63	279.66	+4.92	343.58
	14	56.31	163.67	+ 8.44	132.18	+20.97	+ 2.61	279.65	+4.73	343.98
	18	58.07	126.43	+ 8.89	93.85	+21.41	+ 2.57	279.73	+4.56	344.47
	22	59.82	89.07	+ 9.40	55.52	+21.82	+ 2.53	279.90	+4.39	345.04
	26	61.57	51.60	+ 9.94	17.17	+22.22	+ 2.49	280.14	+4.24	345.69
	30	63.32	14.01	+10.52	338.82	+22.60	+ 2.44	280.44	+4.09	346.41
Apr.	3	65.07	336.32	+11.14	300.46	+22.95	+ 2.38	280.79	+3.95	347.19
	7	66.82	298.54	+11.78	262.08	+23.28	+ 2.33	281.19	+3.81	348.04
	11	68.56	260.67	+12.45	223.71	+23.59	+ 2.27	281.63	+3.69	348.94
	15	70.31	222.72	+13.13	185.32	+23.88	+ 2.21	282.09	+3.57	349.89
	19	72.05	184.69	+13.82	146.92	+24.14	+ 2.15	282.58	+3.45	350.89
	23	73.80	146.59	+14.53	108.52	+24.38	+ 2.10	283.09	+3.35	351.94
	27	75.55	108.42	+15.24	70.12	+24.60	+ 2.04	283.62	+3.25	353.03
May	1	77.29	70.19	+15.95	31.70	+24.79	+ 1.98	284.15	+3.15	354.15
	5	79.04	31.89	+16.66	353.28	+24.96	+ 1.93	284.70	+3.06	355.32
	9	80.79	353.53	+17.37	314.85	+25.11	+ 1.87	285.24	+2.97	356.51
	13	82.54	315.12	+18.07	276.42	+25.23	+ 1.82	285.78	+2.89	357.74
	17	84.30	276.65	+18.76	237.99	+25.32	+ 1.77	286.32	+2.82	359.00
	21	86.05	238.13	+19.43	199.54	+25.39	+ 1.72	286.85	+2.74	0.28
	25	87.81	199.55	+20.09	161.10	+25.44	+ 1.67	287.36	+2.68	1.58
	29	89.57	160.93	+20.73	122.65	+25.46	+ 1.62	287.87	+2.61	2.91
June	2	91.34	122.25	+21.35	84.20	+25.45	+ 1.58	288.36	+2.55	4.25
	6	93.11	83.53	+21.95	45.75	+25.42	+ 1.53	288.83	+2.49	5.62
	10	94.88	44.76	+22.51	7.29	+25.36	+ 1.49	289.29	+2.44	6.99
	14	96.66	5.95	+23.05	328.84	+25.27	+ 1.45	289.72	+2.38	8.38
	18	98.44	327.09	+23.55	290.38	+25.16	+ 1.41	290.13	+2.34	9.78
	22	100.23	288.19	+24.02	251.92	+25.03	+ 1.37	290.52	+2.29	11.18
	26	102.03	249.25	+24.45	213.46	+24.86	+ 1.33	290.88	+2.25	12.59
	30	103.83	210.27	+24.84	175.01	+24.67	+ 1.29	291.22	+2.21	14.00

MARS, 2025

EPHEMERIS FOR PHYSICAL OBSERVATIONS FOR 0ʰ TERRESTRIAL TIME

Date		Light-time	Magnitude	Surface Brightness	Diameter Eq.	Diameter Polar	Phase	Phase Angle	Defect of Illumination
		m		mag./arcsec²	″	″		°	″
June	30	15.95	+1.5	+4.6	4.88	4.86	0.924	32.0	0.37
July	4	16.18	+1.5	+4.6	4.81	4.79	0.926	31.5	0.35
	8	16.41	+1.5	+4.6	4.75	4.72	0.929	31.0	0.34
	12	16.63	+1.5	+4.5	4.68	4.66	0.931	30.4	0.32
	16	16.84	+1.5	+4.5	4.63	4.60	0.934	29.9	0.31
	20	17.04	+1.6	+4.5	4.57	4.55	0.936	29.3	0.29
	24	17.24	+1.6	+4.5	4.52	4.50	0.938	28.7	0.28
	28	17.43	+1.6	+4.5	4.47	4.45	0.941	28.1	0.26
Aug.	1	17.62	+1.6	+4.5	4.42	4.40	0.943	27.5	0.25
	5	17.79	+1.6	+4.5	4.38	4.36	0.946	26.9	0.24
	9	17.97	+1.6	+4.5	4.34	4.31	0.948	26.3	0.22
	13	18.13	+1.6	+4.5	4.30	4.28	0.951	25.7	0.21
	17	18.29	+1.6	+4.4	4.26	4.24	0.953	25.1	0.20
	21	18.44	+1.6	+4.4	4.22	4.20	0.955	24.4	0.19
	25	18.58	+1.6	+4.4	4.19	4.17	0.957	23.8	0.18
	29	18.72	+1.6	+4.4	4.16	4.14	0.960	23.2	0.17
Sept.	2	18.85	+1.6	+4.4	4.13	4.11	0.962	22.5	0.16
	6	18.97	+1.6	+4.4	4.11	4.08	0.964	21.8	0.15
	10	19.09	+1.6	+4.4	4.08	4.06	0.966	21.2	0.14
	14	19.20	+1.6	+4.3	4.06	4.04	0.968	20.5	0.13
	18	19.30	+1.6	+4.3	4.03	4.01	0.970	19.8	0.12
	22	19.40	+1.6	+4.3	4.01	3.99	0.972	19.2	0.11
	26	19.49	+1.6	+4.3	4.00	3.98	0.974	18.5	0.10
	30	19.58	+1.6	+4.3	3.98	3.96	0.976	17.8	0.09
Oct.	4	19.65	+1.6	+4.2	3.96	3.94	0.978	17.1	0.09
	8	19.73	+1.5	+4.2	3.95	3.93	0.980	16.4	0.08
	12	19.79	+1.5	+4.2	3.94	3.91	0.981	15.7	0.07
	16	19.85	+1.5	+4.2	3.92	3.90	0.983	15.0	0.07
	20	19.91	+1.5	+4.2	3.91	3.89	0.984	14.3	0.06
	24	19.96	+1.5	+4.2	3.90	3.88	0.986	13.6	0.05
	28	20.00	+1.5	+4.1	3.89	3.87	0.987	12.9	0.05
Nov.	1	20.04	+1.4	+4.1	3.89	3.87	0.989	12.2	0.04
	5	20.07	+1.4	+4.1	3.88	3.86	0.990	11.5	0.04
	9	20.09	+1.4	+4.1	3.88	3.85	0.991	10.8	0.03
	13	20.12	+1.4	+4.1	3.87	3.85	0.992	10.1	0.03
	17	20.13	+1.4	+4.0	3.87	3.85	0.993	9.4	0.03
	21	20.15	+1.4	+4.0	3.87	3.84	0.994	8.7	0.02
	25	20.15	+1.3	+4.0	3.86	3.84	0.995	8.0	0.02
	29	20.16	+1.3	+4.0	3.86	3.84	0.996	7.3	0.02
Dec.	3	20.16	+1.3	+4.0	3.86	3.84	0.997	6.6	0.01
	7	20.15	+1.3	+3.9	3.86	3.84	0.997	5.8	0.01
	11	20.15	+1.2	+3.9	3.87	3.84	0.998	5.2	0.01
	15	20.13	+1.2	+3.9	3.87	3.85	0.998	4.5	0.01
	19	20.12	+1.2	+3.9	3.87	3.85	0.999	3.8	0.00
	23	20.10	+1.2	+3.8	3.87	3.85	0.999	3.1	0.00
	27	20.08	+1.1	+3.8	3.88	3.86	1.000	2.4	0.00
	31	20.06	+1.1	+3.8	3.88	3.86	1.000	1.7	0.00

EPHEMERIS FOR PHYSICAL OBSERVATIONS FOR 0^h TERRESTRIAL TIME

Date		L_s	Sub-Earth Point		Sub-Solar Point				North Pole	
			Long.	Lat.	Long.	Lat.	Dist.	P.A.	Dist.	P.A.
		°	°	°	°	°	″	°	″	°
June	30	103.83	210.27	+24.84	175.01	+24.67	+ 1.29	291.22	+2.21	14.00
July	4	105.63	171.26	+25.19	136.55	+24.46	+ 1.26	291.53	+2.17	15.42
	8	107.45	132.21	+25.50	98.10	+24.21	+ 1.22	291.81	+2.13	16.82
	12	109.26	93.13	+25.76	59.64	+23.95	+ 1.18	292.06	+2.10	18.22
	16	111.09	54.01	+25.98	21.19	+23.65	+ 1.15	292.28	+2.07	19.60
	20	112.93	14.87	+26.14	342.74	+23.33	+ 1.12	292.47	+2.04	20.97
	24	114.77	335.71	+26.26	304.30	+22.98	+ 1.08	292.62	+2.02	22.32
	28	116.62	296.52	+26.32	265.86	+22.61	+ 1.05	292.75	+2.00	23.65
Aug.	1	118.48	257.31	+26.33	227.42	+22.21	+ 1.02	292.83	+1.97	24.95
	5	120.35	218.08	+26.28	188.98	+21.79	+ 0.99	292.89	+1.96	26.22
	9	122.22	178.84	+26.18	150.55	+21.34	+ 0.96	292.91	+1.94	27.45
	13	124.11	139.59	+26.03	112.12	+20.86	+ 0.93	292.89	+1.92	28.64
	17	126.01	100.33	+25.82	73.70	+20.36	+ 0.90	292.83	+1.91	29.78
	21	127.91	61.06	+25.55	35.28	+19.84	+ 0.87	292.74	+1.90	30.88
	25	129.83	21.79	+25.22	356.86	+19.29	+ 0.85	292.61	+1.89	31.92
	29	131.76	342.52	+24.84	318.45	+18.72	+ 0.82	292.44	+1.88	32.90
Sept.	2	133.70	303.25	+24.40	280.04	+18.13	+ 0.79	292.23	+1.87	33.82
	6	135.65	263.98	+23.90	241.64	+17.51	+ 0.76	291.99	+1.87	34.67
	10	137.61	224.72	+23.35	203.24	+16.87	+ 0.74	291.70	+1.87	35.45
	14	139.58	185.47	+22.75	164.84	+16.20	+ 0.71	291.37	+1.86	36.15
	18	141.57	146.23	+22.09	126.44	+15.52	+ 0.68	291.00	+1.86	36.77
	22	143.57	106.99	+21.38	88.04	+14.81	+ 0.66	290.59	+1.86	37.31
	26	145.58	67.77	+20.62	49.65	+14.08	+ 0.63	290.14	+1.86	37.77
	30	147.61	28.57	+19.81	11.26	+13.33	+ 0.61	289.64	+1.86	38.13
Oct.	4	149.65	349.37	+18.95	332.87	+12.57	+ 0.58	289.11	+1.87	38.40
	8	151.70	310.19	+18.04	294.48	+11.78	+ 0.56	288.53	+1.87	38.58
	12	153.77	271.02	+17.09	256.08	+10.97	+ 0.53	287.92	+1.87	38.66
	16	155.85	231.87	+16.10	217.69	+10.15	+ 0.51	287.27	+1.88	38.65
	20	157.94	192.72	+15.07	179.30	+ 9.31	+ 0.48	286.58	+1.88	38.53
	24	160.05	153.59	+14.00	140.90	+ 8.45	+ 0.46	285.86	+1.88	38.31
	28	162.18	114.47	+12.89	102.50	+ 7.58	+ 0.43	285.10	+1.89	38.00
Nov.	1	164.31	75.36	+11.75	64.09	+ 6.69	+ 0.41	284.32	+1.89	37.58
	5	166.47	36.26	+10.58	25.68	+ 5.79	+ 0.39	283.51	+1.90	37.06
	9	168.64	357.16	+ 9.38	347.26	+ 4.87	+ 0.36	282.69	+1.90	36.44
	13	170.82	318.07	+ 8.16	308.84	+ 3.94	+ 0.34	281.86	+1.91	35.72
	17	173.02	278.98	+ 6.90	270.40	+ 3.00	+ 0.32	281.02	+1.91	34.90
	21	175.23	239.89	+ 5.63	231.96	+ 2.05	+ 0.29	280.19	+1.91	33.99
	25	177.46	200.80	+ 4.34	193.51	+ 1.09	+ 0.27	279.39	+1.92	32.98
	29	179.71	161.70	+ 3.04	155.04	+ 0.13	+ 0.24	278.64	+1.92	31.89
Dec.	3	181.97	122.60	+ 1.72	116.57	− 0.85	+ 0.22	277.96	+1.92	30.70
	7	184.24	83.50	+ 0.39	78.07	− 1.82	+ 0.20	277.39	+1.92	29.43
	11	186.53	44.38	− 0.94	39.57	− 2.81	+ 0.17	276.99	−1.92	28.08
	15	188.84	5.25	− 2.27	1.05	− 3.79	+ 0.15	276.85	−1.92	26.66
	19	191.16	326.10	− 3.61	322.51	− 4.78	+ 0.13	277.13	−1.92	25.16
	23	193.49	286.93	− 4.94	283.95	− 5.77	+ 0.10	278.10	−1.92	23.60
	27	195.84	247.74	− 6.27	245.37	− 6.75	+ 0.08	280.34	−1.92	21.97
	31	198.21	208.52	− 7.58	206.77	− 7.73	+ 0.06	285.28	−1.91	20.29

EPHEMERIS FOR PHYSICAL OBSERVATIONS FOR 0^h TERRESTRIAL TIME

Date		Light-time	Magnitude	Surface Brightness	Diameter Eq.	Diameter Polar	Phase Angle	Defect of Illumination
		m		mag./arcsec^2	″	″	°	″
Jan.	−3	34.61	−2.8	+5.3	47.37	44.30	4.3	0.07
	1	34.85	−2.7	+5.3	47.04	44.00	5.1	0.09
	5	35.13	−2.7	+5.3	46.67	43.65	5.9	0.12
	9	35.44	−2.7	+5.3	46.26	43.27	6.6	0.15
	13	35.78	−2.7	+5.3	45.82	42.86	7.3	0.18
	17	36.16	−2.6	+5.3	45.35	42.41	7.9	0.21
	21	36.56	−2.6	+5.3	44.85	41.95	8.5	0.24
	25	36.98	−2.6	+5.3	44.34	41.47	9.0	0.27
	29	37.43	−2.5	+5.3	43.80	40.97	9.4	0.30
Feb.	2	37.90	−2.5	+5.3	43.26	40.46	9.8	0.32
	6	38.39	−2.5	+5.3	42.71	39.95	10.2	0.34
	10	38.89	−2.4	+5.3	42.16	39.43	10.5	0.35
	14	39.40	−2.4	+5.3	41.61	38.92	10.7	0.36
	18	39.92	−2.4	+5.3	41.07	38.41	10.9	0.37
	22	40.45	−2.4	+5.3	40.53	37.91	11.1	0.38
	26	40.99	−2.3	+5.3	40.00	37.41	11.2	0.38
Mar.	2	41.53	−2.3	+5.3	39.48	36.93	11.2	0.38
	6	42.07	−2.3	+5.3	38.98	36.45	11.2	0.37
	10	42.60	−2.2	+5.3	38.48	35.99	11.1	0.36
	14	43.14	−2.2	+5.3	38.01	35.55	11.0	0.35
	18	43.66	−2.2	+5.3	37.55	35.12	10.9	0.34
	22	44.18	−2.2	+5.3	37.11	34.71	10.7	0.33
	26	44.69	−2.1	+5.3	36.68	34.31	10.5	0.31
	30	45.19	−2.1	+5.3	36.28	33.93	10.3	0.29
Apr.	3	45.68	−2.1	+5.3	35.89	33.57	10.0	0.27
	7	46.15	−2.1	+5.3	35.52	33.22	9.7	0.25
	11	46.61	−2.1	+5.3	35.18	32.90	9.4	0.23
	15	47.05	−2.0	+5.3	34.85	32.59	9.0	0.22
	19	47.48	−2.0	+5.3	34.53	32.30	8.6	0.20
	23	47.88	−2.0	+5.3	34.24	32.02	8.2	0.18
	27	48.27	−2.0	+5.3	33.97	31.77	7.8	0.16
May	1	48.63	−2.0	+5.3	33.71	31.53	7.3	0.14
	5	48.98	−2.0	+5.3	33.48	31.31	6.9	0.12
	9	49.30	−2.0	+5.3	33.26	31.11	6.4	0.10
	13	49.60	−1.9	+5.3	33.06	30.92	5.9	0.09
	17	49.87	−1.9	+5.3	32.88	30.75	5.4	0.07
	21	50.12	−1.9	+5.3	32.71	30.59	4.8	0.06
	25	50.35	−1.9	+5.3	32.57	30.46	4.3	0.05
	29	50.55	−1.9	+5.3	32.44	30.34	3.8	0.04
June	2	50.72	−1.9	+5.3	32.32	30.23	3.2	0.03
	6	50.87	−1.9	+5.3	32.23	30.14	2.7	0.02
	10	51.00	−1.9	+5.3	32.15	30.07	2.1	0.01
	14	51.09	−1.9	+5.3	32.09	30.01	1.5	0.01
	18	51.17	−1.9	+5.3	32.05	29.97	1.0	0.00
	22	51.21	−1.9	+5.3	32.02	29.94	0.4	0.00
	26	51.23	−1.9	+5.3	32.01	29.93	0.2	0.00
	30	51.22	−1.9	+5.3	32.01	29.94	0.8	0.00

JUPITER, 2025

EPHEMERIS FOR PHYSICAL OBSERVATIONS FOR 0^h TERRESTRIAL TIME

Date		L_s	Sub-Earth Point		Sub-Solar Point				North Pole	
			Long.	Lat.	Long.	Lat.	Dist.	P.A.	Dist.	P.A.
		°	°	°	°	°	″	°	″	°
Jan.	−3	120.42	266.28	+3.23	261.93	+3.07	+1.79	261.63	+22.12	353.29
	1	120.77	148.72	+3.21	143.58	+3.06	+2.11	261.74	+21.97	353.09
	5	121.11	31.11	+3.20	25.21	+3.05	+2.40	261.79	+21.80	352.91
	9	121.46	273.43	+3.19	266.82	+3.04	+2.66	261.80	+21.61	352.74
	13	121.81	155.69	+3.17	148.41	+3.03	+2.90	261.80	+21.40	352.60
	17	122.16	37.88	+3.16	29.98	+3.02	+3.11	261.80	+21.18	352.48
	21	122.50	280.00	+3.14	271.53	+3.01	+3.30	261.80	+20.95	352.38
	25	122.85	162.06	+3.12	153.07	+2.99	+3.46	261.80	+20.71	352.31
	29	123.20	44.04	+3.11	34.60	+2.98	+3.59	261.82	+20.46	352.26
Feb.	2	123.54	285.97	+3.09	276.11	+2.97	+3.70	261.85	+20.20	352.23
	6	123.89	167.82	+3.07	157.62	+2.96	+3.78	261.90	+19.95	352.23
	10	124.23	49.61	+3.06	39.11	+2.95	+3.84	261.96	+19.69	352.25
	14	124.58	291.34	+3.04	280.60	+2.94	+3.88	262.04	+19.44	352.29
	18	124.93	173.02	+3.03	162.08	+2.92	+3.89	262.13	+19.18	352.36
	22	125.27	54.63	+3.01	43.56	+2.91	+3.89	262.25	+18.93	352.45
	26	125.62	296.20	+2.99	285.03	+2.90	+3.87	262.38	+18.68	352.56
Mar.	2	125.96	177.71	+2.98	166.51	+2.89	+3.83	262.53	+18.44	352.69
	6	126.31	59.18	+2.96	47.98	+2.87	+3.78	262.70	+18.20	352.85
	10	126.65	300.60	+2.95	289.45	+2.86	+3.72	262.88	+17.98	353.03
	14	127.00	181.99	+2.93	170.93	+2.85	+3.64	263.08	+17.75	353.22
	18	127.34	63.34	+2.92	52.41	+2.83	+3.55	263.29	+17.54	353.43
	22	127.69	304.65	+2.90	293.90	+2.82	+3.46	263.52	+17.33	353.67
	26	128.03	185.93	+2.89	175.39	+2.81	+3.35	263.77	+17.14	353.91
	30	128.37	67.19	+2.87	56.89	+2.79	+3.24	264.03	+16.95	354.18
Apr.	3	128.72	308.42	+2.86	298.39	+2.78	+3.12	264.30	+16.77	354.46
	7	129.06	189.62	+2.84	179.91	+2.77	+3.00	264.59	+16.59	354.75
	11	129.40	70.81	+2.82	61.43	+2.75	+2.86	264.89	+16.43	355.06
	15	129.75	311.98	+2.81	302.96	+2.74	+2.73	265.20	+16.28	355.39
	19	130.09	193.14	+2.79	184.51	+2.73	+2.59	265.52	+16.13	355.72
	23	130.43	74.29	+2.78	66.06	+2.71	+2.45	265.86	+16.00	356.07
	27	130.78	315.43	+2.76	307.63	+2.70	+2.30	266.21	+15.87	356.42
May	1	131.12	196.56	+2.74	189.21	+2.69	+2.15	266.56	+15.75	356.79
	5	131.46	77.68	+2.72	70.81	+2.67	+2.00	266.93	+15.64	357.17
	9	131.80	318.81	+2.71	312.42	+2.66	+1.85	267.31	+15.54	357.55
	13	132.14	199.93	+2.69	194.04	+2.64	+1.70	267.69	+15.44	357.94
	17	132.49	81.05	+2.67	75.67	+2.63	+1.54	268.09	+15.36	358.34
	21	132.83	322.18	+2.65	317.33	+2.61	+1.38	268.50	+15.28	358.75
	25	133.17	203.31	+2.63	198.99	+2.60	+1.22	268.93	+15.21	359.16
	29	133.51	84.45	+2.61	80.67	+2.59	+1.07	269.37	+15.15	359.57
June	2	133.85	325.59	+2.59	322.37	+2.57	+0.91	269.83	+15.10	359.99
	6	134.19	206.74	+2.56	204.08	+2.56	+0.75	270.33	+15.06	0.41
	10	134.53	87.91	+2.54	85.81	+2.54	+0.59	270.88	+15.02	0.84
	14	134.87	329.08	+2.52	327.56	+2.53	+0.43	271.56	+14.99	1.26
	18	135.21	210.27	+2.49	209.32	+2.51	+0.27	272.58	+14.97	1.69
	22	135.55	91.48	+2.47	91.09	+2.50	+0.11	275.46	+14.96	2.12
	26	135.89	332.70	+2.45	332.89	+2.48	+0.05	83.54	+14.95	2.54
	30	136.23	213.93	+2.42	214.70	+2.47	+0.21	90.05	+14.96	2.97

EPHEMERIS FOR PHYSICAL OBSERVATIONS FOR 0^h TERRESTRIAL TIME

Date		Light-time	Magnitude	Surface Brightness	Diameter Eq.	Diameter Polar	Phase Angle	Defect of Illumination
		m		mag./arcsec²	″	″	°	″
June	30	51.22	−1.9	+5.3	32.01	29.94	0.8	0.00
July	4	51.18	−1.9	+5.3	32.03	29.96	1.3	0.00
	8	51.12	−1.9	+5.3	32.07	30.00	1.9	0.01
	12	51.03	−1.9	+5.3	32.13	30.05	2.5	0.01
	16	50.92	−1.9	+5.3	32.20	30.11	3.0	0.02
	20	50.78	−1.9	+5.3	32.29	30.20	3.6	0.03
	24	50.61	−1.9	+5.3	32.39	30.30	4.1	0.04
	28	50.42	−1.9	+5.3	32.52	30.41	4.7	0.05
Aug.	1	50.21	−1.9	+5.3	32.66	30.54	5.2	0.07
	5	49.97	−1.9	+5.3	32.81	30.69	5.7	0.08
	9	49.71	−1.9	+5.3	32.99	30.85	6.2	0.10
	13	49.42	−1.9	+5.3	33.18	31.03	6.7	0.11
	17	49.11	−1.9	+5.3	33.39	31.22	7.1	0.13
	21	48.78	−2.0	+5.3	33.61	31.43	7.6	0.15
	25	48.43	−2.0	+5.3	33.86	31.66	8.0	0.17
	29	48.06	−2.0	+5.3	34.12	31.91	8.4	0.18
Sept.	2	47.67	−2.0	+5.3	34.40	32.17	8.8	0.20
	6	47.26	−2.0	+5.4	34.69	32.45	9.2	0.22
	10	46.83	−2.0	+5.4	35.01	32.74	9.5	0.24
	14	46.39	−2.0	+5.4	35.34	33.05	9.8	0.26
	18	45.94	−2.1	+5.4	35.69	33.38	10.1	0.28
	22	45.47	−2.1	+5.4	36.06	33.72	10.4	0.29
	26	44.99	−2.1	+5.4	36.45	34.08	10.6	0.31
	30	44.50	−2.1	+5.4	36.85	34.46	10.8	0.32
Oct.	4	44.00	−2.1	+5.4	37.27	34.85	10.9	0.34
	8	43.49	−2.2	+5.4	37.70	35.25	11.0	0.35
	12	42.98	−2.2	+5.4	38.15	35.67	11.1	0.35
	16	42.47	−2.2	+5.4	38.61	36.10	11.1	0.36
	20	41.96	−2.2	+5.4	39.08	36.55	11.1	0.36
	24	41.44	−2.3	+5.4	39.56	37.00	11.0	0.36
	28	40.94	−2.3	+5.4	40.05	37.46	10.9	0.36
Nov.	1	40.43	−2.3	+5.4	40.55	37.92	10.7	0.35
	5	39.94	−2.3	+5.4	41.05	38.39	10.5	0.34
	9	39.45	−2.4	+5.4	41.56	38.86	10.2	0.33
	13	38.98	−2.4	+5.4	42.06	39.33	9.9	0.31
	17	38.53	−2.4	+5.4	42.55	39.79	9.5	0.29
	21	38.09	−2.5	+5.4	43.04	40.25	9.1	0.27
	25	37.68	−2.5	+5.4	43.51	40.69	8.6	0.24
	29	37.29	−2.5	+5.4	43.97	41.12	8.1	0.22
Dec.	3	36.93	−2.5	+5.4	44.40	41.52	7.5	0.19
	7	36.59	−2.6	+5.3	44.81	41.90	6.8	0.16
	11	36.29	−2.6	+5.3	45.18	42.25	6.2	0.13
	15	36.02	−2.6	+5.3	45.52	42.57	5.5	0.10
	19	35.78	−2.6	+5.3	45.82	42.85	4.7	0.08
	23	35.58	−2.6	+5.3	46.08	43.09	3.9	0.05
	27	35.43	−2.7	+5.3	46.28	43.28	3.1	0.03
	31	35.31	−2.7	+5.3	46.44	43.43	2.2	0.02

EPHEMERIS FOR PHYSICAL OBSERVATIONS FOR 0h TERRESTRIAL TIME

Date		L_s	Sub-Earth Point		Sub-Solar Point				North Pole	
			Long.	Lat.	Long.	Lat.	Dist.	P.A.	Dist.	P.A.
		°	°	°	°	°	″	°	″	°
June	30	136.23	213.93	+2.42	214.70	+2.47	+0.21	90.05	+14.96	2.97
July	4	136.57	95.19	+2.40	96.52	+2.45	+0.37	91.33	+14.97	3.39
	8	136.91	336.46	+2.37	338.37	+2.44	+0.53	92.07	+14.99	3.82
	12	137.25	217.76	+2.34	220.22	+2.42	+0.69	92.65	+15.01	4.23
	16	137.59	99.07	+2.32	102.10	+2.40	+0.85	93.15	+15.05	4.65
	20	137.93	340.41	+2.29	343.99	+2.39	+1.01	93.62	+15.09	5.06
	24	138.27	221.77	+2.26	225.89	+2.37	+1.16	94.05	+15.14	5.46
	28	138.60	103.16	+2.24	107.81	+2.36	+1.32	94.47	+15.19	5.86
Aug.	1	138.94	344.57	+2.21	349.75	+2.34	+1.47	94.87	+15.26	6.25
	5	139.28	226.01	+2.18	231.70	+2.33	+1.63	95.25	+15.33	6.64
	9	139.62	107.48	+2.15	113.67	+2.31	+1.78	95.63	+15.42	7.01
	13	139.96	348.97	+2.12	355.65	+2.29	+1.93	95.99	+15.50	7.38
	17	140.29	230.50	+2.09	237.64	+2.28	+2.07	96.34	+15.60	7.74
	21	140.63	112.05	+2.07	119.65	+2.26	+2.22	96.68	+15.71	8.09
	25	140.97	353.64	+2.04	1.67	+2.25	+2.36	97.01	+15.82	8.43
	29	141.30	235.26	+2.01	243.70	+2.23	+2.50	97.32	+15.94	8.76
Sept.	2	141.64	116.92	+1.98	125.74	+2.21	+2.64	97.62	+16.08	9.07
	6	141.98	358.61	+1.95	7.80	+2.20	+2.77	97.92	+16.21	9.37
	10	142.31	240.34	+1.93	249.86	+2.18	+2.90	98.19	+16.36	9.67
	14	142.65	122.10	+1.90	131.94	+2.16	+3.02	98.46	+16.52	9.94
	18	142.98	3.91	+1.87	14.02	+2.15	+3.13	98.71	+16.68	10.21
	22	143.32	245.75	+1.85	256.11	+2.13	+3.24	98.94	+16.85	10.45
	26	143.66	127.63	+1.82	138.21	+2.11	+3.34	99.16	+17.03	10.69
	30	143.99	9.56	+1.80	20.32	+2.10	+3.44	99.36	+17.22	10.90
Oct.	4	144.33	251.52	+1.78	262.43	+2.08	+3.52	99.55	+17.42	11.10
	8	144.66	133.53	+1.75	144.54	+2.06	+3.60	99.72	+17.62	11.29
	12	145.00	15.59	+1.73	26.66	+2.04	+3.66	99.87	+17.83	11.45
	16	145.33	257.69	+1.71	268.78	+2.03	+3.71	100.01	+18.04	11.60
	20	145.66	139.83	+1.69	150.90	+2.01	+3.75	100.13	+18.27	11.73
	24	146.00	22.02	+1.67	33.02	+1.99	+3.77	100.22	+18.49	11.84
	28	146.33	264.26	+1.66	275.14	+1.98	+3.78	100.30	+18.72	11.92
Nov.	1	146.67	146.54	+1.64	157.25	+1.96	+3.77	100.35	+18.95	11.99
	5	147.00	28.87	+1.63	39.36	+1.94	+3.74	100.39	+19.19	12.04
	9	147.33	271.25	+1.61	281.46	+1.92	+3.68	100.40	+19.42	12.06
	13	147.67	153.67	+1.60	163.56	+1.91	+3.61	100.39	+19.66	12.07
	17	148.00	36.13	+1.59	45.64	+1.89	+3.52	100.36	+19.89	12.05
	21	148.33	278.64	+1.58	287.72	+1.87	+3.40	100.30	+20.12	12.01
	25	148.66	161.18	+1.58	169.78	+1.85	+3.25	100.23	+20.34	11.95
	29	149.00	43.77	+1.57	51.83	+1.84	+3.08	100.12	+20.55	11.87
Dec.	3	149.33	286.38	+1.57	293.86	+1.82	+2.89	99.99	+20.75	11.77
	7	149.66	169.03	+1.57	175.88	+1.80	+2.67	99.83	+20.94	11.64
	11	149.99	51.70	+1.56	57.87	+1.78	+2.43	99.65	+21.12	11.50
	15	150.33	294.40	+1.56	299.85	+1.76	+2.16	99.43	+21.28	11.34
	19	150.66	177.11	+1.57	181.80	+1.75	+1.87	99.18	+21.42	11.17
	23	150.99	59.83	+1.57	63.73	+1.73	+1.57	98.87	+21.54	10.98
	27	151.32	302.56	+1.57	305.64	+1.71	+1.25	98.47	+21.63	10.77
	31	151.65	185.29	+1.58	187.53	+1.69	+0.91	97.92	+21.71	10.56

EPHEMERIS FOR PHYSICAL OBSERVATIONS FOR 0^h TERRESTRIAL TIME

Date		Light-time	Magnitude	Surface Brightness	Diameter Eq.	Diameter Polar	Phase Angle	Defect of Illumination
		m		mag./arcsec^2	″	″	°	″
Jan.	−3	82.88	+1.0	+6.7	16.68	15.05	5.4	0.04
	1	83.38	+1.0	+6.7	16.58	14.96	5.3	0.03
	5	83.86	+1.0	+6.7	16.48	14.88	5.1	0.03
	9	84.33	+1.1	+6.7	16.39	14.79	4.9	0.03
	13	84.78	+1.1	+6.7	16.30	14.71	4.7	0.03
	17	85.21	+1.1	+6.7	16.22	14.64	4.4	0.02
	21	85.61	+1.1	+6.7	16.15	14.57	4.2	0.02
	25	85.99	+1.1	+6.7	16.07	14.51	3.9	0.02
	29	86.34	+1.1	+6.7	16.01	14.45	3.6	0.02
Feb.	2	86.66	+1.1	+6.7	15.95	14.39	3.3	0.01
	6	86.95	+1.1	+6.7	15.90	14.34	3.0	0.01
	10	87.22	+1.1	+6.7	15.85	14.30	2.7	0.01
	14	87.45	+1.1	+6.7	15.81	14.26	2.3	0.01
	18	87.65	+1.1	+6.7	15.77	14.23	2.0	0.00
	22	87.82	+1.1	+6.7	15.74	14.20	1.7	0.00
	26	87.96	+1.1	+6.7	15.71	14.18	1.3	0.00
Mar.	2	88.06	+1.1	+6.7	15.70	14.16	1.0	0.00
	6	88.13	+1.1	+6.7	15.68	14.15	0.6	0.00
	10	88.17	+1.1	+6.7	15.68	14.14	0.3	0.00
	14	88.17	+1.1	+6.7	15.68	14.14	0.2	0.00
	18	88.14	+1.1	+6.7	15.68	14.15	0.5	0.00
	22	88.08	+1.1	+6.7	15.69	14.16	0.9	0.00
	26	87.98	+1.2	+6.7	15.71	14.17	1.2	0.00
	30	87.85	+1.2	+6.7	15.73	14.19	1.6	0.00
Apr.	3	87.69	+1.2	+6.7	15.76	14.22	1.9	0.00
	7	87.49	+1.2	+6.7	15.80	14.25	2.3	0.01
	11	87.26	+1.2	+6.7	15.84	14.29	2.6	0.01
	15	87.01	+1.2	+6.7	15.89	14.33	2.9	0.01
	19	86.72	+1.2	+6.7	15.94	14.38	3.2	0.01
	23	86.41	+1.2	+6.7	16.00	14.43	3.5	0.01
	27	86.07	+1.2	+6.7	16.06	14.49	3.8	0.02
May	1	85.71	+1.2	+6.7	16.13	14.55	4.1	0.02
	5	85.32	+1.2	+6.7	16.20	14.62	4.4	0.02
	9	84.90	+1.1	+6.7	16.28	14.69	4.6	0.03
	13	84.47	+1.1	+6.7	16.36	14.76	4.9	0.03
	17	84.01	+1.1	+6.7	16.45	14.84	5.1	0.03
	21	83.54	+1.1	+6.7	16.55	14.93	5.3	0.03
	25	83.05	+1.1	+6.7	16.64	15.02	5.5	0.04
	29	82.55	+1.1	+6.7	16.74	15.11	5.6	0.04
June	2	82.03	+1.1	+6.7	16.85	15.20	5.7	0.04
	6	81.50	+1.1	+6.7	16.96	15.30	5.9	0.04
	10	80.96	+1.0	+6.7	17.07	15.41	6.0	0.04
	14	80.42	+1.0	+6.7	17.19	15.51	6.0	0.05
	18	79.87	+1.0	+6.7	17.31	15.62	6.1	0.05
	22	79.31	+1.0	+6.7	17.43	15.73	6.1	0.05
	26	78.76	+1.0	+6.7	17.55	15.84	6.1	0.05
	30	78.21	+0.9	+6.7	17.67	15.95	6.1	0.05

EPHEMERIS FOR PHYSICAL OBSERVATIONS FOR 0^h TERRESTRIAL TIME

Date		L_s	Sub-Earth Point		Sub-Solar Point				North Pole	
			Long.	Lat.	Long.	Lat.	Dist.	P.A.	Dist.	P.A.
		°	°	°	°	°	″	°	″	°
Jan.	−3	175.73	317.66	+5.41	312.84	+2.36	+0.79	248.08	+7.50	5.25
	1	175.86	320.30	+5.23	315.62	+2.29	+0.76	248.20	+7.46	5.23
	5	175.99	322.93	+5.04	318.40	+2.21	+0.73	248.34	+7.41	5.21
	9	176.13	325.55	+4.84	321.20	+2.14	+0.70	248.48	+7.37	5.19
	13	176.26	328.16	+4.63	324.00	+2.07	+0.66	248.64	+7.34	5.17
	17	176.39	330.78	+4.41	326.82	+2.00	+0.62	248.81	+7.30	5.14
	21	176.52	333.39	+4.18	329.65	+1.92	+0.59	249.01	+7.27	5.12
	25	176.65	336.00	+3.94	332.50	+1.85	+0.54	249.23	+7.24	5.09
	29	176.78	338.61	+3.69	335.36	+1.78	+0.50	249.49	+7.21	5.07
Feb.	2	176.91	341.22	+3.44	338.23	+1.71	+0.46	249.81	+7.18	5.04
	6	177.05	343.84	+3.18	341.13	+1.63	+0.41	250.19	+7.16	5.01
	10	177.18	346.47	+2.91	344.04	+1.56	+0.37	250.68	+7.14	4.98
	14	177.31	349.11	+2.64	346.96	+1.49	+0.32	251.30	+7.12	4.95
	18	177.44	351.76	+2.37	349.91	+1.42	+0.28	252.14	+7.11	4.92
	22	177.57	354.41	+2.09	352.87	+1.34	+0.23	253.34	+7.10	4.89
	26	177.70	357.09	+1.81	355.85	+1.27	+0.18	255.19	+7.08	4.86
Mar.	2	177.84	359.77	+1.53	358.85	+1.20	+0.13	258.41	+7.08	4.82
	6	177.97	2.48	+1.25	1.87	+1.12	+0.08	265.29	+7.07	4.79
	10	178.10	5.20	+0.97	4.91	+1.05	+0.04	288.10	+7.07	4.76
	14	178.23	7.93	+0.68	7.96	+0.98	+0.03	11.43	+7.07	4.72
	18	178.36	10.69	+0.40	11.04	+0.91	+0.07	45.01	+7.07	4.69
	22	178.49	13.47	+0.12	14.13	+0.83	+0.12	53.71	+7.08	4.65
	26	178.63	16.26	−0.15	17.24	+0.76	+0.17	57.48	−7.09	4.62
	30	178.76	19.08	−0.43	20.38	+0.69	+0.22	59.57	−7.10	4.58
Apr.	3	178.89	21.92	−0.70	23.53	+0.61	+0.26	60.91	−7.11	4.55
	7	179.02	24.79	−0.96	26.69	+0.54	+0.31	61.84	−7.12	4.52
	11	179.15	27.67	−1.22	29.88	+0.47	+0.36	62.53	−7.14	4.48
	15	179.29	30.59	−1.47	33.08	+0.40	+0.40	63.06	−7.16	4.45
	19	179.42	33.52	−1.72	36.30	+0.32	+0.45	63.49	−7.19	4.42
	23	179.55	36.48	−1.96	39.53	+0.25	+0.49	63.84	−7.21	4.39
	27	179.68	39.47	−2.19	42.78	+0.18	+0.54	64.15	−7.24	4.35
May	1	179.82	42.48	−2.42	46.04	+0.10	+0.58	64.41	−7.27	4.32
	5	179.95	45.52	−2.63	49.32	+0.03	+0.62	64.64	−7.30	4.29
	9	180.08	48.58	−2.84	52.61	−0.04	+0.66	64.85	−7.34	4.27
	13	180.21	51.67	−3.03	55.91	−0.12	+0.69	65.04	−7.37	4.24
	17	180.34	54.79	−3.22	59.23	−0.19	+0.73	65.21	−7.41	4.21
	21	180.48	57.93	−3.39	62.55	−0.26	+0.76	65.38	−7.45	4.19
	25	180.61	61.10	−3.55	65.88	−0.34	+0.79	65.53	−7.50	4.16
	29	180.74	64.29	−3.70	69.22	−0.41	+0.82	65.69	−7.54	4.14
June	2	180.87	67.51	−3.84	72.57	−0.48	+0.84	65.83	−7.59	4.12
	6	181.01	70.76	−3.96	75.93	−0.56	+0.87	65.97	−7.64	4.10
	10	181.14	74.03	−4.07	79.29	−0.63	+0.89	66.11	−7.69	4.08
	14	181.27	77.32	−4.17	82.65	−0.70	+0.90	66.25	−7.74	4.07
	18	181.40	80.64	−4.25	86.02	−0.78	+0.92	66.39	−7.79	4.05
	22	181.54	83.99	−4.32	89.39	−0.85	+0.92	66.53	−7.85	4.04
	26	181.67	87.35	−4.37	92.76	−0.92	+0.93	66.68	−7.90	4.03
	30	181.80	90.74	−4.41	96.12	−0.99	+0.93	66.83	−7.96	4.02

EPHEMERIS FOR PHYSICAL OBSERVATIONS FOR 0^h TERRESTRIAL TIME

Date		Light-time	Magnitude	Surface Brightness	Diameter		Phase Angle	Defect of Illumination
					Eq.	Polar		
		m		mag./arcsec^2	″	″	°	″
June	30	78.21	+0.9	+ 6.7	17.67	15.95	6.1	0.05
July	4	77.66	+0.9	+ 6.7	17.80	16.06	6.0	0.05
	8	77.12	+0.9	+ 6.7	17.92	16.17	5.9	0.05
	12	76.59	+0.9	+ 6.7	18.05	16.29	5.8	0.05
	16	76.07	+0.9	+ 6.7	18.17	16.40	5.7	0.04
	20	75.56	+0.8	+ 6.7	18.29	16.51	5.5	0.04
	24	75.07	+0.8	+ 6.7	18.41	16.61	5.3	0.04
	28	74.60	+0.8	+ 6.7	18.53	16.72	5.1	0.04
Aug.	1	74.15	+0.8	+ 6.7	18.64	16.82	4.8	0.03
	5	73.72	+0.8	+ 6.7	18.75	16.92	4.6	0.03
	9	73.32	+0.7	+ 6.7	18.85	17.01	4.3	0.03
	13	72.95	+0.7	+ 6.7	18.95	17.10	4.0	0.02
	17	72.60	+0.7	+ 6.7	19.04	17.18	3.6	0.02
	21	72.29	+0.7	+ 6.7	19.12	17.25	3.3	0.02
	25	72.01	+0.7	+ 6.7	19.20	17.32	2.9	0.01
	29	71.76	+0.6	+ 6.7	19.26	17.38	2.5	0.01
Sept.	2	71.55	+0.6	+ 6.7	19.32	17.43	2.1	0.01
	6	71.38	+0.6	+ 6.7	19.36	17.47	1.7	0.00
	10	71.24	+0.6	+ 6.7	19.40	17.50	1.3	0.00
	14	71.15	+0.6	+ 6.7	19.43	17.53	0.8	0.00
	18	71.10	+0.6	+ 6.7	19.44	17.54	0.5	0.00
	22	71.08	+0.6	+ 6.7	19.45	17.54	0.3	0.00
	26	71.11	+0.6	+ 6.7	19.44	17.54	0.6	0.00
	30	71.18	+0.6	+ 6.7	19.42	17.52	1.0	0.00
Oct.	4	71.29	+0.6	+ 6.7	19.39	17.49	1.4	0.00
	8	71.43	+0.6	+ 6.7	19.35	17.45	1.8	0.00
	12	71.62	+0.7	+ 6.7	19.30	17.41	2.2	0.01
	16	71.84	+0.7	+ 6.7	19.24	17.35	2.6	0.01
	20	72.10	+0.7	+ 6.7	19.17	17.29	3.0	0.01
	24	72.40	+0.7	+ 6.7	19.09	17.22	3.4	0.02
	28	72.73	+0.7	+ 6.7	19.00	17.14	3.7	0.02
Nov.	1	73.09	+0.8	+ 6.7	18.91	17.06	4.1	0.02
	5	73.48	+0.8	+ 6.7	18.81	16.97	4.4	0.03
	9	73.90	+0.8	+ 6.7	18.70	16.87	4.7	0.03
	13	74.34	+0.8	+ 6.7	18.59	16.77	4.9	0.03
	17	74.81	+0.8	+ 6.7	18.48	16.67	5.1	0.04
	21	75.29	+0.9	+ 6.7	18.36	16.56	5.3	0.04
	25	75.79	+0.9	+ 6.7	18.24	16.45	5.5	0.04
	29	76.31	+0.9	+ 6.7	18.11	16.34	5.6	0.04
Dec.	3	76.84	+0.9	+ 6.7	17.99	16.23	5.8	0.04
	7	77.38	+0.9	+ 6.7	17.86	16.11	5.8	0.05
	11	77.93	+0.9	+ 6.7	17.74	16.00	5.9	0.05
	15	78.48	+1.0	+ 6.7	17.61	15.89	5.9	0.05
	19	79.03	+1.0	+ 6.7	17.49	15.78	5.9	0.05
	23	79.58	+1.0	+ 6.7	17.37	15.67	5.9	0.04
	27	80.12	+1.0	+ 6.7	17.25	15.56	5.8	0.04
	31	80.67	+1.0	+ 6.7	17.13	15.46	5.8	0.04

SATURN, 2025

EPHEMERIS FOR PHYSICAL OBSERVATIONS FOR 0^h TERRESTRIAL TIME

Date		L_s	Sub-Earth Point		Sub-Solar Point				North Pole	
			Long.	Lat.	Long.	Lat.	Dist.	P.A.	Dist.	P.A.
		°	°	°	°	°	″	°	″	°
June	30	181.80	90.74	− 4.41	96.12	− 0.99	+ 0.93	66.83	− 7.96	4.02
July	4	181.93	94.15	− 4.43	99.49	− 1.07	+ 0.93	66.98	− 8.01	4.01
	8	182.07	97.58	− 4.44	102.85	− 1.14	+ 0.92	67.14	− 8.07	4.01
	12	182.20	101.02	− 4.43	106.21	− 1.22	+ 0.91	67.31	− 8.12	4.01
	16	182.33	104.49	− 4.41	109.56	− 1.29	+ 0.90	67.49	− 8.18	4.01
	20	182.47	107.97	− 4.37	112.90	− 1.36	+ 0.88	67.68	− 8.23	4.01
	24	182.60	111.47	− 4.32	116.23	− 1.44	+ 0.85	67.89	− 8.29	4.01
	28	182.73	114.98	− 4.25	119.55	− 1.51	+ 0.82	68.12	− 8.34	4.02
Aug.	1	182.86	118.50	− 4.17	122.86	− 1.58	+ 0.79	68.37	− 8.39	4.03
	5	183.00	122.03	− 4.07	126.16	− 1.66	+ 0.75	68.66	− 8.44	4.04
	9	183.13	125.56	− 3.96	129.44	− 1.73	+ 0.70	68.99	− 8.49	4.05
	13	183.26	129.11	− 3.84	132.71	− 1.80	+ 0.66	69.37	− 8.53	4.06
	17	183.40	132.65	− 3.71	135.96	− 1.88	+ 0.60	69.82	− 8.57	4.08
	21	183.53	136.20	− 3.57	139.20	− 1.95	+ 0.55	70.37	− 8.61	4.09
	25	183.66	139.74	− 3.42	142.41	− 2.02	+ 0.49	71.07	− 8.65	4.11
	29	183.80	143.28	− 3.26	145.61	− 2.10	+ 0.42	71.99	− 8.68	4.13
Sept.	2	183.93	146.81	− 3.09	148.78	− 2.17	+ 0.35	73.25	− 8.70	4.15
	6	184.06	150.34	− 2.92	151.93	− 2.24	+ 0.29	75.12	− 8.73	4.17
	10	184.20	153.84	− 2.75	155.07	− 2.32	+ 0.21	78.24	− 8.74	4.19
	14	184.33	157.34	− 2.57	158.18	− 2.39	+ 0.14	84.47	− 8.76	4.22
	18	184.46	160.82	− 2.39	161.26	− 2.46	+ 0.08	102.28	− 8.76	4.24
	22	184.60	164.27	− 2.21	164.33	− 2.54	+ 0.05	173.00	− 8.77	4.26
	26	184.73	167.71	− 2.03	167.37	− 2.61	+ 0.10	219.79	− 8.76	4.28
	30	184.86	171.12	− 1.85	170.39	− 2.68	+ 0.17	231.40	− 8.76	4.31
Oct.	4	185.00	174.50	− 1.68	173.38	− 2.76	+ 0.24	236.15	− 8.74	4.33
	8	185.13	177.85	− 1.52	176.35	− 2.83	+ 0.31	238.73	− 8.72	4.35
	12	185.26	181.17	− 1.36	179.31	− 2.90	+ 0.38	240.35	− 8.70	4.37
	16	185.40	184.46	− 1.21	182.24	− 2.98	+ 0.44	241.48	− 8.68	4.39
	20	185.53	187.71	− 1.07	185.14	− 3.05	+ 0.51	242.31	− 8.64	4.41
	24	185.66	190.93	− 0.95	188.03	− 3.13	+ 0.57	242.96	− 8.61	4.43
	28	185.80	194.12	− 0.83	190.90	− 3.20	+ 0.62	243.49	− 8.57	4.44
Nov.	1	185.93	197.27	− 0.73	193.76	− 3.27	+ 0.67	243.93	− 8.53	4.46
	5	186.07	200.38	− 0.65	196.59	− 3.35	+ 0.72	244.30	− 8.48	4.47
	9	186.20	203.45	− 0.58	199.41	− 3.42	+ 0.76	244.62	− 8.44	4.48
	13	186.33	206.49	− 0.52	202.22	− 3.49	+ 0.79	244.91	− 8.39	4.49
	17	186.47	209.49	− 0.48	205.01	− 3.57	+ 0.83	245.16	− 8.33	4.50
	21	186.60	212.46	− 0.46	207.80	− 3.64	+ 0.85	245.40	− 8.28	4.50
	25	186.74	215.39	− 0.45	210.57	− 3.71	+ 0.87	245.61	− 8.22	4.51
	29	186.87	218.29	− 0.46	213.33	− 3.79	+ 0.89	245.81	− 8.17	4.51
Dec.	3	187.00	221.15	− 0.49	216.09	− 3.86	+ 0.90	245.99	− 8.11	4.51
	7	187.14	223.99	− 0.54	218.84	− 3.93	+ 0.91	246.17	− 8.06	4.50
	11	187.27	226.80	− 0.60	221.59	− 4.01	+ 0.91	246.33	− 8.00	4.50
	15	187.41	229.58	− 0.67	224.34	− 4.08	+ 0.91	246.49	− 7.94	4.49
	19	187.54	232.33	− 0.76	227.08	− 4.15	+ 0.90	246.65	− 7.89	4.48
	23	187.67	235.06	− 0.87	229.83	− 4.23	+ 0.89	246.80	− 7.83	4.47
	27	187.81	237.77	− 1.00	232.57	− 4.30	+ 0.88	246.95	− 7.78	4.46
	31	187.94	240.46	− 1.13	235.33	− 4.38	+ 0.86	247.11	− 7.73	4.44

EPHEMERIS FOR PHYSICAL OBSERVATIONS
FOR 0h TERRESTRIAL TIME

Date		Light-time	Magnitude	Equatorial Diameter	Phase Angle	L_s	Sub-Earth Lat.	North Pole	
								Dist.	P.A.
		m		″	°	°	°	″	°
Jan.	−3	156.55	+5.7	3.74	2.0	67.81	+ 65.71	+ 0.78	273.39
	5	157.38	+5.7	3.72	2.2	67.90	+ 65.52	+ 0.78	273.20
	13	158.32	+5.7	3.70	2.5	67.99	+ 65.39	+ 0.78	273.07
	21	159.33	+5.7	3.68	2.7	68.08	+ 65.30	+ 0.78	272.98
	29	160.41	+5.7	3.65	2.8	68.17	+ 65.26	+ 0.78	272.95
Feb.	6	161.53	+5.7	3.63	2.9	68.26	+ 65.27	+ 0.77	272.97
	14	162.66	+5.7	3.60	2.9	68.35	+ 65.34	+ 0.76	273.05
	22	163.79	+5.8	3.58	2.9	68.44	+ 65.46	+ 0.75	273.17
Mar.	2	164.89	+5.8	3.55	2.8	68.53	+ 65.63	+ 0.74	273.35
	10	165.94	+5.8	3.53	2.6	68.62	+ 65.84	+ 0.73	273.58
	18	166.93	+5.8	3.51	2.4	68.71	+ 66.09	+ 0.72	273.86
	26	167.83	+5.8	3.49	2.2	68.80	+ 66.39	+ 0.71	274.19
Apr.	3	168.64	+5.8	3.48	1.9	68.90	+ 66.72	+ 0.70	274.56
	11	169.33	+5.8	3.46	1.6	68.99	+ 67.07	+ 0.69	274.97
	19	169.90	+5.8	3.45	1.3	69.08	+ 67.45	+ 0.67	275.42
	27	170.34	+5.8	3.44	1.0	69.17	+ 67.85	+ 0.66	275.91
May	5	170.65	+5.8	3.44	0.6	69.26	+ 68.26	+ 0.65	276.42
	13	170.81	+5.8	3.43	0.2	69.35	+ 68.68	+ 0.63	276.97
	21	170.83	+5.8	3.43	0.1	69.44	+ 69.10	+ 0.62	277.53
	29	170.71	+5.8	3.43	0.5	69.53	+ 69.52	+ 0.61	278.11
June	6	170.44	+5.8	3.44	0.9	69.62	+ 69.93	+ 0.60	278.70
	14	170.04	+5.8	3.45	1.2	69.71	+ 70.33	+ 0.59	279.28
	22	169.51	+5.8	3.46	1.6	69.80	+ 70.71	+ 0.58	279.86
	30	168.86	+5.8	3.47	1.9	69.89	+ 71.06	+ 0.57	280.43
July	8	168.10	+5.8	3.49	2.1	69.98	+ 71.39	+ 0.57	280.97
	16	167.24	+5.8	3.50	2.4	70.07	+ 71.69	+ 0.56	281.47
	24	166.30	+5.8	3.52	2.6	70.17	+ 71.95	+ 0.56	281.92
Aug.	1	165.28	+5.8	3.55	2.8	70.26	+ 72.18	+ 0.55	282.32
	9	164.20	+5.8	3.57	2.9	70.35	+ 72.36	+ 0.55	282.65
	17	163.09	+5.7	3.59	3.0	70.44	+ 72.50	+ 0.55	282.91
	25	161.97	+5.7	3.62	3.0	70.53	+ 72.60	+ 0.55	283.09
Sept.	2	160.84	+5.7	3.64	2.9	70.62	+ 72.64	+ 0.55	283.18
	10	159.74	+5.7	3.67	2.8	70.71	+ 72.65	+ 0.56	283.18
	18	158.68	+5.7	3.69	2.7	70.80	+ 72.60	+ 0.56	283.09
	26	157.68	+5.7	3.72	2.5	70.89	+ 72.51	+ 0.57	282.92
Oct.	4	156.76	+5.7	3.74	2.3	70.98	+ 72.37	+ 0.58	282.67
	12	155.95	+5.6	3.76	2.0	71.07	+ 72.20	+ 0.59	282.35
	20	155.26	+5.6	3.78	1.6	71.17	+ 71.98	+ 0.59	281.97
	28	154.70	+5.6	3.79	1.3	71.26	+ 71.74	+ 0.60	281.55
Nov.	5	154.29	+5.6	3.80	0.9	71.35	+ 71.47	+ 0.61	281.10
	13	154.03	+5.6	3.81	0.5	71.44	+ 71.18	+ 0.63	280.63
	21	153.94	+5.6	3.81	0.0	71.53	+ 70.89	+ 0.63	280.16
	29	154.01	+5.6	3.81	0.4	71.62	+ 70.59	+ 0.64	279.69
Dec.	7	154.25	+5.6	3.80	0.8	71.71	+ 70.30	+ 0.65	279.26
	15	154.65	+5.6	3.79	1.2	71.80	+ 70.02	+ 0.66	278.85
	23	155.20	+5.6	3.78	1.6	71.89	+ 69.77	+ 0.66	278.49
	31	155.89	+5.6	3.76	1.9	71.98	+ 69.55	+ 0.67	278.18
	36	157.38	+5.7	3.72	2.2	67.90	+ 65.52	+ 0.78	273.20

EPHEMERIS FOR PHYSICAL OBSERVATIONS FOR 0^h TERRESTRIAL TIME

Date		Light-time	Magnitude	Equatorial Diameter	Phase Angle	L_s	Sub-Earth Lat.	North Pole	
								Dist.	P.A.
		m		″	°	°	°	″	°
Jan.	−3	249.84	+7.8	2.27	1.9	313.04	−21.58	−1.04	318.26
	5	250.96	+7.8	2.26	1.8	313.09	−21.54	−1.04	318.22
	13	252.04	+7.8	2.25	1.7	313.14	−21.50	−1.04	318.16
	21	253.04	+7.8	2.24	1.6	313.19	−21.45	−1.03	318.09
	29	253.96	+7.8	2.24	1.4	313.23	−21.39	−1.03	318.01
Feb.	6	254.78	+7.8	2.23	1.2	313.28	−21.31	−1.03	317.92
	14	255.47	+7.8	2.22	1.0	313.33	−21.23	−1.02	317.82
	22	256.04	+7.8	2.22	0.8	313.38	−21.14	−1.02	317.72
Mar.	2	256.47	+7.8	2.21	0.6	313.43	−21.05	−1.02	317.61
	10	256.75	+7.8	2.21	0.3	313.48	−20.95	−1.02	317.50
	18	256.88	+7.8	2.21	0.1	313.52	−20.85	−1.02	317.38
	26	256.86	+7.8	2.21	0.2	313.57	−20.75	−1.02	317.27
Apr.	3	256.68	+7.8	2.21	0.4	313.62	−20.64	−1.02	317.16
	11	256.37	+7.8	2.22	0.7	313.67	−20.54	−1.02	317.06
	19	255.91	+7.8	2.22	0.9	313.72	−20.44	−1.03	316.96
	27	255.32	+7.8	2.22	1.1	313.77	−20.35	−1.03	316.87
May	5	254.61	+7.8	2.23	1.3	313.81	−20.26	−1.03	316.78
	13	253.79	+7.8	2.24	1.5	313.86	−20.17	−1.04	316.71
	21	252.88	+7.8	2.25	1.7	313.91	−20.10	−1.04	316.64
	29	251.89	+7.8	2.25	1.8	313.96	−20.03	−1.05	316.58
June	6	250.84	+7.8	2.26	1.9	314.01	−19.98	−1.05	316.54
	14	249.75	+7.8	2.27	1.9	314.06	−19.94	−1.05	316.50
	22	248.63	+7.8	2.28	1.9	314.10	−19.90	−1.06	316.48
	30	247.51	+7.7	2.29	1.9	314.15	−19.88	−1.06	316.47
July	8	246.41	+7.7	2.30	1.9	314.20	−19.88	−1.07	316.47
	16	245.35	+7.7	2.31	1.8	314.25	−19.88	−1.07	316.48
	24	244.34	+7.7	2.32	1.7	314.30	−19.90	−1.08	316.50
Aug.	1	243.40	+7.7	2.33	1.6	314.34	−19.92	−1.08	316.53
	9	242.56	+7.7	2.34	1.4	314.39	19.96	1.09	316.57
	17	241.83	+7.7	2.35	1.2	314.44	−20.01	−1.09	316.63
	25	241.22	+7.7	2.35	1.0	314.49	−20.07	−1.09	316.69
Sept.	2	240.75	+7.7	2.36	0.7	314.54	−20.13	−1.09	316.75
	10	240.42	+7.7	2.36	0.5	314.59	−20.20	−1.09	316.83
	18	240.25	+7.7	2.36	0.2	314.63	−20.28	−1.09	316.90
	26	240.24	+7.7	2.36	0.1	314.68	−20.35	−1.09	316.98
Oct.	4	240.38	+7.7	2.36	0.3	314.73	−20.43	−1.09	317.06
	12	240.69	+7.7	2.36	0.6	314.78	−20.50	−1.09	317.14
	20	241.14	+7.7	2.36	0.9	314.83	−20.57	−1.09	317.21
	28	241.74	+7.7	2.35	1.1	314.88	−20.63	−1.09	317.27
Nov.	5	242.47	+7.7	2.34	1.3	314.92	−20.69	−1.08	317.33
	13	243.32	+7.7	2.33	1.5	314.97	−20.74	−1.08	317.38
	21	244.28	+7.7	2.32	1.6	315.02	−20.78	−1.07	317.42
	29	245.31	+7.7	2.32	1.7	315.07	−20.81	−1.07	317.44
Dec.	7	246.41	+7.7	2.30	1.8	315.12	−20.82	−1.06	317.46
	15	247.54	+7.7	2.29	1.9	315.17	−20.83	−1.06	317.46
	23	248.70	+7.8	2.28	1.9	315.21	−20.82	−1.05	317.44
	31	249.84	+7.8	2.27	1.9	315.26	−20.80	−1.05	317.41
	36	250.96	+7.8	2.26	1.8	313.09	−21.54	−1.04	318.22

FOR 0^h TERRESTRIAL TIME

Date		Mars	Jupiter System I	Jupiter System II	Jupiter System III	Saturn
		°	°	°	°	°
Jan.	0	96.35	57.09	207.76	358.12	229.64
	1	87.54	215.06	358.10	148.72	320.30
	2	78.74	13.03	148.44	299.33	50.96
	3	69.95	170.99	298.77	89.92	141.61
	4	61.17	328.95	89.10	240.52	232.27
	5	52.39	126.90	239.42	31.11	322.93
	6	43.63	284.85	29.74	181.69	53.58
	7	34.86	82.80	180.06	332.28	144.24
	8	26.11	240.74	330.37	122.86	234.89
	9	17.35	38.68	120.68	273.43	325.55
	10	8.60	196.61	270.98	64.00	56.20
	11	359.86	354.54	61.28	214.57	146.86
	12	351.12	152.47	211.58	5.13	237.51
	13	342.38	310.39	1.87	155.69	328.16
	14	333.64	108.31	152.16	306.24	58.82
	15	324.90	266.22	302.44	96.79	149.47
	16	316.16	64.13	92.72	247.34	240.12
	17	307.42	222.03	243.00	37.88	330.78
	18	298.68	19.93	33.27	188.41	61.43
	19	289.93	177.83	183.54	338.95	152.08
	20	281.18	335.72	333.80	129.48	242.73
	21	272.43	133.61	124.06	280.00	333.39
	22	263.68	291.49	274.31	70.52	64.04
	23	254.91	89.37	64.56	221.04	154.69
	24	246.15	247.25	214.81	11.55	245.34
	25	237.37	45.12	5.05	162.06	336.00
	26	228.59	202.99	155.29	312.56	66.65
	27	219.81	0.85	305.52	103.06	157.30
	28	211.01	158.71	95.75	253.55	247.95
	29	202.21	316.56	245.97	44.04	338.61
	30	193.39	114.41	36.19	194.53	69.26
	31	184.57	272.26	186.41	345.01	159.91
Feb.	1	175.74	70.10	336.62	135.49	250.57
	2	166.89	227.94	126.83	285.97	341.22
	3	158.04	25.77	277.04	76.44	71.88
	4	149.18	183.60	67.24	226.90	162.53
	5	140.30	341.42	217.43	17.36	253.19
	6	131.41	139.24	7.62	167.82	343.84
	7	122.51	297.06	157.81	318.27	74.50
	8	113.60	94.88	307.99	108.72	165.16
	9	104.68	252.68	98.17	259.17	255.81
	10	95.74	50.49	248.35	49.61	346.47
	11	86.79	208.29	38.52	200.05	77.13
	12	77.83	6.09	188.69	350.49	167.79
	13	68.86	163.88	338.86	140.92	258.45
	14	59.88	321.67	129.02	291.34	349.11
	15	50.88	119.46	279.18	81.77	79.77

FOR 0^h TERRESTRIAL TIME

Date		Mars	Jupiter			Saturn
			System I	System II	System III	
		°	°	°	°	°
Feb.	15	50.88	119.46	279.18	81.77	79.77
	16	41.87	277.25	69.33	232.19	170.43
	17	32.85	75.03	219.48	22.60	261.09
	18	23.82	232.80	9.63	173.02	351.76
	19	14.77	30.57	159.77	323.43	82.42
	20	5.72	188.34	309.91	113.83	173.08
	21	356.65	346.11	100.05	264.24	263.75
	22	347.57	143.87	250.18	54.63	354.41
	23	338.47	301.63	40.31	205.03	85.08
	24	329.37	99.39	190.44	355.42	175.75
	25	320.25	257.14	340.56	145.81	266.42
	26	311.13	54.89	130.68	296.20	357.09
	27	301.99	212.64	280.80	86.58	87.76
	28	292.84	10.38	70.91	236.96	178.43
Mar.	1	283.68	168.12	221.02	27.34	269.10
	2	274.51	325.86	11.13	177.71	359.77
	3	265.33	123.59	161.24	328.08	90.45
	4	256.13	281.32	311.34	118.45	181.12
	5	246.93	79.05	101.44	268.82	271.80
	6	237.72	236.78	251.54	59.18	2.48
	7	228.49	34.50	41.63	209.54	93.15
	8	219.26	192.22	191.72	359.90	183.83
	9	210.02	349.94	341.81	150.25	274.51
	10	200.77	147.65	131.90	300.60	5.20
	11	191.50	305.37	281.98	90.95	95.88
	12	182.23	103.08	72.06	241.30	186.56
	13	172.96	260.79	222.14	31.65	277.25
	14	163.67	58.49	12.22	181.99	7.93
	15	154.37	216.20	162.29	332.33	98.62
	16	145.07	13.90	312.36	122.67	189.31
	17	135.75	171.60	102.43	273.00	280.00
	18	126.43	329.29	252.50	63.34	10.69
	19	117.11	126.99	42.56	213.67	101.38
	20	107.77	284.68	192.63	4.00	192.08
	21	98.43	82.37	342.69	154.32	282.77
	22	89.07	240.06	132.75	304.65	13.47
	23	79.72	37.75	282.81	94.97	104.16
	24	70.35	195.43	72.86	245.29	194.86
	25	60.98	353.11	222.91	35.61	285.56
	26	51.60	150.80	12.97	185.93	16.26
	27	42.21	308.47	163.02	336.25	106.97
	28	32.82	106.15	313.07	126.56	197.67
	29	23.42	263.83	103.11	276.87	288.38
	30	14.01	61.50	253.16	67.19	19.08
	31	4.60	219.18	43.20	217.50	109.79
Apr.	1	355.18	16.85	193.24	7.80	200.50
	2	345.75	174.52	343.28	158.11	291.21

FOR 0^h TERRESTRIAL TIME

Date		Mars	Jupiter System I	Jupiter System II	Jupiter System III	Saturn
		°	°	°	°	°
Apr.	1	355.18	16.85	193.24	7.80	200.50
	2	345.75	174.52	343.28	158.11	291.21
	3	336.32	332.19	133.32	308.42	21.92
	4	326.88	129.85	283.36	98.72	112.64
	5	317.44	287.52	73.40	249.02	203.35
	6	307.99	85.18	223.43	39.32	294.07
	7	298.54	242.85	13.47	189.62	24.79
	8	289.08	40.51	163.50	339.92	115.51
	9	279.61	198.17	313.53	130.22	206.23
	10	270.14	355.83	103.56	280.52	296.95
	11	260.67	153.49	253.59	70.81	27.67
	12	251.19	311.15	43.62	221.11	118.40
	13	241.70	108.80	193.65	11.40	209.13
	14	232.21	266.46	343.67	161.69	299.86
	15	222.72	64.12	133.70	311.98	30.59
	16	213.22	221.77	283.73	102.28	121.32
	17	203.71	19.42	73.75	252.57	212.05
	18	194.20	177.08	223.77	42.85	302.79
	19	184.69	334.73	13.79	193.14	33.52
	20	175.17	132.38	163.82	343.43	124.26
	21	165.65	290.03	313.84	133.72	215.00
	22	156.12	87.68	103.86	284.00	305.74
	23	146.59	245.33	253.88	74.29	36.48
	24	137.05	42.98	43.90	224.58	127.23
	25	127.51	200.63	193.92	14.86	217.97
	26	117.97	358.27	343.93	165.14	308.72
	27	108.42	155.92	133.95	315.43	39.47
	28	98.87	313.57	283.97	105.71	130.22
	29	89.31	111.21	73.99	255.99	220.97
	30	79.75	268.86	224.00	46.28	311.73
May	1	70.19	66.51	14.02	196.56	42.48
	2	60.62	224.15	164.03	346.84	133.24
	3	51.04	21.80	314.05	137.12	224.00
	4	41.47	179.44	104.06	287.40	314.76
	5	31.89	337.08	254.08	77.68	45.52
	6	22.30	134.73	44.09	227.96	136.28
	7	12.72	292.37	194.11	18.25	227.05
	8	3.13	90.02	344.12	168.53	317.81
	9	353.53	247.66	134.14	318.81	48.58
	10	343.93	45.31	284.15	109.09	139.35
	11	334.33	202.95	74.17	259.37	230.12
	12	324.73	0.60	224.18	49.65	320.90
	13	315.12	158.24	14.20	199.93	51.67
	14	305.50	315.88	164.21	350.21	142.45
	15	295.89	113.53	314.23	140.49	233.23
	16	286.27	271.17	104.24	290.77	324.01
	17	276.65	68.82	254.26	81.05	54.79

FOR 0^h TERRESTRIAL TIME

Date		Mars	Jupiter System I	Jupiter System II	Jupiter System III	Saturn
		°	°	°	°	°
May	17	276.65	68.82	254.26	81.05	54.79
	18	267.02	226.46	44.27	231.33	145.57
	19	257.39	24.11	194.29	21.62	236.36
	20	247.76	181.75	344.30	171.90	327.14
	21	238.13	339.40	134.32	322.18	57.93
	22	228.49	137.04	284.34	112.46	148.72
	23	218.84	294.69	74.35	262.74	239.51
	24	209.20	92.34	224.37	53.03	330.30
	25	199.55	249.98	14.39	203.31	61.10
	26	189.90	47.63	164.40	353.59	151.90
	27	180.24	205.28	314.42	143.88	242.69
	28	170.59	2.93	104.44	294.16	333.49
	29	160.93	160.57	254.46	84.45	64.29
	30	151.26	318.22	44.48	234.73	155.10
	31	141.59	115.87	194.50	25.02	245.90
June	1	131.92	273.52	344.52	175.30	336.71
	2	122.25	71.17	134.54	325.59	67.51
	3	112.57	228.83	284.56	115.88	158.32
	4	102.89	26.48	74.58	266.16	249.13
	5	93.21	184.13	224.60	56.45	339.95
	6	83.53	341.78	14.63	206.74	70.76
	7	73.84	139.44	164.65	357.03	161.57
	8	64.15	297.09	314.68	147.32	252.39
	9	54.45	94.75	104.70	297.62	343.21
	10	44.76	252.40	254.73	87.91	74.03
	11	35.06	50.06	44.75	238.20	164.85
	12	25.36	207.72	194.78	28.49	255.67
	13	15.65	5.38	344.81	178.79	346.50
	14	5.95	163.03	134.84	329.08	77.32
	15	356.24	320.69	284.87	119.38	168.15
	16	346.52	118.35	74.90	269.68	258.98
	17	336.81	276.02	224.93	59.97	349.81
	18	327.09	73.68	14.97	210.27	80.64
	19	317.37	231.34	165.00	0.57	171.48
	20	307.65	29.01	315.03	150.87	262.31
	21	297.92	186.67	105.07	301.17	353.15
	22	288.19	344.34	255.10	91.48	83.99
	23	278.46	142.01	45.14	241.78	174.83
	24	268.73	299.67	195.18	32.08	265.67
	25	258.99	97.34	345.22	182.39	356.51
	26	249.25	255.01	135.26	332.70	87.35
	27	239.51	52.68	285.30	123.00	178.20
	28	229.77	210.36	75.34	273.31	269.04
	29	220.02	8.03	225.39	63.62	359.89
	30	210.27	165.71	15.43	213.93	90.74
July	1	200.52	323.38	165.48	4.24	181.59
	2	190.77	121.06	315.53	154.56	272.44

FOR 0^h TERRESTRIAL TIME

Date		Mars	Jupiter System I	Jupiter System II	Jupiter System III	Saturn
		°	°	°	°	°
July	1	200.52	323.38	165.48	4.24	181.59
	2	190.77	121.06	315.53	154.56	272.44
	3	181.01	278.74	105.57	304.87	3.29
	4	171.26	76.42	255.62	95.19	94.15
	5	161.50	234.10	45.67	245.50	185.00
	6	151.74	31.78	195.73	35.82	275.86
	7	141.97	189.46	345.78	186.14	6.72
	8	132.21	347.15	135.83	336.46	97.58
	9	122.44	144.83	285.89	126.78	188.44
	10	112.67	302.52	75.95	277.11	279.30
	11	102.90	100.21	226.00	67.43	10.16
	12	93.13	257.90	16.06	217.76	101.02
	13	83.35	55.59	166.12	8.08	191.89
	14	73.57	213.28	316.19	158.41	282.75
	15	63.79	10.98	106.25	308.74	13.62
	16	54.01	168.67	256.32	99.07	104.49
	17	44.23	326.37	46.38	249.40	195.36
	18	34.45	124.07	196.45	39.74	286.23
	19	24.66	281.76	346.52	190.07	17.10
	20	14.87	79.47	136.59	340.41	107.97
	21	5.08	237.17	286.66	130.75	198.84
	22	355.29	34.87	76.74	281.09	289.72
	23	345.50	192.58	226.81	71.43	20.59
	24	335.71	350.28	16.89	221.77	111.47
	25	325.91	147.99	166.97	12.11	202.34
	26	316.11	305.70	317.05	162.46	293.22
	27	306.32	103.41	107.13	312.81	24.10
	28	296.52	261.13	257.21	103.16	114.98
	29	286.72	58.84	47.29	253.51	205.86
	30	276.91	216.56	197.38	43.86	296.74
	31	267.11	14.28	347.47	194.21	27.62
Aug.	1	257.31	172.00	137.56	344.57	118.50
	2	247.50	329.72	287.65	134.93	209.38
	3	237.70	127.44	77.74	285.29	300.26
	4	227.89	285.17	227.84	75.65	31.14
	5	218.08	82.89	17.93	226.01	122.03
	6	208.27	240.62	168.03	16.37	212.91
	7	198.46	38.35	318.13	166.74	303.80
	8	188.65	196.08	108.23	317.11	34.68
	9	178.84	353.82	258.34	107.48	125.56
	10	169.03	151.55	48.44	257.85	216.45
	11	159.21	309.29	198.55	48.22	307.34
	12	149.40	107.03	348.66	198.60	38.22
	13	139.59	264.77	138.77	348.97	129.11
	14	129.77	62.51	288.88	139.35	219.99
	15	119.96	220.26	79.00	289.73	310.88
	16	110.14	18.01	229.11	80.11	41.77

FOR 0^h TERRESTRIAL TIME

Date		Mars	Jupiter System I	Jupiter System II	Jupiter System III	Saturn
		°	°	°	°	°
Aug.	16	110.14	18.01	229.11	80.11	41.77
	17	100.33	175.75	19.23	230.50	132.65
	18	90.51	333.50	169.35	20.88	223.54
	19	80.69	131.26	319.47	171.27	314.43
	20	70.88	289.01	109.60	321.66	45.31
	21	61.06	86.77	259.72	112.05	136.20
	22	51.24	244.53	49.85	262.45	227.08
	23	41.42	42.29	199.98	52.84	317.97
	24	31.61	200.05	350.11	203.24	48.86
	25	21.79	357.81	140.25	353.64	139.74
	26	11.97	155.58	290.38	144.04	230.63
	27	2.15	313.35	80.52	294.45	321.51
	28	352.33	111.12	230.66	84.86	52.40
	29	342.52	268.89	20.80	235.26	143.28
	30	332.70	66.67	170.95	25.68	234.17
	31	322.88	224.45	321.10	176.09	325.05
Sept.	1	313.06	22.23	111.24	326.50	55.93
	2	303.25	180.01	261.40	116.92	146.81
	3	293.43	337.79	51.55	267.34	237.69
	4	283.61	135.58	201.71	57.76	328.58
	5	273.80	293.37	351.86	208.19	59.46
	6	263.98	91.16	142.02	358.61	150.34
	7	254.16	248.95	292.19	149.04	241.21
	8	244.35	46.75	82.35	299.47	332.09
	9	234.53	204.54	232.52	89.90	62.97
	10	224.72	2.34	22.69	240.34	153.84
	11	214.91	160.15	172.86	30.78	244.72
	12	205.09	317.95	323.03	181.22	335.59
	13	195.28	115.76	113.21	331.66	66.47
	14	185.47	273.57	263.39	122.10	157.34
	15	175.66	71.38	53.57	272.55	248.21
	16	165.85	229.19	203.75	63.00	339.08
	17	156.04	27.01	353.94	213.45	69.95
	18	146.23	184.83	144.13	3.91	160.82
	19	136.42	342.65	294.32	154.36	251.68
	20	126.61	140.47	84.51	304.82	342.55
	21	116.80	298.30	234.71	95.28	73.41
	22	106.99	96.13	24.90	245.75	164.27
	23	97.19	253.96	175.11	36.22	255.13
	24	87.38	51.79	325.31	186.69	345.99
	25	77.58	209.63	115.52	337.16	76.85
	26	67.77	7.47	265.72	127.63	167.71
	27	57.97	165.31	55.93	278.11	258.56
	28	48.17	323.16	206.15	68.59	349.41
	29	38.37	121.00	356.37	219.07	80.27
	30	28.57	278.85	146.58	9.56	171.12
Oct.	1	18.77	76.71	296.81	160.05	261.96

FOR 0ʰ TERRESTRIAL TIME

Date		Mars	Jupiter			Saturn
			System I	System II	System III	
		°	°	°	°	°
Oct.	1	18.77	76.71	296.81	160.05	261.96
	2	8.97	234.56	87.03	310.54	352.81
	3	359.17	32.42	237.26	101.03	83.65
	4	349.37	190.28	27.49	251.52	174.50
	5	339.57	348.14	177.72	42.02	265.34
	6	329.78	146.01	327.96	192.52	356.18
	7	319.98	303.88	118.19	343.03	87.01
	8	310.19	101.75	268.43	133.53	177.85
	9	300.40	259.62	58.68	284.04	268.68
	10	290.60	57.50	208.92	74.56	359.51
	11	280.81	215.38	359.17	225.07	90.34
	12	271.02	13.26	149.42	15.59	181.17
	13	261.23	171.15	299.68	166.11	272.00
	14	251.44	329.03	89.94	316.63	2.82
	15	241.65	126.93	240.20	107.16	93.64
	16	231.87	284.82	30.46	257.69	184.46
	17	222.08	82.72	180.72	48.22	275.28
	18	212.29	240.62	330.99	198.75	6.09
	19	202.51	38.52	121.27	349.29	96.90
	20	192.72	196.42	271.54	139.83	187.71
	21	182.94	354.33	61.82	290.38	278.52
	22	173.16	152.24	212.10	80.92	9.33
	23	163.37	310.16	2.38	231.47	100.13
	24	153.59	108.07	152.67	22.02	190.93
	25	143.81	265.99	302.96	172.58	281.73
	26	134.03	63.91	93.25	323.14	12.53
	27	124.25	221.84	243.54	113.70	103.33
	28	114.47	19.77	33.84	264.26	194.12
	29	104.69	177.70	184.14	54.83	284.91
	30	94.91	335.63	334.44	205.40	15.70
	31	85.14	133.57	124.75	355.97	106.48
Nov.	1	75.36	291.51	275.06	146.54	197.27
	2	65.58	89.45	65.37	297.12	288.05
	3	55.81	247.40	215.69	87.70	18.83
	4	46.03	45.35	6.00	238.29	109.60
	5	36.26	203.30	156.32	28.87	200.38
	6	26.48	1.25	306.65	179.46	291.15
	7	16.71	159.21	96.97	330.06	21.92
	8	6.93	317.17	247.30	120.65	112.69
	9	357.16	115.13	37.64	271.25	203.45
	10	347.39	273.10	187.97	61.85	294.21
	11	337.61	71.06	338.31	212.45	24.98
	12	327.84	229.04	128.65	3.06	115.73
	13	318.07	27.01	278.99	153.67	206.49
	14	308.30	184.99	69.34	304.28	297.24
	15	298.52	342.96	219.68	94.89	28.00
	16	288.75	140.95	10.04	245.51	118.74

FOR 0^h TERRESTRIAL TIME

Date		Mars	Jupiter System I	Jupiter System II	Jupiter System III	Saturn
		°	°	°	°	°
Nov.	16	288.75	140.95	10.04	245.51	118.74
	17	278.98	298.93	160.39	36.13	209.49
	18	269.21	96.92	310.75	186.75	300.24
	19	259.43	254.91	101.11	337.38	30.98
	20	249.66	52.90	251.47	128.01	121.72
	21	239.89	210.89	41.83	278.64	212.46
	22	230.12	8.89	192.20	69.27	303.19
	23	220.34	166.89	342.57	219.91	33.93
	24	210.57	324.89	132.94	10.54	124.66
	25	200.80	122.90	283.31	161.18	215.39
	26	191.03	280.90	73.69	311.83	306.12
	27	181.25	78.91	224.07	102.47	36.84
	28	171.48	236.93	14.45	253.12	127.57
	29	161.70	34.94	164.83	43.77	218.29
	30	151.93	192.95	315.22	194.42	309.01
Dec.	1	142.16	350.97	105.60	345.07	39.73
	2	132.38	148.99	255.99	135.73	130.44
	3	122.60	307.01	46.38	286.38	221.15
	4	112.83	105.04	196.78	77.04	311.87
	5	103.05	263.06	347.17	227.70	42.58
	6	93.27	61.09	137.57	18.36	133.28
	7	83.50	219.12	287.97	169.03	223.99
	8	73.72	17.15	78.37	319.70	314.69
	9	63.94	175.18	228.77	110.36	45.40
	10	54.16	333.21	19.17	261.03	136.10
	11	44.38	131.25	169.58	51.70	226.80
	12	34.60	289.29	319.98	202.37	317.49
	13	24.81	87.32	110.39	353.05	48.19
	14	15.03	245.36	260.80	143.72	138.88
	15	5.25	43.40	51.21	294.40	229.58
	16	355.46	201.44	201.62	85.08	320.27
	17	345.67	359.49	352.03	235.75	50.96
	18	335.88	157.53	142.44	26.43	141.64
	19	326.10	315.57	292.86	177.11	232.33
	20	316.31	113.62	83.27	327.79	323.01
	21	306.51	271.66	233.68	118.47	53.70
	22	296.72	69.71	24.10	269.15	144.38
	23	286.93	227.75	174.52	59.83	235.06
	24	277.13	25.80	324.93	210.52	325.74
	25	267.33	183.84	115.35	1.20	56.42
	26	257.54	341.89	265.76	151.88	147.09
	27	247.74	139.94	56.18	302.56	237.77
	28	237.94	297.98	206.59	93.24	328.44
	29	228.13	96.03	357.01	243.92	59.11
	30	218.33	254.07	147.43	34.61	149.79
	31	208.52	52.12	297.84	185.29	240.46
	32	198.72	210.16	88.25	335.97	331.13

CONTENTS OF SECTION F

The satellite ephemerides were calculated using $\Delta T = 69.0$ seconds.

SATELLITES: ORBITAL DATA

Satellite		Orbital Period (R = Retrograde)	Max. Elong. at Mean Opposition	Semimajor Axis	Orbital Eccentricity	Inclination of Orbit to Planet's Equator	Motion of Node on Fixed Plane[2,11]
		d	° ′ ″	$\times 10^3$ km		°	°/yr
Earth							
Moon		27.321 661		384.400	0.054 900 489	18.2–28.6	19.34[7]
Mars							
I	Phobos[1]	0.318 9	25	9.380	0.015 1	1.1	158.8
II	Deimos[1]	1.262 4	1 02	23.460	0.000 2	1.8	6.260
Jupiter							
I	Io[1]	1.769 138	2 18	422.000	0.004	0.04	48.6
II	Europa[1]	3.551 181	3 40	671.000	0.009	0.47	12.0
III	Ganymede[1]	7.154 553	5 51	1 070.000	0.002	0.18	2.63
IV	Callisto[1]	16.689 018	10 18	1 883.000	0.007	0.19	0.643
V	Amalthea[1]	0.498 2	59	181.20	0.003	0.4	914.6
VI	Himalia	250.1	1 22 14	11 443.000	0.16	29	524.4
VII	Elara	259.1	1 24 14	11 716.00	0.21	28	506.1
VIII	Pasiphae	744.2 R	2 49 33	23 658.000	0.41	151	185.6
IX	Sinope	753.2 R	2 10 20	23 848.000	0.26	158	181.4
X	Lysithea	258.5	1 03 58	11 700.000	0.12	28	506.9
XI	Carme	726.3 R	2 47 55	23 280.000	0.26	165	187.1
XII	Ananke	624.1 R	2 32 30	21 048.000	0.23	149	215.2
XIII	Leda	240.5	1 20 07	11 150.000	0.16	28	545.4
XIV	Thebe[1]	0.674 5	1 13	221.895	0.015	0.8	
XV	Adrastea[1]	0.298 3	42	128.980	0.002	0.1	
XVI	Metis[1]	0.294 8	42	127.979	0.001	0.02	
XVII	Callirrhoe	748.7 R	2 52 55	23 788.645	0.28	147[9]	
XVIII	Themisto	130.4	53 51	7 450.000	0.24	43[9]	
XIX	Megaclite	734.1 R	2 50 52	23 439.084	0.42	153[9]	
XX	Taygete	650.1 R	2 47 38	21 671.854	0.25	165[9]	
XXI	Chaldene	591.7 R	2 46 20	20 299.459	0.25	165[9]	
XXII	Harpalyke	617.3 R	2 31 27	20 917.717	0.23	149[9]	
XXIII	Kalyke	725.8 R	2 49 05	23 302.374	0.25	165[9]	
XXIV	Iocaste	606.3 R	2 32 38	20 642.860	0.22	149[9]	
XXV	Erinome	661.1 R	2 47 05	21 867.753	0.27	165[9]	
XXVI	Isonoe	704.9 R	2 46 42	22 804.699	0.25	165[9]	
XXVII	Praxidike	624.6 R	2 31 45	21 098.102	0.23	149[9]	
XXVIII	Autonoe	778.0 R	2 52 29	24 413.086	0.32	152[9]	
XXIX	Thyone	610.0 R	2 32 06	20 769.899	0.23	149[9]	
XXX	Hermippe	624.6 R	2 32 49	21 047.986	0.21	151[9]	
XXXI	Aitne	679.3 R	2 47 18	22 274.405	0.26	165[9]	
XXXII	Eurydome	752.4 R	2 46 05	23 830.940	0.28	150[9]	
XXXIII	Euanthe	620.9 R	2 30 58	20 983.136	0.23	149[9]	
XXXVI	Sponde	690.3 R	2 50 42	22 548.244	0.31	151[9]	
XXXVII	Kale	679.4 R	2 47 14	22 300.644	0.26	165[9]	
XXXIX	Hegemone	727.6 R	2 49 09	23 339.942	0.34	154[9]	
XLI	Aoede	747.8 R	2 52 01	23 776.774	0.43	158[9]	
XLIII	Arche	748.7 R	2 47 34	23 765.118	0.25	165[9]	
XLV	Helike	601.4 R	2 31 09	20 540.266	0.15	155[9]	
XLVI	Carpo	455.1	2 02 23	17 056.041	0.43	52[9]	
XLVII	Eukelade	735.3 R	2 47 21	23 485.280	0.26	165[9]	
LIII	Dia	288.5	1 28 14	12 623.008	0.23	29[9]	
LXV	Pandia	251.2	1 03 01	11 479.646	0.18	28[9]	
LXXI	Ersa	248.6	1 02 48	11 398.485	0.09	30[9]	
Saturn							
I	Mimas[1]	0.942 422	30	185.540	0.019 05	1.56	365.0
II	Enceladus[1]	1.370 218	38	238.200	0.004 9	0.03	156.2[8]
III	Tethys[1]	1.887 803	48	294.992	0.0	1.10	72.25
IV	Dione[1]	2.736 916	1 01	377.654	0.002 2	0.01	30.85[8]
V	Rhea[1]	4.517 503	1 25	527.367	0.000 3	0.35	10.16
VI	Titan[1]	15.945 446	3 17	1 221.803	0.029 1	0.30	0.521 3[8]
VII	Hyperion[1]	21.276 673	4 02	1 481.100	0.103 5	0.64	
VIII	Iapetus[1]	79.330 954	9 35	3 561.850	0.028 3	18.5	
IX	Phoebe[1]	546.4 R	34 51	12 893.240	0.175 63	173.73[9]	

[1] Mean orbital data given with respect to the local Laplace plane.
[2] Rate of decrease (or increase) in the longitude of the ascending node.
[3] S = Synchronous, rotation period same as orbital period. C = Chaotic.
[4] $V(\text{Sun}) = -26.75$
[5] $V(1, 0)$ is the visual magnitude of the satellite reduced to a distance of 1 au from both the Sun and Earth and with phase angle of zero.
[6] V_0 is the mean opposition magnitude of the satellite.

Satellite	Mass Ratio (sat./planet)	Radius	Sid. Rot. Per.[3,11]	Geom. Alb. (V)[4]	$V(1,0)$[5,11]	V_0[6]	$B-V$[11]	$U-B$[11]
		km	d					
rth								
oon	0.012 300 037 1	1737.4	S	0.12	+ 0.21	− 12.74	0.92	0.46
ars								
Phobos	1.651×10^{-8}	13.00 × 11.39 × 9.07	S	0.071	+ 11.8	+ 11.9		
Deimos	2.358×10^{-9}	7.8 × 6.0 × 5.1	S	0.068	+ 12.89	+ 12.95	0.65	0.18
piter								
Io	4.704×10^{-5}	1829.7 × 1819.2 × 1815.8	S	0.63	− 1.68	+ 4.85	1.17	1.30
Europa	2.528×10^{-5}	1562.6 × 1560.3 × 1559.5	S	0.64	− 1.41	+ 5.25	0.87	0.52
Ganymede	7.803×10^{-5}	2631.2	S	0.43	− 2.09	+ 4.54	0.83	0.50
Callisto	5.666×10^{-5}	2410.3	S	0.17	− 1.05	+ 5.47	0.86	0.55
Amalthea	1.097×10^{-9}	125 × 73 × 64	S	0.090	+ 6.3	+ 14.1	1.50	
I Himalia	2.210×10^{-9}	75 × 60 × 60	0.40	0.04 :	+ 8.1	+ 14.62	0.67	0.30
II Elara	4.58×10^{-10}	43 :		0.04 :	+ 10.1	+ 16.32	0.69	0.28
III Pasiphae	1.58×10^{-10}	30 :		0.04 :	+ 9.92	+ 17.00	0.74	0.34
X Sinope	3.95×10^{-11}	19 :	0.548	0.04 :	+ 11.56	+ 18.05	0.84	
Lysithea	3.315×10^{-11}	18 :	0.533	0.04 :	+ 11.09	+ 18.25	0.72	
I Carme	6.945×10^{-11}	23 :	0.433	0.04 :	+ 10.91	+ 17.55	0.76	
II Ananke	1.58×10^{-11}	14 :	0.35	0.04 :	+ 11.87	+ 18.75	0.90	
III Leda	5.76×10^{-12}	10 :		0.04 :	+ 13.5	+ 19.50	0.7	
IV Thebe	7.89×10^{-10}	58 × 49 × 42	S	0.047	+ 9.0	+ 16.0	1.3	
V Adrastea	3.95×10^{-12}	10 × 8 × 7	S	0.1	+ 12.4	+ 18.7		
VI Metis	6.31×10^{-11}	30 × 20 × 20	S	0.061	+ 10.8	+ 17.5		
VII Callirrhoe	5.303×10^{-13}	4.5 :		0.04 :	+ 13.92	+ 21.05	0.72	
VIII Themisto	3.488×10^{-13}	3.9 :		0.04 :	+ 12.94	+ 21.00	0.83	
IX Megaclite	2.131×10^{-13}	3.3 :		0.04 :	+ 15.12	+ 22.82	0.94	
X Taygete	1.144×10^{-13}	2.7 :		0.04 :	+ 15.63	+ 22.25	0.56	
XXI Chaldene	7.497×10^{-14}	2.4 :		0.04 :	+ 15.7	+ 22.66		
XXII Harpalyke	8.365×10^{-14}	2.4 :		0.04 :	+ 16.03	+ 22.61		
XXIII Kalyke	1.547×10^{-13}	3.0 :		0.04 :	+ 15.42	+ 22.20	0.94	
XXIV Iocaste	1.397×10^{-13}	2.9 :		0.04 :	+ 15.27	+ 22.21	0.63	
XXV Erinome	3.788×10^{-14}	1.9 :		0.04 :	+ 16.0	+ 22.70		
XXVI Isonoe	6.156×10^{-14}	2.2 :		0.04 :	+ 15.9	+ 22.72		
XXVII Praxidike	2.849×10^{-13}	3.7 :		0.04 :	+ 15.24	+ 21.84	0.77	
XXVIII Autonoe	7.813×10^{-14}	2.4 :		0.04 :	+ 15.4	+ 22.33		
XXIX Thyone	6.945×10^{-14}	2.3 :		0.04 :	+ 15.7	+ 22.56		
XXX Hermippe	1.492×10^{-13}	3.0 :		0.04 :	+ 15.5	+ 22.30		
XXXI Aitne	4.025×10^{-14}	1.9 :		0.04 :	+ 16.1	+ 22.78		
XXXII Eurydome	4.262×10^{-14}	2.0 :		0.04 :	+ 16.1	+ 22.96		
XXXIII Euanthe	4.341×10^{-14}	2.0 :		0.04 :	+ 16.2	+ 23.31		
XXXVI Sponde	2.762×10^{-14}	1.7 :		0.04 :	+ 16.4	+ 23.49		
XXXVII Kale	2.446×10^{-14}	1.6 :		0.04 :	+ 16.4	+ 22.91		
XXXIX Hegemone	3.391×10^{-14}	1.8 :		0.04 :	+ 15.9	+ 22.74		
XLI Aoede	6.471×10^{-14}	2.3 :		0.04 :	+ 15.8	+ 22.48		
XLIII Arche	2.841×10^{-14}	1.7 :		0.04 :	+ 16.4	+ 22.98		
XLV Helike	7.182×10^{-14}	2.3 :		0.04 :	+ 16.0	+ 22.72		
XLVI Carpo	3.394×10^{-14}	1.8 :		0.04 :	+ 15.6	+ 22.94		
XLVII Eukelade	7.103×10^{-14}	2.3 :		0.04 :	+ 15.0	+ 22.62		
LIII Dia	7.89×10^{-15}	2.0 :		0.04 :	+ 16.1	+ 22.4		
LXV Pandia		1.5 :		0.04 :		+ 23.0		
LXXI Ersa		1.5 :		0.04 :		+ 22.9		
Saturn								
I Mimas	6.613×10^{-8}	207.8 × 196.7 × 190.6	S	0.96	+ 3.3	+12.8		
II Enceladus	1.899×10^{-7}	256.6 × 251.4 × 248.3	S	1.38	+ 2.2	+11.8	0.70	0.28
III Tethys	1.086×10^{-6}	538.4 × 528.3 × 526.3	S	1.23	+ 0.7	+10.2	0.73	0.30
IV Dione	1.927×10^{-6}	563.4 × 561.3 × 559.6	S	1.00	+ 0.88	+10.4	0.71	0.31
V Rhea	4.057×10^{-6}	765.0 × 763.1 × 762.4	S	0.95	+ 0.16	+ 9.6	0.78	0.38
VI Titan	2.366×10^{-4}	2574.73	S	0.2	− 1.20	+ 8.4	1.28	0.75
VII Hyperion	9.823×10^{-9}	180.1 × 133.0 × 102.7	C	0.3	+ 4.6	+14.4	0.78	0.33
VIII Iapetus	3.176×10^{-6}	745.7 × 745.7 × 712.1	S	0.6[10]	+ 1.6	+11	0.72	0.30
IX Phoebe	1.459×10^{-8}	109.4 × 108.5 × 101.8	0.4	0.081	+ 6.63	+16.4	0.63	0.34

[7] Motion on the ecliptic plane.
[8] Rate of increase in the longitude of the apse.
[9] Measured from the ecliptic plane.
[10] Bright side, 0.5; faint side, 0.05.
[11] These data are under review.
: Quantity is uncertain.

Satellite		Orbital Period (R = Retrograde)	Max. Elong. at Mean Opposition	Semimajor Axis	Orbital Eccentricity	Inclination of Orbit to Planet's Equator	Motion of Node on Fixed Plane[2,11]
		d	° ′ ″	×10³ km		°	°/yr
Saturn							
X	Janus	0.694 7	24	151.470	0.007	0.14	
XI	Epimetheus	0.694 3	24	151.420	0.009	0.34	
XII	Helene	2.74	1 01	377.400	0.0	0.212	
XIII	Telesto	1.887 8	48	294.660	0.001	1.158	
XIV	Calypso	1.887 8	48	294.660	0.001	1.473	
XV	Atlas	0.602 1	22	137.670	0.002	0.3	
XVI	Prometheus	0.613 2	23	139.350	0.002	0.0	
XVII	Pandora	0.628 5	23	141.700	0.004	0.0	
XVIII	Pan[1]	0.575	22	133.600	0.0	0.0	
XIX	Ymir	1329.5 R	1 02 14	23 305.867	0.374 658 0	172.745 56	
XX	Paaliaq	686.7	40 55	14 985.054	0.461 865 3	45.862 46	
XXI	Tarvos	898.5	49 06	17 977.236	0.612 523 7	34.901 18	
XXII	Ijiraq	452.9	30 42	11 359.250	0.359 235 5	49.177 94	
XXIV	Kiviuq	449.3	30 38	11 319.009	0.165 818 4	48.392 59	
XXVI	Albiorix	792.6	44 07	16 495.933	0.451 550 1	37.403 68	
XXIX	Siarnaq	916.8	48 56	18 201.438	0.380 475 3	45.502 65	
Uranus							
I	Ariel	2.520 379	14	190.945	0.001 2	0.04	6.8
II	Umbriel	4.144 176	20	265.998	0.004 0	0.13	3.6
III	Titania	8.705 867	33	436.298	0.001 4	0.08	2.0
IV	Oberon	13.463 234	44	583.519	0.001 6	0.07	1.4
V	Miranda	1.413 479	10	129.872	0.001 3	4.34	19.8
VII	Ophelia	0.376	4	53.764	0.010 1	0.09	417.9
VIII	Bianca	0.435	4	59.165	0.000 88	0.16	298.7
IX	Cressida	0.464	5	61.767	0.000 23	0.04	256.9
X	Desdemona	0.474	5	62.659	0.000 23	0.16	244.3
XI	Juliet	0.493	5	64.358	0.000 59	0.06	222.5
XII	Portia	0.513	5	66.097	0.000 17	0.09	202.6
XIII	Rosalind	0.558	5	69.927	0.000 09	0.28	166.4
XIV	Belinda	0.624	6	75.255	0.000 11	0.03	128.8
XV	Puck	0.762	7	86.004	0.000 05	0.31	80.91
XVI	Caliban	579.6 R	9 08	7 170.000	0.159	139.8[9]	
XVII	Sycorax	1289.0 R	15 24	12 216.000	0.522	152.7[9]	
Neptune							
I	Triton[1]	5.876 85 R	17	354.759	0.000 02	156.3	0.523 2
II	Nereid[1]	360.135	4 22	5 513.410	0.751	6.68	0.039
V	Despina[1]	0.334 66	2	52.526	0.000 139	0.07	466.0
VI	Galatea[1]	0.428 75	3	61.953	0.000 12	0.05	261.3
VII	Larissa[1]	0.554 65	3	73.548	0.001 39	0.20	143.5
VIII	Proteus[1]	1.122 32	6	117.647	0.000 44	0.04	28.80
Pluto							
I	Charon	6.387	1	19.636	0.008	0.00	

[1] Mean orbital data given with respect to the local Laplace plane.
[2] Rate of decrease (or increase) in the longitude of the ascending node.
[3] S = Synchronous, rotation period same as orbital period. C = Chaotic.
[4] V(Sun) = −26.75
[5] $V(1, 0)$ is the visual magnitude of the satellite reduced to a distance of 1 au from both the Sun and Earth and with phase angle of zero.
[6] V_0 is the mean opposition magnitude of the satellite.

A Note on the Satellite Diagrams

The satellite orbit diagrams have been designed to assist observers in locating many of the shorter period (< 21 days) satellites of the planets. Each diagram depicts a planet and the apparent orbits of its satellites at 0 hours UT on that planet's opposition date, unless no opposition date occurs during the year. In that case, the diagram depicts the planet and orbits at 0 hours UT on January 1 or December 31, depending on which date provides the better view. The diagrams are inverted to reproduce what an observer would normally see through a telescope. Two arrows or text in the diagram indicate the apparent motion of the satellite(s); for most satellites in the solar system, the orbital motion is counterclockwise when viewed from the northern side of the orbital plane. In the case of Jupiter, Saturn, and Uranus, the diagram may have an expanded scale in one direction to better clarify the relative positions of the orbits.

Satellite		Mass Ratio (sat./planet)	Radius	Sid. Rot. Per.[3,11]	Geom. Alb. (V)[4]	$V(1,0)$[5,11]	V_0[6]	$B-V$[11]	$U-B$[11]
			km	d					
aturn									
	Janus	3.334×10^{-9}	101.5 × 92.5 × 76.3	S	0.71	+ 4 :	+14.4		
I	Epimetheus	9.254×10^{-10}	64.9 × 57.0 × 53.1	S	0.73	+ 5.4 :	+15.6		
II	Helene	4.481×10^{-11}	21.7 × 19.1 × 13.0		0.6	+ 8.4 :	+18.4		
III	Telesto	1.265×10^{-11}	16.3 × 11.8 × 10.0		1.0	+ 8.9 :	+18.5		
IV	Calypso	6.326×10^{-12}	15.1 × 11.5 × 7.0		0.7	+ 9.1 :	+18.7		
V	Atlas	1.012×10^{-11}	20.4 × 17.7 × 9.4		0.4	+ 8.4 :	+19.0		
VI	Prometheus	2.814×10^{-10}	67.8 × 39.7 × 29.7	S	0.6	+ 6.4 :	+15.8		
VII	Pandora	2.407×10^{-10}	52.0 × 40.5 × 32.0	S	0.5	+ 6.4 :	+16.4		
VIII	Pan	8.698×10^{-12}	17.2 × 15.7 × 10.4		0.5 :		+19.4		
IX	Ymir	1.387×10^{-11}	9.4 :		0.06 :	+ 12.4	+21.81	0.80	
X	Paaliaq	2.272×10^{-11}	11.0 :		0.06 :	+ 11.8	+21.30	0.86	
XI	Tarvos	5.453×10^{-12}	6.9 :		0.06 :	+ 12.6	+22.34	0.78	
XII	Ijiraq	3.247×10^{-12}	5.8 :		0.06 :	+ 13.6	+22.75	1.05	
XIV	Kiviuq	8.627×10^{-12}	8.0 :		0.06 :	+ 12.7	+22.05	0.92	
XVI	Albiorix	4.362×10^{-11}	13.7 :		0.06 :		+20.83	0.80	
XIX	Siarnaq	2.419×10^{-10}	24.3 :		0.06 :	+ 10.7	+19.92	0.87	
ranus									
	Ariel	1.441×10^{-5}	581.1 × 577.9 × 577.7	S	0.36	+ 1.7	+13.2	0.65	
I	Umbriel	1.469×10^{-5}	584.7	S	0.19	+ 2.6	+14.0	0.68	
II	Titania	3.916×10^{-5}	788.9	S	0.25	+ 1.3	+13.0	0.70	0.28
V	Oberon	3.543×10^{-5}	761.4	S	0.22	+ 1.5	+13.2	0.68	0.20
V	Miranda	7.421×10^{-7}	240.4 × 234.2 × 232.9	S	0.32	+ 3.8	+15.3		
VII	Ophelia	6.213×10^{-10}	27 × 19 × 19		0.065 :	+ 11.1	+22.8		
VIII	Bianca	1.070×10^{-9}	32 × 23 × 23		0.065 :	+ 10.3	+22.0		
X	Cressida	3.952×10^{-9}	46 × 37 × 37		0.069 :	+ 9.5	+21.1		
X	Desdemona	2.054×10^{-9}	45 × 27 × 27		0.084 :	+ 9.8	+21.5		
XI	Juliet	6.420×10^{-9}	75 × 37 × 37		0.075 :	+ 8.8	+20.6		
XII	Portia	1.936×10^{-8}	78 × 63 × 63		0.069 :	+ 8.3	+19.9		
XIII	Rosalind	2.934×10^{-9}	36		0.072 :	+ 9.8	+21.3		
XIV	Belinda	4.107×10^{-9}	64 × 32 × 32		0.067 :	+ 9.4	+21.0		
XV	Puck	3.332×10^{-8}	81		0.104 :	+ 7.5	+19.2		
XVI	Caliban	8.130×10^{-9}	48.3 :		0.04 :	+ 9.7	+21.60		
XVII	Sycorax	4.667×10^{-8}	86.4 :		0.04 :	+ 8.2	+20.30		
Neptune									
I	Triton	6.255×10^{-5}	1354.6 × 1352.8 × 1352.4	S	0.756	− 1.2	+13.472	0.72	0.29
II	Nereid	3.01×10^{-7}	170		0.155	+ 4.0	+19.7	0.65	
V	Despina	2.05×10^{-8}	90 × 74 × 64		0.090	+ 7.9	+22.00		
VI	Galatea	3.66×10^{-8}	102 × 92 × 72		0.079	+ 7.6 :	+21.85		
VII	Larissa	4.83×10^{-8}	108 × 102 × 84		0.091	+ 7.3	+21.49		
VIII	Proteus	4.91×10^{-7}	203.8	S	0.096	+ 5.6	+19.75		
Pluto									
I	Charon	0.1090	606.0	S	0.372	+ 0.9	+17.97	0.71	

[7] Motion on the ecliptic plane.
[8] Rate of increase in the longitude of the apse.
[9] Measured from the ecliptic plane.
[10] Bright side, 0.5; faint side, 0.05.
[11] These data are under review.
: Quantity is uncertain.

A Note on Selection Criteria for the Satellite Data Tables

Due to the recent proliferation of known satellites associated with the gas giant planets, a set of selection criteria has been established under which satellites will be included in the data tables presented on pages F2-F5. These criteria are the following: The value of the visual magnitude of the satellite must not be greater than 23.0, and the satellite must be sanctioned by the IAU with a roman numeral and a name designation. Satellites that have yet to receive IAU approval shall be designated as "works in progress" and shall be included at a later time should such approval be granted, provided their visual magnitudes are not dimmer than 23.0.

APPARENT ORBITS OF THE SATELLITES AT 0^h UNIVERSAL TIME ON JANUARY 16

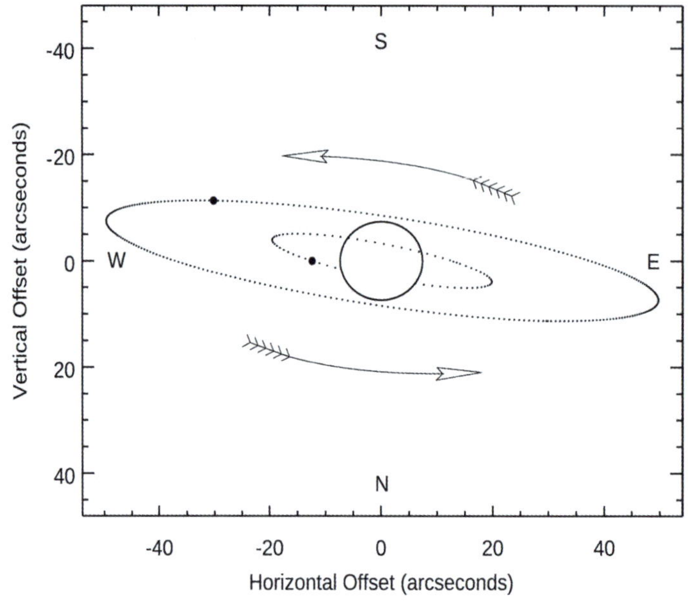

	NAME	MEAN SIDEREAL PERIOD
		d
I	Phobos	0.318 9
II	Deimos	1.262 4

II Deimos

UNIVERSAL TIME OF GREATEST EASTERN ELONGATION

Jan.	Feb.	Mar.	Apr.	May	June	July	Aug.	Sept.	Oct.	Nov.	Dec.
d h	d h	d h	d h	d h	d h	d h	d h	d h	d h	d h	d h
−1 03.8	2 04.9	1 23.3	1 07.0	1 15.2	2 06.0	1 08.3	1 23.5	1 08.5	1 17.4	1 02.3	1 11.2
0 10.1	3 11.2	3 05.6	2 13.3	2 21.5	3 12.3	2 14.6	3 05.9	2 14.9	2 23.7	2 08.7	2 17.5
1 16.3	4 17.5	4 11.9	3 19.6	4 03.8	4 18.7	3 21.1	4 12.3	3 21.2	4 06.1	3 15.1	4 00.0
2 22.7	5 23.7	5 18.2	5 01.9	5 10.2	6 01.0	5 03.4	5 18.6	5 03.6	5 12.5	4 21.4	5 06.4
4 04.9	7 06.0	7 00.5	6 08.3	6 16.5	7 07.4	6 09.8	7 01.0	6 10.0	6 18.9	6 03.8	6 12.7
5 11.2	8 12.3	8 06.8	7 14.7	7 22.8	8 13.7	7 16.2	8 07.4	7 16.3	8 01.3	7 10.1	7 19.1
6 17.4	9 18.5	9 13.2	8 21.0	9 05.3	9 20.1	8 22.5	9 13.8	8 22.7	9 07.7	8 16.5	9 01.4
7 23.7	11 00.9	10 19.5	10 03.3	10 11.6	11 02.5	10 04.9	10 20.2	10 05.0	10 14.0	9 22.9	10 07.8
9 05.9	12 07.2	12 01.8	11 09.6	11 18.0	12 08.9	11 11.2	12 02.5	11 11.4	11 20.4	11 05.3	11 14.2
10 12.3	13 13.4	13 08.1	12 16.0	13 00.3	13 15.2	12 17.6	13 08.9	12 17.9	13 02.7	12 11.7	12 20.5
11 18.5	14 19.7	14 14.4	13 22.3	14 06.6	14 21.6	13 23.9	14 15.2	14 00.2	14 09.1	13 18.0	14 02.9
13 00.7	16 02.0	15 20.7	15 04.6	15 13.0	16 03.9	15 06.4	15 21.6	15 06.6	15 15.5	15 00.4	15 09.3
14 07.0	17 08.3	17 03.0	16 11.0	16 19.3	17 10.3	16 12.8	17 04.0	16 13.0	16 21.8	16 06.7	16 15.7
15 13.2	18 14.5	18 09.3	17 17.4	18 01.7	18 16.6	17 19.1	18 10.3	17 19.3	18 04.3	17 13.1	17 22.1
16 19.5	19 20.9	19 15.7	18 23.7	19 08.0	19 23.0	19 01.5	19 16.8	19 01.7	19 10.6	18 19.5	19 04.4
18 01.8	21 03.2	20 22.0	20 06.0	20 14.4	21 05.3	20 07.8	20 23.1	20 08.0	20 17.0	20 01.8	20 10.8
19 08.1	22 09.5	22 04.3	21 12.4	21 20.8	22 11.8	21 14.2	22 05.5	21 14.4	21 23.4	21 08.2	21 17.1
20 14.3	23 15.8	23 10.6	22 18.7	23 03.1	23 18.2	22 20.6	23 11.9	22 20.8	23 05.7	22 14.6	22 23.5
21 20.5	24 22.0	24 17.0	24 01.0	24 09.5	25 00.5	24 02.9	24 18.2	24 03.2	24 12.1	23 21.0	24 05.9
23 02.8	26 04.3	25 23.3	25 07.4	25 15.8	26 06.9	25 09.3	26 00.6	25 09.6	25 18.4	25 03.4	25 12.2
24 09.0	27 10.6	27 05.6	26 13.7	26 22.2	27 13.2	26 15.7	27 07.0	26 15.9	27 00.8	26 09.7	26 18.6
25 15.3	28 17.0	28 12.0	27 20.0	28 04.5	28 19.6	27 22.1	28 13.3	27 22.3	28 07.2	27 16.1	28 01.1
26 21.6		29 18.3	29 02.5	29 10.9	30 01.9	29 04.5	29 19.7	29 04.7	29 13.6	28 22.4	29 07.4
28 03.9		31 00.6	30 08.8	30 17.3		30 10.8	31 02.1	30 11.0	30 20.0	30 04.8	30 13.8
29 10.1				31 23.7		31 17.2					31 20.2
30 16.4											
31 22.6											

I Phobos

UNIVERSAL TIME OF EVERY THIRD GREATEST EASTERN ELONGATION

Jan.	Feb.	Mar.	Apr.	May	June	July	Aug.	Sept.	Oct.	Nov.	Dec.
d h	d h	d h	d h	d h	d h	d h	d h	d h	d h	d h	d h
−1 20.6	1 09.0	1 02.9	1 16.8	1 08.9	1 23.0	1 15.2	1 06.4	1 20.6	1 12.9	1 04.0	1 19.3
0 19.5	2 07.9	2 01.8	2 15.7	2 07.8	2 21.9	2 14.1	2 05.3	2 19.5	2 11.8	2 03.1	2 18.2
1 18.4	3 06.9	3 00.7	3 14.6	3 06.7	3 20.8	3 13.1	3 04.3	3 18.6	3 10.8	3 02.0	3 17.3
2 17.4	4 05.9	3 23.8	4 13.7	4 05.8	4 19.9	4 12.1	4 03.3	4 17.5	4 09.8	4 01.0	4 16.2
3 16.4	5 04.9	4 22.7	5 12.6	5 04.7	5 18.8	5 11.0	5 02.3	5 16.5	5 08.7	5 00.0	5 15.1
4 15.3	6 03.8	5 21.7	6 11.5	6 03.7	6 17.7	6 10.1	6 01.3	6 15.5	6 07.7	5 22.9	6 14.2
5 14.3	7 02.7	6 20.6	7 10.6	7 02.7	7 16.8	7 09.0	7 00.2	7 14.4	7 06.7	6 22.0	7 13.1
6 13.2	8 01.7	7 19.6	8 09.5	8 01.6	8 15.7	8 07.9	7 23.2	8 13.5	8 05.7	7 20.9	8 12.1
7 12.2	9 00.6	8 18.6	9 08.5	9 00.6	9 14.8	9 07.0	8 22.2	9 12.4	9 04.7	8 19.8	9 11.1
8 11.1	9 23.7	9 17.5	10 07.5	9 23.6	10 13.7	10 05.9	9 21.2	10 11.3	10 03.6	9 18.9	10 10.0
9 10.1	10 22.6	10 16.5	11 06.4	10 22.6	11 12.6	11 04.9	10 20.1	11 10.4	11 02.6	10 17.8	11 09.0
10 09.1	11 21.5	11 15.5	12 05.4	11 21.5	12 11.7	12 03.9	11 19.1	12 09.3	12 01.6	11 16.8	12 08.0
11 08.0	12 20.5	12 14.4	13 04.4	12 20.5	13 10.6	13 02.8	12 18.1	13 08.3	13 00.6	12 15.8	13 06.9
12 07.0	13 19.4	13 13.4	14 03.4	13 19.5	14 09.6	14 01.9	13 17.1	14 07.3	13 23.5	13 14.7	14 06.0
13 05.9	14 18.5	14 12.4	15 02.3	14 18.4	15 08.6	15 00.8	14 16.0	15 06.2	14 22.5	14 13.7	15 04.9
14 04.8	15 17.4	15 11.3	16 01.2	15 17.4	16 07.5	15 23.7	15 15.0	16 05.3	15 21.5	15 12.7	16 03.9
15 03.8	16 16.3	16 10.3	17 00.3	16 16.4	17 06.5	16 22.8	16 14.0	17 04.2	16 20.5	16 11.7	17 02.9
16 02.7	17 15.3	17 09.2	17 23.2	17 15.3	18 05.5	17 21.7	17 13.0	18 03.1	17 19.5	17 10.6	18 01.8
17 01.8	18 14.2	18 08.3	18 22.2	18 14.4	19 04.5	18 20.7	18 11.9	19 02.2	18 18.4	18 09.6	19 00.8
18 00.7	19 13.3	19 07.2	19 21.2	19 13.3	20 03.4	19 19.7	19 10.9	20 01.1	19 17.4	19 08.6	19 23.8
18 23.6	20 12.2	20 06.1	20 20.1	20 12.2	21 02.4	20 18.6	20 09.9	21 00.2	20 16.4	20 07.6	20 22.8
19 22.6	21 11.1	21 05.1	21 19.1	21 11.3	22 01.4	21 17.7	21 08.9	21 23.1	21 15.3	21 06.6	21 21.8
20 21.5	22 10.1	22 04.1	22 18.1	22 10.2	23 00.4	22 16.6	22 07.9	22 22.0	22 14.3	22 05.5	22 20.7
21 20.5	23 09.1	23 03.1	23 17.1	23 09.2	23 23.3	23 15.6	23 06.8	23 21.1	23 13.3	23 04.5	23 19.7
22 19.4	24 08.1	24 02.0	24 16.0	24 08.2	24 22.3	24 14.6	24 05.8	24 20.0	24 12.2	24 03.5	24 18.7
23 18.4	25 07.0	25 01.0	25 15.0	25 07.1	25 21.3	25 13.5	25 04.8	25 19.0	25 11.3	25 02.4	25 17.7
24 17.4	26 05.9	26 00.0	26 14.0	26 06.1	26 20.3	26 12.5	26 03.7	26 18.0	26 10.2	26 01.4	26 16.6
25 16.3	27 04.9	26 22.9	27 12.9	27 05.1	27 19.2	27 11.5	27 02.8	27 16.9	27 09.2	27 00.4	27 15.6
26 15.3	28 03.9	27 21.9	28 11.9	28 04.1	28 18.2	28 10.4	28 01.7	28 16.0	28 08.2	27 23.3	28 14.6
27 14.2		28 20.9	29 10.9	29 03.0	29 17.2	29 09.5	29 00.7	29 14.9	29 07.1	28 22.4	29 13.5
28 13.1		29 19.8	30 09.8	30 02.0	30 16.1	30 08.4	29 23.7	30 13.9	30 06.2	29 21.3	30 12.5
29 12.2		30 18.8		31 01.0		31 07.4	30 22.6		31 05.1	30 20.3	31 11.5
30 11.1		31 17.8		31 23.9			31 21.6				32 10.5
31 10.1											33 09.5

APPARENT ORBITS OF SATELLITES I-IV AT 0^h UNIVERSAL TIME ON THE DATE OF OPPOSITION, DECEMBER 31

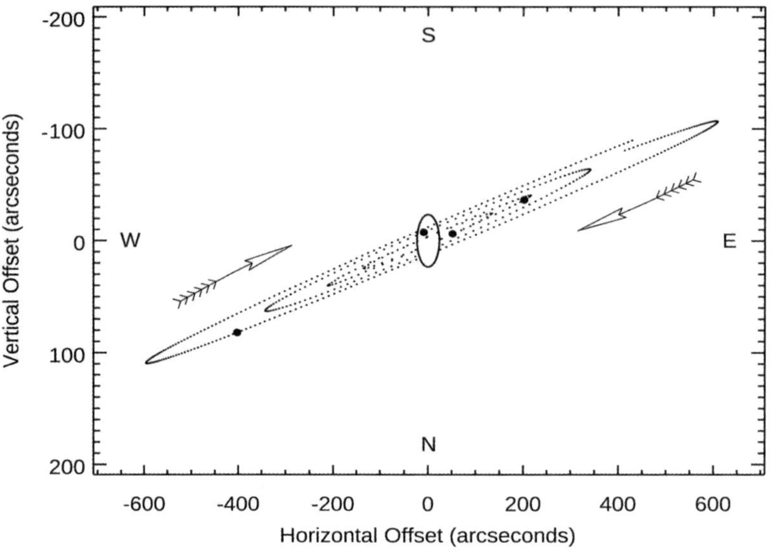

Orbits elongated in ratio of 3.5 to 1 in the North-South direction.

Name	Mean Sidereal Period		Name	Mean Sidereal Period
	d h m s	d		d
V Amalthea	0 11 57 24.480 =	0.498 2	XIII Leda	240.5
I Io	1 18 27 33.523 =	1.769 138	X Lysithea	258.5
II Europa	3 13 13 42.038 =	3.551 181	XII Ananke	624.1 R
III Ganymede	7 03 42 33.379 =	7.154 553	XI Carme	726.3 R
IV Callisto	16 16 32 11.155 =	16.689 018	VIII Pasiphae	744.2 R
VI Himalia		250.1	IX Sinope	753.2 R
VII Elara		259.1		

V Amalthea

UNIVERSAL TIME OF EVERY TWENTIETH GREATEST EASTERN ELONGATION

	d h		d h		d h		d h		d h
Jan.	–1 07.3	Mar.	20 00.6	June	7 18.2	Aug.	26 11.7	Nov.	14 04.8
	9 06.5		29 23.8		17 17.4	Sept.	5 10.9		24 03.9
	19 05.6	Apr.	8 22.9		27 16.6		15 10.0	Dec.	4 03.1
	29 04.7		18 22.1	July	7 15.8		25 09.2		14 02.1
Feb.	8 03.8		28 21.4		17 15.0	Oct.	5 08.4		24 01.2
	18 03.0	May	8 20.6		27 14.2		15 07.5	Dec.	34 00.3
	28 02.2		18 19.8	Aug.	6 13.3		25 06.7		
Mar.	10 01.3		28 18.9		16 12.6	Nov.	4 05.8		

MULTIPLES OF THE MEAN SYNODIC PERIOD

	d	h		d	h		d	h		d	h
1	0	12.0	6	2	23.7	11	5	11.5	16	7	23.3
2	0	23.9	7	3	11.7	12	5	23.5	17	8	11.3
3	1	11.9	8	3	23.7	13	6	11.4	18	8	23.2
4	1	23.8	9	4	11.6	14	6	23.4	19	9	11.2
5	2	11.8	10	4	23.6	15	7	11.4	20	9	23.2

DIFFERENTIAL COORDINATES FOR 0ʰ UNIVERSAL TIME

Date	VI Himalia Δα	VI Himalia Δδ	VII Elara Δα	VII Elara Δδ	Date	VI Himalia Δα	VI Himalia Δδ	VII Elara Δα	VII Elara Δδ
	m s	′	m s	′		m s	′	m s	′
Jan. −3	+ 0 12	− 23.7	1 31	− 10.9	July 4	+ 3 04	+ 9.2	+ 2 56	+ 22.6
1	− 0 11	− 26.2	− 1 53	− 15.1	8	+ 3 08	+ 7.3	+ 2 58	+ 22.2
5	− 0 32	− 28.5	− 2 12	− 19.0	12	+ 3 10	+ 5.3	+ 3 00	+ 21.7
9	− 0 53	− 30.6	− 2 27	− 22.4	16	+ 3 11	+ 3.2	+ 3 01	+ 21.0
13	− 1 12	− 32.4	− 2 39	− 25.4	20	+ 3 11	+ 1.1	+ 3 01	+ 20.2
17	− 1 30	− 33.9	− 2 47	− 27.8	24	+ 3 10	− 1.0	+ 3 00	+ 19.2
21	− 1 47	− 35.1	− 2 52	− 29.6	28	+ 3 07	− 3.1	+ 2 58	+ 18.0
25	− 2 02	− 36.0	− 2 54	− 30.8	Aug. 1	+ 3 04	− 5.2	+ 2 55	+ 16.7
29	− 2 16	− 36.7	− 2 52	− 31.5	5	+ 2 59	− 7.3	+ 2 51	+ 15.2
Feb. 2	− 2 28	− 37.0	− 2 48	− 31.6	9	+ 2 53	− 9.3	+ 2 45	+ 13.5
6	− 2 39	− 37.1	− 2 42	− 31.3	13	+ 2 47	− 11.3	+ 2 37	+ 11.8
10	− 2 48	− 36.8	− 2 34	− 30.6	17	+ 2 39	− 13.3	+ 2 28	+ 9.8
14	− 2 56	− 36.3	− 2 24	− 29.5	21	+ 2 30	− 15.1	+ 2 18	+ 7.8
18	− 3 02	− 35.4	− 2 13	− 28.1	25	+ 2 21	− 16.9	+ 2 05	+ 5.6
22	− 3 06	− 34.3	− 2 01	− 26.4	29	+ 2 10	− 18.5	+ 1 51	+ 3.3
26	− 3 09	− 32.9	− 1 49	− 24.5	Sept. 2	+ 1 59	− 20.1	+ 1 35	+ 1.0
Mar. 2	− 3 10	− 31.3	− 1 36	− 22.4	6	+ 1 47	− 21.4	+ 1 17	− 1.3
6	− 3 10	− 29.4	− 1 23	− 20.2	10	+ 1 34	− 22.7	+ 0 57	− 3.6
10	− 3 09	− 27.3	− 1 10	− 17.9	14	+ 1 20	− 23.8	+ 0 36	− 5.8
14	− 3 06	− 24.9	− 0 57	− 15.6	18	+ 1 06	− 24.8	+ 0 14	− 8.0
18	− 3 01	− 22.4	− 0 44	− 13.2	22	+ 0 51	− 25.6	− 0 09	− 9.9
22	− 2 55	− 19.7	− 0 32	− 10.8	26	+ 0 35	− 26.2	− 0 33	− 11.7
26	− 2 47	− 16.9	− 0 19	− 8.4	30	+ 0 18	− 26.6	− 0 56	− 13.2
30	− 2 38	− 14.0	− 0 07	− 6.1	Oct. 4	+ 0 01	− 26.8	− 1 19	− 14.5
Apr. 3	− 2 28	− 10.9	+ 0 04	− 3.8	8	− 0 17	− 26.9	− 1 42	− 15.4
7	− 2 16	− 7.8	+ 0 16	− 1.5	12	− 0 35	− 26.6	− 2 03	− 16.1
11	− 2 02	− 4.7	+ 0 27	+ 0.7	16	− 0 53	− 26.2	− 2 23	− 16.5
15	− 1 48	− 1.6	+ 0 37	+ 2.8	20	− 1 12	− 25.6	− 2 42	− 16.6
19	− 1 32	+ 1.4	+ 0 48	+ 4.9	24	− 1 31	− 24.7	− 2 58	− 16.4
23	− 1 15	+ 4.2	+ 0 57	+ 6.8	28	− 1 49	− 23.6	− 3 12	− 16.0
27	− 0 57	+ 7.0	+ 1 07	+ 8.7	Nov. 1	− 2 08	− 22.2	− 3 25	− 15.3
May 1	− 0 38	+ 9.5	+ 1 16	+ 10.4	5	− 2 26	− 20.7	− 3 34	− 14.5
5	− 0 19	+ 11.8	+ 1 25	+ 12.1	9	− 2 43	− 18.9	− 3 42	− 13.4
9	+ 0 01	+ 13.7	+ 1 34	+ 13.7	13	− 2 59	− 16.9	− 3 47	− 12.3
13	+ 0 20	+ 15.4	+ 1 42	+ 15.1	17	− 3 14	− 14.7	− 3 50	− 10.9
17	+ 0 39	+ 16.7	+ 1 50	+ 16.4	21	− 3 27	− 12.3	− 3 50	− 9.5
21	+ 0 57	+ 17.7	+ 1 57	+ 17.6	25	− 3 38	− 9.7	− 3 48	− 7.9
25	+ 1 15	+ 18.3	+ 2 04	+ 18.7	29	− 3 47	− 7.0	− 3 44	− 6.3
29	+ 1 31	+ 18.6	+ 2 11	+ 19.7	Dec. 3	− 3 54	− 4.2	− 3 37	− 4.7
June 2	+ 1 47	+ 18.6	+ 2 18	+ 20.5	7	− 3 57	− 1.4	− 3 28	− 2.9
6	+ 2 01	+ 18.2	+ 2 24	+ 21.3	11	− 3 57	+ 1.5	− 3 17	− 1.2
10	+ 2 14	+ 17.6	+ 2 30	+ 21.9	15	− 3 53	+ 4.4	− 3 04	+ 0.6
14	+ 2 26	+ 16.7	+ 2 36	+ 22.3	19	− 3 45	+ 7.2	− 2 49	+ 2.4
18	+ 2 37	+ 15.6	+ 2 41	+ 22.7	23	− 3 33	+ 10.0	− 2 32	+ 4.1
22	+ 2 46	+ 14.2	+ 2 45	+ 22.9	27	− 3 18	+ 12.6	− 2 14	+ 5.9
26	+ 2 53	+ 12.7	+ 2 49	+ 22.9	31	− 2 58	+ 14.9	− 1 54	+ 7.6
30	+ 2 59	+ 11.0	+ 2 53	+ 22.9	35	− 2 36	+ 17.1	− 1 34	+ 9.3

Differential coordinates are given in the sense "satellite minus planet."

DIFFERENTIAL COORDINATES FOR 0^h UNIVERSAL TIME

Date		VIII Pasiphae $\Delta\alpha$	VIII Pasiphae $\Delta\delta$	IX Sinope $\Delta\alpha$	IX Sinope $\Delta\delta$	X Lysithea $\Delta\alpha$	X Lysithea $\Delta\delta$
		m s	′	m s	′	m s	′
Jan.	−5	− 0 44	+ 1.0	+ 11 40	− 37.8	+ 2 00	+ 22.5
	5	− 1 35	+ 4.9	+ 11 19	− 36.4	+ 3 01	+ 18.5
	15	− 2 23	+ 8.4	+ 10 52	− 35.0	+ 3 42	+ 13.1
	25	− 3 06	+ 11.5	+ 10 21	− 33.7	+ 4 03	+ 6.8
Feb.	4	− 3 47	+ 14.1	+ 9 46	− 32.7	+ 4 04	+ 0.2
	14	− 4 24	+ 16.5	+ 9 08	− 31.9	+ 3 50	− 6.1
	24	− 4 58	+ 18.6	+ 8 28	− 31.3	+ 3 24	− 11.8
Mar.	6	− 5 29	+ 20.7	+ 7 46	− 30.9	+ 2 50	− 16.6
	16	− 5 58	+ 22.7	+ 7 03	− 30.6	+ 2 12	− 20.2
	26	− 6 24	+ 24.8	+ 6 19	− 30.4	+ 1 32	− 22.6
Apr.	5	− 6 47	+ 27.0	+ 5 34	− 30.2	+ 0 51	− 23.8
	15	− 7 08	+ 29.3	+ 4 49	− 29.9	+ 0 11	− 23.8
	25	− 7 26	+ 31.8	+ 4 03	− 29.4	− 0 27	− 22.7
May	5	− 7 42	+ 34.4	+ 3 17	− 28.8	− 1 02	− 20.5
	15	− 7 55	+ 37.3	+ 2 30	− 27.9	− 1 34	− 17.5
	25	− 8 05	+ 40.2	+ 1 44	− 26.8	− 2 02	− 13.6
June	4	− 8 13	+ 43.4	+ 0 57	− 25.3	− 2 26	− 9.1
	14	− 8 19	+ 46.6	+ 0 12	− 23.4	− 2 44	− 4.1
	24	− 8 22	+ 49.9	− 0 33	− 21.2	− 2 56	+ 1.1
July	4	− 8 22	+ 53.3	− 1 17	− 18.6	− 3 01	+ 6.3
	14	− 8 20	+ 56.7	− 1 59	− 15.6	− 2 58	+ 11.2
	24	− 8 16	+ 60.1	− 2 39	− 12.2	− 2 48	+ 15.4
Aug.	3	− 8 10	+ 63.5	− 3 16	− 8.5	− 2 28	+ 18.6
	13	− 8 02	+ 66.8	− 3 51	− 4.5	− 2 00	+ 20.2
	23	− 7 53	+ 70.0	− 4 22	− 0.3	− 1 24	+ 20.0
Sept.	2	− 7 42	+ 73.1	− 4 49	+ 4.2	− 0 41	+ 17.8
	12	− 7 30	+ 76.1	− 5 12	+ 8.8	+ 0 06	+ 13.6
	22	− 7 18	+ 79.0	− 5 31	+ 13.4	+ 0 53	+ 7.7
Oct.	2	− 7 06	+ 81.7	− 5 44	+ 18.1	+ 1 38	+ 0.6
	12	− 6 54	+ 84.2	− 5 52	+ 22.5	+ 2 19	− 7.2
	22	− 6 42	+ 86.5	− 5 54	+ 26.8	+ 2 54	− 15.0
Nov.	1	− 6 32	+ 88.5	− 5 50	+ 30.7	+ 3 20	− 22.4
	11	− 6 23	+ 90.2	− 5 39	+ 34.2	+ 3 37	− 28.9
	21	− 6 16	+ 91.4	− 5 23	+ 37.1	+ 3 43	− 34.1
Dec.	1	− 6 10	+ 92.1	− 5 00	+ 39.3	+ 3 38	− 37.6
	11	− 6 05	+ 92.2	− 4 31	+ 40.8	+ 3 19	− 39.2
	21	− 6 01	+ 91.4	− 3 57	+ 41.4	+ 2 48	− 38.8
	31	− 5 56	+ 89.7	− 3 18	+ 41.1	+ 2 05	− 36.4

Differential coordinates are given in the sense “satellite minus planet.”

DIFFERENTIAL COORDINATES FOR 0ʰ UNIVERSAL TIME

Date		XI Carme Δα	XI Carme Δδ	XII Ananke Δα	XII Ananke Δδ	XIII Leda Δα	XIII Leda Δδ
		m s	′	m s	′	m s	′
Jan.	−5	− 3 22	− 2.8	+ 7 45	− 57.4	− 4 37	+ 16.2
	5	− 3 58	− 7.9	+ 7 59	− 55.0	− 4 52	+ 10.1
	15	− 4 30	− 12.7	+ 8 07	− 52.2	− 4 49	+ 3.9
	25	− 4 58	− 17.1	+ 8 10	− 49.0	− 4 30	− 1.9
Feb.	4	− 5 22	− 21.0	+ 8 09	− 45.6	− 3 59	− 7.2
	14	− 5 43	− 24.3	+ 8 04	− 42.4	− 3 19	− 11.6
	24	− 6 00	− 26.9	+ 7 54	− 39.3	− 2 32	− 15.1
Mar.	6	− 6 14	− 28.9	+ 7 42	− 36.4	− 1 42	− 17.6
	16	− 6 23	− 30.2	+ 7 26	− 33.7	− 0 49	− 18.9
	26	− 6 29	− 31.1	+ 7 07	− 31.3	+ 0 02	− 19.2
Apr.	5	− 6 31	− 31.4	+ 6 45	− 29.0	+ 0 50	− 18.2
	15	− 6 28	− 31.3	+ 6 21	− 26.8	+ 1 33	− 15.9
	25	− 6 22	− 30.8	+ 5 54	− 24.8	+ 2 07	− 12.5
May	5	− 6 11	− 30.1	+ 5 24	− 22.6	+ 2 30	− 8.2
	15	− 5 56	− 29.2	+ 4 52	− 20.5	+ 2 41	− 3.2
	25	− 5 38	− 28.2	+ 4 19	− 18.2	+ 2 40	+ 1.9
June	4	− 5 15	− 27.3	+ 3 43	− 15.8	+ 2 28	+ 6.8
	14	− 4 49	− 26.4	+ 3 06	− 13.0	+ 2 07	+ 11.3
	24	− 4 20	− 25.6	+ 2 28	− 10.0	+ 1 40	+ 15.0
July	4	− 3 47	− 25.0	+ 1 49	− 6.7	+ 1 08	+ 18.0
	14	− 3 12	− 24.7	+ 1 09	− 3.0	+ 0 33	+ 20.1
	24	− 2 34	− 24.6	+ 0 30	+ 1.0	− 0 03	+ 21.3
Aug.	3	− 1 54	− 24.8	− 0 10	+ 5.3	− 0 39	+ 21.8
	13	− 1 13	− 25.3	− 0 48	+ 10.1	− 1 15	+ 21.4
	23	− 0 30	− 26.0	− 1 26	+ 15.1	− 1 49	+ 20.3
Sept.	2	+ 0 15	− 27.0	− 2 02	+ 20.3	− 2 22	+ 18.5
	12	+ 1 00	− 28.2	− 2 36	+ 25.8	− 2 51	+ 15.9
	22	+ 1 45	− 29.6	− 3 08	+ 31.4	− 3 17	+ 12.6
Oct.	2	+ 2 31	− 31.1	− 3 38	+ 37.0	− 3 37	+ 8.7
	12	+ 3 16	− 32.5	− 4 05	+ 42.5	− 3 49	+ 4.2
	22	+ 4 01	− 33.7	− 4 29	+ 47.8	− 3 52	− 0.9
Nov.	1	+ 4 45	− 34.8	− 4 50	+ 52.8	− 3 43	− 6.2
	11	+ 5 27	− 35.5	− 5 08	+ 57.3	− 3 18	− 11.6
	21	+ 6 08	− 35.6	− 5 23	+ 61.0	− 2 37	− 16.5
Dec.	1	+ 6 46	− 35.2	− 5 34	+ 63.9	− 1 39	− 20.4
	11	+ 7 20	− 34.1	− 5 41	+ 65.6	− 0 28	− 22.4
	21	+ 7 50	− 32.2	− 5 44	+ 66.2	+ 0 51	− 22.0
	31	+ 8 15	− 29.7	− 5 42	+ 65.4	+ 2 06	− 18.8

Differential coordinates are given in the sense "satellite minus planet."

TERRESTRIAL TIME OF SUPERIOR GEOCENTRIC CONJUNCTION

I Io

	d	h m		d	h m		d	h m		d	h m
Jan.	0	07 34	Mar.	20	22 28	July	31	18 11	Oct.	19	10 16
	2	02 00		22	16 57	Aug.	2	12 41		21	04 44
	3	20 26		24	11 27		4	07 12		22	23 13
	5	14 53		26	05 56		6	01 42		24	17 41
	7	09 19		28	00 26		7	20 12		26	12 09
	9	03 46		29	18 55		9	14 42		28	06 37
	10	22 12		31	13 25		11	09 12		30	01 05
	12	16 39	Apr.	2	07 54		13	03 42		31	19 33
	14	11 06		4	02 24		14	22 12	Nov.	2	14 00
	16	05 33		5	20 54		16	16 42		4	08 28
	18	00 00		7	15 24		18	11 12		6	02 56
	19	18 27		9	09 53		20	05 42		7	21 23
	21	12 54		11	04 23		22	00 12		9	15 51
	23	07 21		12	22 53		23	18 42		11	10 18
	25	01 48		14	17 23		25	13 12		13	04 46
	26	20 15		16	11 53		27	07 41		14	23 13
	28	14 43		18	06 23		29	02 11		16	17 40
	30	09 10		20	00 53		30	20 41		18	12 08
Feb.	1	03 38		21	19 23	Sept.	1	15 11		20	06 35
	2	22 05		23	13 53		3	09 40		22	01 02
	4	16 33		25	08 23		5	04 10		23	19 29
	6	11 01		27	02 53		6	22 40		25	13 56
	8	05 29		28	21 23		8	17 09		27	08 22
	9	23 57		30	15 53		10	11 39		29	02 49
	11	18 25	May	2	10 23		12	06 08		30	21 16
	13	12 53		4	04 54		14	00 38	Dec.	2	15 42
	15	07 21		5	23 24		15	19 07		4	10 09
	17	01 49		7	17 54		17	13 36		6	04 35
	18	20 17		9	12 24		19	08 06		7	23 02
	20	14 46		11	06 54		21	02 35		9	17 28
	22	09 14		13	01 25		22	21 04		11	11 55
	24	03 42		14	19 55		24	15 33		13	06 21
	25	22 11		16	14 25		26	10 02		15	00 47
	27	16 40		18	08 56		28	04 32		16	19 13
Mar.	1	11 08		20	03 26		29	23 01		18	13 40
	3	05 37		21	21 56	Oct.	1	17 30		20	08 06
	5	00 06		23	16 27		3	11 58		22	02 32
	6	18 35		25	10 57		5	06 27		23	20 58
	8	13 04		27	05 27		7	00 56		25	15 24
	10	07 33		..	.. ..		8	19 25		27	09 50
	12	02 02	July	22	21 40		10	13 53		29	04 16
	13	20 31		24	16 10		12	08 22		30	22 41
	15	15 00		26	10 41		14	02 51			
	17	09 29		28	05 11		15	21 19			
	19	03 59		29	23 41		17	15 48			

Jupiter is too close to the Sun for observations between May 28 and July 21.

TERRESTRIAL TIME OF SUPERIOR GEOCENTRIC CONJUNCTION

II Europa

	d	h m		d	h m		d	h m		d	h m
Jan.	1	18 32	Mar.	24	11 36	Aug.	3	03 47	Oct.	23	22 32
	5	07 41		28	00 58		6	17 11		27	11 47
	8	20 51		31	14 21		10	06 34		31	01 02
	12	10 01	Apr.	4	03 44		13	19 57	Nov.	3	14 16
	15	23 13		7	17 07		17	09 20		7	03 30
	19	12 24		11	06 31		20	22 43		10	16 43
	23	01 36		14	19 54		24	12 05		14	05 55
	26	14 49		18	09 19		28	01 27		17	19 07
	30	04 02		21	22 43		31	14 49		21	08 19
Feb.	2	17 16		25	12 07	Sept.	4	04 10		24	21 30
	6	06 31		29	01 32		7	17 31		28	10 40
	9	19 46	May	2	14 57		11	06 52	Dec.	1	23 50
	13	09 03		6	04 22		14	20 13		5	12 59
	16	22 19		9	17 47		18	09 33		9	02 08
	20	11 37		13	07 12		21	22 53		12	15 17
	24	00 54		16	20 38		25	12 12		16	04 25
	27	14 13		20	10 03		29	01 31		19	17 32
Mar.	3	03 31		23	23 28	Oct.	2	14 50		23	06 40
	6	16 51		27	12 54		6	04 08		26	19 47
	10	06 11		..	.. ..		9	17 26		30	08 54
	13	19 32	July	23	11 35		13	06 43			
	17	08 53		27	00 59		16	20 00			
	20	22 14		30	14 23		20	09 16			

III Ganymede

	d	h m		d	h m		d	h m		d	h m
Jan.	2	22 57	Mar.	29	20 52	Aug.	6	04 41		31	06 53
	10	02 22	Apr.	6	01 07		13	09 06	Nov.	7	10 40
	17	05 51		13	05 26		20	13 29		14	14 23
	24	09 24		20	09 47		27	17 50		21	18 00
	31	13 01		27	14 10	Sept.	3	22 09		28	21 32
Feb.	7	16 44	May	4	18 34		11	02 26	Dec.	6	01 00
	14	20 32		11	22 59		18	06 41		13	04 24
	22	00 25		19	03 26		25	10 52		20	07 45
Mar.	1	04 23		26	07 54	Oct.	2	15 00		27	11 03
	8	08 25		..	.. ..		9	19 04			
	15	12 31	July	22	19 47		16	23 04			
	22	16 39		30	00 15		24	03 01			

IV Callisto

	d	h m		d	h m		d	h m		d	h m
Jan.	14	17 22	Apr.	8	09 58	Aug.	21	06 09	Nov.	13	03 00
	31	09 10		25	05 55	Sept.	7	02 04		29	18 54
Feb.	17	02 01	May	12	02 16		23	21 29	Dec.	16	09 52
Mar.	5	19 51		..	.. ..	Oct.	10	16 12			
	22	14 33	Aug.	4	09 49		27	10 05			

Jupiter is too close to the Sun for observations between May 28 and July 21.

UNIVERSAL TIME OF GEOCENTRIC PHENOMENA

JANUARY

d	h m	
0	0 17	II Sh I
	1 40	II Tr E
	2 51	II Sh E
	6 27	I Oc D
	9 14	I Ec R
1	3 35	I Tr I
	4 11	I Sh I
	5 46	I Tr E
	6 23	I Sh E
	17 15	II Oc D
	21 06	II Ec R
2	0 53	I Oc D
	3 43	I Ec R
	21 53	III Oc D
	22 01	I Tr I
	22 40	I Sh I
3	0 00	III Oc R
	0 12	I Tr E
	0 26	III Ec D
	0 52	I Sh E
	2 44	III Ec R
	12 17	II Tr I
	13 35	II Sh I
	14 49	II Tr E
	16 09	II Sh E
	19 20	I Oc D
	22 12	I Ec R
4	16 28	I Tr I
	17 08	I Sh I
	18 39	I Tr E
	19 21	I Sh E
5	6 24	II Oc D
	10 24	II Ec R
	13 46	I Oc D
	16 40	I Ec R
6	10 54	I Tr I
	11 37	I Sh I
	11 45	III Tr I
	13 06	I Tr E
	13 49	I Sh E
	13 51	III Tr E
	14 37	III Sh I
	16 53	III Sh E
7	1 26	II Tr I
	2 53	II Sh I
	3 57	II Tr E
	5 27	II Sh E
	8 13	I Oc D
	11 09	I Ec R
8	5 21	I Tr I

d	h m	
8	6 06	I Sh I
	7 32	I Tr E
	8 18	I Sh E
	19 34	II Oc D
	23 44	II Ec R
9	2 39	I Oc D
	5 38	I Ec R
	23 47	I Tr I
10	0 35	I Sh I
	1 17	III Oc D
	1 59	I Tr E
	2 47	I Sh E
	3 26	III Oc R
	4 27	III Ec D
	6 46	III Ec R
	14 36	II Tr I
	16 10	II Sh I
	17 07	II Tr E
	18 45	II Sh E
	21 06	I Oc D
11	0 07	I Ec R
	18 14	I Tr I
	19 04	I Sh I
	20 26	I Tr E
	21 16	I Sh E
12	8 44	II Oc D
	13 02	II Ec R
	15 33	I Oc D
	18 35	I Ec R
13	12 41	I Tr I
	13 33	I Sh I
	14 52	I Tr E
	15 10	III Tr I
	15 45	I Sh E
	17 18	III Tr E
	18 37	III Sh I
	20 55	III Sh E
14	3 45	II Tr I
	5 28	II Sh I
	6 17	II Tr E
	8 03	II Sh E
	9 59	I Oc D
	13 04	I Ec R
15	7 08	I Tr I
	8 01	I Sh I
	9 19	I Tr E
	10 14	I Sh E
	21 55	II Oc D
16	2 22	II Ec R
	4 26	I Oc D

d	h m	
16	7 33	I Ec R
17	1 35	I Tr I
	2 30	I Sh I
	3 46	I Tr E
	4 42	I Sh E
	4 45	III Oc D
	6 55	III Oc R
	8 27	III Ec D
	10 47	III Ec R
	16 56	II Tr I
	18 46	II Sh I
	19 27	II Tr E
	21 21	II Sh E
	22 53	I Oc D
18	2 02	I Ec R
	20 02	I Tr I
	20 59	I Sh I
	22 13	I Tr E
	23 11	I Sh E
19	11 06	II Oc D
	15 41	II Ec R
	17 20	I Oc D
	20 30	I Ec R
20	14 29	I Tr I
	15 28	I Sh I
	16 41	I Tr E
	17 40	I Sh E
	18 40	III Tr I
	20 50	III Tr E
	22 37	III Sh I
21	0 56	III Sh E
	6 07	II Tr I
	8 04	II Sh I
	8 38	II Tr E
	10 38	II Sh E
	11 47	I Oc D
	14 59	I Ec R
22	8 56	I Tr I
	9 57	I Sh I
	11 08	I Tr E
	12 09	I Sh E
23	0 19	II Oc D
	5 00	II Ec R
	6 14	I Oc D
	9 28	I Ec R
24	3 24	I Tr I
	4 26	I Sh I
	5 35	I Tr E
	6 38	I Sh E
	8 17	III Oc D

d	h m	
24	10 29	III Oc R
	12 28	III Ec D
	14 49	III Ec R
	19 18	II Tr I
	21 22	II Sh I
	21 50	II Tr E
	23 56	II Sh E
25	0 42	I Oc D
	3 57	I Ec R
	21 51	I Tr I
	22 55	I Sh I
26	0 02	I Tr E
	1 07	I Sh E
	13 31	II Oc D
	18 19	II Ec R
	19 09	I Oc D
	22 26	I Ec R
27	16 19	I Tr I
	17 24	I Sh I
	18 30	I Tr E
	19 36	I Sh E
	22 15	III Tr I
28	0 27	III Tr E
	2 38	III Sh I
	4 58	III Sh E
	8 31	II Tr I
	10 40	II Sh I
	11 02	II Tr E
	13 14	II Sh E
	13 36	I Oc D
	16 54	I Ec R
29	10 46	I Tr I
	11 53	I Sh I
	12 57	I Tr E
	14 05	I Sh E
30	2 44	II Oc D
	7 39	II Ec R
	8 04	I Oc D
	11 23	I Ec R
31	5 14	I Tr I
	6 21	I Sh I
	7 25	I Tr E
	8 33	I Sh E
	11 53	III Oc D
	14 08	III Oc R
	16 28	III Ec D
	18 50	III Ec R
	21 43	II Tr I
	23 57	II Sh I

I. Jan. 16	II. Jan. 16	III. Jan. 17	IV. Jan.
$x_2 = +1.7,\ y_2 = +0.3$	$x_2 = +2.2,\ y_2 = +0.4$	$x_1 = +1.4,\ y_1 = +0.8$ $x_2 = +2.7,\ y_2 = +0.7$	no eclipse

NOTE.—I denotes ingress; E, egress; D, disappearance; R, reappearance; Ec, eclipse; Oc, occultation; Tr, transit of the satellite; Sh, transit of the shadow.

CONFIGURATIONS OF SATELLITES I-IV FOR JANUARY

UNIVERSAL TIME

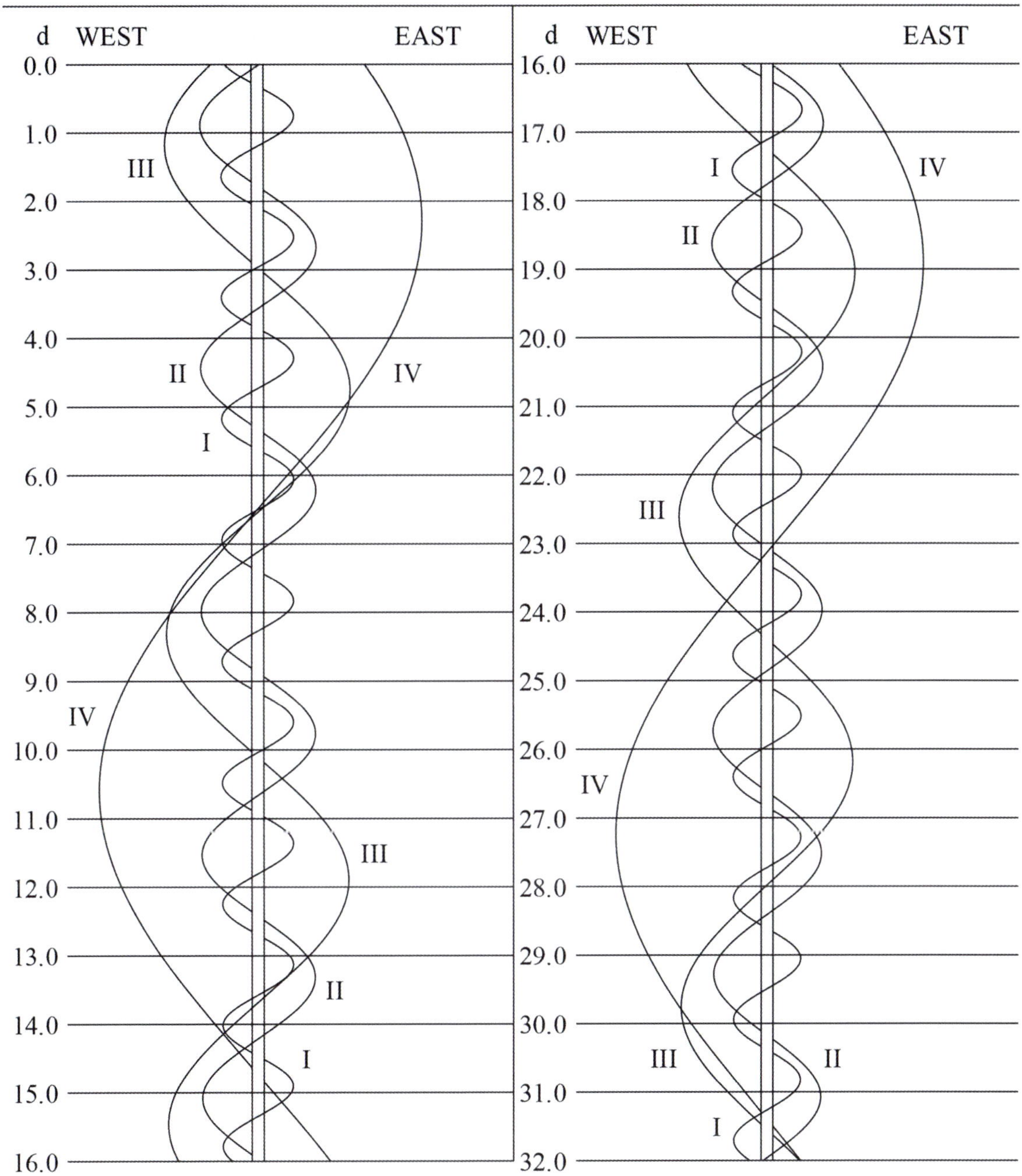

PHASES OF THE ECLIPSES

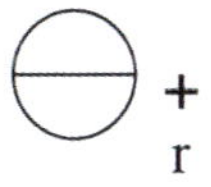

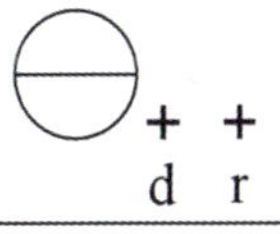

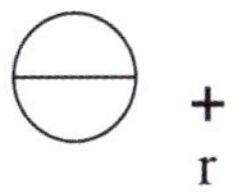

UNIVERSAL TIME OF GEOCENTRIC PHENOMENA

FEBRUARY

d	h m	
1	0 15	II Tr E
	2 31	I Oc D
	2 32	II Sh E
	5 52	I Ec R
	23 41	I Tr I
2	0 50	I Sh I
	1 53	I Tr E
	3 02	I Sh E
	15 58	II Oc D
	20 58	II Ec R
	20 59	I Oc D
3	0 21	I Ec R
	18 09	I Tr I
	19 19	I Sh I
	20 21	I Tr E
	21 31	I Sh E
4	1 56	III Tr I
	4 10	III Tr E
	6 40	III Sh I
	9 01	III Sh E
	10 57	II Tr I
	13 15	II Sh I
	13 29	II Tr E
	15 26	I Oc D
	15 50	II Sh E
	18 49	I Ec R
5	12 37	I Tr I
	13 48	I Sh I
	14 48	I Tr E
	16 00	I Sh E
6	5 13	II Oc D
	9 54	I Oc D
	10 17	II Ec R
	13 18	I Ec R
7	7 05	I Tr I
	8 17	I Sh I
	9 16	I Tr E
	10 29	I Sh E
	15 35	III Oc D
	17 52	III Oc R
	20 27	III Ec D
	22 51	III Ec R
8	0 11	II Tr I
	2 33	II Sh I
	2 43	II Tr E

d	h m	
8	4 22	I Oc D
	5 08	II Sh E
	7 47	I Ec R
9	1 33	I Tr I
	2 46	I Sh I
	3 44	I Tr E
	4 58	I Sh E
	18 28	II Oc D
	22 50	I Oc D
	23 36	II Ec R
10	2 16	I Ec R
	20 01	I Tr I
	21 15	I Sh I
	22 13	I Tr E
	23 27	I Sh E
11	5 41	III Tr I
	7 57	III Tr E
	10 40	III Sh I
	13 02	III Sh E
	13 25	II Tr I
	15 51	II Sh I
	15 57	II Tr E
	17 18	I Oc D
	18 26	II Sh E
	20 45	I Ec R
12	14 29	I Tr I
	15 44	I Sh I
	16 41	I Tr E
	17 56	I Sh E
13	7 44	II Oc D
	11 46	I Oc D
	12 56	II Ec R
	15 13	I Ec R
14	8 57	I Tr I
	10 13	I Sh I
	11 09	I Tr E
	12 25	I Sh E
	19 22	III Oc D
	21 41	III Oc R
15	0 28	III Ec D
	2 40	II Tr I
	2 53	III Ec R
	5 09	II Sh I
	5 12	II Tr E
	6 14	I Oc D

d	h m	
15	7 43	II Sh E
	9 42	I Ec R
16	3 26	I Tr I
	4 42	I Sh I
	5 37	I Tr E
	6 54	I Sh E
	21 00	II Oc D
	23 36	II Oc R
	23 36	II Ec D
17	0 42	I Oc D
	2 15	II Ec R
	4 11	I Ec R
	21 54	I Tr I
	23 11	I Sh I
18	0 06	I Tr E
	1 23	I Sh E
	9 31	III Tr I
	11 48	III Tr E
	14 41	III Sh I
	15 56	II Tr I
	17 04	III Sh E
	18 26	II Sh I
	18 28	II Tr E
	19 11	I Oc D
	21 01	II Sh E
	22 40	I Ec R
19	16 23	I Tr I
	17 40	I Sh I
	18 34	I Tr E
	19 52	I Sh E
20	10 18	II Oc D
	12 54	II Oc R
	12 56	II Ec D
	13 39	I Oc D
	15 35	II Ec R
	17 09	I Ec R
21	10 51	I Tr I
	12 09	I Sh I
	13 03	I Tr E
	14 21	I Sh E
	23 14	III Oc D
22	1 34	III Oc R
	4 28	III Ec D
	5 12	II Tr I
	6 55	III Ec R

d	h m	
22	7 44	II Sh I
	7 45	II Tr E
	8 07	I Oc D
	10 19	II Sh E
	11 37	I Ec R
23	5 20	I Tr I
	6 38	I Sh I
	7 31	I Tr E
	8 50	I Sh E
	23 35	II Oc D
24	2 12	II Oc R
	2 15	II Ec D
	2 36	I Oc D
	4 54	II Ec R
	6 06	I Ec R
	23 48	I Tr I
25	1 07	I Sh I
	2 00	I Tr E
	3 19	I Sh E
	13 25	III Tr I
	15 45	III Tr E
	18 29	II Tr I
	18 41	III Sh I
	21 01	II Tr E
	21 02	II Sh I
	21 04	I Oc D
	21 06	III Sh E
	23 37	II Sh E
26	0 35	I Ec R
	18 17	I Tr I
	19 35	I Sh I
	20 29	I Tr E
	21 48	I Sh E
27	12 54	II Oc D
	15 31	II Oc R
	15 33	I Oc D
	15 35	II Ec D
	18 14	II Ec R
	19 04	I Ec R
28	12 46	I Tr I
	14 04	I Sh I
	14 58	I Tr E
	16 17	I Sh E

I. Feb. 15	II. Feb. 13	III. Feb. 15	IV. Feb.
$x_2 = +2.0$, $y_2 = +0.3$	$x_2 = +2.6$, $y_2 = +0.4$	$x_1 = +2.2$, $y_1 = +0.7$ $x_2 = +3.5$, $y_2 = +0.7$	no eclipse

NOTE.—I denotes ingress; E, egress; D, disappearance; R, reappearance; Ec, eclipse; Oc, occultation; Tr, transit of the satellite; Sh, transit of the shadow.

CONFIGURATIONS OF SATELLITES I-IV FOR FEBRUARY

UNIVERSAL TIME

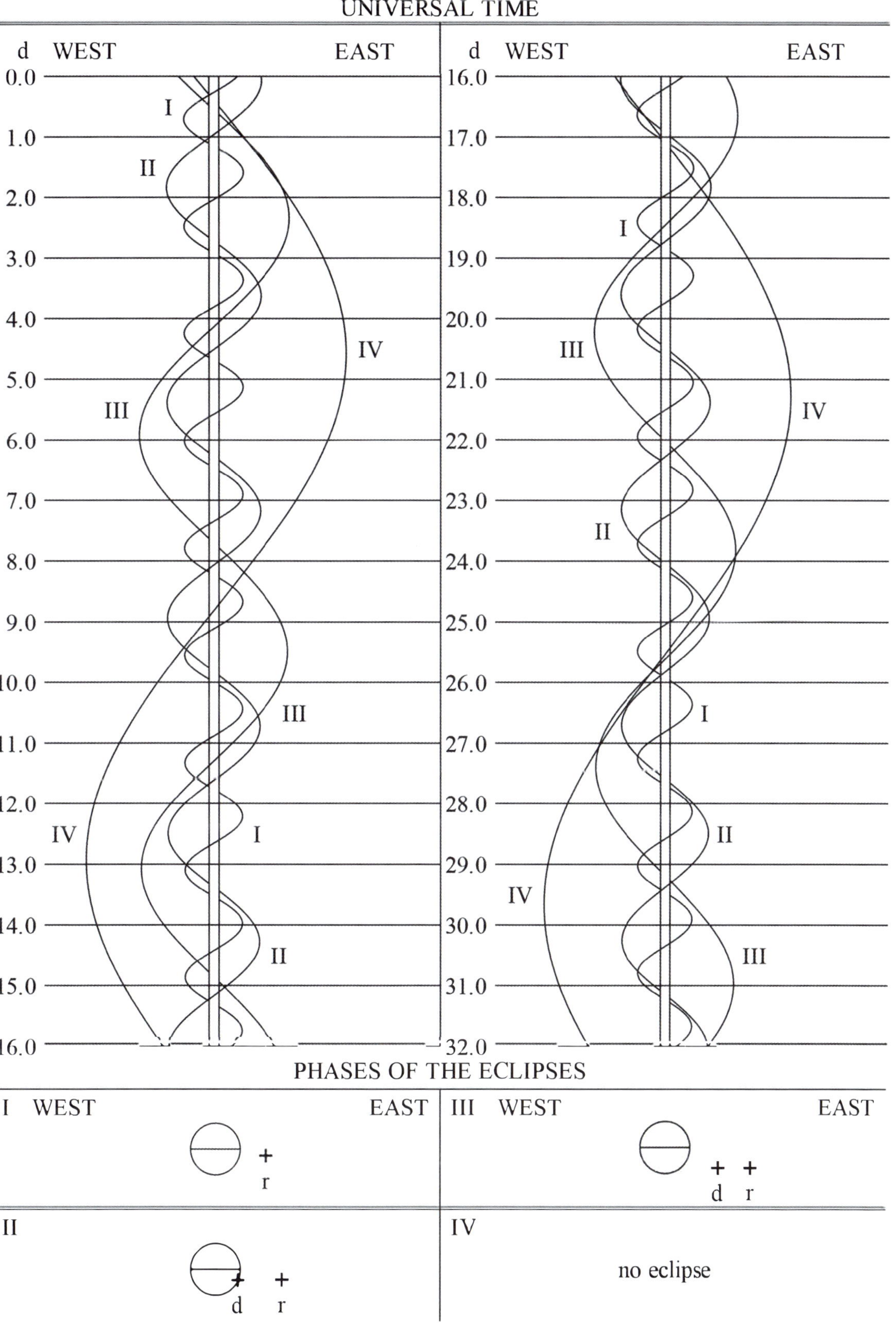

NOTE. – The position d given in box II is not visible from the Earth's surface.

UNIVERSAL TIME OF GEOCENTRIC PHENOMENA

MARCH

d	h m	
1	3 11	III Oc D
	5 34	III Oc R
	7 46	II Tr I
	8 29	III Ec D
	10 02	I Oc D
	10 19	II Tr E
	10 19	II Sh I
	10 57	III Ec R
	12 55	II Sh E
	13 33	I Ec R
2	7 15	I Tr I
	8 33	I Sh I
	9 27	I Tr E
	10 45	I Sh E
3	2 12	II Oc D
	4 30	I Oc D
	4 49	II Oc R
	4 53	II Ec D
	7 33	II Ec R
	8 01	I Ec R
4	1 44	I Tr I
	3 02	I Sh I
	3 56	I Tr E
	5 15	I Sh E
	17 24	III Tr I
	19 45	III Tr E
	21 03	II Tr I
	22 41	III Sh I
	22 59	I Oc D
	23 37	II Tr E
	23 37	II Sh I
5	1 08	III Sh E
	2 13	II Sh E
	2 30	I Ec R
	20 13	I Tr I
	21 31	I Sh I
	22 25	I Tr E
	23 43	I Sh E
6	15 32	II Oc D
	17 28	I Oc D
	18 10	II Oc R
	18 13	II Ec D
	20 53	II Ec R
	20 59	I Ec R
7	14 42	I Tr I
	16 00	I Sh I
	16 54	I Tr E
	18 12	I Sh E
8	7 12	III Oc D
	9 36	III Oc R
	10 21	II Tr I
8	11 57	I Oc D
	12 30	III Ec D
	12 55	II Sh I
	12 55	II Tr E
	14 59	III Ec R
	15 28	I Ec R
	15 31	II Sh E
9	9 11	I Tr I
	10 29	I Sh I
	11 23	I Tr E
	12 41	I Sh E
10	4 52	II Oc D
	6 26	I Oc D
	7 29	II Oc R
	7 32	II Ec D
	9 57	I Ec R
	10 12	II Ec R
11	3 40	I Tr I
	4 58	I Sh I
	5 52	I Tr E
	7 10	I Sh E
	21 27	III Tr I
	23 40	II Tr I
	23 50	III Tr E
12	0 55	I Oc D
	2 13	II Sh I
	2 14	II Tr E
	2 42	III Sh I
	4 25	I Ec R
	4 48	II Sh E
	5 10	III Sh E
	22 09	I Tr I
	23 27	I Sh I
13	0 21	I Tr E
	1 39	I Sh E
	18 12	II Oc D
	19 24	I Oc D
	20 50	II Oc R
	20 51	II Ec D
	22 54	I Ec R
	23 32	II Ec R
14	16 39	I Tr I
	17 56	I Sh I
	18 51	I Tr E
	20 08	I Sh E
15	11 17	III Oc D
	12 59	II Tr I
	13 43	III Oc R
	13 53	I Oc D
	15 30	II Sh I
	15 33	II Tr E
15	16 30	III Ec D
	17 23	I Ec R
	18 06	II Sh E
	19 00	III Ec R
16	11 08	I Tr I
	12 25	I Sh I
	13 20	I Tr E
	14 37	I Sh E
17	7 33	II Oc D
	8 22	I Oc D
	11 52	I Ec R
	12 51	II Ec R
18	5 37	I Tr I
	6 54	I Sh I
	7 50	I Tr E
	9 06	I Sh E
19	1 34	III Tr I
	2 19	II Tr I
	2 52	I Oc D
	3 59	III Tr E
	4 48	II Sh I
	4 53	II Tr E
	6 21	I Ec R
	6 43	III Sh I
	7 24	II Sh E
	9 12	III Sh E
20	0 07	I Tr I
	1 23	I Sh I
	2 19	I Tr E
	3 35	I Sh E
	20 55	II Oc D
	21 21	I Oc D
21	0 49	I Ec R
	2 10	II Ec R
	18 36	I Tr I
	19 52	I Sh I
	20 49	I Tr E
	22 04	I Sh E
22	15 25	III Oc D
	15 38	II Tr I
	15 50	I Oc D
	17 53	III Oc R
	18 06	II Sh I
	18 13	II Tr E
	19 18	I Ec R
	20 30	III Ec D
	20 42	II Sh E
	23 02	III Ec R
23	13 06	I Tr I
	14 21	I Sh I
23	15 18	I Tr E
	16 33	I Sh E
24	10 16	II Oc D
	10 20	I Oc D
	13 47	I Ec R
	15 29	II Ec R
25	7 36	I Tr I
	8 50	I Sh I
	9 48	I Tr E
	11 02	I Sh E
26	4 49	I Oc D
	4 59	II Tr I
	5 46	III Tr I
	7 23	II Sh I
	7 34	II Tr E
	8 12	III Tr E
	8 16	I Ec R
	10 00	II Sh E
	10 45	III Sh I
	13 15	III Sh E
27	2 05	I Tr I
	3 19	I Sh I
	4 17	I Tr E
	5 31	I Sh E
	23 19	I Oc D
	23 38	II Oc D
28	2 45	I Ec R
	4 49	II Ec R
	20 35	I Tr I
	21 48	I Sh I
	22 47	I Tr E
29	0 00	I Sh E
	17 48	I Oc D
	18 19	II Tr I
	19 36	III Oc D
	20 41	II Sh I
	20 54	II Tr E
	21 13	I Ec R
	22 06	III Oc R
	23 18	II Sh E
30	0 30	III Ec D
	3 03	III Ec R
	15 04	I Tr I
	16 17	I Sh I
	17 17	I Tr E
	18 29	I Sh E
31	12 18	I Oc D
	13 00	II Oc D
	15 42	I Ec R
	18 08	II Ec R

I. Mar. 15	II. Mar. 17	III. Mar. 15	IV. Mar.
		$x_1 = +2.2,\ y_1 = +0.7$	
$x_2 = +2.1,\ y_2 = +0.2$	$x_2 = +2.7,\ y_2 = +0.4$	$x_2 = +3.5,\ y_2 = +0.7$	no eclipse

NOTE.–I denotes ingress; E, egress; D, disappearance; R, reappearance; Ec, eclipse; Oc, occultation; Tr, transit of the satellite; Sh, transit of the shadow.

CONFIGURATIONS OF SATELLITES I-IV FOR MARCH

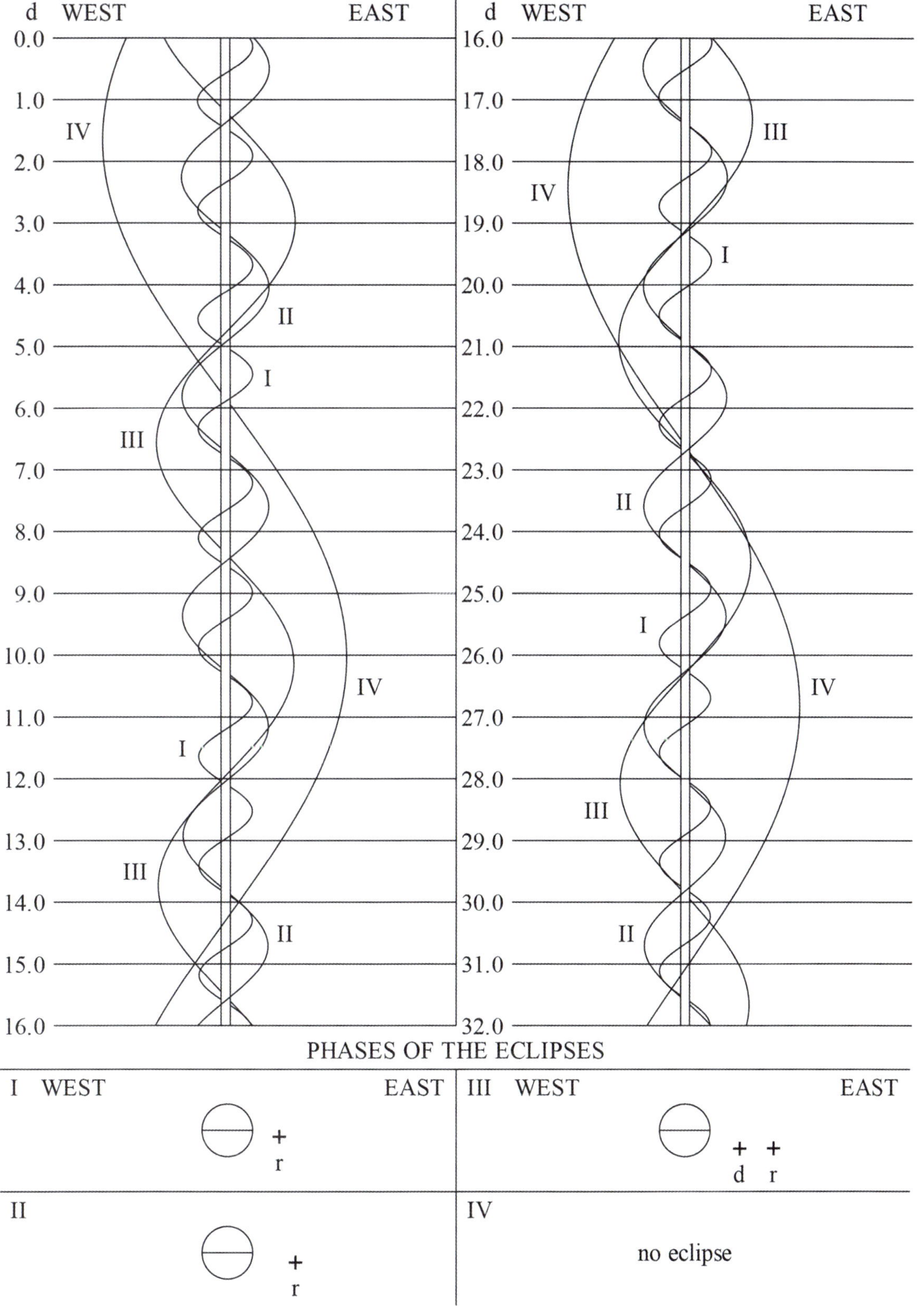

UNIVERSAL TIME OF GEOCENTRIC PHENOMENA

APRIL

d	h m	
1	9 34	I Tr I
	10 45	I Sh I
	11 47	I Tr E
	12 58	I Sh E
2	6 47	I Oc D
	7 40	II Tr I
	9 59	II Sh I
	9 59	III Tr I
	10 11	I Ec R
	10 16	II Tr E
	12 27	III Tr E
	12 36	II Sh E
	14 45	III Sh I
	17 17	III Sh E
3	4 04	I Tr I
	5 14	I Sh I
	6 17	I Tr E
	7 27	I Sh E
4	1 17	I Oc D
	2 24	II Oc D
	4 40	I Ec R
	7 28	II Ec R
	22 34	I Tr I
	23 43	I Sh I
5	0 46	I Tr E
	1 56	I Sh E
	19 47	I Oc D
	21 01	II Tr I
	23 09	I Ec R
	23 16	II Sh I
	23 37	II Tr E
	23 51	III Oc D
6	1 54	II Sh E
	2 22	III Oc R
	4 30	III Ec D
	7 04	III Ec R
	17 04	I Tr I
	18 12	I Sh I
	19 16	I Tr E
	20 25	I Sh E
7	14 17	I Oc D
	15 46	II Oc D
	17 37	I Ec R
	20 47	II Ec R
8	11 34	I Tr I
	12 41	I Sh I
	13 46	I Tr E

d	h m	
8	14 54	I Sh E
9	8 46	I Oc D
	10 23	II Tr I
	12 06	I Ec R
	12 34	II Sh I
	12 59	II Tr E
	14 16	III Tr I
	15 12	II Sh E
	16 46	III Tr E
	18 46	III Sh I
	21 19	III Sh E
10	6 04	I Tr I
	7 10	I Sh I
	8 16	I Tr E
	9 23	I Sh E
11	3 16	I Oc D
	5 10	II Oc D
	6 35	I Ec R
	10 06	II Ec R
12	0 34	I Tr I
	1 39	I Sh I
	2 46	I Tr E
	3 52	I Sh E
	21 46	I Oc D
	23 45	II Tr I
13	1 04	I Ec R
	1 51	II Sh I
	2 21	II Tr E
	4 09	III Oc D
	4 30	II Sh E
	6 41	III Oc R
	8 30	III Ec D
	11 06	III Ec R
	19 04	I Tr I
	20 08	I Sh I
	21 16	I Tr E
	22 21	I Sh E
14	16 16	I Oc D
	18 33	II Oc D
	19 32	I Ec R
	23 25	II Ec R
15	13 34	I Tr I
	14 37	I Sh I
	15 47	I Tr E
	16 50	I Sh E
16	10 46	I Oc D

d	h m	
16	13 07	II Tr I
	14 01	I Ec R
	15 09	II Sh I
	15 44	II Tr E
	17 47	II Sh E
	18 34	III Tr I
	21 06	III Tr E
	22 46	III Sh I
17	1 20	III Sh E
	8 04	I Tr I
	9 06	I Sh I
	10 17	I Tr E
	11 19	I Sh E
18	5 16	I Oc D
	7 58	II Oc D
	8 30	I Ec R
	12 45	II Ec R
19	2 34	I Tr I
	3 35	I Sh I
	4 47	I Tr E
	5 48	I Sh E
	23 46	I Oc D
20	2 29	II Tr I
	2 59	I Ec R
	4 27	II Sh I
	5 06	II Tr E
	7 05	II Sh E
	8 29	III Oc D
	11 03	III Oc R
	12 31	III Ec D
	15 08	III Ec R
	21 04	I Tr I
	22 03	I Sh I
	23 17	I Tr E
21	0 16	I Sh E
	18 16	I Oc D
	21 22	II Oc D
	21 27	I Ec R
22	2 03	II Ec R
	15 34	I Tr I
	16 32	I Sh I
	17 47	I Tr E
	18 45	I Sh E
23	12 46	I Oc D
	15 52	II Tr I
	15 56	I Ec R
	17 44	II Sh I

d	h m	
23	18 29	II Tr E
	20 23	II Sh E
	22 55	III Tr I
24	1 28	III Tr E
	2 46	III Sh I
	5 21	III Sh E
	10 04	I Tr I
	11 01	I Sh I
	12 17	I Tr E
	13 14	I Sh E
25	7 16	I Oc D
	10 25	I Ec R
	10 46	II Oc D
	15 23	II Ec R
26	4 35	I Tr I
	5 30	I Sh I
	6 48	I Tr E
	7 43	I Sh E
27	1 46	I Oc D
	4 54	I Ec R
	5 15	II Tr I
	7 02	II Sh I
	7 53	II Tr E
	9 41	II Sh E
	12 51	III Oc D
	15 27	III Oc R
	16 31	III Ec D
	19 09	III Ec R
	23 05	I Tr I
	23 59	I Sh I
28	1 18	I Tr E
	2 12	I Sh E
	20 16	I Oc D
	23 22	I Ec R
29	0 11	II Oc D
	4 41	II Ec R
	17 35	I Tr I
	18 28	I Sh I
	19 48	I Tr E
	20 41	I Sh E
30	14 46	I Oc D
	17 51	I Ec R
	18 38	II Tr I
	20 20	II Sh I
	21 16	II Tr E
	22 59	II Sh E

I. Apr. 16	II. Apr. 14	III. Apr. 13	IV. Apr.
		$x_1 = +1.7,\ y_1 = +0.7$	no eclipse
$x_2 = +1.9,\ y_2 = +0.2$	$x_2 = +2.4,\ y_2 = +0.4$	$x_2 = +3.1,\ y_2 = +0.7$	

NOTE.—I denotes ingress; E, egress; D, disappearance; R, reappearance; Ec, eclipse; Oc, occultation; Tr, transit of the satellite; Sh, transit of the shadow.

CONFIGURATIONS OF SATELLITES I-IV FOR APRIL

UNIVERSAL TIME

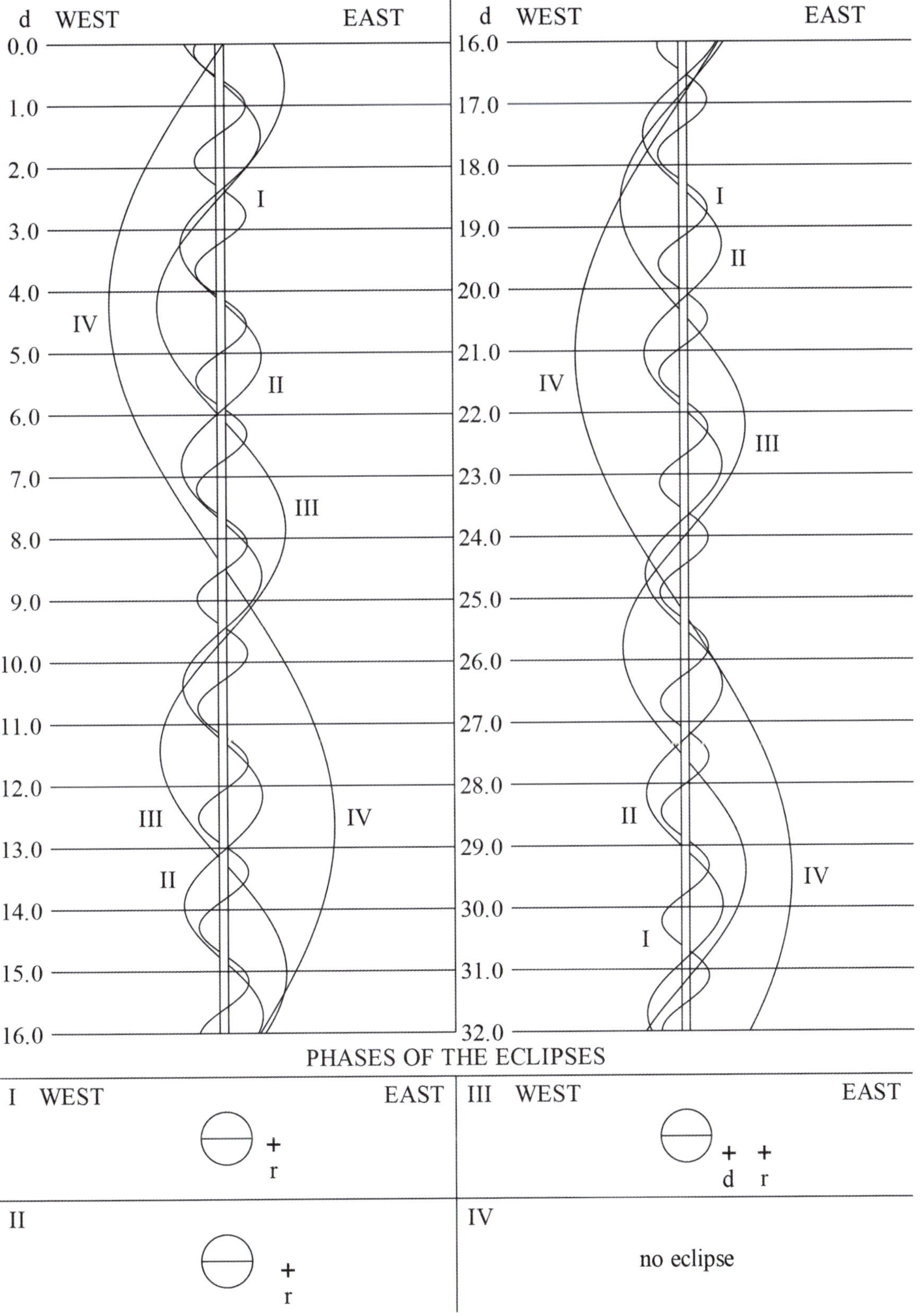

UNIVERSAL TIME OF GEOCENTRIC PHENOMENA

MAY

d	h m	
1	3 18	III Tr I
	5 53	III Tr E
	6 46	III Sh I
	9 23	III Sh E
	12 05	I Tr I
	12 57	I Sh I
	14 19	I Tr E
	15 10	I Sh E
2	9 16	I Oc D
	12 20	I Ec R
	13 36	II Oc D
	18 01	II Ec R
3	6 36	I Tr I
	7 25	I Sh I
	8 49	I Tr E
	9 39	I Sh E
4	3 46	I Oc D
	6 49	I Ec R
	8 01	II Tr I
	9 37	II Sh I
	10 40	II Tr E
	12 17	II Sh E
	17 15	III Oc D
	19 52	III Oc R
	20 31	III Ec D
	23 11	III Ec R
5	1 06	I Tr I
	1 54	I Sh I
	3 19	I Tr E
	4 08	I Sh E
	22 16	I Oc D
6	1 17	I Ec R
	3 00	II Oc D
	7 19	II Ec R
	19 36	I Tr I
	20 23	I Sh I
	21 50	I Tr E
	22 37	I Sh E
7	16 47	I Oc D
	19 46	I Ec R
	21 25	II Tr I
	22 55	II Sh I
8	0 04	II Tr E
	1 35	II Sh E
	7 42	III Tr I
	10 19	III Tr E
	10 46	III Sh I
	13 25	III Sh E
	14 06	I Tr I

d	h m	
8	14 52	I Sh I
	16 20	I Tr E
	17 05	I Sh E
9	11 17	I Oc D
	14 15	I Ec R
	16 26	II Oc D
	20 38	II Ec R
10	8 37	I Tr I
	9 21	I Sh I
	10 50	I Tr E
	11 34	I Sh E
11	5 47	I Oc D
	8 44	I Ec R
	10 48	II Tr I
	12 13	II Sh I
	13 28	II Tr E
	14 53	II Sh E
	21 39	III Oc D
12	0 18	III Oc R
	0 31	III Ec D
	3 07	I Tr I
	3 11	III Ec R
	3 49	I Sh I
	5 21	I Tr E
	6 03	I Sh E
13	0 17	I Oc D
	3 12	I Ec R
	5 50	II Oc D
	9 57	II Ec R
	21 38	I Tr I
	22 18	I Sh I
	23 51	I Tr E
14	0 32	I Sh E
	18 48	I Oc D
	21 41	I Ec R
15	0 12	II Tr I
	1 30	II Sh I
	2 52	II Tr E
	4 11	II Sh E
	12 09	III Tr I
	14 47	III Sh I
	14 47	III Tr E
	16 08	I Tr I
	16 47	I Sh I
	17 27	III Sh E
	18 22	I Tr E
	19 01	I Sh E
16	13 18	I Oc D

d	h m	
16	16 10	I Ec R
	19 16	II Oc D
	23 16	II Ec R
17	10 38	I Tr I
	11 16	I Sh I
	12 52	I Tr E
	13 30	I Sh E
18	7 48	I Oc D
	10 38	I Ec R
	13 36	II Tr I
	14 48	II Sh I
	16 16	II Tr E
	17 29	II Sh E
19	2 05	III Oc D
	5 09	I Tr I
	5 45	I Sh I
	7 12	III Ec R
	7 23	I Tr E
	7 58	I Sh E
20	2 19	I Oc D
	5 07	I Ec R
	8 41	II Oc D
	12 34	II Ec R
	23 39	I Tr I
21	0 13	I Sh I
	1 53	I Tr E
	2 27	I Sh E
	20 49	I Oc D
	23 36	I Ec R
22	3 00	II Tr I
	4 06	II Sh I
	5 41	II Tr E
	6 47	II Sh E
	16 36	III Tr I
	18 10	I Tr I
	18 42	I Sh I
	18 47	III Sh I
	19 16	III Tr E
	20 23	I Tr E
	20 56	I Sh E
	21 28	III Sh E
23	15 19	I Oc D
	18 05	I Ec R
	22 06	II Oc D
24	1 53	II Ec R
	12 40	I Tr I
	13 11	I Sh I
	14 54	I Tr E

d	h m	
24	15 25	I Sh E
25	9 50	I Oc D
	12 33	I Ec R
	16 24	II Tr I
	17 23	II Sh I
	19 05	II Tr E
	20 05	II Sh E
26	6 32	III Oc D
	7 10	I Tr I
	7 40	I Sh I
	9 24	I Tr E
	9 54	I Sh E
	11 13	III Ec R
27	4 20	I Oc D
	7 02	I Ec R
	11 31	II Oc D
	15 11	II Ec R
28	1 41	I Tr I
	2 08	I Sh I
	3 55	I Tr E
	4 22	I Sh E
	22 29	IV Oc D
	22 50	I Oc D
	23 15	IV Oc R
29	1 31	I Ec R
	2 35	IV Ec D
	3 33	IV Ec R
	5 49	II Tr I
	6 41	II Sh I
	8 30	II Tr E
	9 23	II Sh E
	20 11	I Tr I
	20 37	I Sh I
	21 03	III Tr I
	22 25	I Tr E
	22 47	III Sh I
	22 51	I Sh E
	23 45	III Tr E
30	1 30	III Sh E
	17 21	I Oc D
	19 59	I Ec R
31	0 57	II Oc D
	4 30	II Ec R
	14 42	I Tr I
	15 06	I Sh I
	16 56	I Tr E
	17 20	I Sh E

I. May 16	II. May 16	III. May 19	IV. May 29
$x_2 = +1.5,\ y_2 = +0.2$	$x_2 = +1.8,\ y_2 = +0.3$	$x_2 = +2.1,\ y_2 = +0.6$	$x_1 = +1.5,\ y_1 = +0.9$ $x_2 = +1.9,\ y_2 = +0.9$

NOTE.–I denotes ingress; E, egress; D, disappearance; R, reappearance; Ec, eclipse; Oc, occultation; Tr, transit of the satellite; Sh, transit of the shadow.

CONFIGURATIONS OF SATELLITES I-IV FOR MAY

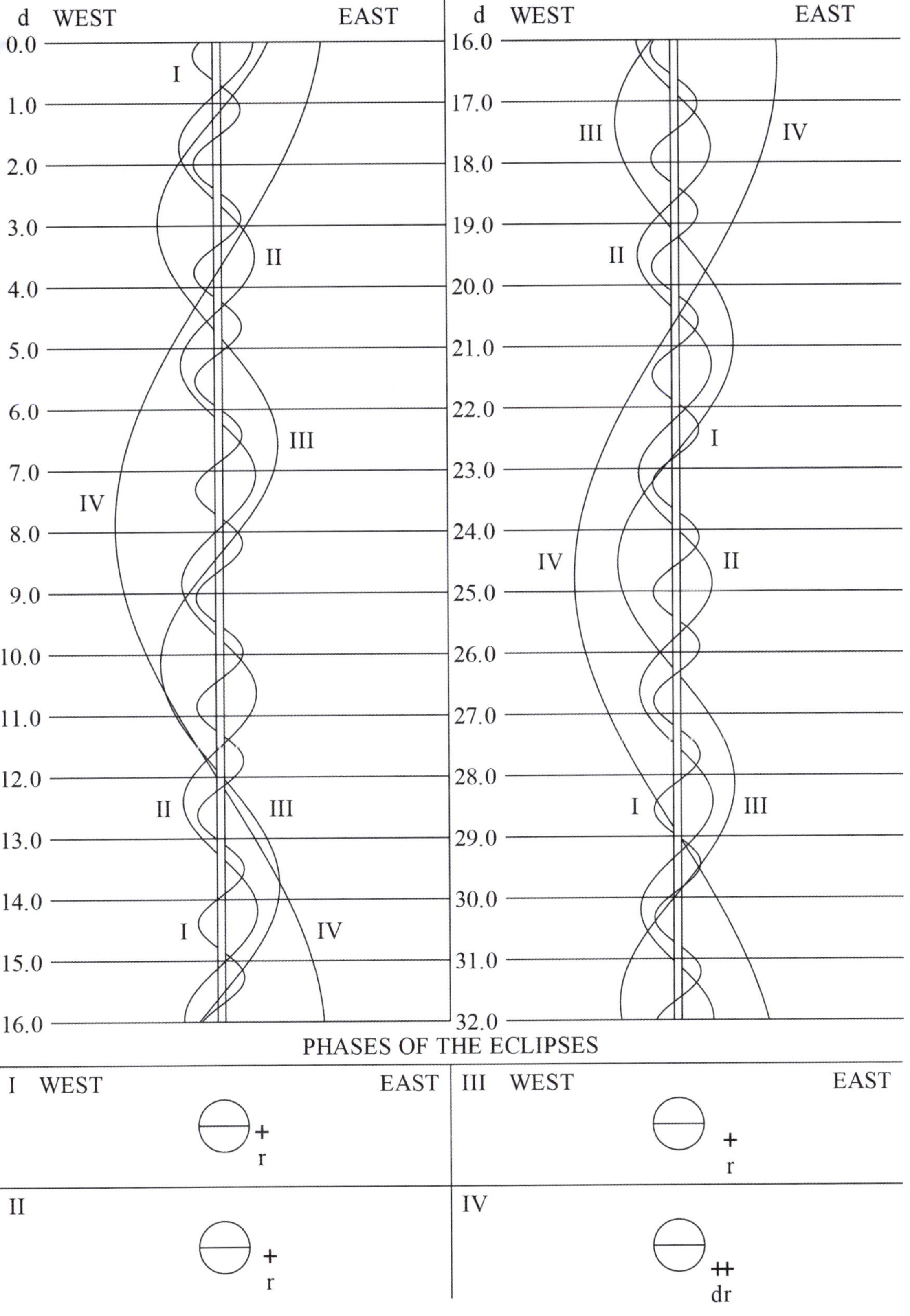

PHASES OF THE ECLIPSES

I WEST	EAST	III WEST	EAST
+ r		+ r	
II		IV	
+ r		++ dr	

UNIVERSAL TIME OF GEOCENTRIC PHENOMENA

JUNE

d	h m	Phenomenon
1	11 51	I Oc D
	14 28	I Ec R
	19 13	II Tr I
	19 59	II Sh I
	21 55	II Tr E
	22 41	II Sh E
2	9 12	I Tr I
	9 35	I Sh I
	11 00	III Oc D
	11 26	I Tr E
	11 49	I Sh E
	15 14	III Ec R
3	6 21	I Oc D
	8 57	I Ec R
	14 22	II Oc D
	17 48	II Ec R
4	3 43	I Tr I
	4 03	I Sh I
	5 57	I Tr E
	6 17	I Sh E
5	0 52	I Oc D
	3 25	I Ec R
	8 38	II Tr I
	9 16	II Sh I
	11 20	II Tr E
	11 59	II Sh E
	22 13	I Tr I
	22 32	I Sh I
6	0 27	I Tr E
	0 46	I Sh E
	1 31	III Tr I
	2 46	III Sh I
	4 15	III Tr E
	5 30	III Sh E
	10 32	IV Tr I
	11 35	IV Tr E
	13 25	IV Sh I
	14 30	IV Sh E
	19 22	I Oc D
	21 54	I Ec R
7	3 48	II Oc D
	7 07	II Ec R
	16 44	I Tr I
	17 01	I Sh I
	18 58	I Tr E
	19 15	I Sh E
8	13 53	I Oc D
	16 23	I Ec R
8	22 03	II Tr I
	22 34	II Sh I
9	0 45	II Tr E
	1 17	II Sh E
	11 14	I Tr I
	11 29	I Sh I
	13 28	I Tr E
	13 44	I Sh E
	15 29	III Oc D
	19 16	III Ec R
10	8 23	I Oc D
	10 51	I Ec R
	17 13	II Oc D
	20 25	II Ec R
11	5 45	I Tr I
	5 58	I Sh I
	7 59	I Tr E
	8 12	I Sh E
12	2 53	I Oc D
	5 20	I Ec R
	11 27	II Tr I
	11 52	II Sh I
	14 10	II Tr E
	14 35	II Sh E
13	0 15	I Tr I
	0 27	I Sh I
	2 29	I Tr E
	2 41	I Sh E
	5 59	III Tr I
	6 45	III Sh I
	8 45	III Tr E
	9 31	III Sh E
	21 24	I Oc D
	23 49	I Ec R
14	6 39	II Oc D
	9 43	II Ec R
	18 45	I Tr I
	18 52	IV Oc D
	18 56	I Sh I
	20 24	IV Oc R
	20 28	IV Ec D
	21 00	I Tr E
	21 10	I Sh E
	21 55	IV Ec R
15	15 54	I Oc D
	18 17	I Ec R
16	0 52	II Tr I
16	1 10	II Sh I
	3 35	II Tr E
	3 53	II Sh E
	13 16	I Tr I
	13 24	I Sh I
	15 30	I Tr E
	15 38	I Sh E
	19 58	III Oc D
	23 17	III Ec R
17	10 25	I Oc D
	12 46	I Ec R
	20 04	II Oc D
	23 01	II Ec R
18	7 46	I Tr I
	7 53	I Sh I
	10 01	I Tr E
	10 07	I Sh E
19	4 55	I Oc D
	7 15	I Ec R
	14 17	II Tr I
	14 28	II Sh I
	17 01	II Tr E
	17 11	II Sh E
20	2 17	I Tr I
	2 21	I Sh I
	4 31	I Tr E
	4 36	I Sh E
	10 27	III Tr I
	10 45	III Sh I
	13 15	III Tr E
	13 32	III Sh E
	23 25	I Oc D
21	1 43	I Ec R
	9 29	II Oc D
	12 20	II Ec R
	20 47	I Tr I
	20 50	I Sh I
	23 02	I Tr E
	23 04	I Sh E
22	17 56	I Oc D
	20 12	I Ec R
23	3 42	II Tr I
	3 45	II Sh I
	6 26	II Tr E
	6 29	II Sh E
	7 01	IV Tr I
	7 19	IV Sh I
	8 45	IV Tr E
23	8 52	IV Sh E
	15 18	I Tr I
	15 19	I Sh I
	17 32	I Tr E
	17 33	I Sh E
24	0 26	III Oc D
	3 17	III Ec R
	12 26	I Oc D
	14 41	I Oc R
	22 54	II Ec D
25	1 39	II Oc R
	9 47	I Sh I
	9 48	I Tr I
	12 02	I Sh E
	12 03	I Tr E
26	6 55	I Ec D
	9 11	I Oc R
	17 03	II Sh I
	17 07	II Tr I
	19 47	II Sh E
	19 51	II Tr E
27	4 16	I Sh I
	4 19	I Tr I
	6 30	I Sh E
	6 33	I Tr E
	14 45	III Sh I
	14 56	III Tr I
	17 32	III Sh E
	17 46	III Tr E
28	1 24	I Ec D
	3 42	I Oc R
	12 12	II Ec D
	15 04	II Oc R
	22 45	I Sh I
	22 49	I Tr I
29	0 59	I Sh E
	1 03	I Tr E
	19 52	I Ec D
	22 12	I Oc R
30	6 21	II Sh I
	6 32	II Tr I
	9 05	II Sh E
	9 17	II Tr E
	17 13	I Sh I
	17 19	I Tr I
	19 27	I Sh E
	19 34	I Tr E

I. June 15	II. June 14	III. June 16	IV. June 14
			$x_1 = +0.3$, $y_1 = +0.9$
$x_2 = +1.1$, $y_2 = +0.2$	$x_2 = +1.2$, $y_2 = +0.3$	$x_2 = +1.0$, $y_2 = +0.6$	$x_2 = +0.9$, $y_2 = +0.9$

NOTE.—I denotes ingress; E, egress; D, disappearance; R, reappearance; Ec, eclipse; Oc, occultation; Tr, transit of the satellite; Sh, transit of the shadow.

CONFIGURATIONS OF SATELLITES I-IV FOR JUNE

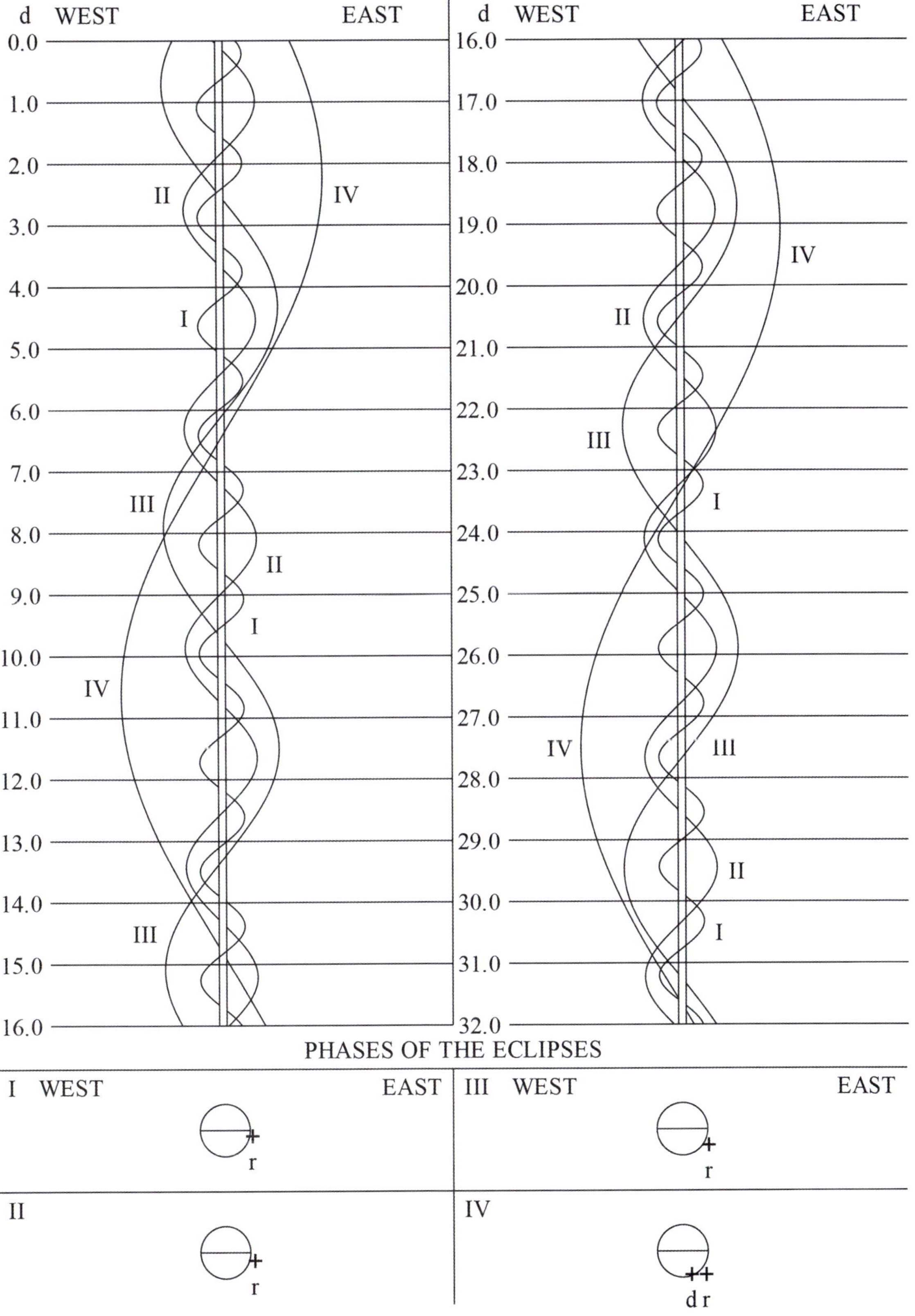

UNIVERSAL TIME OF GEOCENTRIC PHENOMENA

JULY

d	h m	
1	4 28	III Ec D
	7 46	III Oc R
	14 21	I Ec D
	14 25	IV Ec D
	16 42	I Oc R
	17 28	IV Oc R
2	1 29	II Ec D
	4 29	II Oc R
	11 42	I Sh I
	11 50	I Tr I
	13 56	I Sh E
	14 04	I Tr E
3	8 49	I Ec D
	11 13	I Oc R
	19 39	II Sh I
	19 57	II Tr I
	22 23	II Sh E
	22 42	II Tr E
4	6 10	I Sh I
	6 20	I Tr I
	8 25	I Sh E
	8 35	I Tr E
	18 45	III Sh I
	19 25	III Tr I
	21 34	III Sh E
	22 17	III Tr E
5	3 18	I Ec D
	5 43	I Oc R
	14 47	II Ec D
	17 54	II Oc R
6	0 39	I Sh I
	0 50	I Tr I
	2 53	I Sh E
	3 05	I Tr E
	21 46	I Ec D
7	0 14	I Oc R
	8 57	II Sh I
	9 22	II Tr I
	11 41	II Sh E
	12 07	II Tr E
	19 08	I Sh I
	19 21	I Tr I
	21 22	I Sh E
	21 35	I Tr E
8	8 27	III Ec D
	12 16	III Oc R
	16 15	I Ec D
	18 44	I Oc R

d	h m	
9	4 05	II Ec D
	7 19	II Oc R
	13 36	I Sh I
	13 51	I Tr I
	15 50	I Sh E
	16 06	I Tr E
10	1 16	IV Sh I
	3 09	IV Sh E
	3 35	IV Tr I
	5 47	IV Tr E
	10 44	I Ec D
	13 14	I Oc R
	22 15	II Sh I
	22 47	II Tr I
11	0 59	II Sh E
	1 33	II Tr E
	8 05	I Sh I
	8 21	I Tr I
	10 19	I Sh E
	10 36	I Tr E
	22 44	III Sh I
	23 53	III Tr I
12	1 34	III Sh E
	2 47	III Tr E
	5 12	I Ec D
	7 45	I Oc R
	17 23	II Ec D
	20 44	II Oc R
13	2 33	I Sh I
	2 52	I Tr I
	4 48	I Sh E
	5 06	I Tr E
	23 41	I Ec D
14	2 15	I Oc R
	11 32	II Sh I
	12 12	II Tr I
	14 17	II Sh E
	14 58	II Tr E
	21 02	I Sh I
	21 22	I Tr I
	23 16	I Sh E
	23 37	I Tr E
15	12 27	III Ec D
	16 46	III Oc R
	18 09	I Ec D
	20 46	I Oc R
16	6 40	II Ec D
	10 09	II Oc R
	15 30	I Sh I

d	h m	
16	15 52	I Tr I
	17 45	I Sh E
	18 07	I Tr E
17	12 38	I Ec D
	15 16	I Oc R
18	0 50	II Sh I
	1 37	II Tr I
	3 35	II Sh E
	4 23	II Tr E
	8 23	IV Ec D
	9 59	I Sh I
	10 22	I Tr I
	10 28	IV Ec R
	11 59	IV Oc D
	12 13	I Sh E
	12 37	I Tr E
	14 26	IV Oc R
19	2 43	III Sh I
	4 20	III Tr I
	5 34	III Sh E
	7 06	I Ec D
	7 16	III Tr E
	9 46	I Oc R
	19 58	II Ec D
	23 33	II Oc R
20	4 28	I Sh I
	4 53	I Tr I
	6 42	I Sh E
	7 07	I Tr E
21	1 35	I Ec D
	4 17	I Oc R
	14 08	II Sh I
	15 02	II Tr I
	16 53	II Sh E
	17 48	II Tr E
	22 56	I Sh I
	23 23	I Tr I
22	1 10	I Sh E
	1 37	I Tr E
	16 26	III Ec D
	20 04	I Ec D
	21 16	III Oc R
	22 47	I Oc R
23	9 15	II Ec D
	12 58	II Oc R
	17 25	I Sh I
	17 53	I Tr I
	19 39	I Sh E
	20 08	I Tr E

d	h m	
24	14 32	I Ec D
	17 17	I Oc R
25	3 26	II Sh I
	4 27	II Tr I
	6 12	II Sh E
	7 14	II Tr E
	11 53	I Sh I
	12 23	I Tr I
	14 07	I Sh E
	14 38	I Tr E
26	6 41	III Sh I
	8 46	III Tr I
	9 01	I Ec D
	9 34	III Sh E
	11 43	III Tr E
	11 48	I Oc R
	19 14	IV Sh I
	21 24	IV Sh E
	22 33	II Ec D
27	0 05	IV Tr I
	2 22	II Oc R
	2 41	IV Tr E
	6 22	I Sh I
	6 53	I Tr I
	8 36	I Sh E
	9 08	I Tr E
28	3 29	I Ec D
	6 18	I Oc R
	16 44	II Sh I
	17 51	II Tr I
	19 30	II Sh E
	20 38	II Tr E
29	0 50	I Sh I
	1 24	I Tr I
	3 04	I Sh E
	3 38	I Tr E
	20 26	III Ec D
	21 58	I Ec D
30	0 48	I Oc R
	1 45	III Oc R
	11 50	II Ec D
	15 46	II Oc R
	19 19	I Sh I
	19 54	I Tr I
	21 33	I Sh E
	22 08	I Tr E
31	16 26	I Ec D
	19 18	I Oc R

I. July 15	II. July 16	III. July 15	IV. July 18
$x_1 = -1.3,\ y_1 = +0.2$	$x_1 = -1.4,\ y_1 = +0.3$	$x_1 = -1.6,\ y_1 = +0.6$	$x_1 = -2.0,\ y_1 = +0.8$ $x_2 = -1.1,\ y_2 = +0.8$

NOTE.–I denotes ingress; E, egress; D, disappearance; R, reappearance; Ec, eclipse; Oc, occultation; Tr, transit of the satellite; Sh, transit of the shadow.

CONFIGURATIONS OF SATELLITES I-IV FOR JULY

UNIVERSAL TIME

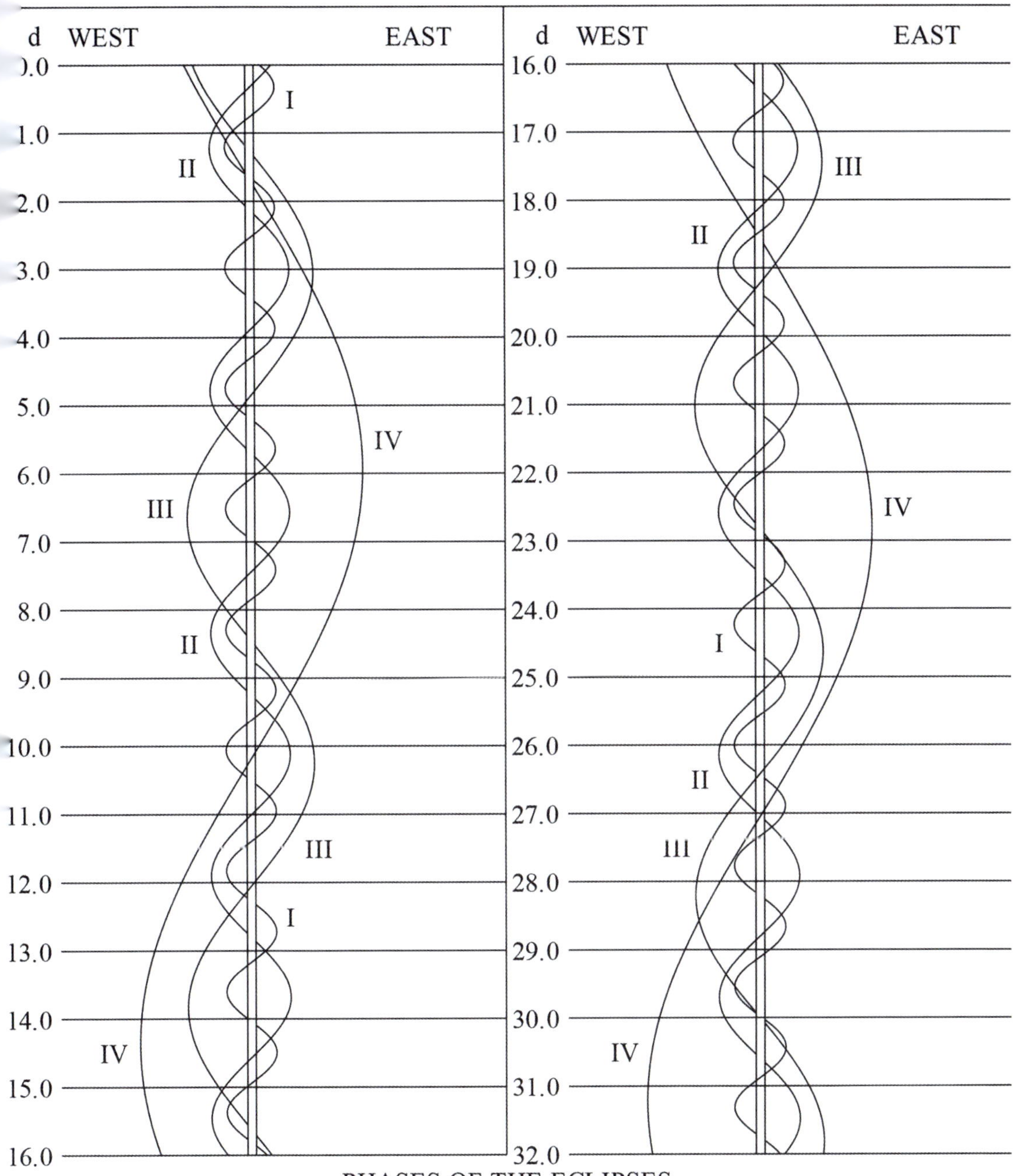

d	WEST	EAST	d	WEST	EAST
0.0			16.0		
1.0			17.0		
2.0			18.0		
3.0			19.0		
4.0			20.0		
5.0			21.0		
6.0			22.0		
7.0			23.0		
8.0			24.0		
9.0			25.0		
10.0			26.0		
11.0			27.0		
12.0			28.0		
13.0			29.0		
14.0			30.0		
15.0			31.0		
16.0			32.0		

PHASES OF THE ECLIPSES

I WEST EAST

d

III WEST EAST

d

II

d

IV

d r

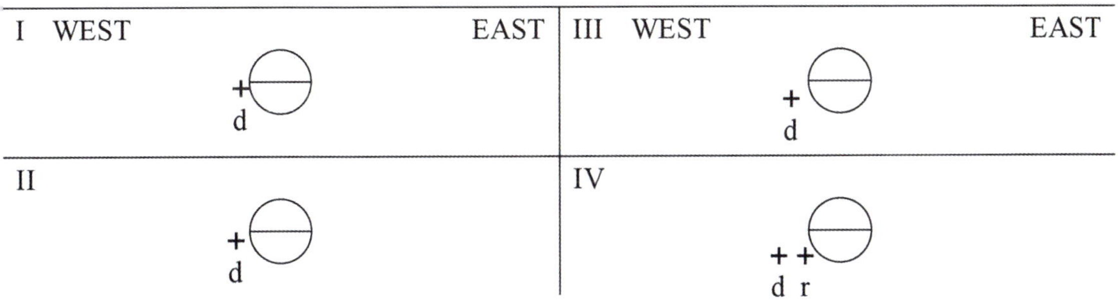

UNIVERSAL TIME OF GEOCENTRIC PHENOMENA

AUGUST

d	h m	
1	6 02	II Sh I
	7 16	II Tr I
	8 48	II Sh E
	10 04	II Tr E
	13 47	I Sh I
	14 24	I Tr I
	16 01	I Sh E
	16 38	I Tr E
2	10 40	III Sh I
	10 55	I Ec D
	13 11	III Tr I
	13 34	III Sh E
	13 49	I Oc R
	16 10	III Tr E
3	1 07	II Ec D
	5 10	II Oc R
	8 16	I Sh I
	8 54	I Tr I
	10 30	I Sh E
	11 08	I Tr E
4	2 21	IV Ec D
	4 42	IV Ec R
	5 23	I Ec D
	8 19	I Oc R
	8 24	IV Oc D
	11 12	IV Oc R
	19 20	II Sh I
	20 40	II Tr I
	22 06	II Sh E
	23 28	II Tr E
5	2 44	I Sh I
	3 24	I Tr I
	4 58	I Sh E
	5 38	I Tr E
	23 52	I Ec D
6	0 25	III Ec D
	2 49	I Oc R
	6 12	III Oc R
	14 24	II Ec D
	18 33	II Oc R
	21 13	I Sh I
	21 54	I Tr I
	23 27	I Sh E
7	0 08	I Tr E
	18 20	I Ec D
	21 19	I Oc R
8	8 39	II Sh I
	10 05	II Tr I
	11 24	II Sh E
	12 53	II Tr E
	15 41	I Sh I
	16 24	I Tr I
	17 55	I Sh E

d	h m	
8	18 38	I Tr E
9	12 49	I Ec D
	14 39	III Sh I
	15 49	I Oc R
	17 34	III Sh E
	17 35	III Tr I
	20 36	III Tr E
10	3 42	II Ec D
	7 57	II Oc R
	10 10	I Sh I
	10 54	I Tr I
	12 24	I Sh E
	13 08	I Tr E
11	7 17	I Ec D
	10 19	I Oc R
	21 56	II Sh I
	23 29	II Tr I
12	0 42	II Sh E
	2 17	II Tr E
	4 38	I Sh I
	5 24	I Tr I
	6 52	I Sh E
	7 38	I Tr E
	13 12	IV Sh I
	15 37	IV Sh E
	20 23	IV Tr I
	23 19	IV Tr E
13	1 46	I Ec D
	4 24	III Ec D
	4 49	I Oc R
	7 20	III Ec R
	7 34	III Oc D
	10 37	III Oc R
	16 59	II Ec D
	21 20	II Oc R
	23 06	I Sh I
	23 54	I Tr I
14	1 20	I Sh E
	2 08	I Tr E
	20 15	I Ec D
	23 19	I Oc R
15	11 15	II Sh I
	12 54	II Tr I
	14 01	II Sh E
	15 42	II Tr E
	17 35	I Sh I
	18 23	I Tr I
	19 49	I Sh E
	20 38	I Tr E
16	14 43	I Ec D
	17 49	I Oc R
	18 38	III Sh I

d	h m	
16	21 34	III Sh E
	21 58	III Tr I
17	1 01	III Tr E
	6 16	II Ec D
	10 43	II Oc R
	12 03	I Sh I
	12 53	I Tr I
	14 17	I Sh E
	15 08	I Tr E
18	9 12	I Ec D
	12 19	I Oc R
19	0 32	II Sh I
	2 17	II Tr I
	3 19	II Sh E
	5 05	II Tr E
	6 32	I Sh I
	7 23	I Tr I
	8 46	I Sh E
	9 37	I Tr E
20	3 40	I Ec D
	6 49	I Oc R
	8 22	III Ec D
	11 20	III Ec R
	11 55	III Oc D
	15 01	III Oc R
	19 33	II Ec D
	20 19	IV Ec D
	22 54	IV Ec R
21	0 05	II Oc R
	1 00	I Sh I
	1 53	I Tr I
	3 14	I Sh E
	4 07	I Tr E
	4 35	IV Oc D
	7 41	IV Oc R
	22 09	I Ec D
22	1 19	I Oc R
	13 51	II Sh I
	15 41	II Tr I
	16 37	II Sh E
	18 30	II Tr E
	19 29	I Sh I
	20 23	I Tr I
	21 42	I Sh E
	22 37	I Tr E
23	16 37	I Ec D
	19 49	I Oc R
	22 38	III Sh I
24	1 34	III Sh E
	2 20	III Tr I
	5 24	III Tr E
	8 50	II Ec D

d	h m	
24	13 28	II Oc R
	13 57	I Sh I
	14 52	I Tr I
	16 11	I Sh E
	17 07	I Tr E
25	11 06	I Ec D
	14 19	I Oc R
26	3 09	II Sh I
	5 04	II Tr I
	5 55	II Sh E
	7 53	II Tr E
	8 25	I Sh I
	9 22	I Tr I
	10 39	I Sh E
	11 36	I Tr E
27	5 34	I Ec D
	8 49	I Oc R
	12 21	III Ec D
	15 19	III Ec R
	16 16	III Oc D
	19 23	III Oc R
	22 07	II Ec D
28	2 50	II Oc R
	2 54	I Sh I
	3 52	I Tr I
	5 08	I Sh E
	6 06	I Tr E
29	0 03	I Ec D
	3 19	I Oc R
	7 11	IV Sh I
	9 49	IV Sh E
	16 23	IV Tr I
	16 27	II Sh I
	18 28	II Tr I
	19 14	II Sh E
	19 34	IV Tr E
	21 17	II Tr E
	21 22	I Sh I
	22 21	I Tr I
	23 36	I Sh E
30	0 36	I Tr E
	18 31	I Ec D
	21 48	I Oc R
31	2 36	III Sh I
	5 34	III Sh E
	6 39	III Tr I
	9 44	III Tr E
	11 24	II Ec D
	15 51	I Sh I
	16 12	II Oc R
	16 51	I Tr I
	18 04	I Sh E
	19 05	I Tr E

I. Aug. 16	II. Aug. 17	III. Aug. 13	IV. Aug. 20
$x_1 = -1.7,\ y_1 = +0.2$	$x_1 = -2.1,\ y_1 = +0.3$	$x_1 = -2.5,\ y_1 = +0.5$ $x_2 = -1.0,\ y_2 = +0.5$	$x_1 = -4.0,\ y_1 = +0.7$ $x_2 = -3.0,\ y_2 = +0.7$

NOTE.—I denotes ingress; E, egress; D, disappearance; R, reappearance; Ec, eclipse; Oc, occultation; Tr, transit of the satellite; Sh, transit of the shadow.

CONFIGURATIONS OF SATELLITES I-IV FOR AUGUST

UNIVERSAL TIME

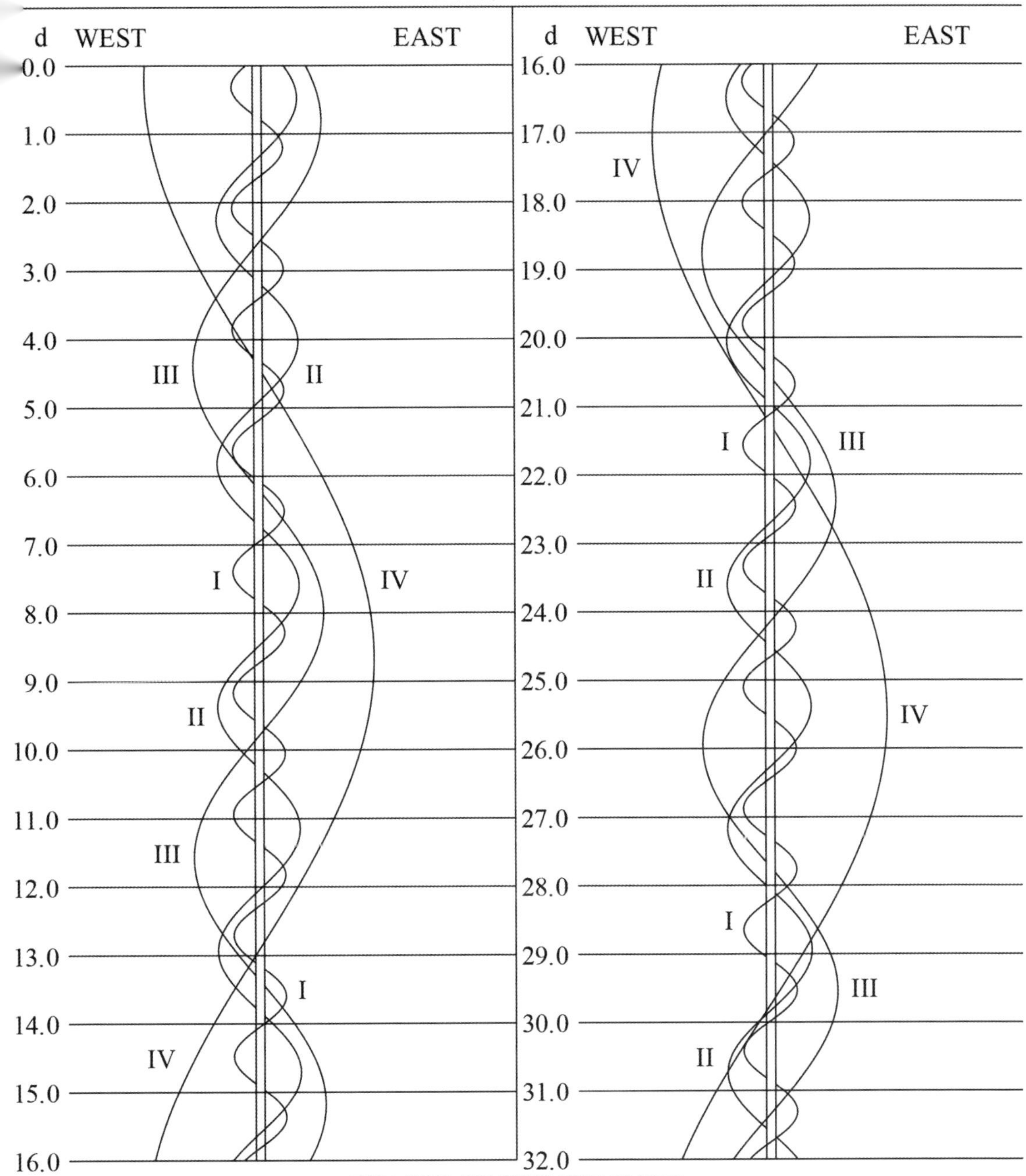

d WEST EAST

0.0 1.0 2.0 3.0 4.0 5.0 6.0 7.0 8.0 9.0 10.0 11.0 12.0 13.0 14.0 15.0 16.0

III II I IV II III I IV

d WEST EAST

16.0 17.0 18.0 19.0 20.0 21.0 22.0 23.0 24.0 25.0 26.0 27.0 28.0 29.0 30.0 31.0 32.0

IV I III II IV I III II

PHASES OF THE ECLIPSES

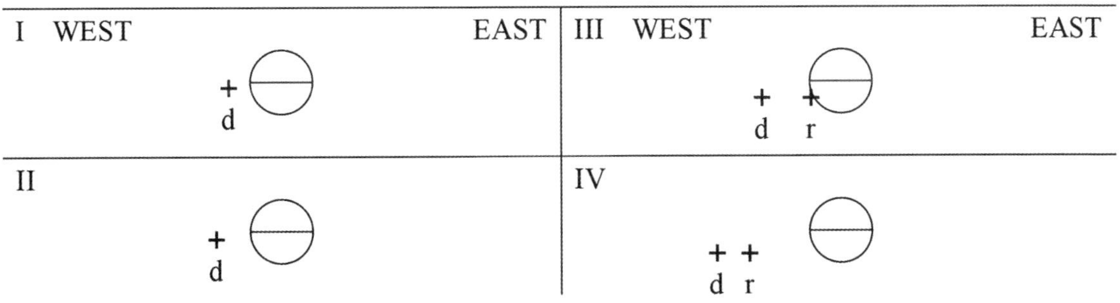

I WEST EAST

+ d

III WEST EAST

+ + d r

II

+ d

IV

+ + d r

UNIVERSAL TIME OF GEOCENTRIC PHENOMENA

SEPTEMBER

d	h m	
1	13 00	I Ec D
	16 18	I Oc R
2	5 45	II Sh I
	7 51	II Tr I
	8 32	II Sh E
	10 19	I Sh I
	10 40	II Tr E
	11 20	I Tr I
	12 33	I Sh E
	13 35	I Tr E
3	7 28	I Ec D
	10 48	I Oc R
	16 20	III Ec D
	19 20	III Ec R
	20 34	III Oc D
	23 43	III Oc R
4	0 40	II Ec D
	4 47	I Sh I
	5 33	II Oc R
	5 50	I Tr I
	7 01	I Sh E
	8 04	I Tr E
5	1 57	I Ec D
	5 18	I Oc R
	19 04	II Sh I
	21 14	II Tr I
	21 50	II Sh E
	23 16	I Sh I
6	0 03	II Tr E
	0 19	I Tr I
	1 30	I Sh E
	2 34	I Tr E
	14 18	IV Ec D
	17 05	IV Ec R
	20 25	I Ec D
	23 47	I Oc R
7	0 23	IV Oc D
	3 45	IV Oc R
	6 35	III Sh I
	9 33	III Sh E
	10 55	III Tr I
	13 57	II Ec D
	14 02	III Tr E
	17 44	I Sh I
	18 49	I Tr I
	18 55	II Oc R
	19 58	I Sh E
	21 03	I Tr E
8	14 54	I Ec D
	18 17	I Oc R

d	h m	
9	8 21	II Sh I
	10 36	II Tr I
	11 08	II Sh E
	12 13	I Sh I
	13 18	I Tr I
	13 25	II Tr E
	14 26	I Sh E
	15 32	I Tr E
10	9 22	I Ec D
	12 46	I Oc R
	20 18	III Ec D
	23 20	III Ec R
11	0 51	III Oc D
	3 14	II Ec D
	4 01	III Oc R
	6 41	I Sh I
	7 47	I Tr I
	8 16	II Oc R
	8 55	I Sh E
	10 02	I Tr E
12	3 50	I Ec D
	7 16	I Oc R
	21 40	II Sh I
	23 59	II Tr I
13	0 27	II Sh E
	1 09	I Sh I
	2 17	I Tr I
	2 48	II Tr E
	3 23	I Sh E
	4 31	I Tr E
	22 19	I Ec D
14	1 45	I Oc R
	10 33	III Sh I
	13 32	III Sh E
	15 09	III Tr I
	16 31	II Ec D
	18 17	III Tr E
	19 38	I Sh I
	20 46	I Tr I
	21 36	II Oc R
	21 51	I Sh E
	23 00	I Tr E
15	1 10	IV Sh I
	3 59	IV Sh E
	11 56	IV Tr I
	15 22	IV Tr E
	16 47	I Ec D
	20 15	I Oc R
16	10 58	II Sh I
	13 20	II Tr I

d	h m	
16	13 45	II Sh E
	14 06	I Sh I
	15 15	I Tr I
	16 10	II Tr E
	16 20	I Sh E
	17 29	I Tr E
17	11 16	I Ec D
	14 44	I Oc R
18	0 18	III Ec D
	3 20	III Ec R
	5 05	III Oc D
	5 48	II Ec D
	8 17	III Oc R
	8 34	I Sh I
	9 44	I Tr I
	10 48	I Sh E
	10 56	II Oc R
	11 58	I Tr E
19	5 44	I Ec D
	9 13	I Oc R
20	0 16	II Sh I
	2 42	II Tr I
	3 03	I Sh I
	3 03	II Sh E
	4 13	I Tr I
	5 16	I Sh E
	5 32	II Tr E
	6 28	I Tr E
21	0 13	I Ec D
	3 43	I Oc R
	14 31	III Sh I
	17 31	III Sh E
	19 04	II Ec D
	19 20	III Tr I
	21 31	I Sh I
	22 30	III Tr E
	22 42	I Tr I
	23 45	I Sh E
22	0 16	II Oc R
	0 57	I Tr E
	18 41	I Ec D
	22 12	I Oc R
23	8 16	IV Ec D
	11 14	IV Ec R
	13 34	II Sh I
	15 59	I Sh I
	16 03	II Tr I
	16 21	II Sh E
	17 11	I Tr I
	18 13	I Sh E

d	h m	
23	18 52	II Tr E
	19 26	I Tr E
	19 41	IV Oc D
	23 15	IV Oc R
24	13 10	I Ec D
	16 41	I Oc R
25	4 16	III Ec D
	7 20	III Ec R
	8 21	II Ec D
	9 15	III Oc D
	10 28	I Sh I
	11 40	I Tr I
	12 28	III Oc R
	12 41	I Sh E
	13 36	II Oc R
	13 55	I Tr E
26	7 38	I Ec D
	11 10	I Oc R
27	2 53	II Sh I
	4 56	I Sh I
	5 24	II Tr I
	5 40	II Sh E
	6 09	I Tr I
	7 10	I Sh E
	8 14	II Tr E
	8 23	I Tr E
28	2 07	I Ec D
	5 39	I Oc R
	18 29	III Sh I
	21 30	III Sh E
	21 38	II Ec D
	23 24	I Sh I
	23 29	III Tr I
29	0 38	I Tr I
	1 38	I Sh E
	2 40	III Tr E
	2 52	I Tr E
	2 55	II Oc R
	20 35	I Ec D
30	0 08	I Oc R
	16 10	II Sh I
	17 53	I Sh I
	18 44	II Tr I
	18 58	II Sh E
	19 07	I Tr I
	20 06	I Sh E
	21 21	I Tr E
	21 34	II Tr E

I. Sept. 15	II. Sept. 14	III. Sept. 18	IV. Sept. 23
$x_1 = -2.0,\ y_1 = +0.2$	$x_1 = -2.5,\ y_1 = +0.2$	$x_1 = -3.4,\ y_1 = +0.5$	$x_1 = -5.4,\ y_1 = +0.6$
		$x_2 = -1.8,\ y_2 = +0.5$	$x_2 = -4.2,\ y_2 = +0.6$

NOTE.—I denotes ingress; E, egress; D, disappearance; R, reappearance; Ec, eclipse; Oc, occultation; Tr, transit of the satellite; Sh, transit of the shadow.

CONFIGURATIONS OF SATELLITES I-IV FOR SEPTEMBER

UNIVERSAL TIME

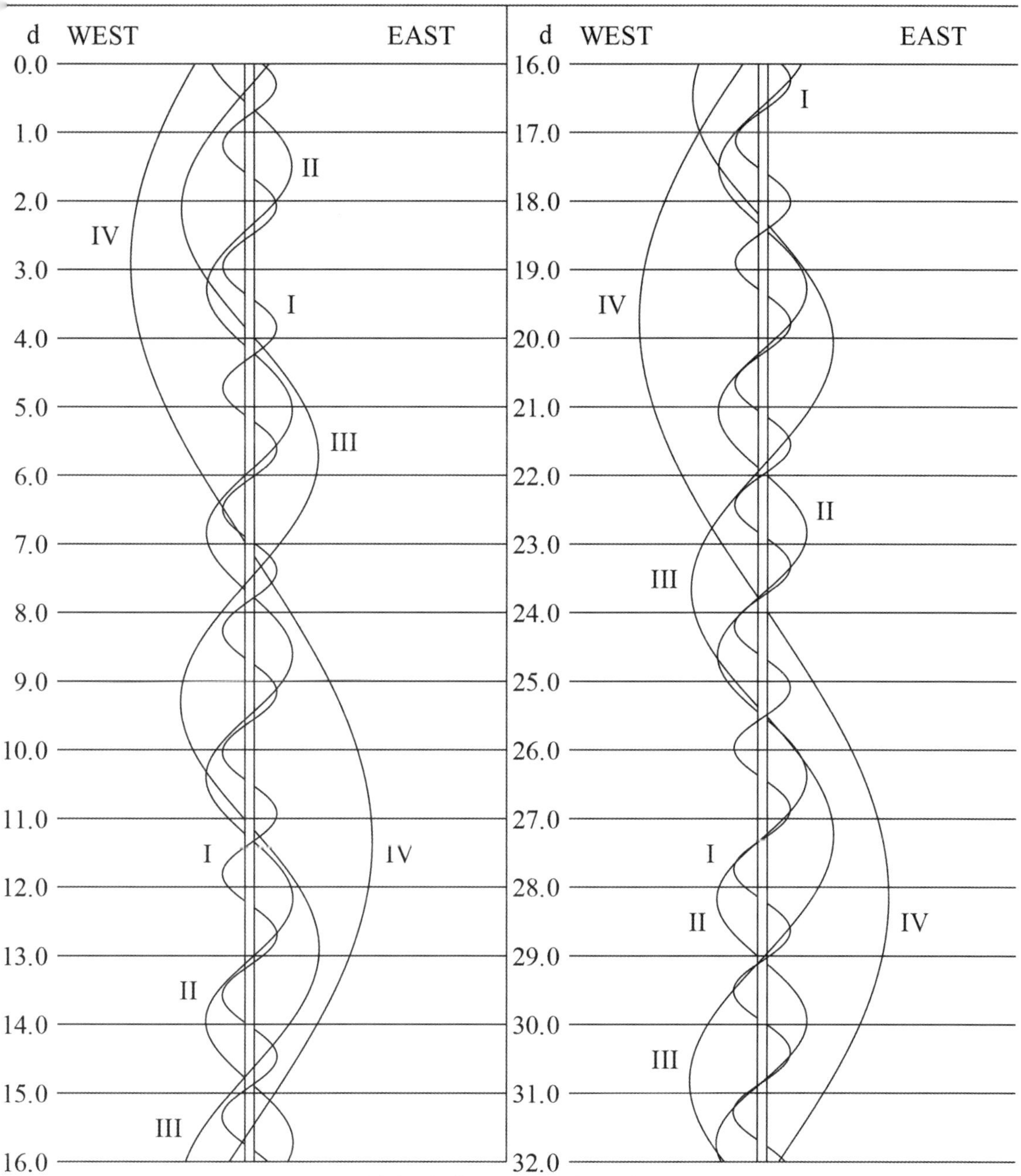

PHASES OF THE ECLIPSES

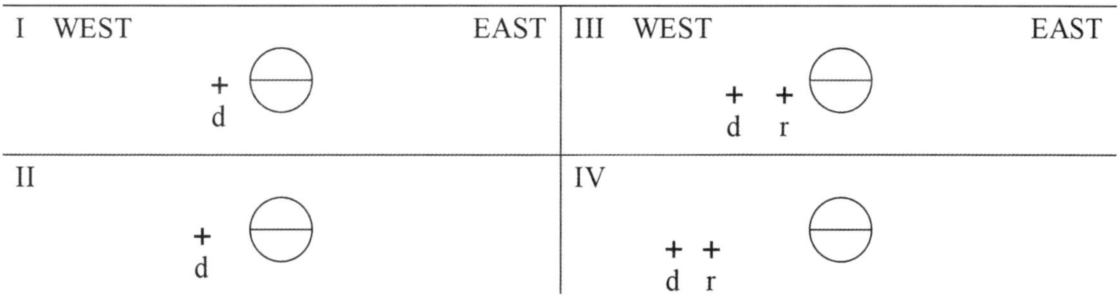

UNIVERSAL TIME OF GEOCENTRIC PHENOMENA

OCTOBER

d	h m	Phenomenon
1	15 04	I Ec D
	18 37	I Oc R
	19 08	IV Sh I
	22 09	IV Sh E
2	6 54	IV Tr I
	8 15	III Ec D
	10 30	IV Tr E
	10 54	II Ec D
	11 19	III Ec R
	12 21	I Sh I
	13 22	III Oc D
	13 36	I Tr I
	14 34	I Sh E
	15 50	I Tr E
	16 13	II Oc R
	16 37	III Oc R
3	9 32	I Ec D
	13 06	I Oc R
4	5 29	II Sh I
	6 49	I Sh I
	8 04	II Tr I
	8 04	I Tr I
	8 17	II Sh E
	9 03	I Sh E
	10 19	I Tr E
	10 54	II Tr E
5	4 01	I Ec D
	7 35	I Oc R
	22 27	III Sh I
6	0 11	II Ec D
	1 17	I Sh I
	1 30	III Sh E
	2 33	I Tr I
	3 31	I Sh E
	3 34	III Tr I
	4 47	I Tr E
	5 32	II Oc R
	6 46	III Tr E
	22 29	I Ec D
7	2 04	I Oc R
	18 47	II Sh I
	19 46	I Sh I
	21 01	I Tr I
	21 23	II Tr I
	21 34	II Sh E
	21 59	I Sh E
	23 16	I Tr E
8	0 13	II Tr E
	16 57	I Ec D
	20 33	I Oc R
9	12 13	III Ec D
9	13 28	II Ec D
	14 14	I Sh I
	15 18	III Ec R
	15 30	I Tr I
	16 28	I Sh E
	17 26	III Oc D
	17 44	I Tr E
	18 49	II Oc R
	20 41	III Oc R
10	2 15	IV Ec D
	5 24	IV Ec R
	11 26	I Ec D
	14 19	IV Oc D
	15 01	I Oc R
	18 04	IV Oc R
11	8 05	II Sh I
	8 42	I Sh I
	9 58	I Tr I
	10 43	II Tr I
	10 53	II Sh E
	10 56	I Sh E
	12 13	I Tr E
	13 33	II Tr E
12	5 54	I Ec D
	9 30	I Oc R
13	2 26	III Sh I
	2 44	II Ec D
	3 11	I Sh I
	4 27	I Tr I
	5 24	I Sh E
	5 29	III Sh E
	6 41	I Tr E
	7 36	III Tr I
	8 07	II Oc R
	10 49	III Tr E
14	0 23	I Ec D
	3 58	I Oc R
	21 23	II Sh I
	21 39	I Sh I
	22 55	I Tr I
	23 53	I Sh E
15	0 01	II Tr I
	0 11	II Sh E
	1 10	I Tr E
	2 51	II Tr E
	18 51	I Ec D
	22 27	I Oc R
16	16 01	II Ec D
	16 07	I Sh I
	16 11	III Ec D
	17 23	I Tr I
	18 21	I Sh E
16	19 18	III Ec R
	19 38	I Tr E
	21 24	II Oc R
	21 25	III Oc D
17	0 42	III Oc R
	13 20	I Ec D
	16 55	I Oc R
18	10 36	I Sh I
	10 42	II Sh I
	11 52	I Tr I
	12 49	I Sh E
	13 07	IV Sh I
	13 19	II Tr I
	13 30	II Sh E
	14 06	I Tr E
	16 09	II Tr E
	16 17	IV Sh E
19	1 08	IV Tr I
	4 52	IV Tr E
	7 48	I Ec D
	11 24	I Oc R
20	5 04	I Sh I
	5 17	II Ec D
	6 20	I Tr I
	6 24	III Sh I
	7 18	I Sh E
	8 34	I Tr E
	9 28	III Sh E
	10 40	II Oc R
	11 33	III Tr I
	14 47	III Tr E
21	2 17	I Ec D
	5 52	I Oc R
	23 32	I Sh I
	23 59	II Sh I
22	0 48	I Tr I
	1 46	I Sh E
	2 36	II Tr I
	2 47	II Sh E
	3 02	I Tr E
	5 27	II Tr E
	20 45	I Ec D
23	0 20	I Oc R
	18 00	I Sh I
	18 34	II Ec D
	19 16	I Tr I
	20 10	III Ec D
	20 14	I Sh E
	21 30	I Tr E
	23 18	III Ec R
	23 56	II Oc R
24	1 22	III Oc D
	4 39	III Oc R
	15 13	I Ec D
	18 48	I Oc R
25	12 29	I Sh I
	13 18	II Sh I
	13 44	I Tr I
	14 42	I Sh E
	15 54	II Tr I
	15 58	I Tr E
	16 06	II Sh E
	18 44	II Tr E
26	9 42	I Ec D
	13 17	I Oc R
	20 13	IV Ec D
	23 32	IV Ec R
27	6 57	I Sh I
	7 51	II Ec D
	8 08	IV Oc D
	8 12	I Tr I
	9 11	I Sh E
	10 22	III Sh I
	10 26	I Tr E
	12 00	IV Oc R
	13 11	II Oc R
	13 27	III Sh E
	15 26	III Tr I
	18 41	III Tr E
28	4 10	I Ec D
	7 45	I Oc R
29	1 25	I Sh I
	2 35	II Sh I
	2 40	I Tr I
	3 39	I Sh E
	4 54	I Tr E
	5 09	II Tr I
	5 24	II Sh E
	8 00	II Tr E
	22 39	I Ec D
30	2 13	I Oc R
	19 53	I Sh I
	21 07	II Ec D
	21 07	I Tr I
	22 07	I Sh E
	23 22	I Tr E
31	0 09	III Ec D
	2 26	II Oc R
	3 17	III Ec R
	5 13	III Oc D
	8 31	III Oc R
	17 07	I Ec D
	20 40	I Oc R

I. Oct. 15	II. Oct. 16	III. Oct. 16	IV. Oct. 10
$x_1 = -2.1,\ y_1 = +0.1$	$x_1 = -2.7,\ y_1 = +0.2$	$x_1 = -3.7,\ y_1 = +0.4$ $x_2 = -2.1,\ y_2 = +0.4$	$x_1 = -5.7,\ y_1 = +0.6$ $x_2 = -4.4,\ y_2 = +0.6$

NOTE.—I denotes ingress; E, egress; D, disappearance; R, reappearance; Ec, eclipse; Oc, occultation; Tr, transit of the satellite; Sh, transit of the shadow.

CONFIGURATIONS OF SATELLITES I-IV FOR OCTOBER

UNIVERSAL TIME

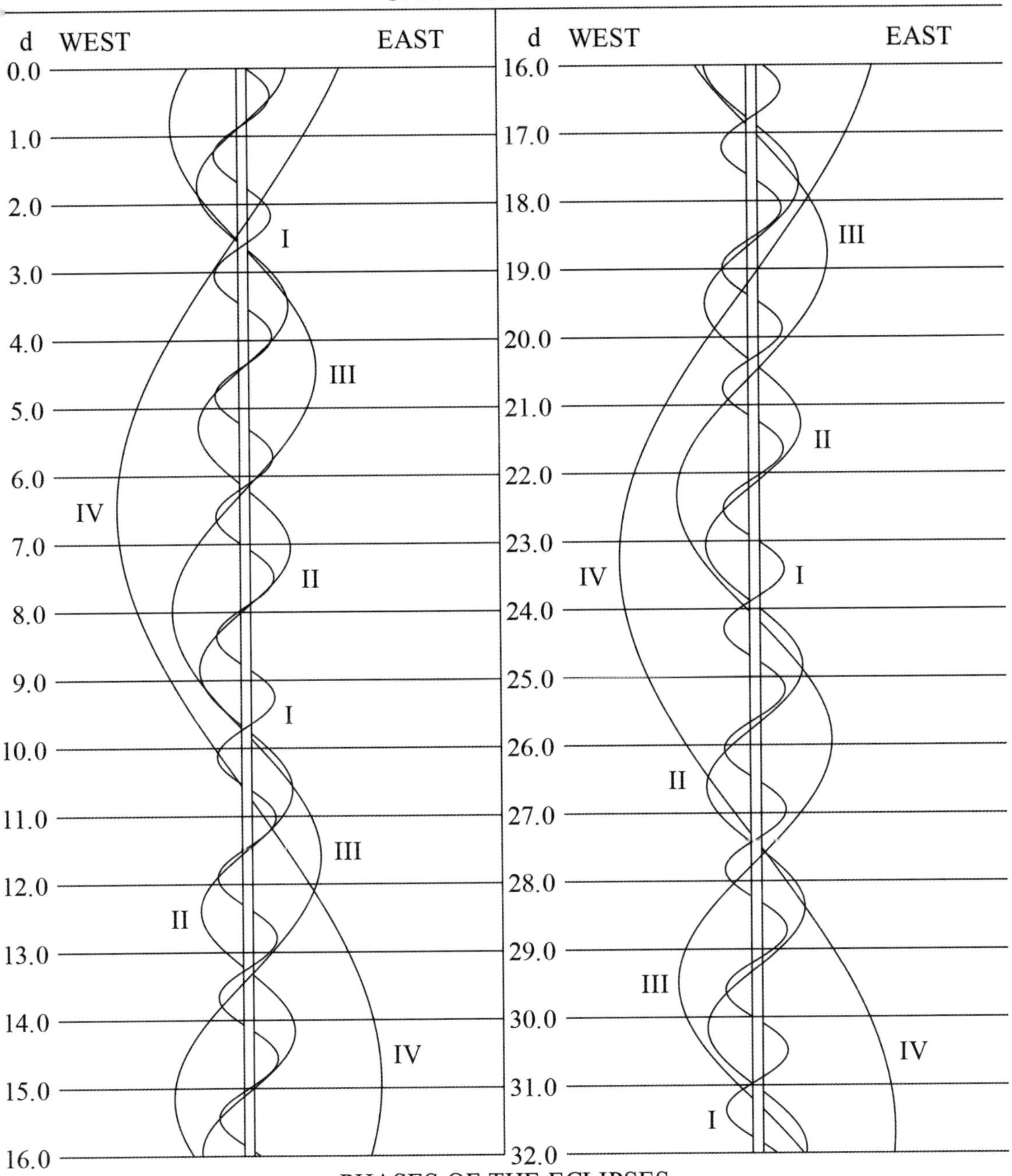

PHASES OF THE ECLIPSES

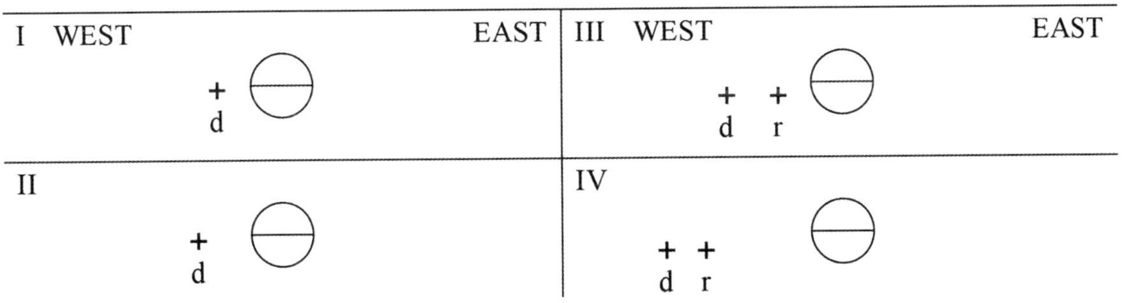

UNIVERSAL TIME OF GEOCENTRIC PHENOMENA

NOVEMBER

d	h m	
1	14 22	I Sh I
	15 35	I Tr I
	15 54	II Sh I
	16 36	I Sh E
	17 50	I Tr E
	18 26	II Tr I
	18 43	II Sh E
	21 16	II Tr E
2	11 36	I Ec D
	15 08	I Oc R
3	8 50	I Sh I
	10 03	I Tr I
	10 24	II Ec D
	11 04	I Sh E
	12 17	I Tr E
	14 19	III Sh I
	15 40	II Oc R
	17 26	III Sh E
	19 15	III Tr I
	22 30	III Tr E
4	6 04	I Ec D
	7 06	IV Sh I
	9 36	I Oc R
	10 25	IV Sh E
	18 30	IV Tr I
	22 20	IV Tr E
5	3 18	I Sh I
	4 30	I Tr I
	5 12	II Sh I
	5 32	I Sh E
	6 45	I Tr E
	7 40	II Tr I
	8 00	II Sh E
	10 31	II Tr E
6	0 33	I Ec D
	4 04	I Oc R
	21 46	I Sh I
	22 58	I Tr I
	23 40	II Ec D
7	0 01	I Sh E
	1 13	I Tr E
	4 08	III Ec D
	4 54	II Oc R
	7 17	III Ec R
	9 01	III Oc D
	12 19	III Oc R
	19 01	I Ec D
	22 31	I Oc R
8	16 15	I Sh I
	17 25	I Tr I
	18 29	I Sh E
8	18 30	II Sh I
	19 40	I Tr E
	20 55	II Tr I
	21 19	II Sh E
	23 46	II Tr E
9	13 30	I Ec D
	16 59	I Oc R
10	10 43	I Sh I
	11 53	I Tr I
	12 57	II Ec D
	12 57	I Sh E
	14 07	I Tr E
	18 07	II Oc R
	18 17	III Sh I
	21 25	III Sh E
	22 58	III Tr I
11	2 14	III Tr E
	7 58	I Ec D
	11 26	I Oc R
12	5 11	I Sh I
	6 20	I Tr I
	7 26	I Sh E
	7 48	II Sh I
	8 35	I Tr E
	10 09	II Tr I
	10 37	II Sh E
	13 00	II Tr E
	14 12	IV Ec D
	17 40	IV Ec R
13	1 01	IV Oc D
	2 27	I Ec D
	4 58	IV Oc R
	5 54	I Oc R
	23 40	I Sh I
14	0 47	I Tr I
	1 54	I Sh E
	2 14	II Ec D
	3 02	I Tr E
	7 20	II Oc R
	8 06	III Ec D
	11 17	III Ec R
	12 42	III Oc D
	16 01	III Oc R
	20 55	I Ec D
15	0 21	I Oc R
	18 08	I Sh I
	19 14	I Tr I
	20 22	I Sh E
	21 06	II Sh I
	21 29	I Tr E
	23 23	II Tr I
15	23 56	II Sh E
16	2 14	II Tr E
	15 24	I Ec D
	18 48	I Oc R
17	12 36	I Sh I
	13 41	I Tr I
	14 51	I Sh E
	15 31	II Ec D
	15 56	I Tr E
	20 32	II Oc R
	22 15	III Sh I
18	1 24	III Sh E
	2 38	III Tr I
	5 55	III Tr E
	9 52	I Ec D
	13 15	I Oc R
19	7 04	I Sh I
	8 08	I Tr I
	9 19	I Sh E
	10 23	I Tr E
	10 24	II Sh I
	12 35	II Tr I
	13 13	II Sh E
	15 26	II Tr E
20	4 20	I Ec D
	7 43	I Oc R
21	1 04	IV Sh I
	1 33	I Sh I
	2 35	I Tr I
	3 47	I Sh E
	4 33	IV Sh E
	4 47	II Ec D
	4 50	I Tr E
	9 43	II Oc R
	10 53	IV Tr I
	12 05	III Ec D
	14 47	IV Tr E
	15 16	III Ec R
	16 19	III Oc D
	19 39	III Oc R
	22 49	I Ec D
22	2 10	I Oc R
	20 01	I Sh I
	21 02	I Tr I
	22 16	I Sh E
	23 17	I Tr E
	23 42	II Sh I
23	1 48	II Tr I
	2 32	II Sh E
	4 39	II Tr E
23	17 17	I Ec D
	20 37	I Oc R
24	14 29	I Sh I
	15 29	I Tr I
	16 44	I Sh E
	17 44	I Tr E
	18 04	II Ec D
	22 54	II Oc R
25	2 13	III Sh I
	5 23	III Sh E
	6 13	III Tr I
	9 30	III Tr E
	11 46	I Ec D
	15 03	I Oc R
26	8 58	I Sh I
	9 56	I Tr I
	11 12	I Sh E
	12 11	I Tr E
	13 00	II Sh I
	14 59	II Tr I
	15 50	II Sh E
	17 50	II Tr E
27	6 14	I Ec D
	9 30	I Oc R
28	3 26	I Sh I
	4 22	I Tr I
	5 41	I Sh E
	6 38	I Tr E
	7 21	II Ec D
	12 04	II Oc R
	16 03	III Ec D
	19 15	III Ec R
	19 52	III Oc D
	23 11	III Oc R
29	0 43	I Ec D
	3 57	I Oc R
	8 12	IV Ec D
	11 48	IV Ec R
	16 54	IV Oc D
	20 53	IV Oc R
	21 54	I Sh I
	22 49	I Tr I
30	0 09	I Sh E
	1 04	I Tr E
	2 18	II Sh I
	4 11	II Tr I
	5 08	II Sh E
	7 02	II Tr E
	19 11	I Ec D
	22 24	I Oc R

I. Nov. 16	II. Nov. 17	III. Nov. 14	IV. Nov. 12
$x_1 = -1.9,\ y_1 = +0.1$	$x_1 = -2.5,\ y_1 = +0.2$	$x_1 = -3.4,\ y_1 = +0.4$ $x_2 = -1.7,\ y_2 = +0.4$	$x_1 = -5.2,\ y_1 = +0.5$ $x_2 = -3.8,\ y_2 = +0.5$

NOTE.—I denotes ingress; E, egress; D, disappearance; R, reappearance; Ec, eclipse; Oc, occultation; Tr, transit of the satellite; Sh, transit of the shadow.

CONFIGURATIONS OF SATELLITES I-IV FOR NOVEMBER

UNIVERSAL TIME

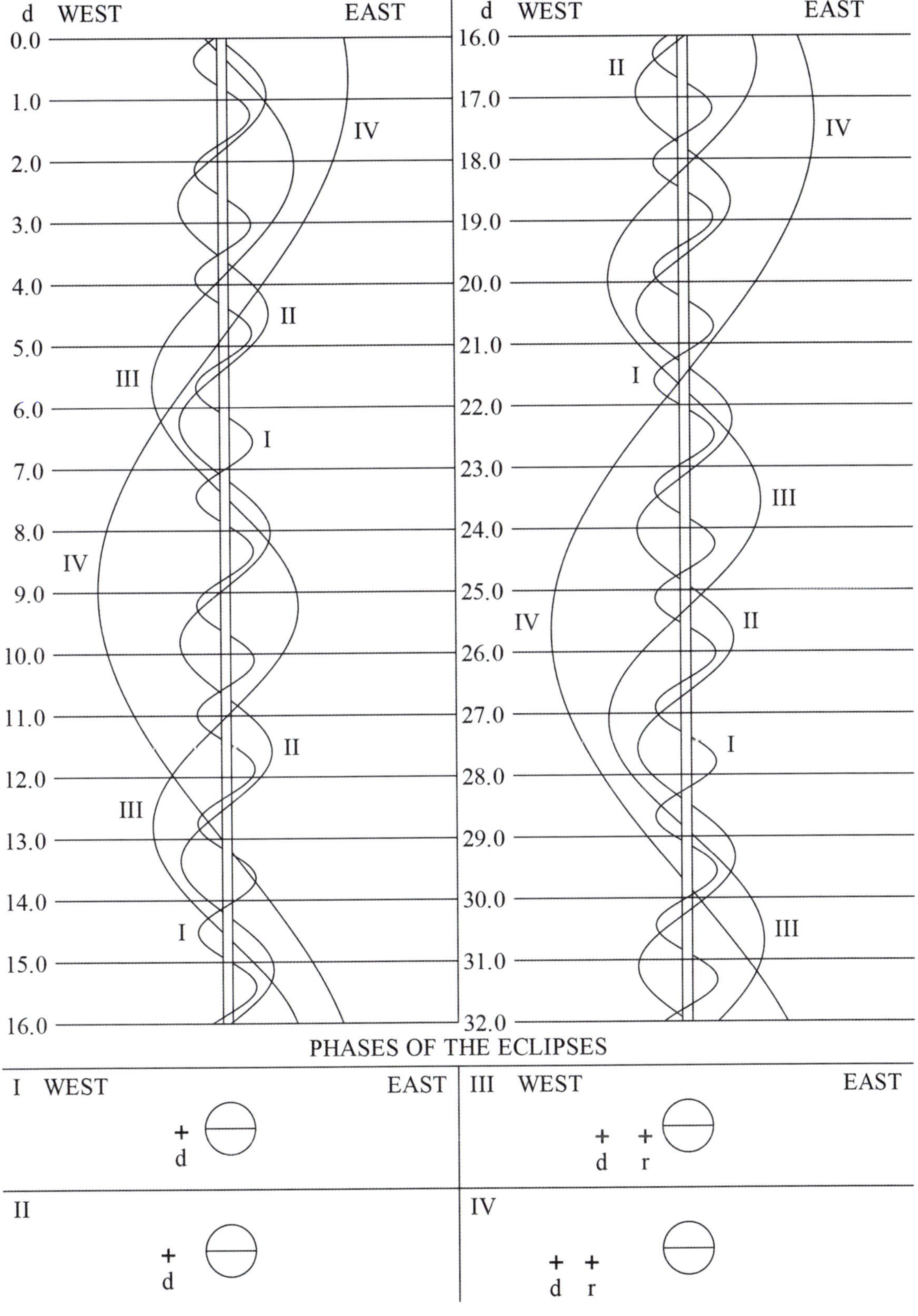

UNIVERSAL TIME OF GEOCENTRIC PHENOMENA

DECEMBER

d	h m	Phenomenon
1	16 23	I Sh I
	17 16	I Tr I
	18 37	I Sh E
	19 31	I Tr E
	20 38	II Ec D
2	1 14	II Oc R
	6 12	III Sh I
	9 23	III Sh E
	9 44	III Tr I
	13 01	III Tr E
	13 40	I Ec D
	16 50	I Oc R
3	10 51	I Sh I
	11 42	I Tr I
	13 06	I Sh E
	13 58	I Tr E
	15 36	II Sh I
	17 21	II Tr I
	18 26	II Sh E
	20 12	II Tr E
4	8 08	I Ec D
	11 17	I Oc R
5	5 19	I Sh I
	6 08	I Tr I
	7 34	I Sh E
	8 24	I Tr E
	9 55	II Ec D
	14 24	II Oc R
	20 01	III Ec D
	23 15	III Ec R
	23 19	III Oc D
6	2 37	I Ec D
	2 39	III Oc R
	5 43	I Oc R
	23 48	I Sh I
7	0 35	I Tr I
	2 03	I Sh E
	2 50	I Tr E
	4 54	II Sh I
	6 31	II Tr I
	7 45	II Sh E
	9 22	II Tr E
	19 02	IV Sh I
	21 05	I Ec D
	22 40	IV Sh E
8	0 10	I Oc R
	2 17	IV Tr I
	6 12	IV Tr E
	18 16	I Sh I
	19 01	I Tr I
	20 31	I Sh E
	21 17	I Tr E

d	h m	Phenomenon
8	23 12	II Ec D
9	3 33	II Oc R
	10 10	III Sh I
	13 10	III Tr I
	13 22	III Sh E
	15 34	I Ec D
	16 27	III Tr E
	18 36	I Oc R
10	12 44	I Sh I
	13 27	I Tr I
	15 00	I Sh E
	15 43	I Tr E
	18 12	II Sh I
	19 40	II Tr I
	21 03	II Sh E
	22 31	II Tr E
11	10 02	I Ec D
	13 02	I Oc R
12	7 13	I Sh I
	7 54	I Tr I
	9 28	I Sh E
	10 09	I Tr E
	12 29	II Ec D
	16 41	II Oc R
13	0 00	III Ec D
	4 31	I Ec D
	6 03	III Oc R
	7 29	I Oc R
14	1 41	I Sh I
	2 20	I Tr I
	3 56	I Sh E
	4 36	I Tr E
	7 31	II Sh I
	8 49	II Tr I
	10 21	II Sh E
	11 41	II Tr E
	23 00	I Ec D
15	1 55	I Oc R
	20 09	I Sh I
	20 46	I Tr I
	22 25	I Sh E
	23 02	I Tr E
16	1 46	II Ec D
	2 11	IV Ec D
	5 49	II Oc R
	5 55	IV Ec R
	7 52	IV Oc D
	11 51	IV Oc R
	14 08	III Sh I
	16 32	III Tr I
	17 21	III Sh E

d	h m	Phenomenon
16	17 28	I Ec D
	19 49	III Tr E
	20 21	I Oc R
17	14 38	I Sh I
	15 12	I Tr I
	16 53	I Sh E
	17 28	I Tr E
	20 48	II Sh I
	21 58	II Tr I
	23 39	II Sh E
18	0 49	II Tr E
	11 57	I Ec D
	14 47	I Oc R
19	9 06	I Sh I
	9 38	I Tr I
	11 22	I Sh E
	11 54	I Tr E
	15 03	II Ec D
	18 57	II Oc R
20	3 59	III Ec D
	6 25	I Ec D
	9 13	I Oc R
	9 24	III Oc R
21	3 35	I Sh I
	4 04	I Tr I
	5 50	I Sh E
	6 20	I Tr E
	10 07	II Sh I
	11 06	II Tr I
	12 57	II Sh E
	13 58	II Tr E
22	0 54	I Ec D
	3 39	I Oc R
	22 03	I Sh I
	22 30	I Tr I
23	0 19	I Sh E
	0 46	I Tr E
	4 20	II Ec D
	8 04	II Oc R
	18 06	III Sh I
	19 22	I Ec D
	19 50	III Tr I
	21 20	III Sh E
	22 05	I Oc R
	23 08	III Tr E
24	13 02	IV Sh I
	16 31	I Sh I
	16 48	IV Sh E
	16 53	IV Tr I
	16 56	I Tr I
	18 47	I Sh E

d	h m	Phenomenon
24	19 12	I Tr E
	20 49	IV Tr E
	23 24	II Sh I
25	0 14	II Tr I
	2 15	II Sh E
	3 05	II Tr E
	13 51	I Ec D
	16 31	I Oc R
26	11 00	I Sh I
	11 22	I Tr I
	13 16	I Sh E
	13 38	I Tr E
	17 37	II Ec D
	21 12	II Oc R
27	7 59	III Ec D
	8 19	I Ec D
	10 57	I Oc R
	12 42	III Oc R
28	5 28	I Sh I
	5 48	I Tr I
	7 44	I Sh E
	8 04	I Tr E
	12 43	II Sh I
	13 22	II Tr I
	15 34	II Sh E
	16 13	II Tr E
29	2 48	I Ec D
	5 23	I Oc R
	23 57	I Sh I
30	0 14	I Tr I
	2 13	I Sh E
	2 30	I Tr E
	6 55	II Ec D
	10 18	II Oc R
	21 17	I Ec D
	22 04	III Sh I
	23 07	III Tr I
	23 49	I Oc R
31	1 20	III Sh E
	2 24	III Tr E
	18 25	I Sh I
	18 40	I Tr I
	20 41	I Sh E
	20 56	I Tr E
32	2 01	II Sh I
	2 29	II Tr I
	4 52	II Sh E
	5 20	II Tr E
	15 45	I Ec D
	18 15	I Oc R
	20 12	IV Ec D

I. Dec. 16	II. Dec. 16	III. Dec. 13	IV. Dec. 16
$x_1 = -1.5,\ y_1 = +0.1$	$x_1 = -1.8,\ y_1 = +0.2$	$x_1 = -2.4,\ y_1 = +0.4$	$x_1 = -3.2,\ y_1 = +0.5$ $x_2 = -1.6,\ y_2 = +0.5$

NOTE.—I denotes ingress; E, egress; D, disappearance; R, reappearance; Ec, eclipse; Oc, occultation; Tr, transit of the satellite; Sh, transit of the shadow.

CONFIGURATIONS OF SATELLITES I-IV FOR DECEMBER

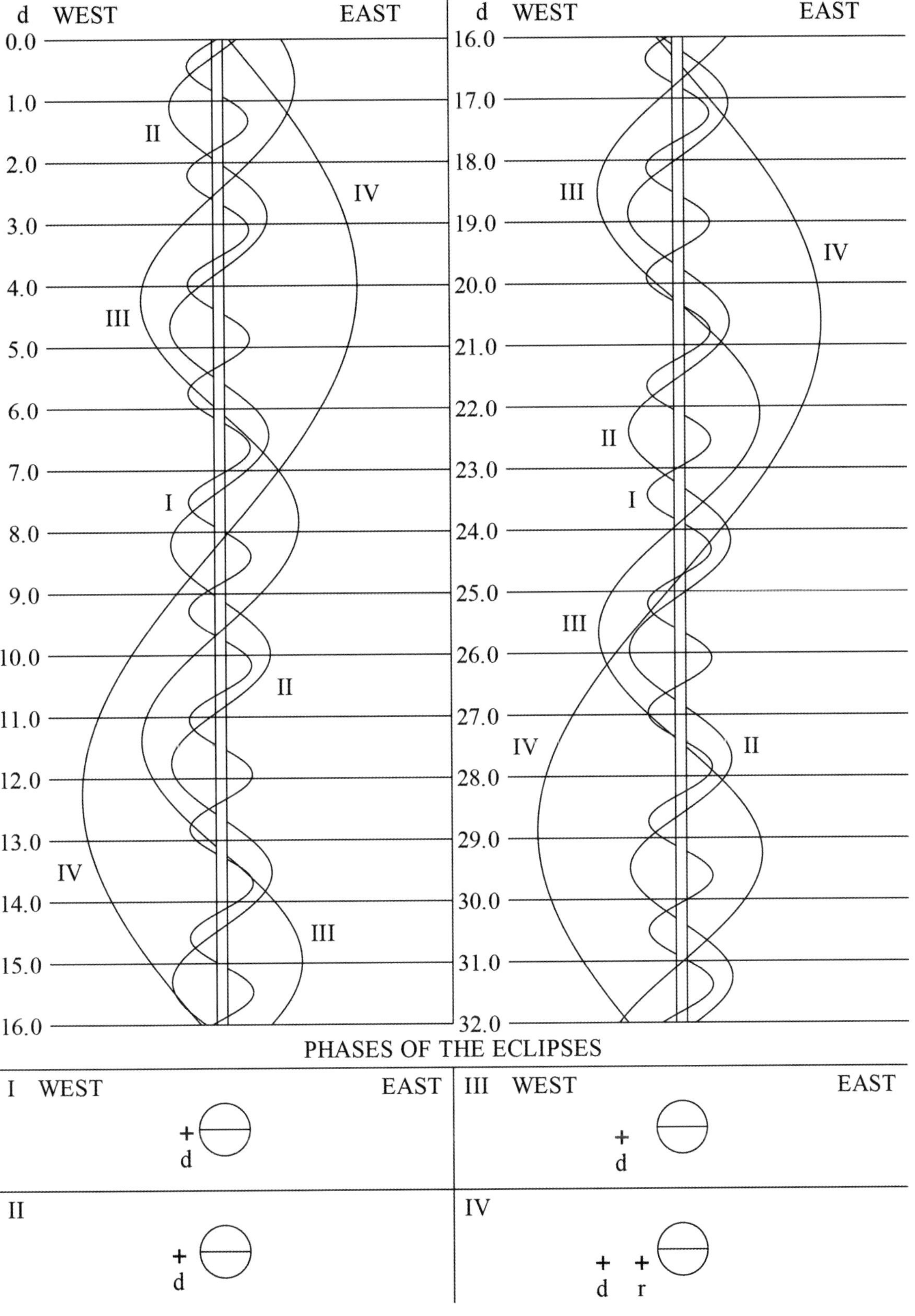

FOR 0^h UNIVERSAL TIME

Date	Axes of outer edge of A ring: Major	Axes of outer edge of A ring: Minor	U	B	P	U'	B'	P'
	″	″	°	°	°	°	°	°
Jan. −3	37.86	2.91	215.026	+ 4.402	+ 5.269	180.776	+ 1.915	+ 28.084
1	37.63	2.79	215.279	+ 4.257	+ 5.251	180.893	+ 1.857	+ 28.083
5	37.41	2.68	215.551	+ 4.102	+ 5.232	181.011	+ 1.798	+ 28.082
9	37.20	2.56	215.841	+ 3.939	+ 5.211	181.128	+ 1.739	+ 28.081
13	37.01	2.43	216.149	+ 3.766	+ 5.189	181.245	+ 1.680	+ 28.080
17	36.82	2.30	216.472	+ 3.586	+ 5.165	181.363	+ 1.621	+ 28.078
21	36.65	2.17	216.811	+ 3.399	+ 5.141	181.480	+ 1.562	+ 28.077
25	36.49	2.04	217.164	+ 3.204	+ 5.115	181.598	+ 1.503	+ 28.075
29	36.34	1.90	217.530	+ 3.003	+ 5.088	181.715	+ 1.443	+ 28.074
Feb. 2	36.20	1.77	217.907	+ 2.796	+ 5.061	181.833	+ 1.384	+ 28.072
6	36.08	1.63	218.296	+ 2.585	+ 5.032	181.950	+ 1.325	+ 28.070
10	35.97	1.49	218.694	+ 2.369	+ 5.002	182.068	+ 1.266	+ 28.068
14	35.88	1.35	219.101	+ 2.149	+ 4.972	182.185	+ 1.207	+ 28.065
18	35.79	1.20	219.515	+ 1.926	+ 4.941	182.303	+ 1.148	+ 28.063
22	35.72	1.06	219.935	+ 1.700	+ 4.909	182.420	+ 1.089	+ 28.060
26	35.67	0.92	220.361	+ 1.472	+ 4.876	182.538	+ 1.029	+ 28.058
Mar. 2	35.63	0.77	220.791	+ 1.243	+ 4.843	182.656	+ 0.970	+ 28.055
6	35.60	0.63	221.225	+ 1.013	+ 4.810	182.773	+ 0.911	+ 28.052
10	35.58	0.49	221.660	+ 0.783	+ 4.776	182.891	+ 0.852	+ 28.049
14	35.58	0.34	222.096	+ 0.553	+ 4.742	183.009	+ 0.792	+ 28.046
18	35.59	0.20	222.532	+ 0.324	+ 4.708	183.126	+ 0.733	+ 28.042
22	35.62	0.06	222.968	+ 0.096	+ 4.674	183.244	+ 0.674	+ 28.039
26	35.66	0.08	223.401	− 0.129	+ 4.640	183.362	+ 0.614	+ 28.035
30	35.71	0.22	223.831	− 0.352	+ 4.605	183.480	+ 0.555	+ 28.032
Apr. 3	35.78	0.36	224.257	− 0.571	+ 4.571	183.598	+ 0.496	+ 28.028
7	35.86	0.49	224.678	− 0.787	+ 4.537	183.716	+ 0.436	+ 28.024
11	35.95	0.63	225.092	− 0.999	+ 4.504	183.833	+ 0.377	+ 28.020
15	36.06	0.76	225.500	− 1.205	+ 4.471	183.951	+ 0.317	+ 28.016
19	36.18	0.89	225.899	− 1.407	+ 4.438	184.069	+ 0.258	+ 28.011
23	36.31	1.02	226.290	− 1.602	+ 4.406	184.187	+ 0.198	+ 28.007
27	36.45	1.14	226.670	− 1.792	+ 4.374	184.305	+ 0.139	+ 28.002
May 1	36.61	1.26	227.039	− 1.974	+ 4.344	184.423	+ 0.079	+ 27.998
5	36.77	1.38	227.396	− 2.149	+ 4.314	184.541	+ 0.020	+ 27.993
9	36.95	1.49	227.740	− 2.316	+ 4.285	184.660	− 0.040	+ 27.988
13	37.14	1.60	228.070	− 2.475	+ 4.258	184.778	− 0.099	+ 27.983
17	37.34	1.71	228.386	− 2.626	+ 4.231	184.896	− 0.159	+ 27.977
21	37.55	1.81	228.685	− 2.767	+ 4.206	185.014	− 0.218	+ 27.972
25	37.78	1.91	228.968	− 2.899	+ 4.182	185.132	− 0.278	+ 27.966
29	38.01	2.00	229.233	− 3.020	+ 4.159	185.251	− 0.338	+ 27.961
June 2	38.25	2.09	229.480	− 3.132	+ 4.138	185.369	− 0.397	+ 27.955
6	38.50	2.17	229.708	− 3.232	+ 4.118	185.487	− 0.457	+ 27.949
10	38.75	2.25	229.915	− 3.322	+ 4.101	185.606	− 0.516	+ 27.943
14	39.01	2.31	230.102	− 3.400	+ 4.084	185.724	− 0.576	+ 27.937
18	39.28	2.38	230.268	− 3.467	+ 4.070	185.842	− 0.636	+ 27.931
22	39.56	2.43	230.412	− 3.522	+ 4.058	185.961	− 0.695	+ 27.924
26	39.83	2.48	230.533	− 3.565	+ 4.047	186.079	− 0.755	+ 27.918
30	40.12	2.52	230.631	− 3.595	+ 4.039	186.198	− 0.815	+ 27.911

Factor by which axes of outer edge of the A ring are to be multiplied to obtain axes of:

Inner edge of the A ring	0.8944	Inner edge of the B ring	0.6724
Outer edge of the B ring	0.8591	Inner edge of the C ring	0.5458

U = The geocentric longitude of Saturn, measured in the plane of the rings eastward from its ascending node on the mean equator of the Earth. The Saturnicentric longitude of the Earth, measured in the same way, is $U + 180°$.

B = The Saturnicentric latitude of the Earth, referred to the plane of the rings, positive toward the north. When B is positive the visible surface of the rings is the northern surface.

P = The geocentric position angle of the northern semiminor axis of the apparent ellipse of the rings, measured eastward from north.

FOR 0^h UNIVERSAL TIME

Date	Axes of outer edge of A ring Major	Minor	U	B	P	U'	B'	P'
	″	″	°	°	°	°	°	°
July 4	40.40	2.55	230.705	− 3.614	+ 4.032	186.316	− 0.875	+ 27.904
8	40.68	2.57	230.756	− 3.619	+ 4.028	186.435	− 0.934	+ 27.897
12	40.96	2.58	230.783	− 3.613	+ 4.026	186.554	− 0.994	+ 27.890
16	41.24	2.59	230.786	− 3.594	+ 4.025	186.672	− 1.054	+ 27.883
20	41.52	2.58	230.765	− 3.563	+ 4.027	186.791	− 1.113	+ 27.875
24	41.79	2.57	230.720	− 3.520	+ 4.031	186.910	− 1.173	+ 27.868
28	42.05	2.54	230.651	− 3.465	+ 4.037	187.028	− 1.233	+ 27.860
Aug. 1	42.31	2.51	230.559	− 3.399	+ 4.045	187.147	− 1.293	+ 27.852
5	42.56	2.47	230.445	− 3.321	+ 4.055	187.266	− 1.353	+ 27.845
9	42.79	2.41	230.310	− 3.234	+ 4.067	187.385	− 1.412	+ 27.837
13	43.01	2.35	230.154	− 3.136	+ 4.080	187.504	− 1.472	+ 27.828
17	43.21	2.28	229.979	− 3.029	+ 4.095	187.623	− 1.532	+ 27.820
21	43.40	2.21	229.785	− 2.913	+ 4.112	187.742	− 1.592	+ 27.812
25	43.57	2.12	229.574	− 2.790	+ 4.130	187.861	− 1.652	+ 27.803
29	43.72	2.03	229.349	− 2.660	+ 4.150	187.980	− 1.712	+ 27.794
Sept. 2	43.85	1.93	229.110	− 2.525	+ 4.170	188.099	− 1.771	+ 27.786
6	43.95	1.83	228.860	− 2.385	+ 4.191	188.218	− 1.831	+ 27.777
10	44.04	1.72	228.601	− 2.241	+ 4.213	188.337	− 1.891	+ 27.768
14	44.09	1.61	228.335	− 2.095	+ 4.236	188.456	− 1.951	+ 27.758
18	44.13	1.50	228.064	− 1.948	+ 4.259	188.576	− 2.011	+ 27.749
22	44.14	1.39	227.790	− 1.801	+ 4.282	188.695	− 2.071	+ 27.740
26	44.12	1.27	227.516	− 1.655	+ 4.305	188.814	− 2.131	+ 27.730
30	44.08	1.16	227.245	− 1.513	+ 4.328	188.933	− 2.191	+ 27.720
Oct. 4	44.01	1.06	226.978	− 1.374	+ 4.350	189.053	− 2.250	+ 27.710
8	43.92	0.95	226.718	− 1.240	+ 4.372	189.172	− 2.310	+ 27.700
12	43.81	0.85	226.467	− 1.112	+ 4.392	189.292	− 2.370	+ 27.690
16	43.67	0.76	226.227	− 0.992	+ 4.412	189.411	− 2.430	+ 27.680
20	43.51	0.67	226.000	− 0.880	+ 4.431	189.531	− 2.490	+ 27.670
24	43.33	0.59	225.788	− 0.777	+ 4.448	189.650	− 2.550	+ 27.659
28	43.14	0.52	225.594	− 0.684	+ 4.464	189.770	− 2.610	+ 27.648
Nov. 1	42.92	0.45	225.418	− 0.603	+ 4.478	189.890	− 2.670	+ 27.638
5	42.70	0.40	225.263	− 0.533	+ 4.491	190.010	− 2.790	+ 27.616
9	42.46	0.35	225.129	− 0.475	+ 4.502	190.129	− 2.790	+ 27.616
13	42.20	0.32	225.017	− 0.430	+ 4.511	190.249	− 2.850	+ 27.604
17	41.94	0.29	224.928	− 0.398	+ 4.518	190.369	− 2.910	+ 27.593
21	41.67	0.28	224.864	− 0.379	+ 4.523	190.489	− 2.970	+ 27.581
25	41.39	0.27	224.824	− 0.374	+ 4.526	190.608	− 3.029	+ 27.570
29	41.11	0.27	224.810	− 0.383	+ 4.527	190.728	− 3.089	+ 27.558
Dec. 3	40.83	0.29	224.820	− 0.405	+ 4.526	190.848	− 3.149	+ 27.546
7	40.54	0.31	224.857	− 0.441	+ 4.523	190.968	− 3.209	+ 27.534
11	40.26	0.34	224.918	− 0.490	+ 4.518	191.089	− 3.269	+ 27.522
15	39.98	0.38	225.004	− 0.552	+ 4.511	191.209	− 3.329	+ 27.510
19	39.70	0.43	225.115	− 0.627	+ 4.502	191.329	− 3.389	+ 27.497
23	39.42	0.49	225.251	− 0.715	+ 4.491	191.449	− 3.449	+ 27.485
27	39.16	0.56	225.410	− 0.815	+ 4.478	191.569	− 3.509	+ 27.472
31	38.89	0.63	225.592	− 0.927	+ 4.463	191.690	− 3.569	+ 27.459
35	38.64	0.71	225.797	− 1.050	+ 4.446	191.810	− 3.629	+ 27.446

Factor by which axes of outer edge of the A ring are to be multiplied to obtain axes of:

Inner edge of the A ring	0.8944	Inner edge of the B ring	0.6724
Outer edge of the B ring	0.8591	Inner edge of the C ring	0.5458

U' = The heliocentric longitude of Saturn, measured in the plane of the rings eastward from its ascending node on the ecliptic. The Saturnicentric longitude of the Sun, measured in the same way is $U' + 180°$.

B' = The Saturnicentric latitude of the Sun, referred to the plane of the rings, positive toward the north. When B′ is positive the northern surface of the rings is illuminated.

P' = The heliocentric position angle of the northern semiminor axis of the rings on the heliocentric celestial sphere, measured eastward from the great circle that passes through Saturn and the poles of the ecliptic.

APPARENT ORBITS OF SATELLITES I–VII AT 0^h UNIVERSAL TIME ON THE DATE OF OPPOSITION, SEPTEMBER 21

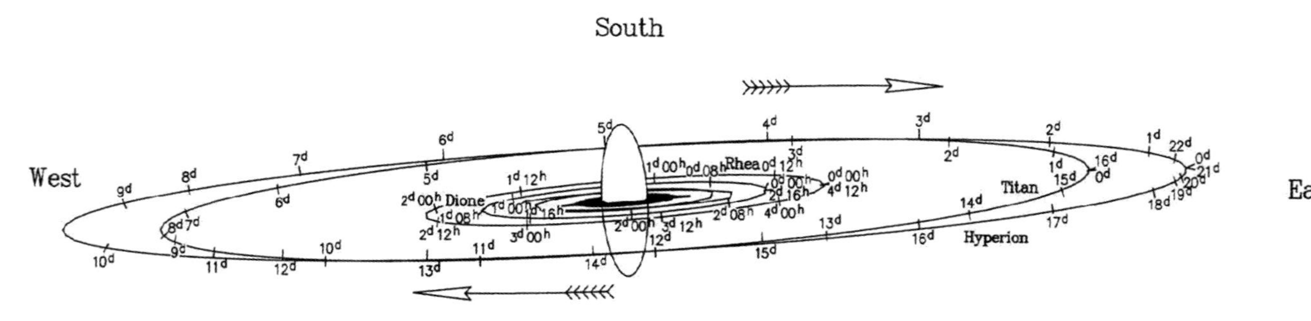

Orbits elongated in ratio of 3 to 1 in the North-South direction.

	Name	Mean Sidereal Period		Name	Mean Sidereal Period
		d			d
I	Mimas.	0.9424	VI	Titan.	15.9454
II	Enceladus.	1.3702	VII	Hyperion	21.2767
III	Tethys	1.8878	VIII	Iapetus	79.3310
IV	Dione.	2.7369	IX	Phoebe.	546.4 R
V	Rhea.	4.5175			

UNIVERSAL TIME OF GREATEST EASTERN ELONGATION

I Mimas

Jan.	Feb.	Mar.	Apr.	May	June	July	Aug.	Sept.	Oct.	Nov.	Dec.
d h	d h	d h	d h	d h	d h	d h	d h	d h	d h	d h	d h
−1 07.0	1 06.9	1 13.6	1 16.3	1 20.2	1 00.1	1 03.8	1 06.1	1 08.3	1 12.0	1 14.3	1 18.1
0 05.6	2 05.5	2 12.3	2 14.9	2 18.8	1 22.7	2 02.5	2 04.7	2 07.0	2 10.6	2 12.9	2 16.8
1 04.2	3 04.1	3 10.9	3 13.5	3 17.4	2 21.4	3 01.1	3 03.3	3 05.6	3 09.2	3 11.6	3 15.4
2 02.9	4 02.7	4 09.5	4 12.1	4 16.1	3 20.0	3 23.7	4 02.0	4 04.2	4 07.8	4 10.2	4 14.0
3 01.5	5 01.3	5 08.1	5 10.8	5 14.8	4 18.6	4 22.3	5 00.6	5 02.8	5 06.5	5 08.8	5 12.6
4 00.1	6 00.0	6 06.7	6 09.4	6 13.4	5 17.2	5 20.9	5 23.2	6 01.4	6 05.1	6 07.4	6 11.2
4 22.7	6 22.6	7 05.4	7 08.0	7 12.0	6 15.8	6 19.6	6 21.8	7 00.1	7 03.7	7 06.0	7 09.9
5 21.3	7 21.2	8 04.1	8 06.6	8 10.6	7 14.5	7 18.2	7 20.4	7 22.7	8 02.3	8 04.7	8 08.5
6 20.0	8 19.9	9 02.7	9 05.3	9 09.2	8 13.1	8 16.8	8 19.1	8 21.3	9 00.9	9 03.3	9 07.1
7 18.6	9 18.5	10 01.3	10 04.0	10 07.9	9 11.7	9 15.4	9 17.7	9 19.9	9 23.6	10 01.9	10 05.7
8 17.2	10 17.2	10 23.9	11 02.6	11 06.5	10 10.3	10 14.0	10 16.3	10 18.4	10 22.2	11 00.5	11 04.3
9 15.8	11 15.8	11 22.6	12 01.2	12 05.1	11 08.9	11 12.7	11 14.9	11 17.1	11 20.8	11 23.1	12 03.0
10 14.4	12 14.4	12 21.2	12 23.8	13 03.7	12 07.6	12 11.3	12 13.5	12 15.7	12 19.4	12 21.8	13 01.6
11 13.1	13 13.0	13 19.8	13 22.4	14 02.3	13 06.2	13 09.9	13 12.1	13 14.3	13 17.9	13 20.4	14 00.2
12 11.8	14 11.6	14 18.4	14 21.0	15 01.0	14 04.8	14 08.4	14 10.8	14 12.9	14 16.6	14 19.0	14 22.8
13 10.4	15 10.3	15 17.0	15 19.7	15 23.6	15 03.4	15 07.0	15 09.3	15 11.5	15 15.2	15 17.6	15 21.4
14 09.0	16 08.9	16 15.7	16 18.3	16 22.2	16 02.0	16 05.7	16 07.9	16 10.2	16 13.8	16 16.2	16 20.1
15 07.6	17 07.5	17 14.3	17 16.9	17 20.8	17 00.6	17 04.3	17 06.5	17 08.8	17 12.4	17 14.9	17 18.7
16 06.2	18 06.1	18 12.9	18 15.5	18 19.4	17 23.3	18 02.9	18 05.1	18 07.4	18 11.0	18 13.5	18 17.3
17 04.9	19 04.7	19 11.5	19 14.1	19 18.1	18 21.8	19 01.5	19 03.8	19 06.0	19 09.7	19 12.1	19 15.9
18 03.5	20 03.4	20 10.1	20 12.8	20 16.7	19 20.4	20 00.1	20 02.4	20 04.6	20 08.3	20 10.7	20 14.5
19 02.1	21 02.0	21 08.7	21 11.4	21 15.3	20 19.0	20 22.8	21 01.0	21 03.3	21 06.9	21 09.3	21 13.2
20 00.7	22 00.7	22 07.5	22 10.0	22 13.9	21 17.6	21 21.4	21 23.6	22 01.9	22 05.5	22 08.0	22 11.8
20 23.3	22 23.3	23 06.1	23 08.6	23 12.5	22 16.3	22 20.0	22 22.2	23 00.5	23 04.1	23 06.6	23 10.4
21 22.0	23 21.9	24 04.7	24 07.2	24 11.2	23 14.9	23 18.6	23 20.9	23 23.1	24 02.7	24 05.2	24 09.0
22 20.6	24 20.5	25 03.3	25 05.9	25 09.8	24 13.5	24 17.2	24 19.5	24 21.7	25 01.4	25 03.8	25 07.7
23 19.2	25 19.2	26 01.9	26 04.5	26 08.4	25 12.1	25 15.9	25 18.1	25 20.3	26 00.0	26 02.4	26 06.3
24 17.8	26 17.8	27 00.6	27 03.1	27 07.0	26 10.7	26 14.5	26 16.7	26 18.9	26 22.6	27 01.0	27 05.0
25 16.5	27 16.4	27 23.2	28 01.7	28 05.6	27 09.4	27 13.1	27 15.3	27 17.5	27 21.2	27 23.7	28 03.6
26 15.2	28 15.0	28 21.8	29 00.3	29 04.3	28 08.0	28 11.7	28 13.9	28 16.1	28 19.8	28 22.3	29 02.2
27 13.8		29 20.4	29 23.0	30 02.9	29 06.6	29 10.3	29 12.5	29 14.7	29 18.5	29 20.9	30 00.8
28 12.4		30 19.0	30 21.6	31 01.5	30 05.2	30 09.0	30 11.1	30 13.4	30 17.1	30 19.5	30 23.4
29 11.0		31 17.7				31 07.5	31 09.7		31 15.7		31 22.1
30 09.6											32 20.7
31 08.3											33 19.3

II Enceladus

Jan.	Feb.	Mar.	Apr.	May	June	July	Aug.	Sept.	Oct.	Nov.	Dec.
d h	d h	d h	d h	d h	d h	d h	d h	d h	d h	d h	d h
−1 19.0	1 16.6	1 02.5	1 15.2	1 18.9	2 07.4	1 02.0	1 14.4	2 02.5	2 05.8	1 09.2	1 12.7
1 03.9	3 01.4	2 11.5	3 00.1	3 03.9	3 16.3	2 11.0	2 23.3	3 11.4	3 14.7	2 18.1	2 21.6
2 12.8	4 10.4	3 20.3	4 09.0	4 12.7	5 01.3	3 19.9	4 08.1	4 20.3	4 23.6	4 02.9	4 06.4
3 21.7	5 19.3	5 05.2	5 17.9	5 21.6	6 10.1	5 04.7	5 17.0	6 05.1	6 08.4	5 11.8	5 15.3
5 06.6	7 04.1	6 14.2	7 02.8	7 06.5	7 19.0	6 13.6	7 01.9	7 14.0	7 17.4	6 20.7	7 00.3
6 15.5	8 13.1	7 23.0	8 11.7	8 15.4	9 03.9	7 22.5	8 10.7	8 23.0	9 02.3	8 05.6	8 09.1
8 00.4	9 22.0	9 07.9	9 20.6	10 00.3	10 12.7	9 07.3	9 19.6	10 07.8	10 11.1	9 14.5	9 18.0
9 09.3	11 06.8	10 16.9	11 05.5	11 09.2	11 21.7	10 16.3	11 04.6	11 16.7	11 20.0	10 23.4	11 02.9
10 18.2	12 15.8	12 01.7	12 14.4	12 18.1	13 06.6	12 01.2	12 13.4	13 01.6	13 04.9	12 08.2	12 11.8
12 03.1	14 00.7	13 10.6	13 23.3	14 03.0	14 15.4	13 10.0	13 22.3	14 10.4	14 13.7	13 17.1	13 20.7
13 11.9	15 09.5	14 19.6	15 08.2	15 11.9	16 00.3	14 18.9	15 07.2	15 19.3	15 22.6	15 02.0	15 05.6
14 20.9	16 18.5	16 04.4	16 17.1	16 20.7	17 09.3	16 03.8	16 16.0	17 04.2	17 07.5	16 10.9	16 14.4
16 05.8	18 03.4	17 13.3	18 01.9	18 05.7	18 18.1	17 12.6	18 00.9	18 13.1	18 16.3	17 19.8	17 23.4
17 14.6	19 12.2	18 22.3	19 10.9	19 14.6	20 03.0	18 21.5	19 09.8	19 21.9	20 01.3	19 04.7	19 08.3
18 23.6	20 21.2	20 07.1	20 19.8	20 23.4	21 11.9	20 06.5	20 18.6	21 06.8	21 10.2	20 13.5	20 17.1
20 08.5	22 06.1	21 16.0	22 04.6	22 08.3	22 20.7	21 15.3	22 03.5	22 15.7	22 19.0	21 22.4	22 02.0
21 17.3	23 14.9	23 01.0	23 13.6	23 17.3	24 05.7	23 00.2	23 12.4	24 00.6	24 03.9	23 07.4	23 11.0
23 02.3	24 23.8	24 09.8	24 22.5	25 02.1	25 14.6	24 09.1	24 21.3	25 09.5	25 12.8	24 16.2	24 19.8
24 11.2	26 08.8	25 18.7	26 07.3	26 11.0	26 23.4	25 18.0	26 06.2	26 18.4	26 21.6	26 01.1	26 04.7
25 20.0	27 17.6	27 03.7	27 16.3	27 19.9	28 08.3	27 02.8	27 15.1	28 03.2	28 06.5	27 10.0	27 13.6
27 05.0		28 12.5	29 01.2	29 04.7	29 17.2	28 11.7	28 23.9	29 12.1	29 15.4	28 18.9	28 22.5
28 13.9		29 21.4	30 10.0	30 13.7		29 20.7	30 08.8	30 21.0	31 00.3	30 03.8	30 07.4
29 22.7		31 06.4		31 22.6		31 05.5	31 17.7				31 16.3
31 07.7											33 01.2

UNIVERSAL TIME OF GREATEST EASTERN ELONGATION

Jan.	Feb.	Mar.	Apr.	May	June	July	Aug.	Sept.	Oct.	Nov.	Dec.
III Tethys											
d h	d h	d h	d h	d h	d h	d h	d h	d h	d h	d h	d h
−1 13.8	2 13.8	1 00.4	2 03.1	2 08.3	1 13.5	1 18.5	2 20.7	2 01.3	2 06.0	1 10.8	1 15.6
1 11.2	4 11.1	2 21.8	4 00.5	4 05.7	3 10.9	3 15.8	4 17.9	3 22.6	4 03.3	3 08.0	3 12.9
3 08.5	6 08.5	4 19.1	5 21.8	6 03.0	5 08.1	5 13.1	6 15.2	5 19.9	6 00.6	5 05.3	5 10.3
5 05.9	8 05.7	6 16.4	7 19.1	8 00.4	7 05.4	7 10.5	8 12.5	7 17.2	7 21.8	7 02.6	7 07.6
7 03.1	10 03.1	8 13.8	9 16.4	9 21.6	9 02.8	9 07.7	10 09.9	9 14.5	9 19.2	9 00.0	9 04.9
9 00.5	12 00.4	10 11.1	11 13.8	11 19.0	11 00.1	11 05.0	12 07.2	11 11.8	11 16.5	10 21.3	11 02.2
10 21.8	13 21.8	12 08.5	13 11.1	13 16.3	12 21.4	13 02.3	14 04.4	13 09.1	13 13.8	12 18.5	12 23.5
12 19.2	15 19.1	14 05.7	15 08.4	15 13.6	14 18.7	14 23.7	16 01.7	15 06.4	15 11.1	14 15.8	14 20.9
14 16.4	17 16.4	16 03.1	17 05.7	17 11.0	16 16.0	16 21.0	17 23.0	17 03.7	17 08.3	16 13.2	16 18.1
16 13.8	19 13.8	18 00.5	19 03.1	19 08.2	18 13.4	18 18.2	19 20.3	19 00.9	19 05.6	18 10.5	18 15.5
18 11.1	21 11.1	19 21.8	21 00.4	21 05.6	20 10.7	20 15.5	21 17.6	20 22.2	21 02.9	20 07.7	20 12.8
20 08.5	23 08.5	21 19.1	22 21.8	23 02.9	22 07.9	22 12.9	23 14.9	22 19.5	23 00.3	22 05.1	22 10.1
22 05.8	25 05.7	23 16.4	24 19.0	25 00.3	24 05.3	24 10.2	25 12.2	24 16.9	24 21.5	24 02.4	24 07.4
24 03.1	27 03.1	25 13.8	26 16.4	26 21.5	26 02.6	26 07.5	27 09.5	26 14.2	26 18.8	25 23.7	26 04.7
26 00.4		27 11.1	28 13.7	28 18.8	27 23.9	28 04.7	29 06.8	28 11.4	28 16.1	27 21.0	28 02.1
27 21.8		29 08.4	30 11.1	30 16.2	29 21.3	30 02.0	31 04.1	30 08.7	30 13.4	29 18.3	29 23.4
29 19.1		31 05.7				31 23.4					31 20.8
31 16.4											
IV Dione											
d h	d h	d h	d h	d h	d h	d h	d h	d h	d h	d h	d h
−2 03.7	2 18.1	2 03.6	1 06.7	1 09.8	3 06.4	3 09.0	2 11.5	1 13.8	1 15.9	3 11.9	3 14.4
0 21.4	5 11.9	4 21.3	4 00.4	4 03.5	6 00.0	6 02.7	5 05.2	4 07.4	4 09.5	6 05.5	6 08.0
3 15.0	8 05.6	7 15.0	6 18.1	6 21.1	8 17.8	8 20.4	7 22.8	7 01.0	7 03.3	8 23.2	9 01.7
6 08.8	10 23.3	10 08.8	9 11.9	9 14.9	11 11.5	11 14.1	10 16.4	9 18.7	9 20.9	11 16.9	11 19.5
9 02.5	13 17.1	13 02.5	12 05.6	12 08.6	14 05.1	14 07.8	13 10.2	12 12.3	12 14.5	14 10.5	14 13.1
11 20.2	16 10.8	15 20.3	14 23.3	15 02.3	16 22.9	17 01.5	16 03.8	15 06.0	15 08.2	17 04.2	17 06.9
14 14.0	19 04.5	18 14.0	17 17.1	17 20.1	19 16.6	19 19.1	18 21.5	17 23.7	18 01.8	19 21.9	20 00.6
17 07.7	21 22.3	21 07.7	20 10.8	20 13.8	22 10.3	22 12.8	21 15.1	20 17.3	20 19.6	22 15.6	22 18.3
20 01.4	24 16.0	24 01.5	23 04.6	23 07.5	25 04.0	25 06.5	24 08.7	23 11.0	23 13.2	25 09.3	25 12.0
22 19.2	27 09.7	26 19.2	25 22.3	26 01.2	27 21.6	28 00.2	27 02.5	26 04.6	26 06.8	28 03.0	28 05.7
25 12.9		29 12.9	28 16.0	28 18.9	30 15.4	30 17.8	29 20.1	28 22.3	29 00.5	30 20.6	30 23.4
28 06.6				31 12.7					31 18.2		33 17.2
31 00.4											
V Rhea											
d h	d h	d h	d h	d h	d h	d h	d h	d h	d h	d h	d h
−2 02.3	3 06.7	2 10.0	3 02.0	4 17.8	5 09.4	2 12.1	3 03.0	3 17.4	5 07.7	1 09.8	3 00.6
2 14.8	7 19.2	6 22.6	7 14.5	9 06.4	9 21.9	7 00.7	7 15.3	8 05.7	9 20.0	5 22.2	7 13.1
7 03.3	12 07.8	11 11.2	12 03.1	13 18.9	14 10.4	11 13.1	12 03.7	12 18.1	14 08.4	10 10.6	12 01.6
11 15.9	16 20.3	15 23.7	16 15.6	18 07.4	18 22.8	16 01.5	16 16.1	17 06.4	18 20.7	14 23.0	16 14.0
16 04.4	21 08.9	20 12.3	21 04.2	22 20.0	23 11.3	20 13.9	21 04.5	21 18.8	23 09.1	19 11.4	21 02.5
20 16.9	25 21.5	25 00.9	25 16.7	27 08.5	27 23.7	25 02.2	25 16.8	26 07.1	27 21.5	23 23.8	25 15.0
25 05.5		29 13.4	30 05.3	31 20.9		29 14.6	30 05.1	30 19.4		28 12.2	30 03.5
29 18.1											34 15.9

UNIVERSAL TIME OF CONJUNCTIONS AND ELONGATIONS

VI Titan

Eastern Elongation		Inferior Conjunction		Western Elongation		Superior Conjunction	
	d h		d h		d h		d h
Jan.	−13 12.3	Jan.	−9 14.1	Jan.	−5 15.6	Jan.	−1 14.1
	3 12.1		7 14.0		11 15.5		15 14.0
	19 12.2		23 14.2		27 15.7		31 14.2
Feb.	4 12.5	Feb.	8 14.6	Feb.	12 16.2	Feb.	16 14.5
	20 13.0		24 15.2		28 16.7	Mar.	4 14.9
Mar.	8 13.6	Mar.	12 15.8	Mar.	16 17.3		20 15.4
	24 14.2		28 16.5	Apr.	1 17.9	Apr.	5 15.8
Apr.	9 14.8	Apr.	13 17.1		17 18.4		21 16.1
	25 15.2		29 17.5	May	3 18.7	May	7 16.2
May	11 15.5	May	15 17.7		19 18.8		23 16.1
	27 15.5		31 17.6	June	4 18.6	June	8 15.8
June	12 15.1	June	16 17.2		20 18.0		24 15.1
	28 14.4	July	2 16.3	July	6 17.1	July	10 14.0
July	14 13.2		18 15.1		22 15.7		26 12.6
	30 11.6	Aug.	3 13.4	Aug.	7 13.9	Aug.	11 10.8
Aug.	15 09.6		19 11.4		23 11.8		27 08.7
	31 07.3	Sept.	4 09.1	Sept.	8 09.4	Sept.	12 06.4
Sept.	16 04.8		20 06.6		24 06.9		28 04.0
Oct.	2 02.3	Oct.	6 04.0	Oct.	10 04.4	Oct.	14 01.6
	17 23.8		22 01.7		26 02.1		29 23.5
Nov.	2 21.7	Nov.	6 23.6	Nov.	11 00.1	Nov.	14 21.7
	18 19.9		22 21.9		26 22.5		30 20.3
Dec.	4 18.5	Dec.	8 20.7	Dec.	12 21.4	Dec.	16 19.2
	20 17.6		24 19.9		28 20.7		32 18.6
	36 17.1		40 19.6		44 20.4		

VII Hyperion

Eastern Elongation		Inferior Conjunction		Western Elongation		Superior Conjunction	
	d h		d h		d h		d h
Jan.	−24 18.2	Jan.	−18 23.5	Jan.	−13 16.3	Jan.	−8 05.8
	− 2 05.1		4 10.7		9 03.8		13 17.8
	19 17.4		25 21.9		30 14.5	Feb.	4 05.1
Feb.	10 06.0	Feb.	16 10.1	Feb.	21 02.2		25 16.7
Mar.	3 18.4	Mar.	9 22.3	Mar.	14 14.5	Mar.	19 05.3
	25 06.8		31 08.8	Apr.	5 00.5	Apr.	9 16.2
Apr.	15 18.5	Apr.	21 19.5		26 10.7	May	1 02.2
May	7 05.0	May	13 05.7	May	17 20.9		22 12.7
	28 14.5	June	3 13.1	June	8 04.0	June	12 20.5
June	18 22.5		24 20.2		29 10.7	July	4 02.9
July	10 04.8	July	16 02.4	July	20 16.9		25 09.1
	31 09.6	Aug.	6 05.6	Aug.	10 20.0	Aug.	15 12.8
Aug.	21 13.1		27 09.0		31 22.8	Sept.	5 15.2
Sept.	11 15.1	Sept.	17 11.5	Sept.	22 01.6		26 18.2
Oct.	2 16.9	Oct.	8 12.7	Oct.	13 02.8	Oct.	17 20.2
	23 19.2		29 15.5	Nov.	3 05.4	Nov.	7 22.6
Nov.	13 21.5	Nov.	19 18.6		24 09.0		29 02.7
Dec.	5 01.4	Dec.	10 22.0	Dec.	15 12.5	Dec.	20 07.3
	26 07.2		32 04.1		36 18.5		41 13.3

VIII Iapetus

Eastern Elongation		Inferior Conjunction		Western Elongation		Superior Conjunction	
	d h		d h		d h		d h
Jan.	−40 00.1	Jan.	−20 03.8	Jan.	0 15.1	Jan.	21 03.0
Feb.	9 16.5	Mar.	2 04.3	Mar.	23 04.6	Apr.	12 09.4
May	2 09.0	May	22 13.4	June	12 10.9	July	1 23.2
July	21 15.1	Aug.	10 06.1	Aug.	30 10.0	Sept.	18 16.2
Oct.	7 14.7	Oct.	27 09.3	Nov.	16 07.2	Dec.	6 06.9
Dec.	25 10.7	Dec.	45 22.8				

DIFFERENTIAL COORDINATES OF VII HYPERION FOR 0^h UNIVERSAL TIME

Date		$\Delta\alpha$	$\Delta\delta$	Date		$\Delta\alpha$	$\Delta\delta$	Date		$\Delta\alpha$	$\Delta\delta$
		s	′			s	′			s	′
Jan.	−1	+15	−0.3	May	1	0	−0.1	Aug.	31	−13	+0.2
	1	+12	−0.4		3	+7	−0.2	Sept.	2	−13	+0.1
	3	+5	−0.3		5	+12	−0.2		4	−7	0.0
	5	−2	−0.2		7	+15	−0.2		6	+2	−0.2
	7	−9	0.0		9	+13	−0.1		8	+10	−0.3
	9	−12	+0.2		11	+8	0.0		10	+16	−0.3
	11	−10	+0.3		13	+1	+0.1		12	+17	−0.2
	13	−3	+0.2		15	−7	+0.2		14	+14	−0.1
	15	+5	+0.1		17	−12	+0.2		16	+7	0.0
	17	+11	−0.1		19	−11	+0.1		18	−2	+0.2
	19	+15	−0.2		21	−6	−0.1		20	−11	+0.2
	21	+14	−0.3		23	+2	−0.2		22	−14	+0.2
	23	+10	−0.3		25	+9	−0.3		24	−11	+0.1
	25	+3	−0.2		27	+14	−0.3		26	−4	−0.1
	27	−4	−0.1		29	+15	−0.2		28	+6	−0.2
	29	−10	+0.1		31	+12	−0.1		30	+13	−0.3
	31	−12	+0.2	June	2	+6	+0.1	Oct.	2	+17	−0.3
Feb.	2	−8	+0.2		4	−2	+0.2		4	+16	−0.2
	4	−1	+0.2		6	−9	+0.2		6	+11	−0.1
	6	+7	0.0		8	−13	+0.2		8	+3	0.0
	8	+12	−0.1		10	−10	0.0		10	−7	+0.2
	10	+14	−0.2		12	−4	−0.1		12	−13	+0.2
	12	+13	−0.3		14	+5	−0.3		14	−14	+0.2
	14	+8	−0.2		16	+11	−0.3		16	−8	+0.1
	16	+2	−0.1		18	+15	−0.2		18	+1	−0.1
	18	−6	0.0		20	+15	−0.1		20	+9	−0.2
	20	−11	+0.1		22	+11	0.0		22	+15	−0.2
	22	−11	+0.2		24	+4	+0.2		24	+17	−0.2
	24	−6	+0.2		26	−5	+0.2		26	+14	−0.2
	26	+1	+0.1		28	−11	+0.2		28	+7	−0.1
	28	+8	−0.1		30	−13	+0.1		30	−2	+0.1
Mar.	2	+13	−0.2	July	2	−8	−0.1	Nov.	1	−10	+0.2
	4	+14	−0.2		4	−1	−0.2		3	−14	+0.2
	6	+12	−0.2		6	+8	−0.3		5	−11	+0.2
	8	+7	−0.2		8	+14	−0.3		7	−4	0.0
	10	0	0.0		10	+16	−0.2		9	+5	−0.1
	12	−7	+0.1		12	+14	−0.1		11	+12	−0.2
	14	−11	+0.2		14	+9	+0.1		13	+16	−0.2
	16	−10	+0.2		16	0	+0.2		15	+16	−0.2
	18	−5	+0.1		18	−8	+0.3		17	+11	−0.2
	20	+3	0.0		20	−13	+0.2		19	+4	0.0
	22	+10	−0.1		22	−12	+0.1		21	−5	+0.1
	24	+14	−0.2		24	−6	−0.1		23	−12	+0.2
	26	+14	−0.2		26	+3	−0.3		25	−13	+0.2
	28	+11	−0.2		28	+11	−0.3		27	−9	+0.1
	30	+5	−0.1		30	+16	−0.3		29	0	0.0
Apr.	1	−2	+0.1	Aug.	1	+16	−0.2	Dec.	1	+8	−0.1
	3	−9	+0.2		3	+13	0.0		3	+14	−0.2
	5	−12	+0.2		5	+6	+0.1		5	+16	−0.2
	7	−9	+0.1		7	−4	+0.2		7	+14	−0.2
	9	−3	0.0		9	−11	+0.3		9	+8	−0.1
	11	+5	−0.1		11	−14	+0.2		11	0	0.0
	13	+11	−0.2		13	−10	0.0		13	−8	+0.1
	15	+14	−0.2		15	−2	−0.2		15	−13	+0.2
	17	+14	−0.2		17	+6	−0.3		17	−11	+0.2
	19	+10	−0.1		19	+13	−0.3		19	−5	0.0
	21	+3	0.0		21	+17	−0.3		21	+3	−0.1
	23	−4	+0.1		23	+16	−0.1		23	+10	−0.2
	25	−10	+0.2		25	+10	0.0		25	+15	−0.2
	27	−12	+0.1		27	+2	+0.1		27	+15	−0.2
	29	−8	0.0		29	−7	+0.2		29	+12	−0.1
May	1	0	−0.1	Aug.	31	−13	+0.2		31	+5	0.0

Differential coordinates are given in the sense "satellite minus planet."

DIFFERENTIAL COORDINATES OF VIII IAPETUS FOR 0^h UNIVERSAL TIME

Date	Δα	Δδ	Date	Δα	Δδ	Date	Δα	Δδ
	s	′		s	′		s	′
Jan. −1	− 33	− 0.9	May 1	+ 31	+ 1.3	Aug. 31	− 38	− 1.8
1	− 33	− 1.0	3	+ 31	+ 1.5	Sept. 2	− 37	− 2.0
3	− 33	− 1.1	5	+ 30	+ 1.7	4	− 35	− 2.1
5	− 31	− 1.2	7	+ 29	+ 1.8	6	− 32	− 2.2
7	− 29	− 1.3	9	+ 27	+ 1.9	8	− 28	− 2.2
9	− 26	− 1.3	11	+ 24	+ 1.9	10	− 24	− 2.1
11	− 23	− 1.3	13	+ 20	+ 1.9	12	− 19	− 2.0
13	− 19	− 1.2	15	+ 17	+ 1.8	14	− 13	− 1.9
15	− 15	− 1.2	17	+ 12	+ 1.8	16	− 7	− 1.7
17	− 10	− 1.1	19	+ 8	+ 1.6	18	− 1	− 1.4
19	− 5	− 0.9	21	+ 3	+ 1.4	20	+ 5	− 1.1
21	0	− 0.8	23	− 2	+ 1.2	22	+ 11	− 0.8
23	+ 5	− 0.6	25	− 7	+ 1.0	24	+ 17	− 0.4
25	+ 10	− 0.4	27	− 12	+ 0.7	26	+ 22	− 0.1
27	+ 15	− 0.2	29	− 16	+ 0.5	28	+ 27	+ 0.3
29	+ 19	0.0	31	− 20	+ 0.2	30	+ 31	+ 0.6
31	+ 22	+ 0.2	June 2	− 24	− 0.1	Oct. 2	+ 34	+ 0.9
Feb. 2	+ 25	+ 0.4	4	− 27	− 0.4	4	+ 36	+ 1.2
4	+ 28	+ 0.6	6	− 30	− 0.7	6	+ 37	+ 1.5
6	+ 30	+ 0.8	8	− 32	− 1.0	8	+ 37	+ 1.7
8	+ 31	+ 1.0	10	− 33	− 1.3	10	+ 36	+ 1.9
10	+ 31	+ 1.1	12	− 33	− 1.5	12	+ 35	+ 2.0
12	+ 30	+ 1.3	14	− 33	− 1.7	14	+ 32	+ 2.1
14	+ 29	+ 1.4	16	− 32	− 1.9	16	+ 29	+ 2.1
16	+ 27	+ 1.4	18	− 30	− 2.0	18	+ 24	+ 2.1
18	+ 24	+ 1.4	20	− 27	− 2.0	20	+ 20	+ 2.0
20	+ 21	+ 1.4	22	− 24	− 2.1	22	+ 14	+ 1.8
22	+ 17	+ 1.4	24	− 20	− 2.0	24	+ 9	+ 1.7
24	+ 13	+ 1.3	26	− 15	− 1.9	26	+ 3	+ 1.4
26	+ 9	+ 1.2	28	− 10	− 1.8	28	− 3	+ 1.2
28	+ 4	+ 1.1	30	− 4	− 1.6	30	− 8	+ 0.9
Mar. 2	0	+ 1.0	July 2	+ 1	− 1.3	Nov. 1	− 14	+ 0.6
4	− 5	+ 0.8	4	+ 7	− 1.0	3	− 19	+ 0.3
6	− 9	+ 0.6	6	+ 12	− 0.7	5	− 24	0.0
8	− 14	+ 0.4	8	+ 17	− 0.4	7	− 28	− 0.3
10	− 17	+ 0.2	10	+ 22	− 0.1	9	− 31	− 0.6
12	− 21	− 0.1	12	+ 26	+ 0.3	11	− 34	− 0.9
14	− 24	− 0.3	14	+ 29	+ 0.6	13	− 35	− 1.1
16	− 27	− 0.5	16	+ 32	+ 1.0	15	− 36	− 1.3
18	− 29	− 0.7	18	+ 34	+ 1.3	17	− 36	− 1.5
20	− 30	− 0.9	20	+ 35	+ 1.6	19	− 35	− 1.7
22	− 31	− 1.1	22	+ 35	+ 1.8	21	− 34	− 1.8
24	− 31	− 1.3	24	+ 34	+ 2.0	23	− 31	− 1.9
26	− 30	− 1.4	26	+ 33	+ 2.1	25	− 28	− 1.9
28	− 29	− 1.5	28	+ 30	+ 2.2	27	− 24	− 1.8
30	− 26	− 1.6	30	+ 27	+ 2.3	29	− 19	− 1.8
Apr. 1	− 24	− 1.6	Aug. 1	+ 23	+ 2.2	Dec. 1	− 14	− 1.6
3	− 20	− 1.6	3	+ 18	+ 2.2	3	− 8	− 1.5
5	− 16	− 1.6	5	+ 13	+ 2.0	5	− 3	− 1.3
7	− 12	− 1.5	7	+ 8	+ 1.9	7	+ 3	− 1.0
9	− 8	− 1.4	9	+ 2	+ 1.6	9	+ 8	− 0.8
11	− 3	− 1.2	11	− 3	+ 1.4	11	+ 14	− 0.5
13	+ 2	− 1.0	13	− 9	+ 1.1	13	+ 18	− 0.2
15	+ 7	− 0.8	15	− 14	+ 0.7	15	+ 23	+ 0.1
17	+ 12	− 0.5	17	− 20	+ 0.4	17	+ 26	+ 0.4
19	+ 16	− 0.3	19	− 24	0.0	19	+ 29	+ 0.7
21	+ 20	0.0	21	− 28	− 0.3	21	+ 32	+ 0.9
23	+ 24	+ 0.3	23	− 32	− 0.7	23	+ 33	+ 1.2
25	+ 26	+ 0.6	25	− 35	− 1.0	25	+ 33	+ 1.4
27	+ 29	+ 0.8	27	− 36	− 1.3	27	+ 33	+ 1.6
29	+ 30	+ 1.1	29	− 37	− 1.5	29	+ 32	+ 1.7
May 1	+ 31	+ 1.3	Aug. 31	− 38	− 1.8	31	+ 30	+ 1.8

Differential coordinates are given in the sense “satellite minus planet.”

DIFFERENTIAL COORDINATES OF IX PHOEBE FOR 0^{h} UNIVERSAL TIME

Date		Δα	Δδ	Date		Δα	Δδ	Date		Δα	Δδ
		m s	′			m s	′			m s	′
Jan.	−1	+ 1 11	+ 4.0	May	1	− 1 23	− 9.3	Sept.	2	− 0 04	+ 2.8
	1	+ 1 09	+ 3.8		3	− 1 24	− 9.3		4	− 0 02	+ 3.1
	3	+ 1 06	+ 3.5		5	− 1 25	− 9.4		6	+ 0 01	+ 3.4
	5	+ 1 03	+ 3.3		7	− 1 26	− 9.4		8	+ 0 04	+ 3.7
	7	+ 1 01	+ 3.0		9	− 1 27	− 9.4		10	+ 0 07	+ 3.9
	9	+ 0 58	+ 2.7		11	− 1 28	− 9.4		12	+ 0 09	+ 4.2
	11	+ 0 55	+ 2.5		13	− 1 29	− 9.4		14	+ 0 12	+ 4.5
	13	+ 0 52	+ 2.2		15	− 1 29	− 9.4		16	+ 0 15	+ 4.8
	15	+ 0 49	+ 1.9		17	− 1 30	− 9.4		18	+ 0 17	+ 5.0
	17	+ 0 47	+ 1.7		19	− 1 30	− 9.3		20	+ 0 20	+ 5.3
	19	+ 0 44	+ 1.4		21	− 1 31	− 9.3		22	+ 0 23	+ 5.6
	21	+ 0 41	+ 1.1		23	− 1 31	− 9.2		24	+ 0 25	+ 5.8
	23	+ 0 38	+ 0.9		25	− 1 31	− 9.2		26	+ 0 28	+ 6.1
	25	+ 0 35	+ 0.6		27	− 1 31	− 9.1		28	+ 0 31	+ 6.4
	27	+ 0 32	+ 0.3		29	− 1 31	− 9.0		30	+ 0 33	+ 6.6
	29	+ 0 29	0.0		31	− 1 31	− 8.9	Oct.	2	+ 0 36	+ 6.9
	31	+ 0 26	− 0.2	June	2	− 1 31	− 8.8		4	+ 0 38	+ 7.1
Feb.	2	+ 0 23	− 0.5		4	− 1 30	− 8.7		6	+ 0 41	+ 7.3
	4	+ 0 21	− 0.8		6	− 1 30	− 8.5		8	+ 0 44	+ 7.6
	6	+ 0 18	− 1.1		8	− 1 30	− 8.4		10	+ 0 46	+ 7.8
	8	+ 0 15	− 1.3		10	− 1 29	− 8.3		12	+ 0 48	+ 8.0
	10	+ 0 12	− 1.6		12	− 1 28	− 8.1		14	+ 0 51	+ 8.2
	12	+ 0 09	− 1.9		14	− 1 28	− 8.0		16	+ 0 53	+ 8.4
	14	+ 0 06	− 2.1		16	− 1 27	− 7.8		18	+ 0 56	+ 8.7
	16	+ 0 03	− 2.4		18	− 1 26	− 7.6		20	+ 0 58	+ 8.9
	18	0 00	− 2.7		20	− 1 25	− 7.4		22	+ 1 00	+ 9.1
	20	− 0 03	− 2.9		22	− 1 24	− 7.2		24	+ 1 03	+ 9.3
	22	− 0 06	− 3.2		24	− 1 22	− 7.0		26	+ 1 05	+ 9.5
	24	− 0 09	− 3.5		26	− 1 21	− 6.8		28	+ 1 07	+ 9.6
	26	− 0 12	− 3.7		28	− 1 20	− 6.6		30	+ 1 09	+ 9.8
	28	− 0 14	− 4.0		30	− 1 18	− 6.4	Nov.	1	+ 1 11	+ 10.0
Mar.	2	− 0 17	− 4.2	July	2	− 1 17	− 6.1		3	+ 1 14	+ 10.2
	4	− 0 20	− 4.5		4	− 1 15	− 5.9		5	+ 1 16	+ 10.3
	6	− 0 23	− 4.7		6	− 1 14	− 5.7		7	+ 1 18	+ 10.5
	8	− 0 26	− 5.0		8	− 1 12	− 5.4		9	+ 1 20	+ 10.7
	10	− 0 28	− 5.2		10	− 1 10	− 5.1		11	+ 1 22	+ 10.8
	12	− 0 31	− 5.4		12	− 1 08	− 4.9		13	+ 1 24	+ 11.0
	14	− 0 34	− 5.7		14	− 1 06	− 4.6		15	+ 1 25	+ 11.1
	16	− 0 36	− 5.9		16	− 1 04	− 4.3		17	+ 1 27	+ 11.3
	18	− 0 39	− 6.1		18	− 1 02	− 4.1		19	+ 1 29	+ 11.4
	20	− 0 42	− 6.3		20	− 1 00	− 3.8		21	+ 1 31	+ 11.5
	22	− 0 44	− 6.5		22	− 0 58	− 3.5		23	+ 1 33	+ 11.7
	24	− 0 47	− 6.7		24	− 0 56	− 3.2		25	+ 1 34	+ 11.8
	26	− 0 49	− 6.9		26	− 0 53	− 2.9		27	+ 1 36	+ 11.9
	28	− 0 52	− 7.1		28	− 0 51	− 2.6		29	+ 1 38	+ 12.0
	30	− 0 54	− 7.3		30	− 0 49	− 2.3	Dec.	1	+ 1 39	+ 12.1
Apr.	1	− 0 56	− 7.5	Aug.	1	− 0 46	− 2.0		3	+ 1 41	+ 12.2
	3	− 0 58	− 7.7		3	− 0 44	− 1.7		5	+ 1 42	+ 12.4
	5	− 1 01	− 7.9		5	− 0 41	− 1.4		7	+ 1 44	+ 12.4
	7	− 1 03	− 8.0		7	− 0 39	− 1.1		9	+ 1 45	+ 12.5
	9	− 1 05	− 8.2		9	− 0 36	− 0.8		11	+ 1 46	+ 12.6
	11	− 1 07	− 8.3		11	− 0 34	− 0.5		13	+ 1 48	+ 12.7
	13	− 1 09	− 8.4		13	− 0 31	− 0.2		15	+ 1 49	+ 12.8
	15	− 1 11	− 8.6		15	− 0 29	+ 0.1		17	+ 1 50	+ 12.9
	17	− 1 12	− 8.7		17	− 0 26	+ 0.4		19	+ 1 51	+ 12.9
	19	− 1 14	− 8.8		19	− 0 23	+ 0.7		21	+ 1 53	+ 13.0
	21	− 1 16	− 8.9		21	− 0 21	+ 1.0		23	+ 1 54	+ 13.1
	23	− 1 17	− 9.0		23	− 0 18	+ 1.3		25	+ 1 55	+ 13.1
	25	− 1 19	− 9.1		25	− 0 15	+ 1.6		27	+ 1 56	+ 13.2
	27	− 1 20	− 9.2		27	− 0 13	+ 1.9		29	+ 1 57	+ 13.2
	29	− 1 22	− 9.2		29	− 0 10	+ 2.2		31	+ 1 58	+ 13.3
May	1	− 1 23	− 9.3		31	− 0 07	+ 2.5		33	+ 1 58	+ 13.3

Differential coordinates are given in the sense "satellite minus planet."

APPARENT ORBITS OF SATELLITES I-V AT 0^h UNIVERSAL TIME ON THE DATE OF OPPOSITION, NOVEMBER 21

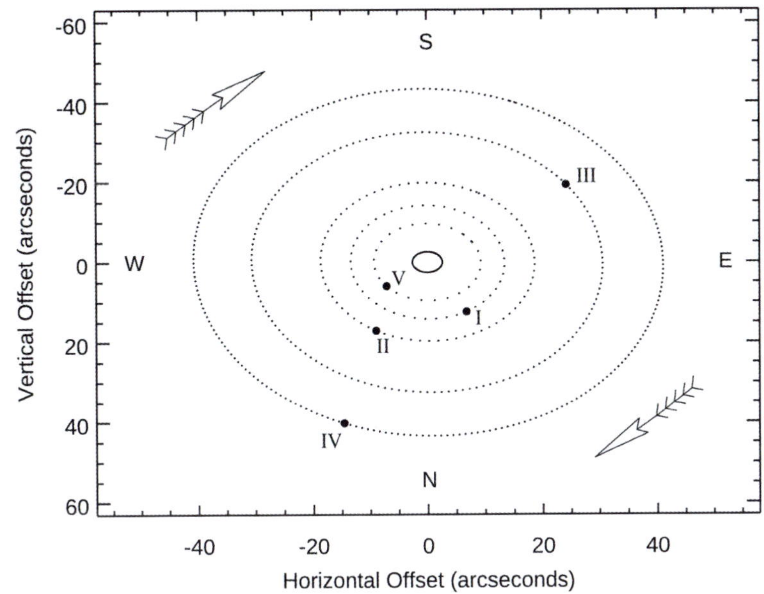

Orbits elongated in ratio of 1.7 to 1 in the East-West direction.

	Name	Mean Sidereal Period
		d
V	Miranda	1.413 479
I	Ariel	2.520 379
II	Umbriel	4.144 176
III	Titania	8.705 867
IV	Oberon	13.463 234

RINGS OF URANUS

Ring	Semimajor Axis	Width	Eccentricity	Inclination	Optical Depth
	km	km		°	
6	41837	1.5	0.00101	0.062	~ 0.3
5	42234	~ 2	0.00190	0.054	~ 0.5
4	42571	~ 2	0.001065	0.032	~ 0.3
α	44718	4 – 10	0.00076	0.015	~ 0.4
β	45661	5 – 11	0.00044	0.005	~ 0.3
η	47176	1.6	—	—	≤ 0.4
γ	47627	1 – 4	0.00109	0.000	≥ 0.3
δ	48300	3 – 7	0.00004	0.001	~ 0.5
λ	50024	~ 2	0.	0.	~ 0.1
ε	51149	20 – 96	0.00794	0.000	0.5 – 2.3

UNIVERSAL TIME OF GREATEST NORTHERN ELONGATION

V Miranda

Jan.	Feb.	Mar.	Apr.	May	June	July	Aug.	Sept.	Oct.	Nov.	Dec.
d h	d h	d h	d h	d h	d h	d h	d h	d h	d h	d h	d h
−2 06.3	1 04.6	1 11.1	1 13.4	1 05.6	1 07.6	2 09.7	1 01.8	1 04.0	2 06.3	2 08.8	2 01.4
−1 16.3	2 14.6	2 21.0	2 23.3	2 15.5	2 17.6	3 19.6	2 11.8	2 13.9	3 16.3	3 18.7	3 11.3
1 02.2	4 00.5	4 07.0	4 09.2	4 01.4	4 03.5	5 05.6	3 21.7	3 23.9	5 02.2	5 04.6	4 21.2
2 12.1	5 10.4	5 16.9	5 19.2	5 11.4	5 13.4	6 15.4	5 07.6	5 09.8	6 12.1	6 14.6	6 07.2
3 22.0	6 20.3	7 02.8	7 05.1	6 21.2	6 23.4	8 01.3	6 17.5	6 19.7	7 22.1	8 00.5	7 17.1
5 08.0	8 06.3	8 12.8	8 14.9	8 07.1	8 09.2	9 11.3	8 03.4	8 05.6	9 8.0	9 10.4	9 03.0
6 17.9	9 16.2	9 22.6	10 00.8	9 17.1	9 19.1	10 21.2	9 13.3	9 15.5	10 17.9	10 20.4	10 13.0
8 03.8	11 02.1	11 08.5	11 10.8	11 03.0	11 05.1	12 07.1	10 23.2	11 01.4	12 03.8	12 06.3	11 22.9
9 13.8	12 12.0	12 18.5	12 20.7	12 12.9	12 15.0	13 17.0	12 09.2	12 11.3	13 13.8	13 16.2	13 08.8
10 23.7	13 21.9	14 04.4	14 06.6	13 22.9	14 00.9	15 02.9	13 19.1	13 21.3	14 23.7	15 02.1	14 18.8
12 09.6	15 07.8	15 14.3	15 16.6	15 08.8	15 10.8	16 12.8	15 05.0	15 07.2	16 09.6	16 12.2	16 04.8
13 19.5	16 17.8	17 00.2	17 02.5	16 18.6	16 20.7	17 22.7	16 14.9	16 17.1	17 19.6	17 22.1	17 14.7
15 05.5	18 03.7	18 10.2	18 12.3	18 04.5	18 06.6	19 08.7	18 00.8	18 03.0	19 05.5	19 08.0	19 00.6
16 15.4	19 13.6	19 20.1	19 22.3	19 14.5	19 16.5	20 18.5	19 10.7	19 13.0	20 15.4	20 18.0	20 10.6
18 01.3	20 23.5	21 06.0	21 08.2	21 00.4	21 02.5	22 04.4	20 20.7	20 22.9	22 01.3	22 03.9	21 20.5
19 11.3	22 09.5	22 16.0	22 18.1	22 10.3	22 12.3	23 14.4	22 06.6	22 08.8	23 11.3	23 13.8	23 06.4
20 21.2	23 19.4	24 01.9	24 04.0	23 20.2	23 22.2	25 00.3	23 16.5	23 18.8	24 21.2	24 23.7	24 16.4
22 07.1	25 05.3	25 11.7	25 14.0	25 06.1	25 08.2	26 10.2	25 02.4	25 04.7	26 07.1	26 09.7	26 02.3
23 17.1	26 15.3	26 21.6	26 23.9	26 16.0	26 18.1	27 20.1	26 12.3	26 14.6	27 17.1	27 19.6	27 12.2
25 03.0	28 01.2	28 07.6	28 09.7	28 02.0	28 04.0	29 06.0	27 22.2	28 00.6	29 03.0	29 05.5	28 22.1
26 12.9		29 17.5	29 19.7	29 11.9	29 13.9	30 15.9	29 08.1	29 10.5	30 12.9	30 15.5	30 08.1
27 22.8		31 03.4		30 21.7	30 23.8		30 18.1	30 20.4	31 22.9		31 18.0
29 08.8											
30 18.7											

I Ariel

Jan.	Feb.	Mar.	Apr.	May	June	July	Aug.	Sept.	Oct.	Nov.	Dec.
d h	d h	d h	d h	d h	d h	d h	d h	d h	d h	d h	d h
-3 13.2	1 20.2	1 13.6	3 07.9	1 01.1	2 19.2	3 00.8	2 06.3	1 12.0	1 17.9	3 12.4	1 06.0
0 01.8	4 08.7	4 02.1	5 20.3	3 13.5	5 07.7	5 13.2	4 18.8	4 00.5	4 06.4	6 00.9	3 18.5
2 14.2	6 21.2	6 14.6	8 08.8	6 02.0	7 20.1	8 01.7	7 07.2	6 13.0	6 18.9	8 13.4	6 07.0
5 02.8	9 09.7	9 03.0	10 21.3	8 14.5	10 08.6	10 14.1	9 19.7	9 01.5	9 07.3	11 01.9	8 19.5
7 15.2	11 22.2	11 15.6	13 09.8	11 03.0	12 21.0	13 02.6	12 08.2	11 13.9	11 19.9	13 14.4	11 08.0
10 03.8	14 10.6	14 04.0	15 22.3	13 15.5	15 09.5	15 15.0	14 20.6	14 02.5	14 08.3	16 02.9	13 20.5
12 16.2	16 23.2	16 16.5	18 10.7	16 03.9	17 21.9	18 03.5	17 09.2	16 14.9	16 20.9	18 15.4	16 09.0
15 04.7	19 11.6	19 05.0	20 23.2	18 16.4	20 10.4	20 16.0	19 21.6	19 03.4	19 09.3	21 03.9	18 21.5
17 17.2	22 00.1	21 17.5	23 11.7	21 04.8	22 22.8	23 04.4	22 10.1	21 15.9	21 21.9	23 16.4	21 10.0
20 05.7	24 12.7	24 06.0	26 00.2	23 17.3	25 11.3	25 16.9	24 22.5	24 04.4	24 10.3	26 04.9	23 22.5
22 18.2	27 01.1	26 18.4	28 12.6	26 05.7	27 23.8	28 05.4	27 11.1	26 16.8	26 22.9	28 17.5	26 11.0
25 06.7		29 07.0		28 18.2	30 12.2	30 17.9	29 23.5	29 05.4	29 11.3		28 23.5
27 19.3		31 19.4		31 06.7					31 23.9		31 12.0
30 07.7											34 00.6

UNIVERSAL TIME OF GREATEST NORTHERN ELONGATION

II Umbriel

Jan.	Feb.	Mar.	Apr.	May	June	July	Aug.	Sept.	Oct.	Nov.	Dec.
d h	d h	d h	d h	d h	d h	d h	d h	d h	d h	d h	d h
−3 06.0	3 13.2	4 13.5	2 13.5	1 13.5	3 16.7	2 16.5	4 19.6	2 19.6	1 20.0	3 23.8	3 00.3
1 09.4	7 16.8	8 16.9	6 17.0	5 16.9	7 20.0	6 19.9	8 23.1	6 23.0	5 23.5	8 03.4	7 03.9
5 13.0	11 20.2	12 20.4	10 20.4	9 20.3	11 23.4	10 23.3	13 02.4	11 02.6	10 02.9	12 06.8	11 07.4
9 16.4	15 23.7	16 23.7	14 23.8	13 23.6	16 02.8	15 02.7	17 05.9	15 06.0	14 06.5	16 10.4	15 10.9
13 19.9	20 03.1	21 03.2	19 03.2	18 03.1	20 06.3	19 06.1	21 09.3	19 09.5	18 09.9	20 13.8	19 14.4
17 23.4	24 06.6	25 06.6	23 06.7	22 06.4	24 09.6	23 09.5	25 12.7	23 13.0	22 13.4	24 17.3	23 18.0
22 02.9	28 10.0	29 10.1	27 10.0	26 09.8	28 13.1	27 12.9	29 16.1	27 16.5	26 16.9	28 20.8	27 21.4
26 06.3				30 13.2		31 16.3			30 20.4		32 01.0
30 09.8											36 04.4

III Titania

Jan.	Feb.	Mar.	Apr.	May	June	July	Aug.	Sept.	Oct.	Nov.	Dec.
d h	d h	d h	d h	d h	d h	d h	d h	d h	d h	d h	d h
−3 03.7	9 16.7	7 19.4	2 21.7	7 16.7	2 18.8	7 13.9	2 16.0	6 11.2	2 13.9	6 10.4	2 13.9
5 20.7	18 09.7	16 12.3	11 14.5	16 09.3	11 11.6	16 06.6	11 08.8	15 04.1	11 07.0	15 03.7	11 07.0
14 13.7	27 02.5	25 05.0	20 07.2	25 02.1	20 04.3	24 23.3	20 01.6	23 20.9	20 00.1	23 20.8	20 00.1
23 06.8			29 00.0		28 21.0		28 18.3		28 17.2		28 17.1
31 23.7											

IV Oberon

Jan.	Feb.	Mar.	Apr.	May	June	July	Aug.	Sept.	Oct.	Nov.	Dec.
d h	d h	d h	d h	d h	d h	d h	d h	d h	d h	d h	d h
0 21.2	10 06.4	9 04.4	5 02.2	1 23.7	11 07.2	8 03.9	4 01.2	13 10.6	10 09.2	6 07.8	3 06.3
14 08.4	23 17.4	22 15.3	18 13.0	15 10.4	24 17.6	21 14.5	17 12.1	26 21.9	23 20.4	19 19.1	16 17.9
27 19.5				28 20.8			30 23.3				30 05.3

APPARENT ORBIT OF I TRITON AT 0^h UNIVERSAL TIME
ON THE DATE OF OPPOSITION, SEPTEMBER 23

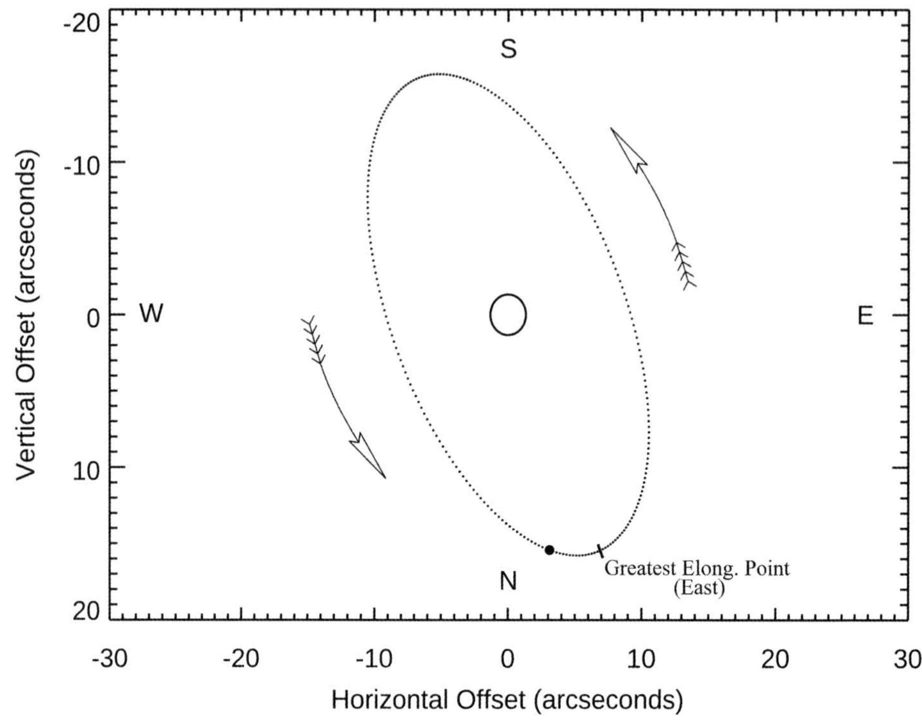

	Name	Mean Sidereal Period
		d
I	Triton	5.876 85 R
II	Nereid	360.135

DIFFERENTIAL COORDINATES OF II NEREID FOR 0^h UNIVERSAL TIME

Date		$\Delta\alpha \cos\delta$	$\Delta\delta$	Date		$\Delta\alpha \cos\delta$	$\Delta\delta$	Date		$\Delta\alpha \cos\delta$	$\Delta\delta$
		′ ″	′ ″			′ ″	′ ″			′ ″	′ ″
Jan.	−5	+1 12.6	+0 26.7	May	5	+4 47.5	+2 45.4	Sept.	12	+6 18.2	+3 14.8
	5	+0 08.0	−0 04.4		15	+5 06.1	+2 54.3		22	+6 07.2	+3 07.4
	15	−0 51.4	−0 28.5		25	+5 23.1	+3 02.2	Oct.	2	+5 52.8	+2 58.2
	25	−0 39.2	−0 13.5	June	4	+5 38.3	+3 09.1		12	+5 34.7	+2 47.3
Feb.	4	+0 06.8	+0 15.3		14	+5 51.9	+3 15.0		22	+5 12.8	+2 34.4
	14	+0 52.4	+0 41.7		24	+6 03.7	+3 19.9	Nov.	1	+4 46.9	+2 19.6
	24	+1 33.6	+1 04.6	July	4	+6 13.7	+3 23.7		11	+4 16.7	+2 02.7
Mar.	6	+2 10.4	+1 24.7		14	+6 21.7	+3 26.5		21	+3 41.6	+1 43.5
	16	+2 43.4	+1 42.3		24	+6 27.6	+3 28.0	Dec.	1	+3 01.0	+1 21.8
	26	+3 13.2	+1 57.9	Aug.	3	+6 31.1	+3 28.3		11	+2 13.8	+0 57.2
Apr.	5	+3 40.1	+2 11.8		13	+6 32.2	+3 27.1		21	+1 18.2	+0 29.1
	15	+4 04.6	+2 24.3		23	+6 30.5	+3 24.6		31	+0 12.4	−0 02.5
	25	+4 27.0	+2 35.4	Sept.	2	+6 25.9	+3 20.5		41	−0 50.3	−0 28.2

I Triton

UNIVERSAL TIME OF GREATEST EASTERN ELONGATION

Jan.	Feb.	Mar.	Apr.	May	June	July	Aug.	Sept.	Oct.	Nov.	Dec.
d h	d h	d h	d h	d h	d h	d h	d h	d h	d h	d h	d h
−3 03.4	1 09.5	2 18.5	1 03.3	6 09.2	4 18.1	4 03.2	2 12.4	6 18.8	6 04.3	4 13.8	3 23.2
3 00.5	7 06.5	8 15.4	7 00.3	12 06.1	10 15.0	10 00.1	8 09.4	12 15.9	12 01.5	10 10.9	9 20.3
8 21.4	13 03.5	14 12.3	12 21.2	18 03.1	16 12.1	15 21.2	14 06.5	18 13.1	17 22.6	16 08.0	15 17.3
14 18.5	19 00.5	20 09.3	18 18.2	24 00.1	22 09.1	21 18.3	20 03.6	24 10.2	23 19.6	22 05.0	21 14.3
20 15.5	24 21.5	26 06.3	24 15.2	29 21.1	28 06.1	27 15.3	26 00.7	30 07.2	29 16.7	28 02.1	27 11.4
26 12.5			30 12.2				31 21.8				33 08.5

SATELLITE OF PLUTO, 2025

APPARENT ORBIT OF I CHARON AT 0^h UNIVERSAL TIME ON THE DATE OF OPPOSITION, JULY 25

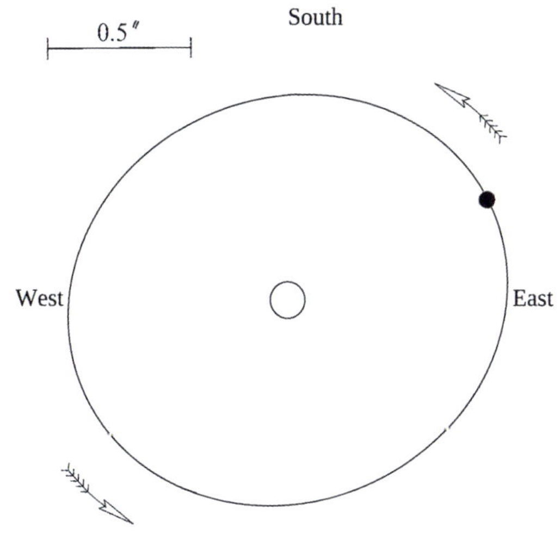

North

NAME	MEAN SIDEREAL PERIOD
	d
I Charon	6.387

I Charon

UNIVERSAL TIME OF GREATEST NORTHERN ELONGATION

Jan.	Feb.	Mar.	Apr.	May	June	July	Aug.	Sept.	Oct.	Nov.	Dec.
d h	d h	d h	d h	d h	d h	d h	d h	d h	d h	d h	d h
−2 08.2	5 15.1	3 03.7	4 01.6	5 23.8	6 22.3	2 11.8	3 10.7	4 09.7	6 08.5	7 06.9	2 19.8
4 17.3	12 00.2	9 12.8	10 10.7	12 09.0	13 07.7	8 21.2	9 20.1	10 19.0	12 17.8	13 16.2	9 05.0
11 02.5	18 09.4	15 22.1	16 20.1	18 18.4	19 17.0	15 06.6	16 05.6	17 04.4	19 03.1	20 01.4	15 14.2
17 11.7	24 18.5	22 07.2	23 05.3	25 03.7	26 02.3	21 15.9	22 14.9	23 13.7	25 12.3	26 10.6	21 23.4
23 20.8		28 16.4	29 14.5	31 13.0		28 01.3	29 00.3	29 23.1	31 21.6		28 08.5
30 05.9											34 17.7

CONTENTS OF SECTION G

Introduction

At the XXVI General Assembly (2006), the IAU defined a new classification scheme for the solar system. This scheme includes definitions for planets, dwarf planets and small solar system bodies (i.e. asteroids, trans-Neptunian objects, comets, and other small bodies). The 2006 IAU resolution B5 (2) classifies a dwarf planet as follows: A "dwarf planet" is a celestial body that (a) is in orbit around the Sun, (b) has sufficient mass for its self gravity to overcome rigid body forces so that it assumes a hydrostatic equilibrium shape, (c) has not cleared the neighbourhood around its orbit, and (d) is not a satellite. Resolution B6 confirmed the re-classification of Pluto as a dwarf planet.

This section includes tabulated data on selected dwarf planets, minor planets, and comets. Solar system bodies classified as planets are tabulated in Section E. See Section L for details about the selection of dwarf and minor planets, the sources of the various data and about the star catalogues used to plot the charts.

Notes on dwarf planets

The current selection of dwarf planets is (1) Ceres, (134340) Pluto and (136199) Eris. When these selected dwarf planets are at opposition between 2025 January 1 and January 31 of the following year more data are provided. Not only is the opposition date and time (nearest hour UT) given but also when the object is stationary in right ascension. Two star charts, one showing the path of the dwarf planet during the year and the other, a more detailed 60-day view on either side of opposition, are provided in order to help with identification. A daily astrometric ephemeris (see page B29) is also tabulated around opposition, which covers the interval when the dwarf planet is within 45° of opposition. Independent of the opposition date the osculating elements and heliocentric coordinates are tabulated for three dates during the year.

A physical ephemeris is tabulated at a ten day interval for those dwarf planets for which reliable data are available; currently (1) Ceres and (134340) Pluto. Information on the use of a physical ephemeris for the planets is given in Section E (see page E3) and can be applied to a dwarf planet ephemeris with the exception that a positive pole, defined as the pole around which the object rotates in a counterclockwise direction, replaces the notion of a north pole.

All dwarf planets acknowledged by the IAU (at the time of production) are listed with their basic physical properties. No reliable, refereed mass estimate is available for Makemake. The topic of dwarf planets in our solar system and small solar system bodies is the subject of ongoing research and new discoveries are being made. This section makes no attempt to provide a complete or definitive list.

Notes on bright minor planets

Pages G12–G24 contain various data on a selection of 92 of the largest and/or brightest minor planets. The first of these tabulate their heliocentric osculating orbital elements for epoch 2025 May 5·0 TT (JD 246 0800·5), with respect to the ecliptic and equinox J2000·0.

The next opposition dates of all the objects are listed in chronological order together with the visual magnitude and apparent declination. A sub-set (printed in bold) of the 14 larger minor planets, consisting of (2) Pallas, (3) Juno, (4) Vesta, (6) Hebe, (7) Iris, (8) Flora, (9) Metis, (10) Hygiea, (15) Eunomia, (16) Psyche, (52) Europa, (65) Cybele, (511) Davida and (704) Interamnia are candidates for a daily ephemeris.

A daily geocentric astrometric ephemeris is tabulated for those of the 14 larger minor planets that have an opposition date occurring between 2025 January 1 and 2026 January 31. The daily ephemeris of each object is centred about the opposition date, which is repeated at the bottom of the first column and at the top of the second column. The highlighted dates indicate when the object is stationary in right ascension. It is very occasionally possible for a stationary date to be outside the period tabulated.

Linear interpolation is sufficient for the magnitude and ephemeris transit, but for the right ascension and declination second differences are significant. The tabulations are similar to those for the dwarf planets, and the use of the data is similar to that for the planets.

Notes on comets

The table of osculating elements (see last page of this section) is for use in the generation of ephemerides by numerical integration. Typically, an ephemeris may be computed from these unperturbed elements to provide positions accurate to one to two arcminutes within a year of the epoch (Osc. epoch). The innate inaccuracy of some of these elements can be more of a problem and are discussed further in that part of Section L that deals with section G.

PHYSICAL PROPERTIES OF DWARF PLANETS

Number	Name	Equat. Radius	Mass	Minimum Geocentric Distance	Sidereal Period of Rotation	Maximum Angular Diameter	Geometric Albedo	Year of Discovery
		km	kg × 10^{20}	au	d	″		
(1)	Ceres	482·2	9·38	1·58865	0·3781	0·837	0·090	1801
(134340)	Pluto	1188·3	130·3	28·6031	6·3872	0·115	0·52	1930
(136108)	Haumea	1161	42	33·8492	0·1631	0·095	0·66	2004
(136199)	Eris	1163	164·66	37·3267	1·0800	0·086	0·96	2005
(136472)	Makemake	717	—	37·2098	0·9511	0·053	0·82	2005

OSCULATING ELEMENTS FOR ECLIPTIC AND EQUINOX J2000·0

Name	Magnitude Parameters *H*	*G*	Mean Diameter	Julian Date	Inclination *i*	Long. of Asc. Node *Ω*	Argument of Perihelion *ω*	Semi-major Axis *a*	Daily Motion *n*	Eccentricity *e*	Mean Anomaly *M*
			km		°	°	°	au	°/d		°
Ceres	3·34	0·15	939·4	2460800·5	10·588	80·252	73·273	2·766	0·2142	0·079	188·7026868
				2460900·5	10·588	80·251	73·276	2·765	0·2142	0·079	210·1300486
				2461000·5	10·588	80·250	73·300	2·765	0·2143	0·079	231·5397344
Pluto	−0·46	0·15	2377	2460800·5	17·172	110·333	113·072	39·297	0·0040	0·246	52·4908293
				2460900·5	17·174	110·335	112·966	39·284	0·0040	0·246	52·9652588
				2461000·5	17·176	110·336	112·869	39·275	0·0040	0·246	53·4211799
Eris	−1·23	0·15	2400	2460800·5	43·822	36·046	150·754	68·013	0·0017	0·436	210·9865180
				2460900·5	43·842	36·038	150·756	67·990	0·0017	0·437	211·2046847
				2461000·5	43·869	36·027	150·773	67·958	0·0017	0·437	211·4009246

USEFUL FORMULAE

Mean Longitude: $L = M + \varpi$

Longitude of perihelion: $\varpi = \omega + \Omega$

True anomaly in radians:
$$\nu = M + (2e - e^3/4)\sin M + (5e^2/4)\sin 2M + (13e^3/12)\sin 3M + \cdots$$

Planet-Sun distance: $r = a(1 - e^2)/(1 + e\cos\nu)$

Heliocentric rectangular coordinates, referred to the ecliptic, may be computed from the elements using:

$$x = r\{\cos(\nu + \omega)\cos\Omega - \sin(\nu + \omega)\cos i \sin\Omega\}$$
$$y = r\{\cos(\nu + \omega)\sin\Omega + \sin(\nu + \omega)\cos i \cos\Omega\}$$
$$z = r\sin(\nu + \omega)\sin i$$

HELIOCENTRIC COORDINATES AND VELOCITY COMPONENTS REFERRED TO THE MEAN EQUATOR AND EQUINOX OF J2000·0

Name	Julian Date	x	y	z	$\dot{x}$	$\dot{y}$	$\dot{z}$
		au	au	au	au/d	au/d	au/d
Ceres	2460800·5	+2·7711316	−0·6693115	−0·8798673	+0·0029910	+0·0084318	+0·0033681
	2460900·5	+2·9108089	+0·1952909	−0·5004918	−0·0002365	+0·0086987	+0·0041511
	2461000·5	+2·7207773	+1·0371287	−0·0647249	−0·0035539	+0·0079680	+0·0044819
Pluto	2460800·5	+18·5701323	−26·5598590	−13·8817744	+0·0027447	+0·0012412	−0·0004414
	2460900·5	+18·8439678	−26·4348852	−13·9254659	+0·0027320	+0·0012582	−0·0004324
	2461000·5	+19·1165315	−26·3082317	−13·9682627	+0·0027193	+0·0012749	−0·0004235
Eris	2460800·5	+85·3289847	+43·0678181	−0·6475557	−0·0004714	+0·0004196	+0·0012021
	2460900·5	+85·2816898	+43·1096631	−0·5273634	−0·0004745	+0·0004173	+0·0012017
	2461000·5	+85·2340995	+43·1512645	−0·4072106	−0·0004773	+0·0004148	+0·0012013

CERES AT OPPOSITION

Date	UT	Mag.
2025 Oct. 2	13^h	+ 7.6

Stationary in right ascension on 2025 August 16 and November 27.

The following diagrams are provided for observers wishing to find the position of Ceres in relation to the stars. The first chart shows the path of the dwarf planet during 2025. The second chart provides a detailed view of the path over 60 days either side of opposition. The V-magnitude scale used is given on each chart.

This space has been intentionally left blank.

CERES, 2025

GEOCENTRIC POSITIONS FOR 0^h TERRESTRIAL TIME

Date	Astrometric R.A.	Astrometric Dec.	Vis. Mag.	Ephemeris Transit	Date	Astrometric R.A.	Astrometric Dec.	Vis. Mag.	Ephemeris Transit
	h m s	° ′ ″		h m		h m s	° ′ ″		h m
2025 Aug. 4	1 19 52·9	− 5 38 59	8·6	4 29·2	**2025 Oct. 2**	0 58 21·6	−10 11 37	7·6	0 15·8
5	1 20 07·8	− 5 41 23	8·6	4 25·5	**3**	0 57 30·9	−10 15 53	7·6	0 11·0
6	1 20 21·5	− 5 43 54	8·6	4 21·8	**4**	0 56 40·0	−10 20 01	7·6	0 06·2
7	1 20 33·9	− 5 46 33	8·5	4 18·1	**5**	0 55 48·9	−10 24 01	7·6	0 01·4
8	1 20 45·0	− 5 49 19	8·5	4 14·4	**6**	0 54 57·8	−10 27 52	7·6	23 51·9
9	1 20 54·9	− 5 52 13	8·5	4 10·6	**7**	0 54 06·5	−10 31 35	7·6	23 47·1
10	1 21 03·5	− 5 55 14	8·5	4 06·8	**8**	0 53 15·3	−10 35 10	7·7	23 42·3
11	1 21 10·9	− 5 58 22	8·5	4 03·0	**9**	0 52 24·1	−10 38 35	7·7	23 37·5
12	1 21 16·9	− 6 01 37	8·5	3 59·1	**10**	0 51 33·0	−10 41 50	7·7	23 32·8
13	1 21 21·6	− 6 04 59	8·4	3 55·3	**11**	0 50 42·1	−10 44 56	7·7	23 28·0
14	1 21 25·0	− 6 08 29	8·4	3 51·4	**12**	0 49 51·4	−10 47 52	7·7	23 23·2
15	1 21 27·0	− 6 12 05	8·4	3 47·5	**13**	0 49 00·9	−10 50 38	7·7	23 18·5
16	1 21 27·7	− 6 15 48	8·4	3 43·6	**14**	0 48 10·7	−10 53 14	7·7	23 13·7
17	1 21 27·0	− 6 19 38	8·4	3 39·6	**15**	0 47 21·0	−10 55 39	7·7	23 09·0
18	1 21 25·0	− 6 23 34	8·4	3 35·7	**16**	0 46 31·6	−10 57 54	7·8	23 04·2
19	1 21 21·6	− 6 27 37	8·3	3 31·7	**17**	0 45 42·7	−10 59 58	7·8	22 59·5
20	1 21 16·8	− 6 31 47	8·3	3 27·7	**18**	0 44 54·3	−11 01 50	7·8	22 54·8
21	1 21 10·7	− 6 36 02	8·3	3 23·6	**19**	0 44 06·5	−11 03 32	7·8	22 50·0
22	1 21 03·1	− 6 40 24	8·3	3 19·6	**20**	0 43 19·3	−11 05 02	7·8	22 45·3
23	1 20 54·2	− 6 44 51	8·3	3 15·5	**21**	0 42 32·8	−11 06 21	7·8	22 40·6
24	1 20 43·9	− 6 49 24	8·3	3 11·4	**22**	0 41 47·0	−11 07 28	7·9	22 36·0
25	1 20 32·2	− 6 54 03	8·2	3 07·3	**23**	0 41 02·0	−11 08 23	7·9	22 31·3
26	1 20 19·1	− 6 58 47	8·2	3 03·1	**24**	0 40 17·8	−11 09 07	7·9	22 26·7
27	1 20 04·6	− 7 03 35	8·2	2 58·9	**25**	0 39 34·4	−11 09 39	7·9	22 22·0
28	1 19 48·8	− 7 08 29	8·2	2 54·7	**26**	0 38 52·0	−11 09 59	7·9	22 17·4
29	1 19 31·6	− 7 13 27	8·2	2 50·5	**27**	0 38 10·5	−11 10 07	7·9	22 12·8
30	1 19 13·0	− 7 18 30	8·1	2 46·3	**28**	0 37 29·9	−11 10 04	8·0	22 08·2
31	1 18 53·1	− 7 23 36	8·1	2 42·0	**29**	0 36 50·4	−11 09 48	8·0	22 03·6
Sept. 1	1 18 31·8	− 7 28 46	8·1	2 37·7	**30**	0 36 11·9	−11 09 21	8·0	21 59·1
2	1 18 09·2	− 7 34 00	8·1	2 33·4	**31**	0 35 34·5	−11 08 42	8·0	21 54·5
3	1 17 45·3	− 7 39 17	8·1	2 29·1	**Nov. 1**	0 34 58·2	−11 07 52	8·0	21 50·0
4	1 17 20·1	− 7 44 37	8·0	2 24·7	**2**	0 34 23·1	−11 06 50	8·0	21 45·5
5	1 16 53·5	− 7 50 00	8·0	2 20·4	**3**	0 33 49·1	−11 05 36	8·1	21 41·1
6	1 16 25·7	− 7 55 25	8·0	2 16·0	**4**	0 33 16·2	−11 04 11	8·1	21 36·6
7	1 15 56·7	− 8 00 52	8·0	2 11·5	**5**	0 32 44·6	−11 02 34	8·1	21 32·2
8	1 15 26·4	− 8 06 21	8·0	2 07·1	**6**	0 32 14·2	−11 00 47	8·1	21 27·7
9	1 14 54·9	− 8 11 52	8·0	2 02·7	**7**	0 31 45·1	−10 58 48	8·1	21 23·3
10	1 14 22·2	− 8 17 24	7·9	1 58·2	**8**	0 31 17·2	−10 56 38	8·2	21 19·0
11	1 13 48·3	− 8 22 56	7·9	1 53·7	**9**	0 30 50·6	−10 54 17	8·2	21 14·6
12	1 13 13·2	− 8 28 29	7·9	1 49·2	**10**	0 30 25·2	−10 51 45	8·2	21 10·3
13	1 12 37·0	− 8 34 02	7·9	1 44·6	**11**	0 30 01·2	−10 49 03	8·2	21 06·0
14	1 11 59·7	− 8 39 36	7·9	1 40·1	**12**	0 29 38·5	−10 46 10	8·2	21 01·7
15	1 11 21·4	− 8 45 08	7·8	1 35·5	**13**	0 29 17·2	−10 43 06	8·2	20 57·4
16	1 10 41·9	− 8 50 40	7·8	1 30·9	**14**	0 28 57·2	−10 39 53	8·3	20 53·2
17	1 10 01·5	− 8 56 10	7·8	1 26·3	**15**	0 28 38·5	−10 36 29	8·3	20 49·0
18	1 09 20·1	− 9 01 39	7·8	1 21·7	**16**	0 28 21·2	−10 32 54	8·3	20 44·8
19	1 08 37·7	− 9 07 05	7·8	1 17·1	**17**	0 28 05·3	−10 29 10	8·3	20 40·6
20	1 07 54·5	− 9 12 29	7·8	1 12·4	**18**	0 27 50·8	−10 25 16	8·3	20 36·4
21	1 07 10·4	− 9 17 51	7·7	1 07·8	**19**	0 27 37·6	−10 21 12	8·3	20 32·3
22	1 06 25·4	− 9 23 08	7·7	1 03·1	**20**	0 27 25·9	−10 16 59	8·4	20 28·2
23	1 05 39·7	− 9 28 23	7·7	0 58·4	**21**	0 27 15·5	−10 12 36	8·4	20 24·1
24	1 04 53·3	− 9 33 33	7·7	0 53·7	**22**	0 27 06·6	−10 08 04	8·4	20 20·0
25	1 04 06·2	− 9 38 38	7·7	0 49·0	**23**	0 26 59·0	−10 03 23	8·4	20 16·0
26	1 03 18·4	− 9 43 39	7·7	0 44·3	**24**	0 26 52·8	− 9 58 32	8·4	20 12·0
27	1 02 30·1	− 9 48 34	7·7	0 39·5	**25**	0 26 48·0	− 9 53 34	8·4	20 08·0
28	1 01 41·3	− 9 53 23	7·7	0 34·8	**26**	0 26 44·6	− 9 48 26	8·5	20 04·0
29	1 00 51·9	− 9 58 07	7·6	0 30·0	**27**	0 26 42·6	− 9 43 10	8·5	20 00·1
30	1 00 02·2	−10 02 44	7·6	0 25·3	**28**	0 26 42·0	− 9 37 46	8·5	19 56·2
Oct. 1	0 59 12·1	−10 07 14	7·6	0 20·5	**29**	0 26 42·7	− 9 32 14	8·5	19 52·3
Oct. 2	0 58 21·6	−10 11 37	7·6	0 15·8	**Nov. 30**	0 26 44·8	− 9 26 33	8·5	19 48·4

Second transit for Ceres 2025 October $5^d\ 23^h\ 56\overset{m}{.}7$

PLUTO AT OPPOSITION

Date	UT	Mag.
2025 July 25	7^h	+ 15.1

Stationary in right ascension on 2025 May 6 and October 14.

The following diagrams are provided for observers wishing to find the position of Pluto in relation to the stars. The first chart shows the path of the dwarf planet during 2025. The second chart provides a detailed view of the path over 60 days either side of opposition. The V-magnitude scale used is given on each chart.

Pluto is in Sagittarius, towards the Galatic Centre. The field of view is therefore crowded with background stars.

This space has been intentionally left blank.

GEOCENTRIC POSITIONS FOR 0^h TERRESTRIAL TIME

Date	Astrometric R.A.	Astrometric Dec.	Vis. Mag.	Ephemeris Transit
	h m s	° ′ ″		h m
2025 May 27	20 26 14·3	−22 55 29	15·2	4 07·8
28	20 26 11·9	−22 55 48	15·2	4 03·9
29	20 26 09·4	−22 56 07	15·2	3 59·9
30	20 26 06·7	−22 56 27	15·2	3 55·9
31	20 26 04·0	−22 56 46	15·2	3 51·9
June 1	20 26 01·2	−22 57 06	15·2	3 48·0
2	20 25 58·3	−22 57 27	15·2	3 44·0
3	20 25 55·2	−22 57 47	15·2	3 40·0
4	20 25 52·1	−22 58 08	15·2	3 36·0
5	20 25 48·9	−22 58 29	15·2	3 32·0
6	20 25 45·6	−22 58 51	15·2	3 28·1
7	20 25 42·2	−22 59 12	15·2	3 24·1
8	20 25 38·7	−22 59 34	15·2	3 20·1
9	20 25 35·1	−22 59 56	15·2	3 16·1
10	20 25 31·4	−23 00 19	15·2	3 12·1
11	20 25 27·6	−23 00 41	15·2	3 08·1
12	20 25 23·8	−23 01 04	15·2	3 04·1
13	20 25 19·8	−23 01 27	15·2	3 00·1
14	20 25 15·8	−23 01 50	15·2	2 56·1
15	20 25 11·7	−23 02 13	15·2	2 52·1
16	20 25 07·5	−23 02 37	15·2	2 48·1
17	20 25 03·3	−23 03 00	15·2	2 44·1
18	20 24 58·9	−23 03 24	15·2	2 40·1
19	20 24 54·5	−23 03 48	15·2	2 36·1
20	20 24 50·0	−23 04 12	15·2	2 32·1
21	20 24 45·5	−23 04 36	15·2	2 28·1
22	20 24 40·8	−23 05 01	15·2	2 24·1
23	20 24 36·1	−23 05 25	15·2	2 20·1
24	20 24 31·3	−23 05 50	15·2	2 16·1
25	20 24 26·5	−23 06 15	15·2	2 12·0
26	20 24 21·6	−23 06 40	15·2	2 08·0
27	20 24 16·6	−23 07 05	15·2	2 04·0
28	20 24 11·6	−23 07 30	15·1	2 00·0
29	20 24 06·5	−23 07 55	15·1	1 56·0
30	20 24 01·4	−23 08 20	15·1	1 52·0
July 1	20 23 56·2	−23 08 46	15·1	1 48·0
2	20 23 50·9	−23 09 11	15·1	1 43·9
3	20 23 45·6	−23 09 36	15·1	1 39·9
4	20 23 40·3	−23 10 02	15·1	1 35·9
5	20 23 34·9	−23 10 27	15·1	1 31·9
6	20 23 29·4	−23 10 53	15·1	1 27·9
7	20 23 23·9	−23 11 19	15·1	1 23·8
8	20 23 18·4	−23 11 44	15·1	1 19·8
9	20 23 12·9	−23 12 10	15·1	1 15·8
10	20 23 07·3	−23 12 35	15·1	1 11·8
11	20 23 01·6	−23 13 01	15·1	1 07·7
12	20 22 56·0	−23 13 26	15·1	1 03·7
13	20 22 50·3	−23 13 52	15·1	0 59·7
14	20 22 44·5	−23 14 17	15·1	0 55·7
15	20 22 38·8	−23 14 43	15·1	0 51·6
16	20 22 33·0	−23 15 08	15·1	0 47·6
17	20 22 27·2	−23 15 34	15·1	0 43·6
18	20 22 21·4	−23 15 59	15·1	0 39·5
19	20 22 15·6	−23 16 24	15·1	0 35·5
20	20 22 09·7	−23 16 49	15·1	0 31·5
21	20 22 03·8	−23 17 14	15·1	0 27·5
22	20 21 58·0	−23 17 39	15·1	0 23·4
23	20 21 52·1	−23 18 04	15·1	0 19·4
24	20 21 46·2	−23 18 29	15·1	0 15·4
July 25	20 21 40·3	−23 18 53	15·1	0 11·3

Date	Astrometric R.A.	Astrometric Dec.	Vis. Mag.	Ephemeris Transit
	h m s	° ′ ″		h m
2025 July 25	20 21 40·3	−23 18 53	15·1	0 11·3
26	20 21 34·4	−23 19 18	15·1	0 07·3
27	20 21 28·4	−23 19 42	15·1	0 03·3
28	20 21 22·5	−23 20 07	15·1	23 55·2
29	20 21 16·6	−23 20 31	15·1	23 51·2
30	20 21 10·7	−23 20 55	15·1	23 47·2
31	20 21 04·9	−23 21 19	15·1	23 43·1
Aug. 1	20 20 59·0	−23 21 42	15·1	23 39·1
2	20 20 53·1	−23 22 06	15·1	23 35·1
3	20 20 47·3	−23 22 29	15·1	23 31·1
4	20 20 41·4	−23 22 52	15·1	23 27·0
5	20 20 35·6	−23 23 15	15·1	23 23·0
6	20 20 29·8	−23 23 38	15·1	23 19·0
7	20 20 24·1	−23 24 00	15·1	23 14·9
8	20 20 18·3	−23 24 22	15·1	23 10·9
9	20 20 12·6	−23 24 44	15·1	23 06·9
10	20 20 07·0	−23 25 06	15·1	23 02·9
11	20 20 01·3	−23 25 28	15·1	22 58·8
12	20 19 55·7	−23 25 49	15·1	22 54·8
13	20 19 50·1	−23 26 10	15·1	22 50·8
14	20 19 44·6	−23 26 31	15·1	22 46·8
15	20 19 39·1	−23 26 52	15·1	22 42·8
16	20 19 33·6	−23 27 12	15·1	22 38·7
17	20 19 28·2	−23 27 32	15·1	22 34·7
18	20 19 22·8	−23 27 52	15·1	22 30·7
19	20 19 17·5	−23 28 11	15·1	22 26·7
20	20 19 12·2	−23 28 31	15·1	22 22·7
21	20 19 07·0	−23 28 50	15·2	22 18·6
22	20 19 01·8	−23 29 08	15·2	22 14·6
23	20 18 56·7	−23 29 27	15·2	22 10·6
24	20 18 51·7	−23 29 45	15·2	22 06·6
25	20 18 46·7	−23 30 03	15·2	22 02·6
26	20 18 41·7	−23 30 20	15·2	21 58·6
27	20 18 36·9	−23 30 37	15·2	21 54·5
28	20 18 32·1	−23 30 54	15·2	21 50·5
29	20 18 27·4	−23 31 10	15·2	21 46·5
30	20 18 22·7	−23 31 27	15·2	21 42·5
31	20 18 18·1	−23 31 42	15·2	21 38·5
Sept. 1	20 18 13·6	−23 31 58	15·2	21 34·5
2	20 18 09·2	−23 32 13	15·2	21 30·5
3	20 18 04·8	−23 32 28	15·2	21 26·5
4	20 18 00·5	−23 32 42	15·2	21 22·5
5	20 17 56·3	−23 32 56	15·2	21 18·5
6	20 17 52·2	−23 33 10	15·2	21 14·5
7	20 17 48·2	−23 33 23	15·2	21 10·5
8	20 17 44·2	−23 33 36	15·2	21 06·5
9	20 17 40·4	−23 33 49	15·2	21 02·5
10	20 17 36·6	−23 34 01	15·2	20 58·5
11	20 17 32·9	−23 34 13	15·2	20 54·5
12	20 17 29·3	−23 34 25	15·2	20 50·5
13	20 17 25·8	−23 34 36	15·2	20 46·6
14	20 17 22·4	−23 34 46	15·2	20 42·6
15	20 17 19·1	−23 34 57	15·2	20 38·6
16	20 17 15·9	−23 35 07	15·2	20 34·6
17	20 17 12·8	−23 35 16	15·2	20 30·6
18	20 17 09·7	−23 35 26	15·2	20 26·6
19	20 17 06·8	−23 35 34	15·2	20 22·7
20	20 17 04·0	−23 35 43	15·2	20 18·7
21	20 17 01·3	−23 35 51	15·2	20 14·7
Sept. 22	20 16 58·7	−23 35 58	15·2	20 10·7

Second transit for Pluto 2025 July 27^d 23^h $59^m.3$

ERIS AT OPPOSITION

Date	UT	Mag.
2025 Oct. 18	7^h	+ 18.7

Stationary in right ascension on 2025 January 17 and July 25.

The following diagrams are provided for observers wishing to find the position of Eris in relation to the stars. The first chart shows the path of the dwarf planet during 2025. The second chart provides a detailed view of the path over 60 days either side of opposition. The V-magnitude scale used is given on each chart.

This space has been intentionally left blank.

ERIS, 2025

GEOCENTRIC POSITIONS FOR 0^{h} TERRESTRIAL TIME

Date	Astrometric R.A.	Astrometric Dec.	Vis. Mag.	Ephemeris Transit
	h m s	° ′ ″		h m
2025 Aug. 20	1 49 17·3	− 0 10 51	18·8	3 55·6
21	1 49 16·3	− 0 11 01	18·8	3 51·7
22	1 49 15·2	− 0 11 11	18·8	3 47·7
23	1 49 14·2	− 0 11 21	18·8	3 43·8
24	1 49 13·0	− 0 11 31	18·8	3 39·8
25	1 49 11·9	− 0 11 42	18·8	3 35·9
26	1 49 10·7	− 0 11 52	18·8	3 31·9
27	1 49 09·5	− 0 12 03	18·8	3 28·0
28	1 49 08·2	− 0 12 14	18·8	3 24·0
29	1 49 06·9	− 0 12 25	18·8	3 20·1
30	1 49 05·6	− 0 12 36	18·8	3 16·1
31	1 49 04·2	− 0 12 47	18·8	3 12·2
Sept. 1	1 49 02·9	− 0 12 58	18·8	3 08·2
2	1 49 01·4	− 0 13 09	18·8	3 04·3
3	1 49 00·0	− 0 13 21	18·8	3 00·3
4	1 48 58·5	− 0 13 32	18·8	2 56·3
5	1 48 57·0	− 0 13 44	18·8	2 52·4
6	1 48 55·5	− 0 13 56	18·8	2 48·4
7	1 48 53·9	− 0 14 07	18·8	2 44·5
8	1 48 52·3	− 0 14 19	18·8	2 40·5
9	1 48 50·7	− 0 14 31	18·8	2 36·6
10	1 48 49·1	− 0 14 43	18·8	2 32·6
11	1 48 47·4	− 0 14 55	18·8	2 28·6
12	1 48 45·7	− 0 15 07	18·8	2 24·7
13	1 48 44·0	− 0 15 19	18·8	2 20·7
14	1 48 42·2	− 0 15 31	18·8	2 16·8
15	1 48 40·5	− 0 15 43	18·8	2 12·8
16	1 48 38·7	− 0 15 55	18·8	2 08·8
17	1 48 36·8	− 0 16 08	18·8	2 04·9
18	1 48 35·0	− 0 16 20	18·8	2 00·9
19	1 48 33·1	− 0 16 32	18·8	1 57·0
20	1 48 31·2	− 0 16 44	18·8	1 53·0
21	1 48 29·3	− 0 16 57	18·8	1 49·0
22	1 48 27·4	− 0 17 09	18·8	1 45·1
23	1 48 25·4	− 0 17 21	18·8	1 41·1
24	1 48 23·5	− 0 17 34	18·7	1 37·1
25	1 48 21·5	− 0 17 46	18·7	1 33·2
26	1 48 19·4	− 0 17 58	18·7	1 29·2
27	1 48 17·4	− 0 18 11	18·7	1 25·2
28	1 48 15·4	− 0 18 23	18·7	1 21·3
29	1 48 13·3	− 0 18 35	18·7	1 17·3
30	1 48 11·2	− 0 18 47	18·7	1 13·3
Oct. 1	1 48 09·1	− 0 18 59	18·7	1 09·4
2	1 48 07·0	− 0 19 12	18·7	1 05·4
3	1 48 04·9	− 0 19 24	18·7	1 01·4
4	1 48 02·8	− 0 19 36	18·7	0 57·5
5	1 48 00·6	− 0 19 48	18·7	0 53·5
6	1 47 58·4	− 0 20 00	18·7	0 49·5
7	1 47 56·3	− 0 20 12	18·7	0 45·6
8	1 47 54·1	− 0 20 23	18·7	0 41·6
9	1 47 51·9	− 0 20 35	18·7	0 37·6
10	1 47 49·7	− 0 20 47	18·7	0 33·7
11	1 47 47·5	− 0 20 59	18·7	0 29·7
12	1 47 45·2	− 0 21 10	18·7	0 25·7
13	1 47 43·0	− 0 21 22	18·7	0 21·8
14	1 47 40·8	− 0 21 33	18·7	0 17·8
15	1 47 38·5	− 0 21 44	18·7	0 13·8
16	1 47 36·3	− 0 21 55	18·7	0 09·9
17	1 47 34·0	− 0 22 06	18·7	0 05·9
Oct. 18	1 47 31·8	− 0 22 17	18·7	0 01·9

Date	Astrometric R.A.	Astrometric Dec.	Vis. Mag.	Ephemeris Transit
	h m s	° ′ ″		h m
2025 Oct. 18	1 47 31·8	− 0 22 17	18·7	0 01·9
19	1 47 29·5	− 0 22 28	18·7	23 54·0
20	1 47 27·3	− 0 22 39	18·7	23 50·0
21	1 47 25·0	− 0 22 50	18·7	23 46·0
22	1 47 22·7	− 0 23 00	18·7	23 42·1
23	1 47 20·5	− 0 23 10	18·7	23 38·1
24	1 47 18·2	− 0 23 21	18·7	23 34·1
25	1 47 15·9	− 0 23 31	18·7	23 30·2
26	1 47 13·7	− 0 23 41	18·7	23 26·2
27	1 47 11·4	− 0 23 51	18·7	23 22·2
28	1 47 09·2	− 0 24 00	18·7	23 18·3
29	1 47 06·9	− 0 24 10	18·7	23 14·3
30	1 47 04·7	− 0 24 19	18·7	23 10·3
31	1 47 02·4	− 0 24 28	18·7	23 06·3
Nov. 1	1 47 00·2	− 0 24 37	18·7	23 02·4
2	1 46 58·0	− 0 24 46	18·7	22 58·4
3	1 46 55·8	− 0 24 55	18·7	22 54·4
4	1 46 53·5	− 0 25 03	18·7	22 50·5
5	1 46 51·3	− 0 25 12	18·7	22 46·5
6	1 46 49·2	− 0 25 20	18·7	22 42·5
7	1 46 47·0	− 0 25 28	18·7	22 38·6
8	1 46 44·8	− 0 25 36	18·7	22 34·6
9	1 46 42·6	− 0 25 43	18·7	22 30·6
10	1 46 40·5	− 0 25 50	18·7	22 26·7
11	1 46 38·4	− 0 25 58	18·7	22 22·7
12	1 46 36·3	− 0 26 05	18·7	22 18·7
13	1 46 34·2	− 0 26 11	18·8	22 14·8
14	1 46 32·1	− 0 26 18	18·8	22 10·8
15	1 46 30·0	− 0 26 24	18·8	22 06·8
16	1 46 27·9	− 0 26 31	18·8	22 02·9
17	1 46 25·9	− 0 26 37	18·8	21 58·9
18	1 46 23·9	− 0 26 42	18·8	21 54·9
19	1 46 21·9	− 0 26 48	18·8	21 51·0
20	1 46 19·9	− 0 26 53	18·8	21 47·0
21	1 46 18·0	− 0 26 58	18·8	21 43·0
22	1 46 16·0	− 0 27 03	18·8	21 39·1
23	1 46 14·1	− 0 27 08	18·8	21 35·1
24	1 46 12·2	− 0 27 12	18·8	21 31·2
25	1 46 10·3	− 0 27 16	18·8	21 27·2
26	1 46 08·5	− 0 27 20	18·8	21 23·2
27	1 46 06·7	− 0 27 24	18·8	21 19·3
28	1 46 04·9	− 0 27 27	18·8	21 15·3
29	1 46 03·1	− 0 27 30	18·8	21 11·4
30	1 46 01·3	− 0 27 33	18·8	21 07·4
Dec. 1	1 45 59·6	− 0 27 36	18·8	21 03·4
2	1 45 57·9	− 0 27 38	18·8	20 59·5
3	1 45 56·3	− 0 27 40	18·8	20 55·5
4	1 45 54·6	− 0 27 42	18·8	20 51·6
5	1 45 53·0	− 0 27 44	18·8	20 47·6
6	1 45 51·4	− 0 27 45	18·8	20 43·6
7	1 45 49·9	− 0 27 46	18·8	20 39·7
8	1 45 48·4	− 0 27 47	18·8	20 35·7
9	1 45 46·9	− 0 27 48	18·8	20 31·8
10	1 45 45·4	− 0 27 48	18·8	20 27·8
11	1 45 44·0	− 0 27 48	18·8	20 23·9
12	1 45 42·6	− 0 27 48	18·8	20 19·9
13	1 45 41·2	− 0 27 48	18·8	20 15·9
14	1 45 39·9	− 0 27 47	18·8	20 12·0
15	1 45 38·6	− 0 27 46	18·8	20 08·0
Dec. 16	1 45 37·4	− 0 27 45	18·8	20 04·1

Second transit for Eris 2025 October 18^{d} 23^{h} 57$^{m}_{.}$9

EPHEMERIS FOR PHYSICAL OBSERVATIONS FOR 0^h TERRESTRIAL TIME

Date		Light Time	Visual Magnitude	Phase Angle	L_s	Sub-Earth Point Longitude	Sub-Earth Point Latitude	Positive Pole P.A.
		m		°	°	°	°	°
Jan.	**−15**	30·53	9·3	12·1	103·22	159·16	+4·59	353·86
	−5	31·23	9·2	10·3	105·06	316·61	+4·00	352·37
	5	31·81	9·2	8·5	106·91	114·04	+3·44	350·91
	15	32·28	9·2	6·6	108·75	271·48	+2·91	349·47
Jan.	**25**	32·62	9·1	4·8	110·59	68·95	+2·41	348·08
Feb.	**4**	32·84	9·0	3·2	112·43	226·47	+1·97	346·75
	14	32·94	9·0	2·4	114·27	24·05	+1·57	345·49
	24	32·91	9·0	3·1	116·10	181·72	+1·23	344·30
Mar.	**6**	32·76	9·1	4·6	117·94	339·48	+0·95	343·20
	16	32·48	9·2	6·3	119·77	137·35	+0·74	342·18
	26	32·09	9·2	8·2	121·60	295·35	+0·59	341·26
Apr.	**5**	31·59	9·3	9·9	123·44	93·48	+0·52	340·43
	15	30·98	9·3	11·7	125·27	251·77	+0·52	339·69
	25	30·27	9·3	13·3	127·11	50·22	+0·60	339·05
May	**5**	29·46	9·3	14·8	128·94	208·85	+0·76	338·50
	15	28·58	9·3	16·2	130·78	7·68	+1·00	338·05
	25	27·62	9·2	17·4	132·62	166·73	+1·32	337·68
June	**4**	26·60	9·2	18·5	134·46	326·03	+1·71	337·38
	14	25·53	9·1	19·3	136·30	125·60	+2·18	337·16
	24	24·42	9·0	19·8	138·14	285·47	+2·72	337·00
July	**4**	23·30	8·9	20·0	139·99	85·67	+3·33	336·89
	14	22·17	8·8	19·9	141·84	246·26	+4·00	336·82
	24	21·07	8·7	19·3	143·70	47·27	+4·71	336·77
Aug.	**3**	20·01	8·5	18·3	145·56	208·74	+5·44	336·74
	13	19·02	8·4	16·8	147·42	10·71	+6·16	336·72
	23	18·14	8·2	14·7	149·29	173·19	+6·83	336·69
Sept.	**2**	17·40	8·0	12·2	151·16	336·17	+7·40	336·68
	12	16·83	7·8	9·4	153·04	139·57	+7·82	336·68
	22	16·46	7·7	6·6	154·92	303·26	+8·02	336·72
Oct.	**2**	16·31	7·6	5·1	156·81	107·05	+7·97	336·81
	12	16·39	7·6	6·2	158·70	270·70	+7·65	336·94
	22	16·70	7·8	8·9	160·61	73·99	+7·09	337·11
Nov.	**1**	17·22	8·0	11·8	162·51	236·73	+6·33	337·28
	11	17·92	8·1	14·4	164·43	38·81	+5·42	337·43
	21	18·77	8·3	16·6	166·35	200·17	+4·45	337·52
Dec.	**1**	19·73	8·5	18·2	168·28	0·84	+3·44	337·55
	11	20·77	8·6	19·2	170·22	160·87	+2·46	337·52
	21	21·86	8·7	19·8	172·17	320·33	+1·52	337·44
	31	22·96	8·8	19·9	174·12	119·31	+0·64	337·31
Dec.	**41**	24·06	8·9	19·6	176·09	277·88	−0·16	337·17

EPHEMERIS FOR PHYSICAL OBSERVATIONS FOR 0^h TERRESTRIAL TIME

Date		Light Time	Visual Magnitude	Phase Angle	L_s	Sub-Earth Point Longitude	Sub-Earth Point Latitude	Positive Pole P.A.
		m		°	°	°	°	°
Jan.	**−15**	298·98	15·3	1·0	262·18	235·89	+59·04	199·06
	−5	299·78	15·2	0·7	262·23	79·96	+59·18	198·54
	5	300·36	15·2	0·5	262·28	284·07	+59·33	197·96
	15	300·70	15·2	0·2	262·33	128·23	+59·49	197·36
Jan.	**25**	300·80	15·2	0·1	262·38	332·41	+59·64	196·74
Feb.	**4**	300·66	15·2	0·4	262·43	176·61	+59·78	196·12
	14	300·28	15·2	0·6	262·48	20·80	+59·91	195·52
	24	299·68	15·3	0·9	262·53	224·98	+60·04	194·94
Mar.	**6**	298·88	15·3	1·1	262·57	69·13	+60·14	194·40
	16	297·89	15·3	1·3	262·62	273·24	+60·23	193·91
	26	296·77	15·3	1·4	262·67	117·29	+60·30	193·50
Apr.	**5**	295·52	15·3	1·5	262·72	321·28	+60·34	193·16
	15	294·21	15·3	1·6	262·77	165·19	+60·37	192·91
	25	292·85	15·3	1·6	262·82	9·02	+60·37	192·74
May	**5**	291·51	15·3	1·6	262·86	212·76	+60·35	192·67
	15	290·21	15·3	1·5	262·91	56·42	+60·31	192·70
	25	288·99	15·2	1·4	262·96	260·00	+60·26	192·81
June	**4**	287·90	15·2	1·3	263·01	103·49	+60·18	193·00
	14	286·96	15·2	1·1	263·06	306·91	+60·09	193·27
	24	286·20	15·2	0·8	263·11	150·26	+59·98	193·60
July	**4**	285·65	15·1	0·6	263·15	353·57	+59·87	193·98
	14	285·33	15·1	0·3	263·20	196·83	+59·75	194·40
	24	285·24	15·1	0·1	263·25	40·06	+59·62	194·83
Aug.	**3**	285·40	15·1	0·3	263·30	243·29	+59·50	195·27
	13	285·79	15·1	0·5	263·35	86·52	+59·38	195·69
	23	286·42	15·2	0·8	263·39	289·76	+59·27	196·09
Sept.	**2**	287·26	15·2	1·0	263·44	133·04	+59·18	196·44
	12	288·29	15·2	1·2	263·49	336·36	+59·10	196·73
	22	289·49	15·2	1·4	263·54	179·73	+59·04	196·96
Oct.	**2**	290·81	15·3	1·5	263·59	23·17	+59·00	197·11
	12	292·23	15·3	1·6	263·63	226·68	+58·99	197·17
	22	293·70	15·3	1·6	263·68	70·27	+59·00	197·15
Nov.	**1**	295·18	15·3	1·6	263·73	273·93	+59·03	197·04
	11	296·64	15·3	1·5	263·78	117·68	+59·09	196·84
	21	298·01	15·3	1·4	263·83	321·51	+59·17	196·56
Dec.	**1**	299·28	15·3	1·3	263·87	165·41	+59·27	196·19
	11	300·40	15·3	1·1	263·92	9·39	+59·38	195·75
	21	301·34	15·3	0·9	263·97	213·43	+59·50	195·25
	31	302·07	15·3	0·6	264·02	57·53	+59·64	194·69
Dec.	**41**	302·58	15·2	0·4	264·07	261·68	+59·77	194·10

HELIOCENTRIC OSCULATING ELEMENTS FOR EPOCH 2025 MAY 5·0 TT, ECLIPTIC AND EQUINOX J2000·0

No.	Name	Magnitude Parameters H	G	Mean Diameter	Inclination i	Long. of Asc. Node Ω	Argument of Perihelion ω	Semi-major Axis a	Daily Motion n	Eccentricity e	Mean Anomaly M
				km	°	°	°	au	°/d		°
(2)	Pallas	4·12	0·15	502	34·924	172·895	310·910	2·7702	0·21377	0·2305	168·799
(3)	Juno	5·18	0·15	250	12·986	169·830	247·860	2·6707	0·22583	0·2559	172·455
(4)	Vesta	3·25	0·15	525	7·144	103·703	151·584	2·3614	0·27161	0·0901	332·451
(5)	Astraea	6·99	0·15	114	5·359	141·453	359·318	2·5768	0·23828	0·1874	86·247
(6)	Hebe	5·61	0·15	193	14·735	138·614	239·670	2·4259	0·26086	0·2023	300·413
(7)	Iris	5·64	0·15	214	5·520	259·498	145·529	2·3863	0·26737	0·2300	8·235
(8)	Flora	6·61	0·15	140	5·890	110·845	285·422	2·2010	0·30183	0·1565	138·542
(9)	Metis	6·34	0·15	201	5·578	68·870	5·855	2·3864	0·26736	0·1226	145·778
(10)	Hygiea	5·64	0·15	434	3·832	283·128	312·705	3·1436	0·17683	0·1096	181·279
(11)	Parthenope	6·73	0·15	153	4·633	125·474	196·372	2·4543	0·25633	0·0998	122·460
(12)	Victoria	7·30	0·15	124	8·374	235·353	69·539	2·3339	0·27642	0·2200	21·647
(13)	Egeria	6·92	0·15	201	16·526	43·188	79·094	2·5771	0·23824	0·0850	353·288
(14)	Irene	6·55	0·15	148	9·130	86·011	98·225	2·5880	0·23673	0·1627	325·608
(15)	Eunomia	5·41	0·15	248	11·761	292·880	98·634	2·6432	0·22935	0·1877	67·713
(16)	Psyche	6·21	0·15	226	3·097	150·019	229·640	2·9221	0·19731	0·1341	1·282
(17)	Thetis	7·94	0·15	83	5·592	125·523	135·782	2·4712	0·25371	0·1320	142·119
(18)	Melpomene	6·35	0·15	162	10·131	150·334	228·057	2·2953	0·28344	0·2181	170·571
(19)	Fortuna	7·50	0·15	211	1·573	211·031	182·648	2·4429	0·25813	0·1579	44·725
(20)	Massalia	6·54	0·15	141	0·709	205·978	257·337	2·4088	0·26364	0·1439	337·170
(21)	Lutetia	7·51	0·15	97	3·065	80·837	249·978	2·4338	0·25958	0·1648	194·850
(22)	Kalliope	6·81	0·15	166	13·702	65·971	358·120	2·9101	0·19854	0·0989	271·066
(23)	Thalia	7·17	0·15	107	10·109	66·491	61·613	2·6290	0·23122	0·2311	123·982
(24)	Themis	7·25	0·15	183	0·737	36·389	109·035	3·1427	0·17691	0·1153	21·457
(25)	Phocaea	7·88	0·15	80	21·608	214·089	90·199	2·4000	0·26508	0·2541	36·207
(26)	Proserpina	7·56	0·15	90	3·555	45·705	195·729	2·6564	0·22765	0·0885	244·351
(27)	Euterpe	7·08	0·15	106	1·583	94·767	356·519	2·3475	0·27402	0·1715	218·186
(28)	Bellona	7·26	0·15	108	9·423	144·152	343·420	2·7771	0·21297	0·1490	22·900
(29)	Amphitrite	5·99	0·15	204	6·078	356·256	61·882	2·5539	0·24149	0·0735	96·828
(30)	Urania	7·59	0·15	95	2·094	307·397	87·137	2·3660	0·27082	0·1268	265·410
(31)	Euphrosyne	6·87	0·15	273	26·316	30·801	61·927	3·1611	0·17537	0·2160	112·873
(32)	Pomona	7·79	0·15	82	5·522	220·361	338·069	2·5868	0·23690	0·0816	194·418
(37)	Fides	7·39	0·15	107	3·068	7·242	62·263	2·6426	0·22943	0·1748	127·034
(39)	Laetitia	5·97	0·15	164	10·370	156·904	210·116	2·7699	0·21380	0·1124	51·120
(40)	Harmonia	6·55	0·15	111	4·256	94·156	269·471	2·2670	0·28876	0·0460	22·937
(41)	Daphne	7·64	0·15	190	15·722	177·727	46·710	2·7699	0·21380	0·2708	245·831
(42)	Isis	7·71	0·15	103	8·511	84·165	237·273	2·4424	0·25821	0·2219	51·565
(43)	Ariadne	7·97	0·15	63	3·471	264·746	16·110	2·2029	0·30145	0·1684	81·241
(44)	Nysa	6·75	0·15	83	3·712	131·486	344·121	2·4222	0·26145	0·1497	296·710
(45)	Eugenia	7·79	0·15	186	6·605	147·579	87·321	2·7200	0·21971	0·0828	162·576
(48)	Doris	7·14	0·15	212	6·558	183·431	251·220	3·1123	0·17951	0·0664	105·979
(51)	Nemausa	7·75	0·15	144	9·973	175·881	2·204	2·3655	0·27090	0·0659	332·437
(52)	Europa	6·66	0·15	315	7·481	128·581	343·005	3·0917	0·18131	0·1118	276·206
(54)	Alexandra	7·99	0·15	143	11·811	313·060	345·971	2·7144	0·22039	0·1973	143·004
(60)	Echo	8·65	0·15	60	3·600	191·527	270·810	2·3923	0·26636	0·1845	74·871
(63)	Ausonia	7·13	0·15	87	5·773	337·685	295·670	2·3949	0·26593	0·1282	4·871
(64)	Angelina	7·80	0·15	50	1·306	308·957	181·026	2·6814	0·22448	0·1264	170·058
(65)	Cybele	6·83	0·15	273	3·564	155·104	103·938	3·4093	0·15657	0·1274	241·485

HELIOCENTRIC OSCULATING ELEMENTS
FOR EPOCH 2025 MAY 5·0 TT, ECLIPTIC AND EQUINOX J2000·0

No.	Name	Magnitude Parameters H	G	Mean Diameter	Inclination i	Long. of Asc. Node Ω	Argument of Perihelion ω	Semi-major Axis a	Daily Motion n	Eccentricity e	Mean Anomaly M
				km	°	°	°	au	°/d		°
(67)	Asia	8·42	0·15	61	6·024	202·329	107·455	2·4235	0·26124	0·1850	133·353
(68)	Leto	6·90	0·15	125	7·961	44·049	304·843	2·7824	0·21236	0·1843	8·231
(69)	Hesperia	7·24	0·15	110	8·584	184·904	288·180	2·9783	0·19176	0·1693	4·389
(71)	Niobe	7·24	0·15	82	23·243	315·909	267·051	2·7546	0·21558	0·1770	18·050
(79)	Eurynome	7·78	0·15	63	4·613	206·503	201·414	2·4441	0·25794	0·1911	75·701
(80)	Sappho	8·07	0·15	66	8·677	218·641	139·640	2·2958	0·28334	0·1996	0·644
(85)	Io	7·96	0·15	177	11·960	203·043	122·894	2·6534	0·22804	0·1932	2·656
(87)	Sylvia	6·96	0·15	273	10·880	73·011	264·990	3·4796	0·15185	0·0942	65·472
(88)	Thisbe	7·30	0·15	212	5·226	276·325	36·938	2·7687	0·21393	0·1645	158·723
(89)	Julia	6·37	0·15	142	16·123	311·520	45·171	2·5513	0·24186	0·1839	310·022
(92)	Undina	6·77	0·15	124	9·923	101·394	236·770	3·1849	0·17341	0·1050	203·391
(94)	Aurora	7·74	0·15	169	7·971	2·537	60·513	3·1544	0·17592	0·0958	335·465
(97)	Klotho	7·84	0·15	85	11·776	159·591	268·401	2·6679	0·22618	0·2577	88·852
(103)	Hera	7·79	0·15	84	5·421	135·973	190·385	2·7045	0·22160	0·0802	121·302
(107)	Camilla	7·13	0·15	255	10·001	172·565	304·426	3·4891	0·15123	0·0658	301·590
(115)	Thyra	7·79	0·15	82	11·587	308·751	96·968	2·3803	0·26838	0·1924	247·639
(121)	Hermione	7·45	0·15	187	7·567	72·873	297·056	3·4562	0·15339	0·1249	197·269
(128)	Nemesis	7·71	0·15	184	6·247	76·159	302·834	2·7495	0·21618	0·1272	188·645
(129)	Antigone	7·01	0·15	125	12·269	135·654	110·573	2·8688	0·20284	0·2131	27·027
(135)	Hertha	8·37	0·15	77	2·303	343·435	340·335	2·4269	0·26069	0·2083	191·001
(185)	Eunike	7·66	0·15	161	23·251	153·736	223·977	2·7390	0·21743	0·1270	303·494
(192)	Nausikaa	7·21	0·15	90	6·796	343·082	30·587	2·4032	0·26456	0·2454	220·457
(194)	Prokne	7·87	0·15	151	18·508	159·241	163·271	2·6166	0·23287	0·2372	67·766
(196)	Philomela	6·73	0·15	145	7·263	72·298	203·941	3·1127	0·17948	0·0142	122·243
(216)	Kleopatra	7·11	0·15	122	13·119	215·318	179·775	2·7945	0·21098	0·2505	175·487
(230)	Athamantis	7·54	0·15	110	9·455	239·771	139·091	2·3826	0·26800	0·0612	254·033
(270)	Anahita	8·93	0·15	49	2·368	254·294	80·845	2·1991	0·30222	0·1503	106·512
(287)	Nephthys	8·31	0·15	60	10·034	142·233	122·870	2·3526	0·27314	0·0236	277·775
(324)	Bamberga	7·23	0·15	227	11·096	327·836	44·205	2·6821	0·22439	0·3406	223·971
(346)	Hermentaria	7·38	0·15	93	8·758	91·848	290·714	2·7946	0·21097	0·1029	144·766
(349)	Dembowska	6·05	0·15	156	8·249	32·196	344·518	2·9251	0·19701	0·0887	219·469
(354)	Eleonora	6·15	0·15	165	18·360	140·211	8·064	2·8004	0·21031	0·1118	74·417
(372)	Palma	7·40	0·15	192	23·781	327·216	115·373	3·1619	0·17530	0·2526	118·569
(387)	Aquitania	7·54	0·15	97	18·146	127·989	157·708	2·7375	0·21761	0·2380	218·704
(389)	Industria	7·99	0·15	74	8·123	282·023	267·850	2·6080	0·23401	0·0663	14·883
(409)	Aspasia	7·69	0·15	180	11·285	242·052	355·765	2·5748	0·23856	0·0732	301·180
(423)	Diotima	7·41	0·15	208	11·243	69·348	199·032	3·0663	0·18356	0·0341	105·403
(433)	Eros	10·41	0·15	15	10·828	304·272	178·923	1·4582	0·55975	0·2227	198·598
(451)	Patientia	6·82	0·15	250	15·206	88·996	337·104	3·0637	0·18380	0·0698	147·847
(471)	Papagena	6·33	0·15	132	15·019	83·771	315·878	2·8885	0·20077	0·2290	326·521
(511)	Davida	6·41	0·15	289	15·947	107·557	336·865	3·1650	0·17504	0·1898	0·083
(532)	Herculina	5·92	0·15	198	16·299	107·411	76·686	2·7704	0·21374	0·1800	93·724
(654)	Zelinda	8·64	0·15	116	18·098	278·325	214·578	2·2967	0·28316	0·2315	237·107
(702)	Alauda	7·50	0·15	192	20·603	289·713	352·866	3·1925	0·17278	0·0156	71·681
(704)	Interamnia	6·35	0·15	332	17·316	280·168	94·125	3·0558	0·18451	0·1554	147·277
( )											

BRIGHT MINOR PLANETS, 2025

NEXT OPPOSITION

	Name	Date			Mag.	Dec.
						° ′
(14)	Irene	2025	Jan.	3	9·3	+27 12
(79)	Eurynome	2025	Jan.	14	10·4	+13 03
(65)	**Cybele**	**2025**	**Jan.**	**14**	**11·9**	**+18 06**
(51)	Nemausa	2025	Jan.	14	10·3	+06 07
(387)	Aquitania	2025	Jan.	16	12·2	+15 27
(28)	Bellona	2025	Jan.	31	9·9	+13 48
(135)	Hertha	2025	Feb.	4	12·1	+17 38
(29)	Amphitrite	2025	Feb.	12	9·0	+18 31
(21)	Lutetia	2025	Feb.	15	11·2	+16 30
(409)	Aspasia	2025	Feb.	22	11·1	−07 02
(24)	Themis	2025	Feb.	26	10·6	+09 34
(704)	**Interamnia**	**2025**	**Feb.**	**27**	**11·1**	**−11 23**
(346)	Hermentaria	2025	Mar.	2	11·4	+18 17
(287)	Nephthys	2025	Mar.	3	11·1	+12 16
(92)	Undina	2025	Mar.	9	11·7	+15 57
(8)	**Flora**	**2025**	**Mar.**	**12**	**9·3**	**+10 59**
(97)	Klotho	2025	Mar.	15	11·3	+06 29
(48)	Doris	2025	Mar.	20	11·1	−00 39
(18)	Melpomene	2025	Mar.	24	10·3	+06 21
(60)	Echo	2025	Mar.	28	10·9	−03 42
(389)	Industria	2025	Apr.	10	11·1	−20 38
(121)	Hermione	2025	Apr.	10	12·8	−00 47
(128)	Nemesis	2025	Apr.	12	11·8	−01 46
(37)	Fides	2025	Apr.	17	11·2	−12 09
(216)	Kleopatra	2025	Apr.	20	12·1	−13 15
(324)	Bamberga	2025	Apr.	24	11·9	−26 19
(451)	Patientia	2025	Apr.	28	11·3	+02 08
(192)	Nausikaa	2025	Apr.	28	11·2	−22 24
(372)	Palma	2025	May	1	12·8	−44 19
(4)	**Vesta**	**2025**	**May**	**2**	**5·6**	**−04 19**
(31)	Euphrosyne	2025	May	4	11·8	−25 00
(9)	**Metis**	**2025**	**May**	**9**	**9·6**	**−14 24**
(349)	Dembowska	2025	May	12	10·2	−22 02
(3)	**Juno**	**2025**	**May**	**14**	**10·2**	**−02 38**
(354)	Eleonora	2025	May	20	10·4	+07 25
(5)	Astraea	2025	June	6	10·4	−14 53
(71)	Niobe	2025	June	14	10·5	−55 26
(23)	Thalia	2025	July	1	11·3	−31 17
(230)	Athamantis	2025	July	3	10·3	−12 00
(115)	Thyra	2025	July	13	10·6	−27 35
(30)	Urania	2025	Aug.	2	10·0	−17 33
(63)	Ausonia	2025	Aug.	2	9·7	−22 23
(129)	Antigone	2025	Aug.	5	10·0	−15 54
(532)	Herculina	2025	Aug.	6	10·1	−27 10
(2)	**Pallas**	**2025**	**Aug.**	**7**	**9·4**	**+14 43**
(89)	Julia	2025	Aug.	11	8·8	−11 27
(64)	Angelina	2025	Aug.	12	11·5	−14 27
(27)	Euterpe	2025	Aug.	13	10·1	−16 14
(6)	**Hebe**	**2025**	**Aug.**	**26**	**7·6**	**−17 12**
(185)	Eunike	2025	Aug.	31	10·5	−11 20
(22)	Kalliope	2025	Sept.	14	10·5	−22 02
(85)	Io	2025	Oct.	16	10·0	+09 06
(702)	Alauda	2025	Oct.	18	12·2	+36 43
(654)	Zelinda	2025	Oct.	27	11·7	+39 29
(433)	Eros	2025	Oct.	29	10·8	+47 11
(12)	Victoria	2025	Nov.	5	9·8	+18 53
(471)	Papagena	2025	Nov.	10	9·4	+02 03
(423)	Diotima	2025	Nov.	14	11·7	+13 35
(52)	**Europa**	**2025**	**Nov.**	**15**	**10·4**	**+07 50**
(68)	Leto	2025	Nov.	20	9·9	+22 57
(25)	Phocaea	2025	Nov.	22	11·3	+04 31
(16)	**Psyche**	**2025**	**Dec.**	**8**	**9·4**	**+18 02**
(32)	Pomona	2025	Dec.	8	11·1	+17 41
(43)	Ariadne	2025	Dec.	8	11·0	+23 36
(196)	Philomela	2025	Dec.	10	10·8	+24 05
(94)	Aurora	2025	Dec.	12	11·6	+34 56
(45)	Eugenia	2025	Dec.	14	11·6	+14 11
(80)	Sappho	2025	Dec.	17	10·5	+11 54
(87)	Sylvia	2025	Dec.	20	11·9	+27 28
(10)	**Hygiea**	**2025**	**Dec.**	**22**	**10·1**	**+24 37**
(107)	Camilla	2025	Dec.	22	11·9	+09 21
(42)	Isis	2025	Dec.	26	11·1	+25 45
(17)	Thetis	2025	Dec.	31	11·4	+19 16
(40)	Harmonia	2026	Jan.	2	9·4	+23 53
(194)	Prokne	2026	Jan.	8	12·2	+01 03
(44)	Nysa	2026	Jan.	23	8·8	+18 21
(39)	Laetitia	2026	Jan.	27	10·1	+10 48
(54)	Alexandra	2026	Feb.	4	12·0	+15 30
(41)	Daphne	2026	Feb.	10	10·5	−00 28
(67)	Asia	2026	Feb.	19	12·1	+04 20
(103)	Hera	2026	Feb.	20	11·5	+12 55
(511)	Davida	2026	Feb.	23	10·4	+26 14
(11)	Parthenope	2026	Feb.	26	10·1	+12 21
(7)	Iris	2026	Feb.	27	8·7	−00 11
(88)	Thisbe	2026	Mar.	6	11·4	−01 13
(270)	Anahita	2026	Mar.	11	11·9	+00 06
(19)	Fortuna	2026	Mar.	13	10·6	+01 34
(20)	Massalia	2026	Mar.	21	8·9	−00 54
(15)	Eunomia	2026	Mar.	25	9·7	−16 55
(26)	Proserpina	2026	Apr.	5	10·5	−03 19
(69)	Hesperia	2026	Apr.	12	10·9	−05 08
(13)	Egeria	2026	Apr.	19	10·0	−04 53

Daily ephemerides of minor planets printed in **bold** are given in this section

PALLAS, 2025
GEOCENTRIC POSITIONS FOR 0^h TERRESTRIAL TIME

Date	Astrometric R.A. (h m s)	Astrometric Dec. (° ′ ″)	Vis. Mag.	Ephemeris Transit (h m)
2025 June 9	21 06 48·3	+16 25 11	10·0	3 56·9
10	21 06 42·0	+16 29 16	10·0	3 52·8
11	21 06 34·6	+16 33 13	10·0	3 48·8
12	21 06 26·0	+16 37 01	9·9	3 44·7
13	21 06 16·3	+16 40 40	9·9	3 40·6
14	21 06 05·5	+16 44 11	9·9	3 36·5
15	21 05 53·5	+16 47 33	9·9	3 32·4
16	21 05 40·4	+16 50 46	9·9	3 28·2
17	21 05 26·2	+16 53 49	9·9	3 24·0
18	21 05 10·8	+16 56 42	9·9	3 19·8
19	21 04 54·3	+16 59 25	9·9	3 15·6
20	21 04 36·7	+17 01 58	9·8	3 11·4
21	21 04 18·0	+17 04 21	9·8	3 07·2
22	21 03 58·1	+17 06 32	9·8	3 02·9
23	21 03 37·1	+17 08 33	9·8	2 58·6
24	21 03 15·1	+17 10 23	9·8	2 54·3
25	21 02 51·9	+17 12 01	9·8	2 50·0
26	21 02 27·7	+17 13 27	9·8	2 45·7
27	21 02 02·4	+17 14 42	9·8	2 41·3
28	21 01 36·0	+17 15 44	9·7	2 36·9
29	21 01 08·6	+17 16 34	9·7	2 32·6
30	21 00 40·2	+17 17 12	9·7	2 28·1
July 1	21 00 10·8	+17 17 36	9·7	2 23·7
2	20 59 40·4	+17 17 48	9·7	2 19·3
3	20 59 09·0	+17 17 46	9·7	2 14·8
4	20 58 36·7	+17 17 32	9·7	2 10·4
5	20 58 03·5	+17 17 04	9·7	2 05·9
6	20 57 29·3	+17 16 22	9·6	2 01·4
7	20 56 54·3	+17 15 26	9·6	1 56·9
8	20 56 18·4	+17 14 17	9·6	1 52·3
9	20 55 41·7	+17 12 53	9·6	1 47·8
10	20 55 04·2	+17 11 15	9·6	1 43·3
11	20 54 25·8	+17 09 23	9·6	1 38·7
12	20 53 46·8	+17 07 17	9·6	1 34·1
13	20 53 06·9	+17 04 56	9·6	1 29·5
14	20 52 26·4	+17 02 20	9·6	1 24·9
15	20 51 45·2	+16 59 29	9·5	1 20·3
16	20 51 03·3	+16 56 24	9·5	1 15·7
17	20 50 20·9	+16 53 03	9·5	1 11·0
18	20 49 37·8	+16 49 28	9·5	1 06·4
19	20 48 54·2	+16 45 37	9·5	1 01·7
20	20 48 10·0	+16 41 31	9·5	0 57·1
21	20 47 25·4	+16 37 11	9·5	0 52·4
22	20 46 40·3	+16 32 34	9·5	0 47·7
23	20 45 54·8	+16 27 43	9·5	0 43·0
24	20 45 08·9	+16 22 36	9·4	0 38·3
25	20 44 22·7	+16 17 14	9·4	0 33·6
26	20 43 36·3	+16 11 37	9·4	0 28·9
27	20 42 49·5	+16 05 45	9·4	0 24·2
28	20 42 02·6	+15 59 39	9·4	0 19·5
29	20 41 15·5	+15 53 17	9·4	0 14·8
30	20 40 28·3	+15 46 40	9·4	0 10·1
31	20 39 41·0	+15 39 50	9·4	0 05·4
Aug. 1	20 38 53·7	+15 32 44	9·4	0 00·7
2	20 38 06·3	+15 25 25	9·4	23 51·2
3	20 37 19·1	+15 17 52	9·4	23 46·5
4	20 36 31·9	+15 10 05	9·4	23 41·8
5	20 35 44·8	+15 02 04	9·4	23 37·1
6	20 34 57·9	+14 53 50	9·4	23 32·4
Aug. 7	20 34 11·3	+14 45 23	9·4	23 27·7

Date	Astrometric R.A. (h m s)	Astrometric Dec. (° ′ ″)	Vis. Mag.	Ephemeris Transit (h m)
2025 Aug. 7	20 34 11·3	+14 45 23	9·4	23 27·7
8	20 33 24·9	+14 36 43	9·4	23 23·0
9	20 32 38·7	+14 27 51	9·4	23 18·3
10	20 31 52·9	+14 18 46	9·4	23 13·6
11	20 31 07·5	+14 09 30	9·4	23 09·0
12	20 30 22·4	+14 00 02	9·4	23 04·3
13	20 29 37·8	+13 50 22	9·4	22 59·6
14	20 28 53·7	+13 40 31	9·4	22 55·0
15	20 28 10·1	+13 30 30	9·4	22 50·3
16	20 27 27·1	+13 20 18	9·4	22 45·7
17	20 26 44·6	+13 09 56	9·4	22 41·1
18	20 26 02·8	+12 59 24	9·4	22 36·5
19	20 25 21·6	+12 48 43	9·4	22 31·9
20	20 24 41·1	+12 37 53	9·4	22 27·3
21	20 24 01·4	+12 26 54	9·4	22 22·7
22	20 23 22·4	+12 15 47	9·4	22 18·1
23	20 22 44·2	+12 04 32	9·4	22 13·6
24	20 22 06·9	+11 53 10	9·4	22 09·0
25	20 21 30·4	+11 41 41	9·4	22 04·5
26	20 20 54·8	+11 30 06	9·4	22 00·0
27	20 20 20·1	+11 18 24	9·4	21 55·5
28	20 19 46·4	+11 06 37	9·4	21 51·1
29	20 19 13·7	+10 54 44	9·5	21 46·6
30	20 18 41·9	+10 42 47	9·5	21 42·2
31	20 18 11·2	+10 30 45	9·5	21 37·7
Sept. 1	20 17 41·5	+10 18 40	9·5	21 33·3
2	20 17 12·9	+10 06 30	9·5	21 28·9
3	20 16 45·3	+ 9 54 18	9·5	21 24·6
4	20 16 18·9	+ 9 42 03	9·5	21 20·2
5	20 15 53·5	+ 9 29 46	9·5	21 15·9
6	20 15 29·3	+ 9 17 27	9·5	21 11·6
7	20 15 06·2	+ 9 05 06	9·5	21 07·3
8	20 14 44·3	+ 8 52 44	9·6	21 03·0
9	20 14 23·5	+ 8 40 22	9·6	20 58·7
10	20 14 03·8	+ 8 27 59	9·6	20 54·5
11	20 13 45·4	+ 8 15 35	9·6	20 50·3
12	20 13 28·1	+ 8 03 13	9·6	20 46·1
13	20 13 12·1	+ 7 50 50	9·6	20 41·9
14	20 12 57·2	+ 7 38 29	9·6	20 37·7
15	20 12 43·6	+ 7 26 09	9·6	20 33·6
16	20 12 31·1	+ 7 13 51	9·7	20 29·5
17	20 12 19·9	+ 7 01 34	9·7	20 25·4
18	20 12 10·0	+ 6 49 20	9·7	20 21·3
19	20 12 01·2	+ 6 37 08	9·7	20 17·2
20	20 11 53·8	+ 6 24 59	9·7	20 13·2
21	20 11 47·5	+ 6 12 54	9·7	20 09·2
22	20 11 42·5	+ 6 00 52	9·7	20 05·2
23	20 11 38·7	+ 5 48 53	9·7	20 01·2
24	20 11 36·2	+ 5 36 59	9·8	19 57·3
Sept. 25	20 11 35·0	+ 5 25 09	9·8	19 53·3
26	20 11 34·9	+ 5 13 24	9·8	19 49·4
27	20 11 36·1	+ 5 01 43	9·8	19 45·5
28	20 11 38·6	+ 4 50 08	9·8	19 41·6
29	20 11 42·3	+ 4 38 38	9·8	19 37·8
30	20 11 47·1	+ 4 27 13	9·8	19 34·0
Oct. 1	20 11 53·2	+ 4 15 54	9·9	19 30·1
2	20 12 00·6	+ 4 04 41	9·9	19 26·4
3	20 12 09·1	+ 3 53 34	9·9	19 22·6
4	20 12 18·8	+ 3 42 33	9·9	19 18·8
Oct. 5	20 12 29·7	+ 3 31 38	9·9	19 15·1

Second transit for Pallas 2025 August 1^d 23^h $56^m.0$

JUNO, 2025

GEOCENTRIC POSITIONS FOR 0^h TERRESTRIAL TIME

Date	Astrometric R.A.	Astrometric Dec.	Vis. Mag.	Ephemeris Transit
	h m s	° ′ ″		h m
2025 Mar. 16	16 08 07·9	− 7 55 59	10·9	4 33·4
17	16 08 15·8	− 7 51 19	10·9	4 29·6
18	16 08 22·4	− 7 46 35	10·9	4 25·8
19	16 08 27·8	− 7 41 46	10·8	4 22·0
20	16 08 31·9	− 7 36 54	10·8	4 18·1
21	16 08 34·8	− 7 31 57	10·8	4 14·2
Mar. 22	16 08 36·4	− 7 26 56	10·8	4 10·3
23	16 08 36·7	− 7 21 52	10·8	4 06·4
24	16 08 35·7	− 7 16 43	10·8	4 02·4
25	16 08 33·4	− 7 11 31	10·8	3 58·4
26	16 08 29·8	− 7 06 15	10·7	3 54·4
27	16 08 25·0	− 7 00 56	10·7	3 50·4
28	16 08 18·8	− 6 55 33	10·7	3 46·4
29	16 08 11·4	− 6 50 08	10·7	3 42·3
30	16 08 02·6	− 6 44 39	10·7	3 38·2
31	16 07 52·6	− 6 39 07	10·7	3 34·1
Apr. 1	16 07 41·2	− 6 33 33	10·7	3 30·0
2	16 07 28·6	− 6 27 56	10·7	3 25·9
3	16 07 14·7	− 6 22 17	10·6	3 21·7
4	16 06 59·5	− 6 16 35	10·6	3 17·5
5	16 06 43·0	− 6 10 51	10·6	3 13·3
6	16 06 25·4	− 6 05 06	10·6	3 09·1
7	16 06 06·4	− 5 59 19	10·6	3 04·8
8	16 05 46·2	− 5 53 30	10·6	3 00·6
9	16 05 24·8	− 5 47 39	10·6	2 56·3
10	16 05 02·2	− 5 41 48	10·5	2 52·0
11	16 04 38·4	− 5 35 55	10·5	2 47·6
12	16 04 13·4	− 5 30 02	10·5	2 43·3
13	16 03 47·2	− 5 24 07	10·5	2 38·9
14	16 03 19·9	− 5 18 13	10·5	2 34·5
15	16 02 51·4	− 5 12 18	10·5	2 30·1
16	16 02 21·8	− 5 06 23	10·5	2 25·7
17	16 01 51·1	− 5 00 28	10·4	2 21·3
18	16 01 19·3	− 4 54 34	10·4	2 16·8
19	16 00 46·4	− 4 48 40	10·4	2 12·3
20	16 00 12·5	− 4 42 46	10·4	2 07·8
21	15 59 37·6	− 4 36 54	10·4	2 03·3
22	15 59 01·6	− 4 31 03	10·4	1 58·8
23	15 58 24·7	− 4 25 14	10·4	1 54·2
24	15 57 46·9	− 4 19 26	10·3	1 49·7
25	15 57 08·1	− 4 13 40	10·3	1 45·1
26	15 56 28·4	− 4 07 57	10·3	1 40·5
27	15 55 47·9	− 4 02 15	10·3	1 35·9
28	15 55 06·5	− 3 56 37	10·3	1 31·3
29	15 54 24·4	− 3 51 02	10·3	1 26·7
30	15 53 41·5	− 3 45 30	10·3	1 22·0
May 1	15 52 58·0	− 3 40 01	10·3	1 17·4
2	15 52 13·7	− 3 34 36	10·2	1 12·7
3	15 51 28·8	− 3 29 16	10·2	1 08·0
4	15 50 43·3	− 3 23 59	10·2	1 03·3
5	15 49 57·3	− 3 18 47	10·2	0 58·6
6	15 49 10·8	− 3 13 40	10·2	0 53·9
7	15 48 23·8	− 3 08 37	10·2	0 49·2
8	15 47 36·4	− 3 03 40	10·2	0 44·5
9	15 46 48·5	− 2 58 48	10·2	0 39·8
10	15 46 00·4	− 2 54 01	10·2	0 35·0
11	15 45 11·9	− 2 49 20	10·2	0 30·3
12	15 44 23·2	− 2 44 46	10·2	0 25·6
13	15 43 34·2	− 2 40 17	10·2	0 20·8
May 14	15 42 45·1	− 2 35 55	10·2	0 16·1

Date	Astrometric R.A.	Astrometric Dec.	Vis. Mag.	Ephemeris Transit
	h m s	° ′ ″		h m
2025 May 14	15 42 45·1	− 2 35 55	10·2	0 16·1
15	15 41 55·8	− 2 31 39	10·2	0 11·3
16	15 41 06·4	− 2 27 30	10·2	0 06·6
17	15 40 17·0	− 2 23 28	10·2	0 01·8
18	15 39 27·5	− 2 19 33	10·2	23 52·3
19	15 38 38·1	− 2 15 45	10·2	23 47·6
20	15 37 48·8	− 2 12 04	10·2	23 42·8
21	15 36 59·6	− 2 08 31	10·2	23 38·1
22	15 36 10·5	− 2 05 06	10·2	23 33·3
23	15 35 21·7	− 2 01 49	10·2	23 28·6
24	15 34 33·1	− 1 58 39	10·2	23 23·9
25	15 33 44·7	− 1 55 38	10·2	23 19·1
26	15 32 56·8	− 1 52 45	10·2	23 14·4
27	15 32 09·1	− 1 50 00	10·2	23 09·7
28	15 31 22·0	− 1 47 24	10·3	23 05·0
29	15 30 35·2	− 1 44 57	10·3	23 00·3
30	15 29 49·0	− 1 42 38	10·3	22 55·6
31	15 29 03·3	− 1 40 28	10·3	22 50·9
June 1	15 28 18·2	− 1 38 26	10·3	22 46·3
2	15 27 33·7	− 1 36 34	10·3	22 41·6
3	15 26 49·8	− 1 34 50	10·3	22 37·0
4	15 26 06·7	− 1 33 15	10·3	22 32·3
5	15 25 24·2	− 1 31 49	10·4	22 27·7
6	15 24 42·5	− 1 30 32	10·4	22 23·1
7	15 24 01·5	− 1 29 24	10·4	22 18·5
8	15 23 21·4	− 1 28 24	10·4	22 13·9
9	15 22 42·1	− 1 27 33	10·4	22 09·3
10	15 22 03·6	− 1 26 51	10·4	22 04·8
11	15 21 26·1	− 1 26 18	10·4	22 00·2
12	15 20 49·4	− 1 25 54	10·5	21 55·7
13	15 20 13·6	− 1 25 38	10·5	21 51·2
14	15 19 38·8	− 1 25 31	10·5	21 46·7
15	15 19 04·9	− 1 25 32	10·5	21 42·2
16	15 18 32·1	− 1 25 42	10·5	21 37·8
17	15 18 00·2	− 1 26 00	10·5	21 33·3
18	15 17 29·4	− 1 26 27	10·5	21 28·9
19	15 16 59·6	− 1 27 02	10·6	21 24·5
20	15 16 30·8	− 1 27 46	10·6	21 20·1
21	15 16 03·1	− 1 28 37	10·6	21 15·7
22	15 15 36·5	− 1 29 37	10·6	21 11·4
23	15 15 11·0	− 1 30 45	10·6	21 07·0
24	15 14 46·6	− 1 32 01	10·6	21 02·7
25	15 14 23·4	− 1 33 25	10·6	20 58·4
26	15 14 01·3	− 1 34 56	10·7	20 54·1
27	15 13 40·3	− 1 36 35	10·7	20 49·9
28	15 13 20·5	− 1 38 22	10·7	20 45·6
29	15 13 01·8	− 1 40 16	10·7	20 41·4
30	15 12 44·3	− 1 42 17	10·7	20 37·2
July 1	15 12 28·0	− 1 44 26	10·7	20 33·0
2	15 12 12·9	− 1 46 41	10·7	20 28·8
3	15 11 59·0	− 1 49 04	10·8	20 24·7
4	15 11 46·2	− 1 51 33	10·8	20 20·6
5	15 11 34·6	− 1 54 09	10·8	20 16·5
6	15 11 24·2	− 1 56 51	10·8	20 12·4
7	15 11 14·9	− 1 59 39	10·8	20 08·3
8	15 11 06·9	− 2 02 34	10·8	20 04·3
9	15 11 00·0	− 2 05 35	10·8	20 00·2
10	15 10 54·3	− 2 08 42	10·8	19 56·2
11	15 10 49·7	− 2 11 55	10·9	19 52·2
July 12	15 10 46·3	− 2 15 13	10·9	19 48·2

Second transit for Juno 2025 May $17^d\ 23^h\ 57^m.1$

VESTA, 2025

GEOCENTRIC POSITIONS FOR 0^h TERRESTRIAL TIME

Date		Astrometric R.A.	Astrometric Dec.	Vis. Mag.	Ephemeris Transit
		h m s	° ′ ″		h m
2025 Mar.	4	15 08 59·3	− 7 27 56	6·8	4 21·7
	5	15 09 32·9	− 7 26 38	6·8	4 18·3
	6	15 10 05·0	− 7 25 14	6·8	4 14·9
	7	15 10 35·4	− 7 23 42	6·8	4 11·5
	8	15 11 04·1	− 7 22 04	6·8	4 08·0
	9	15 11 31·1	− 7 20 18	6·7	4 04·5
	10	15 11 56·4	− 7 18 26	6·7	4 01·0
	11	15 12 20·0	− 7 16 26	6·7	3 57·5
	12	15 12 41·8	− 7 14 20	6·7	3 53·9
	13	15 13 01·9	− 7 12 07	6·7	3 50·3
	14	15 13 20·2	− 7 09 48	6·6	3 46·7
	15	15 13 36·7	− 7 07 22	6·6	3 43·0
	16	15 13 51·3	− 7 04 50	6·6	3 39·3
	17	15 14 04·1	− 7 02 12	6·6	3 35·6
	18	15 14 15·0	− 6 59 27	6·5	3 31·8
	19	15 14 24·1	− 6 56 36	6·5	3 28·0
	20	15 14 31·3	− 6 53 40	6·5	3 24·2
	21	15 14 36·5	− 6 50 38	6·5	3 20·4
	22	15 14 39·8	− 6 47 30	6·5	3 16·5
Mar.	23	15 14 41·2	− 6 44 16	6·4	3 12·6
	24	15 14 40·7	− 6 40 58	6·4	3 08·6
	25	15 14 38·1	− 6 37 34	6·4	3 04·6
	26	15 14 33·6	− 6 34 06	6·4	3 00·6
	27	15 14 27·2	− 6 30 32	6·3	2 56·6
	28	15 14 18·8	− 6 26 55	6·3	2 52·5
	29	15 14 08·4	− 6 23 13	6·3	2 48·4
	30	15 13 56·0	− 6 19 27	6·3	2 44·3
	31	15 13 41·7	− 6 15 37	6·2	2 40·1
Apr.	1	15 13 25·5	− 6 11 45	6·2	2 35·9
	2	15 13 07·3	− 6 07 49	6·2	2 31·7
	3	15 12 47·2	− 6 03 50	6·2	2 27·4
	4	15 12 25·2	− 5 59 49	6·1	2 23·1
	5	15 12 01·4	− 5 55 46	6·1	2 18·8
	6	15 11 35·7	− 5 51 41	6·1	2 14·4
	7	15 11 08·2	− 5 47 34	6·1	2 10·0
	8	15 10 38·9	− 5 43 26	6·1	2 05·6
	9	15 10 07·9	− 5 39 18	6·0	2 01·1
	10	15 09 35·1	− 5 35 08	6·0	1 56·7
	11	15 09 00·6	− 5 30 59	6·0	1 52·2
	12	15 08 24·4	− 5 26 49	6·0	1 47·6
	13	15 07 46·6	− 5 22 40	5·9	1 43·1
	14	15 07 07·3	− 5 18 32	5·9	1 38·5
	15	15 06 26·4	− 5 14 25	5·9	1 33·9
	16	15 05 44·0	− 5 10 20	5·9	1 29·2
	17	15 05 00·1	− 5 06 16	5·8	1 24·6
	18	15 04 14·9	− 5 02 15	5·8	1 19·9
	19	15 03 28·3	− 4 58 16	5·8	1 15·2
	20	15 02 40·4	− 4 54 21	5·8	1 10·5
	21	15 01 51·3	− 4 50 29	5·8	1 05·7
	22	15 01 01·1	− 4 46 41	5·7	1 00·9
	23	15 00 09·7	− 4 42 57	5·7	0 56·2
	24	14 59 17·4	− 4 39 18	5·7	0 51·4
	25	14 58 24·1	− 4 35 44	5·7	0 46·5
	26	14 57 29·9	− 4 32 15	5·7	0 41·7
	27	14 56 34·9	− 4 28 53	5·7	0 36·9
	28	14 55 39·2	− 4 25 37	5·6	0 32·0
	29	14 54 42·9	− 4 22 28	5·6	0 27·1
	30	14 53 46·1	− 4 19 26	5·6	0 22·3
May	1	14 52 48·8	− 4 16 32	5·6	0 17·4
May	2	14 51 51·2	− 4 13 46	5·6	0 12·5

Date		Astrometric R.A.	Astrometric Dec.	Vis. Mag.	Ephemeris Transit
		h m s	° ′ ″		h m
2025 May	2	14 51 51·2	− 4 13 46	5·6	0 12·5
	3	14 50 53·3	− 4 11 08	5·6	0 07·6
	4	14 49 55·2	− 4 08 39	5·6	0 02·7
	5	14 48 57·0	− 4 06 20	5·6	23 52·9
	6	14 47 58·8	− 4 04 09	5·6	23 48·0
	7	14 47 00·7	− 4 02 08	5·6	23 43·1
	8	14 46 02·7	− 4 00 17	5·6	23 38·3
	9	14 45 05·0	− 3 58 36	5·6	23 33·4
	10	14 44 07·6	− 3 57 05	5·7	23 28·5
	11	14 43 10·6	− 3 55 45	5·7	23 23·6
	12	14 42 14·1	− 3 54 36	5·7	23 18·8
	13	14 41 18·1	− 3 53 38	5·7	23 13·9
	14	14 40 22·7	− 3 52 51	5·7	23 09·1
	15	14 39 28·1	− 3 52 15	5·7	23 04·3
	16	14 38 34·2	− 3 51 51	5·8	22 59·4
	17	14 37 41·2	− 3 51 38	5·8	22 54·6
	18	14 36 49·1	− 3 51 37	5·8	22 49·9
	19	14 35 57·9	− 3 51 48	5·8	22 45·1
	20	14 35 07·9	− 3 52 11	5·8	22 40·4
	21	14 34 18·9	− 3 52 45	5·8	22 35·6
	22	14 33 31·1	− 3 53 32	5·9	22 30·9
	23	14 32 44·5	− 3 54 31	5·9	22 26·2
	24	14 31 59·2	− 3 55 42	5·9	22 21·6
	25	14 31 15·3	− 3 57 05	5·9	22 17·0
	26	14 30 32·8	− 3 58 41	5·9	22 12·3
	27	14 29 51·7	− 4 00 29	6·0	22 07·7
	28	14 29 12·2	− 4 02 29	6·0	22 03·2
	29	14 28 34·2	− 4 04 41	6·0	21 58·6
	30	14 27 57·8	− 4 07 05	6·0	21 54·1
	31	14 27 23·0	− 4 09 42	6·0	21 49·7
June	1	14 26 49·9	− 4 12 30	6·1	21 45·2
	2	14 26 18·6	− 4 15 30	6·1	21 40·8
	3	14 25 48·9	− 4 18 42	6·1	21 36·4
	4	14 25 21·0	− 4 22 05	6·1	21 32·0
	5	14 24 54·8	− 4 25 40	6·2	21 27·7
	6	14 24 30·4	− 4 29 25	6·2	21 23·4
	7	14 24 07·9	− 4 33 22	6·2	21 19·1
	8	14 23 47·1	− 4 37 30	6·2	21 14·8
	9	14 23 28·2	− 4 41 48	6·2	21 10·6
	10	14 23 11·1	− 4 46 17	6·3	21 06·4
	11	14 22 55·8	− 4 50 56	6·3	21 02·3
	12	14 22 42·4	− 4 55 45	6·3	20 58·1
	13	14 22 30·8	− 5 00 44	6·3	20 54·0
	14	14 22 21·0	− 5 05 53	6·3	20 50·0
	15	14 22 13·1	− 5 11 12	6·4	20 45·9
	16	14 22 07·1	− 5 16 39	6·4	20 41·9
	17	14 22 02·9	− 5 22 16	6·4	20 38·0
June	18	14 22 00·5	− 5 28 02	6·4	20 34·0
	19	14 21 59·9	− 5 33 57	6·4	20 30·1
	20	14 22 01·2	− 5 40 00	6·5	20 26·2
	21	14 22 04·4	− 5 46 12	6·5	20 22·4
	22	14 22 09·3	− 5 52 32	6·5	20 18·5
	23	14 22 16·0	− 5 59 01	6·5	20 14·7
	24	14 22 24·6	− 6 05 37	6·5	20 11·0
	25	14 22 35·0	− 6 12 21	6·6	20 07·2
	26	14 22 47·1	− 6 19 12	6·6	20 03·5
	27	14 23 01·1	− 6 26 11	6·6	19 59·9
	28	14 23 16·8	− 6 33 17	6·6	19 56·2
	29	14 23 34·2	− 6 40 30	6·6	19 52·6
June	30	14 23 53·4	− 6 47 49	6·6	19 49·0

Second transit for Vesta 2025 May 4^d 23^h $57^m.8$

HEBE, 2025

GEOCENTRIC POSITIONS FOR 0^{h} TERRESTRIAL TIME

Date	Astrometric R.A.	Astrometric Dec.	Vis. Mag.	Ephemeris Transit
	h m s	° ′ ″		h m
2025 June 28	22 35 33·8	− 6 40 50	9·2	4 11·0
29	22 36 14·4	− 6 43 45	9·2	4 07·7
30	22 36 53·6	− 6 46 55	9·2	4 04·4
July 1	22 37 31·5	− 6 50 20	9·1	4 01·1
2	22 38 08·0	− 6 54 01	9·1	3 57·8
3	22 38 43·2	− 6 57 58	9·1	3 54·4
4	22 39 17·0	− 7 02 11	9·1	3 51·0
5	22 39 49·4	− 7 06 40	9·0	3 47·7
6	22 40 20·4	− 7 11 26	9·0	3 44·2
7	22 40 50·0	− 7 16 28	9·0	3 40·8
8	22 41 18·1	− 7 21 47	9·0	3 37·3
9	22 41 44·8	− 7 27 23	8·9	3 33·8
10	22 42 09·9	− 7 33 16	8·9	3 30·3
11	22 42 33·6	− 7 39 27	8·9	3 26·8
12	22 42 55·7	− 7 45 55	8·9	3 23·2
13	22 43 16·3	− 7 52 41	8·8	3 19·6
14	22 43 35·3	− 7 59 45	8·8	3 16·0
15	22 43 52·8	− 8 07 06	8·8	3 12·3
16	22 44 08·6	− 8 14 47	8·7	3 08·7
17	22 44 22·8	− 8 22 45	8·7	3 05·0
18	22 44 35·4	− 8 31 02	8·7	3 01·2
19	22 44 46·3	− 8 39 37	8·7	2 57·5
20	22 44 55·6	− 8 48 31	8·6	2 53·7
21	22 45 03·2	− 8 57 43	8·6	2 49·9
22	22 45 09·1	− 9 07 14	8·6	2 46·1
23	22 45 13·3	− 9 17 03	8·6	2 42·2
24	22 45 15·8	− 9 27 11	8·5	2 38·3
July 25	22 45 16·6	− 9 37 37	8·5	2 34·4
26	22 45 15·7	− 9 48 21	8·5	2 30·4
27	22 45 13·1	− 9 59 23	8·4	2 26·5
28	22 45 08·8	−10 10 43	8·4	2 22·5
29	22 45 02·8	−10 22 20	8·4	2 18·4
30	22 44 55·2	−10 34 15	8·3	2 14·4
31	22 44 45·9	−10 46 26	8·3	2 10·3
Aug. 1	22 44 34·9	−10 58 53	8·3	2 06·2
2	22 44 22·3	−11 11 37	8·3	2 02·0
3	22 44 08·0	−11 24 36	8·2	1 57·8
4	22 43 52·2	−11 37 51	8·2	1 53·7
5	22 43 34·7	−11 51 20	8·2	1 49·4
6	22 43 15·7	−12 05 04	8·1	1 45·2
7	22 42 55·2	−12 19 01	8·1	1 40·9
8	22 42 33·1	−12 33 11	8·1	1 36·6
9	22 42 09·6	−12 47 33	8·0	1 32·3
10	22 41 44·6	−13 02 08	8·0	1 27·9
11	22 41 18·2	−13 16 53	8·0	1 23·6
12	22 40 50·5	−13 31 49	8·0	1 19·2
13	22 40 21·3	−13 46 54	7·9	1 14·8
14	22 39 50·9	−14 02 08	7·9	1 10·3
15	22 39 19·2	−14 17 30	7·9	1 05·9
16	22 38 46·3	−14 33 00	7·8	1 01·4
17	22 38 12·2	−14 48 35	7·8	0 56·9
18	22 37 37·0	−15 04 16	7·8	0 52·4
19	22 37 00·8	−15 20 02	7·7	0 47·9
20	22 36 23·6	−15 35 50	7·7	0 43·3
21	22 35 45·6	−15 51 41	7·7	0 38·8
22	22 35 06·6	−16 07 34	7·7	0 34·2
23	22 34 27·0	−16 23 26	7·7	0 29·6
24	22 33 46·6	−16 39 18	7·6	0 25·0
25	22 33 05·7	−16 55 07	7·6	0 20·4
Aug. 26	22 32 24·2	−17 10 54	7·6	0 15·8

Date	Astrometric R.A.	Astrometric Dec.	Vis. Mag.	Ephemeris Transit
	h m s	° ′ ″		h m
2025 Aug. 26	22 32 24·2	−17 10 54	7·6	0 15·8
27	22 31 42·3	−17 26 36	7·6	0 11·1
28	22 31 00·1	−17 42 13	7·6	0 06·5
29	22 30 17·6	−17 57 44	7·6	0 01·9
30	22 29 34·9	−18 13 08	7·7	23 52·6
31	22 28 52·2	−18 28 24	7·7	23 48·0
Sept. 1	22 28 09·5	−18 43 30	7·7	23 43·3
2	22 27 26·9	−18 58 26	7·7	23 38·7
3	22 26 44·4	−19 13 11	7·7	23 34·1
4	22 26 02·3	−19 27 44	7·7	23 29·4
5	22 25 20·5	−19 42 05	7·8	23 24·8
6	22 24 39·1	−19 56 11	7·8	23 20·2
7	22 23 58·2	−20 10 04	7·8	23 15·6
8	22 23 18·0	−20 23 41	7·8	23 11·0
9	22 22 38·4	−20 37 02	7·9	23 06·5
10	22 21 59·6	−20 50 07	7·9	23 01·9
11	22 21 21·6	−21 02 54	7·9	22 57·4
12	22 20 44·5	−21 15 24	7·9	22 52·8
13	22 20 08·5	−21 27 35	7·9	22 48·3
14	22 19 33·5	−21 39 28	8·0	22 43·8
15	22 18 59·6	−21 51 01	8·0	22 39·4
16	22 18 26·9	−22 02 15	8·0	22 34·9
17	22 17 55·6	−22 13 08	8·0	22 30·5
18	22 17 25·5	−22 23 41	8·1	22 26·1
19	22 16 57·0	−22 33 52	8·1	22 21·7
20	22 16 29·9	−22 43 42	8·1	22 17·3
21	22 16 04·3	−22 53 11	8·1	22 13·0
22	22 15 40·4	−23 02 17	8·1	22 08·7
23	22 15 18·1	−23 11 02	8·2	22 04·4
24	22 14 57·6	−23 19 24	8·2	22 00·2
25	22 14 38·8	−23 27 24	8·2	21 56·0
26	22 14 21·8	−23 35 02	8·2	21 51·8
27	22 14 06·6	−23 42 17	8·3	21 47·6
28	22 13 53·4	−23 49 10	8·3	21 43·5
29	22 13 42·0	−23 55 41	8·3	21 39·4
30	22 13 32·6	−24 01 49	8·3	21 35·4
Oct. 1	22 13 25·2	−24 07 35	8·3	21 31·3
2	22 13 19·7	−24 13 00	8·4	21 27·3
3	22 13 16·2	−24 18 02	8·4	21 23·4
Oct. 4	22 13 14·8	−24 22 43	8·4	21 19·5
5	22 13 15·3	−24 27 02	8·4	21 15·6
6	22 13 17·9	−24 31 00	8·5	21 11·7
7	22 13 22·5	−24 34 36	8·5	21 07·9
8	22 13 29·1	−24 37 52	8·5	21 04·1
9	22 13 37·8	−24 40 48	8·5	21 00·3
10	22 13 48·4	−24 43 22	8·5	20 56·6
11	22 14 01·1	−24 45 37	8·6	20 52·9
12	22 14 15·8	−24 47 32	8·6	20 49·2
13	22 14 32·5	−24 49 06	8·6	20 45·6
14	22 14 51·3	−24 50 22	8·6	20 42·0
15	22 15 12·0	−24 51 18	8·6	20 38·5
16	22 15 34·7	−24 51 55	8·7	20 34·9
17	22 15 59·4	−24 52 12	8·7	20 31·4
18	22 16 26·1	−24 52 12	8·7	20 28·0
19	22 16 54·7	−24 51 53	8·7	20 24·6
20	22 17 25·3	−24 51 16	8·8	20 21·2
21	22 17 57·8	−24 50 21	8·8	20 17·8
22	22 18 32·2	−24 49 08	8·8	20 14·5
23	22 19 08·5	−24 47 38	8·8	20 11·1
Oct. 24	22 19 46·7	−24 45 51	8·8	20 07·9

Second transit for Hebe 2025 August $29^{d}\ 23^{h}\ 57^{m}.2$

GEOCENTRIC POSITIONS FOR 0^h TERRESTRIAL TIME

Date	Astrometric R.A.	Astrometric Dec.	Vis. Mag.	Ephemeris Transit	Date	Astrometric R.A.	Astrometric Dec.	Vis. Mag.	Ephemeris Transit
	h m s	° ′ ″		h m		h m s	° ′ ″		h m
2025 Jan. 12	12 08 52·1	+ 5 05 45	10·4	4 42·5	**2025 Mar. 12**	11 46 17·4	+11 01 01	9·3	0 27·9
13	12 09 17·7	+ 5 07 00	10·4	4 39·0	**13**	11 45 17·5	+11 08 45	9·3	0 23·0
14	12 09 41·7	+ 5 08 26	10·3	4 35·5	**14**	11 44 17·5	+11 16 21	9·3	0 18·1
15	12 10 04·1	+ 5 10 04	10·3	4 31·9	**15**	11 43 17·5	+11 23 50	9·4	0 13·2
16	12 10 24·9	+ 5 11 55	10·3	4 28·3	**16**	11 42 17·5	+11 31 11	9·4	0 08·2
17	12 10 44·0	+ 5 13 57	10·3	4 24·7	**17**	11 41 17·6	+11 38 23	9·4	0 03·3
18	12 11 01·5	+ 5 16 11	10·3	4 21·0	**18**	11 40 17·9	+11 45 26	9·4	23 53·5
19	12 11 17·2	+ 5 18 38	10·3	4 17·4	**19**	11 39 18·5	+11 52 20	9·4	23 48·6
20	12 11 31·3	+ 5 21 16	10·2	4 13·6	**20**	11 38 19·4	+11 59 03	9·4	23 43·7
21	12 11 43·6	+ 5 24 07	10·2	4 09·9	**21**	11 37 20·7	+12 05 37	9·5	23 38·8
22	12 11 54·2	+ 5 27 10	10·2	4 06·2	**22**	11 36 22·5	+12 12 00	9·5	23 33·9
23	12 12 03·0	+ 5 30 26	10·2	4 02·4	**23**	11 35 24·8	+12 18 11	9·5	23 29·0
24	12 12 10·0	+ 5 33 54	10·2	3 58·5	**24**	11 34 27·8	+12 24 11	9·5	23 24·1
25	12 12 15·2	+ 5 37 34	10·2	3 54·7	**25**	11 33 31·4	+12 30 00	9·6	23 19·3
26	12 12 18·7	+ 5 41 26	10·1	3 50·8	**26**	11 32 35·9	+12 35 36	9·6	23 14·5
Jan. 27	12 12 20·3	+ 5 45 30	10·1	3 46·9	**27**	11 31 41·1	+12 41 00	9·6	23 09·6
28	12 12 20·1	+ 5 49 47	10·1	3 43·0	**28**	11 30 47·3	+12 46 11	9·6	23 04·8
29	12 12 18·0	+ 5 54 15	10·1	3 39·0	**29**	11 29 54·4	+12 51 10	9·6	23 00·0
30	12 12 14·1	+ 5 58 55	10·1	3 35·0	**30**	11 29 02·5	+12 55 55	9·7	22 55·3
31	12 12 08·4	+ 6 03 48	10·0	3 31·0	**31**	11 28 11·8	+13 00 27	9·7	22 50·5
Feb. 1	12 12 00·8	+ 6 08 51	10·0	3 26·9	**Apr. 1**	11 27 22·2	+13 04 45	9·7	22 45·8
2	12 11 51·3	+ 6 14 07	10·0	3 22·8	**2**	11 26 33·7	+13 08 49	9·7	22 41·1
3	12 11 40·0	+ 6 19 33	10·0	3 18·7	**3**	11 25 46·6	+13 12 40	9·8	22 36·4
4	12 11 26·9	+ 6 25 11	10·0	3 14·5	**4**	11 25 00·7	+13 16 17	9·8	22 31·7
5	12 11 11·9	+ 6 31 00	10·0	3 10·4	**5**	11 24 16·2	+13 19 40	9·8	22 27·0
6	12 10 55·1	+ 6 36 59	9·9	3 06·1	**6**	11 23 33·0	+13 22 48	9·8	22 22·4
7	12 10 36·4	+ 6 43 08	9·9	3 01·9	**7**	11 22 51·3	+13 25 43	9·9	22 17·8
8	12 10 16·0	+ 6 49 28	9·9	2 57·6	**8**	11 22 11·0	+13 28 24	9·9	22 13·2
9	12 09 53·8	+ 6 55 58	9·9	2 53·3	**9**	11 21 32·2	+13 30 51	9·9	22 08·7
10	12 09 29·7	+ 7 02 37	9·9	2 49·0	**10**	11 20 54·9	+13 33 05	9·9	22 04·2
11	12 09 03·9	+ 7 09 25	9·8	2 44·6	**11**	11 20 19·1	+13 35 04	10·0	21 59·7
12	12 08 36·4	+ 7 16 23	9·8	2 40·2	**12**	11 19 44·9	+13 36 50	10·0	21 55·2
13	12 08 07·1	+ 7 23 29	9·8	2 35·8	**13**	11 19 12·3	+13 38 22	10·0	21 50·7
14	12 07 36·0	+ 7 30 43	9·8	2 31·4	**14**	11 18 41·2	+13 39 40	10·0	21 46·3
15	12 07 03·3	+ 7 38 05	9·8	2 26·9	**15**	11 18 11·8	+13 40 45	10·1	21 41·9
16	12 06 28·9	+ 7 45 35	9·7	2 22·4	**16**	11 17 44·0	+13 41 37	10·1	21 37·6
17	12 05 52·9	+ 7 53 12	9·7	2 17·9	**17**	11 17 17·8	+13 42 16	10·1	21 33·2
18	12 05 15·3	+ 8 00 56	9·7	2 13·3	**18**	11 16 53·2	+13 42 41	10·1	21 28·9
19	12 04 36·0	+ 8 08 46	9·7	2 08·7	**19**	11 16 30·4	+13 42 54	10·1	21 24·6
20	12 03 55·3	+ 8 16 42	9·7	2 04·1	**20**	11 16 09·1	+13 42 53	10·2	21 20·4
21	12 03 13·0	+ 8 24 43	9·6	1 59·5	**21**	11 15 49·6	+13 42 40	10·2	21 16·1
22	12 02 29·2	+ 8 32 48	9·6	1 54·8	**22**	11 15 31·7	+13 42 15	10·2	21 11·9
23	12 01 44·1	+ 8 40 59	9·6	1 50·1	**23**	11 15 15·4	+13 41 37	10·2	21 07·7
24	12 00 57·6	+ 8 49 12	9·6	1 45·4	**24**	11 15 00·9	+13 40 47	10·3	21 03·6
25	12 00 09·7	+ 8 57 29	9·6	1 40·7	**25**	11 14 48·0	+13 39 45	10·3	20 59·5
26	11 59 20·6	+ 9 05 49	9·5	1 36·0	**26**	11 14 36·8	+13 38 31	10·3	20 55·4
27	11 58 30·3	+ 9 14 10	9·5	1 31·2	**27**	11 14 27·3	+13 37 05	10·3	20 51·3
28	11 57 38·8	+ 9 22 33	9·5	1 26·4	**28**	11 14 19·4	+13 35 27	10·3	20 47·3
Mar. 1	11 56 46·3	+ 9 30 57	9·5	1 21·6	**29**	11 14 13·2	+13 33 38	10·4	20 43·3
2	11 55 52·7	+ 9 39 20	9·5	1 16·8	**30**	11 14 08·7	+13 31 38	10·4	20 39·3
3	11 54 58·2	+ 9 47 43	9·4	1 11·9	**May 1**	11 14 05·8	+13 29 27	10·4	20 35·3
4	11 54 02·8	+ 9 56 05	9·4	1 07·1	**May 2**	11 14 04·6	+13 27 04	10·4	20 31·4
5	11 53 06·6	+10 04 25	9·4	1 02·2	**3**	11 14 04·9	+13 24 31	10·4	20 27·5
6	11 52 09·7	+10 12 43	9·4	0 57·4	**4**	11 14 06·9	+13 21 48	10·5	20 23·6
7	11 51 12·2	+10 20 57	9·4	0 52·5	**5**	11 14 10·4	+13 18 54	10·5	20 19·8
8	11 50 14·1	+10 29 08	9·4	0 47·6	**6**	11 14 15·6	+13 15 51	10·5	20 15·9
9	11 49 15·5	+10 37 14	9·4	0 42·7	**7**	11 14 22·2	+13 12 37	10·5	20 12·1
10	11 48 16·4	+10 45 15	9·3	0 37·8	**8**	11 14 30·4	+13 09 14	10·5	20 08·4
11	11 47 17·0	+10 53 11	9·3	0 32·9	**9**	11 14 40·2	+13 05 41	10·6	20 04·6
Mar. 12	11 46 17·4	+11 01 01	9·3	0 27·9	**May 10**	11 14 51·4	+13 01 59	10·6	20 00·9

Second transit for Flora 2025 March 17^d 23^h $58^m.4$

METIS, 2025

GEOCENTRIC POSITIONS FOR 0^h TERRESTRIAL TIME

Date	Astrometric R.A.	Astrometric Dec.	Vis. Mag.	Ephemeris Transit	Date	Astrometric R.A.	Astrometric Dec.	Vis. Mag.	Ephemeris Transit
	h m s	° ′ ″		h m		h m s	° ′ ″		h m
2025 Mar. 11	15 38 14·0	−15 23 57	10·9	4 23·3	**2025 May 9**	15 07 59·5	−14 18 46	9·6	0 01·2
12	15 38 28·7	−15 24 47	10·9	4 19·7	**10**	15 06 58·0	−14 16 34	9·6	23 51·3
13	15 38 41·7	−15 25 31	10·8	4 15·9	**11**	15 05 56·7	−14 14 22	9·6	23 46·3
14	15 38 53·2	−15 26 11	10·8	4 12·2	**12**	15 04 55·4	−14 12 12	9·7	23 41·4
15	15 39 03·0	−15 26 47	10·8	4 08·4	**13**	15 03 54·4	−14 10 04	9·7	23 36·4
16	15 39 11·2	−15 27 17	10·8	4 04·6	**14**	15 02 53·7	−14 07 57	9·7	23 31·5
17	15 39 17·6	−15 27 43	10·8	4 00·8	**15**	15 01 53·2	−14 05 52	9·8	23 26·6
18	15 39 22·5	−15 28 05	10·8	3 56·9	**16**	15 00 53·2	−14 03 49	9·8	23 21·7
19	15 39 25·6	−15 28 21	10·7	3 53·0	**17**	14 59 53·7	−14 01 49	9·8	23 16·7
Mar. 20	15 39 27·0	−15 28 33	10·7	3 49·1	**18**	14 58 54·6	−13 59 51	9·8	23 11·8
21	15 39 26·7	−15 28 41	10·7	3 45·2	**19**	14 57 56·2	−13 57 56	9·9	23 07·0
22	15 39 24·7	−15 28 44	10·7	3 41·2	**20**	14 56 58·4	−13 56 04	9·9	23 02·1
23	15 39 20·9	−15 28 42	10·7	3 37·2	**21**	14 56 01·3	−13 54 15	9·9	22 57·2
24	15 39 15·4	−15 28 36	10·6	3 33·2	**22**	14 55 04·9	−13 52 30	9·9	22 52·4
25	15 39 08·2	−15 28 25	10·6	3 29·1	**23**	14 54 09·4	−13 50 49	10·0	22 47·5
26	15 38 59·2	−15 28 09	10·6	3 25·1	**24**	14 53 14·8	−13 49 11	10·0	22 42·7
27	15 38 48·4	−15 27 49	10·6	3 20·9	**25**	14 52 21·1	−13 47 37	10·0	22 37·9
28	15 38 35·9	−15 27 25	10·6	3 16·8	**26**	14 51 28·4	−13 46 08	10·1	22 33·1
29	15 38 21·6	−15 26 56	10·5	3 12·6	**27**	14 50 36·7	−13 44 44	10·1	22 28·3
30	15 38 05·5	−15 26 23	10·5	3 08·4	**28**	14 49 46·1	−13 43 24	10·1	22 23·6
31	15 37 47·7	−15 25 45	10·5	3 04·2	**29**	14 48 56·7	−13 42 09	10·1	22 18·8
Apr. 1	15 37 28·2	−15 25 03	10·5	2 59·9	**30**	14 48 08·4	−13 40 59	10·1	22 14·1
2	15 37 06·9	−15 24 17	10·5	2 55·7	**31**	14 47 21·4	−13 39 55	10·2	22 09·4
3	15 36 43·9	−15 23 26	10·4	2 51·3	**June 1**	14 46 35·7	−13 38 56	10·2	22 04·8
4	15 36 19·2	−15 22 32	10·4	2 47·0	**2**	14 45 51·2	−13 38 02	10·2	22 00·1
5	15 35 52·8	−15 21 33	10·4	2 42·6	**3**	14 45 08·1	−13 37 14	10·2	21 55·5
6	15 35 24·8	−15 20 31	10·4	2 38·2	**4**	14 44 26·4	−13 36 32	10·3	21 50·9
7	15 34 55·1	−15 19 24	10·4	2 33·8	**5**	14 43 46·0	−13 35 55	10·3	21 46·3
8	15 34 23·7	−15 18 14	10·3	2 29·3	**6**	14 43 07·1	−13 35 25	10·3	21 41·8
9	15 33 50·8	−15 17 00	10·3	2 24·9	**7**	14 42 29·6	−13 35 01	10·3	21 37·2
10	15 33 16·2	−15 15 42	10·3	2 20·3	**8**	14 41 53·6	−13 34 42	10·4	21 32·7
11	15 32 40·1	−15 14 20	10·3	2 15·8	**9**	14 41 19·1	−13 34 30	10·4	21 28·2
12	15 32 02·5	−15 12 55	10·3	2 11·3	**10**	14 40 46·0	−13 34 25	10·4	21 23·8
13	15 31 23·3	−15 11 26	10·2	2 06·7	**11**	14 40 14·5	−13 34 25	10·4	21 19·3
14	15 30 42·7	−15 09 54	10·2	2 02·1	**12**	14 39 44·6	−13 34 32	10·4	21 14·9
15	15 30 00·6	−15 08 18	10·2	1 57·4	**13**	14 39 16·1	−13 34 45	10·5	21 10·6
16	15 29 17·1	−15 06 39	10·2	1 52·8	**14**	14 38 49·2	−13 35 05	10·5	21 06·2
17	15 28 32·2	−15 04 57	10·1	1 48·1	**15**	14 38 23·9	−13 35 31	10·5	21 01·9
18	15 27 46·0	−15 03 12	10·1	1 43·4	**16**	14 38 00·2	−13 36 04	10·5	20 57·6
19	15 26 58·5	−15 01 24	10·1	1 38·7	**17**	14 37 38·0	−13 36 43	10·6	20 53·3
20	15 26 09·8	−14 59 32	10·1	1 33·9	**18**	14 37 17·4	−13 37 29	10·6	20 49·0
21	15 25 19·8	−14 57 38	10·1	1 29·2	**19**	14 36 58·4	−13 38 21	10·6	20 44·8
22	15 24 28·7	−14 55 42	10·0	1 24·4	**20**	14 36 41·0	−13 39 20	10·6	20 40·6
23	15 23 36·4	−14 53 43	10·0	1 19·6	**21**	14 36 25·2	−13 40 25	10·6	20 36·5
24	15 22 43·1	−14 51 41	10·0	1 14·8	**22**	14 36 10·9	−13 41 37	10·7	20 32·3
25	15 21 48·8	−14 49 38	10·0	1 10·0	**23**	14 35 58·3	−13 42 56	10·7	20 28·2
26	15 20 53·6	−14 47 32	9·9	1 05·1	**24**	14 35 47·3	−13 44 21	10·7	20 24·1
27	15 19 57·5	−14 45 24	9·9	1 00·2	**25**	14 35 37·9	−13 45 53	10·7	20 20·0
28	15 19 00·5	−14 43 15	9·9	0 55·4	**26**	14 35 30·1	−13 47 31	10·7	20 16·0
29	15 18 02·8	−14 41 05	9·9	0 50·5	**27**	14 35 23·8	−13 49 15	10·8	20 12·0
30	15 17 04·4	−14 38 53	9·8	0 45·6	**28**	14 35 19·2	−13 51 07	10·8	20 08·0
May 1	15 16 05·4	−14 36 40	9·8	0 40·7	**29**	14 35 16·1	−13 53 04	10·8	20 04·0
2	15 15 05·9	−14 34 27	9·8	0 35·8	**June 30**	14 35 14·7	−13 55 08	10·8	20 00·1
3	15 14 05·8	−14 32 12	9·8	0 30·8	**July 1**	14 35 14·7	−13 57 18	10·8	19 56·2
4	15 13 05·4	−14 29 58	9·7	0 25·9	**2**	14 35 16·4	−13 59 34	10·9	19 52·3
5	15 12 04·6	−14 27 43	9·7	0 21·0	**3**	14 35 19·5	−14 01 57	10·9	19 48·4
6	15 11 03·6	−14 25 28	9·7	0 16·0	**4**	14 35 24·2	−14 04 25	10·9	19 44·6
7	15 10 02·3	−14 23 14	9·7	0 11·1	**5**	14 35 30·4	−14 06 59	10·9	19 40·8
8	15 09 00·9	−14 21 00	9·6	0 06·1	**6**	14 35 38·1	−14 09 39	10·9	19 37·0
May 9	15 07 59·5	−14 18 46	9·6	0 01·2	**July 7**	14 35 47·3	−14 12 25	11·0	19 33·3

Second transit for Metis 2025 May $9^d\ 23^h\ 56^m.2$

HYGIEA, 2025

GEOCENTRIC POSITIONS FOR 0^{h} TERRESTRIAL TIME

Date	Astrometric R.A.	Astrometric Dec.	Vis. Mag.	Ephemeris Transit	Date	Astrometric R.A.	Astrometric Dec.	Vis. Mag.	Ephemeris Transit
	h m s	° ′ ″		h m		h m s	° ′ ″		h m
2025 Oct. 24	6 31 02·8	+24 54 08	11·3	4 21·3	**2025 Dec. 22**	6 02 16·2	+24 37 46	10·1	0 00·7
25	6 31 09·7	+24 53 52	11·3	4 17·5	**23**	6 01 22·6	+24 36 59	10·1	23 51·0
26	6 31 15·2	+24 53 36	11·3	4 13·7	**24**	6 00 28·9	+24 36 10	10·1	23 46·2
27	6 31 19·3	+24 53 21	11·3	4 09·8	**25**	5 59 35·4	+24 35 20	10·2	23 41·4
28	6 31 22·2	+24 53 06	11·2	4 05·9	**26**	5 58 41·9	+24 34 29	10·2	23 36·6
Oct. 29	6 31 23·6	+24 52 52	11·2	4 02·0	**27**	5 57 48·7	+24 33 35	10·2	23 31·8
30	6 31 23·8	+24 52 39	11·2	3 58·1	**28**	5 56 55·7	+24 32 40	10·3	23 27·0
31	6 31 22·5	+24 52 26	11·2	3 54·1	**29**	5 56 03·0	+24 31 43	10·3	23 22·2
Nov. 1	6 31 19·9	+24 52 14	11·2	3 50·2	**30**	5 55 10·7	+24 30 45	10·3	23 17·4
2	6 31 16·0	+24 52 03	11·2	3 46·1	**31**	5 54 18·7	+24 29 46	10·3	23 12·6
3	6 31 10·6	+24 51 51	11·1	3 42·1	**2026 Jan. 1**	5 53 27·2	+24 28 45	10·4	23 07·8
4	6 31 03·9	+24 51 41	11·1	3 38·1	**2**	5 52 36·2	+24 27 42	10·4	23 03·0
5	6 30 55·8	+24 51 31	11·1	3 34·0	**3**	5 51 45·8	+24 26 39	10·4	22 58·3
6	6 30 46·4	+24 51 21	11·1	3 29·9	**4**	5 50 55·9	+24 25 34	10·4	22 53·5
7	6 30 35·5	+24 51 12	11·1	3 25·8	**5**	5 50 06·7	+24 24 28	10·4	22 48·8
8	6 30 23·3	+24 51 03	11·1	3 21·7	**6**	5 49 18·1	+24 23 20	10·5	22 44·1
9	6 30 09·7	+24 50 55	11·0	3 17·5	**7**	5 48 30·2	+24 22 12	10·5	22 39·4
10	6 29 54·7	+24 50 47	11·0	3 13·3	**8**	5 47 43·2	+24 21 03	10·5	22 34·7
11	6 29 38·3	+24 50 39	11·0	3 09·1	**9**	5 46 56·9	+24 19 53	10·5	22 30·0
12	6 29 20·6	+24 50 32	11·0	3 04·9	**10**	5 46 11·4	+24 18 42	10·5	22 25·3
13	6 29 01·4	+24 50 24	11·0	3 00·6	**11**	5 45 26·9	+24 17 31	10·6	22 20·6
14	6 28 40·9	+24 50 17	11·0	2 56·4	**12**	5 44 43·3	+24 16 19	10·6	22 16·0
15	6 28 19·1	+24 50 10	10·9	2 52·1	**13**	5 44 00·6	+24 15 06	10·6	22 11·4
16	6 27 55·8	+24 50 03	10·9	2 47·8	**14**	5 43 19·0	+24 13 53	10·6	22 06·8
17	6 27 31·2	+24 49 57	10·9	2 43·4	**15**	5 42 38·3	+24 12 40	10·6	22 02·2
18	6 27 05·3	+24 49 50	10·9	2 39·0	**16**	5 41 58·8	+24 11 27	10·7	21 57·6
19	6 26 38·1	+24 49 43	10·9	2 34·7	**17**	5 41 20·3	+24 10 13	10·7	21 53·1
20	6 26 09·5	+24 49 35	10·8	2 30·3	**18**	5 40 43·0	+24 09 00	10·7	21 48·5
21	6 25 39·7	+24 49 28	10·8	2 25·8	**19**	5 40 06·9	+24 07 46	10·7	21 44·0
22	6 25 08·6	+24 49 20	10·8	2 21·4	**20**	5 39 31·9	+24 06 32	10·7	21 39·5
23	6 24 36·2	+24 49 12	10·8	2 16·9	**21**	5 38 58·2	+24 05 19	10·7	21 35·1
24	6 24 02·7	+24 49 04	10·8	2 12·4	**22**	5 38 25·7	+24 04 06	10·8	21 30·6
25	6 23 27·9	+24 48 55	10·8	2 07·9	**23**	5 37 54·5	+24 02 53	10·8	21 26·2
26	6 22 51·9	+24 48 45	10·7	2 03·4	**24**	5 37 24·6	+24 01 41	10·8	21 21·8
27	6 22 14·8	+24 48 35	10·7	1 58·8	**25**	5 36 56·0	+24 00 29	10·8	21 17·4
28	6 21 36·6	+24 48 24	10·7	1 54·3	**26**	5 36 28·7	+23 59 18	10·8	21 13·0
29	6 20 57·3	+24 48 12	10·7	1 49·7	**27**	5 36 02·8	+23 58 07	10·9	21 08·7
30	6 20 16·9	+24 48 00	10·7	1 45·1	**28**	5 35 38·2	+23 56 57	10·9	21 04·4
Dec. 1	6 19 35·5	+24 47 46	10·6	1 40·5	**29**	5 35 14·9	+23 55 48	10·9	21 00·1
2	6 18 53·0	+24 47 32	10·6	1 35·8	**30**	5 34 53·1	+23 54 40	10·9	20 55·8
3	6 18 09·7	+24 47 16	10·6	1 31·2	**31**	5 34 32·6	+23 53 32	10·9	20 51·5
4	6 17 25·4	+24 46 59	10·6	1 26·5	**Feb. 1**	5 34 13·5	+23 52 26	10·9	20 47·3
5	6 16 40·2	+24 46 41	10·5	1 21·8	**2**	5 33 55·7	+23 51 20	10·9	20 43·1
6	6 15 54·1	+24 46 22	10·5	1 17·1	**3**	5 33 39·4	+23 50 16	11·0	20 38·9
7	6 15 07·3	+24 46 02	10·5	1 12·4	**4**	5 33 24·5	+23 49 12	11·0	20 34·8
8	6 14 19·6	+24 45 40	10·5	1 07·7	**5**	5 33 11·0	+23 48 10	11·0	20 30·6
9	6 13 31·3	+24 45 16	10·5	1 03·0	**6**	5 32 58·9	+23 47 08	11·0	20 26·5
10	6 12 42·2	+24 44 52	10·4	0 58·2	**7**	5 32 48·2	+23 46 08	11·0	20 22·4
11	6 11 52·5	+24 44 25	10·4	0 53·5	**8**	5 32 38·9	+23 45 09	11·0	20 18·3
12	6 11 02·1	+24 43 57	10·4	0 48·7	**9**	5 32 31·0	+23 44 12	11·1	20 14·3
13	6 10 11·2	+24 43 28	10·4	0 43·9	**10**	5 32 24·5	+23 43 15	11·1	20 10·3
14	6 09 19·8	+24 42 57	10·3	0 39·1	**11**	5 32 19·4	+23 42 20	11·1	20 06·3
15	6 08 27·9	+24 42 24	10·3	0 34·4	**12**	5 32 15·8	+23 41 26	11·1	20 02·3
16	6 07 35·6	+24 41 49	10·3	0 29·6	**13**	5 32 13·5	+23 40 34	11·1	19 58·4
17	6 06 43·0	+24 41 13	10·3	0 24·8	**Feb. 14**	5 32 12·7	+23 39 43	11·1	19 54·4
18	6 05 50·0	+24 40 35	10·2	0 19·9	**15**	5 32 13·2	+23 38 53	11·1	19 50·5
19	6 04 56·8	+24 39 55	10·2	0 15·1	**16**	5 32 15·1	+23 38 04	11·2	19 46·6
20	6 04 03·4	+24 39 14	10·2	0 10·3	**17**	5 32 18·5	+23 37 17	11·2	19 42·8
21	6 03 09·9	+24 38 31	10·1	0 05·5	**18**	5 32 23·2	+23 36 31	11·2	19 39·0
Dec. 22	6 02 16·2	+24 37 46	10·1	0 00·7	**Feb. 19**	5 32 29·2	+23 35 46	11·2	19 35·1

Second transit for Hygiea 2025 December 22^{d} 23^{h} $55^{m}.9$

PSYCHE, 2025

GEOCENTRIC POSITIONS FOR 0^h TERRESTRIAL TIME

Date		Astrometric R.A.	Astrometric Dec.	Vis. Mag.	Ephemeris Transit
		h m s	° ′ ″		h m
2025 Oct.	**10**	5 26 29·1	+19 14 02	10·5	4 12·0
	11	5 26 48·3	+19 12 58	10·5	4 08·4
	12	5 27 05·8	+19 11 53	10·4	4 04·7
	13	5 27 21·7	+19 10 47	10·4	4 01·0
	14	5 27 36·0	+19 09 39	10·4	3 57·3
	15	5 27 48·5	+19 08 31	10·4	3 53·6
	16	5 27 59·4	+19 07 20	10·4	3 49·9
	17	5 28 08·5	+19 06 09	10·4	3 46·1
	18	5 28 16·0	+19 04 57	10·3	3 42·3
	19	5 28 21·7	+19 03 43	10·3	3 38·4
	20	5 28 25·6	+19 02 29	10·3	3 34·5
Oct.	**21**	5 28 27·9	+19 01 14	10·3	3 30·6
	22	5 28 28·3	+18 59 58	10·3	3 26·7
	23	5 28 27·1	+18 58 41	10·3	3 22·8
	24	5 28 24·0	+18 57 23	10·2	3 18·8
	25	5 28 19·2	+18 56 05	10·2	3 14·8
	26	5 28 12·7	+18 54 46	10·2	3 10·7
	27	5 28 04·4	+18 53 27	10·2	3 06·6
	28	5 27 54·3	+18 52 07	10·2	3 02·5
	29	5 27 42·5	+18 50 47	10·1	2 58·4
	30	5 27 29·0	+18 49 26	10·1	2 54·3
	31	5 27 13·7	+18 48 05	10·1	2 50·1
Nov.	**1**	5 26 56·8	+18 46 43	10·1	2 45·8
	2	5 26 38·1	+18 45 22	10·1	2 41·6
	3	5 26 17·7	+18 44 00	10·1	2 37·3
	4	5 25 55·7	+18 42 38	10·0	2 33·0
	5	5 25 32·0	+18 41 15	10·0	2 28·7
	6	5 25 06·6	+18 39 53	10·0	2 24·3
	7	5 24 39·6	+18 38 31	10·0	2 20·0
	8	5 24 11·0	+18 37 08	10·0	2 15·6
	9	5 23 40·8	+18 35 45	9·9	2 11·1
	10	5 23 09·1	+18 34 23	9·9	2 06·7
	11	5 22 35·8	+18 33 00	9·9	2 02·2
	12	5 22 01·0	+18 31 38	9·9	1 57·7
	13	5 21 24·7	+18 30 16	9·9	1 53·1
	14	5 20 47·0	+18 28 54	9·8	1 48·6
	15	5 20 07·9	+18 27 32	9·8	1 44·0
	16	5 19 27·4	+18 26 11	9·8	1 39·4
	17	5 18 45·6	+18 24 50	9·8	1 34·8
	18	5 18 02·5	+18 23 29	9·8	1 30·1
	19	5 17 18·1	+18 22 09	9·7	1 25·4
	20	5 16 32·6	+18 20 50	9·7	1 20·8
	21	5 15 46·0	+18 19 31	9·7	1 16·1
	22	5 14 58·3	+18 18 13	9·7	1 11·3
	23	5 14 09·6	+18 16 56	9·7	1 06·6
	24	5 13 20·0	+18 15 39	9·6	1 01·8
	25	5 12 29·5	+18 14 23	9·6	0 57·1
	26	5 11 38·1	+18 13 09	9·6	0 52·3
	27	5 10 46·0	+18 11 55	9·6	0 47·5
	28	5 09 53·2	+18 10 42	9·6	0 42·7
	29	5 08 59·8	+18 09 31	9·5	0 37·9
	30	5 08 05·8	+18 08 21	9·5	0 33·0
Dec.	**1**	5 07 11·4	+18 07 12	9·5	0 28·2
	2	5 06 16·5	+18 06 04	9·5	0 23·4
	3	5 05 21·3	+18 04 58	9·4	0 18·5
	4	5 04 25·8	+18 03 53	9·4	0 13·7
	5	5 03 30·1	+18 02 50	9·4	0 08·8
	6	5 02 34·2	+18 01 49	9·4	0 04·0
	7	5 01 38·3	+18 00 49	9·4	23 54·2
Dec.	**8**	5 00 42·3	+17 59 51	9·4	23 49·4

Date		Astrometric R.A.	Astrometric Dec.	Vis. Mag.	Ephemeris Transit
		h m s	° ′ ″		h m
2025 Dec.	**8**	5 00 42·3	+17 59 51	9·4	23 49·4
	9	4 59 46·5	+17 58 55	9·4	23 44·5
	10	4 58 50·7	+17 58 01	9·4	23 39·7
	11	4 57 55·1	+17 57 10	9·4	23 34·8
	12	4 56 59·8	+17 56 20	9·4	23 30·0
	13	4 56 04·8	+17 55 33	9·5	23 25·1
	14	4 55 10·3	+17 54 48	9·5	23 20·3
	15	4 54 16·2	+17 54 06	9·5	23 15·5
	16	4 53 22·7	+17 53 26	9·5	23 10·7
	17	4 52 29·7	+17 52 49	9·6	23 05·9
	18	4 51 37·5	+17 52 15	9·6	23 01·1
	19	4 50 46·0	+17 51 44	9·6	22 56·3
	20	4 49 55·3	+17 51 16	9·6	22 51·6
	21	4 49 05·4	+17 50 51	9·7	22 46·8
	22	4 48 16·5	+17 50 29	9·7	22 42·1
	23	4 47 28·6	+17 50 10	9·7	22 37·4
	24	4 46 41·7	+17 49 55	9·7	22 32·7
	25	4 45 55·9	+17 49 43	9·8	22 28·0
	26	4 45 11·3	+17 49 34	9·8	22 23·4
	27	4 44 27·9	+17 49 30	9·8	22 18·7
	28	4 43 45·7	+17 49 28	9·8	22 14·1
	29	4 43 04·7	+17 49 31	9·9	22 09·5
	30	4 42 25·1	+17 49 37	9·9	22 05·0
	31	4 41 46·9	+17 49 46	9·9	22 00·4
2026 Jan.	**1**	4 41 10·0	+17 50 00	9·9	21 55·9
	2	4 40 34·5	+17 50 17	10·0	21 51·4
	3	4 40 00·5	+17 50 38	10·0	21 46·9
	4	4 39 28·0	+17 51 03	10·0	21 42·5
	5	4 38 56·9	+17 51 32	10·0	21 38·1
	6	4 38 27·3	+17 52 05	10·1	21 33·7
	7	4 37 59·3	+17 52 41	10·1	21 29·3
	8	4 37 32·9	+17 53 22	10·1	21 24·9
	9	4 37 08·0	+17 54 06	10·1	21 20·6
	10	4 36 44·7	+17 54 55	10·2	21 16·3
	11	4 36 23·0	+17 55 47	10·2	21 12·1
	12	4 36 02·9	+17 56 43	10·2	21 07·8
	13	4 35 44·5	+17 57 43	10·2	21 03·6
	14	4 35 27·7	+17 58 47	10·2	20 59·4
	15	4 35 12·5	+17 59 55	10·3	20 55·3
	16	4 34 59·0	+18 01 07	10·3	20 51·1
	17	4 34 47·2	+18 02 23	10·3	20 47·0
	18	4 34 37·1	+18 03 42	10·3	20 43·0
	19	4 34 28·6	+18 05 05	10·4	20 38·9
	20	4 34 21·8	+18 06 32	10·4	20 34·9
	21	4 34 16·6	+18 08 03	10·4	20 30·9
	22	4 34 13·2	+18 09 37	10·4	20 26·9
Jan.	**23**	4 34 11·4	+18 11 14	10·4	20 23·0
	24	4 34 11·2	+18 12 55	10·5	20 19·1
	25	4 34 12·7	+18 14 40	10·5	20 15·2
	26	4 34 15·9	+18 16 28	10·5	20 11·3
	27	4 34 20·7	+18 18 19	10·5	20 07·5
	28	4 34 27·1	+18 20 13	10·5	20 03·7
	29	4 34 35·1	+18 22 10	10·6	19 59·9
	30	4 34 44·7	+18 24 10	10·6	19 56·2
	31	4 34 55·9	+18 26 13	10·6	19 52·4
Feb.	**1**	4 35 08·7	+18 28 19	10·6	19 48·8
	2	4 35 23·0	+18 30 28	10·6	19 45·1
	3	4 35 38·8	+18 32 39	10·7	19 41·4
	4	4 35 56·1	+18 34 53	10·7	19 37·8
Feb.	**5**	4 36 15·0	+18 37 09	10·7	19 34·2

Second transit for Psyche 2025 December 6^d 23^h $59^m.1$

GEOCENTRIC POSITIONS FOR 0^h TERRESTRIAL TIME

Date	Astrometric R.A. (h m s)	Astrometric Dec. (° ′ ″)	Vis. Mag.	Ephemeris Transit (h m)
2025 Sept. 17	3 53 48·3	+10 47 04	11·4	4 09·9
18	3 54 04·1	+10 45 02	11·4	4 06·2
19	3 54 18·5	+10 42 55	11·4	4 02·5
20	3 54 31·6	+10 40 44	11·4	3 58·8
21	3 54 43·4	+10 38 28	11·4	3 55·0
22	3 54 53·8	+10 36 09	11·3	3 51·3
23	3 55 02·8	+10 33 45	11·3	3 47·5
24	3 55 10·4	+10 31 17	11·3	3 43·7
25	3 55 16·6	+10 28 46	11·3	3 39·8
26	3 55 21·4	+10 26 11	11·3	3 36·0
27	3 55 24·8	+10 23 32	11·3	3 32·1
Sept. 28	3 55 26·8	+10 20 49	11·2	3 28·2
29	3 55 27·3	+10 18 02	11·2	3 24·3
30	3 55 26·5	+10 15 13	11·2	3 20·3
Oct. 1	3 55 24·2	+10 12 20	11·2	3 16·4
2	3 55 20·5	+10 09 23	11·2	3 12·4
3	3 55 15·3	+10 06 24	11·1	3 08·3
4	3 55 08·7	+10 03 21	11·1	3 04·3
5	3 55 00·7	+10 00 16	11·1	3 00·2
6	3 54 51·3	+ 9 57 08	11·1	2 56·1
7	3 54 40·4	+ 9 53 57	11·1	2 52·0
8	3 54 28·1	+ 9 50 43	11·0	2 47·9
9	3 54 14·3	+ 9 47 27	11·0	2 43·7
10	3 53 59·1	+ 9 44 09	11·0	2 39·5
11	3 53 42·6	+ 9 40 48	11·0	2 35·3
12	3 53 24·6	+ 9 37 25	11·0	2 31·1
13	3 53 05·1	+ 9 34 01	10·9	2 26·8
14	3 52 44·3	+ 9 30 34	10·9	2 22·6
15	3 52 22·1	+ 9 27 06	10·9	2 18·3
16	3 51 58·6	+ 9 23 37	10·9	2 13·9
17	3 51 33·6	+ 9 20 06	10·9	2 09·6
18	3 51 07·3	+ 9 16 34	10·8	2 05·2
19	3 50 39·7	+ 9 13 01	10·8	2 00·8
20	3 50 10·8	+ 9 09 28	10·8	1 56·4
21	3 49 40·6	+ 9 05 54	10·8	1 52·0
22	3 49 09·2	+ 9 02 19	10·8	1 47·5
23	3 48 36·5	+ 8 58 45	10·7	1 43·0
24	3 48 02·7	+ 8 55 11	10·7	1 38·5
25	3 47 27·6	+ 8 51 37	10·7	1 34·0
26	3 46 51·5	+ 8 48 04	10·7	1 29·5
27	3 46 14·3	+ 8 44 31	10·7	1 25·0
28	3 45 36·0	+ 8 41 00	10·6	1 20·4
29	3 44 56·6	+ 8 37 30	10·6	1 15·8
30	3 44 16·3	+ 8 34 01	10·6	1 11·2
31	3 43 35·1	+ 8 30 34	10·6	1 06·6
Nov. 1	3 42 53·0	+ 8 27 09	10·6	1 02·0
2	3 42 10·0	+ 8 23 46	10·5	0 57·3
3	3 41 26·3	+ 8 20 25	10·5	0 52·7
4	3 40 41·7	+ 8 17 07	10·5	0 48·0
5	3 39 56·5	+ 8 13 52	10·5	0 43·3
6	3 39 10·5	+ 8 10 40	10·5	0 38·6
7	3 38 24·0	+ 8 07 31	10·4	0 33·9
8	3 37 36·9	+ 8 04 26	10·4	0 29·2
9	3 36 49·3	+ 8 01 24	10·4	0 24·5
10	3 36 01·1	+ 7 58 26	10·4	0 19·7
11	3 35 12·6	+ 7 55 32	10·4	0 15·0
12	3 34 23·7	+ 7 52 43	10·4	0 10·3
13	3 33 34·5	+ 7 49 58	10·4	0 05·5
14	3 32 45·0	+ 7 47 18	10·4	0 00·8
Nov. 15	3 31 55·4	+ 7 44 43	10·4	23 51·2

Date	Astrometric R.A. (h m s)	Astrometric Dec. (° ′ ″)	Vis. Mag.	Ephemeris Transit (h m)
2025 Nov. 15	3 31 55·4	+ 7 44 43	10·4	23 51·2
16	3 31 05·5	+ 7 42 13	10·4	23 46·5
17	3 30 15·7	+ 7 39 49	10·4	23 41·7
18	3 29 25·7	+ 7 37 31	10·4	23 37·0
19	3 28 35·9	+ 7 35 19	10·4	23 32·2
20	3 27 46·1	+ 7 33 12	10·4	23 27·5
21	3 26 56·5	+ 7 31 13	10·4	23 22·7
22	3 26 07·1	+ 7 29 19	10·4	23 18·0
23	3 25 18·0	+ 7 27 33	10·4	23 13·2
24	3 24 29·2	+ 7 25 53	10·4	23 08·5
25	3 23 40·8	+ 7 24 20	10·4	23 03·8
26	3 22 52·8	+ 7 22 54	10·5	22 59·0
27	3 22 05·4	+ 7 21 36	10·5	22 54·3
28	3 21 18·5	+ 7 20 25	10·5	22 49·6
29	3 20 32·3	+ 7 19 22	10·5	22 44·9
30	3 19 46·7	+ 7 18 27	10·5	22 40·3
Dec. 1	3 19 01·8	+ 7 17 39	10·5	22 35·6
2	3 18 17·6	+ 7 16 59	10·6	22 31·0
3	3 17 34·3	+ 7 16 27	10·6	22 26·3
4	3 16 51·8	+ 7 16 03	10·6	22 21·7
5	3 16 10·2	+ 7 15 46	10·6	22 17·1
6	3 15 29·5	+ 7 15 38	10·6	22 12·5
7	3 14 49·8	+ 7 15 38	10·7	22 07·9
8	3 14 11·0	+ 7 15 47	10·7	22 03·4
9	3 13 33·4	+ 7 16 03	10·7	21 58·8
10	3 12 56·7	+ 7 16 27	10·7	21 54·3
11	3 12 21·2	+ 7 17 00	10·7	21 49·8
12	3 11 46·9	+ 7 17 41	10·7	21 45·3
13	3 11 13·7	+ 7 18 31	10·8	21 40·9
14	3 10 41·7	+ 7 19 28	10·8	21 36·4
15	3 10 11·0	+ 7 20 34	10·8	21 32·0
16	3 09 41·5	+ 7 21 48	10·8	21 27·6
17	3 09 13·3	+ 7 23 10	10·8	21 23·2
18	3 08 46·4	+ 7 24 41	10·9	21 18·8
19	3 08 20·9	+ 7 26 20	10·9	21 14·5
20	3 07 56·7	+ 7 28 06	10·9	21 10·2
21	3 07 33·9	+ 7 30 01	10·9	21 05·9
22	3 07 12·5	+ 7 32 04	10·9	21 01·6
23	3 06 52·5	+ 7 34 15	10·9	20 57·4
24	3 06 34·0	+ 7 36 34	11·0	20 53·2
25	3 06 16·8	+ 7 39 00	11·0	20 49·0
26	3 06 01·2	+ 7 41 34	11·0	20 44·8
27	3 05 47·0	+ 7 44 16	11·0	20 40·7
28	3 05 34·2	+ 7 47 05	11·0	20 36·6
29	3 05 22·9	+ 7 50 01	11·1	20 32·5
30	3 05 13·1	+ 7 53 04	11·1	20 28·4
31	3 05 04·8	+ 7 56 15	11·1	20 24·3
2026 Jan. 1	3 04 58·0	+ 7 59 33	11·1	20 20·3
2	3 04 52·6	+ 8 02 57	11·1	20 16·3
3	3 04 48·7	+ 8 06 28	11·1	20 12·3
4	3 04 46·2	+ 8 10 06	11·2	20 08·4
Jan. 5	3 04 45·2	+ 8 13 50	11·2	20 04·5
6	3 04 45·7	+ 8 17 40	11·2	20 00·6
7	3 04 47·6	+ 8 21 37	11·2	19 56·7
8	3 04 51·0	+ 8 25 40	11·2	19 52·8
9	3 04 55·9	+ 8 29 49	11·2	19 49·0
10	3 05 02·2	+ 8 34 03	11·2	19 45·2
11	3 05 09·9	+ 8 38 24	11·3	19 41·4
12	3 05 19·0	+ 8 42 50	11·3	19 37·6
Jan. 13	3 05 29·6	+ 8 47 22	11·3	19 33·9

Second transit for Europa 2025 November 14^d 23^h $56^m.0$

CYBELE, 2025

GEOCENTRIC POSITIONS FOR 0^h TERRESTRIAL TIME

Date	Astrometric R.A.	Astrometric Dec.	Vis. Mag.	Ephemeris Transit
	h m s	° ′ ″		h m
2024 Nov. 16	8 08 07·2	+17 01 58	13·0	4 26·6
17	8 08 11·2	+17 01 20	13·0	4 22·7
18	8 08 14·0	+17 00 45	13·0	4 18·8
19	8 08 15·8	+17 00 14	13·0	4 14·9
Nov. 20	8 08 16·4	+16 59 47	13·0	4 11·0
21	8 08 15·8	+16 59 24	13·0	4 07·1
22	8 08 14·1	+16 59 04	12·9	4 03·1
23	8 08 11·2	+16 58 48	12·9	3 59·1
24	8 08 07·2	+16 58 37	12·9	3 55·1
25	8 08 02·0	+16 58 29	12·9	3 51·1
26	8 07 55·7	+16 58 25	12·9	3 47·1
27	8 07 48·1	+16 58 26	12·9	3 43·0
28	8 07 39·5	+16 58 30	12·8	3 38·9
29	8 07 29·6	+16 58 38	12·8	3 34·8
30	8 07 18·5	+16 58 51	12·8	3 30·7
Dec. 1	8 07 06·3	+16 59 07	12·8	3 26·6
2	8 06 53·0	+16 59 28	12·8	3 22·4
3	8 06 38·4	+16 59 52	12·8	3 18·2
4	8 06 22·8	+17 00 21	12·7	3 14·0
5	8 06 05·9	+17 00 54	12·7	3 09·8
6	8 05 47·9	+17 01 31	12·7	3 05·6
7	8 05 28·8	+17 02 12	12·7	3 01·3
8	8 05 08·6	+17 02 57	12·7	2 57·1
9	8 04 47·2	+17 03 46	12·7	2 52·8
10	8 04 24·8	+17 04 39	12·6	2 48·5
11	8 04 01·3	+17 05 35	12·6	2 44·2
12	8 03 36·6	+17 06 36	12·6	2 39·8
13	8 03 11·0	+17 07 40	12·6	2 35·5
14	8 02 44·2	+17 08 48	12·6	2 31·1
15	8 02 16·5	+17 10 00	12·5	2 26·7
16	8 01 47·7	+17 11 16	12·5	2 22·3
17	8 01 17·9	+17 12 35	12·5	2 17·9
18	8 00 47·1	+17 13 58	12·5	2 13·4
19	8 00 15·4	+17 15 24	12·5	2 09·0
20	7 59 42·7	+17 16 54	12·4	2 04·5
21	7 59 09·1	+17 18 27	12·4	2 00·0
22	7 58 34·6	+17 20 03	12·4	1 55·5
23	7 57 59·1	+17 21 43	12·4	1 51·0
24	7 57 22·9	+17 23 25	12·4	1 46·4
25	7 56 45·8	+17 25 11	12·3	1 41·9
26	7 56 07·8	+17 27 00	12·3	1 37·3
27	7 55 29·1	+17 28 51	12·3	1 32·8
28	7 54 49·7	+17 30 46	12·3	1 28·2
29	7 54 09·6	+17 32 43	12·2	1 23·6
30	7 53 28·7	+17 34 42	12·2	1 19·0
31	7 52 47·2	+17 36 44	12·2	1 14·4
2025 Jan. 1	7 52 05·1	+17 38 49	12·2	1 09·7
2	7 51 22·5	+17 40 55	12·2	1 05·1
3	7 50 39·3	+17 43 04	12·1	1 00·4
4	7 49 55·6	+17 45 15	12·1	0 55·8
5	7 49 11·4	+17 47 27	12·1	0 51·1
6	7 48 26·9	+17 49 41	12·1	0 46·5
7	7 47 41·9	+17 51 57	12·0	0 41·8
8	7 46 56·6	+17 54 15	12·0	0 37·1
9	7 46 11·1	+17 56 33	12·0	0 32·4
10	7 45 25·2	+17 58 53	11·9	0 27·7
11	7 44 39·2	+18 01 14	11·9	0 23·0
12	7 43 53·0	+18 03 36	11·9	0 18·3
13	7 43 06·7	+18 05 59	11·9	0 13·6
Jan. 14	7 42 20·2	+18 08 23	11·9	0 08·9
2025 Jan. 14	7 42 20·2	+18 08 23	11·9	0 08·9
15	7 41 33·7	+18 10 47	11·9	0 04·2
16	7 40 47·2	+18 13 12	11·9	23 54·8
17	7 40 00·8	+18 15 37	11·9	23 50·1
18	7 39 14·4	+18 18 02	11·9	23 45·4
19	7 38 28·1	+18 20 28	11·9	23 40·7
20	7 37 41·9	+18 22 54	12·0	23 36·0
21	7 36 56·0	+18 25 20	12·0	23 31·4
22	7 36 10·3	+18 27 45	12·0	23 26·7
23	7 35 24·9	+18 30 11	12·0	23 22·0
24	7 34 39·8	+18 32 36	12·1	23 17·3
25	7 33 55·1	+18 35 01	12·1	23 12·7
26	7 33 10·8	+18 37 25	12·1	23 08·0
27	7 32 27·0	+18 39 48	12·1	23 03·3
28	7 31 43·6	+18 42 11	12·2	22 58·7
29	7 31 00·7	+18 44 33	12·2	22 54·1
30	7 30 18·5	+18 46 54	12·2	22 49·4
31	7 29 36·8	+18 49 15	12·2	22 44·8
Feb. 1	7 28 55·8	+18 51 34	12·2	22 40·2
2	7 28 15·5	+18 53 52	12·3	22 35·7
3	7 27 35·9	+18 56 08	12·3	22 31·1
4	7 26 57·0	+18 58 24	12·3	22 26·5
5	7 26 19·0	+19 00 38	12·3	22 22·0
6	7 25 41·7	+19 02 50	12·3	22 17·4
7	7 25 05·3	+19 05 01	12·4	22 12·9
8	7 24 29·8	+19 07 11	12·4	22 08·4
9	7 23 55·1	+19 09 19	12·4	22 03·9
10	7 23 21·4	+19 11 25	12·4	21 59·4
11	7 22 48·7	+19 13 30	12·4	21 55·0
12	7 22 16·9	+19 15 32	12·5	21 50·5
13	7 21 46·1	+19 17 33	12·5	21 46·1
14	7 21 16·3	+19 19 33	12·5	21 41·7
15	7 20 47·5	+19 21 30	12·5	21 37·3
16	7 20 19·8	+19 23 25	12·5	21 32·9
17	7 19 53·2	+19 25 19	12·5	21 28·6
18	7 19 27·6	+19 27 11	12·6	21 24·2
19	7 19 03·2	+19 29 00	12·6	21 19·9
20	7 18 39·8	+19 30 48	12·6	21 15·6
21	7 18 17·6	+19 32 33	12·6	21 11·3
22	7 17 56·6	+19 34 17	12·6	21 07·1
23	7 17 36·7	+19 35 58	12·6	21 02·8
24	7 17 17·9	+19 37 38	12·7	20 58·6
25	7 17 00·4	+19 39 15	12·7	20 54·4
26	7 16 44·0	+19 40 50	12·7	20 50·2
27	7 16 28·9	+19 42 23	12·7	20 46·0
28	7 16 14·9	+19 43 54	12·7	20 41·9
Mar. 1	7 16 02·2	+19 45 22	12·7	20 37·8
2	7 15 50·7	+19 46 48	12·8	20 33·7
3	7 15 40·4	+19 48 12	12·8	20 29·6
4	7 15 31·3	+19 49 34	12·8	20 25·5
5	7 15 23·5	+19 50 53	12·8	20 21·5
6	7 15 16·9	+19 52 11	12·8	20 17·4
7	7 15 11·5	+19 53 25	12·8	20 13·4
8	7 15 07·3	+19 54 38	12·8	20 09·5
9	7 15 04·4	+19 55 48	12·9	20 05·5
Mar. 10	7 15 02·7	+19 56 56	12·9	20 01·5
11	7 15 02·2	+19 58 01	12·9	19 57·6
12	7 15 02·9	+19 59 04	12·9	19 53·7
13	7 15 04·8	+20 00 05	12·9	19 49·8
Mar. 14	7 15 07·9	+20 01 03	12·9	19 46·0

Second transit for Cybele 2025 January $15^d\ 23^h\ 59^m.5$

INTERAMNIA, 2025
GEOCENTRIC POSITIONS FOR 0^h TERRESTRIAL TIME

Date	Astrometric R.A.	Astrometric Dec.	Vis. Mag.	Ephemeris Transit
	h m s	° ′ ″		h m
2024 Dec. 30	10 45 20·6	− 9 08 01	11·9	4 10·2
31	10 45 16·7	− 9 14 36	11·9	4 06·2
2025 Jan. 1	10 45 11·6	− 9 21 05	11·9	4 02·2
2	10 45 05·3	− 9 27 27	11·9	3 58·1
3	10 44 57·7	− 9 33 42	11·8	3 54·1
4	10 44 49·0	− 9 39 50	11·8	3 50·0
5	10 44 39·0	− 9 45 51	11·8	3 45·9
6	10 44 27·8	− 9 51 44	11·8	3 41·8
7	10 44 15·4	− 9 57 30	11·8	3 37·6
8	10 44 01·7	−10 03 08	11·8	3 33·5
9	10 43 46·9	−10 08 39	11·8	3 29·3
10	10 43 30·9	−10 14 01	11·7	3 25·1
11	10 43 13·6	−10 19 16	11·7	3 20·9
12	10 42 55·2	−10 24 22	11·7	3 16·6
13	10 42 35·6	−10 29 19	11·7	3 12·4
14	10 42 14·8	−10 34 08	11·7	3 08·1
15	10 41 52·8	−10 38 48	11·7	3 03·8
16	10 41 29·6	−10 43 20	11·7	2 59·5
17	10 41 05·3	−10 47 42	11·6	2 55·1
18	10 40 39·8	−10 51 55	11·6	2 50·8
19	10 40 13·2	−10 55 59	11·6	2 46·4
20	10 39 45·5	−10 59 53	11·6	2 42·0
21	10 39 16·6	−11 03 38	11·6	2 37·6
22	10 38 46·6	−11 07 12	11·6	2 33·2
23	10 38 15·5	−11 10 37	11·5	2 28·7
24	10 37 43·4	−11 13 52	11·5	2 24·3
25	10 37 10·2	−11 16 56	11·5	2 19·8
26	10 36 36·0	−11 19 50	11·5	2 15·3
27	10 36 00·8	−11 22 33	11·5	2 10·8
28	10 35 24·6	−11 25 06	11·5	2 06·2
29	10 34 47·4	−11 27 28	11·4	2 01·7
30	10 34 09·3	−11 29 40	11·4	1 57·1
31	10 33 30·3	−11 31 40	11·4	1 52·5
Feb. 1	10 32 50·4	−11 33 30	11·4	1 47·9
2	10 32 09·7	−11 35 08	11·4	1 43·3
3	10 31 28·1	−11 36 36	11·4	1 38·7
4	10 30 45·8	−11 37 52	11·4	1 34·1
5	10 30 02·8	−11 38 58	11·3	1 29·4
6	10 29 19·1	−11 39 52	11·3	1 24·8
7	10 28 34·7	−11 40 35	11·3	1 20·1
8	10 27 49·6	−11 41 07	11·3	1 15·4
9	10 27 04·0	−11 41 29	11·3	1 10·7
10	10 26 17·8	−11 41 39	11·3	1 06·0
11	10 25 31·1	−11 41 38	11·3	1 01·3
12	10 24 44·0	−11 41 26	11·2	0 56·6
13	10 23 56·4	−11 41 03	11·2	0 51·9
14	10 23 08·4	−11 40 30	11·2	0 47·2
15	10 22 20·0	−11 39 46	11·2	0 42·4
16	10 21 31·3	−11 38 51	11·2	0 37·7
17	10 20 42·4	−11 37 45	11·2	0 33·0
18	10 19 53·2	−11 36 29	11·2	0 28·2
19	10 19 03·9	−11 35 03	11·2	0 23·5
20	10 18 14·4	−11 33 26	11·2	0 18·7
21	10 17 24·8	−11 31 39	11·1	0 14·0
22	10 16 35·2	−11 29 42	11·1	0 09·2
23	10 15 45·5	−11 27 36	11·1	0 04·4
24	10 14 55·9	−11 25 20	11·1	23 54·9
25	10 14 06·4	−11 22 54	11·1	23 50·2
26	10 13 17·1	−11 20 19	11·1	23 45·4
Feb. 27	10 12 27·9	−11 17 36	11·1	23 40·7
2025 Feb. 27	10 12 27·9	−11 17 36	11·1	23 40·7
28	10 11 38·9	−11 14 43	11·1	23 36·0
Mar. 1	10 10 50·2	−11 11 42	11·1	23 31·2
2	10 10 01·9	−11 08 33	11·1	23 26·5
3	10 09 13·9	−11 05 16	11·1	23 21·8
4	10 08 26·3	−11 01 51	11·1	23 17·1
5	10 07 39·2	−10 58 19	11·2	23 12·4
6	10 06 52·6	−10 54 39	11·2	23 07·7
7	10 06 06·6	−10 50 53	11·2	23 03·0
8	10 05 21·1	−10 47 01	11·2	22 58·3
9	10 04 36·2	−10 43 02	11·2	22 53·6
10	10 03 52·0	−10 38 58	11·2	22 49·0
11	10 03 08·4	−10 34 48	11·2	22 44·4
12	10 02 25·6	−10 30 33	11·2	22 39·7
13	10 01 43·6	−10 26 13	11·2	22 35·1
14	10 01 02·3	−10 21 48	11·3	22 30·5
15	10 00 21·9	−10 17 19	11·3	22 25·9
16	9 59 42·3	−10 12 46	11·3	22 21·3
17	9 59 03·6	−10 08 09	11·3	22 16·8
18	9 58 25·8	−10 03 29	11·3	22 12·2
19	9 57 48·9	− 9 58 45	11·3	22 07·7
20	9 57 12·9	− 9 53 59	11·4	22 03·2
21	9 56 38·0	− 9 49 11	11·4	21 58·7
22	9 56 04·1	− 9 44 20	11·4	21 54·2
23	9 55 31·1	− 9 39 27	11·4	21 49·8
24	9 54 59·3	− 9 34 33	11·4	21 45·3
25	9 54 28·5	− 9 29 38	11·4	21 40·9
26	9 53 58·8	− 9 24 41	11·5	21 36·5
27	9 53 30·2	− 9 19 44	11·5	21 32·1
28	9 53 02·7	− 9 14 47	11·5	21 27·7
29	9 52 36·4	− 9 09 49	11·5	21 23·4
30	9 52 11·2	− 9 04 52	11·5	21 19·0
31	9 51 47·2	− 8 59 55	11·5	21 14·7
Apr. 1	9 51 24·4	− 8 54 59	11·6	21 10·4
2	9 51 02·8	− 8 50 05	11·6	21 06·2
3	9 50 42·4	− 8 45 11	11·6	21 01·9
4	9 50 23·2	− 8 40 20	11·6	20 57·7
5	9 50 05·2	− 8 35 30	11·6	20 53·5
6	9 49 48·5	− 8 30 42	11·6	20 49·3
7	9 49 32·9	− 8 25 57	11·7	20 45·1
8	9 49 18·6	− 8 21 14	11·7	20 41·0
9	9 49 05·5	− 8 16 35	11·7	20 36·8
10	9 48 53·6	− 8 11 58	11·7	20 32·7
11	9 48 42·9	− 8 07 24	11·7	20 28·6
12	9 48 33·5	− 8 02 54	11·7	20 24·6
13	9 48 25·2	− 7 58 27	11·8	20 20·5
14	9 48 18·2	− 7 54 04	11·8	20 16·5
15	9 48 12·4	− 7 49 45	11·8	20 12·5
16	9 48 07·8	− 7 45 29	11·8	20 08·5
17	9 48 04·4	− 7 41 18	11·8	20 04·5
18	9 48 02·2	− 7 37 12	11·8	20 00·5
Apr. 19	9 48 01·2	− 7 33 09	11·9	19 56·6
20	9 48 01·3	− 7 29 12	11·9	19 52·7
21	9 48 02·7	− 7 25 19	11·9	19 48·8
22	9 48 05·2	− 7 21 31	11·9	19 44·9
23	9 48 08·9	− 7 17 47	11·9	19 41·1
24	9 48 13·7	− 7 14 09	11·9	19 37·2
25	9 48 19·7	− 7 10 37	12·0	19 33·4
26	9 48 26·9	− 7 07 09	12·0	19 29·6
Apr. 27	9 48 35·2	− 7 03 47	12·0	19 25·8

Second transit for Interamnia 2025 February 23^d 23^h $59^m.7$

OSCULATING ELEMENTS FOR ECLIPTIC AND EQUINOX OF J2000·0

Designation/Name	Perihelion Time T	Perihelion Distance q	Eccen-tricity e	Period P	Arg. of Perihelion ω	Long. of Asc. Node Ω	Inclin-ation i	Osc. Epoch
		au		years	°	°	°	
136P/Mueller	Jan. 3·237 19	2·958 3548	0·293 0508	8·56	225·276 15	137·421 11	9·427 39	Jan. 5
367P/Catalina	Jan. 11·555 44	2·527 9600	0·280 0319	6·58	172·638 60	58·714 27	8·458 87	Jan. 5
105P/Singer Brewster	Jan. 22·760 74	2·052 0931	0·409 0660	6·47	46·333 43	192·397 45	9·167 54	Jan. 5
366P/Spacewatch	Jan. 30·894 24	2·279 9675	0·348 5704	6·55	152·960 07	70·760 54	8·856 58	Feb. 14
249P/LINEAR	Feb. 1·695 24	0·499 5032	0·819 3446	4·60	65·743 26	239·042 71	8·385 37	Feb. 14
236P/LINEAR	Feb. 3·812 33	1·828 0916	0·509 1431	7·19	119·418 52	245·569 10	16·355 77	Feb. 14
48P/Johnson	Mar. 2·645 46	2·006 5892	0·426 6043	6·55	216·775 61	110·063 95	12·201 79	Feb. 14
229P/Gibbs	Mar. 5·771 28	2·440 3591	0·377 9221	7·77	224·212 11	157·882 91	26·097 15	Feb. 14
302P/Lemmon-PANSTARRS	Mar. 9·418 88	3·288 6290	0·229 3997	8·82	208·630 04	121·714 33	6·035 65	Mar. 26
323P/SOHO	Mar. 14·076 14	0·039 7534	0·984 6136	4·15	353·126 55	324·279 96	5·326 79	Mar. 26
21P/Giacobini-Zinner	Mar. 25·238 39	1·008 9487	0·711 0009	6·52	172·933 29	195·331 63	32·051 00	Mar. 26
351P/Wiegert-PANSTARRS	Mar. 26·179 74	3·131 9486	0·294 7209	9·36	352·562 97	283·386 18	12·779 06	Mar. 26
49P/Arend-Rigaux	Apr. 10·616 56	1·431 3506	0·599 0776	6·75	332·933 40	118·791 67	19·059 06	Mar. 26
289P/Blanpain	Apr. 14·309 40	0·954 3388	0·686 4757	5·31	9·877 79	68·892 40	5·900 49	Mar. 26
456P/PANSTARRS	Apr. 15·022 38	2·802 2479	0·116 0790	5·64	233·021 70	243·147 70	16·965 70	May 5
341P/Gibbs	Apr. 22·707 74	2·506 4420	0·415 0634	8·87	312·362 38	29·952 71	3·796 33	May 5
250P/Larson	May 16·742 90	2·272 3288	0·398 4693	7·34	45·709 09	73·304 04	13·152 29	May 5
217P/LINEAR	May 24·944 36	1·226 3737	0·689 0647	7·83	247·035 75	125·371 62	12·865 47	May 5
164P/Christensen	May 27·412 52	1·675 1012	0·541 3276	6·98	325·952 52	88·268 94	16·277 37	June 14
65P/Gunn	June 16·480 77	2·926 2550	0·248 1413	7·68	213·673 20	61·976 99	9·175 15	June 14
60P/Tsuchinshan	July 20·607 69	1·645 7063	0·533 7789	6·63	216·911 20	267·397 53	3·579 84	July 24
306P/LINEAR	Aug. 1·647 39	1·272 9638	0·592 5557	5·52	0·910 27	341·340 22	8·301 78	July 24
43P/Wolf-Harrington	Aug. 4·553 83	2·442 6314	0·436 1307	9·02	223·803 48	243·989 63	9·329 74	July 24
195P/Hill	Aug. 5·745 71	4·440 5388	0·310 7942	16·35	250·617 49	243·095 49	36·415 85	July 24
294P/LINEAR	Aug. 11·191 88	1·273 0415	0·600 9326	5·70	237·585 69	309·600 52	17·742 98	July 24
340P/Boattini	Aug. 29·220 79	3·058 0621	0·279 8371	8·75	36·139 27	291·600 04	2·078 93	Sept. 2
441P/PANSTARRS	Sept. 9·330 62	3·327 8744	0·194 5565	8·40	178·858 79	143·591 05	2·574 84	Sept. 2
248P/Gibbs	Sept. 14·925 77	2·157 7427	0·639 4109	14·64	209·992 26	207·795 92	6·351 69	Sept. 2
171P/Spahr	Sept. 25·053 68	1·766 3904	0·502 9304	6·70	347·084 91	101·694 21	21·954 92	Oct. 12
414P/STEREO	Sept. 26·326 75	0·524 1566	0·812 2971	4·67	210·708 94	257·816 90	23·406 20	Oct. 12
198P/ODAS	Oct. 9·695 28	1·994 8507	0·445 0114	6·81	69·405 89	358·137 66	1·338 26	Oct. 12
47P/Ashbrook-Jackson	Oct. 28·002 99	2·807 4603	0·318 0507	8·35	357·917 82	356·880 90	13·039 25	Oct. 12
317P/WISE	Oct. 30·861 83	1·266 6207	0·572 0565	5·09	334·887 40	275·472 12	11·974 77	Oct. 12
172P/Yeung	Nov. 2·374 56	3·358 1894	0·205 0723	8·68	208·871 16	30·880 82	11·222 01	Nov. 21
40P/Väisälä	Nov. 12·016 75	1·823 7719	0·631 0901	10·99	52·057 29	128·900 48	11·640 35	Nov. 21
210P/Christensen	Nov. 22·727 57	0·524 4178	0·834 0760	5·62	345·950 59	93·796 26	10·287 31	Nov. 21
313P/Gibbs	Dec. 2·784 56	2·421 5850	0·234 3101	5·62	254·998 00	105·925 61	10·981 12	Nov. 21
240P/NEAT	Dec. 20·001 57	2·121 6141	0·450 5114	7·59	352·079 68	74·913 80	23·536 42	Dec. 31
235P/LINEAR	Dec. 22·684 08	1·978 0481	0·425 9458	6·40	352·194 62	200·172 19	9·811 17	Dec. 31
331P/Gibbs	Dec. 25·498 89	2·878 3897	0·041 4315	5·20	185·785 61	216·741 75	9·741 04	Dec. 31
261P/Larson	Dec. 27·423 62	2·014 2045	0·422 6502	6·52	67·366 71	291·050 52	6·073 41	Dec. 31

Up-to-date elements of the comets currently observable may be found at the web site of the IAU Minor Planet Center (see page x for web address).

CONTENTS OF SECTION H

Except for the table of ICRF radio sources, positions tabulated in Section H are referred to the mean equator and equinox of J2025.5 = 2025 July 2.375 = JD 246 0858.875. The positions of the ICRF radio sources, including Galactic abberation, provide a practical realization of the ICRS and are given for the epoch 2015.0 = JD 245 7023.5. When present, notes associated with a table are found on the table's last page.

Data for subsections previously included in Section H (i.e., selected UBVRI Landolt standards, RV standards, variable sources, star clusters, bright galaxies, radio flux calibrators, X-ray sources, quasars, pulsars, and gamma ray sources) will now be available at the following link: **https://aa.usno.navy.mil/publications/asa.**

Designation	BS=HR No.	WDS No.	Right Ascension	Declination	V	$B-V$	Spectral Type	Notes
			h m s	° ′ ″				
α And	15	00084+2905	00 09 42.7	+29 13 52	2.06	−0.11	B9p Hg Mn	dbn01
β Cas	21	00092+5909	00 10 33.3	+59 17 25	2.27	+0.34	F2 III	svb
γ Peg	39	00132+1511	00 14 33.1	+15 19 31	2.84	−0.23	B2 IV	svdb
β Hyi	98		00 27 03.3	-77 06 39	2.79	+0.62	G1 IV	
α Phe	99		00 27 32.4	-42 10 03	2.38	+1.09	K0 IIIb	bn02
α Cas	168	00405+5632	00 41 58.3	+56 40 36	2.23	+1.17	K0⁻ IIIa	dn03
β Cet	188		00 44 52.1	-17 50 49	2.01	+1.01	G9 III CH−1 CN 0.5 Ca 1	n04
γ Cas	264	00567+6043	00 58 16.2	+60 51 15	2.39	+2.10	B0 IVnpe (shell)	db
β And	337	01097+3537	01 11 10.1	+35 45 18	2.05	+1.57	M0⁺ IIIa	ad
δ Cas	403	01258+6014	01 27 30.4	+60 22 01	2.68	+0.13	A5 IV	sb
α Eri	472		01 38 39.6	-57 06 29	0.46	−0.16	B3 Vnp (shell)	n05
β Ari	553	01546+2049	01 56 03.3	+20 55 54	2.65	+0.13	A4 V	db
α Hyi	591		01 59 34.4	-61 26 47	2.84	+0.29	F0n III−IV	
γ And	603	02039+4220	02 05 28.6	+42 27 03	2.10	+2.20	K3⁻ IIb	dbm
α Ari	617		02 08 37.0	+23 34 54	2.01	+1.16	K2 IIIab	abn06
β Tri	622	02095+3459	02 11 04.2	+35 06 24	3.00	+0.14	A5 IV	db
θ Eri	897	02583-4018	02 59 13.7	-40 12 13	2.88	+0.13	A5 IV	pdbmn07
α Cet	911		03 03 36.9	+04 11 18	2.53	+1.64	M1.5 IIIa	n08
α UMi	424	02318+8916	03 05 11.7	+89 22 10	2.02	+2.60	F5−8 Ib	vdbn58
β Per	936	03082+4057	03 09 50.3	+41 03 07	2.12	−0.05	B8 V + F:	cvdb
α Per	1017	03243+4952	03 26 09.4	+49 56 59	1.79	+0.48	F5 Ib	asn09
η Tau	1165	03475+2406	03 49 00.3	+24 10 55	2.87	−0.09	B7 IIIn	d
ζ Per	1203	03541+3153	03 55 44.5	+31 57 26	2.85	+0.12	B1 Ib	sdb
ϵ Per	1220	03579+4001	03 59 34.4	+40 04 54	2.89	−0.18	B0.5 IV	sdb
γ Eri	1231	03580-1331	03 59 13.2	-13 26 15	2.94	+2.60	M0.5 IIIb Ca−1	d
α Tau	1457	04359+1631	04 37 23.2	+16 33 30	0.86	+1.54	K5⁺ III	sdbn10
ι Aur	1577		04 58 39.5	+33 12 14	2.69	+1.53	K3 II	a
β Eri	1666	05078-0505	05 09 06.3	-05 03 19	2.79	+0.13	A3 IVn	d
β Ori	1713	05145-0812	05 15 45.9	-08 10 27	0.13	−0.03	B8 Ia	vdasbn11
α Aur	1708	05167+4600	05 18 34.6	+46 01 16	0.08	+0.80	G6 III + G2 III	cdbn12
γ Ori	1790	05251+0621	05 26 30.0	+06 22 15	1.64	−0.22	B2 III	dbn13
β Tau	1791	05263+2836	05 27 54.4	+28 37 35	1.65	−0.13	B7 III	sdn14
β Lep	1829	05282-2046	05 29 20.3	-20 44 27	2.84	+0.82	G5 II	d
δ Ori	1852	05320-0018	05 33 18.6	-00 16 56	2.41	−0.39	O9.5 II	dvbm
α Lep	1865	05327-1749	05 33 51.4	-17 48 21	2.57	+2.20	F0 Ib	das
ι Ori	1899	05354-0555	05 36 40.9	-05 53 42	2.77	−0.24	O9 III	sb
ϵ Ori	1903	05362-0112	05 37 30.5	-01 11 15	1.69	−0.18	B0 Ia	asbn15
ζ Tau	1910		05 39 10.2	+21 09 21	3.03	−0.19	B2 IIIpe (shell)	sb
α Col	1956	05396-3404	05 40 34.4	-34 03 43	2.65	−0.12	B7 IV	d
ζ Ori	1948	05407-0157	05 42 02.8	-01 55 52	1.77	−0.21	O9.5 Ib	pdbm
κ Ori	2004		05 48 58.0	-09 39 45	2.06	−0.18	B0.5 Ia	
α Ori	2061	05552+0724	05 56 33.2	+07 24 35	0.42	+1.85	M1−M2 Ia−Iab	vadbn16
β Aur	2088	05595+4457	06 01 24.0	+44 56 50	1.90	+0.03	A1 IV	vdb
θ Aur	2095	05597+3713	06 01 27.6	+37 12 42	2.62	−0.08	A0p Si	vdb
β CMa	2294	06227-1757	06 23 49.4	-17 58 13	1.97	−0.24	B1 II−III	svb
α Car	2326		06 24 31.1	-52 42 38	-0.74	+0.15	A9 II	n17
γ Gem	2421	06377+1624	06 39 11.0	+16 22 30	1.92	+1.00	A1 IVs	db
α CMa	2491	06451-1643	06 46 15.9	-16 45 13	-1.46	−1.00	A0m A1 Va	odbn18
τ Pup	2553		06 50 34.1	-50 38 45	2.93	+2.20	K1 III	b
ϵ CMa	2618	06586-2858	06 59 37.7	-29 00 30	1.50	−0.21	B2 II	dn19

Designation	BS=HR No.	WDS No.	Right Ascension	Declination	V	$B-V$	Spectral Type	Notes
			h m s	° ′ ″				
o CMa	2653		07 04 05.4	-23 52 20	3.02	−0.08	B3 Ia	vasb
δ CMa	2693	07084-2624	07 09 25.7	-26 26 07	1.84	+0.68	F8 Ia	dasb
π Pup	2773	07171-3706	07 18 02.6	-37 08 40	2.70	+1.62	K3 Ib	dm
η CMa	2827	07241-2918	07 25 06.3	-29 21 15	2.45	−0.08	B5 Ia	das
β CMi	2845	07272+0817	07 28 32.0	+08 14 09	2.89	−0.09	B8 V	db
σ Pup	2878	07292-4318	07 30 02.4	-43 21 15	3.25	+1.52	K5 III	vdb
α Gem	2891	07346+3153	07 36 13.1	+31 49 46	1.58	+0.04	A1m A2 Va	podbm
α CMi	2943	07393+0514	07 40 38.1	+05 09 26	0.37	+0.42	F5 IV−V	osdbn20
β Gem	2990	07453+2802	07 46 52.4	+27 57 45	1.14	+1.00	K0 IIIb	an21
ζ Pup	3165		08 04 28.9	-40 04 34	2.25	−0.27	O5 Iafn	s
ρ Pup	3185	08075-2418	08 08 37.8	-24 22 45	2.81	+0.43	F5 (Ib−II)p	vdb
γ Vel	3207	08095-4720	08 10 19.1	-47 24 46	1.83	−0.25	WC8 + O9I:	cdb
ϵ Car	3307	08225-5931	08 23 02.1	-59 35 32	1.86	+1.27	K3: III + B2: V	pdcmn22
δ Vel	3485	08447-5443	08 45 24.5	-54 48 11	1.93	+0.04	A1 Va	dm
ι UMa	3569	08592+4803	09 00 56.5	+47 56 24	3.14	+0.19	A7 IVn	db
λ Vel	3634	09080-4326	09 08 56.1	-43 32 11	2.21	+1.65	K4.5 Ib	dn23
β Car	3685		09 13 28.2	-69 49 21	1.69	+1.00	A1 III	n24
ι Car	3699		09 17 46.3	-59 22 58	2.26	+0.18	A7 Ib	
κ Vel	3734		09 22 54.3	-55 07 13	2.47	−0.15	B2 IV−V	b
α Hya	3748	09276-0840	09 28 50.4	-08 46 13	1.97	+1.45	K3 II−III	dn25
N Vel	3803		09 31 59.9	-57 08 51	3.14	+1.55	K5 III	
ϵ Leo	3873		09 47 17.6	+23 39 20	2.98	+0.81	G1 II	
α Leo	3982	10084+1158	10 09 43.6	+11 50 30	1.40	−0.16	B7 Vn	dbn26
γ Leo	4057	10200+1950	10 21 22.5	+19 42 42	2.37	+1.42	K1$^-$ IIIb Fe−0.5	pdbm
θ Car	4199		10 43 52.4	-64 31 42	2.76	−0.22	B0.5 Vp	b
μ Vel	4216	10468-4925	10 47 52.3	-49 33 20	2.69	+2.90	G5 III + F8: V	cdbm
β UMa	4295		11 03 21.8	+56 14 43	2.37	−0.02	A0m A1 IV−V	b
α UMa	4301	11037+6145	11 05 16.8	+61 36 47	1.79	+1.07	K0$^-$ IIIa	dbmn27
ψ UMa	4335		11 11 05.2	+44 21 35	3.01	+1.14	K1 III	
δ Leo	4357	11141+2031	11 15 27.7	+20 23 01	2.53	+0.15	A4 IV	d
β Leo	4534	11491+1434	11 50 21.5	+14 25 46	2.13	+0.09	A3 Va	dn28
γ UMa	4554	11538+5342	11 55 09.7	+53 33 11	2.44	+0.01	A0 Van	adb
δ Cen	4621	12084-5043	12 09 41.4	-50 51 52	2.52	−0.13	B2 IVne	d
γ Crv	4662		12 17 07.3	-17 41 00	2.58	−0.11	B8p Hg Mn	bn29
α Cru	4730	12266-6306	12 28 02.2	-63 14 25	0.77	−0.24	B0.5 IV	pcdbmn30
γ Cru	4763	12312-5707	12 32 35.8	-57 15 20	1.64	+1.59	M3.5 III	n31
β Crv	4786		12 35 43.9	-23 32 15	2.64	+0.88	G5 IIb	
α Mus	4798	12372-6908	12 38 44.0	-69 16 32	2.65	−0.17	B2 IV−V	d
γ Cen	4819	12415-4858	12 42 56.2	-49 05 58	2.17	−0.01	A1 IV	dbm
γ Vir	4825	12417-0127	12 42 57.2	-01 35 21	2.74	+0.36	F1 V	pocdbm
β Cru	4853	12477-5941	12 49 13.8	-59 49 40	1.25	−0.23	B0.5 III	vdb
ϵ UMa	4905	12540+5558	12 55 08.6	+55 49 19	1.77	−0.02	A0p Cr	dvbn32
α CVn	4915	12560+3819	12 57 13.0	+38 10 52	2.88	−0.12	A0p Si Eu	vd
ϵ Vir	4932	13022+1058	13 03 26.8	+10 49 22	2.79	+0.92	G8 IIIab	as
ι Cen	5028		13 22 02.4	-36 50 46	2.73	+0.03	A2 Va	
ζ UMa	5054	13239+5456	13 24 56.9	+54 47 34	2.23	+0.06	A1 Va$^+$ (Si)	db
α Vir	5056	13252-1110	13 26 32.4	-11 17 37	0.97	−0.23	B1 V	vdbn33
ϵ Cen	5132	13399-5328	13 41 31.2	-53 35 42	2.30	−0.22	B1 III	d
η UMa	5191		13 48 32.6	+49 11 12	1.86	−0.19	B3 V	abn34
η Boo	5235	13547+1824	13 55 53.9	+18 16 15	2.68	+0.57	G0 IV	asb

Designation	BS=HR No.	WDS No.	Right Ascension	Declination	V	$B-V$	Spectral Type	Notes
			h m s	° ′ ″				
ζ Cen	5231		13 57 08.6	-47 24 46	2.55	−0.22	B2.5 IV	b
β Cen	5267	14038-6022	14 05 38.8	-60 29 41	0.58	+0.20	B1 III	dbmn35
θ Cen	5288	14067-3622	14 08 11.5	-36 29 39	2.05	+0.99	K0− IIIb	dn36
α Boo	5340	14157+1911	14 16 49.5	+19 03 02	-0.05	+1.23	K1.5 III Fe−0.5	mn37
γ Boo	5435	14321+3818	14 33 06.2	+38 11 52	3.02	+0.19	A7 IV+	d
η Cen	5440		14 37 08.2	-42 16 06	2.31	−0.19	B1.5 IVpne (shell)	v
α Cen	5459	14396-6050	14 41 20.8	-60 56 28	-0.10	−0.50	G2 V	odbn38
α Lup	5469	14419-4723	14 43 38.3	-47 29 46	2.29	−0.16	B1.5 III	vdb
ϵ Boo	5506	14450+2704	14 46 06.0	+26 58 04	2.39	+0.97	K0− II–III	dm
β UMi	5563	14507+7409	14 50 39.5	+74 03 04	2.08	+1.47	K4− III	n40
α Lib	5531	14509-1603	14 52 17.6	-16 08 47	2.75	+0.15	A3 III–IV	dbn39
β Lup	5571		15 00 12.8	-43 14 06	2.68	−0.22	B2 IV	
β Lib	5685		15 18 23.0	-09 28 31	2.62	−0.11	B8 IIIn	b
γ UMi	5735		15 20 42.5	+71 44 36	3.00	+0.06	A3 III	
γ TrA	5671		15 21 19.7	-68 46 15	2.89	+2.00	A1 III	
α CrB	5793		15 35 46.1	+26 37 49	2.24	−0.02	A0 IV	bn41
γ Lup	5776	15351-4110	15 36 51.0	-41 15 01	2.77	−0.18	B2 IVn	dvbm
α Ser	5854	15443+0626	15 45 31.5	+06 20 49	2.63	+1.17	K2 IIIb CN 1	d
β TrA	5897	15551-6326	15 57 24.8	-63 30 24	2.85	+0.29	F0 IV	d
π Sco	5944	15589-2607	16 00 24.0	-26 11 08	2.91	+2.20	B1 V + B2 V	cvdb
δ Sco	5953	16003-2237	16 01 50.8	-22 41 32	2.32	−0.12	B0.3 IV	dbm
β Sco	5984	16054-1948	16 06 55.4	-19 52 24	2.50	−0.07	B0.5 V	db
δ Oph	6056	16143-0342	16 15 41.1	-03 45 29	2.75	+1.59	M0.5 III	
η Dra	6132	16240+6131	16 24 20.5	+61 27 25	2.74	+0.91	G8− IIIab	db
α Sco	6134	16294-2626	16 30 58.5	-26 29 11	0.91	+1.84	M1.5 Iab–Ib	vdbn42
β Her	6148	16302+2129	16 31 19.0	+21 26 08	2.77	+0.93	G7 IIIa Fe−0.5	db
τ Sco	6165		16 37 28.5	-28 16 00	2.81	−0.25	B0 V	s
ζ Oph	6175		16 38 33.9	-10 37 00	2.56	+0.02	O9.5 Vn	
ζ Her	6212	16413+3136	16 42 14.9	+31 33 28	2.80	+0.63	G0 IV	dbm
α TrA	6217	16487-6902	16 51 23.3	-69 04 14	1.88	+1.45	K2 IIb–IIIa	n43
ϵ Sco	6241		16 51 49.2	-34 20 14	2.29	+1.16	K2 III	
ζ Ara	6285		17 00 44.4	-56 01 38	3.08	+1.62	K4 III	
η Oph	6378	17104-1544	17 11 50.6	-15 45 15	2.42	+0.05	A2 Va+ (Sr)	pdbmn44
α Her	6406	17146+1423	17 15 48.7	+14 21 47	2.78	+1.16	M5 Ib–II	pvsdm
β Ara	6461		17 27 25.5	-55 33 03	2.85	+1.46	K3 Ib–IIa	
β Dra	6536	17304+5218	17 31 00.6	+52 17 00	2.81	+0.98	G2 Ib–IIa	sd
υ Sco	6508		17 32 30.0	-37 18 49	2.65	−0.17	B2 IV	b
α Ara	6510		17 33 49.0	-49 53 36	2.95	−0.17	B2 Vne	b
λ Sco	6527	17336-3706	17 35 20.5	-37 07 11	1.63	−0.14	B1.5 IV	vdbn45
α Oph	6556	17349+1234	17 36 07.1	+12 32 36	2.07	+0.15	A5 Vnn	dbn46
θ Sco	6553	17373-4300	17 39 09.2	-43 00 41	1.85	+0.44	F1 III	bdm
κ Sco	6580		17 44 15.2	-39 02 26	2.39	−0.17	B1.5 III	vb
β Oph	6603		17 44 44.0	+04 33 31	2.75	+1.18	K2 III CN 0.5	
γ Dra	6705	17566+5129	17 57 12.0	+51 29 13	2.23	+1.53	K5 III	asdn47
γ Sgr	6746		18 07 26.8	-30 25 17	2.99	+1.01	K0+ III	b
δ Sgr	6859	18210-2950	18 22 37.6	-29 48 53	2.67	+2.40	K2.5 IIIa CN 0.5	d
ϵ Sgr	6879	18242-3423	18 25 51.8	-34 22 12	1.81	+0.01	A0 II−n (shell)	dn48
λ Sgr	6913	18280-2525	18 29 32.6	-25 24 19	2.81	+1.04	K1 IIIb	d
α Lyr	7001	18369+3846	18 37 48.2	+38 48 32	0.03	+0.00	A0 Va	asdn49
σ Sgr	7121	18553-2618	18 56 50.7	-26 15 46	2.07	−0.14	B3 IV	dn50

Designation	BS=HR No.	WDS No.	Right Ascension	Declination	V	$B-V$	Spectral Type	Notes
			h m s	° ′ ″				
ζ Sgr	7194	19026-2953	19 04 13.9	-29 50 29	2.59	+2.10	A2 IV–V	dbm
ζ Aql	7235	19054+1352	19 06 34.9	+13 54 11	2.99	+0.01	A0 Vann	db
π Sgr	7264		19 11 16.7	-20 58 51	2.88	+0.34	F2 II–III	
β Cyg	7417	19307+2758	19 31 45.0	+28 00 53	3.08	+1.13	K3 II + B9.5 V	cdm
δ Cyg	7528	19450+4508	19 45 46.3	+45 11 39	2.87	−0.02	B9.5 III	dbm
γ Aql	7525	19463+1037	19 47 28.3	+10 40 37	2.72	+1.51	K3 II	d
α Aql	7557	19508+0852	19 52 01.6	+08 56 15	0.76	+0.22	A7 Vnn	dvn51
γ Cyg	7796		20 23 08.7	+40 20 22	2.23	+0.67	F8 Ib	as
α Pav	7790	20256-5644	20 27 38.9	-56 39 03	1.92	−0.13	B2.5 V	dbn52
α Ind	7869	20376-4717	20 39 21.0	-47 12 02	3.11	+3.00	K0 III CN−1	d
α Cyg	7924	20414+4517	20 42 18.1	+45 22 21	1.25	+0.09	A2 Ia	asdbn53
ϵ Cyg	7949	20462+3358	20 47 14.7	+34 04 01	2.48	+1.04	K0 III	adb
α Cep	8162		21 19 11.2	+62 41 39	2.46	+0.22	A7 V^{+}n	
β Aqr	8232	21316-0534	21 32 54.0	-05 27 28	2.89	+0.82	G0 Ib	asd
ϵ Peg	8308		21 45 26.3	+09 59 35	2.39	+1.52	K2 Ib–II	sn54
δ Cap	8322		21 48 26.7	-16 00 38	2.83	+0.29	F2m	vb
α Gru	8425		22 09 49.7	-46 50 11	1.71	−0.13	B7 Vn	n55
α Tuc	8502		22 20 13.5	-60 07 53	2.82	+1.36	K3 III	b
β Gru	8636		22 44 10.7	-46 45 02	2.11	+1.62	M4.5 III	
α PsA	8728	22577-2937	22 59 03.2	-29 29 12	1.16	+0.09	A3 Va	adbn56
β Peg	8775		23 05 00.9	+28 13 18	2.42	+1.67	M2.5 II–III	
α Peg	8781		23 06 02.0	+15 20 34	2.48	−0.04	A0 III–IV	bn57
γ Cep	8974	23393+7738	23 40 25.2	+77 46 28	3.21	+1.04	K1 III–IV CN 1	ads

Notes to Table

a anchor point for the MK system
b spectroscopic binary
c composite or combined spectrum
d confirmed or suspected multiple system with details given in the Washington Double Star (WDS) Catalog
m magnitude and color refer to combined light of two or more stars
n navigational star followed by its star number in *The Nautical Almanac*
o orbital position generated using FK5 center-of-mass position and proper motion
p potentially problematic for navigational use as companions are marginally separated (1-10") and relatively similar in brightness (dmag <2)
s MK standard star
v variable star

Name	BS=HR No.	Right Ascension	Declination	V	Spectral Type	Note[1]
		h m s	° ′ ″			
HD 224926	9087	00 03 07.88	−02 53 08.3	5.12	B7III	
G 158−100		00 35 12.04	−11 59 38.7	14.89	dG−K	
HD 3360	153	00 38 24.41	+54 02 12.8	3.66	B2IV	
CD−34 241		00 43 01.14	−33 30 46.8	11.23	F	
BPM 16274		00 51 12.84	−51 59 55.8	14.20	DA2	Model
LTT 1020		01 56 00.75	−27 21 14.1	11.52	G	
HD 15318	718	02 29 31.11	+08 34 22.8	4.28	B9III	
EGGR 21 1		03 10 45.52	−68 30 21.9	11.38	DA	
LTT 1788		03 49 18.21	−39 04 05.9	13.16	F	
GD 50		03 50 08.31	−00 54 00.9	14.06	DA2	
SA 95−42		03 55 02.03	−00 00 09.9	15.61	DA	
HZ 4		03 56 45.74	+09 51 41.4	14.52	DA4	
LB 227		04 10 56.83	+17 11 49.5	15.34	DA4	
HZ 2		04 14 08.44	+11 55 36.0	13.86	DA3	
HD 30739	1544	04 52 00.24	+08 56 30.7	4.36	A1V	
G 191−B2B		05 07 32.78	+52 51 47.7	11.78	DA1	
HD 38666	1996	05 46 56.82	−32 17 53.7	5.17	O9V	Model
GD 71		05 53 55.86	+15 53 24.0	13.03	DA1	
LTT 2415		05 57 25.60	−27 51 29.4	12.21		
HILT 600		06 46 33.02	+02 06 33.0	10.44	B1	
HD 49798		06 48 50.56	−44 20 45.5	8.30	O6	Model
HD 60753		07 34 07.66	−50 38 26.5	6.70	B3IV	Model
G 193−74		07 55 24.33	+52 25 20.6	15.70	DA0	
BD+75 325		08 13 53.93	+74 53 19.1	9.54	O5p	
LTT 3218		08 42 31.75	−33 01 30.6	11.86	DA	
HD 74280	3454	08 44 33.37	+03 18 20.1	4.30	B3V	
AGK+81°266		09 25 04.51	+81 36 50.3	11.92	sdO	
GD 108		10 02 03.34	−07 40 55.0	13.56	sdB	
LTT 3864		10 33 22.37	−35 45 36.5	12.17	F	
Feige 34		10 41 06.02	+42 58 08.2	11.18	DO	
HD 93521		10 49 49.88	+37 26 06.4	7.04	O9Vp	
HD 100889	4468	11 37 58.64	−09 56 36.6	4.70	B9.5V	
LTT 4364		11 47 07.71	−64 58 52.1	11.50	C2	
HD 103287	4554	11 55 09.68	+53 33 10.5	2.44	A0V	Model
Feige 56		12 08 05.40	+11 31 41.6	11.06	B5p	
HZ 21		12 15 13.10	+32 48 02.6	14.68	DO2	
Feige 66		12 38 39.32	+24 55 35.2	10.50	sdO	
LTT 4816		12 40 15.00	−49 56 10.6	13.79	DA	
Feige 67		12 43 08.22	+17 22 56.6	11.81	sdO	
GD 153		12 58 17.27	+21 53 33.0	13.35	DA1	
G 60−54		13 01 26.22	+03 20 06.1	15.81	DC	
HD 114330	4963	13 11 16.36	−05 40 28.2	4.38	A1IV	
HZ 43		13 17 33.73	+28 57 50.3	12.91	DA1	
HZ 44		13 24 44.63	+36 00 02.7	11.66	sdO	
GRW+70°5824		13 39 27.13	+70 09 23.0	12.77	DA3	

Name	BS=HR No.	Right Ascension	Declination	*V*	Spectral Type	Note[1]
		h m s	° ′ ″			
HD 120315	5191	13 48 32.58	+49 11 12.1	1.86	B3V	Model
CD−32 9927		14 13 16.88	−33 10 22.1	10.42	A0	
HD 129956	5501	14 46 48.29	+00 36 39.5	5.68	B9.5V	
LTT 6248		15 40 32.85	−28 40 34.9	11.80	A	
BD+33 2642		15 52 59.55	+32 52 24.4	10.81	B2IV	
EGGR 274		16 25 17.88	−39 17 13.2	11.03	DA	
G 138−31		16 29 06.73	+09 08 45.9	16.14	DC	
HD 172167	7001	18 37 48.17	+38 48 31.6	0.00	A0V	
LTT 7379		18 38 16.76	−44 17 18.1	10.23	G0	
HD 188350	7596	19 56 03.12	+00 20 31.4	5.62	A0III	
LTT 7987		20 12 31.21	−30 08 35.1	12.23	DA	
G 24−9		20 15 10.90	+06 47 23.7	15.72	DC	
HD 198001	7950	20 49 03.23	−09 24 03.1	3.78	A1V	
LDS 749B		21 33 35.25	+00 22 04.8	14.67	DB4	
BD+28 4211		21 52 19.38	+28 59 02.0	10.51	Op	
G 93−48		21 53 43.07	+02 30 26.5	12.74	DA3	
BD+25 4655		22 00 51.84	+26 33 19.2	9.76	O	
NGC 7293		22 31 01.96	−20 42 21.4	13.51	V.Hot	
HD 214923	8634	22 42 44.08	+10 57 54.4	3.40	B8V	
LTT 9239		22 54 03.25	−20 27 31.2	12.07	F	
LTT 9491		23 20 56.02	−16 57 04.8	14.11	DC	
Feige 110		23 21 17.31	−05 01 32.8	11.82	DOp	
GD 248		23 27 23.50	+16 08 42.4	15.09	DC	

Notes to Table

[1] Model data for the optical range; only suitable as a standard in the ultraviolet range.

IERS Designation	Right Ascension	Declination	Type	z	V	G
	h m s	° ′ ″				
0002−478	00 04 35.6554 8526	−47 36 19.6040 054	AQ	0.8800	19.0	19.7
0007+106	00 10 31.0059 0413	+10 58 29.5042 981	A1	0.0893	15.0	16.1
0009−148	00 11 40.4558 4973	−14 34 04.6348 040	AQ	1.3000		19.7
0010+405	00 13 31.1301 9909	+40 51 37.1441 374	A1	0.2550	18.0	19.3
0013−005	00 16 11.0885 5044	+00 15 12.4454 125	AQ	1.5763	20.0	19.7
0016+731	00 19 45.7863 7230	+73 27 30.0176 020	AQ	1.7810	19.0	18.3
0017+200	00 19 37.8544 9305	+20 21 45.6446 105	AL	3.9300	20.6	19.2
0035−252	00 38 14.7355 0152	−24 59 02.2352 926	AQ	0.4981	17.5	19.1
0038−326	00 40 30.6548 5223	−32 25 20.3298 466	AL	0.5240		
0044−846	00 44 26.6892 3207	−84 22 39.9875 303	AQ	1.0320	18.5	19.5
0046+316	00 48 47.1414 7900	+31 57 25.0845 702	A2	0.0150	14.3	17.9
0047+023	00 49 43.2359 3957	+02 37 03.7785 936	AL	1.4400	18.5	18.2
0048−097	00 50 41.3173 8216	−09 29 05.2103 418	AL	0.6350	16.0	15.7
0054+161	00 56 55.2943 2895	+16 25 13.3409 138	AL	0.2060	18.5	19.8
0059+581	01 02 45.7623 7340	+58 24 11.1366 164	AQ	0.6440	19.2	17.9
0104−408	01 06 45.1079 6439	−40 34 19.9603 733	AQ	0.5840	19.0	19.6
0107−610	01 09 15.4751 9907	−60 49 48.4601 187	AQ		19.0	
0110+495	01 13 27.0068 0467	+49 48 24.0432 101	AQ	0.3890	18.4	18.2
0133+476	01 36 58.5948 0326	+47 51 29.1000 720	AQ	0.8590	18.0	18.3
0149+218	01 52 18.0590 4204	+22 07 07.6997 943	AQ	1.3200	18.0	18.4
0159+723	02 03 33.3849 5695	+72 32 53.6673 482	AL	0.3900	19.2	18.8
0202−172	02 04 57.6743 3267	−17 01 19.8408 671	AQ	1.7395	18.0	17.4
0202+319	02 05 04.9253 6206	+32 12 30.0954 703	AQ	1.4660	17.9	17.6
0208−512	02 10 46.2004 2049	−51 01 01.8919 205	AL	0.9990	16.9	16.7
0215+015	02 17 48.9547 5095	+01 44 49.6990 271	AQ	1.7150	16.1	18.8
0221+067	02 24 28.4281 8961	+06 59 23.3415 566	AQ	0.5110	20.0	18.0
0227−369	02 29 28.4490 5708	−36 43 56.8223 412	AQ	2.1150	19.0	19.6
0230−790	02 29 34.9465 9694	−78 47 45.6017 623	AQ	1.0700	18.9	19.3
0227+403	02 30 45.7107 8259	+40 32 53.0685 846	AQ	1.0190	19.0	18.6
0234−301	02 36 31.1694 1522	−29 53 55.5405 598	A	2.1034	18.0	18.4
0235−618	02 36 53.2457 4011	−61 36 15.1835 463	AQ	0.4650	18.5	19.6
0235+164	02 38 38.9301 0450	+16 36 59.2745 528	AL	0.9400	17.5	17.4
0237−027	02 39 45.4722 7239	−02 34 40.9145 702	AQ	1.1160	19.4	19.7
0239+175	02 42 24.2682 6371	+17 42 58.8491 818	AL	0.5510	21.3	20.2
0256−005	02 59 28.5161 5658	+00 19 59.9753 897	AL	2.0012	17.6	17.3
0300+470	03 03 35.2422 1958	+47 16 16.2754 726	AL	0.4750	16.6	16.9
0302+625	03 06 42.6595 5141	+62 43 02.0241 670	R			
0305+039	03 08 26.2238 0005	+04 06 39.3007 808	A1	0.0287	13.5	17.1
0308−611	03 09 56.0991 4475	−60 58 39.0564 095	AQ	1.4800	18.5	18.4
0307+380	03 10 49.8799 2240	+38 14 53.8378 761	AL	0.8160	19.7	20.0
0312+100	03 15 21.1398 1265	+10 12 43.0838 933	AL	0.2220	18.3	19.0
0316−444	03 17 57.6794 6154	−44 14 17.1632 318	AQ	0.0761		20.6
0322+222	03 25 36.8143 5345	+22 24 00.3656 161	AQ	2.0600	18.9	19.1
0332−403	03 34 13.6544 8823	−40 08 25.3979 928	AL	1.4450	18.5	17.8
0334−131	03 36 35.0358 1609	−13 02 04.6600 312	AQ	1.3030	19.0	20.4
0346−279	03 48 38.1445 7039	−27 49 13.5657 855	AQ	0.9910	19.4	19.0
0347−211	03 49 57.8266 7348	−21 02 47.7416 093	AQ	2.9440	20.9	20.1
0346+800	03 54 46.1259 9356	+80 09 28.8472 674	AB			20.6
0355−669	03 55 47.8834 3322	−66 45 33.8173 093	AQ	0.7753		18.5
0400−319	04 02 21.2659 9921	−31 47 25.9455 847	AQ	1.2880		20.0
0402−362	04 03 53.7499 0003	−36 05 01.9131 880	AQ	1.4228	17.2	17.0
0403−132	04 05 34.0033 9116	−13 08 13.6909 309	AL	0.5706	17.1	16.8

IERS Designation	Right Ascension	Declination	Type	z	V	G
	h m s	° ′ ″				
0406−127	04 09 05.7697 2871	−12 38 48.1438 174	AQ	1.5630	18.5	18.5
0415+398	04 19 22.5495 1530	+39 55 28.9775 938	V			
0420+022	04 22 52.2146 5085	+02 19 26.9307 480	AQ	2.2770	19.5	19.5
0430+289	04 33 37.8298 5981	+29 05 55.4770 576	AL	0.9700	17.8	20.4
0437−454	04 39 00.8546 6368	−45 22 22.5631 875	AQ	2.0170	20.6	19.7
0454−810	04 50 05.4402 1015	−81 01 02.2314 265	AQ	0.4440	19.2	19.2
0454−234	04 57 03.1792 2481	−23 24 52.0203 248	AQ	1.0030	18.5	16.8
0458−020	05 01 12.8098 8538	−01 59 14.2564 557	AQ	2.2860	18.5	18.7
0506−612	05 06 43.9887 4900	−61 09 40.9939 787	AQ	1.0930	16.9	17.2
0454+844	05 08 42.3635 1222	+84 32 04.5441 733	AL	1.3400	18.3	19.3
0506+101	05 09 27.4570 6676	+10 11 44.6001 432	AQ	0.6210	17.8	19.4
0507+179	05 10 02.3691 2937	+18 00 41.5815 635	AQ	0.4160	19.0	17.6
0510+559	05 14 18.6996 0090	+56 02 11.0530 616	AQ	2.1900		
0515+208	05 18 03.8245 1380	+20 54 52.4973 957	AQ	2.5790		21.0
0522−611	05 22 34.4254 7703	−61 07 57.1337 711	AQ	1.4000	18.1	18.6
0524−485	05 26 16.6713 1784	−48 30 36.7919 695	AQ	1.3000	20.0	18.2
0524+034	05 27 32.7054 4208	+03 31 31.5165 613	AL	0.9000	20.0	19.7
0530−727	05 29 30.0421 7573	−72 45 28.5075 004	AQ	1.3400		19.6
0529+483	05 33 15.8657 9115	+48 22 52.8077 787	AQ	1.1620	19.9	18.4
0534−340	05 36 28.4323 6164	−34 01 11.4684 065	AQ	0.6825	18.3	17.9
0536+145	05 39 42.3659 9322	+14 33 45.5616 887	AQ	2.6900		20.6
0537−286	05 39 54.2814 7904	−28 39 55.9481 236	AQ	3.1040	19.1	19.0
0539−057	05 41 38.0833 6552	−05 41 49.4283 917	AQ	0.8390	20.4	20.8
0544+273	05 47 34.1489 2156	+27 21 56.8425 747	I			
0548+084	05 51 11.2293 4426	+08 29 11.2218 668	AL			19.4
0552+398	05 55 30.8056 1419	+39 48 49.1649 683	AQ	2.3650	18.0	17.6
0556+238	05 59 32.0331 3313	+23 53 53.9267 334	I			
0605−085	06 07 59.6992 4014	−08 34 49.9783 246	AL	0.8720	16.7	18.7
0607−157	06 09 40.9495 4062	−15 42 40.6727 537	AQ	0.3226	18.0	18.5
0613+570	06 17 16.9225 6638	+57 01 16.4232 088	AL		17.5	17.1
0615+820	06 26 03.0062 3818	+82 02 25.5679 443	AQ	0.7100	17.5	18.1
0627−199	06 29 23.7618 6296	−19 59 19.7236 825	AL	1.7240	18.6	19.9
0641+392	06 44 53.7095 9953	+39 14 47.5339 198	AQ	1.2660	20.3	19.2
0642−349	06 44 25.2810 3832	−34 59 41.9491 795	AQ	2.1650	18.5	17.6
0646−306	06 48 14.0964 6706	−30 44 19.6597 807	AQ	0.4550	20.4	18.9
0648−165	06 50 24.5818 5949	−16 37 39.7255 562	AQ			
0657+172	07 00 01.5255 4306	+17 09 21.7013 068	AQ	1.0800		18.5
0700−465	07 01 34.5465 8767	−46 34 36.6251 872	AQ	0.8220	19.5	18.8
0700−197	07 02 42.9006 6398	−19 51 22.0355 917	AQ	0.1000		18.1
0716+714	07 21 53.4484 7569	+71 20 36.3634 294	AL	0.3000	13.7	13.5
0727−115	07 30 19.1124 7452	−11 41 12.6006 642	AQ	1.5910	20.3	19.5
0738−674	07 38 56.4962 4352	−67 35 50.8260 320	AQ	1.6630	19.8	19.7
0736+017	07 39 18.0338 9906	+01 37 04.6177 501	AQ	0.1894	16.5	17.0
0738+491	07 42 02.7489 5098	+49 00 15.6089 311	AQ	2.3180	21.8	20.4
0742−562	07 43 20.4852 3465	−56 19 32.9587 169	AQ	2.3190		19.4
0743−006	07 45 54.0823 2685	+00 44 17.5399 048	AQ	0.9940	17.1	17.0
0743+259	07 46 25.8741 8071	+25 49 02.1347 101	AQ	2.9875	19.7	19.5
0743+277	07 46 40.4323 1234	+27 34 59.0470 434	AQ	2.6250		20.0
0748+126	07 50 52.0457 3865	+12 31 04.8282 079	AQ	0.8890	17.3	17.4
0749+540	07 53 01.3845 7270	+53 52 59.6370 830	AL	0.2000	17.5	18.2
0759+183	08 02 48.0319 7175	+18 09 49.2493 330	AQ	1.5860	20.7	20.3
0800+618	08 05 18.1795 6222	+61 44 23.7005 580	AQ	3.0330		19.9

IERS Designation	Right Ascension	Declination	Type	*z*	*V*	*G*
	h m s	° ′ ″				
0802−010	08 05 12.8884 8306	−01 11 13.7952 408	AQ	1.3880		18.9
0804−267	08 06 12.7226 1243	−26 52 33.3085 062	AQ	1.2302		18.5
0804+499	08 08 39.6662 8970	+49 50 36.5304 041	AQ	1.4352	19.2	18.6
0805+410	08 08 56.6520 4477	+40 52 44.8888 932	AQ	1.4200	19.4	18.6
0808+019	08 11 26.7073 1711	+01 46 52.2201 568	AL	1.1480	18.0	18.0
0809−493	08 11 08.8032 2300	−49 29 43.5114 798	AQ			
0818−128	08 20 57.4476 2374	−12 58 59.1692 275	AL	0.0740	15.0	19.1
0826−373	08 28 04.7802 3133	−37 31 06.2815 112	AQ			
0829+089	08 31 55.0915 0458	+08 47 43.6518 657	AQ	0.9409	20.1	20.5
0834−201	08 36 39.2152 5204	−20 16 59.5042 773	AQ	2.7520	19.4	19.1
0834+250	08 37 40.2456 8929	+24 54 23.1214 722	AQ	1.1264	17.9	17.9
0847−120	08 50 09.6356 3375	−12 13 35.3761 390	AQ	0.5660	19.3	18.1
0855−716	08 55 11.7698 5589	−71 49 06.4572 052	AQ	1.8560		18.3
0912+297	09 15 52.4016 4472	+29 33 24.0429 125	AL	0.1010	16.2	16.0
0918−534	09 19 44.0394 6690	−53 40 06.4476 712	AQ	0.6000		18.6
0920+390	09 23 14.4529 3735	+38 49 39.9100 905	V			
0926−039	09 28 33.4693 7078	−04 09 08.8470 898	AQ	0.6000		20.0
0930−080	09 33 17.0953 9312	−08 19 10.8504 430	AQ	0.9030		20.8
0943+105	09 46 35.0699 5887	+10 17 06.1344 498	AQ	1.0045	19.7	19.0
0951+268	09 54 39.7965 2916	+26 39 24.5433 239	V			
0954+658	09 58 47.2451 1333	+65 33 54.8180 376	AL	0.3680	16.8	16.3
0955+476	09 58 19.6716 4698	+47 25 07.8424 065	AQ	1.8821	18.6	18.3
1004−217	10 06 46.4136 8347	−21 59 20.4102 018	A1	0.3300	16.9	16.6
1004−500	10 06 14.0093 1655	−50 18 13.4707 354	AQ			20.0
1012+232	10 14 47.0654 6648	+23 01 16.5707 383	A1	0.5664	17.8	17.3
1015+057	10 18 27.8482 8610	+05 30 29.9620 200	AQ	1.9453	19.3	20.0
1016−311	10 18 28.7535 0173	−31 23 53.8497 307	AQ	0.7940		17.7
1022−665	10 23 43.5331 9662	−66 46 48.7176 018	AQ		17.9	20.6
1022+194	10 24 44.8095 9654	+19 12 20.4155 021	AQ	0.8275	17.8	19.0
1027−186	10 29 33.0976 9855	−18 52 50.2889 530	AQ	1.7840	19.0	18.6
1034−374	10 36 53.4396 0110	−37 44 15.0658 359	AQ	1.8210	19.5	18.8
1036−529	10 38 40.6571 7784	−53 11 43.2702 782	AQ	1.4500		18.5
1040+244	10 43 09.0357 8135	+24 08 35.4094 642	AL	0.5634	17.3	18.6
1042+071	10 44 55.9112 4811	+06 55 38.2624 955	AQ	0.6896	19.4	20.2
1053+704	10 56 53.6175 0640	+70 11 45.9155 652	AQ	2.4920	18.5	18.8
1059+282	11 02 14.2884 6235	+27 57 08.6894 771	AQ	1.8646	19.6	18.9
1101−536	11 03 52.2216 8463	−53 57 00.6966 389	AL		17.9	18.0
1111+149	11 13 58.6950 8613	+14 42 26.9526 507	AQ	0.8674	17.6	17.4
1116−462	11 18 26.9576 6041	−46 34 15.0014 696	AQ	0.7130	17.0	17.0
1124−186	11 27 04.3924 5388	−18 57 17.4418 445	AQ	1.0500		17.8
1130+009	11 33 20.0557 9109	+00 40 52.8371 482	AQ	1.6400		19.6
1133−032	11 36 24.5769 3472	−03 30 29.4966 741	AQ	1.6480	19.5	19.6
1143−696	11 45 53.6241 8068	−69 54 01.7975 812	A1	0.2440	16.7	16.4
1143−245	11 46 08.1033 1974	−24 47 32.8964 951	AQ	1.9400	18.0	17.3
1143−332	11 46 28.4517 6683	−33 28 42.6323 932	AL	0.2940		20.2
1144+402	11 46 58.2979 1724	+39 58 34.3043 988	AQ	1.0901	18.1	18.0
1144−379	11 47 01.3707 1212	−38 12 11.0235 229	AL	1.0480	16.2	17.7
1149−084	11 52 17.2095 1637	−08 41 03.3139 769	AQ	2.3700	18.5	19.2
1150+497	11 53 24.4666 3994	+49 31 08.8301 372	AQ	0.3337	17.7	17.5
1219+044	12 22 22.5496 2606	+04 13 15.7760 715	AQ	0.9660	18.0	17.8
1221+809	12 23 40.4937 5661	+80 40 04.3404 140	AL		19.0	19.1
1222+131	12 25 03.7433 3922	+12 53 13.1392 138	A2	0.0034	10.6	

IERS Designation	Right Ascension	Declination	Type	z	V	G
	h m s	° ′ ″				
1226+373	12 28 47.4236 7714	+37 06 12.0958 131	AQ	1.5169	18.3	18.1
1227+255	12 30 14.0893 5178	+25 18 07.1361 158	AL	0.1350	14.5	15.5
1236+077	12 39 24.5883 3099	+07 30 17.1890 748	AQ	0.4000	20.1	18.0
1243−160	12 45 53.7422 7041	−16 16 45.7052 308	AQ	0.2000		20.3
1243−072	12 46 04.2321 1565	−07 30 46.5746 985	AQ	1.2860	20.1	19.8
1244−255	12 46 46.8020 3943	−25 47 49.2889 822	AQ	0.6330	17.4	17.3
1245−457	12 48 28.4951 5071	−45 59 47.1796 776	AQ	1.0200		17.1
1251−713	12 54 59.9214 8599	−71 38 18.4366 378	AQ			19.4
1300+580	13 02 52.4652 8286	+57 48 37.6093 029	AQ	1.0880	19.8	20.4
1306−395	13 09 48.4883 1525	−39 48 33.0864 996	AQ	1.8280		
1308+328	13 10 59.4027 3257	+32 33 34.4495 500	AQ	1.6348	16.8	18.8
1312−533	13 15 04.1811 3270	−53 34 35.8740 743	AB			19.7
1313−333	13 16 07.9859 4757	−33 38 59.1726 741	AQ	1.2100	20.0	18.2
1324+224	13 27 00.8613 1319	+22 10 50.1628 385	AQ	1.4000	18.9	18.9
1325+126	13 27 54.6829 9830	+12 23 09.1783 574	AQ	0.9500	19.0	20.8
1325−558	13 29 01.1449 1196	−56 08 02.6655 453	AQ			18.7
1330+022	13 32 53.2705 3616	+02 00 45.6991 690	A1	0.2156	18.5	19.1
1330+476	13 32 45.2464 2464	+47 22 22.6677 558	AQ	0.6691	17.9	18.5
1334−127	13 37 39.7827 8132	−12 57 24.6933 925	AQ	0.5390	18.5	17.9
1348+308	13 50 52.7362 2485	+30 34 53.5906 894	AQ	0.7115	18.3	19.1
1351−018	13 54 06.8953 2721	−02 06 03.1904 962	AQ	3.7070	19.9	19.6
1357+769	13 57 55.3715 4275	+76 43 21.0509 950	AQ	1.5850	19.0	
1406−076	14 08 56.4812 0623	−07 52 26.6665 312	AQ	1.4940	18.4	18.9
1406−267	14 09 50.1697 8505	−26 57 36.9804 663	AQ	2.4300		20.9
1412−368	14 15 26.0163 3738	−37 05 26.9704 854	V			
1418+546	14 19 46.5974 0979	+54 23 14.7870 963	AL	0.1526	15.6	15.7
1420−679	14 24 55.5573 9084	−68 07 58.0945 831	AQ			
1423+146	14 25 49.0180 1221	+14 24 56.9018 642	AQ	0.7800	18.0	18.9
1424−418	14 27 56.2975 6617	−42 06 19.4376 238	AQ	1.5220	17.7	17.1
1428+370	14 30 40.5836 9349	+36 49 03.8887 684	AL	0.5674	19.7	19.9
1435−218	14 38 09.4694 0207	−22 04 54.7484 420	AQ	1.1870	17.9	18.3
1443−162	14 45 53.3763 0149	−16 29 01.6191 263	AQ			19.6
1448+762	14 48 28.7790 7399	+76 01 11.5972 341	AQ	0.8990	22.3	
1448−648	14 52 39.6791 8743	−65 02 03.4332 326	G			
1451−400	14 54 32.9123 7565	−40 12 32.5143 755	AQ	1.8100	18.5	19.1
1502+106	15 04 24.9797 8391	+10 29 39.1985 309	AQ	1.8383	17.8	17.4
1504+377	15 06 09.5299 7529	+37 30 51.1325 012	A2	0.6715	21.2	
1508+572	15 10 02.9223 7321	+57 02 43.3759 220	AQ	4.3087	20.2	20.5
1510−089	15 12 50.5329 3048	−09 05 59.8297 908	AQ	0.3600	16.9	15.9
1511−476	15 14 40.0246 0253	−47 48 29.8576 501	AQ	1.5512		19.3
1511−558	15 15 12.6729 0705	−55 59 32.8381 627	R			
1514+197	15 16 56.7961 6460	+19 32 12.9919 519	AL	1.0700	18.7	18.5
1520+437	15 21 49.6138 7806	+43 36 39.2681 695	AQ	2.1746	18.9	19.0
1519−273	15 22 37.6759 9511	−27 30 10.7855 131	AL	1.2940	18.2	18.8
1520+319	15 22 09.9917 3254	+31 44 14.3819 383	AQ	1.4870	19.9	19.1
1538+149	15 40 49.4915 1924	+14 47 45.8846 989	AL	0.6050	17.7	18.3
1555+001	15 57 51.4339 7121	+00 01 50.4137 827	AQ	1.7700	19.7	19.8
1556−245	15 59 41.4090 8144	−24 42 38.8322 303	AQ	2.8130	18.7	18.5
1557+032	15 59 30.9726 1910	+03 04 48.2567 339	AQ	3.8910	19.8	20.3
1600−445	16 04 31.0207 4903	−44 41 31.9734 699	AB			19.9
1602−115	16 05 17.5316 5742	−11 39 26.8311 169	V	0.9000		19.6
1606+106	16 08 46.2031 8700	+10 29 07.7757 424	AQ	1.2260	18.0	18.4

IERS Designation	Right Ascension	Declination	Type	z	V	G
	h m s	° ′ ″				
1606−398	16 10 21.8790 9104	−39 58 58.3294 463	AQ	0.5180		19.3
1608+243	16 10 42.0267 7563	+24 14 49.0115 848	AQ	1.4490	20.3	19.7
1619−680	16 24 18.4370 0381	−68 09 12.4965 744	AQ	1.3600	17.2	16.3
1623+578	16 24 24.8075 6989	+57 41 16.2809 410	AQ	0.7890	19.5	20.0
1624−617	16 28 54.6898 0334	−61 52 36.3980 187	AQ	2.5780		19.1
1636+473	16 37 45.1305 5568	+47 17 33.8311 081	AQ	0.7400	19.0	19.4
1639−062	16 42 02.1777 1463	−06 21 23.6950 367	AL	1.5140	20.9	20.1
1642+690	16 42 07.8485 1261	+68 56 39.7563 611	AQ	0.7510	19.2	20.4
1647−296	16 50 39.5441 2547	−29 43 46.9547 609	AQ	0.8000		19.6
1657−261	17 00 53.1540 6418	−26 10 51.7253 944	AQ			18.0
1659+399	17 01 24.6348 1525	+39 54 37.0915 503	AL	0.5074	17.1	17.1
1705+018	17 07 34.4152 7083	+01 48 45.6993 042	AQ	2.5680	18.5	18.4
1706−174	17 09 34.3453 9302	−17 28 53.3650 596	AQ		17.5	20.4
1717+178	17 19 13.0484 8035	+17 45 06.4371 847	AL	0.1370	19.1	17.2
1718−259	17 21 55.9791 4608	−25 58 40.6931 367	X			
1725+044	17 28 24.9527 2284	+04 27 04.9138 307	A1	0.2960	17.1	17.9
1730−130	17 33 02.7057 8907	−13 04 49.5482 119	AQ	0.9020	18.5	18.3
1737−081	17 40 01.5661 9684	−08 11 14.7817 717	V			21.0
1741−038	17 43 58.8561 3537	−03 50 04.6167 326	AQ	1.0540	18.5	18.1
1745+624	17 46 14.0341 3499	+62 26 54.7383 195	AQ	3.8890	19.5	19.1
1746+470	17 47 26.6472 7228	+46 58 50.9262 456	AL	1.4840	21.3	
1749+096	17 51 32.8185 7326	+09 39 00.7284 066	AL	0.3220	17.3	16.9
1751+288	17 53 42.4736 4223	+28 48 04.9388 788	AQ	1.1150		19.2
1753+204	17 55 35.5209 8108	+20 23 57.1371 713	AQ	1.4200	18.0	18.0
1754+155	17 56 53.1021 3899	+15 35 20.8265 134	V	2.0600		20.3
1758+388	18 00 24.7653 6016	+38 48 30.6974 570	AQ	2.0920	17.8	17.7
1759−396	18 02 42.6800 5300	−39 40 07.9081 646	AB	0.2960		18.5
1806−458	18 09 57.8717 4351	−45 52 41.0141 114	AL	0.0697	15.7	18.3
1815−553	18 19 45.3995 1531	−55 21 20.7453 837	AQ	1.6292	16.0	
1823+689	18 23 32.8539 0331	+68 57 52.6125 366	AL	2.1430		19.8
1831−711	18 37 28.7149 6089	−71 08 43.5546 170	AQ	1.3560	17.5	17.1
1846+322	18 48 22.0885 7099	+32 19 02.6037 977	AQ	0.7980		18.2
1849+670	18 49 16.0722 8484	+67 05 41.6802 599	A1	0.6570	18.6	18.9
1908+484	19 09 46.5627 0767	+48 34 31.8201 871	AQ	0.5130	19.0	20.5
1908−201	19 11 09.6528 9294	−20 06 55.1090 664	AQ	1.1190	18.4	18.6
1909+161	19 11 58.2574 0170	+16 11 46.8652 526	I			
1921−293	19 24 51.0559 5254	−29 14 30.1210 248	AL	0.3526	18.2	17.7
1925−610	19 30 06.1600 8387	−60 56 09.1841 871	AQ	3.2540		19.9
1929+226	19 31 24.9167 7020	+22 43 31.2585 148	R			
1929−457	19 32 44.8877 4432	−45 36 37.9289 309	AQ	0.6520	19.5	19.0
1936+046	19 38 30.6695 4887	+04 48 11.6142 608	V			20.7
1936−155	19 39 26.6577 5171	−15 25 43.0584 711	AQ	1.6570	19.4	19.3
1937−101	19 39 57.2565 7102	−10 02 41.5206 043	AL	3.7870	18.1	17.0
1935−692	19 40 25.5281 5148	−69 07 56.9717 355	AQ	3.1540	18.8	18.3
1949−052	19 51 47.4684 6027	−05 09 43.9624 421	AQ	1.0830		19.5
1951+355	19 53 30.8757 1313	+35 37 59.3592 795	AL			19.6
1954−388	19 57 59.8192 7491	−38 45 06.3558 881	AQ	0.6300	17.1	17.5
2000+148	20 02 41.9992 3145	+15 01 14.5740 653	AQ			20.6
2000+472	20 02 10.4182 4494	+47 25 28.7737 471	AQ	2.2660		19.3
2002−375	20 05 55.0708 9847	−37 23 41.4779 107	V			
2008−159	20 11 15.7109 2555	−15 46 40.2537 406	AQ	1.1800	17.2	16.9
2017+745	20 17 13.0792 9657	+74 40 47.9999 016	AQ	2.1870	18.1	18.2

IERS Designation	Right Ascension	Declination	Type	z	V	G
	h m s	° ′ ″				
2022−077	20 25 40.6604 0313	−07 35 52.6889 470	AL	1.3880		18.1
2029+121	20 31 54.9942 6552	+12 19 41.3401 260	AL	1.2150	18.5	19.8
2036−034	20 39 09.9848 8939	−03 17 14.4169 978	AQ	1.5510		19.6
2037+216	20 39 34.8083 0863	+21 52 09.6829 032	AQ			18.8
2037−253	20 40 08.7729 1682	−25 07 46.6634 680	AQ	1.5740	18.5	18.9
2052−474	20 56 16.3598 0507	−47 14 47.6277 179	AQ	1.4890	19.1	17.7
2059+034	21 01 38.8341 5344	+03 41 31.3207 714	AQ	1.0130	17.8	17.5
2111+400	21 13 29.4862 5383	+40 12 51.3877 999	R			
2113+293	21 15 29.4134 5155	+29 33 38.3669 390	AQ	1.5140	19.5	18.7
2109−811	21 16 30.8456 5873	−80 53 55.2229 061	AQ			20.9
2121+547	21 23 05.3134 5329	+55 00 27.3252 330	I			
2142+110	21 45 18.7750 6615	+11 15 27.3123 630	AL	0.5480	18.2	18.0
2143−156	21 46 22.9793 2711	−15 25 43.8856 539	A1	0.6980	17.3	17.2
2142−758	21 47 12.7306 3669	−75 36 13.2249 063	AQ	1.1390	17.3	17.2
2149+056	21 51 37.8754 9026	+05 52 12.9545 152	A1	0.7400	22.1	
2155+312	21 57 28.8238 8667	+31 27 01.3517 551	AQ	1.4860	18.6	20.5
2155−304	21 58 52.0651 1983	−30 13 32.1182 492	AL	0.1160	13.4	13.7
2209+236	22 12 05.9663 1459	+23 55 40.5438 259	AQ	1.1250	18.3	19.2
2210−257	22 13 02.4979 8123	−25 29 30.0806 026	AQ	1.8330	19.0	19.0
2214+350	22 16 20.0098 9880	+35 18 14.1799 033	AL	0.5100	18.5	18.2
2215+150	22 18 10.9139 0230	+15 20 35.7174 349	AQ	2.3350	18.6	18.4
2216−038	22 18 52.0377 2044	−03 35 36.8795 441	AQ	0.9010	16.6	16.3
2220−351	22 23 05.9305 5963	−34 55 47.1778 251	A1	0.2980	17.5	16.0
2227−088	22 29 40.0843 3313	−08 32 54.4355 294	AQ	1.5605	17.4	17.6
2229+695	22 30 36.4697 3826	+69 46 28.0769 147	AL	1.4130	19.6	20.0
2232−488	22 35 13.2365 7823	−48 35 58.7945 202	AQ	0.5058	17.2	17.5
2236−572	22 39 12.0758 9936	−57 01 00.8395 331	AQ	0.5686		21.0
2244−372	22 47 03.9173 2859	−36 57 46.3041 035	AQ	2.2520	19.0	19.2
2245−328	22 48 38.6857 3790	−32 35 52.1881 477	AQ	2.2680	18.7	18.6
2250+190	22 53 07.3691 6889	+19 42 34.6286 731	AL	0.2840	16.8	16.4
2254+074	22 57 17.3031 1778	+07 43 12.3025 633	AL	0.1900	16.5	17.8
2318+049	23 20 44.8565 9166	+05 13 49.9526 016	AQ	0.6220	19.0	18.1
2319+317	23 21 54.9559 8750	+32 04 07.6225 103	AQ	1.4890	18.0	19.4
2319+444	23 22 20.3580 8015	+44 45 42.3536 071	AQ	1.3100		20.5
2325−150	23 27 47.9642 6891	−14 47 55.7511 114	AQ	2.4650	19.0	19.3
2331−240	23 33 55.2378 2715	−23 43 40.6581 980	AL	0.0477	17.0	17.0
2335−027	23 37 57.3390 7021	−02 30 57.6293 054	AQ	1.0720	19.3	18.8
2336+598	23 39 21.1251 9661	+60 10 11.8495 795	V			
2353−686	23 56 00.6814 2337	−68 20 03.4720 105	AQ	1.7160	17.0	17.1
2353+816	23 56 22.7939 1486	+81 52 52.2550 985	AQ	1.3440	20.3	20.6
2355−534	23 57 53.2660 5016	−53 11 13.6895 021	AL	1.0060	17.8	18.8
2355−106	23 58 10.8823 9662	−10 20 08.6114 174	AQ	1.6363	18.9	18.2
2356+385	23 59 33.1807 9487	+38 50 42.3182 764	AQ	2.7040	18.0	18.9

Notes to Table

A AGN including unspecified QSO in NED
AB Blazar (replaced by other AGN class when known)
AL BL Lac type
AQ Quasar
A1 Seyfert 1 galaxy
A2 Seyfert 2 galaxy
G Radio galaxy
I IR source
R Radio source
V Visual source
X X-ray source

CONTENTS OF SECTION J

NOTES AND EXPLANATION

Lunar Reference Systems

The Lunar Celestial Reference System (LCRS) is a system of space-time coordinates, within the framework of General Relativity, with origin at the center of mass of the Moon. The LCRS is defined in the same way as the Geocentric Celestial Reference System (GCRS) specified by the IAU 2000 Resolution B1.3, with parameter values related to the Moon replacing those related to Earth. The transformation between the spatial coordinates of the Barycentric Celestial Reference System (BCRS) and those of the LCRS contains no rotation component, so that the LCRS is kinematically non-rotating with respect to BCRS. In this way, the spatial orientation of the LCRS is derived from that of the BCRS. (See page L2.)

To determine the positions of celestial objects relative to the Moon, as well as to express the orientation parameters of the Moon in the BCRS system, it is also necessary to define a Lunar Reference System (LRS) comprising three lunar-body-fixed coordinate axes having their origin at the center of mass of the Moon and rotating with the Moon. The changing orientation of the LRS — that is, of the solid body of the Moon — is then parameterized, in the BCRS, by three Euler angles.

There are two coordinate systems used for the Lunar Reference System that are widely used:

The Mean Earth/Polar Axis (ME) system is normally employed for cartographic purposes and surface navigation. NASA has standardized on the Jet Propulsion Laboratory's DE421 ME frame as its practical realization. In this realization, the z-axis points from the origin towards the mean rotational pole. The prime meridian (corresponding to zero longitude) is defined by the mean Earth direction. The intersection of the lunar equator and prime meridian is called the "mean sub-Earth point".

The Principal Axis (PA) system is practical for dynamical studies, and for spacecraft trajectories and gravity field determination. This is a coordinate system whose axes coincide with the principal axes of inertia of the Moon. Each PA axis differs from its ME counterpart by about 860 m at the lunar surface (Archinal et al. 2018).

Sun and Planets in the Lunarcentric Celestial Reference System

The tables on pages J4 – J39 provide the LCRS apparent right ascension and apparent declination, as well as the true lunarcentric distance (that is, the Euclidean distance at the tabular time), of the Sun and planets, including Earth. These parameters' daily values are given for 0^h Barycentric Dynamical Time (TBD). These coordinates are based on the JPL DE440 ephemeris (Park, et al. 2021) and are fully corrected for light-time, gravitational deflection of light, and aberration. They are expressed with respect to the LCRS, rather than a lunar equatorial system, because there is no convention specifying a right ascension origin on the lunar celestial equator. Similarly, the tabular time is TDB because there is no convention on a lunar time scale.

Lunar Orientation Parameters

The tables on pages J40 – J47 provide the lunar orientation parameters (Euler angles) defining, with respect to the BCRS, the orientation of both the PA and ME Lunar Reference Systems. These angles' daily values are given for 0^h TDB. The angles for the PA system are taken directly from the JPL DE440 ephemeris, and those for the ME system are derived from the transformation between the PA and ME systems given in Park, et al. (2021) for use with the DE440 ephemeris.

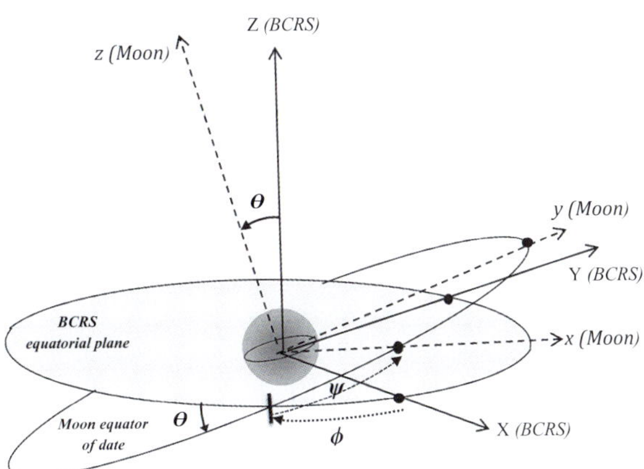

Figure 1: The Lunar Reference System (LRS) and the Lunar Celestial Reference System (LCRS), both having origin at the center of mass of the Moon. The LCRS is defined through the BCRS so that the transformation between the BCRS and LCRS spatial coordinate axes contains no rotation component. The LRS spatial coordinates can be represented either by the Mean Earth/Polar Axis (ME) system or by the Principal Axis (PA) system. The Euler angles ϕ, θ, ψ parameterize the orientation of the LRS spatial axes relative to the LCRS. For the Moon, ϕ is always a small angle and can be either positive or negative. A negative ϕ value is shown. The angle θ is always close to 22° degrees, and ψ can take on any value as the Moon rotates.

The first two Euler angles, ϕ and θ, specify the direction of the Moon's rotation axis (north celestial pole), and the third, ψ, measures the rotational angle of the Moon. Specifically, $\alpha_0 = \phi - 90°$, $\delta_0 = 90° - \theta$, and $W = \psi$, using the notation of Archinal et. al (2018) for the coordinates of the Moon's celestial pole in the BCRS and the rotational angle measured from the ascending node of the Moon's equator on the BCRS XY-plane. See Fig. 1 above and also Fig. 1 in Archinal et al. (2018).

Lunar South Pole Navigation Parameters

To facilitate navigation and other applications near the lunar south pole, the tables on pages J48 – J53 provide the apparent azimuth and altitude for the bright planets (Mercury through Saturn) and several bright stars, as would be seen from the ME system south pole. Altitude is measured from the horizon plane orthogonal to the ME system z-axis at the south pole, i.e., at z = −1737.4 km (the adopted radius of the Moon). Azimuth is measured eastward from the direction of the ME system prime meridian. The values of both azimuth and altitude are given for 0^{h} Barycentric Dynamical Time every four days.

The tabulated coordinates reflect the fact that the lunar south celestial pole is only about $1.5°$ from the south ecliptic pole, so that the ecliptic plane almost coincides with the south pole horizon. Coordinates are not listed for planets that remain below the horizon for the entire year. The sidereal rotation rate of the Moon is $13.1764°$/day, which is the daily decrease in azimuth for stars seen at the lunar south pole. The Sun and planets, however, have their own motions with respect to the stars, so that their azimuths decrease at somewhat different rates, which vary with time. The motions of the Earth in the lunar sky result from the librations tabulated in Section D.

LCRS COORDINATES FOR 0^h BARYCENTRIC DYNAMICAL TIME

Date	Apparent Right Ascension	Apparent Declination	True Lunarcentric Distance	Date	Apparent Right Ascension	Apparent Declination	True Lunarcentric Distance
	°	°	au		°	°	au
Jan. 0	280.272727	−23.087285	0.980 8030	Feb. 15	328.505625	−12.761155	0.990 0647
1	281.343485	−23.014552	0.980 8759	16	329.501693	−12.405477	0.989 9993
2	282.414746	−22.935132	0.981 0652	17	330.491057	−12.047711	0.989 8580
3	283.487982	−22.848820	0.981 3647	18	331.473109	−11.688408	0.989 6545
4	284.564553	−22.755341	0.981 7622	19	332.447389	−11.328066	0.989 4043
5	285.645604	−22.654372	0.982 2402	20	333.413580	−10.967118	0.989 1242
6	286.731969	−22.545569	0.982 7763	21	334.371514	−10.605934	0.988 8323
7	287.824107	−22.428595	0.983 3449	22	335.321172	−10.244804	0.988 5480
8	288.922053	−22.303148	0.983 9183	23	336.262711	−9.883929	0.988 2918
9	290.025411	−22.168998	0.984 4690	24	337.196492	−9.523394	0.988 0849
10	291.133367	−22.026001	0.984 9706	25	338.123116	−9.163149	0.987 9490
11	292.244739	−21.874127	0.985 4004	26	339.043458	−8.802981	0.987 9047
12	293.358054	−21.713464	0.985 7401	27	339.958681	−8.442503	0.987 9700
13	294.471655	−21.544219	0.985 9773	28	340.870214	−8.081152	0.988 1582
14	295.583811	−21.366700	0.986 1059	Mar. 1	341.779676	−7.718230	0.988 4761
15	296.692838	−21.181303	0.986 1259	2	342.688755	−7.352960	0.988 9217
16	297.797185	−20.988475	0.986 0429	3	343.599047	−6.984578	0.989 4848
17	298.895507	−20.788698	0.985 8667	4	344.511920	−6.612413	0.990 1472
18	299.986691	−20.582458	0.985 6106	5	345.428400	−6.235957	0.990 8849
19	301.069865	−20.370232	0.985 2901	6	346.349129	−5.854907	0.991 6709
20	302.144387	−20.152473	0.984 9221	7	347.274369	−5.469166	0.992 4769
21	303.209823	−19.929605	0.984 5241	8	348.204044	−5.078838	0.993 2759
22	304.265935	−19.702013	0.984 1145	9	349.137799	−4.684197	0.994 0433
23	305.312663	−19.470040	0.983 7119	10	350.075058	−4.285660	0.994 7577
24	306.350133	−19.233977	0.983 3352	11	351.015085	−3.883751	0.995 4013
25	307.378662	−18.994049	0.983 0037	12	351.957031	−3.479082	0.995 9604
26	308.398782	−18.750406	0.982 7362	13	352.899980	−3.072318	0.996 4257
27	309.411258	−18.503099	0.982 5510	14	353.842988	−2.664153	0.996 7914
28	310.417108	−18.252066	0.982 4648	15	354.785119	−2.255292	0.997 0559
29	311.417594	−17.997117	0.982 4912	16	355.725468	−1.846425	0.997 2213
30	312.414186	−17.737935	0.982 6390	17	356.663194	−1.438214	0.997 2926
31	313.408486	−17.474087	0.982 9114	18	357.597525	−1.031279	0.997 2781
Feb. 1	314.402114	−17.205057	0.983 3043	19	358.527779	−0.626186	0.997 1885
2	315.396574	−16.930297	0.983 8062	20	359.453365	−0.223442	0.997 0367
3	316.393127	−16.649277	0.984 3991	21	0.373793	+0.176511	0.996 8380
4	317.392695	−16.361547	0.985 0597	22	1.288685	+0.573307	0.996 6096
5	318.395801	−16.066771	0.985 7613	23	2.197795	+0.966669	0.996 3709
6	319.402564	−15.764759	0.986 4759	24	3.101034	+1.356423	0.996 1432
7	320.412722	−15.455481	0.987 1760	25	3.998519	+1.742523	0.995 9496
8	321.425676	−15.139066	0.987 8363	26	4.890621	+2.125081	0.995 8142
9	322.440560	−14.815791	0.988 4345	27	5.778017	+2.504390	0.995 7608
10	323.456306	−14.486069	0.988 9529	28	6.661730	+2.880940	0.995 8113
11	324.471720	−14.150420	0.989 3785	29	7.543115	+3.255404	0.995 9828
12	325.485554	−13.809444	0.989 7031	30	8.423794	+3.628592	0.996 2850
13	326.496573	−13.463794	0.989 9240	31	9.305522	+4.001364	0.996 7185
14	327.503614	−13.114141	0.990 0426	Apr. 1	10.190008	+4.374529	0.997 2744
15	328.505625	−12.761155	0.990 0647	2	11.078749	+4.748750	0.997 9353

LCRS COORDINATES FOR 0^h BARYCENTRIC DYNAMICAL TIME

Date	Apparent Right Ascension	Apparent Declination	True Lunarcentric Distance	Date	Apparent Right Ascension	Apparent Declination	True Lunarcentric Distance
	°	°	au		°	°	au
Apr. 1	10.190008	+4.374529	0.997 2744	May 17	53.786161	+19.289331	1.012 9510
2	11.078749	+4.748750	0.997 9353	18	54.797077	+19.515518	1.012 7208
3	11.972915	+5.124483	0.998 6776	19	55.804905	+19.734237	1.012 4314
4	12.873294	+5.501951	0.999 4745	20	56.808808	+19.945428	1.012 1021
5	13.780300	+5.881155	1.000 2985	21	57.808154	+20.149123	1.011 7557
6	14.694025	+6.261912	1.001 1234	22	58.802588	+20.345458	1.011 4176
7	15.614291	+6.643887	1.001 9251	23	59.792110	+20.534674	1.011 1152
8	16.540712	+7.026633	1.002 6827	24	60.777152	+20.717109	1.010 8761
9	17.472742	+7.409625	1.003 3785	25	61.758618	+20.893180	1.010 7258
10	18.409707	+7.792277	1.003 9979	26	62.737870	+21.063351	1.010 6849
11	19.350844	+8.173972	1.004 5298	27	63.716634	+21.228077	1.010 7670
12	20.295317	+8.554073	1.004 9664	28	64.696830	+21.387755	1.010 9763
13	21.242244	+8.931942	1.005 3031	29	65.680365	+21.542675	1.011 3077
14	22.190719	+9.306950	1.005 5386	30	66.668947	+21.692991	1.011 7480
15	23.139829	+9.678499	1.005 6748	31	67.663948	+21.838720	1.012 2780
16	24.088677	+10.046022	1.005 7165	June 1	68.666350	+21.979755	1.012 8754
17	25.036397	+10.409007	1.005 6718	2	69.676748	+22.115894	1.013 5163
18	25.982174	+10.766993	1.005 5514	3	70.695393	+22.246868	1.014 1774
19	26.925261	+11.119591	1.005 3689	4	71.722247	+22.372364	1.014 8364
20	27.865005	+11.466487	1.005 1408	5	72.757035	+22.492050	1.015 4730
21	28.800877	+11.807460	1.004 8864	6	73.799280	+22.605588	1.016 0685
22	29.732513	+12.142393	1.004 6276	7	74.848335	+22.712643	1.016 6061
23	30.659776	+12.471299	1.004 3887	8	75.903394	+22.812898	1.017 0712
24	31.582819	+12.794340	1.004 1959	9	76.963508	+22.906057	1.017 4511
25	32.502159	+13.111840	1.004 0752	10	78.027590	+22.991859	1.017 7355
26	33.418724	+13.424293	1.004 0510	11	79.094431	+23.070079	1.017 9168
27	34.333855	+13.732333	1.004 1429	12	80.162712	+23.140545	1.017 9906
28	35.249227	+14.036679	1.004 3629	13	81.231043	+23.203139	1.017 9558
29	36.166700	+14.338054	1.004 7139	14	82.297992	+23.257810	1.017 8155
30	37.088123	+14.637094	1.005 1887	15	83.362138	+23.304572	1.017 5768
May 1	38.015147	+14.934273	1.005 7714	16	84.422126	+23.343513	1.017 2514
2	38.949089	+15.229869	1.006 4402	17	85.476731	+23.374789	1.016 8552
3	39.890875	+15.523957	1.007 1699	18	86.524924	+23.398617	1.016 4083
4	40.841051	+15.816436	1.007 9345	19	87.565951	+23.415269	1.015 9346
5	41.799823	+16.107062	1.008 7089	20	88.599402	+23.425050	1.015 4606
6	42.767119	+16.395491	1.009 4700	21	89.625284	+23.428285	1.015 0146
7	43.742643	+16.681306	1.010 1969	22	90.644072	+23.425282	1.014 6245
8	44.725917	+16.964040	1.010 8716	23	91.656711	+23.416311	1.014 3161
9	45.716313	+17.243202	1.011 4785	24	92.664578	+23.401571	1.014 1098
10	46.713077	+17.518286	1.012 0049	25	93.669360	+23.381166	1.014 0195
11	47.715343	+17.788782	1.012 4405	26	94.672899	+23.355101	1.014 0507
12	48.722147	+18.054189	1.012 7780	27	95.676998	+23.323281	1.014 2004
13	49.732447	+18.314027	1.013 0129	28	96.683274	+23.285529	1.014 4585
14	50.745141	+18.567845	1.013 1440	29	97.693039	+23.241615	1.014 8095
15	51.759089	+18.815231	1.013 1732	30	98.707261	+23.191277	1.015 2342
16	52.773140	+19.055826	1.013 1059	July 1	99.726566	+23.134244	1.015 7119
17	53.786161	+19.289331	1.012 9510	2	100.751266	+23.070253	1.016 2213

LCRS COORDINATES FOR 0ʰ BARYCENTRIC DYNAMICAL TIME

Date	Apparent Right Ascension	Apparent Declination	True Lunarcentric Distance	Date	Apparent Right Ascension	Apparent Declination	True Lunarcentric Distance
	°	°	au		°	°	au
July 1	99.726566	+23.134244	1.015 7119	Aug. 16	145.511108	+13.779532	1.012 7641
2	100.751266	+23.070253	1.016 2213	17	146.442847	+13.462151	1.012 0177
3	101.781412	+22.999064	1.016 7416	18	147.365964	+13.144239	1.011 2896
4	102.816825	+22.920463	1.017 2527	19	148.281066	+12.825796	1.010 6064
5	103.857135	+22.834273	1.017 7356	20	149.189063	+12.506652	1.009 9917
6	104.901796	+22.740356	1.018 1724	21	150.091101	+12.186487	1.009 4642
7	105.950099	+22.638623	1.018 5463	22	150.988485	+11.864867	1.009 0371
8	107.001172	+22.529040	1.018 8422	23	151.882590	+11.541281	1.008 7178
9	108.053983	+22.411638	1.019 0466	24	152.774780	+11.215181	1.008 5081
10	109.107342	+22.286517	1.019 1485	25	153.666338	+10.886026	1.008 4043
11	110.159925	+22.153858	1.019 1400	26	154.558414	+10.553309	1.008 3983
12	111.210299	+22.013921	1.019 0171	27	155.451996	+10.216579	1.008 4787
13	112.256977	+21.867046	1.018 7805	28	156.347900	+9.875460	1.008 6315
14	113.298480	+21.713643	1.018 4360	29	157.246772	+9.529650	1.008 8408
15	114.333420	+21.554176	1.017 9947	30	158.149099	+9.178927	1.009 0895
16	115.360578	+21.389135	1.017 4733	31	159.055218	+8.823148	1.009 3596
17	116.378991	+21.219017	1.016 8929	Sept. 1	159.965319	+8.462250	1.009 6322
18	117.388021	+21.044285	1.016 2788	2	160.879443	+8.096257	1.009 8878
19	118.387414	+20.865340	1.015 6585	3	161.797474	+7.725287	1.010 1064
20	119.377332	+20.682489	1.015 0608	4	162.719109	+7.349573	1.010 2677
21	120.358367	+20.495915	1.014 5133	5	163.643840	+6.969471	1.010 3520
22	121.331507	+20.305667	1.014 0407	6	164.570928	+6.585483	1.010 3409
23	122.298068	+20.111651	1.013 6628	7	165.499397	+6.198256	1.010 2189
24	123.259592	+19.913644	1.013 3933	8	166.428058	+5.808576	1.009 9752
25	124.217713	+19.711320	1.013 2385	9	167.355572	+5.417329	1.009 6055
26	125.174029	+19.504286	1.013 1978	10	168.280545	+5.025448	1.009 1130
27	126.129990	+19.292125	1.013 2644	11	169.201656	+4.633839	1.008 5086
28	127.086827	+19.074423	1.013 4265	12	170.117778	+4.243307	1.007 8107
29	128.045513	+18.850804	1.013 6688	13	171.028074	+3.854497	1.007 0432
30	129.006762	+18.620939	1.013 9738	14	171.932054	+3.467856	1.006 2334
31	129.971045	+18.384561	1.014 3228	15	172.829584	+3.083623	1.005 4096
Aug. 1	130.938622	+18.141461	1.014 6966	16	173.720872	+2.701834	1.004 5997
2	131.909561	+17.891496	1.015 0761	17	174.606425	+2.322346	1.003 8290
3	132.883759	+17.634589	1.015 4419	18	175.486996	+1.944866	1.003 1197
4	133.860953	+17.370728	1.015 7753	19	176.363528	+1.568982	1.002 4895
5	134.840714	+17.099980	1.016 0577	20	177.237102	+1.194202	1.001 9518
6	135.822445	+16.822498	1.016 2712	21	178.108876	+0.819984	1.001 5151
7	136.805362	+16.538530	1.016 3992	22	178.980034	+0.445771	1.001 1833
8	137.788500	+16.248434	1.016 4270	23	179.851742	+0.071021	1.000 9559
9	138.770709	+15.952680	1.016 3430	24	180.725106	−0.304768	1.000 8285
10	139.750694	+15.651847	1.016 1400	25	181.601150	−0.682045	1.000 7934
11	140.727069	+15.346608	1.015 8162	26	182.480796	−1.061187	1.000 8399
12	141.698437	+15.037695	1.015 3762	27	183.364855	−1.442499	1.000 9552
13	142.663493	+14.725859	1.014 8310	28	184.254024	−1.826206	1.001 1246
14	143.621124	+14.411818	1.014 1981	29	185.148881	−2.212454	1.001 3315
15	144.570494	+14.096206	1.013 5004	30	186.049883	−2.601301	1.001 5579
16	145.511108	+13.779532	1.012 7641	Oct. 1	186.957346	−2.992714	1.001 7841

LCRS COORDINATES FOR 0^h BARYCENTRIC DYNAMICAL TIME

Date	Apparent Right Ascension	Apparent Declination	True Lunarcentric Distance	Date	Apparent Right Ascension	Apparent Declination	True Lunarcentric Distance
	°	°	au		°	°	au
Oct. 1	186.957346	−2.992714	1.001 7841	Nov. 16	231.246508	−18.672581	0.987 2090
2	187.871424	−3.386554	1.001 9892	17	232.256787	−18.912896	0.986 6455
3	188.792075	−3.782558	1.002 1510	18	233.266666	−19.147324	0.986 1681
4	189.719008	−4.180320	1.002 2469	19	234.277116	−19.376158	0.985 7854
5	190.651651	−4.579275	1.002 2552	20	235.289189	−19.599667	0.985 5032
6	191.589114	−4.978692	1.002 1565	21	236.303988	−19.818085	0.985 3238
7	192.530205	−5.377700	1.001 9366	22	237.322644	−20.031600	0.985 2467
8	193.473497	−5.775328	1.001 5881	23	238.346286	−20.240347	0.985 2682
9	194.417446	−6.170591	1.001 1125	24	239.376013	−20.444402	0.985 3813
10	195.360552	−6.562573	1.000 5202	25	240.412867	−20.643779	0.985 5761
11	196.301511	−6.950513	0.999 8296	26	241.457799	−20.838420	0.985 8395
12	197.239328	−7.333853	0.999 0648	27	242.511641	−21.028198	0.986 1555
13	198.173378	−7.712260	0.998 2530	28	243.575063	−21.212913	0.986 5052
14	199.103401	−8.085609	0.997 4221	29	244.648516	−21.392288	0.986 8666
15	200.029471	−8.453957	0.996 5988	30	245.732174	−21.565970	0.987 2153
16	200.951949	−8.817505	0.995 8072	Dec. 1	246.825848	−21.733537	0.987 5251
17	201.871424	−9.176560	0.995 0685	2	247.928917	−21.894506	0.987 7697
18	202.788667	−9.531505	0.994 4000	3	249.040269	−22.048355	0.987 9242
19	203.704590	−9.882770	0.993 8156	4	250.158317	−22.194566	0.987 9686
20	204.620205	−10.230809	0.993 3252	5	251.281084	−22.332664	0.987 8899
21	205.536588	−10.576074	0.992 9349	6	252.406383	−22.462270	0.987 6845
22	206.454851	−10.919004	0.992 6473	7	253.532038	−22.583131	0.987 3583
23	207.376106	−11.259999	0.992 4614	8	254.656097	−22.695135	0.986 9257
24	208.301443	−11.599414	0.992 3732	9	255.776975	−22.798299	0.986 4068
25	209.231905	−11.937546	0.992 3754	10	256.893519	−22.892748	0.985 8254
26	210.168469	−12.274624	0.992 4583	11	258.004993	−22.978675	0.985 2060
27	211.112033	−12.610807	0.992 6094	12	259.111031	−23.056320	0.984 5725
28	212.063399	−12.946177	0.992 8140	13	260.211570	−23.125938	0.983 9473
29	213.023257	−13.280733	0.993 0550	14	261.306795	−23.187785	0.983 3506
30	213.992154	−13.614384	0.993 3132	15	262.397090	−23.242105	0.982 8007
31	214.970461	−13.946939	0.993 5670	16	263.483010	−23.289119	0.982 3134
Nov. 1	215.958319	−14.278090	0.993 7928	17	264.565257	−23.329018	0.981 9024
2	216.955571	−14.607399	0.993 9661	18	265.644668	−23.361957	0.981 5793
3	217.961700	−14.934293	0.994 0622	19	266.722194	−23.388047	0.981 3529
4	218.975777	−15.258064	0.994 0587	20	267.798886	−23.407349	0.981 2294
5	219.996467	−15.577901	0.993 9379	21	268.875870	−23.419872	0.981 2117
6	221.022098	−15.892947	0.993 6895	22	269.954311	−23.425566	0.981 2996
7	222.050820	−16.202374	0.993 3126	23	271.035380	−23.424326	0.981 4892
8	223.080793	−16.505463	0.992 8159	24	272.120207	−23.415986	0.981 7728
9	224.110387	−16.801665	0.992 2166	25	273.209832	−23.400329	0.982 1389
10	225.138315	−17.090629	0.991 5377	26	274.305160	−23.377094	0.982 5722
11	226.163694	−17.372193	0.990 8051	27	275.406898	−23.345985	0.983 0536
12	227.186038	−17.646355	0.990 0454	28	276.515500	−23.306685	0.983 5608
13	228.205216	−17.913240	0.989 2841	29	277.631095	−23.258880	0.984 0685
14	229.221389	−18.173057	0.988 5445	30	278.753422	−23.202281	0.984 5496
15	230.234956	−18.426072	0.987 8469	31	279.881772	−23.136654	0.984 9765
16	231.246508	−18.672581	0.987 2090	32	281.014962	−23.061858	0.985 3236

LCRS COORDINATES FOR 0^h BARYCENTRIC DYNAMICAL TIME

Date	Apparent Right Ascension	Apparent Declination	True Lunarcentric Distance	Date	Apparent Right Ascension	Apparent Declination	True Lunarcentric Distance
	°	°	au		°	°	au
Jan. 0	257.291316	−21.648705	1.128 2602	Feb. 15	333.308455	−12.929932	1.356 2064
1	258.620114	−21.894254	1.145 9397	16	335.055472	−12.191480	1.345 9710
2	259.985566	−22.130785	1.163 0930	17	336.795724	−11.432418	1.334 6894
3	261.385620	−22.356747	1.179 7084	18	338.527431	−10.653990	1.322 3318
4	262.818355	−22.570680	1.195 7720	19	340.248584	−9.857621	1.308 8704
5	264.281889	−22.771203	1.211 2679	20	341.956897	−9.044946	1.294 2805
6	265.774304	−22.957027	1.226 1789	21	343.649740	−8.217845	1.278 5419
7	267.293603	−23.126953	1.240 4875	22	345.324092	−7.378470	1.261 6409
8	268.837683	−23.279889	1.254 1773	23	346.976501	−6.529271	1.243 5722
9	270.404338	−23.414858	1.267 2339	24	348.603054	−5.673011	1.224 3414
10	271.991277	−23.531010	1.279 6465	25	350.199373	−4.812777	1.203 9669
11	273.596164	−23.627626	1.291 4083	26	351.760634	−3.951962	1.182 4822
12	275.216672	−23.704121	1.302 5178	27	353.281606	−3.094253	1.159 9368
13	276.850548	−23.760040	1.312 9790	28	354.756701	−2.243598	1.136 3969
14	278.495682	−23.795042	1.322 8011	Mar. 1	356.180030	−1.404180	1.111 9447
15	280.150163	−23.808884	1.331 9978	2	357.545448	−0.580390	1.086 6779
16	281.812314	−23.801402	1.340 5862	3	358.846589	+0.223192	1.060 7084
17	283.480711	−23.772484	1.348 5858	4	0.076912	+1.001820	1.034 1613
18	285.154172	−23.722056	1.356 0171	5	1.229758	+1.750613	1.007 1740
19	286.831739	−23.650062	1.362 9004	6	2.298453	+2.464607	0.979 8945
20	288.512649	−23.556456	1.369 2557	7	3.276430	+3.138819	0.952 4800
21	290.196307	−23.441190	1.375 1018	8	4.157388	+3.768320	0.925 0940
22	291.882261	−23.304209	1.380 4563	9	4.935452	+4.348313	0.897 9034
23	293.570194	−23.145444	1.385 3356	10	5.605330	+4.874197	0.871 0755
24	295.259912	−22.964807	1.389 7549	11	6.162470	+5.341630	0.844 7748
25	296.951352	−22.762180	1.393 7277	12	6.603201	+5.746582	0.819 1605
26	298.644585	−22.537410	1.397 2662	13	6.924875	+6.085395	0.794 3845
27	300.339829	−22.290295	1.400 3802	14	7.126008	+6.354839	0.770 5898
28	302.037453	−22.020570	1.403 0765	15	7.206430	+6.552191	0.747 9096
29	303.737962	−21.727910	1.405 3576	16	7.167433	+6.675330	0.726 4668
30	305.441973	−21.411920	1.407 2206	17	7.011916	+6.722850	0.706 3735
31	307.150158	−21.072148	1.408 6557	18	6.744517	+6.694190	0.687 7303
Feb. 1	308.863176	−20.708105	1.409 6457	19	6.371708	+6.589771	0.670 6265
2	310.581592	−20.319296	1.410 1658	20	5.901849	+6.411143	0.655 1397
3	312.305804	−19.905254	1.410 1845	21	5.345181	+6.161103	0.641 3350
4	314.035996	−19.465571	1.409 6645	22	4.713746	+5.843797	0.629 2649
5	315.772115	−18.999930	1.408 5647	23	4.021238	+5.464773	0.618 9691
6	317.513867	−18.508121	1.406 8414	24	3.282793	+5.030987	0.610 4735
7	319.260741	−17.990053	1.404 4501	25	2.514702	+4.550735	0.603 7902
8	321.012036	−17.445761	1.401 3460	26	1.734082	+4.033520	0.598 9157
9	322.766885	−16.875405	1.397 4857	27	0.958475	+3.489833	0.595 8301
10	324.524291	−16.279267	1.392 8269	28	0.205372	+2.930840	0.594 4950
11	326.283150	−15.657751	1.387 3291	29	359.491638	+2.367968	0.594 8519
12	328.042277	−15.011381	1.380 9540	30	358.832858	+1.812407	0.596 8209
13	329.800424	−14.340782	1.373 6649	31	358.242654	+1.274567	0.600 3016
14	331.556279	−13.646685	1.365 4269	Apr. 1	357.732109	+0.763588	0.605 1763
15	333.308455	−12.929932	1.356 2064	2	357.309403	+0.286984	0.611 3157

LCRS COORDINATES FOR 0^h BARYCENTRIC DYNAMICAL TIME

Date	Apparent Right Ascension	Apparent Declination	True Lunarcentric Distance	Date	Apparent Right Ascension	Apparent Declination	True Lunarcentric Distance
	°	°	au		°	°	au
Apr. 1	357.732109	+0.763588	0.605 1763	May 17	39.449679	+13.689177	1.230 0093
2	357.309403	+0.286984	0.611 3157	18	41.288875	+14.407669	1.241 9830
3	356.979762	−0.149519	0.618 5850	19	43.166780	+15.124176	1.253 3482
4	356.745667	−0.541941	0.626 8509	20	45.083842	+15.836691	1.264 0459
5	356.607275	−0.887863	0.635 9860	21	47.040389	+16.543073	1.274 0141
6	356.562896	−1.186173	0.645 8730	22	49.036598	+17.241039	1.283 1880
7	356.609486	−1.436782	0.656 4061	23	51.072453	+17.928161	1.291 5005
8	356.743063	−1.640368	0.667 4919	24	53.147705	+18.601859	1.298 8833
9	356.959060	−1.798154	0.679 0493	25	55.261818	+19.259407	1.305 2664
10	357.252600	−1.911726	0.691 0088	26	57.413888	+19.897929	1.310 5795
11	357.618705	−1.982892	0.703 3122	27	59.602540	+20.514410	1.314 7521
12	358.052462	−2.013565	0.715 9111	28	61.825803	+21.105718	1.317 7165
13	358.549133	−2.005677	0.728 7666	29	64.080998	+21.668651	1.319 4097
14	359.104246	−1.961119	0.741 8482	30	66.364686	+22.200049	1.319 7780
15	359.713652	−1.881687	0.755 1325	31	68.672695	+22.696692	1.318 7809
16	0.373563	−1.769052	0.768 6029	June 1	71.000002	+23.155771	1.316 3942
17	1.080570	−1.624744	0.782 2482	2	73.341184	+23.574673	1.312 6124
18	1.831656	−1.450132	0.796 0620	3	75.690366	+23.951182	1.307 4493
19	2.624196	−1.246422	0.810 0422	4	78.041463	+24.283534	1.300 9373
20	3.455961	−1.014652	0.824 1899	5	80.388355	+24.570457	1.293 1254
21	4.325123	−0.755689	0.838 5093	6	82.725036	+24.811172	1.284 0762
22	5.230267	−0.470220	0.853 0066	7	85.045739	+25.005391	1.273 8636
23	6.170403	−0.158752	0.867 6890	8	87.345022	+25.153280	1.262 5686
24	7.144981	+0.178384	0.882 5636	9	89.617822	+25.255426	1.250 2770
25	8.153878	+0.541019	0.897 6352	10	91.859480	+25.312786	1.237 0765
26	9.197359	+0.929103	0.912 9042	11	94.065741	+25.326642	1.223 0546
27	10.275983	+1.342634	0.928 3644	12	96.232737	+25.298549	1.208 2974
28	11.390454	+1.781560	0.944 0010	13	98.356963	+25.230296	1.192 8884
29	12.541452	+2.245683	0.959 7903	14	100.435241	+25.123861	1.176 9080
30	13.729481	+2.734574	0.975 7010	15	102.464697	+24.981379	1.160 4334
May 1	14.954772	+3.247544	0.991 6965	16	104.442733	+24.805110	1.143 5389
2	16.217280	+3.783652	1.007 7377	17	106.367012	+24.597404	1.126 2965
3	17.516729	+4.341756	1.023 7853	18	108.235458	+24.360678	1.108 7756
4	18.852709	+4.920575	1.039 8018	19	110.046263	+24.097384	1.091 0442
5	20.224761	+5.518747	1.055 7515	20	111.797923	+23.809979	1.073 1689
6	21.632454	+6.134870	1.071 6011	21	113.489277	+23.500884	1.055 2149
7	23.075434	+6.767528	1.087 3185	22	115.119565	+23.172451	1.037 2455
8	24.553457	+7.415308	1.102 8728	23	116.688481	+22.826913	1.019 3207
9	26.066401	+8.076797	1.118 2330	24	118.196187	+22.466352	1.001 4959
10	27.614267	+8.750584	1.133 3676	25	119.643286	+22.092669	0.983 8198
11	29.197176	+9.435254	1.148 2442	26	121.030735	+21.707581	0.966 3329
12	30.815358	+10.129373	1.162 8286	27	122.359709	+21.312632	0.949 0665
13	32.469146	+10.831483	1.177 0847	28	123.631448	+20.909228	0.932 0431
14	34.158958	+11.540093	1.190 9739	29	124.847119	+20.498675	0.915 2774
15	35.885286	+12.253661	1.204 4547	30	126.007715	+20.082216	0.898 7778
16	37.648671	+12.970582	1.217 4826	July 1	127.113992	+19.661066	0.882 5485
17	39.449679	+13.689177	1.230 0093	2	128.166445	+19.236436	0.866 5903

LCRS COORDINATES FOR 0^h BARYCENTRIC DYNAMICAL TIME

Date	Apparent Right Ascension	Apparent Declination	True Lunarcentric Distance	Date	Apparent Right Ascension	Apparent Declination	True Lunarcentric Distance
	°	°	au		°	°	au
July 1	127.113992	+19.661066	0.882 5485	Aug. 16	127.239625	+17.150288	0.818 7392
2	128.166445	+19.236436	0.866 5903	17	127.915823	+17.280557	0.842 7755
3	129.165295	+18.809548	0.850 9023	18	128.705361	+17.378500	0.867 6364
4	130.110498	+18.381654	0.835 4824	19	129.607214	+17.440841	0.893 2210
5	131.001737	+17.954042	0.820 3280	20	130.619451	+17.464405	0.919 4116
6	131.838415	+17.528058	0.805 4363	21	131.739119	+17.446211	0.946 0740
7	132.619637	+17.105116	0.790 8049	22	132.962175	+17.383572	0.973 0588
8	133.344175	+16.686725	0.776 4319	23	134.283463	+17.274200	1.000 2036
9	134.010433	+16.274512	0.762 3169	24	135.696748	+17.116289	1.027 3370
10	134.616413	+15.870250	0.748 4619	25	137.194818	+16.908593	1.054 2826
11	135.159679	+15.475889	0.734 8721	26	138.769640	+16.650475	1.080 8638
12	135.637362	+15.093572	0.721 5575	27	140.412559	+16.341935	1.106 9091
13	136.046184	+14.725657	0.708 5347	28	142.114535	+15.983604	1.132 2562
14	136.382536	+14.374709	0.695 8280	29	143.866382	+15.576719	1.156 7566
15	136.642605	+14.043484	0.683 4710	30	145.659004	+15.123072	1.180 2788
16	136.822558	+13.734886	0.671 5076	31	147.483614	+14.624935	1.202 7102
17	136.918775	+13.451905	0.659 9922	Sept. 1	149.331907	+14.084988	1.223 9585
18	136.928133	+13.197526	0.648 9904	2	151.196197	+13.506224	1.243 9520
19	136.848321	+12.974626	0.638 5774	3	153.069499	+12.891869	1.262 6385
20	136.678176	+12.785849	0.628 8369	4	154.945574	+12.245303	1.279 9840
21	136.418016	+12.633470	0.619 8591	5	156.818926	+11.569988	1.295 9716
22	136.069918	+12.519264	0.611 7371	6	158.684771	+10.869415	1.310 5994
23	135.637908	+12.444400	0.604 5640	7	160.538993	+10.147043	1.323 8796
24	135.128030	+12.409363	0.598 4289	8	162.378094	+9.406255	1.335 8370
25	134.548263	+12.413930	0.593 4141	9	164.199161	+8.650306	1.346 5083
26	133.908323	+12.457188	0.589 5929	10	165.999840	+7.882268	1.355 9410
27	133.219379	+12.537594	0.587 0281	11	167.778325	+7.104982	1.364 1915
28	132.493730	+12.653046	0.585 7720	12	169.533346	+6.321015	1.371 3235
29	131.744477	+12.800972	0.585 8665	13	171.264144	+5.532633	1.377 4050
30	130.985212	+12.978412	0.587 3437	14	172.970423	+4.741788	1.382 5057
31	130.229719	+13.182095	0.590 2265	15	174.652289	+3.950150	1.386 6952
Aug. 1	129.491691	+13.408519	0.594 5290	16	176.310217	+3.159122	1.390 0402
2	128.784455	+13.654026	0.600 2569	17	177.944969	+2.369853	1.392 6035
3	128.120710	+13.914877	0.607 4079	18	179.557532	+1.583279	1.394 4432
4	127.512291	+14.187322	0.615 9723	19	181.149064	+0.800160	1.395 6113
5	126.969968	+14.467666	0.625 9330	20	182.720850	+0.021111	1.396 1542
6	126.503286	+14.752328	0.637 2672	21	184.274258	−0.753373	1.396 1117
7	126.120479	+15.037880	0.649 9466	22	185.810702	−1.522881	1.395 5178
8	125.828446	+15.321070	0.663 9392	23	187.331608	−2.287069	1.394 4006
9	125.632814	+15.598822	0.679 2107	24	188.838389	−3.045633	1.392 7827
10	125.538060	+15.868209	0.695 7252	25	190.332422	−3.798295	1.390 6819
11	125.547697	+16.126408	0.713 4463	26	191.815040	−4.544790	1.388 1114
12	125.664469	+16.370637	0.732 3367	27	193.287517	−5.284858	1.385 0803
13	125.890540	+16.598087	0.752 3574	28	194.751066	−6.018235	1.381 5941
14	126.227619	+16.805871	0.773 4657	29	196.206835	−6.744648	1.377 6547
15	126.677018	+16.990982	0.795 6125	30	197.655901	−7.463810	1.373 2608
16	127.239625	+17.150288	0.818 7392	Oct. 1	199.099254	−8.175409	1.368 4073

LCRS COORDINATES FOR 0ʰ BARYCENTRIC DYNAMICAL TIME

Date	Apparent Right Ascension	Apparent Declination	True Lunarcentric Distance	Date	Apparent Right Ascension	Apparent Declination	True Lunarcentric Distance
	°	°	au		°	°	au
Oct. 1	199.099254	−8.175409	1.368 4073	Nov. 16	241.372460	−21.768575	0.696 8760
2	200.537782	−8.879098	1.363 0857	17	240.273306	−21.239089	0.686 9708
3	201.972235	−9.574479	1.357 2843	18	239.045638	−20.660326	0.679 7781
4	203.403182	−10.261084	1.350 9880	19	237.725442	−20.043324	0.675 5617
5	204.830959	−10.938358	1.344 1797	20	236.355711	−19.402866	0.674 5194
6	206.255617	−11.605647	1.336 8414	21	234.983676	−18.756789	0.676 7657
7	207.676886	−12.262192	1.328 9565	22	233.657290	−18.124716	0.682 3199
8	209.094175	−12.907154	1.320 5123	23	232.421553	−17.526369	0.691 1024
9	210.506615	−13.539644	1.311 5018	24	231.315324	−16.979830	0.702 9405
10	211.913144	−14.158777	1.301 9251	25	230.369110	−16.500056	0.717 5820
11	213.312610	−14.763719	1.291 7899	26	229.604062	−16.097931	0.734 7139
12	214.703867	−15.353728	1.281 1094	27	229.032099	−15.779927	0.753 9841
13	216.085836	−15.928166	1.269 9012	28	228.656888	−15.548307	0.775 0219
14	217.457532	−16.486502	1.258 1851	29	228.475310	−15.401707	0.797 4567
15	218.818065	−17.028300	1.245 9811	30	228.479095	−15.335923	0.820 9325
16	220.166614	−17.553195	1.233 3089	Dec. 1	228.656386	−15.344729	0.845 1189
17	221.502399	−18.060876	1.220 1865	2	228.993094	−15.420643	0.869 7192
18	222.824647	−18.551067	1.206 6299	3	229.474018	−15.555570	0.894 4749
19	224.132562	−19.023506	1.192 6531	4	230.083736	−15.741326	0.919 1687
20	225.425285	−19.477933	1.178 2680	5	230.807305	−15.970029	0.943 6248
21	226.701867	−19.914075	1.163 4840	6	231.630786	−16.234361	0.967 7065
22	227.961225	−20.331631	1.148 3085	7	232.541601	−16.527724	0.991 3127
23	229.202103	−20.730260	1.132 7470	8	233.528704	−16.844285	1.014 3716
24	230.423025	−21.109570	1.116 8033	9	234.582591	−17.178949	1.036 8344
25	231.622254	−21.469106	1.100 4800	10	235.695200	−17.527289	1.058 6696
26	232.797735	−21.808338	1.083 7787	11	236.859736	−17.885458	1.079 8583
27	233.947052	−22.126657	1.066 7007	12	238.070487	−18.250105	1.100 3908
28	235.067366	−22.423357	1.049 2476	13	239.322654	−18.618297	1.120 2640
29	236.155355	−22.697629	1.031 4212	14	240.612204	−18.987457	1.139 4794
30	237.207136	−22.948546	1.013 2248	15	241.935758	−19.355314	1.158 0426
31	238.218169	−23.175040	0.994 6633	16	243.290488	−19.719854	1.175 9612
Nov. 1	239.183130	−23.375880	0.975 7440	17	244.674048	−20.079283	1.193 2448
2	240.095753	−23.549643	0.956 4783	18	246.084503	−20.431992	1.209 9036
3	240.948642	−23.694671	0.936 8837	19	247.520269	−20.776527	1.225 9476
4	241.733077	−23.809047	0.916 9871	20	248.980061	−21.111558	1.241 3863
5	242.438866	−23.890554	0.896 8296	21	250.462834	−21.435857	1.256 2275
6	243.054290	−23.936674	0.876 4719	22	251.967732	−21.748277	1.270 4770
7	243.566224	−23.944585	0.856 0003	23	253.494038	−22.047734	1.284 1385
8	243.960455	−23.911194	0.835 5312	24	255.041122	−22.333196	1.297 2126
9	244.222196	−23.833182	0.815 2145	25	256.608395	−22.603671	1.309 6974
10	244.336763	−23.707069	0.795 2352	26	258.195260	−22.858204	1.321 5878
11	244.290415	−23.529319	0.775 8127	27	259.801070	−23.095874	1.332 8761
12	244.071359	−23.296504	0.757 2002	28	261.425082	−23.315797	1.343 5520
13	243.670955	−23.005572	0.739 6815	29	263.066407	−23.517133	1.353 6029
14	243.085108	−22.654243	0.723 5667	30	264.723967	−23.699094	1.363 0154
15	242.315780	−22.241560	0.709 1855	31	266.396464	−23.860961	1.371 7762
16	241.372460	−21.768575	0.696 8760	32	268.082376	−24.002103	1.379 8738

LCRS COORDINATES FOR 0^h BARYCENTRIC DYNAMICAL TIME

Date	Apparent Right Ascension	Apparent Declination	True Lunarcentric Distance	Date	Apparent Right Ascension	Apparent Declination	True Lunarcentric Distance
	°	°	au		°	°	au
Jan. 0	329.170536	−14.078688	0.756 3994	Feb. 15	4.127396	+6.345972	0.428 0653
1	330.157014	−13.657959	0.748 7015	16	4.576513	+6.736452	0.421 6069
2	331.129450	−13.235724	0.741 0909	17	5.002196	+7.119151	0.415 1086
3	332.089249	−12.811659	0.733 5820	18	5.400854	+7.492211	0.408 5765
4	333.038092	−12.385265	0.726 1845	19	5.768806	+7.853696	0.402 0206
5	333.977847	−11.955902	0.718 9023	20	6.102320	+8.201599	0.395 4546
6	334.910456	−11.522841	0.711 7323	21	6.397660	+8.533851	0.388 8959
7	335.837805	−11.085323	0.704 6654	22	6.651153	+8.848337	0.382 3659
8	336.761602	−10.642627	0.697 6861	23	6.859303	+9.142930	0.375 8898
9	337.683258	−10.194133	0.690 7739	24	7.018968	+9.415556	0.369 4971
10	338.603787	−9.739382	0.683 9043	25	7.127608	+9.664299	0.363 2216
11	339.523726	−9.278128	0.677 0505	26	7.183595	+9.887547	0.357 1000
12	340.443102	−8.810375	0.670 1855	27	7.186551	+10.084165	0.351 1709
13	341.361426	−8.336385	0.663 2836	28	7.137632	+10.253675	0.345 4723
14	342.277753	−7.856671	0.656 3222	Mar. 1	7.039659	+10.396375	0.340 0380
15	343.190758	−7.371959	0.649 2831	2	6.896999	+10.513361	0.334 8946
16	344.098851	−6.883143	0.642 1533	3	6.715193	+10.606412	0.330 0586
17	345.000280	−6.391229	0.634 9249	4	6.500386	+10.677766	0.325 5357
18	345.893221	−5.897290	0.627 5947	5	6.258700	+10.729834	0.321 3208
19	346.775843	−5.402427	0.620 1639	6	5.995695	+10.764925	0.317 4001
20	347.646345	−4.907746	0.612 6371	7	5.715990	+10.785022	0.313 7538
21	348.502972	−4.414347	0.605 0221	8	5.423060	+10.791643	0.310 3585
22	349.344017	−3.923311	0.597 3292	9	5.119174	+10.785764	0.307 1894
23	350.167824	−3.435705	0.589 5714	10	4.805445	+10.767790	0.304 2228
24	350.972801	−2.952566	0.581 7639	11	4.481931	+10.737575	0.301 4371
25	351.757445	−2.474890	0.573 9249	12	4.147796	+10.694453	0.298 8143
26	352.520398	−2.003600	0.566 0751	13	3.801487	+10.637305	0.296 3407
27	353.260529	−1.539503	0.558 2380	14	3.440940	+10.564630	0.294 0075
28	353.977049	−1.083229	0.550 4393	15	3.063800	+10.474638	0.291 8112
29	354.669629	−0.635159	0.542 7061	16	2.667638	+10.365355	0.289 7537
30	355.338526	−0.195364	0.535 0653	17	2.250166	+10.234730	0.287 8420
31	355.984640	+0.236445	0.527 5419	18	1.809431	+10.080739	0.286 0881
Feb. 1	356.609520	+0.660918	0.520 1562	19	1.343988	+9.901496	0.284 5084
2	357.215257	+1.079022	0.512 9226	20	0.853061	+9.695354	0.283 1237
3	357.804305	+1.491957	0.505 8473	21	0.336682	+9.461011	0.281 9581
4	358.379257	+1.901031	0.498 9291	22	359.795844	+9.197625	0.281 0393
5	358.942605	+2.307538	0.492 1587	23	359.232655	+8.904941	0.280 3977
6	359.496527	+2.712646	0.485 5207	24	358.650509	+8.583437	0.280 0657
7	0.042727	+3.117298	0.478 9946	25	358.054266	+8.234500	0.280 0768
8	0.582312	+3.522154	0.472 5569	26	357.450395	+7.860590	0.280 4643
9	1.115722	+3.927538	0.466 1827	27	356.847020	+7.465382	0.281 2583
10	1.642701	+4.333422	0.459 8473	28	356.253769	+7.053804	0.282 4827
11	2.162306	+4.739422	0.453 5276	29	355.681335	+6.631914	0.284 1518
12	2.672953	+5.144820	0.447 2036	30	355.140722	+6.206543	0.286 2670
13	3.172491	+5.548595	0.440 8589	31	354.642262	+5.784749	0.288 8151
14	3.658301	+5.949473	0.434 4819	Apr. 1	354.194643	+5.373173	0.291 7690
15	4.127396	+6.345972	0.428 0653	2	353.804194	+4.977461	0.295 0903

LCRS COORDINATES FOR 0^h BARYCENTRIC DYNAMICAL TIME

Date	Apparent Right Ascension	Apparent Declination	True Lunarcentric Distance	Date	Apparent Right Ascension	Apparent Declination	True Lunarcentric Distance
	°	°	au		°	°	au
Apr. 1	354.194643	+5.373173	0.291 7690	May 17	10.824798	+3.582416	0.578 9012
2	353.804194	+4.977461	0.295 0903	18	11.618135	+3.806233	0.586 2662
3	353.474586	+4.601898	0.298 7342	19	12.411965	+4.031878	0.593 6813
4	353.206961	+4.249300	0.302 6534	20	13.206697	+4.259655	0.601 1682
5	353.000341	+3.921108	0.306 8024	21	14.003154	+4.490092	0.608 7480
6	352.852157	+3.617618	0.311 1395	22	14.802581	+4.723930	0.616 4401
7	352.758757	+3.338239	0.315 6288	23	15.606645	+4.962103	0.624 2605
8	352.715845	+3.081750	0.320 2402	24	16.417372	+5.205676	0.632 2202
9	352.718811	+2.846513	0.324 9502	25	17.237036	+5.455764	0.640 3229
10	352.762982	+2.630643	0.329 7408	26	18.067959	+5.713407	0.648 5636
11	352.843803	+2.432147	0.334 6002	27	18.912275	+5.979434	0.656 9278
12	352.956977	+2.249035	0.339 5217	28	19.771681	+6.254342	0.665 3932
13	353.098563	+2.079410	0.344 5034	29	20.647268	+6.538229	0.673 9313
14	353.265061	+1.921537	0.349 5482	30	21.539453	+6.830795	0.682 5109
15	353.453460	+1.773903	0.354 6628	31	22.448030	+7.131398	0.691 1011
16	353.661280	+1.635261	0.359 8574	June 1	23.372291	+7.439150	0.699 6737
17	353.886594	+1.504659	0.365 1451	2	24.311178	+7.753013	0.708 2042
18	354.128036	+1.381466	0.370 5414	3	25.263415	+8.071882	0.716 6725
19	354.384811	+1.265387	0.376 0637	4	26.227621	+8.394642	0.725 0629
20	354.656704	+1.156478	0.381 7308	5	27.202370	+8.720208	0.733 3634
21	354.944094	+1.055163	0.387 5621	6	28.186233	+9.047544	0.741 5658
22	355.247979	+0.962248	0.393 5772	7	29.177801	+9.375678	0.749 6647
23	355.569987	+0.878939	0.399 7941	8	30.175693	+9.703702	0.757 6580
24	355.912364	+0.806828	0.406 2284	9	31.178566	+10.030785	0.765 5465
25	356.277891	+0.747852	0.412 8906	10	32.185124	+10.356178	0.773 3340
26	356.669698	+0.704179	0.419 7838	11	33.194146	+10.679224	0.781 0275
27	357.090957	+0.678021	0.426 9019	12	34.204505	+10.999371	0.788 6371
28	357.544468	+0.671380	0.434 2283	13	35.215211	+11.316184	0.796 1760
29	358.032252	+0.685790	0.441 7365	14	36.225447	+11.629359	0.803 6607
30	358.555243	+0.722116	0.449 3924	15	37.234616	+11.938729	0.811 1102
May 1	359.113188	+0.780474	0.457 1583	16	38.242384	+12.244272	0.818 5456
2	359.704748	+0.860279	0.464 9961	17	39.248717	+12.546107	0.825 9896
3	0.327752	+0.960387	0.472 8709	18	40.253917	+12.844493	0.833 4656
4	0.979487	+1.079272	0.480 7524	19	41.258647	+13.139809	0.840 9964
5	1.656963	+1.215189	0.488 6160	20	42.263940	+13.432535	0.848 6028
6	2.357117	+1.366308	0.496 4425	21	43.271182	+13.723216	0.856 3023
7	3.076943	+1.530800	0.504 2178	22	44.282068	+14.012418	0.864 1071
8	3.813566	+1.706895	0.511 9325	23	45.298495	+14.300665	0.872 0224
9	4.564288	+1.892919	0.519 5813	24	46.322425	+14.588371	0.880 0456
10	5.326605	+2.087311	0.527 1625	25	47.355709	+14.875789	0.888 1659
11	6.098221	+2.288643	0.534 6782	26	48.399918	+15.162959	0.896 3652
12	6.877064	+2.495632	0.542 1337	27	49.456222	+15.449705	0.904 6202
13	7.661296	+2.707154	0.549 5374	28	50.525329	+15.735654	0.912 9047
14	8.449338	+2.922257	0.556 9008	29	51.607498	+16.020275	0.921 1921
15	9.239885	+3.140178	0.564 2378	30	52.702601	+16.302931	0.929 4569
16	10.031934	+3.360351	0.571 5651	July 1	53.810206	+16.582934	0.937 6765
17	10.824798	+3.582416	0.578 9012	2	54.929660	+16.859576	0.945 8310

LCRS COORDINATES FOR 0^h BARYCENTRIC DYNAMICAL TIME

Date	Apparent Right Ascension	Apparent Declination	True Lunarcentric Distance	Date	Apparent Right Ascension	Apparent Declination	True Lunarcentric Distance
	°	°	au		°	°	au
July 1	53.810206	+16.582934	0.937 6765	Aug. 16	109.649956	+21.469645	1.260 3021
2	54.929660	+16.859576	0.945 8310	17	110.897334	+21.361844	1.266 1298
3	56.060154	+17.132161	0.953 9038	18	112.140419	+21.245540	1.272 0031
4	57.200771	+17.400024	0.961 8812	19	113.380163	+21.120683	1.277 9377
5	58.350514	+17.662535	0.969 7519	20	114.617617	+20.987139	1.283 9434
6	59.508322	+17.919113	0.977 5076	21	115.853853	+20.844704	1.290 0239
7	60.673072	+18.169224	0.985 1423	22	117.089888	+20.693121	1.296 1768
8	61.843591	+18.412389	0.992 6527	23	118.326613	+20.532108	1.302 3946
9	63.018668	+18.648192	1.000 0386	24	119.564752	+20.361378	1.308 6651
10	64.197071	+18.876287	1.007 3031	25	120.804832	+20.180665	1.314 9728
11	65.377583	+19.096405	1.014 4533	26	122.047178	+19.989735	1.321 3000
12	66.559056	+19.308366	1.021 5000	27	123.291921	+19.788404	1.327 6279
13	67.740461	+19.512081	1.028 4583	28	124.539027	+19.576541	1.333 9373
14	68.920962	+19.707556	1.035 3471	29	125.788315	+19.354068	1.340 2094
15	70.099971	+19.894880	1.042 1884	30	127.039486	+19.120966	1.346 4258
16	71.277206	+20.074218	1.049 0064	31	128.292139	+18.877274	1.352 5689
17	72.452723	+20.245786	1.055 8264	Sept. 1	129.545784	+18.623087	1.358 6218
18	73.626934	+20.409831	1.062 6729	2	130.799840	+18.358564	1.364 5684
19	74.800595	+20.566594	1.069 5688	3	132.053637	+18.083932	1.370 3937
20	75.974773	+20.716290	1.076 5328	4	133.306404	+17.799490	1.376 0844
21	77.150782	+20.859073	1.083 5790	5	134.557275	+17.505619	1.381 6292
22	78.330088	+20.995010	1.090 7147	6	135.805288	+17.202782	1.387 0203
23	79.514194	+21.124069	1.097 9403	7	137.049415	+16.891520	1.392 2546
24	80.704516	+21.246109	1.105 2493	8	138.288610	+16.572431	1.397 3347
25	81.902272	+21.360888	1.112 6286	9	139.521881	+16.246146	1.402 2701
26	83.108390	+21.468078	1.120 0605	10	140.748375	+15.913284	1.407 0770
27	84.323472	+21.567294	1.127 5239	11	141.967457	+15.574407	1.411 7777
28	85.547785	+21.658117	1.134 9964	12	143.178770	+15.229982	1.416 3985
29	86.781300	+21.740122	1.142 4555	13	144.382253	+14.880352	1.420 9676
30	88.023730	+21.812901	1.149 8800	14	145.578132	+14.525730	1.425 5131
31	89.274588	+21.876070	1.157 2499	15	146.766875	+14.166201	1.430 0603
Aug. 1	90.533228	+21.929286	1.164 5474	16	147.949140	+13.801739	1.434 6311
2	91.798876	+21.972251	1.171 7563	17	149.125713	+13.432227	1.439 2426
3	93.070651	+22.004717	1.178 8623	18	150.297460	+13.057486	1.443 9070
4	94.347579	+22.026487	1.185 8529	19	151.465274	+12.677291	1.448 6313
5	95.628588	+22.037425	1.192 7174	20	152.630034	+12.291402	1.453 4176
6	96.912521	+22.037457	1.199 4476	21	153.792573	+11.899580	1.458 2634
7	98.198135	+22.026580	1.206 0381	22	154.953648	+11.501609	1.463 1622
8	99.484124	+22.004864	1.212 4870	23	156.113928	+11.097308	1.468 1042
9	100.769157	+21.972457	1.218 7966	24	157.273976	+10.686544	1.473 0769
10	102.051927	+21.929578	1.224 9744	25	158.434254	+10.269239	1.478 0660
11	103.331232	+21.876509	1.231 0333	26	159.595121	+9.845371	1.483 0555
12	104.606048	+21.813575	1.236 9913	27	160.756844	+9.414978	1.488 0288
13	105.875612	+21.741115	1.242 8711	28	161.919603	+8.978151	1.492 9684
14	107.139470	+21.659460	1.248 6982	29	163.083495	+8.535042	1.497 8567
15	108.397510	+21.568896	1.254 4997	30	164.248536	+8.085861	1.502 6755
16	109.649956	+21.469645	1.260 3021	Oct. 1	165.414658	+7.630880	1.507 4064

LCRS COORDINATES FOR 0^h BARYCENTRIC DYNAMICAL TIME

Date	Apparent Right Ascension	Apparent Declination	True Lunarcentric Distance	Date	Apparent Right Ascension	Apparent Declination	True Lunarcentric Distance
	°	°	au		°	°	au
Oct. 1	165.414658	+7.630880	1.507 4064	Nov. 16	218.995477	−14.010695	1.652 0459
2	166.581693	+7.170443	1.512 0311	17	220.204851	−14.414639	1.653 9542
3	167.749359	+6.704971	1.516 5315	18	221.417337	−14.812598	1.655 9082
4	168.917248	+6.234974	1.520 8913	19	222.633593	−15.204613	1.657 9124
5	170.084811	+5.761050	1.525 0964	20	223.854287	−15.590702	1.659 9682
6	171.251369	+5.283880	1.529 1374	21	225.080090	−15.970852	1.662 0744
7	172.416150	+4.804202	1.533 0112	22	226.311663	−16.345017	1.664 2270
8	173.578349	+4.322768	1.536 7222	23	227.549644	−16.713110	1.666 4191
9	174.737222	+3.840290	1.540 2834	24	228.794634	−17.075008	1.668 6415
10	175.892173	+3.357386	1.543 7148	25	230.047180	−17.430540	1.670 8822
11	177.042825	+2.874534	1.547 0421	26	231.307769	−17.779494	1.673 1269
12	178.189051	+2.392060	1.550 2934	27	232.576801	−18.121608	1.675 3588
13	179.330972	+1.910139	1.553 4970	28	233.854576	−18.456576	1.677 5589
14	180.468918	+1.428821	1.556 6790	29	235.141260	−18.784043	1.679 7059
15	181.603386	+0.948055	1.559 8621	30	236.436855	−19.103606	1.681 7768
16	182.734993	+0.467726	1.563 0652	Dec. 1	237.741155	−19.414817	1.683 7477
17	183.864440	−0.012327	1.566 3025	2	239.053711	−19.717190	1.685 5954
18	184.992473	−0.492285	1.569 5845	3	240.373811	−20.010218	1.687 2990
19	186.119866	−0.972333	1.572 9174	4	241.700492	−20.293396	1.688 8430
20	187.247397	−1.452650	1.576 3038	5	243.032601	−20.566256	1.690 2195
21	188.375830	−1.933388	1.579 7427	6	244.368899	−20.828396	1.691 4294
22	189.505904	−2.414672	1.583 2301	7	245.708184	−21.079506	1.692 4826
23	190.638318	−2.896588	1.586 7589	8	247.049399	−21.319375	1.693 3963
24	191.773723	−3.379175	1.590 3198	9	248.391704	−21.547884	1.694 1926
25	192.912716	−3.862425	1.593 9011	10	249.734494	−21.764989	1.694 8954
26	194.055832	−4.346280	1.597 4895	11	251.077387	−21.970697	1.695 5290
27	195.203543	−4.830628	1.601 0698	12	252.420186	−22.165047	1.696 1161
28	196.356253	−5.315304	1.604 6255	13	253.762844	−22.348093	1.696 6775
29	197.514289	−5.800086	1.608 1387	14	255.105425	−22.519892	1.697 2314
30	198.677888	−6.284694	1.611 5900	15	256.448083	−22.680497	1.697 7940
31	199.847179	−6.768777	1.614 9590	16	257.791046	−22.829950	1.698 3789
Nov. 1	201.022160	−7.251910	1.618 2247	17	259.134603	−22.968276	1.698 9978
2	202.202660	−7.733589	1.621 3662	18	260.479098	−23.095485	1.699 6601
3	203.388323	−8.213224	1.624 3641	19	261.824923	−23.211563	1.700 3728
4	204.578592	−8.690152	1.627 2028	20	263.172509	−23.316471	1.701 1402
5	205.772733	−9.163666	1.629 8727	21	264.522314	−23.410141	1.701 9641
6	206.969892	−9.633054	1.632 3722	22	265.874803	−23.492478	1.702 8429
7	208.169194	−10.097652	1.634 7089	23	267.230437	−23.563355	1.703 7718
8	209.369849	−10.556899	1.636 8986	24	268.589640	−23.622616	1.704 7428
9	210.571245	−11.010364	1.638 9640	25	269.952783	−23.670080	1.705 7444
10	211.772998	−11.457757	1.640 9313	26	271.320157	−23.705544	1.706 7614
11	212.974961	−11.898913	1.642 8275	27	272.691938	−23.728790	1.707 7755
12	214.177200	−12.333764	1.644 6784	28	274.068161	−23.739594	1.708 7654
13	215.379954	−12.762313	1.646 5074	29	275.448683	−23.737741	1.709 7072
14	216.583594	−13.184605	1.648 3344	30	276.833144	−23.723034	1.710 5752
15	217.788589	−13.600708	1.650 1761	31	278.220940	−23.695321	1.711 3435
16	218.995477	−14.010695	1.652 0459	32	279.611207	−23.654506	1.711 9883

LCRS COORDINATES FOR 0^h BARYCENTRIC DYNAMICAL TIME

Date	Apparent Right Ascension	Apparent Declination	True Lunarcentric Distance	Date	Apparent Right Ascension	Apparent Declination	True Lunarcentric Distance
	°	°	au		°	°	au
Jan. 0	101.547814	+27.961269	0.002 5760	Feb. 15	354.364948	−2.784802	0.002 6757
1	116.287285	+25.922714	0.002 5518	16	4.982091	+3.003898	0.002 6917
2	130.593808	+22.385152	0.002 5305	17	15.579548	+8.623447	0.002 7024
3	144.263205	+17.585639	0.002 5128	18	26.401346	+13.906776	0.002 7065
4	157.301582	+11.832819	0.002 4988	19	37.677732	+18.684686	0.002 7029
5	169.876952	+5.456990	0.002 4881	20	49.608960	+22.770700	0.002 6910
6	182.254026	−1.214073	0.002 4806	21	62.332641	+25.952438	0.002 6708
7	194.742518	−7.855673	0.002 4760	22	75.875121	+27.996896	0.002 6431
8	207.656789	−14.133494	0.002 4744	23	90.106089	+28.677321	0.002 6093
9	221.268202	−19.690614	0.002 4762	24	104.737250	+27.821446	0.002 5714
10	235.731228	−24.150423	0.002 4818	25	119.397846	+25.364574	0.002 5323
11	250.987029	−27.153442	0.002 4920	26	133.762867	+21.381032	0.002 4951
12	266.701178	−28.434147	0.002 5070	27	147.658271	+16.080115	0.002 4629
13	282.328023	−27.907912	0.002 5270	28	161.090596	+9.776391	0.002 4384
14	297.314451	−25.706348	0.002 5513	Mar. 1	174.212910	+2.853582	0.002 4238
15	311.305533	−22.127472	0.002 5787	2	187.267671	−4.266650	0.002 4196
16	324.212237	−17.537651	0.002 6077	3	200.530828	−11.149083	0.002 4257
17	336.151127	−12.287717	0.002 6360	4	214.256540	−17.364670	0.002 4405
18	347.349488	−6.671889	0.002 6616	5	228.611059	−22.510824	0.002 4619
19	358.076259	−0.922582	0.002 6823	6	243.595296	−26.241082	0.002 4876
20	8.607717	+4.775519	0.002 6963	7	258.989344	−28.310172	0.002 5155
21	19.215305	+10.264051	0.002 7024	8	274.381214	−28.623222	0.002 5438
22	30.161109	+15.388130	0.002 6998	9	289.304358	−27.257509	0.002 5712
23	41.688802	+19.975107	0.002 6885	10	303.407644	−24.433260	0.002 5970
24	53.999290	+23.818522	0.002 6691	11	316.545881	−20.448253	0.002 6209
25	67.203730	+26.674188	0.002 6431	12	328.763239	−15.614130	0.002 6427
26	81.260785	+28.278887	0.002 6123	13	340.224658	−10.218378	0.002 6623
27	95.934308	+28.398912	0.002 5790	14	351.151658	−4.511966	0.002 6794
28	110.827959	+26.898212	0.002 5460	15	1.782893	+1.287659	0.002 6937
29	125.514143	+23.792751	0.002 5158	16	12.355705	+6.987069	0.002 7045
30	139.687164	+19.258220	0.002 4906	17	23.098393	+12.405434	0.002 7109
31	153.244422	+13.591233	0.002 4719	18	34.223666	+17.363153	0.002 7120
Feb. 1	166.272896	+7.153571	0.002 4605	19	45.915509	+21.672109	0.002 7069
2	178.987731	+0.327263	0.002 4563	20	58.303865	+25.130385	0.002 6947
3	191.669796	−6.509540	0.002 4586	21	71.427412	+27.526167	0.002 6752
4	204.615862	−12.988976	0.002 4662	22	85.197659	+28.655811	0.002 6483
5	218.090781	−18.751022	0.002 4778	23	99.393084	+28.356316	0.002 6149
6	232.265287	−23.444845	0.002 4922	24	113.709868	+26.542525	0.002 5763
7	247.137607	−26.749032	0.002 5087	25	127.859925	+23.232613	0.002 5349
8	262.474454	−28.419776	0.002 5267	26	141.665408	+18.552184	0.002 4936
9	277.840061	−28.353457	0.002 5461	27	155.102244	+12.722821	0.002 4557
10	292.742268	−26.623651	0.002 5668	28	168.288368	+6.048125	0.002 4246
11	306.813561	−23.459499	0.002 5886	29	181.442618	−1.096405	0.002 4035
12	319.905513	−19.177627	0.002 6113	30	194.835857	−8.273492	0.002 3943
13	332.068394	−14.110439	0.002 6341	31	208.736072	−15.002339	0.002 3977
14	343.477272	−8.560636	0.002 6560	Apr. 1	223.336033	−20.792019	0.002 4129
15	354.364948	−2.784802	0.002 6757	2	238.659923	−25.194758	0.002 4380

LCRS COORDINATES FOR 0^h BARYCENTRIC DYNAMICAL TIME

Date	Apparent Right Ascension	Apparent Declination	True Lunarcentric Distance	Date	Apparent Right Ascension	Apparent Declination	True Lunarcentric Distance
	°	°	au		°	°	au
Apr. 1	223.336033	−20.792019	0.002 4129	May 17	105.893558	+27.448869	0.002 6399
2	238.659923	−25.194758	0.002 4380	18	119.660557	+25.036026	0.002 6133
3	254.483921	−27.878104	0.002 4699	19	133.030649	+21.328456	0.002 5830
4	270.350451	−28.696400	0.002 5058	20	145.951551	+16.500497	0.002 5500
5	285.722213	−27.719682	0.002 5426	21	158.517448	+10.765416	0.002 5153
6	300.189792	−25.191423	0.002 5781	22	170.934246	+4.365796	0.002 4811
7	313.585014	−21.439680	0.002 6106	23	183.481971	−2.417969	0.002 4496
8	325.959096	−16.796036	0.002 6391	24	196.480822	−9.247748	0.002 4239
9	337.497256	−11.552970	0.002 6630	25	210.247987	−15.708955	0.002 4066
10	348.441863	−5.955711	0.002 6823	26	225.020726	−21.312159	0.002 3999
11	359.047538	−0.212115	0.002 6971	27	240.831110	−25.540156	0.002 4052
12	9.561617	+5.492101	0.002 7076	28	257.377904	−27.956823	0.002 4222
13	20.216986	+10.978808	0.002 7139	29	274.031238	−28.347513	0.002 4496
14	31.226483	+16.065822	0.002 7159	30	290.064444	−26.798010	0.002 4848
15	42.770935	+20.559300	0.002 7134	31	304.964460	−23.639208	0.002 5246
16	54.975721	+24.252142	0.002 7059	June 1	318.569143	−19.303420	0.002 5655
17	67.876608	+26.931694	0.002 6930	2	330.996715	−14.199329	0.002 6047
18	81.387636	+28.399722	0.002 6743	3	342.509163	−8.656391	0.002 6396
19	95.297326	+28.502893	0.002 6496	4	353.412485	−2.923635	0.002 6683
20	109.316682	+27.163496	0.002 6191	5	4.008999	+2.807510	0.002 6898
21	123.170196	+24.395753	0.002 5837	6	14.581637	+8.375544	0.002 7038
22	136.684263	+20.301231	0.002 5447	7	25.389676	+13.624176	0.002 7103
23	149.830251	+15.052110	0.002 5043	8	36.661904	+18.383269	0.002 7100
24	162.717630	+8.878011	0.002 4654	9	48.577788	+22.457768	0.002 7038
25	175.560634	+2.065565	0.002 4313	10	61.232303	+25.628789	0.002 6927
26	188.639043	−5.031601	0.002 4053	11	74.591585	+27.672236	0.002 6776
27	202.254819	−11.983641	0.002 3902	12	88.466013	+28.396449	0.002 6596
28	216.669480	−18.291856	0.002 3879	13	102.538453	+27.688580	0.002 6393
29	232.004776	−23.429740	0.002 3986	14	116.459029	+25.547040	0.002 6171
30	248.121667	−26.928848	0.002 4211	15	129.961968	+22.081008	0.002 5935
May 1	264.565140	−28.495238	0.002 4531	16	142.938601	+17.480268	0.002 5685
2	280.687316	−28.097403	0.002 4912	17	155.442700	+11.977490	0.002 5427
3	295.914669	−25.955909	0.002 5321	18	167.654216	+5.823485	0.002 5166
4	309.952579	−22.437125	0.002 5727	19	179.836409	−0.717229	0.002 4911
5	322.800037	−17.930497	0.002 6103	20	192.301492	−7.353843	0.002 4676
6	334.645252	−12.774880	0.002 6431	21	205.378326	−13.747979	0.002 4480
7	345.757703	−7.239817	0.002 6700	22	219.361270	−19.496576	0.002 4341
8	356.423386	−1.537893	0.002 6905	23	234.415986	−24.139483	0.002 4279
9	6.917466	+4.152907	0.002 7047	24	250.445946	−27.218245	0.002 4308
10	17.495963	+9.667292	0.002 7129	25	267.003708	−28.394860	0.002 4433
11	28.391677	+14.834939	0.002 7156	26	283.388913	−27.579449	0.002 4651
12	39.804215	+19.468588	0.002 7134	27	298.938575	−24.967699	0.002 4946
13	51.877517	+23.360169	0.002 7067	28	313.283535	−20.949910	0.002 5294
14	64.664111	+26.288611	0.002 6960	29	326.389573	−15.968530	0.002 5667
15	78.087962	+28.042718	0.002 6813	30	338.444978	−10.417027	0.002 6036
16	91.934031	+28.457118	0.002 6626	July 1	349.735285	−4.604528	0.002 6372
17	105.893558	+27.448869	0.002 6399	2	0.567309	+1.236409	0.002 6655

LCRS COORDINATES FOR 0^h BARYCENTRIC DYNAMICAL TIME

Date	Apparent Right Ascension	Apparent Declination	True Lunarcentric Distance	Date	Apparent Right Ascension	Apparent Declination	True Lunarcentric Distance
	°	°	au		°	°	au
July 1	349.735285	−4.604528	0.002 6372	Aug. 16	226.378763	−22.230694	0.002 4715
2	0.567309	+1.236409	0.002 6655	17	241.330518	−26.003428	0.002 4778
3	11.237314	+6.924877	0.002 6867	18	256.955658	−28.151033	0.002 4873
4	22.021336	+12.304064	0.002 6998	19	272.820964	−28.485261	0.002 4999
5	33.169773	+17.216957	0.002 7047	20	288.367042	−27.015389	0.002 5156
6	44.893970	+21.488218	0.002 7017	21	303.124688	−23.948582	0.002 5345
7	57.336966	+24.916003	0.002 6916	22	316.862618	−19.621109	0.002 5564
8	70.528981	+27.279693	0.002 6757	23	329.590592	−14.409174	0.002 5808
9	84.345951	+28.368941	0.002 6555	24	341.476905	−8.665322	0.002 6066
10	98.509174	+28.030815	0.002 6326	25	352.763287	−2.691173	0.002 6325
11	112.656554	+26.216313	0.002 6085	26	3.711445	+3.264320	0.002 6568
12	126.463792	+23.000284	0.002 5844	27	14.577862	+8.993813	0.002 6777
13	139.746091	+18.564329	0.002 5613	28	25.602892	+14.315709	0.002 6935
14	152.490682	+13.157637	0.002 5399	29	37.001707	+19.057917	0.002 7025
15	164.830165	+7.060061	0.002 5205	30	48.948101	+23.044581	0.002 7037
16	176.995642	+0.561962	0.002 5031	31	61.546538	+26.089906	0.002 6965
17	189.275691	−6.037608	0.002 4881	Sept. 1	74.796363	+28.004138	0.002 6808
18	201.983300	−12.419788	0.002 4757	2	88.566379	+28.615177	0.002 6575
19	215.416156	−18.230818	0.002 4664	3	102.608474	+27.802495	0.002 6277
20	229.788896	−23.076925	0.002 4611	4	116.625379	+25.530351	0.002 5935
21	245.127731	−26.549835	0.002 4607	5	130.367780	+21.864652	0.002 5575
22	261.167625	−28.300780	0.002 4661	6	143.709436	+16.968270	0.002 5224
23	277.359415	−28.148573	0.002 4780	7	156.669127	+11.083451	0.002 4909
24	293.059603	−26.155532	0.002 4964	8	169.388751	+4.513403	0.002 4656
25	307.791310	−22.605596	0.002 5206	9	182.094067	−2.391332	0.002 4482
26	321.376358	−17.900276	0.002 5495	10	195.054070	−9.242920	0.002 4395
27	333.893432	−12.449042	0.002 5809	11	208.537103	−15.626626	0.002 4394
28	345.566634	−6.605558	0.002 6127	12	222.750891	−21.117041	0.002 4469
29	356.674908	−0.650904	0.002 6424	13	237.758528	−25.308791	0.002 4606
30	7.503874	+5.195780	0.002 6678	14	253.393873	−27.870376	0.002 4787
31	18.326768	+10.755828	0.002 6870	15	269.247155	−28.614593	0.002 4996
Aug. 1	29.396735	+15.867789	0.002 6985	16	284.784631	−27.550021	0.002 5221
2	40.936952	+20.366915	0.002 7016	17	299.552436	−24.871984	0.002 5453
3	53.119167	+24.071084	0.002 6961	18	313.320039	−20.894228	0.002 5687
4	66.026936	+26.778270	0.002 6827	19	326.088584	−15.967038	0.002 5920
5	79.612391	+28.281780	0.002 6623	20	338.015119	−10.421812	0.002 6148
6	93.674700	+28.405626	0.002 6368	21	349.330790	−4.549165	0.002 6370
7	107.895992	+27.050785	0.002 6080	22	0.287646	+1.401323	0.002 6580
8	121.939823	+24.230666	0.002 5782	23	11.132499	+7.212109	0.002 6769
9	135.563373	+20.076837	0.002 5494	24	22.095234	+12.686352	0.002 6928
10	148.681154	+14.815901	0.002 5237	25	33.380032	+17.637270	0.002 7043
11	161.363145	+8.735240	0.002 5023	26	45.151423	+21.880081	0.002 7103
12	173.795242	+2.154677	0.002 4862	27	57.511209	+25.229038	0.002 7096
13	186.234168	−4.589114	0.002 4754	28	70.469337	+27.502877	0.002 7014
14	198.968564	−11.146665	0.002 4697	29	83.922786	+28.540903	0.002 6851
15	212.278773	−17.153469	0.002 4687	30	97.664778	+28.227174	0.002 6609
16	226.378763	−22.230694	0.002 4715	Oct. 1	111.437778	+26.513750	0.002 6295

LCRS COORDINATES FOR 0^h BARYCENTRIC DYNAMICAL TIME

Date	Apparent Right Ascension	Apparent Declination	True Lunarcentric Distance	Date	Apparent Right Ascension	Apparent Declination	True Lunarcentric Distance
	°	°	au		°	°	au
Oct. 1	111.437778	+26.513750	0.002 6295	Nov. 16	5.547724	+4.384885	0.002 6792
2	125.014426	+23.432367	0.002 5926	17	16.311530	+9.931948	0.002 6965
3	138.267160	+19.091538	0.002 5524	18	27.334831	+15.078176	0.002 7086
4	151.197377	+13.666617	0.002 5116	19	38.809480	+19.641156	0.002 7158
5	163.925719	+7.393308	0.002 4736	20	50.863110	+23.426013	0.002 7185
6	176.662865	+0.569037	0.002 4418	21	63.528261	+26.234400	0.002 7169
7	189.675127	−6.441769	0.002 4189	22	76.715185	+27.886770	0.002 7109
8	203.243756	−13.207563	0.002 4069	23	90.213302	+28.253633	0.002 7003
9	217.604120	−19.245580	0.002 4065	24	103.741159	+27.283342	0.002 6848
10	232.851873	−24.064649	0.002 4172	25	117.033478	+25.011509	0.002 6641
11	248.835380	−27.241876	0.002 4372	26	129.922280	+21.547165	0.002 6380
12	265.116174	−28.520679	0.002 4640	27	142.374814	+17.046037	0.002 6068
13	281.090512	−27.882032	0.002 4949	28	154.486761	+11.687685	0.002 5713
14	296.230927	−25.533235	0.002 5275	29	166.454071	+5.667681	0.002 5328
15	310.266370	−21.817281	0.002 5596	30	178.544626	−0.792745	0.002 4934
16	323.195041	−17.107704	0.002 5900	Dec. 1	191.075314	−7.423130	0.002 4560
17	335.191784	−11.743135	0.002 6177	2	204.383934	−13.874165	0.002 4238
18	346.510104	−6.007797	0.002 6422	3	218.771451	−19.697157	0.002 4000
19	357.421063	−0.138807	0.002 6635	4	234.386125	−24.359783	0.002 3876
20	8.185179	+5.657555	0.002 6816	5	251.059910	−27.332454	0.002 3881
21	19.041287	+11.189949	0.002 6963	6	268.217690	−28.248931	0.002 4017
22	30.198932	+16.270003	0.002 7074	7	285.037709	−27.058219	0.002 4272
23	41.825529	+20.705733	0.002 7145	8	300.819766	−24.038164	0.002 4619
24	54.024260	+24.301958	0.002 7169	9	315.244867	−19.654797	0.002 5023
25	66.805841	+26.869750	0.002 7140	10	328.358943	−14.391698	0.002 5450
26	80.068091	+28.245551	0.002 7049	11	340.415439	−8.652362	0.002 5867
27	93.605275	+28.315884	0.002 6891	12	351.738904	−2.740651	0.002 6246
28	107.160391	+27.037612	0.002 6663	13	2.654072	+3.118335	0.002 6568
29	120.504930	+24.443392	0.002 6366	14	13.460110	+8.746645	0.002 6822
30	133.507749	+20.630881	0.002 6008	15	24.423006	+13.984615	0.002 7004
31	146.164636	+15.745502	0.002 5606	16	35.768138	+18.669343	0.002 7114
Nov. 1	158.590388	+9.969866	0.002 5181	17	47.662884	+22.622876	0.002 7159
2	170.993215	+3.527225	0.002 4765	18	60.186372	+25.653236	0.002 7146
3	183.646886	−3.301895	0.002 4393	19	73.294953	+27.571557	0.002 7084
4	196.860893	−10.157719	0.002 4098	20	86.807402	+28.224455	0.002 6981
5	210.933363	−16.587888	0.002 3911	21	100.438377	+27.531082	0.002 6842
6	226.062817	−22.063385	0.002 3853	22	113.883246	+25.506244	0.002 6673
7	242.212649	−26.047238	0.002 3927	23	126.915060	+22.256197	0.002 6474
8	258.995655	−28.122342	0.002 4124	24	139.443289	+17.951490	0.002 6246
9	275.726726	−28.129810	0.002 4419	25	151.518349	+12.794637	0.002 5990
10	291.697094	−26.218276	0.002 4780	26	163.303181	+6.998727	0.002 5707
11	306.467050	−22.756468	0.002 5175	27	175.039788	+0.783337	0.002 5404
12	319.949753	−18.183137	0.002 5572	28	187.023922	−5.613500	0.002 5091
13	332.309791	−12.896906	0.002 5946	29	199.584301	−11.911868	0.002 4783
14	343.827196	−7.216924	0.002 6280	30	213.049287	−17.762938	0.002 4504
15	354.808655	−1.390052	0.002 6564	31	227.674043	−22.734109	0.002 4279
16	5.547724	+4.384885	0.002 6792	32	243.508584	−26.335142	0.002 4133

LCRS COORDINATES FOR 0ʰ BARYCENTRIC DYNAMICAL TIME

Date	Apparent Right Ascension	Apparent Declination	True Lunarcentric Distance	Date	Apparent Right Ascension	Apparent Declination	True Lunarcentric Distance
	°	°	au		°	°	au
Jan. 0	125.002478	+23.537839	0.661 6838	Feb. 15	108.988999	+26.280559	0.758 4212
1	124.722989	+23.632747	0.659 2638	16	108.849729	+26.270341	0.765 5232
2	124.434469	+23.727713	0.656 9000	17	108.735312	+26.256443	0.772 7808
3	124.134280	+23.823330	0.654 5925	18	108.645500	+26.238965	0.780 1640
4	123.819699	+23.920193	0.652 3502	19	108.579632	+26.218046	0.787 6438
5	123.488150	+24.018837	0.650 1908	20	108.536693	+26.193862	0.795 1924
6	123.137450	+24.119674	0.648 1402	21	108.515342	+26.166617	0.802 7840
7	122.766029	+24.222938	0.646 2311	22	108.513946	+26.136548	0.810 3949
8	122.373127	+24.328648	0.644 5012	23	108.530594	+26.103920	0.818 0044
9	121.958926	+24.436580	0.642 9908	24	108.563119	+26.069035	0.825 5956
10	121.524620	+24.546267	0.641 7395	25	108.609130	+26.032226	0.833 1566
11	121.072398	+24.657020	0.640 7841	26	108.666086	+25.993858	0.840 6820
12	120.605341	+24.767971	0.640 1554	27	108.731420	+25.954312	0.848 1744
13	120.127222	+24.878132	0.639 8763	28	108.802715	+25.913966	0.855 6455
14	119.642252	+24.986474	0.639 9603	Mar. 1	108.877925	+25.873164	0.863 1161
15	119.154786	+25.091995	0.640 4112	2	108.955591	+25.832184	0.870 6145
16	118.669057	+25.193786	0.641 2241	3	109.034995	+25.791208	0.878 1744
17	118.188953	+25.291071	0.642 3859	4	109.116213	+25.750307	0.885 8307
18	117.717874	+25.383235	0.643 8780	5	109.200048	+25.709443	0.893 6162
19	117.258652	+25.469824	0.645 6772	6	109.287877	+25.668481	0.901 5583
20	116.813526	+25.550542	0.647 7573	7	109.381458	+25.627213	0.909 6779
21	116.384148	+25.625236	0.650 0907	8	109.482737	+25.585383	0.917 9875
22	115.971608	+25.693877	0.652 6487	9	109.593679	+25.542709	0.926 4922
23	115.576451	+25.756551	0.655 4028	10	109.716145	+25.498901	0.935 1896
24	115.198689	+25.813441	0.658 3245	11	109.851787	+25.453678	0.944 0711
25	114.837801	+25.864826	0.661 3866	12	110.001990	+25.406777	0.953 1221
26	114.492738	+25.911069	0.664 5639	13	110.167824	+25.357963	0.962 3240
27	114.161927	+25.952612	0.667 8343	14	110.350023	+25.307034	0.971 6545
28	113.843310	+25.989965	0.671 1801	15	110.548980	+25.253828	0.981 0889
29	113.534441	+26.023689	0.674 5902	16	110.764755	+25.198220	0.990 6013
30	113.232635	+26.054364	0.678 0613	17	110.997102	+25.140130	1.000 1652
31	112.935209	+26.082555	0.681 5992	18	111.245497	+25.079517	1.009 7546
Feb. 1	112.639746	+26.108764	0.685 2194	19	111.509170	+25.016378	1.019 3446
2	112.344379	+26.133389	0.688 9456	20	111.787141	+24.950752	1.028 9114
3	112.048016	+26.156693	0.692 8080	21	112.078240	+24.882715	1.038 4336
4	111.750467	+26.178788	0.696 8406	22	112.381129	+24.812383	1.047 8917
5	111.452471	+26.199637	0.701 0777	23	112.694313	+24.739913	1.057 2694
6	111.155620	+26.219080	0.705 5510	24	113.016154	+24.665506	1.066 5538
7	110.862208	+26.236855	0.710 2876	25	113.344890	+24.589410	1.075 7367
8	110.575045	+26.252636	0.715 3075	26	113.678678	+24.511913	1.084 8158
9	110.297238	+26.266070	0.720 6231	27	114.015662	+24.433338	1.093 7960
10	110.031984	+26.276802	0.726 2384	28	114.354098	+24.354022	1.102 6907
11	109.782359	+26.284509	0.732 1492	29	114.692506	+24.274286	1.111 5222
12	109.551151	+26.288914	0.738 3437	30	115.029835	+24.194397	1.120 3203
13	109.340720	+26.289807	0.744 8034	31	115.365605	+24.114530	1.129 1202
14	109.152907	+26.287045	0.751 5049	Apr. 1	115.699953	+24.034746	1.137 9584
15	108.988999	+26.280559	0.758 4212	2	116.033588	+23.954982	1.146 8687

LCRS COORDINATES FOR 0^h BARYCENTRIC DYNAMICAL TIME

Date	Apparent Right Ascension	Apparent Declination	True Lunarcentric Distance	Date	Apparent Right Ascension	Apparent Declination	True Lunarcentric Distance
	°	°	au		°	°	au
Apr. 1	115.699953	+24.034746	1.137 9584	May 17	135.864680	+18.577273	1.568 8090
2	116.033588	+23.954982	1.146 8687	18	136.385809	+18.410111	1.577 8068
3	116.367653	+23.875067	1.155 8789	19	136.909269	+18.240609	1.586 6577
4	116.703557	+23.794748	1.165 0091	20	137.434120	+18.069087	1.595 3533
5	117.042802	+23.713722	1.174 2709	21	137.959372	+17.895903	1.603 8904
6	117.386853	+23.631661	1.183 6681	22	138.484014	+17.721445	1.612 2724
7	117.737046	+23.548236	1.193 1975	23	139.007074	+17.546109	1.620 5096
8	118.094540	+23.463130	1.202 8504	24	139.527678	+17.370276	1.628 6201
9	118.460283	+23.376051	1.212 6136	25	140.045143	+17.194272	1.636 6296
10	118.835009	+23.286734	1.222 4700	26	140.559058	+17.018333	1.644 5700
11	119.219226	+23.194952	1.232 3999	27	141.069344	+16.842570	1.652 4767
12	119.613226	+23.100515	1.242 3817	28	141.576279	+16.666955	1.660 3850
13	120.017087	+23.003276	1.252 3921	29	142.080449	+16.491324	1.668 3265
14	120.430681	+22.903134	1.262 4076	30	142.582670	+16.315406	1.676 3261
15	120.853690	+22.800033	1.272 4044	31	143.083877	+16.138861	1.684 4006
16	121.285616	+22.693964	1.282 3593	June 1	143.585028	+15.961319	1.692 5589
17	121.725800	+22.584967	1.292 2505	2	144.087030	+15.782410	1.700 8025
18	122.173437	+22.473128	1.302 0577	3	144.590694	+15.601787	1.709 1270
19	122.627591	+22.358582	1.311 7628	4	145.096714	+15.419140	1.717 5232
20	123.087205	+22.241513	1.321 3504	5	145.605663	+15.234195	1.725 9787
21	123.551115	+22.122150	1.330 8087	6	146.117999	+15.046722	1.734 4780
22	124.018070	+22.000773	1.340 1302	7	146.634064	+14.856533	1.743 0037
23	124.486751	+21.877704	1.349 3126	8	147.154094	+14.663484	1.751 5364
24	124.955826	+21.753300	1.358 3604	9	147.678212	+14.467474	1.760 0554
25	125.424021	+21.627931	1.367 2859	10	148.206433	+14.268455	1.768 5387
26	125.890222	+21.501955	1.376 1095	11	148.738653	+14.066430	1.776 9639
27	126.353603	+21.375676	1.384 8598	12	149.274651	+13.861460	1.785 3082
28	126.813738	+21.249303	1.393 5711	13	149.814085	+13.653665	1.793 5500
29	127.270664	+21.122919	1.402 2802	14	150.356493	+13.443228	1.801 6686
30	127.724877	+20.996469	1.411 0223	15	150.901303	+13.230391	1.809 6464
May 1	128.177243	+20.869770	1.419 8271	16	151.447848	+13.015453	1.817 4687
2	128.628863	+20.742546	1.428 7167	17	151.995382	+12.798760	1.825 1258
3	129.080937	+20.614459	1.437 7048	18	152.543106	+12.580696	1.832 6131
4	129.534642	+20.485152	1.446 7966	19	153.090206	+12.361666	1.839 9324
5	129.991056	+20.354268	1.455 9905	20	153.635890	+12.142077	1.847 0924
6	130.451117	+20.221473	1.465 2793	21	154.179442	+11.922312	1.854 1090
7	130.915604	+20.086464	1.474 6515	22	154.720276	+11.702700	1.861 0053
8	131.385132	+19.948974	1.484 0921	23	155.258001	+11.483484	1.867 8103
9	131.860163	+19.808777	1.493 5835	24	155.792462	+11.264797	1.874 5569
10	132.341002	+19.665686	1.503 1061	25	156.323770	+11.046641	1.881 2788
11	132.827807	+19.519560	1.512 6389	26	156.852283	+10.828890	1.888 0081
12	133.320589	+19.370303	1.522 1599	27	157.378570	+10.611311	1.894 7717
13	133.819215	+19.217868	1.531 6463	28	157.903332	+10.393594	1.901 5898
14	134.323411	+19.062262	1.541 0757	29	158.427335	+10.175385	1.908 4752
15	134.832767	+18.903543	1.550 4260	30	158.951344	+9.956324	1.915 4336
16	135.346743	+18.741824	1.559 6767	July 1	159.476073	+9.736066	1.922 4645
17	135.864680	+18.577273	1.568 8090	2	160.002166	+9.514294	1.929 5623

LCRS COORDINATES FOR 0^h BARYCENTRIC DYNAMICAL TIME

Date	Apparent Right Ascension	Apparent Declination	True Lunarcentric Distance	Date	Apparent Right Ascension	Apparent Declination	True Lunarcentric Distance
	°	°	au		°	°	au
July 1	159.476073	+9.736066	1.922 4645	Aug. 16	185.077634	−1.728696	2.195 8962
2	160.002166	+9.514294	1.929 5623	17	185.662641	−1.994107	2.200 1062
3	160.530180	+9.290730	1.936 7177	18	186.246303	−2.258189	2.204 1960
4	161.060585	+9.065138	1.943 9178	19	186.828374	−2.520804	2.208 1938
5	161.593768	+8.837318	1.951 1477	20	187.408777	−2.781911	2.212 1289
6	162.130033	+8.607117	1.958 3900	21	187.987597	−3.041557	2.216 0308
7	162.669600	+8.374421	1.965 6255	22	188.565069	−3.299871	2.219 9265
8	163.212603	+8.139163	1.972 8332	23	189.141555	−3.557048	2.223 8393
9	163.759080	+7.901328	1.979 9910	24	189.717518	−3.813328	2.227 7881
10	164.308965	+7.660960	1.987 0755	25	190.293477	−4.068978	2.231 7863
11	164.862076	+7.418165	1.994 0632	26	190.869986	−4.324273	2.235 8421
12	165.418111	+7.173117	2.000 9317	27	191.447599	−4.579477	2.239 9586
13	165.976647	+6.926061	2.007 6601	28	192.026851	−4.834839	2.244 1347
14	166.537151	+6.677303	2.014 2314	29	192.608248	−5.090580	2.248 3652
15	167.098996	+6.427204	2.020 6329	30	193.192256	−5.346891	2.252 6417
16	167.661495	+6.176162	2.026 8579	31	193.779298	−5.603935	2.256 9529
17	168.223933	+5.924593	2.032 9064	Sept. 1	194.369752	−5.861839	2.261 2846
18	168.785612	+5.672907	2.038 7855	2	194.963946	−6.120698	2.265 6201
19	169.345895	+5.421480	2.044 5097	3	195.562148	−6.380566	2.269 9399
20	169.904254	+5.170632	2.050 0997	4	196.164553	−6.641452	2.274 2219
21	170.460305	+4.920602	2.055 5821	5	196.771263	−6.903309	2.278 4418
22	171.013848	+4.671528	2.060 9870	6	197.382261	−7.166024	2.282 5735
23	171.564882	+4.423436	2.066 3462	7	197.997394	−7.429412	2.286 5905
24	172.113604	+4.176245	2.071 6905	8	198.616350	−7.693212	2.290 4678
25	172.660389	+3.929772	2.077 0474	9	199.238662	−7.957090	2.294 1841
26	173.205747	+3.683761	2.082 4394	10	199.863733	−8.220663	2.297 7244
27	173.750276	+3.437906	2.087 8828	11	200.490879	−8.483520	2.301 0816
28	174.294610	+3.191882	2.093 3877	12	201.119390	−8.745263	2.304 2572
29	174.839382	+2.945368	2.098 9578	13	201.748593	−9.005530	2.307 2617
30	175.385190	+2.698060	2.104 5920	14	202.377905	−9.264026	2.310 1124
31	175.932580	+2.449686	2.110 2846	15	203.006871	−9.520534	2.312 8324
Aug. 1	176.482042	+2.200007	2.116 0265	16	203.635184	−9.774920	2.315 4483
2	177.034004	+1.948820	2.121 8055	17	204.262689	−10.027132	2.317 9878
3	177.588834	+1.695961	2.127 6071	18	204.889383	−10.277192	2.320 4790
4	178.146834	+1.441303	2.133 4142	19	205.515396	−10.525184	2.322 9480
5	178.708242	+1.184759	2.139 2075	20	206.140978	−10.771244	2.325 4186
6	179.273219	+0.926290	2.144 9656	21	206.766478	−11.015545	2.327 9108
7	179.841835	+0.665911	2.150 6653	22	207.392322	−11.258285	2.330 4408
8	180.414054	+0.403700	2.156 2822	23	208.018986	−11.499671	2.333 0201
9	180.989718	+0.139803	2.161 7913	24	208.646977	−11.739911	2.335 6561
10	181.568538	−0.125555	2.167 1690	25	209.276813	−11.979204	2.338 3520
11	182.150090	−0.392080	2.172 3941	26	209.909006	−12.217730	2.341 1069
12	182.733830	−0.659413	2.177 4503	27	210.544052	−12.455650	2.343 9166
13	183.319126	−0.927153	2.182 3275	28	211.182422	−12.693098	2.346 7734
14	183.905301	−1.194880	2.187 0228	29	211.824557	−12.930184	2.349 6668
15	184.491678	−1.462184	2.191 5415	30	212.470862	−13.166985	2.352 5830
16	185.077634	−1.728696	2.195 8962	Oct. 1	213.121696	−13.403550	2.355 5056

LCRS COORDINATES FOR 0^h BARYCENTRIC DYNAMICAL TIME

Date	Apparent Right Ascension	Apparent Declination	True Lunarcentric Distance	Date	Apparent Right Ascension	Apparent Declination	True Lunarcentric Distance
	°	°	au		°	°	au
Oct. 1	213.121696	−13.403550	2.355 5056	Nov. 16	246.104024	−22.158123	2.419 1225
2	213.777360	−13.639890	2.358 4146	17	246.872030	−22.280565	2.419 1485
3	214.438078	−13.875971	2.361 2872	18	247.640265	−22.399403	2.419 2081
4	215.103968	−14.111707	2.364 0978	19	248.409090	−22.514716	2.419 3154
5	215.775013	−14.346951	2.366 8188	20	249.178920	−22.626574	2.419 4810
6	216.451024	−14.581488	2.369 4222	21	249.950207	−22.735038	2.419 7128
7	217.131630	−14.815038	2.371 8820	22	250.723434	−22.840152	2.420 0151
8	217.816275	−15.047264	2.374 1773	23	251.499099	−22.941947	2.420 3886
9	218.504259	−15.277801	2.376 2947	24	252.277703	−23.040432	2.420 8306
10	219.194807	−15.506285	2.378 2303	25	253.059732	−23.135597	2.421 3348
11	219.887142	−15.732387	2.379 9900	26	253.845652	−23.227411	2.421 8910
12	220.580563	−15.955836	2.381 5883	27	254.635884	−23.315820	2.422 4856
13	221.274500	−16.176434	2.383 0462	28	255.430791	−23.400747	2.423 1009
14	221.968534	−16.394060	2.384 3888	29	256.230656	−23.482094	2.423 7156
15	222.662411	−16.608661	2.385 6429	30	257.035644	−23.559740	2.424 3049
16	223.356026	−16.820241	2.386 8355	Dec. 1	257.845773	−23.633543	2.424 8409
17	224.049409	−17.028853	2.387 9925	2	258.660871	−23.703349	2.425 2944
18	224.742709	−17.234586	2.389 1374	3	259.480547	−23.768994	2.425 6365
19	225.436174	−17.437553	2.390 2914	4	260.304187	−23.830323	2.425 8421
20	226.130135	−17.637884	2.391 4723	5	261.130977	−23.887196	2.425 8926
21	226.824988	−17.835716	2.392 6947	6	261.959980	−23.939510	2.425 7787
22	227.521182	−18.031189	2.393 9693	7	262.790228	−23.987199	2.425 5015
23	228.219195	−18.224437	2.395 3034	8	263.620817	−24.030243	2.425 0715
24	228.919530	−18.415580	2.396 7005	9	264.450985	−24.068658	2.424 5069
25	229.622692	−18.604726	2.398 1605	10	265.280142	−24.102492	2.423 8302
26	230.329180	−18.791961	2.399 6800	11	266.107881	−24.131807	2.423 0665
27	231.039481	−18.977350	2.401 2522	12	266.933959	−24.156681	2.422 2410
28	231.754053	−19.160936	2.402 8668	13	267.758272	−24.177189	2.421 3779
29	232.473323	−19.342732	2.404 5105	14	268.580832	−24.193407	2.420 5000
30	233.197669	19.522726	2.406 1664	15	269.401747	−24.205402	2.419 6280
31	233.927404	−19.700870	2.407 8142	16	270.221207	−24.213233	2.418 7809
Nov. 1	234.662748	−19.877083	2.409 4302	17	271.039471	−24.216946	2.417 9751
2	235.403797	−20.051237	2.410 9874	18	271.856865	−24.216573	2.417 2249
3	236.150484	−20.223162	2.412 4572	19	272.673772	−24.212131	2.416 5419
4	236.902539	−20.392639	2.413 8107	20	273.490623	−24.203618	2.415 9349
5	237.659478	−20.559415	2.415 0217	21	274.307888	−24.191013	2.415 4094
6	238.420616	−20.723210	2.416 0702	22	275.126065	−24.174274	2.414 9670
7	239.185120	−20.883749	2.416 9447	23	275.945658	−24.153341	2.414 6057
8	239.952097	−21.040783	2.417 6444	24	276.767162	−24.128135	2.414 3192
9	240.720688	−21.194111	2.418 1782	25	277.591043	−24.098557	2.414 0969
10	241.490150	−21.343590	2.418 5632	26	278.417711	−24.064500	2.413 9238
11	242.259897	−21.489139	2.418 8222	27	279.247501	−24.025842	2.413 7810
12	243.029521	−21.630727	2.418 9808	28	280.080640	−23.982464	2.413 6456
13	243.798779	−21.768367	2.419 0654	29	280.917221	−23.934247	2.413 4912
14	244.567578	−21.902103	2.419 1016	30	281.757168	−23.881090	2.413 2894
15	245.335948	−22.031996	2.419 1133	31	282.600211	−23.822917	2.413 0109
16	246.104024	−22.158123	2.419 1225	32	283.445871	−23.759691	2.412 6282

LCRS COORDINATES FOR 0^h BARYCENTRIC DYNAMICAL TIME

Date	Apparent Right Ascension	Apparent Declination	True Lunarcentric Distance	Date	Apparent Right Ascension	Apparent Declination	True Lunarcentric Distance
	°	°	au		°	°	au
Jan. 0	71.641513	+21.757058	4.185 397	Feb. 15	69.586528	+21.662711	4.753 757
1	71.533125	+21.747333	4.192 662	16	69.627540	+21.672167	4.769 988
2	71.425926	+21.737539	4.200 098	17	69.673417	+21.682197	4.786 231
3	71.319644	+21.727666	4.207 724	18	69.723958	+21.692742	4.802 462
4	71.214092	+21.717723	4.215 567	19	69.778923	+21.703742	4.818 656
5	71.109191	+21.707739	4.223 655	20	69.838037	+21.715133	4.834 797
6	71.004984	+21.697764	4.232 020	21	69.900994	+21.726853	4.850 867
7	70.901644	+21.687865	4.240 691	22	69.967465	+21.738841	4.866 856
8	70.799465	+21.678127	4.249 698	23	70.037100	+21.751038	4.882 757
9	70.698853	+21.668642	4.259 062	24	70.109533	+21.763390	4.898 568
10	70.600297	+21.659509	4.268 800	25	70.184397	+21.775849	4.914 294
11	70.504340	+21.650823	4.278 918	26	70.261339	+21.788379	4.929 948
12	70.411542	+21.642673	4.289 414	27	70.340047	+21.800959	4.945 548
13	70.322440	+21.635133	4.300 278	28	70.420283	+21.813586	4.961 120
14	70.237517	+21.628260	4.311 490	Mar. 1	70.501911	+21.826279	4.976 695
15	70.157168	+21.622091	4.323 023	2	70.584920	+21.839078	4.992 308
16	70.081693	+21.616642	4.334 847	3	70.669431	+21.852039	5.007 990
17	70.011283	+21.611912	4.346 931	4	70.755685	+21.865230	5.023 769
18	69.946036	+21.607885	4.359 240	5	70.844006	+21.878721	5.039 663
19	69.885956	+21.604529	4.371 743	6	70.934770	+21.892579	5.055 684
20	69.830976	+21.601808	4.384 408	7	71.028365	+21.906861	5.071 832
21	69.780964	+21.599674	4.397 209	8	71.125157	+21.921608	5.088 099
22	69.735736	+21.598079	4.410 120	9	71.225473	+21.936849	5.104 471
23	69.695058	+21.596967	4.423 119	10	71.329582	+21.952595	5.120 928
24	69.658659	+21.596281	4.436 188	11	71.437692	+21.968845	5.137 443
25	69.626225	+21.595964	4.449 310	12	71.549937	+21.985582	5.153 990
26	69.597412	+21.595955	4.462 477	13	71.666384	+22.002777	5.170 539
27	69.571850	+21.596200	4.475 682	14	71.787034	+22.020394	5.187 059
28	69.549156	+21.596647	4.488 928	15	71.911823	+22.038386	5.203 522
29	69.528959	+21.597256	4.502 223	16	72.040629	+22.056701	5.219 901
30	69.510925	+21.598001	4.515 582	17	72.173282	+22.075282	5.236 168
31	69.494790	+21.598876	4.529 028	18	72.309570	+22.094073	5.252 302
Feb. 1	69.480391	+21.599894	4.542 590	19	72.449247	+22.113015	5.268 284
2	69.467687	+21.601093	4.556 299	20	72.592037	+22.132052	5.284 098
3	69.456769	+21.602530	4.570 186	21	72.737646	+22.151128	5.299 732
4	69.447849	+21.604278	4.584 278	22	72.885758	+22.170193	5.315 178
5	69.441243	+21.606418	4.598 599	23	73.036047	+22.189199	5.330 433
6	69.437340	+21.609032	4.613 162	24	73.188181	+22.208105	5.345 499
7	69.436569	+21.612200	4.627 974	25	73.341831	+22.226878	5.360 384
8	69.439367	+21.615993	4.643 033	26	73.496685	+22.245495	5.375 103
9	69.446154	+21.620467	4.658 330	27	73.652472	+22.263947	5.389 677
10	69.457303	+21.625664	4.673 845	28	73.808988	+22.282241	5.404 134
11	69.473124	+21.631606	4.689 556	29	73.966126	+22.300399	5.418 507
12	69.493851	+21.638300	4.705 434	30	74.123900	+22.318462	5.432 832
13	69.519631	+21.645735	4.721 449	31	74.282449	+22.336483	5.447 142
14	69.550529	+21.653885	4.737 567	Apr. 1	74.442027	+22.354522	5.461 464
15	69.586528	+21.662711	4.753 757	2	74.602968	+22.372636	5.475 817

LCRS COORDINATES FOR 0^h BARYCENTRIC DYNAMICAL TIME

Date	Apparent Right Ascension	Apparent Declination	True Lunarcentric Distance	Date	Apparent Right Ascension	Apparent Declination	True Lunarcentric Distance
	°	°	au		°	°	au
Apr. 1	74.442027	+22.354522	5.461 464	May 17	83.860578	+23.111850	5.998 887
2	74.602968	+22.372636	5.475 817	18	84.099636	+23.122680	6.006 427
3	74.765647	+22.390874	5.490 208	19	84.338812	+23.133043	6.013 680
4	74.930431	+22.409273	5.504 637	20	84.577839	+23.142942	6.020 659
5	75.097656	+22.427856	5.519 092	21	84.816478	+23.152392	6.027 383
6	75.267601	+22.446630	5.533 557	22	85.054533	+23.161410	6.033 877
7	75.440484	+22.465589	5.548 008	23	85.291874	+23.170026	6.040 171
8	75.616458	+22.484717	5.562 421	24	85.528450	+23.178273	6.046 298
9	75.795610	+22.503987	5.576 768	25	85.764310	+23.186187	6.052 293
10	75.977968	+22.523365	5.591 022	26	85.999606	+23.193807	6.058 188
11	76.163505	+22.542811	5.605 156	27	86.234591	+23.201164	6.064 011
12	76.352141	+22.562283	5.619 143	28	86.469586	+23.208283	6.069 777
13	76.543748	+22.581734	5.632 958	29	86.704950	+23.215179	6.075 496
14	76.738158	+22.601116	5.646 578	30	86.941034	+23.221851	6.081 164
15	76.935165	+22.620382	5.659 984	31	87.178152	+23.228290	6.086 768
16	77.134530	+22.639485	5.673 159	June 1	87.416556	+23.234479	6.092 289
17	77.335993	+22.658384	5.686 089	2	87.656430	+23.240390	6.097 705
18	77.539270	+22.677037	5.698 766	3	87.897891	+23.245997	6.102 989
19	77.744069	+22.695410	5.711 184	4	88.140994	+23.251268	6.108 116
20	77.950086	+22.713474	5.723 345	5	88.385739	+23.256174	6.113 059
21	78.157020	+22.731205	5.735 253	6	88.632080	+23.260683	6.117 796
22	78.364577	+22.748590	5.746 919	7	88.879928	+23.264768	6.122 301
23	78.572487	+22.765623	5.758 360	8	89.129157	+23.268402	6.126 555
24	78.780520	+22.782309	5.769 598	9	89.379604	+23.271564	6.130 536
25	78.988508	+22.798666	5.780 664	10	89.631071	+23.274233	6.134 230
26	79.196373	+22.814722	5.791 591	11	89.883331	+23.276395	6.137 621
27	79.404143	+22.830517	5.802 413	12	90.136130	+23.278042	6.140 702
28	79.611969	+22.846096	5.813 165	13	90.389195	+23.279169	6.143 465
29	79.820104	+22.861508	5.823 875	14	90.642240	+23.279780	6.145 911
30	80.028882	+22.876793	5.834 560	15	90.894975	+23.279886	6.148 046
May 1	80.238673	+22.891985	5.845 228	16	91.147122	+23.279503	6.149 880
2	80.449837	+22.907102	5.855 875	17	91.398428	+23.278656	6.151 430
3	80.662697	+22.922150	5.866 491	18	91.648673	+23.277372	6.152 719
4	80.877512	+22.937122	5.877 056	19	91.897693	+23.275687	6.153 773
5	81.094477	+22.952001	5.887 547	20	92.145390	+23.273635	6.154 623
6	81.313717	+22.966763	5.897 938	21	92.391748	+23.271252	6.155 304
7	81.535299	+22.981378	5.908 205	22	92.636843	+23.268571	6.155 846
8	81.759231	+22.995812	5.918 319	23	92.880854	+23.265614	6.156 282
9	81.985474	+23.010031	5.928 255	24	93.124116	+23.262350	6.156 636
10	82.213942	+23.023997	5.937 990	25	93.366085	+23.258837	6.156 924
11	82.444508	+23.037673	5.947 499	26	93.608678	+23.255269	6.157 152
12	82.677006	+23.051025	5.956 762	27	93.851216	+23.251312	6.157 318
13	82.911239	+23.064017	5.965 762	28	94.094158	+23.247058	6.157 410
14	83.146975	+23.076620	5.974 483	29	94.337768	+23.242481	6.157 408
15	83.383961	+23.088807	5.982 915	30	94.582231	+23.237551	6.157 291
16	83.621924	+23.100556	5.991 050	July 1	94.827662	+23.232236	6.157 032
17	83.860578	+23.111850	5.998 887	2	95.074112	+23.226506	6.156 607

LCRS COORDINATES FOR 0^h BARYCENTRIC DYNAMICAL TIME

Date	Apparent Right Ascension	Apparent Declination	True Lunarcentric Distance	Date	Apparent Right Ascension	Apparent Declination	True Lunarcentric Distance
	°	°	au		°	°	au
July 1	94.827662	+23.232236	6.157 032	Aug. 16	105.718521	+22.589111	5.913 152
2	95.074112	+23.226506	6.156 607	17	105.929488	+22.569238	5.903 184
3	95.321578	+23.220333	6.155 990	18	106.138236	+22.549440	5.893 160
4	95.570012	+23.213695	6.155 157	19	106.345035	+22.529702	5.883 098
5	95.819320	+23.206570	6.154 086	20	106.550186	+22.509996	5.873 009
6	96.069375	+23.198945	6.152 756	21	106.754002	+22.490284	5.862 897
7	96.320012	+23.190810	6.151 150	22	106.956780	+22.470520	5.852 756
8	96.571032	+23.182159	6.149 251	23	107.158789	+22.450658	5.842 575
9	96.822204	+23.172994	6.147 046	24	107.360247	+22.430650	5.832 336
10	97.073269	+23.163325	6.144 527	25	107.561315	+22.410454	5.822 020
11	97.323943	+23.153167	6.141 690	26	107.762094	+22.390034	5.811 602
12	97.573929	+23.142545	6.138 537	27	107.962626	+22.369362	5.801 058
13	97.822928	+23.131490	6.135 074	28	108.162897	+22.348419	5.790 367
14	98.070655	+23.120040	6.131 316	29	108.362843	+22.327193	5.779 504
15	98.316855	+23.108237	6.127 283	30	108.562356	+22.305682	5.768 449
16	98.561323	+23.096127	6.123 001	31	108.761289	+22.283894	5.757 184
17	98.803916	+23.083755	6.118 500	Sept. 1	108.959458	+22.261844	5.745 693
18	99.044569	+23.071161	6.113 813	2	109.156642	+22.239557	5.733 961
19	99.283299	+23.058382	6.108 972	3	109.352586	+22.217067	5.721 978
20	99.520210	+23.045443	6.104 011	4	109.547000	+22.194419	5.709 739
21	99.755486	+23.032360	6.098 956	5	109.739564	+22.171669	5.697 241
22	99.989380	+23.019134	6.093 831	6	109.929936	+22.148883	5.684 490
23	100.222194	+23.005755	6.088 648	7	110.117772	+22.126135	5.671 497
24	100.454250	+22.992201	6.083 413	8	110.302743	+22.103507	5.658 283
25	100.685867	+22.978439	6.078 122	9	110.484566	+22.081077	5.644 875
26	100.917330	+22.964433	6.072 764	10	110.663035	+22.058920	5.631 308
27	101.148873	+22.950143	6.067 321	11	110.838040	+22.037094	5.617 619
28	101.380670	+22.935532	6.061 770	12	111.009581	+22.015642	5.603 847
29	101.612831	+22.920563	6.056 088	13	111.177761	+21.994584	5.590 028
30	101.845403	+22.905209	6.050 250	14	111.342773	+21.973919	5.576 192
31	102.078379	+22.889445	6.044 231	15	111.504876	+21.953626	5.562 364
Aug. 1	102.311706	+22.873255	6.038 008	16	111.664370	+21.933671	5.548 559
2	102.545285	+22.856626	6.031 559	17	111.821570	+21.914006	5.534 786
3	102.778983	+22.839555	6.024 865	18	111.976789	+21.894577	5.521 044
4	103.012628	+22.822045	6.017 907	19	112.130312	+21.875327	5.507 327
5	103.246014	+22.804105	6.010 672	20	112.282388	+21.856201	5.493 623
6	103.478903	+22.785753	6.003 148	21	112.433220	+21.837147	5.479 915
7	103.711022	+22.767017	5.995 325	22	112.582951	+21.818120	5.466 183
8	103.942072	+22.747933	5.987 203	23	112.731668	+21.799085	5.452 406
9	104.171737	+22.728547	5.978 783	24	112.879398	+21.780015	5.438 560
10	104.399698	+22.708910	5.970 076	25	113.026113	+21.760896	5.424 623
11	104.625651	+22.689084	5.961 098	26	113.171733	+21.741725	5.410 575
12	104.849332	+22.669129	5.951 874	27	113.316131	+21.722510	5.396 396
13	105.070538	+22.649105	5.942 433	28	113.459138	+21.703268	5.382 069
14	105.289146	+22.629068	5.932 809	29	113.600546	+21.684028	5.367 579
15	105.505121	+22.609059	5.923 037	30	113.740111	+21.664830	5.352 916
16	105.718521	+22.589111	5.913 152	Oct. 1	113.877550	+21.645723	5.338 072

LCRS COORDINATES FOR 0^h BARYCENTRIC DYNAMICAL TIME

Date	Apparent Right Ascension	Apparent Declination	True Lunarcentric Distance	Date	Apparent Right Ascension	Apparent Declination	True Lunarcentric Distance
	°	°	au		°	°	au
Oct. 1	113.877550	+21.645723	5.338 072	Nov. 16	116.677566	+21.297694	4.645 564
2	114.012551	+21.626770	5.323 041	17	116.659272	+21.303849	4.632 652
3	114.144768	+21.608042	5.307 826	18	116.639017	+21.310271	4.619 894
4	114.273835	+21.589625	5.292 434	19	116.616799	+21.316938	4.607 269
5	114.399382	+21.571610	5.276 880	20	116.592556	+21.323844	4.594 758
6	114.521060	+21.554092	5.261 188	21	116.566173	+21.330993	4.582 343
7	114.638570	+21.537164	5.245 389	22	116.537478	+21.338406	4.570 009
8	114.751707	+21.520906	5.229 521	23	116.506254	+21.346115	4.557 743
9	114.860379	+21.505377	5.213 626	24	116.472240	+21.354165	4.545 536
10	114.964630	+21.490610	5.197 746	25	116.435141	+21.362612	4.533 383
11	115.064623	+21.476606	5.181 920	26	116.394634	+21.371522	4.521 285
12	115.160622	+21.463340	5.166 177	27	116.350378	+21.380968	4.509 245
13	115.252953	+21.450764	5.150 540	28	116.302022	+21.391031	4.497 275
14	115.341971	+21.438817	5.135 023	29	116.249222	+21.401793	4.485 392
15	115.428027	+21.427428	5.119 629	30	116.191658	+21.413337	4.473 619
16	115.511449	+21.416526	5.104 355	Dec. 1	116.129066	+21.425740	4.461 987
17	115.592527	+21.406041	5.089 193	2	116.061263	+21.439064	4.450 535
18	115.671500	+21.395908	5.074 129	3	115.988190	+21.453350	4.439 303
19	115.748556	+21.386071	5.059 146	4	115.909940	+21.468603	4.428 336
20	115.823822	+21.376484	5.044 224	5	115.826768	+21.484795	4.417 676
21	115.897367	+21.367112	5.029 342	6	115.739085	+21.501856	4.407 360
22	115.969201	+21.357933	5.014 480	7	115.647411	+21.519686	4.397 412
23	116.039276	+21.348936	4.999 617	8	115.552324	+21.538165	4.387 848
24	116.107489	+21.340125	4.984 734	9	115.454394	+21.557163	4.378 669
25	116.173690	+21.331515	4.969 812	10	115.354149	+21.576556	4.369 869
26	116.237680	+21.323136	4.954 838	11	115.252037	+21.596229	4.361 434
27	116.299221	+21.315025	4.939 799	12	115.148424	+21.616084	4.353 346
28	116.358036	+21.307236	4.924 687	13	115.043591	+21.636041	4.345 583
29	116.413817	+21.299830	4.909 497	14	114.937737	+21.656035	4.338 123
30	116.466223	+21.292881	4.894 230	15	114.830990	+21.676016	4.330 944
31	116.514890	+21.286472	4.878 891	16	114.723407	+21.695952	4.324 023
Nov. 1	116.559443	+21.280694	4.863 491	17	114.614985	+21.715825	4.317 339
2	116.599507	+21.275645	4.848 051	18	114.505660	+21.735628	4.310 872
3	116.634741	+21.271422	4.832 596	19	114.395309	+21.755372	4.304 605
4	116.664864	+21.268115	4.817 163	20	114.283758	+21.775078	4.298 522
5	116.689703	+21.265795	4.801 792	21	114.170786	+21.794782	4.292 614
6	116.709221	+21.264506	4.786 528	22	114.056131	+21.814530	4.286 873
7	116.723535	+21.264256	4.771 415	23	113.939504	+21.834376	4.281 297
8	116.732904	+21.265016	4.756 492	24	113.820599	+21.854385	4.275 888
9	116.737699	+21.266727	4.741 790	25	113.699110	+21.874622	4.270 657
10	116.738350	+21.269303	4.727 327	26	113.574748	+21.895157	4.265 618
11	116.735305	+21.272650	4.713 113	27	113.447259	+21.916053	4.260 793
12	116.728985	+21.276667	4.699 148	28	113.316448	+21.937369	4.256 209
13	116.719768	+21.281261	4.685 425	29	113.182204	+21.959150	4.251 897
14	116.707968	+21.286345	4.671 931	30	113.044522	+21.981421	4.247 895
15	116.693839	+21.291843	4.658 651	31	112.903533	+22.004184	4.244 240
16	116.677566	+21.297694	4.645 564	32	112.759516	+22.027412	4.240 973

LCRS COORDINATES FOR 0h BARYCENTRIC DYNAMICAL TIME

Date	Apparent Right Ascension	Apparent Declination	True Lunarcentric Distance	Date	Apparent Right Ascension	Apparent Declination	True Lunarcentric Distance
	°	°	au		°	°	au
Jan. 0	346.134191	−8.076369	10.009 206	Feb. 15	350.324733	−6.247061	10.524 253
1	346.201299	−8.046298	10.023 651	16	350.435810	−6.199148	10.530 353
2	346.269137	−8.015996	10.038 059	17	350.547158	−6.151176	10.536 097
3	346.337796	−7.985410	10.052 451	18	350.658652	−6.103211	10.541 497
4	346.407399	−7.954476	10.066 841	19	350.770178	−6.055310	10.546 565
5	346.478089	−7.923116	10.081 236	20	350.881636	−6.007523	10.551 316
6	346.550020	−7.891248	10.095 636	21	350.992942	−5.959893	10.555 769
7	346.623345	−7.858790	10.110 031	22	351.104027	−5.912452	10.559 947
8	346.698208	−7.825667	10.124 404	23	351.214845	−5.865220	10.563 874
9	346.774727	−7.791816	10.138 730	24	351.325369	−5.818207	10.567 575
10	346.852988	−7.757192	10.152 977	25	351.435605	−5.771405	10.571 079
11	346.933038	−7.721770	10.167 108	26	351.545588	−5.724789	10.574 413
12	347.014878	−7.685549	10.181 088	27	351.655392	−5.678315	10.577 603
13	347.098467	−7.648550	10.194 879	28	351.765127	−5.631918	10.580 670
14	347.183722	−7.610817	10.208 448	Mar. 1	351.874934	−5.585519	10.583 628
15	347.270530	−7.572408	10.221 766	2	351.984973	−5.539028	10.586 480
16	347.358753	−7.533395	10.234 810	3	352.095406	−5.492356	10.589 219
17	347.448240	−7.493854	10.247 564	4	352.206380	−5.445425	10.591 829
18	347.538839	−7.453866	10.260 020	5	352.318010	−5.398172	10.594 284
19	347.630398	−7.413507	10.272 174	6	352.430373	−5.350558	10.596 553
20	347.722773	−7.372851	10.284 026	7	352.543503	−5.302567	10.598 604
21	347.815833	−7.331965	10.295 584	8	352.657394	−5.254207	10.600 402
22	347.909456	−7.290910	10.306 857	9	352.771999	−5.205505	10.601 918
23	348.003535	−7.249739	10.317 857	10	352.887245	−5.156505	10.603 123
24	348.097975	−7.208500	10.328 601	11	353.003029	−5.107268	10.603 995
25	348.192702	−7.167229	10.339 110	12	353.119221	−5.057857	10.604 516
26	348.287658	−7.125952	10.349 404	13	353.235684	−5.008326	10.604 672
27	348.382811	−7.084683	10.359 509	14	353.352304	−4.958740	10.604 458
28	348.478158	−7.043418	10.369 451	15	353.468950	−4.909192	10.603 872
29	348.573729	−7.002138	10.379 257	16	353.585478	−4.859760	10.602 916
30	348.669592	−6.960803	10.388 951	17	353.701754	−4.810512	10.601 600
31	348.765848	−6.919354	10.398 554	18	353.817657	−4.761510	10.599 934
Feb. 1	348.862630	−6.877718	10.408 079	19	353.933080	−4.712807	10.597 936
2	348.960088	−6.835812	10.417 532	20	354.047929	−4.664449	10.595 623
3	349.058379	−6.793552	10.426 907	21	354.162127	−4.616472	10.593 017
4	349.157649	−6.750857	10.436 193	22	354.275617	−4.568905	10.590 142
5	349.258022	−6.707662	10.445 365	23	354.388358	−4.521762	10.587 025
6	349.359591	−6.663917	10.454 398	24	354.500336	−4.475046	10.583 693
7	349.462412	−6.619594	10.463 257	25	354.611564	−4.428744	10.580 173
8	349.566499	−6.574684	10.471 909	26	354.722086	−4.382824	10.576 495
9	349.671830	−6.529201	10.480 320	27	354.831981	−4.337238	10.572 684
10	349.778342	−6.483179	10.488 458	28	354.941367	−4.291917	10.568 760
11	349.885946	−6.436666	10.496 295	29	355.050391	−4.246776	10.564 738
12	349.994525	−6.389724	10.503 807	30	355.159218	−4.201721	10.560 619
13	350.103946	−6.342426	10.510 978	31	355.268018	−4.156662	10.556 395
14	350.214064	−6.294846	10.517 795	Apr. 1	355.376938	−4.111516	10.552 048
15	350.324733	−6.247061	10.524 253	2	355.486093	−4.066227	10.547 548

LCRS COORDINATES FOR 0^h BARYCENTRIC DYNAMICAL TIME

Date	Apparent Right Ascension	Apparent Declination	True Lunarcentric Distance	Date	Apparent Right Ascension	Apparent Declination	True Lunarcentric Distance
	°	°	au		°	°	au
Apr. 1	355.376938	−4.111516	10.552 048	May 17	359.902971	−2.276940	10.101 030
2	355.486093	−4.066227	10.547 548	18	359.980850	−2.247210	10.086 487
3	355.595548	−4.020761	10.542 863	19	0.057105	−2.218273	10.071 870
4	355.705323	−3.975114	10.537 960	20	0.131781	−2.190094	10.057 206
5	355.815391	−3.929303	10.532 805	21	0.204955	−2.162623	10.042 522
6	355.925690	−3.883366	10.527 370	22	0.276734	−2.135793	10.027 841
7	356.036130	−3.837357	10.521 631	23	0.347257	−2.109523	10.013 178
8	356.146601	−3.791337	10.515 569	24	0.416685	−2.083721	9.998 541
9	356.256978	−3.745376	10.509 172	25	0.485189	−2.058291	9.983 928
10	356.367130	−3.699547	10.502 431	26	0.552939	−2.033145	9.969 329
11	356.476920	−3.653924	10.495 344	27	0.620079	−2.008209	9.954 719
12	356.586214	−3.608580	10.487 913	28	0.686713	−1.983433	9.940 069
13	356.694877	−3.563584	10.480 144	29	0.752889	−1.958801	9.925 345
14	356.802786	−3.519004	10.472 050	30	0.818603	−1.934324	9.910 512
15	356.909825	−3.474897	10.463 644	31	0.883799	−1.910041	9.895 542
16	357.015892	−3.431315	10.454 947	June 1	0.948382	−1.886011	9.880 407
17	357.120900	−3.388300	10.445 979	2	1.012231	−1.862305	9.865 090
18	357.224779	−3.345884	10.436 765	3	1.075210	−1.839000	9.849 581
19	357.327481	−3.304088	10.427 332	4	1.137176	−1.816176	9.833 872
20	357.428976	−3.262919	10.417 706	5	1.197985	−1.793911	9.817 965
21	357.529264	−3.222372	10.407 917	6	1.257494	−1.772281	9.801 864
22	357.628370	−3.182425	10.397 994	7	1.315568	−1.751356	9.785 580
23	357.726349	−3.143039	10.387 963	8	1.372076	−1.731203	9.769 126
24	357.823294	−3.104158	10.377 850	9	1.426900	−1.711879	9.752 521
25	357.919327	−3.065708	10.367 673	10	1.479933	−1.693437	9.735 784
26	358.014602	−3.027602	10.357 444	11	1.531083	−1.675917	9.718 942
27	358.109289	−2.989743	10.347 165	12	1.580281	−1.659347	9.702 021
28	358.203557	−2.952041	10.336 825	13	1.627479	−1.643743	9.685 052
29	358.297558	−2.914415	10.326 403	14	1.672657	−1.629104	9.668 065
30	358.391400	−2.876811	10.315 871	15	1.715827	−1.615413	9.651 093
May 1	358.485144	−2.839202	10.305 193	16	1.757031	−1.602634	9.634 165
2	358.578796	−2.801593	10.294 335	17	1.796346	−1.590716	9.617 309
3	358.672313	−2.764012	10.283 267	18	1.833880	−1.579590	9.600 551
4	358.765618	−2.726508	10.271 959	19	1.869768	−1.569175	9.583 907
5	358.858604	−2.689144	10.260 393	20	1.904172	−1.559379	9.567 389
6	358.951149	−2.651988	10.248 552	21	1.937264	−1.550105	9.551 001
7	359.043119	−2.615116	10.236 428	22	1.969222	−1.541259	9.534 736
8	359.134377	−2.578604	10.224 018	23	2.000208	−1.532756	9.518 578
9	359.224786	−2.542524	10.211 321	24	2.030356	−1.524533	9.502 503
10	359.314208	−2.506951	10.198 345	25	2.059755	−1.516550	9.486 480
11	359.402515	−2.471951	10.185 100	26	2.088442	−1.508801	9.470 477
12	359.489582	−2.437589	10.171 600	27	2.116397	−1.501308	9.454 461
13	359.575298	−2.403919	10.157 864	28	2.143550	−1.494118	9.438 405
14	359.659566	−2.370988	10.143 913	29	2.169795	−1.487299	9.422 285
15	359.742304	−2.338833	10.129 772	30	2.194999	−1.480929	9.406 087
16	359.823451	−2.307480	10.115 468	July 1	2.219016	−1.475090	9.389 802
17	359.902971	−2.276940	10.101 030	2	2.241696	−1.469865	9.373 430

LCRS COORDINATES FOR 0^h BARYCENTRIC DYNAMICAL TIME

Date	Apparent Right Ascension	Apparent Declination	True Lunarcentric Distance	Date	Apparent Right Ascension	Apparent Declination	True Lunarcentric Distance
	°	°	au		°	°	au
July 1	2.219016	−1.475090	9.389 802	Aug. 16	1.552685	−1.979723	8.737 903
2	2.241696	−1.469865	9.373 430	17	1.503248	−2.004893	8.728 366
3	2.262891	−1.465334	9.356 972	18	1.453373	−2.030078	8.719 130
4	2.282458	−1.461570	9.340 439	19	1.403153	−2.055242	8.710 163
5	2.300265	−1.458642	9.323 844	20	1.352633	−2.080378	8.701 435
6	2.316189	−1.456611	9.307 204	21	1.301804	−2.105508	8.692 915
7	2.330119	−1.455527	9.290 539	22	1.250616	−2.130674	8.684 577
8	2.341963	−1.455434	9.273 874	23	1.198978	−2.155938	8.676 400
9	2.351645	−1.456361	9.257 236	24	1.146773	−2.181374	8.668 368
10	2.359112	−1.458325	9.240 656	25	1.093868	−2.207062	8.660 473
11	2.364343	−1.461326	9.224 165	26	1.040124	−2.233081	8.652 713
12	2.367347	−1.465345	9.207 796	27	0.985407	−2.259507	8.645 093
13	2.368170	−1.470344	9.191 582	28	0.929590	−2.286406	8.637 622
14	2.366898	−1.476265	9.175 553	29	0.872561	−2.313837	8.630 314
15	2.363650	−1.483031	9.159 735	30	0.814226	−2.341846	8.623 187
16	2.358579	−1.490552	9.144 148	31	0.754509	−2.370468	8.616 262
17	2.351862	−1.498726	9.128 805	Sept. 1	0.693355	−2.399726	8.609 563
18	2.343690	−1.507447	9.113 711	2	0.630731	−2.429628	8.603 116
19	2.334255	−1.516612	9.098 862	3	0.566631	−2.460168	8.596 950
20	2.323738	−1.526130	9.084 246	4	0.501080	−2.491322	8.591 093
21	2.312295	−1.535924	9.069 840	5	0.434137	−2.523048	8.585 577
22	2.300043	−1.545942	9.055 620	6	0.365904	−2.555278	8.580 433
23	2.287052	−1.556161	9.041 553	7	0.296528	−2.587925	8.575 687
24	2.273339	−1.566586	9.027 609	8	0.226198	−2.620876	8.571 363
25	2.258869	−1.577250	9.013 758	9	0.155143	−2.654004	8.567 475
26	2.243561	−1.588208	8.999 975	10	0.083617	−2.687172	8.564 030
27	2.227301	−1.599532	8.986 241	11	0.011879	−2.720244	8.561 022
28	2.209952	−1.611303	8.972 544	12	359.940172	−2.753098	8.558 436
29	2.191366	−1.623606	8.958 881	13	359.868708	−2.785633	8.556 249
30	2.171397	−1.636521	8.945 251	14	359.797650	−2.817780	8.554 430
31	2.149900	−1.650125	8.931 663	15	359.727108	−2.849497	8.552 945
Aug. 1	2.126744	−1.664487	8.918 128	16	359.657137	−2.880774	8.551 761
2	2.101809	−1.679665	8.904 663	17	359.587742	−2.911627	8.550 845
3	2.074992	−1.695710	8.891 288	18	359.518884	−2.942096	8.550 169
4	2.046202	−1.712662	8.878 025	19	359.450487	−2.972237	8.549 709
5	2.015373	−1.730547	8.864 900	20	359.382448	−3.002118	8.549 446
6	1.982458	−1.749381	8.851 943	21	359.314647	−3.031814	8.549 369
7	1.947439	−1.769160	8.839 185	22	359.246955	−3.061403	8.549 472
8	1.910330	−1.789865	8.826 658	23	359.179246	−3.090957	8.549 756
9	1.871185	−1.811452	8.814 395	24	359.111398	−3.120544	8.550 227
10	1.830100	−1.833857	8.802 428	25	359.043304	−3.150221	8.550 896
11	1.787212	−1.856994	8.790 785	26	358.974875	−3.180034	8.551 778
12	1.742698	−1.880759	8.779 488	27	358.906040	−3.210019	8.552 889
13	1.696767	−1.905034	8.768 550	28	358.836751	−3.240194	8.554 252
14	1.649640	−1.929696	8.757 978	29	358.766985	−3.270567	8.555 889
15	1.601543	−1.954628	8.747 767	30	358.696741	−3.301132	8.557 824
16	1.552685	−1.979723	8.737 903	Oct. 1	358.626049	−3.331865	8.560 083

LCRS COORDINATES FOR 0^h BARYCENTRIC DYNAMICAL TIME

Date	Apparent Right Ascension	Apparent Declination	True Lunarcentric Distance	Date	Apparent Right Ascension	Apparent Declination	True Lunarcentric Distance
	°	°	au		°	°	au
Oct. 1	358.626049	−3.331865	8.560 083	Nov. 16	356.307927	−4.234431	8.982 965
2	358.554966	−3.362726	8.562 691	17	356.290649	−4.238044	8.997 027
3	358.483588	−3.393657	8.565 676	18	356.274686	−4.241128	9.011 129
4	358.412050	−3.424576	8.569 062	19	356.259929	−4.243741	9.025 280
5	358.340526	−3.455384	8.572 870	20	356.246282	−4.245929	9.039 492
6	358.269236	−3.485958	8.577 115	21	356.233672	−4.247726	9.053 781
7	358.198428	−3.516166	8.581 803	22	356.222047	−4.249152	9.068 165
8	358.128369	−3.545866	8.586 932	23	356.211380	−4.250216	9.082 663
9	358.059319	−3.574930	8.592 484	24	356.201666	−4.250911	9.097 295
10	357.991511	−3.603245	8.598 434	25	356.192929	−4.251217	9.112 082
11	357.925126	−3.630735	8.604 748	26	356.185221	−4.251098	9.127 043
12	357.860282	−3.657354	8.611 387	27	356.178618	−4.250505	9.142 197
13	357.797035	−3.683094	8.618 311	28	356.173226	−4.249374	9.157 560
14	357.735385	−3.707977	8.625 484	29	356.169180	−4.247628	9.173 143
15	357.675283	−3.732046	8.632 873	30	356.166637	−4.245179	9.188 955
16	357.616645	−3.755363	8.640 450	Dec. 1	356.165781	−4.241929	9.204 994
17	357.559363	−3.777999	8.648 195	2	356.166806	−4.237774	9.221 254
18	357.503312	−3.800033	8.656 093	3	356.169907	−4.232618	9.237 716
19	357.448363	−3.821542	8.664 136	4	356.175261	−4.226378	9.254 351
20	357.394384	−3.842601	8.672 321	5	356.183001	−4.218994	9.271 121
21	357.341253	−3.863280	8.680 650	6	356.193206	−4.210443	9.287 982
22	357.288856	−3.883640	8.689 131	7	356.205885	−4.200739	9.304 888
23	357.237095	−3.903733	8.697 774	8	356.220984	−4.189925	9.321 798
24	357.185893	−3.923596	8.706 596	9	356.238397	−4.178075	9.338 673
25	357.135194	−3.943257	8.715 613	10	356.257981	−4.165275	9.355 485
26	357.084964	−3.962727	8.724 846	11	356.279578	−4.151618	9.372 213
27	357.035196	−3.982005	8.734 315	12	356.303024	−4.137197	9.388 845
28	356.985907	−4.001074	8.744 042	13	356.328157	−4.122099	9.405 375
29	356.937142	−4.019904	8.754 049	14	356.354827	−4.106404	9.421 801
30	356.888976	−4.038448	8.764 359	15	356.382895	−4.090183	9.438 128
31	356.841517	−4.056641	8.774 992	16	356.412240	−4.073498	9.454 364
Nov. 1	356.794906	−4.074402	8.785 965	17	356.442753	−4.056401	9.470 521
2	356.749317	−4.091633	8.797 293	18	356.474345	−4.038932	9.486 613
3	356.704961	−4.108221	8.808 983	19	356.506946	−4.021119	9.502 657
4	356.662070	−4.124042	8.821 033	20	356.540509	−4.002979	9.518 671
5	356.620883	−4.138976	8.833 430	21	356.575008	−3.984516	9.534 677
6	356.581629	−4.152912	8.846 151	22	356.610445	−3.965717	9.550 694
7	356.544495	−4.165764	8.859 161	23	356.646848	−3.946559	9.566 742
8	356.509610	−4.177482	8.872 419	24	356.684270	−3.927002	9.582 842
9	356.477035	−4.188055	8.885 881	25	356.722793	−3.906993	9.599 008
10	356.446764	−4.197505	8.899 504	26	356.762522	−3.886468	9.615 255
11	356.418733	−4.205885	8.913 250	27	356.803583	−3.865354	9.631 589
12	356.392841	−4.213263	8.927 086	28	356.846122	−3.843568	9.648 013
13	356.368958	−4.219723	8.940 990	29	356.890296	−3.821027	9.664 522
14	356.346942	−4.225348	8.954 944	30	356.936264	−3.797647	9.681 102
15	356.326646	−4.230224	8.968 937	31	356.984178	−3.773354	9.697 732
16	356.307927	−4.234431	8.982 965	32	357.034165	−3.748088	9.714 381

LCRS COORDINATES FOR 0^h BARYCENTRIC DYNAMICAL TIME

Date	Apparent Right Ascension	Apparent Declination	True Lunarcentric Distance	Date	Apparent Right Ascension	Apparent Declination	True Lunarcentric Distance
	°	°	au		°	°	au
Jan. 0	50.993715	+18.355355	18.860 974	Feb. 15	50.673609	+18.292278	19.576 997
1	50.969403	+18.349661	18.872 911	16	50.688521	+18.296490	19.594 475
2	50.945470	+18.344024	18.884 991	17	50.704579	+18.300977	19.611 848
3	50.921878	+18.338439	18.897 242	18	50.721723	+18.305717	19.629 095
4	50.898611	+18.332907	18.909 689	19	50.739887	+18.310688	19.646 199
5	50.875677	+18.327439	18.922 363	20	50.758999	+18.315865	19.663 148
6	50.853110	+18.322052	18.935 292	21	50.778983	+18.321224	19.679 932
7	50.830971	+18.316773	18.948 503	22	50.799760	+18.326742	19.696 548
8	50.809341	+18.311629	18.962 013	23	50.821250	+18.332397	19.712 997
9	50.788320	+18.306657	18.975 837	24	50.843374	+18.338166	19.729 286
10	50.768019	+18.301891	18.989 979	25	50.866054	+18.344031	19.745 427
11	50.748554	+18.297367	19.004 432	26	50.889223	+18.349978	19.761 439
12	50.730034	+18.293114	19.019 184	27	50.912830	+18.355998	19.777 349
13	50.712561	+18.289160	19.034 212	28	50.936842	+18.362091	19.793 185
14	50.696216	+18.285524	19.049 487	Mar. 1	50.961256	+18.368264	19.808 980
15	50.681061	+18.282216	19.064 977	2	50.986100	+18.374535	19.824 765
16	50.667132	+18.279241	19.080 645	3	51.011429	+18.380928	19.840 566
17	50.654444	+18.276597	19.096 458	4	51.037325	+18.387473	19.856 403
18	50.642992	+18.274275	19.112 382	5	51.063880	+18.394202	19.872 283
19	50.632754	+18.272261	19.128 387	6	51.091193	+18.401145	19.888 205
20	50.623695	+18.270539	19.144 445	7	51.119360	+18.408328	19.904 158
21	50.615768	+18.269092	19.160 533	8	51.148462	+18.415774	19.920 123
22	50.608917	+18.267897	19.176 631	9	51.178568	+18.423496	19.936 075
23	50.603082	+18.266935	19.192 724	10	51.209728	+18.431504	19.951 987
24	50.598193	+18.266181	19.208 798	11	51.241972	+18.439800	19.967 826
25	50.594177	+18.265614	19.224 847	12	51.275313	+18.448380	19.983 560
26	50.590959	+18.265211	19.240 869	13	51.309745	+18.457236	19.999 158
27	50.588459	+18.264949	19.256 867	14	51.345247	+18.466355	20.014 589
28	50.586603	+18.264810	19.272 850	15	51.381783	+18.475720	20.029 825
29	50.585322	+18.264777	19.288 834	16	51.419301	+18.485309	20.044 840
30	50.584561	+18.264841	19.304 842	17	51.457744	+18.495102	20.059 614
31	50.584286	+18.264998	19.320 902	18	51.497043	+18.505074	20.074 130
Feb. 1	50.584486	+18.265254	19.337 043	19	51.537124	+18.515202	20.088 374
2	50.585181	+18.265624	19.353 296	20	51.577911	+18.525461	20.102 338
3	50.586417	+18.266129	19.369 686	21	51.619322	+18.535827	20.116 018
4	50.588266	+18.266797	19.386 237	22	51.661277	+18.546278	20.129 414
5	50.590815	+18.267660	19.402 960	23	51.703696	+18.556793	20.142 532
6	50.594165	+18.268749	19.419 860	24	51.746500	+18.567351	20.155 383
7	50.598417	+18.270097	19.436 933	25	51.789617	+18.577937	20.167 983
8	50.603669	+18.271730	19.454 165	26	51.832987	+18.588539	20.180 355
9	50.610008	+18.273672	19.471 537	27	51.876561	+18.599152	20.192 526
10	50.617508	+18.275939	19.489 021	28	51.920316	+18.609776	20.204 528
11	50.626222	+18.278542	19.506 588	29	51.964255	+18.620423	20.216 395
12	50.636185	+18.281483	19.524 202	30	52.008413	+18.631112	20.228 159
13	50.647410	+18.284759	19.541 831	31	52.052853	+18.641868	20.239 845
14	50.659892	+18.288362	19.559 440	Apr. 1	52.097663	+18.652722	20.251 471
15	50.673609	+18.292278	19.576 997	2	52.142941	+18.663706	20.263 042

LCRS COORDINATES FOR 0^h BARYCENTRIC DYNAMICAL TIME

Date	Apparent Right Ascension	Apparent Declination	True Lunarcentric Distance	Date	Apparent Right Ascension	Apparent Declination	True Lunarcentric Distance
	°	°	au		°	°	au
Apr. 1	52.097663	+18.652722	20.251 471	May 17	54.648407	+19.252967	20.542 914
2	52.142941	+18.663706	20.263 042	18	54.709031	+19.266204	20.542 609
3	52.188789	+18.674848	20.274 552	19	54.769720	+19.280146	20.541 971
4	52.235293	+18.686171	20.285 985	20	54.830056	+19.293595	20.541 026
5	52.282529	+18.697691	20.297 320	21	54.889971	+19.306893	20.539 803
6	52.330548	+18.709417	20.308 528	22	54.949461	+19.320058	20.538 333
7	52.379385	+18.721352	20.319 580	23	55.008529	+19.333100	20.536 649
8	52.429052	+18.733494	20.330 446	24	55.067203	+19.346037	20.534 786
9	52.479546	+18.745833	20.341 096	25	55.125536	+19.358891	20.532 771
10	52.530848	+18.758358	20.351 499	26	55.183603	+19.371688	20.530 627
11	52.582922	+18.771052	20.361 631	27	55.241499	+19.384455	20.528 365
12	52.635723	+18.783897	20.371 466	28	55.299327	+19.397222	20.525 987
13	52.689194	+18.796872	20.380 985	29	55.357184	+19.410011	20.523 481
14	52.743268	+18.809954	20.390 171	30	55.415153	+19.422840	20.520 829
15	52.797873	+18.823119	20.399 010	31	55.473295	+19.435718	20.518 002
16	52.852931	+18.836345	20.407 494	June 1	55.531644	+19.448646	20.514 973
17	52.908362	+18.849607	20.415 620	2	55.590213	+19.461621	20.511 711
18	52.964083	+18.862884	20.423 388	3	55.648995	+19.474634	20.508 188
19	53.020014	+18.876154	20.430 804	4	55.707963	+19.487671	20.504 377
20	53.076076	+18.889399	20.437 879	5	55.767078	+19.500717	20.500 257
21	53.132196	+18.902603	20.444 627	6	55.826289	+19.513754	20.495 808
22	53.188309	+18.915753	20.451 070	7	55.885537	+19.526762	20.491 014
23	53.244363	+18.928841	20.457 233	8	55.944753	+19.539721	20.485 862
24	53.300320	+18.941866	20.463 147	9	56.003864	+19.552610	20.480 345
25	53.356166	+18.954833	20.468 844	10	56.062791	+19.565409	20.474 458
26	53.411914	+18.967754	20.474 357	11	56.121450	+19.578096	20.468 202
27	53.467606	+18.980649	20.479 719	12	56.179756	+19.590653	20.461 583
28	53.523314	+18.993546	20.484 954	13	56.237628	+19.603060	20.454 611
29	53.579127	+19.006474	20.490 077	14	56.294986	+19.615304	20.447 303
30	53.635149	+19.019464	20.495 091	15	56.351759	+19.627371	20.439 680
May 1	53.691479	+19.032541	20.499 987	16	56.407886	+19.639254	20.431 768
2	53.748203	+19.045725	20.504 746	17	56.463322	+19.650949	20.423 595
3	53.805388	+19.059030	20.509 345	18	56.518038	+19.662459	20.415 195
4	53.863078	+19.072460	20.513 755	19	56.572029	+19.673789	20.406 601
5	53.921292	+19.086015	20.517 944	20	56.625310	+19.684955	20.397 847
6	53.980033	+19.099686	20.521 884	21	56.677922	+19.695974	20.388 963
7	54.039284	+19.113464	20.525 546	22	56.729928	+19.706868	20.379 973
8	54.099015	+19.127332	20.528 906	23	56.781412	+19.717664	20.370 898
9	54.159182	+19.141275	20.531 939	24	56.832469	+19.728387	20.361 743
10	54.219733	+19.155273	20.534 627	25	56.883198	+19.739062	20.352 507
11	54.280603	+19.169305	20.536 952	26	56.933693	+19.749709	20.343 177
12	54.341724	+19.183349	20.538 903	27	56.984029	+19.760341	20.333 733
13	54.403018	+19.197382	20.540 472	28	57.034259	+19.770964	20.324 147
14	54.464408	+19.211383	20.541 654	29	57.084414	+19.781578	20.314 391
15	54.525813	+19.225330	20.542 450	30	57.134496	+19.792176	20.304 435
16	54.587158	+19.239202	20.542 867	July 1	57.184491	+19.802748	20.294 254
17	54.648407	+19.252967	20.542 914	2	57.234365	+19.813279	20.283 823

LCRS COORDINATES FOR 0^h BARYCENTRIC DYNAMICAL TIME

Date	Apparent Right Ascension	Apparent Declination	True Lunarcentric Distance	Date	Apparent Right Ascension	Apparent Declination	True Lunarcentric Distance
	°	°	au		°	°	au
July 1	57.184491	+19.802748	20.294 254	Aug. 16	58.821249	+20.133551	19.624 802
2	57.234365	+19.813279	20.283 823	17	58.837426	+20.136649	19.607 916
3	57.284071	+19.823752	20.273 123	18	58.852762	+20.139618	19.591 139
4	57.333554	+19.834150	20.262 136	19	58.867357	+20.142480	19.574 468
5	57.382747	+19.844453	20.250 852	20	58.881303	+20.145252	19.557 894
6	57.431579	+19.854641	20.239 260	21	58.894677	+20.147945	19.541 397
7	57.479973	+19.864695	20.227 358	22	58.907535	+20.150566	19.524 955
8	57.527848	+19.874596	20.215 145	23	58.919914	+20.153113	19.508 544
9	57.575118	+19.884323	20.202 626	24	58.931826	+20.155582	19.492 136
10	57.621699	+19.893861	20.189 811	25	58.943263	+20.157963	19.475 708
11	57.667509	+19.903192	20.176 715	26	58.954196	+20.160242	19.459 236
12	57.712471	+19.912306	20.163 361	27	58.964584	+20.162403	19.442 703
13	57.756518	+19.921192	20.149 774	28	58.974370	+20.164429	19.426 094
14	57.799599	+19.929846	20.135 984	29	58.983492	+20.166301	19.409 398
15	57.841682	+19.938272	20.122 027	30	58.991880	+20.168001	19.392 611
16	57.882755	+19.946474	20.107 937	31	58.999460	+20.169511	19.375 731
17	57.922832	+19.954466	20.093 750	Sept. 1	59.006156	+20.170812	19.358 761
18	57.961950	+19.962266	20.079 498	2	59.011888	+20.171889	19.341 709
19	58.000168	+19.969895	20.065 209	3	59.016579	+20.172726	19.324 587
20	58.037564	+19.977376	20.050 902	4	59.020153	+20.173309	19.307 412
21	58.074230	+19.984734	20.036 591	5	59.022538	+20.173628	19.290 209
22	58.110264	+19.991994	20.022 279	6	59.023675	+20.173675	19.273 007
23	58.145759	+19.999175	20.007 959	7	59.023517	+20.173450	19.255 839
24	58.180803	+20.006293	19.993 616	8	59.022042	+20.172956	19.238 745
25	58.215461	+20.013358	19.979 228	9	59.019257	+20.172205	19.221 765
26	58.249780	+20.020374	19.964 770	10	59.015195	+20.171214	19.204 937
27	58.283779	+20.027336	19.950 215	11	59.009925	+20.170007	19.188 297
28	58.317458	+20.034238	19.935 533	12	59.003536	+20.168611	19.171 872
29	58.350793	+20.041065	19.920 702	13	58.996137	+20.167053	19.155 679
30	58.383745	+20.047804	19.905 700	14	58.987843	+20.165361	19.139 727
31	58.416263	+20.054436	19.890 509	15	58.978767	+20.163558	19.124 015
Aug. 1	58.448285	+20.060944	19.875 116	16	58.969011	+20.161663	19.108 531
2	58.479742	+20.067309	19.859 513	17	58.958663	+20.159690	19.093 261
3	58.510561	+20.073511	19.843 695	18	58.947792	+20.157647	19.078 183
4	58.540662	+20.079532	19.827 660	19	58.936444	+20.155535	19.063 273
5	58.569964	+20.085354	19.811 414	20	58.924646	+20.153353	19.048 506
6	58.598384	+20.090959	19.794 965	21	58.912402	+20.151093	19.033 857
7	58.625839	+20.096331	19.778 328	22	58.899698	+20.148742	19.019 304
8	58.652248	+20.101459	19.761 521	23	58.886503	+20.146288	19.004 827
9	58.677542	+20.106331	19.744 571	24	58.872772	+20.143714	18.990 410
10	58.701661	+20.110942	19.727 509	25	58.858449	+20.141003	18.976 041
11	58.724567	+20.115292	19.710 371	26	58.843473	+20.138136	18.961 714
12	58.746243	+20.119388	19.693 193	27	58.827775	+20.135096	18.947 425
13	58.766700	+20.123243	19.676 015	28	58.811287	+20.131866	18.933 176
14	58.785975	+20.126873	19.658 871	29	58.793936	+20.128430	18.918 973
15	58.804131	+20.130301	19.641 792	30	58.775652	+20.124773	18.904 828
16	58.821249	+20.133551	19.624 802	Oct. 1	58.756368	+20.120883	18.890 755

LCRS COORDINATES FOR 0^h BARYCENTRIC DYNAMICAL TIME

Date	Apparent Right Ascension	Apparent Declination	True Lunarcentric Distance	Date	Apparent Right Ascension	Apparent Declination	True Lunarcentric Distance
	°	°	au		°	°	au
Oct. 1	58.756368	+20.120883	18.890 755	Nov. 16	57.146520	+19.796845	18.515 627
2	58.736019	+20.116749	18.876 775	17	57.104376	+19.788368	18.514 503
3	58.714550	+20.112364	18.862 914	18	57.062415	+19.779903	18.513 599
4	58.691918	+20.107725	18.849 202	19	57.020588	+19.771433	18.512 900
5	58.668096	+20.102835	18.835 675	20	56.978840	+19.762944	18.512 399
6	58.643085	+20.097701	18.822 372	21	56.937112	+19.754420	18.512 092
7	58.616913	+20.092341	18.809 333	22	56.895343	+19.745846	18.511 980
8	58.589646	+20.086779	18.796 597	23	56.853474	+19.737209	18.512 067
9	58.561377	+20.081042	18.784 195	24	56.811446	+19.728497	18.512 364
10	58.532229	+20.075163	18.772 148	25	56.769210	+19.719703	18.512 885
11	58.502332	+20.069173	18.760 468	26	56.726722	+19.710820	18.513 648
12	58.471822	+20.063102	18.749 155	27	56.683950	+19.701847	18.514 675
13	58.440822	+20.056972	18.738 198	28	56.640875	+19.692786	18.515 993
14	58.409435	+20.050801	18.727 579	29	56.597498	+19.683645	18.517 629
15	58.377745	+20.044600	18.717 277	30	56.553836	+19.674436	18.519 616
16	58.345811	+20.038373	18.707 265	Dec. 1	56.509936	+19.665178	18.521 983
17	58.313668	+20.032120	18.697 518	2	56.465869	+19.655897	18.524 762
18	58.281333	+20.025835	18.688 009	3	56.421740	+19.646624	18.527 976
19	58.248802	+20.019509	18.678 716	4	56.377675	+19.637394	18.531 643
20	58.216054	+20.013131	18.669 617	5	56.333821	+19.628243	18.535 769
21	58.183055	+20.006685	18.660 693	6	56.290330	+19.619205	18.540 348
22	58.149759	+20.000155	18.651 932	7	56.247340	+19.610309	18.545 360
23	58.116113	+19.993526	18.643 323	8	56.204971	+19.601575	18.550 778
24	58.082057	+19.986779	18.634 862	9	56.163310	+19.593015	18.556 568
25	58.047527	+19.979900	18.626 547	10	56.122411	+19.584633	18.562 694
26	58.012458	+19.972872	18.618 383	11	56.082302	+19.576426	18.569 122
27	57.976789	+19.965683	18.610 378	12	56.042985	+19.568385	18.575 819
28	57.940458	+19.958320	18.602 545	13	56.004441	+19.560498	18.582 757
29	57.903412	+19.950775	18.594 901	14	55.966642	+19.552753	18.589 910
30	57.865603	+19.943040	18.587 468	15	55.929542	+19.545134	18.597 259
31	57.826995	+19.935113	18.580 273	16	55.893094	+19.537625	18.604 787
Nov. 1	57.787566	+19.926997	18.573 346	17	55.857239	+19.530210	18.612 484
2	57.747313	+19.918698	18.566 722	18	55.821917	+19.522873	18.620 341
3	57.706261	+19.910232	18.560 436	19	55.787067	+19.515599	18.628 356
4	57.664464	+19.901618	18.554 526	20	55.752624	+19.508374	18.636 530
5	57.622009	+19.892886	18.549 025	21	55.718528	+19.501186	18.644 870
6	57.579016	+19.884069	18.543 958	22	55.684724	+19.494025	18.653 387
7	57.535625	+19.875202	18.539 339	23	55.651164	+19.486886	18.662 096
8	57.491987	+19.866321	18.535 173	24	55.617813	+19.479765	18.671 015
9	57.448247	+19.857454	18.531 448	25	55.584648	+19.472664	18.680 169
10	57.404530	+19.848626	18.528 145	26	55.551663	+19.465591	18.689 581
11	57.360938	+19.839851	18.525 239	27	55.518874	+19.458556	18.699 279
12	57.317543	+19.831136	18.522 700	28	55.486315	+19.451577	18.709 289
13	57.274392	+19.822485	18.520 497	29	55.454045	+19.444675	18.719 635
14	57.231506	+19.813891	18.518 602	30	55.422148	+19.437878	18.730 340
15	57.188887	+19.805348	18.516 986	31	55.390730	+19.431217	18.741 420
16	57.146520	+19.796845	18.515 627	32	55.359914	+19.424724	18.752 881

LCRS COORDINATES FOR 0^h BARYCENTRIC DYNAMICAL TIME

Date	Apparent Right Ascension	Apparent Declination	True Lunarcentric Distance	Date	Apparent Right Ascension	Apparent Declination	True Lunarcentric Distance
	°	°	au		°	°	au
Jan. 0	357.703133	−2.396652	30.091 296	Feb. 15	358.714818	−1.936001	30.729 935
1	357.714909	−2.390960	30.107 660	16	358.746258	−1.921996	30.739 083
2	357.726988	−2.385160	30.124 015	17	358.777932	−1.907909	30.747 861
3	357.739392	−2.379241	30.140 384	18	358.809792	−1.893764	30.756 274
4	357.752153	−2.373183	30.156 786	19	358.841794	−1.879586	30.764 331
5	357.765315	−2.366962	30.173 233	20	358.873897	−1.865394	30.772 043
6	357.778928	−2.360551	30.189 732	21	358.906064	−1.851207	30.779 427
7	357.793045	−2.353919	30.206 279	22	358.938265	−1.837041	30.786 502
8	357.807721	−2.347038	30.222 862	23	358.970474	−1.822908	30.793 291
9	357.823004	−2.339880	30.239 461	24	359.002672	−1.808814	30.799 818
10	357.838938	−2.332425	30.256 047	25	359.034852	−1.794764	30.806 111
11	357.855552	−2.324655	30.272 586	26	359.067015	−1.780752	30.812 200
12	357.872863	−2.316563	30.289 042	27	359.099177	−1.766769	30.818 112
13	357.890873	−2.308148	30.305 374	28	359.131366	−1.752797	30.823 872
14	357.909570	−2.299419	30.321 546	Mar. 1	359.163626	−1.738809	30.829 497
15	357.928929	−2.290389	30.337 523	2	359.196006	−1.724778	30.834 995
16	357.948914	−2.281080	30.353 277	3	359.228563	−1.710672	30.840 364
17	357.969481	−2.271514	30.368 785	4	359.261348	−1.696461	30.845 592
18	357.990584	−2.261717	30.384 031	5	359.294408	−1.682121	30.850 655
19	358.012174	−2.251717	30.399 004	6	359.327776	−1.667634	30.855 525
20	358.034202	−2.241539	30.413 699	7	359.361471	−1.652990	30.860 169
21	358.056622	−2.231208	30.428 116	8	359.395497	−1.638187	30.864 552
22	358.079388	−2.220748	30.442 258	9	359.429846	−1.623232	30.868 643
23	358.102460	−2.210180	30.456 134	10	359.464498	−1.608135	30.872 410
24	358.125799	−2.199524	30.469 757	11	359.499423	−1.592915	30.875 828
25	358.149372	−2.188797	30.483 140	12	359.534582	−1.577591	30.878 874
26	358.173150	−2.178013	30.496 305	13	359.569932	−1.562188	30.881 533
27	358.197114	−2.167181	30.509 274	14	359.605425	−1.546733	30.883 793
28	358.221251	−2.156307	30.522 072	15	359.641013	−1.531252	30.885 648
29	358.245560	−2.145389	30.534 726	16	359.676645	−1.515772	30.887 099
30	358.270054	−2.134418	30.547 264	17	359.712275	−1.500321	30.888 150
31	358.294756	−2.123379	30.559 708	18	359.747859	−1.484927	30.888 811
Feb. 1	358.319706	−2.112251	30.572 077	19	359.783346	−1.469628	30.889 094
2	358.344949	−2.101005	30.584 382	20	359.818646	−1.454434	30.889 017
3	358.370539	−2.089613	30.596 622	21	359.853771	−1.439276	30.888 599
4	358.396527	−2.078045	30.608 790	22	359.888746	−1.424233	30.887 863
5	358.422964	−2.066275	30.620 867	23	359.923518	−1.409334	30.886 836
6	358.449888	−2.054280	30.632 828	24	359.958062	−1.394576	30.885 545
7	358.477329	−2.042047	30.644 642	25	359.992376	−1.379954	30.884 018
8	358.505304	−2.029566	30.656 275	26	0.026465	−1.365461	30.882 287
9	358.533814	−2.016837	30.667 691	27	0.060351	−1.351084	30.880 378
10	358.562850	−2.003866	30.678 855	28	0.094066	−1.336799	30.878 315
11	358.592389	−1.990666	30.689 735	29	0.127656	−1.322582	30.876 116
12	358.622399	−1.977256	30.700 303	30	0.161175	−1.308400	30.873 786
13	358.652839	−1.963658	30.710 537	31	0.194681	−1.294222	30.871 322
14	358.683661	−1.949897	30.720 417	Apr. 1	0.228228	−1.280017	30.868 706
15	358.714818	−1.936001	30.729 935	2	0.261859	−1.265762	30.865 914

LCRS COORDINATES FOR 0^h BARYCENTRIC DYNAMICAL TIME

Date	Apparent Right Ascension	Apparent Declination	True Lunarcentric Distance	Date	Apparent Right Ascension	Apparent Declination	True Lunarcentric Distance
	°	°	au		°	°	au
Apr. 1	0.228228	−1.280017	30.868 706	May 17	1.606705	−0.706182	30.461 299
2	0.261859	−1.265762	30.865 914	18	1.629228	−0.697258	30.446 977
3	0.295603	−1.251443	30.862 912	19	1.651166	−0.688613	30.432 554
4	0.329470	−1.237055	30.859 668	20	1.672531	−0.680239	30.418 060
5	0.363457	−1.222600	30.856 148	21	1.693347	−0.672120	30.403 523
6	0.397547	−1.208089	30.852 322	22	1.713649	−0.664235	30.388 967
7	0.431711	−1.193539	30.848 164	23	1.733482	−0.656557	30.374 409
8	0.465914	−1.178969	30.843 653	24	1.752899	−0.649058	30.359 860
9	0.500112	−1.164403	30.838 775	25	1.771957	−0.641704	30.345 319
10	0.534261	−1.149866	30.833 517	26	1.790713	−0.634465	30.330 776
11	0.568312	−1.135384	30.827 876	27	1.809218	−0.627315	30.316 210
12	0.602216	−1.120982	30.821 853	28	1.827509	−0.620235	30.301 591
13	0.635926	−1.106687	30.815 451	29	1.845606	−0.613217	30.286 886
14	0.669395	−1.092521	30.808 680	30	1.863511	−0.606262	30.272 062
15	0.702580	−1.078509	30.801 555	31	1.881207	−0.599380	30.257 087
16	0.735442	−1.064668	30.794 093	June 1	1.898665	−0.592589	30.241 936
17	0.767945	−1.051017	30.786 316	2	1.915849	−0.585911	30.226 591
18	0.800063	−1.037568	30.778 247	3	1.932712	−0.579371	30.211 040
19	0.831772	−1.024331	30.769 913	4	1.949210	−0.572994	30.195 278
20	0.863058	−1.011312	30.761 342	5	1.965295	−0.566805	30.179 305
21	0.893916	−0.998511	30.752 565	6	1.980921	−0.560829	30.163 125
22	0.924349	−0.985924	30.743 610	7	1.996044	−0.555090	30.146 750
23	0.954372	−0.973540	30.734 508	8	2.010621	−0.549609	30.130 192
24	0.984010	−0.961342	30.725 286	9	2.024615	−0.544405	30.113 470
25	1.013303	−0.949308	30.715 964	10	2.037991	−0.539495	30.096 606
26	1.042299	−0.937409	30.706 557	11	2.050719	−0.534893	30.079 625
27	1.071054	−0.925613	30.697 069	12	2.062778	−0.530609	30.062 555
28	1.099628	−0.913888	30.687 493	13	2.074152	−0.526649	30.045 427
29	1.128072	−0.902206	30.677 810	14	2.084835	−0.523012	30.028 272
30	1.156428	−0.890544	30.667 992	15	2.094832	−0.519695	30.011 123
May 1	1.184721	−0.878891	30.658 006	16	2.104157	−0.516686	29.994 012
2	1.212955	−0.867246	30.647 817	17	2.112836	−0.513970	29.976 966
3	1.241122	−0.855615	30.637 394	18	2.120903	−0.511524	29.960 012
4	1.269196	−0.844013	30.626 708	19	2.128403	−0.509324	29.943 168
5	1.297143	−0.832460	30.615 738	20	2.135389	−0.507339	29.926 446
6	1.324923	−0.820978	30.604 467	21	2.141918	−0.505538	29.909 851
7	1.352490	−0.809593	30.592 886	22	2.148048	−0.503890	29.893 377
8	1.379798	−0.798329	30.580 990	23	2.153834	−0.502367	29.877 008
9	1.406800	−0.787213	30.568 780	24	2.159321	−0.500945	29.860 721
10	1.433448	−0.776268	30.556 260	25	2.164541	−0.499610	29.844 486
11	1.459696	−0.765519	30.543 442	26	2.169507	−0.498357	29.828 270
12	1.485503	−0.754987	30.530 338	27	2.174217	−0.497191	29.812 041
13	1.510827	−0.744694	30.516 967	28	2.178652	−0.496125	29.795 771
14	1.535636	−0.734654	30.503 352	29	2.182778	−0.495179	29.779 437
15	1.559899	−0.724884	30.489 516	30	2.186556	−0.494376	29.763 025
16	1.583593	−0.715391	30.475 489	July 1	2.189942	−0.493741	29.746 526
17	1.606705	−0.706182	30.461 299	2	2.192887	−0.493300	29.729 937

LCRS COORDINATES FOR 0^h BARYCENTRIC DYNAMICAL TIME

Date	Apparent Right Ascension	Apparent Declination	True Lunarcentric Distance	Date	Apparent Right Ascension	Apparent Declination	True Lunarcentric Distance
	°	°	au		°	°	au
July 1	2.189942	−0.493741	29.746 526	Aug. 16	1.791760	−0.705817	29.085 864
2	2.192887	−0.493300	29.729 937	17	1.772658	−0.714779	29.076 134
3	2.195348	−0.493077	29.713 265	18	1.753437	−0.723750	29.066 702
4	2.197281	−0.493096	29.696 516	19	1.734127	−0.732718	29.057 538
5	2.198644	−0.493378	29.679 706	20	1.714742	−0.741679	29.048 612
6	2.199402	−0.493941	29.662 850	21	1.695282	−0.750637	29.039 892
7	2.199521	−0.494802	29.645 970	22	1.675733	−0.759604	29.031 352
8	2.198973	−0.495974	29.629 091	23	1.656069	−0.768597	29.022 971
9	2.197737	−0.497468	29.612 239	24	1.636255	−0.777637	29.014 732
10	2.195798	−0.499287	29.595 446	25	1.616253	−0.786747	29.006 627
11	2.193151	−0.501434	29.578 743	26	1.596021	−0.795951	28.998 652
12	2.189801	−0.503901	29.562 164	27	1.575518	−0.805272	28.990 813
13	2.185762	−0.506680	29.545 741	28	1.554707	−0.814732	28.983 116
14	2.181064	−0.509751	29.529 504	29	1.533554	−0.824347	28.975 577
15	2.175744	−0.513091	29.513 481	30	1.512029	−0.834134	28.968 211
16	2.169851	−0.516674	29.497 690	31	1.490109	−0.844104	28.961 039
17	2.163442	−0.520467	29.482 146	Sept. 1	1.467775	−0.854266	28.954 084
18	2.156577	−0.524437	29.466 854	2	1.445018	−0.864625	28.947 372
19	2.149317	−0.528551	29.451 809	3	1.421832	−0.875180	28.940 931
20	2.141720	−0.532781	29.436 998	4	1.398223	−0.885928	28.934 789
21	2.133836	−0.537101	29.422 402	5	1.374205	−0.896858	28.928 977
22	2.125704	−0.541492	29.407 993	6	1.349805	−0.907954	28.923 527
23	2.117347	−0.545946	29.393 741	7	1.325062	−0.919193	28.918 464
24	2.108773	−0.550462	29.379 614	8	1.300030	−0.930544	28.913 813
25	2.099974	−0.555047	29.365 583	9	1.274773	−0.941972	28.909 590
26	2.090927	−0.559718	29.351 623	10	1.249363	−0.953438	28.905 802
27	2.081598	−0.564494	29.337 714	11	1.223875	−0.964902	28.902 444
28	2.071947	−0.569400	29.323 844	12	1.198380	−0.976327	28.899 503
29	2.061930	−0.574460	29.310 009	13	1.172942	−0.987683	28.896 957
30	2.051504	−0.579699	29.296 209	14	1.147610	−0.998946	28.894 775
31	2.040625	−0.585141	29.282 452	15	1.122418	−1.010102	28.892 926
Aug. 1	2.029254	−0.590806	29.268 749	16	1.097384	−1.021146	28.891 376
2	2.017356	−0.596712	29.255 116	17	1.072511	−1.032080	28.890 092
3	2.004901	−0.602875	29.241 573	18	1.047790	−1.042913	28.889 046
4	1.991863	−0.609308	29.228 142	19	1.023200	−1.053662	28.888 214
5	1.978221	−0.616020	29.214 849	20	0.998710	−1.064344	28.887 577
6	1.963964	−0.623015	29.201 722	21	0.974287	−1.074982	28.887 122
7	1.949085	−0.630295	29.188 792	22	0.949890	−1.085599	28.886 843
8	1.933590	−0.637854	29.176 092	23	0.925483	−1.096215	28.886 740
9	1.917494	−0.645682	29.163 654	24	0.901027	−1.106853	28.886 818
10	1.900827	−0.653759	29.151 509	25	0.876490	−1.117531	28.887 086
11	1.883630	−0.662063	29.139 685	26	0.851841	−1.128264	28.887 559
12	1.865954	−0.670562	29.128 205	27	0.827059	−1.139065	28.888 255
13	1.847862	−0.679223	29.117 082	28	0.802125	−1.149942	28.889 192
14	1.829422	−0.688009	29.106 322	29	0.777028	−1.160899	28.890 393
15	1.810700	−0.696885	29.095 920	30	0.751766	−1.171939	28.891 883
16	1.791760	−0.705817	29.085 864	Oct. 1	0.726342	−1.183056	28.893 687

LCRS COORDINATES FOR 0^h BARYCENTRIC DYNAMICAL TIME

Date	Apparent Right Ascension	Apparent Declination	True Lunarcentric Distance	Date	Apparent Right Ascension	Apparent Declination	True Lunarcentric Distance
	°	°	au		°	°	au
Oct. 1	0.726342	−1.183056	28.893 687	Nov. 16	359.787495	−1.575804	29.301 473
2	0.700768	−1.194242	28.895 831	17	359.776173	−1.580037	29.315 587
3	0.675069	−1.205484	28.898 343	18	359.765246	−1.584108	29.329 760
4	0.649278	−1.216761	28.901 249	19	359.754682	−1.588035	29.343 999
5	0.623443	−1.228046	28.904 570	20	359.744449	−1.591833	29.358 316
6	0.597624	−1.239305	28.908 323	21	359.734524	−1.595515	29.372 726
7	0.571890	−1.250502	28.912 519	22	359.724890	−1.599088	29.387 245
8	0.546318	−1.261594	28.917 156	23	359.715534	−1.602557	29.401 893
9	0.520986	−1.272542	28.922 220	24	359.706455	−1.605921	29.416 690
10	0.495964	−1.283311	28.927 688	25	359.697657	−1.609176	29.431 657
11	0.471310	−1.293874	28.933 529	26	359.689154	−1.612313	29.446 814
12	0.447064	−1.304214	28.939 704	27	359.680966	−1.615319	29.462 181
13	0.423247	−1.314323	28.946 176	28	359.673125	−1.618174	29.477 774
14	0.399863	−1.324204	28.952 908	29	359.665671	−1.620857	29.493 609
15	0.376903	−1.333867	28.959 868	30	359.658653	−1.623338	29.509 695
16	0.354345	−1.343326	28.967 028	Dec. 1	359.652128	−1.625588	29.526 034
17	0.332160	−1.352602	28.974 366	2	359.646160	−1.627573	29.542 621
18	0.310312	−1.361716	28.981 867	3	359.640812	−1.629259	29.559 440
19	0.288766	−1.370689	28.989 521	4	359.636148	−1.630616	29.576 465
20	0.267481	−1.379545	28.997 324	5	359.632218	−1.631619	29.593 660
21	0.246421	−1.388304	29.005 278	6	359.629056	−1.632255	29.610 981
22	0.225551	−1.396985	29.013 389	7	359.626676	−1.632521	29.628 383
23	0.204840	−1.405606	29.021 668	8	359.625071	−1.632424	29.645 822
24	0.184263	−1.414179	29.030 128	9	359.624217	−1.631983	29.663 259
25	0.163800	−1.422714	29.038 787	10	359.624078	−1.631220	29.680 663
26	0.143438	−1.431218	29.047 664	11	359.624607	−1.630162	29.698 012
27	0.123171	−1.439692	29.056 780	12	359.625757	−1.628837	29.715 289
28	0.103001	−1.448133	29.066 158	13	359.627480	−1.627271	29.732 486
29	0.082938	−1.456536	29.075 820	14	359.629730	−1.625489	29.749 601
30	0.063000	−1.464888	29.085 790	15	359.632465	−1.623514	29.766 636
31	0.043215	−1.473173	29.096 089	16	359.635645	−1.621366	29.783 595
Nov. 1	0.023622	−1.481368	29.106 736	17	359.639235	−1.619062	29.800 491
2	0.004272	−1.489445	29.117 750	18	359.643207	−1.616617	29.817 334
3	359.985224	−1.497372	29.129 138	19	359.647537	−1.614041	29.834 143
4	359.966547	−1.505111	29.140 904	20	359.652207	−1.611341	29.850 933
5	359.948317	−1.512623	29.153 037	21	359.657208	−1.608521	29.867 725
6	359.930606	−1.519872	29.165 518	22	359.662538	−1.605578	29.884 540
7	359.913476	−1.526826	29.178 314	23	359.668203	−1.602506	29.901 398
8	359.896975	−1.533465	29.191 387	24	359.674221	−1.599295	29.918 318
9	359.881132	−1.539779	29.204 693	25	359.680613	−1.595928	29.935 316
10	359.865952	−1.545767	29.218 190	26	359.687414	−1.592387	29.952 408
11	359.851425	−1.551442	29.231 840	27	359.694664	−1.588647	29.969 602
12	359.837528	−1.556819	29.245 609	28	359.702411	−1.584682	29.986 902
13	359.824226	−1.561920	29.259 473	29	359.710706	−1.580464	30.004 304
14	359.811481	−1.566769	29.273 412	30	359.719604	−1.575964	30.021 796
15	359.799251	−1.571389	29.287 414	31	359.729158	−1.571154	30.039 356
16	359.787495	−1.575804	29.301 473	32	359.739417	−1.566013	30.056 956

FOR 0^h BARYCENTRIC DYNAMICAL TIME

Date		Principal Axis System			Mean Earth System		
		ϕ	θ	ψ	ϕ	θ	ψ
		°	°	°	°	°	°
Jan.	0	−0.168283	+21.861972	105.231732	−0.153093	+21.883086	105.198787
	1	−0.181580	+21.869468	118.420824	−0.153872	+21.888736	118.376264
	2	−0.189073	+21.878408	131.604359	−0.150320	+21.894814	131.549551
	3	−0.189866	+21.888129	144.781513	−0.142119	+21.900812	144.718363
	4	−0.183687	+21.897890	157.952052	−0.129466	+21.906183	157.882896
	5	−0.170931	+21.906964	171.116363	−0.113089	+21.910434	171.043850
	6	−0.152586	+21.914730	184.275394	−0.094160	+21.913195	184.202340
	7	−0.130064	+21.920742	197.430484	−0.074115	+21.914284	197.359731
	8	−0.104967	+21.924767	210.583158	−0.054428	+21.913725	210.517425
	9	−0.078854	+21.926779	223.734901	−0.036373	+21.911733	223.676643
	10	−0.053049	+21.926914	236.886977	−0.020855	+21.908654	236.838262
	11	−0.028528	+21.925405	250.040335	−0.008314	+21.904889	250.002733
	12	−0.005924	+21.922511	263.195593	+0.001245	+21.900815	263.170095
	13	+0.014397	+21.918459	276.353123	+0.008136	+21.896724	276.340084
	14	+0.032196	+21.913421	289.513165	+0.012828	+21.892790	289.512287
	15	+0.047233	+21.907522	302.675951	+0.015768	+21.889080	302.686298
	16	+0.059178	+21.900871	315.841784	+0.017264	+21.885587	315.861827
	17	+0.067599	+21.893599	329.011051	+0.017436	+21.882279	329.038750
	18	+0.072008	+21.885902	342.184181	+0.016231	+21.879143	342.217091
	19	+0.071954	+21.878058	355.361560	+0.013497	+21.876216	355.396959
	20	+0.067134	+21.870426	8.543435	+0.009077	+21.873600	8.578464
	21	+0.057493	+21.863437	21.729815	+0.002899	+21.871460	21.761632
	22	+0.043310	+21.857556	34.920403	−0.004937	+21.870007	34.946331
	23	+0.025243	+21.853245	48.114547	−0.014106	+21.869467	48.132219
	24	+0.004340	+21.850915	61.311237	−0.024030	+21.870053	61.318719
	25	−0.017992	+21.850875	74.509132	−0.033883	+21.871918	74.505032
	26	−0.040068	+21.853287	87.706638	−0.042642	+21.875125	87.690179
	27	−0.060049	+21.858125	100.902024	−0.049178	+21.879607	100.873087
	28	−0.076117	+21.865153	114.093589	−0.052384	+21.885144	114.052716
	29	−0.086679	+21.873918	127.279851	−0.051348	+21.891366	127.228217
	30	−0.090586	+21.883787	140.459752	−0.045530	+21.897775	140.399097
	31	−0.087304	+21.894011	153.632819	−0.034903	+21.903803	153.565352
Feb.	1	−0.077003	+21.903818	166.799245	−0.020019	+21.908902	166.727527
	2	−0.060520	+21.912521	179.959844	−0.001946	+21.912631	179.886653
	3	−0.039187	+21.919600	193.115899	+0.017906	+21.914732	193.044085
	4	−0.014588	+21.924751	206.268928	+0.038031	+21.915160	206.201264
	5	+0.011694	+21.927880	219.420441	+0.057085	+21.914070	219.359484
	6	+0.038286	+21.929065	232.571754	+0.074066	+21.911762	232.519712
	7	+0.064122	+21.928490	245.723887	+0.088415	+21.908600	245.682502
	8	+0.088465	+21.926376	258.877554	+0.099990	+21.904944	258.848013
	9	+0.110826	+21.922931	272.033226	+0.108974	+21.901082	272.016097
	10	+0.130861	+21.918325	285.191237	+0.115721	+21.897208	285.186436
	11	+0.148246	+21.912687	298.351890	+0.120606	+21.893412	298.358687
	12	+0.162597	+21.906131	311.515536	+0.123904	+21.889712	311.532589
	13	+0.173433	+21.898789	324.682606	+0.125714	+21.886090	324.708036
	14	+0.180206	+21.890851	337.853587	+0.125968	+21.882541	337.885068
	15	+0.182384	+21.882587	351.028944	+0.124477	+21.879105	351.063832

FOR 0ʰ BARYCENTRIC DYNAMICAL TIME

Date		Principal Axis System ϕ	Principal Axis System θ	Principal Axis System ψ	Mean Earth System ϕ	Mean Earth System θ	Mean Earth System ψ
		°	°	°	°	°	°
Feb.	15	+0.182384	+21.882587	351.028944	+0.124477	+21.879105	351.063832
	16	+0.179554	+21.874358	4.209025	+0.121027	+21.875888	4.244489
	17	+0.171541	+21.866606	17.393953	+0.115481	+21.873069	17.427130
	18	+0.158503	+21.859822	30.583540	+0.107870	+21.870879	30.611683
	19	+0.140994	+21.854507	43.777233	+0.098465	+21.869575	43.797856
	20	+0.119984	+21.851120	56.974092	+0.087809	+21.869405	56.985105
	21	+0.096830	+21.850029	70.172817	+0.076712	+21.870565	70.172640
	22	+0.073205	+21.851459	83.371821	+0.066207	+21.873163	83.359468
	23	+0.050981	+21.855459	96.569336	+0.057468	+21.877184	96.544468
	24	+0.032071	+21.861865	109.763563	+0.051690	+21.882466	109.726508
	25	+0.018235	+21.870298	122.952852	+0.049939	+21.888690	122.904583
	26	+0.010874	+21.880178	136.135900	+0.052979	+21.895392	136.077981
	27	+0.010829	+21.890774	149.311937	+0.061108	+21.902010	149.246437
	28	+0.018240	+21.901285	162.480863	+0.074040	+21.907955	162.410243
Mar.	1	+0.032516	+21.910950	175.643271	+0.090904	+21.912705	175.570253
	2	+0.052451	+21.919152	188.800338	+0.110362	+21.915901	188.727764
	3	+0.076466	+21.925489	201.953594	+0.130867	+21.917404	201.884279
	4	+0.102908	+21.929791	215.104640	+0.150948	+21.917296	215.041226
	5	+0.130296	+21.932080	228.254907	+0.169460	+21.915831	228.199727
	6	+0.157469	+21.932501	241.405521	+0.185701	+21.913351	241.360482
	7	+0.183595	+21.931247	254.557291	+0.199412	+21.910200	254.523769
	8	+0.208098	+21.928502	267.710772	+0.210664	+21.906663	267.689543
	9	+0.230540	+21.924416	280.866383	+0.219716	+21.902933	280.857578
	10	+0.250510	+21.919109	294.024508	+0.226855	+21.899111	294.027606
	11	+0.267535	+21.912690	307.185574	+0.232287	+21.895228	307.199430
	12	+0.281059	+21.905291	320.350082	+0.236062	+21.891284	320.372984
	13	+0.290458	+21.897099	333.518585	+0.238072	+21.887285	333.548344
	14	+0.295111	+21.888385	346.691628	+0.238089	+21.883281	346.725693
	15	+0.294503	+21.879513	359.869654	+0.235845	+21.879389	359.905240
	16	+0.288341	+21.870935	13.052896	+0.231137	+21.875800	13.087134
	17	+0.276657	+21.863168	26.241282	+0.223928	+21.872766	26.271369
	18	+0.259890	+21.856750	39.434362	+0.214423	+21.870576	39.457711
	19	+0.238914	+21.852192	52.631283	+0.203116	+21.869517	52.645659
	20	+0.215031	+21.849921	65.830797	+0.190797	+21.869831	65.834441
	21	+0.189894	+21.850231	79.031329	+0.178506	+21.871676	79.023050
	22	+0.165401	+21.853241	92.231084	+0.167459	+21.875087	92.210326
	23	+0.143540	+21.858859	105.428184	+0.158926	+21.879954	105.395057
	24	+0.126205	+21.866779	118.620844	+0.154097	+21.886010	118.576113
	25	+0.115005	+21.876482	131.807554	+0.153917	+21.892837	131.752598
	26	+0.111063	+21.887280	144.987264	+0.158934	+21.899899	144.923998
	27	+0.114860	+21.898379	158.159536	+0.169160	+21.906599	158.090308
	28	+0.126141	+21.908971	171.324630	+0.184012	+21.912362	171.252091
	29	+0.143958	+21.918341	184.483473	+0.202361	+21.916727	184.410444
	30	+0.166838	+21.925968	197.637498	+0.222711	+21.919435	197.566817
	31	+0.193077	+21.931566	210.788364	+0.243495	+21.920457	210.722745
Apr.	1	+0.221047	+21.935080	223.937662	+0.263370	+21.919978	223.879553
	2	+0.249421	+21.936611	237.086702	+0.281431	+21.918309	237.038160

FOR 0^h BARYCENTRIC DYNAMICAL TIME

Date		Principal Axis System			Mean Earth System		
		ϕ	θ	ψ	ϕ	θ	ψ
		°	°	°	°	°	°
Apr.	1	+0.221047	+21.935080	223.937662	+0.263370	+21.919978	223.879553
	2	+0.249421	+21.936611	237.086702	+0.281431	+21.918309	237.038160
	3	+0.277237	+21.936334	250.236437	+0.297254	+21.915791	250.199021
	4	+0.303830	+21.934418	263.387528	+0.310800	+21.912714	263.362214
	5	+0.328698	+21.931000	276.540467	+0.322250	+21.909274	276.527600
	6	+0.351358	+21.926179	289.695709	+0.331825	+21.905571	289.694983
	7	+0.371260	+21.920043	302.853761	+0.339659	+21.901637	302.864232
	8	+0.387752	+21.912710	316.015213	+0.345736	+21.897474	316.035348
	9	+0.400106	+21.904360	329.180713	+0.349876	+21.893095	329.208471
	10	+0.407593	+21.895259	342.350908	+0.351786	+21.888561	342.383843
	11	+0.409580	+21.885779	355.526348	+0.351129	+21.884000	355.561739
	12	+0.405649	+21.876383	8.707382	+0.347633	+21.879618	8.742373
	13	+0.395702	+21.867611	21.894058	+0.341180	+21.875693	21.925808
	14	+0.380050	+21.860039	35.086045	+0.331905	+21.872542	35.111878
	15	+0.359460	+21.854228	48.282585	+0.320240	+21.870493	48.300136
	16	+0.335156	+21.850670	61.482502	+0.306939	+21.869839	61.489841
	17	+0.308760	+21.849730	74.684249	+0.293041	+21.870791	74.679989
	18	+0.282187	+21.851599	87.886011	+0.279796	+21.873440	87.869382
	19	+0.257490	+21.856261	101.085846	+0.268548	+21.877730	101.056737
	20	+0.236684	+21.863478	114.281855	+0.260595	+21.883440	114.240818
	21	+0.221546	+21.872794	127.472361	+0.257036	+21.890198	127.420580
	22	+0.213431	+21.883569	140.656089	+0.258616	+21.897499	140.595314
	23	+0.213107	+21.895034	153.832313	+0.265596	+21.904759	153.764763
	24	+0.220656	+21.906372	167.000962	+0.277681	+21.911381	166.929207
	25	+0.235450	+21.916810	180.162636	+0.294014	+21.916843	180.089456
	26	+0.256258	+21.925721	193.318517	+0.313289	+21.920777	193.246763
	27	+0.281462	+21.932691	206.470168	+0.333973	+21.923031	206.402608
	28	+0.309358	+21.937548	219.619248	+0.354601	+21.923680	219.558431
	29	+0.338436	+21.940319	232.767245	+0.374041	+21.922969	232.715369
	30	+0.367541	+21.941148	245.915317	+0.391643	+21.921227	245.874112
May	1	+0.395877	+21.940203	259.064276	+0.407209	+21.918757	259.034916
	2	+0.422870	+21.937619	272.214708	+0.420833	+21.915772	272.197750
	3	+0.447999	+21.933480	285.367127	+0.432695	+21.912381	285.362476
	4	+0.470672	+21.927853	298.522095	+0.442897	+21.908608	298.529014
	5	+0.490162	+21.920823	311.680278	+0.451367	+21.904446	311.697422
	6	+0.505641	+21.912546	324.842428	+0.457857	+21.899896	324.867915
	7	+0.516253	+21.903272	338.009312	+0.461983	+21.895017	338.040818
	8	+0.521225	+21.893365	351.181611	+0.463321	+21.889941	351.216492
	9	+0.519992	+21.883300	4.359812	+0.461499	+21.884888	4.395242
	10	+0.512309	+21.873634	17.544100	+0.456311	+21.880153	17.577217
	11	+0.498344	+21.864978	30.734276	+0.447801	+21.876084	30.762334
	12	+0.478739	+21.857939	43.929703	+0.436324	+21.873049	43.950218
	13	+0.454615	+21.853071	57.129296	+0.422576	+21.871388	57.140182
	14	+0.427537	+21.850813	70.331562	+0.407573	+21.871370	70.331242
	15	+0.399411	+21.851433	83.534693	+0.392579	+21.873144	83.522186
	16	+0.372342	+21.854996	96.736701	+0.378999	+21.876714	96.711676
	17	+0.348447	+21.861334	109.935588	+0.368232	+21.881914	109.898379

FOR 0^h BARYCENTRIC DYNAMICAL TIME

Date		Principal Axis System			Mean Earth System		
		ϕ	θ	ψ	ϕ	θ	ψ
		°	°	°	°	°	°
May	17	+0.348447	+21.861334	109.935588	+0.368232	+21.881914	109.898379
	18	+0.329658	+21.870057	123.129532	+0.361515	+21.888412	123.081122
	19	+0.317526	+21.880571	136.317071	+0.359760	+21.895735	136.259034
	20	+0.313058	+21.892141	149.497254	+0.363432	+21.903317	149.431667
	21	+0.316608	+21.903954	162.669744	+0.372461	+21.910556	162.599076
	22	+0.327841	+21.915215	175.834854	+0.386233	+21.916897	175.761833
	23	+0.345797	+21.925230	188.993489	+0.403663	+21.921907	188.920959
	24	+0.369054	+21.933488	202.147002	+0.423362	+21.925334	202.077775
	25	+0.395969	+21.939696	215.296968	+0.443876	+21.927141	215.233680
	26	+0.424952	+21.943778	228.444931	+0.463951	+21.927481	228.389908
	27	+0.454677	+21.945814	241.592201	+0.482726	+21.926630	241.547335
	28	+0.484174	+21.945953	254.739760	+0.499801	+21.924887	254.706416
	29	+0.512755	+21.944332	267.888319	+0.515139	+21.922491	267.867260
	30	+0.539861	+21.941042	281.038455	+0.528872	+21.919571	281.029801
	31	+0.564888	+21.936133	294.190763	+0.541095	+21.916160	294.193986
June	1	+0.587087	+21.929659	307.345951	+0.551733	+21.912234	307.359900
	2	+0.605562	+21.921735	320.504846	+0.560496	+21.907773	320.527808
	3	+0.619347	+21.912578	333.668329	+0.566928	+21.902814	333.698114
	4	+0.627521	+21.902527	346.837224	+0.570500	+21.897477	346.871282
	5	+0.629355	+21.892049	0.012174	+0.570728	+21.891980	0.047725
	6	+0.624432	+21.881712	13.193527	+0.567287	+21.886629	13.227706
	7	+0.612754	+21.872150	26.381240	+0.560109	+21.881795	26.411247
	8	+0.594811	+21.864013	39.574819	+0.549450	+21.877880	39.598068
	9	+0.571599	+21.857911	52.773298	+0.535925	+21.875269	52.787558
	10	+0.544589	+21.854352	65.975271	+0.520494	+21.874285	65.978784
	11	+0.515648	+21.853685	79.178967	+0.504410	+21.875140	79.170548
	12	+0.486899	+21.856058	92.382381	+0.489111	+21.877902	92.361480
	13	+0.460541	+21.861384	105.583440	+0.476079	+21.882463	105.550173
	14	+0.438645	+21.869341	118.780196	+0.466677	+21.888543	118.735336
	15	+0.422947	+21.879390	131.971016	+0.461979	+21.895703	131.915950
	16	+0.414668	+21.890827	145.154751	+0.462630	+21.903393	145.091401
	17	+0.414393	+21.902853	158.330846	+0.468748	+21.911012	158.261568
	18	+0.422028	+21.914659	171.499389	+0.479912	+21.917984	171.426841
	19	+0.436846	+21.925516	184.661060	+0.495217	+21.923834	184.588063
	20	+0.457627	+21.934845	197.817010	+0.513424	+21.928247	197.746404
	21	+0.482862	+21.942269	210.968670	+0.533163	+21.931101	210.903163
	22	+0.510993	+21.947613	224.117527	+0.553165	+21.932462	224.059561
	23	+0.540624	+21.950874	237.264934	+0.572462	+21.932535	237.216555
	24	+0.570651	+21.952151	250.411981	+0.590485	+21.931586	250.374736
	25	+0.600256	+21.951566	263.559493	+0.607046	+21.929854	263.534346
	26	+0.628804	+21.949215	276.708120	+0.622191	+21.927495	276.695407
	27	+0.655676	+21.945145	289.858488	+0.636001	+21.924558	289.857890
	28	+0.680130	+21.939394	303.011312	+0.648420	+21.921021	303.021880
	29	+0.701257	+21.932037	316.167453	+0.659168	+21.916843	316.187650
	30	+0.718021	+21.923243	329.327867	+0.667755	+21.912027	329.355651
July	1	+0.729378	+21.913311	342.493503	+0.673570	+21.906664	342.526432
	2	+0.734431	+21.902680	355.665168	+0.676012	+21.900954	355.700523

FOR 0^h BARYCENTRIC DYNAMICAL TIME

Date		Principal Axis System			Mean Earth System		
		ϕ	θ	ψ	ϕ	θ	ψ
		°	°	°	°	°	°
July	1	+0.729378	+21.913311	342.493503	+0.673570	+21.906664	342.526432
	2	+0.734431	+21.902680	355.665168	+0.676012	+21.900954	355.700523
	3	+0.732579	+21.891911	8.843386	+0.674622	+21.895198	8.878315
	4	+0.723632	+21.881652	22.028296	+0.669195	+21.889781	22.059962
	5	+0.707903	+21.872584	35.219570	+0.659862	+21.885128	35.245302
	6	+0.686229	+21.865366	48.416389	+0.647131	+21.881665	48.433825
	7	+0.659964	+21.860571	61.617462	+0.631881	+21.879765	61.624676
	8	+0.630898	+21.858626	74.821088	+0.615320	+21.879702	74.816697
	9	+0.601136	+21.859764	88.025281	+0.598888	+21.881608	88.008519
	10	+0.572928	+21.863988	101.227919	+0.584125	+21.885446	101.198681
	11	+0.548467	+21.871053	114.426945	+0.572506	+21.890993	114.385790
	12	+0.529665	+21.880485	127.620561	+0.565264	+21.897855	127.568680
	13	+0.517962	+21.891618	140.807419	+0.563230	+21.905504	140.746570
	14	+0.514172	+21.903667	153.986758	+0.566712	+21.913338	153.919165
	15	+0.518422	+21.915812	167.158462	+0.575460	+21.920763	167.086698
	16	+0.530180	+21.927293	180.323033	+0.588718	+21.927265	180.249882
	17	+0.548393	+21.937482	193.481468	+0.605357	+21.932478	193.409780
	18	+0.571676	+21.945939	206.635077	+0.624082	+21.936223	206.567618
	19	+0.598542	+21.952417	219.785272	+0.643648	+21.938500	219.724587
	20	+0.627603	+21.956839	232.933385	+0.663048	+21.939451	232.881661
	21	+0.657695	+21.959243	246.080543	+0.681623	+21.939297	246.039501
	22	+0.687908	+21.959714	259.227637	+0.699066	+21.938256	259.198440
	23	+0.717524	+21.958330	272.375387	+0.715325	+21.936486	272.358578
	24	+0.745876	+21.955138	285.524450	+0.730432	+21.934054	285.519927
	25	+0.772222	+21.950165	298.675550	+0.744336	+21.930948	298.682568
	26	+0.795656	+21.943460	311.829546	+0.756785	+21.927120	311.846755
	27	+0.815117	+21.935153	324.987429	+0.767294	+21.922548	325.012944
	28	+0.829482	+21.925493	338.150230	+0.775211	+21.917287	338.181729
	29	+0.837715	+21.914878	351.318893	+0.779843	+21.911505	351.353736
	30	+0.839030	+21.903845	4.494119	+0.780599	+21.905484	4.529483
	31	+0.833036	+21.893041	17.676237	+0.777126	+21.899608	17.709265
Aug.	1	+0.819843	+21.883168	30.865110	+0.769407	+21.894318	30.893061
	2	+0.800110	+21.874926	44.060088	+0.757819	+21.890072	44.080484
	3	+0.775039	+21.868946	57.260018	+0.743135	+21.887291	57.270777
	4	+0.746316	+21.865731	70.463299	+0.726492	+21.886305	70.462848
	5	+0.715996	+21.865597	83.667990	+0.709303	+21.887314	83.655352
	6	+0.686345	+21.868638	96.871953	+0.693135	+21.890351	96.846804
	7	+0.659646	+21.874703	110.073044	+0.679552	+21.895264	110.035725
	8	+0.637982	+21.883392	123.269309	+0.669940	+21.901718	123.220807
	9	+0.623018	+21.894095	136.459186	+0.665328	+21.909220	136.401082
	10	+0.615829	+21.906050	149.641677	+0.666247	+21.917178	149.576053
	11	+0.616788	+21.918425	162.816440	+0.672651	+21.924974	162.745768
	12	+0.625571	+21.930423	175.983792	+0.683937	+21.932049	175.910802
	13	+0.641271	+21.941362	189.144601	+0.699073	+21.937982	189.072137
	14	+0.662595	+21.950742	202.300101	+0.716804	+21.942534	202.230972
	15	+0.688104	+21.958256	215.451665	+0.735882	+21.945653	215.388503
	16	+0.716423	+21.963771	228.600613	+0.755270	+21.947434	228.545736

FOR 0^h BARYCENTRIC DYNAMICAL TIME

Date		Principal Axis System			Mean Earth System		
		ϕ	θ	ψ	ϕ	θ	ψ
		°	°	°	°	°	°
Aug.	16	+0.716423	+21.963771	228.600613	+0.755270	+21.947434	228.545736
	17	+0.746371	+21.967271	241.748085	+0.774254	+21.948058	241.703376
	18	+0.776996	+21.968796	254.895005	+0.792455	+21.947715	254.861820
	19	+0.807519	+21.968395	268.042136	+0.809743	+21.946551	268.021225
	20	+0.837221	+21.966093	281.190177	+0.826091	+21.944633	281.181652
	21	+0.865325	+21.961904	294.339873	+0.841421	+21.941954	294.343196
	22	+0.890912	+21.955858	307.492092	+0.855480	+21.938466	307.506108
	23	+0.912901	+21.948054	320.647840	+0.867794	+21.934134	320.670832
	24	+0.930120	+21.938703	333.808198	+0.877697	+21.928988	333.837978
	25	+0.941428	+21.928162	346.974207	+0.884438	+21.923162	347.008227
	26	+0.945884	+21.916934	0.146718	+0.887320	+21.916916	0.182201
	27	+0.942903	+21.905653	13.326241	+0.885849	+21.910619	13.360327
	28	+0.932386	+21.895031	26.512834	+0.879852	+21.904721	26.542729
	29	+0.914792	+21.885799	39.706034	+0.869558	+21.899705	39.729158
	30	+0.891153	+21.878643	52.904847	+0.855618	+21.896031	52.918972
	31	+0.863025	+21.874133	66.107789	+0.839075	+21.894087	66.111165
Sept.	1	+0.832388	+21.872671	79.312988	+0.821294	+21.894136	79.304435
	2	+0.801492	+21.874441	92.518321	+0.803841	+21.896283	92.497293
	3	+0.772677	+21.879383	105.721583	+0.788339	+21.900449	105.688202
	4	+0.748162	+21.887191	118.920687	+0.776298	+21.906368	118.875733
	5	+0.729832	+21.897326	132.113866	+0.768942	+21.913603	132.058731
	6	+0.719038	+21.909070	145.299852	+0.767047	+21.921591	145.236464
	7	+0.716458	+21.921597	158.478019	+0.770825	+21.929704	158.408737
	8	+0.722039	+21.934071	171.648432	+0.779897	+21.937339	171.575914
	9	+0.735063	+21.945745	184.811785	+0.793371	+21.944006	184.738854
	10	+0.754335	+21.956041	197.969233	+0.810033	+21.949387	197.898725
	11	+0.778430	+21.964584	211.122150	+0.828602	+21.953366	211.056770
	12	+0.805947	+21.971185	224.271895	+0.847967	+21.955992	224.214077
	13	+0.835671	+21.975787	237.419652	+0.867342	+21.957416	237.371432
	14	+0.866620	+21.978395	250.566382	+0.886284	+21.957811	250.529298
	15	+0.897987	+21.979024	263.712879	+0.904614	+21.957305	263.687885
	16	+0.929021	+21.977667	276.859870	+0.922262	+21.955954	276.847290
	17	+0.958906	+21.974310	290.008132	+0.939112	+21.953742	290.007641
	18	+0.986682	+21.968956	303.158567	+0.954886	+21.950612	303.169207
	19	+1.011226	+21.961675	316.312215	+0.969088	+21.946520	316.332449
	20	+1.031303	+21.952647	329.470210	+0.981027	+21.941478	329.497995
	21	+1.045686	+21.942195	342.633675	+0.989904	+21.935599	342.666569
	22	+1.053298	+21.930795	355.803581	+0.994939	+21.929121	355.838869
	23	+1.053384	+21.919060	8.980599	+0.995517	+21.922399	9.015434
	24	+1.045646	+21.907706	22.164970	+0.991322	+21.915884	22.196521
	25	+1.030339	+21.897489	35.356420	+0.982432	+21.910076	35.382021
	26	+1.008312	+21.889142	48.554123	+0.969359	+21.905476	48.571418
	27	+0.980973	+21.883300	61.756733	+0.953042	+21.902520	61.763801
	28	+0.950204	+21.880445	74.962464	+0.934780	+21.901534	74.957927
	29	+0.918219	+21.880847	88.169224	+0.916120	+21.902693	88.152324
	30	+0.887384	+21.884543	101.374781	+0.898717	+21.905990	101.345417
Oct.	1	+0.860017	+21.891314	114.576950	+0.884174	+21.911230	114.535689

FOR 0^h BARYCENTRIC DYNAMICAL TIME

Date	Principal Axis System			Mean Earth System		
	ϕ	θ	ψ	ϕ	θ	ψ
	°	°	°	°	°	°
Oct. 1	+0.860017	+21.891314	114.576950	+0.884174	+21.911230	114.535689
2	+0.838179	+21.900708	127.773790	+0.873871	+21.918042	127.721828
3	+0.823476	+21.912069	140.963786	+0.868805	+21.925909	140.902886
4	+0.816899	+21.924604	154.146007	+0.869463	+21.934221	154.078398
5	+0.818728	+21.937465	167.320191	+0.875751	+21.942355	167.248451
6	+0.828532	+21.949847	180.486757	+0.887012	+21.949756	180.413668
7	+0.845293	+21.961081	193.646685	+0.902161	+21.956016	193.575096
8	+0.867638	+21.970699	206.801308	+0.919912	+21.960926	206.733980
9	+0.894111	+21.978435	219.952045	+0.939057	+21.964469	219.891515
10	+0.923411	+21.984186	233.100182	+0.958678	+21.966760	233.048629
11	+0.954490	+21.987936	246.246767	+0.978234	+21.967964	246.205901
12	+0.986515	+21.989676	259.392638	+0.997494	+21.968206	259.363609
13	+1.018733	+21.989375	272.538541	+1.016371	+21.967533	272.521884
14	+1.050321	+21.986981	285.685271	+1.034740	+21.965913	285.680872
15	+1.080289	+21.982454	298.833760	+1.052300	+21.963266	298.840868
16	+1.107456	+21.975824	311.985105	+1.068521	+21.959523	312.002365
17	+1.130506	+21.967232	325.140514	+1.082659	+21.954675	325.166041
18	+1.148101	+21.956966	338.301208	+1.093846	+21.948815	338.332681
19	+1.159032	+21.945478	351.468281	+1.101214	+21.942162	351.503063
20	+1.162379	+21.933366	4.642555	+1.104035	+21.935061	4.677828
21	+1.157655	+21.921343	17.824445	+1.101860	+21.927963	17.857356
22	+1.144919	+21.910186	31.013858	+1.094620	+21.921385	31.041674
23	+1.124825	+21.900668	44.210147	+1.082687	+21.915855	44.230394
24	+1.098621	+21.893485	57.412114	+1.066881	+21.911861	57.422715
25	+1.068073	+21.889195	70.618078	+1.048418	+21.909788	70.617467
26	+1.035337	+21.888156	83.826000	+1.028811	+21.909879	83.813207
27	+1.002782	+21.890492	97.033641	+1.009730	+21.912198	97.008346
28	+0.972796	+21.896079	110.238748	+0.992843	+21.916619	110.201300
29	+0.947572	+21.904544	123.439249	+0.979647	+21.922835	123.390645
30	+0.928919	+21.915306	136.633437	+0.971313	+21.930383	136.575261
31	+0.918094	+21.927621	149.820118	+0.968558	+21.938691	149.754459
Nov. 1	+0.915694	+21.940659	162.998720	+0.971559	+21.947141	162.928055
2	+0.921619	+21.953593	176.169333	+0.979940	+21.955148	176.096393
3	+0.935131	+21.965685	189.332651	+0.992843	+21.962234	189.260280
4	+0.955021	+21.976364	202.489830	+1.009097	+21.968089	202.420834
5	+0.979855	+21.985264	215.642260	+1.027465	+21.972601	215.579262
6	+1.008237	+21.992208	228.791311	+1.046890	+21.975823	228.736620
7	+1.038999	+21.997147	241.938158	+1.066675	+21.977899	241.893646
8	+1.071236	+22.000066	255.083733	+1.086488	+21.978966	255.050742
9	+1.104191	+22.000930	268.228816	+1.106222	+21.979083	268.208084
10	+1.137079	+21.999658	281.374195	+1.125781	+21.978212	281.365823
11	+1.168934	+21.996168	294.520804	+1.144896	+21.976247	294.524245
12	+1.198554	+21.990428	307.669770	+1.163031	+21.973078	307.683863
13	+1.224548	+21.982522	320.822383	+1.179395	+21.968653	320.845407
14	+1.245457	+21.972689	333.979977	+1.193034	+21.963032	334.009746
15	+1.259917	+21.961343	347.143794	+1.202969	+21.956406	347.177762
16	+1.266829	+21.949061	0.314820	+1.208346	+21.949107	0.350215

FOR 0ʰ BARYCENTRIC DYNAMICAL TIME

Date		Principal Axis System ϕ	Principal Axis System θ	Principal Axis System ψ	Mean Earth System ϕ	Mean Earth System θ	Mean Earth System ψ
		°	°	°	°	°	°
Nov.	16	+1.266829	+21.949061	0.314820	+1.208346	+21.949107	0.350215
	17	+1.265511	+21.936554	13.493651	+1.208572	+21.941582	13.527618
	18	+1.255818	+21.924611	26.680384	+1.203428	+21.934359	26.710135
	19	+1.238207	+21.914039	39.874555	+1.193139	+21.927994	39.897517
	20	+1.213747	+21.905589	53.075132	+1.178392	+21.923017	53.089084
	21	+1.184064	+21.899891	66.280563	+1.160302	+21.919872	66.283761
	22	+1.151229	+21.897388	79.488887	+1.140324	+21.918865	79.480157
	23	+1.117590	+21.898294	92.697884	+1.120120	+21.920133	92.676689
	24	+1.085576	+21.902574	105.905261	+1.101402	+21.923621	105.871730
	25	+1.057483	+21.909941	119.108850	+1.085759	+21.929083	119.063769
	26	+1.035279	+21.919882	132.306790	+1.074498	+21.936110	132.251560
	27	+1.020431	+21.931712	145.497688	+1.068509	+21.944171	145.434244
	28	+1.013794	+21.944637	158.680727	+1.068183	+21.952672	158.611432
	29	+1.015555	+21.957835	171.855715	+1.073385	+21.961025	171.783232
	30	+1.025269	+21.970536	185.023054	+1.083497	+21.968717	184.950207
Dec.	1	+1.041974	+21.982103	198.183646	+1.097543	+21.975371	198.113268
	2	+1.064378	+21.992074	211.338714	+1.114377	+21.980784	211.273503
	3	+1.091097	+22.000178	224.489589	+1.132910	+21.984925	224.431971
	4	+1.120869	+22.006300	237.637513	+1.152312	+21.987884	237.589512
	5	+1.152674	+22.010406	250.783519	+1.172102	+21.989793	250.746658
	6	+1.185702	+22.012465	263.928452	+1.192101	+21.990737	263.903671
	7	+1.219201	+22.012402	277.073094	+1.212237	+21.990699	277.060703
	8	+1.252285	+22.010108	290.218337	+1.232321	+21.989567	290.217999
	9	+1.283809	+22.005494	303.365286	+1.251887	+21.987194	303.376036
	10	+1.312371	+21.998567	316.515262	+1.270157	+21.983468	316.535557
	11	+1.336420	+21.989493	329.669704	+1.286121	+21.978389	329.697498
	12	+1.354437	+21.978623	342.830004	+1.298684	+21.972099	342.862858
	13	+1.365125	+21.966496	355.997339	+1.306841	+21.964896	356.032544
	14	+1.367585	+21.953804	9.172511	+1.309835	+21.957215	9.207224
	15	+1.361448	+21.941340	22.355825	+1.307277	+21.949585	22.387223
	16	+1.346955	+21.929937	35.547020	+1.299227	+21.942584	35.572445
	17	+1.324975	+21.920393	48.745250	+1.286221	+21.936776	48.762352
	18	+1.296970	+21.913401	61.949119	+1.269249	+21.932656	61.955987
	19	+1.264892	+21.909486	75.156775	+1.249679	+21.930595	75.152040
	20	+1.231032	+21.908953	88.366053	+1.229137	+21.930801	88.348963
	21	+1.197832	+21.911857	101.574649	+1.209352	+21.933289	101.545114
	22	+1.167665	+21.917999	114.780324	+1.191983	+21.937883	114.738917
	23	+1.142630	+21.926941	127.981095	+1.178449	+21.944227	127.929021
	24	+1.124372	+21.938055	141.175406	+1.169787	+21.951831	141.114434
	25	+1.113953	+21.950586	154.362245	+1.166554	+21.960129	154.294611
	26	+1.111789	+21.963731	167.541204	+1.168797	+21.968539	167.469487
	27	+1.117678	+21.976716	180.712458	+1.176089	+21.976539	180.639443
	28	+1.130889	+21.988870	193.876678	+1.187634	+21.983719	193.805213
	29	+1.150324	+21.999672	207.034892	+1.202427	+21.989819	206.967733
	30	+1.174713	+22.008773	220.188298	+1.219446	+21.994738	220.127974
	31	+1.202810	+22.015982	233.338091	+1.237835	+21.998501	233.286770
	32	+1.233530	+22.021214	246.485334	+1.257018	+22.001205	246.444710

COORDINATES FOR 0^h BARYCENTRIC DYNAMICAL TIME

Date		Sun Az.	Sun Alt.	Mercury Az.	Mercury Alt.	Venus Az.	Venus Alt.	Earth Az.	Earth Alt.
		°	°	°	°	°	°	°	°
Jan.	0	174.4	+1.5279	153.1	+0.2397	221.4	+2.3652	355.2	−6.7290
	4	125.6	+1.4933	105.6	+0.8133	172.8	+1.9768	356.9	−3.1379
	8	77.0	+1.4641	58.5	+1.3693	124.1	+1.5427	0.2	+3.0705
	12	28.4	+1.4392	11.6	+1.8839	75.5	+1.0715	3.9	+6.3009
	16	339.9	+1.4006	324.9	+2.3282	26.8	+0.5553	5.0	+3.8559
	20	291.4	+1.3487	278.4	+2.6947	338.1	−0.0057	1.2	−1.4930
	24	242.7	+1.2906	231.9	+2.9781	289.2	−0.5978	356.0	−5.9297
	28	194.0	+1.2213	185.5	+3.1615	240.0	−1.2173	354.6	−6.5297
Feb.	1	145.2	+1.1375	139.3	+3.2315	190.4	−1.8716	357.9	−1.8637
	5	96.5	+1.0516	93.3	+3.1897	140.5	−2.5580	2.2	+4.3488
	9	47.9	+0.9674	47.6	+3.0278	90.4	−3.2698	4.8	+6.3647
	13	359.4	+0.8750	2.1	+2.7216	40.2	−4.0156	4.3	+2.9683
	17	310.8	+0.7785	316.8	+2.2570	349.8	−4.7925	0.1	−2.5920
	21	262.2	+0.6865	271.6	+1.6262	298.9	−5.5771	354.9	−6.5449
	25	213.4	+0.5912	226.2	+0.8187	247.3	−6.3454	353.5	−6.2228
Mar.	1	164.6	+0.4813	180.3	−0.1559	194.7	−7.0679	357.9	−0.7338
	5	115.8	+0.3639	133.4	−1.2291	141.5	−7.6926	3.8	+5.3076
	9	67.1	+0.2461	85.1	−2.2798	87.7	−8.1850	6.1	+6.1471
	13	18.5	+0.1247	34.9	−3.1655	33.7	−8.5431	4.2	+1.9885
	17	329.9	+0.0086	342.5	−3.7226	339.4	−8.7410	359.4	−3.5660
	21	281.2	−0.0917	288.1	−3.7994	284.7	−8.7179	354.3	−6.9119
	25	232.5	−0.1855	232.1	−3.3439	229.4	−8.4216	352.6	−5.7089
	29	183.6	−0.2911	175.8	−2.4631	173.9	−7.8401	357.1	+0.2774
Apr.	2	134.7	−0.4082	120.3	−1.3764	118.8	−7.0354	4.5	+5.8883
	6	85.9	−0.5283	66.4	−0.3054	64.7	−6.1451	7.2	+5.6049
	10	37.2	−0.6489	14.0	+0.6185	11.5	−5.2675	4.4	+0.8841
	14	348.5	−0.7571	323.0	+1.3618	319.0	−4.4137	359.1	−4.4309
	18	299.8	−0.8392	273.0	+1.9230	266.9	−3.5728	354.3	−7.0005
	22	251.1	−0.9043	223.8	+2.2879	215.1	−2.7616	352.4	−4.8964
	26	202.2	−0.9772	175.3	+2.4410	163.6	−2.0145	356.3	+1.3001
	30	153.2	−1.0648	127.5	+2.3931	112.7	−1.3569	4.2	+6.1641
May	4	104.3	−1.1584	80.4	+2.1670	62.4	−0.8025	7.7	+4.7922
	8	55.5	−1.2524	33.9	+1.7844	12.5	−0.3371	4.5	−0.3249
	12	6.8	−1.3300	347.9	+1.2749	323.0	+0.0757	359.0	−5.2065
	16	318.1	−1.3737	302.4	+0.6639	273.5	+0.4559	354.7	−6.8355
	20	269.3	−1.3914	257.4	−0.0389	224.1	+0.7883	353.0	−3.7796
	24	220.4	−1.4121	212.9	−0.8208	174.7	+1.0470	356.2	+2.4277
	28	171.4	−1.4498	168.7	−1.6292	125.5	+1.2276	3.6	+6.2553
June	1	122.4	−1.4973	124.7	−2.3782	76.5	+1.3399	7.3	+3.8182
	5	73.5	−1.5472	80.7	−2.9854	27.8	+1.4045	4.2	−1.5717
	9	24.7	−1.5807	36.4	−3.3832	339.3	+1.4524	358.8	−5.8942
	13	336.0	−1.5764	351.6	−3.5312	290.7	+1.4986	355.2	−6.4764
	17	287.2	−1.5389	306.2	−3.4317	242.2	+1.5241	354.2	−2.4457
	21	238.3	−1.5003	260.1	−3.1259	193.6	+1.4988	357.0	+3.6290
	25	189.3	−1.4800	213.2	−2.6565	145.0	+1.4177	3.3	+6.2317
	29	140.3	−1.4734	165.6	−2.0447	96.5	+1.2930	6.5	+2.7882
July	3	91.3	−1.4730	117.2	−1.3115	48.2	+1.1428	3.5	−2.7699

COORDINATES FOR 0^h BARYCENTRIC DYNAMICAL TIME

Date	Sun		Mercury		Venus		Earth	
	Az.	Alt.	Az.	Alt.	Az.	Alt.	Az.	Alt.
	°	°	°	°	°	°	°	°
July 3	91.3	−1.4730	117.2	−1.3115	48.2	+1.1428	3.5	−2.7699
7	42.5	−1.4598	68.1	−0.4705	0.0	+0.9966	358.3	−6.4713
11	353.7	−1.4086	18.2	+0.4753	311.9	+0.8724	355.4	−5.9906
15	304.9	−1.3201	327.2	+1.4982	263.7	+0.7541	355.7	−1.0367
19	256.1	−1.2272	275.0	+2.5040	215.5	+0.6098	358.7	+4.7687
23	207.1	−1.1532	221.3	+3.3476	167.2	+0.4315	3.5	+6.0726
27	158.1	−1.0962	166.3	+3.8706	119.0	+0.2290	5.6	+1.7587
31	109.1	−1.0505	110.6	+3.9450	70.9	+0.0161	2.5	−3.8400
Aug. 4	60.3	−0.9985	55.1	+3.5540	22.9	−0.1803	357.5	−6.8916
8	11.5	−0.9126	0.6	+2.8058	334.9	−0.3377	355.2	−5.4234
12	322.7	−0.7880	307.5	+1.8428	287.0	−0.4657	356.9	+0.2991
16	273.9	−0.6568	256.1	+0.7805	239.0	−0.5966	0.8	+5.6803
20	225.0	−0.5444	206.4	−0.2564	190.9	−0.7420	4.5	+5.6987
24	176.1	−0.4511	158.5	−1.1377	142.9	−0.8955	5.0	+0.7260
28	127.1	−0.3745	112.0	−1.7728	94.9	−1.0494	1.5	−4.7331
Sept. 1	78.3	−0.3004	66.6	−2.1145	47.1	−1.1822	356.5	−7.0940
5	29.5	−0.2007	21.6	−2.1583	359.2	−1.2682	354.3	−4.7689
9	340.8	−0.0644	336.7	−1.9486	311.5	−1.3090	357.4	+1.4604
13	292.1	+0.0799	291.7	−1.5666	263.6	−1.3352	2.8	+6.2392
17	243.3	+0.2068	246.3	−1.0800	215.8	−1.3620	5.9	+5.0375
21	194.4	+0.3144	200.7	−0.5278	167.9	−1.3871	4.8	−0.3487
25	145.4	+0.4012	154.7	+0.0550	120.0	−1.4101	0.7	−5.4415
29	96.6	+0.4752	108.5	+0.6455	72.2	−1.4175	355.7	−7.0248
Oct. 3	47.9	+0.5630	62.1	+1.2444	24.5	−1.3834	353.3	−3.9619
7	359.2	+0.6808	15.6	+1.8557	336.8	−1.3009	357.0	+2.4414
11	310.6	+0.8069	328.9	+2.4555	289.1	−1.1960	4.1	+6.4158
15	261.9	+0.9184	282.0	+3.0131	241.3	−1.0858	7.2	+4.0793
19	213.0	+1.0142	234.7	+3.5126	193.5	−0.9713	5.0	−1.4953
23	164.2	+1.0879	187.0	+3.9264	145.7	−0.8599	0.3	−5.9915
27	115.4	+1.1396	138.9	+4.2192	98.0	−0.7484	355.3	−6.6689
31	66.7	+1.1909	90.3	+4.3681	50.3	−0.6145	352.5	−2.9229
Nov. 4	18.0	+1.2617	40.9	+4.3488	2.6	−0.4442	356.0	+3.3348
8	329.5	+1.3385	350.2	+4.0908	315.0	−0.2549	4.2	+6.2913
12	280.9	+1.4049	297.5	+3.4850	267.3	−0.0618	8.0	+2.9028
16	232.2	+1.4628	242.1	+2.4555	219.6	+0.1337	5.3	−2.6962
20	183.4	+1.5027	184.3	+1.0930	171.8	+0.3180	0.2	−6.4199
24	134.6	+1.5156	126.4	−0.2009	124.1	+0.4828	355.4	−6.0692
28	85.9	+1.5148	70.9	−0.9921	76.4	+0.6427	352.6	−1.6382
Dec. 2	37.3	+1.5203	18.4	−1.2073	28.7	+0.8156	355.3	+4.2461
6	348.8	+1.5272	328.4	−1.0290	341.1	+0.9950	3.5	+6.0083
10	300.2	+1.5275	279.8	−0.6350	293.5	+1.1718	7.9	+1.6566
14	251.6	+1.5293	231.9	−0.1303	245.8	+1.3486	5.3	−3.8739
18	202.9	+1.5232	184.5	+0.4053	198.1	+1.5106	0.1	−6.7452
22	154.1	+1.4916	137.5	+0.9186	150.4	+1.6387	355.7	−5.3165
26	105.4	+1.4374	90.6	+1.3934	102.7	+1.7367	353.4	−0.2066
30	56.8	+1.3772	43.9	+1.8301	55.0	+1.8222	355.5	+5.1676
34	8.3	+1.3121	357.4	+2.2161	7.4	+1.8977	2.5	+5.6526

COORDINATES FOR 0^h BARYCENTRIC DYNAMICAL TIME

Date		Mars Az.	Mars Alt.	Saturn Az.	Saturn Alt.	Sirius Az.	Sirius Alt.	Canopus Az.	Canopus Alt.
		°	°	°	°	°	°	°	°
Jan.	0	16.8	−5.2340	239.1	+2.4583	358.8	+38.0897	358.7	+74.3013
	4	323.0	−5.3534	186.7	+2.4282	306.1	+38.1144	306.0	+74.3261
	8	268.9	−5.4617	134.3	+2.3838	253.3	+38.1287	253.2	+74.3404
	12	214.5	−5.5789	82.0	+2.3507	200.6	+38.1215	200.4	+74.3333
	16	160.0	−5.6831	29.6	+2.3311	147.9	+38.1085	147.6	+74.3204
	20	105.6	−5.7544	337.3	+2.3189	95.2	+38.0964	94.9	+74.3085
	24	51.4	−5.7829	285.0	+2.3144	42.5	+38.0903	42.3	+74.3025
	28	357.4	−5.7575	232.7	+2.3053	349.8	+38.1025	349.6	+74.3149
Feb.	1	303.6	−5.6883	180.4	+2.2736	297.1	+38.1286	296.9	+74.3410
	5	249.8	−5.6137	128.1	+2.2302	244.4	+38.1407	244.1	+74.3531
	9	196.1	−5.5478	75.9	+2.1989	191.6	+38.1330	191.3	+74.3454
	13	142.5	−5.4754	23.6	+2.1798	138.9	+38.1202	138.6	+74.3327
	17	89.3	−5.3899	331.4	+2.1701	86.2	+38.1069	85.8	+74.3195
	21	36.4	−5.2837	279.2	+2.1700	33.5	+38.1011	33.2	+74.3139
	25	343.8	−5.1458	227.0	+2.1636	340.8	+38.1164	340.5	+74.3293
Mar.	1	291.3	−4.9894	174.7	+2.1331	288.1	+38.1434	287.8	+74.3563
	5	238.9	−4.8505	122.5	+2.0927	235.4	+38.1535	235.0	+74.3663
	9	186.6	−4.7354	70.3	+2.0645	182.7	+38.1456	182.2	+74.3584
	13	134.5	−4.6302	18.1	+2.0478	129.9	+38.1322	129.5	+74.3450
	17	82.5	−4.5271	325.9	+2.0433	77.2	+38.1170	76.8	+74.3298
	21	30.8	−4.4119	273.7	+2.0500	24.5	+38.1119	24.1	+74.3249
	25	339.3	−4.2699	221.5	+2.0484	331.8	+38.1303	331.4	+74.3433
	29	287.9	−4.1150	169.2	+2.0214	279.1	+38.1577	278.7	+74.3706
Apr.	2	236.4	−3.9812	117.0	+1.9860	226.4	+38.1662	225.9	+74.3789
	6	185.0	−3.8723	64.8	+1.9621	173.7	+38.1583	173.1	+74.3708
	10	133.7	−3.7762	12.5	+1.9496	121.0	+38.1435	120.4	+74.3560
	14	82.5	−3.6848	320.3	+1.9525	68.3	+38.1262	67.7	+74.3387
	18	31.4	−3.5804	268.1	+1.9679	15.6	+38.1224	15.0	+74.3350
	22	340.5	−3.4466	215.8	+1.9725	322.9	+38.1438	322.4	+74.3564
	26	289.6	−3.2984	163.5	+1.9510	270.2	+38.1710	269.6	+74.3835
	30	238.7	−3.1688	111.2	+1.9223	217.4	+38.1782	216.8	+74.3903
May	4	187.7	−3.0618	58.9	+1.9039	164.7	+38.1703	164.0	+74.3822
	8	136.8	−2.9685	6.6	+1.8972	112.0	+38.1538	111.3	+74.3655
	12	86.1	−2.8818	314.3	+1.9093	59.3	+38.1349	58.6	+74.3466
	16	35.4	−2.7816	261.9	+1.9342	6.6	+38.1333	6.0	+74.3451
	20	344.7	−2.6500	209.5	+1.9455	313.9	+38.1576	313.3	+74.3694
	24	294.2	−2.5018	157.1	+1.9304	261.2	+38.1839	260.5	+74.3954
	28	243.5	−2.3688	104.7	+1.9096	208.5	+38.1899	207.7	+74.4010
June	1	192.9	−2.2560	52.3	+1.8977	155.7	+38.1819	154.9	+74.3927
	5	142.3	−2.1580	359.9	+1.8983	103.0	+38.1636	102.2	+74.3742
	9	91.7	−2.0694	307.4	+1.9205	50.3	+38.1442	49.5	+74.3547
	13	41.2	−1.9687	254.9	+1.9543	357.6	+38.1458	356.9	+74.3565
	17	350.8	−1.8364	202.4	+1.9711	304.9	+38.1726	304.2	+74.3832
	21	300.4	−1.6859	149.8	+1.9622	252.2	+38.1974	251.5	+74.4076
	25	250.0	−1.5475	97.2	+1.9493	199.5	+38.2023	198.7	+74.4121
	29	199.5	−1.4266	44.7	+1.9436	146.8	+38.1939	145.9	+74.4032
July	3	149.1	−1.3216	352.0	+1.9518	94.1	+38.1739	93.1	+74.3830

Jupiter is below the horizon the entire year.

COORDINATES FOR 0^h BARYCENTRIC DYNAMICAL TIME

Date		Mars		Saturn		Sirius		Canopus	
		Az.	Alt.	Az.	Alt.	Az.	Alt.	Az.	Alt.
		°	°	°	°	°	°	°	°
July	3	149.1	−1.3216	352.0	+1.9518	94.1	+38.1739	93.1	+74.3830
	7	98.7	−1.2295	299.4	+1.9834	41.4	+38.1550	40.5	+74.3641
	11	48.3	−1.1285	246.7	+2.0239	348.7	+38.1606	347.9	+74.3699
	15	358.0	−0.9969	194.0	+2.0433	296.0	+38.1895	295.2	+74.3987
	19	307.8	−0.8468	141.3	+2.0383	243.3	+38.2123	242.4	+74.4211
	23	257.5	−0.7057	88.5	+2.0305	190.6	+38.2162	189.6	+74.4245
	27	207.2	−0.5791	35.7	+2.0289	137.8	+38.2069	136.8	+74.4147
	31	156.9	−0.4694	342.9	+2.0430	85.1	+38.1851	84.1	+74.3927
Aug.	4	106.6	−0.3766	290.1	+2.0810	32.4	+38.1677	31.4	+74.3754
	8	56.4	−0.2794	237.3	+2.1232	339.7	+38.1777	338.8	+74.3856
	12	6.2	−0.1541	184.4	+2.1400	287.0	+38.2081	286.1	+74.4159
	16	316.1	−0.0104	131.5	+2.1341	234.3	+38.2289	233.3	+74.4362
	20	266.0	+0.1273	78.5	+2.1263	181.6	+38.2320	180.5	+74.4388
	24	215.8	+0.2536	25.6	+2.1239	128.9	+38.2209	127.8	+74.4273
	28	165.6	+0.3625	332.7	+2.1397	76.2	+38.1973	75.0	+74.4034
Sept.	1	115.4	+0.4503	279.7	+2.1788	23.5	+38.1819	22.4	+74.3883
	5	65.3	+0.5366	226.7	+2.2156	330.8	+38.1964	329.8	+74.4031
	9	15.3	+0.6473	173.7	+2.2231	278.1	+38.2278	277.1	+74.4344
	13	325.3	+0.7756	120.7	+2.2101	225.4	+38.2470	224.3	+74.4531
	17	275.3	+0.9010	67.7	+2.1953	172.6	+38.2493	171.5	+74.4549
	21	225.2	+1.0188	14.6	+2.1866	119.9	+38.2358	118.7	+74.4409
	25	175.1	+1.1195	321.6	+2.1993	67.2	+38.2102	66.0	+74.4152
	29	125.1	+1.1948	268.6	+2.2331	14.5	+38.1975	13.3	+74.4029
Oct.	3	75.1	+1.2618	215.6	+2.2580	321.8	+38.2162	320.7	+74.4219
	7	25.2	+1.3475	162.6	+2.2510	269.1	+38.2482	268.0	+74.4538
	11	335.3	+1.4495	109.6	+2.2260	216.4	+38.2662	215.2	+74.4713
	15	285.4	+1.5518	56.6	+2.1996	163.7	+38.2678	162.4	+74.4724
	19	235.4	+1.6512	3.7	+2.1815	110.9	+38.2513	109.6	+74.4554
	23	185.5	+1.7351	310.7	+2.1883	58.2	+38.2241	56.9	+74.4283
	27	135.6	+1.7902	257.8	+2.2134	5.6	+38.2147	4.3	+74.4195
	31	85.7	+1.8297	204.9	+2.2235	312.9	+38.2372	311.7	+74.4424
Nov.	4	35.9	+1.8804	152.0	+2.2014	260.1	+38.2692	258.9	+74.4743
	8	346.1	+1.9449	99.1	+2.1643	207.4	+38.2864	206.1	+74.4910
	12	296.3	+2.0123	46.3	+2.1261	154.7	+38.2871	153.3	+74.4911
	16	246.5	+2.0828	353.5	+2.0999	102.0	+38.2675	100.5	+74.4711
	20	196.7	+2.1415	300.8	+2.1015	49.3	+38.2398	47.9	+74.4436
	24	146.8	+2.1699	248.0	+2.1181	356.6	+38.2343	355.2	+74.4388
	28	97.1	+2.1758	195.3	+2.1154	303.9	+38.2601	302.6	+74.4651
Dec.	2	47.3	+2.1846	142.6	+2.0820	251.2	+38.2914	249.9	+74.4963
	6	357.7	+2.2027	89.9	+2.0365	198.5	+38.3077	197.1	+74.5121
	10	308.0	+2.2257	37.3	+1.9904	145.7	+38.3072	144.2	+74.5110
	14	258.3	+2.2581	344.7	+1.9599	93.0	+38.2850	91.5	+74.4884
	18	208.6	+2.2847	292.1	+1.9594	40.3	+38.2580	38.8	+74.4618
	22	158.9	+2.2822	239.5	+1.9702	347.6	+38.2571	346.2	+74.4617
	26	109.2	+2.2522	187.0	+1.9589	294.9	+38.2853	293.5	+74.4904
	30	59.5	+2.2172	134.5	+1.9198	242.2	+38.3152	240.8	+74.5201
	34	9.9	+2.1860	82.0	+1.8707	189.5	+38.3305	188.0	+74.5349

Jupiter is below the horizon the entire year.

COORDINATES FOR 0^h BARYCENTRIC DYNAMICAL TIME

Date		α Cen		Antares		Fomalhaut		Rigel	
		Az.	Alt.	Az.	Alt.	Az.	Alt.	Az.	Alt.
		°	°	°	°	°	°	°	°
Jan.	0	133.6	+43.9046	144.6	+6.0100	229.3	+21.8697	332.0	+29.6206
	4	80.9	+43.8892	91.9	+5.9914	176.6	+21.8518	279.3	+29.6413
	8	28.2	+43.8971	39.2	+5.9939	123.9	+21.8232	226.6	+29.6427
	12	335.5	+43.9186	346.5	+6.0132	71.2	+21.8100	173.9	+29.6257
	16	282.8	+43.9345	293.8	+6.0295	18.5	+21.8110	121.2	+29.6098
	20	230.1	+43.9431	241.1	+6.0397	325.8	+21.8188	68.5	+29.5990
	24	177.4	+43.9397	188.4	+6.0387	273.1	+21.8313	15.8	+29.5983
	28	124.7	+43.9213	135.7	+6.0209	220.4	+21.8342	323.0	+29.6155
Feb.	1	72.0	+43.9072	83.0	+6.0028	167.7	+21.8130	270.3	+29.6360
	5	19.3	+43.9176	30.3	+6.0079	115.0	+21.7847	217.6	+29.6347
	9	326.6	+43.9386	337.6	+6.0268	62.3	+21.7728	164.9	+29.6179
	13	273.9	+43.9546	284.9	+6.0430	9.6	+21.7735	112.2	+29.6020
	17	221.2	+43.9638	232.2	+6.0539	316.9	+21.7824	59.5	+29.5903
	21	168.5	+43.9586	179.5	+6.0512	264.2	+21.7963	6.8	+29.5911
	25	115.8	+43.9380	126.8	+6.0308	211.5	+21.7973	314.1	+29.6110
Mar.	1	63.1	+43.9255	74.1	+6.0136	158.7	+21.7730	261.4	+29.6309
	5	10.4	+43.9381	21.4	+6.0209	106.0	+21.7452	208.6	+29.6274
	9	317.7	+43.9589	328.7	+6.0395	53.4	+21.7338	155.9	+29.6106
	13	265.0	+43.9759	276.0	+6.0566	0.7	+21.7342	103.2	+29.5939
	17	212.3	+43.9857	223.2	+6.0683	307.9	+21.7451	50.5	+29.5809
	21	159.6	+43.9780	170.5	+6.0635	255.2	+21.7607	357.8	+29.5836
	25	106.9	+43.9554	117.8	+6.0404	202.5	+21.7596	305.1	+29.6062
	29	54.2	+43.9446	65.1	+6.0244	149.8	+21.7329	252.4	+29.6252
Apr.	2	1.5	+43.9587	12.4	+6.0333	97.1	+21.7056	199.7	+29.6200
	6	308.8	+43.9795	319.7	+6.0518	44.4	+21.6941	147.0	+29.6033
	10	256.1	+43.9981	267.0	+6.0704	351.7	+21.6946	94.2	+29.5849
	14	203.4	+44.0082	214.3	+6.0828	299.0	+21.7082	41.5	+29.5709
	18	150.7	+43.9976	161.6	+6.0752	246.3	+21.7251	348.8	+29.5760
	22	98.0	+43.9733	108.9	+6.0499	193.6	+21.7217	296.1	+29.6011
	26	45.3	+43.9643	56.2	+6.0353	140.9	+21.6932	243.4	+29.6189
	30	352.6	+43.9793	3.5	+6.0452	88.2	+21.6666	190.7	+29.6125
May	4	299.9	+44.0003	310.8	+6.0637	35.5	+21.6549	138.0	+29.5957
	8	247.2	+44.0204	258.1	+6.0839	342.8	+21.6561	85.3	+29.5756
	12	194.5	+44.0299	205.4	+6.0962	290.1	+21.6725	32.6	+29.5613
	16	141.8	+44.0160	152.7	+6.0853	237.4	+21.6900	339.9	+29.5696
	20	89.1	+43.9906	100.0	+6.0584	184.7	+21.6836	287.2	+29.5965
	24	36.4	+43.9837	47.3	+6.0457	132.0	+21.6539	234.5	+29.6126
	28	343.7	+43.9992	354.6	+6.0562	79.3	+21.6285	181.8	+29.6054
June	1	291.0	+44.0203	301.9	+6.0749	26.6	+21.6166	129.0	+29.5884
	5	238.3	+44.0415	249.2	+6.0964	333.9	+21.6191	76.3	+29.5669
	9	185.6	+44.0493	196.5	+6.1075	281.2	+21.6381	23.6	+29.5534
	13	132.9	+44.0318	143.7	+6.0929	228.5	+21.6550	330.9	+29.5654
	17	80.2	+44.0063	91.0	+6.0652	175.7	+21.6450	278.2	+29.5935
	21	27.5	+44.0019	38.3	+6.0550	123.0	+21.6147	225.5	+29.6072
	25	334.8	+44.0176	345.6	+6.0660	70.3	+21.5905	172.8	+29.5994
	29	282.1	+44.0390	292.9	+6.0851	17.6	+21.5788	120.1	+29.5821
July	3	229.4	+44.0607	240.2	+6.1074	325.0	+21.5832	67.4	+29.5595

COORDINATES FOR 0^h BARYCENTRIC DYNAMICAL TIME

Date		α Cen Az.	α Cen Alt.	Antares Az.	Antares Alt.	Fomalhaut Az.	Fomalhaut Alt.	Rigel Az.	Rigel Alt.
		°	°	°	°	°	°	°	°
July	3	229.4	+44.0607	240.2	+6.1074	325.0	+21.5832	67.4	+29.5595
	7	176.7	+44.0657	187.5	+6.1162	272.2	+21.6044	14.7	+29.5480
	11	124.0	+44.0448	134.8	+6.0978	219.5	+21.6194	322.0	+29.5639
	15	71.3	+44.0202	82.1	+6.0704	166.8	+21.6055	269.3	+29.5924
	19	18.6	+44.0185	29.4	+6.0629	114.1	+21.5749	216.6	+29.6035
	23	325.9	+44.0343	336.7	+6.0743	61.4	+21.5519	163.9	+29.5951
	27	273.2	+44.0564	284.0	+6.0943	8.7	+21.5407	111.1	+29.5769
	31	220.5	+44.0780	231.3	+6.1171	316.0	+21.5477	58.4	+29.5536
Aug.	4	167.8	+44.0796	178.6	+6.1228	263.3	+21.5706	5.7	+29.5450
	8	115.1	+44.0555	125.9	+6.1008	210.6	+21.5828	313.0	+29.5648
	12	62.4	+44.0325	73.2	+6.0744	157.9	+21.5649	260.3	+29.5929
	16	9.7	+44.0333	20.5	+6.0695	105.2	+21.5344	207.6	+29.6014
	20	317.0	+44.0496	327.8	+6.0816	52.5	+21.5121	154.9	+29.5924
	24	264.3	+44.0730	275.1	+6.1032	359.8	+21.5018	102.2	+29.5726
	28	211.6	+44.0941	222.4	+6.1261	307.1	+21.5120	49.5	+29.5487
Sept.	1	158.9	+44.0916	169.7	+6.1281	254.4	+21.5363	356.8	+29.5436
	5	106.2	+44.0648	117.0	+6.1030	201.7	+21.5454	304.1	+29.5671
	9	53.5	+44.0436	64.3	+6.0778	149.0	+21.5240	251.4	+29.5944
	13	0.8	+44.0466	11.6	+6.0752	96.3	+21.4934	198.7	+29.6008
	17	308.1	+44.0637	318.9	+6.0883	43.6	+21.4711	146.0	+29.5909
	21	255.4	+44.0890	266.2	+6.1121	350.9	+21.4623	93.2	+29.5688
	25	202.7	+44.1091	213.5	+6.1349	298.2	+21.4762	40.5	+29.5447
	29	150.0	+44.1022	160.7	+6.1328	245.5	+21.5018	347.8	+29.5435
Oct.	3	97.3	+44.0731	108.0	+6.1048	192.8	+21.5075	295.1	+29.5703
	7	44.6	+44.0539	55.3	+6.0811	140.0	+21.4831	242.4	+29.5966
	11	351.9	+44.0584	2.6	+6.0802	87.3	+21.4525	189.7	+29.6014
	15	299.2	+44.0768	309.9	+6.0946	34.6	+21.4299	137.0	+29.5903
	19	246.5	+44.1041	257.2	+6.1209	341.9	+21.4230	84.3	+29.5655
	23	193.8	+44.1226	204.5	+6.1429	289.2	+21.4410	31.6	+29.5418
	27	141.1	+44.1112	151.8	+6.1364	236.5	+21.4670	338.9	+29.5450
	31	88.4	+44.0804	99.1	+6.1061	183.8	+21.4691	286.2	+29.5745
Nov.	4	35.7	+44.0631	46.4	+6.0841	131.1	+21.4426	233.5	+29.5995
	8	343.0	+44.0688	353.7	+6.0845	78.4	+21.4119	180.7	+29.6032
	12	290.3	+44.0886	301.0	+6.1003	25.7	+21.3890	128.0	+29.5907
	16	237.6	+44.1177	248.3	+6.1288	333.0	+21.3845	75.3	+29.5635
	20	184.9	+44.1337	195.6	+6.1490	280.3	+21.4062	22.6	+29.5411
	24	132.1	+44.1178	142.9	+6.1379	227.6	+21.4317	329.9	+29.5489
	28	79.4	+44.0863	90.1	+6.1063	174.9	+21.4299	277.2	+29.5803
Dec.	2	26.8	+44.0713	37.4	+6.0864	122.1	+21.4019	224.5	+29.6035
	6	334.1	+44.0779	344.7	+6.0876	69.4	+21.3714	171.8	+29.6063
	10	281.4	+44.0992	292.0	+6.1050	16.7	+21.3485	119.1	+29.5923
	14	228.7	+44.1292	239.3	+6.1349	324.0	+21.3470	66.3	+29.5634
	18	176.0	+44.1418	186.6	+6.1521	271.3	+21.3715	13.6	+29.5435
	22	123.2	+44.1219	133.9	+6.1367	218.6	+21.3949	320.9	+29.5558
	26	70.5	+44.0911	81.2	+6.1050	165.9	+21.3889	268.2	+29.5878
	30	17.9	+44.0786	28.5	+6.0875	113.2	+21.3602	215.5	+29.6088
	34	325.2	+44.0861	335.8	+6.0897	60.5	+21.3302	162.8	+29.6105

CONTENTS OF SECTION K

CONVERSION FOR PRE–JANUARY AND POST–DECEMBER DATES

Tabulated Date	Equivalent Date in Previous Year	Tabulated Date	Equivalent Date in Previous Year	Tabulated Date	Equivalent Date in Subsequent Year	Tabulated Date	Equivalent Date in Subsequent Year
Jan. −39	Nov. 22	Jan. −19	Dec. 12	Dec. 32	Jan. 1	Dec. 52	Jan. 21
−38	23	−18	13	33	2	53	22
−37	24	−17	14	34	3	54	23
−36	25	−16	15	35	4	55	24
−35	26	−15	16	36	5	56	25
Jan. −34	Nov. 27	Jan. −14	Dec. 17	Dec. 37	Jan. 6	Dec. 57	Jan. 26
−33	28	−13	18	38	7	58	27
−32	29	−12	19	39	8	59	28
−31	30	−11	20	40	9	60	29
−30	1	−10	21	41	10	61	30
Jan. −29	Dec. 2	Jan. − 9	Dec. 22	Dec. 42	Jan. 11	Dec. 62	Jan. 31
−28	3	− 8	23	43	12	63	Feb. 1
−27	4	− 7	24	44	13	64	2
−26	5	− 6	25	45	14	65	3
−25	6	− 5	26	46	15	66	4
Jan. −24	Dec. 7	Jan. − 4	Dec. 27	Dec. 47	Jan. 16	Dec. 67	Feb. 5
−23	8	− 3	28	48	17	68	6
−22	9	− 2	29	49	18	69	7
−21	10	− 1	30	50	19	70	8
−20	11	Jan. 0	Dec. 31	51	20	71	9

JULIAN DAY NUMBER, 1950–2000

OF DAY COMMENCING AT GREENWICH NOON ON:

Year	Jan. 0	Feb. 0	Mar. 0	Apr. 0	May 0	June 0	July 0	Aug. 0	Sept. 0	Oct. 0	Nov. 0	Dec. 0
1950	243 3282	3313	3341	3372	3402	3433	3463	3494	3525	3555	3586	3616
1951	3647	3678	3706	3737	3767	3798	3828	3859	3890	3920	3951	3981
1952	4012	4043	4072	4103	4133	4164	4194	4225	4256	4286	4317	4347
1953	4378	4409	4437	4468	4498	4529	4559	4590	4621	4651	4682	4712
1954	4743	4774	4802	4833	4863	4894	4924	4955	4986	5016	5047	5077
1955	243 5108	5139	5167	5198	5228	5259	5289	5320	5351	5381	5412	5442
1956	5473	5504	5533	5564	5594	5625	5655	5686	5717	5747	5778	5808
1957	5839	5870	5898	5929	5959	5990	6020	6051	6082	6112	6143	6173
1958	6204	6235	6263	6294	6324	6355	6385	6416	6447	6477	6508	6538
1959	6569	6600	6628	6659	6689	6720	6750	6781	6812	6842	6873	6903
1960	243 6934	6965	6994	7025	7055	7086	7116	7147	7178	7208	7239	7269
1961	7300	7331	7359	7390	7420	7451	7481	7512	7543	7573	7604	7634
1962	7665	7696	7724	7755	7785	7816	7846	7877	7908	7938	7969	7999
1963	8030	8061	8089	8120	8150	8181	8211	8242	8273	8303	8334	8364
1964	8395	8426	8455	8486	8516	8547	8577	8608	8639	8669	8700	8730
1965	243 8761	8792	8820	8851	8881	8912	8942	8973	9004	9034	9065	9095
1966	9126	9157	9185	9216	9246	9277	9307	9338	9369	9399	9430	9460
1967	9491	9522	9550	9581	9611	9642	9672	9703	9734	9764	9795	9825
1968	243 9856	9887	9916	9947	9977	*0008	*0038	*0069	*0100	*0130	*0161	*0191
1969	244 0222	0253	0281	0312	0342	0373	0403	0434	0465	0495	0526	0556
1970	244 0587	0618	0646	0677	0707	0738	0768	0799	0830	0860	0891	0921
1971	0952	0983	1011	1042	1072	1103	1133	1164	1195	1225	1256	1286
1972	1317	1348	1377	1408	1438	1469	1499	1530	1561	1591	1622	1652
1973	1683	1714	1742	1773	1803	1834	1864	1895	1926	1956	1987	2017
1974	2048	2079	2107	2138	2168	2199	2229	2260	2291	2321	2352	2382
1975	244 2413	2444	2472	2503	2533	2564	2594	2625	2656	2686	2717	2747
1976	2778	2809	2838	2869	2899	2930	2960	2991	3022	3052	3083	3113
1977	3144	3175	3203	3234	3264	3295	3325	3356	3387	3417	3448	3478
1978	3509	3540	3568	3599	3629	3660	3690	3721	3752	3782	3813	3843
1979	3874	3905	3933	3964	3994	4025	4055	4086	4117	4147	4178	4208
1980	244 4239	4270	4299	4330	4360	4391	4421	4452	4483	4513	4544	4574
1981	4605	4636	4664	4695	4725	4756	4786	4817	4848	4878	4909	4939
1982	4970	5001	5029	5060	5090	5121	5151	5182	5213	5243	5274	5304
1983	5335	5366	5394	5425	5455	5486	5516	5547	5578	5608	5639	5669
1984	5700	5731	5760	5791	5821	5852	5882	5913	5944	5974	6005	6035
1985	244 6066	6097	6125	6156	6186	6217	6247	6278	6309	6339	6370	6400
1986	6431	6462	6490	6521	6551	6582	6612	6643	6674	6704	6735	6765
1987	6796	6827	6855	6886	6916	6947	6977	7008	7039	7069	7100	7130
1988	7161	7192	7221	7252	7282	7313	7343	7374	7405	7435	7466	7496
1989	7527	7558	7586	7617	7647	7678	7708	7739	7770	7800	7831	7861
1990	244 7892	7923	7951	7982	8012	8043	8073	8104	8135	8165	8196	8226
1991	8257	8288	8316	8347	8377	8408	8438	8469	8500	8530	8561	8591
1992	8622	8653	8682	8713	8743	8774	8804	8835	8866	8896	8927	8957
1993	8988	9019	9047	9078	9108	9139	9169	9200	9231	9261	9292	9322
1994	9353	9384	9412	9443	9473	9504	9534	9565	9596	9626	9657	9687
1995	244 9718	9749	9777	9808	9838	9869	9899	9930	9961	9991	*0022	*0052
1996	245 0083	0114	0143	0174	0204	0235	0265	0296	0327	0357	0388	0418
1997	0449	0480	0508	0539	0569	0600	0630	0661	0692	0722	0753	0783
1998	0814	0845	0873	0904	0934	0965	0995	1026	1057	1087	1118	1148
1999	1179	1210	1238	1269	1299	1330	1360	1391	1422	1452	1483	1513
2000	245 1544	1575	1604	1635	1665	1696	1726	1757	1788	1818	1849	1879

OF DAY COMMENCING AT GREENWICH NOON ON:

Year	Jan. 0	Feb. 0	Mar. 0	Apr. 0	May 0	June 0	July 0	Aug. 0	Sept. 0	Oct. 0	Nov. 0	Dec. 0
2000	245 1544	1575	1604	1635	1665	1696	1726	1757	1788	1818	1849	1879
2001	1910	1941	1969	2000	2030	2061	2091	2122	2153	2183	2214	2244
2002	2275	2306	2334	2365	2395	2426	2456	2487	2518	2548	2579	2609
2003	2640	2671	2699	2730	2760	2791	2821	2852	2883	2913	2944	2974
2004	3005	3036	3065	3096	3126	3157	3187	3218	3249	3279	3310	3340
2005	245 3371	3402	3430	3461	3491	3522	3552	3583	3614	3644	3675	3705
2006	3736	3767	3795	3826	3856	3887	3917	3948	3979	4009	4040	4070
2007	4101	4132	4160	4191	4221	4252	4282	4313	4344	4374	4405	4435
2008	4466	4497	4526	4557	4587	4618	4648	4679	4710	4740	4771	4801
2009	4832	4863	4891	4922	4952	4983	5013	5044	5075	5105	5136	5166
2010	245 5197	5228	5256	5287	5317	5348	5378	5409	5440	5470	5501	5531
2011	5562	5593	5621	5652	5682	5713	5743	5774	5805	5835	5866	5896
2012	5927	5958	5987	6018	6048	6079	6109	6140	6171	6201	6232	6262
2013	6293	6324	6352	6383	6413	6444	6474	6505	6536	6566	6597	6627
2014	6658	6689	6717	6748	6778	6809	6839	6870	6901	6931	6962	6992
2015	245 7023	7054	7082	7113	7143	7174	7204	7235	7266	7296	7327	7357
2016	7388	7419	7448	7479	7509	7540	7570	7601	7632	7662	7693	7723
2017	7754	7785	7813	7844	7874	7905	7935	7966	7997	8027	8058	8088
2018	8119	8150	8178	8209	8239	8270	8300	8331	8362	8392	8423	8453
2019	8484	8515	8543	8574	8604	8635	8665	8696	8727	8757	8788	8818
2020	245 8849	8880	8909	8940	8970	9001	9031	9062	9093	9123	9154	9184
2021	9215	9246	9274	9305	9335	9366	9396	9427	9458	9488	9519	9549
2022	9580	9611	9639	9670	9700	9731	9761	9792	9823	9853	9884	9914
2023	245 9945	9976	*0004	*0035	*0065	*0096	*0126	*0157	*0188	*0218	*0249	*0279
2024	246 0310	0341	0370	0401	0431	0462	0492	0523	0554	0584	0615	0645
2025	246 0676	0707	0735	0766	0796	0827	0857	0888	0919	0949	0980	1010
2026	1041	1072	1100	1131	1161	1192	1222	1253	1284	1314	1345	1375
2027	1406	1437	1465	1496	1526	1557	1587	1618	1649	1679	1710	1740
2028	1771	1802	1831	1862	1892	1923	1953	1984	2015	2045	2076	2106
2029	2137	2168	2196	2227	2257	2288	2318	2349	2380	2410	2441	2471
2030	246 2502	2533	2561	2592	2622	2653	2683	2714	2745	2775	2806	2836
2031	2867	2898	2926	2957	2987	3018	3048	3079	3110	3140	3171	3201
2032	3232	3263	3292	3323	3353	3384	3414	3445	3476	3506	3537	3567
2033	3598	3629	3657	3688	3718	3749	3779	3810	3841	3871	3902	3932
2034	3963	3994	4022	4053	4083	4114	4144	4175	4206	4236	4267	4297
2035	246 4328	4359	4387	4418	4448	4479	4509	4540	4571	4601	4632	4662
2036	4693	4724	4753	4784	4814	4845	4875	4906	4937	4967	4998	5028
2037	5059	5090	5118	5149	5179	5210	5240	5271	5302	5332	5363	5393
2038	5424	5455	5483	5514	5544	5575	5605	5636	5667	5697	5728	5758
2039	5789	5820	5848	5879	5909	5940	5970	6001	6032	6062	6093	6123
2040	246 6154	6185	6214	6245	6275	6306	6336	6367	6398	6428	6459	6489
2041	6520	6551	6579	6610	6640	6671	6701	6732	6763	6793	6824	6854
2042	6885	6916	6944	6975	7005	7036	7066	7097	7128	7158	7189	7219
2043	7250	7281	7309	7340	7370	7401	7431	7462	7493	7523	7554	7584
2044	7615	7646	7675	7706	7736	7767	7797	7828	7859	7889	7920	7950
2045	246 7981	8012	8040	8071	8101	8132	8162	8193	8224	8254	8285	8315
2046	8346	8377	8405	8436	8466	8497	8527	8558	8589	8619	8650	8680
2047	8711	8742	8770	8801	8831	8862	8892	8923	8954	8984	9015	9045
2048	9076	9107	9136	9167	9197	9228	9258	9289	9320	9350	9381	9411
2049	9442	9473	9501	9532	9562	9593	9623	9654	9685	9715	9746	9776
2050	246 9807	9838	9866	9897	9927	9958	9988	*0019	*0050	*0080	*0111	*0141

JULIAN DAY NUMBER, 2050–2100

OF DAY COMMENCING AT GREENWICH NOON ON:

Year		Jan. 0	Feb. 0	Mar. 0	Apr. 0	May 0	June 0	July 0	Aug. 0	Sept. 0	Oct. 0	Nov. 0	Dec. 0
2050	246	9807	9838	9866	9897	9927	9958	9988	*0019	*0050	*0080	*0111	*0141
2051	247	0172	0203	0231	0262	0292	0323	0353	0384	0415	0445	0476	0506
2052		0537	0568	0597	0628	0658	0689	0719	0750	0781	0811	0842	0872
2053		0903	0934	0962	0993	1023	1054	1084	1115	1146	1176	1207	1237
2054		1268	1299	1327	1358	1388	1419	1449	1480	1511	1541	1572	1602
2055	247	1633	1664	1692	1723	1753	1784	1814	1845	1876	1906	1937	1967
2056		1998	2029	2058	2089	2119	2150	2180	2211	2242	2272	2303	2333
2057		2364	2395	2423	2454	2484	2515	2545	2576	2607	2637	2668	2698
2058		2729	2760	2788	2819	2849	2880	2910	2941	2972	3002	3033	3063
2059		3094	3125	3153	3184	3214	3245	3275	3306	3337	3367	3398	3428
2060	247	3459	3490	3519	3550	3580	3611	3641	3672	3703	3733	3764	3794
2061		3825	3856	3884	3915	3945	3976	4006	4037	4068	4098	4129	4159
2062		4190	4221	4249	4280	4310	4341	4371	4402	4433	4463	4494	4524
2063		4555	4586	4614	4645	4675	4706	4736	4767	4798	4828	4859	4889
2064		4920	4951	4980	5011	5041	5072	5102	5133	5164	5194	5225	5255
2065	247	5286	5317	5345	5376	5406	5437	5467	5498	5529	5559	5590	5620
2066		5651	5682	5710	5741	5771	5802	5832	5863	5894	5924	5955	5985
2067		6016	6047	6075	6106	6136	6167	6197	6228	6259	6289	6320	6350
2068		6381	6412	6441	6472	6502	6533	6563	6594	6625	6655	6686	6716
2069		6747	6778	6806	6837	6867	6898	6928	6959	6990	7020	7051	7081
2070	247	7112	7143	7171	7202	7232	7263	7293	7324	7355	7385	7416	7446
2071		7477	7508	7536	7567	7597	7628	7658	7689	7720	7750	7781	7811
2072		7842	7873	7902	7933	7963	7994	8024	8055	8086	8116	8147	8177
2073		8208	8239	8267	8298	8328	8359	8389	8420	8451	8481	8512	8542
2074		8573	8604	8632	8663	8693	8724	8754	8785	8816	8846	8877	8907
2075	247	8938	8969	8997	9028	9058	9089	9119	9150	9181	9211	9242	9272
2076		9303	9334	9363	9394	9424	9455	9485	9516	9547	9577	9608	9638
2077	247	9669	9700	9728	9759	9789	9820	9850	9881	9912	9942	9973	*0003
2078	248	0034	0065	0093	0124	0154	0185	0215	0246	0277	0307	0338	0368
2079		0399	0430	0458	0489	0519	0550	0580	0611	0642	0672	0703	0733
2080	248	0764	0795	0824	0855	0885	0916	0946	0977	1008	1038	1069	1099
2081		1130	1161	1189	1220	1250	1281	1311	1342	1373	1403	1434	1464
2082		1495	1526	1554	1585	1615	1646	1676	1707	1738	1768	1799	1829
2083		1860	1891	1919	1950	1980	2011	2041	2072	2103	2133	2164	2194
2084		2225	2256	2285	2316	2346	2377	2407	2438	2469	2499	2530	2560
2085	248	2591	2622	2650	2681	2711	2742	2772	2803	2834	2864	2895	2925
2086		2956	2987	3015	3046	3076	3107	3137	3168	3199	3229	3260	3290
2087		3321	3352	3380	3411	3441	3472	3502	3533	3564	3594	3625	3655
2088		3686	3717	3746	3777	3807	3838	3868	3899	3930	3960	3991	4021
2089		4052	4083	4111	4142	4172	4203	4233	4264	4295	4325	4356	4386
2090	248	4417	4448	4476	4507	4537	4568	4598	4629	4660	4690	4721	4751
2091		4782	4813	4841	4872	4902	4933	4963	4994	5025	5055	5086	5116
2092		5147	5178	5207	5238	5268	5299	5329	5360	5391	5421	5452	5482
2093		5513	5544	5572	5603	5633	5664	5694	5725	5756	5786	5817	5847
2094		5878	5909	5937	5968	5998	6029	6059	6090	6121	6151	6182	6212
2095	248	6243	6274	6302	6333	6363	6394	6424	6455	6486	6516	6547	6577
2096		6608	6639	6668	6699	6729	6760	6790	6821	6852	6882	6913	6943
2097		6974	7005	7033	7064	7094	7125	7155	7186	7217	7247	7278	7308
2098		7339	7370	7398	7429	7459	7490	7520	7551	7582	7612	7643	7673
2099		7704	7735	7763	7794	7824	7855	7885	7916	7947	7977	8008	8038
2100	248	8069	8100	8128	8159	8189	8220	8250	8281	8312	8342	8373	8403

The Julian date (JD) corresponding to any instant is the interval in mean solar days elapsed since 4713 BC January 1 at Greenwich mean noon (12^h UT). To determine the JD at 0^h UT for a given Gregorian calendar date, sum the values from Table A for century, Table B for year and Table C for month; then add the day of the month. Julian dates for the current year are given on page B3.

A. Julian date at January 0^d 0^h UT of centurial year

Year	1600†	1700	1800	1900	2000†	2100
Julian date	230 5447·5	234 1971·5	237 8495·5	241 5019·5	245 1544·5	248 8068·5

† Centurial years that are exactly divisible by 400 are leap years in the Gregorian calendar. To determine the JD for any date in such a year, subtract 1 from the JD in Table A and use the leap year portion of Table C. (For 1600 and 2000 the JDs tabulated in Table A are actually for January 1^d 0^h.)

B. Addition to give Julian date for January 0^d 0^h UT of year

Year	Add	Year	Add	Year	Add	Year	Add
0	0	25	9131	50	18262	75	27393
1	365	26	9496	51	18627	76*	27758
2	730	27	9861	52*	18992	77	28124
3	1095	28*	10226	53	19358	78	28489
4*	1460	29	10592	54	19723	79	28854
5	1826	30	10957	55	20088	80*	29219
6	2191	31	11322	56*	20453	81	29585
7	2556	32*	11687	57	20819	82	29950
8*	2921	33	12053	58	21184	83	30315
9	3287	34	12418	59	21549	84*	30680
10	3652	35	12783	60*	21914	85	31046
11	4017	36*	13148	61	22280	86	31411
12*	4382	37	13514	62	22645	87	31776
13	4748	38	13879	63	23010	88*	32141
14	5113	39	14244	64*	23375	89	32507
15	5478	40*	14609	65	23741	90	32872
16*	5843	41	14975	66	24106	91	33237
17	6209	42	15340	67	24471	92*	33602
18	6574	43	15705	68*	24836	93	33968
19	6939	44*	16070	69	25202	94	34333
20*	7304	45	16436	70	25567	95	34698
21	7670	46	16801	71	25932	96*	35063
22	8035	47	17166	72*	26297	97	35429
23	8400	48*	17531	73	26663	98	35794
24*	8765	49	17897	74	27028	99	36159

* Leap years

Examples

a. 1981 November 14

Table A	
1900 Jan. 0	241 5019·5
+ Table B	+ 2 9585
1981 Jan. 0	244 4604·5
+ Table C (n.y.)	+ 304
1981 Nov. 0	244 4908·5
+ Day of Month	+ 14
1981 Nov. 14	244 4922·5

b. 2000 September 24

Table A	
2000 Jan. 1	245 1544·5
− 1 (for 2000)	− 1
2000 Jan. 0	245 1543·5
+ Table B	+ 0
2000 Jan. 0	245 1543·5
+ Table C (l.y.)	+ 244
2000 Sept. 0	245 1787·5
+ Day of Month	+ 24
2000 Sept. 24	245 1811·5

c. 2006 June 21

Table A	
2000 Jan. 1	245 1544·5
+ Table B	+ 2191
2006 Jan. 0	245 3735·5
+ Table C (n.y.)	+ 151
2006 June 0	245 3886·5
+ Day of Month	+ 21
2006 June 21	245 3907·5

C. Addition to give Julian date for beginning of month (0^d 0^h UT)

	Jan.	Feb.	Mar.	Apr.	May	June	July	Aug.	Sept.	Oct.	Nov.	Dec.
Normal year	0	31	59	90	120	151	181	212	243	273	304	334
Leap year	0	31	60	91	121	152	182	213	244	274	305	335

WARNING: prior to 1925 Greenwich mean noon (i.e. 12^h UT) was usually denoted by 0^h GMT in astronomical publications.

Conversions between Calendar dates and Julian dates may be performed using the USNO utility which is located under "Data Services" on the Astronomical Applications web pages (see page x).

Selected Astronomical Constants

The IAU 2009 System of Astronomical Constants (1) published in the IAU WG report on Numerical Standards for Fundamental Astronomy (NSFA, 2011) and updated by resolution B2 of the IAU XXVIII General Assembly (2012), (2) planetary equatorial radii, from the IAU WG report on Cartographic Coordinates and Rotational Elements: 2015 (2018), and (3) other useful constants. Tabulated for each quantity is its description, symbol and value, and, as appropriate, its uncertainty in units in which the quantity is given. Further information is given at the foot of the table on the next page.

1 IAU 2009/2012 System of Astronomical Constants[1]

1.1 Natural Defining Constant:

Description	Value	Uncertainty
Speed of light	$c = 299\,792\,458$ m s^{-1}	

1.2 Auxiliary Defining Constants:

Description	Value	Uncertainty
Astronomical unit[2]	$au = 149\,597\,870\,700$ m	
$1 - d(TT)/d(TCG)$	$L_G = 6{\cdot}969\,290\,134 \times 10^{-10}$	
$1 - d(TDB)/d(TCB)$	$L_B = 1{\cdot}550\,519\,768 \times 10^{-8}$	
TDB − TCB at $T_0 = 244\,3144{\cdot}5003\,725$(TCB)	$TDB_0 = -6{\cdot}55 \times 10^{-5}$ s	
Earth rotation angle (ERA) at J2000·0 UT1	$\theta_0 = 0{\cdot}779\,057\,273\,2640$ revolutions	
Rate of advance of ERA	$\dot{\theta} = 1{\cdot}002\,737\,811\,911\,354\,48$ revolutions UT1-day^{-1}	

1.3 Natural Measurable Constant:

Description	Value	Uncertainty
Constant of gravitation	$G = 6{\cdot}674\,28 \times 10^{-11}$ m^3 kg^{-1} s^{-2}	$\pm 6{\cdot}7 \times 10^{-15}$

1.4 Other Constants:

Description	Value	Uncertainty
Average value of $1 - d(TCG)/d(TCB)$	$L_C = 1{\cdot}480\,826\,867\,41 \times 10^{-8}$	$\pm 2 \times 10^{-17}$

1.5 Body Constants:

Description	Value	Uncertainty
Solar mass parameter[2]	$GM_S = 1{\cdot}327\,124\,420\,99 \times 10^{20}$ m^3 s^{-2} (TCB)	$\pm 1 \times 10^{10}$
	$= 1{\cdot}327\,124\,400\,41 \times 10^{20}$ m^3 s^{-2} (TDB)	$\pm 1 \times 10^{10}$
Equatorial radius for Earth	$a_E = a_e = 6\,378\,136{\cdot}6$ m (TT)	$\pm 0{\cdot}1$
Dynamical form-factor for the Earth	$J_2 = 0{\cdot}001\,082\,635\,9$	$\pm 1 \times 10^{-10}$
Time rate of change in J_2	$\dot{J}_2 = -3{\cdot}0 \times 10^{-9}$ cy^{-1}	$\pm 6 \times 10^{-10}$
Geocentric gravitational constant	$GM_E = 3{\cdot}986\,004\,418 \times 10^{14}$ m^3 s^{-2} (TCB)	$\pm 8 \times 10^5$
	$= 3{\cdot}986\,004\,415 \times 10^{14}$ m^3 s^{-2} (TT)	$\pm 8 \times 10^5$
	$= 3{\cdot}986\,004\,356 \times 10^{14}$ m^3 s^{-2} (TDB)	$\pm 8 \times 10^5$
Potential of the geoid	$W_0 = 6{\cdot}263\,685\,34 \times 10^7$ m^2 s^{-2}	$\pm 0{\cdot}5$
Nominal mean angular velocity of the Earth	$\omega = 7{\cdot}292\,115 \times 10^{-5}$ rad s^{-1} (TT)	
Mass Ratio: Moon to Earth	$M_M/M_E = 1{\cdot}230\,003\,71 \times 10^{-2}$	$\pm 4 \times 10^{-10}$

Ratio of the mass of the Sun to the mass of the Body

Description	Value	Uncertainty
Mass Ratio: Sun to Mercury[3]	$M_S/M_{Me} = 6{\cdot}023\,6 \times 10^6$	$\pm 3 \times 10^2$
Mass Ratio: Sun to Venus	$M_S/M_{Ve} = 4{\cdot}085\,237\,19 \times 10^5$	$\pm 8 \times 10^{-3}$
Mass Ratio: Sun to Mars	$M_S/M_{Ma} = 3{\cdot}098\,703\,59 \times 10^6$	$\pm 2 \times 10^{-2}$
Mass Ratio: Sun to Jupiter	$M_S/M_J = 1{\cdot}047\,348\,644 \times 10^3$	$\pm 1{\cdot}7 \times 10^{-5}$
Mass Ratio: Sun to Saturn	$M_S/M_{Sa} = 3{\cdot}497\,9018 \times 10^3$	$\pm 1 \times 10^{-4}$
Mass Ratio: Sun to Uranus[3]	$M_S/M_U = 2{\cdot}290\,298 \times 10^4$	$\pm 3 \times 10^{-2}$
Mass Ratio: Sun to Neptune	$M_S/M_N = 1{\cdot}941\,226 \times 10^4$	$\pm 3 \times 10^{-2}$
Mass Ratio: Sun to (134340) Pluto[3]	$M_S/M_P = 1{\cdot}365\,66 \times 10^8$	$\pm 2{\cdot}8 \times 10^4$
Mass Ratio: Sun to (136199) Eris	$M_S/M_{Eris} = 1{\cdot}191 \times 10^8$	$\pm 1{\cdot}4 \times 10^6$

Ratio of the mass of the Body to the mass of the Sun

Description	Value	Uncertainty
Mass Ratio: (1) Ceres to Sun[3]	$M_{Ceres}/M_S = 4{\cdot}72 \times 10^{-10}$	$\pm 3 \times 10^{-12}$
Mass Ratio: (2) Pallas to Sun	$M_{Pallas}/M_S = 1{\cdot}03 \times 10^{-10}$	$\pm 3 \times 10^{-12}$
Mass Ratio: (4) Vesta to Sun[3]	$M_{Vesta}/M_S = 1{\cdot}35 \times 10^{-10}$	$\pm 3 \times 10^{-12}$

All values of the masses from Mars to Eris are the sum of the masses of the celestial body and its satellites.

1.6 Initial Values at J2000·0:

Description	Value	Uncertainty
Mean obliquity of the ecliptic	$\epsilon_{J2000{\cdot}0} = \epsilon_0 = 23^\circ\ 26'\ 21''{\cdot}406 = 84\,381''{\cdot}406$	$\pm 0''{\cdot}001$

Selected Astronomical Constants (continued)

2 Constants from IAU WG on Cartographic Coordinates and Rotational Elements 2015

Equatorial radii in km:

Mercury	2 440·53	±0·04	Jupiter	71 492 ± 4	(134340) Pluto	1 188·3	±1·6
Venus	6 051·8	±1·0	Saturn	60 268 ± 4			
Earth	6 378·1366	±0·0001	Uranus	25 559 ± 4	Moon (mean)	1 737·4	±1
Mars	3 396·19	±0·1	Neptune	24 764 ±15	Sun	695 700[4]	

3 Other Constants

Light-time for unit distance[2]	$\tau_A = au/c = 499^s.004\,783\,84$	
	$1/\tau_A = 173{\cdot}144\,632\,674$ au/d	
Mass Ratio: Earth to Moon	$M_E/M_M = 1/\mu = 81{\cdot}300\,568$	$\pm 3 \times 10^{-6}$
Mass Ratio: Sun to Earth	$GM_S/GM_E = 332\,946{\cdot}0487$	$\pm 7 \times 10^{-4}$
Mass of the Sun	$M_S = S = GM_S/G = 1{\cdot}9884 \times 10^{30}$ kg	$\pm 2 \times 10^{26}$
Mass of the Earth	$M_E = E = GM_E/G = 5{\cdot}9722 \times 10^{24}$ kg	$\pm 6 \times 10^{20}$
Mass Ratio: Sun to Earth + Moon	$(S/E)/(1+\mu) = 328\,900{\cdot}5596$	$\pm 7 \times 10^{-4}$
Earth, reciprocal of flattening (IERS 2010)	$1/f = 298{\cdot}256\,42$	$\pm 1 \times 10^{-5}$
Rates of precession at J2000·0 (IAU 2006)		
General precession in longitude	$p_A = 5028''.796\,195$ per Julian century (TDB)	
Rate of change in obliquity	$\dot{\epsilon} = -46''.836\,769$ per Julian century (TDB)	
Precession of the equator in longitude	$\dot{\psi} = 5038''.481\,507$ per Julian century (TDB)	
Precession of the equator in obliquity	$\dot{\omega} = -0''.025\,754$ per Julian century (TDB)	
Constant of nutation at epoch J2000·0	$N = 9''.2052\,331$	
Solar parallax	$\pi_\odot = \sin^{-1}(a_e/au) = 8''.794\,143$	
Constant of aberration at epoch J2000·0	$\kappa = 20''.495\,51$	

Masses of the larger natural satellites: mass satellite/mass of the planet (see pages F3, F5)

Jupiter	Io	$4{\cdot}705 \times 10^{-5}$	**Uranus**	Ariel	$1{\cdot}441 \times 10^{-5}$
	Europa	$2{\cdot}528 \times 10^{-5}$		Umbriel	$1{\cdot}469 \times 10^{-5}$
	Ganymede	$7{\cdot}805 \times 10^{-5}$		Titania	$3{\cdot}916 \times 10^{-5}$
	Callisto	$5{\cdot}667 \times 10^{-5}$		Oberon	$3{\cdot}543 \times 10^{-5}$
Saturn	Titan	$2{\cdot}367 \times 10^{-4}$	**Neptune**	Triton	$2{\cdot}089 \times 10^{-4}$

The IAU Working Group on Numerical Standards for Fundamental Astronomy maintains a website, https://iau-a3.gitlab.io/NSFA/index.html, containing an agreed list of **Current Best Estimates**, with detailed information about the constants and relevant references. See footnotes below for more details.

This almanac, in certain circumstances, may not use constants from this list. The reasons and those constants used will be given at the end of Section L *Notes and References*.

The units meter (m), kilogram (kg), and SI second (s) are the units of length, mass and time in the International System of Units (SI).

The astronomical unit of time is a time interval of one day (D) of 86400 seconds. An interval of 36525 days is one Julian century. Some constants that involve time, either directly or indirectly need to be compatible with the underlying time scales, for example TDB-compatible. To specify the time scale that the value of the constant is compatible with, (TDB), (TCB) or (TT) is included after the unit.

[1] The IAU 2009 System of Astronomical Constants classifies the constants into the groups shown. This may be redefined and users should check the NSFA website for updates.

[2] The astronomical unit of length (au) in metres is re-defined as a conventional unit of length (resolution B2, IAU XXVIII GA 2012) in agreement with the value adopted by IAU 2009 Resolution B2; it is to be used with all time scales such as TCB, TDB, TCG, TT, etc. Also the heliocentric gravitational constant GM_S is renamed the solar mass parameter. Further details are given in Section L *Notes and References*.

[3] In May 2015 new best estimates were agreed. Values printed here are those of the IAU 2009 System of Astronomical Constants.

[4] The value given here is that from the report of the IAU WG on Cartographic Coordinates and Rotational Elements 2015 (2018). However, computation of the phenomena in this almanac use a value of 696,000 km. Further details are given in Section L *Notes and References* for Section K.

$\Delta T = \mathrm{ET} - \mathrm{UT}$

Year	ΔT	Year	ΔT	Year	ΔT	Year	ΔT	Year	ΔT	Year	ΔT
	s		s		s		s		s		s
1620·0	+124	**1665·0**	+32	**1710·0**	+10	**1755·0**	+14	**1800·0**	+13·7	**1845·0**	+6·3
1621	+119	**1666**	+31	**1711**	+10	**1756**	+14	**1801**	+13·4	**1846**	+6·5
1622	+115	**1667**	+30	**1712**	+10	**1757**	+14	**1802**	+13·1	**1847**	+6·6
1623	+110	**1668**	+28	**1713**	+10	**1758**	+15	**1803**	+12·9	**1848**	+6·8
1624	+106	**1669**	+27	**1714**	+10	**1759**	+15	**1804**	+12·7	**1849**	+6·9
1625·0	+102	**1670·0**	+26	**1715·0**	+10	**1760·0**	+15	**1805·0**	+12·6	**1850·0**	+7·1
1626	+ 98	**1671**	+25	**1716**	+10	**1761**	+15	**1806**	+12·5	**1851**	+7·2
1627	+ 95	**1672**	+24	**1717**	+11	**1762**	+15	**1807**	+12·5	**1852**	+7·3
1628	+ 91	**1673**	+23	**1718**	+11	**1763**	+15	**1808**	+12·5	**1853**	+7·4
1629	+ 88	**1674**	+22	**1719**	+11	**1764**	+15	**1809**	+12·5	**1854**	+7·5
1630·0	+ 85	**1675·0**	+21	**1720·0**	+11	**1765·0**	+16	**1810·0**	+12·5	**1855·0**	+7·6
1631	+ 82	**1676**	+20	**1721**	+11	**1766**	+16	**1811**	+12·5	**1856**	+7·7
1632	+ 79	**1677**	+19	**1722**	+11	**1767**	+16	**1812**	+12·5	**1857**	+7·7
1633	+ 77	**1678**	+18	**1723**	+11	**1768**	+16	**1813**	+12·5	**1858**	+7·8
1634	+ 74	**1679**	+17	**1724**	+11	**1769**	+16	**1814**	+12·5	**1859**	+7·8
1635·0	+ 72	**1680·0**	+16	**1725·0**	+11	**1770·0**	+16	**1815·0**	+12·5	**1860·0**	+7·88
1636	+ 70	**1681**	+15	**1726**	+11	**1771**	+16	**1816**	+12·5	**1861**	+7·82
1637	+ 67	**1682**	+14	**1727**	+11	**1772**	+16	**1817**	+12·4	**1862**	+7·54
1638	+ 65	**1683**	+14	**1728**	+11	**1773**	+16	**1818**	+12·3	**1863**	+6·97
1639	+ 63	**1684**	+13	**1729**	+11	**1774**	+16	**1819**	+12·2	**1864**	+6·40
1640·0	+ 62	**1685·0**	+12	**1730·0**	+11	**1775·0**	+17	**1820·0**	+12·0	**1865·0**	+6·02
1641	+ 60	**1686**	+12	**1731**	+11	**1776**	+17	**1821**	+11·7	**1866**	+5·41
1642	+ 58	**1687**	+11	**1732**	+11	**1777**	+17	**1822**	+11·4	**1867**	+4·10
1643	+ 57	**1688**	+11	**1733**	+11	**1778**	+17	**1823**	+11·1	**1868**	+2·92
1644	+ 55	**1689**	+10	**1734**	+12	**1779**	+17	**1824**	+10·6	**1869**	+1·82
1645·0	+ 54	**1690·0**	+10	**1735·0**	+12	**1780·0**	+17	**1825·0**	+10·2	**1870·0**	+1·61
1646	+ 53	**1691**	+10	**1736**	+12	**1781**	+17	**1826**	+ 9·6	**1871**	+0·10
1647	+ 51	**1692**	+ 9	**1737**	+12	**1782**	+17	**1827**	+ 9·1	**1872**	−1·02
1648	+ 50	**1693**	+ 9	**1738**	+12	**1783**	+17	**1828**	+ 8·6	**1873**	−1·28
1649	+ 49	**1694**	+ 9	**1739**	+12	**1784**	+17	**1829**	+ 8·0	**1874**	−2·69
1650·0	+ 48	**1695·0**	+ 9	**1740·0**	+12	**1785·0**	+17	**1830·0**	+ 7·5	**1875·0**	−3·24
1651	+ 47	**1696**	+ 9	**1741**	+12	**1786**	+17	**1831**	+ 7·0	**1876**	−3·64
1652	+ 46	**1697**	+ 9	**1742**	+12	**1787**	+17	**1832**	+ 6·6	**1877**	−4·54
1653	+ 45	**1698**	+ 9	**1743**	+12	**1788**	+17	**1833**	+ 6·3	**1878**	−4·71
1654	+ 44	**1699**	+ 9	**1744**	+13	**1789**	+17	**1834**	+ 6·0	**1879**	−5·11
1655·0	+ 43	**1700·0**	+ 9	**1745·0**	+13	**1790·0**	+17	**1835·0**	+ 5·8	**1880·0**	−5·40
1656	+ 42	**1701**	+ 9	**1746**	+13	**1791**	+17	**1836**	+ 5·7	**1881**	−5·42
1657	+ 41	**1702**	+ 9	**1747**	+13	**1792**	+16	**1837**	+ 5·6	**1882**	−5·20
1658	+ 40	**1703**	+ 9	**1748**	+13	**1793**	+16	**1838**	+ 5·6	**1883**	−5·46
1659	+ 38	**1704**	+ 9	**1749**	+13	**1794**	+16	**1839**	+ 5·6	**1884**	−5·46
1660·0	+ 37	**1705·0**	+ 9	**1750·0**	+13	**1795·0**	+16	**1840·0**	+ 5·7	**1885·0**	−5·79
1661	+ 36	**1706**	+ 9	**1751**	+14	**1796**	+15	**1841**	+ 5·8	**1886**	−5·63
1662	+ 35	**1707**	+ 9	**1752**	+14	**1797**	+15	**1842**	+ 5·9	**1887**	−5·64
1663	+ 34	**1708**	+10	**1753**	+14	**1798**	+14	**1843**	+ 6·1	**1888**	−5·80
1664·0	+ 33	**1709·0**	+10	**1754·0**	+14	**1799·0**	+14	**1844·0**	+ 6·2	**1889·0**	−5·66

For years 1620 to 1955 the table is based on an adopted value of $-26''/\mathrm{cy}^2$ for the tidal term ($\dot{n}$) in the mean motion of the Moon from the results of analyses of observations of lunar occultations of stars, eclipses of the Sun, and transits of Mercury (see F. R. Stephenson and L. V. Morrison, *Phil. Trans. R. Soc. London*, 1984, A **313**, 47-70).

To calculate the values of ΔT for a different value of the tidal term ($\dot{n}'$), add to the tabulated value of ΔT

$$-0{\cdot}000\,091\,(\dot{n}' + 26)\,(\text{year} - 1955)^2 \text{ seconds}$$

For 1956 through 1997 the table is derived from the direct comparison between TAI and UT1 taken from the Annual Reports of the BIH and from the IERS Bulletin B for 1988 onwards.

1890–1983, ΔT = ET − UT
1984–2000, ΔT = TDT − UT
From 2001, ΔT = TT − UT

Year	ΔT	Year	ΔT	Year	ΔT
	s		s		s
1890·0	− 5·87	**1935·0**	+23·93	**1980·0**	+50·54
1891	− 6·01	**1936**	+23·73	**1981**	+51·38
1892	− 6·19	**1937**	+23·92	**1982**	+52·17
1893	− 6·64	**1938**	+23·96	**1983**	+52·96
1894	− 6·44	**1939**	+24·02	**1984**	+53·79
1895·0	− 6·47	**1940·0**	+24·33	**1985·0**	+54·34
1896	− 6·09	**1941**	+24·83	**1986**	+54·87
1897	− 5·76	**1942**	+25·30	**1987**	+55·32
1898	− 4·66	**1943**	+25·70	**1988**	+55·82
1899	− 3·74	**1944**	+26·24	**1989**	+56·30
1900·0	− 2·72	**1945·0**	+26·77	**1990·0**	+56·86
1901	− 1·54	**1946**	+27·28	**1991**	+57·57
1902	− 0·02	**1947**	+27·78	**1992**	+58·31
1903	+ 1·24	**1948**	+28·25	**1993**	+59·12
1904	+ 2·64	**1949**	+28·71	**1994**	+59·98
1905·0	+ 3·86	**1950·0**	+29·15	**1995·0**	+60·78
1906	+ 5·37	**1951**	+29·57	**1996**	+61·63
1907	+ 6·14	**1952**	+29·97	**1997**	+62·29
1908	+ 7·75	**1953**	+30·36	**1998**	+62·97
1909	+ 9·13	**1954**	+30·72	**1999**	+63·47
1910·0	+10·46	**1955·0**	+31·07	**2000·0**	+63·83
1911	+11·53	**1956**	+31·35	**2001**	+64·09
1912	+13·36	**1957**	+31·68	**2002**	+64·30
1913	+14·65	**1958**	+32·18	**2003**	+64·47
1914	+16·01	**1959**	+32·68	**2004**	+64·57
1915·0	+17·20	**1960·0**	+33·15	**2005·0**	+64·69
1916	+18·24	**1961**	+33·59	**2006**	+64·85
1917	+19·06	**1962**	+34·00	**2007**	+65·15
1918	+20·25	**1963**	+34·47	**2008**	+65·46
1919	+20·95	**1964**	+35·03	**2009**	+65·78
1920·0	+21·16	**1965·0**	+35·73	**2010·0**	+66·07
1921	+22·25	**1966**	+36·54	**2011**	+66·32
1922	+22·41	**1967**	+37·43	**2012**	+66·60
1923	+23·03	**1968**	+38·29	**2013**	+66·91
1924	+23·49	**1969**	+39·20	**2014**	+67·28
1925·0	+23·62	**1970·0**	+40·18	**2015·0**	+67·64
1926	+23·86	**1971**	+41·17	**2016**	+68·10
1927	+24·49	**1972**	+42·23	**2017**	+68·59
1928	+24·34	**1973**	+43·37	**2018**	+68·97
1929	+24·08	**1974**	+44·49	**2019**	+69·22
1930·0	+24·02	**1975·0**	+45·48	**2020·0**	+69·36
1931	+24·00	**1976**	+46·46	**2021**	+69·36
1932	+23·87	**1977**	+47·52	**2022**	+69·29
1933	+23·95	**1978**	+48·53	**2023**	+69·20
1934·0	+23·86	**1979·0**	+49·59	**2024**	+69·18

From 1990 onwards, ΔT is for January 1 0^h UTC.

Page B6 gives a summary of the notation for time scales.

Extrapolated Values

Year	ΔT
	s
2025	+69·2
2026	+69
2027	+69
2028	+69
2029	+69

TAI − UTC

Date	ΔAT
	s
1972 Jan. 1	+10·00
1972 July 1	+11·00
1973 Jan. 1	+12·00
1974 Jan. 1	+13·00
1975 Jan. 1	+14·00
1976 Jan. 1	+15·00
1977 Jan. 1	+16·00
1978 Jan. 1	+17·00
1979 Jan. 1	+18·00
1980 Jan. 1	+19·00
1981 July 1	+20·00
1982 July 1	+21·00
1983 July 1	+22·00
1985 July 1	+23·00
1988 Jan. 1	+24·00
1990 Jan. 1	+25·00
1991 Jan. 1	+26·00
1992 July 1	+27·00
1993 July 1	+28·00
1994 July 1	+29·00
1996 Jan. 1	+30·00
1997 July 1	+31·00
1999 Jan. 1	+32·00
2006 Jan. 1	+33·00
2009 Jan. 1	+34·00
2012 July 1	+35·00
2015 July 1	+36·00
2017 Jan. 1	+37·00

In critical cases descend

$$\begin{array}{l}\Delta \mathbf{ET}\\ \Delta \mathbf{TT}\end{array} = \Delta \mathrm{AT} + 32^{s}.184$$

WITH RESPECT TO THE INTERNATIONAL TERRESTRIAL REFERENCE SYSTEM (ITRS)

Date	x	y	x	y	x	y	x	y	x	y
	1980		**1990**		**2000**		**2010**		**2020**	
	″	″	″	″	″	″	″	″	″	″
Jan. 1	+0·129	+0·251	−0·132	+0·165	+0·043	+0·378	+0·099	+0·193	+0·077	+0·282
Apr. 1	+0·014	+0·189	−0·154	+0·469	+0·075	+0·346	−0·061	+0·319	+0·051	+0·401
July 1	−0·044	+0·280	+0·161	+0·542	+0·110	+0·280	+0·061	+0·483	+0·167	+0·432
Oct. 1	−0·006	+0·338	+0·297	+0·243	−0·006	+0·247	+0·234	+0·366	+0·194	+0·324
	1981		**1991**		**2001**		**2011**		**2021**	
Jan. 1	+0·056	+0·361	+0·023	+0·069	−0·073	+0·400	+0·131	+0·203	+0·069	+0·304
Apr. 1	+0·088	+0·285	−0·217	+0·281	+0·091	+0·490	−0·033	+0·279	+0·082	+0·412
July 1	+0·075	+0·209	−0·033	+0·560	+0·254	+0·308	+0·044	+0·436	+0·205	+0·419
Oct. 1	−0·045	+0·210	+0·250	+0·436	+0·065	+0·118	+0·180	+0·377	+0·220	+0·280
	1982		**1992**		**2002**		**2012**		**2022**	
Jan. 1	−0·091	+0·378	+0·182	+0·168	−0·177	+0·294	+0·119	+0·263	+0·055	+0·277
Apr. 1	+0·093	+0·431	−0·083	+0·162	−0·031	+0·541	−0·010	+0·313	+0·043	+0·427
July 1	+0·231	+0·239	−0·142	+0·378	+0·228	+0·462	+0·094	+0·409	+0·230	+0·461
Oct. 1	+0·036	+0·060	+0·055	+0·503	+0·199	+0·200	+0·169	+0·334	+0·281	+0·260
	1983		**1993**		**2003**		**2013**		**2023**	
Jan. 1	−0·211	+0·249	+0·208	+0·359	−0·088	+0·188	+0·075	+0·290	+0·063	+0·201
Apr. 1	−0·069	+0·538	+0·115	+0·170	−0·133	+0·436	+0·051	+0·375	−0·019	+0·405
July 1	+0·269	+0·436	−0·062	+0·209	+0·131	+0·539	+0·143	+0·391	+0·184	+0·508
Oct. 1	+0·235	+0·069	−0·095	+0·370	+0·259	+0·304	+0·133	+0·294	+0·301	+0·334
	1984		**1994**		**2004**		**2014**		**2024**	
Jan. 1	−0·125	+0·089	+0·010	+0·476	+0·031	+0·154	+0·039	+0·319	+0·135	+0·203
Apr. 1	−0·211	+0·410	+0·174	+0·391	−0·140	+0·321	+0·044	+0·421	−0·013	+0·341
July 1	+0·119	+0·543	+0·137	+0·212	−0·008	+0·510	+0·171	+0·415		
Oct. 1	+0·313	+0·246	−0·066	+0·199	+0·199	+0·432	+0·189	+0·289		
	1985		**1995**		**2005**		**2015**			
Jan. 1	+0·051	+0·025	−0·154	+0·418	+0·149	+0·238	+0·031	+0·281		
Apr. 1	−0·196	+0·220	+0·032	+0·558	−0·029	+0·243	+0·014	+0·396		
July 1	−0·044	+0·482	+0·280	+0·384	−0·040	+0·397	+0·142	+0·448		
Oct. 1	+0·214	+0·404	+0·138	+0·106	+0·059	+0·417	+0·210	+0·316		
	1986		**1996**		**2006**		**2016**			
Jan. 1	+0·187	+0·072	−0·176	+0·191	+0·053	+0·383	+0·051	+0·257		
Apr. 1	−0·041	+0·139	−0·152	+0·506	+0·103	+0·374	−0·008	+0·421		
July 1	−0·075	+0·324	+0·179	+0·546	+0·128	+0·300	+0·152	+0·484		
Oct. 1	+0·062	+0·395	+0·267	+0·227	+0·033	+0·252	+0·234	+0·331		
	1987		**1997**		**2007**		**2017**			
Jan. 1	+0·146	+0·315	−0·023	+0·095	−0·049	+0·347	+0·080	+0·263		
Apr. 1	+0·096	+0·212	−0·191	+0·329	+0·023	+0·479	+0·005	+0·378		
July 1	−0·003	+0·208	+0·019	+0·536	+0·209	+0·412	+0·156	+0·449		
Oct. 1	−0·053	+0·295	+0·221	+0·379	+0·134	+0·206	+0·224	+0·303		
	1988		**1998**		**2008**		**2018**			
Jan. 1	−0·023	+0·414	+0·103	+0·175	−0·081	+0·258	+0·059	+0·248		
Apr. 1	+0·134	+0·407	−0·110	+0·252	−0·064	+0·490	+0·032	+0·394		
July 1	+0·171	+0·253	−0·068	+0·439	+0·211	+0·498	+0·163	+0·430		
Oct. 1	+0·011	+0·132	+0·125	+0·445	+0·265	+0·220	+0·211	+0·331		
	1989		**1999**		**2009**		**2019**			
Jan. 1	−0·159	+0·316	+0·139	+0·296	−0·017	+0·146	+0·086	+0·271		
Apr. 1	+0·028	+0·482	+0·026	+0·241	−0·119	+0·406	+0·049	+0·384		
July 1	+0·238	+0·369	−0·032	+0·310	+0·130	+0·534	+0·159	+0·421		
Oct. 1	+0·167	+0·106	+0·006	+0·379	+0·266	+0·331	+0·198	+0·312		

The orientation of the ITRS is consistent with the former BIH system (and the previous IPMS and ILS systems). The angles, x y, are defined on page B84. From 1988 their values have been taken from the IERS Bulletin B, published by the IERS Central Bureau, Bundesamt für Kartographie und Geodäsie, Richard-Strauss-Allee 11, 60598 Frankfurt am Main, Germany.

Introduction

In the reduction of astrometric observations of high precision, it is necessary to distinguish between several different systems of terrestrial coordinates used to specify the positions of points on or near the surface of the Earth. The formulae on page B84 for the reduction for polar motion give the relationships between representations of a geocentric vector referred to either the equinox-based celestial reference system of the true equator and equinox of date, or the Celestial Intermediate Reference System, and the current terrestrial reference system, realized by the International Terrestrial Reference Frame, ITRF2020 (Institut national de l'information geographique et forestier, https://itrf.ign.fr/en/solutions/itrf2020).

ITRF realizations have been published at intervals since 1989 in the form of the geocentric rectangular coordinates and velocities of observing sites around the world. ITRF2020 is a rigorous combination of space geodesy solutions from the techniques of VLBI, SLR, LLR, GPS and DORIS from more than 1500 stations located at nearly one thousand sites. Following the innovation first reported in ITRF2014, ITRF2020 is also generated with an enhanced modelling of non-linear station motions, including seasonal (annual and semi-annual) signals of station positions and post-seismic deformation for sites that were subject to major earthquakes. The ITRF2020 origin is defined by the Earth-system centre of mass sensed by SLR and its scale by the mean scale of the VLBI and SLR solutions. Following improved and recently implemented modelling for the SLR solutions, agreement between these two estimates of scale is now better than a few millimetres.

The ITRF axes are consistent with the axes of the former BIH Terrestrial System (BTS) to within ±0.″005, and the BTS was consistent with the earlier Conventional International Origin to within ±0.″03. The use of rectangular coordinates is precise and unambiguous, but for some purposes it is more convenient to represent the position by its longitude, latitude and height referred to a reference spheroid (the term "spheroid" is used here in the sense of an ellipsoid whose equatorial section is a circle and for which each meridional section is an ellipse).

The precise transformation between these coordinate systems is given below. The spheroid is defined by two parameters, its equatorial radius and flattening (usually the reciprocal of the flattening is given). The values used should always be stated with any tabulation of spheroidal positions, but in case they should be omitted a list of the parameters of some commonly used spheroids is given in the table on page K13. For work such as mapping gravity anomalies, it is convenient that the reference spheroid should also be an equipotential surface of a reference body that is in hydrostatic equilibrium, and has the equatorial radius, gravitational constant, dynamical form factor and angular velocity of the Earth. This is referred to as a Geodetic Reference System (rather than just a reference spheroid). It provides a suitable approximation to mean sea level (i.e. to the geoid), but may differ from it by up to 100m in some regions.

Reduction from geodetic to geocentric coordinates

The position of a point relative to a terrestrial reference frame may be expressed in three ways:

(i) geocentric equatorial rectangular coordinates, x, y, z;
(ii) geocentric longitude, latitude and radius, λ, ϕ', ρ;
(iii) geodetic longitude, latitude and height, λ, ϕ, h.

The geodetic and geocentric longitudes of a point are the same, while the relationship between the geodetic and geocentric latitudes of a point is illustrated in the figure on page K12, which represents a meridional section through the reference spheroid. The geocentric radius ρ is usually expressed in units of the equatorial radius of the reference spheroid. The following relationships hold between the geocentric and geodetic coordinates:

$$\begin{aligned} x &= a\,\rho\,\cos\phi'\cos\lambda = (aC+h)\cos\phi\,\cos\lambda \\ y &= a\,\rho\,\cos\phi'\sin\lambda = (aC+h)\cos\phi\,\sin\lambda \\ z &= a\,\rho\,\sin\phi' \qquad\quad\;\, = (aS+h)\sin\phi \end{aligned}$$

where a is the equatorial radius of the spheroid and C and S are auxiliary functions that depend on the geodetic latitude and on the flattening f of the reference spheroid. The polar radius b and the eccentricity e of the ellipse are given by:

$$b = a\,(1-f) \qquad e^2 = 2f - f^2 \qquad \text{or} \qquad 1 - e^2 = (1-f)^2$$

It follows from the geometrical properties of the ellipse that:

$$C = \{\cos^2\phi + (1-f)^2\sin^2\phi\}^{-1/2} \qquad S = (1-f)^2 C$$

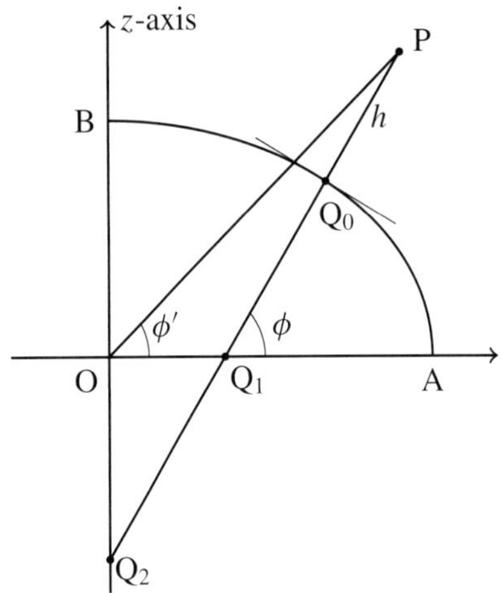

O is centre of Earth
OA = equatorial radius, a
OB = polar radius, b
$= a(1 - f)$
OP = geocentric radius, $a\rho$
PQ_0 is normal to the reference spheroid
$Q_0Q_1 = aS$
$Q_0Q_2 = aC$
ϕ = geodetic latitude
ϕ' = geocentric latitude

Geocentric coordinates may be calculated directly from geodetic coordinates. The reverse calculation of geodetic coordinates from geocentric coordinates can be done in closed form (see for example, Borkowski, *Bull. Geod.* **63**, 50-56, 1989), but it is usually done using an iterative procedure.

An iterative procedure for calculating λ, ϕ, h from x, y, z is as follows:

Calculate: $\lambda = \tan^{-1}(y/x)$ $\quad r = (x^2 + y^2)^{1/2}$ $\quad e^2 = 2f - f^2$

Calculate the first approximation to ϕ from: $\phi = \tan^{-1}(z/r)$

Then perform the following iteration until ϕ is unchanged to the required precision:

$$\phi_1 = \phi \qquad C = (1 - e^2 \sin^2 \phi_1)^{-1/2} \qquad \phi = \tan^{-1}((z + aCe^2 \sin \phi_1)/r)$$

Then:

$$h = r/\cos\phi - aC$$

Series expressions and tables are available for certain values of f for the calculation of C and S and also of ρ and $\phi - \phi'$ for points on the spheroid ($h = 0$). The quantity $\phi - \phi'$ is sometimes known as the "reduction of the latitude" or the "angle of the vertical", and it is of the order of $10'$ in mid-latitudes. To a first approximation when h is small the geocentric radius is increased by h/a and the angle of the vertical is unchanged. The height h refers to a height above the reference spheroid and differs from the height above mean sea level (i.e. above the geoid) by the "undulation of the geoid" at the point.

Other geodetic reference systems

In practice, most geodetic positions are referred either (a) to a regional geodetic datum that is represented by a spheroid that approximates to the geoid in the region considered or (b) to a global reference system, ideally the ITRF2020 or earlier versions. Data for the reduction of regional geodetic coordinates or those in earlier versions of the ITRF to ITRF2020 are available in the relevant geodetic publications, but it is hoped that the following notes, formulae and data will be useful.

(a) Each regional geodetic datum is specified by the size and shape of an adopted spheroid and by the coordinates of an "origin point". The principal axis of the spheroid is generally close to the mean axis of rotation of the Earth, but the centre of the spheroid may not coincide with the centre of mass of the Earth. The offset is usually represented by the geocentric rectangular coordinates (x_0, y_0, z_0) of the centre of the regional spheroid. The reduction from the regional geodetic coordinates (λ, ϕ, h) to the geocentric rectangular coordinates referred to the ITRF (and hence to the geodetic coordinates relative to a reference spheroid) may then be made by using the expressions:

$$x = x_0 + (aC + h)\cos\phi\cos\lambda$$
$$y = y_0 + (aC + h)\cos\phi\sin\lambda$$
$$z = z_0 + (aS + h)\sin\phi$$

(b) The global reference systems defined by the various versions of ITRF differ slightly due to an evolution in the multi-technique combination and constraints philosophy as well as through observational and modelling improvements, although all versions give good approximations to the latest reference frame. The transformations from the latest to previous ITRF solutions involve coordinate and velocity translations, rotations and scaling, and all of these are given online (see https://itrf.ign.fr/en/solutions/transformations) for the ITRF2020 frame. For example, translation parameters T_1 , T_2 and T_3 from ITRF2020 to ITRF2014 are (−1·4, −0·9, +1·4) millimetres, with scale difference −0·42 parts per billion, at epoch 2015.

The space techniques of the multi-constellation global navigation satellite systems (GNSS) such as GPS, GLONASS and Galileo are now widely used for position determination. Since January 1987 the broadcast orbits of the GPS satellites have been referred to the WGS84 terrestrial frame, and so positions determined directly using these orbits will also be referred to this frame, which at the level of a few centimetres is close to the ITRF. The parameters of the spheroid used are listed below, and the frame is defined to agree with the BIH frame. However, with the ready availability of data from a large number of geodetic sites whose coordinates and velocities are rigorously defined within ITRF2020, and with GNSS orbital solutions also being referred by the International GNSS Service (IGS) analysis centres to the same frame, it is straightforward to determine new sites' coordinates within ITRF2020.

GEODETIC REFERENCE SPHEROIDS

Name and Date	Equatorial Radius, a	Reciprocal of Flattening, $1/f$	Gravitational Constant, GM	Dynamical Form Factor, J_2	Ang. Velocity of earth, ω
	m		10^{14}m^{3}s^{-2}		10^{-5}rad s^{-1}
WGS 84	637 8137	298·257 223 563	3·986 005	0·001 082 63	7·292 115
GRS 80 (IUGG, 1980)†	8137	298·257 222	3·986 005	0·001 082 63	7·292 115
IAU 1976	8140	298·257	3·986 005	0·001 082 63	—
GRS 67 (IUGG, 1967)	8160	298·247 167	3·986 03	0·001 082 7	7·292 115 146 7
IAU 1964	8160	298·25	3·986 03	0·001 082 7	7·292 1
International 1924 (Hayford)	8388	297	—	—	—
Clarke 1866	8206·4	294·978 698	—	—	—
Airy 1830	637 7563·396	299·324 964	—	—	—

†H. Moritz, Geodetic Reference System 1980, *Bull. Géodésique,* **58**(3), 388-398, 1984.

Astronomical coordinates

Many astrometric observations that historically were used in the determination of the terrestrial coordinates of the point of observation used the local vertical, which defines the zenith, as a principal reference axis; the coordinates so obtained are called "astronomical coordinates". The local vertical is in the direction of the vector sum of the acceleration due to the gravitational field of the Earth and of the apparent acceleration due to the rotation of the Earth on its axis. The vertical is normal to the equipotential (or level) surface at the point, but it is inclined to the normal to the geodetic reference spheroid; the angle of inclination is known as the "deflection of the vertical".

The astronomical coordinates of an observatory may differ significantly (e.g. by as much as 1′) from its geodetic coordinates, which are required for the determination of the geocentric coordinates of the observatory for use in computing, for example, parallax corrections for solar system observations. The size and direction of the deflection may be estimated by studying the gravity field in the region concerned. The deflection may affect both the latitude and longitude, and hence local time. Astronomical coordinates also vary with time because they are affected by polar motion (see page B84).

Introduction and notation

The interpolation methods described in this section, together with the accompanying tables, are usually sufficient to interpolate to full precision the ephemerides in this volume. Additional notes, formulae and tables are given in the booklets *Interpolation and Allied Tables* and *Subtabulation* and in many textbooks on numerical analysis.

f_p denotes the value of the function $f(t)$ at the time $t = t_0 + ph$, where h is the interval of tabulation, t_0 is a tabular argument, and $p = (t - t_0)/h$ is known as the interpolating factor. The notation for the differences of the tabular values is shown in the following table; it is derived from the use of the central-difference operator δ, which is defined by:

$$\delta f_p = f_{p+1/2} - f_{p-1/2}$$

The symbol for the function is usually omitted in the notation for the differences. Tables are given for use with Bessel's interpolation formula for p in the range 0 to +1. The differences may be expressed in terms of function values for convenience in the use of programmable calculators or computers.

Arg.	Function	Differences 1st	2nd	3rd	4th	Differences in terms of Function Values
t_{-2}	f_{-2}		δ^2_{-2}			$\delta_{1/2} = f_1 - f_0$
		$\delta_{-3/2}$		$\delta^3_{-3/2}$		$\delta^2_0 = \delta_{1/2} - \delta_{-1/2}$
t_{-1}	f_{-1}		δ^2_{-1}		δ^4_{-1}	$= f_1 - 2f_0 + f_{-1}$
		$\delta_{-1/2}$		$\delta^3_{-1/2}$		$\delta^2_0 + \delta^2_1 = f_2 - f_1 - f_0 + f_{-1}$
t_0	f_0		δ^2_0		δ^4_0	$\delta^3_{1/2} = \delta^2_1 - \delta^2_0$
		$\delta_{1/2}$		$\delta^3_{1/2}$		$= f_2 - 3f_1 + 3f_0 - f_{-1}$
t_{+1}	f_{+1}		δ^2_1		δ^4_1	$\delta^4_0 = \delta^3_{1/2} - \delta^3_{-1/2}$
		$\delta_{3/2}$		$\delta^3_{3/2}$		$= f_2 - 4f_1 + 6f_0 - 4f_{-1} + f_{-2}$
t_{+2}	f_{+2}		δ^2_2			$\delta^4_0 + \delta^4_1 = f_3 - 3f_2 + 2f_1 + 2f_0 - 3f_{-1} + f_{-2}$

$$p \equiv \text{the interpolating factor} = (t - t_0)/(t_1 - t_0) = (t - t_0)/h$$

Bessel's interpolation formula

In this notation, Bessel's interpolation formula is:

$$f_p = f_0 + p\,\delta_{1/2} + B_2\,(\delta^2_0 + \delta^2_1) + B_3\,\delta^3_{1/2} + B_4\,(\delta^4_0 + \delta^4_1) + \cdots$$

where $B_2 = p\,(p-1)/4 \qquad B_3 = p\,(p-1)\,(p-\tfrac{1}{2})/6$

$B_4 = (p+1)\,p\,(p-1)\,(p-2)/48$

The maximum contribution to the truncation error of f_p, for $0 < p < 1$, from neglecting each order of difference is less than 0·5 in the unit of the end figure of the tabular function if

$$\delta^2 < 4 \qquad \delta^3 < 60 \qquad \delta^4 < 20 \qquad \delta^5 < 500.$$

The critical table of B_2 opposite provides a rapid means of interpolating when δ^2 is less than 500 and higher-order differences are negligible or when full precision is not required. The interpolating factor p should be rounded to 4 decimals, and the required value of B_2 is then the tabular value opposite the interval in which p lies, or it is the value above and to the right of p if p exactly equals a tabular argument. B_2 is always negative. The effects of the third and fourth differences can be estimated from the values of B_3 and B_4, given in the last column.

Inverse interpolation

Inverse interpolation to derive the interpolating factor p, and hence the time, for which the function takes a specified value f_p is carried out by successive approximations. The first estimate p_1 is obtained from:

$$p_1 = (f_p - f_0)/\delta_{1/2}$$

This value of p is used to obtain an estimate of B_2, from the critical table or otherwise, and hence an improved estimate of p from:

$$p = p_1 - B_2\,(\delta_0^2 + \delta_1^2)/\delta_{1/2}$$

This last step is repeated until there is no further change in B_2 or p; the effects of higher-order differences may be taken into account in this step.

CRITICAL TABLE FOR BESSEL'S INTERPOLATION FORMULA COEFFICIENTS

p	B_2	p	B_2	p	B_2	p	B_2	p	B_2
	−		−		−		−		−
0·0000		0·1101		0·2719		0·7280		0·8898	
	·000		·025		·050		·049		·024
0·0020		0·1152		0·2809		0·7366		0·8949	
	·001		·026		·051		·048		·023
0·0060		0·1205		0·2902		0·7449		0·9000	
	·002		·027		·052		·047		·022
0·0101		0·1258		0·3000		0·7529		0·9049	
	·003		·028		·053		·046		·021
0·0142		0·1312		0·3102		0·7607		0·9098	
	·004		·029		·054		·045		·020
0·0183		0·1366		0·3211		0·7683		0·9147	
	·005		·030		·055		·044		·019
0·0225		0·1422		0·3326		0·7756		0·9195	
	·006		·031		·056		·043		·018
0·0267		0·1478		0·3450		0·7828		0·9242	
	·007		·032		·057		·042		·017
0·0309		0·1535		0·3585		0·7898		0·9289	
	·008		·033		·058		·041		·016
0·0352		0·1594		0·3735		0·7966		0·9335	
	·009		·034		·059		·040		·015
0·0395		0·1653		0·3904		0·8033		0·9381	
	·010		·035		·060		·039		·014
0·0439		0·1713		0·4105		0·8098		0·9427	
	·011		·036		·061		·038		·013
0·0483		0·1775		0·4367		0·8162		0·9472	
	·012		·037		·062		·037		·012
0·0527		0·1837		0·5632		0·8224		0·9516	
	·013		·038		·061		·036		·011
0·0572		0·1901		0·5894		0·8286		0·9560	
	·014		·039		·060		·035		·010
0·0618		0·1966		0·6095		0·8346		0·9604	
	·015		·040		·059		·034		·009
0·0664		0·2033		0·6264		0·8405		0·9647	
	·016		·041		·058		·033		·008
0·0710		0·2101		0·6414		0·8464		0·9690	
	·017		·042		·057		·032		·007
0·0757		0·2171		0·6549		0·8521		0·9732	
	·018		·043		·056		·031		·006
0·0804		0·2243		0·6673		0·8577		0·9774	
	·019		·044		·055		·030		·005
0·0852		0·2316		0·6788		0·8633		0·9816	
	·020		·045		·054		·029		·004
0·0901		0·2392		0·6897		0·8687		0·9857	
	·021		·046		·053		·028		·003
0·0950		0·2470		0·7000		0·8741		0·9898	
	·022		·047		·052		·027		·002
0·1000		0·2550		0·7097		0·8794		0·9939	
	·023		·048		·051		·026		·001
0·1050		0·2633		0·7190		0·8847		0·9979	
	·024		·049		·050		·025		·000
0·1101		0·2719		0·7280		0·8898		1·0000	

p	B_3
0·0	0·000
0·1	+0·006
0·2	+0·008
0·3	+0·007
0·4	+0·004
0·5	0·000
0·6	−0·004
0·7	−0·007
0·8	−0·008
0·9	−0·006
1·0	0·000

p	B_4
0·0	0·000
0·1	+0·004
0·2	+0·007
0·3	+0·010
0·4	+0·011
0·5	+0·012
0·6	+0·011
0·7	+0·010
0·8	+0·007
0·9	+0·004
1·0	0·000

In critical cases ascend. B_2 is always negative.

Polynomial representations

It is sometimes convenient to construct a simple polynomial representation of the form

$$f_p = a_0 + a_1\,p + a_2\,p^2 + a_3\,p^3 + a_4\,p^4 + \cdots$$

which may be evaluated in the nested form

$$f_p = (((a_4\,p + a_3)\,p + a_2)\,p + a_1)\,p + a_0$$

Expressions for the coefficients a_0, a_1, ... may be obtained from Stirling's interpolation formula, neglecting fifth-order differences:

$$a_4 = \delta_0^4/24 \qquad a_2 = \delta_0^2/2 - a_4 \qquad a_0 = f_0$$

$$a_3 = (\delta_{1/2}^3 + \delta_{-1/2}^3)/12 \qquad a_1 = (\delta_{1/2} + \delta_{-1/2})/2 - a_3$$

This is suitable for use in the range $-\frac{1}{2} \le p \le +\frac{1}{2}$, and it may be adequate in the range $-2 \le p \le 2$, but it should not normally be used outside this range. Techniques are available in the literature for obtaining polynomial representations which give smaller errors over similar or larger intervals. The coefficients may be expressed in terms of function values rather than differences.

Examples

To find (a) the declination of the Sun at $16^{\mathrm{h}}\ 23^{\mathrm{m}}\ 14^{\mathrm{s}}.8$ TT on 1984 January 19, (b) the right ascension of Mercury at $17^{\mathrm{h}}\ 21^{\mathrm{m}}\ 16^{\mathrm{s}}.8$ TT on 1984 January 8, and (c) the time on 1984 January 8 when Mercury's right ascension is exactly $18^{\mathrm{h}}\ 04^{\mathrm{m}}$.

Difference tables for the Sun and Mercury are constructed as shown below, where the differences are in units of the end figures of the function. Second-order differences are sufficient for the Sun, but fourth-order differences are required for Mercury.

Sun

Jan.	Dec.	δ	δ^2
	° ′ ″		
18	−20 44 48·3		
		+7212	
19	−20 32 47·1		+233
		+7445	
20	−20 20 22·6		+230
		+7675	
21	−20 07 35·1		

Mercury

Jan.	R.A.	δ	δ^2	δ^3	δ^4
	h m s				
6	18 10 10·12				
		−18709			
7	18 07 03·03		+4299		
		−14410		−16	
8	18 04 38·93		+4283		−104
		−10127		−120	
9	18 02 57·66		+4163		−76
		−5964		−196	
10	18 01 58·02		+3967		
		−1997			
11	18 01 38·05				

(a) *Use of Bessel's formula*

The tabular interval is one day, hence the interpolating factor is 0·68281. From the critical table, $B_2 = -0{\cdot}054$, and

$$f_p = -20^\circ\ 32'\ 47''.1 + 0{\cdot}68281\,(+744''.5) - 0{\cdot}054\,(+23''.3 + 23''.0)$$
$$= -20^\circ\ 24'\ 21''.2$$

(b) *Use of polynomial formula*

Using the polynomial method, the coefficients are:

$a_4 = -1^{\mathrm{s}}.04/24 = -0^{\mathrm{s}}.043$

$a_3 = (-1^{\mathrm{s}}.20 - 0^{\mathrm{s}}.16)/12 = -0^{\mathrm{s}}.113$

$a_2 = +42^{\mathrm{s}}.83/2 + 0^{\mathrm{s}}.043 = +21^{\mathrm{s}}.458$

$a_1 = (-101^{\mathrm{s}}.27 - 144^{\mathrm{s}}.10)/2 + 0^{\mathrm{s}}.113 = -122^{\mathrm{s}}.572$

$a_0 = 18^{\mathrm{h}} + 278^{\mathrm{s}}.93$

where an extra decimal place has been kept as a guarding figure. Then with interpolating factor $p = 0{\cdot}72311$

$$f_p = 18^{\mathrm{h}} + 278^{\mathrm{s}}.93 - 122^{\mathrm{s}}.572\,p + 21^{\mathrm{s}}.458\,p^2 - 0^{\mathrm{s}}.113\,p^3 - 0^{\mathrm{s}}.043\,p^4$$
$$= 18^{\mathrm{h}}\ 03^{\mathrm{m}}\ 21^{\mathrm{s}}.46$$

(c) *Inverse interpolation*

Since $f_p = 18^{\mathrm{h}}\ 04^{\mathrm{m}}$ the first estimate for p is:

$$p_1 = (18^{\mathrm{h}}\ 04^{\mathrm{m}} - 18^{\mathrm{h}}\ 04^{\mathrm{m}}\ 38^{\mathrm{s}}.93)/(-101^{\mathrm{s}}.27) = 0{\cdot}38442$$

From the critical table, with $p = 0{\cdot}3844$, $B_2 = -0{\cdot}059$. Also

$$(\delta_0^2 + \delta_1^2)/\delta_{1/2} = (+42{\cdot}83 + 41{\cdot}63)/(-101{\cdot}27) = -0{\cdot}834$$

The second approximation to p is:

$$p = 0{\cdot}38442 + 0{\cdot}059\,(-0{\cdot}834) = 0{\cdot}33521 \quad \text{which gives } t = 8^{\mathrm{h}}\ 02^{\mathrm{m}}\ 42^{\mathrm{s}};$$

as a check, using the polynomial found in (b) with $p = 0{\cdot}33521$ gives

$$f_p = 18^{\mathrm{h}}\ 04^{\mathrm{m}}\ 00^{\mathrm{s}}.25.$$

The next approximation is $B_2 = -0{\cdot}056$ and $p = 0{\cdot}38442 + 0{\cdot}056(-0{\cdot}834) = 0{\cdot}33772$ which gives $t = 8^{\mathrm{h}}\ 06^{\mathrm{m}}\ 19^{\mathrm{s}}$: using the polynomial in (b) with $p = 0{\cdot}33772$ gives

$$f_p = 18^{\mathrm{h}}\ 03^{\mathrm{m}}\ 59^{\mathrm{s}}.98.$$

Subtabulation

Coefficients for use in the systematic interpolation of an ephemeris to a smaller interval are given in the following table for certain values of the ratio of the two intervals. The table is entered for each of the appropriate multiples of this ratio to give the corresponding decimal value of the interpolating factor p and the Bessel coefficients. The values of p are exact or recurring decimal numbers. The values of the coefficients may be rounded to suit the maximum number of figures in the differences.

BESSEL COEFFICIENTS FOR SUBTABULATION

Ratio of intervals											Bessel Coefficients			
$\frac{1}{2}$	$\frac{1}{3}$	$\frac{1}{4}$	$\frac{1}{5}$	$\frac{1}{6}$	$\frac{1}{8}$	$\frac{1}{10}$	$\frac{1}{12}$	$\frac{1}{20}$	$\frac{1}{24}$	$\frac{1}{40}$	p	B_2	B_3	B_4
										1	0·025	−0·006094	0·00193	0·0010
									1		0·0416	−0·009983	0·00305	0·0017
								1		2	0·050	−0·011875	0·00356	0·0020
										3	0·075	−0·017344	0·00491	0·0030
							1		2		0·0833	−0·019097	0·00530	0·0033
						1		2		4	0·100	−0·022500	0·00600	0·0039
					1				3	5	0·125	−0·027344	0·00684	0·0048
								3		6	0·150	−0·031875	0·00744	0·0057
				1			2		4		0·1666	−0·034722	0·00772	0·0062
										7	0·175	−0·036094	0·00782	0·0064
			1			2		4		8	0·200	−0·040000	0·00800	0·0072
									5		0·2083	−0·041233	0·00802	0·0074
										9	0·225	−0·043594	0·00799	0·0079
		1			2		3	5	6	10	0·250	−0·046875	0·00781	0·0085
										11	0·275	−0·049844	0·00748	0·0091
									7		0·2916	−0·051649	0·00717	0·0095
						3		6		12	0·300	−0·052500	0·00700	0·0097
										13	0·325	−0·054844	0·00640	0·0101
	1			2			4		8		0·3333	−0·055556	0·00617	0·0103
								7		14	0·350	−0·056875	0·00569	0·0106
					3				9	15	0·375	−0·058594	0·00488	0·0109
			2			4		8		16	0·400	−0·060000	0·00400	0·0112
							5		10		0·4166	−0·060764	0·00338	0·0114
										17	0·425	−0·061094	0·00305	0·0114
								9		18	0·450	−0·061875	0·00206	0·0116
									11		0·4583	−0·062066	0·00172	0·0116
										19	0·475	−0·062344	0·00104	0·0117
1		2		3	4	5	6	10	12	20	0·500	−0·062500	0·00000	0·0117
										21	0·525	−0·062344	−0·00104	0·0117
									13		0·5416	−0·062066	−0·00172	0·0116
								11		22	0·550	−0·061875	0 00206	0·0116
										23	0·575	−0·061094	−0·00305	0·0114
							7		14		0·5833	−0·060764	−0·00338	0·0114
			3			6		12		24	0·600	−0·060000	−0·00400	0·0112
					5				15	25	0·625	−0·058594	−0·00488	0·0109
								13		26	0·650	−0·056875	−0·00569	0·0106
	2			4			8		16		0·6666	−0·055556	−0·00617	0·0103
										27	0·675	−0·054844	−0·00640	0·0101
						7		14		28	0·700	−0·052500	−0·00700	0·0097
									17		0·7083	−0·051649	−0·00717	0·0095
										29	0·725	−0·049844	−0·00748	0·0091
		3			6		9	15	18	30	0·750	−0·046875	−0·00781	0·0085
										31	0·775	−0·043594	−0·00799	0·0079
									19		0·7916	−0·041233	−0·00802	0·0074
			4			8		16		32	0·800	−0·040000	−0·00800	0·0072
										33	0·825	−0·036094	−0·00782	0·0064
				5			10		20		0·8333	−0·034722	−0·00772	0·0062
								17		34	0·850	−0·031875	−0·00744	0·0057
					7				21	35	0·875	−0·027344	−0·00684	0·0048
						9		18		36	0·900	−0·022500	−0·00600	0·0039
							11		22		0·9166	−0·019097	−0·00530	0·0033
										37	0·925	−0·017344	−0·00491	0·0030
								19		38	0·950	−0·011875	−0·00356	0·0020
									23		0·9583	−0·009983	−0·00305	0·0017
										39	0·975	−0·006094	−0·00193	0·0010

The following are some useful formulae involving vectors and matrices.

Position vectors

Positions or directions on the sky can be represented as column vectors in a specific celestial coordinate system with components that are Cartesian (rectangular) coordinates. The relationship between a position vector **r** its three components r_x, r_y, r_z, and its right ascension (α), declination (δ) and distance (d) from the specified origin have the general form

$$\mathbf{r} = \begin{bmatrix} r_x \\ r_y \\ r_z \end{bmatrix} = \begin{bmatrix} d \cos\alpha \cos\delta \\ d \sin\alpha \cos\delta \\ d \sin\delta \end{bmatrix} \quad \text{and} \quad \begin{aligned} \alpha &= \tan^{-1}\left(r_y/r_x\right) \\ \delta &= \tan^{-1} r_z/\sqrt{(r_x^2 + r_y^2)} \\ d &= |\mathbf{r}| = \sqrt{(r_x^2 + r_y^2 + r_z^2)} \end{aligned}$$

where α is measured counterclockwise as viewed from the positive side of the z-axis. A two-argument arctangent function (e.g., atan2) will return the correct quadrant for α if r_y and r_x are provided separately. The above is written in terms of equatorial coordiates (α, δ), however they are also valid, for example, for ecliptic longitude and latitude (λ, β) and geocentric (but not geodetic) longitude and latitude (λ, ϕ').

Unit vectors are often used; the unit vector $\hat{\mathbf{r}}$ is a vector with distance (magnitude) equal to one, and may be calculated thus;

$$\hat{\mathbf{r}} = \frac{\mathbf{r}}{|\mathbf{r}|}$$

For stars and other objects "at infinity" (beyond the solar system), d is often set to 1.

Vector dot and cross products

The dot or scalar product ($\mathbf{r}_1 \cdot \mathbf{r}_2$) of two vectors $\mathbf{r}_1$ and $\mathbf{r}_2$ is the sum of the products of their corresponding components in the same Cartesian coordinate system, thus

$$\mathbf{r}_1 \cdot \mathbf{r}_2 = x_1\, x_2 + y_1\, y_2 + z_1\, z_2$$

The angle (θ) between two unit vectors $\hat{\mathbf{r}}_1$ and $\hat{\mathbf{r}}_2$ is given by

$$\hat{\mathbf{r}}_1 \cdot \hat{\mathbf{r}}_2 = \cos\theta$$

Note, also, that the magnitude (d) of **r** is given by

$$d = |\mathbf{r}| = \sqrt{(\mathbf{r} \cdot \mathbf{r})} = \sqrt{r_x^2 + r_y^2 + r_z^2}$$

The cross or vector product ($\mathbf{r}_1 \times \mathbf{r}_2$) of two vectors $\mathbf{r}_1$ and $\mathbf{r}_2$ is a vector that is perpendicular to the plane containing both $\mathbf{r}_1$ and $\mathbf{r}_2$ in the direction given by a right-handed screw, and

$$\mathbf{r}_1 \times \mathbf{r}_2 = \begin{bmatrix} y_1\, z_2 - y_2\, z_1 \\ x_2\, z_1 - x_1\, z_2 \\ x_1\, y_2 - x_2\, y_1 \end{bmatrix}$$

where $\mathbf{r}_1$ and $\mathbf{r}_2$ have column vectors (x_1, y_1, z_1) and (x_2, y_2, z_2), respectively. A cross product is not commutative since

$$\mathbf{r}_1 \times \mathbf{r}_2 = -\mathbf{r}_2 \times \mathbf{r}_1$$

The magnitude of the cross product of two unit vectors is the sine of the angle between them

$$|\hat{\mathbf{r}}_1 \times \hat{\mathbf{r}}_2| = \sin\theta \qquad \text{and} \qquad 0 \le \theta \le \pi$$

The vector triple product

$$(\mathbf{r}_1 \times \mathbf{r}_2) \times \mathbf{r}_3 = (\mathbf{r}_1 \cdot \mathbf{r}_3)\, \mathbf{r}_2 - (\mathbf{r}_2 \cdot \mathbf{r}_3)\, \mathbf{r}_1$$

is a vector in the same plane as $\mathbf{r}_1$ and $\mathbf{r}_2$. Note the position of the brackets. The latter is used on page B67 in step 3 where $\mathbf{r}_1 = \mathbf{q}$, $\mathbf{r}_2 = \mathbf{e}$ and $\mathbf{r}_3 = \mathbf{p}$.

Matrices and matrix multiplication

The general form of a 3×3 matrix **M** used with 3-vectors is usually specified

$$\mathbf{M} = \begin{bmatrix} m_{11} & m_{12} & m_{13} \\ m_{21} & m_{22} & m_{23} \\ m_{31} & m_{32} & m_{33} \end{bmatrix}$$

If each element of **M** (m_{ij}) is the result of multiplying matrices **A** and **B**, i.e. **M** = **A B**, then **M** is calculated from

$$m_{ij} = \sum_{k=1}^{3} a_{ik}\, b_{kj} \qquad \text{thus} \qquad \mathbf{M} = \begin{bmatrix} \sum a_{1k}\, b_{k1} & \sum a_{1k}\, b_{k2} & \sum a_{1k}\, b_{k3} \\ \sum a_{2k}\, b_{k1} & \sum a_{2k}\, b_{k2} & \sum a_{2k}\, b_{k3} \\ \sum a_{3k}\, b_{k1} & \sum a_{3k}\, b_{k2} & \sum a_{3k}\, b_{k3} \end{bmatrix}$$

where $i = 1, 2, 3$, $j = 1, 2, 3$ and k is summed from 1 to 3. Note that matrix multiplication is associative, i.e. $\mathbf{A}\,(\mathbf{B}\,\mathbf{C}) = (\mathbf{A}\,\mathbf{B})\,\mathbf{C}$, but it is **not** commutative i.e. $\mathbf{A}\,\mathbf{B} \neq \mathbf{B}\,\mathbf{A}$.

Rotation matrices

The rotation matrix $\mathbf{R}_n(\phi)$, for $n = 1, 2$ and 3 transforms column 3-vectors from one Cartesian coordinate system to another. The final system is formed by rotating the original system about its own n^{th}-axis (i.e. the x, y, or z-axis) by the angle ϕ, counterclockwise as viewed from the $+x$, $+y$ or $+z$ direction, respectively.

The two columns below give $\mathbf{R}_n(\phi)$ and its inverse $\mathbf{R}_n^{-1}(\phi)$ (see below), respectively,

$$\mathbf{R}_1(\phi) = \begin{bmatrix} 1 & 0 & 0 \\ 0 & \cos\phi & \sin\phi \\ 0 & -\sin\phi & \cos\phi \end{bmatrix} \qquad \mathbf{R}_1^{-1}(\phi) = \begin{bmatrix} 1 & 0 & 0 \\ 0 & \cos\phi & -\sin\phi \\ 0 & \sin\phi & \cos\phi \end{bmatrix}$$

$$\mathbf{R}_2(\phi) = \begin{bmatrix} \cos\phi & 0 & -\sin\phi \\ 0 & 1 & 0 \\ \sin\phi & 0 & \cos\phi \end{bmatrix} \qquad \mathbf{R}_2^{-1}(\phi) = \begin{bmatrix} \cos\phi & 0 & \sin\phi \\ 0 & 1 & 0 \\ -\sin\phi & 0 & \cos\phi \end{bmatrix}$$

$$\mathbf{R}_3(\phi) = \begin{bmatrix} \cos\phi & \sin\phi & 0 \\ -\sin\phi & \cos\phi & 0 \\ 0 & 0 & 1 \end{bmatrix} \qquad \mathbf{R}_3^{-1}(\phi) = \begin{bmatrix} \cos\phi & -\sin\phi & 0 \\ \sin\phi & \cos\phi & 0 \\ 0 & 0 & 1 \end{bmatrix}$$

Generally, a rotation matrix **R** is a matrix formed from products of the above rotational matricies $\mathbf{R}_n(\phi)$ that implements a transformation from one Cartesian coordinate system to another, the two systems sharing a common origin. Any such matrix is orthogonal; that is, the transpose $\mathbf{R}^{\mathrm{T}}$ (where rows are replaced by columns) equals the inverse, $\mathbf{R}^{-1}$. Therefore

$$\mathbf{R}^{\mathrm{T}}\,\mathbf{R} = \mathbf{R}^{-1}\,\mathbf{R} = \mathbf{I}$$

where **I** is the unit (identity) matrix. Sometimes $\mathbf{R}^{\mathrm{T}}$ is denoted $\mathbf{R}'$. It is also worth noting the following relationships

$$\mathbf{R}_n^{-1}(\phi) = \mathbf{R}_n^{\mathrm{T}}(\phi) = \mathbf{R}_n(-\phi)$$

which is shown in the right-hand column above. The initial and final Cartesian coordinate systems are right handed ($\hat{\mathbf{e}}_x \times \hat{\mathbf{e}}_y = \hat{\mathbf{e}}_z$), where $\hat{\mathbf{e}}_n$ are the unit vectors along the axes. Matrices interconnecting such systems have their determinant equal to +1 and are called *proper orthogonal matrices* or *proper rotation matrices*. Such a matrix can always be represented as a product of three matrices of the types $\mathbf{R}_n(\phi)$.

Example: The transformation between a geocentric position with respect to the Geocentric Celestial Reference System $\mathbf{r}_{\text{GCRS}}$ and a position with respect to the true equator and equinox of date $\mathbf{r}_t$, and vice versa, is given by:

$$\mathbf{r}_t = \mathbf{N}\,\mathbf{P}\,\mathbf{B}\,\mathbf{r}_{\text{GCRS}}$$

$$\mathbf{B}^{-1}\mathbf{P}^{-1}\mathbf{N}^{-1}\mathbf{r}_t = \mathbf{B}^{-1}\,[\mathbf{P}^{-1}\,(\mathbf{N}^{-1}\mathbf{N})\,\mathbf{P}]\,\mathbf{B}\,\mathbf{r}_{\text{GCRS}}$$

Rearranging gives $$\mathbf{r}_{\text{GCRS}} = \mathbf{B}^{-1}\,\mathbf{P}^{-1}\,\mathbf{N}^{-1}\,\mathbf{r}_t = \mathbf{B}^{\mathrm{T}}\,\mathbf{P}^{\mathrm{T}}\,\mathbf{N}^{\mathrm{T}}\,\mathbf{r}_t$$

where **B**, **P** and **N** are the frame bias, precession and nutation matrices, respectively, and are all proper rotation matrices. Note that the order the transformations are applied is crucial.

CONTENTS OF SECTION L

This section specifies the sources for the theories and data used to construct the ephemerides in this volume, explains the basic concepts required to use the ephemerides, and where appropriate states the precise meaning of tabulated quantities. Definitions of individual terms appear in the Glossary (Section M). The *Explanatory Supplement to the Astronomical Almanac* (Urban and Seidelmann, 2012) contains additional information about the theories and data used.

Some of the information printed in this volume as well as closely related data can also be found online. The URL [1] for the website in the US is https://aa.usno.navy.mil/publications/asa.html and in the UK is https://asa.hmnao.com .

To the greatest extent possible, *The Astronomical Almanac* is prepared using standard data sources and models recommended by the International Astronomical Union (IAU). The data prepared in the United States rely heavily on the US Naval Observatory's NOVAS software package [2]. Data prepared in the United Kingdom utilize the IAU Standards of Fundamental Astronomy (SOFA) library [3]. Although NOVAS and SOFA were written independently, the underlying scientific bases are the same. Resulting computations typically are in agreement at the microarcsecond level.

Fundamental Reference System

The fundamental reference system for astronomical applications is the International Celestial Reference System (ICRS), as adopted by the IAU General Assembly (GA) in 1997 (Resolution B2, IAU, 1999). At the same time, the IAU specified that the practical realization of the ICRS in the radio regime is the International Celestial Reference Frame (ICRF), a space-fixed frame based on high accuracy radio positions of extragalactic sources measured by Very Long Baseline Interferometry (VLBI); see Ma et al. (1998). Beginning in 2019, the ICRS is realized in the radio by the ICRF3 catalog (Gordon, 2018); also available at [4]. The ICRS is realized in the optical regime by the Hipparcos Celestial Reference Frame (HCRF), consisting of the *Hipparcos Catalogue* (ESA, 1997) with certain exclusions (Resolution B1.2, IAU, 2001). Although the directions of the ICRS coordinate axes are not defined by the kinematics of the Earth, the ICRS axes (as implemented by the ICRF and HCRF) closely approximate the axes that would be defined by the mean Earth equator and equinox of J2000.0 (to within 0.1 arcsecond).

In 2000, the IAU defined a system of space-time coordinates for the solar system, and the Earth, within the framework of General Relativity, by specifying the form of the metric tensors for each and the 4-dimensional space-time transformation between them. The former is called the Barycentric Celestial Reference System (BCRS), and the latter, the Geocentric Celestial Reference System (GCRS) (Resolution B1.3, IAU, 2001). The ICRS can be considered a specific implementation of the BCRS; the ICRS defines the spatial axis directions of the BCRS. The GCRS axis directions are derived from those of the BCRS (ICRS); the GCRS can be considered to be the "geocentric ICRS," and the coordinates of stars and planets in the GCRS are obtained from basic ICRS reference data by applying the algorithms for proper place (*e.g.*, for stars, correcting the ICRS-based catalog position for proper motion, parallax, gravitational deflection of light, and aberration).

Precession and Nutation Models

The IAU Resolution B1 adopts the IAU 2006 precession theory (Capitaine, Wallace, and Chapront, 2003) recommended by the Working Group on Precession and the Ecliptic (Hilton et al., 2006) and the IAU 2000A nutation theory (IAU 2000 Resolution B1.6) based on the transfer functions of Matthews et al. (2002), MHB2000. However, at the highest precision (μas), implementing these precession and nutation theories will not agree with the combined precession-nutation approach using the X,Y of the CIP as implemented by the IERS Conventions (IERS, 2010, Chapter 5, and the updates at [5]). This is due to some very small adjustments that are needed in a few of the IAU

2000A nutation amplitudes in order to ensure compatibility with the IAU 2006 values for ϵ_0 and the J_2 rate (see IERS (2010), 5.6.3).

Sections C, E, F use IAU 2000A nutation without the adjustments (see USNO Circular 179, Kaplan (2005) available at [6]) and Sections A, B, D and G use IAU SOFA software, which includes the adjustments. Note that these adjustments are well below the precision printed. These IAU recommendations have been implemented into this almanac since the 2009 edition.

Section B describes the transformation (rotations for precession and nutation) from the GCRS to the "of date" system. This includes the offsets of the ICRS axes from the axes of the dynamical system (mean equator and equinox of J2000.0, termed frame bias). Users are reminded that both variants of formulation, with and without frame bias, are often given, and the difference matters.

Timescales

Two fundamentally different types of time scales are used in astronomy: coordinate timescales such as International Atomic Time (TAI), Terrestrial Time (TT), and Barycentric Dynamical Time (TDB), and those based on the rotation of the Earth such as Universal Time (UT) and sidereal time.

A coordinate timescale is one associated with a coordinate system. To be of use, a coordinate timescale must be related to the proper time of an actual clock. This connection is made from the proper times of an ensemble of atomic clocks on the geoid, through a relativistic transformation, to define the TAI coordinate timescale. The realization of TAI is the responsibility of the Bureau International de Poids et Mesures (BIPM).

The Earth is subject to external torques and changes to its internal structure. Thus, the Earth's rotation rate varies with time. And those timescales, such as UT, that are based on the Earth's rotation do not have a fixed relationship to coordinate timescales.

The fundamental unit of time in a coordinate time scale is the SI second defined as 9 192 631 770 cycles of the radiation corresponding to the ground state hyperfine transition of Cesium 133. As a simple count of cycles of an observable phenomenon, the SI second can be implemented, at least in principle, by an observer anywhere. According to relativity theory, clocks advancing by SI seconds according to a co-moving observer (*i.e.*, an observer moving with the clock) may not, in general, appear to advance by SI seconds to an observer on a different space-time trajectory from that of the clock. Thus, a coordinate time scale defined for use in a particular reference system is related to the coordinate time scale defined for a second reference system by a rather complex formula that depends on the relative space-time trajectories of the two reference systems. Simply stated, different astronomical reference systems use different time scales. However, the universal use of SI units allows the values of fundamental physical constants determined in one reference system to be used in another reference system without scaling.

The IAU has recommended relativistic coordinate time scales based on the SI second for theoretical developments using the Barycentric Celestial Reference System or the Geocentric Celestial Reference System. These time scales are, respectively, Barycentric Coordinate Time (TCB) and Geocentric Coordinate Time (TCG). Neither TCB nor TCG appear explicitly in this volume (except here and in the Glossary), but may underlie the physical theories that contribute to the data, and are likely to be more widely used in the future.

International Atomic Time (TAI) is a commonly used time scale with a mean rate equal, to a high level of accuracy, to the mean rate of the proper time of an observer situated on the Earth's surface (the rotating geoid). TAI is the most precisely determined time scale that is now available for astronomical use. This scale results from analyses, by the BIPM in Sèvres, France, of data from atomic time standards of many countries. Although TAI was not officially introduced until 1972, atomic time scales have been available since 1956, and TAI may be extrapolated backwards to the period 1956–1971 (for a history of TAI, see Nelson et al. (2001)). TAI is readily available as an integral number of seconds offset from UTC, which is extensively disseminated. UTC is discussed at the end of this section.

The astronomical time scale called Terrestrial Time (TT), used widely in this volume, is an idealized form of TAI with an epoch offset. In practice it is TT = TAI + $32\overset{s}{.}184$. TT was so defined to preserve continuity with previously used (now obsolete) "dynamical" time scales, Terrestrial Dynamical Time (TDT) and Ephemeris Time (ET).

Barycentric Dynamical Time (TDB, defined by the IAU in 1976 and 1979 and modified in 2006 by Resolution B3) is defined such that it is linearly related to TCB and, at the geocenter, remains close to TT. Barycentric and heliocentric data are therefore often tabulated with TDB shown as the time argument. Values of parameters involving TDB (see pages K6–K7), which are not based on the SI second, will, in general, require scaling to convert them to SI-based values (dimensionless quantities such as mass ratios are unaffected).

The coordinate time scale TDB is used as the independent argument of various fundamental solar system ephemerides. In particular, it is the coordinate time scale of the Jet Propulsion Laboratory (JPL) ephemerides DE440/DE441 and of their preceding version DE430/DE431. Older JPL ephemerides, *e.g.* DE405/LE405, used the coordinate time scale $\mathrm{T_{eph}}$ (see Glossary). The DE440 ephemerides are the basis for many of the tabulations in this volume (see the Ephemerides Section on page L5). They were computed in the Barycentric Celestial Reference System. The linear drift between TDB and TCB (of about 10^{-8} s yr^{-1}) is such that the rates of TDB and TT are as close as possible for the time span covered by the particular ephemeris (Resolution B3, IAU, 2008).

The second group of time scales, which is also used in this volume, is based on the (variable) rotation of the Earth. In 2000, the IAU (Resolution B1.8, IAU, 2001) defined UT1 (Universal Time) to be linearly proportional to the Earth rotation angle (ERA) (see page B8), which is the geocentric angle between two directions in the equatorial plane called, respectively, the celestial intermediate origin (CIO) and the terrestrial intermediate origin (TIO). The TIO rotates with the Earth, while the motion of the CIO has no component of instantaneous motion along the celestial equator, thus ERA is a direct measure of the Earth's rotation.

Greenwich sidereal time is the hour angle of the equinox measured with respect to the Greenwich meridian. Local sidereal time is the local hour angle of the equinox, or the Greenwich sidereal time plus the longitude (east positive) of the observer, expressed in time units. Sidereal time appears in two forms, apparent and mean, the difference being the *equation of the equinoxes*; apparent sidereal time includes the effect of nutation on the location of the equinox. Greenwich (or local) sidereal time can be observationally obtained from the equinox-based right ascensions of celestial objects transiting the Greenwich (or local) meridian. The current form of the expression for Greenwich mean sidereal time (GMST) in terms of ERA (which is a function of UT1) and the accumulated precession in right ascension (which is a function of TDB or TT), was first adopted for the 2006 edition of the almanac. The current expression for GMST is given on page B8.

Universal Time (formerly Greenwich Mean Time) is widely used in astronomy, and in this volume always means UT1. The expression for UT1 is in terms of GMST (consistent with the IAU 2006 precession) as in Capitaine et al. (2005). No discontinuities in any time scale resulted from any of the changes in the definition of UT1.

UT1 and sidereal time are affected by variations in the Earth's rate of rotation (length of day), which are unpredictable. The lengths of the sidereal and UT1 seconds are therefore not constant when expressed in a uniform time scale such as TT. The accumulated difference in time measured by a clock keeping SI seconds on the geoid from that measured by the rotation of the Earth is ΔT = TT − UT1. In preparing this volume, an assumption had to be made about the value(s) of ΔT during the tabular year; a table of observed and extrapolated values of ΔT is given on page K9. Calculations of positions relative to the terrestrial frame, such as precise transit times and hour angles, are often referred to the *ephemeris meridian*, which is 1.002 738 ΔT east of the Greenwich meridian, and thus independent of the Earth's actual rotation. Only when ΔT is specified can such predictions be referred to the Greenwich meridian. Essentially, the ephemeris meridian rotates at a uniform rate corresponding to the SI second on the geoid, rather than at the variable (and generally slower) rate of the real Earth.

The worldwide system of civil time is based on Coordinated Universal Time (UTC), which is now ubiquitous and tightly synchronized. UTC is a hybrid time scale, using the SI second on the geoid as its fundamental unit, but subject to occasional 1-second adjustments to keep it within $0^{s}.9$ of UT1. Such adjustments, called "leap seconds," are normally introduced at the end of June or December, when necessary, by international agreement. Tables of the differences UT1 − UTC, called ΔUT made available by the International Earth Rotation and Reference System Service's *Bulletin B*. DUT1, an approximation to UT1 − UTC, is transmitted in code with some radio time signals, such as those from WWV. As previously noted, UTC and TAI differ by an integral number of seconds, which increases by 1 whenever a positive leap second is introduced into UTC. Only positive leap seconds have ever been introduced. The TAI − UTC difference is referred to as ΔAT, tabulated on page K9. Therefore TAI = UTC + ΔAT and TT = UTC + ΔAT + $32^{s}.184$.

From 2016, in order to provide UT1 directly via a time server rather than only UTC, the Time and Frequency Division of the US National Institute of Standards and Technology (NIST) transmits UT1 time in the Network Time Protocol format [7]. The time difference between UT1 and UTC is updated every day at 0^{h}UTC from IERS Bulletin A. The accuracy of UT1(NIST) at the server is approximately 4 ms, and is determined by the uncertainty in the prediction of the difference UT1-UTC. The accuracy of the time received by a user will usually be further limited by the stability of the network delay from the user's system to the time server.

In many astronomical applications multiple time scales must be used. In the astronomical system of units, the unit of time is the day of 86400 seconds. For long periods, however, the Julian century of 36525 days is used. With the increasing precision of various quantities it is now often necessary not only to specify the date but also the time scale. Thus the standard epoch for astrometric reference data designated J2000.0 is 2000 January 1, 12^{h} TT (JD 245 1545.0 TT). The use of time scales based on the tropical year and Besselian epochs was discontinued in 1984. Other information on time scales and the relationships between them may be found on pages B6–B12.

Ephemerides

The fundamental ephemerides of the Sun, Moon, and major planets were calculated by numerical integration at the Jet Propulsion Laboratory (JPL). These ephemerides, designated DE440, provide barycentric equatorial rectangular coordinates for the period JD2287184.5 (1549 Dec. 21.0) through JD2688976.5 (2650 Jan. 25.0) (Park et al., 2021). *The Astronomical Almanac* for 2024 is the first edition that uses the DE440 ephemerides; the volumes for 2015 through 2023 used the ephemerides designated DE430 (Folkner et al., 2014); the volumes for 2003 through 2014 used DE405/LE405 (Standish, 1998). Optical, radar, laser, and spacecraft observations are analyzed to determine starting conditions for the numerical integration and values of fundamental constants such as the planetary masses and the length of the astronomical unit in meters. The reference frame for the basic ephemerides is the ICRF; the alignment onto this frame has an estimated accuracy of 1 − 2 milliarcseconds. As described above, the JPL DE440 ephemerides have been developed in a barycentric reference system using a barycentric coordinate time scale TDB.

The geocentric ephemerides of the Sun, Moon, and planets tabulated in this volume have been computed from the basic JPL ephemerides in a manner consistent with the rigorous reduction methods presented in Section B. For each planet, the ephemerides represent the position of the center of mass, which includes any satellites, not the center of figure or center of light. The precession-nutation model used in the computation of geocentric positions follows the IAU resolutions adopted in 2000 and 2006; see the Precession and Nutation Models section above.

Section A: Summary of Principal Phenomena

In 2006, the IAU agreed on resolution 5B, which provides the definition for "planet" and also introduces the new class of "dwarf planets". Following those resolutions, only eight solar system objects – Mercury, Venus, Earth, Mars, Jupiter, Saturn, Uranus, and Neptune – classify as planets. Along with Pluto, Ceres is now in the new class of dwarf planets.

The lunations given on page A1 are numbered in continuation of E.W. Brown's series, of which No. 1 commenced on 1923 January 16 (Brown, 1933).

The list of occultations of planets and bright stars by the Moon starting on page A2 gives the approximate times and areas of visibility for the planets, the dwarf planets Ceres and Pluto, the minor planets Pallas, Juno, and Vesta, and the five bright stars *Aldebaran*, *Antares*, *Regulus*, *Pollux* and *Spica*. However, due primarily to precession, it is known that *Pollux* has not, nor will be, occulted by the Moon for hundreds of years. Maps of the area of visibility of these occultations and for the minor planets published in Section G are available in *The Astronomical Almanac*. IOTA, the International Occultation Timing Association [8], is responsible for the predictions and reductions of timings of lunar occultations of stars by the Moon.

Times tabulated on page A3 for the stationary points of the planets are the instants at which the planet is stationary in apparent geocentric right ascension; but for elongations of the planets from the Sun, the tabular times are for the geometric configurations. From inferior conjunction to superior conjunction for Mercury or Venus, or from conjunction to opposition for a superior planet, the elongation from the Sun is west; from superior to inferior conjunction, or from opposition to conjunction, the elongation is east. Because planetary orbits do not lie exactly in the ecliptic plane, elongation passages from west to east or from east to west do not in general coincide with oppositions and conjunctions. For the selected dwarf planets Pluto and Ceres and minor planets Pallas, Juno and Vesta conjunctions, oppositions and stationary points are tabulated at the bottom of page A4 while their magnitudes, every 40 days, are given on page A5.

Dates of heliocentric phenomena are given on page A3. Since they are determined from the actual perturbed motion, these dates generally differ from dates obtained by using the elements of the mean orbit. The date on which the radius vector is a minimum may differ considerably from the date on which the heliocentric longitude of a planet is equal to the longitude of perihelion of the mean orbit. Similarly, when the heliocentric latitude of a planet is zero, the heliocentric longitude may not equal the longitude of the mean node.

The magnitudes and elongations of the planets are tabulated on pages A4–A5. For Mercury and Venus (page A4) they are tabulated every 5 days and the expressions for the magnitudes are given by Mallama and Hilton (2018). Magnitudes are not tabulated for a few dates around inferior and superior conjunction. In terms of the phase angle (ϕ) magnitudes are given for Mercury when $2.^\circ1 < \phi < 169.^\circ5$, and for Venus when $2.^\circ2 < \phi < 179.^\circ0$. For the other planets (page A5), the elongations and magnitudes are given every 10 days. These magnitude expressions are due to Mallama and Hilton (2018). Daily tabulations are given in Section E.

Configurations of the Sun, Moon and planets (pages A9–A11) are a chronological listing, with times to the nearest hour, of geocentric phenomena. Included are eclipses; lunar perigees, apogees and phases; phenomena in apparent geocentric longitude of the planets, dwarf planets Ceres and

Pluto and the minor planets Pallas, Juno and Vesta; times when these planets are stationary in right ascension and when the geocentric distance to Mars is a minimum; and geocentric conjunctions in apparent right ascension of the planets with the Moon, with each other, and with the five bright stars *Aldebaran*, *Regulus*, *Spica*, *Pollux* and *Antares*, provided these conjunctions are considered to occur sufficiently far from the Sun to permit observation. Thus conjunctions in right ascension are excluded if they occur within 20° of the Sun for Uranus and Neptune; 15° for the Moon, Mars and Saturn; within 10° for Venus and Jupiter; and within approximately 10° for Mercury, depending on Mercury's brightness. For Venus the occasion of its greatest illuminated extent is included. The occurrence of occultations of planets and bright stars is indicated by "Occn."; the areas of visibility are given in the list on page A2 while the maps are available in *The Astronomical Almanac*. Geocentric phenomena differ from the actually observed configurations by the effects of the geocentric parallax at the place of observation, which for configurations with the Moon may be quite large.

The explanation for the tables of sunrise and sunset, twilight, moonrise and moonset is given on page A12; examples are given on page A13.

Eclipses

The elements and circumstances are computed according to Bessel's method from apparent right ascensions and declinations of the Sun and Moon based on the JPL ephemerides DE440. Semidiameters of the Sun and Moon used in the calculation of eclipses do not include irradiation. Given the uncertainty of the radius of the Sun and the need to use a value at an appropriate optical depth, the adopted semidiameter of the Sun at unit distance is 15′ 59″.64 from the IAU (1976) Astronomical Constants (IAU, 1977). The apparent semidiameter of the Moon is equal to arcsin(k sin π), where π is the Moon's horizontal parallax and k is an adopted constant. In 1982, the IAU adopted $k = 0.272\,5076$ (IAU, 1983, pp. 51–53), corresponding to the mean radius of the Watts' datum (Watts, 1963) as determined by observations of occultations and to the adopted radius of the Earth. Corrections to the ephemerides, if any, are noted in the beginning of the eclipse section.

In calculating lunar eclipses, the radius of the geocentric shadow of the Earth is increased by one-fiftieth part to allow for the effect of the atmosphere. Refraction is neglected in calculating solar and lunar eclipses. Because the circumstances of eclipses are calculated for the surface of the ellipsoid, refraction is not included in Besselian elements. For local predictions, corrections for refraction are unnecessary; they are required only in precise comparisons of theory with observation in which many other refinements are also necessary.

Descriptions of the maps and use of Besselian elements are given on pages A78–A83, while maps of the areas of visibility are available in *The Astronomical Almanac*.

Section B: Timescales and Coordinate Systems

Calendar

Over extended intervals civil time is ordinarily reckoned according to conventional calendar years and adopted historical eras; in constructing and regulating civil calendars and fixing ecclesiastical calendars, a number of auxiliary cycles and periods are used. In particular the Islamic calendar printed is determined from an algorithm that approximates the lunar cycle and is independent of location. In practice the dates of Islamic fasts and festivals are determined by an actual sighting of the appropriate new crescent moon.

To facilitate chronological reckoning, the system of Julian day (JD) numbers maintains a continuous count of astronomical days, beginning with JD 0 on 1 January 4713 B.C., Julian proleptic calendar. Julian day numbers for the current year are given on page B3 and in the Universal and Sidereal Times pages, B13–B20, and the Universal Time and Earth rotation angle table on pages

B21–B24. To determine JD numbers for other years on the Gregorian calendar, consult the Julian Day Number tables on pages K2–K5.

Note that the Julian day begins at noon, whereas the calendar day begins at the preceding midnight. Thus the Julian day system is consistent with astronomical practice before 1925, with the astronomical day being reckoned from noon. The Julian date should include a specification as to the time scale being used, e.g., JD 245 1545.0 TT or JD 245 1545.5 UT1.

At the bottom of pages B4–B5, dates are given for various chronological cycles, eras, and religious calendars. Note that the beginning of a cycle or era is an instant in time; the date given is the Gregorian day on which the period begins. Religious holidays, unlike the beginning of eras, are not instants in time but typically run an entire day. The tabulated date of a religious festival is the Gregorian day on which it is celebrated. When converting to other calendars whose days begin at different times of day (*e.g.*, sunset rather than midnight), the convention utilized is to tabulate the day that contains noon in both calendars.

For a discussion on time scales, see page L3 of this section.

Universal and Sidereal Times and Earth Rotation Angle

The tabulations of Greenwich mean sidereal time (GMST) at 0^{h} UT1 are calculated from the defining relation between the Earth rotation angle (ERA), which is a function of UT1, and the accumulated precession (P03, see reference above) in right ascension, which is a function of TDB or TT (see pages B8 and L3).

The tabulations of Greenwich apparent sidereal time (GAST, or GST as it is designated in the papers above), is calculated from ERA and the equation of the origins. The latter is a function of the CIO locator s and precession and nutation (see Capitaine and Wallace (2006) and Wallace and Capitaine (2006)). This formulation ensures that whichever paradigm is used, equinox or CIO based, the resulting hour angles will be identical. Greenwich mean and apparent sidereal times and the equation of the equinoxes are tabulated on pages B13–B20, while ERA and equation of the origins are tabulated on pages B21–B24.

The IAU SOFA library has been used in the software that has generated the data in this section. The code is available from the IAU Standards Of Fundamental Astronomy (SOFA) website [3] and contains code for all the fundamental quantities related to various systems (e.g. IAU 2006, IAU 2000).

Bias, Precession and Nutation

The report of the IAU Working Group on Precession and the Ecliptic (WGPE) (Hilton et al., 2006) is implemented in this section. Table 1 of this report gives a useful list of "The polynomial coefficients for the precession angles". The WGPE adopted the precession theory designated P03 (Capitaine et al., 2003). The papers of Capitaine and Wallace (2006) and Wallace and Capitaine (2006) have also been used. The WGPE stated that the choice of the precession parameters should be left to the user. It should be noted that the effect of the frame bias (see page B50), the offset of the ICRS from the J2000.0 system, is not related to precession. However, the Fukushima-Williams angles (see page B56), which are used by SOFA, and the series method (see page B46) of calculating the ICRS-to-date matrix, have the frame bias offset included. Chapter 5 of the IERS (2010), available from their website [5] , describes the ITRS to GCRS conversion. In addition to updated precession angles, the WGPE report includes updates to Greenwich mean sidereal time and other related quantities.

The formulae given on page B54 using the precessional constants M, N, a, b, c and c' for the reduction of precession that transform positions and orbital elements from and to J2000.0 are approximate. For the position formulae (α, δ, λ, β) they are accurate to $0\overset{\prime\prime}{.}5$ within half a century of

J2000.0 and to $1''$ within one century of J2000.0. For the orbital element formulae, they are accurate to $0''.5$ within half a century of J2000.0 and to $1''.5$ within one century of J2000.0. These differences were found, in the case of transforming positions, by comparing values of right ascension such that $0^\circ \leq \alpha \leq 360^\circ$ in steps of 30° and declination such that $-75^\circ \leq \alpha \leq +75^\circ$ in steps of 5° every 10 days. In the case of transforming orbital elements the differences were found by comparing values for each of the planets every 10 days.

The formulae given at the bottom of the page B54 which are for the approximate reduction from the mean equinox and equator or ecliptic of the middle of the year (e.g. mean places of stars) to a date within the year (i.e.$-0.5 \leq \tau \leq +0.5$) were compared daily with a similar range of positions as above. These formulae use the annual rates m, n, p, π for the middle of the year, which are given at the top of the following page. The years analyzed were 1950 to 2050 and the formulae are accurate to $0''.002$ for right ascension and declination and accurate to $0''.006$ for ecliptic longitude and latitude. All these traditional approximate formulae break down near the poles.

Reduction of Celestial Coordinates

Formulae and methods are given showing the various stages of the reduction from an International Celestial Reference System (ICRS) position to an "of date" position consistent with the IAU 2012 resolution B2 (IAU, 2015). This reduction may be achieved either by using the long-standing equinox approach or the CIO-based method, thus generating apparent or intermediate places, respectively. The examples also show the calculation of Greenwich hour angle using GAST or ERA as appropriate. The matrices for the transformation from the GCRS to the "of date" position for each method are tabulated on pages B30–B45. The Earth's position and velocity components (tabulated on pages B76-B83) are extracted from the JPL ephemeris DE440, which is described on page L5.

The determination of latitude using the position of Polaris or σ Octantis may be performed using the methods and tables on pages B87-B92.

Section C: The Sun

The formulae for the Sun's orbital elements found on page C1 — the geometric mean longitude (λ), the mean longitude of perigee (ϖ), the mean anomaly (l') and the eccentricity (e) — are computed using the values from Simon et al. (1994): λ, the expression $\lambda = F + \Omega - D$ is used where F and D are the Delaunay arguments found in § 3.5b and Ω is the longitude of the Moon's node found in § 3.4 3.b; the expression $\varpi = \lambda - l'$ is used, where l' is taken from § 3.5b; e is taken directly from § 5.8.3. Mean obliquity, ε, is from Capitaine, Wallace, and Chapront (2003), Eq. 39 with ε_0 from Eq. 37. Rates for these mean orbital elements are the time derivatives of the above expressions.

The lengths of the principal years are computed using the rates of the orbital elements as describe in the previous paragraph. They are:

- Tropical year: the period of time for the ecliptic longitude of the Sun to increase 360 degrees. The tropical year is then $360^\circ/\dot{\lambda}$.
- Sidereal year: the period of revolution of the Earth around the Sun in a fixed reference frame, computed as $360^\circ/(\dot{\lambda} - \dot{P})$ where $\dot{P}$ is the precession rate found in Simon et al. (1994), Eq. 5.
- Anomalistic year: the period between successive passages of the Earth through perihelion; it is computed as $360^\circ/\dot{l}'$.
- Eclipse year: the period between successive passages of the Sun—as seen from the geocenter—through the same lunar node. The mean eclipse year is $360^\circ/(\dot{\lambda} - \dot{\Omega})$.

The coefficients for the equation of time formula are computed using Smart (1956), § 90; in that formula the value for L is the same as λ (explained above) but corrected for aberration and rounded for ease of computation.

The rotation elements listed on page C3 are due to Carrington (1863). The synodic rotation numbers tabulated on page C4 are in continuation of Carrington's Greenwich photoheliographic series of which Number 1 commenced on November 9, 1853.

Low precision formulae for the Sun are given on page C5. The position are apparent places; that is, they are given with respect to the equator and equinox of date.

The JPL DE440 ephemeris, which is described on page L5, is the basis of the various tabular data for the Sun on pages C6–C25. Given the uncertainty of the radius of the Sun and the need to use a value at an appropriate optical depth, the value of the equatorial radius of the Sun used throughout this almanac is the IAU 1976 value (IAU, 1977).

Daily geocentric coordinates of the Sun are given on the even pages of C6–C20; the tabular argument is Terrestrial Time (TT). The ecliptic longitudes and latitudes are referred to the mean equinox and ecliptic of date. These values are geometric, that is they are not antedated for light-time, aberration, etc. The apparent equatorial coordinates, right ascension and declination, are referred to the true equator and equinox of date and are antedated for light-time and have aberration applied. The true geocentric distance is given in astronomical units and is the value at the tabular time; that is, the values are not antedated.

Daily physical ephemeris data are found on the odd pages of C7–C21 and are computed using the techniques outlined in *The Explanatory Supplement to the Astronomical Almanac* (Urban and Seidelmann, 2012); the tabular argument is TT. The solar rotation parameters are from *Report of the IAU Group on Cartographic Coordinates and Rotational Elements: 2015* (Archinal et al., 2018); the data are based on Carrington (1863). Prior to *The Astronomical Almanac* for 2009, neither light-time correction nor aberration were applied to the solar rotation because they were presumably already in Carrington's meridian. Since the Earth-Sun distance is relatively constant, this is possible only for the Sun. At the 2006 IAU General Assembly, the Working Group on Cartographic Coordinates and Rotational Elements decided to make the physical ephemeris computations for the Sun consistent with the other major solar system bodies. The W_0 value for the Sun was "foredated" by about 499s; using the new value, the computation must take into account the light travel time. To further unify the process with other solar system objects, aberration is now explicitly corrected. Differences between the pre-2009 technique and the current recommendation are negligible at the Earth; for *The Astronomical Almanac*, differences of one in the least significant digit are occasionally seen in P, B_0 and L_0 with no other values being affected.

The Sun's daily ephemeris transit times are given on the odd pages of C7–C21. An ephemeris transit is the passage of the Sun across the *ephemeris meridian*, defined as a fictitious meridian that rotates independently of the Earth at the uniform rate. The ephemeris meridian is 1.002738 $\times \Delta T$ east of the Greenwich meridian.

Geocentric rectangular coordinates, in au, are given on pages C22–C25. These are referred to the ICRS axes, which are within a few tens of milliarcseconds of the mean equator and equinox of J2000.0. The time argument is TT and the coordinates are geometric, that is there is no correction for light-time, aberration, etc.

Section D: The Moon

The geocentric and physical ephemerides of the Moon are based on the JPL DE440 numerical integration described on page L5, with the tabular argument being TT. Additional formulae and data pertaining to the Moon are given on pages D1–D5 and D22.

For high precision calculations, a polynomial ephemeris (ASCII or PDF) is available at *The Astronomical Almanac*, along with the necessary procedures for its evaluation. Daily apparent ecliptic latitude and longitude (to nearest second of arc) and apparent geocentric right ascension and declination (to $0.''1$) are given on the even numbered pages D6–D20. Although the tabular apparent right ascension and declination are antedated for light-time, the true distance and the horizontal parallax are the geometric values for the tabular time. The horizontal parallax is derived from $\arcsin(a_E/r)$, where r is the true distance and $a_E = 6378.1366$ km is the Earth's equatorial radius (see page K6).

The semidiameter s is computed from $s = \arcsin(R_M/r)$, where r is the true distance and $R_M = 1737.4$ km is the mean radius of the Moon (see page K7). The semidiameter is tabulated on odd pages D7–D21.

The values for the librations of the Moon are calculated using rigorous formulae. The optical librations are based on the mean lunar elements of Simon et al. (1994) while the total librations are computed from the DE440 rotation angles. The rotation angles have been transformed from the Principal Moment of Inertia system used in the JPL ephemeris to librations that are defined in the mean-Earth direction, mean pole of rotation system given in Section D, by means of specific rotations provided by Park et al. (2021) and Williams et al. (2013). The value of $1^\circ\ 32'\ 33''\!.6$ for the inclination of the mean lunar equator to the ecliptic (also given on page D2) has been taken from Newhall and Williams (1996). Since apparent coordinates of the Sun and Moon are used in the calculations, aberration is fully included, except for the inappreciable difference between the light-time from the Sun to the Moon and from the Sun to the Earth. A detailed description of this process can found in *NAO Technical Note*, No. 74 (Taylor, D. B. et al., 2010).

The selenographic coordinates of the Earth and Sun specify the points on the lunar surface where the Earth and Sun, respectively, are in the selenographic zenith. The selenographic longitude and latitude of the Earth are the total geocentric (optical and physical) librations with respect to the coordinate system in which the x-axis is the mean direction towards the geocenter and the z-axis is the mean pole of lunar rotation. When the longitude is positive, the mean central point is displaced eastward on the celestial sphere, exposing to view a region on the west limb. When the latitude is positive, the mean central point is displaced toward the south, exposing to view the north limb.

The tabulated selenographic colongitude of the Sun is the east selenographic longitude of the morning terminator. It is calculated by subtracting the selenographic longitude of the Sun from 90° or 450°. Colongitudes of 270°, 0°, 90° and 180° approximately correspond to New Moon, First Quarter, Full Moon and Last Quarter, respectively.

The position angles of the axis of rotation and the midpoint of the bright limb are measured counterclockwise around the disk from the north point. The position angle of the terminator may be obtained by adding 90° to the position angle of the bright limb before Full Moon and by subtracting 90° after Full Moon.

For precise reduction of observations, the tabular librations and position angle of the axis must be reduced to topocentric values via the formulae by Atkinson (1951) that are given on page D5.

Section E: Planets

Rotational elements on E5 and the mean equatorial radius, flattening and sidereal period of rotation, found on E6, are based on the Archinal et al. (2018), *Report of the IAU Working Group on Cartographic Coordinates and Rotational Elements: 2015*. This report contains tables giving the dimensions, directions of the north poles of rotation and the prime meridians of the planets, Pluto, some of the satellites, and asteroids.

The orientation of the pole of a planet is specified by the right ascension α_0 and declination δ_0 of the north pole, with respect to the ICRS. According to the IAU, the north pole is defined as the pole that lies on the north side of the invariable plane of the solar system. Because of precession and nutation of a planet's axis, α_0 and δ_0 may vary with time (see Table 1 of Archinal et al., 2018); values for the current year are given on page E5.

The apparent disk of an oblate planet is always elliptical, with an oblateness less than or equal to that of the planet itself, depending on the apparent tilt of the planet's axis. Archinal et al. (2018)

gives two values for the polar radii of Mars because there is a difference along its axis between its center of figure and center of mass.

Except for the Earth, the period of rotation is the time required for a point on the equator of the planet to twice cross the XY-plane of the ICRS. The length of the sidereal day is given for the Earth, because its equator is nearly coincident with the XY-plane (see B9). A negative sign indicates that the rotation is retrograde with respect to the pole that lies north of the invariable plane of the solar system. The period is measured in days of 86 400 SI seconds.

For the four gas giant planets, the apparent rate of rotation is a function of both latitude and distance from the center of mass. The primary rotation rate is defined by the periodicity of radio emissions, which are presumably modulated by the planet's internal magnetic field; this is referred to as "System III" rotation. For Jupiter, "System I" and "System II" rotations have also been defined, which correspond to the apparent rotations of the equatorial and mid-latitude cloud tops, respectively, in the visual band. For Neptune, the rotation is defined as "System II" which refers to observed features in the Neptunian atmosphere. Cassini spacecraft observations provide evidence that the variation in the radio emissions of Saturn are not anchored in its bulk, and show variation in its period on the order of 1% over a time span of several years (Gurnett et al., 2007). This casts doubt on the reliability of the current methods to predict Saturn's rotation parameters. The influence of Saturn's moon Enceladus may also be affecting the results.

The rotation rates of Uranus and Neptune are determined from the Voyager mission encounters in 1986 and 1989. The uncertainty of those rotation rates are large enough that the uncertainties in their rotation angles are greater than a complete rotation.

The physical and photometric data for planets on E6 include the geometric flattening, which is the ratio of the difference of the mean equatorial and polar radii to the equatorial radius from Table 4 of Archinal et al. (2018). The flattening of Mars, is calculated using the average polar radius.

The planetary masses include their atmospheres but not the masses of their satellites. They are calculated using the values for GM_S and the masses of the planet-satellite systems, found on K6, and the planet-satellite mass ratios found on pages F3 and F5.

The tabulated maximum angular diameter of planets is based on the equatorial diameter when the planet is at the tabulated minimum geocentric distance during the interval 1950-2050.

Konopliv et al. (2020) provides the coefficients of the potential for Mercury; Konopliv et al. (1999) provides those for Venus. The coefficients of the potential for the Earth and Moon are those used in constructing DE440 (Park et al., 2021), the planetary ephemeris used for this volume. Cheng et al. (2011) is the source for the Earth's J_2 and Pavlis et al. (2012) for its J_3 and J_4 values. Konopliv et al. (2016) provides the coefficients of the potential for Mars; SSD JPL (2020, internal document) those for Jupiter and Saturn; Jacobson (2014) those for Uranus; and Jacobson (2009) those for Neptune.

Mallama et al. (2017) provides the geometric albedos of the planets. It is the ratio of the illumination of a planet at zero phase angle to the illumination produced by a plane, perfectly white Lambert surface of the same radius and position as the planet. The quantity $V(1,0)$ is the visual magnitude of a planet reduced to a distance of 1 au from both the Sun and Earth and with phase angle zero. The $V(1,0)$ values on page E6 are taken from Mallama and Hilton (2018). V_0 is the magnitude at mean opposition.

The heliocentric and geocentric ephemerides of the planets are based on the numerical integration DE440 described on page L5. These data are given in TDB. The values for heliocentric positions and elements, and the geocentric coordinates are for the planet-satellite barycenters. The longitude of perihelion for both Venus and Neptune is given to a lower degree of precision because they have nearly circular orbits, so the longitude of perihelion is poorly defined.

The apparent right ascension and declination are antedated for light-time, but the true geocentric distance is the geometric distance at the tabular time.

The physical ephemerides of the planets are based on the fundamental solar system ephemerides DE440 described on page L5. The apparent equatorial and polar diameters are separately tabulated for planets with significant oblateness. The apparent visual magnitudes of the planets are calculated using the Mallama and Hilton (2018) algorithms.

- Mercury and Venus values are valid for a sub-range of possible phase angles (see page E3).
- The apparent magnitude of Mercury does not include variations from albedo markings which may cause variations up to approximately 0.08 magnitudes.
- The apparent magnitude of Mars includes a seasonal correction but does not include sub-longitude or dust storm corrections. These may cause variations up to approximately 0.10 magnitudes.
- The apparent magnitude of Saturn is for the combination of its disk and rings, but the surface brightness is for the disk only.

The tabulated latitudes and longitudes are planetographic.

All tabulated quantities in the physical ephemeris tables are corrected for light-time, so the given values apply to the disk that is visible at the tabular time. Except for planetographic longitudes, all tabulated quantities vary so slowly that they remain unchanged if the time argument is considered to be UT rather than TT. Conversion from TT to UT affects the tabulated planetographic longitudes by several tenths of a degree for all but Mercury and Venus.

Section F: Natural Satellites

The data given in Section F for the positions of the satellites at specific times in their orbits are intended only for search and identification, not for the exact comparison of theory with observation; they are calculated only to the accuracy sufficient for facilitating observations. The positions and reference planes for the satellite orbits are based on the individual theories cited below. They are corrected for light-time. The value of ΔT used to prepare the ephemerides is given on page F1.

Beginning with the 2013 edition of *The Astronomical Almanac*, the orbital data given for the planetary satellites of Mars, Jupiter (satellites I - XVI), Saturn (satellites I - IX), and Neptune (satellites I - VIII) in the table on pages F2 and F4 are given with respect to the local Laplace Plane. The Laplace Plane is an auxiliary concept convenient for describing the orbital plane evolution of a satellite in a nearly circular orbit within the "star - oblate planet - weightless satellite" setting, provided the orbit is not too close to polar. In an ideal situation where a planet is perfectly spherical and its satellite feels no influence from the Sun, the orbital plane of that satellite would be coplanar with the planet's equatorial plane with its normal vector parallel to the spin axis of the planet. In a real situation, however, planets are oblate and the gravitational influence of the Sun cannot be ignored. The oblateness of the planet and the gravitational influence of the Sun causes the satellite's orbital normal vector to precess in an elliptical pattern about another vector which serves as the normal vector to the Laplace Plane. For satellite orbits close to the planet, the Laplace Plane lies close to the planet's equatorial plane; for satellite orbits high above the planet, the Laplace Plane lies close the planet's equatorial to the planet's orbital plane.

Beginning with the 2006 edition of *The Astronomical Almanac*, a set of selection criteria has been instituted to determine which satellites are included in the table; those criteria appear on page F5. As a result, many newer satellites of Jupiter, Saturn, and Uranus have been included. However, some satellites that were included in previous editions have now been excluded. The following sources were used to update the data presented in this table: Jacobson et al. (1989); the Jupiter Planet Satellite and Moon Page at [9]; the JPL Planetary Satellite Mean Orbital Parameters at [10], and references therein; Nicholson (2008); Jacobson (2000); Owen, Jr. et al. (1991).

Ephemerides, elongation times, and phenomena for planetary satellites are computed using data from a mixed function solution for twenty short-period planetary satellite orbits presented in Taylor (1995). The printed apparent satellite orbits are projections of their true orbits in three dimensions onto the two dimensional plane of the sky. The time of greatest eastern (or northern) elongation of an orbit is when the separation between satellite and planet is at a maximum on the eastern (or northern) side of the orbit. Starting with the 2007 edition, the offset data generated are used to produce satellite diagrams for Mars, Jupiter, Uranus, and Neptune. Beginning with the 2010 edition the paths of the satellites are computed at six minute intervals for Mars, eighty minute intervals for Jupiter, eighty-one minute intervals for Uranus, and thirty-five minute intervals for Neptune. As a consequence of these choices, the paths of the satellites for these planets appear as dotted lines in the satellite diagrams. The new diagrams give a scale (in arcseconds) of the orbit of the satellites as seen from Earth. Approximate formulae for calculating differential coordinates of satellites are given with the relevant tables.

Satellites of Mars

The Phobos and Deimos ephemerides are computed via the orbital elements from Sinclair (1989).

Satellites of Jupiter

The ephemerides of Satellites I–IV are based on the theory presented in Lieske (1977), with constants from Arlot (1982).

Elongations of Satellite V are computed from circular orbital elements given in Sudbury (1969). The differential coordinates of Satellites VI–XIII are computed by numerical integration, using starting coordinates and velocities calculated at the U.S. Naval Observatory (Rohde and Sinclair, 1992).

The use of ".. .. .." for the Terrestrial Time of Superior Geocentric Conjunction data for satellites I–IV indicates times of the year when Jupiter is too close to the Sun for any conjunctions to be observed, which occurs when the angular separation between Jupiter and the Sun is less than 20 degrees.

The actual geocentric phenomena of Satellites I–IV, are not instantaneous. Since the tabulated times are for the middle of the phenomena, a satellite is usually observable after the tabulated time of eclipse disappearance (Ec D) and before the time of eclipse reappearance (Ec R). In the case of Satellite IV, the difference is sometimes quite large. Light curves of eclipse phenomena are discussed in Harris (1961).

To facilitate identification, approximate configurations of Satellites I–IV are shown in graphical form on pages facing the tabular ephemerides of the geocentric phenomena. Time is shown by the vertical scale, with horizontal lines denoting 0^{h} UT. For any time the curves specify the relative positions of the satellites in the equatorial plane of Jupiter. The width of the central band, which represents the disk of Jupiter, is scaled to the planet's equatorial diameter.

For eclipses, the points d of immersion into the shadow and points r of emersion from the shadow are shown pictorially at the foot of the right-hand pages for the superior conjunctions nearest the middle of each month. At the foot of the left-hand pages, rectangular coordinates of these points are given in units of the equatorial radius of Jupiter. The x-axis lies in Jupiter's equatorial plane, positive toward the east; the y-axis is positive toward the north pole of Jupiter. The subscript 1 refers to the beginning of an eclipse, subscript 2 to the end of an eclipse.

Galilean Satellites

The configuration of Galilean satellites and the tables of geocentric phenomena are supplied by the Institut de Mécanique Céleste et de Calcul des Éphémérides (IMCCE).

About every six years the Earth's orbit crosses the orbital planes of the four Galilean satellites. This results in a significant number of observable occultations and eclipses involving these satellites. These data were provided by Dr. Kaare Aksnes of the Institute for Theoretical Astrophysics in Oslo, Norway.

Satellites and Rings of Saturn

The apparent dimensions of the outer edge of ring A and the factors for computing relative dimensions of rings B and C were originally from Esposito et al. (1984). Observations from the Cassini spacecraft have provided updated values [11]. The appearance of the rings depends upon the Saturnicentric positions of the Earth and Sun. The ephemeris of the rings is corrected for light-time.

The positions of Mimas, Enceladus, Tethys and Dione are based upon orbital theories presented in Kozai (1957), elements from Taylor and Shen (1988), with mean motions and secular rates from Kozai (1957) and Garcia (1972). The positions of Rhea and Titan are based upon orbital theories given in Sinclair (1977) with elements from Taylor and Shen (1988), mean motions and secular rates by Garcia (1972). The theory and elements for Hyperion are from Taylor (1984). The theory for Iapetus is from Sinclair (1974) with additional terms from Harper et al. (1988) and elements from Taylor and Shen (1988). The orbital elements used for Phoebe are from Zadunaisky (1954).

For Satellites I–V times of eastern elongation are tabulated; for Satellites VI–VIII times of all elongations and conjunctions are tabulated. On the diagram of the orbits of Satellites I–VII, points of eastern elongation are marked "0^d". From the tabular times of these elongations the apparent position of a satellite at any other time can be marked on the diagram by setting off on the orbit the elapsed interval since last eastern elongation. For Hyperion, Iapetus, and Phoebe, ephemerides of differential coordinates are also included.

Solar perturbations are not included in calculating the tables of elongations and conjunctions, distances and position angles for Satellites I–VIII. For Satellites I–IV, the orbital eccentricity e is neglected.

Satellites and Rings of Uranus

Data for the Uranian rings are from NASA's Planetary Data System archive [12] and references presented there. Ephemerides of the satellites are calculated from orbital elements determined in Laskar and Jacobson (1987).

Satellites of Neptune

The ephemerides of Triton and Nereid are calculated from elements given in Jacobson (1990). The differential coordinates of Nereid are apparent positions with respect to the true equator and equinox of date.

Satellite of Pluto

The ephemeris of Charon is calculated from the elements given in Tholen (1985). The remaining satellites' mean opposition magnitudes (> 23.0) are deemed too faint for inclusion.

Section G: Dwarf Planets and Small Solar System Bodies

This section contains data on a selection of 5 dwarf planets, 92 minor planets and short period comets.

Astrometric positions for selected dwarf planets and minor planets are given daily at 0^h TT for 60 days on either side of an opposition occurring between January 1 of the current year and January 31 of the following year. Also given are the apparent visual magnitude and the time of ephemeris transit over the ephemeris meridian. The dates when the object is stationary in apparent right ascension are indicated by shading. It is occasionally possible for a stationary date to be outside the period tabulated. Linear interpolation is sufficient for the magnitude and ephemeris transit, but for the astrometric right ascension and declination second differences may be significant.

Astrometric ephemerides (right ascension and declination) of these objects are tabulated, so their position can be directly comparable with the catalogue positions of background stars in the same area of the sky, after the star positions are updated for proper motion and parallax.

Dwarf Planets

The dwarf planets are those acknowledged by the IAU in the year of production (see IAU website [13]). For the edition for 2021, these are the following objects: (1) Ceres, (134340) Pluto, (136108) Haumea, (136199) Eris and (136472) Makemake.

From those five, we currently provide more detailed information for Ceres, Pluto and Eris. Ceres and Pluto have been chosen due to their long observational history and the availability of high quality positions, which make the published ephemeris reliable. While Eris may be seen as the object which (historically) had a major influence on the process of reclassification within the solar system, it can also be targeted by amateur astronomers. In addition to these three objects, Makemake and Haumea are included in this list of dwarf planets, and their physical properties are tabulated.

Osculating elements are tabulated for ecliptic and equinox J2000.0 for Ceres, Pluto and Eris for three dates per year (100 day dates). For any of these three objects that are at opposition during the year, like the minor planets, an astrometric ephemeris is tabulated daily for a 120-day window centered on the opposition date, 60 days on either side of opposition. Two star charts are also provided, one showing the astrometric positions around opposition and the other the path during the year. The stars plotted with Ceres and any dwarf planet brighter than magnitude V=10.0 are from a hybrid catalogue (Urban, 2010 private communication) that was generated from the *Tycho 2 Catalogue* (Høg et al., 2000) and *Hipparcos Catalogue* (ESA, 1997). For other fainter dwarf planets (*i.e.*, trans-Neptunian objects), the stars that are plotted are taken from the NOMAD database (Zacharias et al., 2004). This selection of stars is related to the opposition magnitude of the particular dwarf planet and includes all those stars whose magnitudes are at least brighter than the opposition magnitude. Depending on the density of the stars, other selection criteria may be used. The magnitude range has thus been chosen to fit with each object and is given at the bottom of each chart. All of the charts show astrometric J2000.0 positions.

The astrometric positions of Pluto are based on the JPL DE440 ephemeris, while those of Ceres and Eris are based on data from JPL Horizons [14]. Pluto's positions based on data from JPL Horizons may differ significantly from those based on the JPL DE440 ephemeris. A physical ephemeris is also included for those dwarf planets for which reliable data are available; currently (1) Ceres and (134340) Pluto. The data are taken from Archinal et al. (2018). Basic physical properties are listed for all five dwarf planets. Data have been collected from several sources:

- Ceres: values as published in earlier editions of *The Astronomical Almanac*; mass as given in Konopliv et al. (2018)
- Pluto: values as published previously in Section E of the 2013 edition of *The Astronomical Almanac*; the minimum Earth distance has been taken from the JPL Small-Body Database [15]
- Eris: values as given in Brown et al. (2005); Brown (2008).
- Makemake: period of rotation from Heinze and de Lahunta (2009); see JPL Small-Body Database [15] and the IAU Minor Planet Center [16] for other parameters.
- Haumea: period of rotation from Lacerda et al. (2008); see JPL Small-Body Database [15] and the IAU Minor Planet Center [16] for other parameters.

The absolute visual magnitude at zero phase angle (H) and the slope parameter for magnitude (G) are taken from the Minor Planet Center database. For Ceres, the values are the same as used previously, and were taken from the Minor Planet Ephemerides produced by the Institute of Applied Astronomy, St. Petersburg.

For Pluto, the visual magnitude is that of the Pluto and Charon combined system as many photometric observations include a significant contribution from Charon. Predicting the apparent visual magnitude is difficult for several reasons. Pluto has significant, possibly dynamic, albedo markings. Its pole of rotation is close to the plane of the ecliptic. Finally, Pluto has been observed for less than half of its orbital period. Consequently, the values of H and G, taken from the Minor Planet Center database, may fluctuate from year to year.

Minor Planets

The 92 minor planets are divided into two sets. The main set of the fourteen largest minor planets are (2) Pallas, (3) Juno, (4) Vesta, (6) Hebe, (7) Iris, (8) Flora, (9) Metis, (10) Hygiea, (15) Eunomia, (16) Psyche, (52) Europa, (65) Cybele, (511) Davida, and (704) Interamnia. Their astrometric ephemerides are based on data from JPL Horizons [14]. These particular minor planets were chosen because they are large ($>$ 300 km in diameter), have well observed histories, and/or are the largest member of their taxonomic class. The remaining 78 minor planets constitute the set with opposition magnitudes < 11, or < 12 if the diameter ≥ 200 km. Their positions are also based on data from JPL Horizons [14]. The absolute visual magnitude at zero phase angle (H) and the slope parameter (G), which depends on the albedo, are from the Minor Planet Ephemerides produced by the Institute of Applied Astronomy, St. Petersburg. The purpose of the selection of objects is to encourage observation of the most massive, largest and brightest of the minor planets.

A chronological list of the opposition dates of all the objects is given together with their visual magnitude and apparent declination. Those oppositions printed in bold also have a sixty-day ephemeris around opposition. All phenomena (dates of opposition and dates of stationary points) are calculated to the nearest hour (UT1). It must be noted, as with phenomena for all objects, that opposition dates are determined from the apparent longitude of the Sun and the object, with respect to the mean ecliptic of date. Stationary points, on the other hand, are defined to occur when the rate of change of the apparent right ascension is zero.

Osculating orbital elements for all the minor planets are tabulated with respect to the ecliptic and equinox J2000.0 for, usually, a 400-day epoch. Also tabulated are the H and G parameters for magnitude and the diameters. The masses of most of the objects have been set to an arbitrary value of 1×10^{-12} $M_{\odot}$. The masses of 13 minor planets tabulated by Hilton (2002) have been used. However, the masses of Pallas and Vesta have been updated with the adopted IAU 2009 Best Estimates [17] which are taken from Pitjeva and Standish (2009).

Periodic Comets

The osculating elements for periodic comets returning to perihelion in the year have been supplied by Daniel W. E. Green, Department of Earth and Planetary Sciences, Harvard University, with collaboration from S. Nakano, Sumoto, Japan.

The innate inaccuracy of some of the elements of the Periodic Comets tabulated on the last page of section G can be more of a problem, particularly for those comets that have been observed for no more than a few months in the past (*i.e.*, those without a number in front of the P). It is important to note that elements for numbered comets may be prone to uncertainty due to non-gravitational forces that affect their orbits. In some cases, these forces have a degree of predictability. However, calculations of these non-gravitational effects can never be absolute, and their effects, in common with short-arc uncertainties, mainly affect the perihelion time.

Up-to-date elements of the comets currently observable may be found at the web site of the IAU Minor Planet Center [22].

Section H: Stars and Stellar Systems

Positions tabulated in Section H are barycentric (mean places) and in reference to the mean equator and equinox of J2025.5 = 2025 July 2.375 = JD 246 0858.875, except for the tables of ICRF radio sources which are in reference to the epoch 2015.0 = JD 245 7023.5. The positions of the ICRF radio sources, including Galactic aberration, provide a practical realization of the ICRS. When present, notes associated with a table are found on the table's last page.

Navigational Stars

The (new as of 2025) list of bright stars corresponds to the 173 navigational stars currently used in the Nautical Almanac.

Positions and proper motions are taken from the *Hipparcos Catalogue* and converted to epoch, equator, and equinox of the middle of the current year; radial velocities are included in the calculation where available. However, FK5 positions and proper motions are used for a few wide binary stars given the requirement for center of mass positions to generate their orbital positions. Orbital elements for these stars are taken from the *Sixth Catalog of Orbits of Visual Binary Stars* at [18]. See also the *Fifth Catalog of Orbits of Visual Binary Stars* (Hartkopf et al., 2001). Stars marked as spectroscopic binaries are those identified as such in the BSC.

The V magnitudes and color indices $B-V$ and $V-I$ are taken from the Hipparcos Catalogue. Spectral types were provided by W.P. Bidelman and updated by R.F. Garrison. Codes in the Notes column are explained at the end of the table (page H31). Stars marked as MK Standards are from either of the two spectral atlases listed above. Stars marked as MK Standards are from either of the two spectral atlases listed above. Stars marked as anchor points to the MK System are a subset of standard stars that represent the most stable points in the system (Garrison, 1994).

Photometric Standards

The spectrophotometric standard stars are suitable for the reduction of astronomical spectroscopic observations in the optical and ultraviolet wavelengths. As recommended by the IAU Standard Stars Working Group, data for the spectrophotometric standard stars listed here are taken from the European Southern Observatory's (ESO) site at [20] except for the positions taken from the NOMAD database as described above. Finding charts for the sources and explanation are found on the website.

The standards on the ESO list are from four sources. The ultraviolet standards are from the Hubble Space Telescope (HST) ultraviolet spectrophotometric standards which are based on International Ultraviolet Explorer (IUE) and optical spectra and calibrated by the primary white dwarf standards (Turnshek et al., 1990; Bohlin et al., 1990). The optical standards are based on Hale 5m observations in the 7 to 16 magnitude range (Oke, 1990) and CTIO observations of southern hemisphere secondary and tertiary standard stars (Hamuy et al., 1992, 1994). Some of the Hamuy standards were misidentified in the original reference and have since been corrected. Data for four white dwarf primary spectrophotometric standards in the 11–13 magnitude range based on model atmospheres and HST Faint Object Spectrograph (FOS) observations in 10Å to 3 microns are also included (Bohlin et al., 1995).

Radio Sources

Beginning in 2019, the fundamental reference system in astronomy, ICRS, is actualized by the second realization of the International Celestial Reference Frame, ICRF3 (see Fundamental Reference System section on page L2; IAU (2018), Res. B2). The ICRF3 contains positions for 4536 extragalactic sources, measured at 8.4 GHz, 303 of which, uniformly distributed on the sky, are identified as defining sources, which define the axes of the frame. Positions at 8.4 GHz are supplemented with positions of 824 sources at 24 GHz and 678 sources at 32 GHz. In all, 600 sources have three-frequency positions available. The positions were estimated independently at each of the frequencies to preserve the underlying astrophysical content. The frame is aligned onto the International Celestial Reference System to within the accuracy of ICRF3. Positions are reported for epoch 2015.0. High accuracy applications must apply a galactocentric acceleration of 0.0058 mas yr^{-1} for observations at other epochs. Individual source coordinates have a noise floor of 0.030 mas. The 303 defining sources are presented in the table. Positions of all ICRF3 sources are available at [4].

Section J: Lunarcentric Celestial Objects

Section J provides astronomical data for scientific operations on or near the Moon. All of the coordinates listed are based on the fundamental positions and velocities of solar system bodies, and the orientation of the Moon, provided by the Jet Propulsion Laboratory DE440 ephemeris (see pages L5-L6). The time scale for the tabulations is Barycentric Dynamical Time (TDB). Three types of data are provided. Pages J4-J39 list the apparent coordinates of the Sun and planets (including the Earth) at daily intervals with respect to the Lunar Celestial Reference System (LCRS), which is the lunar analog of the Geocentric Celestial Reference System (GCRS) that is the basis for the apparent coordinates of celestial bodies as seen from the Earth (see page L2). The coordinates listed are corrected for light-time, gravitational deflection of light, and aberration, as computed for a fictitious observer at the Moon's center of mass. Pages J40-J47 list the daily orientation angles of two Moon-body-fixed coordinate systems (i.e., systems that rotate with the Moon) with respect to the Barycentric Celestial Reference System (BCRS) axes. The angles are described on pages J2-J3; those on the left side of each page refer to the Principal Axis (PA) system and those on the right refer to the Mean Earth (ME) system, as described in Archinal et al. (2018). Pages J48-J53 list apparent topocentric coordinates — azimuth and angular altitude — for the bright planets and a few bright stars as would be seen by an observer at the lunar south pole, at 4-day intervals. The lunar south pole is here assumed to be at $Z = -1737.4$ km in the ME system.

Section K: Tables and Data

Astronomical constants are a topic that is in the purview of the IAU Working Group on Numerical Standards for Fundamental Astronomy [17]. At the 2009 XXVII GA, Resolution B2 on "Current Best Estimates of Astronomical Constants" was adopted. This list of constants (Luzum et al., 2011), modified by the re-definition of the astronomical unit, is tabulated in items 1 and 2 of pages K6–K7.

Resolution B2 passed at the IAU XXVIII General Assembly (2012), recommends

1. that the astronomical unit be redefined as a conventional unit of length equal to 149 597 870 700 m exactly, in agreement with the value adopted in the IAU 2009 Resolution B2,
2. that this definition of the astronomical unit be used with all time scales such as TCB, TDB, TCG, TT, etc.,
3. that the Gaussian gravitational constant k be deleted from the system of astronomical constants,
4. that the value of the solar mass parameter (previously known as the heliocentric gravitational constant), GM_S, be determined observationally in SI units, and
5. that the unique symbol "au" be used for the astronomical unit.

The NSFA, via their website at [17] will be keeping the list of "Current Best Estimates" up-to-date, together with detailed notes and references.

Given the uncertainty of the radius of the Sun and the need to use a value at an appropriate optical depth, the value of the equatorial radius of the Sun used throughout this almanac is that taken from the *Report of the IAU Working Group on Cartographic Coordinates and Rotational Elements: 2015* (Archinal et al., 2018).

The ΔT values provided on pages K8–K9 are not necessarily those used in the production of *The Astronomical Almanac* or its predecessors. They are tabulated primarily for those involved in historical research. Estimates of ΔT are derived from data published in Bulletins B and C of the International Earth Rotation and Reference Systems Service [21].

Since 2003, the pole is the Celestial Intermediate Pole. However, the coordinates of the celestial pole tabulated on page K10 are with respect to the celestial pole definition for the relevant year. The orientation of the ITRS is consistent with the former BIH system and the previous IPMS and ILS systems (1974-1987). Prior to 1988, values were taken from Circular D of the BIH, while since 1988 the values have been taken from the IERS Bulletin B.

Pages K11–K13, on "Reduction of Terrestrial Coordinates", which include information on the International Terrestrial Reference Frame [23], have been updated by G. Appleby, Head of the UK Space Geodesy Facility at Herstmonceux. At the 2018 IAU XXX GA, Resolution B1, "on Geocentric and International Terrestrial Reference Systems and Frames", was adopted. This resolution recommends that the ITRS be adopted as the preferred GTRS (Geocentric Terrestrial Reference System) for scientific and technical applications.

Section M: Glossary

The definitions in the glossary are composed by staff members of Her Majesty's Nautical Almanac Office and the US Naval Observatory's Astronomical Applications Department. Various astronomical dictionaries and encyclopedia are used to ensure correctness and to develop particular phrasing.

Definitions of some glossary entries contain terms that are defined elsewhere in the section. These are given in italics.

Entries marked (*OBSOLETE*) are no longer in common use and will be dropped beginning with the glossary in the 2025 edition of The Astronomical Almanac. Similarly, those marked (*Obsolete*) will be dropped beginning with the glossary in the 2026 edition of The Astronomical Almanac, and those marked (*obsolete*) will be dropped beginning with the glossary in the 2027 edition of *The Astronomical Almanac*.

The glossary is not intended to be a complete astronomical reference, but instead clarify terms used within *The Astronomical Almanac*.

References

[1]. USNO Astronomical Almanac Website
https://aa.usno.navy.mil/publications/asa.html .

[2]. USNO Vector Astrometry Software (NOVAS)
https://aa.usno.navy.mil/software/novas_info.html.

[3]. IAU Standards of Fundamental Astronomy (SOFA)
https://www.iausofa.org.

[4]. ICRS Product Center
https://hpiers.obspm.fr/icrs-pc/newwww/.

[5]. IERS Earth Orientation Data
https://www.iers.org/IERS/EN/DataProducts/EarthOrientationData/eop.html.

[6]. USNO Publications
https://aa.usno.navy.mil/publications/.

[7]. NIST note on UT1 NTP Time Dissemination
https://www.nist.gov/time-and-frequency-services/ut1-ntp-time-dissemination/.

[8]. The International Occultation Timing Association (IOTA)
http://lunar-occultations.com/iota.

[9]. Scott Sheppard's Jupiter Satellite Page
https://sites.google.com/carnegiescience.edu/sheppard/moons .

[10]. JPL Planetary Satellite Mean Orbital Parameters
https://ssd.jpl.nasa.gov/sats/elem/.

[11]. Saturnian Rings Fact Sheet
https://nssdc.gsfc.nasa.gov/planetary/factsheet/satringfact.html.

[12]. NASA's Planetary Data System Uranian Rings Page
https://pds-rings.seti.org/uranus/.

[13]. IAU, Pluto and the Developing Landscape of Our Solar System
https://www.iau.org/public/pluto/.

[14]. JPL Horizons
https://ssd.jpl.nasa.gov/horizons/app.html#/.

[15]. JPL Small-Body Database
https://ssd.jpl.nasa.gov/sb/.

[16]. IAU Minor Planet Center Dwarf Planets
https://www.minorplanetcenter.net/dwarf_planets/.

[17]. IAU Numerical Standards for Fundamental Astronomy (NSFA)
Please see https://iau-a3.gitlab.io/NSFA/index.html.

[18]. USNO Sixth Catalog of Orbits of Visual Binary Stars
https://crf.usno.navy.mil/wds-orb6?pageid=data-products-page/.

[19]. USNO Washington Double Star Catalog
https://crf.usno.navy.mil/wdstext.

[20]. ESO Optical and UV Spectrophotometric Standard Stars
https://www.eso.org/sci/observing/tools/standards/spectra.html.

[21]. IERS Conventions 2010
http://iers-conventions.obspm.fr/.

[22]. IAU Minor Planet Center Elements of Periodic Comets
https://www.minorplanetcenter.net/iau/Ephemerides/Comets/index.html.

[23]. ITRF 2020
https://itrf.ign.fr/en/solutions/itrf2020.

Aoki, S., H. Kinoshita, B. Guinot, G. H. Kaplan, D. D. McCarthy, and P. K. Seidelmann (1982). The New Definition of Universal Time. *Astronomy & Astrophysics* **105**, 359–361.

Archinal, B. A., C. H. Acton, M. F. A'Hearn, A. Conrad, G. J. Consolmagno, T. Duxbury, D. Hestroffer, J. L. Hilton, R. L. Kirk, S. A. Klioner, D. McCarthy, K. Meech, J. Oberst, J. Ping, P. K. Seidelmann, D. J. Tholen, P. C. Thomas, and I. P. Williams (2018). Report of the IAU Working Group on Cartographic Coordinates and Rotational Elements: 2015. *Celestial Mechanics and Dynamical Astronomy* **130**, doi:10.1007/s10569–017–9805–5.

Arlot, J. -E. (1982). New Constants for Sampson-Lieske Theory of the Galilean Satellites of Jupiter. *Astronomy & Astrophysics* **107**, 305–310.

Atkinson, R. d'E. (1951). The Computation of Topocentric Librations. *Monthly Notices of the Royal Astronomical Society* **111**, 448–454.

Baars, J. W. M., R. Genzel, I. I. K. Pauliny-Toth, and A. Witzel (1977). The Absolute Spectrum of CAS A; An Accurate Flux Density Scale and a Set of Secondary Calibrators. *Astronomy & Astrophysics* **61**, 99–106.

Bird, A. J., A. Bazzano, L. Bassani, F. Capitanio, M. Fiocchi, A. B. Hill, A. Malizia, V. A. McBride, S. Scaringi, V. Sguera, J. B. Stephen, P. Ubertini, A. J. Dean, F. Lebrun, R. Terrier, M. Renaud, F. Mattana, D. Götz, J. Rodriguez, G. Belanger, R. Walter, and C. Winkler (2010). The Fourth IBIS/ISGRI Soft Gamma-ray Survey Catalog. *The Astrophysical Journal Supplement Series* **186**, 1–9.

Bohlin, R. C., L. Colina, and D. S. Finley (1995). White Dwarf Standard Stars: G191-B2B, GD 71, GD 153, HZ 43. *Astronomical Journal* **110**, 1316–1325.

Bohlin, R. C., A. W. Harris, A. V. Holm, and C. Gry (1990). The Ultraviolet Calibration of the Hubble Space Telescope. IV. Absolute IUE Fluxes of Hubble Space Telescope Standard Stars. *Astrophysical Journal Supplement Series* **73**, 413–439.

Bradt, H. V. D. and J. E. McClintock (1983). The Optical Counterparts of Compact Galactic X-ray Sources. *Annual Review of Astronomy & Astrophysics* **21**, 13–66.

Brown, E. W. (1933). Theory and Tables of the Moon: The Motion of the Moon, 1923-31. *Monthly Notices of the Royal Astronomical Society* **93**, 603–619.

Brown, M. E. (2008). The Largest Kuiper Belt Objects. In M. A. Barucci, H. Boehnhardt, D. P. Cruikshank, A. Morbidelli, and R. Dotson (Eds.), *The Solar System Beyond Neptune*, pp. 335–344.

Brown, M. E., C. A. Trujillo, and D. L. Rabinowitz (2005). Discovery of a Planetary-sized Object in the Scattered Kuiper Belt. *The Astrophysical Journal* **635**, L97–L100.

Capitaine, N. and P. T. Wallace (2006). High Precision Methods for Locating the Celestial Intermediate Pole and Origin. *Astronomy & Astrophysics* **450**, 855–872.

Capitaine, N., P. T. Wallace, and J. Chapront (2003). Expressions for IAU 2000 Precession Quantities. *Astronomy & Astrophysics* **412**, 567–586.

Capitaine, N., P. T. Wallace, and J. Chapront (2005). Improvement of the IAU 2000 Precession Model. *Astronomy & Astrophysics* **432**, 355–367.

Capitaine, N., P. T. Wallace, and D. D. McCarthy (2003). Expressions to Implement the IAU 2000 Definition of UT1. *Astronomy & Astrophysics* **406**, 1135–1149.

Carretta, E. and R. G. Gratton (1997). Abundances for Globular Cluster Giants. I. Homogeneous Metallicities for 24 Clusters. *Astronomy & Astrophysics Supplement* **121**, 95–112.

Carrington, R. C. (1863). *Observations of the Spots on the Sun: From November 9, 1853, to March 24, 1861, Made at Redhill.* London: Williams and Norgate.

Charlot, P., C. S. Jacobs, D. Gordon, S. Lambert, A. de Witt, J. Böhm, A. L. Fey, R. Heinkelmann, E. Skurikhina, O. Titov, E. F. Arias, S. Bolotin, G. Bourda, C. Ma, Z. Malkin, A. Nothnagel, D. Mayer, D. S. MacMillan, T. Nilsson, and R. Gaume (2021). The Third Realization of the International Celestial Reference Frame by Very Long Baseline Interferometry. *Astronomy & Astrophysics* **644**, A159.

Cheng, M. K., J. C. Ries, and B. D. Tapley (2011). Variations of the Earth's Figure Axis from Satellite Laser Ranging and GRACE. *Journal of Geophysical Research* **116**, doi:10.1029/2010JB000850.

de Vaucouleurs, G. (1959). Classification and Morphology of External Galaxies. *Handbuch der Physik* **53**, 275–310.

de Vaucouleurs, G. (1963). Revised Classification of 1500 Bright Galaxies. *Astrophysical Journal Supplement* **8**, 31–97.

de Vaucouleurs, G. and H. D. Ables (1968). Integrated Magnitudes and Color Indices of the Fornax Dwarf Galaxy. *Astrophysical Journal* **151**, 105–116.

de Vaucouleurs, G., A. de Vaucouleurs, H. Corwin, R. J. Buta, G. Paturel, and P. Fouque (1991). *Third Reference Catalogue of Bright Galaxies (RC3).* New York: Springer-Verlag.

Dias, W. S., B. S. Alessi, A. Moitinho, and J. R. D. Lepine (2002). New Catalog of Optically Visible Open Clusters and Candidates. *Astronomy & Astrophysics* **389**, 871–873.

Downes, R., R. F. Webbink, and M. M. Shara (1997). A Catalog and Atlas of Cataclysmic Variables-Second Edition. *Publications of the Astronomical Society of the Pacific* **109**, 345–440.

ESA (1997). *The Hipparcos and Tycho Catalogues.* Noordwijk, Netherlands: European Space Agency. SP-1200 (17 volumes).

Esposito, L. W., J. N. Cuzzi, J. H. Holberg, E. A. Marouf, G. L. Tyler, and C. C. Porco (1984). *Saturn*, Chapter Saturn's Rings: Structure, Dynamics, and Particle Properties, pp. 463–545. Tucson, AZ: University of Arizona Press.

Folkner, W. M., J. G. Williams, D. H. Boggs, R. S. Park, and P. Kuchynka (2014). The Planetary and Lunar Ephemerides DE430 and DE431. *Interplanetary Network Progress Report* 42-196, 1–81.

Forman, W., C. Jones, L. Cominsky, P. Julien, S. Murray, G. Peters, H. Tananbaum, and R. Giacconi (1978). The Fourth Uhuru Catalog of X-ray Sources. *Astrophysical Journal Supplement Series* **38**, 357–412.

Fricke, W., H. Schwan, T. Lederle, U. Bastian, R. Bien, G. Burkhardt, B. Du Mont, R. Hering, R. Jährling, H. Jahreiß, S. Röser, H. M. Schwerdtfeger, and H. G. Walter (1988). *Fifth Fundamental Catalogue Part I.* Heidelberg: Veroeff. Astron. Rechen-Institut.

Garcia, H. A. (1972). The Mass and Figure of Saturn by Photographic Astrometry of Its Satellites. *Astronomical Journal* **77**, 684–691.

Garrison, R. F. (1994). A Hierarchy of Standards for the MK Process. *Astronomical Society of the Pacific Conference Series* **60**, 3–14.

Gordon, D. (2018). ICRF3: A New Realization of the International Celestial Reference Frame. *American Geophysical Union, Fall Meeting 2018*, G42A–01.

Gurnett, D. A., A. M. Persoon, W. S. Kurth, J. B. Groene, T. F. Averkamp, M. K. Dougherty, and D. J. Southwood (2007). The Variable Rotation Period of the Inner Region of Saturn's Plasma Disk. *Science* **316**, 442–445.

Hamuy, M., N. Suntzeff, S. R. Heathcote, A. R. Walker, P. Gigoux, and M. M. Phillips (1994). Southern Spectrophotometric Standards, 2. *Publications of the Astronomical Society of the Pacific* **106**, 566–589.

Hamuy, M., A. R. Walker, N. B. Suntzeff, P. Gigoux, S. R. Heathcote, and M. M. Phillips (1992). Southern Spectrophotometric Standards. *Publications of the Astronomical Society of the Pacific* **104**, 533–552.

Harper, D., D. B. Taylor, A. T. Sinclair, and K. X. Shen (1988). The Theory of the Motion of Iapetus. *Astronomy & Astrophysics* **191**, 381–384.

Harris, D. L. (1961). Photometry and Colorimetry of Planets and Satellites. In G. P. Kuiper and B. M. Middlehurst (Eds.), *Planets and Satellites*, pp. 327–340. Chicago, IL.

Harris, W. E. (1996). A Catalog of Parameters for Globular Clusters in the Milky Way. *Astronomical Journal* **112**, 1487–1488.

Hartkopf, W. I., B. D. Mason, and C. E. Worley (2001). The 2001 US Naval Observatory Double Star CD-ROM. II. The Fifth Catalog of Orbits of Visual Binary Stars. *Astronomical Journal* **122**, 3472–3479.

Healey, S. E., R. W. Romani, G. B. Taylor, E. M. Sadler, R. Ricci, T. Murphy, J. S. Ulvestad, and J. N. Winn (2007). CRATES: An All-Sky Survey of Flat-Spectrum Radio Sources. *The Astrophysical Journal Supplement Series* **171**, 61–71.

Heinze, A. N. and D. de Lahunta (2009). The Rotation Period and Light-Curve Amplitude of Kuiper Belt Dwarf Planet 136472 Makemake (2005 FY9). *Astronomical Journal* **138**, 428–438.

Hilton, J. L. (2002). Asteroid Masses and Densities. In *Asteroids III*, pp. 103–112.

Hilton, J. L., N. Capitaine, J. Chapront, J. M. Ferrandiz, A. Fienga, T. Fukushima, J. Getino, P. Mathews, J. L. Simon, M. Soffel, J. Vondrak, P. T. Wallace, and J. Williams (2006). Report of the International Astronomical Union Division I Working Group on Precession and the Ecliptic. *Celestial Mechanics and Dynamical Astronomy* **94**, 351–367.

Hirshfeld, A. and R. W. Sinnott (1997). *Sky catalogue 2000.0. Volume 2: Double Stars, Variable Stars and Nonstellar Objects.* Cambridge, UK: Cambridge University Press.

Hodge, P. W. (1977). The Structure and Content of NGC 6822. *Astrophysical Journal Supplement* **33**, 69–82.

Hodge, P. W. and D. W. Smith (1974). The Structure of the Fornax Dwarf Galaxy. *Astrophysical Journal* **188**, 19–26.

Hoffleit, E. D. and W. Warren (1991). *The Bright Star Catalogue (5th edition).* New Haven: Yale University Observatory.

Høg, E., C. Fabricius, V. V. Makarov, S. Urban, T. Corbin, G. Wycoff, U. Bastian, P. Schwekendiek, and A. Wicenec (2000). The Tycho-2 Catalog of the 2.5 Million Brightest Stars. *Astronomy & Astrophysics* **355**, L27–L30.

IAU (1977). Report of Joint Meetings of Commissions 4, 8 and 31 on the New System of Astronomical Constants. In *Transactions of the International Astronomical Union*, Volume XVIB, Dordrecht, Holland. Reidel.

IAU (1983). In R. M. West (Ed.), *Transactions of the International Astronomical Union*, Volume XVIIIB, Dordrecht, Holland. Reidel. Proc. 18th General Assembly, Patras, 1982.

IAU (1999). In J. Andersen (Ed.), *Transactions of the International Astronomical Union*, Volume XXIIIB, Dordrecht. Kluwer. Proc. 23rd General Assembly, Kyoto, 1997.

IAU (2001). In H. Rickman (Ed.), *Transactions of the International Astronomical Union*, Volume XXIVB, San Francisco. Astronomical Society of the Pacific. Proc. 24th General Assembly, Manchester, 2000.

IAU (2008). In K. van der Hucht (Ed.), *Transactions of the International Astronomical Union*, Volume XXVIB, San Francisco. Astronomical Society of the Pacific. Proc. 26th General Assembly, Prague, 2006.

IAU (2015). In T. Montmerle (Ed.), *Transactions of the International Astronomical Union*, Volume XXVIIIB, Cambridge, UK. Cambridge University Press. Proc. 28th General Assembly, Beijing, China, 2012.

IAU (2018). In T. Lago (Ed.), *Transactions of the International Astronomical Union*, Volume XXXB. Proc. 30th General Assembly, Vienna, Austria, 2018.

Ibata, R. A., R. F. G. Wyse, G. Gilmore, M. J. Irwin, and N. B. Suntzeff (1997). The Kinematics, Orbit, and Survival of the Sagittarius Dwarf Spheroidal Galaxy. *Astrophysical Journal* **113**, 634–655.

IERS (2010). Conventions (2010). Technical Note 36, International Earth Rotation Service, Frankfurt am Main. Verlag des Bundesamts für Kartographie und Geodäsie, G. Petit and B. Luzum (Eds.).

Iess, L., W. M. Folkner, D. Durante, M. Parisi, Y. Kaspi, E. Galanti, T. Guillot, W. B. Hubbard, D. J. Stevenson, J. D. Anderson, D. R. Buccino, L. G. Casajus, A. Milani, R. Park, P. Racioppa, D. Serra, P. Tortora, M. Zannoni, H. Cao, R. Helled, J. I. Lunine, Y. Miguel, B. Militzer, S. Wahl, J. E. P. Connerney, S. M. Levin, and S. J. Bolton (2018). Measurement of Jupiter's Asymmetric Gravity Field. *Nature* **555**, 220–222.

Iess, L., B. Militzer, Y. Kaspi, P. Nicholson, D. Durante, P. Racioppa, A. Anabtawi, E. Galanti, W. Hubbard, M. J. Mariani, P. Tortora, S. Wahl, and M. Zannoni (2019). Measurement and Implications of Saturn's Gravity Field and Ring Mass. *Science* **364**, 1046–1054.

Irwin, M. and D. Hatzidimitriou (1995). Structural Parameters for the Galactic Dwarf Spheroidals. *Monthly Notices of the Royal Astronomical Society* **277**, 1354–1378.

Jacobson, R. A. (1990). The Orbits of the Satellites of Neptune. *Astronomy & Astrophysics* **231**, 241–250.

Jacobson, R. A. (2000). The Orbits of the Outer Jovian Satellites. *Astronomical Journal* **120**, 2679–2686.

Jacobson, R. A. (2009). The Orbits of the Neptunian Satellites and the Orientation of the Pole of Neptune. *Astronomical Journal* **137**, 4322–4329.

Jacobson, R. A. (2014). The Orbits of the Uranian Satellites and Rings, the Gravity Field of the Urania System, and the Orientation of the Pole of Uranus. *Astronomical Journal* **148**, 76.

Jacobson, R. A., S. P. Synnott, and J. K. Campbell (1989). The Orbits of the Satellites of Mars from Spacecraft and Earthbased Observations. *Astronomy & Astrophysics* **225**, 548–554.

Jarrett, T. H., T. Chester, R. Cutri, S. Schneider, M. Skrutskie, and J. P. Huchra (2000). 2MASS Extended Source Catalog: Overview and Algorithms. *Astronomical Journal* **119**, 2498–2531.

Jordi, C., M. Gebran, J. M. Carrasco, J. de Bruijne, H. Voss, C. Fabricius, J. Knude, A. Vallenari, R. Kohley, and A. Mora (2010). *Gaia* Broad Band Photometry. *Astronomy & Astrophysics* **523**, A48.

Kaplan, G. H. (2005). The IAU Resolutions on Astronomical Reference Systems, Time Scales, and Earth Rotation Models : Explanation and Implementation. *U.S. Naval Observatory Circulars* **179**.

Keenan, P. C. and R. C. McNeil (1976). *Atlas of Spectra of the Cooler Stars: Types G, K, M, S, and C.* Ohio: Ohio State University Press.

Kholopov, P. N., N. N. Samus, M. S. Frolov, V. P. Goranskij, N. A. Gorynya, N. N. Kireeva, N. P. Kukarkina, N. E. Kurochkin, G. I. Medvedeva, and N. B. Perova (1996). *General Catalogue of Variable Stars, 4th edition.* Moscow: Nauka Publishing House.

Konopliv, A. S., W. B. Banerdt, and W. L. Sjogren (1999). Venus Gravity: 180th Degree and Order Model. *Icarus* **139**, 3–18.

Konopliv, A. S., R. S. Park, and A. I. Ermakov (2020). The Mercury gravity field, orientation, love number, and ephemeris from the MESSENGER radiometric tracking data. *Icarus* **335**, 113386.

Konopliv, A. S., R. S. Park, and W. M. Folkner (2016). An improved JPL Mars gravity field and orientation from Mars orbiter and lander tracking data. *Icarus* **274**, 253–260.

Konopliv, A. S., R. S. Park, D.-N. Yuan, S. W. Asmar, M. M. Watkins, J. G. Williams, E. Fahnestock, G. Kruizinga, M. Paik, D. Strekalov, N. Harvey, D. E. Smith, and M. T. Zuber (2013). The JPL lunar gravity field to spherical harmonic degree 660 from the GRAIL Primary Mission. *Journal of Geophysical Research (Planets)* **118**, 1415–1434.

Konopliv, A. S., R. S. Park, A. T. Vaughan, B. G. Bills, S. W. Asmar, A. I. Ermakov, N. Rambaux, C. A. Raymond, J. C. Castillo-Rogez, C. T. Russell, D. E. Smith, and M. T. Zuber (2018). The Ceres gravity field, spin pole, rotation period and orbit from the Dawn radiometric tracking and optical data. *Icarus* **299**, 411–429.

Kozai, Y. (1957). On the Astronomical Constants of Saturnian Satellites System. *Annals of the Tokyo Observatory, Series 2* **5**, 73–106.

Lacerda, P., D. Jewitt, and N. Peixinho (2008). High-Precision Photometry of Extreme KBO 2003 EL_{61}. *Astronomical Journal* **135**, 1749–1756.

Landolt, A. U. (1992). UBVRI Photometric Standard Stars in the Magnitude Range 11.5-16.0 Around the Celestial Equator. *Astronomical Journal* **104**, 340–371.

Landolt, A. U. (2009). UBVRI Photometric Standard Stars Around the Celestial Equator: Updates and Additions. *Astronomical Journal* **137**, 4186–4269.

Laskar, J. and R. A. Jacobson (1987). GUST 86. An Analytical Ephemeris of the Uranian Satellites. *Astronomy & Astrophysics* **188**, 212–224.

Lieske, J. H. (1977). Theory of Motion of Jupiter's Galilean Satellites. *Astronomy & Astrophysics* **56**, 333–352.

Liu, Q. Z., J. van Paradijs, and E. P. J. van den Heuvel (2000). A Catalogue of High-Mass X-ray Binaries. *Astronomy & Astrophysics Supplement* **147**, 25–49.

Liu, Q. Z., J. van Paradijs, and E. P. J. van den Heuvel (2001). A Catalog of Low-Mass X-ray Binaries. *Astronomy & Astrophysics* **368**, 1021–1054.

Luzum, B., N. Capitaine, A. Fienga, W. Folkner, T. Fukushima, J. Hilton, C. Hohenkerk, G. Krasinsky, G. Petit, E. Pitjeva, M. Soffel, and P. Wallace (2011). The IAU 2009 System of Astronomical Constants: The Report of the IAU Working Group on Numerical Standards for Fundamental Astronomy. *Celestial Mechanics and Dynamical Astronomy* **110**, 293–304.

Lyngå, G. (1981). The Lund – Strasourg Catalogue of Open Cluster Data. *Astronomical Data Center Bulletin 1*(2), 90–93. NSSDC/WDC-A-R&S 81-09 T. A. Nagy, W. H. Warren, Jr. and J. M. Mead (Eds.).

Ma, C., E. F. Arias, T. M. Eubanks, A. L. Fey, A. M. Gontier, C. S. Jacobs, O. J. Sovers, B. A. Archinal, and P. Charlot (1998). The International Celestial Reference Frame as Realized by Very Long Baseline Interferometry. *Astronomical Journal* **116**, 516–546.

Mainzer, A., J. Bauer, R. Cutri, T. Grav, E. Kramer, J. Masiero, S. Sonnett, and E. Wright (Eds.) (2019). *NEOWISE Diameters and Albedos V2.0*, Volume NEOWISE Diameters and Albedos V2.0. NASA Planetary Data System.

Malkin, Z. M. (2016). The Second Version of the OCARS Catalog of Optical Characteristics of Astrometric Radio Sources. *Astronomy Reports 60*(11), 996–1005.

Mallama, A. and J. L. Hilton (2018). Computing Apparent Planetary Magnitudes for *The Astronomical Almanac*. *Astronomy and Computing* **25**, 10–24.

Mallama, A., B. Krobusek, and H. Pavlov (2017). Comprehensive Wide-Band Magnitudes and Albedos for the Planets, with Applications to Exo-Planets and Planet Nine. *Icarus* **282**, 19–33.

Manchester, R. N., G. B. Hobbs, A. Teoh, and M. Hobbs (2005). The Australia Telescope National Facility Pulsar Catalogue. *Astronomical Journal* **129**, 1993–2006.

Masiero, J., A. K. Mainzer, T. Grav, J. M. Bauer, R. M. Cutri, J. Dailey, P. R. M. Eisenhardt, R. S. McMillan, T. B. Spahr, M. F. Skrutskie, D. Tholen, R. G. Walker, E. L. Wright, E. DeBaun, D. Elsbury, T. Gautier, IV, S. Gomillion, and A. Wilkins (2011). Main Belt Asteroids with WISE/NEOWISE. I. Preliminary Albedos and Diameters. *Astrophysical Journal* **741**, 68.

Mason, B. D., G. L. Wycoff, W. I. Hartkopf, G. Douglass, and C. E. Worley (2001). The Washington Double Star Catalog. *Astronomical Journal* **122**, 3466–3471.

Matthews, P. M., T. A. Herring, and B. A. Buffett (2002). Modeling of Nutation and Precession: New Nutation Series for Nonrigid Earth and Insights into the Earth's Interior. *Journal of Geophysical Research* **107(B4)**, doi:10.1029/2001JB000390.

Morgan, W. W., H. A. Abt, and J. W. Tapschott (1978). *Revised MK Spectral Atlas for Stars Earlier than the Sun*. Williams Bay, WI and Tucson, AZ: Yerkes Obs. and Kitt Peak Nat. Obs.

Nelson, R. A., D. D. McCarthy, S. Malys, J. Levine, B. Guinot, H. F. Fliegel, R. L. Beard, and T. R. Bartholomew (2001). The Leap Second: its History and Possible Future. *Metrologia* **38**, 509 529.

Newhall, X X. and J. G. Williams (1996). Estimation of the Lunar Physical Librations. *Celestial Mechanics and Dynamical Astronomy* **66**, 21–30.

Nicholson, P. D. (2008). *Natural Satellites of the Planets*. Toronto, Ontario, Canada: University of Toronto Press.

Oke, J. B. (1990). Faint Spectrophotometric Standard Stars. *Astronomical Journal* **99**, 1621–1631.

Owen, Jr., W. M., R. M. Vaughan, and S. P. Synnott (1991). Orbits of the Six New Satellites of Neptune. *Astronomical Journal* **101**, 1511–1515.

Park, R. S., W. M. Folkner, J. G. Williams, and D. H. Boggs (2021). The Planetary and Lunar Ephemerides DE440 and DE441. *The Astronomical Journal* **161**, 105.

Pavlis, N. K., S. A. Holmes, S. C. Kenyon, and J. K. Factor (2012). The Development and Evaluation of the Earth Gravitational Model 2008 (EGM2008). *Journal of Geophysical Research* **117**, doi:10.1002/2011JB008916.

Pitjeva, E. V. and E. M. Standish (2009). Proposals for the Masses of the Three Largest Asteroids, the Moon-Earth Mass Ratio and the Astronomical Unit. *Celestial Mechanics and Dynamical Astronomy* **103**, 365–372.

Rohde, J. R. and A. T. Sinclair (1992). Orbital Ephemerides and Rings of Satellites. In P. K. Seidelmann (Ed.), *Explanatory Supplement to The Astronomical Almanac*, pp. 353. Mill Valley, CA: University Science Books.

Rutledge, G. A., J. E. Hesser, and P. B. Stetson (1997). Galactic Globular Cluster Metallicity Scale from the Ca II Triplet II. Rankings, Comparisons, and Puzzles. *Publications of the Astronomical Society of the Pacific* **109**, 907–919.

Simon, J. L., P. Bretagnon, J. Chapront, M. Chapront-Touzé, G. Francou, and J. Laskar (1994). Numerical Expressions for Precession Formulae and Mean Elements for the Moon and the Planets. *Astronomy & Astrophysics* **282**, 663–683.

Sinclair, A. T. (1974). A Theory of the Motion of Iapetus. *Monthly Notices of the Royal Astronomical Society* **169**, 591–605.

Sinclair, A. T. (1977). The Orbits of Tethys, Dione, Rhea, Titan and Iapetus. *Monthly Notices of the Royal Astronomical Society* **180**, 447–459.

Sinclair, A. T. (1989). The Orbits of the Satellites of Mars Determined from Earth-based and Spacecraft Observations. *Astronomy & Astrophysics* **220**, 321–328.

Smart, W. M. (1956). *Text-Book on Spherical Astronomy*. Cambridge, UK: Cambridge University Press.

Soubiran, C., G. Jasniewicz, L. Chemin, F. Crifo, S. Udry, D. Hestroffer, and D. Katz (2013). The Catalogue of Radial Velocity Standard Stars for Gaia. Pre-Launch Release. *Astronomy & Astrophysics* **552**, A64.

Souchay, J., A. H. Andrei, C. Barache, S. Bouquillon, A.-M. Gontier, S. B. Lambert, C. Le Poncin-Lafitte, F. Taris, E. F. Arias, D. Suchet, and M. Baudin (2009). The Construction of the Large Quasar Astrometric Catalogue (LQAC). *Astronomy & Astrophysics* **494**, 799–815.

Souchay, J., C. Gattano, A. Andrei, D. Souami, B. Coehlo, C. Barache, F. Taris, N. Secrest, and A. Berthereau (2019). LQAC-5: The fifth release of the Large Quasar Astrometric Catalogue. *Astronomy & Astrophysics* **624**, A145.

Standish, E. M. (1998). JPL Planetary and Lunar Ephemerides, DE405/LE405. Technical Report JPL IOM 312.F-98-048.

Stickel, M., J. W. Fried, and H. Kuehr (1989). Optical Spectroscopy of 1 Jy BL Lacertae Objects and Flat Spectrum Radio Sources. *Astronomy & Astrophysics Supplement* **80**, 103–114.

Stickel, M. and H. Kuehr (1994). An Update of the Optical Identification Status of the S4 Radio Source Catalogue. *Astronomy & Astrophysics Supplement* **103**, 349–363.

Sudbury, P. V. (1969). The Motion of Jupiter's Fifth Satellite. *Icarus* **10**, 116–143.

Taylor, D. B. (1984). A Comparison of the Theory of the Motion of Hyperion with Observations Made During 1967-1982. *Astronomy & Astrophysics* **141**, 151–158.

Taylor, D. B. (1995). Compact Ephemerides for Differential Tangent Plane Coordinates of Planetary Satellites. *NAO Technical Note* **No. 68**.

Taylor, D. B. and K. X. Shen (1988). Analysis of Astrometric Observations from 1967 to 1983 of the Major Satellites of Saturn. *Astronomy & Astrophysics* **200**, 269–278.

Taylor, D. B., Bell, S. A., Hilton, J. L., and Sinclair, A. T. (2010). Computation of the Quantities Describing the Lunar Librations in The Astronomical Almanac. Technical Report NAO Technical Note No. 74.

Tholen, D. J. (1985). The Orbit of Pluto's Satellite. *Astronomical Journal* **90**, 2353–2359.

Trager, S. C., S. Djorgovski, and I. R. King (1993). Structural Parameters of Galactic Globular Clusters. In S. G. Djorgovski and G. Meylan (Eds.), *Structure and Dynamics of Globular Clusters*, Volume 50 of *Astronomical Society of the Pacific Conference Series*, pp. 347–355.

Trager, S. C., I. R. King, and S. Djorgovski (1995). Catalogue of Galactic Globular-Cluster Surface-Brightness Profiles. *Astronomical Journal* **109**, 218–241.

Trumpler, R. J. (1930). Preliminary Results on the Distances, Dimensions and Space Distribution of Open Star Clusters. *Lick Observatory Bulletin* **XIV**, 154–188.

Turnshek, D. A., R. C. Bohlin, R. L. Williamson, O. L. Lupie, J. Koornneef, and D. H. Morgan (1990). An Atlas of Hubble Space Telescope Photometric, Spectrophotometric, and Polarimetric Calibration Objects. *Astronomical Journal* **99**, 1243–1261.

Urban, S. E. and P. K. Seidelmann (Eds.) (2012). *Explanatory Supplement to The Astronomical Almanac*, Mill Valley, CA. University Science Books.

van Paradijs, J. (1995). A Catalogue of X-Ray Binaries. In W. H. G. Lewin, J. van Paradijs, and E. P. J. van den Heuvel (Eds.), *X-ray Binaries*, pp. 536–577. University of Chicago Press. Volume IX of Stars and Stellar Systems.

Verma, A. and J.-L. Margot (2016). Mercury's Gravity, Tides, and Spin from MESSENGER Radio Science Data. *Journal of Geophysical Research* **121**, 1627–1640.

Véron-Cetty, M. P. and P. Véron (2006). A Catalogue of Quasars and Active Nuclei: 12th edition. *Astronomy & Astrophysics* **455**, 773–777.

Wallace, P. T. and N. Capitaine (2006). Precession-Nutation Procedures Consistent with IAU 2006 Resolutions. *Astronomy & Astrophysics* **459**, 981–985.

Watts, C. B. (1963). The Marginal Zone of the Moon. In *Astronomical Papers of the American Ephemeris and Nautical Almanac*, Volume 17. Washington, DC: U.S. Government Printing Office.

Williams, J. G., D. H. Boggs, and W. M. Folkner (2013). DE430 lunar orbit, physical librations, and surface coordinates. Technical Report JPL IOM 335-JW,DB,WF-20080314-001.

Zacharias, N., D. G. Monet, S. E. Levine, S. E. Urban, R. Gaume, and G. L. Wycoff (2004). The Naval Observatory Merged Astrometric Dataset (NOMAD). In *American Astronomical Society Meeting Abstracts*, Volume 36 of *Bulletin of the American Astronomical Society*, pp. 1418.

Zadunaisky, P. E. (1954). A Determination of New Elements of the Orbit of Phoebe, Ninth Satellite of Saturn. *Astronomical Journal* **59**, 1–6.

Zinn, R. and M. J. West (1984). The Globular Cluster System of the Galaxy. III - Measurements of Radial Velocity and Metallicity for 60 Clusters and a Compilation of Metallicities for 121 Clusters. *Astrophysical Journal Supplement Series* **55**, 45–66.

ΔT: the difference between *Terrestrial Time (TT)* and *Universal Time (UT)*: $\Delta T = TT - UT1$.

ΔUT1 (or ΔUT): the value of the difference between *Universal Time (UT)* and *Coordinated Universal Time (UTC)*: $\Delta UT1 = UT1 - UTC$.

aberration (of light): the relativistic apparent angular displacement of the observed position of a celestial object from its *geometric position*, caused by the motion of the observer in the reference system in which the trajectories of the observed object and the observer are described. (See *aberration, planetary.*)

aberration, annual: the component of *stellar aberration* resulting from the motion of the Earth about the Sun. (See *aberration, stellar.*)

aberration, diurnal: the component of *stellar aberration* resulting from the observer's *diurnal motion* about the center of the Earth due to Earth's rotation. (See *aberration, stellar.*)

aberration, galactic: the apparent angular displacement of the observed position of an extra-galactic celestial object from its *geometric position*, arising from the motion of the solar system about the galactic center.

aberration, planetary: the apparent angular displacement of the observed position of a solar system body from its instantaneous geometric direction as would be seen by an observer at the geocenter. This displacement is produced by the combination of *aberration of light* and *light-time displacement.*

aberration, secular: the component of *stellar aberration* resulting from the essentially uniform and almost rectilinear motion of the entire solar system in space. Secular *aberration* is usually disregarded. (See *aberration, stellar.*)

aberration, stellar: the apparent angular displacement of the observed position of a celestial body resulting from the motion of the observer. Stellar *aberration* is divided into diurnal, annual, and secular components. (See *aberration, annual; aberration, diurnal; aberration, secular.*)

altitude: the angular distance of a celestial body above or below the *horizon*, measured along the great circle passing through the body and the *zenith*. Altitude is 90° minus the *zenith distance*.

annual parallax: see *parallax, heliocentric.*

anomalistic year: see: *year, anomalistic*

anomaly: the angular separation of a body in its *orbit* from its *pericenter*.

anomaly, eccentric: in undisturbed elliptic motion, the angle measured at the center of the *orbit* ellipse from *pericenter* to the point on the circumscribing auxiliary circle from which a perpendicular to the major axis would intersect the orbiting body. (See *anomaly, mean; anomaly, true.*)

anomaly, mean: the product of the *mean motion* of an orbiting body and the interval of time since the body passed the *pericenter*. Thus, the mean *anomaly* is the angle from the pericenter of a hypothetical body moving with a constant angular speed that is equal to the mean motion. In realistic computations, with disturbances taken into account, the mean anomaly is equal to its initial value at an *epoch* plus an integral of the mean motion over the time elapsed since the epoch. (See *anomaly, eccentric; anomaly, mean at epoch; anomaly, true.*)

anomaly, mean at epoch: the value of the *mean anomaly* at a specific *epoch*, i.e., at some fiducial moment of time. It is one of the six *Keplerian elements* that specify an *orbit*. (See *Keplerian elements; orbital elements.*)

anomaly, true: the angle, measured at the focus nearest the *pericenter* of an *elliptical orbit*, between the pericenter and the *radius vector* from the focus to the orbiting body; one of the standard *orbital elements*. (See *anomaly, eccentric; anomaly, mean; orbital elements.*)

aphelion: the point in an *orbit* that is the most distant from the Sun.

apocenter: the point in an *orbit* that is farthest from the origin of the reference system. (See *aphelion; apogee.*)

apogee: the point in an *orbit* that is the most distant from the Earth. Apogee is sometimes used with reference to the apparent orbit of the Sun around the Earth.

apparent place (or position): the *proper place* of an object expressed with respect to the *true (intermediate) equator and equinox* of date.

apparent solar time: see *solar time, apparent.*

appulse: the least apparent distance between two celestial objects from the observer's point of view. The time of appulse is close to that of *conjunction* in *ecliptic longitude* for objects moving on or near the *ecliptic*.

Aries, First point of: another name for the *vernal equinox*.

aspect: the position of any of the *planets* or the Moon relative to the Sun, as seen from the Earth.

asteroid: a *small solar system body* orbiting the Sun that is not massive enough to be a *dwarf planet*. Unlike a *comet*, asteroids rarely exhibit the ejection of volatile material. The term "asteroid" is sometimes restricted to bodies with orbital *semimajor axes* less than or approximately equal to that of Jupiter, and is often used interchangeably with the term *"minor planet"*.

astrometric ephemeris: an *ephemeris* of a solar system body in which the tabulated positions are *astrometric places*. Values in an astrometric ephemeris are essentially comparable to catalog *mean places* of stars after the star positions have been updated for *proper motion* and *parallax*.

astrometric place (or position): the position of a solar system body formed by applying corrections for *light-time displacement* to the *geometric position*. This position is directly comparable with the catalog positions of nearby background stars after those positions have been updated for *proper motion* and *parallax*. There is no correction for *aberration* or *deflection of light*. It is assumed that these correction are nearly identical for both the solar system body and background stars.

astronomical coordinates: the longitude and latitude of the point on Earth relative to the *geoid*. These coordinates are influenced by local gravity anomalies. (See *latitude, terrestrial; longitude, terrestrial; zenith.*)

astronomical refraction: see *refraction, astronomical.*

astronomical unit (au): a conventional unit of length equal to 149 597 870 700 m exactly. Prior to 2012, it was defined as the radius of a circular *orbit* in which a body of negligible mass, and free of *perturbations*, would revolve around the Sun in $2\pi/\mathrm{k}$ *days*, k being the *Gaussian gravitational constant*. This is slightly less than the orbital *semimajor axis* of the Earth's orbit.

astronomical zenith: see *zenith, astronomical.*

atomic second: see *second, Système International (SI).*

augmentation: the increase in the *topocentric* apparent *semidiameter* of a celestial body compared to its apparent semidiameter when viewed from the geocenter.

autumnal equinox: see *equinox, autumnal.*

azimuth: the angular distance measured eastward along the *horizon* from a specified reference point (usually north). Azimuth is measured to the point where the great circle determining the *altitude* of an object meets the horizon.

barycenter: the center of mass of a system of bodies; *e.g.*, the center of mass of the solar system or the Earth-Moon system.

barycentric: with reference to, or pertaining to, the *barycenter* (usually of the solar system).

Barycentric Celestial Reference System (BCRS): a system of *barycentric* space-time coordinates for the solar system within the framework of General Relativity, with its geometric origin at the solar system barycenter. The metric tensor to be used in the system is specified by the *IAU* 2000 resolution B1.3. For all practical applications, unless otherwise stated, the BCRS is assumed to be oriented according to the *ICRS* axes. (See *Barycentric Coordinate Time (TCB).*)

Barycentric Coordinate Time (TCB): the coordinate time of the *Barycentric Celestial Reference System (BCRS)*, which advances by *SI seconds* within that system. TCB is related to *Geocentric Coordinate Time (TCG)* and *Terrestrial Time (TT)* by relativistic transformations that include a secular term. (See *second, Système International (SI).*)

Barycentric Dynamical Time (TDB): a time scale defined by the *IAU* in 1976, named in 1979, and revised in 2006 for use as an independent argument of *barycentric ephemerides* and equations of motion. TDB is a linear function of *Barycentric Coordinate Time (TCB)* that on average tracks *TT* for an extended time period around the current standard *epoch*, JD 245 1545.0. The difference between TT and TDB remains less than 2 ms for several thousand *years* around the this *epoch*. (See *second, Système International (SI).*)

Besselian elements: quantities tabulated for the calculation of accurate predictions of an *eclipse* or *occultation* for any point on or above the surface of the Earth.

Besselian year: see: *year, Besselian*. OBSOLETE.

calendar: a system of reckoning time in units of solar *days*. The days are enumerated according to their position in cyclic patterns usually involving the motions of the Sun and/or the Moon.

calendar, Gregorian: The *calendar* introduced by Pope Gregory XIII in 1582 to replace the *Julian calendar*. This calendar is now used as the civil calendar in most countries. In the Gregorian calendar, every *year* that is exactly divisible by four is a leap year, except for centurial years, which must be exactly divisible by 400 to be leap years. Thus 2000 was a leap year, but 1900 and 2100 are not leap years.

calendar, Julian: the *calendar* introduced by Julius Caesar in 46 B.C. to replace the Roman calendar. In the Julian calendar a common *year* is defined to comprise 365 *days*, and every fourth year is a leap year comprising 366 days. The Julian calendar was superseded by the *Gregorian calendar*.

calendar, proleptic: the extrapolation of a *calendar* prior to its date of introduction.

calendar year: see *year, calendar.*

catalog equinox: see *equinox, catalog.*

celestial equator: the plane perpendicular to the *Celestial Intermediate Pole (CIP)*. Colloquially, the projection onto the *celestial sphere* of the Earth's *equator*. (See *mean equator and equinox; true equator and equinox.*)

Celestial Intermediate Origin (CIO): the nonrotating origin of the *Celestial Intermediate Reference System*.

Celestial Intermediate Origin Locator (CIO Locator): denoted by s, is the difference between the *Geocentric Celestial Reference System (GCRS) right ascension* and the intermediate right ascension of the intersection of the GCRS and intermediate *equators*.

Celestial Intermediate Pole (CIP): the reference pole of the P03 *precession* and *IAU* 2000A *nutation* models. The motions of the CIP are those of the *Tisserand mean axis* of the Earth with *periods* longer than two *days*. (See *nutation; precession.*)

Celestial Intermediate Reference System: a *geocentric* reference system related to the *Geocentric Celestial Reference System (GCRS)* by time-dependent rotations for *precession* and *nutation*. It is defined by the intermediate *equator* of the *Celestial Intermediate Pole (CIP)* and the *Celestial Intermediate Origin (CIO)* at a specific *epoch*.

celestial pole: see *pole, celestial*.

celestial sphere: an imaginary sphere of arbitrary radius upon which celestial bodies may be considered to be located. As circumstances require, the celestial sphere may be centered at the observer, at the Earth's center, or at any other location.

Centaur: a *small solar system body* orbiting the Sun that is not massive enough to be a *dwarf planet* with a *perihelion* greater than Jupiter's orbital *semimajor axis* and an orbital *semimajor axis* less than Neptune's.

center of figure: that point so situated relative to the apparent figure of a body that any line drawn through it divides the figure into two parts having equal apparent areas. If the body is oddly shaped, the center of figure may lie outside the figure itself.

center of light: same as *center of figure* except referring only to the illuminated portion.

central meridian: see *meridian* central.

century: a period of 100 years.

century, Julian: a period of *100 Julian years*.

comet: a *small solar system body* that normally exhibits the ejection of volatile material for some part of its orbital *period*.

conjunction: the phenomenon in which two bodies have the same apparent *ecliptic longitude* or *right ascension* as viewed from a third body. Conjunctions are usually tabulated as *geocentric* phenomena. For Mercury and Venus, geocentric inferior conjunctions occur when the *planet* is between the Earth and Sun, and superior conjunctions occur when the Sun is between the planet and Earth. (See *longitude, ecliptic*.)

constellation: 1. A grouping of stars, usually with pictorial or mythical associations, that serves to identify an area of the *celestial sphere*. **2.** One of the precisely defined areas of the celestial sphere, associated with a grouping of stars, that the *International Astronomical Union (IAU)* has designated as a constellation.

Coordinated Universal Time (UTC): the time scale available from broadcast time signals, and serving as the basis of the worldwide system of civil time. UTC differs from *International Atomic Time (TAI)* by an integral number of *SI seconds*; it is maintained within $\pm0\overset{s}{.}9$ seconds of *UT1* by the introduction of *leap seconds*. (See *International Atomic Time (TAI); leap second; Universal Time (UT)*.)

culmination: the passage of a celestial object across the observer's *meridian*; also called "meridian passage".

culmination, lower: (also called "*culmination* below pole" for circumpolar stars and the Moon) is the crossing farther from the observer's *zenith*.

culmination, upper: (also called "*culmination* above pole" for circumpolar stars and the Moon) or *transit* is the crossing closer to the observer's *zenith*.

day: an interval of 86 400 *SI seconds*, unless otherwise indicated. (See *second, Système International (SI)*.)

declination: angular distance on the *celestial sphere* north or south of the *celestial equator*. It is measured along the *hour circle* passing through the celestial object. Declination is usually given in combination with *right ascension* or *hour angle*.

defect of illumination: (sometimes, greatest defect of illumination): the maximum angular width of the unilluminated portion of the apparent disk of a solar system body measured along a radius.

deflection of light: the angle by which the direction of a light ray is altered from a straight line by the gravitational field of the Sun or other massive object. As seen from the Earth, objects appear to be deflected radially away from the Sun by up to 1″.75 at the Sun's *limb*. Correction for this effect, which is independent of wavelength, is included in the transformation from *mean place* to *apparent place*.

deflection of the vertical: the angle between the astronomical *vertical* and the geodetic vertical. (See *astronomical coordinates; geodetic coordinates; zenith.*)

delta T: see **ΔT**.

delta UT1: see **ΔUT1** *(or* **ΔUT***)*.

direct motion (prograde motion): for orbital motion in the solar system, motion that is counterclockwise in the *orbit* as seen from the north pole of the *ecliptic*; for an object observed on the *celestial sphere*, motion that is from west to east, resulting from the relative motion of the object and the Earth.

diurnal motion: the apparent daily motion, caused by the Earth's rotation, of celestial bodies across the sky from east to west.

diurnal parallax: see *parallax, geocentric.*

dwarf planet: a celestial body that is in *orbit* around the Sun, has sufficient mass for its self-gravity to overcome rigid body forces so that it assumes a hydrostatic equilibrium (nearly round) shape, has not cleared the neighbourhood around its orbit, and is not a satellite. (See *planet.*)

dynamical equinox: the ascending *node* of the Earth's mean *orbit* on the Earth's *true equator*; i.e., the intersection of the *ecliptic* with the *celestial equator* at which the Sun's *declination* changes from south to north. (See *catalog equinox; equinox; true equator and equinox.*)

dynamical time: the family of time scales introduced in 1984 to replace *ephemeris time (ET)* as the independent argument of dynamical theories and *ephemerides*. (See *Barycentric Dynamical Time (TDB); Terrestrial Time (TT).*)

Earth Rotation Angle (ERA): the angle, θ, measured along the *equator* of the *Celestial Intermediate Pole (CIP)* between the direction of the *Celestial Intermediate Origin (CIO)* and the *Terrestrial Intermediate Origin (TIO)*. It is a linear function of *UT1*; its time derivative is the Earth's angular velocity.

eccentricity: **1.** A parameter that specifies the shape of a conic section. **2.** One of the standard *orbital elements*, usually denoted by e, used to describe an *elliptical orbit* or a *hyperbolic orbit*. For an *elliptical orbit*, $e = \sqrt{1 - (b^2/a^2)}$, where a and b are the lengths of the *semimajor* and semiminor axes, respectively; for a parabolic orbit $e = 1$; and for a hyperbolic orbit, the quantity $e = \sqrt{1 + (b^2/a^2)}$. (See *orbital elements.*)

eclipse: the obscuration of a celestial body caused by its passage through the shadow cast by another body.

eclipse, annular: a *solar eclipse* in which the solar disk is not completely covered but is seen as an annulus or ring at maximum *eclipse*. An annular eclipse occurs when the apparent disk of the Moon is smaller than that of the Sun. (See *eclipse, solar.*)

eclipse, lunar: an *eclipse* in which the Moon passes through the shadow cast by the Earth. The eclipse may be total (the Moon passing completely through the Earth's *umbra*), partial (the Moon passing partially through the Earth's umbra at maximum eclipse), or penumbral (the Moon passing only through the Earth's *penumbra*).

eclipse, solar: actually an *occultation* of the Sun by the Moon in which the Earth passes through the shadow cast by the Moon. It may be total (observer in the Moon's *umbra*), partial (observer in the Moon's *penumbra*), annular, or annular-total. (See *eclipse, annular.*)

eclipse year: see *year, eclipse.*

ecliptic: **1.** The mean plane of the *orbit* of the Earth-Moon *barycenter* around the solar system barycenter. **2.** The apparent path of the Sun around the *celestial sphere.*

ecliptic latitude: see *latitude, ecliptic.*

ecliptic longitude: see *longitude, ecliptic.*

elements: a set of parameters used to describe the position and motion or orientation (attitude) of an astronomical object.

elements, Besselian: see *Besselian elements.*

elements, Keplerian: see *Keplerian elements.*

elements, mean: see *mean elements.*

elements, orbital: see *orbital elements.*

elements, osculating: see *osculating elements.*

elements, rotational: see *rotational elements.*

ellipsoid: a quadratic surface defined by three mutually perpendicular semiaxes. If two of the semiaxes are equal then the figure is called a spheroid, and if all three are the same it is called a sphere.

elliptical orbit: see *orbit, elliptical.*

elongation: the *geocentric* angle between two celestial objects.

elongation, greatest: **1.** For satellites, the maximum value of a *satellite elongation* during an *orbit* about its primary. Often a general direction is given. For example, greatest eastern *elongation* is the maximum value of a satellite elongation that occurs on the eastern half of the apparent orbit. **2.** For bodies that orbit the Sun, the maximum value of elongation during an orbit about the Sun.

elongation, planetary: the usually *geocentric* angle between a *planet* and the Sun. Planetary *elongations* are measured from 0° to 180°, east or west of the Sun.

elongation, satellite: the *geocentric* angle between a satellite and its primary. The *elongation* is usually designated as being east or west of the primary, but on rare occasions could be designated north or south.

epact: **1.** The age of the Moon. **2.** The number of *days* since new moon, diminished by one day, on January 1 in the Gregorian ecclesiastical lunar cycle. (See *calendar, Gregorian; lunar phases.*)

ephemeris: a time-ordered sequence of the location, velocity or sometimes the physical properties of a celestial object.

ephemeris hour angle: an *hour angle* referred to the *ephemeris meridian.*

ephemeris longitude: longitude measured eastward from the *ephemeris meridian.* (See *longitude, terrestrial.*)

ephemeris meridian: see *meridian, ephemeris.*

ephemeris, physical: an *ephemeris* of properties such as the apparent size, *phase*, *apparent magnitude*, and orientation of an extended object, for use in planning and analyzing observations.

ephemeris time (ET): the time scale used prior to 1984 as the independent variable in gravitational theories of the solar system. In 1984, ET was replaced by *dynamical time.*

ephemeris transit: the passage of a celestial body or point across the *ephemeris meridian.*

epoch: an arbitrary fixed instant of time or date used as a chronological reference datum for *calendars*, celestial reference systems, star catalogs, or orbital motions. (See *calendar; orbit.*)

equation of the equinoxes: the difference apparent *sidereal time* minus mean sidereal time, due to the effect of *nutation* in longitude on the location of the *equinox*. Equivalently, the difference between the *right ascensions* of the true and *mean equinoxes*, expressed in time units. (See *sidereal time*.)

equation of the origins: the arc length, measured positively eastward, from the *Celestial Intermediate Origin (CIO)* to the *equinox* along the intermediate *equator*; alternatively the difference between the *Earth Rotation Angle (ERA)* and *Greenwich Apparent Sidereal Time (GAST)*, namely, (*ERA* - GAST).

equation of time: the difference *apparent solar time* minus *mean solar time*.

equator: the great circle on the surface of a body formed by the intersection of its surface with the plane passing through the center of the body perpendicular to the axis of rotation. (See *celestial equator*.)

equinox: 1. Either of the two points on the *celestial sphere* at which the *ecliptic* intersects the *celestial equator*. **2.** The instant at which the center of the Sun crosses the Earth's equator. At these times, the apparent *ecliptic longitude* of the Sun is approximately either 0° or 180°. **3.** The *vernal equinox*. (See *mean equator and equinox; true equator and equinox*.)

equinox, autumnal: 1. The decending *node* of the *ecliptic* on the *celestial sphere*. **2.** The time which the apparent *ecliptic longitude* of the Sun is 180°.

equinox, dynamical: the ascending *node* of the *ecliptic* on the Earth's *true equator*.

equinox, vernal: 1. The ascending *node* of the *ecliptic* on the *celestial equator*. **2.** The time at which the apparent *ecliptic longitude* of the Sun is 0°.

era: a system of chronological notation reckoned from a specific event.

ERA: see *Earth Rotation Angle (ERA)*.

flattening: a parameter that specifies the degree by which a *planet*'s figure differs from that of a sphere; the ratio $f = (a - b)/a$, where a is the equatorial radius and b is the polar radius.

frame bias: the orientation of the *mean equator and equinox* of J2000.0 with respect to the *Geocentric Celestial Reference System (GCRS)*. It is defined by three small and constant angles, two of which describe the offset of the mean pole at J2000.0 and the other is the GCRS *right ascension* of the mean inertial *equinox* of J2000.0.

frequency: the number of *periods* of a regular, cyclic phenomenon in a given measure of time, such as a *second* or a *year*. (See *period; second, Système International (SI); year*.)

frequency standard: a generator whose output is used as a precise *frequency* reference; a primary frequency standard is one whose frequency corresponds to the adopted definition of the *second*, with its specified accuracy achieved without calibration of the device. (See *second, Système International (SI)*.)

GAST: see *Greenwich Apparent Sidereal Time (GAST)*.

geocentric: with reference to, or pertaining to, the center of mass of the Earth.

Geocentric Celestial Reference System (GCRS): a system of *geocentric* space-time coordinates within the framework of General Relativity, with origin at the geocenter. The metric tensor used in the system is specified by the *IAU* 2000 resolutions. The GCRS is defined such that its spatial coordinates are kinematically nonrotating with respect to those of the *Barycentric Celestial Reference System (BCRS)*. (See *Geocentric Coordinate Time (TCG)*.)

Geocentric Coordinate Time (TCG): the coordinate time of the *Geocentric Celestial Reference System (GCRS)*, which advances by *SI seconds* within that system. TCG is related to *Barycentric Coordinate Time (TCB)* and *Terrestrial Time (TT)* by relativistic transformations that include a secular term. (See *second, Système International (SI)*.) When compared to *TT*, it has a rate difference of about 0.02 s/yr. The rate difference between *TT* and TCG is named L_G and is provided on page K6.

geocentric coordinates: 1. The latitude and longitude of a point on the Earth's surface relative to the center of the Earth. **2.** Celestial coordinates given with respect to the center of the Earth. (See *latitude, terrestrial; longitude, terrestrial; zenith.*)

geocentric zenith: see *zenith, geocentric.*

geodetic coordinates: the latitude and longitude of a point on the Earth's surface determined from the geodetic *vertical* (normal to the reference ellipsoid). (See *latitude, terrestrial; longitude, terrestrial; zenith.*)

geodetic zenith: see *zenith, geodetic.*

geoid: an equipotential surface that coincides with mean sea level in the open ocean. On land, it is the level surface that would be assumed by water in an imaginary network of frictionless channels connected to the ocean.

geometric position: the position of an object defined by a straight line (vector) between the center of the Earth (or the observer) and the object at a given time, without any corrections for *light-time*, *aberration*, etc.

GHA: see *Greenwich Hour Angle (GHA).*

GMST: see *Greenwich Mean Sidereal Time (GMST).*

greatest defect of illumination: see *defect of illumination.*

Greenwich Apparent Sidereal Time (GAST): the *Greenwich hour angle* of the *true equinox* of date.

Greenwich Hour Angle (GHA): angular distance on the *celestial sphere* measured westward along the *celestial equator* from the *Greenwich meridian* to the *hour circle* that passes through a celestial object or point.

Greenwich Mean Sidereal Time (GMST): the *Greenwich hour angle* of the *mean equinox* of date.

Greenwich meridian: see *meridian, Greenwich.*

Greenwich sidereal date (GSD): the number of *sidereal days* elapsed at Greenwich since the beginning of the Greenwich sidereal *day* that was in progress at the *Julian date (JD)* 0.0.

Greenwich sidereal day number: the integral part of the *Greenwich sidereal date (GSD).*

Gregorian calendar: see *calendar, Gregorian.*

height: the distance above or below a reference surface such as mean sea level on the Earth or a planetographic reference surface on another solar system *planet.*

heliocentric: with reference to, or pertaining to, the center of the Sun.

heliocentric parallax: see *parallax, heliocentric.*

horizon: 1. A plane perpendicular to the line from an observer through the *zenith.* **2.** The observed border between Earth and the sky.

horizon, astronomical: the plane perpendicular to the line from an observer to the *astronomical zenith* that passes through the point of observation.

horizon, geocentric: the plane perpendicular to the line from an observer to the *geocentric zenith* that passes through the center of the Earth.

horizon, natural: the border between the sky and the Earth as seen from an observation point.

horizontal parallax: see *parallax, horizontal.*

horizontal refraction: see *refraction, horizontal.*

hour angle: angular distance on the *celestial sphere* measured westward along the *celestial equator* from the *meridian* to the *hour circle* that passes through a celestial object.

hour circle: a great circle on the *celestial sphere* that passes through the *celestial poles* and is therefore perpendicular to the *celestial equator.*

hyperbolic orbit: see *orbit, hyperbolic.*

IAU: see *International Astronomical Union (IAU).*

illuminated extent: the illuminated area of an apparent planetary disk, expressed as a solid angle.

inclination: **1.** The angle between two planes or their poles. **2.** Usually, the angle between an orbital plane and a reference plane. **3.** One of the standard *orbital elements* that specifies the orientation of the *orbit*. (See *orbital elements.*)

instantaneous orbit: see *orbit, instantaneous.*

intercalate: to insert an interval of time (e.g., a *day* or a *month*) within a *calendar*, usually so that it is synchronized with some natural phenomenon such as the seasons or *lunar phases*.

intermediate place (or position): the *proper place* of an object expressed with respect to the true (intermediate) *equator* and *CIO* of date.

International Astronomical Union (IAU): an international nongovernmental organization that promotes the science of astronomy. The IAU is composed of both national and individual members. In the field of positional astronomy, the IAU, among other activities, recommends standards for data analysis and modeling, usually in the form of resolutions passed at General Assemblies held every three *years*.

International Atomic Time (TAI): the continuous time scale resulting from analysis by the Bureau International des Poids et Mesures of atomic time standards in many countries. The fundamental unit of TAI is the *SI second* on the *geoid*, and the *epoch* is 1958 January 1. (See *second, Système International (SI).*)

International Celestial Reference Frame (ICRF): **1.** A set of extragalactic objects whose adopted positions and uncertainties realize the *International Celestial Reference System (ICRS)* axes and give the uncertainties of those axes. **2.** The name of the radio catalog whose defining sources serve as fiducial points to fix the axes of the ICRS, recommended by the *International Astronomical Union (IAU)*. The first such catalog was adopted for use beginning in 1997. The third catalog, termed ICRF3, was adopted for use beginning in 2020.

International Celestial Reference System (ICRS): a time-independent, kinematically nonrotating *barycentric* reference system recommended by the *International Astronomical Union (IAU)* in 1997. The directional axes of the ICRS are defined to be those of the *ICRF*.

international meridian: see *meridian, Greenwich.*

International Terrestrial Reference Frame (ITRF): a set of reference points on the surface of the Earth whose adopted positions and velocities fix the rotating axes of the *International Terrestrial Reference System (ITRS)*.

International Terrestrial Reference System (ITRS): a time-dependent, noninertial reference system co-moving with the geocenter and rotating with the Earth. The ITRS is the recommended system in which to express positions on the Earth.

invariable plane: the plane through the center of mass of the solar system perpendicular to the angular momentum vector of the solar system.

irradiation: an optical effect of contrast that makes bright objects viewed against a dark background appear to be larger than they really are.

Julian calendar: see *calendar, Julian.*

Julian century: see *century, Julian.*

Julian date (JD): the interval of time in *days* and fractions of a day, since 4713 B.C. January 1, Greenwich noon, Julian *proleptic calendar*. In precise work, the timescale, e.g., *Terrestrial Time (TT)* or *Universal Time (UT)*, should be specified.

Julian date, modified (MJD): the *Julian date (JD)* minus 2400000.5.

Julian day number: the integral part of the *Julian date (JD)*.

Julian year: see *year, Julian.*

Keplerian elements: a certain set of six *orbital elements*, sometimes referred to as the Keplerian set. Historically, this set included the *mean anomaly* at the *epoch*, the orbital *semimajor axis*, the *eccentricity* and three Euler angles: the *longitude of the ascending node*, the *inclination*, and the *argument of pericenter*. The time of *pericenter* passage is often used as part of the Keplerian set instead of the mean *anomaly* at the epoch. Sometimes the longitude of pericenter (which is the sum of the longitude of the ascending *node* and the argument of pericenter) is used instead of the argument of pericenter.

Laplacian plane: **1.** For *planets*, see *invariable plane*. **2.** For a system of satellites, the fixed plane relative to which the vector sum of the disturbing forces has no orthogonal component.

latitude, celestial: see *latitude, ecliptic*.

latitude, ecliptic: angular distance on the *celestial sphere* measured north or south of the *ecliptic* along the great circle passing through the poles of the ecliptic and the celestial object. Also referred to as *celestial latitude*.

latitude, terrestrial: angular distance on the Earth measured north or south of the *equator* along the *meridian* of a geographic location.

leap second: a *second* inserted as the 61st second of a minute at announced times to keep *UTC* within $0^{s}.9$ of *UT1*. Generally, leap seconds are added at the end of June or December as necessary, but may be inserted at the end of any *month*. Although it has never been utilized, it is possible to have a negative leap second in which case the 60th second of a minute would be removed. (See *Coordinated Universal Time (UTC); second, Système International (SI); Universal Time (UT)*.)

libration: the physical (real) or optical (apparent) oscillations in the rotation of a celestial body, or the positional oscillations of an orbiting celestial body around a reference point moving in a similar *orbit*.

libration, physical: real periodic variations in the orientation of a celestial body in inertial space, both forced (due to external torques) and unforced (comparable to the Eulerian free precession).

libration, optical: apparent periodic changes in the orientation of a celestial body as seen from a specific reference point (e.g. the Moon as seen by an observer on Earth) due to periodic changes in the viewing geometry. For the Moon, these variations occur over the course of its orbital *period* and, to a lesser extent, over the course of a *day*. During an *orbit*, the viewing angle to a specific point on the lunar surface changes due to the *inclination* of the Moon's equator with respect to its orbital plane and the variations in the Moon's rate of orbital motion. During a day, the viewing angle changes as the Earth's rotation alters the observer's position with respect to the geocenter. For the Moon, the optical librations are much larger than the physical librations.

libration, orbital: the positional oscillations of the third body in the restricted three-body problem about a moving reference point (often the L_4 or L_5 Lagrange points) with the same average orbital period.

light, deflection of: see *deflection of light*.

light-time: the interval of time required for light to travel from a celestial body to the Earth.

light-time displacement: the difference between the geometric and *astrometric place* of a solar system body. It is caused by the motion of the body during the interval it takes light to travel from the body to Earth.

light-year: the distance that light traverses in a vacuum during one *year*. Since there are various ways to define a year, there is an ambiguity in the exact distance; the *IAU* recommends using the *Julian year* as the time basis. A light-year is approximately 9.46×10^{12} km, 5.88×10^{12} statute miles, 6.32×10^{4} *au*, and 3.07×10^{-1} *parsecs*. Often distances beyond the solar system are given in parsecs. (See *parsec (pc)*.)

limb: the apparent edge of the Sun, Moon, or a *planet* or any other celestial body with a detectable disk.

limb correction: generally, a small angle (positive or negative) that is added to the tabulated apparent *semidiameter* of a body to compensate for local topography at a specific point along the *limb*. Specifically for the Moon, the angle taken from the Watts lunar limb data (Watts, C. B., APAE XVII, 1963) that is used to correct the semidiameter of the Watts mean limb. The correction is a function of position along the limb and the apparent *libration*. The Watts mean limb is a circle whose center is offset by about 0.″6 from the direction of the Moon's center of mass and whose radius is about 0.″4 greater than the semidiameter of the Moon that is computed based on its *IAU* adopted radius in kilometers.

local place: a *topocentric place* of an object expressed with respect to the *Geocentric Celestial Reference System (GCRS)* axes.

local sidereal time: the *hour angle* of the *vernal equinox* with respect to the local *meridian*.

longitude of the ascending node: given an *orbit* and a reference plane through the primary body (or center of mass): the angle, Ω, at the primary, between a fiducial direction in the reference plane and the point at which the orbit crosses the reference plane from south to north. Equivalently, Ω is one of the angles in the reference plane between the fiducial direction and the line of *nodes*. It is one of the six *Keplerian elements* that specify an orbit. For planetary orbits, the primary is the Sun, the reference plane is usually the *ecliptic*, and the fiducial direction is usually toward the *equinox*. (See *node; orbital elements*.)

longitude, celestial: see *longitude, ecliptic*.

longitude, ecliptic: angular distance on the *celestial sphere* measured eastward along the *ecliptic* from the *dynamical equinox* to the great circle passing through the poles of the ecliptic and the celestial object. Also referred to as *celestial longitude*.

longitude, terrestrial: angular distance measured along the Earth's *equator* from the *Greenwich meridian* to the *meridian* of a geographic location.

luminosity class: distinctions in intrinsic brightness among stars of the same *spectral type*, typically given as a Roman numeral. It denotes if a star is a supergiant (Ia or Ib), giant (II or III), subgiant (IV), or main sequence — also called dwarf (V). Sometimes subdwarfs (VI) and white dwarfs (VII) are regarded as luminosity classes. (See *spectral types or classes*.)

lunar phases: cyclically recurring apparent forms of the Moon. The principal phases: new moon, first quarter, full moon and last quarter are defined as the times at which the excess of the apparent *ecliptic longitude* of the Moon over that of the Sun is 0°, 90°, 180° and 270°, respectively. (See *longitude, ecliptic*.)

lunation: the *period* of time between two consecutive new moons.

magnitude of a lunar eclipse: the fraction of the lunar diameter obscured by the shadow of the Earth at the greatest *phase* of a *lunar eclipse*, measured along the common diameter. (See *eclipse, lunar*.)

magnitude of a solar eclipse: the fraction of the solar diameter obscured by the Moon at the greatest *phase* of a *solar eclipse*, measured along the common diameter. (See *eclipse, solar*.)

magnitude: a measure on a logarithmic scale of the brightness of a celestial object. Since brightness varies with wavelength, often a wavelength band is specified. A factor of 100 in brightness is equivalent to a change of 5 in stellar magnitude, and brighter sources have lower magnitudes. For example, the bright star Sirius has a visual-band magnitude of −1.46 whereas the faintest stars detectable with an unaided eye under ideal conditions have visual-band magnitudes of about 6.0.

magnitude, absolute: 1. The *magnitude* of a self-luminous celestial object such as a star or galaxy at a distance of 10 parsecs from the observer. **2.** The *magnitude* of a nonself-luminous celestial object such as a *planet* or *asteroid* at a distance of 1 au from both the observer and the illuminating body, usually the Sun, at a *phase angle* of 0 degrees.

magnitude, apparent: the observed *magnitude* of a celestial body.

magnitude, bolometric: the *absolute magnitude* of a celestial object where the wavelength band is the entire electromagnetic spectrum.

mean distance: an average distance between the primary and the secondary gravitating body. The meaning of the mean distance depends upon the chosen method of averaging (i.e., averaging over the time, or over the *true anomaly*, or the *mean anomaly*. It is also important what power of the distance is subject to averaging.) In this volume the mean distance is defined as the inverse of the time-averaged reciprocal distance: $(\int r^{-1}\,\mathrm{d}t)^{-1}$. In the two body setting, when the disturbances are neglected and the *orbit* is elliptic, this formula yields the orbital *semimajor axis*, a, which plays the role of mean distance.

mean elements: average values of the *orbital elements* over some section of the *orbit* or over some interval of time. They are interpreted as the *elements* of some reference (mean) orbit that approximates the actual one and, thus, may serve as the basis for calculating orbit *perturbations*. The values of mean elements depend upon the chosen method of averaging and upon the length of time over which the averaging is made.

mean equator and equinox: the celestial coordinate system defined by the orientation of the Earth's equatorial plane on some specified date together with the direction of the *dynamical equinox* on that date, neglecting *nutation*. Thus, the mean *equator* and *equinox* moves in response only to *precession*. Positions in a star catalog have traditionally been referred to a catalog *equator* and equinox that approximate the mean equator and equinox of a *standard epoch*. (See *catalog equinox; true equator and equinox.*)

mean motion: defined for bound *orbits* only. **1.** The rate of change of the *mean anomaly*. **2.** The value $\sqrt{Gm/a^3}$, where G is Newton's gravitational constant, m is the sum of the masses of the primary and secondary bodies, and a is the orbital *semimajor axis* of the relative orbit. For unperturbed elliptic or circular orbits, these definitions are equivalent; the mean motion is related to the *period* through $nT = 2\pi$ where n is the mean motion and T is the period. For perturbed bound orbits, the two definitions yield, in general, different values of n, both of which are time dependent.

mean place: coordinates of a star or other celestial object (outside the solar system) at a specific date, in the *Barycentric Celestial Reference System (BCRS)*. Conceptually, the coordinates represent the direction of the object as it would hypothetically be observed from the solar system *barycenter* at the specified date, with respect to a fixed coordinate system (e.g., the axes of the *International Celestial Reference Frame (ICRF)*), if the masses of the Sun and other solar system bodies were negligible.

mean solar time: see *solar time, mean.*

meridian: a great circle passing through the *celestial poles* and through the *zenith* of any location on Earth. For planetary observations a meridian is half the great circle passing through the *planet*'s poles and through any location on the planet.

meridian, central (planetary): half of the great circle passing through the *planet*'s poles and through the *sub-earth point)*. This is the same as the longitude of the sub-earth point. Do not confuse with planetary *prime meridian*. See diagram on page E4.

meridian, ephemeris: a fictitious *meridian* that rotates independently of the Earth at the uniform rate implicitly defined by *Terrestrial Time (TT)*. The *ephemeris* meridian is 1.002 738 ΔT east of the *Greenwich meridian*, where $\Delta T = TT - UT1$.

meridian, Greenwich: (also called international or *prime meridian*) is a generic reference to one of several origins of the Earth's longitude coordinate (zero-longitude). In *The Astronomical Almanac*, it is the plane defining the astronomical zero *meridian*; it contains the geocenter, the *Celestial Intermediate Pole* and the *Terrestrial Intermediate Origin*. Other definitions are: the x-z plane of the *International Terrestrial Reference System (ITRS)*; the zero-longitude meridian of the World Geodetic System 1984 (WGS-84); and the meridian that passes through the *transit* circle at the Royal Observatory, Greenwich. Note that the latter meridian is about 100 m west of the others.

meridian, international: see *meridian, Greenwich*.

meridian, prime: on Earth, same as *Greenwich meridian*. On other solar system objects, the zero-longitude *meridian*, typically defined via international convention by an observable surface feature or *rotational elements*.

minor planet: a loosely defined term generally meaning a small solar system body that is orbiting the Sun, does not show a comet-like appearance, and is not massive enough to be a *dwarf planet*. The term is often used interchangeably with *"asteroid"*, although there is no implicit constraint that a minor *planet* be interior to Jupiter's *orbit*.

month: a calendrical unit that approximates the *period* of revolution of the Moon. Also, the period of time between the same dates in successive *calendar* months.

month, sidereal: the *period* of revolution of the Moon about Earth (or the Earth-Moon *barycenter*) in a nonrotating reference frame. It is the mean period of revolution with respect to the background stars. The mean length of the sidereal *month* is approximately 27.322 *days*.

month, synodic: the *period* between successive new moons (as seen from the geocenter). The mean length of the synodic *month* is approximately 29.531 *days*.

moonrise, moonset: the times at which the apparent upper *limb* of the Moon is on the *astronomical horizon*. In *The Astronomical Almanac*, they are computed as the times when the true *zenith distance*, referred to the center of the Earth, of the central point of the Moon's disk is $90° 34' + s - \pi$, where s is the Moon's *semidiameter*, π is the *horizontal parallax*, and $34'$ is the adopted value of *horizontal refraction*.

nadir: the point on the *celestial sphere* diametrically opposite to the *zenith*.

Near Earth Object (NEO): any *small solar system body*, including *comets*, whose *orbit* brings it near the Earth. A small solar system body is conventionally considered an NEO if its *orbit* enters the volume of space between 0.983 au and 1.3 au (147 000 000 km to 195 000 000 km) from the Sun.

node: either of the points on the *celestial sphere* at which the plane of an *orbit* intersects a reference plane. The position of one of the nodes (the *longitude of the ascending node*) is traditionally used as one of the standard *orbital elements*.

nutation: oscillations in the motion of the rotation pole of a freely rotating body that is undergoing torque from external gravitational forces. Nutation of the Earth's pole is specified in terms of components in *obliquity* and longitude.

obliquity: in general, the angle between the equatorial and orbital planes of a body or, equivalently, between the rotational and orbital poles. For the Earth, the obliquity of the *ecliptic* is the angle between the planes of the *equator* and the ecliptic; its value is approximately 23°.44.

occultation: the obscuration of one celestial body by another of greater apparent diameter; especially the passage of the Moon in front of a star or *planet*, or the disappearance of a satellite behind the disk of its primary. If the primary source of illumination of a reflecting body is cut off by the occultation, the phenomenon is also called an *eclipse*. The occultation of the Sun by the Moon is a *solar eclipse*. (See *eclipse, solar.*)

opposition: the phenomenon whereby two bodies have apparent *ecliptic longitudes* or *right ascensions* that differ by 180° as viewed by a third body. Oppositions are usually tabulated as *geocentric* phenomena.

orbit: the path in space followed by a celestial body, as a function of time. (See *orbital elements.*)

orbit, elliptical: a closed *orbit* with an *eccentricity* less than 1.

orbit, hyperbolic: an open *orbit* with an *eccentricity* greater than 1.

orbit, instantaneous: the unperturbed two-body *orbit* that a body would follow if *perturbations* were to cease instantaneously. Each orbit in the solar system (and, more generally, in any perturbed two-body setting) can be represented as a sequence of instantaneous ellipses or hyperbolae whose parameters are called *orbital elements*. If these *elements* are chosen to be osculating, each instantaneous orbit is tangential to the physical orbit. (See *orbital elements; osculating elements.*)

orbit, parabolic: an open *orbit* with an *eccentricity* of 1.

orbital elements: a set of six independent parameters that specifies an *instantaneous orbit*. Every real *orbit* can be represented as a sequence of instantaneous ellipses or hyperbolae sharing one of their foci. At each instant of time, the position and velocity of the body is characterised by its place on one such instantaneous curve. The evolution of this representation is mathematically described by evolution of the values of orbital *elements*. Different sets of geometric parameters may be chosen to play the role of orbital elements. The set of *Keplerian elements* is one of many such sets. When the Lagrange constraint (the requirement that the instantaneous orbit is tangential to the actual orbit) is imposed upon the orbital elements, they are called *osculating elements*.

osculating elements: a set of parameters that specifies the instantaneous position and velocity of a celestial body in its perturbed *orbit*. Osculating *elements* describe the unperturbed (two-body) orbit that the body would follow if *perturbations* were to cease instantaneously. (See *orbit, instantaneous; orbital elements.*)

parallax: the difference in apparent direction of an object as seen from two different locations; conversely, the angle at the object that is subtended by the line joining two designated points.

parallax, annual: see *parallax, heliocentric.*

parallax, diurnal: see *parallax, geocentric.*

parallax, geocentric: the angular difference between the *topocentric* and *geocentric* directions toward an object. Also called *diurnal parallax*.

parallax, heliocentric: the angular difference between the *geocentric* and *heliocentric* directions toward an object; it is the angle subtended at the observed object. Also called *annual parallax*.

parallax, horizontal: the angular difference between the *topocentric* and a *geocentric* direction toward an object when its topocentric position is on the *astronomical horizon*.

parallax, solar: the angular width subtended by the Earth's equatorial radius when the Earth is at a distance of 1 *astronomical unit (au)*. The value for the solar *parallax* is 8.794143 arcseconds.

parallax in altitude: the angular difference between the *topocentric* and *geocentric* direction toward an object when the object is at a given *altitude*.

parsec (pc): the distance at which one *astronomical unit (au)* subtends an angle of one arcsecond; equivalently the distance to an object having an *annual parallax* of one arcsecond. One parsec is $1/\sin(1'') = 206264.806$ au, or about 3.26 *light-years*.

penumbra: **1.** The portion of a shadow in which light from an extended source is partially but not completely cut off by an intervening body. **2.** The area of partial shadow surrounding the *umbra*.

pericenter: the point in an *orbit* that is nearest to the origin of the reference system. (See *perigee; perihelion.*)

pericenter, argument of: one of the *Keplerian elements*. It is the angle measured in the *orbit* plane from the ascending *node* of a reference plane (usually the *ecliptic*) to the *pericenter*.

perigee: the point in an *orbit* that is nearest to the Earth. Perigee is sometimes used with reference to the apparent orbit of the Sun around the Earth.

perihelion: the point in an *orbit* that is nearest to the Sun.

period: the interval of time required to complete one revolution in an *orbit* or one cycle of a periodic phenomenon, such as a cycle of *phases*. (See *phase.*)

perturbations: **1.** Deviations between the actual *orbit* of a celestial body and an assumed reference orbit. **2.** The forces that cause deviations between the actual and reference orbits. Perturbations, according to the first meaning, are usually calculated as quantities to be added to the coordinates of the reference orbit to obtain the precise coordinates.

phase: **1.** The name applied to the apparent degree of illumination of the disk of the Moon or a *planet* as seen from Earth (crescent, gibbous, full, etc.). **2.** The ratio of the illuminated area of the apparent disk of a celestial body to the entire area of the apparent disk; i.e., the fraction illuminated. **3.** Used loosely to refer to one *aspect* of an *eclipse* (partial phase, annular phase, etc.). (See *lunar phases.*)

phase angle: the angle measured at the center of an illuminated body between the light source and the observer.

photometry: a measurement of the intensity of light, usually specified for a specific wavelength range.

physical ephemeris: see *ephemeris, physical.*

planet: a celestial body that is in *orbit* around the Sun, has sufficient mass for its self-gravity to overcome rigid body forces so that it assumes a hydrostatic-equilibrium (near-spherical) shape, and has cleared the neighbourhood around its orbit. (See *dwarf planet.*)

planetocentric coordinates: coordinates for general use, where the z-axis is the mean axis of rotation, the x-axis is the intersection of the planetary *equator* (normal to the z-axis through the center of mass) and an arbitrary *prime meridian*, and the y-axis completes a right-hand coordinate system. Longitude of a point is measured positive to the prime *meridian* as defined by *rotational elements*. Latitude of a point is the angle between the planetary equator and a line to the center of mass. The radius is measured from the center of mass to the surface point.

planetographic coordinates: coordinates for cartographic purposes dependent on an equipotential surface as a reference surface. Longitude of a point is measured in the direction opposite to the rotation (positive to the west for direct rotation) from the cartographic position of the *prime meridian* defined by a clearly observable surface feature. Latitude of a point is the angle between the planetary *equator* (normal to the z-axis and through the center of mass) and normal to the reference surface at the point. The *height* of a point is specified as the distance above a point with the same longitude and latitude on the reference surface.

polar motion: the quasi-periodic motion of the Earth's pole of rotation with respect to the Earth's solid body. More precisely, the angular excursion of the *CIP* from the *ITRS* z-axis. (See *Celestial Intermediate Pole (CIP); International Terrestrial Reference System (ITRS).*)

polar wobble: see *wobble, polar.*

pole, celestial: either of the two points projected onto the *celestial sphere* by the Earth's axis. Usually, this is the axis of the *Celestial Intermediate Pole (CIP)*, but it may also refer to the instantaneous axis of rotation, or the angular momentum vector. All of these axes are within $0\overset{''}{.}1$ of each other. If greater accuracy is desired, the specific axis should be designated.

pole, Tisserand mean: the angular momentum pole for the Earth about which the total internal angular momentum of the Earth is zero. The motions of the *Celestial Intermediate Pole (CIP)* (described by the conventional theories of *precession* and *nutation*) are those of the Tisserand mean pole with *periods* greater than two *days* in a celestial reference system (specifically, the *Geocentric Celestial Reference System (GCRS)*).

precession: the smoothly changing orientation (secular motion) of an orbital plane or the *equator* of a rotating body. Applied to rotational dynamics, precession comprises two components — free precession and forced precession. Free precession may be excited by a singular event, such as a collision, a progenitor's disruption, or a tidal interaction at a close approach. Forced precession is caused by continuous torques from other solar system bodies, or from jetting, in the case of comets. The main torques changing the Earth's rotation are exerted on the Earth's equatorial bulge by the Sun, Moon, and planets. These torques'action results in the precession of the equator with respect to inertial space (formerly called lunisolar precession, because the accuracy was too low to recognize the input from planets). In the case of orbital dynamics, the gravitational pull of celestial bodies other than the Sun causes a slow evolution in the orientation of the Earth's orbital plane with respect to inertial space. This evolution is called precession of the *ecliptic* (formerly known as planetary precession). The combination of both motions — that is, the total motion of the equator with respect to the ecliptic — is called general precession.

prime meridian: see *meridian, prime.*

prograde motion: see *direct motion.*

proleptic calendar: see *calendar, proleptic.*

proper motion: the projection onto the *celestial sphere* of the space motion of a star relative to the solar system; thus the transverse component of the space motion of a star with respect to the solar system. Proper motion is usually tabulated in star catalogs as changes in *right ascension* and *declination* per *year* or century.

proper place: direction of an object in the *Geocentric Celestial Reference System (GCRS)* that takes into account orbital or space motion and *light-time* (as applicable), light deflection, and *annual aberration*. Thus, the position (*geocentric right ascension* and *declination*) at which the object would actually be seen from the center of the Earth if the Earth were transparent, nonrefracting, and massless. Unless otherwise stated, the coordinates are expressed with respect to the GCRS axes, which are derived from those of the *ICRS*.

quadrature: a configuration in which two celestial bodies have apparent longitudes that differ by 90° as viewed from a third body. Quadratures are usually tabulated with respect to the Sun as viewed from the center of the Earth. (See *longitude, ecliptic.*)

radial velocity: the rate of change of the distance to an object, usually corrected for the Earth's motion with respect to the solar system *barycenter*.

radius vector: an imaginary line from the center of one body to another, often from the heliocenter. Sometimes only the length of the vector is given.

refraction: the change in direction of travel (bending) of a light ray as it passes obliquely from one medium to another. The media may differ in composition, temperature, pressure, or a combination of all three.

refraction, astronomical: the change in direction of travel (bending) of a light ray as it passes obliquely through the atmosphere. As a result of *refraction* the observed *altitude* of a celestial object is greater than its geometric altitude. The amount of refraction depends on the altitude of the object and on atmospheric conditions.

refraction, horizontal: the *astronomical refraction* at the *astronomical horizon*; often, an adopted value of 34′ is used in computations for sea level observations.

retrograde motion: for orbital motion in the solar system, motion that is clockwise in the *orbit* as seen from the north pole of the *ecliptic*; for an object observed on the *celestial sphere*, motion that is from east to west, resulting from the relative motion of the object and the Earth. (See *direct motion.*)

right ascension: angular distance on the *celestial sphere* measured eastward along the *celestial equator* from the *equinox* to the *hour circle* passing through the celestial object. Right ascension is usually given in combination with *declination*.

rotational elements: typically, a set of six time-dependent parameters used to describe the instantaneous orientation (attitude) and the instantaneous spin (angular velocity) of a celestial body. When the orientation and spin are described in inertial space, the set of rotational *elements* is often chosen to comprise the two angular coordinates of the direction of the north (or positive) pole and the location of the *prime meridian* at a *standard epoch*, and the time derivatives of each of those three angles. Additional parameters may be required when the object is a nonrigid body.

second, Système International (SI): the duration of 9 192 631 770 cycles of radiation corresponding to the transition between two hyperfine levels of the ground state of cesium 133.

selenocentric: with reference to, or pertaining to, the center of the Moon.

semidiameter: half a diameter, radius. Semidiameter is often used in place of radius when the object is mildly elliptical to refer to a semiaxis of interest (*e.g.* the vertical semidiameter of the Sun or the semidiameter of the greatest *defect of illumination* of Saturn).

semimajor axis: **1.** Half the length of the major axis of an ellipse. **2.** A standard orbital element used to describe an *elliptical orbit* or a *hyperbolic orbit*. (The orbital semimajor axis is negative for a hyperbolic *orbit*.)) **3.** Half the length of the longest axis of an *ellipsoid*.

SI second: see *second, Système International (SI).*

sidereal day: the *period* between successive *transits* of the *equinox*. The mean sidereal *day* is approximately 23 hours, 56 minutes, 4.091 *SI seconds*. (See *sidereal time.*)

sidereal hour angle: angular distance on the *celestial sphere* measured westward along the *celestial equator* from the *equinox* to the *hour circle* passing through the celestial object. It is equal to 360° minus *right ascension* in degrees.

sidereal month: see *month, sidereal.*

sidereal time: the *hour angle* of the *equinox*. If the *mean equinox* is used, the result is mean sidereal time; if the *true equinox* is used, the result is apparent sidereal time. The hour angle can be measured with respect to the local *meridian* or the *Greenwich meridian*, yielding, respectively, local or Greenwich (mean or apparent) sidereal times.

sidereal year: see *year, sidereal.*

small solar system body: a body orbiting the Sun that is not massive enough to be a *dwarf planet* and is not a *comet.*

solar parallax: see *parallax, solar.*

solar time: the measure of time based on the *diurnal motion* of the Sun.

solar time, apparent: the measure of time based on the *diurnal motion* of the true Sun. The rate of diurnal motion undergoes seasonal variation caused by the *obliquity* of the *ecliptic* and by the *eccentricity* of the Earth's *orbit*. Additional small variations result from irregularities in the rotation of the Earth on its axis.

solar time, mean: a measure of time based conceptually on the *diurnal motion* of a fiducial point, called the fictitious mean Sun, with uniform motion along the *celestial equator*.

solar year: see *year, solar.*

solstice: either of the two points on the *ecliptic* at which the apparent longitude of the Sun is 90° or 270°; also the time at which the Sun is at either point. (See *longitude, ecliptic.*)

spectral types or classes: categorization of stars according to their spectra, primarily due to differing temperatures of the stellar atmosphere. From hottest to coolest, the commonly used Morgan-Keenan spectral types are O, B, A, F, G, K and M. Some other extended spectral types include W, L, T, S, D and C.

standard epoch: a date and time that specifies the reference system to which celestial coordinates are referred. (See *mean equator and equinox.*)

stationary point: the time or position at which the rate of change of the apparent *right ascension* of a *planet* is momentarily zero. (See *apparent place (or position).*)

sub-earth point: the point on a body's surface that lies directly beneath the Earth on the line (geodesic) connecting the body's center to the geocenter. For spherical bodies, the Earth would be at the zenith for an observer at the sub-earth point. As viewed from the Earth, a body's sub-earth point appears at the center of the body's disk. In *The Astronomical Almanac*, the sub-earth point is typically described by a planetographic longitude and latitude. See diagram on page E4.

sub-solar point: the point on a body's surface that lies directly beneath the Sun on the line (geodesic) connecting the body's center to the heliocenter. For spherical bodies, the Sun would be at the zenith for an observer at the sub-solar point. In *The Astronomical Almanac*, the sub-solar point of a *planet* is typically described by a planetographic longitude and latitude, its distance from the *sub-earth point* (center of disk), and its position angle (north through east). See diagram on page E4.

sunrise, sunset: the times at which the apparent upper *limb* of the Sun is on the *astronomical horizon*. In *The Astronomical Almanac* they are computed as the times when the true *zenith distance*, referred to the center of the Earth, of the central point of the disk is 90° 50′, based on adopted values of 34′ for *horizontal refraction* and 16′ for the Sun's *semidiameter*.

surface brightness: the visual *magnitude* of an average square arcsecond area of the illuminated portion of the apparent disk of the Moon or a *planet*.

synodic month: see *month, synodic.*

synodic period: the mean interval of time between successive *conjunctions* of a pair of *planets*, as observed from the Sun; or the mean interval between successive conjunctions of a satellite with the Sun, as observed from the satellite's primary.

synodic time: pertaining to successive *conjunctions*; successive returns of a *planet* to the same *aspect* as determined by Earth.

syzygy: 1. A configuration where three or more celestial bodies are positioned approximately in a straight line in space. Often the bodies involved are the Earth, Sun and either the Moon or a *planet*. **2.** The times of the new moon and full moon.

T_{eph}: the independent argument of the JPL planetary and lunar *ephemerides* DE405/LE405; in the terminology of General Relativity, a *barycentric* coordinate time scale. T_{eph} is a linear function of *Barycentric Coordinate Time (TCB)* and has the same rate as *Terrestrial Time (TT)* over the time span of the ephemeris. T_{eph} is regarded as functionally equivalent to *Barycentric Dynamical Time (TDB)*. (See *Barycentric Coordinate Time (TCB); Barycentric Dynamical Time (TDB); Terrestrial Time (TT).*) OBSOLETE

TAI: see *International Atomic Time (TAI).*

TCB: see *Barycentric Coordinate Time (TCB).*

TCG: see *Geocentric Coordinate Time (TCG).*

TDB: see *Barycentric Dynamical Time (TDB).*

TNO: see *trans-Neptunian Object (TNO).*

terminator: the boundary between the illuminated and dark areas of a celestial body.

Terrestrial Intermediate Origin (TIO): the nonrotating origin of the *Terrestrial Intermediate Reference System (TIRS)*, established by the *International Astronomical Union (IAU)* in 2000. The TIO was originally set at the *International Terrestrial Reference Frame (ITRF)* origin of longitude and throughout 1900-2100 stays within 0.1 mas of the ITRF zero-*meridian*.

Terrestrial Intermediate Reference System (TIRS): a *geocentric* reference system defined by the intermediate *equator* of the *Celestial Intermediate Pole (CIP)* and the *Terrestrial Intermediate Origin (TIO)* on a specific date. It is related to the *Celestial Intermediate Reference System* by a rotation of the *Earth Rotation Angle*, θ, around the Celestial Intermediate Pole.

Terrestrial Time (TT): an idealized form of *International Atomic Time (TAI)* with an *epoch* offset; in practice TT = TAI + $32^{s}.184$. TT thus advances by *SI seconds* on the *geoid*. Used as an independent argument for apparent *geocentric ephemerides*. (See *second, Système International (SI).*)

Tisserand mean axis: the axis of a rotating deformable body chosen such that the contribution to angular momentum arising from its deformation integrated over its volume is 0.

topocentric: with reference to, or pertaining to, a point on the surface of the Earth.

topocentric place (or position): the *proper place* of an object computed for a specific location on or near the surface of the Earth (ignoring atmospheric *refraction*) and expressed with respect to either the *true (intermediate) equator and equinox* of date or the true *equator* and *CIO* of date. In other words, it is similar to an apparent or *intermediate place*, but with corrections for *geocentric parallax* and *diurnal aberration*. (See *aberration, diurnal; parallax, geocentric.*)

transit: 1. The passage of the apparent center of the disk of a celestial object across a *meridian*. **2.** The passage of one celestial body in front of another of greater apparent diameter (e.g., the passage of Mercury or Venus across the Sun or Jupiter's satellites across its disk); however, the passage of the Moon in front of the larger apparent Sun is called an *annular eclipse*. (See *eclipse, annular; eclipse, solar.*)

transit, shadow: The passage of a body's shadow across another body; however, the passage of the Moon's shadow across the Earth is called a *solar eclipse*.

trans-Neptunian Object (TNO): a solar system body with a semimajor axis greater than Neptune's.

tropical year: see *year, tropical.*

true equator and equinox: the celestial coordinate system defined by the orientation of the Earth's equatorial plane on some specified date together with the direction of the *dynamical equinox* on that date. The true *equator* and *equinox* are affected by both *precession* and *nutation*. (See *mean equator and equinox; nutation; precession.*)

TT: see *Terrestrial Time (TT).*

twilight: the interval before *sunrise* and after sunset during which the scattering of sunlight by the Earth's atmosphere provides significant illumination. The qualitative descriptions of astronomical, civil and *nautical twilight* will match the computed beginning and ending times for an observer near sea level, with good weather conditions, and a level *horizon*. (See *sunrise, sunset.*)

twilight, astronomical: the illumination level at which scattered light from the Sun exceeds that from starlight and other natural sources before *sunrise* and after sunset. Astronomical *twilight* is defined to begin or end when the geometric *zenith distance* of the central point of the Sun, referred to the center of the Earth, is 108°.

twilight, civil: the illumination level sufficient that most ordinary outdoor activities can be done without artificial lighting before *sunrise* or after sunset. Civil *twilight* is defined to begin or end when the geometric *zenith distance* of the central point of the Sun, referred to the center of the Earth, is 96°.

twilight, nautical: the illumination level at which the *horizon* is still visible even on a moonless night allowing mariners to take reliable star sights for navigational purposes before *sunrise* or after sunset. Nautical *twilight* is defined to begin or end when the geometric *zenith distance* of the central point of the Sun, referred to the center of the Earth, is 102°.

umbra: the portion of a shadow cone in which none of the light from an extended light source (ignoring *refraction*) can be observed.

Universal Time (UT): a generic reference to one of several time scales that approximate the mean *diurnal motion* of the Sun; loosely, *mean solar time* on the *Greenwich meridian* (previously referred to as Greenwich Mean Time). In current usage, UT refers either to a time scale called UT1 or to *Coordinated Universal Time (UTC)*; in this volume, UT always refers to UT1. UT1 is formally defined by a mathematical expression that relates it to *sidereal time*. Thus, UT1 is observationally determined by the apparent diurnal motions of celestial bodies, and is affected by irregularities in the Earth's rate of rotation. UTC is an atomic time scale but is maintained within $0^{s}.9$ of UT1 by the introduction of 1-*second* steps when necessary. (See *leap second.*)

UT0: a rarely used local approximation to *Universal Time*; not corrected for *polar motion*.

UT1: see *Universal Time (UT).*

UTC: see *Coordinated Universal Time (UTC).*

vernal equinox: see *equinox, vernal.*

vertical: the apparent direction of gravity at the point of observation (normal to the plane of a free level surface).

week: an arbitrary *period* of *days*, usually seven days; approximately equal to the number of days counted between the four principal *phases of the Moon*. (See *lunar phases.*)

wobble, polar: **1.** In current practice, including the phraseology used in *The Astronomical Almanac*, it is identical to *polar motion*. **2.** In certain contexts, it can refer to specific components of polar motion, *e.g.* Chandler wobble or annual wobble. (See *polar motion.*)

year: the time taken for Earth to complete one orbit about the Sun.

year, anomalistic: the time between two consecutive passages of Earth through *perihelion*. Its duration is approximately 365 days 6 hours 13 minutes 53 *seconds*.

year, Besselian: the *period* of one complete revolution in *right ascension* of the fictitious mean Sun, as defined by Newcomb. Its length is shorter than a *tropical year* by 0.148×T *seconds*, where T is centuries since 1900.0. The beginning of the Besselian *year* occurs when the fictitious mean Sun is at mean right ascension 18h 40m. OBSOLETE.

year, calendar: the *period* between two dates with the same name in a *calendar*, either 365 or 366 *days*. The *Gregorian calendar*, now universally used for civil purposes, is based on the *tropical year*.

year, eclipse: the *period* between successive passages of the Sun (as seen from the geocenter) through the same lunar *node* (one of two points where the Moon's *orbit* intersects the *ecliptic*). It is approximately 346.62 *days*.

year, Julian: a unit of measurement of time defined as exactly 365.25 days of 86400 *SI seconds* each.

year, sidereal: the time taken for the Earth to complete one orbit about the Sun, as measured against the fixed stars.

year, solar: see: *year, tropical*

year, tropical: the time that the Sun takes to return to the same position in the sky along the *ecliptic*, relative to the *equinox*, as viewed from the Earth – which is the time between two consecutive passages of the Earth through the *ascending node* of its orbital plane on the Earth's *equator*. Variations in the length of the tropical year are due to the perturbations by the Moon and planets acting on the Earth, and also due to Earth's nutation. Presently, the tropical year is shorter than the sidereal year by approximately 20 min 24.5 *seconds*.

zenith: in general, the point directly overhead on the *celestial sphere*.

zenith, astronomical: the extension to infinity of a plumb line from an observer's location.

zenith, geocentric: The point projected onto the *celestial sphere* by a line that passes through the geocenter and an observer.

zenith, geodetic: the point projected onto the *celestial sphere* by the line normal to the Earth's geodetic ellipsoid at an observer's location.

zenith distance: angular distance on the *celestial sphere* measured along the great circle from the *zenith* to the celestial object. Zenith distance is 90° minus *altitude*.

Definitions of astronomical terms are provided in the Glossary, Section M. Entries in the Glossary are not cited in the Index.

Definitions of astronomical terms are provided in the Glossary, Section M. Entries in the Glossary are not cited in the Index.

Definitions of astronomical terms are provided in the Glossary, Section M. Entries in the Glossary are not cited in the Index.

Definitions of astronomical terms are provided in the Glossary, Section M. Entries in the Glossary are not cited in the Index.

Definitions of astronomical terms are provided in the Glossary, Section M. Entries in the Glossary are not cited in the Index.

Definitions of astronomical terms are provided in the Glossary, Section M. Entries in the Glossary are not cited in the Index.

Definitions of astronomical terms are provided in the Glossary, Section M. Entries in the Glossary are not cited in the Index.

Definitions of astronomical terms are provided in the Glossary, Section M. Entries in the Glossary are not cited in the Index.

Definitions of astronomical terms are provided in the Glossary, Section M. Entries in the Glossary are not cited in the Index.

Definitions of astronomical terms are provided in the Glossary, Section M. Entries in the Glossary are not cited in the Index.

Definitions of astronomical terms are provided in the Glossary, Section M. Entries in the Glossary are not cited in the Index.

Definitions of astronomical terms are provided in the Glossary, Section M. Entries in the Glossary are not cited in the Index.

Definitions of astronomical terms are provided in the Glossary, Section M. Entries in the Glossary are not cited in the Index.

Definitions of astronomical terms are provided in the Glossary, Section M. Entries in the Glossary are not cited in the Index.

Definitions of astronomical terms are provided in the Glossary, Section M. Entries in the Glossary are not cited in the Index.

Definitions of astronomical terms are provided in the Glossary, Section M. Entries in the Glossary are not cited in the Index.

Definitions of astronomical terms are provided in the Glossary, Section M. Entries in the Glossary are not cited in the Index.

NOTES

NOTES

NOTES

NOTES

NOTES

NOTES

NOTES

NOTES